October 12–16, 2013
Hong Kong, China

Association for
Computing Machinery

Advancing Computing as a Science & Profession

RecSys'13

Proceedings of the 7th ACM Conference on Recommender Systems

Sponsored by:

ACM SIGCHI

In-cooperation with:

ACM SIGART, ACM SIGIR, ACM SIGCKDD, ACM SIGWEB, and ACM SIGecom

Supported by:

Huawei Noah's Ark Lab, City University of Hong Kong, KC Wong Education Foundation, Alimama.com, IBM, Yelp!, VeriGuide, CINTEC, The Chinese University of Hong Kong, and The Baptist University of Hong Kong Most

Association for
Computing Machinery

Advancing Computing as a Science & Profession

The Association for Computing Machinery
2 Penn Plaza, Suite 701
New York, New York 10121-0701

Notice to Past Authors of ACM-Published Articles
ACM intends to create a complete electronic archive of all articles and/or other material previously published by ACM. If you have written a work that has been previously published by ACM in any journal or conference proceedings prior to 1978, or any SIG Newsletter at any time, and you do NOT want this work to appear in the ACM Digital Library, please inform permissions@acm.org, stating the title of the work, the author(s), and where and when published.

ISBN: 978-1-4503-2409-0 (Digital)

ISBN: 978-1-4503-2678-0 (Print)

Additional copies may be ordered prepaid from:

ACM Order Department
PO Box 30777
New York, NY 10087-0777, USA

Phone: 1-800-342-6626 (USA and Canada)
+1-212-626-0500 (Global)
Fax: +1-212-944-1318
E-mail: acmhelp@acm.org
Hours of Operation: 8:30 am – 4:30 pm ET

Printed in the USA

Program Chairs' Welcome

It is our great pleasure to welcome you to the 7th ACM Recommender Systems Conference (ACM RecSys 2013), held in Hong Kong on October 12-16. As RecSys enters the second half of its first decade, it has clearly established itself as the premier international venue for research and development in the field of Recommender Systems, where leading researchers and practitioners from around the world meet and discuss their latest results and solutions.

The growing prestige of the conference is reflected by the significant increase in the number of papers that were submitted to the technical program. The overall number of paper submissions went up 20% as compared to last year, with a total of 222 submissions. We received 136 full paper submissions, from which 32 were accepted (23.5%) for oral presentation and 18 were accepted as short papers and poster presentations. We received 80 short paper submissions, from which 24 were accepted (28.75%). Seven of these short papers were selected for short oral presentation and the remaining for poster presentation. For the first time this year, in addition to full and short papers, we also had a new category of submissions consisting of full-length industry papers. We received six papers in this category, out of which two papers were accepted and were presented during the industrial research session. To accommodate the large number of high-quality papers that we received and accepted, the number of research sessions has been increased to eight from the previous year's five sessions.

Besides the technical program, the conference's overall program also includes tutorials, workshops, a doctoral symposium, and demonstrations. The tutorial program includes four exciting tutorials covering state-of-the-art methods for building recommender systems and emerging application areas. The workshop program includes eight different one-day workshops that take place the two days prior to the main conference. The doctoral symposium showcases the work of six PhD students, whose work has been selected after a rigorous review process. Finally, the demonstration program contains five different demonstrations covering various aspects of recommender systems.

The conference program also includes three keynotes, one from an academic perspective by Oren Etzioni (University of Washington) and two from an industrial perspective by Dou Shen (Baidu) and Mu Yan (Beihe). Finally, continuing with the tradition of the conference, there is a strong integration of the research with its commercial applications. This is reflected through the strong participation of industry at the workshops, demonstrations, and technical program, as well as a special industrial session containing presentations of the accepted industry papers, invited talks, and panel discussions.

Pearl Pu
Program Co-chair
Computer and Communication Sciences
Ecole Polytechnique Fédérale de Lausanne
Lausanne, Switzerland

George Karypis
Program Co-chair
Department of Computer Science & Engineering
University of Minnesota
Minneapolis, USA

Table of Contents

Technical Session 4: Media Recommendation

Session Chair: Bamshad Mobasher *(DePaul University)*

Technical Session 5: User Experience

Session Chair: Dietmar Jannach *(Technical University of Dortmund)*

Technical Session 6: Beyond Ratings

Session Chair: Martin Ester *(Fraser University)*

Technical Session 7: Methods, Algorithms, and Theory II

Session Chair: Alexandros Karatzoglou *(Telefonica Research)*

Technical Session 8: Scalability

Session Chair: Paolo Cremonesi *(Politecnico di Milano)*

Session 9: Industry

Session Chair: Tao Zhou *(Beifendian Inc.)*

Session 10: Poster

Session 11: Doctoral Symposium

Session Chair: Yi Zhang *(University of California Santa Cruz)*

Session 12: Demonstrations

Session Chair: Rong Zheng *(Hong Kong University of Science and Technology)*

Session 13: Workshops

Session 14: Tutorials

ACM RecSys 2013 Conference Organization

General Chairs: Qiang Yang *(Huawei Noah Ark Research Lab, China)*
Irwin King *(Chinese University of Hong Kong, China)*
Qing Li *(City University of Hong Kong, China)*

Program Chairs: Pearl Pu *(Ecole Polytechnique Fédérale de Lausanne, Switzerland)*
George Karypis *(University of Minnesota, USA)*

Workshop Chairs: Shlomo Berkovsky *(NICTA, Australia)*
Jie Tang *(Tsinghua University, China)*
Paolo Cremonesi *(Politecnico di Milano, Italy)*

Doctoral Symposium Chair: Yi Zhang *(University of California Santa Cruz, USA)*

Demo Chair: Rong Zheng *(Hong Kong University of Science and Technology, China)*

Tutorial Chair: Dietmar Jannach *(Technical University of Dortmund, Germany)*

Industrial Chairs: Christian Posse *(Google, USA)*
Tao Zhou *(Beifendian Inc., China)*

Publicity Chairs: Mi Zhang *(Fudan University, China)*
Simon Dooms *(Ghent University, Belgium)*
Tim Hussein *(University of Duisburg-Essen, Germany)*
Qian Xu *(Baidu Inc., China)*

Local Chairs: Li Chen *(Hong Kong Baptist University, China)*
Chi Yin Chow *(City University of Hong Kong, China)*

Finance/Registration Chair: Hong Cheng *(The Chinese University of Hong Kong, China)*

Steering Committee:

Alexander Tuzhilin *(New York University Stern School of Business)*
Alexander Felfernig *(Graz University of Technology)*
Barry Smyth *(University College Dublin)*
Lawrence Bergman *(IBM Research)*
Dietmar Jannach *(TU Dortmund, Germany)*
Derek Bridge *(University College Cork)*
Francesco Ricci *(Free University of Bozen-Bolzano)*
Gediminas Adomavicious *(University of Minnesota)*
Jon Sanders *(Netflix)*
Irwin King *(Chinese University of Hong Kong)*
Alfred Kobsa *(University of California Irvine)*
Joseph Konstan *(University of Minnesota)*
Markus Zanker *(Alpen-Adria-Universitaet Klagenfurt)*
Bamshad Mobasher *(DePaul University)*
Michelle X Zhou *(IBM Research)*
Neil Hurley *(University College Dublin)*
Padraig Cunningham *(University College Dublin)*
Paul Lamere *(The Echo Nest)*
Pearl Pu *(Ecole Polytechnique Fédérale de Lausanne)*
Qiang Yang *(Huawei Noah Ark Research Lab)*
Robin Burke *(DePaul University)*
Sarabjot Anand *(Algorithmic Insight)*
Lars Schmidt-Thieme *(University of Hildesheim)*
Marc Torrens *(Stands Inc.)*
Xavier Amatrian *(Netflix)*
Yehuda Koren *(Google Research)*
George Karypis *(University of Minnesota)*
Li Qing *(City University of Hong Kong)*
Ido Guy *(IBM Research)*

Senior Program Committee

Gediminas Adomavicius *(University of Minnesota)*
Sarabjot Anand *(Algorithmic Insight)*
Shlomo Berkovsky *(NICTA)*
Robin Burke *(DePaul University)*
Li Chen *(Hong Kong Baptist University)*
Paolo Cremonesi *(Politecnico di Milano)*
Martin Ester Simon *(Fraser University)*
Alexander Felfernig *(Graz University of Technology)*
Jill Freyne *(CSIRO)*
Jennifer Golbeck *(University of Maryland, College Park)*
Ido Guy *(IBM Research)*
Rong Hu *(Swiss Federal Institute of Technology in Lausanne)*
Alejandro Jaimes *(Yahoo! Research)*
Dietmar Jannach *(Technical University of Dortmund)*
Alexandros Karatzoglou *(Telefonica Research)*
Tsvi Kuflik *(The University of Haifa)*
Bamshad Mobasher *(DePaul University)*
Alexandros Nanopoulos *(University of Hildesheim)*
Olfa Nasraoui *(University of Louisville)*
Wolfgang Nejdl *(L3S and University of Hannover)*
Naren Ramakrishnan *(Virginia Tech)*
Francesco Ricci *(Free University of Bozen-Bolzano)*
Lars Schmidt-Thieme *(University of Hildesheim)*
Bracha Shapira *(Ben-Gurion University)*
Barry Smyth *(University College Dublin)*
Panagiotis Symeonidis *(Aristotle University of Thessaloniki)*
Jie Tang *(Tsinghua University)*
Xing Xie *(Microsoft Research Asia)*
Markus Zanker *(Alpen-Adria-Universitaet Klagenfurt)*

Program Committee: Albert Ching-Man Au-Yeung *(Huawei Noah's Ark Lab)*
Leandro Balby Marinho *(Federal University of Campina Grande)*
Linas Baltrunas *(Telefonica Research)*
Alejandro Bellogin *(Universidad Autonoma de Madrid)*
Derek Bridge *(University College Cork)*
Peter Brusilovsky *(University of Pittsburgh)*
Olga C. Santos *(UNED)*
Ivan Cantador *(Universidad Autonoma de Madrid)*
Sylvain Castagnos *(LORIA)*
Pablo Castells *(Universidad Autonoma de Madrid)*
Jilin Chen *(IBM Research)*
Wen-Huang Cheng *(Academia Sinica)*
Dan Cosley *(Cornell)*
Claudiu Cristian Musat *(Ecole Polytechnique Fédérale de Lausanne)*
Marco De Gemmis *(University of Bari)*
Christian Desrosiers *(Ecole de Technologie Superieure)*
Ernesto Diaz-Aviles *(Leibniz University of Hannover)*
Guiguang Ding *(Tsinghua University)*
Casey Dugan *(IBM T.J. Watson Research)*
Zeno Gantner *(Nokia)*
Florent Garcin *(Ecole Polytechnique Fédérale de Lausanne)*
Fatih Gedikli *(Technical University of Dortmund)*
Aristides Gionis *(Y!R)*
Andreas Hotho *(University of Wuerzburg)*
Tim Hussein *(University of Duisburg-Essen)*
Mohsen Jamali *(University of British Columbia)*
Robert Jaschke *(L3S Research Center)*
Georgia Koutrika *(Stanford University)*
Artus Krohn-Grimberghe *(University of Paderborn)*
Antonio Krueger *(DFKI)*
Daniel Lemire *(Universite du Quebec a Montreal)*
Cane Leung *(Huawei Noah's Ark Lab)*
Gang Li *(Deakin University)*
Tao Li *(Florida International University)*
Pasquale Lops *(University of Bari)*
Nikos Manouselis *(Agro-Know Technologies)*
Judith Masthoff *(University of Aberdeen)*
Kevin McCarthy *(University College Dublin)*
Lorraine McGinty *(University College Dublin)*
Stuart Middleton *(University of Southampton)*
Xia Ning *(NEC Research)*
Shimei Pan *(IBM Research)*
Weike Pan *(Hong Kong Baptist University)*
Seung-Taek Park *(Samsung Electronics)*
Bruno Pradel *(Laboratoire d'Informatique de Paris 6)*

Program Committee (continued):

Li Pu *(EPFL)*
Daniele Quercia *(Yahoo! Labs)*
Steffen Rendle *(University of Konstanz)*
Haggai Roitman *(IBM Research Haifa)*
Lior Rokach *(BGU)*
Inbal Ronen *(IBM Research Haifa)*
Alan Said *(Technische Universitat Berlin)*
Kostyantyn Shchekotykhin *(Alpen-Adria University)*
Yue Shi *(Delft University of Technology)*
Yangqiu Song *(Hong Kong University of Science and Technology)*
Myra Spiliopoulou *(University of Magdeburg)*
Markus Strohmaier *(Graz University of Technology)*
Andrea Tagarelli *(University of Calabria)*
Loren Terveen *(University of Minnesota)*
Nava Tintarev *(University of Aberdeen)*
Mitul Tiwari *(LinkedIn)*
Nicolas Usunier *(LIP6)*
Jun Wang *(University College London)*
Markus Weimer *(Microsoft)*
Martijn Willemsen *(Eindhoven University of Technology)*
Ernesto William De Luca *(Technical University of Berlin)*
Daniel Xiaodan Zhou *(University of Michigan)*
Jierui Xie *(Oracle)*
Guandong Xu *(University of Technology Sydney)*
Robbie Yan *(Two Sigma Investments)*
Quan Yuan *(IBM Research)*
Jiyong Zhang *(Swiss Federal Institute of Technology in Lausanne)*
Mi Zhang *(Fudan University)*
Ying Zhao *(Tsinghua University)*
Tingshao Zhu *(Chinese Academy of Sciences)*

RecSys 2013 Sponsor & Supporters

Sponsor: SIGCHI

In-Cooperation with: SIGART, SIGIR (Special Interest Group on Information Retrieval), KDD.org, sigweb, SIGecom

Gold Supporters:
Huawei Noah's Ark Lab
City University of Hong Kong

Silver Supporter:
KC Wong Education Foundation
Alimama.com
IBM

Bronze Supporter:
Yelp!

Technical Supporters:
VeriGuide
CINTEC
The Chinese University of Hong Kong
The Baptist University of Hong Kong Most

Context-Aware Review Helpfulness Rating Prediction

Jiliang Tang, Huiji Gao, Xia Hu and Huan Liu
Computer Science and Engineering, Arizona State University, Tempe, AZ, USA
{jiliang.tang, huiji.gao, xia.hu, huan.liu}@asu.edu

ABSTRACT

Online reviews play a vital role in the decision-making process for online users. Helpful reviews are usually buried in a large number of unhelpful reviews, and with the consistently increasing number of reviews, it becomes more and more difficult for online users to find helpful reviews. Therefore most online review websites allow online users to rate the helpfulness of a review and a global helpfulness score is computed for the review based on its available ratings. However, in reality, user-specified helpfulness ratings for reviews are very sparse - a few reviews attract large numbers of helpfulness ratings while most reviews obtain few or even no helpfulness ratings. The available helpfulness ratings are too sparse for online users to assess the helpfulness of reviews. Also the helpfulness of a review is not necessarily equally useful for all users and users with different background may treat the helpfulness of a review very differently. The user idiosyncracy of review helpfulness motivates us to study the problem of review helpfulness rating prediction in this paper. We first identify various types of context information, model them mathematically, and propose a context-aware review helpfulness rating prediction framework CAP. Experimental results demonstrate the effectiveness of the proposed framework and the importance of context awareness in solving the review helpfulness rating prediction problem.

Categories and Subject Descriptors

H.3.3 [**Information Search and Retrieval**]: Information filtering; J.4 [**Computer Application**]: Social and Behavioral Sciences

Keywords

Review Rating Prediction, Social Context, Review Recommendation, Content Context

1. INTRODUCTION

Reviews, providing experiences with and opinions about products or services from other users, play a crucial role in online communities such as e-commerce and product review sites, where users rely on reviews in their decision-making process. For example, users will select restaurants with good reviews in Yelp, and reviews about products in eBay are important sources of information for users to make purchases. However, helpful reviews are usually buried in large numbers of useless reviews [15], and with the availability of massive reviews, it becomes increasingly difficult for online users to find helpful reviews.

In an attempt to help online users identify helpful reviews, most online review websites implement a mechanism to allow users to rate the helpfulness of a review and then a global helpfulness score is computed for the review such as "20 out of 30 people found the following review helpful" in eBay and a score from 0 to 5 in Ciao. In reality, a large proportion of reviews obtain few or no helpfulness ratings, particularly the more recent ones and the available helpfulness ratings are too sparse for online users to assess the helpfulness of reviews [15]. For example, it is difficult for users to assess the helpfulness of a review in eBay with a score of "1 out of 1 people found review helpful". There is recent work automatically predicting a global helpfulness score for a review [9, 13, 15]. However, a review is not necessarily equally useful for all users. For example, in eBay, a review's helpfulness can have a score of "500 out of 1000 people found the following review helpful", which indicates that the other half do not think the review helpful or are indifferent. This user idiosyncracy of review helpfulness motivates us to study if we can predict review helpfulness rating for each user.

We choose a product review site, a classical type of online review websites, to investigate if review helpfulness rating prediction can help mitigate the problem caused by user idiosyncracy. Figure 1(a) gives an overview of product review sites where users have four different behaviors - connecting to other users, writing reviews, rating the helpfulness of reviews, and rating items. Figure 1(b) depicts the user helpfulness rating behavior and there are two types of ratings including item ratings and review helpfulness ratings. The review helpfulness rating is fundamentally different from the item rating. The former indicates "how does a user X rate a review from another user Y?" while the latter denotes "how does a user X rate an item?". These differences not only are useful to differ our studied problem from item rating prediction problem, but also present unique opportunities for us to investigate the review helpfulness rating prediction problem. First, the texts of reviews can affect how users rate the helpfulness of reviews [13], thus provide content context about reviews. Second, users play two roles in review helpfulness rating: authors - users who write reviews, and raters - users who rate reviews. Both raters and authors can rate items,

RecSys'13, October 12–16, 2013, Hong Kong, China.
Copyright 2013 ACM 978-1-4503-2409-0/13/10 ...$15.00.
http://–enter the whole DOI string from rightsreview form confirmation.

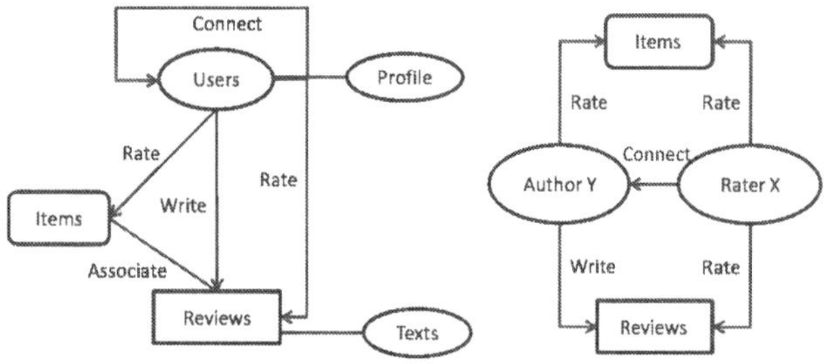

(a) An Overview (b) Helpfulness Rating

Figure 1: An Overview of Product Review Sites and the User Helpfulness Rating Behavior.

and raters may be related to authors such as raters may connect to authors. Raters, authors and their relations provide rich social context about reviews. For example, authors with high reputations are likely to write helpful reviews [4], and raters might think of reviews from their connected authors more helpful. Therefore the dual roles of users expand the horizon of social context in helpfulness rating, providing a new perspective to exploit social context.

The availability of content context and social context provides unique opportunities but also brings about new challenges: (1) what types of social context can be extracted from the dual roles of users in helpfulness rating, and (2) how to model content context and various types of social context mathematically for prediction. Addressing these two challenges, we propose a framework for the helpfulness rating prediction problem by exploiting context information. Our contributions are summarized next.

- Defining the problem of review helpfulness rating prediction with context awareness formally;
- Analyzing various types of social context and providing a way to formulate them mathematically;
- Proposing a **C**ontext-**A**ware helpfulness rating **P**rediction framework (CAP) that exploits content context with various types of social context; and
- Evaluating the framework in Ciao, a real-world product review site, to understand the working of CAP and the importance of context awareness in the problem of review helpfulness rating prediction.

The rest of this paper is organized as follows. Section 2 defines our problem formally. Section 3 describes the dataset and analyzes various types of social context. Section 4 introduces how to formulate context information mathematically and a context-aware helpfulness rating prediction framework. Section 5 presents experimental results and our observations. Section 6 briefly reviews related work. Section 7 concludes this study with future work.

2. PROBLEM STATEMENT

Typically there are three types of objects on product review sites. Let $\mathcal{U} = \{u_1, u_2, \ldots, u_n\}$ be the set of users, $\mathcal{P} = \{p_1, p_2, \ldots, p_m\}$ be the set of items, and $\mathcal{R} = \{r_1, r_2, \ldots, r_N\}$ be the set of reviews where n, m and N are the numbers of users, items and reviews, respectively. Users in product review websites have four behaviors. First, users can connect to each other and we use $\mathbf{T} \in \mathbb{R}^{n\times n}$ to represent their social relations where $\mathbf{T}_{ij} = 1$ if u_j creates a connection to u_i and zero otherwise. Second, users can rate items and $\mathbf{R} \in \mathbb{R}^{n\times m}$ is introduced to denote item rating where $\mathbf{R}_{ij}$ is the item rating if u_i gives p_j a rating. Third, users can rate the helpfulness of reviews and $\mathbf{H} \in \mathbb{R}^{n\times N}$ is employed to represent helpfulness rating where $\mathbf{H}_{ij}$ is the helpfulness rating if u_i gives r_j a rating. For both $\mathbf{R}$ and $\mathbf{H}$, we adopt a symbol "?" to represent unknown ratings. Finally, users can write reviews and we use $\mathbf{A} \in \mathbb{R}^{n\times N}$ to denote the author-review relations where $\mathbf{A}_{ij} = 1$ indicates that r_j is written by u_i and zero otherwise. For the j-th review r_j, we use $\mathbf{x}_j$ to represent its textual feature vector. We use $\mathcal{O} = \{\langle u_i, r_j, u_k\rangle | \mathbf{H}_{ij} \neq ?\}$ and $\mathcal{Q} = \{\langle u_i, r_j, u_k\rangle | \mathbf{H}_{ij} = ?\}$ to denote the set of known and unknown helpfulness ratings respectively, where u_k is the author of r_j. Although we choose product view sites to study the problem, the framework proposed in this paper can be applied to other online review websites.

With the notations above, our problem can be stated as: *given the known helpfulness rating set $\mathcal{O}$ and its contextual awareness including the social network $\mathbf{T}$, the item ratings $\mathbf{R}$, the author-review relations $\mathbf{A}$, and the review content $\{\mathbf{x}_j\}_{j=1}^N$, we aim to predict unknown helpful ratings for triples $\langle u_i, r_j, u_k\rangle$ in $\mathcal{Q}$ by exploiting the known helpfulness rating set $\mathcal{O}$ and context information $\{\mathbf{T}, \mathbf{R}, \mathbf{A}, \{\mathbf{x}_j\}_{j=1}^N\}$.*

3. SOCIAL CONTEXT ANALYSIS

The dual roles of users in the studied problem bring about unique challenges and opportunities to exploit social context. In this section, we conduct preliminary social context analysis to seek a solution to the first challenge - what types of social context can be extracted.

3.1 Dataset

For the purpose of this study, we crawled a data set from Ciao, a popular product review site. We started with a set of the most active users and then did breadth-first search until no new users could be found. For each user, we collect his/her profile, social networks and item rating entities. For each item rating entity, we collected the time point when this entity was created, item name, the category of the item, the rating score and the associated review. For each review, we collected its textual content, raters, their helpfulness ratings to the review and the time points when helpfulness ratings were created. We filter users giving no helpfulness ratings and reviews receiving no helpfulness ratings. Some statistics about the dataset are shown in Table 1 where the number of item ratings is the same as that of reviews since they are one-to-one correspondences.

Table 1: Statistics of the Dataset

# of Users	43,666
# of Reviews	302,232
# of Items	112,804
# of Item Ratings	302,232
# of Helpfulness Ratings	8,894,899
Ave Rating Score per Review	3.9126
# of Connections	145,528

In Ciao, users give scores from 0 to 5 to indicate the helpfulness of reviews, and we find that the majority (80.74%) of helpfulness ratings are 3 and 4. We compute the number of helpfulness ratings given by each user and the distribution suggests a power-law-like distribution: a few users con-

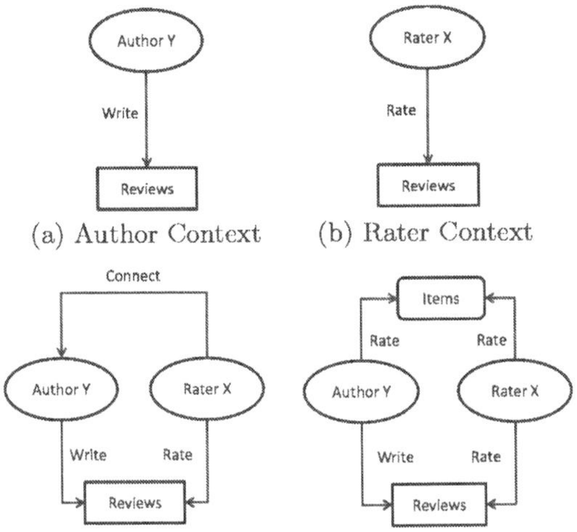

(a) Author Context (b) Rater Context

(c) Connection Context (d) Preference Context

Figure 2: Four Types of Social Context

tribute a large number of helpfulness ratings, and most users give few helpfulness ratings. We also compute the number of helpfulness ratings received by each review, and the distribution also suggests a power-law-like distribution.

3.2 Various Types of Social Context

Authors, raters and their relations provide rich social context about reviews. From Figure 1(b), we extract two types of *individual context*, i.e., author context in Figure 2(a) and rater context in Figure 2(b), and two types of *relation context*, i.e., connection context in Figure 2(c) and preference context in Figure 2(d)).

- *Author Context.* Author context is defined to capture context information from the authors of reviews. For example, raters are likely to think of reviews from authors with high reputation more helpful [4], and the helpfulness of reviews from the same authors is likely to be consistent [15].
- *Rater Context.* Rater context is extracted to capture context information from raters. For example, raters are likely to rate the helpfulness of a review similarly to how their trust networks do [17] and some users have a propensity to rate reviews higher or lower [5].
- *Connection Context.* If raters connect to the author of a review, how will they think of the helpfulness of the review? Connection context is employed to capture context information about social relations between raters and authors.
- *Preference Context.* If raters have similar preferences with the author of a review, how will they think of the helpfulness of the review? Preference context is introduced to exploit the context information of raters and authors of reviews with similar preferences.

Most existing tasks exploiting social context only consider users as either authors [15, 12] or raters [10, 16]. For example, author context is exploited as the social features in review quality prediction problem [12], while rater context is widely exploited in the item rating prediction problem [10, 1]. Author context and rater context are seldom both investigated in one problem, while our problem naturally involves both of them. There are recent studies exploiting relations between users [11, 17]. Only considering one role of users, they utilize relations between two raters [11, 17] or two authors [15]. However, we consider relations between raters and authors in our problem, which is rarely studied before. In the following two subsections, we focus our attention on the analysis of connection context and preference context.

3.3 Connection Context Analysis

Given that raters connect to the author of a review, we investigate how the raters will rate the helpfulness of the review. For each review, we divide its raters into two groups: connection group $\mathcal{G}_t$ - containing raters who have connections with its author, and non-connection group $\mathcal{G}_r$ - containing raters without relations with its author. To analyze connection context, we select reviews with both $\mathcal{G}_t$ and $\mathcal{G}_r$ not null, including 74.45% of all reviews. This observation suggests that most reviews involve connection context. On average, 33.17% of helpfulness ratings for a review are from the connection group $\mathcal{G}_t$.

For the j-th review r_j, we use connection rating T_j and non-connection rating R_j to represent the average helpfulness ratings from raters in $\mathcal{G}_t$ and $\mathcal{G}_r$, respectively. Assume that $\mathbf{t}$ and $\mathbf{r}$ are the vectors of all connection ratings (T_is) and non-connection ratings (R_is), respectively. We check the means of $\mathbf{t}$ and $\mathbf{r}$ and find that the mean of $\mathbf{t}$ **3.9627** is larger than that of $\mathbf{r}$ **3.7734**. To study the significance, we also conduct a two-sample t-test on the vectors $\mathbf{t}$ and $\mathbf{r}$. The null hypothesis is H_0: $\mathbf{t} \leq \mathbf{r}$, and the alternative hypothesis is H_1: $\mathbf{t} > \mathbf{r}$. The result show that there is strong evidence to reject the null hypothesis with significance level $\alpha = 0.01$, indicating $\mathbf{t}$ is significantly larger than $\mathbf{r}$. With the evidence from the means and t-test result, we conclude **Observation 1** - raters are likely to think of reviews from their connected authors more helpful.

Users may have heterogeneous connection strengths with their social networks [22]. For each review, we further divide the connection group $\mathcal{G}_t$ equally into strong connection group and weak connection group based on the metric introduced in [22]. We do similar analysis on these two groups to that on $\mathcal{G}_t$ and $\mathcal{G}_r$. To save space, we ignore the detailed results and directly give **Observation 2** - the more strongly raters connect to an author, the more helpful raters consider the reviews from the author.

3.4 Preference Context Analysis

Given that raters have similar preferences to the author of a review, we investigate how the raters will think of the helpfulness of the review. To answer this question, we first need to define the measure of preference similarity between raters and authors. In the context of product review sites, user preferences can be extracted from the item rating behavior [23]. For example, if two users rate the same items similarly, they have similar preferences or opinions. Therefore we use item rating similarity to measure preference similarity between the raters and authors. For the i-th user u_i, we first calculate his/her cosine item rating similarities with other users s_{ik}, $\forall k \neq i$, and then we choose j-th user u_j as u_i's preference similar user if $s_{ij} > \frac{1}{n-1}\sum_k s_{ik}$ where $\frac{1}{n-1}\sum_k s_{ik}$ is the average item similarity between u_i and other users. Let $\mathbf{P} \in \mathbb{R}^{n \times n}$ denote the preference relation matrix where $\mathbf{P}(i, j) = 1$ if u_j is a preference similar user of u_i and zero otherwise.

Similar to connection context analysis, for each review, we split its raters into two groups: preference group $\mathcal{G}_o$ - the group of raters who are the preference similar users of the author, and non-preference group $\mathcal{G}_s$ - the group of users who are not the preference similar users of the author. To conduct preference context analysis, we choose reviews with both $\mathcal{G}_o$ and $\mathcal{G}_s$ not null, including 89.08% of all reviews. On average, 48.93% of helpfulness ratings for a review are from the preference group $\mathcal{G}_t$. These observations reveal that most reviews have preference context. For each review, we check the rater overlap between preference group $\mathcal{G}_o$ and connection group $\mathcal{G}_t$ in connection context analysis and find that the average overlap is 9.23%. This observation suggests that preference context is very different from connection context and it is necessary to study them separately.

For the i-th review, we use preference rating O_i and non-preference rating S_i to denote the average helpfulness ratings from $\mathcal{G}_o$ and $\mathcal{G}_s$, respectively. Let $\mathbf{o}$ and $\mathbf{s}$ be the set of preference ratings (O_is) and non-preference ratings (S_is) respectively, and the mean of **o 3.8440** is larger than that of **s 3.7468**. We also conduct a two-sample t-test on the vectors $\mathbf{o}$ and $\mathbf{s}$. The null hypothesis is H_0: $\mathbf{o} \leq \mathbf{s}$, and the alternative hypothesis is H_1: $\mathbf{o} > \mathbf{s}$. The result show that there is strong evidence to reject the null hypothesis with significance level $\alpha = 0.01$. With the evidence from the means and t-test result, we conclude **Observation 3** - raters are likely to consider the reviews from their preference similar authors more helpful.

For each review, based on the item similarities between raters and its author, we further divide $\mathcal{G}_o$ equally into high preference similar group and low preference similar group. By analyzing these two groups as similar to $\mathcal{G}_o$ and $\mathcal{G}_s$, we find **Observation 4** - the more similar the preferences of raters and an author are, the more helpful raters consider the reviews from the author.

4. OUR FRAMEWORK

With social context analysis in the last section, we are ready to introduce our context-aware helpfulness rating prediction framework CAP to address the second challenge - how to model content context and various types of social context for the prediction problem.

4.1 Modeling Context Awareness

We use $\hat{\mathbf{H}}_{ij}$ to denote the estimated helpfulness rating from u_i to r_j. Before modeling contextual information, we first introduce our basic model based on probabilistic matrix factorization, and the helpfulness rating $\mathbf{H}_{ij}$ can be estimated as,

$$\mathbf{H}_{ij} \sim \mathcal{N}(\hat{\mathbf{H}}_{ij}, \sigma_H^2), \;\; \hat{\mathbf{H}}_{ij} = \mathbf{u}_i^\top \mathbf{v}_j. \quad (1)$$

where $\mathbf{u}_i \in \mathbb{R}^K$ and $\mathbf{v}_j \in \mathbb{R}^K$ are latent factors of u_i and r_j to capture the preference of u_i and the characteristics of r_j where K is the number of latent factors.

Modeling Content Context : Different from the item rating prediction problem, in the review helpfulness rating prediction problem, the texts of reviews provide content context about reviews. We introduce a latent factor β_j to exploit the review content of r_j as,

$$\beta_j \sim \mathcal{N}(\mathbf{g}^\top \mathbf{x}_j, \sigma_\beta^2),$$

where the latent factor β_j has a linear relation with the textual features from review content [14] with coefficients $\mathbf{g}$ and we use similar textual features to these in [15]. Following the common assumption on the loss or error function, we further assume Gaussian error between β_j and $\mathbf{g}^\top \mathbf{x}_j$ [1, 4].

Modeling Individual Context : Individual context contains author context and rater context. For the helpfulness rating of u_i to r_j from the author u_k, we introduce two latent factors ξ_k and α_i to capture author context and rater context, respectively. According to the observations from [15], author context is usually related to the characteristics of authors such as their reputations and statuses. Assume that there is an author feature vector $\mathbf{z}_k$ for u_k,. Similar to modeling review content, we consider a linear relation between author context ξ_k and the characteristics of the author $\mathbf{z}_k$ with Gaussian error, and then author context can be formulated as,

$$\xi_k \sim \mathcal{N}(\mathbf{b}^\top \mathbf{z}_k, \sigma_\xi^2).$$

A similar strategy can be applied to rater context. Assume that for the rater u_i, there is a rater feature vector $\mathbf{y}_i$, and then rater context is formally defined as,

$$\alpha_i \sim \mathcal{N}(\mathbf{d}^\top \mathbf{y}_i, \sigma_\alpha^2).$$

Modeling Relation Context : Relation context includes connection context and preference context. Different from individual context, relation context only exists when raters and authors have connections or preference relations. Therefore for the helpfulness rating of u_i to r_j from the author u_k, we define two indicator functions: (1) δ_1 is defined for preference context where $\delta_1(i,k) = 1$ if u_i is the preference similar user of u_k ($\mathbf{P}_{ik} = 1$) and zero otherwise; (2) δ_2 is defined for connection context where $\delta_2(i,k) = 1$ if u_i trusts u_k ($\mathbf{T}_{ik} = 1$) and zero otherwise. To model connection context and preference context, we introduce two latent factors λ_i^k and γ_i^k to model them, respectively. Based on **Observation 2**, connection context is related to the connection strengths between raters and authors. Therefore for the pair of users $\langle u_i, u_k \rangle$, we define a connection strength feature vector $\mathbf{q}_i^k$, and then the latent factor λ_i^k for connection context is formulated as,

$$\lambda_i^k \sim \mathcal{N}(f(\mathbf{h}^\top \mathbf{q}_i^k), \sigma_\lambda^2).$$

where we use an active function f on $\mathbf{h}^\top \mathbf{q}_i^k$ to ensure that the effect from connection context is positive according to **Observation 1** and we find that a sigmoid function works well in this paper. Similarly, based on **Observation 3** and **Observation 4**, the latent factor γ_i^k is formally defined as,

$$\gamma_i^k \sim \mathcal{N}(f(\mathbf{r}^\top \mathbf{p}_i^k), \sigma_\gamma^2).$$

where $\mathbf{p}_i^k$ is a preference similar feature vector for the pair of users $\langle u_i, u_k \rangle$.

We use similar author feature vector $\mathbf{z}_k$ as in [15], and the definitions of the rater features for $\mathbf{y}_i$, the preference similar features for $\mathbf{p}_i^k$ and the connection strength features for $\mathbf{q}_i^k$ can be found in **Appendix**. Exploiting content context and various types of social context, our context-aware helpfulness rating prediction framework CAP will estimate the helpfulness rating $\mathbf{H}_{ij}$ as

$$\mathbf{H}_{ij} \sim \mathcal{N}(\hat{\mathbf{H}}_{ij}, \sigma_H^2),$$
$$\hat{\mathbf{H}}_{ij} = \mathbf{u}_i^\top \mathbf{v}_j + \beta_j + \alpha_i + \xi_k + \delta_1(i,k)\gamma_i^k + \delta_2(i,k)\lambda_i^k$$
$$\beta_j \sim \mathcal{N}(\mathbf{g}^\top \mathbf{x}_j, \sigma_\beta^2),\ \alpha_i \sim \mathcal{N}(\mathbf{d}^\top \mathbf{y}_i, \sigma_\alpha^2),\ \xi_k \sim \mathcal{N}(\mathbf{b}^\top \mathbf{z}_k, \sigma_\xi^2)$$
$$\gamma_i^k \sim \mathcal{N}(f(\mathbf{r}^\top \mathbf{p}_i^k), \sigma_\gamma^2),\ \lambda_i^k \sim \mathcal{N}(f(\mathbf{h}^\top \mathbf{q}_i^k), \sigma_\lambda^2)$$
$$\mathbf{u}_i \sim \mathcal{MVN}(\mathbf{W}\mathbf{y}_i, \mathbf{A}_u),\ \ \mathbf{v}_j \sim \mathcal{MVN}(\mathbf{V}\mathbf{x}_j, \mathbf{A}_v), \tag{2}$$

where we also relate the latent factors of $\mathbf{u}_i$ and $\mathbf{v}_j$ to observed features of u_i and r_j with coefficients $\mathbf{W}$ and $\mathbf{V}$ respectively, and $\mathcal{MVN}$ denotes multivariate normal distribution.

Predicting Helpfulness Rating: After learning the latent factors Ω and prior parameters Θ from known ratings $\mathcal{O}$, an unknown rating of $u_{i'}$ to $r_{j'}$ from $u_{k'}$ can be predicted as,

$$\hat{\mathbf{H}}_{i',j'} = \mathbf{u}_{i'}^\top \mathbf{v}_{j'} + \beta_{j'} + \alpha_{i'} + \xi_{k'} + \delta_1(i',k')\gamma_{i'}^{k'} + \delta_2(i',a_{k'})\lambda_{i'}^{k'},$$

product review sites are highly dynamic systems where new users and new reviews are continuously added [23]. For new users and reviews, we do not have any historical helpfulness ratings (cold-start problem) and we cannot get their latent factors directly. However, the parameters Θ are independent of any specific users or reviews, and their latent factors can be estimated via Θ with their observed features as,

$$\alpha_{i'} = \mathbf{d}^\top \mathbf{y}_{i'},\ \ \beta_{j'} = \mathbf{g}^\top \mathbf{x}_{j'},\ \ \xi_{k'} = \mathbf{b}^\top \mathbf{z}_{k'},\ \ \gamma_{i'}^{j'} = f(\mathbf{r}^\top \mathbf{p}_{i'}^{k'})$$
$$\lambda_{i'}^{k'} = f(\mathbf{V}^\top \mathbf{q}_{i'}^{k'}),\ \ \mathbf{u}_{i'} = \mathbf{W}\mathbf{y}_{i'},\ \ \mathbf{v}_{j'} = \mathbf{V}\mathbf{x}_{j'}.$$

The proposed framework CAP has several nice properties. First, CAP allows us to incorporate the observed features of review content, authors, raters and their relations by modeling the effects of content context and various types of social context information on the helpfulness rating prediction problem. Usually the more we observe the data, a better model we can learn from the data [1, 4]. Second, the parameters Θ in CAP are independent of any specific users or reviews and can be applied to new users or new reviews. Therefore, it provides a unique framework to address both cold and warm start problems in the review helpfulness rating prediction problem. In reality, this property is very important as online review systems are highly dynamic with new users and reviews consistently added.

4.2 Learning Parameters

In this paper, we adopt Monte Carlo EM algorithm [3] to learn latent factors and prior parameters for CAP from the data automatically. The Monte Carlo EM algorithm maximizes the marginal log-likelihood by iterating through expectation (E) and maximization (M) steps until convergence. Let $\hat{\Theta}^t$ denote the t-th estimate of the set of prior parameters Θ at the t-th iteration.

E-step: We take the expectation of the complete data log likelihood with respect to the posterior of latent factors Ω conditional on the observation data $\mathcal{O}$ as,

$$g_t(\Theta) = E_{\Omega \sim P(\Omega|\mathcal{O},\hat{\Theta}^t)}[L(\Omega, \Theta)], \tag{3}$$

where $L(\Omega, \Theta)$ is the data log-likelihood and the expectation is taken over the posterior distribution $P(\Omega|\mathcal{O}, \hat{\Theta}^t)$. The E-step in our model is not in close form due to the multiplicative terms $\mathbf{u}_i^\top \mathbf{v}_j$, thus approximated by Monte Carlo mean. We use a Gibbs sampler to draw ℓ samples of the latent factors and compute the Monte Carlo means and variances of latent factors.

Computing Monte Carlo mean and variance of α_i: Now considering that all the other factors are given, we use *Rest* to denote all other factors except α_i. Assume that $L(\alpha_i)$ is the function including terms involving α_i in $L(\Omega, \Theta)$. Let $L'(\alpha_i)$ and $L''(\alpha_i)$ denote the first-order and second-order derivatives of $L(\alpha_i)$, respectively. Suppose that $\hat{\alpha}_i$ is the minimizer of $L(\alpha_i)$ satisfying the equation $L'(\alpha_i) = 0$. Then approximations of the mean and variance of α_i are $\hat{\alpha}_i$ and $L''(\alpha_i)(\hat{\alpha}_i)^{-1}$, respectively [3]. We first take the derivation of $L(\Omega, \Theta)$ w.r.t. α_i as,

$$\frac{\partial L}{\partial \alpha_i} = (\sum_{j \in I(i)} \frac{a_{ij}}{\sigma_H^2} + \frac{\mathbf{d}^\top \mathbf{y}_i}{\sigma_\alpha^2}) - (\sum_{j \in I(i)} \frac{1}{\sigma_H^2} + \frac{1}{\sigma_\alpha^2})\alpha_i,$$

where $a_{ij} = \mathbf{H}_{ij} - \beta_j - \delta_1(i,k)\gamma_i^k - \delta_2(i,k)\lambda_i^k - \mathbf{u}_i^\top \mathbf{v}_j - \xi_k$ and $I(i)$ is the set of helpfulness ratings from u_i. Then given *Rest*, the Monte Carlo mean and variance of α_i are,

$$V[\alpha_i|Rest] = (\sum_{j \in I(i)} \frac{1}{\sigma_H^2} + \frac{1}{\sigma_\alpha^2})^{-1}$$
$$E[\alpha_i|Rest] = V[\alpha_i|Rest](\sum_{j \in I(i)} \frac{a_{ij}}{\sigma_H^2} + \frac{\mathbf{d}^\top \mathbf{y}_i}{\sigma_\alpha^2}). \tag{4}$$

Similar to α_i, we can compute the Monte Carlo means and variances of β_j, ξ_k, $\mathbf{u}_i$, $\mathbf{v}_j$, γ_i^k and λ_i^k and we ignore the details to save space.

M-step: We maximize the expected complete log likelihood from the E-step to update Θ as,

$$\hat{\Theta}^{t+1} = \arg\max_{\Theta} g_t(\Theta). \tag{5}$$

where we consider $\mathbf{A}_u = \sigma_u^2 \mathbf{I}$ and $\mathbf{A}_v = \sigma_v^2 \mathbf{I}$.

Estimating (σ_α^2, $\mathbf{d}$): Setting zeros to the derivations of $E_{\Omega \sim P(\Omega|\mathcal{O},\hat{\Theta}^t)}[L(\Omega, \Theta)]$ with respective to σ_α^2 and $\mathbf{d}$, we obtain,

$$\sigma_\alpha^2 = \frac{\sum_i (E[\alpha_i] - \mathbf{d}^\top \mathbf{y}_i)^2 + V[\alpha_i]}{n},$$
$$\mathbf{d} = (\eta \mathbf{I} + \mathbf{Y}^\top \mathbf{Y})^{-1} \mathbf{Y} \mathbf{a}^\top,\ \ where$$
$$\mathbf{Y} = [\mathbf{y}_1, \ldots, \mathbf{y}_n], \mathbf{a} = [E[\alpha_1], \ldots, E[\alpha_n]].$$

where $E[\alpha_i]$ and $V[\alpha_i]$ are the Monte Carlo mean and variance of α_i obtained in the E-step, respectively.

Similarly, we can obtain other prior parameters $\{\sigma_H^2, \sigma_u^2, \sigma_\beta^2, \sigma_v^2, \sigma_\gamma^2, \sigma_\lambda^2, \mathbf{W}, \mathbf{p}, \mathbf{V}\}$. For $\mathbf{r}$ and $\mathbf{h}$, we use the Newton-Raphson method to update them as,

$$\mathbf{r}^{t+1} = \mathbf{r}^t - \frac{\partial E}{\partial \mathbf{r}} / \frac{\partial^2 E}{\partial \mathbf{r} \partial \mathbf{r}^\top}$$
$$\mathbf{h}^{t+1} = \mathbf{h}^t - \frac{\partial E}{\partial \mathbf{h}} / \frac{\partial^2 E}{\partial \mathbf{h} \partial \mathbf{h}^\top}, \tag{6}$$

where $\frac{\partial E}{\partial \mathbf{r}}$ and $\frac{\partial^2 E}{\partial \mathbf{r} \partial \mathbf{r}^\top}$ are the first-order and second-order partial derivations of $E_{\Omega \sim P(\Omega|\mathcal{O},\hat{\Theta}^t)}[L(\Omega, \Theta)]$ in terms of $\mathbf{r}$, respectively.

5. EXPERIMENTS

In this section, we conduct experiments to answer the following questions (1) Does context awareness help to improve the performance of helpfulness rating prediction as expected? (2) If it does, is it necessary to exploit every type of contextual information? To answer the first question, we compare our proposed framework CAP with representative baseline methods. To answer the second question, we investigate the effects of content context and various types of social context on CAP.

5.1 Experimental Setting

We first rank all helpfulness ratings according to the time points when they are published in chronological order, and then equally split the whole data set into two parts - 50% of them as the training set and 50% of them as the testing set. For the testing set, we further divide it into two parts: (1) *cold-start* - including helpfulness ratings where the raters or authors are newly added users or the reviews are newly written reviews; and (2) *warm-start* - containing ratings where the raters and the reviews exist in the training set. We examine the data and find that *cold-start* includes 44.72% of the testing set. A large proportion of review helpfulness ratings are cold-start ratings, further demonstrating the significance of finding a unique framework for the problem of review helpfulness rating prediction with both cold-start and warm-start settings. A common metric Root Mean Squared Error is used to evaluate performance.

5.2 Comparison of Different Predictors

We compare the proposed framework CAP to various baseline methods, which can be grouped into three categories.

Methods in the first category are totally based on simple statistics from the training set and they are: **ST:Mean** - predicting the helpfulness of a review as the mean of the helpfulness ratings in the training set; **ST:Review** - predicting the helpfulness of a review as the average helpfulness rating the review received in the training set; **ST:Author** - predicting the helpfulness of a review from an author as the average helpfulness rating of the reviews from the author in the training set and **ST:Rater** - predicting the helpfulness rating from a specific rater as the average rating given by the rater in the training set.

The second category covers the state-of-the-art predictors in the item rating prediction problem and they are: **IRP:MF** - performing a low-rank matrix factorization on helpfulness rating matrix **H** [10, 26]; **IRP:Neighbor** - predicting the helpfulness rating of a review from a rater as the average weighted rating of the review from the rater's trust network or similar users; and **IRP:MF+Neighbor** - this predictor exploits both rating and social information [17]. Note that we do not compare our framework CAP with methods based on tensor factorization [8, 18]: (1) the focus of this paper is to investigate whether exploiting context-aware information can improve the prediction performance and we can choose tensor factorization based methods instead of matrix factorization based methods as our basic models; and (2) the high time and space complexities of tensor factorization limit their applications to large-scale data sets. We also do not compare CAP with feature-based factorization methods [25] in this subsection since they are special cases of CAP, which is discussed in later subsection.

The methods in the third category are review quality predictors and they are: **RQP:Text** - performing linear regression on textual features from the review content; **RQP:Author** - performing linear regression on author features, referred as the social features of reviews in [15]; and **RQP:Text+Author** - performing linear regression on the features with both textual features and author features. *The predictors in this category will compute a global helpfulness score for a review over all users, while ignore the user idiosyncracy of review helpfulness.*

Table 2: Performance of Different Predictors in terms of RMSE.

Algorithms	*warm-start*	*cold-start*
ST:Mean	0.5227	0.7371
ST:Review	0.4835	0.7158
ST:Author	0.4653	0.7009
ST:Rater	0.4969	0.7144
IRP:MF	0.3616	N.A.
IRP:Neighbor	0.4102	0.5737
IRP:MF+Neighbor	0.3270	0.5737
RQP:Text	0.3758	0.5519
RQP:Author	0.5441	0.6922
RQP:Text+Author	0.3584	0.5004
CAP	0.2342	0.3165

The parameters in baseline methods are pruned via cross validation and the comparison results are shown in Table 2. We have the following observations from the *warm-start* data set,

- Baseline methods based on simple statistics perform well and sometimes their performance is even better than **THP:Author**. As reported in Section 2, more than 80% of helpfulness ratings are 3 or 4; therefore, the majority of helpfulness is close to the average helpfulness. **ST:Rater** obtains better performance than **ST:Mean**, suggesting that different raters may think of the helpfulness of the same review differently. The quality of reviews from the same author is likely to be consistent [15] and **ST:Author** obtains the best performance in this category.

- A combination of **IRP:MF** and **IRP:Neighbor** obtains the best performance in that category, indicating that users' historical helpfulness ratings and ratings from their neighborhood are complementary to each other.

- **RQP:Text+Author** performs the best among review quality predictors, suggesting the importance of the effect from author context. However only considering the effect from author context is not enough to be a good predictor and sometimes the performance is even worse than those based on simple statistics.

- CAP always outperforms all baseline methods. Compared to the best performance of baseline methods, CAP obtains 28.38% relative improvement in terms of RMSE. There are two major reasons: (1) CAP incorporates observed features of review content, raters, authors and their relations; and (2) CAP considers the effects of content context and various types of social context. We will investigate the contributors to the improvement in the next subsection.

In *cold-start*, we have similar observations. However, content context plays a more important role in the cold-start problem. The methods considering the review content always outperform those ignoring it. CAP also obtains the best performance, indicating the ability of the proposed framework CAP to solve the cold-start problem.

With these observations, we can draw an answer to the first question - Exploiting context awareness, our proposed framework gains significant performance improvement in the problem of review helpfulness rating prediction with both warm-start and cold-start settings.

5.3 Impact of Different Components

Empirical study shows that CAP significantly helps improve the helpfulness rating prediction performance by exploiting context awareness. In this subsection, we investigate the effect of content context and various types of social context on CAP. Except the basic model from the item rating prediction problem ($\mathbf{u}_i^\top \mathbf{v}_j$), our proposed framework CAP exploits content context (β_j) and four types of social context (α_i, ξ_k, γ_i^k and λ_i^k). To answer the second question, we eliminate the effects of content context and four types of social context systematically from the proposed framework CAP by defining the following variants of CAP: (1) *CAP\Author* - eliminating the effect of author context from CAP; (2) *CAP\Rater* - eliminating the effect of rater context from CAP; (3) *CAP\Connection* - eliminating the effect of connection context from CAP; (4) *CAP\Preference* - eliminating the effect of preference context from CAP; (5) *CAP\ARCP* - eliminating the effects of four types of social context from CAP; (6) *CAP\Text* - eliminating the effect of content context of reviews from CAP; and (7) *CAP\Text\ARCP* - eliminating the effects from content context and four types of context information from CAP. This variant is a feature-based matrix factorization method [25].

The results are demonstrated in Figures 3(a) and 3(b) in *warm-start* and *cold-start*, respectively. When we eliminate each type of social context from CAP, the performance degrades. Compared to CAP, on average, the performance of *CAP\Author*, *CAP\Rater*, *CAP\Connection* and *CAP\Preference* relatively reduces 14.86% and 7.22% in terms of RMSE in *warm-start* and *cold-start* respectively, indicating that social context information can help improve the performance. When eliminating four types of social context simultaneously, the performance of *CAP\ARCP* is worse than that of variants which eliminate one type of social context, indicating that the four types of social context contain complementary information to each other. When we eliminate the effect of content context, the performance reduces more than 20% in both *warm-start* and *cold-start* data sets and the content of reviews plays an important role in the prediction process, especially for the cold-start problem. *CAP\Text\ARCP* performs worst, suggesting the importance of content context and various types of social context information for CAP. However, *CAP\Text\ARCP* obtains performance improvement over **IRP:MF**. Both of them consider the interactions between the latent factors of raters and reviews, while *CAP\Text\ARCP* also incorporates observed features of raters and reviews, suggesting that observed features are very important and can help improve prediction performance. Besides the performance improvement, another advantage of *CAP\Text\ARCP* over **IRP:MF** is that it enables to solve the cold-start problem in the review helpfulness rating prediction problem.

With these observations, we can answer the second question that the contributors to the performance improvement in CAP include: (1) considering content context, (2) exploiting various types of social context, and (3) incorporating observed features of raters and reviews.

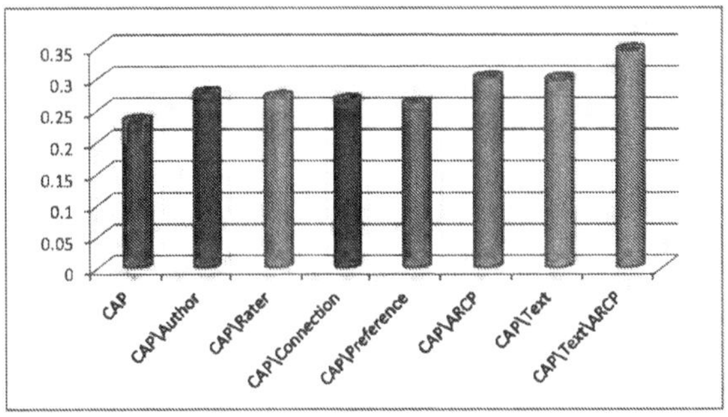

(a) *warm-start*

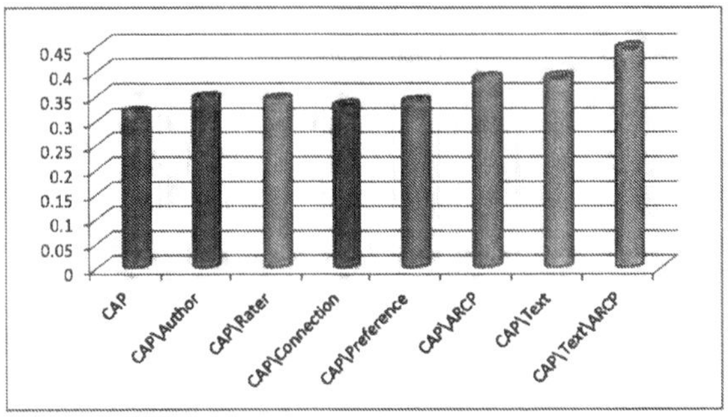

(b) *cold-start*

Figure 3: The Performance of Variants of Our Framework in terms of RMSE.

6. RELATED WORK

6.1 Review Quality Prediction

Helpful reviews are usually buried among large amounts of useless reviews and automatically assessing the quality of a review attracts increasing attention in recent years. Most previous work considers the quality prediction problem as a classification or regression problem [24, 9, 13, 14, 19, 15, 12]. [24, 9, 13, 14] utilize textual features such as the length of the review, percentages of nouns and adjectives, the subjectivity of the review and so on, while methods like [19, 15, 12] expand textual features with social features (the characteristic features of authors) such as the reputations of authors, the number of past reviews by the author, past average ratings etc. The results show that incorporating the characteristics of authors with textual features can significantly improve prediction performance [15, 12]. There are also other studies indicating that the helpfulness of reviews is not necessarily strongly correlated with certain measures about the quality of reviews [13, 5].

6.2 Item Rating Prediction

Collaborative filter is one of the most popular techniques for item rating prediction, roughly categorized into neighborhood approaches and latent factor models [10, 21]. The neighborhood-based approaches can be further divided into user-oriented methods [6] and item-oriented methods [20]. User-oriented methods infer an unknown rating from a user to an item as the weighted average of all the ratings from his correlated users to the item, while item-oriented approaches product the rating from a user to an item based on the average ratings of similar or correlated items by the same user.

Latent factor models consider the interactions between latent features of users and items by projecting them to the same latent factor space. Matrix factorization methods are very competitive methods in this category [10, 7, 17]. They assume that a few latent patterns influence user rating behaviors and perform a low-rank matrix factorization on the user-item rating matrix. Recently, high-dimensional tensor factorization based methods were proposed to allow adding additional dimensions to the user-item matrix [8, 18]. However, the limitations of the high-dimensional tensor factorization based methods are their high time and space complexities.

7. CONCLUSION

In this paper we study the problem of review helpfulness rating prediction by exploiting context awareness to infer unknown helpfulness ratings automatically. We extract four types of social context, i.e., author context, rater context, connection context and preference context, formulate them mathematically, and propose a context-aware helpfulness prediction framework CAP which exploits content context and various types of social context. Experimental results demonstrate that our proposed framework outperforms the state-of-the-art baseline methods with both cold-start and warm-start settings, and further experiments are conducted to understand the importance of context awareness in the proposed framework.

There are several directions needing further investigation. First, we will study how to model context awareness in the tensor factorization based models. Second, user preferences are likely to change over time and it is interesting to exploit temporal effects in CAP. Finally, users may need helpful reviews associating with the recommended items to help them make decisions. Recommending items and the helpful reviews simultaneously will be a promising direction.

Acknowledgments

We thank the useful comments from Atish Das Sarma and anonymous reviewers. This work is, in part, supported by ARO (#025071) and NSF (#IIS-1217466).

8. REFERENCES

[1] D. Agarwal and B. Chen. Regression-based latent factor models. *KDD*, 2009.

[2] C. Yeung and T. Iwata. Strength of social influence in trust networks in product review sites. WSDM, 2011.

[3] J. Booth and J. Hobert. Maximizing generalized linear mixed model likelihoods with an automated monte carlo em algorithm. *JRSS*, 1999.

[4] B. Chen, J. Guo, B. Tseng, and J. Yang. User reput ation in a comment rating environment. *KDD*, 2011.

[5] C. Danescu-Niculescu-Mizil, G. Kossinets, J. Kleinberg, and L. Lee. How opinions are received by online communities: a case study on amazon com helpfulness votes. WWW, 2009.

[6] J. Herlocker, J. Konstan, A. Borchers, and J. Riedl. An algorithmic framework for performing collaborative filtering. *SIGIR*, 1999.

[7] M. Jamali and M. Ester. A matrix factorization technique with trust propagation for recommendation in social networks. *RecSys*, 2010.

[8] A. Karatzoglou, X. Amatriain, L. Baltrunas, and N. Oliver. Multiverse recommendation: n-dimensional tensor factorization for context-aware collaborative filtering. *RecSys*, 2010.

[9] S. Kim, P. Pantel, T. Chklovski, and M. Pennacchiotti. Automatically assessing review helpfulness. *EMNLP*, 2006.

[10] Y. Koren. Factorization meets the neighborhood: a multifaceted collaborative filtering model. *KDD*, 2008.

[11] Y. Koren. Collaborative filtering with temporal dynamics. *Communications of the ACM*, 2010.

[12] E. Lim, V. Nguyen, N. Jindal, B. Liu, and H. Lauw. Detecting product review spammers using rating behaviors. *CIKM*, 2010.

[13] J. Liu, Y. Cao, C. Lin, Y. Huang, and M. Zhou. Low-quality product review detection in opinion summarization. *EMNLP-CoNLL*,2007.

[14] Y.Liu, X.Huang, A.An, and X.Yu. Modeling and pred icting the helpfulness of online reviews. *ICDM*, 2008.

[15] Y. Lu, P. Tsaparas, A. Ntoulas, and L. Polanyi. Exploiting social context for review quality prediction. *WWW*, 2010.

[16] H. Ma, I. King, and M. Lyu. Learning to recommend with social trust ensemble. *SIGIR*, 2009.

[17] H.Ma, D.Zhou, C.Liu, M.Lyu, and I.King. Recommen der systems with social regularization. *WSDM*, 2011.

[18] S. Moghaddam, M. Jamali, and M. Ester. etf: extended tensor factorization model for personalizing prediction of review helpfulness. *WSDM*, 2012.

[19] M. O'Mahony and B. Smyth. Learning to recommend helpful hotel reviews. *RecSys*, 2009.

[20] B. Sarwar, G. Karypis, J. Konstan, and J. Riedl. Item-based collaborative filtering recommendation algorithms. *WWW*, 2001.

[21] X. Su and T. Khoshgoftaar. A survey of collaborative filtering techniques. *Advances in AI*, 2009.

[22] J. Tang, H. Gao, and H. Liu. mTrust: Discerning multi-faceted trust in a connected world. *WSDM*,2012.

[23] J.Tang, H.Gao, H.Liu, A. Sarma. eTrust: Understa nding trust evolution in an online world. *KDD*, 2012.

[24] Z. Zhang and B. Varadarajan. Utility scoring of product reviews. *CIKM*, 2006.

[25] K. Zhou, S. Yang, and H. Zha. Functional matrix factorizations for cold-start recommendation. *SIGIR*,2011.

[26] M. Andriy, and S. Ruslan. Probabilistic matrix factorization. *NIPS*,2011.

APPENDIX

Rater Features : # of trustors, # of trustees, pagerank score, average item rating, average item rating from the social network, average item rating from similar users, average helpfulness rating, average helpfulness rating from the trust network, average helpfulness rating from similar users

Preference Similar Features : # of commonly rated items, Jaccard's coefficient on rated items, Cosine similarity of item ratings, Pearson similarity of item ratings, difference of average item rating scores, difference of maximal item rating scores, difference of minimal item rating scores

Connection Strength Features : Jaccard's coefficient on common out-degrees, Jaccard's coefficient on common in-degrees, Adamic/Adar score on common out-degrees, Adamic /Adar score on in-degrees, Katz score.

Query-Driven Context Aware Recommendation

Negar Hariri
DePaul University
College of Computing and Digital Media
Chicago, IL 60604, USA
nhariri@cs.depaul.edu

Bamshad Mobasher
DePaul University
College of Computing and Digital Media
Chicago, IL 60604, USA
mobasher@cs.depaul.edu

Robin Burke
DePaul University
College of Computing and Digital Media
Chicago, IL 60604, USA
rburke@cs.depaul.edu

ABSTRACT

Context aware recommender systems go beyond the traditional personalized recommendation models by incorporating a form of situational awareness. They provide recommendations that not only correspond to a user's preference profile, but that are also tailored to a given situation or context. We consider the setting in which contextual information is represented as a subset of an item feature space describing short-term interests or needs of a user in a given situation. This contextual information can be provided by the user in the form of an explicit query, or derived implicitly.

We propose a unified probabilistic model that integrates user profiles, item representations, and contextual information. The resulting recommendation framework computes the conditional probability of each item given the user profile and the additional context. These probabilities are used as recommendation scores for ranking items. Our model is an extension of the Latent Dirichlet Allocation (LDA) model that provides the capability for joint modeling of users, items, and the meta-data associated with contexts. Each user profile is modeled as a mixture of the latent topics. The discovered latent topics enable our system to handle missing data in item features. We demonstrate the application of our framework for article and music recommendation. In the latter case, the set of popular tags from social tagging Web sites are used for context descriptions. Our evaluation results show that considering context can help improve the quality of recommendations.

Keywords

Context-aware recommendation, Collaborative filtering, Graphical models, Latent Dirichlet Allocation

Categories and Subject Descriptors

H.3.3 [**Information Search and Retrieval**]: Information filtering

RecSys'13, October 12–16, 2013, Hong Kong, China.

ACM 978-1-4503-2409-0/13/10 ...$15.00.
http://dx.doi.org/10.1145/2507157.2507187 .

1. INTRODUCTION

Despite the their wide-spread use in many domains, recommender systems still tend to use models that fail to consider the context in which users are interacting with the system. This omission may result in recommendations that, while consistent with general interests of a user, may be inappropriate for the user's current situation or environment. To address this issue, the notion of context-aware recommender systems (CARS) has been introduced.

Although there is no universal agreement on the precise definition of context, one of the most commonly used definitions, proposed by Abowd et al. [1], defines context as: "any information that can be used to characterize the situation of an entity," and by entity they mean "a person, place, or object that is considered relevant to the interaction between a user and an application, including the user and applications themselves".

A context-aware recommender system uses the available contextual information in addition to the users' profiles in order to generate recommendations best suited to their current situations. Many variations of context-aware recommender systems have been proposed and studied, including those that rely on an explicit representation of contextual factors [3], as well as those that use behavioral cues from users to derive contextual states [5, 13]. A variety of architectural frameworks and ontological categorizations of context aware recommender systems have been considered [2].

Context aware recommender systems may obtain contextual information relevant to a situation or a task in a variety of ways. In this paper, we consider a typical setting in which contextual information is not pre-specified, but rather is obtained in the course of a user's interaction with the system. This information can be *explicitly* acquired by directly asking users or by eliciting it *implicitly* through other means at particular episodes during the interaction. For example, the user of a music recommender system can specify his/her current interest in a specific genre of music by providing that information in the form of a query. Considering both the queried context and the previously established user profile, the system may then recommend songs that best match the user's short-term situational needs as well as the his or her long-term interests. On the other hand, to recommend restaurants to a user, a context-aware restaurant recommender may implicitly consider variables such as time of the day or the location of the user in addition to the user's history of preferences.

We propose a unified probabilistic model that integrates user profiles, item descriptions, and contextual information.

We assume that contextual information can be represented using the same feature space underlying the representation of items. Our model is an extension of the Latent Dirichlet Allocation (LDA) where each user profile is modeled as a mixture of the latent topics. These topics capture the feature associations as well as the item co-occurrence relations in user profiles. Our contextual modeling recommendation framework enables us to systematically optimize the recommendations for the given context. Given a user's profile p, and context q, our model computes the recommendation score for each item i as $p(i|p,q)$ and ranks items based on these scores. We focus on the special case where item features are available (but may not necessarily be complete) and the given context may contain any arbitrary features from the space of items features. Also, we assume that the only data available for each user is the set of items in which he/she has previously expressed interest.

We investigate the application of this model in both music and document recommendation. For document recommendation, we use words in the documents as features. For music recommendation, popular tags are retrieved from social Web sites for all the songs and are used as songs features. For illustration, let us consider an example from the music recommendation domain. Table 1 shows typical user profile (in this case a playing session) consisting of the set of songs that the user likes. A sample of popular tags for each song is also presented. Although users assign different and sometimes contradictory tags to a given song, popular tags are less prone to noise and are descriptive of different characteristics of songs such as genre, mood, theme, era, etc. Set of features common between these songs includes *rock*, *happy*, *2000s*. If the user specifies *80s* as the context, ideal recommendations should match the user's previous interests (*happy* and *rock music*) as well as the queried context (80s music).

The high dimensionality of this feature space can be a problem for many of the popular context-aware recommendation methods such as item-splitting [7], or user-splitting [21]. For the music recommendation example, if context is expressed in terms of a multitude of factors such as genre category, the era, mood, theme, and others, "splitting" approaches can cause sparsity problems as these features may not be available for all the songs. As a result, songs with incomplete feature representations would have low chance of being recommended. More generally, sparsity can be a problem if context vocabulary is large. This situation is especially common when the contextual variables are represented using subsets of item features. One of the advantages of our approach is that the associations between features are captured by the latent factors, and therefore, are integral part of the trained model. As a result, our recommendation approach has a better chance of overcoming the sparsity problem.

2. CONTEXT-AWARE RECOMMENDATION FRAMEWORK

We propose a latent factor probabilistic model which integrates users, items and the context in a single framework. In this paper, we focus on a special setting where context can be represented by a subset of the features associated with items. However, our model can potentially be used for the cases where contextual variables are not related to the items features. For a given user p and a context q, our model computes the recommendation score for each item i as $p(i|p,q)$ and ranks items based on these scores.

Our model is an extension of the *Latent Dirichlet Allocation* (LDA) model [8], which was originally proposed for modeling text documents. LDA is a generative probabilistic model of a corpus. It models each document as a mixture of latent *topics* where each topic is a distribution over the vocabulary. LDA has been used for various applications such as document modeling, document classification, and document retrieval [23]. Also, LDA and similar methods such as PLSA [14] can be applied for the task of item recommendation. Looking at user profiles as documents and items as words, the probability of each item for a given user can be computed and used for ranking the items. However, as items features (or the contextual variables) are not part of the model, it is not possible to compute the conditional item probability for a given user and a specific context. Therefore, our extension to the original LDA model is to include the items features in the model.

We model each user as a mixture of topics where topic probabilities for each user are inferred according to the set of items which she/he has previously liked and their features. The topics in our model capture the feature associations as well as the items co-occurrence relations in the users profiles.

We will first review the LDA model and then introduce our extension. Finally, we will present the context-aware recommendation algorithm that uses this extended model.

2.1 Latent Dirichlet Allocation

The plate diagram of the LDA model for modeling documents is shown in Figure 1. In the standard form of graphical models, nodes indicates random variables. Shaded nodes are observed random variables and unshaded nodes are latent random variables. A plate is shown as a box around a random variable and indicates replication. The edges between the nodes represent dependency between the variables.

In Figure 1, the outer plate corresponds to the documents in the corpus and is replicated N times, where N is the number of documents. The inner plate corresponds to words in each document and is replicated as many as the number of words in the document (M times). The LDA model can be viewed in terms of a generative process for documents. The complete notation used in Figure 1 is as follows:

θ_i represents the topic distribution for document i
z_{ij} denotes the topic for the jth word in document i
ϕ_k represents the word distribution for topic k.
w_{ij} denotes the jth word in document i.

In this model, θ is a Dirichlet random variable with parameter α:

$$P(\theta|\alpha) = \frac{\Gamma\left(\sum_{i=1}^{k}\alpha_i\right)}{\prod_{i=1}^{k}\Gamma(\alpha_i)}\theta^{\alpha_1 - 1}\dots\theta_k^{\alpha_k - 1}$$
$$\text{and } \theta_i \geq 0, \sum_{i=1}^{k}\theta_i = 1 \quad (1)$$

Where α is a k-dimensional vector with elements $\alpha_i > 0$ and $\Gamma(x)$ is the gamma function.

Table 1: An example playlist

Artist	Song	A Sample of Popular Tags
Luce	Good day	rock, 2000s, happy, playful, feel good music, music from the oc
Ben Howard	Keep your head up	acoustic, British, folk, indie, singer-songwriter, 2000s, alternative rock
Nada Surf	Always love	Alternative, indie rock, 2000s, happy
Vega 4	Life is beautiful	Alternative, 2000s, indie rock, Greyś anatomy, happy
Imagine Dragons	On top of the world	Alternative, indie rock, 10s, happy, cheerful chill easy listening
State Radio	Right me up	reggae-rock, chill, indie, happiness, fun, mellow, summer

The variable ϕ is a $K \cdot V$ random matrix where K is the number of topics and V is the vocabulary size. Each row of this matrix is independently drawn from an exchangeable Dirichlet distribution with parameter β and denotes the word distribution of a topic.

The document generation is based on the idea that each document is a mixture of topics, where a topic is a probability distribution over words.

To generate a new document d, first the distribution over topics shown as $\theta_{(d)}$ should be specified. For each word in the document a topic z is selected based on $\theta_{(d)}$. According to ϕ_z a word is picked and is added to the document.

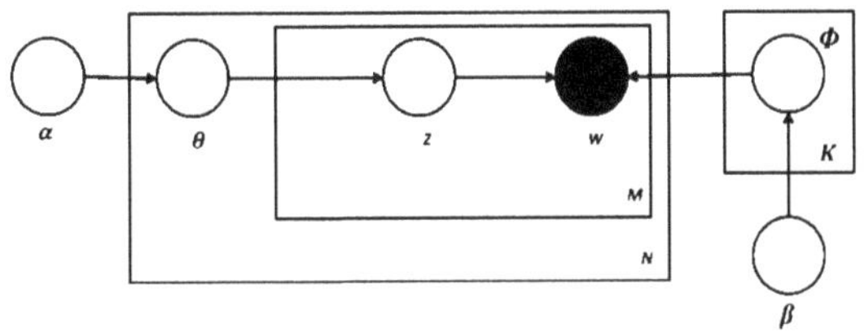

Figure 1: Graphical representation of the LDA model

Given the LDA model with K topics, the probability of a word w given a document d can be computed as in Equation 2. In this formula, $p(\theta|d)$ represents the inferred probability of θ given the observed words in the document d. The computed $p(w|d)$ can be used for ranking documents given the query w. Also, if documents corresponds to user profiles and words represent the items, this probability can be to rank items for recommendation.

$$p(w|d) = \sum_{z=1}^{K} \left(p(w|z) \cdot \int_{\theta} p(z|\theta)p(\theta|d)d\theta \right) \tag{2}$$

2.2 Context-aware Recommendation Model

The graphical representation of our model, which we call the context-aware recommendation model, is shown in Figure 2. The outermost plate corresponds to users which is replicated N times where N is the number of users. The inner plate, which is replicated M times, correspond to M items that the user likes. The innermost plate, which is replicated W times, indicates the W features of the item.

Each user is modeled as a multinomial distribution over a set of topics where each topic has a distribution over the set of items and features. The random variables in this model are as follows:

θ_i represents the topic distribution for user i
z_{ij} denotes the topic for the jth item in i^{th} user profile.
s_{ij} denotes the jth item in the profile of user i.
t_{ijk} denotes the kth feature for the jth item in the ith user profile.
μ_k represents the item distribution for topic k.
ϕ_k represents the feature distribution for topic k.

Similar to LDA, we assume that θ is a k-dimensional Dirichlet random variable with parameter α, where k is the number of topics.

The variable μ is a $K \cdot U$ random matrix where K is the number of topics and U is the number of unique items. Each row of this matrix is independently drawn from an exchangeable Dirichlet distribution with parameter β and denotes the item distribution for a topic. Similarly, the variable ϕ is a $K \cdot X$ random matrix where X is the size of the feature space. Each row of this matrix is independently drawn from an exchangeable Dirichlet distribution with parameter γ and denotes the feature distribution for a topic.

An item s with W features is assumed to be generated by first choosing a value for z and then sampling the item according to μ_z, and also sampling W features according to ϕ_z. Therefore, it is assumed that each item and its features are generated from the same topic.

More formally, the process for generating a user's profile is as follows:

1. Choose $\theta_p \sim Dir(\alpha)$.
2. Choose $\phi_k \sim Dir(\gamma)$, for each topic k
3. Choose $\mu_k \sim Dir(\beta)$, for each topic k
4. For each of the M items, s_i, in the user's profile:
   (a) Choose $z_i \sim Multinomial(\theta_p)$
   (b) Choose $s_i \sim Multinomial(\mu_{z_i})$
   (c) For each of the W features, t_j, associated with s_i
      i. Choose $t_j \sim Multinomial(\phi_{z_i})$

Given μ and ϕ, the joint distribution of topic mixtures θ, topics Z, features T, and items S is computed as follows:

$$p(S, T, Z, \theta|\mu, \phi) = \tag{3}$$
$$\prod_{p=1}^{N} p(\theta_p|\alpha) \prod_{i=1}^{M} \left(p(z_i|\theta_p) p(s_i|z_i, \mu) \cdot \prod_{j=1}^{W} p(t_j|z_i, \phi) \right)$$

Intuitively, for each user profile, θ_p represents the user's taste, reflected in previous items that the user has liked and their associated features.

As the exact inference is not possible for learning the parameters of our model, we use variational message passing for approximate inference. In our implementation we

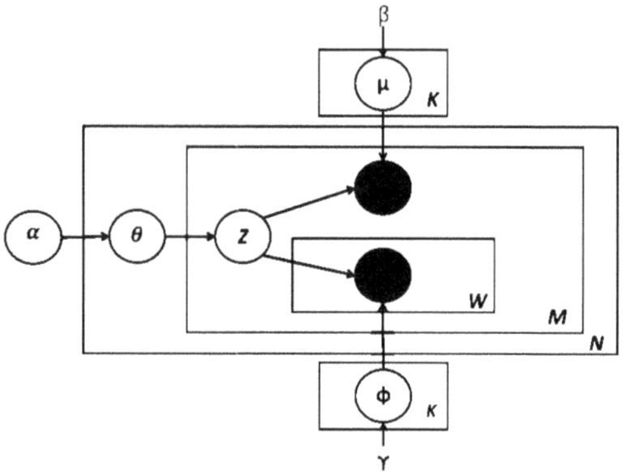

Figure 2: Graphical representation of the context-aware recommendation model

used Infer.Net [20] which provides a framework for running Bayesian inference in graphical models and contains various inference algorithms.

2.3 The Contextual Recommendation Algorithm

This section describes application of our model for context-aware recommendation. Consider a user's profile p with n items. Let $q = \{t_1, t_2, ..., t_w\}$ represent the given context consisting of w features t_i. The goal of the context-aware recommendation algorithm is to provide personalized recommendations for the given context.

Given our model, for an item s, context q and user p, $p(s|q,p)$ is computed and is used as a ranking score. According to Bayes rule:

$$p(s|q,p) \propto p(q|s,p)p(s|p) \tag{4}$$

After we get the posterior estimates of θ, μ, and ϕ, shown as $\hat{\theta}$, $\hat{\mu}$, and $\hat{\phi}$, we have:

$$p\left(s|q,p,\hat{\theta},\hat{\mu},\hat{\phi}\right) \propto p\left(q|s,p,\hat{\theta},\hat{\mu},\hat{\phi}\right) p\left(s|p,\hat{\theta},\hat{\mu}\right) \tag{5}$$

Where, $p(s|p,\hat{\theta},\hat{\mu})$ is computed as follows:

$$p\left(s|p,\hat{\theta},\hat{\mu}\right) = \sum_{j=1}^{k} p\left(s|z_j\right) p\left(z_j|p\right) = \sum_{j=1}^{k} \hat{\mu}_{s,j}\hat{\theta}_{j,p} \tag{6}$$

In equation 5, $p(q|s,p,\hat{\theta},\hat{\mu},\hat{\phi})$ can be compnted as:

$$p\left(q|s,p,\hat{\theta},\hat{\mu},\hat{\phi}\right) = \prod_{t_i \in q} p\left(t_i|s,p,\hat{\theta},\hat{\mu},\hat{\phi}\right) \tag{7}$$

According to the graphical representation of our model shown in Figure 2:

$$\begin{aligned} p\left(t_i|s,p,\hat{\theta},\hat{\mu},\hat{\phi}\right) &= \sum_{j=1}^{k} p\left(t_i|z_j,\hat{\phi}\right) \cdot p\left(z_j|s,p,\hat{\theta},\hat{\mu}\right) \\ &= \sum_{j=1}^{k} \hat{\phi_{i,j}} \cdot p\left(z_j|s,p,\hat{\theta},\hat{\mu}\right) \end{aligned} \tag{8}$$

$$\begin{aligned} p\left(z_j|s,p,\hat{\theta},\hat{\mu}\right) &= \frac{p\left(z_j,s,p\right)}{p\left(s,p\right)} = \frac{p(s|z_j) \cdot p(z_j|p)}{\sum_{y=1}^{k} p(s|z_y) \cdot p(z_y|p)} \\ &= \frac{\hat{\mu_{s,j}} \cdot \hat{\theta_{j,p}}}{\sum_{y=1}^{k} \hat{\mu_{s,y}} \cdot \hat{\theta_{y,p}}} \end{aligned} \tag{9}$$

Using equations 6 and 7, equation 5 can be simplified as follows:

$$\begin{aligned} &p\left(s|q,p,\hat{\theta},\hat{\mu},\hat{\phi}\right) \\ &\propto \left(\sum_{j=1}^{k} \left(\hat{\mu_{s,j}}\hat{\theta_{j,p}}\right)\right) \cdot \prod_{t_i \in q} \sum_{j=1}^{k} \frac{\hat{\phi_{i,j}} \cdot \hat{\mu_{s,j}} \cdot \hat{\theta_{j,p}}}{\sum_{y=1}^{k} \hat{\mu_{s,y}} \cdot \hat{\theta_{y,p}}} \end{aligned} \tag{10}$$

As suggested in [24], and also confirmed in our evaluations, performance can be improved if the probabilities computed in equation 8 are further smoothed by linearly combining them with probabilities computed by the *Bayesian smoothing using Dirichlet priors* [25]; This model computes the probability of t_i given item s, shown as $p_{bd}(t_i|s)$, as follows:

$$p_{bd}(t_i|s) = \frac{c(t_i;s) + \delta p(t_i|c)}{\sum_{t \in s} c(t;s) + \delta} \tag{11}$$

Where δ is the smoothing parameter and $c(t_i;s)$ is the frequency of feature t_i in the description for item s and $p(t_i|c)$ indicates the probability of t_i in the whole collection of items descriptions.

For user p and item s, the probability of t_i computed by our model, shown as p_{cr}, is then linearly combined with p_{bd}:

$$p(t_i|s,p) = (1-\lambda)\frac{c(t_i;s) + \delta p(t_i|c)}{\sum_{t \in s} c(t;s) + \delta} + \lambda p_{cr}(t_i|s,p) \tag{12}$$

Note that while $p_{bd}(t_i|s)$ is conditioned only on the item, $p_{cr}(t_i|s,p)$ is conditioned on both the item and the current user.

The smoothing step can improve the results as topic models are too coarse to be used directly for recommendation and better performance can be achieved by combining them with methods that directly model documents without having latent factors.

3. EVALUATION OF THE RECOMMENDATIONS

3.1 Datasets

For our evaluations, we used two different datasets that we describe in this section.

Playlists.

This dataset has 28,963 user-contributed playlists from *Art of the Mix* website[1] in January 2003. It consists of 218,261 distinct songs for 48,169 unique artists. The average number of songs per playlist is 19.8 and the average number of artists in playlists is 17.1. Top tags (with frequency of at least 4) were retrieved from the last.fm Website for about 73,045 songs in our database. For the rest of the songs either a match was not found or there were no popular tags available for that song. For our evaluations,

[1] http://www.artofthemix.org/

about 8,769 playlists, each containing more than 10 songs that have tags, were selected. The selected playlists contain 86,262 unique songs.

CiteULike.

Another dataset which we used in our evaluations is the CiteULike *Who-posted-what* dataset[2]. This dataset consists of the set of articles posted by each user, the time and date of posting, and the tags that the user used to post it. The data is available from 2007-05-30 onwards. We pruned the data to contain only users with more than 4 postings and articles with frequency of at least 4. The number of users and articles after pruning were 11,533 and 67,335 respectively. Among the set of articles, we were able to retrieve abstracts for 8,494 articles.

3.2 Experiments

We used 5-fold cross-validation for evaluation. In each run of the algorithm, 20% of the items in each user's profile were put aside for testing, while the remaining 80% items (with their features) were used for training the model. In each run, those items in the test data that have no features were removed from the test set and were added to the train set. For each user's profile p, hold-out item s, and context $q = \{t_1, t_2, ..., t_w\}$ (consisting of w features t_j), each of the competing algorithms provides a ranking over all of the candidate items. As discussed in section 2.3, our model computes the recommendation score for each item i as $p(i|p, q)$ and ranks items based on these scores. The following baseline methods were used in our experiments:

Simple Filtering: For a given context q, this model filters out the items that does not contain q in their list of features. The remaining items are then ranked randomly.

User-Based kNN: This approach ignores the given context and recommend items only based on the users' profiles using the k-nearest-neighbor approach.

LDA: This is a non-personalized, but context-sensitive method, which ignores the users' preference histories and recommends items that best match the given context. We trained the LDA model for the items; assuming that each item is a document and the item features are the words in the document. We used the variational message passing approach, explained in section 2, to learn the parameters of the model. For context $q = \{t_1, t_2, ..., t_w\}$, and each candidate item i, we used equation 2 to compute the conditional probability of each contextual feature t_j given i, shown as $p(t_j|i)$. The same approach as in section 2.3 was applied for smoothing these probabilities. For item i, $p(q|i)$ is then computed as the multiplication of smoothed probabilities for all the contextual features. The computed $p(q|i)$ is used as the recommendation score for item i. The items are then ranked based on these scores.

Bayesian Smoothing: This baseline algorithm is also non-personalized but context-sensitive. It uses Bayesian Smoothing with Dirichlet prior as a language model. Using this model, for an item i and a context $q = \{t_1, t_2, ..., t_w\}$, $p(t_j|i)$ is computed according to equation 11 for each contextual feature t_j. For item i, $p(q|i)$ is then computed as the multiplication of the probabilities for all the contextual features. The computed $p(q|i)$ is used as the recommendation score for item i. The items are then ranked based on these scores.

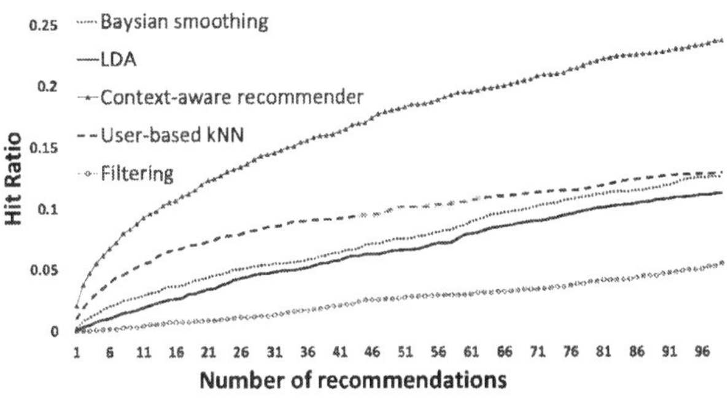

Figure 3: Hit ratio for different number of recommendations for the playlists dataset

The parameters used for each of the algorithms are included in Table 2. We tuned the parameters for each method to achieve the best results.

In our evaluations for the playlists dataset, we assume that each playlist correspond to a user's profile. Also, we used frequent tags for each song as its features. The context for each test song was selected as a randomly-chosen member of its frequent tags set. For example, let song s be a held-out song from playlist p with popular tags T = {"rock", "happy", "80s"}. Any of "rock", "happy", or "80s" could be used as a simulated context when recommending items to include in playlist p. Note that this simulation of context is consistent with our previous assumption that context given to the system is a subset of the features for the desired item.

To compare different algorithms in their ability to provide personalized recommendations for the given context, we look at how well they recover the held-out songs in the test data. For each removed song, its rank in the overall recommendation list is recorded, as top recommendations are more valuable for the user. The results for the cross validation were evaluated by computing the *Hit Ratio*, which computes the probability that the removed song is recommended as part of the top N recommendations. Formally, we will denote the top N recommendations for a given playlist, p, as $R_N(p)$. If the removed target song, s_p, is part of $R_N(p)$, then it is considered a *hit*. For any given rank N, the hit ratio for the recommendation algorithm is computed as: $h(N) = |p \in testset : s_p \in R_N(p)|/|testset|$.

Figure 3 compares the hit ratio results of our approach with the other baselines for the first 100 recommendations. As can be seen, our approach achieves significantly better hit ratio at all ranks. At recommendation rank 10, the hit ratio achieved by our method is 3.5% higher than user-based kNN, 5.7% higher than the Bayesian smoothing approach, 7% higher than LDA, and finally 8.4% higher than simple filtering method.

We used the same five-fold cross-validation approach to evaluate our method based on the CiteULike dataset that was earlier introduced. Each user profile contains the postings by that user. The words in each article abstract were

[2]http://www.citeulike.org/faq/data.adp

Table 2: Parameters used for each method

Method	Playlists dataset	CiteULike dataset
Context-aware recommender	topics = 50, iterations = 100, α = 5, β = 0.01, γ = 0.01, δ= 1000, λ= 0.7	topics = 70, iterations = 150, α = 3.57, β = 0.01, γ = 0.01, δ= 1000, λ= 0.7
User-based kNN	Number of neighbors=10	Number of neighbors=30
Bayesian smoothing	δ= 1000	δ= 1000
LDA	topics = 50, iterations = 100, α = 5, β = 0.01, δ= 1000, λ= 0.7	topics = 70, iterations = 150, α = 3.57, β = 0.01, δ= 1000, λ= 0.7
Simple filtering	-	-

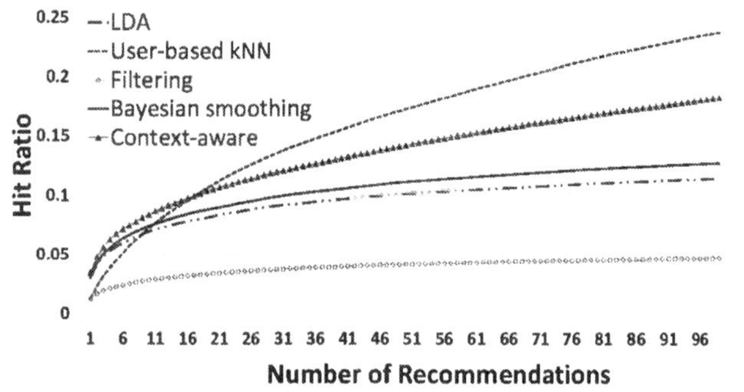

Figure 4: Hit ratio for different number of recommendations for the CiteULike dataset

used as the article features. The context for each test article was selected as the set of tags that the user used to post that article. Note that these tags were not used for training the model as our model is trained based on user profiles and article abstracts.

Figure 4 shows the hit ratio results for this experiment. Our approach achieves the best hit ratio in higher ranks (less than 17) in comparison to the other methods.

The hit ratio of our approach at rank 5 is 2.2% higher in comparison to user-based kNN (that is an improvement of 50%). Also at this rank, the hit ratio of the context-aware recommender is 0.8% (13% improvement), 1% (17% improvement), and 4.5% (197% improvement) higher in comparison to Bayesian smoothing, LDA, and simple filtering method respectively.

4. ANALYSIS OF THE TOPICS

The latent topics in our model can capture the co-occurrence relations among the features of items as well as the associations among items. This section describes a preliminary analysis of some of these associations.

Table 3 presents a few examples of the generated topics for the playlist dataset, showing the top 10 tags, those with the highest probability given the topic. These topics have a clear connection to the genre and, in some cases, the mood of a song. For example, frequent terms in topic# 3 are related to R&B/soul music while topic#4 are mostly describing quirky / humorous songs.

The topics learned from our model can also capture the associations between songs, or similarly, the artists. Using last.fm API, the similar artist for any given artist can be retrieved. We selected the set of 244 artists with at least 50 songs in our dataset of playlists. For each of these artists, the set of similar artists were retrieved from last.fm. We used the similarity data from last.fm as the ground truth and evaluated our model as a representation of artist similarity.

For a model with k topics, each song can be represented as a k-dimensional vector where the jth dimension of the vector represents the probability of the song given the jth topic. After normalizing the song vectors to unit length, they were transformed into binary representation such that each dimension is set to one if its value in the normalized song vector is greater than a pre-specified threshold (that was 0.05 for 50 topics). The elements with the value of one are thereby the *dominant* topics for each song.

We represent each artist as an aggregate of his/her songs vectors. An artist vector representation is generated as the sum of all the binary vectors of the songs for that artist. We compute the similarity of any two artists as the cosine similarity of their corresponding vectors. The artist similarity graph can then be generated. In this graph nodes correspond to the artists and the weight of each edge connecting two artists indicates their cosine similarity.

Given the similarity data from last.fm as the ground truth, the precision of artists' neighbors (in the artist graph) at level X can be computed as the ratio of the number of edges having weight of at least X that are correct to the total number of edges having weight greater than X. An edge connecting artists a and b is counted as correct if b is listed as a similar artist for a (or the reverse) in the last.fm data. Figure 5 shows the precision of artists' neighbors at different thresholds. Figure 6 shows the number of links at each threshold level (> 0.5). As can be seen in Figure 5, the precision of correct neighbors increases by increasing the similarity threshold. When the similarity threshold is equal to zero (that is when the edges are selected randomly), the precision is as low as 5.8%. Precision reaches to 60% when similarity of the artists are greater than 0.95 (which includes 138 links) showing the correlation between topic-based similarities and the true artist neighborhood. Note that for larger threshold values the number of edges become very small (at threshold level of 0.99, only 2 links remains) and the computed precision is not representative of true precision in a larger dataset. so, we did not include them in the precision graph.

5. RELATED WORK

Several researchers have previously investigated the use of contextual information in various recommender systems applications. In [19] a context-aware playlist recommendation system is proposed which provides users opportunity to browse their music by mood. This system uses a combina-

Table 3: **A sample of topics generated by the context-aware recommendation model for the playlists dataset**

Topic#1	Topic#2	Topic#3	Topic#4	Topic#5	Topic#6
electronic	alternative	soul	rock	metal	rock
electronica	indie	rnb	comedy	rock	britpop
alternative	rock	pop	alternative	industrial	british
experimental	shoegaze	dance	funny	hardcore	indie
ambient	upbeat	electronic	punk	alternative	jazz
indie	nostalgia	rap	pop	metalcore	swing
rock	amazing	funk	indie	dance	alternative
chillout	pop	chillout	fun	german	pop
psychedelic	punk	jazz	quirky	pop	oldies
pop	noise	americana	silly	punk	beatles

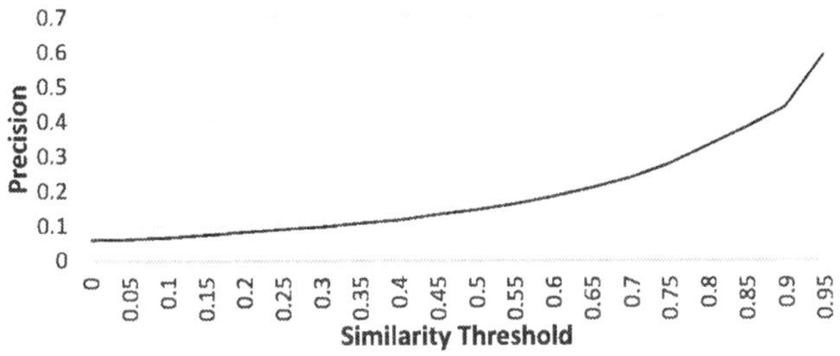

Figure 5: Precision at different similarity levels

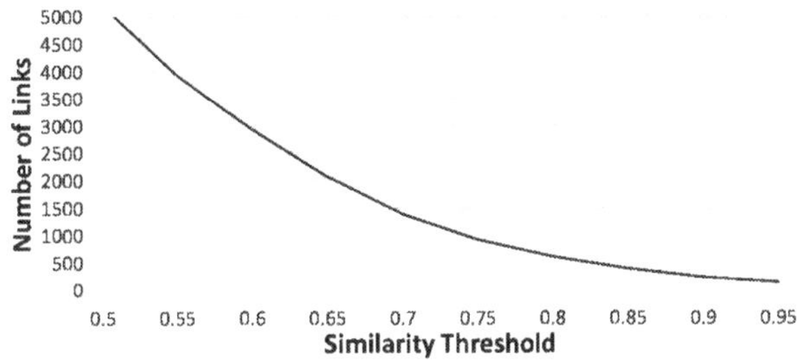

Figure 6: Number of links at different similarity levels

tion of audio and lyric content to classify music by mood. Our approach is different from [19] as the contextual information is not pre-specified in our system.

The system described in [6] focuses on social context and proposes Poolcasting as a method to customize musical sequences for groups of listeners. [11] defines context in music recommendation as the context of selecting and ordering the songs in the playlist. They generate playlists using both acoustic and social-network data. Unlike [6], the focus of this paper is not on capturing and incorporating the social context. The approach presented in this paper is different from [11] as we are assuming that contextual information is obtained as part of a user's interaction with the system.

In [17] a method is introduced for learning song transition probabilities from audio features extracted from songs played in professional radio station playlists. These transition probabilities are used to compute the similarity of different songs. Given a seed song, the playlist is generated based on songs similarities and also a tag cloud (with 360 tag) that the user is able to manipulate to guide the playlist generation process. A content-based *autotagger* is used to tag all the tracks in the database and to provide the similarity of the tag cloud for each track and the given tag cloud by the user. Unlike [17], the queried features in our system are not limited to a fixed set of tags, as a result the user are not forced to explore the tag cloud to express their interests. Another major difference is that, the recommendations for the next song are generated based on *all* the songs in the playing session or the user's profile as opposed to a single seed song.

There exist fair amount of research work on modeling music playlists. A latent factor model of playlists is proposed in [4]. The model captures the temporal dynamics in the system, such as changes of music type by the time of the day, or similarity of adjacently played tracks. For a given playlist, the model can predict the probability distribution of the next song. In [9] playlists are modeled as Markov chains in some latent space and each song is represented as one or multiple points in this space. The proposed method called Logistic Markov Embedding (LME) can capture the sequential and directed nature of playlists and has been evaluated for the task of playlist prediction. While context is not part of the model in [4] and [9], we are using the given context to adapt the recommendations for the most recent preferences of the users.

Several mixture models have been studied and applied for collaborative filtering. The Bayesian clustering, which is the simplest form of mixture models, discovers latent clusters of users with similar preferences and assumes that each user belongs to a single cluster. The aspect model also finds latent factors representing user clusters but unlike Bayesian cluster models, it assumes that different ratings (or preference feedbacks) of the same user can be explained by different latent causes. The LDA model [8] introduced in Section 2.1 is a generative model in which the proportion of latent factors (also called topics) for each user profile is a random random variable with Dirichlet prior. [16] provides a survey and comparison of various mixture models including Bayesian Clustering [10], the Aspect Model [15], the Flexible Mixture Model [22], and the Joint Mixture Model [22] for collaborative filtering. Adaptations or extensions of the aforementioned mixture models have been applied for a variety of problems. In [18], a generative graphical model was introduced for rating-based collaborative filtering. This model is very similar to LDA but it is specially designed to model rating profiles of users instead of binary interactions. Similarly, a graphical model called *session model* was introduced in [26] which captures the listening moods of users. Unlike the LDA model, the session model differentiate different playing sessions in users profiles and assumes that there is a latent mood which guides the choice of songs. Thus, beside the overall tastes of users, another latent variable is included in the model to model the mood of the session. In [12], a generative probabilistic model of web browsing sessions was introduced. The model creates clusters of similar sessions and uses contextual session information such as time, referrer domain, and link locations to assign a session probabilistically to multiple clusters.

6. CONCLUSION

This paper presented a novel approach for context-aware recommendation. We introduced a unified probabilistic latent factor model that integrates user profiles, item representations, and contextual information. We discussed how our model can be used to compute the conditional probability of each item given the user profile and the additional context.

The findings reported in this paper introduce numerous additional questions and areas of future work. In this paper, we evaluated our model for a special setting in which contextual information is represented as a subset of feature space for the items. However, our proposed model can be extended to handle other types of observable contextual information. In our future work, we plan to generalize this framework and evaluate it in application domains where the representation of context is unrelated to the item features.

7. REFERENCES

[1] G. Abowd, A. Dey, P. Brown, N. Davies, M. Smith, and P. Steggles. Towards a better understanding of context and context-awareness. *Handheld and Ubiquitous Computing*, 1707(2):304–307, 1999.

[2] G. Adomavicius, B. Mobasher, F. Ricci, and A. Tuzhilin. Context-aware recommender systems. *AI Magazine*, 32(3):67–80, 2011.

[3] G. Adomavicius and A. Tuzhilin. Context-aware recommender systems. In *Proceedings of the ACM conference on Recommender Systems*. ACM, 2008.

[4] N. Aizenberg, Y. Koren, and O. Somekh. Build your own music recommender by modeling internet radio streams. In *Proceedings of the 21st international conference on World Wide Web*, pages 1–10. ACM.

[5] S. S. Anand and B. Mobasher. Contextual recommendation. In *Lecture Notes In Artificial Intelligence*, volume 4737, pages 142–160. Springer-Verlag, Berlin, Heidelberg, 2007.

[6] C. Baccigalupo. *Poolcasting: an intelligent technique to customise music programmes for their audience.* PhD thesis, Universitat Autonoma de Barcelona, 2009.

[7] L. Baltrunas and F. Ricci. Context-based splitting of item ratings in collaborative filtering. In *Proceedings of the third ACM conference on Recommender systems*. ACM, 2009.

[8] D. Blei, A. Ng, and M. Jordan. Latent dirichlet allocation. *Journal of machine Learning Research*, 3:993–1022, 2003.

[9] S. Chen, J. L. Moore, D. Turnbull, and T. Joachims. Playlist prediction via metric embedding. In *Proceedings of the 18th ACM SIGKDD international conference on Knowledge discovery and data mining*, pages 714–722. ACM, 2012.

[10] Y.-H. Chien and E. George. A bayesian model for collaborative filtering. In *Proceedings of the 7th International Workshop on Artificial Intelligence and Statistics*, 1999.

[11] B. Fields. *Contextualize Your Listening:The Playlist as Recommendation Engine.* PhD thesis, University of London, 2011.

[12] P. Haider, L. Chiarandini, U. Brefeld, and A. Jaimes. Dynamic contextual models for user interaction on the web. In *ECML/PKDD Workshop on Mining and Exploiting Interpretable Local Patterns (I-PAT)*, 2012.

[13] N. Hariri, B. Mobasher, and R. Burke. Context-aware music recommendation based on latenttopic sequential patterns. In *Proceedings of the sixth ACM conference on Recommender systems*, pages 131–138. ACM, 2012.

[14] T. Hofmann. Probabilistic latent semantic indexing. In *Proceedings of Uncertainty in Artificial Intelligence*, 1999.

[15] T. Hofmann and J. Puzicha. Latent class models for collaborative filtering. In *Proceedings of the Sixteenth International Joint Conference on Artificial Intelligence*, pages 688–693, 1999.

[16] R. Jin, L. Si, and C. Zhai. A study of mixture models for collaborative filtering. *Information Retrieval*, 9(3):357–382, 2006.

[17] F. Maillet, D. Eck, G. Desjardins, and P. Lamere. Steerable playlist generation by learning song similarity from radio station playlists. In *ISMIR*, pages 345–350. International Society for Music Information Retrieval, 2009.

[18] B. Marlin. Collaborative Filtering: A Machine Learning Perspective. Master's thesis, University of Toronto, 2004.

[19] O. Meyers. A mood-based music classification and exploration system. Master's thesis, Massachusetts Institute of Technology, 2007.

[20] T. Minka, J. Winn, J. Guiver, and D. Knowles. Infer.NET 2.5, 2012. Microsoft Research Cambridge. http://research.microsoft.com/infernet.

[21] A. Said and E. De Luca. Inferring contextual user profiles - improving recommender performance. In *Context-aware Recommender Systems Workshop at Recsys11*. ACM, 2011.

[22] L. Si and R. Jin. Flexible mixture model for collaborative filtering. In *Proceedings of the international conference on machine learning*, pages 704–711. AAAI Press, 2003.

[23] A. L. Wang. An industrial-strength audio search algorithm. In *Proceedings of the 4th Symposium Conference on Music Information Retrieval*, pages 7–13, 2003.

[24] X. Wei and B. W. Croft. Lda-based document models for ad-hoc retrieval. In *Proceedings of the 29th annual international ACM SIGIR conference on Research and development in information retrieval*, pages 178–185, New York, NY, USA, 2006. ACM Press.

[25] C. Zhai and J. D. Lafferty. A study of smoothing methods for language models applied to ad hoc information retrieval. In W. B. Croft, D. J. Harper, D. H. Kraft, and J. Zobel, editors, *Proceedings of the annual international ACM SIGIR conference on Research and development in information retrieval*, pages 334–342. ACM, 2001.

[26] E. Zheleva, J. Guiver, E. Mendes Rodrigues, and N. Milić-Frayling. Statistical models of music-listening sessions in social media. In *Proceedings of the 19th international conference on World wide web*, WWW '10, pages 1019–1028. ACM, 2010.

Location-Aware Music Recommendation Using Auto-Tagging and Hybrid Matching

Marius Kaminskas
Free University of Bozen-Bolzano
Faculty of Computer Science
Bozen-Bolzano, Italy
mkaminskas@unibz.it

Francesco Ricci
Free University of Bozen-Bolzano
Faculty of Computer Science
Bozen-Bolzano, Italy
fricci@unibz.it

Markus Schedl
Johannes Kepler University
Department of Computational Perception
Linz, Austria
markus.schedl@jku.at

ABSTRACT

We propose a novel approach to context-aware music recommendation – recommending music suited for places of interest (POIs). The suggested hybrid approach combines two techniques – one based on representing both POIs and music with tags, and the other based on the knowledge of the semantic relations between the two types of items.

We show that our approach can be scaled up using a novel music auto-tagging technique and we compare it in a live user study to: two non-hybrid solutions, either based on tags or on semantic relations; and to a context-free but personalized recommendation approach. In the considered scenario, i.e., a situation defined by a context (the POI), we show that personalization (via music preference) is not sufficient and it is important to implement effective adaptation techniques to the user's context. In fact, we show that the users are more satisfied with the recommendations generated by combining the tag-based and knowledge-based context adaptation techniques, which exploit orthogonal types of relations between places and music tracks.

Categories and Subject Descriptors

H.3.3 [**Information Storage and Retrieval**]: Information Search and Retrieval—*Information Filtering*

General Terms

Algorithms, Design, Experimentation, Human Factors

Keywords

Music recommendation; context-aware recommendation; hybrid recommendation; auto-tagging; tag prediction

1. INTRODUCTION

Music recommender systems are decision support tools that reduce information overload by retrieving relevant music items based on a user's profile [8]. However, most of the available music recommenders suggest music without taking into consideration the user's context, e.g., her mood, current location, activity, or any other contextual condition that might influence the user's perception or evaluation of music [1]. In response to these observations, in recent years a new research topic of contextual music retrieval and recommendation has emerged [12]. In this work we address a particular type of context-aware music recommendation – recommending music suited for places of interest (POIs). Finding music items that suit POIs can be exploited in a number of engaging information services. In particular, we have considered a scenario in which a mobile city guide provides an enhanced presentation of a place for a tourist by playing music that is related to the place, i.e., music that is culturally or emotionally associated with the place (e.g., a Mozart sonata in Salzburg or a Bach fugue in a Gothic Cathedral) [6].

The main challenge to face when addressing the above mentioned goal is related to the fact that POIs and music are two rather different domains, and there is no obvious way to match such heterogeneous items. In previous works [6, 11], we have developed two alternative techniques to solve the problem of matching music and POIs – one based on a common representation of both types of items, and the other exploiting semantic relations between the items.

The first technique represents items in the two domains with a common set of features – user-assigned tags describing the emotional properties of music and POIs [6]. We decided to use tags that describe emotional properties of the items, since music and places can both raise emotions, and the commonality of these emotions could provide the base for establishing a degree of match between a place and a music track. The tag-based representation allows matching music tracks and POIs by comparing the tag profiles of the items.

The second technique is based on extracting explicit knowledge about items in the two domains [11]. Obtaining such knowledge automatically has become possible with the advent of the Semantic Web and specifically with its reference implementation in the Linked Data initiative [5]. We have exploited the DBpedia Linked Data repository to build a framework in which semantic networks linking items from music and POI domains are automatically created. These networks are represented as graphs, on which a graph-based algorithm is run to rank the items in the music domain with respect to their relatedness to an item in the POI domain.

RecSys'13, October 12–16, 2013, Hong Kong, China.
ACM 978-1-4503-2409-0/13/10.
http://dx.doi.org/10.1145/2507157.2507180.

These two techniques – *tag-based* and *knowledge-based* – represent two complementary ways of establishing a match between a place and a music track: a track may "feel right" for a POI or it can be linked to a POI by factual relations (e.g., belonging to the same cultural era or composed by someone whose life is related to the POI). In previous works, we have evaluated the two techniques independently on different datasets and against a simple baseline (random recommendations). In this paper, we take some next steps toward location-aware music recommendation by (i) proposing a hybrid recommendation approach which combines the *tag-based* and *knowledge-based* techniques using rank aggregation, (ii) proposing an extension to the *tag-based* technique to scale up the tagging process for the music tracks employing a state-of-the-art *auto-tagger*, and (iii) evaluating the performance of these techniques on a dataset of POIs and music tracks against personalized recommendations. We have validated the research hypothesis that the combination of *knowledge-based* and *tag-based* techniques is preferred by the users over the recommendations produced by each technique separately and over the classical personalization approach.

The remainder of the paper is structured as follows. In Section 2 we overview works related to location-aware music recommendation and music auto-tagging. Section 3 describes the used dataset of music tracks and POIs. In Section 4 we describe the automatic tag prediction technique that we have used for tagging music tracks. Section 5 describes the user study to evaluate the proposed recommendation approach. Finally, we summarize the findings of the evaluation and define future work directions in Section 6.

2. RELATED WORK

Finding music that suits a POI can be viewed as a *context-aware recommendation* problem [1], the place being the context for consuming the recommendations (music). There are several works on context-aware music recommendation that exploit location-related context information. Reddy and Mascia [18] present a mobile music recommender system Lifetrak that generates a playlist using the user's music library based on the current context of the user (location, time, weather, and activity information). Similarly to our tag-based approach [6], Lifetrak requires the user to label songs with tags from a controlled vocabulary. However, in contrast to our approach, the tags in the vocabulary directly represent the values of the previously mentioned context parameters. So for instance, songs have to be labeled with a ZIP code of a certain area to be recommended for that location.

More recently, Ankolekar and Sandholm [2] presented a mobile audio application that plays audio content associated with a particular location with the goal of enhancing the sense of being in a place by creating its emotional atmosphere. Instead of establishing relations between music and location automatically, the presented approach relies on crowd-sourcing – users are allowed to assign audio pieces (either a music track or a sound clip) to a specific location (represented by the geographic coordinates).

Our research is also related to *music auto-tagging*, the process of automatically assigning labels to music pieces. This task is typically performed employing a supervised learning approach; based on a training set of music content features and semantic labels, a classifier is trained and subsequently used to predict tags for unseen pieces. Rhythm or timbre descriptors are frequently used as content features [16] and sometimes high-level features are included [23].

Recent work in music auto-tagging includes [23], where Sordo proposed a simple though efficient algorithm based on a weighted vote k-Nearest Neighbour (kNN) classifier to propagate tags from training data to unseen music items. Moreover, in order to increase the computational efficiency, he used *feature selection* and *dimensionality reduction* of the input feature vectors before training the classifier. A similar approach is suggested in [13] for auto-tagging artists. Kim et al. analyzed artist similarity functions based on different data sources: artist co-occurrences in Last.fm playlists, Last.fm tags, web pages about the artists, and music content features. It is found that the similarity measure based on Last.fm co-occurrences performs best in terms of precision and recall. Mandel et al. [16] used conditional Restricted Boltzmann Machines [22] to learn tag language models over three sets of vocabularies: annotations by users of Amazon's Mechanical Turk, of the tagging game MajorMiner [15], and of Last.fm. Theses models are learned on the level of song segments. Optionally, track level and user level annotations are considered.

A recent trend in music auto-tagging is adopting two-stage algorithms. In the first stage, such algorithms infer higher-level information from content features, such as term weight vector representations. These representations are then fed into a machine learning algorithm to learn semantic labels [9, 17]. For instance, Miotto et al. [17] first model semantic multinomials over tags based on music content features. To account for co-occurrence relations between tags, they subsequently learn a Dirichlet mixture model of the semantic space, which eventually yields a contextual multinomial used for tag prediction.

In this work, we employ a variant of the auto-tagger presented in [19], where Seyerlehner et al. proposed a combination of different audio features described within their block-level framework [21]. This tagger showed superior performance in the "Audio Tag Classification" and the "Audio Tag Affinity Estimation" tasks, run at the 2012 Music Information Retrieval Evaluation eXchange (MIREX)[1]. We extended the set proposed in [21] with two additional audio features.

3. THE DATASET

In order to evaluate the proposed hybrid recommendation approach, we required a dataset of POIs and music tracks on which both *tag-based* and *knowledge-based* techniques could be applied. Since the ground truth relatedness of music and POIs can only be assessed by subjective users' evaluations, and the users cannot perform a large number of judgments during an evaluation session, we have limited the size of the dataset to 25 well-known POIs from 17 major city tourism destinations in Europe (Madrid, Berlin, Florence, Paris, etc.).

Acquiring music tracks related to the selected POIs was performed by retrieving the top-5 musicians for each POI using the *knowledge-based* technique [11], and aggregating them into a single set. This resulted in a collection of 123 musicians (there were two repetitions in the initial list of 125 musicians). Subsequently, we retrieved 3 music tracks

[1] `http://www.music-ir.org/mirex`

Table 1: The controlled vocabulary used for tag-based matching of music and POIs

Tags	*Type*
Affectionate, Agitated, Animated, Bouncy, Calm, Energetic, Melancholic, Sad, Sentimental, Serene, Spiritual, Strong, Tender, Thrilling	GEMS
Ancient, Modern, Bright, Dark, Colorful, Heavy, Lightweight, Open, Cold, Warm	Physical

for each musician by taking the top-ranked results returned by the YouTube search interface. Doing so ensured the collected tracks to be representative of the musicians in our dataset. Eventually, a set of 369 music tracks belonging to 9 music genres was obtained: Classical, Medieval, Opera, Folk, Electronic, Hip Hop, Jazz, Pop, and Rock.

We note that using the *knowledge-based* technique, which retrieves musicians from the DBpedia knowledge base [11], allowed us to avoid the *popularity bias*, i.e. selecting only well-known musicians. In fact, the collected dataset covers a wide variety of less-known musicians from the so-called "long tail" of music content [7].

In order to evaluate the *tag-based* approach on this dataset, the POIs and music tracks had to be tagged using the controlled tag vocabulary as described in [6]. While tagging the 25 POIs was easily performed through a tagging survey, tagging 369 music tracks required substantial user effort and was not practical. Therefore, to address this issue we have selected a third of the music tracks (123 tracks – one random track per musician) to be tagged through a survey. The collected annotations were used as training data for automatically tagging the remaining tracks in the dataset (see next section).

The tagging survey was performed through a web interface where the users were asked to annotate POIs and music tracks using a controlled vocabulary consisting of adjectives from the GEMS emotion model [26] and adjectives describing physical characteristics of items (Table 1). In [6] we have shown that this tag vocabulary is suitable for annotating both music and POIs and performs well for establishing relations between the two types of items. Compared to our previous research, in this work we have used a revised version of the vocabulary. In fact, by analyzing the data collected during the previous tagging surveys [6], we observed that certain tags were rarely used and therefore were marginally providing useful information when recommending music for POIs. We therefore discarded the tags that in the previous surveys were applied to less than 1% of the items. The revision allowed us to reduce the size of the vocabulary from 46 to 24 tags, which was beneficial for the music auto-tagging procedure, in which a separate classifier is trained for each tag (see next section).

The tagging procedure was performed by 10 volunteers recruited via email – students and researchers from the Free University of Bolzano and other European universities. We note that the tagging of music and POIs is a subjective task and users may disagree whether certain tags apply to an item [24]. Consequently, aggregating tags provided by different users into items' tag profiles may result in contradicting tags. Therefore, to ensure the quality of the acquired tags, we considered the agreement between users, which is a standard measure of quality for user-generated tags [14]. We cleaned the data by keeping for each item only the tags on which at least 2 taggers agreed. As a result, we obtained an average of 5.1 distinct tags for the POIs and 2.5 for the music tracks. The lower number of tags for music tracks can be explained by the large number of items and the small number of taggers – on average a music track was tagged by 2 users. However, the quality of the acquired data was more important than the quantity, since it was crucial to train the music auto-tagger on reliable data. In the next section we will show how the evaluation of the auto-tagging algorithm allowed us to collect more tagging data for the music tracks.

4. MUSIC AUTO-TAGGING

We used a variant of the high-performance, state-of-the-art auto-tagger proposed in [19]. It was applied in the data acquisition phase, to reduce the human effort required in the annotation process, and to scale up tagging. We hence used the tags manually obtained for a third of the music dataset to train the auto-tagger, and automatically label the remaining 246 music tracks.

Our auto-tagger is based on a set of audio features defined within the *block-level framework* (BLF) [21]. This framework describes a music piece by first modeling it as overlapping blocks of the Cent spectrum representation of the audio signal. More precisely, a window size of 2048 samples and a hop size of 512 samples are used. The Short Time Fourier Transform (STFT) is then computed on the Hanning-windowed samples of the audio signal. To account for the musical nature of the audio under consideration, the resulting magnitude spectrum with linear frequency resolution is mapped onto the logarithmic Cent scale.

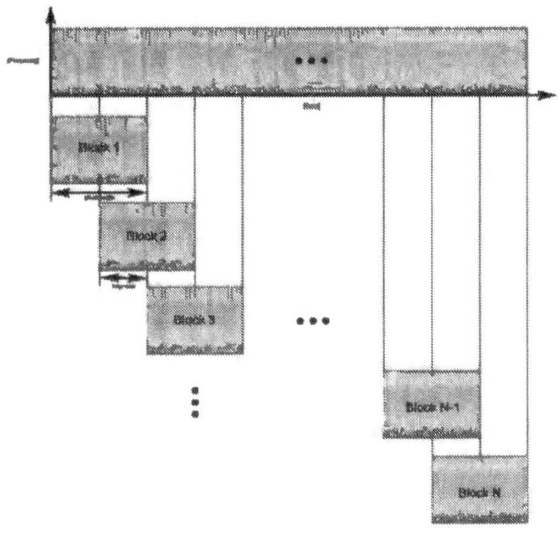

Figure 1: Overview of the block-level framework.

Based on these Cent spectrum representations, we defined several features that are computed on blocks of frames (Figure 1). The features which describe a single block were eventually aggregated over all blocks of the piece under consideration, using a summarization function. This yielded the following music descriptors used in the auto-tagger: *Spectral Pattern* (SP) characterizes the frequency content, *Delta Spectral Pattern* (DSP) emphasizes note onsets, *Variance Delta Spectral Pattern* (VDSP) aims at capturing variations of onsets over time, *Logarithmic Fluctuation Pattern* (LFP) describes the periodicity of beats, *Correlation Pattern* (CP) models the correlation between different frequency bands, and *Spectral Contrast Pattern* (SCP) uses the difference between spectral peaks and valleys to identify tonal and percussive components. Figure 2 illustrates the different feature values for a Jazz piece. The y-axis represents the frequency bands and the x-axis the sorted temporal components of the blocks. In addition to these block-level descriptors, we further included two variants of Mel Frequency Cepstral Coefficient (MFCC) features, which are commonly used to capture music timbre [25, 3], although they originate from speech processing. Finally, the song level feature vectors resulting from these individual music descriptors were concatenated and associations between songs and tags learned using a *Random Forest* classifier. We used a RF classifier because in previous experiments its performance was among the best and comparable to that of a Support Vector Machine classifier using Principal Component Analysis. Moreover, RF has a much better computational performance [20].

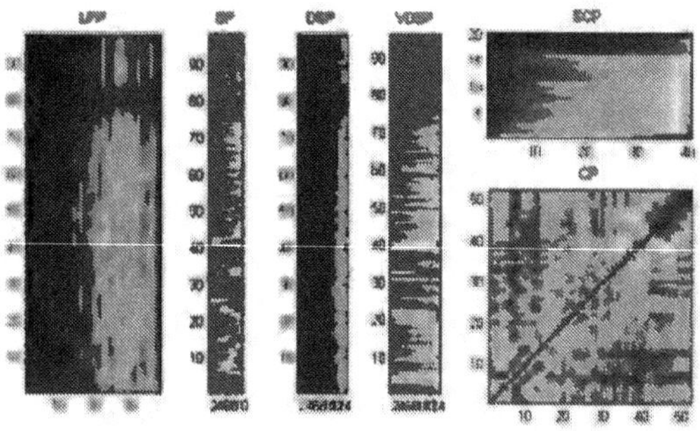

Figure 2: BLF features for a Jazz piece.

4.1 Music Auto-Tagger Evaluation

As described in Section 3, the set of 123 music tracks was initially tagged by a small number of human taggers to acquire data for training the music auto-tagger. Following this initial data acquisition survey, which resulted in 2.5 tags per track on average, we evaluated the auto-tagger on the 123 tracks using leave-one-out train/test data split and cross-validation. The results showed that the auto-tagger can accurately predict the small number of tags for the tracks. However, more rich tagging data had to be obtained before the auto-tagger could be trained and applied to the untagged portion of the dataset.

Therefore, we conducted a second tagging survey on the same set of 123 music tracks, aimed to measure how much the users agree with predictions generated by the auto-tagger and to acquire more tagging data. Figure 3 shows the interface of the web application used in this user study. The participants of the study were asked to tag the music tracks using the controlled tag vocabulary, with 6 of the usable tags pre-selected by the system: 3 tags predicted for the music track by the auto-tagger and 3 tags randomly selected from the remaining 21 tags in the vocabulary.

31 users participated in the study. There was no overlap with the users involved in the initial tagging of the tracks. On average, each music track was tagged by 2.6 users. The participants of the study were informed about the nature of pre-selected tags: "*Note that some tags are pre-selected by a recommender system and some at random. If you disagree with any of the suggestions, please de-select them*". This

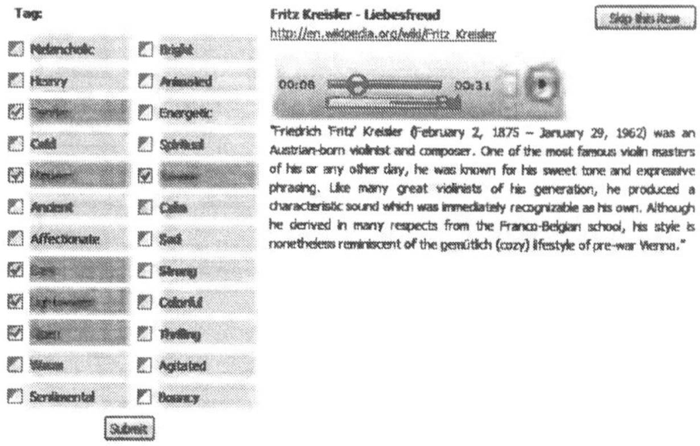

Figure 3: Interface of the experiment on automatic tag prediction.

information was provided to encourage the users' critical thinking when assessing the pre-selected tags.

In total the users performed 318 evaluation sessions (i.e., tagged a music track) assigning on average 5.29 tags to a track per session. Out of 1683 acquired music annotations, 652 were those predicted by the auto-tagger, 377 randomly pre-selected, and 654 newly assigned by the users. This shows that the users were active in assigning new tags, instead of merely revising the pre-selected tags.

We have calculated the probability for a predicted/random tag to be accepted by a user as the ratio of the number of times such tags were selected by users over the total number of times they were displayed by the system. The results (Table 2) show a higher selection probability for the predicted tags compared to random tags to be accepted. Note that the probability for a random tag to be selected by a user is still relatively large, which can be explained by two facts. Firstly, due to the large number of tags assigned to a music track per session, the baseline probability for any tag in the vocabulary to be selected by a user is large: $5.29/24 = 0.22$. Secondly, by suggesting certain tags we created a presentation bias – the users were paying more attention to the pre-selected tags, even those at random. Nevertheless, the difference between the two obtained probabilities is statistically significant with $p < 0.001$ in a two-proportion z-test. Therefore, this result confirms that the users agree with the tag predictions produced by the auto-tagger.

Table 2: Selection probabilities of predicted and randomly pre-selected tags.

Predicted tags	*Random tags*
0.683	0.395

In addition to validating the effectiveness of the auto-tagger, the described experiment also allowed us to collect more tagging data for music tracks, since the study participants not only reviewed the predicted tags, but also added new ones. Upon the completion of the user study we had the 123 tracks tagged with 5.8 distinct tags on average.

Finally, having acquired sufficient tagging data for the 123 tracks and validated the effectiveness of the auto-tagging algorithm, we ran the auto-tagger on the full set of 369 tracks, training it on the 123 tagged tracks considered so far.

The auto-tagger outputs a probability for each tag in the vocabulary to be relevant for a track. However, the Jaccard similarity metric between sets of tags, which we use for the *tag-based* music-to-POI similarity computation, requires to compute the intersection and union of the items' tag profiles [6]. Therefore, we decided to generate binary tag assignments based on the probabilistic output of the auto-tagger by applying a threshold to the tag prediction probabilities. The standard value for the binarization threshold is 0.5, although it can be set higher or lower to trade precision with recall [20]. Typically, an optimal threshold value is determined using cross-validation (e.g., in [20] the authors report an optimal value of 0.25). However, in our research, the performance of the auto-tagger is defined by the quality of music-to-POI recommendations which have to be assessed by users. As it was not feasible to conduct multiple user studies with different binarization threshold values, we determined the threshold value based on the average size of items' tag profiles it produced. Empirical analysis showed that a threshold of 0.4 produced an average tag profile of 5.2 tags which is in accordance with the average profile size of manually tagged items (5.1 tags for POIs and 5.8 for music tracks).

5. EVALUATION AND RESULTS

As described in the previous sections, we have collected a dataset of 25 POIs and 369 music tracks from 9 music genres. Both *tag-based* and *knowledge-based* techniques can be applied to this dataset, since the music tracks and POIs were tagged using the controlled tag vocabulary, and the tracks belong to musicians semantically related to the POIs.

We designed an evaluation study to compare the performance of the two techniques and evaluate their combination. Additionally, we wanted to compare the performance of *tag-based* music recommendations obtained with manually vs. automatically tagged music tracks. Therefore, we considered two variants of the *tag-based* technique: one using only the manually annotated 123 tracks, and the other using the full set of 369 auto-tagged tracks. Moreover, we implemented a baseline approach which exploits only the users' music genre preferences. Hence, in total we considered five approaches to recommend music for POIs, which we describe in the next section.

5.1 Music Recommendation Approaches

5.1.1 Genre-based

The genre-based music recommendation approach implements a basic personalization technique: the music tracks are recommended based on the users' genre preferences. We aimed to compare a personalized music recommendation approach with the *knowledge-based* and *tag-based* approaches, which are not personalized, but rather directly match music with the users' context (i.e., POIs). We did not implement a more sophisticated personalization approach since the users were requested to evaluate if the proposed music tracks suit the presented POI and therefore it was not necessary and even deleterious to totally match the detailed user's music preferences in this particular contextual situation.

In order to obtain the users' preferences, we asked the study participants to select their preferred music genres prior to performing the evaluation. The genre taxonomy was based on the music tracks in our dataset, and included: Classical, Medieval, Opera, Folk, Electronic, Hip Hop, Jazz, Pop, and Rock. For each displayed POI, the *genre-based* track is randomly selected from the whole set of music tracks belonging to the user's preferred genres.

5.1.2 Knowledge-based

The *knowledge-based* music recommendation approach employs the technique presented in [11]. Given a POI, this approach ranks musicians by their relatedness to the POI. The relatedness is computed from the semantic relations between the POI and musicians extracted from the DBpedia knowledge base[2].

To extract relations between POIs and musicians, we considered only a subspace of DBpedia by identifying classes and relations belonging to the two domains of interest – places and music. We identified three types of relations that are useful for matching POIs with musicians: location relations (e.g., POI *located in* City, City *birthplace of* Musician), time relations (e.g., POI *construction* Date, Musician *active* Date), and relations through historical/cultural eras (e.g., POI *has category* Architecture Style, Musician *has category* Music Genre). Subsequently, for each POI, we built a network consisting of a directed acyclic graph whose nodes represent the identified classes, and edges represent the selected relations. We assigned relevance weights to nodes and edges of the graph, and performed a weight spreading algorithm over the graph to compute relatedness scores for musician nodes in the graph.

As explained in Section 3, we have downloaded three representative music tracks for each musician in the dataset. Using this approach, we implicitly assume that there are no major differences between these tracks of the same musician. Therefore, for each POI, the *knowledge-based* track is randomly selected from the three music tracks by the top-ranked musician.

5.1.3 Tag-based

The *tag-based* music recommendation approach uses the technique presented in [6] and is applied to the previously described set of 123 manually tagged tracks. This approach computes the weighted Jaccard similarity between a POI u and a music track v as:

$$\text{JaccardSim}(u,v) = \frac{\sum_{t\in X_u \cap X_v} log\ f(t)}{\sum_{t\in X_u \cup X_v} log\ f(t)} \quad (1)$$

where X_u and X_v are the items' tag profiles and $f(t)$ is the fraction of items in our dataset (both POIs and music tracks) annotated with the tag t. For each POI, the *tag-based* approach recommends the top-ranked music track.

5.1.4 Auto-tag-based

The *auto-tag-based* approach is applied to the full dataset of 369 music tracks which are auto-tagged using the subset of 123 manually tagged tracks for training (see Section 4).

Given the tag vocabulary of size K (in our case $K = 24$), for each music track v the auto-tagger produces a tag affinity vector:

$$a_v = (p(t_1), ..., p(t_K))$$

[2] http://dbpedia.org/

where $p(t_i)$ denotes the probability for a tag t_i to be relevant for the track. Then, the track's tag profile X_v is defined as:

$$X_v = \{t_i \mid p(t_i) \geq 0.4\},\ i = \{1, \ldots, K\}.$$

The similarity between a POI u and a music track v is computed using Equation 1. For each POI, the *auto-tag-based* approach recommends the top-ranked music track.

5.1.5 Combined

This music recommendation approach is a hybrid combination of the *knowledge-based* and *auto-tag-based* techniques, employing a rank aggregation technique [10]. Since the music-to-POI similarities produced by the two techniques have different value ranges, we used the normalized Borda count rank aggregation method to give equal importance to the two. This method is also applied in other recommender systems [4] and works as follows: Given a POI u, the *knowledge-based* and *auto-tag-based* approaches produce the rankings of music tracks σ_u^{kb} and σ_u^{tb}. We denote the position of a track v in these rankings as $\sigma_u^{kb}(v)$ and $\sigma_u^{tb}(v)$ respectively. Then we compute the combined score of the track v for the POI u as:

$$\text{CombinedScore}(u, v) = \frac{N_{kb} - \sigma_u^{kb}(v) + 1}{N_{kb}} + \frac{N_{tb} - \sigma_u^{tb}(v) + 1}{N_{tb}}$$

where N_{kb} and N_{tb} are the total number of tracks in the corresponding rankings. Finally, for each POI the *combined* approach recommends the top-scored music track.

5.2 Web-based Evaluation

To determine which approach produces better music recommendations we designed a web-based interface (Figure 4) for collecting the users' subjective assessments of whether a music track suits a POI. The participants of the experiment were repeatedly asked to consider a POI, and while looking at its images and description, to listen to the recommended music tracks. They were asked to check all the tracks that in their opinion suit that POI. During each evaluation step, the music recommendations for a POI were selected using the proposed five approaches described above – the personalized baseline approach and the four context-aware approaches. The order of the recommendations was randomized, and the user was not aware of the algorithms that were used to generate the recommendations. In total, a maximum of five tracks corresponding to the top-ranked tracks given by each approach were suggested for each POI, but sometimes less tracks were shown as the tracks selected by the different approaches may overlap.

5.3 Results

A total of 58 users participated in the evaluation study, performing 564 evaluation sessions: viewing a POI, listening to the suggested music tracks, and providing feedback. 764 music tracks were selected by the users as well-suited for POIs. Figure 5 shows the performance of the recommendation approaches, computed as the ratio of the number of times a track produced by each approach was considered as well-suited over the total number of evaluation sessions. All context-aware approaches perform significantly better than the personalized *genre-based* track selection ($p < 0.001$ in a two-proportion z-test). This result shows that in a situation defined by a context (i.e., a POI), it is not sufficient to recommend a music track liked by the user, but it is important to adapt music recommendations to the user's context.

Among the four context-aware approaches, the *combined* approach produced the best results, outperforming the others with statistical significance at $p < 0.01$. These results confirm our hypothesis that the users are more satisfied with the recommendations when combining the *tag-based* and *knowledge-based* techniques, which represent orthogonal types of relations between a place and a music track.

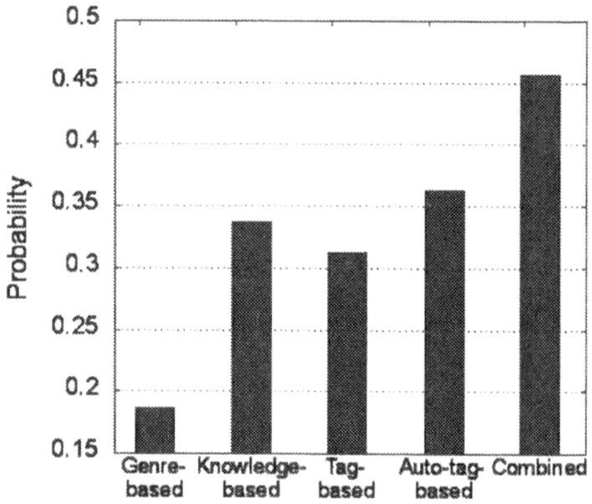

Figure 5: Selection probabilities of the different music recommendation approaches.

While our research hypothesis is supported by the users' feedback averaged across the full set of POIs, it is also interesting to look at the users' judgments of music appropriateness for the individual POIs. Figure 6 shows two interesting cases. For the POI Casa Batlló, the *knowledge-based* approach outperforms both *tag-based* approaches, while for the Royal Palace of Brussels, the *tag-based* approaches perform better. These results can be explained by analyzing the tag profiles of the items. We observe the differences of tag distributions in the profiles of the two POIs. Casa Batlló is tagged as [`Modern, Spiritual, Energetic, Warm, Colorful, Animated, Lightweight`], with over half of the tags in the profile being very frequent in our dataset (among both music tracks and POIs). Instead, the Royal Palace is tagged as [`Calm, Heavy, Strong, Ancient, Open`], with most of the tags being quite rare in the dataset. Note that the Jaccard similarity metric, used in the *tag-based* approach, weights the tags with respect to their frequency in the dataset (by assigning more weight to rare tags, see Equation 1). Therefore, the approach is better at identifying a good match for a POI tagged with a smaller set of tags unique in the set of music tracks compared to a POI tagged with a large number of common tags.

Furthermore, the different performance of the *knowledge-based* approach for the two POIs suggests that for certain POIs the technique fails to provide a relevant recommendation. In fact, we observe that for the Royal Palace of Brussels, the approach recommends a modern music piece by a Brussels-born composer, however, not fitting the nature of this particular POI. Notwithstanding the shortcomings of each individual technique discussed above, the obtained results suggest that the proposed hybrid *combined* approach can effectively balance the effects of the two alternative techniques and therefore produce better recommendations.

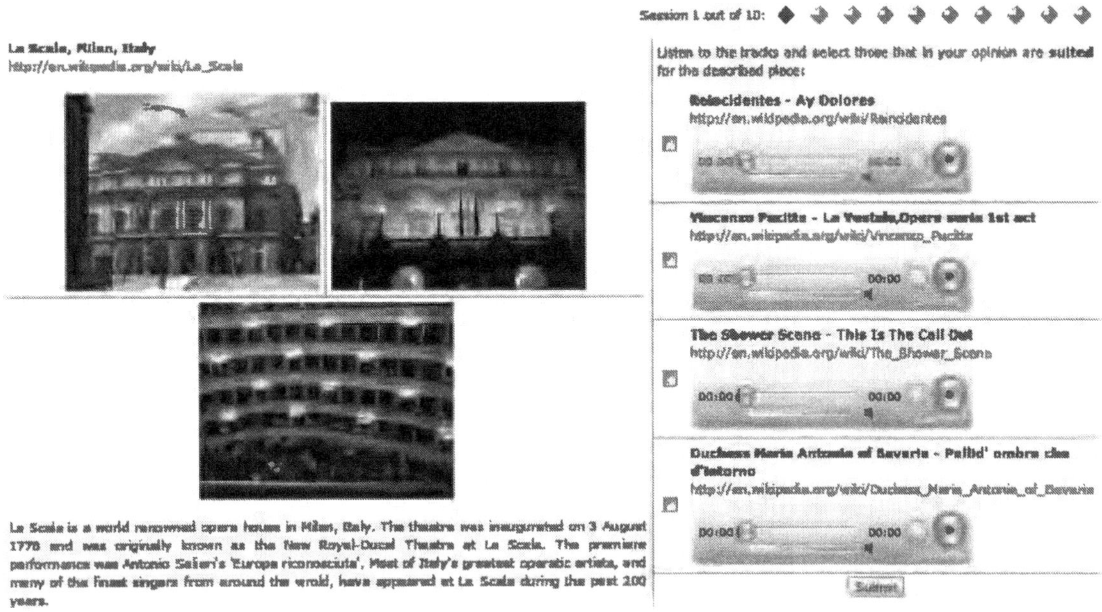

Figure 4: Screenshot of the web application used to evaluate the different music recommendation approaches.

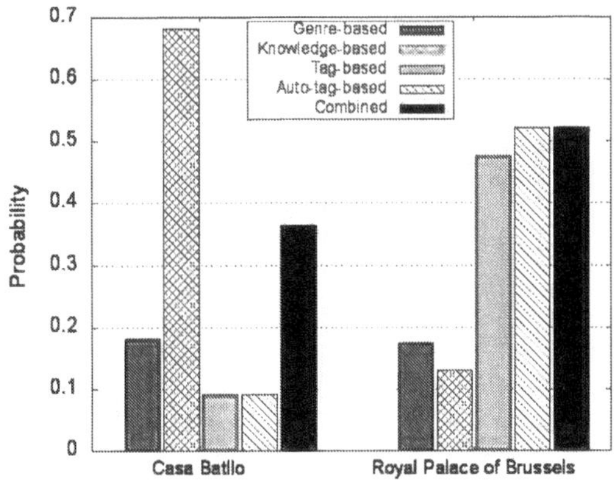

Figure 6: Selection probabilities of the different music recommendation approaches for two individual POIs.

Finally, the evaluation results suggest that the *tag-based* music recommendation approach can be successfully scaled up using automatic tag prediction techniques. The *auto-tag-based* approach even outperformed the *tag-based* approach with marginal significance ($p = 0.078$). This can be explained by the larger variety of music in the auto-tagged music dataset using the *auto-tag-based* approach the recommendations were selected from the full set of 369 music tracks, while the *tag-based* approach used only the subset of 123 manually annotated tracks. Scaling up the process of tag generation without harming performance is hence the vital advantage of using the auto-tagger.

6. CONCLUSIONS AND FUTURE WORK

In this paper, we have presented a novel hybrid approach to recommend music related to POIs. This approach is based on combining two music recommendation techniques: a *tag-based* one and a *knowledge-based* one [6, 11].

Since the *tag-based* technique was previously assessed on a manually tagged dataset of limited size [6], in this work we have shown that it can scale up employing a music auto-tagging technique. In fact, in a user study we have demonstrated that music auto-tagging can be successfully applied in tag-based music recommendation for POIs. Subsequently, we have presented a user study where the proposed approach was evaluated on a dataset of POIs and music tracks and was compared with a personalized recommendation approach that considers users' music genre preferences and does not adapt music to the POIs. The different recommendation techniques were evaluated in a web-based user study where the users were required to evaluate the appropriateness of the music selected by the system for a set of 25 POIs. The results of the evaluation study confirm our hypothesis that the combination of the *tag-based* and *knowledge-based* techniques produces better recommendations. We believe that these findings provide a solid base for the implementation of real-life location-aware music recommenders.

We stress that the ultimate goal of this research is a location-aware music delivery service that combines the *tag-based* and the *knowledge-based* music recommendation techniques. While in this work we demonstrate the effectiveness of such combination through a web-based evaluation, it is important to evaluate the approach in real-life settings and with a larger music/POI dataset to confirm our findings. Moreover, additional evaluation would help us understand which type of associations between music and POIs – emotion-based or knowledge-based – the users prefer in different recommendation scenarios (e.g., sightseeing, choosing a holiday destination, or acquiring knowledge about a destination).

Other important future work directions include automatically acquiring tags describing POIs (using web mining techniques and folksonomy datasets like Flickr as sources of tagging information); analyzing the importance of individual audio features when automatically tagging music tracks; using more complex hybrid recommendation strategies to combine our music recommendations with, e.g., those produced by Last.fm. Finally, we believe that the designed context-aware recommendation solutions may be adapted to other types of content, for instance, recommending music content that fits movies, books, or paintings.

7. ACKNOWLEDGMENTS

This research is supported by the Austrian Science Fund (FWF): P22856 and P25655; and by the EU FP7/2007-2013 through the PHENICX project under grant agreement no. 601166. The authors would further like to thank Klaus Seyerlehner for providing source code and expertise on music auto-tagging.

8. REFERENCES

[1] G. Adomavicius, B. Mobasher, F. Ricci, and A. Tuzhilin. Context-aware recommender systems. *AI Magazine*, 32(3):67–80, 2011.

[2] A. Ankolekar and T. Sandholm. Foxtrot: a soundtrack for where you are. In *Proceedings of Interacting with Sound Workshop: Exploring Context-Aware, Local and Social Audio Applications*, pages 26–31, 2011.

[3] J.-J. Aucouturier and F. Pachet. Improving Timbre Similarity: How High is the Sky? *Journal of Negative Results in Speech and Audio Sciences*, 1(1):1–13, 2004.

[4] L. Baltrunas, T. Makcinskas, and F. Ricci. Group recommendations with rank aggregation and collaborative filtering. In *Proceedings of the 4th ACM Conference on Recommender Systems (RecSys)*, pages 119–126, 2010.

[5] C. Bizer, T. Heath, and T. Berners-Lee. Linked data - the story so far. *International Journal on Semantic Web and Information Systems*, 5(3):1–22, 2009.

[6] M. Braunhofer, M. Kaminskas, and F. Ricci. Location-aware music recommendation. *International Journal of Multimedia Information Retrieval*, 2(1):31–44, 2013.

[7] Ò. Celma. *Music Recommendation and Discovery in the Long Tail.* PhD thesis, Universitat Pompeu Fabra, Barcelona, Spain, 2008.

[8] Ò. Celma and P. Lamere. If you like radiohead, you might like this article. *AI Magazine*, 32(3):57–66, 2011.

[9] E. Coviello, A. B. Chan, and G. Lanckriet. Time Series Models for Semantic Music Annotation. *IEEE Transactions on Audio, Speech, and Language Processing*, 19(5):1343–1359, 2011.

[10] C. Dwork, R. Kumar, M. Naor, and D. Sivakumar. Rank aggregation methods for the web. In *Proceedings of the 10th international conference on World Wide Web (WWW)*, pages 613–622, 2001.

[11] I. Fernández-Tobías, I. Cantador, M. Kaminskas, and F. Ricci. Knowledge-based music retrieval for places of interest. In *Proceedings of the 2nd International Workshop on Music Information Retrieval with User-Centered and Multimodal Strategies (MIRUM)*, pages 19–24, 2012.

[12] M. Kaminskas and F. Ricci. Contextual Music Information Retrieval and Recommendation: State of the Art and Challenges. *Computer Science Review*, 6:89–119, 2012.

[13] J. H. Kim, B. Tomasik, and D. Turnbull. Using Artist Similarity to Propagate Semantic Information. In *Proceedings of the 10th International Society for Music Information Retrieval Conference (ISMIR)*, pages 375–380, 2009.

[14] E. Law, L. Von Ahn, R. Dannenberg, and M. Crawford. Tagatune: A game for music and sound annotation. In *Proceedings of the 8th International Society for Music Information Retrieval Conference (ISMIR)*, pages 361–364, 2007.

[15] M. I. Mandel and D. P. W. Ellis. A Web-Based Game for Collecting Music Metadata. *Journal of New Music Research*, 37(2):151–165, 2008.

[16] M. I. Mandel, R. Pascanu, D. Eck, Y. Bengio, L. M. Aiello, R. Schifanella, and F. Menczer. Contextual Tag Inference. *ACM Transactions on Multimedia Computing, Communications and Applications*, 7S(1):1–18, 2011.

[17] R. Miotto, L. Barrington, and G. Lanckriet. Improving Auto-tagging by Modeling Semantic Co-occurrences. In *Proceedings of the 11th International Society for Music Information Retrieval Conference (ISMIR)*, 2010.

[18] S. Reddy and J. Mascia. Lifetrak: music in tune with your life. In *Proceedings of the 1st ACM International Workshop on Human-centered Multimedia (HCM)*, pages 25–34, 2006.

[19] K. Seyerlehner, M. Schedl, P. Knees, and R. Sonnleitner. A Refined Block-Level Feature Set for Classification, Similarity and Tag Prediction. *Extended Abstract to the Music Information Retrieval Evaluation eXchange (MIREX)*, 2011.

[20] K. Seyerlehner, M. Schedl, T. Pohle, and P. Knees. Using block-level features for genre classification, tag classification and music similarity estimation. *Extended Abstract to the Music Information Retrieval Evaluation eXchange (MIREX)*, 2010.

[21] K. Seyerlehner, G. Widmer, M. Schedl, and P. Knees. Automatic Music Tag Classification based on Block-Level Features. In *Proceedings of the 7th Sound and Music Computing Conference (SMC)*, pages 126–133, 2010.

[22] P. Smolensky. Information Processing in Dynamical Systems: Foundations of Harmony Theory. In *Parallel Distributed Processing: Explorations in the Microstructure of Cognition*, pages 194–281, 1986.

[23] M. Sordo. *Semantic Annotation of Music Collections: A Computational Approach.* PhD thesis, Universitat Pompeu Fabra, Barcelona, Spain, 2012.

[24] D. Turnbull, L. Barrington, and G. Lanckriet. Five approaches to collecting tags for music. In *Proceedings of the 9th International Society for Music Information Retrieval Conference (ISMIR)*, pages 225–230, 2008.

[25] G. Tzanetakis and P. Cook. Musical Genre Classification of Audio Signals. *IEEE Transactions on Speech and Audio Processing*, 10(5):293–302, 2002.

[26] M. Zentner, D. Grandjean, and K. R. Scherer. Emotions evoked by the sound of music: Characterization, classification, and measurement. *Emotion*, 8(4):494–521, 2008.

Spatial Topic Modeling in Online Social Media for Location Recommendation

Bo Hu
School of Computing Science
Simon Fraser University
Burnaby, BC, Canada
boh@cs.sfu.ca

Martin Ester
School of Computing Science
Simon Fraser University
Burnaby, BC, Canada
ester@cs.sfu.ca

ABSTRACT

Mobile networks enable users to post on social media services (e.g., Twitter) from anywhere. The activities of mobile users involve three major entities: user, post, and location. The interaction of these entities is the key to answer questions such as **who** will post a message **where** and on **what** topic? In this paper, we address the problem of profiling mobile users by modeling their activities, i.e., we explore topic modeling considering the spatial and textual aspects of user posts, and predict future user locations. We propose the first **ST** (**S**patial **T**opic) model to capture the correlation between users' movements and between user interests and the function of locations. We employ the sparse coding technique which greatly speeds up the learning process. We perform experiments on two real life data sets from Twitter and Yelp. Through comprehensive experiments, we demonstrate that our proposed model consistently improves the average precision@1,5,10,15,20 for location recommendation by at least 50% (Twitter) and 300% (Yelp) against existing state-of-the-art recommendation algorithms and geographical topic models.

Categories and Subject Descriptors

H.2 [**Database Management**]: Database Applications-Data Mining

General Terms

Algorithms, Design, Measurement, Experimentation

Keywords

Spatial Topic Model, Mobile Users, Location Recommendation

1. INTRODUCTION

With the rapid growth of mobile network users, the way users consume Web 2.0 is changing substantially. Mobile networks enable users to post on social media services (e.g., Twitter or Yelp) from anywhere. This new phenomenon led to the emergence of a new line of research to mine the behavior of social media users taking into account the spatial aspects of their engagement with online social media.

The activities of mobile users can typically be represented as follows: a user appears at a certain location (with a pair of latitude and longitude coordinates), and leaves a post (e.g., tweet or review) which is likely semantically related to the user and/or the location. These activities involve three major entities: user, post, and location. The interaction of these entities is the key to answer questions such as **who** will post a message **where** and on **what** topic? In this paper, we address the problem of profiling mobile users by modeling their activities, i.e., we explore topic modeling considering the spatial and textual aspects of user posts, and predict future user locations.

Several works in the literature have addressed some of the above aspects. In recommender systems, [20, 2, 13] have proposed probabilistic matrix factorization models mining latent user and location preferences to predict user locations, but they totally ignore one of the key components: user posts. Another line of works [18, 21] has focused on user posts and proposed topic models to analyze geographical topics. Most recently, Hong et. al. [10] proposed a geographical topic model to capture language patterns of different regions and different users. Note that the users' distributions over regions are assumed to be independent from each other.

We observe that user movements sometimes correlate if two users have similar lifestyle or living routine. For example, many students from New York University live in the same neighborhood near the campus, and their movement trajectories correlate to each other. They may go to the same restaurants, coffee shops and grocery stores. Therefore, we argue that considering the movements of different users independently as in [10] is not the best way, and that we can predict a user's movement more accurately taking into account the movements of similar users. This idea underlies the paradigm of collaborative filtering.

A second observation is that user interest affects user movement not at the "syntactic" level of 2-dimensional coordinates but at the "semantic" level of places with a certain function. Existing spatial topic models with 2-dimensional coordinates do not distinguish the following two scenarios: 1) two users appear in the same location, like a hockey themed bar, and 2) two users appear in two different locations that are adjacent to each other, where one is a hockey

RecSys'13, October 12–16, 2013, Hong Kong, China.
Copyright 2013 ACM 978-1-4503-2409-0/13/10 ...$15.00.
http://dx.doi.org/10.1145/2507157.2507174.

themed bar and the other one is a facial salon. Intuitively, male users who are interested in sports often go to sport bars and watch games, while female users often go to facial salons. Two users in the first scenario share the same interest, while two users have totally different interests in the second scenario. As a result, without considering the fact that user movements are influenced not only by the coordinates of a location but also by its function, the predictive ability of the model will be greatly reduced.

Motivated by the above observations, this paper explores the following two questions:

1. How are user movements correlated to each other?

2. How does user interest affect user movement at the "semantic" level of locations?

We propose a spatial topic model, called **ST** (Spatial Topic), that takes the correlation of users' movements, and the correlation of user movement and user interest into account. As in existing models, a post is represented as an unordered collection of words (a bag-of-words assumption) associated with user and location, which are all considered as observed random variables. Different from existing works [18, 21, 10], a location in this paper is defined as a place with a semantic functionality and with its 2D coordinates. A set of latent random variables is also defined, i.e., regions and topics are latent, and each post is assigned to a region and a topic. We assume that each location is assigned to one and only one region, and its coordinates are generated by a 2-dimensional Gaussian distribution. For example, in New York City, regions could be areas that corresponded to community districts, such as Manhattan, Brooklyn, and Queens etc. Different from existing models, in order to generate a location of a post by a particular user, the model considers the user's interest and the locations of "similar" users. We develop a MCEM (Monte Carlo Expectation Maximization) method to learn the latent random variables and parameters that maximize the likelihood of the observed random variables, and the sparse coding technique is used to improve the efficiency of the learning method.

We perform experiments on two real life data sets from Twitter and Yelp. All posts (tweets and reviews) in the data sets are annotated with corresponding users and locations. We evaluate the effectiveness of our proposed model and of state-of-the-art models in terms of accuracy of location prediction, i.e., given a post and its author, we recommend top-k locations to the user.

The major contributions of this paper are as follows:

- We propose the first spatial topic model to capture the correlation between users' movements and between user interests and the function of locations.

- We employ the sparse coding technique which greatly speeds up the learning process.

- Through comprehensive experiments, we demonstrate that our proposed model consistently improves the average precision@1,5,10,15,20 for location recommendation by at least 50% (Twitter) and 300% (Yelp) compared to existing state-of-the-art recommendation algorithms and geographical topic models.

2. RELATED WORK

In this section, we briefly review related work. There are three lines of related work, which are geographical topic modeling, location recommendation, and user movement analysis.

Geographical Topic Modeling. Topic modeling is a classic task to enable text analysis at a semantic level. A topic model assumes that each document in a given data set is associated with a topic distribution, and each topic with a word distribution. The most representative models are PLSA [9] and LDA [1]. Recently, there are many works [19, 18, 21, 10] in the area of geographical topic modeling, which detect geographical regions and topics from documents that are associated with locations.

Yin et al. [21] and Eisenstein et al. [7] propose similar models, where the coordinates in each document are drawn from a 2D Gaussian distribution and the region is drawn from a Multinomial distribution over all regions.

Recently, Hong et al. [10] propose a model, called GT (Geographical Topic), assuming that each user has a distribution over all regions, i.e., users tend to appear in a small subset of all regions, and each user has a distribution over all topics, i.e., users tend to have different interests on different topics. They conduct extensive experiments on a large scale Twitter data set and their model achieves better location prediction performance than existing models.

Although all the above works discover regions and geographical topics, they do not consider the correlation of users' movements. Additionally, they assume that users' interests influence users' regional preferences directly but influence users' locations only indirectly. Finally, these models ignore the functionality of locations, which greatly reduces the predictive ability of the model as will be shown in our experiments.

Location Recommendation. In the classic framework of recommender systems, we have a user-item matrix and each element in the matrix represents the user's rating of that item. To put it in the context of location recommendation, locations can be viewed as items, and binary user item ratings can represent whether a user has visited the corresponding locations. Particularly, the user-location matrix can be computed by the user and location latent factors through MF (Matrix Factorization) techniques [11, 12]. Recent works [20, 22, 2, 13] extend PMF (Probabilistic Matrix Factorization) [16] for location recommendation by considering the distance between users and locations, i.e., closer locations are recommended with higher probabilities.

The authors of [2] have proposed a MF model considering geographical influence for POI (Point-Of-Interest) recommendation in location-based social networks. Their model detects multiple centers for each user based on their history of locations, and each center has 2-dimensional coordinates. Motivated by the effect of geographical influence, the probability of recommending a location is inversely proportional to the distance between the location and the nearest user center. Similarly, a recent work [13] has proposed GLDA (Geo Latent Dirichlet Allocation) to capture users' location preferences by combining LDA and geographical influence.

Note that all these methods ignore the text of posts which is an essential component in our problem definition.

User Movement Analysis. Some works [8, 3, 4, 5] have been studying user movements in location-based social networks. Since most user posts are not associated with coordinates, these works address the following problem: given a set of geo-tagged posts from many users, learn a model of region specific words, and apply this model to predict the user location of un-tagged posts based on their content. This is different from the problem in this paper, which is to predict the location of posts by users with many geographical posts. Cheng et al. [3, 4] develop probabilistic methods to identify local words in tweets, and they predict user locations based on the local words in their tweets. Similarly, [8] proposes a Multinomial Naive Bayes model to predict the Twitter user profile's location at the granularity of the city level.

[5] studies the problem of modeling human mobility in social networks, and one of their interesting findings is that users tend to move within a small number of regions, e.g., around their home and office. Another interesting finding is that a user's movement trajectory correlates to that of their friends. Furthermore, a recent work [15] presents a probabilistic model incorporating social networks and achieves better performance for tweet location prediction. This type of work focuses on the impact of social networks on user movements, while we do not use social networks.

3. SPATIAL TOPIC MODEL

In this section, we first introduce the problem definition and then present our proposed **ST** (Spatial Topic) model.

3.1 Problem Def nition

On social media sites, such as Twitter or Yelp, a large number of users generate content. These user generated posts can consist of personal information, news, comments or reviews. We are in particular interested in the text and location of the posts. More precisely, we assume that a post has the following attributes: text, author, and location. An example of publicly available tweets is as follows:

- Close to the equator, perfect soil and high elevation make @CafeDAltamira produce the perfect cup of Coffee!! # Honduras # Coffee | @XXX | 37.38 -121.90 | San Jose | CA | United States | 0befbacea94beb06.

This tweet states that a Twitter user from San Jose, California compliments the coffee at a coffee shop, where "37.38, -121.90" are the latitude and longitude coordinates, and "0befbacea94beb06" is the unique label of the coffee shop.

We assume that all the documents are authored by a user from a fixed set of size U and all the words are from a fixed vocabulary of size V. We associate each user with a set of posts, and the number of posts of user u is denoted as D_u. Each post is represented by a set of words (the number of its words is denoted as $N_{u,d}$), and a pair of latitude and longitude coordinates. For convenience, we consider "tweet", "review", "post" and "document" as synonyms in this paper. Formally, a document d is defined by $d = \{\mathbf{w}, u, i\}$, where w, u, i represents set of (index of) words, the index of user and location respectively. l_i represents the coordinates of location i. A document collection $\mathcal{D}$ is defined as a set of documents from all users. We assume that there is a set of latent topics and a set of latent regions in the document collection $\mathcal{D}$. Each document d is assigned to one of the topics z_d and regions r_d. We use Z and R to denote the number of topics and number of regions, respectively.

A semantically coherent topic in the document collection $\mathcal{D}$ is associated with a probability distribution over all words in the vocabulary, and a probability distribution over all locations. A region has a geographical center, and it is comprised of a set of documents, which are coherent in topics and close to the center geographically. We assume that different users show different distributions over topics and regions. All notations described above are listed in Table 1.

Table 1: Notations of input and output data

Variable	Interpretation
$w_{u,d,n}$	n^{th} word of the dth document posted by the uth user
$i_{u,d}$	location index of the dth document posted by the uth user
l_i	latitude and longitude coordinates of the ith location
$z_{u,d}$	topic assignment of the dth document posted by the uth user
$r_{u,d}$	region assignment of the dth document posted by the uth user
Z	number of topics
R	number of regions
U	number of users
I	number of locations
D_u	number of documents of user u
$N_{u,d}$	number of words in document d of user u
V	size of the vocabulary

Based on the above definitions, we formalize our research problem as follows:

PROBLEM 1 (SPATIAL TOPIC MODELING). *Given a document collection $\mathcal{D}$, and numbers Z of topics and R of regions, the task is to model and extract a set of topics and a set of regions.*

3.2 Model

To address our research problem, we introduce the ST model. Figure 1 shows the graphical model of ST.

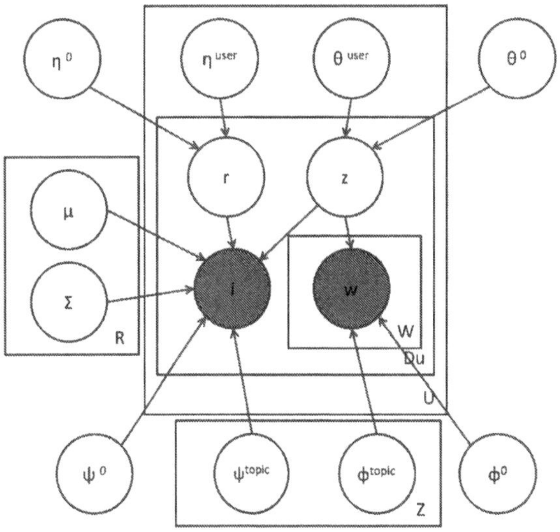

Figure 1: The graphical model of ST

We first introduce the notations of our model and listed in Table 1. Our input data, i.e., words and locations, are modeled as observed random variables, shown as shaded circles in Figure 1, and we use $w_{u,d,n}$ and $i_{u,d}$ to denote them.

l_i is a pair of latitude and longitude real values of ith location. Similar to existing models as in [21, 10], the topic and region index of documents are considered as latent random variables, which are denoted as $z_{u,d}$ and $r_{u,d}$ respectively. Users are associated with topic and region distributions, i.e., θ^{user} and η^{user}, from which the topics and regions of posts are sampled. Topics are associated with word distributions ϕ^{topic}. Given the sampled topic, words are drawn from the word distribution of that topic. The background distributions of words, topics, and regions are denoted as ϕ^0, θ^0, and η^0. All parameters are listed in Table 2.

Table 2: Notations of parameters

Variable	Interpretation
θ^0	topic distribution of the background
θ_u^{user}	topic distribution of the uth user
ϕ^0	word distribution of the background
ϕ_z^{topic}	word distribution of the zth topic
η^0	region distribution of the background
η_u^{user}	region distribution of the uth user
ψ^0	location distribution of the background
ψ_z^{topic}	location distribution of the zth topic
μ_r	region mean location of the rth region
Σ_r	region location covariance of the rth region

An important change from existing models is that instead of generating the coordinates of posts, ST generates the index of the location of posts. Another major change is that, to model the impact of user interest on user movement, ST assumes that the location depends not only on the region but also on the topic. Consequently, it adds a location distribution ψ^{topic} for each topic. Existing models assume that the 2D Gaussian distribution with center μ and covariance Σ of the sampled region governs the choice of locations visited, i.e., the closer a location to the center, the higher the probability of visiting that location, and ST has the same assumption. Additionally, ST assumes that another important reason why the user visits the location can be attributed to the user interests. Since locations with different functions can have very similar coordinates, this assumption is much more meaningful when considering "semantic" locations.

Particularly, users have different topic distributions, and topics have different location distributions, so that the dependency between user interests and user locations is transferred through the topic. ST captures the correlation between movements of different users, such that users who have similar movements share the same topics. Note that the topics serve a similar role as the latent factors in MF (Matrix Factorization). Different from the existing MF methods [2, 13], ST associates a word distribution with a topic so that it can describe the latent user and location factors. Intuitively, collaborative filtering assumes that locations A and B should both have high probabilities in location distributions of some topic(s) in our case if many users frequently co-occur in both A and B. Location A and B do not necessarily have the same functionality. However, ST further assumes that locations with high probabilities for the same topic should be cohesive in their functions, e.g., a topic with high probabilities for words like "coffee", "Java", and "mocha" should have high probability only for coffee shops. This design enables ST to detect users with similar interests and locations with similar functions, and enables ST to better deal with "cold start" users, i.e., users who have very few posts, since the words of their few posts are more informative than their locations.

Next, we describe the generative process of the ST model for a single document d.

- Draw a region index $r_{u,d}$
  - $r_{u,d} \sim p(r_{u,d}|u, \eta^0, \eta^{user})$
- Draw a topic index $z_{u,d}$
  - $z_{u,d} \sim p(z_{u,d}|u, \theta^0, \theta^{user})$
- Draw a location index $i_{u,d}$, given the region index $r_{u,d}$ and topic index $z_{u,d}$
  - $i_{u,d} \sim p(i_{u,d}|r_{u,d}, z_{u,d}, \psi^0, \psi^{topic}, \mu, \Sigma)$
- Draw each word in d given the topic index $z_{u,d}$
  - $w_{u,d,n} \sim p(w_{u,d,n}|z_{u,d}, \phi^0, \phi^{topic})$

For each document, the ST model generates the location and words consecutively. To generate a location, the model first samples a region from the set of regions. To generate a region r, we use a multinomial distribution as follows:

$$p(r_{u,d}|u, \eta^0, \eta^{user}) = p(r_{u,d}|\eta^0 + \eta_u^{user}) \quad (1)$$

where η^0 is the global distribution of regions and η_u^{user} is the region distribution of user u. To simplify the notations, we use $p(r|\eta^0 + \eta_u^{user}) = \beta_{u,r}$ as shown in Equation 6 (see Figure 2). This approach employs the sparse coding technique introduced in the SAGE (Sparse Additive Generative) model [6]. The major advantage of SAGE is that it does not require additional latent "switching" variables when the model needs to take multiple factors into account. For example, in order to model topics, based on the background word distribution, for each topic SAGE models the difference in log-frequencies from the background word distribution instead of the log-frequencies themselves.

Each location i is drawn depending on its corresponding region r and corresponding topic z. Given the sampled topic z and sampled region r, ST draws the location $i_{u,d}$ as follows:

$$\begin{aligned} i_{u,d} \sim\ & p(i_{u,d}|r_{u,d}, z_{u,d}, \psi^0, \psi^{topic}, \mu, \Sigma) \\ & = p(i_{u,d}|\psi^0 + \psi_{z_{u,d}}^{topic}) \times p(l_{i_{u,d}}|\mu_{r_{u,d}}, \Sigma_{r_{u,d}}) \end{aligned} \quad (2)$$

where $p(i|\psi^0 + \psi_z^{topic}) = \delta_{z,i}$ is shown in Equation 6, and $p(l_i|\mu_r, \Sigma_r) = \mathcal{N}(l_i|r, \mu, \Sigma)$, which is the PDF of the Multivariate Gaussian distribution. This is the product of the probability of drawing the coordinates of the location from the 2D Gaussian distribution μ_r, Σ_r of that region, and the probability of drawing the index of the location from the location distribution ψ_z^{topic} of that topic.

Similarly, for generating the topic and word index, the model uses a multinomial distribution considering the background and user topic distributions together, and the background and topic word distributions together, respectively as follows:

$$p(z_{u,d}|u, \theta^0, \theta_u^{user}) = p(z_{u,d}|\theta^0 + \theta_u^{user}) \quad (3)$$

$$p(w_{u,d,n}|z_{u,d}, \phi^0, \phi^{topic}) = p(w_{u,d,n}|\phi^0 + \phi_{z_{u,d}}^{topic}) \quad (4)$$

where $p(z|\theta^0 + \theta_u^{user}) = \alpha_{u,z}$ and $p(w_{u,d,n}|\phi^0 + \phi_z^{topic}) = \gamma_{z,w}$ are shown in Equation 6.

$$
\begin{aligned}
p(\mathbf{z},\mathbf{r},\mathbf{w},\mathbf{i}|\Theta) &= p(\mathbf{z}|\theta^0,\theta^{user}) \times p(\mathbf{r}|\eta^0,\eta^{user}) \times p(\mathbf{w}|\mathbf{z},\phi^0,\phi^{topic}) \times p(\mathbf{i}|\mathbf{r},\mathbf{z},\mu,\Sigma,\psi^0,\psi^{topic}) \\
&= \prod_{u=1}^{U}\prod_{d=1}^{D_u}\alpha_{u,z_{u,d}} \times \prod_{u=1}^{U}\prod_{d=1}^{D_u}\beta_{u,r_{u,d}} \times \prod_{u=1}^{U}\prod_{d=1}^{D_u}\prod_{n=1}^{N_{u,d}}\gamma_{z_{u,d},w_{u,d,n}} \times \prod_{u=1}^{U}\prod_{d=1}^{D_u}\delta_{z_{u,d},i_{u,d}} \\
&\quad \times \prod_{u=1}^{U}\prod_{d=1}^{D_u}\mathcal{N}(l_{i_{u,d}}|r_{u,d},\mu,\Sigma)
\end{aligned} \tag{5}
$$

$$
\alpha_{u,z} = \frac{\exp(\theta_z^0+\theta_{u,z}^{user})}{\sum_{zz=1}^{Z}\exp(\theta_{zz}^0+\theta_{u,zz}^{user})}, \beta_{u,r} = \frac{\exp(\eta_r^0+\eta_{u,r}^{user})}{\sum_{rr=1}^{R}\exp(\eta_{rr}^0+\eta_{u,rr}^{user})}, \gamma_{z,w} = \frac{\exp(\phi_w^0+\phi_{z,w}^{topic})}{\sum_{ww=1}^{V}\exp(\phi_{ww}^0+\phi_{z,ww}^{topic})}, \delta_{z,i} = \frac{\exp(\psi_i^0+\psi_{z,i}^{topic})}{\sum_{ii=1}^{I}\exp(\psi_{ii}^0+\psi_{z,ii}^{topic})} \tag{6}
$$

Figure 2: The joint probability of random variables given parameters in the ST model

3.3 Parameter Learning

Our goal is to learn parameters that maximize the marginal log-likelihood of the observed random variables $\mathbf{i},\mathbf{w}$. The marginalization is performed with respect to the latent random variables $\mathbf{z},\mathbf{r}$, and it is hard to be maximized directly. Therefore, we apply the MCEM (Monte Carlo Expectation Maximization) algorithm to maximize the complete data likelihood $p(\mathbf{z},\mathbf{r},\mathbf{w},\mathbf{i}|\Theta)$ in Equation 5 (see Figure 2), where $\Theta = \{\mu,\Sigma,\theta^0,\theta^{user},\phi^0,\phi^{topic},\eta^0,\eta^{user},\psi^0,\psi^{topic}\}$.

According to the MCEM method, we sample the latent variables $\mathbf{r},\mathbf{z}$ in the E step and maximize the parameters Θ in the M step. To sample a single variable $r_{u,d}$ given all other variables fixed, we use Equation 7. After $\mathbf{r}$ is sampled, we sample $z_{u,d}$ similarly according to Equation 8.

$$
p(r_{u,d}|\mathbf{z},\mathbf{r}_{-u,d},\mathbf{w},\mathbf{i},\Theta) \propto \beta_{u,r_{u,d}} \times \delta_{z_{u,d},i_{u,d}} \times \mathcal{N}(l_i|r,\mu,\Sigma) \tag{7}
$$

$$
p(z_{u,d}|\mathbf{z}_{-u,d},\mathbf{r},\mathbf{w},\mathbf{i},\Theta) \propto \alpha_{u,z_{u,d}} \times \prod_{n=1}^{N_{u,d}}\gamma_{z_{u,d},w_{u,d,n}} \times \delta_{z_{u,d},i_{u,d}} \times \mathcal{N}(l_i|r,\mu,\Sigma) \tag{8}
$$

Figure 3: The sampling formulas for latent variables r,z in the ST model

In the M step, fixing all the latent variables $\mathbf{r},\mathbf{z}$ that are sampled in the E step, we maximize the log likelihood of Equation 5 with respect to the parameters Θ. For variables μ and Σ, to obtain the maximum likelihood estimate, we take the derivative of its log likelihood with respect to μ_r and Σ_r, and set it to zero. Only one term in Equation 5 contains μ_r, so we use Equation 9 to update μ_r, where $\mathcal{I}(.)$ is an identity function, i.e. one where $r_{u,d}$ equals to r and zero otherwise, and $d(r)$ represents the number of documents assigned to region r. μ_r denotes the mean coordinates of locations of the documents assigned to region r in the E step. We use Equation 10 to update the parameter Σ_r.

$$
\mu_r = \frac{1}{d(r)}\sum_{u=1}^{U}\sum_{d=1}^{D_u}\mathcal{I}(r_{u,d}==r)l_{i_{u,d}} \tag{9}
$$

$$
\Sigma_r = \frac{1}{d(r)-1}\sum_{u=1}^{U}\sum_{d=1}^{D_u}\mathcal{I}(r_{u,d}==r)(l_{i_{u,d}}-\mu_r)^T(l_{i_{u,d}}-\mu_r) \tag{10}
$$

To update the other parameters, we use the gradient descent learning algorithm PSSG (Projected Scaled Sub-Gradient) [17], which is designed to solve optimization problems with L1 regularization on the parameters. More importantly, PSSG is scalable because it uses the quasi-Newton strategy with line search that is robust to common functions. According to the limited-memory BFGS [14] updates for the quasi-Newton method, the partial derivative functions of the parameters η^0,η^{user} are provided in the following Equations 11 and 12, where $d(u,r)$ represents the number of documents assigned to region r by user u, and $d(u)$ represents the number of documents by user u.

$$
\frac{\partial L}{\partial \eta_r^0} = \sum_{u=1}^{U} d(u,r) - \sum_{u=1}^{U}\Big(d(u)\times\beta_{u,r}\Big) \tag{11}
$$

$$
\frac{\partial L}{\partial \eta_{u,r}^{user}} = d(u,r) - d(u)\times\beta_{u,r} \tag{12}
$$

Similarly, we get derivative functions for the remaining parameters, which are omitted because of the page limit.

3.4 Location Recommendation

The ST model can be employed for location recommendation as follows. Given a document with a user, our task is to recommend top-k "new " locations, i.e., the locations that the user has not visited in the training data set, which that user will visit. More precisely, given the words and author of a document d, the probability that author u visits location i is computed as in Equation 13:

$$
\begin{aligned}
p(i|\mathbf{w},\Theta) &\propto \sum_{r}^{R}\sum_{z}^{Z} p(\mathbf{w},i,z,r|\Theta) \\
&= \sum_r^R\sum_z^Z p(z|\theta^0,\theta^{user}) \times p(r|\eta^0,\eta^{user}) \\
&\quad \times p(\mathbf{w}|z,\phi^0,\phi^{topic}) \times p(i|z,r,\mu,\Sigma,\psi^0,\psi^{topic})
\end{aligned} \tag{13}
$$

We rank the locations in descending order of $p(i|\mathbf{w},\Theta)$.

4. EXPERIMENTS

In this section, we experimentally evaluate the effectiveness of the ST (Spatial Topic) model, and we compare it against some baseline methods, one of the state-of-the-art location recommendation methods [13], and one of the state-of-the-art geographical topic models [10]. We report our experimental results on Twitter and Yelp data sets, using the top-k average precision of location recommendation for measuring the quality.

4.1 Data Sets

We report our experimental results on a Twitter data set downloaded from [4][1]. We extract a data set from a rep-

[1] http://infolab.tamu.edu/data/

resentative city in the US: NYC (New York City), where all tweets contain a location label and geographical coordinates. To determine the coordinates of the location, we use the mean of the coordinates of all tweets associated with a location. Hence each location corresponds to a unique mean coordinate, and each tweet of that location has the same coordinates. Another data set is from Yelp, and it is publicly available[2]. It is from a US city – Phoenix. In the Yelp data set, each review has a location (being reviewed) that is associated with a unique pair of latitude and longitude coordinates. Note that Twitter users often check in at the same location multiple times, while Yelp users write reviews for a location only once.

In the pre-processing steps, texts are processed by tokenizing on whitespace and punctuations, while we remove the URLs starting with "http" and user names starting with "@". Then we remove all texts with non-latin characters, followed by removing stop words, and the words with occurrences less than 100. To reduce noise, we remove both users and locations with less than 10 posts. Some statistics about the data sets are presented in Table 3.

Table 3: Statistics of data sets from New York City on Twitter and Phoenix on Yelp.

#	Twitter	Yelp
Unique users	9,508	3,963
Posts	607,885	107,981
Locations	3,518	2,951
Avg. posts/user	64.93	27.24
Avg. posts/location	172.79	36.59

Note that our data sets are much larger than the ones used in [13]. Another related work [10] uses data sets from all over the world, while our data sets are at the city level. From this point of view, the size of these two data sets is comparable or larger than the ones in [10].

4.2 Experimental Setup

In our data sets, we randomly select 70% of observed data for each user as the training data, and the remaining 30% as the test data. We focus on the task of location recommendation for users based on each document, which is by far the most commonly used performance measure for spatial topic model in the literature [20, 2, 13]. In particular, we train models in the training data set, and recommend the locations based on posts by users in the test data set.

Evaluation Metric. Precision@k (top-k average precision) is used to evaluate the methods as follows. The top-k precision for a test post is $\frac{1}{k}$ if its location is among the top-k recommendations, and zero otherwise. The precision@k is the average top-k precision over all test posts.

Comparison Partners. In our experiments, we evaluate the following comparison partners, which all model (can predict) either the coordinates or index of locations:

- *PMF* (Probabilistic Matrix Factorization). This is a well-known model in matrix factorization in [16].
- *GLDA* (Geo Latent Dirichlet Allocation). This is the modified LDA model, which is one of the state-of-the-art methods for location recommendation proposed in [13].
- *GT* (Geographical Topic). This is one of the state-of-the-art geographical topic models proposed in [10].
- $ST_{location}$ (ST_{loc} for short). This is a simplified version of the ST model, where we remove the posts, and the only observed variable is the index of locations **i** and the only latent variable is the topic **z**. Note that this model is equivalent to an LDA model that generates index of locations instead of words.
- $ST_{coordinate}$ (ST_{coo} for short). This is a simplified version of the ST model. Similar to ST_{loc}, we remove the posts from the data. Instead of generating the index of locations, ST_{coo} generates the coordinates of locations **l**, and the only latent variable is the region **r**.
- $ST_{coordinate+location}$ ($ST_{loc+coo}$ for short). This is another simplified version of the ST model, that generates both the coordinates and index of locations, and the latent variables are the topic **z** and region **r**. The only difference between this model and the full ST model is the lack of words.
- *ST*. This is the spatial topic model proposed in this paper.

Note that there are other existing models [19, 18, 21] proposed for geographical topic modeling. We do not compare against them because the GT model proposed in [10] is a generalization of the existing models, and it performs better than the existing models in terms of location prediction in the experiments of [10]. We do not compare against [2], since it is similar to GLDA, which is the most recent work [13] on location recommendation.

4.3 Experimental Results

For location recommendation, Figure 4(a) and 4(b) show the precision@1,5,10,15,20 results of the comparison partners in the Twitter and Yelp data sets. Note that the number of topics and regions is set to 30 and 20. We observe that our ST model consistently and drastically outperforms all other models on both data sets. Compared to the state-of-the-art methods, GLDA and GT, in the areas of recommender systems and geographical topic modeling, ST improves the precision@20 by 50% (Twitter) and 300% (Yelp), and the gain is even higher for smaller values of **k**. This indicates that modeling the user interests and the correlation of user movements can help improve the accuracy of location recommendation.

We also observe that the precision difference between ST and other models on Yelp is much larger than on Twitter. We argue that this is because 1) the posts on Yelp are much longer than on Twitter; 2) the words used on Yelp are more formal than on Twitter. As a result, it is easier to capture the user interests on Yelp than on Twitter.

We further analyze the contributions of different components in ST, by comparing the performance of ST and its simplified versions: ST_{loc}, ST_{coo}, and $ST_{loc+coo}$. We observe that modeling the index (semantics) of locations in ST_{loc} is much more precise than modeling the coordinates of locations in ST_{coo}. Comparing *ST* and $ST_{loc+coo}$, we see that the user interests expressed in the posts indeed enable more accurate location recommendation. Furthermore, we observe that $ST_{loc+coo}$ clearly outperforms ST_{coo}, demonstrating the contribution of exploiting the correlation of user movements.

[2]https://www.yelp.com/dataset_challenge/

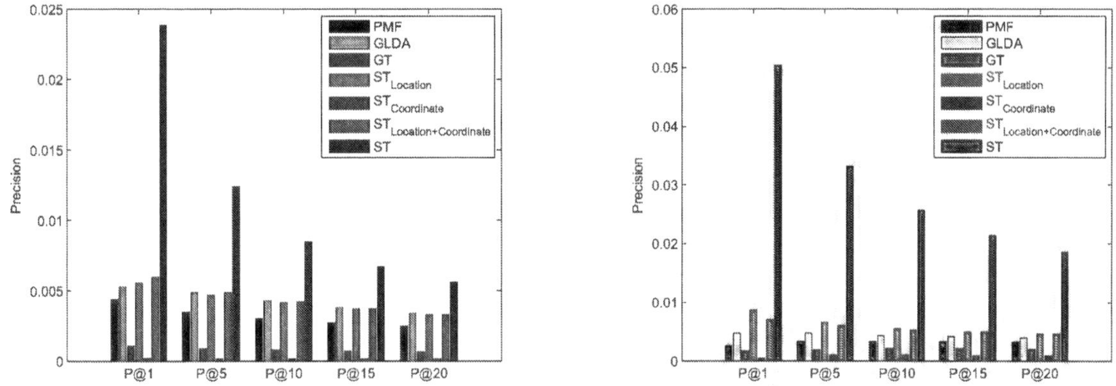

(a) Twitter data set.

(b) Yelp data set.

Figure 4: Precision@1,5,10,15,20 of comparison partners.

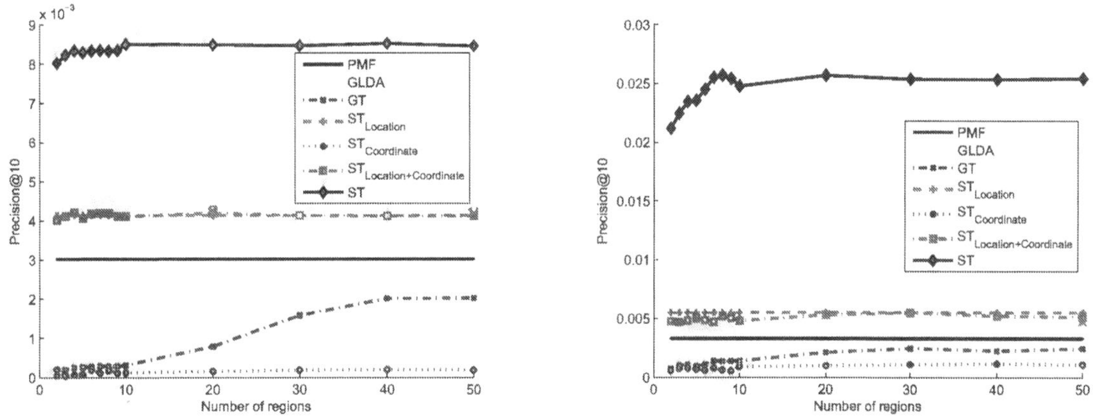

(a) Twitter data set.

(b) Yelp data set.

Figure 5: Precision@10 of the comparison partners for different number of regions. The number of topics is set to 30.

To analyze the impact of the input parameters, we show the precision@10 of the comparison partners for different numbers of regions (see Figure 5(a) and 5(b)) and topics (see Figure 6(a) and 6(b)). The results for precision@1,5,15,20 are similar to the results for precision@10. We observe that ST consistently outperforms the other comparison partners for all number of regions and topics. Furthermore, as the number of regions increases, the precision@10 of ST and GT increases and reaches a peak at first, and it plateaus when the number of regions reaches 10 or 20. Similarly, as the number of topics increases, the precision of ST increases. Some models, such as PMF, $GLDA$ and ST_{loc}, do not take the number of regions as their input, so that their precision is constant in Figure 5. Overall, the results of ST are relatively robust to the choice of the input parameters.

5. CONCLUSION AND FUTURE WORK

In this paper, we address the problem of spatial topic modeling in online social media, such as Twitter and Yelp, for user-generated content with location. Previous work has explored topic models and recommendation algorithms that model either user and location, or user and post, but they do not consider all of them together. We propose the first spatial model to capture spatial and textual aspects of posts, as well as user profiles in a single topic model, called Spatial Topic (ST) model. ST exploits the interdependencies between user movements, and between user interests and user movements. More specifically, ST is based on the intuition that 1) users' movements correlate with each other; 2) users' interests affect the movements of users. We argue that taking the correlation of users' movements, and the correlation of user movement and user interest into account enables a more accurate discovery of relevant regions and topics. We present the graphical model of ST and a corresponding method of parameter learning. We perform an experimental evaluation on Twitter and Yelp data sets from New York City and Phoenix. We compare ST against a state-of-the-art geographical topic model and a state-of-the-art recommendation method in terms of location recommendation. Our

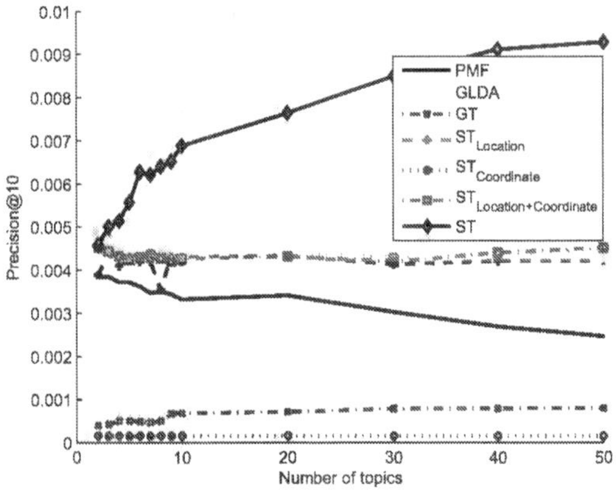

(a) Twitter data set.

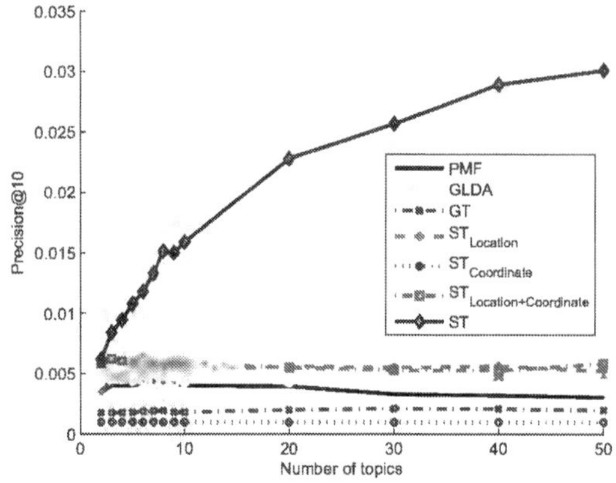

(b) Yelp data set.

Figure 6: Precision@10 of the comparison partners for different number of topics. The number of regions is set to 20.

experiments demonstrate drastically improved performance in location recommendation.

An interesting direction for future work is to integrate other aspects that may impact user locations, i.e. ratings and time, into the spatial topic model. Open questions are in particular how ratings of locations attract users, as well as if and how time (hour, day, week, year) influences user locations.

6. REFERENCES

[1] D. M. Blei, A. Ng, and M. Jordan. Latent dirichlet allocation. *JMLR*, 3:993–1022, 2003.

[2] C. Cheng, H. Yang, I. King, and M. R. Lyu. Fused matrix factorization with geographical and social influence in location-based social networks. AAAI, 2012.

[3] Z. Cheng, J. Caverlee, and K. Lee. You are where you tweet: a content-based approach to geo-locating twitter users. CIKM, pages 759–768, 2010.

[4] Z. Cheng, J. Caverlee, K. Lee, and D. Z. Sui. Exploring millions of footprints in location sharing services. ICWSM, 2011.

[5] E. Cho, S. A. Myers, and J. Leskovec. Friendship and mobility: user movement in location-based social networks. KDD, pages 1082–1090, 2011.

[6] J. Eisenstein, A. Ahmed, and E. P. Xing. Sparse additive generative models of text. ICML, pages 1041–1048, 2011.

[7] J. Eisenstein, B. O'Connor, N. A. Smith, and E. P. Xing. A latent variable model for geographic lexical variation. EMNLP, pages 1277–1287, 2010.

[8] B. Hecht, L. Hong, B. Suh, and E. H. Chi. Tweets from justin bieber's heart: the dynamics of the location field in user profiles. In *CHI*, pages 237–246, 2011.

[9] T. Hofmann. Probilistic latent semantic analysis. In *UAI*, 1999.

[10] L. Hong, A. Ahmed, S. Gurumurthy, A. J. Smola, and K. Tsioutsiouliklis. Discovering geographical topics in the twitter stream. WWW, pages 769–778, 2012.

[11] Y. Koren. Factorization meets the neighborhood: a multifaceted collaborative filtering model. KDD, pages 426–434, 2008.

[12] Y. Koren, R. Bell, and C. Volinsky. Matrix factorization techniques for recommender systems. *Computer*, 42:30–37, 2009.

[13] T. Kurashima, T. Iwata, T. Hoshide, N. Takaya, and K. Fujimura. Geo topic model: joint modeling of user's activity area and interests for location recommendation. WSDM, pages 375–384, 2013.

[14] D. C. Liu, J. Nocedal, D. C. Liu, and J. Nocedal. On the limited memory bfgs method for large scale optimization. *Mathematical Programming*, pages 503–528, 1989.

[15] A. Sadilek, H. Kautz, and J. P. Bigham. Finding your friends and following them to where you are. WSDM, pages 723–732, 2012.

[16] R. Salakhutdinov and M. Andriy. Probabilistic matrix factorization. NIPS, pages 1257–1264, 2008.

[17] M. Schmidt, A. Niculescu-Mizil, and K. Murphy. Learning graphical model structure using l1-regularization paths. AAAI, pages 1278–1283, 2007.

[18] S. Sizov. Geofolk: latent spatial semantics in web 2.0 social media. WSDM, pages 281–290, 2010.

[19] C. Wang, J. Wang, X. Xie, and W.-Y. Ma. Mining geographic knowledge using location aware topic model. GIR, pages 65–70, 2007.

[20] M. Ye, P. Yin, and W.-C. Lee. Location recommendation for location-based social networks. GIS, pages 458–461, 2010.

[21] Z. Yin, L. Cao, J. Han, C. Zhai, and T. Huang. Geographical topic discovery and comparison. WWW, pages 247–256, 2011.

[22] V. W. Zheng, Y. Zheng, X. Xie, and Q. Yang. Collaborative location and activity recommendations with gps history data. WWW, pages 1029–1038, 2010.

Orthogonal Query Recommendation

Hossein Vahabi *
Microblr
London, UK
pvahabi@microblr.com

Margareta Ackerman
Caltech
Pasadena, California, USA
mackerma@caltech.edu

David Loker
University of Waterloo
Waterloo, Canada
dloker@cs.uwaterloo.ca

Ricardo Baeza-Yates
Yahoo! Research Labs
Barcelona, Spain
rbaeza@acm.org

Alejandro Lopez-Ortiz
University of Waterloo
Waterloo, Canada
alopez-o@uwaterloo.ca

ABSTRACT

One important challenge of current search engines is to satisfy the users' needs when they provide a poorly formulated query. When the pages matching the user's original keywords are judged to be unsatisfactory, query recommendation techniques are used to propose alternative queries and alter the result set. These techniques search for queries that are *semantically similar* to the user's original query, often searching for keywords that are similar to the keywords given by the user. However, when the original query is sufficiently ill-posed, the user's informational need is best met using entirely different keywords, and a substantially different query may be necessary.

We propose a novel approach that is not based on the keywords of the original query. We intentionally seek out *orthogonal queries*, which are related queries that have (almost) no common terms with the user's query. This allows an orthogonal query to satisfy the user's informational need when small perturbations of the original keyword set are insufficient. By using this technique to generate query recommendations, we outperform several known approaches, being the best for long tail queries.

Categories and Subject Descriptors

H.4 [**Information Systems Applications**]: Miscellaneous; H.3.3 [**Information Storage and Retrieval**]: Information Search and Retrieval—*Query formulation*

General Terms

Algorithms, Experimentation, Measurement

Keywords

Query Recommendation, Knowledge Extraction

*This work was partially done at CNR,Pisa, Italy.

RecSys'13, October 12–16, 2013, Hong Kong, China.
Copyright 2013 ACM 978-1-4503-2409-0/13/09 ...$15.00.
http://dx.doi.org/10.1145/2507157.2507159.

1. INTRODUCTION

Over the last seventeen years there has been enormous progress on Web search. Starting from the text-based ranking algorithms of 1994, we now have complex ranking algorithms that use hundreds of features and many functionalities based on usage data, such as spelling correction, query completion and query recommendation. Due to these advances, search engines usually satisfy a user's informational need on well-formulated queries. However, an important remaining challenge is to satisfy the users' informational need when they provide vague, poorly formulated or long tail queries.

When the pages matching the user's original keywords are judged to be unsatisfactory, query recommendation algorithms are a common method for helping users find the information they need. These algorithms aim to provide queries that are, at least somewhat, *similar* to the original [2].

Another approach is to use query expansion [2], where the goal is to find keywords that, while syntactically different to varying degrees, have the same semantics as the keywords in the original query. Query recommendation can be seen as query expansion where we limit the query universe to those queries that have been previously input by some user.

Using these approaches, the new result set is a perturbation of the original result set. When the query is sufficiently well composed a small perturbation would be sufficient; in those cases, there is a highly ranked page relevant to the user's needs that appears in the result set of the new query, whereas the result set of the original query did not contain such results. Traditional approaches to query recommendation play an important and necessary role in helping correct queries that require minor adjustment.

However, users cannot always pick the most appropriate keywords. This is not surprising, because some queries are launched precisely because users wish to learn a subject with which they have little familiarity. When the query is sufficiently ill-posed, the user's informational need is best met using entirely different keywords, and a small perturbation of the original result set is bound to fail. Interestingly, in this case, the higher the query similarity used for the perturbation, the less likely that the recommendation would succeed.

We propose a new approach that does not directly rely on the original keyword set, and indeed does not rely on queries that are syntactically similar to the original. We intention-

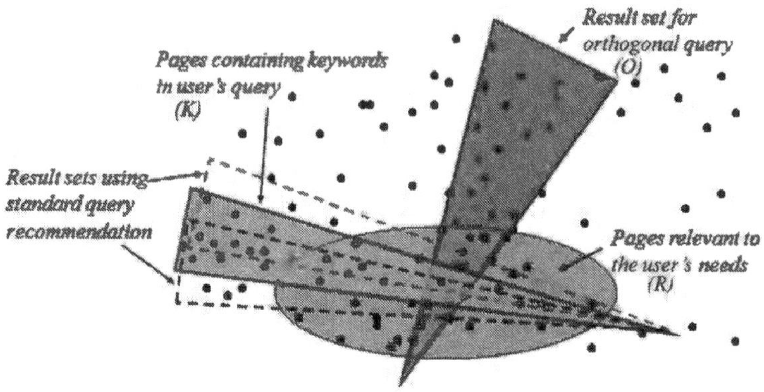

Figure 1: A graphical illustration of the difference between traditional query recommendation and orthogonal query recommendation. The dots represent webpages. The oval represents the set of pages that are relevant to the user's needs. The pages containing the user's keywords are represented in the green, nearly-horizontal stab. Results sets using traditional query recommendation are shown using the dashed stabs. An orthogonal result set is represented using the orange stab, appearing perpendicular to the original result set.

ally seek out *orthogonal queries*, which are related queries that have *no common terms* with the user's query. That is, orthogonal queries contain terms that are *syntactically* different from the terms in the original query, but that are still *semantically similar*. Hence, they provide insightful alternative interpretations that are not reachable by using small variations on the original keyword set.

Orthogonal query recommendation is complementary to traditional query recommendation, each technique may succeed when the other fails. Traditional approaches explore adjacent meanings of the user's query, whereas orthogonal query recommendation considers relevant interpretations that are more distant. See Figure 1 for an illustration of our main idea. Orthogonal queries tap into the space of relevant pages in a radically different way than is possible through traditional query recommendation techniques, allowing them to detect high quality pages that cannot be found by using previous techniques. Observe that if the original query is sufficiently ill posed, no small perturbation will succeed in capturing high value pages. In addition, an orthogonal query can access the user's informational need while consisting of keywords that are mostly distinct from those in the original query.

The challenge is to find orthogonal queries in a computationally efficient manner that proves useful in practice. We find orthogonal queries by taking advantage of the vast amounts of data that search engines collect, finding queries with low result similarity in an *ad-hoc* query recommendation answer cache. The use of an answer cache enables us to take advantage of temporal locality, and hence the query recommendations automatically reflect current events and trends, thus further increasing the likelihood that the user's informational need is met.

We illustrate the effectiveness of this approach by proposing a query recommendation method derived from these observations, and demonstrate its effectiveness on a large query log against other existing query recommendation techniques. As a result of our evaluation, to the best of our knowledge, we present the most extensive comparison of query recommendation algorithms.

Finally, we perform a user study using the standard TREC Web diversification task test bed. We compare orthogonal query recommendation against six previous approaches, including several that are substantially more computationally extensive. Orthogonal query recommendation outperforms all previous methods. In addition, our method outperforms previous approaches by a substantial margin on queries that were not previously seen.

The rest of this paper is organized as follows. In Section 2, we discuss prior approaches to query recommendation. In Section 3, we introduce our notion of orthogonal queries in a formal manner and we discuss how we compute those queries using a particular notion of query similarity. In Section 4, we evaluate the effectiveness of our query recommendation algorithm with respect to others and conclude in Section 5.

2. PREVIOUS WORK

Query recommendation algorithms address the problem of recommending good queries to Web search engine users, and thus the solutions and evaluation metrics are tailored to the Web search domain. Recently, many different approaches have arisen to solve this problem, but they all share a common element: the exploitation of usage information recorded in query logs [13].

One subset of these recommendation algorithms use clustering to determine groups of similar queries that lead users to related documents [14, 1]. In the case of [1], the recommended queries might have completely different terms to the original query, like the algorithm proposed in this paper, as they use term similarity over of clicked answers (and not the queries). Additional approaches include exploiting chains of queries stored in query logs [10], or improving the retrieval accuracy of difficult queries [11].

Baeza-Yates and Tiberi [3] exploit click-through data as a way to provide recommendations. The method is based on the concept of Cover Graph (CG). A CG is a bipartite graph of queries and URLs, where a query q and an URL u are connected if a user issued q and clicked on u that was an answer for the query.

Another approach, similar to the previous one, called user frequency-inverse query frequency (UF-IQF), was introduced by Deng *et al.* [9] and is based on entropy models. The same year, Silvestri *et al.* [7] introduced a new recommendation algorithm: *search short cuts* (SC).

Zaiane and Strilets [15] exploit query traces to find similar queries (SQ), the queries with similar terms and results are scored higher,which is the opposite of our method.

The last four algorithms described above (CG, UF-IQF, SC, SQ) are used as baselines in our experimental comparison. Finally, as part of our user study, we compare our orthogonal query approach with two other graph based query recommendation algorithms that are not that efficient: Query Flow Graph (QFG) [5] and *Term-Query Graph* (TQG) [6].

Our method differs from previous approaches in that we deliberately seek out queries that are only *slightly* similar to the user's original query. In this way, we avoid the pitfall of recommending queries that are simple reformulations of the original, as this would do very little to bring the user closer to their informational need if the original query was poorly formed or has few results, as is the case with long tail queries.

3. ORTHOGONAL QUERIES

In our model, the objective of a search engine is to retrieve at least one highly ranked page that is relevant to the user's needs. The purpose of an orthogonal query is to satisfy the user's information need when they are not met by the original results.

Formally, let $\mathcal{R}$ denote the set of web-pages that are relevant to the user's needs. Let $\mathcal{K}$ denote the set of pages that contain the keywords comprising the user's query. Search engines rely on the existence of some highly ranked pages in $\mathcal{R} \cap \mathcal{K}$, since these would be the top results returned to the user.

As such, the main limitation of the current approach to searching is its restricted capacity to access pages in $\mathcal{R}$. We introduce orthogonal queries as a means of accessing $\mathcal{R}$ in a manner that is not as dependent on the particular keyword choices made by the user.

We refer to $\mathcal{K}$ as a *stab* of $\mathcal{R}$. An *orthogonal stab* is a set $\mathcal{O}$ such that $\mathcal{O} \cap \mathcal{K}$ is small. In particular, we are interested in orthogonal stabs so that $\mathcal{R} \cap \mathcal{O}$ contains some highly ranked pages. See Figure 1 for an illustration. *Orthogonal results* denote pages in $\mathcal{O}$ that do no occur in $\mathcal{K}$.

Orthogonal queries and their results may be useful when $\mathcal{R} \cap \mathcal{K}$ is unsatisfactory; for instance when $\mathcal{R} \cap \mathcal{K}$ does not contain enough highly ranked pages. Orthogonal query recommendation is also useful when the top results in $\mathcal{R} \cap \mathcal{K}$ address the same interpretation of the user's query, allowing orthogonal queries to capture alternative interpretations (or in other words, diversify the results). Orthogonal queries and their results may satisfy the user information needs on poorly formulated queries, by going beyond the scope of the provided keywords. These results are also able to provide relevant information that is entirely new to the user, where the user could not have searched for it directly.

To characterize orthogonal queries we use a similarity measure based in the query terms. Let the *term overlap* between queries p and q be

$$termOverlap(p, q) = \frac{|terms(p) \cap terms(q)|}{|terms(p) \cup terms(q)|}.$$

Query 1	Query 2	T.O.	R.O.
european+rabbit	*European rabbit*	1	0.575
lyrics office space	*office space lyrics*	1	0.4084
car-price	*bluebook cars*	0	0.06
discount travel	*cheap airfares*	0	0.105
Daisy Duke	*"catherine bach"*	0	0.02

Table 2: Examples of query pairs and their Term Overlap (T.O.) and Result Overlap (R.O.) scores.

Using this similarity measure, we can define initially orthogonal queries as those having *termOverlap* equal to zero. However, we will relax this definition later and allow orthogonal queries to have very low *termOverlap*, i.e. we should call them quasi-orthogonal.

3.1 Interesting Orthogonal Queries

Our orthogonal query recommendation technique relies on a measure of similarity that goes beyond keyword comparisons, and is at the same time computationally efficient so that the similarity score can be computed in real-time.

Let *resultSet*(p) denote the set of URLs returned by a search engine on query p. The *result overlap* between queries p and q is,

$$resultOverlap(p, q) = \frac{|resultSet(p) \cap resultSet(q)|}{|resultSet(p) \cup resultSet(q)|}.$$

See, for example, Balfe *et al.* [4].

We found that queries with a large result overlap score yield results that are similar to the original query's results, and thus do not address alternative interpretations. We use the result overlap score to further determine when a query is orthogonal, and build a set of interesting orthogonal queries to be used as recommendations.

In order to find a range of result overlap that leads to interesting orthogonal queries, we compare result overlap with term overlap. We first provide a high level description of the relationship between term overlap and result overlap, and discuss later how this relationship enables us to identify a range of result overlap that leads to orthogonal queries.

Very high values of result overlap tend to indicate that the queries are composed of similar terms. The most similar queries are slight syntactic variants composed of the *same* terms. For instance, the queries *european+rabbit* and *European rabbit* have result overlap 0.575. As our algorithm compares the top 100 results from both queries, a result overlap score of 0.575 indicates that 73 of the top 100 results match. Queries that are word permutations of each other, as in *lyrics office space* and *office space lyrics* also have a high result overlap score, in this case 0.4084. Many other queries with high result overlap score often have significant overlap in their term bags.

When both the result overlap and term overlap scores are high, incorporating highly ranked results from such a query into the original result set does not significantly alter the original result set. Hence, to find pages that satisfy the needs of users when their informational needs are not met by the original highly ranked results, we look for similar queries (according to the result overlap score) that include entirely different keywords. Indeed, the most interesting results occur at a low range of result overlap. Surprisingly, we

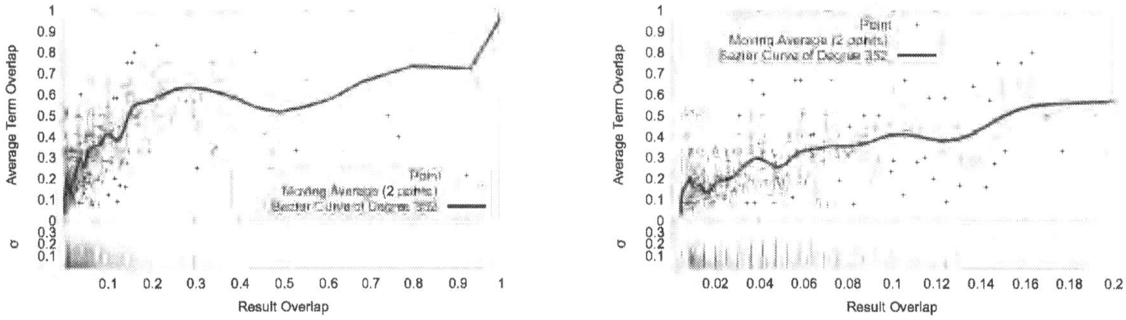

Figure 2: Result overlap versus average term overlap in a query log of 5,000 queries. At the right we show the result overlap values in the range (0,1], while at the left the result overlap values in the range (0,0.2]. The lines represents the moving average of period two, and the Bézier curve of degree 352. We also show the standard deviation σ. The graphs show a positive correlation between result and term overlap.

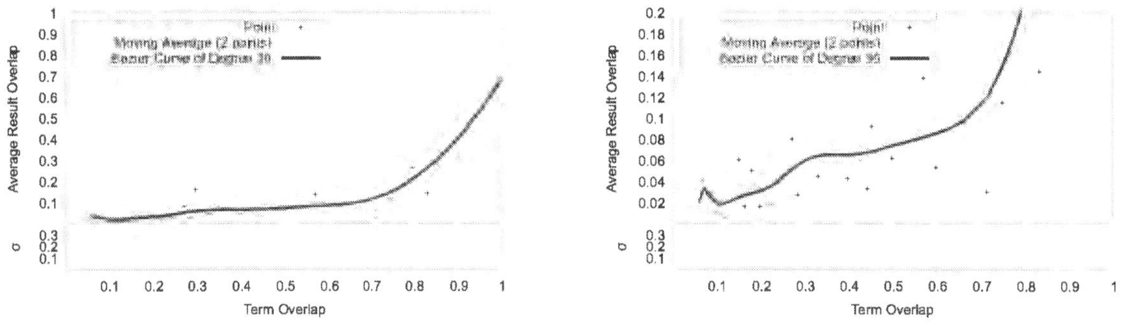

Figure 3: Term overlap versus average result overlap in a query log of 5,000 queries. At the right we show the average result overlap values in the range (0,1], while at the left the values in the range (0,0.2]. The lines represents the moving average of period two, and the Bézier curve of degree 36. We also show the standard deviation σ. The graphs show a positive correlation between results and term overlap.

did not find an instance where two queries have result overlap beyond score 0.01 and yet are semantically dissimilar.

The result overlap measure of query similarity can detect semantic similarity when there are *no common* terms, without the use of complicated natural language processing techniques. For example, the queries `students with reading difficulties` and `dyslexia help` have result overlap 0.0102, and `car-price` and `bluebook cars` have a 0.06 result overlap. A surprising relationship was caught in the comparison of the queries `Daisy Duke` and `"Catherine Bach"` with a result overlap value of 0.02. Further investigation revealed that Catherine Bach played character Daisy Duke in The Dukes of Hazard.

3.2 Finding Interesting Orthogonal Queries

Now we perform a more formal comparison of result overlap with term overlap in order to identify the most appropriate range of result overlap for finding orthogonal queries. For this we compute the result overlap and term overlap scores for each distinct pair of queries in a query log of 5,000 entries. We computed term overlap while ignoring very common stop words (such as "a" and "the"), otherwise many dissimilar pairs of queries would have high term overlap. In addition, we reduce all letters to lower case, and treat words as sequences of alpha-numerical characters (i.e., then *european+rabbit* and *European rabbit* have term overlap 1.)

The Pearson correlation coefficient between result overlap and average term overlap is 0.567(352 data points), indicating a positive correlation. Figure 2 shows result overlap values in the range (0,1] and (0,0.2] with the corresponding average term overlap values. The lines in Figure 2 represent a moving average with a period of two, and a Bézier curve of degree n. We also report the standard deviation of term overlap for each result overlap. Since we were using a real query log, it is not surprising that the number of queries decreases as result overlap increases.

We obtain further evidence of the positive correlation between the two measures of similarity by looking at term overlap versus average result overlap. The Pearson correlation coefficient between them reveals a strong positive correlation of 0.686 (36 data points). Figure 3 shows term overlap values with the corresponding average result overlap values in the range (0,1] and (0,0.2], similarly to the previous figure.

We would like to identify a range of result overlap where term overlap is low, as most queries have very few terms. In a study of 285 million Internet users, we found that over 87% of search queries consist of 4 or fewer terms [12]. A term overlap score below 0.333, on two queries of length at most 4, indicates that the queries overlap on at most one term. With the goal of introducing as little noise as possible, and only presenting those results that are most likely to be orthogonal to, and not similar to, the results of the original query, we want to avoid having large term overlap. To this end, we set a threshold so that we expect to have at most one overlapping term.

Taking into account the size of the Web, and thus the number of possibilities of the first 100 results, a non-zero result overlap is actually very meaningful. Indeed, the probability of a false match can be estimated in the range of 10^{-5} to 10^{-9}. We found that in practice a non-zero result overlap score in most cases represents some semantic similarity.

We would also like the queries to have little term overlap, so that the corresponding result set is orthogonal. Thus, we would like the term overlap to be below 0.333. Figure 2 (right) shows that until result overlap of 0.06, the running average is dominantly below 0.333.

Hence, we chose to use queries with a result overlap score in the range $(0, 0.06]$ *to find interesting orthogonal queries.*

Note that this threshold depends on the data set and should tuned for each search engine depending on the query stream.

3.3 Algorithm

To find orthogonal queries we use result overlap scores to compute query similarity between an incoming query and all queries currently in an *ad-hoc* answers cache. As just discussed, we have determined that a result overlap similarity score in the interval $(0, 0.06]$ is most beneficial for finding good orthogonal queries. Thus, we say that in practice a query A is *orthogonal* to query B if its result overlap similarity score is within this range.[1] Given a user's query, A, we construct the set of all such orthogonal queries B from the cache.

By using this cache, our algorithm is only looking at queries that have been issued within the recent past. This gives our algorithm two desirable properties. First, it can be computed online and efficiently [8] while queries are being executed, as we would not be able to compute similarity scores and present results for incoming queries if we had to run our algorithm over all previously seen queries. Second, and perhaps more importantly, our algorithm reacts to temporal changes in users' query habits. If users are currently interested in searching for `Michael Jackson died`, instead of `Michael Jackson thriller`, the orthogonal queries will reflect this fact.

4. SESSION BASED EFFECTIVENESS

In this section we aim to evaluate the effectiveness of our query recommendation algorithm with respect to others by using a large query log. Our idea is to use the sessions extracted from a query log for the evaluation purpose, where a session is a sequence of queries $q_1, q_2, ..., q_n$ submitted by a user, in a fixed amount of time t, which we will vary. That is, our training data is based in real users and not expert users.

To the best of our knowledge, this is the first time that a large scale analysis has been performed to evaluate the effectiveness of query recommendation algorithms.[2] In fact, while the use of a large scale query log has been widely proposed for training purposes, evaluation is usually done based on user judgements. We generated 7 million query recommendations for evaluation purposes, with more than 2.4 million (600 thousand for each baseline) of them for the comparison itself.

We will proceed by describing our data set, the experimental setup, the best cache policy, and the effectiveness of orthogonal query recommendation when compared with other state-of-the-art query recommendation algorithms.

4.1 Experimental Setup

We used a large search engine query log containing approximately 22 million queries from USA. We used 80% of the query log for training purposes and the rest for testing. In particular, we sessionized the testing set by using four different values for t = 1, 10, 20, and 30 minutes. We then consider only the *satisfied sessions with retype*, that is, sessions where the last query, q_n, is the only query that has received a click, and $n \geq 2$ (i.e. the first query of the session was not satisfactory). Furthermore, we removed sessions where q_n is not present in the training set. Table 3 reports more detailed statistics of the query log.

Number of queries	21,562,727
Number of queries with frequency = 1	4,467,362
Test corpus - number of queries	4,312,545
Training corpus - number of queries	17,250,182
Number of unique URL downloaded	34,228,300
Test Session of 1 min S-1min	99,833
Test Session of 10 min S-10min	157,747
Test Session of 20 min S-20min	170,720
Test Session of 30 min S-30min	177,183

Table 3: Statistics of the query log.

The *satisfied sessions with retype* are interesting because they simulate a real case where a user would need a recommendation. In fact, in this type of session, the user is initially unsatisfied by the URL results of q_1, and consequently, s/he tries to find an alternative query which ends in a click. We base our evaluation methodology on predicting the last query of the session. Predicting the exact last query by simply using the first query of a session is very difficult. Consider that even a single character variation between the recommended query and the last query of a session will not be considered a useful recommendation.

For evaluation purposes, we adopted the *average success at rank k* , denoted S@k, which we define to be the probability of finding at least one relevant query among the top-k recommended queries. Hence, our ground truth is very exigent. Formally, given a set of sessions $\mathcal{S}$, a session $s = (q_1, q_2, \ldots, q_n) \in \mathcal{S}$, and a set R_q of recommended queries for q_1, we define $\mathsf{S_q@k} = \begin{cases} 1, & \text{if } \{q_n\} \cap R_q \neq \emptyset \\ 0, & \text{if } \{q_n\} \cap R_q = \emptyset \end{cases}$, and with $|R_q| = k$, we define $\mathsf{S@k} = \frac{\sum_{s \in \mathcal{S}} \mathsf{S_q@k}}{|\mathcal{S}|}$.

4.2 Cache Policy

Before describing the effectiveness of orthogonal query recommendations, we discuss our static cache policy. Our goal is to keep in the cache those queries that could potentially be the final query of a *satisfied session with retype.*

While other query recommendation algorithms can benefit from the entire query log as training set for recommendation

[1] Thus, in practice, orthogonal queries are quasi-orthogonal queries in both, term overlap and result overlap.

[2] In [7, 9, 3] automated approaches are proposed, but the evaluation was based on samples of a few hundred queries.

	S-1min	S-10min	S-20min	S-30min
MCQ	**55,59**	**56,98**	**57,56**	**57,85**
MFQ	53,08	54,75	55,35	55,64
MFFQS	51,00	52,59	53,12	53,36
MRQ	34,56	36,27	36,81	37,08

Table 4: Last session query hits percentage, normalized by the maximum number of hits per session for an infinite cache. Columns are different types of sessions, rows the techniques used to fill the cache.

purposes, orthogonal query recommendation is based on a finite set of queries in the cache. In other words, a query that is recommended by the orthogonal query recommendation algorithm is, by definition, in the cache, while the other recommendation algorithms could potentially recommend a query that is chosen from the entire training set. Hence, in this sense our technique is at a disadvantage.

As we discussed in the experimental setup, we want to predict the last query of a session. Formally, given a set of queries in cache C, a session $s = (q_1, q_2, \ldots, q_n) \in S$, and a set R_q of recommended queries for q_1, we define a *cache hit* if $q_n \in C$, and a *cache miss* otherwise. We selected four different features extracted from the query log: *query freshness*, *query frequency*, *query click* and *last session query likelihood*. Based on the selected features, we define:

- MCQ (*Most Clicked Query*): The most clicked queries in the training set are kept in the cache;
- MFQ (*Most Frequent Query*): The most frequent queries in the training set are kept in the cache;
- MFFQS (*Most Frequent Final Query in Session*): The query training set is sessionized, and we select the final query of each session. We keep those final queries that occur most often. Here we use sessions with $t = 30$ minutes;
- MRQ (*Most Recent Query*): The most recent queries are kept in the cache;

To avoid introducing queries into the cache that were not available during the training of the baseline algorithms, we use only the training data to determine the best cache policy. We used 80% of the query log to fill the cache to a particular size based on each policy, and we sessionized the remaining 20% for cache testing purposes.

Table 4 reports the normalized hit ratio for different cache policies and session tests by using a cache size of 80,000 query entries. The normalization factor is obtained by considering the cache to have infinite size. The cache policy with the highest hit ratio is MCQ. Thus, the probability of having the last session of a query in the cache is higher if we adopt this policy.

Figure 4 shows the percentage of normalized query hits for different types of cache policies with varied cache sizes. The larger the cache size, the higher the hit ratio. MCQ is almost always better than any other cache policy. Sessions of 1, 10 and 20 minutes follow the same trend.

After discovering that MCQ is the cache policy with the highest hit ratio (in terms of last query of a session), we further investigate the effectiveness of the orthogonal query recommendation algorithm. We investigate the quality of the

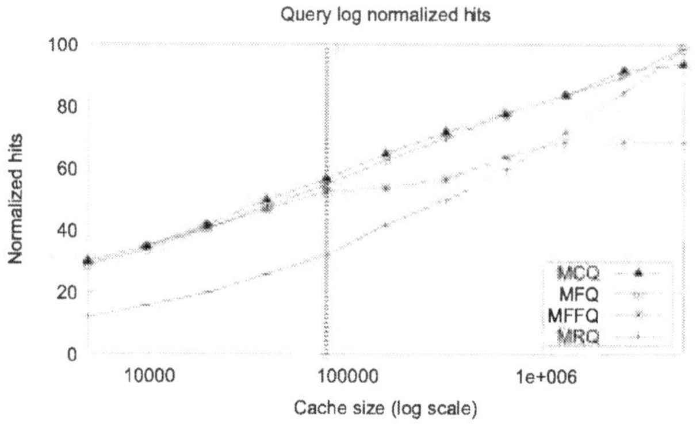

Figure 4: Percentage of S-30min query hits, normalized by the maximum number of hits reachable with a cache of infinite size.

Cache size	10,000	20,000	40,000	80,000
	Sessions of 1 minute			
MCQ	2.66	**3.42**	**4.22**	**4.97**
MFQ	2.46	3.11	3.80	4.51
MFFQS	**2.78**	3.40	4.13	4.48
MRQ	0.18	0.36	0.68	1.43
	Sessions of 30 minutes			
MCQ	1.95	**2.52**	**3.08**	**3.64**
MFQ	1.84	2.29	2.80	3.34
MFFQS	**2.04**	2.47	3.01	3.42
MRQ	0.14	0.27	0.51	1.05

Table 5: S@10 in percentage of orthogonal query recommendations for S-1min and S-30min. Columns indicate different cache sizes and rows the different policies used to fill the cache.

recommended orthogonal queries for different cache policies and cache sizes.

For each cache policy, the same criteria that was used to fill the cache is used to impose an order on the orthogonal queries obtained by our recommendation method.

Table 5 reports the S@10 of orthogonal query recommendations by varying the cache size and the cache policy for S-1min and S-30min. Almost always, the prediction for short session times ($t = 1$ minute) is better. This is probably due to the fact that by considering a shorter session length, the probability that the user's intent changes during the session is lower. The best cache policy is MCQ with S@10 $= 4.97$ for S-1min and S@10 $= 3.64$ for S-30min, with a cache size of 80,000 query entries. MFFQS seems to be a good cache policy for small cache size, with a S@10 $= 2.78$ for S-1min and 2.04 for S-30min.

In conclusion, we could say that the best cache policy is MCQ, as it performs best for short term (S-1min) and long term prediction (S-30min). We note that using short term sessions (S-1min), S@10 in percentage of orthogonal query recommendations for policy MCQ appears to increase by a constant (0.75) as we double the cache size. For longer term sessions (S-30min), we see a similar trend with a smaller constant (0.56). However, as the number of queries increase and we reach the long tail, this trend will end.

Sessions	S-1min	S-10min	S-20min	S-30min
		Overall		
UF-IQF	5.87	4.83	4.54	4.40
OQ	4.97	4.07	3.72	3.64
SC	3.46	2.48	2.32	2.25
SQ	1.47	1.05	0.60	0.58
CG	0.64	0.49	0.46	0.43
		Unseen queries		
OQ	3.54	3.61	3.65	4.16
SC	0.78	0.80	0.79	0.79
SQ	0.74	0.72	0.72	0.71
UF-IQF	0.00	0.00	0.00	0.00
CG	0.00	0.00	0.00	0.00

Table 6: S@10 as a percentage, both for all queries and for long tail queries. In each case, the techniques are sorted in order of effectiveness.

4.3 Comparison

Having found that the best cache policy is MCQ, we now focus on comparing the effectiveness of orthogonal query recommendations w.r.t. state-of-art algorithms for query recommendation. Hereinafter, we will adopt a cache of 80,000 query entries and the MCQ policy for producing orthogonal query recommendations. Before describing our baseline algorithms, it is worth mentioning that we needed to generate approximately 600 thousand recommendations for each baseline. Hence, we selected recommendation algorithms with low computational cost.

As baselines, we used four different well-known recommendation algorithms: CG (*Cover Graph*) [3], UF-IQF (*User Frequency-Inverse Query Frequency*) [9], SC (*Short Cuts*) [7], and SQ (*Similar Queries*) [15].

Recall that these algorithms use all the queries to find the best query recommendations and our algorithm only uses the queries in the cache. Hence, our algorithm is in *disadvantage* with respect to all the baselines. However we trade-off this disadvantage with time efficiency.

Table 6 reports the S@10 as a percentage of orthogonal query recommendations compared to our baselines, for different test session lengths.[3] We report the overall results, and the results of unseen queries separately. In fact, around 21% (Table 3) of the queries in our query log are unseen queries (that is, their frequency is one).

Note that the best results are obtained with S-30min, in the case of unseen queries, and S-1min in the overall case. In the case of unseen queries, the effectiveness of OQ is higher than all of the baselines, showing its effectiveness for long tail queries. Notice that in this case, the second best algorithm is SC and not UF-IFQ, which is not able to provide recommendation for unseen queries.

The effectiveness of OQ is always higher than CG, SQ and SC. However, UF-IQF performs better than OQ when we consider the entire set of sessions. We further investigate this issue by reporting in Table 7 the percentage of the recommended queries that overlap between OQ and our baselines. That is, what percentage of the recommended queries are the same. We want to know whether the queries recommended

[3]Results for S@5 and S@1 were omitted, however we did not notice any difference of order in terms of effectiveness between OQ and the baselines.

Sessions	S-1min	S-10min	S-20min	S-30min
CG	1%	1%	1%	1%
UF-IQF	14%	14%	14%	13%
SC	5%	5%	5%	4%
SQ	2%	2%	2%	2%

Table 7: Overlap of the successful orthogonal recommendations w.r.t. the successful baseline query recommendations. Columns indicate the different types of session lengths and rows are our baselines.

Judgment	useful	somewhat	not useful
	Overall		
OQ	20%	25%	55%
TQG	18%	23%	59%
UF-IQF	20%	20%	60%
CG	16%	22%	62%
SC	14%	16%	70%
QFG	13%	12%	75%
SQ	6%	4%	90%
	Unseen queries		
OQ	25%	8%	67%
TQG	8%	13%	79%
SC	5%	3%	92%
UF-IQF	0%	0%	100%
CG	0%	0%	100%
QFG	0%	0%	100%
SQ	0%	0%	100%

Table 8: User study results, which compare the effectiveness of OQ with the baseline techniques, sorted in order of effectiveness (useful + somewhat).

by the classical query recommendation algorithms contain the orthogonal queries that we recommend. We restrict the test sessions to the successful sessions of each method. As we can see, only 14% of the successful recommended queries of OQ are contained in the successful recommended queries of UF-IQF. This means that the two recommendation algorithms are almost "orthogonal" in terms of recommended queries, and therefore they could be combined. The percentage of overlap with other baselines is even lower as those are not very effective; a maximum of 5% with SC, 2% with SQ, and 1% with CG.

Note that OQ is not always going to be useful. Specifically, if the user's original query gives poor results, but their informational need can only be satisfied by slight variations on the original query (high result overlap), then OQ will not detect these queries. On the other hand, because OQ is the most effective method for unseen queries, in comparison with other recommendation algorithms, and as detecting such queries in the cache is trivial, it would be easy to implement OQ in conjunction with any of the other methods leading to substantial improvement in overall performance.

4.4 User Study Evaluation

In addition to the automated evaluation shown above, we also tested the effectiveness of OQ by running a user study. We experimented with the following methods: OQ, CG, UF-IQF, SQ, and SC. In addition, we introduced two other baselines: QFG (*Query Flow Graph*) [5], TQG (*Term-Query Graph*) [6]. QFG and TQG make use of *Random Walk with Restart* for query suggestions.

The high computation time of the *Random Walk with Restart* ($\Omega(|E| + |V|)$, where $|E|$ is the number of edges of the graph and $|V|$ is the number of nodes, is why QFG and TQG have not been introduced until now.

The user study was conducted on the 50 queries from the standard TREC Web diversification task test bed.

The assessment was conducted by a group of 10 assessors. The assessors were researchers unaware of the used algorithms, and not working on related topics. We generated the top-5 recommendations per query for each technique evaluated: OQ, CG, UF-IQF, SC, SQ, QFG, and TQG.

Using a web interface, each assessor was provided with a random query from the test bed, followed by a list of recommended queries (the top-5 for each of the 7 methods) selected by the different methods. Recommendations were randomly shuffled, so that the assessors could not distinguish which method produced them. Each assessor was asked to assess each recommended query using the following scale: *useful*, *somewhat useful*, and *not useful*.[4] We gave assessors the possibility of observing the search engine results for the original query and the recommended query that was being evaluated. The user study finished when each assessor had assessed all recommendations for all 50 queries in the test bed.

Table 8 reports the results of the user study. The overall results and the results of unseen queries are reported separately. Overall, for OQ, 45% of the recommendations were judged *useful* or *somewhat* useful. This table shows that the quality of the queries recommended by OQ are higher than our baselines, and strictly higher in the *somewhat* category, which demonstrates the orthogonality of our technique. UF-IQF shows lower overall effectiveness, while only 25% of QFG recommendations were judged *useful* or *somewhat* useful. One reason for QFG's recommendation failure is the presence of high in-degree nodes. Also, QFG does not provide recommendations for unseen queries, while TQG solves this issue. In fact, for TQG, 41% of the recommendations were judged *useful* or *somewhat* useful, making it second-best in our user study. For unseen queries, 25% of OQ recommendation were judged *useful*, while for TQG only 8% were judged *useful*. In both cases, OQ was judged to be more useful than all other methods.

5. CONCLUSIONS

We presented a new query recommendation technique based on identifying orthogonal queries in an *ad-hoc* query answer cache. In contrast to previous approaches, we intentionally seek out queries that are only moderately similar to the original. Orthogonal queries aim to detect different interpretations of the user's query that go beyond the scope of the user-provided keywords.

Our approach requires no training, is computationally efficient, and can be easily integrated into any search engine with an answer cache (as answer caches are large, they can be used as a proxy cache for our algorithm).

Our experimental results show that if the user is not satisfied with the original URL results of a query (i.e., he is not going to click on them), orthogonal query recommendations can satisfy the user's informational need, better than several previous approaches. Also, orthogonal query recommendation is shown to be the best technique for long tail queries, performing better than all previous techniques considered.

In the user study with the standard TREC Web diversification task test bed, orthogonal query recommendation also outperforms six known query recommendation methods, including approaches that are notably more computationally extensive. Orthogonal queries have the potential to improve other aspects of web search. Future work will investigate how they can be used in diversification of the web search results.

6. REFERENCES

[1] R. Baeza-Yates, C. Hurtado, and M. Mendoza. Query recommendation using query logs in search engines. In *Proc. EDBT'04*.

[2] R. Baeza-Yates and B. Ribeiro-Neto. *Modern Information Retrieval: the concepts and technology behind search*. Addison-Wesley, 2 edition, 2011.

[3] R. Baeza-Yates and A. Tiberi. Extracting semantic relations from query logs. In *Proc. KDD'07*.

[4] E. Balfe and B. Smyth. A comparative analysis of query similarity metrics for community-based web search. *LNCS*, 3620:63, 2005.

[5] P. Boldi, F. Bonchi, C. Castillo, D. Donato, and S. Vigna. Query suggestions using query-flow graphs. In *Proc. WSCD'09*.

[6] F. Bonchi, F. Silvestri, R. Perego, H. Vahabi, and R. Venturini. Efficient query recommendations in the long tail via center-piece subgraphs. In *Proc. SIGIR'12*.

[7] D. Broccolo, L. Marcon, F. Nardini, R. Perego, and F. Silvestri. Generating suggestions for queries in the long tail with an inverted index. *I.P.M.*, 2011.

[8] A. Broder. On the resemblance and containment of documents. In *Proc. SEQUENCES'97*.

[9] H. Deng, I. King, and M. R. Lyu. Entropy-biased models for query representation on the click graph. In *Proc. SIGIR'09*.

[10] B. Fonseca, P. Golgher, B. Pôssas, B. Ribeiro-Neto, and N. Ziviani. Concept-based interactive query expansion. In *Proc. CIKM'05*.

[11] M. Karimzadehgan and C. Zhai. Improving retrieval accuracy of difficult queries through generalizing negative document language models. In *Proc. CIKM'11*.

[12] C. Silverstein, H. Marais, M. Henzinger, and M. Moricz. Analysis of a very large web search engine query log. *SIGIR Forum*, 33(1):6–12, Sept. 1999.

[13] F. Silvestri. Mining query logs: Turning search usage data into knowledge. *FTIR*, 4(1-2):1–174, 2009.

[14] J. Wen, J. Nie, and H. Zhang. Clustering user queries of a search engine. In *Proc. WWW'01*.

[15] O. R. Zaïane and A. Strilets. Finding similar queries to satisfy searches based on query traces. In *Proc. OOIS'02*.

[4] Each assessor was given the following instructions: A *useful* recommendation is a query such that if it were submitted to a search engine, it would provide URL results that were not available using the original query, and it would reflect the user's intent from the original query.

Understanding and Improving Relational Matrix Factorization in Recommender Systems

Li Pu
Artificia Intelligence Laboratory, EPFL
INR240, EPFL-IC-LIA, Station 14
CH-1015, Lausanne, Switzerland
li.pu@epfl.c

Boi Faltings
Artificia Intelligence Laboratory, EPFL
INR230, EPFL-IC-LIA, Station 14
CH-1015, Lausanne, Switzerland
boi.faltings@epfl.c

ABSTRACT

Matrix factorization techniques such as the singular value decomposition (SVD) have had great success in recommender systems. We present a new perspective of SVD for constructing a latent space from the training data, which is justified by the theory of hypergraph model. We show that the vectors representing the items in the latent space can be grouped into (approximately) orthogonal clusters which correspond to the vertex clusters in the co-rating hypergraph, and the lengths of the vectors are indicators of the representativeness of the items. These properties are used for making top-N recommendations in a two-phase algorithm. In this work, we provide a new explanation for the significantly better performance of the asymmetric SVD approaches and a novel algorithm for better diversity in top-N recommendations.

Categories and Subject Descriptors

H.3.3 [**Information Storage and Retrieval**]: Information Search and Retrieval—*information filtering*

Keywords

recommender system, matrix factorization, hypergraph

1. INTRODUCTION

In a recommender system, there are two types of entities, i.e. users and items. The users give weighted connections, or ratings, to the items. These connections can be modeled as a rating matrix $\boldsymbol{R}$ where the rows represent the users and the columns represent the items. The entry $\boldsymbol{R}(i,k)$ is the rating given by user i to item k (if the rating exists). The goal of the recommender system is to predict unseen items that might be rated with high scores. A common assumption for making predictions is that certain latent factors are associated with each user and each item, and a user gives ratings according to her latent factors and the latent factors of the items.

RecSys'13, October 12–16, 2013, Hong Kong, China.

http://dx.doi.org/10.1145/2507157.2507178.

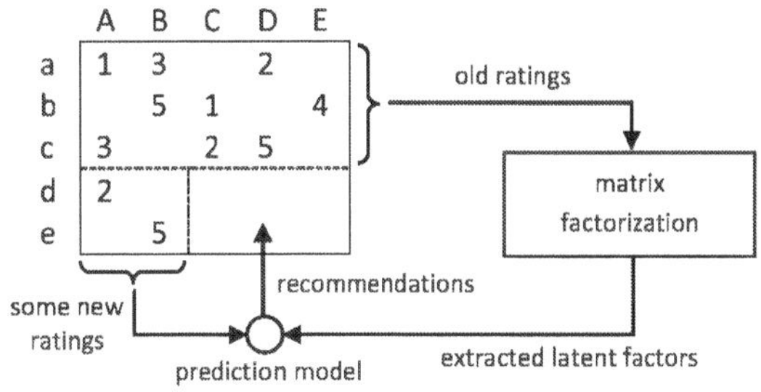

Figure 1: Recommender system using matrix factorizations.

For example, in the `Lastfm` dataset, the items are the artists in a music website. The latent factors could be the music genres. The recommender system first obtains the genres of the artists, and the users' interests on different genres. Then the system makes recommendations by aligning the user's interests to the genres of the artists.

For ratings modeled as the matrix $\boldsymbol{R}$, various matrix factorization techniques have been applied to extract the latent factors and make recommendations. Figure 1 shows a typical recommender system using matrix factorization. The old ratings given by existing users are first decomposed into multiple matrices to extract the latent factors. When new users come into the system, their ratings are combined with the extracted latent factors to make recommendations.

Sarwar et al. [17] proposed one of the early works that use the low-rank Singular Value Decomposition (SVD) approximation to replace the missing values in the original rating matrix, i.e. $\boldsymbol{R} \approx \boldsymbol{U}_l \boldsymbol{S}_l \boldsymbol{V}_l^\top$ where the sizes of the matrices are $\boldsymbol{R}$: $m \times n$, $\boldsymbol{U}_l$: $m \times l$, $\boldsymbol{S}_l$: $l \times l$, and $\boldsymbol{V}_l$: $n \times l$. The diagonal matrix $\boldsymbol{S}_l$ contains the l biggest singular values of $\boldsymbol{R}$, and this low-rank approximation is also called the *truncated SVD*. This approach relies on the fact that the rank-l truncated SVD approximation $\hat{\boldsymbol{R}} = \boldsymbol{U}_l \boldsymbol{S}_l \boldsymbol{V}_l^\top$ minimizes the Frobenius norm $\|\hat{\boldsymbol{R}} - \boldsymbol{R}\|_F$ among all the rank-l matrices, and we hope that the matrix $\hat{\boldsymbol{R}}$ would generalize the correct ratings to the missing entries in $\boldsymbol{R}$. Note that imputation of missing values is implicitly required when computing the truncated SVD. We can represent user i with the vector $\bar{\boldsymbol{u}}_i = \boldsymbol{S}_l^{-1/2} \boldsymbol{U}_l(i,\cdot)^\top$ and item k with the vector $\bar{\boldsymbol{v}}_k = \boldsymbol{S}_l^{-1/2} \boldsymbol{V}_l(i,\cdot)^\top$. The predicted rating from user i to item k is then $\hat{\boldsymbol{R}}(i,k) = \bar{\boldsymbol{u}}_i^\top \bar{\boldsymbol{v}}_k$, where $\bar{\boldsymbol{u}}_i$ and $\bar{\boldsymbol{v}}_k$ can be considered as latent vectors.

During the Netflix prize competition, Funk [5] proposed an iterative way to compute the low-rank SVD approximation on a very big matrix that minimizes only the Frobenius norm on the non-empty entries in the original rating matrix. Based on Funk's work, Paterek [14] suggested a new model to reduce the number of parameters that need to be stored in the recommender system. In Paterek's approach, a truncated SVD is computed as before, but only the right singular vectors in V_l are taken into the second step. In the second step, item k is represented by v_k which is the k-th column of $V_l^\top$, while user i's latent vector is computed by a linear combination of the v_k's whose corresponding items are rated by user i. Finally the rating prediction is the inner product of a user's latent vector and an item's latent vector. Koren [9] pointed out that this "asymmetric SVD" which takes only the right singular vectors actually works better in prediction accuracy. However, besides the empirical studies, the reason of such improvement for asymmetric SVD is not clear.

The **main contributions** of this paper include **(1)** a new explanation of the (approximate) orthogonal structure of the latent space constructed from the asymmetric SVD, which is used as an intermediate step in a top-N recommender system, and **(2)** a novel algorithm based on a hypergraph formulation that brings more diversity in the recommendations by applying normalizations in the asymmetric SVD.

In the reminder of the paper, we start with the hypergraph representation and the normalized hypergraph cut. We show that the asymmetric SVD approach follows the hypergraph learning scheme, and there is an (approximate) orthogonal structure associated with the right singular vectors. Based on the lengths of the latent vectors obtained from the right singular vectors, the items can be categorized into anchor items and non-anchor items. Finally we present a top-N recommendation algorithm that utilizes the above structures, and conduct experiments to compare our algorithm with the state-of-the-art approaches.

2. PRELIMINARIES

Suppose we have two sets of entities: the user set $Y = \{y_1, y_2, ..., y_m\}$ of size m, and the item set $Z = \{z_1, z_2, ..., z_n\}$ of size n. The items in set Z belong to s clusters $\{C_1, C_2, ..., C_s\}$. Each cluster C_j is a subset of Z and $C_j \cap C_{j'} = \emptyset$ for $j \neq j'$.

Taking the `Lastfm` dataset as an example again, let the set Y be the set of users and the set Z be the set of artists. Clusters or partitions over Z can be established according to the genres of the artists. For example, C_1 includes the rock music artists, while all the country music artists are in C_2. Each user in the set Y, on the other hand, is assumed to have a preference over music genres. If the user likes rock music, she would listen to the artists from C_1 with high probability. If the user does not like country music, she would rarely listen to the artists from C_2.

The mutually exclusion between clusters of items is the basic assumption in our analysis. Each cluster can be considered as a latent factor by which the ratings are generated. In some cases, however, an artist could play in multiple genres. This does not pose a problem to our basic assumption, because we can create a cluster (latent factor) that corresponds to a combination of genres. In fact, if the intuition behind the latent factors follows some categorical attributes, e.g. genres, languages, professions, etc., or a combination of categorical attributes, our basic assumption always holds.

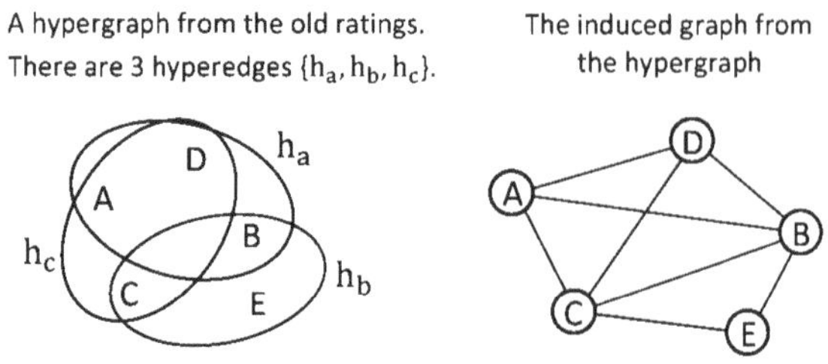

Figure 2: The hypergraph representation of the ratings in Figure 1 and the induced graph.

2.1 From Ratings to Relations

The matrix $\boldsymbol{R}$ contains the ratings between the users and the items, which can be seen as relations between two sets. For simplicity, we assume that all the ratings are bigger than zero, thus the empty entries in the $m \times n$ rating matrix $\boldsymbol{R}$ can be represented by zeros. If we ignore the actual ratings in $\boldsymbol{R}$, we can obtain a binary matrix $\boldsymbol{X} = (\boldsymbol{R} > 0)$ that represents only the relations, i.e. $\boldsymbol{X}(i,k) = 1$ if $\boldsymbol{R}(i,k) > 0$, otherwise $\boldsymbol{X}(i,k) = 0$, and the resulting matrix $\boldsymbol{X}$ can be precisely represented by a hypergraph.

A *hypergraph* is an extension of a graph for modeling relations. In a graph, an edge connects exactly two vertices, while in a hypergraph a *hyperedge* connects any number of vertices. For a binary relation matrix $\boldsymbol{X}$, the items are considered as the vertices of a hypergraph, and a user is represented by a hyperedge which contains all the items (vertices) that have been rated by the user. Following the tradition of visualizing a hypergraph in literatures, Figure 2 shows an example of the hypergraph representation. The matrix $\boldsymbol{X}$ is also called the *incident matrix* of the hypergraph. The *vertex degree* (of an item) is the sum of the k-th column of $\boldsymbol{X}$, i.e. $\deg(z_k) = \sum_i \boldsymbol{X}(i,k)$. The *hyperedge degree* (of a user) is the sum of the i-th row of $\boldsymbol{X}$, i.e. $\deg(y_i) = \sum_k \boldsymbol{X}(i,k)$.

Recall that we assume there are some clusters of items, and these clusters correspond to the latent factors. Thus extracting the latent factors is equivalent to finding clusters of items (vertices) in the hypergraph. There is a wide range of studies for clustering the vertices in a hypergraph [8, 1, 22]. In this paper, we focus on one particular line of studies that convert a hypergraph into an approximated graph so that the graph clustering algorithms can be applied to the hypergraph. Zhou et al. proposed a transformation to convert a hypergraph into a graph based on the *Normalized Hypergraph Cut* (NHC) [22] (others include the clique-expansion, the start-expansion [1], and the hyperedge-expansion [15]). We denote the transformation proposed in [22] as "NHC", and use it to find clusters in the hypergraph.

By applying the NHC transformation, the vertices of the hypergraph are copied into a new graph. Then each hyperedge is converted into a clique of weighted edges in the new graph that connect all the vertices in the original hyperedge. The weights of the edges in the clique are normalized by the hyperedge degree so that the contribution of each hyperedge to the new graph is the same. With a linear combination of all the cliques from all the hyperedges, the new graph can be seen as an approximation of the hypergraph in the sense that any two vertices connected by some hyperedges are also connected in the new graph. We call this new graph the *induced graph* (see Figure 2).

One can show that the adjacency matrix of the induced graph is $\boldsymbol{X}^\top \boldsymbol{D}_e^{-1}\boldsymbol{X}$, where $\boldsymbol{X}^\top$ is the transpose of $\boldsymbol{X}$ and $\boldsymbol{D}_e = \text{diag}(\boldsymbol{X}\mathbf{1})$ is the hyperedge degree matrix. $\boldsymbol{D}_e$ is actually the diagonal matrix of row sums of $\boldsymbol{X}$, and $\mathbf{1}$ is an all-ones vector of proper length. With the NHC transformation, it is proposed to use the normalized Laplacian of the induced graph to find clusters of vertices [22], where the normalized Laplacian matrix $\boldsymbol{L}$ is defined as

$$\boldsymbol{L} = \boldsymbol{I} - \boldsymbol{D}_v^{-1/2}\boldsymbol{X}^\top \boldsymbol{D}_e^{-1}\boldsymbol{X}\boldsymbol{D}_v^{-1/2}. \tag{1}$$

Matrix $\boldsymbol{I}$ is an identity matrix, and $\boldsymbol{D}_v = \text{diag}\left(\mathbf{1}^\top \boldsymbol{X}\right)$ is the vertex degree matrix.

As in standard spectral graph theory [4], the clustering algorithm involves computing the leading (smallest) l eigenvalues $\{\lambda_1, \lambda_2, ..., \lambda_l\}$ of $\boldsymbol{L}$ and the corresponding eigenvectors $[\boldsymbol{f}_1, \boldsymbol{f}_2, ..., \boldsymbol{f}_l] = \boldsymbol{F}$. Then a vertex (or an item z_k) can be represented by a vector $\boldsymbol{\alpha}_k$ that is the k-th column of $\boldsymbol{F}^\top$ (note that $\boldsymbol{F}$ is of size $n \times l$). We call the l-dimensional vector $\boldsymbol{\alpha}_k$ the *latent vector*, and the l-dimensional space the *latent space*. Once the latent vectors are computed, one can apply any clustering algorithm (such as k-means) in the latent space to find clusters of vertices.

This scheme of spectral technique (the list of eigenvalues are often called the *spectrum* of the matrix) has been widely used in many areas. It has close connections to the Principal Component Analysis (PCA), SVD, and many other matrix factorization techniques. In the next section, we show that the NHC transformation of a hypergraph is equivalent to a SVD, and under certain conditions there is a structure with the resulting latent vectors. Note that although the actual ratings are ignored in the hypergraph representation, they will be used again in the top-N recommendation algorithm presented in Section 4.

3. HYPERGRAPH LEARNING USING SVD

The normalized Laplacian $\boldsymbol{L}$ is a symmetric matrix. Let

$$\bar{\boldsymbol{X}} = \boldsymbol{D}_e^{-1/2}\boldsymbol{X}\boldsymbol{D}_v^{-1/2}. \tag{2}$$

We can rewrite $\boldsymbol{L} = \boldsymbol{I} - \bar{\boldsymbol{X}}^\top \bar{\boldsymbol{X}}$. The biggest l eigenvalues of $\bar{\boldsymbol{X}}^\top \bar{\boldsymbol{X}}$ are exactly $\{1-\lambda_1, 1-\lambda_2, ..., 1-\lambda_l\}$, while the corresponding eigenvectors are still $[\boldsymbol{f}_1, \boldsymbol{f}_2, ..., \boldsymbol{f}_l] = \boldsymbol{F}$. Then we decompose the matrix $\bar{\boldsymbol{X}}$ by the full SVD $\bar{\boldsymbol{X}} = \boldsymbol{U}\boldsymbol{S}\boldsymbol{V}^\top$, where $\boldsymbol{U}$ and $\boldsymbol{V}$ are unitary matrices, and $\boldsymbol{S}$ is a rectangular diagonal matrix. The biggest l singular values in $\boldsymbol{S}$ are exactly $\{\sqrt{1-\lambda_1}, \sqrt{1-\lambda_2}, ..., \sqrt{1-\lambda_l}\}$, and the columns of $\boldsymbol{V}$ (right-singular vectors) are the eigenvectors of $\bar{\boldsymbol{X}}^\top \bar{\boldsymbol{X}}$. Therefore, instead of computing the eigen-decomposition of $\boldsymbol{L}$, we can obtain $\boldsymbol{F}$ from the SVD of $\bar{\boldsymbol{X}}$, i.e. $\boldsymbol{F}$ is the submatrix of the first l columns of $\boldsymbol{V}$.

Since we are looking for the right singular vectors of $\bar{\boldsymbol{X}}$ associated with the largest l singular values, computing $\boldsymbol{F}$ can be done by the truncated SVD $\bar{\boldsymbol{X}} \approx \boldsymbol{U}_l\boldsymbol{S}_l\boldsymbol{V}_l^\top = \boldsymbol{U}_l\boldsymbol{S}_l\boldsymbol{F}^\top$. Thus the NHC transformation is equivalent to the asymmetric truncated SVD of $\bar{\boldsymbol{X}}$. We call the column vectors in $\bar{\boldsymbol{X}}$ the "profiles" of the items.

There are many advantages of using SVD to compute the $\boldsymbol{\alpha}_k$'s (latent vectors) rather than the eigen-decomposition of $\boldsymbol{L}$. Firstly, the matrix $\bar{\boldsymbol{X}}$ is usually sparse, but $\bar{\boldsymbol{X}}^\top \bar{\boldsymbol{X}}$ might be non-sparse. When n is large, the computational cost and storage cost of the eigen-decomposition might be impractical. Secondly, there are existing approaches to implement SVD incrementally, which allows us to just compute the minor changes when modifying $\bar{\boldsymbol{X}}$.

3.1 A Special Case

We first consider a special case where all the items in one cluster are rated by the same set of users. In other words, each cluster C_j is associated with a subset of users and these users have rated all the items in C_j. We call this special case the "full concentrated case" because it can be modeled with a beta distribution with a small concentration parameter. If there are s clusters, the matrix $\bar{\boldsymbol{X}}$ can be written as

$$\bar{\boldsymbol{X}} = [\underbrace{\bar{\boldsymbol{x}}_1 \cdots \bar{\boldsymbol{x}}_1}_{|C_1| \text{ vectors}}\ \underbrace{\bar{\boldsymbol{x}}_2 \cdots \bar{\boldsymbol{x}}_2}_{|C_2| \text{ vectors}}\ \cdots\ \underbrace{\bar{\boldsymbol{x}}_s \cdots \bar{\boldsymbol{x}}_s}_{|C_s| \text{ vectors}}], \tag{3}$$

where the column vectors in one cluster are all the same. We call the items in the s clusters the *anchor items* because they define the cluster centers and remain clustered in the latent space.

In spectral graph theory, if the graph contains s disconnected components, one can show that the latent vectors obtained from the first s eigenvectors of the graph Laplacian are aligned with the axes of the s-dimensional latent space [13]. When the disconnected components are connected by some weak links, the latent vectors are still aligned with s approximately orthogonal lines [20]. However, the induced graph of a hypergraph usually does not consist of more than one connected component. Figure 3 shows an example of a hypergraph in full concentrated case. The adjacency matrix of the induced graph is not a diagonal block matrix (not even approximately), so we need to develop a new analysis to support the clustering algorithm for hypergraphs.

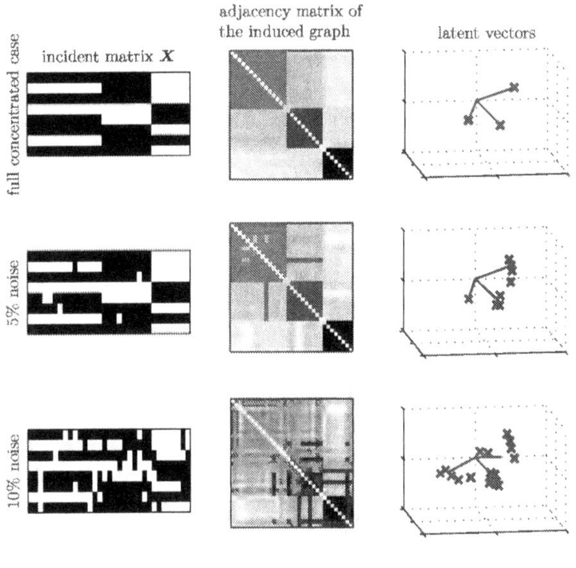

Figure 3: Examples of the incident matrix and the latent vectors with the full concentrated case and noisy cases. The noises are added by randomly flipping some entries of X. Approximately orthogonal structures can be observed in the noisy cases. In the charts of latent vectors, the gray lines are from the origin to the cluster centers.

If the rank of $\bar{\boldsymbol{X}}$ is s, i.e. the anchor item profiles $\bar{\boldsymbol{x}}_j$'s are linearly independent, the truncated SVD $\bar{\boldsymbol{X}} = \boldsymbol{U}_l\boldsymbol{S}_l\boldsymbol{V}_l^\top$ is an exact decomposition when $l = s$. Recall that the latent vectors in $\boldsymbol{F}$ can be obtained from $\boldsymbol{F} = \boldsymbol{V}_l$. The following statement shows the structure of $\boldsymbol{F}$.

PROPOSITION 1. *If $\bar{\boldsymbol{X}}$ is in the form of Eq. (3) and $\bar{\boldsymbol{x}}_j$'s are linearly independent, the latent vectors $\boldsymbol{F} = [\boldsymbol{\alpha}_1 \cdots \boldsymbol{\alpha}_n]^\top$ given by the truncated SVD $\bar{\boldsymbol{X}} = \boldsymbol{U}_s \boldsymbol{S}_s \boldsymbol{F}^\top$ (columns of $\boldsymbol{F}$ are normalized to 1) can be grouped by the clusters $\boldsymbol{\alpha}_k = \boldsymbol{\beta}_j$ for $\forall z_k \in C_j$. The $\boldsymbol{\alpha}_k$'s from the same cluster are identical (denoted as $\boldsymbol{\beta}_j$). Furthermore, we have $\boldsymbol{\beta}_j^\top \boldsymbol{\beta}_{j'} = 0$ for $\forall j \neq j'$, and $\boldsymbol{\beta}_j^\top \boldsymbol{\beta}_j = |C_j|^{-1}$ for $\forall j \in \{1, 2, ..., s\}$. (See appendix for proof.)*

If all the items are anchor items, i.e. in the form of Eq. (3) and having linearly independent $\bar{\boldsymbol{x}}_j$'s, the latent vectors would be in exactly s clusters whose centers are orthogonal to each other (see Figure 3). The length of the latent vector is the reciprocal of the cluster size. Unlike the graph case, the latent vectors computed from a hypergraph are usually not aligned with the axes of the latent space, but up to a rotation that depends on the cluster sizes and the distribution of non-zero entries in $\bar{\boldsymbol{X}}$. Nevertheless, the orthogonal structure of the latent vectors still provides us a similar theoretical foundation for clustering vertices as in the standard spectral graph theory.

3.2 More General Case

The assumption that all the items are anchor items is too strict. We usually have some item profiles which are combinations of some other item profiles. For example, there are pure "SciFi" books and pure "romance" books that attract distinct sets of readers (the anchor items). But one book might have the "SciFi" element and the "romance" element at the same time, so it could attract readers from both sets. The item profile of this book is apparently a combination of two profiles.

Besides the anchor items, we now consider the *non-anchor items* that are combinations of anchor items. We assume that the weights of the combinations are always non-negative, which implies that only additions of profiles are allowed, but not subtractions. If there are n' non-anchor items and s clusters of anchor items, $\bar{\boldsymbol{X}}$ can be rewritten as

$$\bar{\boldsymbol{X}} = [\underbrace{\bar{\boldsymbol{x}}'_1 \cdots\cdots \bar{\boldsymbol{x}}'_{n'}}_{n' \text{ vectors}}\ \underbrace{\bar{\boldsymbol{x}}_1 \cdots \bar{\boldsymbol{x}}_1}_{|C_1| \text{ vectors}}\ \underbrace{\bar{\boldsymbol{x}}_2 \cdots \bar{\boldsymbol{x}}_2}_{|C_2| \text{ vectors}}\ \cdots\ \underbrace{\bar{\boldsymbol{x}}_s \cdots \bar{\boldsymbol{x}}_s}_{|C_s| \text{ vectors}}], \quad (4)$$

where the profile of non-anchor item z'_k is denoted as $\bar{\boldsymbol{x}}'_k$ ($k \in \{1, 2, ..., n'\}$), and the profile of an anchor item from cluster C_j is still denoted as $\bar{\boldsymbol{x}}_j$. Note that $\bar{\boldsymbol{x}}'_k$ is not an exact linear combination of the anchor items, because when combining the profiles of the anchor items, there might be redundant entries. For example, if $\bar{\boldsymbol{x}}_1 = [1\,1\,0\,0]^\top$, $\bar{\boldsymbol{x}}_2 = [0\,1\,1\,0]^\top$ and $\bar{\boldsymbol{x}}'_k$ is a combination of $\bar{\boldsymbol{x}}_1$ and $\bar{\boldsymbol{x}}_2$, $\bar{\boldsymbol{x}}'_k$ would be $[1\,1\,1\,0]^\top$ instead of $[1\,2\,1\,0]^\top$ because the incident matrix $\boldsymbol{X}$ is always a binary matrix (normalizations are ignored in this example for simplicity). Thus we need to subtract the redundant entries when summing the anchor item profiles:

$$\bar{\boldsymbol{x}}'_k = \sum_{j \in I(z'_k)} \sqrt{\frac{\deg(z_j)}{\deg(z'_k)}} \bar{\boldsymbol{x}}_j - \boldsymbol{r}, \quad (5)$$

where $I(z'_k)$ is the set of anchor items from which z'_k is constructed, and $\boldsymbol{r}$ denotes the column vector that consists of the redundant entries in the profiles of the anchor items. Obviously all entries of $\boldsymbol{r}$ are non-negative.

Denote the latent vector of an anchor item from cluster C_j as $\boldsymbol{\beta}_j$, and the latent vector of a non-anchor item z'_k as $\boldsymbol{\beta}'_k$. By the SVD on $\bar{\boldsymbol{X}}$, $\boldsymbol{\beta}'_k$ can be expressed by the combination

$$\boldsymbol{\beta}'_k = \sum_{j \in I(z'_k)} \sqrt{\frac{\deg(z_j)}{\deg(z'_k)}} \boldsymbol{\beta}_j - \boldsymbol{S}_l^{-1} \boldsymbol{U}^\top \boldsymbol{r}. \quad (6)$$

If the entries in $\boldsymbol{r}$ are small enough to be considered as residuals, or in other words the anchor items are associated with disjoint sets of users, we could still expect approximately orthogonal structure between the latent vectors of the anchor items.

PROPOSITION 2. *If the anchor items are associated with disjoint sets of users, i.e. $\bar{\boldsymbol{x}}_j^\top \bar{\boldsymbol{x}}_{j'} = 0$ for $\forall j, j' \in \{1, 2, ..., s\}$, $j \neq j'$, the latent vectors of the anchor items are approximately orthogonal $\boldsymbol{\beta}_j^\top \boldsymbol{\beta}_{j'} \approx 0$ for $\forall j \neq j'$.*

The conclusion of Proposition 2 follows from the fact that $\bar{\boldsymbol{x}}_j^\top \bar{\boldsymbol{x}}_{j'} = \boldsymbol{\beta}_j^\top \boldsymbol{S}_l^2 \boldsymbol{\beta}_{j'} = 0$, and the first l singular values in $\boldsymbol{S}_l$ are approximately the same when the cluster sizes are similar.

In practice, we can consider the anchor items as the most representative items of each cluster. For example, the pure "SciFi" books are the anchor items of the "SciFi" cluster, because they have the most unique features that define what is "SciFi". The anchor items are not necessarily the most popular items or the most informative items in each cluster, but the items that are most distant from all the other clusters and attract a very unique group of users. Usually the anchor items are in the long-tail part, i.e. less popular.

Although the anchor items exhibit the approximately orthogonal structure, we do not know which items are the anchor items. The following result suggests that it is possible to distinguish the anchor items and the non-anchor items by examining the length of the latent vectors.

PROPOSITION 3. *For a non-anchor item z'_k, denote $I(z'_k)$ the set of anchor items from which z'_k is constructed. Suppose that the anchor items in $I(z'_k)$ are non-overlapping, i.e. $\bar{\boldsymbol{x}}_j^\top \bar{\boldsymbol{x}}_{j'} = 0$ for $\forall j, j' \in I(z'_k), j \neq j'$, and the cluster sizes of the anchor items are similar, i.e. the lengths of the anchor latent vectors are similar (denoted as $\|\boldsymbol{\beta}_j\|_2 \approx b_0$ for $\forall j \in I(z'_k)$, where $\|\cdot\|_2$ is the l_2 norm). We have $\|\boldsymbol{\beta}'_k\|_2 < b_0$. (See appendix for proof.)*

This result states that the length of a non-anchor latent vector is smaller than the lengths of the anchor latent vectors from which the former is constructed. Therefore, we can find the anchor items by sorting the lengths of the latent vectors in descending order.

In order to verify the conclusions in Propositions 2 and 3, we compute the latent vectors by the rank-l truncated SVD of $\bar{\boldsymbol{X}}$, and select $10 \cdot l$ items whose latent vectors have the longest lengths. Then the selected latent vectors are grouped into clusters by the k-means algorithm. By the conclusions of the Propositions, the cluster centers of the selected latent vectors should be approximately orthogonal. In Figure 4, we show the results from a real dataset with NHC and SVD. Because there is no hyperedge-degree and vertex-degree normalizations in SVD, the longest latent vectors are not necessarily the anchor items. We can observe that there exists an approximately orthogonal structure in the NHC results, while such structure is less clear with SVD.

There are existing works about the categorization of the items or users based on their impact on the recommender system, e.g. [12]. Our classification of anchor and non-anchor items provides a new perspective in the context of latent space. In summary, **(1)** if the latent vectors are all orthogonal, each corresponds to a different anchor item (the full concentrated case). **(2)** if they are not, there is an orthogonal subset such that each latent vector in this subset corresponds to a different anchor item, and all the others (non-anchor items) are approximately in the subspace spanned by the orthogonal subset. **(3)** generally, the anchor items are rated by different groups of users.

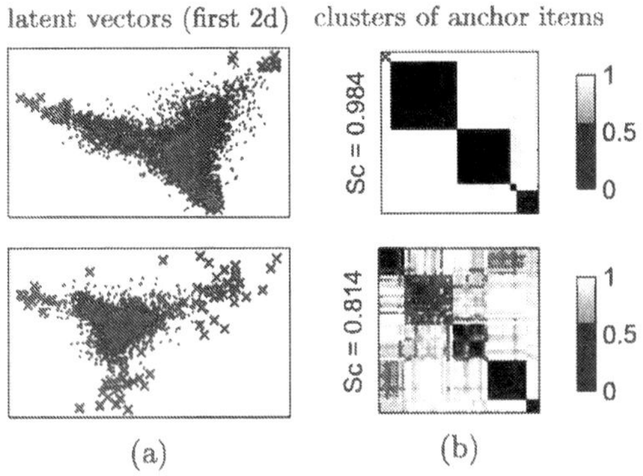

Figure 4: The selected anchor items with longer latent vector lengths in the dataset BookCrossing (see Section 6 for the description of the dataset). (a) The anchor items are shown in red x-markers. (b) The cosine distance matrix of the clustered anchor items. Sc is the sum of average distances between clusters minus the sum of average distances within clusters, normalized by the largest possible value with a perfect orthogonal structure. A Sc value close to 1 suggests a better orthogonal structure.

4. THE NORMALIZED RELATIONAL SVD

We now present a new algorithm based on the NHC Laplacian and the above analysis. Once the latent vectors are computed for the items, we model the user y_i's interests (or latent profile) as another vector $\boldsymbol{\theta}_i$ in the same latent space. The predicted score for user y_i on item z_k is $P(y_i, z_k) = \boldsymbol{\theta}_i^\top \boldsymbol{\alpha}_k$, and the vector $\boldsymbol{\theta}_i$ should take the values such that the predictor P coincides with the existing ratings (or as close as possible).

In order to simulate the scenario where the recommendations are made for new users and evaluate the algorithm, we split the rating matrix $\boldsymbol{R}$ into three parts

$$\boldsymbol{R} = \begin{bmatrix} \boldsymbol{R}_m \\ \boldsymbol{R}_{tr}, \boldsymbol{R}_{te} \end{bmatrix} \begin{matrix} \}\text{subset } Y_m \\ \}\text{subset } Y_t \end{matrix} . \tag{7}$$

Firstly the users are separated into two subsets. Y_m is the subset of old users, and Y_t is the subset of new users. The sub-matrix $\boldsymbol{R}_m$ contains all the ratings from the users in Y_m, and the ratings in $\boldsymbol{R}_m$ are used for constructing the hypergraph and computing the latent vectors. The ratings from the users in Y_t are further split into two parts: $\boldsymbol{R}_{tr}$ and $\boldsymbol{R}_{te}$. $\boldsymbol{R}_{tr}$ contains the "known" ratings of the new users. Based on $\boldsymbol{R}_{tr}$ and the latent vectors, we can predict or recommend more items for the users in Y_t. Then the predictions are evaluated by the ratings in $\boldsymbol{R}_{te}$. Note that only $\boldsymbol{R}_m$ and $\boldsymbol{R}_{tr}$ are taken as the inputs of the algorithm. $\boldsymbol{R}_{te}$ is used for evaluation.

Since our algorithm works with the hypergraph transformation and SVD, we call it HSVD, which contains the following steps:

Step 1: Compute the l-dimensional NHC transformation $\boldsymbol{F}$ by the truncated SVD $\bar{\boldsymbol{X}}_m \approx \boldsymbol{U}_l \boldsymbol{S}_l \boldsymbol{F}^\top$, where $\bar{\boldsymbol{X}}_m$ is computed from the binary matrix $\boldsymbol{X}_m = (\boldsymbol{R}_m > 0)$ (see Eq. (2)). Normalize each of the l columns of $\boldsymbol{F}$ to 1 (l_2 norm).

Step 2: For each user $y_i \in Y_t$, we choose the $\boldsymbol{\theta}_i$ that minimizes the error $\|\boldsymbol{R}_{tr}(i, \cdot) - \boldsymbol{\theta}_i^\top \boldsymbol{F}^\top\|_2^2$. The predicted score vector is $\hat{\boldsymbol{r}}_i = \boldsymbol{\theta}_i^\top \boldsymbol{F}^\top$. In matrix form, the full prediction matrix is $\hat{\boldsymbol{R}}_{te} = \boldsymbol{\Theta}^\top \boldsymbol{F}^\top$, where $\boldsymbol{\Theta}$ is obtained by solving the linear system $\boldsymbol{F}\boldsymbol{\Theta} = \boldsymbol{R}_{tr}^\top$ in a least-squares sense.

Step 3: For each user $y_i \in Y_t$, recommend the top-N unrated items with the highest scores in $\hat{\boldsymbol{R}}_{te}$.

There are several normalizations in the HSVD algorithm which did not exist in previous matrix factorization methods. When computing $\bar{\boldsymbol{X}}_m$ in step 1, the hyperedge-degree normalization (from the induced graph transformation itself) and the vertex-degree normalization (from the normalized Laplacian of the induced graph) ensure that the anchor latent vectors would have longer lengths. By Proposition 1, the normalization of the columns of $\boldsymbol{F}$ in step 1 is also indispensable for producing an (approximately) orthogonal structure in the latent space.

When computing the $\boldsymbol{\theta}_i$ in step 2, two parts are actually taken into consideration, which is illustrated in Figure 5. Firstly we consider the latent vectors of the items which are rated by user y_i (the triangle points in Figure 5). We would like to choose a $\boldsymbol{\theta}_i$ that is close to these rated $\boldsymbol{\alpha}_k$'s. Since the row vector $\boldsymbol{R}(i, \cdot)$ is weighted by the ratings, $\boldsymbol{\theta}_i$ should be even closer to the $\boldsymbol{\alpha}_k$'s with higher ratings, which can be expressed as $\boldsymbol{\theta}_i = \arg\min_{\boldsymbol{\theta}} \sum_{k, \boldsymbol{R}(i,k)>0} \left(\boldsymbol{R}(i,k) - \boldsymbol{\theta}_i^\top \boldsymbol{\alpha}_k\right)^2$. Because every non-anchor item is approximately a linear combination of some anchor items (e.g. $\boldsymbol{\alpha}_3$ is a combination of $\boldsymbol{\alpha}_1$ and $\boldsymbol{\alpha}_5$ in Figure 5), $\boldsymbol{\theta}_i$ should be in the subspace spanned by the latent vectors of the underlying anchor items. Secondly, for those $\boldsymbol{\alpha}_k$'s that are not rated by user y_i (the circle points in Figure 5), $\boldsymbol{\theta}_i$ should stay as far from them as possible, ideally orthogonal to these unrated latent vectors. The orthogonality between the cluster centers of the anchor items suggests that it is possible to find a $\boldsymbol{\theta}_i$ which is orthogonal to the anchor items that the user y_i is not interested in. This can be expressed as $\boldsymbol{\theta}_i = \arg\min_{\boldsymbol{\theta}} \sum_{k, \boldsymbol{R}(i,k)=0} \left(\boldsymbol{\theta}_i^\top \boldsymbol{\alpha}_k\right)^2$. Putting the two parts together, it suggests that in matrix form the $\boldsymbol{\theta}_i$'s can be obtained by solving the linear system $\boldsymbol{F}\boldsymbol{\Theta} = \boldsymbol{R}_{tr}^\top$ in a least-squares sense, which is in the step 2 of the HSVD algorithm.

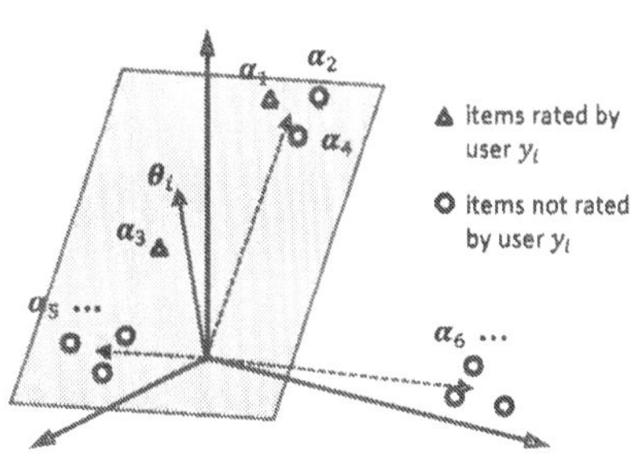

Figure 5: Illustration of the HSVD algorithm in 3d latent space. The dashed lines are cluster centers of the anchor items.

Proposition 3 shows that the lengths of the anchor latent vectors are longer than the non-anchor latent vectors, even if the anchor items are less popular. For a fixed $\boldsymbol{\theta}_i$, because the score $\hat{\boldsymbol{R}}_{te}(i,k)$ is simply the inner product of $\boldsymbol{\theta}_i$ and $\boldsymbol{\alpha}_k$, the anchor items of longer length would have bigger chance to be selected in the top-N recommendations. This would allow us to diversify the recommendation list and recommend more less-popular items.

4.1 Scalability

The main computational cost of our algorithm comes from the truncated SVD routine. Usually the numerical method for truncated SVD on matrix $\bar{\boldsymbol{X}}$ is in an iterative manner, and operated as an eigen-decomposition of the Hermitian matrix $\bar{\boldsymbol{X}}^\top\bar{\boldsymbol{X}}$. The running time of the latter problem depends on the complexity of each iteration and the total number of iterations. In each iteration the basic operation contains two matrix vector multiplications $\bar{\boldsymbol{X}}^\top\bar{\boldsymbol{X}}\boldsymbol{v}$ where $\boldsymbol{v}$ is a dense vector. If the number of non-zero entries in $\bar{\boldsymbol{X}}$ (or the number of ratings in $\boldsymbol{R}$) is M, the complexity of each iteration would be $O(M)$. On the other hand, the total number of iterations to converge depends on the gap between the l largest singular value and the $l+1$ largest singular value. A bigger gap leads to a smaller number of iterations [6, 11]. If the number of iterations is n_I, the overall complexity of the HSVD algorithm is $O(n_I M)$, which is linear to the number of ratings. The parameter l (dimensionality of the truncated SVD) is considered as a constant, which can be determined by cross-validation in practice.

5. RELATED WORK

In the introduction, we have mentioned the SVD [17], the SVD on non-empty entries [5], and the asymmetric SVD [14, 9] for recommender systems. Another matrix factorization technique that is widely used in recommender systems is the *non-negative matrix factorization* (NMF). In NMF, the rating matrix is approximately decomposed into two low-rank, sparse and non-negative matrices $\boldsymbol{R} \approx \boldsymbol{G}\boldsymbol{H}^\top$ such that $\|\boldsymbol{R} - \boldsymbol{G}\boldsymbol{H}^\top\|^2$ is minimized [7, 16]. The idea behind NMF is that the set of orthogonal latent factors controls the values in $\boldsymbol{R}$, and each latent factor takes one axis in the latent space. This idea is essentially similar to the HSVD since we have shown that the anchor items also exhibit an orthogonal structure in the latent space, although they are not aligned to the axes.

In order to compare our algorithm with the existing approaches, we adapt the SVD and the NMF into our setting, i.e. split the rating matrix into three parts as in Eq. (7) and use the sub-matrix $\boldsymbol{R}' = [\boldsymbol{R}_m^\top \boldsymbol{R}_{tr}^\top]^\top$ to compute the SVD or NMF, then evaluate the results on $\boldsymbol{R}_{te}$. The SVD and NMF algorithms in this setting are denoted as SVDR and NMFR.

To make a better baseline, we also apply the SVDR and NMFR on $\boldsymbol{R}_m$ and predict with $\boldsymbol{R}_{tr}$ in an asymmetric manner, i.e. follow the same procedures in Section 4 but replace $\bar{\boldsymbol{X}}_m$ with $\boldsymbol{R}_m$ (or replace $\boldsymbol{F}$ with the matrix $\boldsymbol{H}$ in NMF). These methods are denoted as ASVDR and ANMFR, where the leading "A" means "asymmetric".

We use the routine implemented by TimelyDevelopment for computing the SVD on non-empty entries [18], which is denoted as SVDN. Note that SVDN is exactly the same as SVDR except for the SVD computation routine.

For the asymmetric SVD, we use the approach proposed in [14]. In this approach, a decomposition is first computed by SVDN $\boldsymbol{R} \approx \boldsymbol{U}_l\boldsymbol{S}_l\boldsymbol{V}_l^\top$, where $\boldsymbol{V}_l = [\boldsymbol{\alpha}_1 \cdots \boldsymbol{\alpha}_n]^\top$. Then a user y_i is represented by the currently rated items: $\boldsymbol{\theta}_i = \sum_{k,\boldsymbol{R}(i,k)>0} \boldsymbol{\alpha}_k$. Finally a score is computed by the rule $\hat{\boldsymbol{R}}(i,k) = a_k + \boldsymbol{\theta}_i^\top\boldsymbol{\alpha}_k$ for each unrated item, where a_k is the average rating of item z_k. We call this method ASVDN.

6. EXPERIMENTAL RESULTS

In a top-N recommender system, the primary goal is to discover the unrated items that might be liked by a user [3]. We first test the algorithm's ability to discover the unrated items, which is denoted as the scenario PREDICT-ALL. The rating matrix is split into three parts as in Eq. (7), and we randomly select $\boldsymbol{R}_{tr}$ to have 5 ratings in each row (for each user). The remaining ratings in the Y_t part are assigned to $\boldsymbol{R}_{te}$. This setting simulates the situation where new users just come into the system with only a few ratings, which is denoted as PREDICT-ON-5. Similarly, we create another setting PREDICT-ON-20 where each row of $\boldsymbol{R}_{tr}$ has 20 ratings to simulate the users with more available ratings. Thus in the scenario PREDICT-ALL, there are two settings, namely PREDICT-ON-5 and PREDICT-ON-20. Note that all the items in $\boldsymbol{R}_{te}$ (rated or unrated) could be recommended in the top-N recommendation list. In all the experiments, $\boldsymbol{R}_{tr}$ and $\boldsymbol{R}_{te}$ are randomly selected in 5 different runs.

To test the results, we check if the set of recommended items coincides with the liked items (ratings higher than the median) for each user in the corresponding row of $\boldsymbol{R}_{te}$. Let $\hat{R}_i^N$ and R_i denote these two sets for user y_i. We measure the average precision

$$\text{precision} = (1/|Y_t|) \sum_{y_i \in Y_t} \left(|\hat{R}_i^N \cap R_i| / |\hat{R}_i^N| \right). \tag{8}$$

	Lastfm		YahooMusic		BookCrossing	
SVDR	0.113	0.083	0.237	0.207	0.078	0.063
ASVDR	0.114	0.087	0.237	0.210	0.078	0.062
NMFR	0.114	0.090	0.218	0.189	0.073	0.054
ANMFR	0.110	0.089	0.211	0.190	0.071	0.056
SVDN	0.002	0.003	0.001	0.001	0.005	0.003
ASVDN	0.003	0.002	0.007	0.005	0.005	0.003
HSVD	**0.180**	**0.158**	**0.258**	**0.227**	0.075	0.065

Table 1: Average precisions in PREDICT-ALL. The left column of each dataset: PREDICT-ON-5, the right column: PREDICT-ON-20. The bold number indicates the method that performs significantly better than the others (p-value < 0.05 in paired t-test).

	Lastfm		YahooMusic		BookCrossing	
SVDR	0.198	0.140	0.490	0.418	0.743	0.744
ASVDR	0.198	0.139	0.496	0.435	0.743	0.745
NMFR	**0.541**	**0.545**	0.763	0.774	0.731	0.740
ANMFR	0.279	0.222	0.579	0.496	0.743	0.745
SVDN	0.177	0.244	0.249	0.224	0.389	0.165
ASVDN	0.537	0.531	0.755	**0.783**	0.696	0.714
HSVD	0.515	0.524	0.765	0.766	**0.745**	**0.747**

Table 2: Average precisions in RANK-CANDIDATES. (see the caption of Table 1 for more details)

In the scenario PREDICT-ALL, any item which is not in $\boldsymbol{R}_{tr}$ can be considered in the recommendation list. But sometimes we already know a set of candidate items that a user has suggested implicitly. For example, a user has viewed a list of pages of artists, but did not make any further actions like purchase a CD or download a track. In this case, we can limit our recommendations on the candidate items and only pick up the items that are truly liked by the user, which could be simulated by only recommending the rated items in $\boldsymbol{R}_{te}$. We try to rank these items such that the liked ones are ranked higher. This scenario is denoted as RANK-CANDIDATES. The same measure (precision defined in Eq. (8)) is evaluated in RANK-CANDIDATES.

We have tested all the methods listed in Section 5 with the above settings on three datasets. Lastfm [1] contains the relations between users and artists collected from last.fm, and the ratings in Lastfm are the actual counts of plays with which a user has listened to an artist. YahooMusic [2] is also in the music domain, but includes relations between users and tracks. The ratings in YahooMusic are in the range of 1 to 100. The last dataset BookCrossing contains ratings from users to books [23]. The range of ratings in BookCrossing is from 1 to 10. In each dataset, we take a subset such that the induced graph of the hypergraph representation is connected. When the dataset contains a hypergraph with multiple connected components, we could simply apply the algorithm to each connected component respectively.

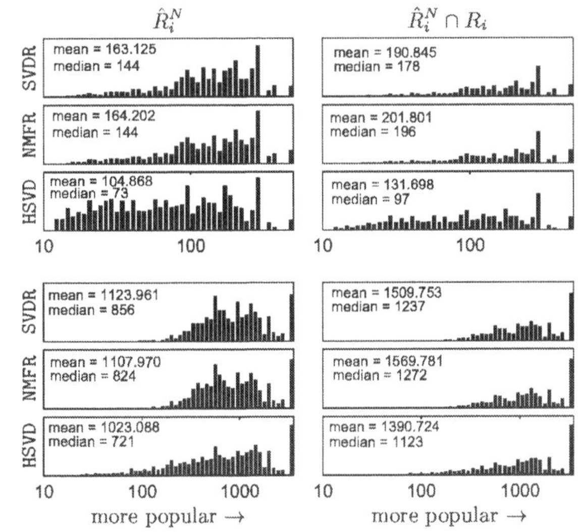

Figure 6: The distribution of popularity of the items (in the PREDICT-ALL scenario with $N = 20$). The x-axis (popularity) is in log-scale. The mean and median of the popularity of the items are also shown in each sub-figure. Top: BookCrossing. Bottom: YahooMusic.

Table 1 and Table 2 show the results of PREDICT-ALL and RANK-CANDIDATES respectively (with $N = 20$). In the first case, our proposed method performs best within the music domain, and shows results as good as the best methods with BookCrossing. The approaches ignoring the empty values (SVDN and ASVDN) does not perform very well. These methods are originally designed to minimize the root mean squared error on a testing set of known ratings, which is not fully compatible with the scenario PREDICT-ALL. In the RANK-CANDIDATES, no method performs significantly better than the others over all datasets. But the NMF-based method NMFR and two asymmetric methods ASVDN and HSVD are always as good as the best one.

In recommender systems, we are mainly interested in recommending non-popular (long-tail) items, because the users are usually already aware of the popular items from other sources [19]. For the purpose of diversifying recommendations, we measure the popularity distribution of the items in $\hat{R}_i^N$ and $\hat{R}_i^N \cap R_i$, i.e. the set of all recommended items and the set of successfully recommended items (Figure 6). The popularity of an item z_k is the number of ratings in the k-th column of the rating matrix, i.e. $\deg(z_k)$. We observe that HSVD produces more diverse recommendations with the same (or better) level of precision. Especially with BookCrossing, there are much more less-popular recommendations from HSVD compared to SVDR and NMFR.

Figure 7 explains why our approach produces more diverse recommendations. By using SVD without normalization, the lengths of the anchor items are not necessarily the longest ones. In fact, we can observe that there is a strong correlation between the popularity and the length of the latent vector with ASVDR, which would promote the popular items in the recommendations. In our approach HSVD, the longest latent vectors correspond to the anchor items of smaller popularity.

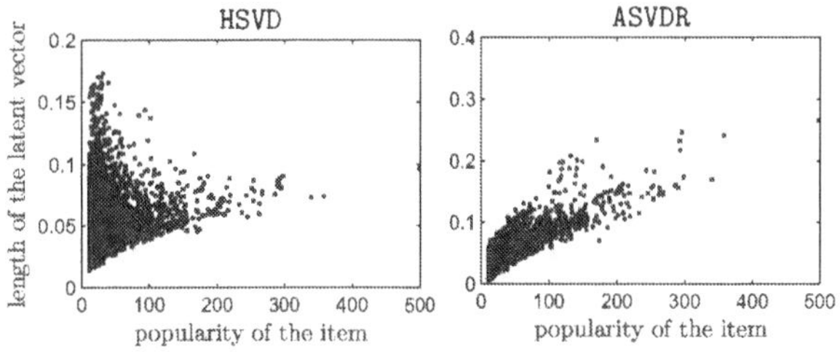

Figure 7: The length of the latent vectors and the popularity of all the items in BookCrossing.

7. CONCLUSION

In this work, we present a new perspective of SVD for constructing a latent space from the training data, which is justified by the transformation of normalized hypergraph cut. We show that the latent vectors representing the items in the latent space can be grouped into (approximately) orthogonal clusters, and the lengths of the vectors can be used to distinguish the anchor items and the non-anchor items. These properties are then utilized for making top-N recommendations in the proposed algorithm HSVD. Instead of explicitly constructing the clusters, the recommendations are generated by solving a linear system. We provide new explanations for the significantly better performance of the asymmetric SVD approaches and better diversity in top-N recommendations. Experiments conducted with three dataset on two domains also confirm our analysis.

Future works could include further studies of the latent space structures, and engineering methods that exploit such structures. For example, we can explicitly extract the anchor items to construct some clusters, and analyze the features of a non-anchor item by studying the underlying anchor clusters. It is also possible to include additional information,

[1] Available at http://mtg.upf.edu/node/1671

[2] Yahoo! Webscope dataset ydata-ymusic-kddcup-2011-track2 http://labs.yahoo.com/Academic_Relations

e.g. contextual information [2] and social information [21], or rating bias corrections [10] into our scheme for further improvements.

8. REFERENCES

[1] S. Agarwal, K. Branson, and S. Belongie. Higher order learning with graphs. In *ICML*, 2006.

[2] L. Baltrunas, B. Ludwig, and F. Ricci. Matrix factorization techniques for context aware recommendation. In *Recsys*, 2011.

[3] P. G. Campos, F. Díez, and M. Sánchez-Montañés. Towards a more realistic evaluation: testing the ability to predict future tastes of matrix factorization-based recommenders. In *Recsys*, 2011.

[4] F. Chung. *Spectral Graph Theory*. American Mathematical Society, 1997.

[5] S. Funk. Netflix update: Try this at home, `http://sifter.org/~simon/journal/20061211.html`. 2006.

[6] G. H. Golub and C. F. Van Loan. *Matrix computations*. Johns Hopkins University Press, 1996.

[7] P. Hoyer. Non-negative matrix factorization with sparseness constraints. *Journal of Machine Learning Research*, 5:1457–1469, 2004.

[8] G. Karypis, R. Aggarwal, V. Kumar, and S. Shekhar. Multilevel hypergraph partitioning: Application in vlsi domain. In *Proc. of the 34th annual Design Automation Conference*, 1997.

[9] Y. Koren. Factorization meets the neighborhood: a multifaceted collaborative filtering model. In *SIGKDD*, 2008.

[10] Y. Koren, R. Bell, and C. Volinsky. Matrix factorization techniques for recommender systems. *Computer*, 42(8):30–37, 2009.

[11] D. Mavroeidis. Mind the eigen-gap, or how to accelerate semi-supervised spectral learning algorithms. In *IJCAI*, 2011.

[12] B. K. Mohan, B. J. Keller, and N. Ramakrishnan. Scouts, promoters, and connectors: The roles of ratings in nearest-neighbor collaborative filtering. *ACM Transactions on the Web*, 1(2):8, 2007.

[13] A. Y. Ng, M. I. Jordan, Y. Weiss, et al. On spectral clustering: Analysis and an algorithm. In *NIPS*, 2002.

[14] A. Paterek. Improving regularized singular value decomposition for collaborative filtering. In *Proc. of KDD Cup and Workshop*, 2007.

[15] L. Pu and B. Faltings. Hypergraph learning with hyperedge expansion. In *ECML-PKDD*, 2012.

[16] S. Rendle and L. Schmidt-Thieme. Online-updating regularized kernel matrix factorization models for large-scale recommender systems. In *Recsys*, 2008.

[17] B. Sarwar, G. Karypis, J. Konstan, and J. Riedl. Application of dimensionality reduction in recommender system-a case study. In *WebKDD*, 2000.

[18] TimelyDevelopment. `http://www.timelydevelopment.com/demos/NetflixPrize.aspx`. 2006.

[19] S. Vargas and P. Castells. Rank and relevance in novelty and diversity metrics for recommender systems. In *Recsys*, 2011.

[20] L. Wu, X. Ying, X. Wu, and Z. Zhou. Line orthogonality in adjacency eigenspace with application to community partition. In *IJCAI*, 2011.

[21] Q. Yuan, L. Chen, and S. Zhao. Factorization vs. regularization: fusing heterogeneous social relationships in top-n recommendation. In *Recsys*, 2011.

[22] D. Zhou, J. Huang, and B. Scholkopf. Learning with hypergraphs: Clustering, classification, and embedding. In *NIPS*, 2007.

[23] C. Ziegler, S. McNee, J. Konstan, and G. Lausen. Improving recommendation lists through topic diversification. In *WWW*, 2005.

APPENDIX

Proof for Proposition 1:

Firstly, it can be shown that $\boldsymbol{\alpha}_k = \boldsymbol{\alpha}_{k'}$ if $z_k, z_{k'} \in C_j$, because the k-th column and the k'-th column of $\boldsymbol{S}_s\boldsymbol{F}^\top$ must be the same to obtain the same $\tilde{\boldsymbol{x}}_k$ and $\tilde{\boldsymbol{x}}_{k'}$, which implies that $\boldsymbol{\alpha}_k = \boldsymbol{\alpha}_{k'}$. Secondly, we consider the full SVD of $\boldsymbol{X}$ and list the rows of $\boldsymbol{V}$ corresponding to items in C_j:

$$\boldsymbol{V}_{(j)}^\top = \begin{bmatrix} \boldsymbol{\beta}_j & \boldsymbol{\beta}_j & \cdots & \boldsymbol{\beta}_j \\ \gamma_1 & \gamma_2 & \cdots & \gamma_{|C_j|} \end{bmatrix}. \tag{9}$$

It is always possible to find a linear combination of the first s columns of $\boldsymbol{V}$ (denoted as $[\boldsymbol{f}_1, \boldsymbol{f}_2, ..., \boldsymbol{f}_s] = \boldsymbol{F}$) such that $\boldsymbol{F}\boldsymbol{t}_j = \left[\boldsymbol{0}^\top \cdots \boldsymbol{1}^\top \cdots \boldsymbol{0}^\top\right]^\top$, where $\boldsymbol{t}_j$ are the coefficients, and the 1's on the right hand side correspond to the items in C_j. Because all the columns in $\boldsymbol{V}$ are orthogonal to each other, a column is also orthogonal to a linear combination of some other columns (e.g. $\boldsymbol{F}\boldsymbol{t}_j$). Thus the entries in each dimension of the vectors $\{\gamma_1, ..., \gamma_{|C_j|}\}$ sum up to 0. In other words, $\sum_{k=\{1,2,...,|C_j|\}} \gamma_k = 0$, and $\boldsymbol{V}_{(j)}^\top \boldsymbol{1} = |C_j| \left[\boldsymbol{\beta}_j^\top \, \boldsymbol{0}^\top\right]^\top$. Since all the rows in $\boldsymbol{V}$ are also orthogonal to each other, we have $\left(\boldsymbol{V}_{(j)}^\top \boldsymbol{1}\right)^\top \left(\boldsymbol{V}_{(j')}^\top \boldsymbol{1}'\right) = 0$, which implies that $\boldsymbol{\beta}_j^\top \boldsymbol{\beta}_{j'} = 0$.

Proof for Proposition 3:

By Eq. (6) we know that $\boldsymbol{\beta}'_k = \sum_{j \in I(z'_k)} \sqrt{\frac{\deg(z_j)}{\deg(z'_k)}} \boldsymbol{\beta}_j$ (the residual $\boldsymbol{r}$ is zero because the involved anchor items are non-overlapping). Thus $\|\boldsymbol{\beta}'_k\|_2^2 = \sum_{j \in I(z'_k)} \frac{\deg(z_j)}{\deg(z'_k)} \|\boldsymbol{\beta}_j\|_2^2 + \sum_{j,j' \in I(z'_k), j \neq j'} 2\frac{\sqrt{\deg(z_j)\deg(z_{j'})}}{\deg(z'_k)} \boldsymbol{\beta}_j^\top \boldsymbol{\beta}_{j'}$. Since the anchor items are non-overlapping, we have $\sum_{j \in I(z'_k)} \deg(z_j) = \deg(z'_k)$. The above equation can be written as

$$\|\boldsymbol{\beta}'_k\|_2^2 = b_0^2 + \sum_{j,j' \in I(z'_k), j \neq j'} 2\frac{\sqrt{\deg(z_j)\deg(z_{j'})}}{\deg(z'_k)} \boldsymbol{\beta}_j^\top \boldsymbol{\beta}_{j'}. \tag{10}$$

Following the proof for Proposition 1, it can be shown that

$$\boldsymbol{\beta}_j^\top \boldsymbol{\beta}_{j'} = \frac{-1}{|C_j||C_{j'}|} \left(\sum_{p \in I^{-1}(j)} \sqrt{\frac{\deg(z_j)}{\deg(z'_p)}} \boldsymbol{\beta}'_p\right)^\top \left(\sum_{q \in I^{-1}(j')} \sqrt{\frac{\deg(z_{j'})}{\deg(z'_q)}} \boldsymbol{\beta}'_q\right), \tag{11}$$

where $I^{-1}(j)$ is the set of non-anchor items that contain a fraction of an anchor item in cluster C_j. Since each $\boldsymbol{\beta}'_p$ is a linear combination of the $\boldsymbol{\beta}_j$'s of the anchor items, and we know from Proposition 2 that $\boldsymbol{\beta}_j^\top \boldsymbol{\beta}_{j'} \approx 0$ for $\forall j \neq j'$, it is easy to show that $\boldsymbol{\beta}_j^\top \boldsymbol{\beta}_{j'} < 0$. Applying this result to Eq. (10), it concludes to $\|\boldsymbol{\beta}'_k\|_2 < b_0$.

Retargeted Matrix Factorization for Collaborative Filtering

Oluwasanmi Koyejo
Electrical and Computer Engineering Dept.,
University Of Texas, Austin.
sanmi.k@utexas.edu

Sreangsu Acharyya
Electrical and Computer Engineering Dept.,
University Of Texas, Austin.
sreangsu@utexas.edu

Joydeep Ghosh
Electrical and Computer Engineering Dept.,
University Of Texas, Austin.
ghosh@ece.utexas.edu

ABSTRACT

This paper introduces retargeted matrix factorization (R-MF); a novel approach for learning the user-wise ranking of items in the context of collaborative filtering. R-MF learns to rank by "retargeting" the item ratings of each user, searching for a monotonic transformation of the ratings that results in a better fit while preserving the ranked order of each user's ratings. The retargeting is combined with an underlying matrix factorization regression model that couples the user-wise rankings to exploit shared low dimensional structure. We show that R-MF recovers a unique solution under mild conditions, and propose a simple and efficient optimization scheme that alternates between retargeting the ratings subject to ordering constraints, and matrix factorization regression. The retargeting step is independent for each user, and is trivially parallelized. The ranking performance of retargeted matrix factorization is evaluated on benchmark movie recommendation datasets and results in superior ranking performance compared to collaborative filtering algorithms specifically designed to optimize ranking metrics.

Categories and Subject Descriptors

H3.3 [**Information Search and Retrieval**]: Information filtering—*Collaborative Filtering*; G3 [**Probability and Statistics**]: Correlation and regression analysis

General Terms

Algorithms, Experimentation

Keywords

Matrix factorization; Collaborative filtering; Learning to rank

1. INTRODUCTION

The focus of research in the recommender systems literature has begun to shift from algorithms and metrics for optimizing *regression* accuracy to learning and measuring the *ranking* of items for each user. Learned rating scores are not shown in most practical deployments of recommender systems. Instead, the user is shown a few of the top items as ordered by the recommender system. This means that although regression metrics such as root mean square error (RMSE) and mean absolute error (MAE) are easier to optimize, ranking metrics such as normalized discounted cumulative gain (NDCG) and expected reciprocal return (ERR) [18] are a more accurate reflection of how recommender systems are used in practice [9].

This paper proposes retargeted matrix factorization (R-MF), a novel approach for learning the user-wise ranking of items inspired by the study of learning to rank (LETOR) in the the information retrieval literature [18]. There, initial approaches using point-wise ranking models [8] were replaced by *pair-wise* models [10], and are now being superseded by *list-wise* ranking models [6, 2]. The list-wise approach learns a ranking model for the entire set of items and has gained prominence in the LETOR literature with strong theoretical guarantees and superior empirical performance [19]. Retargeted matrix factorization (R-MF) transforms the matrix factorization (MF) model into a user-wise ranking model by adjusting the rating values based on the regression fit. These adjustments are constrained to monotonic transformations that preserve the order of the user ratings. We show that R-MF inherits useful statistical and optimization theoretic properties when the loss function for the matrix factorization is a *Bregman divergence* [4], a family of divergences that includes such popular loss functions such as squared loss, Kullback-Leibler (KL) divergence and the I-divergence (also known as the generalized KL divergence). In the context of learning to rank, Bregman divergences are further motivated as the *unique* family of cost functions that are strongly consistent with the NDCG metric [19].

The main contributions of this paper are as follows:

- We propose retargeted matrix factorization (R-MF), a user-wise ranking model for collaborative filtering based on list-wise learning to rank. R-MF jointly searches over monotonic transformations of ratings for each user and an underlying matrix factorization regression that exploits shared structure in the user lists.
- We show that when squared loss is used as the regression loss function, the solution of the retargeted matrix factorization is unique in terms of retargeted scores and the regression matrix under verifiable conditions.
- We propose a simple optimization scheme that alternates between the retargeting step and the regression step. The retargeting step is independent for each user and can be solved in parallel. The user and item factors can be estimated using any number of matrix factorization algorithms.

RecSys'13, October 12–16, 2013, Hong Kong, China.
Copyright 2013 ACM 978-1-4503-2409-0/13/10 ...$15.00.
http://dx.doi.org/10.1145/2507157.2507185.

- Retargeted matrix factorization is evaluated on benchmark movie recommendation datasets and compared to collaborative filtering algorithms specifically designed to optimize ranking metrics.

This paper is organized as follows, we begin with an overview of related work in Section 1.1. This is followed by a discussion of the modeling approach and some of the resulting properties in Section 2. We propose a simple alternating optimization scheme in Section 3. Experimental results are discussed in Section 4 and we conclude in Section 5.

Notation: Vectors are denoted by bold lower case letters, matrices are capitalized. $\boldsymbol{x}^\top$ denotes the transpose of the vector $\boldsymbol{x}$, $||\boldsymbol{x}||$ denotes the L_2 norm. A vector $\boldsymbol{x}$ is defined to be in *descending order* if $x_i \geq x_j$ when $i > j$, the set of such vectors is denoted by $\mathcal{R}_\downarrow$. Vector $\boldsymbol{x}$ is isotonic with $\boldsymbol{y}$ if $x_i \geq x_j$ implies $y_i \geq y_j$. The unit simplex is denoted by Δ and Δ_ϵ denotes the subset of an unit simplex such that each of its members are component-wise bounded away from 0 by ϵ. The positive orthant is denoted by $\mathcal{R}^d_+$ and $\mathcal{R}^d_\epsilon$ denotes its subset such that each of its members are component-wise bounded away from 0 by ϵ.

1.1 Related Work

Models for user-wise ranking have been studied by several researchers in the recommender systems literature. Point-wise models applied to collaborative filtering predict user ratings using regression or classification methods, the final ranking is defined by the ordering of the regression scores. It is often difficult to extract a clear relationship between the regression scores and the item rankings. Cremonesi et al. [9] showed that methods trained to optimize regression metrics may not be effective for top-k recommendation. Steck et al. [24] proposed modifications of matrix factorization methods motivated by top-k ranking performance. A related class of point-wise ordinal regression models have also been proposed. These models are optimized so that user ratings are correctly placed in ordered bins corresponding to the different rating levels. For instance, maximum margin matrix factorization (MMMF) [23] jointly optimized the matrix factorization and the user rating bins using the Hinge loss, COFI^{RANK}-ordinal [26] used bundle methods with squared loss for fast optimization of the user and item factors and ordinal regression bins, and Ordrec [14] combined ordinal logistic regression with matrix factorization.

Ranking performance may be improved further by using a pairwise approach. In this case, the model is trained to order each pair of items [17]. Balakrishnan et al. [3] proposed a pairwise classification approach for collaborative ranking. The authors showed effective ranking performance as measured using the NDCG metric. Pair-wise ranking results in a model with computational cost that is quadratic in the number of items to be ranked. This is a significant increase in computational cost and may be prohibitive in large scale recommender systems with millions of ratings[1]. The learned pairwise orders must also be converted into a fully ordered list (at additional computational cost). Of significant concern is the fact that pair-wise orders are not necessarily transitive. Hence, orders over pairs of items may not directly translate into an ordered list. For example, given three items $\{a, b, c\}$, there is no consistent ordered list if the pair-wise relations are given by $\{a > b\}, \{b > c\}, \{c > a\}$.

List-wise approaches avoid the computational and consistency hazards of pair-wise methods. In addition, list-wise methods often have stronger statistical and optimization theoretic guarantees [19, 2], and superior empirical performance. List-wise models applied to collaborative filtering are known as user-wise ranking models. COFI^{RANK} [25], a popular approach for user-wise collaborative filtering, trains a matrix factorization model to optimize a bound of the NDCG metric. Shi et al. [21] adapted the list-wise ranking algorithm proposed in [6] to collaborative filtering by replacing the underlying linear regression model with a matrix factorization regression model.

The outlined related work is focused on models for optimizing top-k ranking performance and not on regression metrics such as RMSE / MAE [13]. Further, there is a large literature on the use of side information such as features [5] and graphs [15] for recommender systems. The use of such side information enables the model to be used for *cold start* i.e. predicting the rankings of users with no training ratings. Such extensions are not discussed here in detail and are left as a subject for future work.

The proposed framework includes a choice of loss function in the family of Bregman divergences. A unified approach for matrix factorization with Bregman divergence loss functions was proposed by Singh and Gordon [22], showing that several well known methods such as non-negative matrix factorization (NMF), weighted singular value decomposition (SVD), maximum margin matrix factorization (MMMF), probabilistic latent semantic indexing (pLSI) and other related models can be posed as special cases of this framework.

[1]Sub-sampling has been proposed as an approach to reduce this computational burden [3]. However, we note that any computational savings also apply to competing approaches.

Table 1: Examples of identically separable (IS) Bregman divergences. Squared loss (top) and KL divergence (bottom).

$\phi(\boldsymbol{x})$	$D_\phi(\boldsymbol{x}\|\|\boldsymbol{y})$
$\frac{1}{2}\|\|\boldsymbol{x}\|\|^2_W$	$\frac{1}{2}\|\|\boldsymbol{x}-\boldsymbol{y}\|\|^2_2$
$\sum_i x_i \log x_i,\ x \in \Delta$	$\mathrm{KL}(x\|\|y) = \sum_i x_i \log(\frac{x_i}{y_i})$

1.2 Preliminaries

Let $\phi : \Theta \mapsto \mathbb{R}$, $\Theta = \mathrm{dom}\,\phi \subseteq \mathbb{R}^d$ be a strictly convex, closed function, differentiable on $\mathrm{int}\,\Theta$. The corresponding *Bregman divergence* $D_\phi(\cdot\|\cdot) : \mathrm{dom}(\phi) \times \mathrm{int}(\mathrm{dom}(\phi)) \mapsto \mathbb{R}_+$ is defined as $D_\phi(\boldsymbol{x}\|\boldsymbol{y}) \triangleq \phi(\boldsymbol{x}) - \phi(\boldsymbol{y}) - \langle \boldsymbol{x}-\boldsymbol{y}, \nabla\phi(\boldsymbol{y})\rangle$. From strict convexity it follows that $D_\phi(\boldsymbol{x}\|\boldsymbol{y}) \geq 0$ and $D_\phi(\boldsymbol{x}\|\boldsymbol{y}) = 0$ iff. $\boldsymbol{x} = \boldsymbol{y}$. Bregman divergences are (strictly) convex in their first argument, but not necessarily convex in their second.

In this paper we only consider functions of the form $\boldsymbol{\phi}(\cdot) : \mathbb{R}^n \ni \boldsymbol{x} \mapsto \sum_i \phi(x_i)$ that are sums of *identical* scalar convex functions applied to each component. We refer to this class as *identically separable* (**IS**). This class has properties particularly suited to ranking. Squared loss and Kullback-Leibler divergence (KL) are members of this family (Table 1).

The *Legendre conjugate* $\psi(\cdot)$ of the function $\phi(\cdot)$ is defined as $(\phi)^*(\boldsymbol{x}) \triangleq \psi(\boldsymbol{x}) \triangleq \sup_{\boldsymbol{\lambda}}(\langle\boldsymbol{\lambda}, \boldsymbol{x}\rangle - \phi(\boldsymbol{\lambda}))$. If $\phi(\cdot)$ is a convex function of Legendre type [20] (as will always be the case in this paper), $(()^*)^*(\cdot) = \phi(\cdot)$ and $(\nabla\phi(\cdot))^{-1} = \nabla\psi(\cdot)$ is a one to one mapping.

2. LEARNING TO RECOMMEND

Let w_{ij} be a binary variable that denotes whether user i has rated item j ($w_{ij} = 1$) or not ($w_{ij} = 0$). We denote the true ratings by Y_{ij} and predicted ratings by $\hat{Y}_{ij}$. Let $\mathcal{U}$ and $\mathcal{V}$ denote the set of users and items respectively. Let $\mathcal{V}_i$ denote the set of items rated by user i and $|\mathcal{V}_i|$ its cardinality. The item recommendation task

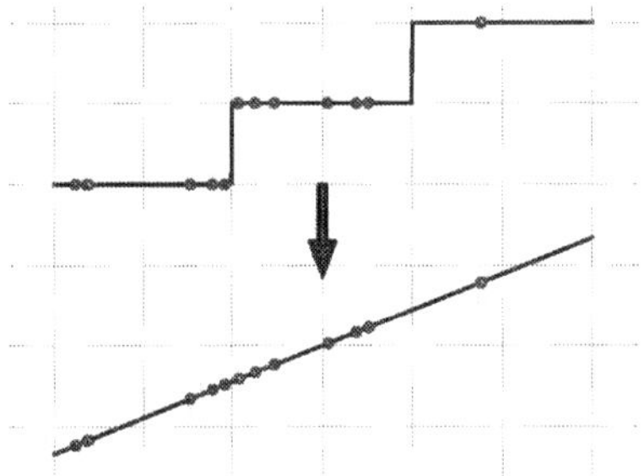

Figure 1: Monotone retargeting [2] searches for an order preserving transformation of the target scores that may be easier for the regressor to fit.

consists of learning the user's taste from the training ratings. A popular technique for item recommendation is matrix factorization (MF) [13]. In MF, the predictions take the form:

$$\hat{Y}_{ij} = \langle \boldsymbol{u}_i, \boldsymbol{v}_j \rangle , \tag{1}$$

where $\boldsymbol{u}_i \in \mathbb{R}^d$ is called a user factor for user i and $\boldsymbol{v}_j \in \mathbb{R}^d$ is the item factor for item j. Further, let $U \in \mathbb{R}^{|\mathcal{U}|\times d}$ with $U(i) = \boldsymbol{u}_i$ represent the collected user factors and let $V \in \mathbb{R}^{|\mathcal{V}|\times d}$ with $V(j) = \boldsymbol{v}_j$ represent the collected item factors. Note that this factorization constrains the rank of the matrix $\hat{Y}$ to be upper-bounded by d. For reasons of scalability, this matrix should never be explicitly maintained. Its entries can be generated dynamically from the user and item factors as needed.

In MF, the factors are learned by minimizing the squared Euclidean distance between the actual ratings and the predicted ratings as:

$$\min_{U,V} \sum_{i\in\mathcal{U}, j\in\mathcal{V}} \frac{1}{2} w_{ij}(Y_{ij} - \hat{Y}_{ij})^2. \tag{2}$$

For recommender systems, making the model predictions close to the ratings is only a means to an end. The true objective is to facilitate the ordering of the items according to the users preference. On one hand the objective (2) is solving a harder problem, and on the other hand, in its goal to keep the predicted $\hat{Y}_{ij}$ *point-wise* close to the observed Y_{ij} the regressor may generate predictions close in squared Euclidean sense with estimated scores that induce an incorrect order, thereby misdirecting the algorithm [9]. This is particularly true when one uses a regressor of limited function-fitting capacity. In this context the cost function (2) is unnecessarily strict.

These drawbacks are now well recognized and have inspired several ranking based approaches to the the recommendation problem. The newer approaches replace (2) by other cost functions that depend not on the predicted scores themselves, but on the order induced by them. Examples of such cost functions include the normalized cumulative discounted gain (NDCG), expected reciprocal return (ERR) and mean absolute precision (MAP) [18]. However, the domain of these cost functions is the space of permutations of the list of items. This is not only a discrete (combinatorial) space, but also one whose size grows exponentially with the number of items. This makes training with respect to these cost functions difficult.

In this paper we adapt a list-wise learning to rank (LETOR) algorithm called monotone retargeting (MR) [2], developed recently by the authors, to the recommendation task. MR introduces a new family of cost functions that have desirable computational and statistical properties. It uses a cost function that is truly a function of the order and not of the predicted values, therefore well suited for ranking. The key observations that motivates the MR is that (i) the combinatorial problem of LETOR can be transformed into a problem of searching over the space of all monotonic transformations and (ii) it is possible to design an efficient, convergent technique to solve the challenging task of minimizing over this infinite function space without sacrificing generality. A pictorial representation of MR is shown in Fig. 1.

2.1 Retargeted Matrix Factorization

Given any loss function $D : \mathbb{R} \times \mathbb{R} \mapsto \mathbb{R}_+$, we may define a pointwise LETOR based MF problem by:

$$\min_{U,V} \sum_i \sum_j w_{ij} D(Y_{ij}, f(\langle \boldsymbol{u}_i, \boldsymbol{v}_j \rangle))$$

where $f : \mathbb{R} \mapsto \mathbb{R}$ is some regression function with parameters $\boldsymbol{u}_i$ and $\boldsymbol{v}_j$. As discussed earlier, this is unnecessarily stringent for ranking. A conceptually better alternative is:

$$\min_{U,V,\{\Upsilon_i \in \mathcal{M}\}} \sum_i \sum_j w_{ij} D(Y_{ij}, \Upsilon_i \circ f(\langle \boldsymbol{u}_i, \boldsymbol{v}_j \rangle)),$$

where $\Upsilon_i : \mathbb{R} \mapsto \mathbb{R}$ is a monotonic increasing transformation and $\mathcal{M}$ is the class of all such transformations. With no loss in generality of modeling, we may apply the monotonic transform to Y_{ij} instead. This avoids the minimization over the function composition, but the need for minimizing over the set of all monotone functions remains.

As noted in [2] the optimization over the infinite space of functions $\mathcal{M}$ can be converted into one over finite dimensional vector spaces provided we have a finite characterization of the constraint set $\mathcal{R}{\downarrow_i}$. Without loss of generality, the monotone transformation can be applied to the left hand side i.e. to the sorted ratings. Let $Y_{i,*}$ represent the item ratings for user i arranged in (non-unique) sorted order. Further, let $V_i \in \mathbb{R}^{|\mathcal{V}_i|\times d}$ represent the subset of item factors corresponding to the items rated by user i, sorted to match the ratings $Y_{i,*}$. The resulting cost function is:

$$\min_{U,V,\{\boldsymbol{r}_i \in \mathcal{R}{\downarrow_i}\}} \sum_i D(\boldsymbol{r}_i, f(V_i \boldsymbol{u}_i)) \tag{3}$$
$$\text{where } \mathcal{R}{\downarrow_i} = \{\boldsymbol{r} \,|\, {}^{\exists M \in \mathcal{M}}_{M(Y_{i,*})=\boldsymbol{r}}\} \; \forall i,$$

$f(\cdot)$ is applied element-wise to result of the matrix vector product $V_i \boldsymbol{u}_i$, and $\mathcal{R}{\downarrow_i}$ represents all vectors that are sorted in decreasing order. Hence $\mathcal{R}{\downarrow_i}$ includes vectors $\boldsymbol{r} \in \mathbb{R}^{|\mathcal{V}_i|}$ such that $r_{k+1} = r_k$ for some k. Since the vectors $\boldsymbol{r}$ are the targets given to the regressor to fit, it is more robust to enforce separation between the components, i.e. maintain $r_k \geq r_{k+1} + \epsilon$. We indicate the set of all such ϵ separated decreasing ordered sets by $\mathcal{R}_\epsilon{\downarrow_i}$. We now characterize these sets.

The Set $\mathcal{R}{\downarrow_i}$: The convex composition $\boldsymbol{r} = \alpha \boldsymbol{r}_1 + (1-\alpha)\boldsymbol{r}_2$ of two isotonic vectors $\boldsymbol{r}_1$ and $\boldsymbol{r}_2$ preserves isotonicity, as does the scaling $\alpha \boldsymbol{r}$ for any $\alpha \in \mathbb{R}_+$. Hence the set $\mathcal{R}{\downarrow_i}$ is a convex cone. Clearly the same holds for $\mathcal{R}_\epsilon{\downarrow_i}$. Convex-conicity makes the problem computationally tractable because the set can be described entirely by its extreme rays, or by the extreme rays of its polar. $\mathcal{R}{\downarrow_i}$ can be expressed as the image of the set $\{\mathbb{R}_+\}^{|\mathcal{V}_i|-1} \times \mathbb{R}$ under a linear transformation by a particular upper triangular matrix S with positive entries. The matrix S is not unique and can be generated from any vector $\boldsymbol{v} \in {\mathbb{R}_+}^{|\mathcal{V}_i|}$, but since any member from the allowed class of S is sufficient for a *exhaustive* representation of $\mathcal{R}{\downarrow_i}$ we use the vector $\mathbf{1}$ to generate S. The property is stated formally in the following lemma:

LEMMA 1. *The set $\mathcal{R}\downarrow_i$ of all vectors in $\mathbb{R}^{|\mathcal{V}_i|}$ that are sorted in a descending order is given by $S\boldsymbol{x}$ s.t. $\boldsymbol{x} \in \{\mathbb{R}_+\}^{|\mathcal{V}_i|-1} \times \mathbb{R}$ where S is a triangular matrix generated from a vector $\mathbf{1}$ such that the kth row $S(k,:)$ is $\{0\}^{k-1} \times \mathbf{1}(k:)$*

The proof of Lemma 1 appears in [2]. In addition, the following lemma defining $\mathcal{R}_\epsilon\downarrow_i$ follows directly from Lemma 1 and is stated without proof.

LEMMA 2. *The set $\mathcal{R}_\epsilon\downarrow_i$ of all vectors in $\mathbb{R}^{|\mathcal{V}_i|}$ that are sorted in a descending order and whose consecutive components are separated by ϵ is given by $S\boldsymbol{x}$ s.t. $\boldsymbol{x} \in \{\mathbb{R}_\epsilon\}^{|\mathcal{V}_i|-1} \times \mathbb{R}$ where S is a triangular matrix generated from a vector $\mathbf{1}$ such that the kth row $S(k,:)$ is $\{0\}^{k-1} \times \mathbf{1}(k:)$*

In addition to these sets we shall make frequent use of the set of all discrete probability distributions that are in descending order, i.e. $\mathcal{R}\downarrow_i \cap \Delta_i$ that we represent by $\Delta\downarrow_i$. We give a similar representation of this set by generating an upper triangular matrix T from the vector $\boldsymbol{v}_{\Delta_i} = \{1, \frac{1}{2}, \cdots \frac{1}{i} \cdots \frac{1}{|\mathcal{V}_i|}\}$ and considering $\boldsymbol{x} \in \Delta_i$. This is formally stated in the following lemma:

LEMMA 3. *The set $\Delta\downarrow_i$ of all discrete probability distributions of dimension $|\mathcal{V}_i|$ that are in descending order is the image $T\boldsymbol{x}$ such that $\boldsymbol{x} \in \Delta_i$ where T is an upper triangular matrix generated from the vector $\boldsymbol{v}_{\Delta_i} = \{1, \frac{1}{2} \cdots \frac{1}{|\mathcal{V}_i|}\}$ such that $T(k,:) = \{0\}^{k-1} \times \boldsymbol{v}_\Delta(k:)$*

The proof of Lemma 3 appears in [2]. Similar to the set $\mathcal{R}_\epsilon\downarrow_i$ we will use a well separated version of $\Delta\downarrow_i$ denoted by $\Delta_\epsilon\downarrow_i$ that consists of discrete probability distributions sorted in decreasing order but also satisfying $r_i > r_{i+1} + \frac{\epsilon}{i}$. Note that vectors in $\Delta_\epsilon\downarrow_i$ are not only sorted but have an increasing gap between consecutive components. The motivation for such a construction is that even if the regressor is inaccurate, if the inaccuracy is more or less uniform across the components, the top entries of the predictions will be less prone to order reversal than the bottom ones: a desirable feature for ranking. The following lemma formally states the representation for $\Delta_\epsilon\downarrow_i$.

LEMMA 4. *The set $\Delta_\epsilon\downarrow_i$ of all discrete probability distributions of dimension $|\mathcal{V}_i|$ that are in descending order is the image $T\boldsymbol{x}$ s.t. $\boldsymbol{x} \in \Delta_{\epsilon_i}$ where T is an upper triangular matrix generated from the vector $\boldsymbol{v}_{\Delta_i} = \{1, \frac{1}{2} \cdots \frac{1}{|\mathcal{V}_i|}\}$ such that $T(k,:) = \{0\}^{k-1} \times \boldsymbol{v}_\Delta(k:)$*

The prof of Lemma 4 follows directly from Lemma 3.

2.2 Cost function

With appropriate choices of the distance like function $D(\cdot,\cdot)$ and the curve fitting function $f(\cdot)$ we can transform (3) into a bi-convex optimization problem over a product of convex sets. We choose $D(\cdot,\cdot)$ to be a Bregman divergence $D_\phi(\cdot||\cdot)$ as defined in Section 1.2, and $f(V_i\boldsymbol{u}_i) = (\nabla\phi)^{-1}(V_i\boldsymbol{u}_i)$. To simplify the notation, we define $C_\phi(\boldsymbol{a}||\boldsymbol{b}) = D_\phi(\boldsymbol{a}||(\nabla\phi)^{-1}(\boldsymbol{b}))$. The resulting cost function is given by:

$$\min_{U,V,\{\boldsymbol{r}_i \in \mathcal{R}\downarrow_i\}} \sum_i C_\phi(\boldsymbol{r}_i||V_i\boldsymbol{u}_i). \tag{4}$$

Let $\boldsymbol{y}_i = (\nabla\phi)^{-1}(V_i\boldsymbol{u}_i)$ with represent the vector of predicted ratings of user i. Using Legendre duality one recognizes that equation (4) quantifies the gap in the Fenchel-Young inequality[2]

$$D_\phi(\boldsymbol{r}_i||(\nabla\phi)^{-1}(\boldsymbol{y}_i)) = \psi(\boldsymbol{y}_i) + \phi(\boldsymbol{r}_i) - \langle \boldsymbol{r}_i, \boldsymbol{y}_i \rangle,$$

where ψ is the Legendre conjugate of ϕ. Although this clarifies the issue of separate convexity in $\boldsymbol{r}_i$ and $\boldsymbol{y}_i$, the conditions under which joint convexity is obtained are not obvious.

2.3 Joint Convexity and Global Minimum

Joint convexity, if ensured, guarantees global minimum even for a coordinate-wise minimization because our constraint set is a product of convex sets. This important question is resolved in the following theorem from [2] (Theorem 2).

THEOREM 1. *The gap in the Fenchel-Young inequality: $\psi(\boldsymbol{y}) + \phi(\boldsymbol{x}) - \langle \boldsymbol{x}, \boldsymbol{w} \rangle$ for any twice differentiable strictly convex $\phi(\cdot)$ with a differentiable conjugate $(\phi)^*(\cdot) = \psi(\cdot)$ is jointly convex if and only if $\phi(\boldsymbol{x}) = c||\boldsymbol{x}||^2$ for all $c > 0$.*

We note that since we maintain explicit representation of the factor matrices U and V, the optimization problem is no longer convex with respect to these factors. However, the following proposition from [1] (Proposition 5) shows conditions under which all local minima in terms of U and V are global, and correspond to the same regression matrix $\hat{Y} = UV^\top$.

PROPOSITION 1. *Let G be a twice differentiable convex function on matrices of size $p \times q$ with compact level sets. Let $d > 1$ and $(U, V) \in \mathbb{R}^{p\times d} \times \mathbb{R}^{q\times d}$ a local optimum of the function $H : \mathbb{R}^{p\times d} \times \mathbb{R}^{q\times d} \mapsto \mathbb{R}$ defined by $H(U,V) = G(UV^\top)$, that is U such that $\nabla H(U,V) = 0$ and the Hessian of H at (U,V) is positive semi-definite. If U or V is rank deficient, then $N = UV^\top$ is a global optimum of G, that is $\nabla G(N) = 0$.*

Combining Theorem 1 and Proposition 1, it follows that under mild conditions, R-MF using squared loss recovers a unique solution. Proposition 1 applied to other Bregman divergences can only provide local optimality guarantees.

2.4 Optimality of Sorting

For any sorted vector $\boldsymbol{r}$, finding the permutation of $\boldsymbol{y}$ that minimizes $D_\phi(\boldsymbol{r}||\boldsymbol{y})$ shows up as a sub-problem in our formulation that needs to be solved in an inner loop. Thus solving it efficiently is critical and this is yet another instance where Bregman divergences are very useful.

For an arbitrary divergence function the search over the optimal permutation is a *non-linear assignment* problem that can be solved only by exhaustive enumeration. For an arbitrary separable divergence the optimal permutation may be found by solving a linear assignment problem, which is an integer linear program and hence also expensive to solve (especially in an inner loop, as required in our algorithm).[3]

On the other hand, if $\phi(\cdot)$ is IS, the solution is remarkably simple, as shown in Lemma 5 where $\left[\frac{r_1}{r_2}\right]$ denotes a vector in $\mathbb{R}^2$ with components r_1 and r_2.

[2]The **Fenchel-Young** inequality:

$$\psi(\boldsymbol{w}) + \phi(\boldsymbol{x}) - \langle \boldsymbol{w}, \boldsymbol{x} \rangle \geq 0.$$

[3]One of our baseline tools, COFI^{RANK}-NDCG [25] does need to solve such an assignment problem in each iteration. Speed comparisons are included in Section 4.

LEMMA 5. *If $r_1 \geq r_2$ and $y_1 \geq y_2$ and $\phi(\cdot)$ is IS, then:*

$$D_\phi\left(\begin{bmatrix} r_1 \\ r_2 \end{bmatrix} \middle\| \begin{bmatrix} y_1 \\ y_2 \end{bmatrix}\right) \leq D_\phi\left(\begin{bmatrix} r_1 \\ r_2 \end{bmatrix} \middle\| \begin{bmatrix} y_2 \\ y_1 \end{bmatrix}\right) \quad \text{and}$$

$$D_\phi\left(\begin{bmatrix} y_1 \\ y_2 \end{bmatrix} \middle\| \begin{bmatrix} r_1 \\ r_2 \end{bmatrix}\right) \leq D_\phi\left(\begin{bmatrix} y_2 \\ y_1 \end{bmatrix} \middle\| \begin{bmatrix} r_1 \\ r_2 \end{bmatrix}\right).$$

Lemma 5 is trivially extended by induction to the vector case.

3. FORMULATION AND ALGORITHM

We safeguard against overfitting by adding squared Frobenius norm regularization for the matrices U and V. Note that the cost function (4) is not invariant to scale. For example squared Euclidean distance and KL divergence are homogeneous functions of degree 2 and 1 respectively. Thus the cost can be reduced just by scaling its arguments down, without actually learning the task. To remedy this, we restrict the $\boldsymbol{r}_i$'s from shrinking below a predefined size. This is accomplished by constraining $\boldsymbol{r}_i$'s to lie in an appropriate closed convex set not only separated from the origin but also to a set of vectors whose adjacent components are separated from each other. For the latter we use the set $\Delta_{\epsilon\downarrow}$ as defined before. After these modifications we obtain the final formulation[4] as:

$$\min_{U,V,\{\boldsymbol{r}_i \in \Delta_{\epsilon\downarrow i}\}} \sum_i C_\phi(\boldsymbol{r}_i \| V_i \boldsymbol{u}_i) + \frac{\lambda_u}{2}\sum_i ||\boldsymbol{u}_i||^2 + \frac{\lambda_v}{2}\sum_j ||\boldsymbol{v}_j||^2 \quad (5)$$

In our formulation we assume that the true movie ratings are totally ordered, though the finer ordering between similar items is not visible to the ranking algorithm. Let $P_j = \{P_{jk}\}_{k=1}^{k_j}$ be a partition of the index set of $\mathcal{V}_j$, such that all items in P_{jk} have the same training score. (for example the set of all movies rated 5 by a particular user). The sets $\mathcal{V}_j$ effectively get partitioned further into $\{P_{jk}\}_{k=1}^{k_j}$. Though the ratings provide an order between movies from any two different sets P_{jk} and P_{jl}, the order within any set P_{jk} remains unknown. To retrieve the total order we introduce a block-diagonally restricted permutation matrix $\mathbb{P}_j$ that can permute indices in each P_{jk} independently. Since the items in P_{jk} are not equivalent they are available for re-ordering as long as that minimizes the cost (5). IS Bregman divergences have the special property that sorting minimizes the divergence over all permutations (Lemma 5). Thus update (6) can be accomplished by sorting.

The combined algorithm for R-MF is given in Fig. 2. We cycle through all three update steps until convergence. The update (7) can be solved using any of a number of constrained convex optimization algorithms. We implemented (7) using the exponentiated gradient (EG) algorithm [12], a proximal gradient method for simplex constrained vectors. EG requires simple multiplicative updates using the function gradient followed by a normalization step. Update (6) is a parallel sort. The user and item factors (8) can be updated using any number of matrix factorization algorithms [22].

4. EXPERIMENTS

[4]To apply the results of Proposition 1 to the regularized case, we will require the variational representation of the matrix trace norm $||\cdot||_*$ under similar rank deficient conditions for the mapping between the cost function $G(N)$ and $H(U, V)$:

$$||N||_* = \min_{U,V \mid N=UV^\top} \frac{1}{2}\left(\sum_i ||\boldsymbol{u}_i||^2 + \sum_j ||\boldsymbol{v}_j||^2\right)$$

$$\mathbb{P}_i^{t+1} = \operatorname*{Argmin}_{\pi} C_\phi(T\boldsymbol{x}_i^t \| \pi V_i \boldsymbol{u}_i) \quad \forall i \text{ in parallel} \quad (6)$$

$$\boldsymbol{x}_i^{t+1} = \operatorname*{Argmin}_{\boldsymbol{x} \in \Delta_{\epsilon\downarrow}} C_\phi(T\boldsymbol{x} \| \mathbb{P}_i^{t+1} V_i \boldsymbol{u}_i) \quad \forall i \text{ in parallel} \quad (7)$$

$$U^{t+1}, V^{t+1} = \operatorname*{Argmin}_{U,V} \sum_i C_\phi(T\boldsymbol{x}_i^{t+1} \| \mathbb{P}_i^{t+1} V\boldsymbol{u}) + \frac{\lambda_u}{2}\sum_i ||\boldsymbol{u}_i||^2 + \frac{\lambda_v}{2}\sum_j ||\boldsymbol{v}_j||^2 \quad (8)$$

Figure 2: Algorithm for optimizing R-MF

Table 2: Data sizes after preprocessing to remove users with less than 30 ratings

Dataset	# Users	# Items	# Ratings
Movielens 100K	744	1,682	95,269
Movielens 1M	5,289	3,701	982,040
Movielens 10M	57,534	10,675	9,704,223
Flixster	30,277	48,146	7,580,563

We evaluated R-MF on four publicly available recommendation datasets:

- Movielens[5] is a movie recommendation website administered by GroupLens Research. GroupLens Research has made available three ratings datasets of varying sizes[6]. We used the movielens 100K, movielens 1M and movielens 10M datasets. Ratings in Movielens 100K and movielens 1M take one of 5 values in the set $\{1.0, 2.0, \ldots, 5.0\}$. Ratings in movielens 10M take one of 10 values in the set $\{0.5, 1, 1.5, \ldots, 5.0\}$
- Flixster[7] is a website where users share film reviews and ratings. We used the flixster dataset provided by [11] with timestamps. Ratings in Flixster take one of 10 values in the set $\{0.5, 1, 1.5, \ldots, 5.0\}$.

Data preprocessing: First, we removed all users with less than 30 ratings. Each of the evaluated datasets contains the time-stamp of the user rating. For each user, we selected the last third of the ratings sorted by user-time as the test set, the middle third as the validation set, and any left over ratings were selected as the training set. This partitioning scheme ensures that each user has at least 10 ratings in the validation and test sets so we are able to compute the top-k performance metrics for at least 10 retrieved items per user. Details of the dataset sizes after preprocessing are provided in table Table 2.

We experimented with R-MF using squared loss motivated by the optimization theoretic guarantees discussed in Section 2.3. Further experiments with other Bregman divergences will be implemented in an extended version of this manuscript. We also evaluated the performance of COFI^RANK -NDCG [25] and COFI^RANK -ordinal [26] as baseline models using the C++ implementation provided by the authors[8]. For all models, we selected the regularization parameter $\lambda = \lambda_u = \lambda_v$ from the set $10^{\{-2,-1.5,-1,\ldots,2\}}$.

The models are scored using metrics commonly used for evaluating ranking models [18]. We plot normalized discounted cumulative gain (NDCG) and precision in Fig. 3 while varying the number of retrieved items $k = \{1, \ldots 10\}$. Further results with

[5]movielens.umn.edu

[6]www.grouplens.org/node/73

[7]www.flixster.com

[8]available at www.cofirank.org

Table 3: **Expected reciprocal return (ERR) results on recommender system datasets. "–" represents datasets where CoFi^{Rank}-NDCG did not finish after running for more than seven days.**

	R-MF	CoFi^{Rank}-NDCG	CoFi^{Rank}-ORD.
Movielens 100K			
Rank 10	**0.779**	0.702	0.722
Rank 20	**0.777**	0.697	0.709
Movielens 1M			
Rank 10	**0.819**	0.726	0.774
Rank 20	**0.816**	0.728	0.756
Movielens 10M			
Rank 10	**0.780**	0.687	0.763
Rank 20	**0.781**	–	0.753
Flixster			
Rank 10	**0.771**	–	0.743
Rank 20	**0.771**	–	0.737

other ranking metrics were also computed including expected reciprocal return (ERR) in Table 3, mean average precision (MAP) in Table 4, and NDCG of the full list in Table 5. For the precision and MAP metrics, a movie was labelled as relevant if its rating was greater than 4.

Our experiments show that R-MF improves ranking performance over CoFi^{Rank}-NDCG and CoFi^{Rank}-ordinal as measured by all the metrics that we computed. We note that CoFi^{Rank}-ordinal [26] has been shown to outperform several state of the art models including maximum margin matrix factorization [23] and Gaussian process ordinal regression [7]. The results were even more striking when we compared the NDCG performance of R-MF to CoFi^{Rank}-NDCG, though the algorithm is specifically designed to optimize NDCG. Our results confirm the observation of other authors, including the authors of CoFi^{Rank} that CoFi^{Rank}-ordinal seems to out-perform CoFi^{Rank}-NDCG. It is unclear why this is the case. We found that CoFi^{Rank} to be susceptible to overfitting when we compared the test performance with the training NDCG values. This might explain some of the performance gap. Our results were qualitatively very similar for rank 10 and rank 20 models.

R-MF was implemented in Python/Numpy. Cython was used to implement the parallel retargeting updates (7) and parallel sorting (6). The matrix factorization step (8) was solved using alternating least squares. The code was executed on a 2.4GHz quad-core Intel Xeon processor. Timing on the larger movie datasets are shown in Table 6 and compared to CoFi^{Rank}. We found that R-MF exhibited much better scaling behavior as the size data increased. We suspect that the large observed runtimes of CoFi^{Rank}-NDCG are due to the cost of the linear assignment problem that must be solved for each user at every iteration. The linear assignment can be solved using a number of efficient algorithms [16], but the computational requirements scale cubically with the number of ratings per user. R-MF is able to avoid solving this linear assignment problem as we prove that sorting recovers the optimal ordering (Section 2.4).

Our experience suggests that the speed of the method can be significantly improved by (i) implementation using a faster language e.g c++ (ii) matrix factorization using stochastic gradient descent or other scalable solvers (iii) interleaving the factorization and retargeting steps, as the matrix factorization is the most computationally intensive portion of the algorithm. We leave such implementation improvements to future work.

Table 4: Mean absolute precision (MAP) results on recommender system datasets. Relevant ratings have a value greater than 4. "–" represents datasets where CoFi^{Rank}-NDCG did not finish after running for more than seven days.

	R-MF	CoFi^{Rank}-NDCG	CoFi^{Rank}-ORD.
Movielens 100K			
Rank 10	**0.425**	0.335	0.364
Rank 20	**0.427**	0.333	0.348
Movielens 1M			
Rank 10	**0.485**	0.358	0.435
Rank 20	**0.482**	0.360	0.408
Movielens 10M			
Rank 10	**0.472**	0.353	0.453
Rank 20	**0.470**	–	0.439
Flixster			
Rank 10	**0.513**	–	0.488
Rank 20	**0.509**	–	0.480

Table 5: NDCG Results on recommender system datasets. "–" represents datasets where CoFi^{Rank}-NDCG did not finish after running for more than seven days.

	R-MF	CoFi^{Rank}-NDCG	CoFi^{Rank}-ORD.
Movielens 100K			
Rank 10	**0.883**	0.839	0.854
Rank 20	**0.882**	0.838	0.844
Movielens 1M			
Rank 10	**0.896**	0.846	0.877
Rank 20	**0.895**	0.847	0.867
Movielens 10M			
Rank 10	**0.892**	0.843	0.883
Rank 20	**0.891**	–	0.878
Flixster			
Rank 10	**0.888**	–	0.877
Rank 20	**0.887**	–	0.874

Table 6: Average training time (mins) on the larger recommender system datasets. "–" represents datasets where CoFi^{Rank}-NDCG did not finish after running for more than seven days. The Movielens 10M (rank 20) result of CoFi^{Rank}-NDCG is based on the average runtime for a subset of the parameters, as the full parameter sweep did not finish running.

	R-MF	CoFi^{Rank}-NDCG	CoFi^{Rank}-ORD.
Movielens 1M			
Rank 10	121.025	**329.889**	41.641
Rank 20	259.051	**340.569**	30.276
Movielens 10M			
Rank 10	396.900	**2912.179**	1391.249
Rank 20	663.889	**7609.683**	820.579
Flixster			
Rank 10	1657.314	**-**	2459.418
Rank 20	2203.207	**-**	897.989

5. CONCLUSION AND FUTURE WORK

In this paper, we proposed retargeted matrix factorization (R-MF), a novel approach for learning the user-wise ranking of items for collaborative filtering. Retargeted matrix factorization improves

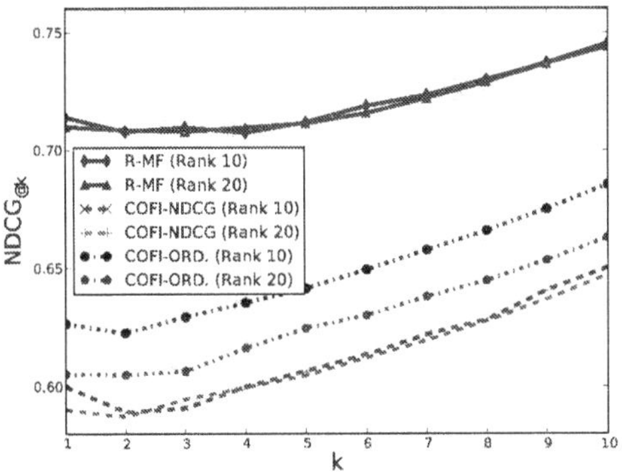

(a) Movielens 100K NDCG

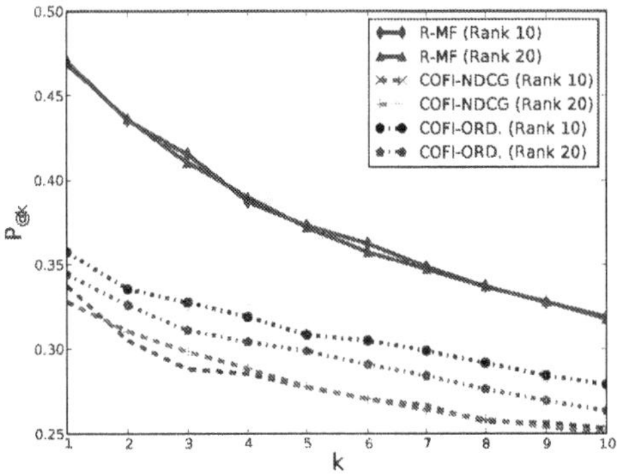

(b) Movielens 100K Precision

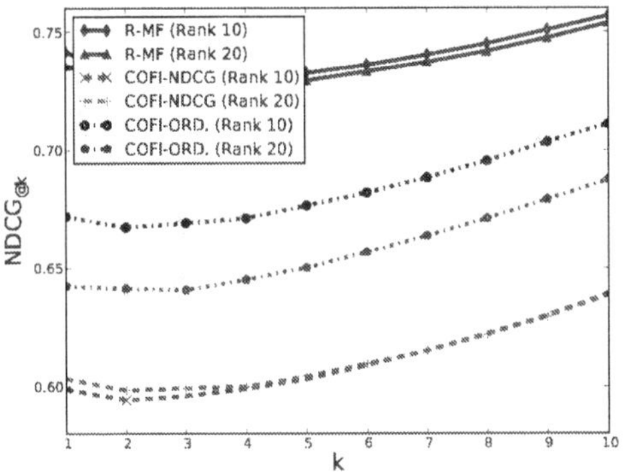

(c) Movielens 1M NDCG

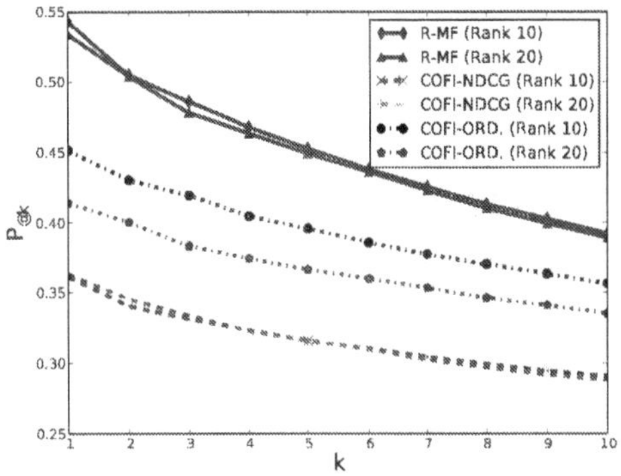

(d) Movielens 1M Precision

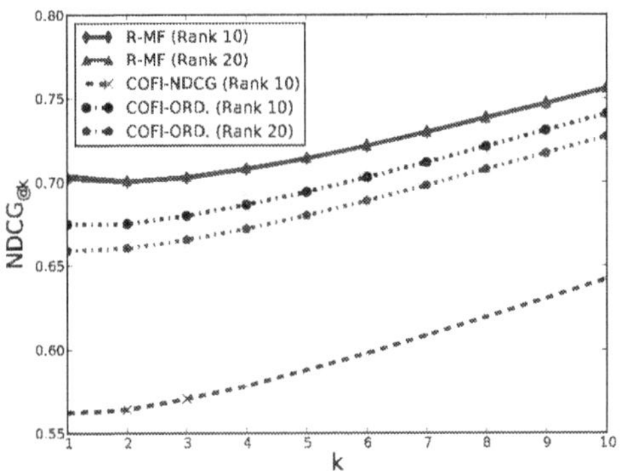

(e) Movielens 10M NDCG

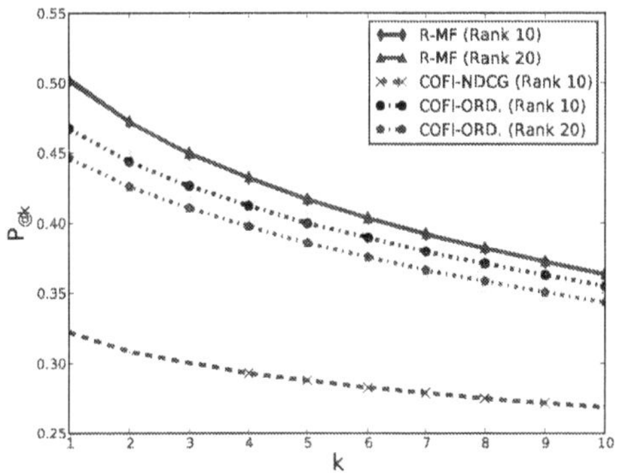

(f) Movielens 10M Precision

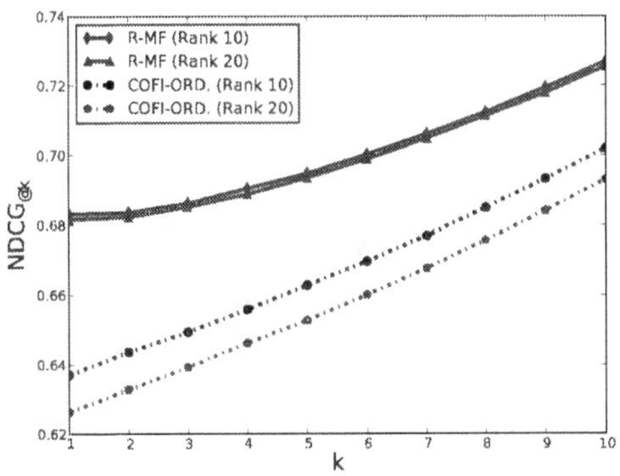

(g) Flixster NDCG

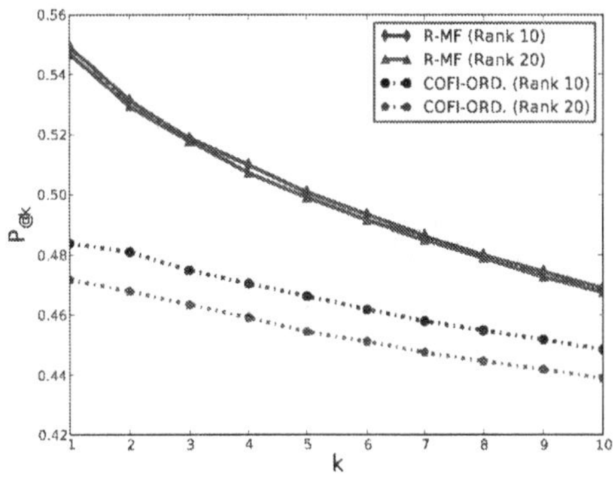

(h) Flixster Precision

Figure 3: Performance results: $\mathrm{NDCG}_{@k}$ **and** $\mathrm{P}_{@k}$ **at** $@k = 1, 2, \ldots, 10$. **Relevant ratings have a value greater than 4. CoFi^{RANK}-ordinal [26] has been shown to outperform several state of the art models including maximum margin matrix factorization [23] and Gaussian process ordinal regression [7].**

the ranking performance by searching for a monotonic transformation of the ratings that results in a better fit while preserving their ranked order. R-MF was compared to the ranking and ordinal regression variants of CoFi^{RANK} and evaluated on benchmark movie recommendation datasets. Our results show that retargeted matrix factorization results in superior ranking performance compared to CoFi^{RANK}, though CoFi^{RANK} is specifically designed to optimize NDCG. Our results also highlight the scalability of R-MF in comparison to CoFi^{RANK}. We plan to explore scalability and implementation concerns in more detail in future work. Although the unique solution is only guaranteed for squared loss, the performance results presented in [2] provide some motivation for experimenting with other Bregman divergences in future work.

6. ACKNOWLEDGMENTS

Authors acknowledge support from NSF grant IIS 1016614

7. REFERENCES

[1] J. Abernethy, F. Bach, T. Evgeniou, and J.-P. Vert. A new approach to collaborative filtering: Operator estimation with spectral regularization. *JMLR*, 10:803–826, 2009.

[2] S. Acharyya, O. Koyejo, and J. Ghosh. Learning to rank with Bregman divergences and monotone retargeting. In *Proceedings of the 28th conference on Uncertainty in artificial intelligence*, UAI '12, 2012.

[3] S. Balakrishnan and S. Chopra. Collaborative ranking. In *Proceedings of the fifth ACM international conference on Web search and data mining*, WSDM '12, pages 143–152, New York, NY, USA, 2012. ACM.

[4] A. Banerjee, S. Merugu, I. Dhillon, and J. Ghosh. Clustering with Bregman divergences. *Journal of Machine Learning Research*, 6:1705–1749, 2005.

[5] J. Basilico and T. Hofmann. Unifying collaborative and content-based filtering. In *ICML '04: Proceedings of the twenty-first international conference on Machine learning*, page 9, New York, NY, USA, 2004. ACM.

[6] Z. Cao, T. Qin, T.-Y. Liu, M.-F. Tsai, and H. Li. Learning to rank: from pairwise approach to listwise approach. In *ICML '07: Proceedings of the 24th international conference on Machine learning*, pages 129–136, New York, NY, USA, 2007. ACM.

[7] W. Chu and Z. Ghahramani. Gaussian processes for ordinal regression. *Journal of Machine Learning Research*, 6:2005, 2004.

[8] K. Crammer and Y. Singer. Pranking with ranking. In *Advances in Neural Information Processing Systems 14*, pages 641–647. MIT Press, 2001.

[9] P. Cremonesi, Y. Koren, and R. Turrin. Performance of recommender algorithms on top-n recommendation tasks. In *Proceedings of the fourth ACM conference on Recommender systems*, RecSys '10, pages 39–46. ACM, 2010.

[10] Y. Freund, R. Iyer, R. E. Schapire, and Y. Singer. An efficient boosting algorithm for combining preferences. *J. Mach. Learn. Res.*, 4:933–969, 2003.

[11] M. Jamali and M. Ester. A matrix factorization technique with trust propagation for recommendation in social networks. In *RecSys*, pages 135–142, 2010.

[12] J. Kivinen and M. K. Warmuth. Exponentiated gradient versus gradient descent for linear predictors. *Information and Computation*, 132, 1995.

[13] Y. Koren, R. Bell, and C. Volinsky. Matrix factorization techniques for recommender systems. *Computer*, 42:30–37, 2009.

[14] Y. Koren and J. Sill. Ordrec: an ordinal model for predicting personalized item rating distributions. In B. Mobasher, R. D. Burke, D. Jannach, and G. Adomavicius, editors, *RecSys*, pages 117–124. ACM, 2011.

[15] O. Koyejo and J. Ghosh. A kernel-based approach to exploiting interaction-networks in heterogeneous information sources for improved recommender systems. In *HetRec '11*, pages 9–16, 2011.

[16] H. Kuhn. The Hungarian method for the assignment problem. *Naval research logistics quarterly*, 2(1-2):83–97, 1955.

[17] N. N. Liu, M. Zhao, and Q. Yang. Probabilistic latent preference analysis for collaborative filtering. In *Proceedings of the 18th ACM conference on Information and knowledge management*, CIKM '09, pages 759–766, New York, NY, USA, 2009. ACM.

[18] T. Liu. *Learning to Rank for Information Retrieval.* Information retrieval. Springer, 2011.

[19] P. Ravikumar, A. Tewari, and E. Yang. On NDCG consistency of listwise ranking methods. In *Proceedings of 14th International Conference on Artificial Intelligence and Statistics*, AISTATS, 2011.

[20] R. T. Rockafellar. *Convex Analysis (Princeton Landmarks in Mathematics and Physics).* Princeton University Press, December 1996.

[21] Y. Shi, M. Larson, and A. Hanjalic. List-wise learning to rank with matrix factorization for collaborative filtering. In *Proceedings of the fourth ACM conference on Recommender systems*, RecSys '10, pages 269–272, New York, NY, USA, 2010. ACM.

[22] A. P. Singh and G. J. Gordon. A unified view of matrix factorization models. In *Machine Learning and Knowledge Discovery in Databases, European Conference (ECML/PKDD)*, 2008.

[23] N. Srebro, J. D. M. Rennie, and T. S. Jaakola. Maximum-margin matrix factorization. In *Advances in Neural Information Processing Systems 17*, pages 1329–1336. MIT Press, 2005.

[24] H. Steck. Training and testing of recommender systems on data missing not at random. In *Proceedings of the 16th ACM SIGKDD international conference on Knowledge discovery and data mining*, KDD '10, pages 713–722, New York, NY, USA, 2010. ACM.

[25] M. Weimer, A. Karatzoglou, Q. V. Le, and A. Smola. Cofirank, maximum margin matrix factorization for collaborative ranking. In *NIPS*, volume 20, 2007.

[26] M. Weimer, A. Karatzoglou, and A. J. Smola. Improving maximum margin matrix factorization. *Machine Learning*, 72(3):263–276, 2008.

Trading-off Among Accuracy, Similarity, Diversity, and Long-tail: A Graph-based Recommendation Approach

Lei Shi
Baidu.com, Inc.
P. R. China
shilei06@baidu.com

ABSTRACT

Improving recommendation accuracy is the mostly focused target of recommendation systems, while it has been increasingly recognized that accuracy is not enough as the only quality criterion. More concepts have been proposed recently to augment the evaluation dimensions, such as similarity, diversity, long-tail, etc. Simultaneously considering multiple criteria leads to a multi-task recommendation. In this paper, a graph-based recommendation approach is proposed to effectively and flexibly trade-off among them.

Our approach is considered based a 1st order Markovian graph with transition probabilities between user-item pairs. A "cost flow" concept is proposed over the graph, so that items with lower costs are stronger recommended to a user. The cost flows are formulated in a recursive dynamic form, whose stability is proved to be guaranteed by appropriately lower-bounding the transition costs. Furthermore, a mixture of transition costs is designed by combining three ingredients related to long-tail, focusing degree and similarity. To evaluate the ingredients, we propose an orthogonal-sparse-orthogonal nonnegative matrix tri-factorization model and an efficient multiplicative algorithm. Empirical experiments on real-world data show promising results of our approach, which could be regarded as a general framework for other affects if transition costs are designed in various ways.

Categories and Subject Descriptors

H.3.3 [**Information Storage and Retrieval**]: Information Search and Retrieval—*Information Filtering*

General Terms

Algorithm, Proof, Experimentation, Performance

Keywords

Collaborative filtering, graph-based cost flow, fixed point stability, contraction mapping, orthogonal-sparse-orthogonal nonnegative matrix tri-factorization

ACM RecSys '2013 Hong Kong
Copyright 2013 ACM 978-1-4503-2409-0/13/10 ...$15.00.
http://dx.doi.org/10.1145/2507157.2507165.

1. INTRODUCTION

With extensive recommendation system technologies developed over the past decade, there emerge lots of successful efforts in both academia and industry, taking the well-known applications by Amazon and Netflix for example. The most common formulation of a recommendation problem adopts the notion of user-to-item ratings, with boolean, integer, or ordinal values. A recommendation system typically tries to predict the values (or orders) of the ratings of unrated items[1] for each user, with a satisfactory ranking [2, 5, 10].

The major existing efforts in the literature focused on improving the recommendation accuracy, as exemplified by the Netflix Prize competition [20]. However, it has been increasingly recognized that it is not sufficient to have accuracy as the only criterion during measuring the recommendation quality. Recently, more concepts have been considered as alternative evaluation dimensions to the recommended items, such as similarity, diversity, novelty, trust, long-tail, etc., to generate results that are not only accurate but also valuable with additional properties [2, 5, 10, 23, 25, 27].

If considering accuracy together with some of these additional targets, we encounter a multi-task recommendation and need to seek a solution that trades-off among them. Particularly, four evaluation concepts are chosen as our focus:

- **Accuracy** (*Acc*) of the predicted ratings or ranked recommendation list on unrated items are usually evaluated based on a held-out testing set, e.g., RMSE or MAE as the measure on ratings, Normalized Distance-based Performance Measure (NDPM) or Mean Reciprocal Rank (MRR) as the measure on ranking [14].
- **Similarity** (*Sim*) measures how similar the recommended items are (usually in semantics or topics) to the user or the user's rated items [27].
- **Diversity** (*Div*) describes the difference of recommended lists throughout all users [10].
- **Long-tail** (*Lt*) encourages the long-tail items, i.e., those have been rated seldom, to be recommended [2].

In different application scenarios, these four evaluation perspectives play different roles. First, accuracy should be the fundamental target in any recommendation systems. Moreover, as listed in Table 1 for example, the remaining three metrics tend be also valuable for recommendation on consumable goods. However, for the non-consumable goods, the similarity measure might be not that important because,

[1]Following existing recommendation studies, here and throughout this paper, "user" and "item" are not limited to their names, whereas they generally stand for the subjective side and the objective side, respectively.

e.g., a person bought a TV set is unlikely to buy another soon even if they are extremely similar. Moreover for food recommendation, accuracy and similarity that indicate the taste of a user become important, whereas diverse/long-tail items without qualified ratings are not preferred.

Table 1: Evaluations for recommendations. Symbol "✓" or "?" indicates an evaluation is or may be not important for the corresponding scenario

Example scenarios	*Acc*	*Sim*	*Div*	*Lt*
consumable goods	✓	✓	✓	✓
non-consumable goods	✓	?	✓	✓
movie/book/restaurant	✓	✓	✓	?
food	✓	✓	?	?

From another point of view, we'd like to discuss about the "satisfaction" of a recommendation system. Ideally, a recommendation system should receive satisfactions from not only the user-side but also the platform-side (e.g., Amazon, Netflix). Table 2 lists four types of feelings that involve satisfaction. First, highly related to accuracy and similarity, feeling a recommendation *matched* with users' need/tastes is important to both user-side and platform-side. Second, the novelty is usually contributed by diversity and long-tail, is the similarity is guaranteed. Third, to widely cover each user's interest, we'd better to enhance the similarity and diversity. Fourth, a platform is satisfactory and attractive to retailers if the item coverage throughout all users is wide, which concerns the diversity and long-tail factors.

Table 2: Satisfactions to recommendations. Different feelings are important on either or both of user-and-platform sides, which should have different key evaluation metrics (as indicated by ✓)

feeling	important to	*Acc*	*Sim*	*Div*	*Lt*
matched	user+platform	✓	✓	–	–
novel	user+platform	–	✓	✓	✓
user-cover	user	–	✓	✓	–
platform-cover	platform	–	–	✓	✓

Focusing on *Acc*, *Sim*, *Div* and *Lt*, this paper proposes a graph-based recommendation approach that can effectively and flexibly trade-off among them. At the beginning, we construct a directed graph with 1st order Markovian, whose transition probabilities are calculated based on rating weights. Given a user, a cost flow concept is proposed on this graph, and items with lower cost are stronger recommended. The costs are formulated in a recursive dynamic form. Thereafter, based on fixed point theorem, we prove that the stability of the dynamics is guaranteed by appropriately lower-bounding the transition cost of each edge. Accordingly, a mixed version of transition costs is designed by combining three ingredients related to long-tail, focusing degree and similarity. In order to evaluate the latter two ingredients, an orthogonal-sparse-orthogonal nonnegative matrix tri-factorization (OSO-NMTF) model is proposed, together with an efficient multiplicative algorithm with the help of gradients on Stiefel manifold. Empirical experiments on real-world data show promising results of our approach.

The remainder of this paper is organized as follows. In Section 2, we briefly review related efforts in the literature. Based on a directed graph representation, Section 3 introduces the cost flow formulation, provides the stability analysis, and proposes a mixture construction to the transition costs. The specification and learning algorithm are described in Section 4. After reporting experimental results in Section 5, we finally draw concluding remarks in Section 6.

2. RELATED WORKS

Among a large number of recommendation techniques that have been developed over the past decade, collaborative filtering (CF) techniques represent most widely used and well-performing algorithms. Aiming to directly predict the ratings, two representative CF techniques are neighborhood-based CF algorithms and matrix factorization based CF algorithms [14, 20, 21]. Moreover, there exist a stream of graph-based recommendation approaches, aiming to propagate information throughout a graph and mostly predict the ranking of the ratings [1, 3, 11, 15], taking the well-known PageRank and related algorithms for example.

Besides the differences on implementation algorithms, existing efforts also take different objective functions to be optimized. Most approaches that directly predict the ratings [14] adopt the estimation errors (e.g., RMSE, MAE) or further ranking accuracies (e.g., MRR, NDPM). Since it is increasingly recognized that merely caring about accuracy is not enough [23], papers [3, 11] further considered the similarity between items and users' tastes. The authors of [1, 10, 17, 22] focused on optimizing diversity, so that not only the redundancy of recommended items to each user is low, but also the coverage of recommended items to all users is large. Moreover, researchers also observed that most of existing recommender systems, especially CF based methods, can not recommend tail products due to the data sparsity issue. On the other, the success of "infinite-inventory" retailers such as Amazon and Netflix is greatly attributed to a long-tail phenomenon, where tail product availability is able to boost head sales by offering the shopping convenience for both mainstream and niche tastes. Under this motivation, recently several efforts [2, 5, 25, 27, 29] turned to take the long-tail effects into consideration. However, to the best of our knowledge, there is still no effort that considers these criteria simultaneously under a unified framework. This paper is thus motivated for such a study.

3. GRAPH-BASED COST FLOW FOR RECOMMENDATION

In this section, we introduce the graph representation of the user-item relation and the cost flow concept. Then, after proposing the flow dynamics, we proceed to analyze its stability and the transition cost composed of multiple effects.

3.1 Graph Construction

In recommendation scenarios, the user-item relationship is usually represented by an edge-weighted undirected bipartite graph $G'(V, E, \rho)$ as illustrated in Fig. 1(a), where V represents the set of vertices, E represents the set of edges, and ρ represents the weights on the edges. With V_u and V_i denoting the sets of user-vertices and item-vertices respectively, there is no edge between any two user-vertices or between two item-vertices. Clearly $V = V_u \cup V_i$, and the number of users is $N_u = |V_u|$ and of items is $N_i = |V_i|$. The edge set E has element $e(u, i)$ if and only if user $u \in V_u$ touches item $i \in V_i$ (e.g., rating in user-movie scenario, click in query-). Since the graph is undirected, the edge weights

$\rho(u,i) = \rho(i,u)$ are symmetric, and indicate the strength of the relation between the user-item pair (u,i).

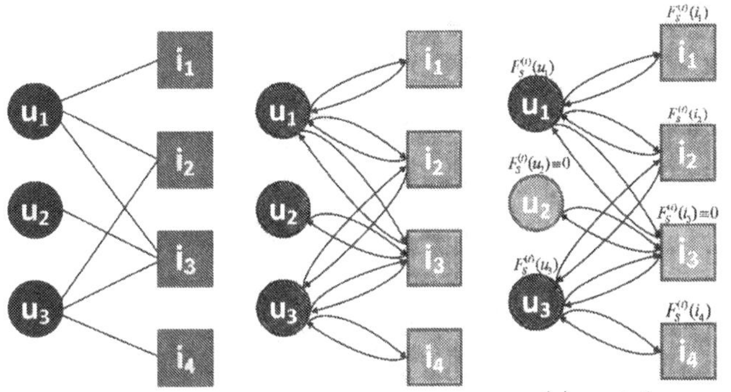

(a) undirected (b) directed (c) cost flow

Figure 1: User(circle)-item(square) relation expressed in bipartite graphs. (a) undirected graph: each edge is associated with symmetric weights ρ. (b) directed graph: each edge is associated with asymmetric transition probability. (c) cost flow: each edge is associated with transition probability and cost; given absorbing nodes $S = S_u \cup S_i$, at time t each vertex j has a cost $F_S^{(t)}(j)$ to reach S, with $S_u = \{u_2\}$ and $S_i = \{i_3\}$ highlighted for instance

Like many existing works on random walk and Markov chain [18, 22, 24, 27], we convert the undirected $G'(V,E,\rho)$ into directed graph $G''(V,E,P)$ as illustrated in Fig. 1(b), where P is the set of transition probabilities on the edges. In graph $G''(V,E,P)$, every undirected edge in $G'(V,E,\rho)$ is converted into two directed edges with opposite directions. In $P = \{p_{iu}, p_{ui}\}$, the p_{ui} denotes the transition probability from user-u to item-i, and p_{iu} is the transition probability from item-i to user-u, both obtained by normalization on ρ:

$$p_{ui} = \frac{\rho(u,i)}{\sum_i \rho(i,u)}, \qquad p_{iu} = \frac{\rho(i,u)}{\sum_u \rho(i,u)}. \tag{1}$$

3.2 Cost Flow for Recommendation

In the recommendation scenario, given a single user or a user set S_u and its connected item set S_i, our target is to output a ranking list on all items based on some objective/criterion and recommend them to S_u.

Consider a random flow (walk) on graph $G''(V,E,P)$, we define $S = S_u \cup S_i$ as the absorbing/sink nodes, i.e., the flow stops when any node in S is reached. Moreover, we assume that each edge $e(j,\ell)$ has a nonnegative one-step transition cost $C(j|\ell)$ when a flow passes through. Finally, we have the cost flow graph $G(V,E,P,C)$, with an additional one-step transition costs C. An example is illustrated in Fig. 1(c). We define the long-term cost of flowing from a vertex j to be absorbed as $F_S(j)$, and $F_S(\ell) = 0$ for $\forall \ell \in S$ by definition. Also, we require the vector $\boldsymbol{F}_S$ to locate in a simplex $\mathbb{S}$, i.e., nonnegative and sum equal to 1. Given $G(V,E,P,C)$ with appropriately defined C, we can output the ranking of $\boldsymbol{F}_S$ given $S = S_u \cup S_i$ as the recommendation list to user set S_u, where item-i with a smaller $F_S(i)$ is more preferred.

However, directly evaluating the flow cost F_S is quite difficult. Instead, we formulate it into the dynamic recursion $\boldsymbol{F}_S^{(t+1)} = f(\boldsymbol{F}_S^{(t)})$ w.r.t. the iteration time t as below.

Definition 1. (Cost flow dynamics). At iteration t, the cost to reach the set $S = S_u \cup S_i$ is defined as $\boldsymbol{F}_S^{(t)} = [F_S^{(t)}(1), \ldots, F_S^{(t)}(N)]$, and it flows in the graph specified by $\{p_{iu}\} \cup \{p_{ui}\}$ in the following dynamic way as t increases:

$$\begin{aligned}
\boldsymbol{F}_S^{(t+1)} &= f(\boldsymbol{F}_S^{(t)}), \quad \text{with } F_S^{(t+1)}(j) = \frac{g^{(t)}(j)}{\sum_j g^{(t)}(j)} \\
g^{(t)}(i) &= \begin{cases} 0, & i \in S_i, \\ \sum_{u'} p_{iu'}\left[C(u'|i) + F_S^{(t)}(u')\right], & i \notin S_i, \end{cases} \\
g^{(t)}(u) &= \begin{cases} 0, & u \in S_u, \\ \sum_{i'} p_{ui'}\left[C(i'|u) + F_S^{(t)}(i')\right], & u \notin S_u, \end{cases}
\end{aligned} \tag{2}$$

where $C(u|i)$ describes the one-step *non-negative* transition cost from item-i to user-u, and vice versa for $C(i|u)$.

Remember that we start from a simplex initialization $\boldsymbol{F}_S^{(0)} \in \mathbb{S}$. First, the above dynamics capture the one-step cost flow in the user-item bipartite graph. Second, at any time t, it not only guarantees $F_S^{(t)}(j) = 0$ for $\forall j \in S$, but also ensures each $F_S^{(t)}(j) \geq 0$ and $\sum_j F_S^{(t)}(j) = 1$, i.e., $\boldsymbol{x} \in \mathbb{S} \Rightarrow f(\boldsymbol{x}) \in \mathbb{S}$.

3.3 Stability Analysis of Flow Dynamics

One crucial analysis of the dynamics in Eq. (2) is to check its stability, i.e., whether it can converge to a unique equilibrium with any random initialization. This part introduces a sufficient condition that guarantees the stability.

Our analysis begins with the *Banach Fixed Point Theorem* as restated in Theorem 1, and Theorem 2 relates the contraction mapping with its Jacobian matrix [12, 19].

THEOREM 1. *Consider a set $\mathcal{D} \in \mathbb{R}^n$ and a function $f: \mathcal{D} \to \mathbb{R}^n$, if (1) $\mathcal{D}$ is a closed set; (2) $\boldsymbol{x} \in \mathcal{D} \Longrightarrow f(\boldsymbol{x}) \in \mathcal{D}$; (3) $f(\cdot)$ is a contraction mapping on $\mathcal{D}$, then:*
(1) there is one unique $\boldsymbol{x}^* \in \mathcal{D}$ s.t. $f(\boldsymbol{x}^*) = \boldsymbol{x}^*$; (2) iteration $\boldsymbol{x}^{(t+1)} = f(\boldsymbol{x}^{(t)})$ from $\forall \boldsymbol{x}^{(0)} \in \mathcal{D}$ converges to $\boldsymbol{x}^*$ as $t \to \infty$.

THEOREM 2. *Assume $\mathcal{D} \in \mathbb{R}^n$ is convex and $f: \mathcal{D} \to \mathbb{R}^n$ has continuous partial derivatives in $\mathcal{D}$. Denote $f'(\boldsymbol{x})$ as the Jacobian matrix. If $\exists\, q < 1$ s.t.,*

$$\forall \boldsymbol{x} \in \mathcal{D}, \quad \left|\left|f'(\boldsymbol{x})\right|\right| \leq q$$

for some matrix norm $||\cdot||$, then f is a contraction mapping.

Based on these theorems, we analyze the mapping $\boldsymbol{F}_S^{(t+1)} = f(\boldsymbol{F}_S^{(t)})$ in Eq. (2) and obtain the Jacobian matrix

$$\boldsymbol{J}(\boldsymbol{F}_S^{(t)}) = \begin{bmatrix} \frac{\partial F_S^{(t+1)}(1)}{\partial F_S^{(t)}(1)} & \cdots & \frac{\partial F_S^{(t+1)}(1)}{\partial F_S^{(t)}(N)} \\ \vdots & \ddots & \vdots \\ \frac{\partial F_S^{(t+1)}(N)}{\partial F_S^{(t)}(1)} & \cdots & \frac{\partial F_S^{(t+1)}(N)}{\partial F_S^{(t)}(N)} \end{bmatrix}, \tag{3}$$

with the following elements

$$\begin{cases}
\frac{\partial F_S^{(t+1)}(u)}{\partial F_S^{(t)}(u')} = \frac{-F_S^{(t+1)}(u)\sum_{i'} p_{i'u'}}{\sum_j g^{(t)}(j)}, \\
\frac{\partial F_S^{(t+1)}(u)}{\partial F_S^{(t)}(i')} = \frac{p_{ui'} - F_S^{(t+1)}(u)\sum_{u'} p_{u'i'}}{\sum_j g^{(t)}(j)}, \\
\frac{\partial F_S^{(t+1)}(i)}{\partial F_S^{(t)}(i')} = \frac{-F_S^{(t+1)}(i)\sum_{u'} p_{u'i'}}{\sum_j g^{(t)}(j)}, \\
\frac{\partial F_S^{(t+1)}(i)}{\partial F_S^{(t)}(u')} = \frac{p_{iu'} - F_S^{(t+1)}(i)\sum_{i'} p_{i'u'}}{\sum_j g^{(t)}(j)}.
\end{cases} \tag{4}$$

In the below, we show that simply lower-bounding all one-step transition costs $\{C(u|i), C(i|u)\}_{i,u}$ appropriately is sufficient to guarantee the flow dynamics' stability.

THEOREM 3. *(Lower-bounded transition cost.) If all one-step transition costs are lower-bounded by 1, i.e,:*

$$C(u|i) \geq 1, \quad C(i|u) \geq 1, \quad \forall i, u,$$

then the Jacobian matrix in Eq. (3) has a bounded infinite-norm $||\boldsymbol{J}||_\infty \leq q < 1$. *Consequently,* $f(\cdot)$ *is a contraction mapping, and there exists a unique equilibrium* $\boldsymbol{F}_S^* \in \mathbb{S}$, *s.t. iterating Eq. (2) from* $\forall \boldsymbol{F}_S^{(0)} \in \mathbb{S}$ *converges to* $\boldsymbol{F}_S^*$ *as* $t \to \infty$.

The proof of Theorem 3 is sketched in Appendix A.

3.4 Mixed Transition Cost

We proceed to design the detailed one-step transition cost $C(u|i)$ and $C(i|u)$ for each linked user-item pair (u, i). It should be noted that, the transition cost is a general concept and not limited to the designs presented below, choices alternative to which deserve study interests in future.

Particularly, we consider three factors that encourage **similarity**, **long tail**, and **focusing degree**, respectively. All of them are nonnegative costs.

- **Similarity.** The intuition is that, a transition should have small/large cost if the current user-item pair is similar/diverse. We define $C_{sim}(u|i)$ as the similarity cost for item-to-user transition and $C_{sim}(i|u)$ for user-to-item transition.
- **Long tail.** As discussed in Section 1, recommending the long-tail items may bring amazing benefits in many recommendation scenarios. We are thus motivated to define the long tail cost $C_{lt}(i)$ on item-i when transiting from some user to item-i. The larger sum of weights connected to item-i, the larger $C_{lt}(i)$ should be. We choose the simplest choice:

$$C_{lt}(i) \propto \sum_u \rho(i, u). \tag{5}$$

  The long tail on the user side does not seem quite meaningful and is not considered, or say $C_{lt}(u) \equiv 0$.
- **Focusing degree.** Suppose there are two users, u_1 and u_2. User u_1 has a wide range of interest types, while user u_2 centers on few specific tastes. Then the information shared by the specific user u_2 may be more important to distinguish the specificity of the items than the ambiguous user u_1. Based on this intuition and following [27], we use the latent topic/cluster to evaluate the focusing degree. Suppose we have clustered users into K_u clusters and items into K_i clusters, the focusing degree cost when transiting to a vertex is chosen as the posterior entropy:

$$C_{foc}(i) = -\sum_{k=1}^{K_i} p(k|i) \log p(k|i),$$
$$C_{foc}(u) = -\sum_{k=1}^{K_u} p(k|u) \log p(k|u). \tag{6}$$

Combining the above three factors, we summarize our final one-step transition cost $C(u|i)$ and $C(i|u)$ as below:

$$\begin{aligned} C(u|i) &= 1 + \pi_{sim} C_{sim}(u|i) + \pi_{foc} C_{foc}(u), \\ C(i|u) &= 1 + \pi_{sim} C_{sim}(i|u) + \pi_{lt} C_{lt}(i) + \pi_{foc} C_{foc}(i), \\ \text{with} \quad & \pi_{sim}, \pi_{lt}, \pi_{foc} \geq 0, \quad \pi_{sim} + \pi_{lt} + \pi_{foc} = 1, \end{aligned} \tag{7}$$

which is a linear mixture of the three factors. The constant 1 is added for stability due to Theorem 3, which also serves as a basic cost similar to the "Absorbing Time" method [27].

Connected Subgraph v.s. Smoothed Full Graph. In implementation, we find that the iteration by Eq. (2) converges very fast, e.g., almost always within 5 rounds. However, each iteration has a complexity of $\mathcal{O}(|E|)$ with $|E|$ being the number of edges. In order to scale the graph size and improve the efficiency, given the absorbing set S, we consider to iteratively extract a connected subgraph G_S:

- (Step 0) Set $G_S = S$;
- (Step 1) For $\tau = 1, \ldots, \lambda$:
  - (1.1) Find $AccG_S = \{\text{node } \ell : \ \ell \text{ is connected to } G_S\}$;
  - (1.2) Accumulate the set by $G_S = G_S \cup AccG_S$;

and then propagate the flow costs by Eq. (2) only through the connected subgraph G_S. This is based on a reasonable intuition: a group of users and items they like are connected. The round number is chosen as $\lambda = 2$ and enough to provide desired results based on our experiences. On the other extreme, some works [22] also smooth the graph by adding edges between each pair of users, resulting in a wholly connected full graph. We do not follow that way for efficiency.

Up till now, we still have not explained the detailed designs on C_{foc} and C_{sim}. First, the computation of C_{foc} in Eq. (6) requires clustering both users and items. In the next section, we will propose a model named as OSO-NMTF that clusters both sides simultaneously. Second, one can certainly evaluate the user-item similarity based on meta features if available (e.g., text description or genre of users and items). However for applications with no or limited meta information, the problem is how to measure the user-item similarity C_{sim} given only the graph weights, for which a novel similarity measure is proposed based on the OSO-NMTF model.

4. OSO-NMTF MODELING

There are extensive studies under the name of topic models in the literature [26], which show promising performances on finding meaningful latent topics. Intuitively, with each topic representing a cluster, the topic based recommendation or ranking [15, 27] owe its success to the abstracted high-level topic features, which are more robust and meaningful than the raw low-level features. Nevertheless, most of existing works only focus on clustering either one of users or items. Aiming to not only implement user-item bi-clustering but also extract user-item similarity simultaneously, we adopt the nonnegative matrix tri-factorization (NMTF) formulation [8, 28]. This section introduces the OSO-NMTF model that assigns orthogonal-sparse-orthogonal constraints, and proposes a multiplicative learning algorithm. Thereafter, we construct the *similarity* cost C_{sim} and *focusing degree* cost C_{foc} in Eq. (7) based on OSO-NMTF.

4.1 The OSO-NMTF Model

In our user-item scenario, a nonnegative matrix $\boldsymbol{X} \in \mathbb{R}_+^{N_u \times N_i}$ is constructed with $x_{ij} = \rho(i, j)$, where $\rho(i, j)$ is the graph weight in Eq. (1). Given $\boldsymbol{X}$, NMTF decomposes it into a product of three nonnegative factors $\boldsymbol{W} \in \mathbb{R}_+^{N_u \times K_u}$, $\boldsymbol{A} \in \mathbb{R}_+^{K_u \times K_i}$, and $\boldsymbol{H} \in \mathbb{R}_+^{N_i \times K_i}$, such that $\boldsymbol{X} \approx \boldsymbol{WAH}^T$. Further imposing orthogonality on both $\boldsymbol{W}$ and $\boldsymbol{H}$ leads to the orthogonal NMTF [8, 28], which can be achieved via solving the following optimization:

$$\begin{aligned} \min_{\boldsymbol{W},\boldsymbol{A},\boldsymbol{H} \geq 0} \quad & \frac{1}{2} \left\| \boldsymbol{X} - \boldsymbol{WAH}^T \right\|_F^2, \\ s.t. \quad & \boldsymbol{W}^T\boldsymbol{W} = \boldsymbol{I}, \ \boldsymbol{H}^T\boldsymbol{H} = \boldsymbol{I}, \end{aligned} \tag{8}$$

where $||\cdot||_F$ denotes the matrix Frobenius norm. Nonnegativity plus strict orthogonality on $\boldsymbol{W}$ and $\boldsymbol{H}$ are difficult to be ensured during optimization, because it will leads each row in both $\boldsymbol{W}$ and $\boldsymbol{H}$ to be all zeros except only one element equals 1, i.e., a typical combinatorial optimization. In consequence, paper [8] proposes a multiplicative algorithm based on an approximate Lagrange, and [28] uses gradients on Stiefel manifold [9] for an approximate updating.

Bi-Clustering Interpretation. From a clustering perspective, the O-NMTF formulation in Eq. (8) corresponds to the simultaneous clustering of the rows (users) and columns (items) of $\boldsymbol{X}$ [7, 8]. Particularly, there are K_u user-clusters and K_i item-clusters, $\boldsymbol{W}$ is the cluster indicator matrix for clustering users, $\boldsymbol{H}$ is the cluster indicator matrix for clustering items, $\boldsymbol{A}$ is the association weight matrix between user-clusters and item-clusters. It should be noted that, despite the approximate orthogonality on $\boldsymbol{W}$ and $\boldsymbol{H}$, they can be still regarded proportional to the *soft*-clustering posteriors. More interpretations and relations to other clustering methods are referred to [7, 13, 16, 21].

The Orthogonal-Sparse-Orthogonal Constraints. As a revised extension to O-NMTF in Eq. (8), we further assume that the association matrix $\boldsymbol{A}$ is sparse. Albeit this tiny revision, it brings the following three main benefits:

- **More interpretable associations.** Constraining $\boldsymbol{A}$ to be sparse encourages the noisy associations between user-clusters and item-clusters to shrink, and thus the learned $\boldsymbol{A}$ is more robust and interpretable [16].
- **Relieve indeterminacy.** Although the uniqueness of exact O-NMTF is claimed in [8], the have-to-be approximate updating in [8, 28] cannot guarantee the uniqueness. Consider a solution $\boldsymbol{WAH}^T$ with $\boldsymbol{W}^T\boldsymbol{W} \approx \boldsymbol{I}$, we may find a rotation matrix $\boldsymbol{\phi}$ with small rotation angle to remain nonnegativity, and let $\widetilde{\boldsymbol{W}} = \boldsymbol{W}\boldsymbol{\phi}$ and $\widetilde{\boldsymbol{A}} = \boldsymbol{\phi}^T\boldsymbol{A}$. As a result, $\widetilde{\boldsymbol{W}}^T\widetilde{\boldsymbol{W}} = \boldsymbol{W}^T\boldsymbol{W}$ and $\boldsymbol{WA} = \widetilde{\boldsymbol{W}}\widetilde{\boldsymbol{A}}$ still hold without changing the objective in Eq. (8), i.e., it is ill-posed with indeterminacy, which can be relived by imposing sparsity on $\boldsymbol{A}$.
- **Model complexity adaptation.** The determination of cluster numbers K_u and K_i is a typical model selection problem [4]. As another by-product, the sparsity also encourages the rows/columns in $\boldsymbol{A}$ to approach zeros, if the corresponding user-clusters/item-clusters are redundant, leading to an adaptive model complexity determination and desired generalization ability.

Mathematically, orthogonal-sparse-orthogonal NMTF (OSO-NMTF) is formulated into the following optimization:

$$\min_{\boldsymbol{W},\boldsymbol{H},\boldsymbol{A}\geq 0} \quad \frac{1}{2}\left|\left|\boldsymbol{X} - \boldsymbol{WAH}^T\right|\right|_F^2 + \lambda\sum_{i,j} A_{ij},$$
$$s.t. \quad \boldsymbol{W}^T\boldsymbol{W} = \boldsymbol{I}, \quad \boldsymbol{H}^T\boldsymbol{H} = \boldsymbol{I}, \tag{9}$$

where $\lambda > 0$ is the Lagrange multiplier, and the second term is the classic L_1-norm for sparsity [16].

4.2 Multiplicative Updating Algorithm

To solve the constrained optimization of OSO-NMTF in Eq. (9), one may augment it into an approximate Lagrangian similar to [8], and determine three Lagrange multipliers on $\boldsymbol{W}$, $\boldsymbol{H}$, $\boldsymbol{A}$, respectively. In contrast, the orthogonality constraint on $\boldsymbol{W}$ and $\boldsymbol{H}$ indicates the Stiefel manifold, the geometry of which was systematically studied in [9]. Employing the gradient on Stiefel manifold similar to [28], we obtain the following multiplicative updates:

$$\boldsymbol{W} \longleftarrow \boldsymbol{W} \circ \frac{[(\boldsymbol{X} + \boldsymbol{WAH}^T)\boldsymbol{HA}^T]}{[\boldsymbol{WAH}^T(\boldsymbol{HA}^T + \boldsymbol{X}^T\boldsymbol{W})]},$$
$$\boldsymbol{H} \longleftarrow \boldsymbol{H} \circ \frac{[(\boldsymbol{X}^T + \boldsymbol{HA}^T\boldsymbol{W}^T)\boldsymbol{WA}]}{[\boldsymbol{HA}^T\boldsymbol{W}^T(\boldsymbol{WA} + \boldsymbol{XH})]},$$
$$\boldsymbol{A} \longleftarrow \boldsymbol{A} \circ \frac{[\boldsymbol{W}^T\boldsymbol{XH}]}{[\lambda + \boldsymbol{W}^T\boldsymbol{WAH}^T\boldsymbol{H}]}, \tag{10}$$

where operator $\circ$ denotes the Hadamard (element-wise) product, operator $\frac{[\cdot]}{[\cdot]}$ is the Hadamard (element-wise) division. The derivation of this algorithm is sketched in Appendix B. In experiments, this updating converges quickly and effectively preserves a rough orthogonality, with low generalization errors when missing values are predicted.

4.3 User-Item Bi-Clustering and Similarity

Once an OSO-NMTF model is learned, the *focusing degree* cost C_{foc} and the *similarity* cost C_{sim} in Eq. (7) can be obtained. Remember the bi-clustering properties of OSO-NMTF discussed in Section 4.1, $\boldsymbol{W}$ and $\boldsymbol{H}$ describe the user-cluster and item-cluster posteriors, respectively. Intuitively, a user or item should have a smaller/larger cost C_{foc} if its cluster posteriors are shaper/smoother. More concretely, we employ entropy for the quantification:

$$C_{foc}(u) \propto -\sum_{k=1}^{K_u} \bar{W}_{uk}\log\bar{W}_{uk}, \text{ with } \bar{\boldsymbol{W}} = \text{normalize}(\boldsymbol{W}),$$
$$C_{foc}(i) \propto -\sum_{k=1}^{K_i} \bar{H}_{ik}\log\bar{H}_{ik}, \text{ with } \bar{\boldsymbol{H}} = \text{normalize}(\boldsymbol{H}), \tag{11}$$

where normalize$(\cdot)$ is the row normalization operator such that each row in $\bar{\boldsymbol{W}}$ and $\bar{\boldsymbol{H}}$ has a posterior-over-clusters form. Again, paper [27] only focuses on clustering users by Latent Dirichlet Allocation, while our C_{foc} is constructed by clustering both items and users simultaneously.

For the user-item similarity C_{sim} in Eq. (7), here we introduce a novel user-item similarity measure based on OSO-NMTF. Consider an item i and a user u, they are represented by a column $\boldsymbol{X}_{*i} \in \mathbb{R}_+^{N_u}$ and a row $\boldsymbol{X}_{u*} \in \mathbb{R}_+^{N_i}$, respectively. Using the normalized $\bar{\boldsymbol{W}}$ and $\bar{\boldsymbol{H}}$ as in Eq. (11), we can explain $\boldsymbol{\alpha}_i = \bar{\boldsymbol{W}}^T\boldsymbol{X}_{*i}$ as the accumulated posteriors over the *user-clusters* contributed by this *item* i. The case is similar for $\boldsymbol{\beta}_u = \bar{\boldsymbol{H}}^T\boldsymbol{X}_{u*}^T$. Given the association $\boldsymbol{A}$, we thus transfer to measure the similarity between $\boldsymbol{\alpha}_i$ and $\boldsymbol{\beta}_u$:

$$C_{sim}(i|u) = C_{sim}(u|i) \propto \frac{1}{\boldsymbol{\alpha}_i^T\boldsymbol{A}\boldsymbol{\beta}_u / \sum_{ij} A_{ij}}, \tag{12}$$

where a symmetric similarity is assumed in our implementations. In case of some applications, one may want to use asymmetric to differentiate the bi-directions. In that case, one possible alternative choice would be:

$$C_{sim}(i|u) \propto \frac{1}{\boldsymbol{\alpha}_i^T\text{normalize}(\boldsymbol{A})\boldsymbol{\beta}_u},$$
$$C_{sim}(u|i) \propto \frac{1}{\boldsymbol{\alpha}_i^T[\text{normalize}(\boldsymbol{A}^T)]^T\boldsymbol{\beta}_u}. \tag{13}$$

That is, normalizing the association matrix $\boldsymbol{A}$ by row will get the transition probability from user-clusters to item-clusters, and vice versa for normalization by column. Moreover, one may also consider to normalize $\boldsymbol{\alpha}_i$ and $\boldsymbol{\beta}_u$ before product, in order to balance the different weights of users and items.

5. EMPIRICAL EXPERIMENTS

5.1 Data Description

In experiments, we consider two real world tagging/rating datasets: `Movielens100K` and `Last.fm`. Collected by the GroupLens Research Project at the University of Minnesota, the `Movielens100K` dataset[2] consists of user-to-movie ratings (in the range of $1 \sim 5$), together with basic tag information of both users and movies. Collected from Last.fm online music system, the `Last.fm` dataset[3] contains user-to-artist tagging (i.e., binary ratings), together with the tagged properties and user social network information.

We preprocess the datasets as follows. For `Movielens100K`, we filter out ratings that are less than 4 (i.e., neutral or negative), and then filter out users who have rated less than 10 items. Moreover, each movie has a genre tag out of 18 possible values. In order to evaluate performance *during testing*, for each user, his/her user-tag vector is obtained by accumulating the genre tags of items rated by him/her. For `Last.fm`, we filter out users who have tagged less than 10 items. Moreover, a user tagged an artist by description phrases. Similarly, we accumulate all tags posted by each user as his/her user-tag vector, and all tags received as the item-tag vector for each item. Thereafter, each tag-vector is normalized so that elements' sum equals to 1. We denote $\boldsymbol{\eta}_u$ and $\boldsymbol{\chi}_i$ as tag-vectors to a user u and an item i, respectively.

Table 3: Description of preprocessed datasets

	`Movielens100K`	`Last.fm`
#users	886	718
#items	1,004	11,924
#ratings	10,514	51,999
sparsity	1.18%	0.61%
#user/item tags	18	8,746
#train : #test	2 : 8	8 : 2

Several key statistics of the data after preprocessing are summarized in Table 3. In order to further decrease the sparsity in `Movielens100K`, we randomly pick 20% ratings for training and leave the remaining 80% for testing, while the training v.s. testing ratio for `Last.fm` is 80% v.s. 20%.

5.2 Performance Evaluation

For each user u, we are given a list of truly rated item set $\boldsymbol{\psi}_u$ based on the testing data. During recommendation, once an algorithm proposes a ranked list $\boldsymbol{\zeta}_u$ of all unrated items (in the training data) by each user u, we use $\zeta_u(\ell)$ to denote the ℓ-th most strongly recommended item, and $\boldsymbol{\zeta}_u^{10}$ to represent the set of top 10 recommended items. Four metrics [6] are chosen for evaluating experimental performances:

- **Accuracy**: The accuracy given testing data is evaluated by the Mean Reciprocal Rank (MRR) of all users:

$$\mathcal{MRR} = \frac{1}{N_u}\sum_{u=1}^{N_u} RR_u,$$
$$RR_u = \max_{\ell} \frac{1}{\ell} \cdot \mathbf{1}\left[\text{item } \zeta_u(\ell) \in \boldsymbol{\psi}_u\right]. \quad (14)$$

Therein, $\mathbf{1}[x]$ denotes the indicator function and equals to 1 (or 0) if expression x is true (or false). A larger $\mathcal{MRR}$ value indicates better accuracy.

- **Similarity**: The similarity score for each user u is measured by comparing the tag vectors of items in $\boldsymbol{\zeta}_u^{10}$ with the tag vector of user u:

$$\mathcal{SIM} = \frac{1}{N_u}\sum_{u=1}^{N_u}\sum_{\ell\in\boldsymbol{\zeta}_u^{10}} \boldsymbol{\eta}_u^T \boldsymbol{\chi}_\ell \quad , \quad (15)$$

which uses the inner-products between the strongly recommended items in $\boldsymbol{\zeta}_u^{10}$ with the user. The tag vectors $\boldsymbol{\eta}$ and $\boldsymbol{\chi}$ are described in Section 5.1. A larger $\mathcal{SIM}$ value represents a better result in similarity.

- **Diversity**: The diversity metric is evaluated as

$$\mathcal{DIV} = \left|\cup_{u=1}^{N_u} \boldsymbol{\zeta}_u^{10}\right|, \quad (16)$$

which describes the coverage size of the recommended item sets throughout all users. A larger $\mathcal{DIV}$ corresponds to a more diverse recommendation result.

- **Long-tail**: We measure the long-tail score by

$$\mathcal{LT} = \frac{1}{N_u}\sum_{u=1}^{N_u}\sum_{\ell\in\boldsymbol{\zeta}_u^{10}} w_\ell, \quad w_\ell = \frac{\sum_{u=1}^{N_u}\rho(\ell,u)}{\sum_{\ell=1}^{N_i}\sum_{u=1}^{N_u}\rho(\ell,u)}, \quad (17)$$

where $\rho(\cdot,\cdot)$ is rating weight same as in Eq. (1). A smaller $\mathcal{LT}$ value indicates a larger long-tail coverage proportion of the top 10 recommendation sets.

5.3 Experimental Results

In order to investigate how each performance metric changes as the mixing weights $(\pi_{sim}, \pi_{lt}, \pi_{foc})$ in Eq. (7) vary, we traverse on grids of the three weights' configurations within the 3-dimensional simplex, as illustrated in Fig. 2. This enumeration is implemented on both `Movielens100K` and `Last.fm` datasets. Two representative CF methods are considered in comparison, namely Matrix Factorization (MF) [20] and Nonnegative Matrix Factorization (NMF) [21]. The latent bi-dimensionalities of OSO-NMTF model are set as $K_u = 30$ and $K_v = 50$, and the latent dimensionalities of MF and N-MF are both fixed as 30 for a fair comparison.

Once OSO-NMTF has been trained, the three ingredients of transition costs are computed according to Eqs. (5&11&12). Enumerating through *hundreds of* gridded configurations of $(\pi_{sim}, \pi_{lt}, \pi_{foc})$ in the simplex, we perform our cost flow approach with each configuration. Finally, the performances on `Movielens100K` and `Last.fm` are reported in Fig. 3 and Fig. 4, respectively, where each subfigure illustrates one metric's values over the simplex same as in Fig. 2. The max and min values of each simplex are reported in Table 4, compared with the results by MF and NMF.

As shown by Figs. 3&4, each metric varies smoothly within the simplex, and the tendencies are similar on the two data. Interestingly, the cost ingredients C_{lt} and C_{sim} play correlated roles in some extent: large weights on them encourage relatively large $\mathcal{MRR}$ (high accuracy), small $\mathcal{DIV}$ (low diversity), and large $\mathcal{LT}$ (low long-tail ratio). Even more, the "focusing-degree" cost C_{foc} brings forward much more diverse and long-tailed results than the "long-tail" cost C_{lt}. Roughly, the "best" values for all metrics are provided with only two cost ingredients combined (i.e., locate near to the simplex edges). Particularly, the best $\mathcal{MRR}$ comes from combining C_{lt} and C_{sim}, while all the best values of $\mathcal{SIM}$, $\mathcal{DIV}$ and $\mathcal{LT}$ result from combining C_{foc} and C_{sim}. We may imagine C_{sim} as a *bridge* that connects C_{lt} and C_{foc} to slither among good environments for different metrics.

[2] http://movielens.umn.edu
[3] http://ir.ii.uam.es/hetrec2011

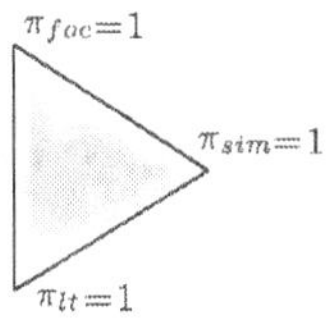

Figure 2: The simplex

Table 4: Results comparison. For each metric on each data, the "best" is bolded

datasets	`Movielens100K`				`Last.fm`			
evaluation metrics	$\mathcal{MRR}$	$\mathcal{SIM}$	$\mathcal{DIV}$	$\mathcal{LT}$	$\mathcal{MRR}$	$\mathcal{SIM}$	$\mathcal{DIV}$	$\mathcal{LT}$
MF	0.493	1.05	19	0.059	0.121	0.105	35	0.015
NMF	0.512	1.04	17	0.060	0.127	0.109	32	0.016
max value in the simplex	**0.632**	**1.23**	**535**	0.056	**0.205**	**0.182**	**1041**	0.014
min value in the simplex	0.120	1.04	73	**0.014**	0.064	0.111	588	**0.003**

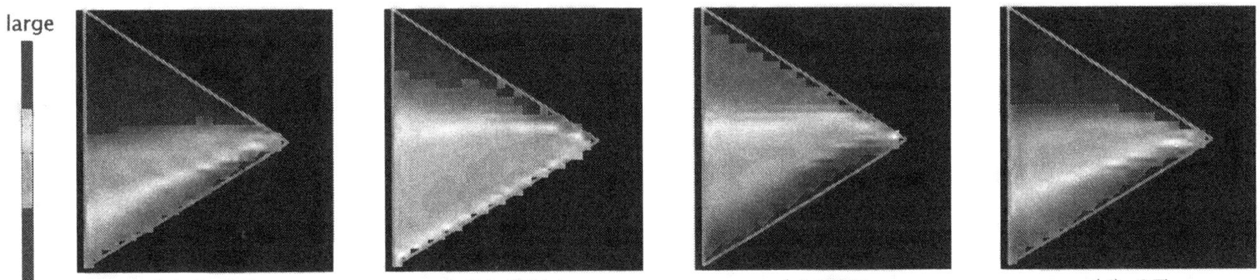

(a) $\mathcal{MRR}$ (b) $\mathcal{SIM}$ (c) $\mathcal{DIV}$ (d) $\mathcal{LT}$

Figure 3: Performances of our approach on `Movielens100K` within the simplex of Fig. 2 (best viewed in color)

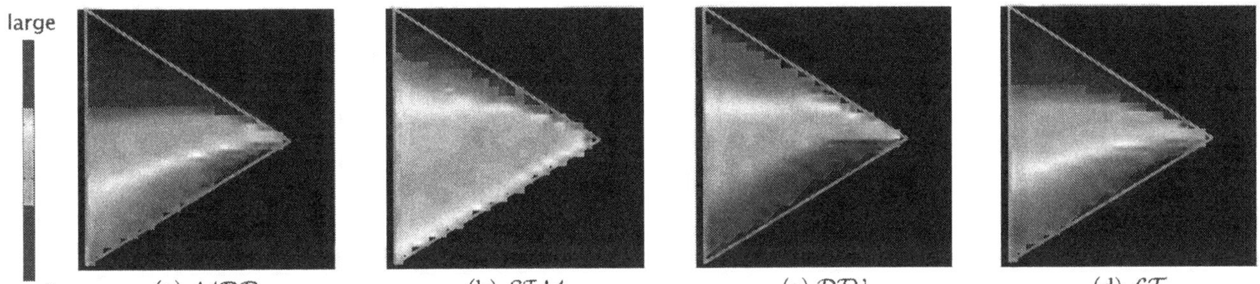

(a) $\mathcal{MRR}$ (b) $\mathcal{SIM}$ (c) $\mathcal{DIV}$ (d) $\mathcal{LT}$

Figure 4: Performances of our approach on `Last.fm` within the simplex of Fig. 2 (best viewed in color)

In Table 4, all the "best" performances of each metric over the simplex are much better than those by MF and NMF. Moreover, even the "worst" performances, except $\mathcal{MRR}$, are better than or at least comparable to MF and NMF. Specifically, MF and NMF tend to recommend top items with small $\mathcal{DIV}$ and large $\mathcal{LT}$. In contrast, in the simplex not only the smallest $\mathcal{DIV}$ is higher, but also the largest $\mathcal{LT}$ is smaller than MF/NMF. That is, our approach performs robust with much better similarity, diversity and long-tail measures.

Time cost. Once transition costs are calculated, our approach includes no training phase. The average prediction time per user is within 0.2 second on `Movielens100K` and within 3 seconds on `Last.fm`, implemented in Python and using an Intel Xeon 2.4G single core CPU.

6. CONCLUSIONS

It is increasingly recognized that accuracy is not enough as the only quality criterion to a recommendation system, and more concepts have been proposed recently as additional evaluation dimensions. Simultaneously considering accuracy, similarity, diversity, and long-tail, this paper proposes a graph-based recommendation approach that effectively and flexibly trades-off among them. Particularly, a cost flow concept is proposed based on a 1st order Markovian graph with transition probabilities between user-item pairs. The costs are further formulated in a recursive dynamic form, whose stability is proved to be guaranteed if the transition costs are appropriately lower-bounded. Furthermore, a mixed version of transition costs is designed by combining three ingredients related to long-tail, focusing degree and similarity. To evaluate the ingredients, we propose an orthogonal-sparse-orthogonal nonnegative matrix tri-factorization model and an efficient multiplicative updating algorithm. Experiments on real-world data show valid performances of our approach.

Consequently, for applications with a specific composition of different objectives, we can easily adjust the mixing weights in Eq. (7) appropriately, hinted by Figs. 3&4. Additionally, although in experiments we only consider the recommendation task to a single user, the extension to a group of users can be obtained by revising the absorbing node set to include those users. More applications and systematic comparisons with other collaborative filtering methods are expected in future. Last but not the least, our approach could be regarded as a general framework with different affects if alternative schemes are considered and designed directly in place of Eq. (7) and the transition costs therein.

7. REFERENCES

[1] G. Adomavicius and Y. Kwon. Maximizing aggregate recommendation diversity: A graph-theoretic approach. In *Proc. Workshop on Novelty and Diversity in Recommender Systems, held in conjunction with ACM RecSys*, pages 3–10, 2011.

[2] C. Anderson. *The Long Tail: Why the Future of Business is Selling Less of More*. Hyperion, 2006.

[3] M. Brand. A random walks perspective on maximizing satisfaction and profit. In *SIAM International Conference on Data Mining*, pages 12–19, 2005.

[4] K. P. Burnham and D. Anderson. *Model Selection and Multi-Model Inference.* Springer, July 2002.

[5] O. Celma. *Music Recommendation and Discovery in the Long Tail.* Springer, 2010.

[6] P. Cremonesi, Y. Koren, and R. Turrin. Performance of recommender algorithms on top-n recommendation tasks. In *Proc. ACM RecSys*, pages 39–46, 2010.

[7] C. Ding, X. He, H. Zha, and H. Simon. On the equivalence of nonnegative matrix factorization and spectral clustering. In *Proc. SIAM Data Mining*, 2005.

[8] C. Ding, T. Li, W. Peng, and H. Park. Orthogonal nonnegative matrix tri-factorizations for clustering. In *Proc. 12th ACM SIGKDD*, pages 126–135, 2006.

[9] A. Edelman, T. Arias, and S. Smith. The geometry of algorithms with orthogonality constraints. *SIAM J. Matrix Anal. Appl.*, 20(2):303–353, 1998.

[10] D. M. Fleder and K. Hosanagar. Recommender systems and their impact on sales diversity. In *Proc. 8th ACM Conf. Electronic Commerce (EC'2007)*, pages 192–199, 2007.

[11] F. Fouss, A. Pirotte, and M. Saerens. A novel way of computing similarities between nodes of a graph, with application to collaborative recommendation. In *Proc. IEEE/WIC/ACM WI'2005*, pages 550–556, 2005.

[12] D. J. H. Garling. *Inequalities: A Journey into Linear Analysis.* Cambridge, 2007.

[13] E. Gaussier and C. Goutte. Relation between PLSA and NMF and implications. In *Proc. SIGIR*, 2005.

[14] A. Gunawardana and G. Shani. A survey of accuracy evaluation metrics of recommendation tasks. *JMLR*, 10:2935–2962, 2009.

[15] T. H. Haveliwala. Topic-sensitive pagerank. In *Proc. WWW*, pages 517–526, 2002.

[16] P. O. Hoyer. Non-negative matrix factorization with sparseness constraints. *Journal of Machine Learning Research*, 5:1457–1469, 2004.

[17] N. Hurley and M. Zhang. Novelty and diversity in top-n recommendation – analysis and evaluation. *ACM Trans. Internet Technol.*, 10(4):14:1–14:30, 2011.

[18] J. G. Kemeny and J. L. Snell. *Finite Markov Chains.* Springer-Verlag, 1976.

[19] W. A. Kirk and M. A. Khamsi. *An Introduction to Metric Spaces and Fixed Point Theory.* John Wiley, New York, 2001.

[20] Y. Koren, R. Bell, and C. Volinsky. Matrix factorization techniques for recommender systems. *Computer*, 42(8):30–37, 2009.

[21] D. D. Lee and H. S. Seung. Learning the parts of objects by non-negative matrix factorization. *Nature*, 401:788–791, 1999.

[22] H. Ma, M. R. Lyu, and I. King. Diversifying query suggestion results. In *Proc. AAAI*, 2010.

[23] S. M. McNee, J. Riedl, and J. A. Konstan. Being accurate is not enough: how accuracy metrics have hurt recommender systems. In *Proc. CHI EA'06*, pages 1097–1101, 2006.

[24] J. Norris. *Markov Chains.* Cambridge University Press, 1997.

[25] Y.-J. Park and A. Tuzhilin. The long tail of recommender systems and how to leverage it. In *Proc. ACM RecSys*, pages 11–18, 2008.

[26] M. Steyvers and T. Griffiths. *Probabilistic Topic Models.* Lawrence Erlbaum Associates, 2007.

[27] H. Yin, B. Cui, J. Li, J. Yao, and C. Chen. Challenging the long tail recommendation. In *Proc. VLDB'2012*, volume 5, pages 896–907. 2012.

[28] J. Yoo and S. Choi. Nonnegative matrix factorization with orthogonality constraints. *Journal of Computing Science and Engineering*, 4(2):97–109, 2010.

[29] M. Zhang and N. Hurley. Avoiding monotony: improving the diversity of recommendation lists. In *Proc. ACM RecSys*, pages 123–130, 2008.

APPENDIX

A. PROOF OF THEOREM 3

According to Theorem 1, since $f(\cdot)$ in Eq. (2) satisfies $f : \mathbb{S} \to \mathbb{S}$ and the simplex $\mathbb{S}$ is closed convex, we need to find one sufficient condition such that $f(\cdot)$ is a contraction mapping, which leads to the stability.

Based on Theorem 2, we evaluate the infinite matrix-norm $||\boldsymbol{J}||_\infty = \max_i \sum_j |J_{ij}|$, i.e., the maximum absolute row sum. Specifically, we derive

$$\sum_j |J_{ij}| \le \frac{1 + N \cdot F_{\mathbb{S}}^{(t+1)}(i)}{\sum_j g^{(t)}(j)}, \quad \text{for } \forall i,$$
$$\Longrightarrow ||\boldsymbol{J}||_\infty = \max_i \sum_j |J_{ij}| \le \sum_{i,j} |J_{ij}| = \frac{1+N}{\sum_j g^{(t)}(j)}, \quad (18)$$

where the first inequality is based on $|a-b| \le |a| + |b|$ with $a, b \ge 0$. To let $||\boldsymbol{J}||_\infty \le q < 1$, our target becomes to find the condition that can ensure $\sum_j g^{(t)}(j) > 1 + N$.

On the other side, if we lower-bound each one-step transition cost $C(u|i)$ and $C(i|u)$ by $C_{lb} \ge 0$, we have

$$\sum_j g^{(t)}(j) \ge 1 + N \cdot C_{lb}, \quad (19)$$

based on the definition in Eq. (2).

In consequence, a necessary condition to $||\boldsymbol{J}||_\infty \le q < 1$ is letting the lower-bound $C_{lb} \ge 1$, which completes the proof.

B. DERIVATION OF EQ. (10)

For the optimization task in Eq. (9), we denote $\mathcal{L} = 0.5||\boldsymbol{X} - \boldsymbol{WAH}^T||_F^2 + \lambda \sum_{i,j} A_{ij}$, the partial derivatives w.r.t. parameters $\boldsymbol{W}$, $\boldsymbol{H}$ and $\boldsymbol{A}$ are given as

$$\begin{aligned}
\frac{\partial \mathcal{L}}{\partial \boldsymbol{W}} &= -\boldsymbol{HA}^T\boldsymbol{X} + \boldsymbol{HA}^T\boldsymbol{WAH}^T, \\
\frac{\partial \mathcal{L}}{\partial \boldsymbol{H}} &= -\boldsymbol{X}^T\boldsymbol{WA} + \boldsymbol{HA}^T\boldsymbol{W}^T\boldsymbol{WA}, \\
\frac{\partial \mathcal{L}}{\partial \boldsymbol{A}} &= -\boldsymbol{W}^T\boldsymbol{XH} + \boldsymbol{W}^T\boldsymbol{WAH}^T\boldsymbol{H}.
\end{aligned}$$

Due to the orthogonality $\boldsymbol{W}^T\boldsymbol{W} = \boldsymbol{I}$ and $\boldsymbol{H}^T\boldsymbol{H} = \boldsymbol{I}$, we employ the gradients $\nabla \boldsymbol{W}$ and $\nabla \boldsymbol{H}$ on Stiefel manifold [9]:

$$\begin{aligned}
\nabla \boldsymbol{W} &= \frac{\partial \mathcal{L}}{\partial \boldsymbol{W}} - \boldsymbol{W}\left(\frac{\partial \mathcal{L}}{\partial \boldsymbol{W}}\right)^T \boldsymbol{W} \\
&= \boldsymbol{WAH}^T(\boldsymbol{HA}^T + \boldsymbol{X}^T\boldsymbol{W}) - (\boldsymbol{X} + \boldsymbol{WAH}^T)\boldsymbol{HA}^T, \\
\nabla \boldsymbol{H} &= \frac{\partial \mathcal{L}}{\partial \boldsymbol{H}} - \boldsymbol{H}\left(\frac{\partial \mathcal{L}}{\partial \boldsymbol{H}}\right)^T \boldsymbol{H} \\
&= \boldsymbol{HA}^T\boldsymbol{W}^T(\boldsymbol{WA} + \boldsymbol{XH}) - (\boldsymbol{X} + \boldsymbol{WAH}^T)^T\boldsymbol{WA}.
\end{aligned}$$

The above yields the multiplicative updates in Eq. (10).

Nonlinear Latent Factorization by Embedding Multiple User Interests

[Extended Abstract]

Jason Weston
Google Inc.
76 9th Avenue, New York
New York, NY 10011 USA
jweston@google.com

Ron J. Weiss
Google Inc.
76 9th Avenue, New York
New York, NY 10011 USA
ronw@google.com

Hector Yee
Google Inc.
901 Cherry Avenue,
San Bruno, CA 94066 USA
hyee@google.com

ABSTRACT

Classical matrix factorization approaches to collaborative filtering learn a latent vector for each user and each item, and recommendations are scored via the similarity between two such vectors, which are of the same dimension. In this work, we are motivated by the intuition that a user is a much more complicated entity than any single item, and cannot be well described by the same representation. Hence, the variety of a user's interests could be better captured by a more complex representation. We propose to model the user with a richer set of functions, specifically via a set of latent vectors, where each vector captures one of the user's latent interests or tastes. The overall recommendation model is then nonlinear where the matching score between a user and a given item is the maximum matching score over each of the user's latent interests with respect to the item's latent representation. We describe a simple, general and efficient algorithm for learning such a model, and apply it to large scale, real-world datasets from YouTube and Google Music, where our approach outperforms existing techniques.

Categories and Subject Descriptors

H.4 [**Information Systems Applications**]: Miscellaneous

Keywords

collaborative filtering, learning to rank, matrix factorization, nonlinear models

1. INTRODUCTION

Standard latent models for recommendation are linear factorizations of the user-item matrix of preferences. These models are then applied at test time for recommendations of new items. For example, singular value decomposition (SVD) and its variants, such as SVD++ (see [2] for a good review), factorize the user-item matrix in a least-squares sense where the matrix elements are considered to be ratings. Methods like CofiRank [8], CLiMF [6] or Wsabie [10] optimize a ranking loss instead with the goal of ranking higher valued user-item pairs above lower-scoring items for the given user, but the model still has the same linear form. In a linear factorization both a given user and a given item are assigned an m-dimensional vector of latent features, where typically m is small, between ten and a few hundred dimensions. To score each item one scores its m dimensional "embedding" against the m-dimensional user embedding, and orders the items by this score. This means that the representation of the user has the same capacity as the representation of a single item.

In this work we challenge the use of that common modeling approach as we believe a user should have a much richer latent representation. Intuitively, the model of a user should be able to encode that they may have many different tastes concerning different items, whereas a single item representation only has to encode a single item. If the item set to be recommended is a large, diverse set, we believe this limitation will have a larger impact. For example, consider the set of all products sold by an online store like Amazon. There is likely only very weak correlation between the user's tastes in different product areas, e.g. between the movies they might like, and the household products they wish to purchase. Yet, the standard factorization models forces that all these interests are encoded in the m latent factors, and diverse topics are forced to share these features. Even within a more focused recommendation area, such as music or movies the issue may be the same, for example a user's interest in history documentaries may have little correlation with their interest in romantic comedies. One could argue that one can simply increase the item embedding dimensionality to capture more interests in the user representation, but there are reasons not to do this (both practical, and generalization-based, especially for the long tail). Practically, the model becomes larger in memory which can be an issue in production. Secondly, as it is larger it would take longer to train well, and may overfit as the item representations have also become larger. We believe that employing a nonlinearity and a higher capacity user model, and keeping the item representation small, makes more sense as we will describe.

Our solution is to model a user with T latent vectors, each of dimension m, that model the user's latent tastes. Each item still has a single m-dimensional latent feature vector. The score between a user and a given item is the maximum match between the user tastes and the given item. The re-

RecSys'13, October 12–16, 2013, Hong Kong, China.
Copyright 2013 ACM 978-1-4503-2409-0/13/10 ...$15.00.
http://dx.doi.org/10.1145/2507157.2507209.

mainder of the paper is as follows. We first describe previous work in Section 2. We then present our model in Section 3, detailing the objective function and learning procedure to train such a model by gradient descent. Experimental results on large scale recommendation tasks from Google Music and YouTube are reported in Section 4. We finally sketch some directions for future work in Section 5.

2. RELATED WORK

We have already talked about the most related linear factorization models in the introduction, but the method we propose in this work generalizes those to a nonlinear model. Several types of nonlinear models have been tried before for recommendation. The authors of [3] proposed a nonlinear matrix factorization approach with Gaussian processes by using a kernelized form for the model. They report very good results on 1M MovieLens and EachMovie, however their approach may have scalability issues for larger problems. The authors of [5] applied Restricted Boltzmann machines for collaborative filtering, which is a kind of neural network that introduces nonlinearities via Gaussian hidden units. They obtained results slightly better than SVD, and an ensemble of the two methods performs very well. Our method can also be considered to be a particular kind of neural network, utilizing max nonlinearities rather than the standard sigmoids, although it is quite different from that of [5].

Other machine learning models consider max-based nonlinearities as we do, e.g. convolutional networks for image tasks use max-pooling [4]. To the best of our knowledge, however, they have not been used in latent models as in our approach, and have similarly not been applied to recommendation tasks.

Perhaps closest to our approach is the work of [1] where multiple profiles for user modeling (micro-profiling) are used for context-aware recommendation.

3. MAX INTEREST LATENT FACTORS

Standard linear user-item factorizations are of the form:

$$f(u,d) = U_u^\top V_d \tag{1}$$

where u is the given user, $u \in \{1,\dots,|\mathcal{U}|\}$, and d is an item to be recommended, $d \in \{1,\dots,|\mathcal{D}|\}$. The score assigned for the given user and item, $f(u,d) = S_{ud} = U_u^\top V_d$, can be seen as the prediction of a missing element of the (full rank) matrix S of dimension $|\mathcal{U}| \times |\mathcal{D}|$, which is approximated by the low rank factorization of S by U and V. The matrix U, which is of size $m \times |\mathcal{U}|$, encodes the latent factors for the users, and a $m \times |\mathcal{D}|$ matrix V encodes those of the items. Hence, every user and every item has m latent factors.

The key idea of the proposed model is to define T interest vectors per user, where the user part of the model is written as $\hat{U}$ which is an $m \times |\mathcal{U}| \times T$ tensor. Hence, we also write $\hat{U}_{iu} \in \mathbb{R}^m$ as the m-dimensional vector that represents the ith of T possible interests for user u. The item part of the model is the same as in the classical user-item factorization models, and is still denoted as a $m \times |\mathcal{D}|$ matrix V. The new scoring model is defined as:

$$f(u,d) = \max_{i=1,\dots,T} \hat{U}_{iu}^\top V_d. \tag{2}$$

For any given item, we are now computing T dot products, rather than one, when comparing it to the user, and taking the highest scoring. The intuition here is that the user is modeled with T differing tastes and the item matches with one of them best, captured via the max function. Said differently, for each user, the set of items is partitioned into T subsets, where the partitioning can vary across users. For each partition a different scoring function is applied.

Algorithm 1 MaxMF SGD algorithm.

Initialize model parameters (we use mean 0, standard deviation $\frac{1}{\sqrt{m}}$), unless parameters are already initialized during MapReduce (Algorithm 2).
repeat
  For user u randomly pick a positive item $d \in \mathcal{D}_u$.
  Compute $f(u,d)$.
  Set $N = 0$.
  repeat
    Pick a random item $\bar{d} \in \mathcal{D} \setminus \mathcal{D}_u$.
    $N = N + 1$.
  until $f(u,\bar{d}) > f(u,d) - 1$ or $N \geq |\mathcal{D} \setminus \mathcal{D}_u|$
  if $f(u,\bar{d}) > f(u,d) - 1$ **then**
    Make a gradient step to minimize:
      $L(\frac{|\mathcal{D}\setminus\mathcal{D}_u|}{N}) \max(0, 1 + f(u,\bar{d}) - f(u,d))$.
    (i.e. equations (3)-(6) for $f(u,d)$ defined by (2)).
    Project weights to enforce constraints, e.g. if $||V_i|| > C$ then set $V_i \leftarrow (CV_i)/||V_i||$ (and similar for U).
  end if
until validation error does not improve.

Algorithm 2 MaxMF MapReduce algorithm.

Initialize V randomly (mean 0, standard deviation $\frac{1}{\sqrt{m}}$).
Define model $f_1(u,d) = \frac{1}{|\mathcal{D}_u|}\sum_{i \in \mathcal{D}_u} V_i^\top V_d$.
Train $f_1(u,d)$ using Algorithm 1.
Define $f_2(u,d) = \max_i \hat{U}_{iu}^\top V_d^*$, where $V^* = V$ from f_1.
for each user u (in parallel) **do**
  Train $\hat{U}_u$, but keep V^* fixed, i.e. run Algorithm 1 but only invoke the gradient updates (3)-(4) and not (5)-(6).
end for

Stochastic Gradient Descent Training.

Now that we have described the model, the next step is to describe how to train it. We could learn such a model using a regression (least squares) approach such as in SVD, but in this work we focus on learning to rank as it has been observed to perform well on several recommendation tasks previously [6, 10]. Our starting point is the objective of the linear factorization model, Wsabie [9], which learns the model parameters by minimizing:

$$\sum_{u \in \mathcal{U}} \sum_{d \in \mathcal{D}} \sum_{\bar{d} \notin \mathcal{D}_u} L(rank_d(u)) \max(0, 1 + f(u,\bar{d}) - f(u,d)).$$

Here $\mathcal{D}_u$ denotes the set of items that the user has purchased / watched / listened to (depending on the context) which we refer to as positive items, i.e. we are in a binary rating setting rather than the real-valued rating setting e.g. of the Netflix challenge. In fact, the binary setting is a very common one in real-world problems, in our experience more common than the rating-based one. In the absence of negative data, the above objective tries to rank all the positive items as highly as possible. Here, $rank_d(u)$ is the rank of the positive item d relative to all the negative items:

$$rank_d(u) = \sum_{\bar{d} \notin \mathcal{D}_u} I(f(u,d) \geq 1 + f(u,\bar{d})),$$

and $L(\eta)$ converts the rank to a weight. Choosing $L(\eta) = C\eta$ for any positive constant C optimizes the mean rank, whereas a weighting such as $L(\eta) = \sum_{i=1}^{\eta} 1/i$ optimizes the top of the ranked list, as described in [7]. To train with such an objective, stochastic gradient has previously been employed. For speed the computation of $rank_d(u)$ is then replaced with a sampled approximation: sample N items $\bar{d}$ until a violation is found, i.e. $\max(0, 1+f(u,\bar{d})-f(u,d))) > 0$ and then approximate the rank with $|\mathcal{D} \setminus \mathcal{D}_u|/N$.

Although our model is nonlinear, we can still use almost the same procedure as used for the linear model in [10], we just need to compute the relevant gradients for our model. Specifically, for a given triple $(u, d, \bar{d})$, let us denote the maximum scoring user interest vector for d as $\hat{U}_{ut}$ and $\hat{U}_{u\bar{t}}$ for $\bar{d}$, where

$$\forall j \neq t : \hat{U}_{tu}^{\top} V_d > \hat{U}_{ju}^{\top} V_d, \quad \forall j \neq t : \hat{U}_{\bar{t}u}^{\top} V_d > \hat{U}_{ju}^{\top} V_{\bar{d}}.$$

For a violating triple we then need to update for the user model:

$$\hat{U}_{tu} \leftarrow \hat{U}_{tu} + \lambda L(\tfrac{|\mathcal{D} \setminus \mathcal{D}_u|}{N}) V_d, \quad (3)$$

$$\hat{U}_{\bar{t}u} \leftarrow \hat{U}_{\bar{t}u} - \lambda L(\tfrac{|\mathcal{D} \setminus \mathcal{D}_u|}{N}) V_{\bar{d}}, \quad (4)$$

and for the item model:

$$\hat{V}_d \leftarrow \hat{V}_d + \lambda L(\tfrac{|\mathcal{D} \setminus \mathcal{D}_u|}{N}) \hat{U}_{ut}, \quad (5)$$

$$\hat{V}_{\bar{d}} \leftarrow \hat{V}_d - \lambda L(\tfrac{|\mathcal{D} \setminus \mathcal{D}_u|}{N}) \hat{U}_{u\bar{t}}, \quad (6)$$

where λ is the learning rate. At each step, one typically also enforces that $||U_{ij}|| \leq C$ and $||V_i|| \leq C$, for all i and j, as a means of regularization.

The whole procedure is outlined in Algorithm 1, and is scalable to medium-size datasets, where the model fits in memory. Unfortunately, there is a major problem when the dataset becomes large. For example if we would like to apply this method to a dataset with 1 billion users (more than 1 billion unique users visit YouTube each month) and latent dimension $m = 64$, this gives a model of size > 238GB (even for $T = 1$). This is too big for most machines, and even if it did fit, it might also be very slow to train. We therefore consider a MapReduce-based training solution to deal with this issue.

MapReduce Training.

Our solution to scale this algorithm is to consider an alternating optimization: first optimize over the item embeddings V and then train the user embeddings U. In the first phase where we train V, the user model U is unknown. One option would be to initialize U to random values, however V is unlikely to be trained well unless the process is iterated enough to allow U to also converge (but similarly U will be training with an impoverished V in early iterations). Instead, in the first phase we build a model that factors out U completely:

$$f_1(u,d) = \frac{1}{|\mathcal{D}_u|} \sum_{i \in \mathcal{D}_u} V_i^{\top} V_d.$$

i.e. we consider that $U_u \triangleq \frac{1}{|\mathcal{D}_u|} \sum_{i \in \mathcal{D}_u} V_i$. Note that this is reminiscent of the item-based embedding of the user employed in SVD++ [2]. We then train using the stochastic gradient descent (SGD) approach of Algorithm 1 which is now tractable, at least if the number of items is say less than a few million. This gives us a good initialization for the item embeddings V. In the second phase we fix V to V^* and train the user models only:

$$f_2(u,d) = \max_{i,\ldots,T} \hat{U}_{iu}^{\top} V_d^*,$$

This decouples the parameters for each user, allowing them to be trained independently. We thus train all users in parallel using MapReduce: the mappers collect and emit the relevant training triples keyed by user, and the reducers train each user independently without requiring a single machine to have access to the entire model. The reducers can then emit their $\hat{U}_u$ vectors to save the entire model to disk for further training iterations. I.e. one can then go back and retrain V given fixed U and so on, although we only considered a two-phase setup in our experiments. In the two-phase case we do not even need to save the user model to disk if we are interested in batch offline predictions. We can both train each user and perform the ranking of items in the reduce phase and output the recommendations to disk instead, hence the user model is never actually stored.

Table 1: Recommendation Datasets

Dataset	Music: Artists	Music: Tracks	YouTube
Number of Items	≈75k	≈700k	≈500k
Train Users	Millions		
Test Users	Tens of Thousands		

Table 2: Google Music Artist Recommendation. Our baseline model is WSABIE and mean rank (Rank), precision at 1 and 10 (P@N) and recall at 1 and 10 (R@N) metrics are given relative to that model. Decreases in rank and increases in R@N and P@N indicate improvements.

Method	Rank	P@1	P@10	R@1	R@10
SVD	+26%	-7.9%	-1.5%	-6.7%	-0.75%
WSABIE	-	-	-	-	-
MAXMF T=3	-3.9%	-3.1%	-0.18%	-4.4%	-0.15%
MAXMF T=5	-8%	-0.46%	+1.3%	-0.63%	+1.9%
MAXMF T=10	-11%	+0.33%	+3.1%	+0.33%	+3.2%

Table 3: Google Music Track Recommendation

Method	Rank	P@1	R@1	P@10	R@10
WSABIE	-	-	-	-	-
MAXMF T=2	-7.7%	+10%	+9.8%	+12%	+10%
MAXMF T=3	-12%	+20%	+20%	+21%	+20%
MAXMF T=5	-15%	+24%	+28%	+26%	+30%
MAXMF T=10	-17%	+30%	+33%	+32%	+34%

Table 4: YouTube Video Recommendation

Method	Rank	P@1	p@10	R@1	R@10
SVD	+56%	-54%	-57%	-54%	-96%
WSABIE	-	-	-	-	-
MAXMF T=2	-3.2%	+8.8%	+13%	+9.9%	+14%
MAXMF T=3	-6.2%	+16%	+18%	+17%	+19%
MAXMF T=5	-9%	+22%	+23%	+23%	+23%
MAXMF T=10	-11%	+26%	+26%	+28%	+26%

4. EXPERIMENTS

We conducted experiments on three large scale, real world tasks: music recommendation using proprietary data from Google Music[1], of both artists and individual tracks, and video recommendation from YouTube[2]. In all cases, the datasets consist of a large set of anonymized users, where for each user there is a set of associated items based on their watch/listen history. The user-item matrix is hence a sparse binary matrix. The sizes of the datasets are given in Table 1.

To construct evaluation data, we randomly selected 5 items for testing per user, and kept them apart from training. At prediction time, for the test users we then ranked all unrated items (i.e. items that they have not watched/listened to that are present in the training set) and observe where the 5 test items are in the ranked list of recommendations. We then evaluate the following metrics: rank (the position in the ranked list, averaged over all test items), precision at 1 and 10 (P@1 and P@10), and recall at 1 and 10 (R@1 and R@10).

Hyperparameters (λ, C) were chosen using a portion of the training set for validation, although for memory and speed reasons we limited the embedding dimension to be $m = 64$. As we trained our model, MaxMF (Max-nonlinearity Matrix Factorization), with a ranking criteria, we consider our baseline to be the same type of model, but without nonlinearity, which is the Wsabie model of [10]. So we used the same λ and C that are optimal for Wsabie and then report results for different values of T for MaxMF with those settings, using the MapReduce based training scheme. On Google Music Artist Recommendation and the YouTube tasks we also compare to SVD (L2-optimal matrix factorization for the complete matrix with log-odds weighting on the columns, which downweights the importance of the popular features, as that worked better than uniform weights). (For YouTube, we trained the SVD on a (large) subset due to scalabilty issues.) Note, however, that SVD was shown to be inferior to Wsabie on several datasets previously [10]. Hence, as Wsabie is our main baseline, we report relative changes in metrics when using other methods compared to it. Results on the three datasets are given in Tables 2, 3 and 4.

The first dataset, Google Music artist recommendation (Table 2), MaxMF gave only relatively small gains compared to Wsabie. SVD performed worse in all metrics. Note that a strongly performing model has a small mean rank, and large precision and recall values, hence we are looking for negative percentage changes in mean rank but positive changes in the other metrics. SVD likely underperforms since we are measuring ranking based metrics, which it does not optimize at training time. In other respects, the models are very similar. For MaxMF, as we increased the number of user interests T that we model, mean rank decreases from 3.9%, 8% and 11% compared to Wsabie, for $T = 3$, $T = 5$ and $T = 10$ respectively. Changes in precision and recall are smaller. We hypothesize that the relatively small size of this dataset compared to the other two is the reason why MaxMF has smaller gains.

The second dataset, Google Music track recommendation, is comprised of the same set of anonymized users, but with items represented at the track rather than the artist level. That means there are more items to rank, ≈700k rather than ≈75k, and correspondingly more items per user. This means the task is harder, since there are more items to rank. However, per user there are more items, which might mean that training nonlinear interest models per user is less likely to overfit, since there is more data for training. As is shown in Table 3 we get considerable gains using our method on this dataset compared to the Wsabie baseline, up to ≈30% gains in precision and recall using $T = 10$ user interest vectors.

The third dataset, YouTube video recommendation, requires us to rank 500k videos. As shown in Table 4 the gains are also quite large, up to around 25% improvement in recall and precision compared to the baseline model.

[1] http://music.google.com
[2] http://www.youtube.com

5. CONCLUSIONS

In this paper, we have introduced a highly scalable method for learning a nonlinear latent factorization. Experiments on three large scale, real-world datasets indicate the efficacy of the approach.

Further work could try explore further algorithms, and to analyse and understand these results further. For example, we could explore whether we can learn the optimal number of tastes T per user rather than leaving this parameter fixed.

6. REFERENCES

[1] L. Baltrunas and X. Amatriain. Towards time-dependant recommendation based on implicit feedback. In *Workshop on context-aware recommender systems (CARSâĂŽ09)*, 2009.

[2] Y. Koren and R. Bell. Advances in collaborative filtering. In *Recommender Systems Handbook*, pages 145–186. Springer, 2011.

[3] N. D. Lawrence and R. Urtasun. Non-linear matrix factorization with gaussian processes. In *Proceedings of the 26th Annual International Conference on Machine Learning*, pages 601–608. ACM, 2009.

[4] Y. LeCun and Y. Bengio. Convolutional networks for images, speech, and time series. *The handbook of brain theory and neural networks*, 3361, 1995.

[5] R. Salakhutdinov, A. Mnih, and G. Hinton. Restricted boltzmann machines for collaborative filtering. In *Proceedings of the 24th international conference on Machine learning*, pages 791–798. ACM, 2007.

[6] Y. Shi, A. Karatzoglou, L. Baltrunas, M. Larson, N. Oliver, and A. Hanjalic. Climf: learning to maximize reciprocal rank with collaborative less-is-more filtering. In *Proceedings of the sixth ACM conference on Recommender systems*, pages 139–146. ACM, 2012.

[7] N. Usunier, D. Buffoni, and P. Gallinari. Ranking with ordered weighted pairwise classification. *ICML*, 2009.

[8] M. Weimer, A. Karatzoglou, Q. Le, A. Smola, et al. Cofirank-maximum margin matrix factorization for collaborative ranking. *NIPS*, 2007.

[9] J. Weston, S. Bengio, and N. Usunier. Wsabie: Scaling up to large vocabulary image annotation. In *Intl. Joint Conf. Artificial Intelligence, (IJCAI)*, pages 2764–2770, 2011.

[10] J. Weston, C. Wang, R. Weiss, and A. Berenzweig. Latent collaborative retrieval. *ICML*, 2012.

Diffusion-aware Personalized Social Update Recommendation

Ye Pan[1], Feng Cong[2], Kailong Chen[1], Yong Yu[1]
[1]Shanghai Jiao Tong University, 800 Dongchuan Road, Shanghai China
{yepan,chenkl,yyu}@apex.sjtu.edu.cn
[2]Sino-US Global Logistics Institute, Shanghai Jiao Tong University
cfier@sjtu.edu.cn

ABSTRACT

Many Internet users have encountered serious information overload problem on social networks such as Facebook and Twitter, where users can consume the streams of social updates from their social connections. Traditional methods solving this problem include collaborative filtering and information diffusion modeling. Both methods answer the "who will adopt what" question from different perspective, while either of them only captures single-faceted knowledge of evidences. In this paper, we solve the personalized social update recommendation problem by proposing a framework which integrates the advantages of collaborative filtering and the characteristics of diffusion processes. The main contributions of this paper are three folds. First, we propose a plenty of diffusion features which capture the characteristics of diffusion processes. Second, we build a joint model which takes the advantages of both collaborative filtering and the characteristics of diffusion processes for recommendation. Finally, experiments on two real-world datasets show that our joint model outperforms the methods capturing single-faceted knowledge and several other baselines.

Categories and Subject Descriptors

H.3.3 [**Information Systems**]: Information Search and Retrieval—*Information filtering*

Keywords

Collaborative Filtering, Information Diffusion, Social Updates, Personalized Recommendation

1. INTRODUCTION

Many Internet users have encountered serious information overload problem on information-driven social networks, such as Facebook [23], Twitter[8], LinkedIn[18]. The most distinguishing feature of information-driven social networks is that they allow users to share their updates with their neighbors, and users can consume the streams of social updates from their connections via customized news feeds in their homepages. However, this characteristic is a double-edged sword in a way [23]. On one hand, it accelerates the propagation of information, because some popular information will reach more users via the sharing mechanism. On the other hand, this leads to hundreds or even thousands of updates posted to many users every day. It is very inconvenient for many users, especially those who are active and have many neighbors to find what they want, as personally useful social updates may be flooded by many others.

Some recent works have tried to tackle information overload problem via developing social update recommendation techniques in different social networks [8, 19]. Collaborative filtering, as a promising technology for recommender systems, has played an important role in solving information overload problem [11]. Collaborative filtering has attracted much attention since the Netflix Prize [5] in the academia and also been applied in some successful commercial systems, including Amazon [28], Netflix and Google News [11]. Collaborative filtering aims to build a recommender system by learning users' preferences based on the community data. It infers the unobserved user preferences by discovering the correlation between users and items based on observed user preferences. The most popular collaborative filtering method nowadays is the latent factor model, as it has helped winning prizes in a lot of competitions.

On the other hand, some research works have accomplished the recommendation task on social networks in the view of information diffusion [36, 25], as information access behaviors of social network users can be modeled as an information diffusion issue. Research works on information diffusion mainly focus on examining the characteristics of diffusion processes [6] and modeling the diffusion by detecting the factors that influencing the diffusion processes [14, 38]. Social networks play important roles in determining whether a user will adopt an item [17, 3], as user behaviors are confounding results driven by homophily [31], social influence and some other external influence [32, 1].

Collaborative filtering and information diffusion modeling on social networks have many internal correlations, as they are targeting the similar problem to some extent in different views. As a technique for recommender systems, collaborative filtering tries to answer whether a user will adopt or give positive feedback for a specific item. Once whether a user will adopt an item is well predicted, the details of information diffusion process can be well described, such as

RecSys'13, October 12–16, 2013, Hong Kong, China.
Copyright 2013 ACM 978-1-4503-2409-0/13/10 ...$15.00.
http://dx.doi.org/10.1145/2507157.2507177 .

whether an item will generate a large cascade [4, 37], what is the depth and the width of dissemination trees [27]. Both collaborative filtering and information diffusion modeling focus on answering the "who will adopt what" question, but they are based on different assumptions. As collaborative filtering assumes users who agreed in the past are likely to agree again in the future, it infers individual preferences from those people with similar tastes. Collaborative filtering actually used the similarity ties [9] as information sources for predicting users' adoption. On the other hand, information diffusion modeling often use the social ties as information sources for dictating users' behaviors [14, 3], as the actions of neighbors in a social network are highly correlated. The emphasis of diffusion model is usually the relationships between users in diffusion graph.

In this paper, we solve the personalized social update recommendation problem by proposing a framework which takes the advantages of collaborative filtering and the characteristics of diffusion processes. As we see, social ties and similarity ties play different roles for predicting future behaviors, and this suggests combining them in a hybrid recommender system will become a promising approach [9]. Our proposed model caters for this intuition by integrating collaborative filtering and the characteristics of diffusion processes, as the former captures the predicting power from similarity ties and the latter captures predicting power from social ties. Some previous works have used the social network structure to help improve the collaborative filtering recommender systems, but they only considered the social relations rather than the dynamic diffusion processes. Some other previous works have used information diffusion processes for recommendation, but the knowledge inside each node of the diffusion graph is ignored.

The main contributions of this paper are three folds. (1)We propose plenty of diffusion features which are helpful for prediction by capturing the characteristics of diffusion processes; (2)We propose a joint model which naturally embeds the the diffusion features in the traditional collaborative filtering model to simultaneously capture the predicting power of collaborative filtering and diffusion features. As far as we know, this is the first work to combine the two parts together; (3)We examine our method on two real-world datasets, Twitter and Sina Weibo. The evaluation results verify that our joint model utilizing all the diffusion features outperforms several baselines.

2. RELATED WORKS

2.1 Information Diffusion Analysis and Characteristics

Information diffusion, or information dissemination, information propagation in online social networks has attracted much attention in research field of online social network mining. Information diffusion in social network is mainly driven by word-of-mouth spread via social ties and social networks represent a fundamental medium. As more and more online social networks such as Facebook, Twitter, Flickr have provided much real world data, research works on information diffusion have become easier to study[24, 35].

Discovering the characteristics of diffusion processes is a central issue on information diffusion in online social networks and many experimental results of qualitative and quantitative analyses across different networks have been proposed. Cha [6] analyzed large-scale traces of information diffusion in the Flickr social network and found that even popular photos spread narrowly and slowly. Romero [35] explored the diffusions of hash tags on Twitter and found that according to their types and topics they exhibited different mechanics, which was interpreted as"stickiness" and "persistence". After examining the characteristics of the diffusion processes, diffusion models were proposed to mimic diffusion processes that had characteristics consistent with the real data [27, 13]. Though most online social networks are user-centric, they may have totally different diffusion characteristics, as the behaviors of users and the social relations shaped by different mechanisms of networks are semantically different.

Some other research works tried to infer and recover the complete and exact diffusion process when the underlying propagation networks were unobserved [15], or when some confounding factors such as homophily, external influence made it difficult to measure the spread of information sharing behaviors [15, 2, 32]. In our experiments, we use the retweeting actions of microblog users to construct the explicit diffusion networks and do not introduce many confounding factors.

2.2 Personalized Social Update Recommendation

Recommender systems have enjoyed a surge of interest in academia since Netflix Prize competition and been adopted in many commercial systems [5, 21]. Towards building a personalized recommender system, collaborative filtering is a promising technology by learning users' preferences based on the community data [21, 34]. It works by discovering the correlation between users and items based on observed user preferences so that unobserved user preferences can be inferred. Collaborative filtering methods have been very popular methods since they help win many open competition including Netfix Prize and KDDCUP.

Social update recommendation has recently attracted much attention to solve the information overload problems in social networks [23, 8, 19, 10, 7]. Different from previous recommendation problems, social update recommendations focus more on incorporating some other special characteristics, such as the sharing behaviors of users, social influence and correlations. The most related category of research works are personalized social recommendation [20, 30, 16, 40, 41]. Most of these works were based on the intuition that user tastes were highly correlated to the ones of their friends or people they trusted then used this to make more accurate guess of user behaviors for improving recommendation. But their works only considered the user-neighbor interaction rather than the characteristics of information diffusion process, which revealed the dynamics of user adoption behaviors and help improve recommendation experimentally. Some other previous works used information diffusion for recommendation [36], but they did not take the similarity ties into consideration, which were the main information source of making collaborative filtering effective for recommendation. Our method takes advantage of collaborative filtering and information diffusion characteristics to deal with the recommendation problem to greatly improve the personalized social update recommendation performance.

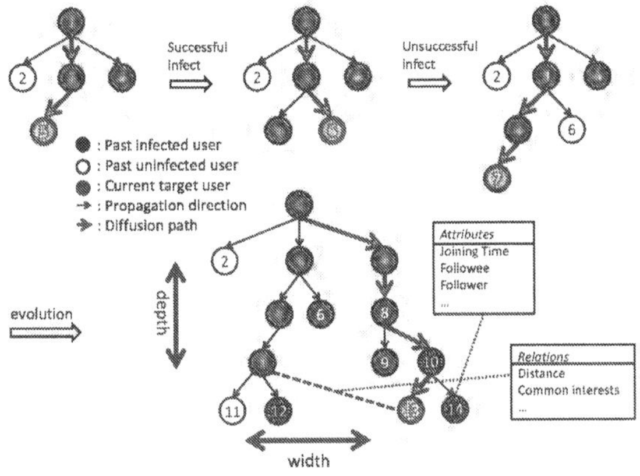

Figure 1: Evolution and features of cascades.

3. DIFFUSION-AWARE MODEL

In this section, we first introduce the diffusion features used in our work. We then propose the joint model which integrates collaborative filtering and diffusion processes in social update recommendation.

3.1 Diffusion Features in Diffusion Process

Previous works solving personalized social update recommendation ignore the effect of information cascades. Cascades are subgraph of the social networks which are consisted of the infected users. However, cascades contain lots of important information, which can greatly influence users' behavior. For example, users are more likely to adopt the information when the cascade contains lots of people they are interested in. Diffusion features are usually varied by the time and are different for each user. Figure 1 shows the evolution of the cascades. The user number is ordered by the time each user received this information. Each time there is only one user who is currently receiving the information. As the time passed, some users are infected while some are not and the cascade becomes bigger and more complex. Each user in the cascade has own attributes such as the time joined into the cascade, number of followees and number of followers. What's more, users in the cascade or path also have strong relations between each other such as distance between them and their common interests. These attributes and relations inside the cascade and path can be used to help predicting the users' behaviour more accurately. In the following, we propose all the features of cascades and propagations paths which are used in our work.

3.1.1 Popularity related features

Popularity related features refer to those features which are highly relevant to the popularity of cascades. General speaking, users in social networks tend to adopt more popular information.

- Cascade size: The size of a cascade equals to the number of infected users in the past and reveals the popularity of the information. Bigger cascade size usually leads to a more popular information, which will be accepted by more users.
- Cascade depth and width: The depth of a cascade is defined as the length of the longest path in the diffusion tree. The width of a cascade is defined as the number of leaves in the diffusion tree.
- Length of propagation path: Length of the propagation path is defined as the length of the path from the root user to the target user in a diffusion tree. Length of a propagation path shows the penetrating power of the information. In common situations, users are more likely to be infected by the information which has longer propagation path.
- Temporal popularity of topics : Some hot topics spread very fast in a certain period of time. Users are more likely to adopt these topics during the beginning eruptible time, but have less interests when these topics are not popular. This feature estimates the temporal popularity of a topic after a period of time:

$$Temporal(i,u) = \frac{|C_{i,u}|}{t_{u,i} - t_p} \quad (1)$$

, where $C_{i,u}$ represents the cascade of information i when user u receives the information. t_u represents the time that user u receives information i and t_p represents the time that the publisher sends out information i.

- Number of influenced users: If at least one of a user's followee posted or reposted the information, the user is influenced by the information no matter whether this user will adopt the information. Popular information usually has a large sum of influenced users.
- Celebrity Score: If more celebrities have agreed on an opinion, the opinion will be adopted by more people. One reason is that celebrities usually have stronger influence. Another reason is that celebrities have more followees but less followers,which leads to the fact that the information flowed from them can be seen by more people. This feature estimates the power of celebrity effect:

$$Celebrity(i,u) = \sum_{v \in C_{i,u}} \frac{|FER(v)|}{|FEE(v)|} \quad (2)$$

, where $C_{i,u}$ represents the cascade of information i when user u receives the information. $FER(v)$ refers to the follower set of user v and $FEE(v)$ refers to the followee set of user v. Considering propagation path instead of the cascade, this feature can also be defined as following:

$$CelebrityPath(i,u) = \sum_{v \in P_{i,u}} \frac{|FER(v)|}{|FEE(v)|} \quad (3)$$

, where $P_{i,u}$ represents the propagation path of information i when user u receives the information.

3.1.2 Neighbor related features

Neighbor related features measure the relation between target user and infected neighbors of target user in cascades. Here neighbors are refer to users who are close to target user in distance or have similar interests. If cascades are highly related to neighbors of the target user, the target user will more easily adopt the information. Unlike popularity related features, neighbor related features are personalized.

- Number of adopted followees: Users get all the information from their followees. If there are many infected followees in the cascades or in the propagation path, the user will be surrounded by this information, which makes the user easier to adopt the information.

- Number of adopted friends: If two users follow each other, we say these two users are friends. Friends are special relationship between two users in social network. Unlike unidirectional following, relationship of friends shows the relation of two users are very close. If many friends have been infected in the cascade or the propagation path, the user will more likely be infected.

- Brotherhood Score: In social network, two users who have more common followers tend to be more similar. This feature estimates the power of this relationship:

$$Brother(i,u) = log(\frac{\sum_{v \in C_{i,u}} |FER_{u,v}|}{|C_{i,u}|} + 1) \quad (4)$$

, where $FER_{u,v}$ represents the number of common followers of u and v. $C_{i,u}$ represents the cascade of information i when user u receives the information. By same strategy of celebrity score, this feature can be defined on propagation path.

- Co-father relationship Score: People follow another people in a social network as he/she appreciates one of their specialties or hobbies. If two people share a lot of common followers, they are more likely to be similar users. This feature estimates the power of this relationship:

$$CF(i,u) = log(\sum_{v \in C_{i,u}} \sum_{w \in FER_{u,v}} \frac{1}{|FEE(w)|+1} + 1) \quad (5)$$

, where $FEE(w)$ refers to the followee set of user w. $FER_{u,v}$ represents the number of common followers of u and v. $C_{i,u}$ represents the cascade of information i when user u receives the information. By same strategy of celebrity score, this feature can be defined on propagation path.

- Grandfather-grandchild relationship Score: If many followee of one user are another user's follower, they are more likely to be similar users. This feature estimates the power of this relationship:

$$G(i,u) = log(\sum_{v \in C_{i,u}} \sum_{w \in S} \frac{1}{|FEE(w)|+1} + 1) \quad (6)$$

$$S = FEE(u) \bigcap FER(v) \quad (7)$$

, where $FEE(u)$ and $FEE(w)$ refer to the followee set of user u and user w respectively. $FER(v)$ refers to the follower set of user v. $C_{i,u}$ represents the cascade of information i when user u receives the information. By same strategy of celebrity score, this feature can be defined on propagation path.

Combining all these cascades features showed above, regression models can be used to predict the extent of preference toward the information given its cascade.

3.2 Diffusion-aware Social Update Recommendation Model

In the previous part, we introduce the diffusion features in diffusion processes. In this part, we will show how we utilize these features in our joint model. The joint model is an extension of our previous work[8]. In the following, we will propose the principle of this diffusion-aware model and explain the parameters. We divide this joint model into several parts for introduction. In the first place , we propose the diffusion level decomposition strategy in the joint model. We then introduce the method incorporating all diffusion based explicit features. Finally, we introduce the collaborative ranking methods for model training.

3.2.1 Diffusion level decomposition

Our previous model[8] improves traditional collaborative filtering by decomposing the latent factor of items. It works well especially when the latent factor of words and publishers are very closed to the latent factor of items. However, our previous model loses a lot of information from the perspective of diffusion. When we need to recommend an item to a user, it is highly related to who have adopted the same or similar items. It leads to a great influence from the past users who have adopted this item. For example, the decision of a user to adopt an item will be influenced by his friends who have already adopted. From the view of diffusion graph and collaborative filtering, if a user adopts an item, the latent factor of this user should be very similar to the users who have already adopted the item in the past. If a user adopts an item, we decompose the latent factor of a user into a combination of latent factors of similar users, to get the following factorization model:

$$\hat{y}_{u,i} = bias + \left(p_u^T + \sum_{s \in C_i} \alpha_s p_s^T \right) q_i \quad (8)$$

Here bias denotes any form of possible bias, C_i is the cascade of tweet i in the past, p_s represents the latent factor of each infected user in C_i and α_s denotes the weight parameter of each user in the cascade. As the influence of people who have adopted the information differs from each other, the weight α_s is usually different for each C_i. For instance, the publisher of an information and the neighbours are usually the most important influencers to a user whom we want to recommend item to.

In many cases, if we want to select part of users in cascade as the influencers, we can make α_s of the other users equal 0. In the final joint model, we make $\alpha_s = 1$ if and only if user s is the direct sender of user i. That's to say we only use the user who delivers the information instead of all users who have adopted the information in the past. The most important reason is that we found users are usually influenced by their closest users in the cascade. This observation makes sense in many social networks such as Twitter and Sina Weibo. The direct sender of the information in a cascade is the followee even the friend of user i who is particular in the cascade. While the rest of users in a cascade usually have less relationship with the user i.

This decomposition strategy matches our intuition well. Firstly, it gets more opinions at diffusion level, which helps collaborative filtering based methods get better performance. What's more, it overcomes the problem of data scarcity for analyzing users. The latent factor of an unknown user can be estimated from the infective in the past. Moreover, this model not only considers the details inside a node but also leverages the global dynamics of diffusion graph, which unifies the recommendation and diffusion process together.

3.2.2 *Explicit features of diffusion*

Besides the latent factors, all the features of the diffusion tree shown in 3.1 are considered in this part. These features directly measure whether an information will be accepted. We use a linear combination of these features to get the bias prediction:

$$\hat{y}_{u,i} = \sum_j b_j \gamma_j^d \tag{9}$$

, where b is a weight parameter vector and γ^d is a diffusion explicit feature we extracted.

Combining two strategies shown above, we get the final joint model as following:

$$\hat{y}_{u,i} = \sum_j b_j \gamma_j^d + \left(p_u^T + \sum_{s \in C_i} \alpha_s p_s^T\right)\left(\frac{1}{Z}\sum_{w_j \in T_i} q_{w_j} + \alpha d_{p(i)}\right) \tag{10}$$

, where T_i is the term set of tweet i, Z is the normalization term for features and $d_{p(i)}$ is a latent factor of the publisher of tweet i.

3.2.3 *Model training*

Ranking-oriented personalized recommendation has attracted much attention in recent years [39, 29, 22, 33]. To adapt to the scenario that rank results of items are presented to users, the idea of ranking-oriented methods is more natural and better than the traditional collaborative filtering methods which aims at predicting the ratings of users [21]. Most of these methods take advantages of the learning to rank techniques [26, 12] to optimize the final ranking criterion for personalized recommendation results.

Under the scenario of social update recommendation, we also introduce optimizing the ranking criterion and collaborative ranking for personalized tweet recommendation. Collaborative ranking is a ranking version of collaborative filtering and provides item ranking results according to relative preference rather than user rating estimation. The collaborative ranking method we used here is an extension of the latent factor model with ranking optimization criterion. In the latent factor model, each user u and item i have a low dimensional representation $p_u \in R^d$ and $q_i \in R^d$ in the latent feature space. The rating score is predicted by measuring the affinity between user and item:

$$\hat{y}_{u,i} = \mu + b_u + b_i + p_u^T q_i \tag{11}$$

Where y is the predicted preference of user u for item i. μ is the overall average rating, and b_u and b_i are user bias and item bias on rating score.

To adapt to the scenario of tweet ranking, we modify the model for the collaborative ranking setting according to ranking optimization criterion. Give a user u and two items k and h the pairwise ranking model for preference is defined as follows:

$$P(r(k) > r(h)|u) = \frac{1}{1 + e^{-(\hat{y}_{u,k} - \hat{y}_{u,h})}} \tag{12}$$

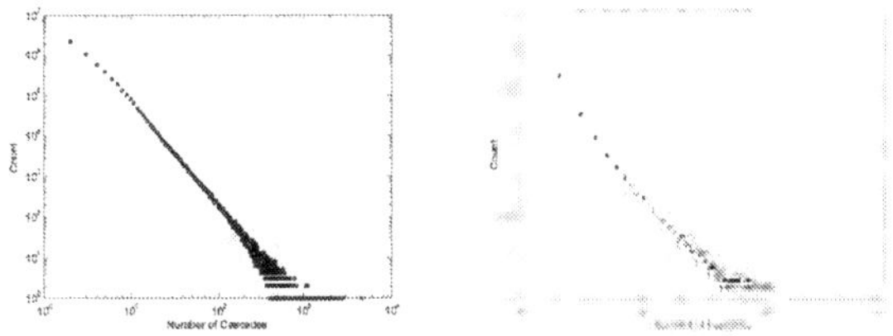

(a) Cascade count distribution over cascade size in Sina Weibo (b) Cascade count distribution over cascade size in Twitter

Figure 2: Overview of the dataset

, where $\hat{y}_{u,k}$ is the predicted preference of user u for tweet k, r is short notation for rank order. Equation 12 models the probability of item pairs' rank orders for a given user. We can get preference pair of items for a given user by assuming a user prefer the tweets he retweeted to the rest of tweets. Formally, we define rank preference set $\mathcal{D}$ as follows:

$$\mathcal{D} = \{< u, k, h > | k \in Re(u), h \notin Re(u)\} \tag{13}$$

, where $Re(u)$ is the set of tweets user u retweeted. Because the number of possible choices of negative sample h is large, we use sampling techniques to get negative samples in the training procedure. To learn the model, we maximize the log-likelihood over the $\mathcal{D}$ to estimate parameters. The maximizing procedure is converted to solve the objective below:

$$\min \sum_{<u,k,h> \in \mathcal{D}} \ln\left(1 + e^{-(\hat{y}_{u,k} - \hat{y}_{u,h})}\right) + \text{regularization} \tag{14}$$

L2 regularization is used as the default choice of regularization term. It can be considered as involving the prior probability for model parameters in a Bayesian view.

4. EXPERIMENTS

4.1 Dataset

We evaluate our model in two datasets, Sina Weibo and Twitter. Sina Weibo is the most popular social network in China. Just like posting tweets, users of Sina Weibo share their updates by posting weibos. The data of Sina Weibo is downloaded from WISE 2012 Challenge. We randomly select users who posted more than 1000 weibos. After randomly selecting 11786 qualified users, we got 36311395 weibos in our database. We then randomly split these weibos into training set with possibility of 0.8 and test set with possibility of 0.2. Finally the dataset is split into a training set with 29054037 weibos and test set with 7257358 weibos. The forwarded weibos are regarded as positive samples and the others are negative samples in experiments. With one positive, we have another 20 negatives in both training set and test set. Figure 2(a) shows the real cascade size with count of cascades in Sina Weibo dataset. From the figure, we can see that most of the cascades are very small, which makes diffusion-based recommendation more difficult.

To create the Twitter data set, we began with a randomly selected user and expanded the user-base by following their followers and followees' links. After following several steps of links, we got 28925 users in our base and downloaded all the statuses they had posted. The retweeted tweets are regarded as positive samples and the others are negative samples in experiments. To simulate the timeline of a user, we get one positive sample with another nineteen negative samples from the scanned tweets and sort them in chronological order. We performed standard data preprocessing including stop word removal and stemming on the raw text. Then we randomly split the samples into test set and training set with possibility of 0.2 into test set and possibility of 0.8 into training set. Each of them had about 199 messages on average. Finally the dataset is split into a training set with 4601966 tweets and test set with 1149389 tweets. Figure 2(b) shows the real cascade size in our dataset. Every tweet in cascade can be found in our base. From the figure, we can see that most tweets are not retweeted or are only retweeted a few times, which shows the sparsity of the dataset. It also shows the fact that most of the cascades are very small as the dataset of Sina Weibo.

Each dataset has its own characteristic. Among two datasets, Sina Weibo is more suitable for cascades evaluations as this dataset records the diffusion path of each weibo. While on Twitter, we can only guess the diffusion path by looking for which followee posted the tweet with same source tweet ID, as each tweet only records the source tweet ID but not the diffusion path. If more than one followees have posted a tweet with same source tweet ID, we can't make sure which one among them exactly delivered this tweet to the user. In this case, we assume that the user is influenced by all these followees. Though having the data of diffusion path, the dataset of Sina Weibo is lack of content data. The dataset of Twitter offsets this drawback and makes it possible to compare our joint model with the best baseline.

4.2 Evaluation Metric

In the evaluations, tweet ratings are considered binary in our scenario. Retweeting a tweet corresponds to a 1 rating, while not retweeting correspond to a 0 rating. We use Mean Average Precision (MAP), a popular rank evaluation method to evaluate the proposed model. For a single user, average precision is defined as the average of the standard $P@n$ values for all retweeted tweets:

$$AP = \frac{\sum_{n=1}^{N} P@n \times retweet(n)}{|R|} \tag{15}$$

, where n is the number of tweets; $|R|$ is the total number of retweeted tweets for the given user; $retweet(n)$ is a binary function to describe whether the user has retweeted the nth tweet in the result list. Finally, MAP can be obtained by averaging the AP values of all the users.

We also use P@n to evaluate our model. As there are limited positives in our Twitter dateset, we modify the standard P@n to show more obvious results. We define the P@n as following:

$$P@n = \frac{TP_n}{R_n} \tag{16}$$

, where TP_n is known as the number of true positives in top n tweets and R_n is number of retweeted Tweets in top n tweets.

4.3 Evaluations on Sina Weibo

4.3.1 Method Comparison

In this part, we compare our models to several others. As lots of baseline methods such as RankSVM, LDA and JointMF have been beaten by CTR model, we only list some important baselines here. The detailed implementations are listed below:

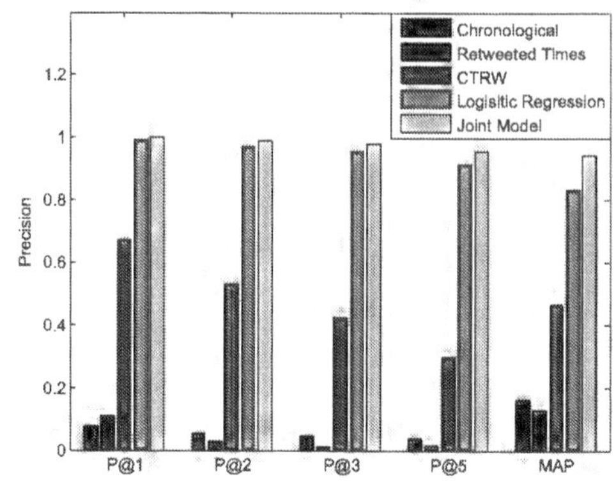

Figure 3: Methods Comparison in Sina Weibo

- CHRONOLOGICAL: The tweets are ranked in chronological order. Without any interventions by algorithms, this strategy indicates the default user experience on social networks.
- RETWEETED TIMES: Retweeted Times is an estimate of the popularity of a weibo in the history. Tweets with more retweeted times are more possibly to be liked by people. This ranking strategy ignores personalization and assumes the user's interests are the same as general public's.
- CTRW: Collaborative tweet ranking model integrating social relations and explicit features proposed in our previous work[8]. As the dataset of Sina Weibo doesn't have content information, here CTR model is degraded into a version without term factors. All the other parts are as same as CTR model. Stochastic gradient descent is used for parameter estimation. In experiments, the number of latent factors is set to 32, as the bigger number will bring little improvement on performance. The normalization term Z for term factors is set as $|T_i|^{\frac{1}{2}}$ according to the experimental results. As far as we known, this is one of the best models to solve this problem. We regard it as the most important baseline.
- LOGISTIC REGRESSION: Excluding the latent factors, we get the logistic regression model which utilizes all of cascades features listed in 3.1. We train logistic regression model on the training data and then evaluate the model by the test data. All the parameters use the default settings.
- JOINT MODEL: The joint model integrates collaborative filtering ,information diffusion factor, social factor and all other explicit features together. The joint model here is also degraded into the version without term factors like CTRW. The parameter configurations are as same as CTRW model.

Figure 3 shows the performance comparison results of each model mentioned above. Although lack of term factor, the performance of CTRW model are still better than

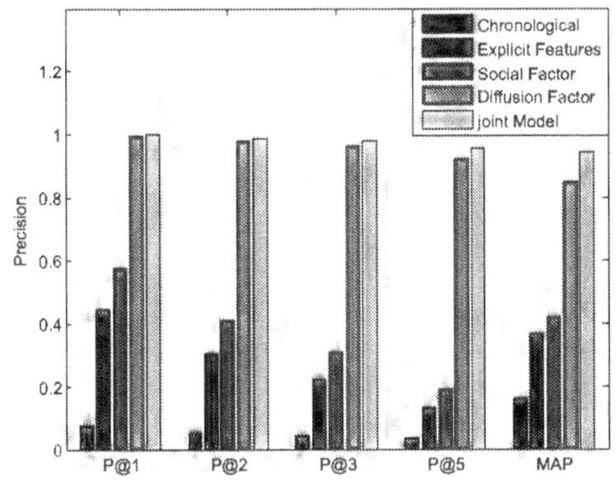

Figure 4: Components Comparison of the Joint Model in Sina Weibo

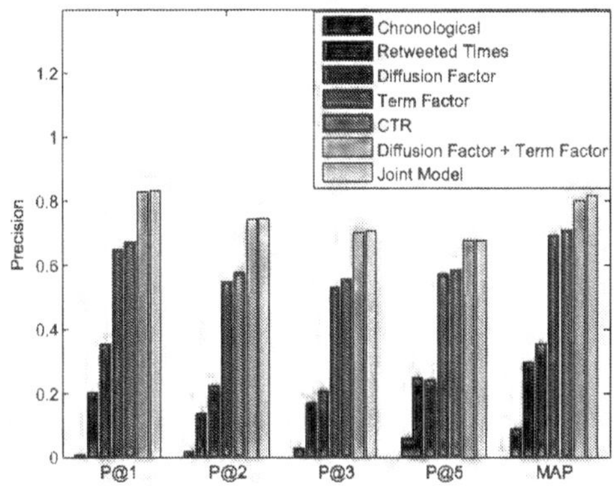

Figure 5: Evaluation results in Twitter

the chronological and retweeted times. The main reason is that the model of chronological and retweeted times don't take personalized knowledge into consideration. On the other hand, CTRW and the joint model gets the MAP value of 0.465351 and 0.945481 respectively. The performance of CTRW is much lower than the joint model. The most possible reason is that the joint model improves the personalized collaborative filtering by considering in the background of information diffusion. By leveraging collaborative filtering and information diffusion, the joint model captures users' interests both from the personal features inside a user node and the global dynamic in the diffusion graph. What's more, using all of diffusion features in this work, logistic regression model achieves the MAP value of 0.831853. The performance is much better than CTRW, but lower than the joint model. The joint model improves logistic regression model by combining collaborative filtering model. This result shows that the latent factor parts do bring improvement on the performance.

Also it is interesting to know which part of our joint model affords the most contribution. We evaluate each part of the joint model and show the effectiveness of each component in Figure 4. The latent factor number of all three components are set to 32. Here the chronological model and the joint model are used as references. From the figure, we can see that the MAP value of explicit features is 0.368272, which is better than the chronological model. It proves these explicit features are useful. The social factor achieves the MAP value of 0.420642, which is a little better than explicit features. The performance of diffusion factors is 0.851439, which stands out among all the components in the final model. This reflects the fact that the influence of the specific followees are quite enormous in social update recommendation. In addition, combining all three parts, the joint model achieves the best MAP value, which verifies our intuition that combining diffusion processes and collaborative filtering are meaningful.

4.4 Evaluations on Twitter

Although our model integrating diffusion process and collaborative filtering achieves good performance, the Sina Weibo dataset does not have contents. It is unknown whether our combined model can beat CTR model when considering content of the information. The dataset of Twitter overcomes this drawback. In this part, we evaluate our model on Twitter and compare our model with the complete CTR model and some other baselines. The parameters setting of CTR model is as same as CTRW which is shown in 4.3.1.

Figure 5 shows the performance comparison results of CTR, the joint model and some other models mentioned above. As what have showed in our previous work, it is not surprising that the performance of CTR model are better than the chronological and retweeted times. Unlike Sina Weibo, the performance of retweeted time is much better in the dataset of Twitter. This is due to the API of Twitter can exactly return the retweeted time of each tweet, while this value in Sina Weibo can only be estimated by counting the number of weibos in incomplete cascades. On the other hand, CTR and the joint model gets the MAP value of 0.709184 and 0.809394 respectively. The performance of CTR is lower than the joint model. This shows the result that our joint model can still beat CTR when considering the influence of social content in the meantime.

We also compare the term factor and diffusion factor in this graph. The diffusion factor and term factor achieves the MAP value of 0.355297 and 0.691963 respectively. The performance of diffusion factor is lower than the term factor. The most probable reason is that the dataset of Twitter is not suitable for cascades evaluation. As explained in 4.1, we can't get the exact information sender and diffusion path in Twitter. Another reason is that there are 3080 weibos for each user in Sina Weibo dataset on average, while only 199 tweets in Twitter. The diffusion part of the joint model may not be sufficiently trained in Twitter. On the other hand, this may be also caused by the fact that the preference of the users to the tweets are mainly determined by the contents of the tweets instead of who delivers the information. However, the performance of the term factors can be greatly improved by combining diffusion factor, which still verifies our intuition that information diffusion modeling and collaborative filtering capture different kind of characteristics in personalized social update recommendation.

5. CONCLUSION AND FUTURE WORK

Information diffusion modeling and collaborative filtering on social networks are highly related. In this paper, we propose a plenty of meaningful diffusion features which capture the characteristics of diffusion processes. What's more, we introduce a joint model leveraging collaborative filtering and information diffusion. Our approach both takes the advantages of information diffusion characteristics and collaborative filtering. Experiments on two real-world datasets show that the diffusion part of our model achieves good performance and our joint model outperforms several baseline methods.

One of our future work is to take time into consideration. The time information can help recommendation system to recommend right thing at right time, which makes the recommendation more suitable. Also it can make diffusion prediction more accurate considering when and where will a specific information flow to. Since the framework of our model is generic, it will be convenient to incorporate other information.

Another interesting issue is to solve cold start problem. New users or inactive users usually have few information for our methods to detect their interests. One possible approach is to transfer the actions of users from other domains. For instance, users who are not active in Twitter may be active in Facebook. Thus the actions of users in Facebook may help improving the recommendation in Twitter.

6. REFERENCES

[1] A. Anagnostopoulos, R. Kumar, and M. Mahdian. Influence and correlation in social networks. In *SIGKDD*, 2008.

[2] S. Aral, L. Muchnik, and A. Sundararajan. Distinguishing influence-based contagion from homophily-driven diffusion in dynamic networks. *PNAS*, 2009.

[3] E. Bakshy, D. Eckles, R. Yan, and I. Rosenn. Social influence in social advertising: evidence from field experiments. In *EC*, 2012.

[4] E. Bakshy, J. Hofman, W. Mason, and D. Watts. Everyone's an influencer: quantifying influence on twitter. In *WSDM*, 2011.

[5] J. Bennett and S. Lanning. The netflix prize. In *Proceedings of KDD Cup and Workshop*, 2007.

[6] M. Cha, A. Mislove, and K. Gummadi. A measurement-driven analysis of information propagation in the flickr social network. In *WWW*, 2009.

[7] J. Chen, R. Nairn, L. Nelson, M. Bernstein, and E. Chi. Short and tweet: experiments on recommending content from information streams. In *CHI*, 2010.

[8] K. Chen, T. Chen, G. Zheng, O. Jin, E. Yao, and Y. Yu. Collaborative personalized tweet recommendation. In *SIGIR*, 2012.

[9] D. Crandall, D. Cosley, D. Huttenlocher, J. Kleinberg, and S. Suri. Feedback effects between similarity and social influence in online communities. In *SIGKDD*, 2008.

[10] P. Cui, F. Wang, S. Liu, M. Ou, S. Yang, and L. Sun. Who should share what?: item-level social influence prediction for users and posts ranking. In *SIGIR*, 2011.

[11] A. Das, M. Datar, A. Garg, and S. Rajaram. Google news personalization: scalable online collaborative filtering. In *WWW*, 2007.

[12] P. Donmez, K. Svore, and C. Burges. On the local optimality of lambdarank. In *SIGIR*, 2009.

[13] M. Götz, J. Leskovec, M. McGlohon, and C. Faloutsos. Modeling blog dynamics. In *ICWSM*, 2009.

[14] A. Goyal, F. Bonchi, and L. Lakshmanan. Learning influence probabilities in social networks. In *WSDM*, 2010.

[15] D. Gruhl, R. Guha, D. Liben-Nowell, and A. Tomkins. Information diffusion through blogspace. In *WWW*, 2004.

[16] I. Guy, N. Zwerdling, I. Ronen, D. Carmel, and E. Uziel. Social media recommendation based on people and tags. In *SIGIR*, 2010.

[17] S. Hill, F. Provost, and C. Volinsky. Network-based marketing: Identifying likely adopters via consumer networks. *Statistical Science*, 2006.

[18] L. Hong, R. Bekkerman, J. Adler, and B. Davison. Learning to rank social update streams. In *SIGIR*, 2012.

[19] L. Hong, R. Bekkerman, J. Adler, and B. D. Davison. Learning to rank social update streams. In *SIGIR*, 2012.

[20] M. Jamali and M. Ester. Trustwalker: a random walk model for combining trust-based and item-based recommendation. In *SIGKDD*, 2009.

[21] Y. Koren. Factorization meets the neighborhood: a multifaceted collaborative filtering model. In *SIGKDD*, 2008.

[22] Y. Koren and J. Sill. Ordrec: an ordinal model for predicting personalized item rating distributions. In *RecSys*.

[23] K. Koroleva, H. Krasnova, and O. Günther. Stop spamming me!-exploring information overload on facebook. In *AMCIS*, 2010.

[24] D. Lazer, A. Pentland, L. Adamic, S. Aral, A. Barabasi, D. Brewer, N. Christakis, N. Contractor, J. Fowler, M. Gutmann, et al. Life in the network: the coming age of computational social science. *Science (New York, NY)*, 2009.

[25] J. Leskovec, L. Adamic, and B. Huberman. The dynamics of viral marketing. *EC*, 2006.

[26] P. Li, C. Burges, and Q. Wu. Learning to rank using classification and gradient boosting. In *NIPS*, 2007.

[27] D. Liben-Nowell and J. Kleinberg. Tracing information flow on a global scale using internet chain-letter data. *PNAS*, 2008.

[28] G. Linden, B. Smith, and J. York. Amazon. com recommendations: Item-to-item collaborative filtering. *Internet Computing, IEEE*, 2003.

[29] N. Liu and Q. Yang. Eigenrank: a ranking-oriented approach to collaborative filtering. In *SIGIR*, 2008.

[30] H. Ma, H. Yang, M. Lyu, and I. King. Sorec: social recommendation using probabilistic matrix factorization. In *CIKM*, 2008.

[31] M. McPherson, L. Smith-Lovin, and J. Cook. Birds of a feather: Homophily in social networks. *Annual review of sociology*, 2001.

[32] S. Myers, C. Zhu, and J. Leskovec. Information diffusion and external influence in networks. In *SIGKDD*, 2012.

[33] S. Rendle, C. Freudenthaler, Z. Gantner, and L. Schmidt-Thieme. Bpr: Bayesian personalized ranking from implicit feedback. *UAI*, 2009.

[34] S. Rendle, Z. Gantner, C. Freudenthaler, and L. Schmidt-Thieme. Fast context-aware recommendations with factorization machines. In *SIGIR*, 2011.

[35] D. Romero, B. Meeder, and J. Kleinberg. Differences in the mechanics of information diffusion across topics: Idioms, political hashtags, and complex contagion on twitter. In *WWW*, 2011.

[36] X. Song, Y. Chi, K. Hino, and B. Tseng. Information flow modeling based on diffusion rate for prediction and ranking. In *WWW*, 2007.

[37] E. Sun, I. Rosenn, C. Marlow, and T. Lento. Gesundheit! modeling contagion through facebook news feed. In *ICWSM*, 2009.

[38] J. Tang, J. Sun, C. Wang, and Z. Yang. Social influence analysis in large-scale networks. In *SIGKDD*, 2009.

[39] M. Weimer, A. Karatzoglou, Q. Le, A. Smola, et al. Cofirank-maximum margin matrix factorization for collaborative ranking. In *NIPS*, 2007.

[40] S. Yang, B. Long, A. Smola, N. Sadagopan, Z. Zheng, and H. Zha. Like like alike: joint friendship and interest propagation in social networks. In *WWW*, 2011.

[41] M. Ye, X. Liu, and W. Lee. Exploring social influence for recommendation: a generative model approach. In *SIGIR*, 2012.

Recommending Branded Products from Social Media

Yongzheng Zhang
eBay Inc.
2065 Hamilton Ave
San Jose, CA, USA 95125
ytzhang@ebay.com

Marco Pennacchiotti
eBay Inc.
2065 Hamilton Ave
San Jose, CA, USA 95125
mpennacchiotti@ebay.com

ABSTRACT

E-commerce companies are increasingly encouraging their users to connect to social media venues such as Facebook and Pinterest. The main strategic goal of such social connections is to boost user interaction and adoption on social media. However only a few efforts have been focused so far on leveraging users' social profiles to personalize the e-commerce experience and to recommend products of interest. In this paper, we start exploring this topic by investigating if a user's social media profile can be used to predict and recommend what type of products and what brands the social user is more likely to buy. More specifically, we study the correlation between the brands liked by the user on social media sites and those purchased on an e-commerce site. We then leverage these correlations in a brand prediction system, showing that social media can be effectively used to recommend branded products when user-user collaborative filtering techniques are used.

Categories and Subject Descriptors

K.4.4 [**Computers and Society**]: Electronic Commerce; H.3.4 [**Information Storage and Retrieval**]: Systems and Software—*Information networks*; H.3.5 [**Information Storage and Retrieval**]: Online Information Services; I.2.6 [**Artificial Intelligence**]: Learning

General Terms

Algorithms, Design, Experimentation

Keywords

E-commerce, recommender systems, brands recommendation, social media, social commerce

1. INTRODUCTION

In recent years many e-commerce companies such as eBay and Amazon have been moving into the social commerce domain by allowing users to interact with social media sites (e.g. Facebook). The main strategic goal of social media interaction is to provide users with a more engaging and social experience, thus increasing user retention and adoption. Such interactions are typically made possible by dedicated API services that connect a user's social media and e-commerce accounts. For example, eBay users can connect to their Facebook account, thus sharing with eBay the set of liked pages and other basic social information.

The social media profile information may be used by the e-commerce companies for social-driven applications. Some typical examples of these applications comprehend sharing purchases and "likes" with social media friends and social gifting. However, e-commerce companies have surprisingly not fully developed technologies to leverage social media information to improve product recommendation and to better predict users' purchase behaviors. Such technologies could not only help improve recommendation for existing e-commerce users, but also and more importantly solve the *cold start* problem, i.e. providing an engaging and personalized experience to new users.

In this paper we show that social media information alone, namely Facebook "likes" and user demographics, provide useful information for recommending personalized branded products. We explore several unsupervised algorithms showing that social recommendation works best in a two-stage setting. First, domains of interests (e.g. fashion) are inferred for each user [25]. Then, the user is recommended brands from the domains of interest using collaborative filtering techniques.

1.1 Problem Statement

We deal with the problem of recommending branded products to social media users. More specifically, we aim at predicting which brands (e.g. *Nike*, *Coach*) the user will buy using solely information derived from the social network. Such a recommendation system would help in several practical scenarios, including: (1) build a *cold start* recommender system, by providing branded product recommendations to social media users who join the e-commerce website as new users and opt to connect to their social media accounts; (2) improve existing product recommendation algorithms by providing social priors; and (3) provide e-commerce companies (e.g. eBay) with tools for targeted social media campaigns.

We choose Facebook as the social network, and eBay as the e-commerce website. We focus on the restricted set of Facebook information that users are typically required to share with the e-commerce website when they connect

RECSYS '13, October 12 - 16 2013, Hong Kong, China
Copyright 2013 ACM 978-1-4503-2409-0/13/10 ...$15.00.
http://dx.doi.org/10.1145/2507157.2507170.

to their social accounts: demographic information and the pages that they have liked on Facebook. As regards the set of brands we want to predict, we use a list of 4,445 brands included in the eBay database.

The paper has two main goals. The first goal is to explore if brands liked on Facebook correlate to brands purchased on eBay. The second goal is to leverage these correlations to recommend branded products using a user-user collaborative filtering system.

1.2 Main Contributions

Our paper has the following main contributions:

- We provide an extensive analysis of user purchase behaviors on branded products and Facebook information over a dataset of 9,398 users. We show that a subset of Facebook features correlates with purchase behaviors with statistical significance.
- Building on the category prediction system presented in our previous work [25], we build and evaluate a brand recommender system that uses Facebook information alone. We show that the recommendation task can be successfully solved with promising accuracy.

To our knowledge this is the first work that systematically analyzes the correlation between brands in social media profiles and brands purchase behaviors on e-commerce websites and that implements a brand recommendation system based on social information.

The rest of the paper is organized as follows: Section 2 reviews relevant previous work. Section 3 reports various statistics of our dataset. In Section 4 we describe different algorithms for recommending branded products from social media information. We present experimental results for these algorithms in Section 5. Finally, Section 6 concludes our work and describes future research directions.

2. RELATED WORK

2.1 Product Recommendation

Recommender systems have been widely studied in the past [17, 5, 18, 13, 7] and applied to various domains. E-commerce is a typical application for these systems, where they are used to predict or recommend product purchases. Two main techniques are most used: collaborative filtering and content-based.

Collaborative Filtering Methods. The underlying assumption of collaborative filtering methods is that users who carry similar characteristics tend to like similar products. In user-user systems, users are typically represented in a vector space which summarizes their characteristics (e.g. demographics, purchased products, review scores assigned to products). These systems suggest new products to a user by selecting a set of products that similar users have bought or reviewed in the past, but the user has not [21]. Sarwar et al. [19] apply nearest neighbor collaborative filtering for recommending purchases and predicting movie ratings, showing that dimensionality reduction techniques solve scaling issues on large-data without losing accuracy. Some studies [18, 13] have focused on the problem of *sparsity*.

Item-Item collaborative filtering, on the other hand, makes product recommendations directly based on users' past behaviors on e-commerce websites. Sarwar et al. [20] propose a system that models item to item relationships and demonstrate that such systems deliver good quality recommendations in sparse data situations. The item-item method is also promising for incremental modeling and has big performance gain over user-user modelling.

In this paper, we apply the k nearest neighbor algorithm similar to [19] to the brand recommendation task. Our system explicitly integrates collaborative filtering techniques in the feature selection phase. Our selection method for Facebook likes is inspired by model-based approaches to collaborative filtering discussed among others by Breese et al. [4].

Content-based Methods. In contrast to collaborative filtering methods, content-based methods often utilize the vast overload of information on the web, such as product reviews, customer opinions, and social media (e.g. blogs, tweets) to directly make product recommendations. In recent years, such systems have become more popular. Wietsma and Ricci [23] propose a system that structures product reviews to help rate and recommend products in a mobile decision aid scenario. Aciar et al. [2] develop a recommender system based on consumer product reviews. The authors apply text mining techniques to extract useful information from review comments and then define an ontology to translate the review information into a form suitable for utilization by a recommendation system. Sen et al. [22] use users' tag preferences to predict movie preferences and demonstrate that such content-based systems are more effective than collaborative filtering methods.

2.2 Social Media Recommendation

Recommendation on social media is a fairly new topic. Most work focuses on suggesting interesting content items (e.g. URLs, pictures, posts) or new friends. Social recommender systems differ from classical ones in that they often leverage existing social relations to boost the recommendations.

Though some interest has focused on collaborative filtering [9], most popular are **content-based methods.** These systems assume that the content that users share on the social network reflects their own interests, thus recommending new items that are similar to their own shared content [16, 15]. Abel et al. [1] represent users by a frequency vector of the hashtags and entities that they mention in their tweets. A similar vector is built for URLs shared in Twitter by analyzing the content of their links. Users are then recommended URLs whose vector is most similar to theirs. Similarly, Chen et al. [6] represent users with the bag-of-words of all terms of their tweets, and the URLs with the terms of the tweets that mention them. Unlike these methods, we do not have access to the social content (e.g. Facebook posts) due to the current scope of eBay's Facebook Connect.

Community-based methods make the assumption that the content coming from a user's friends or authoritative users is more likely to be interesting for a user than the rest. This assumption is usually combined with content-based and collaborative filtering approaches. Yan et al. [24] select personalized tweets using random-walks on a graph that joins the user's friends and tweets. The walk is bootstrapped by selecting with higher probability the tweets whose content is similar to what was previously posted by the user. Jamali and Ester [12] also use a random-walk approach, but they integrate collaborative filtering instead of content-based techniques to estimate the probability of a graph transition.

Jiang et al. [14] combine user topic preferences and social influence into a probabilistic matrix factorization model, recommending items that are both topically similar to the previous user's preferences and authored by people who are trusted by the user. Community-based systems show better performance with respect to purely content-based and collaborative filtering methods. In our work we cannot use community-based techniques since we do not have access to the social graph.

2.3 Social Networks and Purchase Behaviors

Some research has investigated the broader topic of how social network influences users in their purchases. Bhatt et al. [3] empirically demonstrate that a user's friends exercise 'peer pressure': if friends widely adopt a product, the user is more likely to buy it. Guo et al. [8] study the trading dynamics on the e-commerce social network Taobao. They show that buyers are more likely to purchase from sellers that friends in their network have already bought from (information passing). They prove that when a buyer has to decide from which seller to buy a product, the social network has a bigger influence on the decision than the sellers' ratings and the price. Similar findings are found in [10, 11].

All these studies assume that the e-commerce site and the social network are integrated into one platform (e.g. Taobao), or that the e-commerce site has holistic access to the social network. To the best of our knowledge, our work is the first to focus on a more practical and common scenario, where the system (e.g. e-commerce companies such as Amazon and eBay) has limited access to the social network information.

3. FACEBOOK-EBAY DATASET

In this paper we use a set of 9,398 eBay users that connected their account to the Facebook profile. The set is derived from a bigger set of 13,619 users described in [25], from which we select only those users who have liked and purchased at least one of 4,445 brands contained in the eBay database [1]. These brands are organized in nine eBay meta-categories[2] which refer to four different verticals, as shown in Table 1. Note that some brands may appear in multiple categories/verticals, e.g. *3M* appears both in the *Consumer Electronics* and in the *Home & Garden* meta-categories.

For each user in the dataset we select the brand pages that the user has liked on Facebook and we retain those brands that also appear in the eBay database. We also extract the items that the user bought on eBay, if the brand of the item is in the eBay database. For each user in the dataset we hence store the following information:

- List of Facebook likes and the associated Facebook category (for example *Starbucks* is in the Facebook category *Food / Beverage*).
- List of purchased items with their associated brand.
- Demographic information (age, gender).

[1] As we shall see later in the paper, this constraint in practice is not a must have. Using the k nearest neighbor and collaborative filtering algorithms, brand recommendation can be done based on social media profile even when the user has not liked any brands.

[2] Complete eBay category structure is available at `http://www.ebay.com/sch/allcategories/all-categories`.

Table 1: Number of Brands in Each Meta-category.

Vertical	eBay meta-category	#Brands
Electronics	Cameras & Photo	207
	Cell Phones & Accessories	85
	Computers & Networking	523
	Consumer Electronics	304
Fashion	Clothing, Shoes & Accessories	3,419
	Health & Beauty	346
	Jewelry & Watches	298
Home	Home & Garden	602
Sports	Sporting Goods	441

Table 2: Statistics of Our Dataset.

Users	9,398
Brands	4,445
Facebook categories	214
Facebook pages	1,373,984
Facebook likes	4,165,690
eBay meta-categories	9
eBay branded purchases	174,190

Basic statistics for the final dataset are summarized in Table 2.

3.1 Distribution of Brands

Figure 1 reports the distribution of brand pages liked on Facebook for our users, i.e., it indicates how many users have liked a given number of brands. The function is a perfect power law, meaning that most users like few brands, and few users like many brands (max is 373, average is 12, and the median is 6 brands). While not surprising, this indicates that our task is inherently hard: for most users we have to rely on scarce Facebook information for recommending brands for purchases.

Figure 2 reports the distribution of likes for brands, i.e., it indicates how many brands have a given number of likes. The function follows a power law with only a few outlier fluctuations, showing that most of the brands have few likes and only a few brands receive many likes (max is 2814, average is 38, and the median is 5 likes). The fact that users' likes are so sparse poses a great challenge for our recommendation task when likes are used as features.

As regards user purchase behaviors on eBay, the distribution of purchased brands is also power law, as shown in Figure 3, indicating that most users tend to buy a limited number of brands (max is 222, average is 8, and the median is 5 brands).

Similar to what we found out in our previous study, we notice that our dataset has a prevalence of women (64.9% of all users) and of people aged between 25 and 44 (57% of all users). In Section 3.2 we will explore if users in different demographic groups have distinctive purchase behaviors.

3.2 Demographic Differences

In this section we explore if different gender/age groups have peculiar preferences when they buy branded products on eBay or like brands on Facebook.

We first compute for each group the percentage of users who buy in each brand, and then perform a t-test. Results of the t-test for the women/men distinction show that the

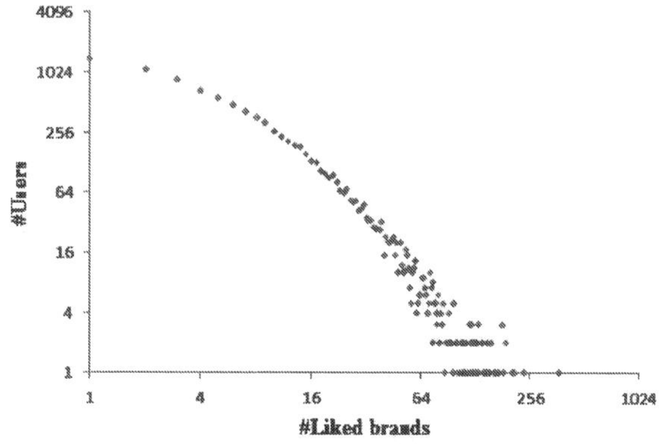

Figure 1: Distribution of liked brands for users.

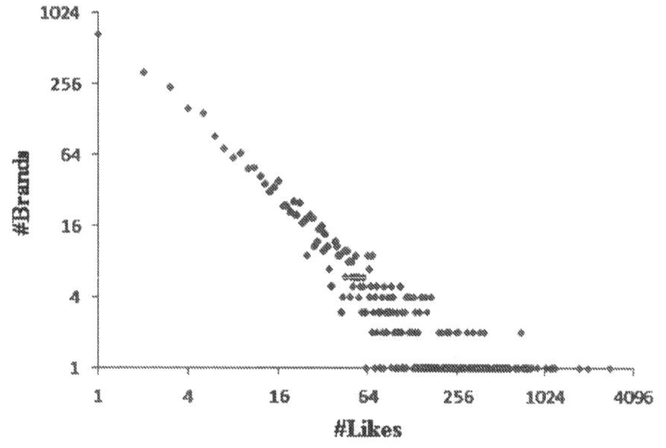

Figure 2: Distribution of likes for brands.

difference in percentage is statistically significant[3] for a large set of brands. Women buy significantly more than men in 795 brands with a statistical significance of $p = 0.99$. The most female-polarized brands, e.g. *Chanel* and *Cuisinart*, are mostly in *Fashion* and *Home* verticals. Men buy significantly more than women in 104 brands, e.g. *Nokia* and *Wilson*, mostly in *Electronics* and *Sports* verticals. For the remaining 3546 brands we do not observe any significant difference. These results show that purchase behavior strongly varies across genders.

Differences across age groups are less strong. For example, only 600 brands show a significant difference between age groups 25-34 and 45-54. In general we observe that young people (25-34) tend to be prevalent in *Sports*, while older people (45+) are prevalent in *Electronics* and *Home* brands.

The overall demographic study suggests that gender and age are important signals for recommending brands for social media users. In Section 4.2.2 we will explain how this information is utilized.

We also study gender and age differences on Facebook. Similarly to purchase behaviors, we observe the same demographic differences. It is worth noting that these results refer to our dataset of 9K Facebook-connected eBay users, and may not generalize to the general population of eBay users or to the whole e-commerce spectrum.

[3]We do 10-fold cross-validation where percentage difference in each fold is taken as a sample of size 10.

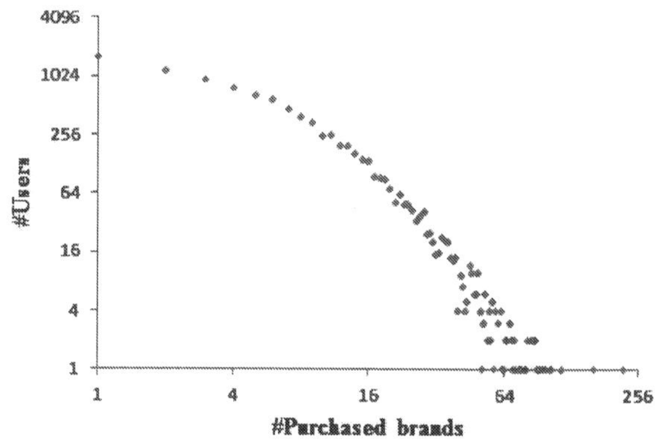

Figure 3: Distribution of purchased brands for users.

3.3 Focus on Purchases and Likes

In this section we explore how focused users are when they purchase from e-commerce web sites (*purchase focus*) and when they like brands on Facebook (*like focus*).

As regards *purchase focus*, let us represent with $P(u)_k$ the ranked probability with which a user u buys from the kth favorite brand. This rank is obtained by first estimating the probability $P(u, b)$ of a user u buying in each brand b, and by successively ranking the probabilities:

$$P(u, b) = \frac{purc(u, b)}{purc(u, B)} \tag{1}$$

where $purc(u, b)$ is the number of purchases of u for brand b, and B is the set of all brands.

To have an estimation of the overall purchase focus we average the $P(u)_k$ across all users U. We thus obtain the probability distribution for the event of an average user buying in the top k ranked brands:

$$P(U)_k = \frac{1}{|U|} \cdot \sum_{u \in U} P(u)_k \tag{2}$$

The hypothesis of a chaotic world where a user buys randomly from different brands would be proved if the distribution was fitted by a uniform distribution. To check the fit, we apply the Kolmogorov-Smirnov (K-S) goodness-of-fit test. The result of the test shows that the hypothesis is rejected. As expected, users do not buy brands randomly.

More specifically, more than 45% of the times an average user buys from the first preferred brand and 18% of the times from the second preferred brand. The top 5 brands collectively account for about 85% of a user's purchases of branded products.

Similarly to the above, we also applied the K-S test to check the *like focus*. We again verified that users do not like brands on Facebook in a random function, and that they have a limited set of brands that they like: on average a Facebook user's most favorite category accounts for 49% of all liked brands, the second about 21%. The top 5 categories collectively account for about 92% of a user's liked brands on Facebook.

Overall, the results above prove that users express strong personal interests for certain brands on Facebook and are highly focused when purchasing branded products online.

Table 3: Examples of Correlated Brands.

Purchased brands	Liked brands	*pmi*
Victoria's Secret	Paul Frank	1.35
	Soda	1.32
	Designer Skin	1.29
	Too Faced	1.24
	Derek Heart	1.23
HTC	Sony Ericsson	1.62
	HTC	1.50
	Galaxy	1.17
	T-mobile	1.12
	Monster	1.10
Pottery Barn	Talbots	3.46
	Banana Republic	2.32
	MAC	1.84
	Bath & Body Works	1.61
	Vera Bradley	1.58
Nike	Supreme	3.02
	Air Jordan	2.67
	NBA	2.44
	59Fifty	2.17
	New Era	2.07

Note that the results reported for 'brands' in this section are in line with those reported in [25], where we showed that users are also very focused at the higher level of 'category' (e.g. Fashion, Electronics).

3.4 Correlation between Likes and Purchases

In this section we study the correlation between brands' pages liked on Facebook and brands purchased on eBay. At the end of the study we would expect that for example users who like many luxury handbag brands are likely to buy items from *Salvatore Ferragamo* or *Burberry* and alike.

Let us define two variables b_l and b_p: b_l is defined on the space of users who like brand b on Facebook; and b_p is the set of users who have bought at least one item in brand b on eBay. We compute association and predictability for pairs (b_l, b_p) using Pointwise Mutual Information (PMI), which measures the degree of association between two events. The higher the *pmi* score, the stronger the correlation. We estimate PMI as follows:

$$pmi(b_l, b_p) = \log \frac{|b_l, b_p| \cdot |U|}{|b_l| \cdot |b_p|} \qquad (3)$$

where $|b_l, b_p|$ is the number of users who have liked and purchased brand b; $|b_p|$ and $|b_l|$ are respectively the number of users liking and buying brand b; and $|U|$ is the total number of users. Table 3 reports the top five correlated brands for four example brands.

These results are very promising. The large number of discovered correlations suggests that purchased brands may be predicted and recommended by looking at the Facebook brands liked by the user[4]. We will discuss various algorithms to utilize user's liked brands on Facebook for recommendation in the next section.

[4]The HTC to HTC mapping indicates that many users who like HTC indeed buy HTC products.

4. BRAND RECOMMENDATION

In the previous section we have shown that users have focused behaviors when buying branded products online. We have also shown that basic information from Facebook (namely demographics and liked brands) have promising correlation with purchase behaviors. In this section we leverage this information to build a recommendation system, whose goal is to predict/recommend brands for purchases using Facebook likes and demographic information as sole features. This setting fits well a cold-start situation in which a social media user for the first time joins the e-commerce web site and shares the social media profile, and the web site wants to provide interesting recommendations from day zero.

Our system is a pipeline of two different modules. The first module selects a large set of candidate brands by exploring user interests at a general level. The second module applies accurate heuristics to select the final brands to recommend among those output brands from the fist module. The core intuition of the two-module pipeline is that applying the *Brand Selection Module* alone, i.e. without pre-filtering, would produce noisy and inaccurate results. Indeed, it often happens that Facebook users 'like' pages without a real interest. Our intuition is that these 'uninteresting' likes can be filtered out by selecting only pages that refer to the domain of passion of the user (*Log-Reg Module*). We describe the two modules here below in more details.

4.1 Logistic Regression Module

This module uses a Logistic Regression (LR) classifier to estimate the probability of a user buying in a specific eBay meta-category (e.g. *Sporting Goods*). The classifier uses as features the likes of the user and the demographic profile. Full details of the system are presented in [25]. For each user, the classifier outputs a purchase probability for each meta-category. In the current study, we use this output to pre-filter the brands to recommend in the second module by applying a threshold on the probability. For example, suppose that for a given user the classifier assigns 0.6 probability for the meta-category *Sporting Goods* and 0.1 for *Home & Garden*. Suppose also that we apply a probability threshold of 0.5. In this case, the module would output only brands from the *Sporting Goods* meta-category.

4.2 Brand Selection Module

This module applies specific strategies to select brands to recommend from the output of the Log-Reg module. In the rest of this section we present different strategies, ranging from simple heuristic methods to collaborative filtering approaches.

4.2.1 Baseline Selection

One reasonable and intuitive way to select brands to recommend is to rank all brands according to their *popularity*, i.e., the number of users in a training set who have bought products from the brand. Then the top brands will be recommended to all users in a testing set, without using any personalization. In our experiments we will refer to this strategy as B_1 and we will empirically recommend the top eight brands, because in our dataset users on average buy from eight brands.

Another naive baseline strategy uses the intuition that users buy what they like, i.e. the strategy selects the brands that the user has liked on Facebook. In the experiments we will refer to this strategy as B_2 and we will rank the selected brands using the popularity score described above.

4.2.2 KNN Selection

The K Nearest Neighbors (KNN) algorithm has been widely and successfully used in recommender systems in the past years (e.g. [19]). We here apply KNN by representing each user in a boolean vectorial space, where dimensions correspond to likes of Facebook pages. If a user likes a specific page the corresponding dimension is set to 1, otherwise to 0. Note that by including all likes, and not only brand likes, allows us to perform effective recommendations even for users who have not liked a brand, but still have many likes in other domains.

For each user, we find the top-k nearest neighbors by computing cosine similarity between the user and all other users. In our experiments we empirically set $k = 5$. Once the top-k neighbors are found we select the brands to recommend following either of the two strategies below:

Like-based KNN. In the first strategy, referred as L_{knn} in the experiments, we select and rank brands by performing a majority voting among the top-k neighbors' liked brands. For example if two of the top-k neighbors liked *Nike*, Nike will receive a score of two and will be ranked accordingly.

Purchase-based KNN. This strategy, referred as P_{knn} in the experiments, selects the brands that are most purchased by the top-k neighbors. More in detail, each brand purchased by any of the top-k neighbors is assigned the following score:

$$score(u, b) = \sum_{v \in topK(u)} cos(u, v) \cdot \frac{purch(v, b)}{purch(v, B)} \quad (4)$$

where $topK(u)$ is the set of top-k neighbors of user u; $cos(u, v)$ is the cosine similarity between the target user u and a user v; $purch(v, b)$ and $purch(v, B)$ are respectively the number of items from brand b bought by user v and the number of items from any brand bought by user v. This score gives a higher weight to brands that are most purchased by closest neighbors. In our experiment we empirically set $k = 5$.

4.2.3 Improving Recommendation with Related Brands

In this section we explore user-user collaborative filtering to improve the recall of the selection strategies proposed earlier in this section. Suppose that for a given user the top brand output from P_{KNN} is *Burberry*. Even though none of the top-k neighbors bought *Louis Vuitton* and *Prada*, it would make sense to recommend these two brands as well, as they target the same segment of users.

In order to capture this intuition, we compute a database of 'related brands', i.e. for each of the 4,445 brands in our dataset we discover the list of most related brands according to the purchase history on eBay, as follows.

We collect a dataset of all purchases of any of our 4,445 brands done by eBay users in 2012. This accounts for hundreds of millions of purchases done by tens of millions users. We then compute the relatedness between any pair of brands b_1 and b_2 using the Jaccard Index as follows:

$$rel(b_1, b_2) = \frac{|b_1 \cap b_2|}{|b_1 \cup b_2|} \quad (5)$$

Table 4: Summary of Recommendation Algorithms.

Algorithm	Recommendation
B_1	most popular brands purchased by users
B_2	brands liked by current user
L_{knn}	brands liked by k nearest neighbors
P_{knn}	brands purchased by k nearest neighbors
$B_1 + R$	most popular brands + related brands
$B_2 + R$	liked brands + related brands
$L_{knn} + R$	brands liked by knn + related brands
$P_{knn} + R$	brands purchased by knn + related brands

Table 5: Confusion Matrix of Purchased and Recommended Brands.

	Recommended	Not recommended
Purchased	tp: true positive	fn: false negative
Not purchased	fp: false positive	tn: true negative

where $|b_1 \cap b_2|$ is the set of users who have purchased both brands and $|b_1 \cup b_2|$ is the set of users who have purchased either brand or both.

The relatedness scores are then normalized to the $[0, 1]$ interval by dividing by the maximum score. Finally, brands that are highly related to the original selected brands are also included in the recommendation set using the following policy: the top-5 related brands are selected for each original brand unless the relatedness score is below 0.30 (i.e. the score is less than 30% of the top-related brand's score). These parameters have been heuristically selected for our experiments. We do not report the details of the tuning process for lack of space. As an example, the top 10 related brands for *Burberry* are: *Gucci*, *Prada*, *Louis Vuitton*, *Dolce Gabbana*, *Tory Burch*, *Fendi*, *Chanel*, *Salvatore Ferragamo*, *Hugo Boss*, and *Lacoste*.

In summary, the brand selection module provides four different selection methods (two baselines and two KNN-based algorithms) and one method to expand the set of recommended brands. Table 4 summarizes the possible combinations of these systems and the notation that will be used in the experimental section.

5. EXPERIMENTS AND EVALUATION

5.1 Experimental Setup

As for gold standard dataset for the experiments we use the 9,398 eBay users who connected to Facebook, as described in Section 3. For each user u the task is to recommend brands that users have actually bought.

As for evaluation measures we use **Precision** and **Recall** to evaluate the recommendation models. Precision measures the fraction of recommended brands that are actually purchased by the user, and recall measures the fraction of purchased brands that are recommended by the algorithm. F_1 combines the two. Given the confusion matrix in Table 5, precision is defined as $P = \frac{tp}{tp+fp}$, recall is defined as $R = \frac{tp}{tp+fn}$, and $F_1 = \frac{2PR}{P+R}$.

We evaluate our models using 10-fold cross validation in order to reliably compute statistical significance values. For each fold we use 90% of the users as training and 10% as testing. We compute the above measures for each fold by averaging the measures over all testing users.

Table 6: Evaluation Results of Algorithms.

Algorithm	*Precision*	*Recall*	F_1	User%
B_1	0.137	0.231	0.172	100%
B_2	0.165	0.238	0.195	100%
L_{knn}	0.143	0.286	0.191	100%
P_{knn}	0.336†	0.410†	0.369†	100%
B_1+R	0.123	0.349†	0.182	100%
B_2+R	0.155	0.357†	0.216	100%
L_{knn}+R	0.138	0.428†	0.209	100%
P_{knn}+R	0.315†	0.582†	0.409†	100%
P_{knn}+R+LR(0.5)	0.407†	0.631†	0.495†	61.5%
P_{knn}+R+LR(0.8)	0.688†	0.739†	0.713†	15.9%

† indicates statistical significance at 0.95 level with respect to baseline methods B_1 and B_2.

5.2 Experimental Results

Table 6 presents the overall results of our experiments. The first eight rows of the table report results by using the brand selection module alone (Section 4.2), while the last two lines report results for the full pipeline that includes the logistic regression module (Section 4.1). This allows us to better study the effect of pre-filtering the user's domains of interest. The LR module is applied with two different probability threshold: 0.5 (the second last line in the table) and 0.8 (the last line in the table).

Results show that our **full pipeline** largely outperforms all other systems both in terms of precision and recall, at the cost of a lower user coverage, i.e. recommendation is provided only for those users that are inferred to have a high interest in a given meta-category. The decrease in user coverage is expected, and we argue that in practical settings it is not as relevant as precision and recall. Indeed, a production recommendation system mostly aims at providing accurate recommendations to a limited set of users than providing inaccurate recommendations to all users.

The **KNN algorithm** performs best in its P_{knn} configuration, i.e. when the recommendation comes from the brands purchased by the neighbors instead of their liked brands. P_{knn} is better than the baselines with statistical significance while L_{knn} is not. This underlines that purchase signals are much stronger than like signals, even when used indirectly as in this case.

Overall, all systems that integrate **related brands** are better than both baselines with statistical significance in terms of recall. The use of related brand proves successful in increasing the recall of the system, with a small (expected) cost in precision.

The experimental results show that both our intuitions are correct. From one side, we showed that a successful system for recommending brands and products from social media should integrate a pre-filtering stage, where the general interests of the users are inferred (e.g. Sport). Only then the social likes can provide useful and un-noised information. From the other side, we showed that user-user collaborative filtering is necessary to expand the recommendations, as social media information may be at times too sparse.

Demographics. Demographic information (gender and age) have been leveraged in the Logistic Regression module as features. As reported in our previous work [25] this improves the accuracy of the Regression model. However, we also tested the use of demographic information in the KNN-based brand selection models, by computing cosine similarity only across users in the same gender and age group, instead of all users. Results (not reported here for lack of space) show improvements both in precision and recall, though with no statistical significance.

5.2.1 *Logistic Regression Threshold*

In table 6 we reported results for the Logistic Regression model only at two specific thresholds, namely 0.5 and 0.8. Figure 4 and Figure 5 report the full spectrum of results for both user coverage and precision/recall at all levels of probability threshold.

The figures show that as the probability threshold increases, the number of qualified users drops significantly (Figure 4) while, as expected, both precision and recall increase substantially.

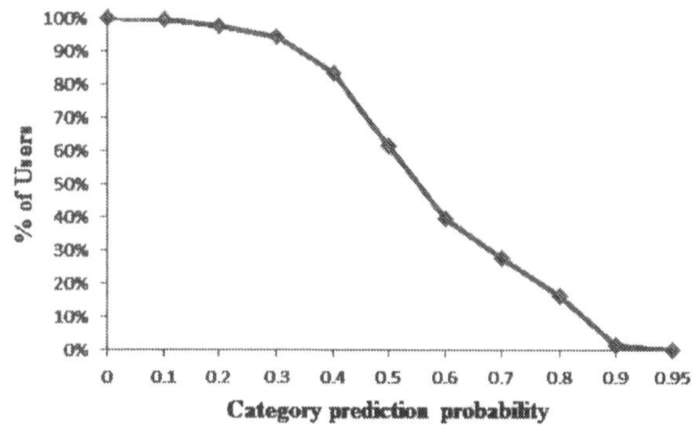

Figure 4: Percentage of users covered in evaluation.

When the threshold increases up to 70%, the number of users drops to 2570. The precision is 0.598, recall is 0.705, and F_1 is 0.647. This indicates that about 70.5% of users' purchased brands (almost 3 out 4) are captured and 59.8% of the recommendations (almost 3 out 5) are actually what users have bought. This result is very promising as 2570 / 9398 > 1/4, i.e. the recommendation algorithm is effective for more than a quarter of the users.

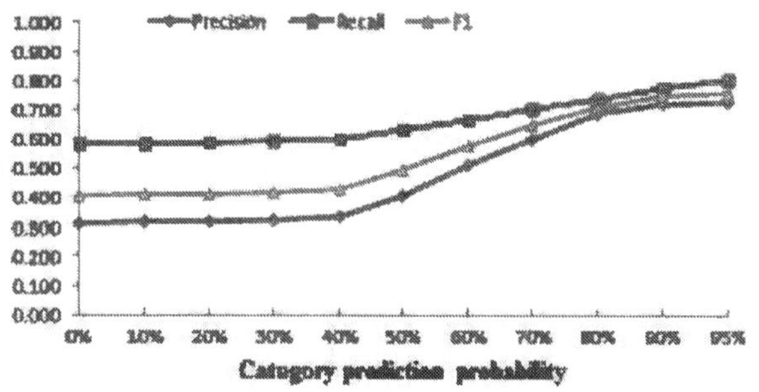

Figure 5: $P_{knn}+R$ using category prediction probability.

6. CONCLUSIONS

In this paper we studied interactions between social media profiles and purchase behaviors on e-commerce websites. We showed that there are significant correlations between social media information and online purchases at the brand level. We presented a two-stage pipeline system that uses Facebook likes for solving the task of branded products recommendation. Results on a large dataset of eBay users who connected to Facebook show that brands recommendation can be successfully accomplished using social media information alone. We also showed that pre-filtering based on broad user interests is necessary for achieving good performance and that user-user collaborative methods improve the recall of the system.

In the future we will explore several research directions, including the following: (1) we will integrate our models into production systems to offer a personalized experience for cold-start social media users, and to improve existing product recommendation systems that rely on purchase history; (2) we will extend our feature sets to include other types of features, such as clusters of likes automatically inferred using topic models; (3) we will investigate how to improve our method by focusing also on recommendation diversity; (4) finally, we will compare our algorithm to other state-of-the-art algorithms such as those based on matrix factorization.

To the best of our knowledge our study is the first attempt to predict e-commerce behaviors using only social media information. It is our hope that it will help and inspire e-commerce companies to develop better and new recommendation engines that leverage social media features, in a time when the issue of monetizing social media information is being more and more debated.

7. REFERENCES

[1] F. Abel, Q. Gao, G.-J. Houben, and K. Tao. Analyzing temporal dynamics in twitter profiles for personalized recommendations in the social web. In *WebSci'11 Conference Proceedings*, 2011.

[2] S. Aciar, D. Zhang, S. Simoff, and J. Debenham. Recommender system based on consumer product reviews. In *WI'06 Conference Proceedings*, pages 719–723, 2006.

[3] R. Bhatt, V. Chaoji, and R. Parekh. Predicting product adoption in large-scale social networks. In *CIKM'10 Conference Proceedings*, 2010.

[4] J. S. Breese, D. Heckerman, and C. Kadie. Empirical analysis of predictive algorithms for collaborative filtering. In *Proceedings of the 14th Conference on Uncertainty in Artificial Intelligence*, 1998.

[5] R. Burke. Hybrid recommender systems: Survey and experiments. *User Modeling and User-Adapted Interation*, 12(4):331–370, 2002.

[6] J. Chen, R. Nairn, L. Nelson, M. Bernstein, and E. Chi. Short and tweet: experiments on recommending content from information streams. In *CHI'10 Conference Proceedings*, 2010.

[7] M. D. Ekstrand, J. T. Riedl, and J. A. Konstan. Collaborative filtering recommender systems. *Foundations and Trends in Human-Computer Interaction*, 4(2), 2011.

[8] S. Guo, M. Wang, and J. Leskovec. The role of social networks in online shopping: information passing, price of trust, and consumer choice. In *ACM EC'11 Conference Proceeding*, pages 157–166, 2011.

[9] J. Hannon, M. Bennett, and B. Smyth. Recommending twitter users to follow using content and collaborative filtering approaches. In *ACM RecSys'10 Conference Proceedings*, pages 199–206, Barcelona, Spain, 2010.

[10] S. Hill, F. Provost, and C. Volinsky. Network-based marketing: Identifying likely adopters via consumer networks. *Statistical Science*, 21(2):256–276, 2006.

[11] R. Iyengar, S. Han, and S. Gupta. Do friends influence purchases in a social network? Working paper, Harvard Business School, 2009.

[12] M. Jamali and M. Ester. Trustwalker: a random walk model for combining trust-based and item-based recommendation. In *KDD'09 Conference Proceedings*, pages 397–406, 2009.

[13] D. Jannach. *Recommender Systems : an Introduction.* Cambridge University Press, 2011.

[14] M. Jiang, P. Cui, R. Liu, Q. Yang, F. Wang, W. Zhu, and S. Yang. Social contextual recommendation. In *CIKM'12 Conference Proceedings*, pages 45–54, 2012.

[15] M. Pennacchiotti and S. Gurumurthy. Investigating topic models for social media user recommendation. In *WWW'11 Conference Proceedings*, 2011.

[16] D. Ramage, S. Dumais, , and D. Liebling. Characterizing microblogs with topic models. In *AAAI ICWSM'10 Conference Proceedings*, 2010.

[17] P. Resnick and H. R. Varian. Recommender systems. *Special Issue of the Communications of the ACM*, 40(3), 1997.

[18] F. Ricci, L. Rokach, B. Shapira, and P. B. Kantor. Recommender systems handbook. *Media*, 54(3):217–253, 2011.

[19] B. Sarwar, G. Karypis, J. Konstan, and J. Riedl. Analysis of recommendation algorithms for e-commerce. In *EC'00 Conference Proceedings*, 2000.

[20] B. Sarwar, G. Karypis, J. Konstan, and J. Riedl. Item-based collaborative filtering recommendation algorithms. In *WWW'01 Conference Proceeding*, 2001.

[21] J. Schafer, J. Konstan, and J. Riedi. Recommender systems in e-commerce. In *ACM EC'99 Conference Proceedings*, 1999.

[22] S. Sen, J. Vig, and J. Riedl. Tagommenders: connecting users to items through tags. In *WWW'09 Conference Proceedings*, pages 671–680, 2009.

[23] R. T. A. Wietsma and F. Ricci. Product reviews in mobile decision aid systems. In *Proceedings of the PERMID*, pages 15–18, Munich, Germany, 2005.

[24] R. Yan, M. Lapata, and X. Li. Tweet recommendation with graph co-ranking. In *ACL'12 Conference Proceedings*, volume 1, 2012.

[25] Y. Zhang and M. Pennacchiotti. Predicting Purchase Behaviors from Social Media. In *WWW'13 Conference Proceedings*, Rio de Janeiro, Brazil, May 2013.

Top-N Recommendations from Implicit Feedback leveraging Linked Open Data

Vito Claudio Ostuni, Tommaso Di Noia, Eugenio Di Sciascio, Roberto Mirizzi
Polytechnic University of Bari – Via Orabona, 4 – 70125 Bari, Italy
{ostuni,mirizzi}@deemail.poliba.it, {t.dinoia,disciascio}@poliba.it

ABSTRACT

The advent of the **Linked Open Data** (LOD) initiative gave birth to a variety of open knowledge bases freely accessible on the Web. They provide a valuable source of information that can improve conventional recommender systems, if properly exploited. In this paper we present **SPrank**, a novel hybrid recommendation algorithm able to compute *top-N* item recommendations from implicit feedback exploiting the information available in the so called Web of Data. We leverage **DBpedia**, a well-known knowledge base in the LOD compass, to extract semantic *path-based* features and to eventually compute recommendations using a *learning to rank* algorithm.
Experiments with datasets on two different domains show that the proposed approach outperforms in terms of prediction accuracy several state-of-the-art *top-N* recommendation algorithms for implicit feedback in situations affected by different degrees of data sparsity.

Categories and Subject Descriptors

H.3.3 [**Information Systems**]: Information Search and Retrieval

Keywords

Hybrid Recommender System; Top-N Recommendations; Implicit Feedback; Learning to Rank; Linked Data; DBpedia

1. INTRODUCTION

Information overload in the current Web challenges users in their decision-making tasks. Recommender systems have become essential tools in assisting users to find what is relevant for them in increasingly complex information spaces. The *Linking Open Data* project [3] started as a community effort in 2007, and helped to produce billions of RDF[1] statements that are now published on the Web. The result of this initiative is a huge decentralized knowledge base, commonly known as the **Linked Open Data** (LOD) cloud, wherein each "piece of little knowledge" is enriched by links to related data. The development of a global information space consisting not only of linked documents but also of linked data has resulted in the emergence of the Web of Data as a subset of the World Wide Web.
With the increased availability of this freely available knowledge, there is a great interest in taking advantage of such information to improve the quality of conventional recommender systems. Although recommender systems leverage well established technologies and tools, new challenges arise when they exploit the huge amount of interlinked data coming from the Web of Data.
In the past, several works on *ontological recommender systems* have been proposed. These works introduced the usage of ontologies and semantic technologies to boost collaborative filtering (CF) systems [2, 5, 16] or to build smarter content-based (CB) systems [21]. In particular they have been shown to be very effective in solving some drawbacks of collaborative methods such as cold start and data sparsity. Most of the works on ontological recommender systems are related to the rating prediction task. However, in the last few years a significant interest has grown towards ranking-oriented approaches as they seem to better approximate the *top-N* recommendation task [7, 23]. Differently from rating prediction, in *top-N* recommendations the goal of the system is to find a few specific items which are supposed to be the most appealing to the user instead of accurately predict all the missing ratings.
Together with the *top-N* recommendation problem, great attention has been gained by implicit feedback scenarios and many recent works have addressed both these issues [20, 22]. Even though the case of explicit feedback where users express their preferences through ratings is the most known in the literature, the implicit feedback case has attracted increasing interest because in many real-world situations explicit ratings are not available and implicit feedback requires no extra feedback on the user side.

In this paper we present **SPrank** (***S**emantic **P**ath-based **rank**ing*), a novel hybrid recommendation algorithm able to compute *top-N* item recommendations from implicit feedback that effectively incorporates ontological knowledge belonging to the Web of Data with collaborative user preferences in a graph-based setting. While several works have been proposed in the last recent years to address *top-N* recommendations and implicit feedback in the literature of collaborative filtering, for ontological recommender systems

[1] `http://www.w3.org/TR/rdf-concepts/`

RecSys'13, October 12–16, 2013, Hong Kong, China.

http://dx.doi.org/10.1145/2507157.2507172.

these issues mostly have not been investigated yet. In SPrank, the ontological knowledge describing the items has been extracted from DBpedia[2], a well-known encyclopedic knowledge base belonging to the LOD cloud. From the analysis of the DBpedia semantic graph we extract *path-based* features and use a *learning to rank* algorithm for computing the *top-N* recommendations as a ranking problem. We remark that previous work on semantic-aware and ontological recommender systems neither addresses the *top-N* item recommendation task nor deals with implicit feedback datasets. Here we show how SPrank is able to compute accurate recommendations in scenarios where collaborative filtering algorithms notoriously are not very effective, such as the ones affected by data sparsity. To the best of our knowledge, this is the first work proposed to address the *top-N* recommendation task as a ranking problem from implicit feedback by leveraging the Web Of Data. Main contributions of this paper are:

- combination of semantic item descriptions from the Web of Data and implicit feedback for the *top-N* recommendation task;
- formulation of a hybrid recommendation problem in a learning to rank setting;
- mining of the semantic graph of LOD datasets through path-based features to capture complex and not trivial relationships between items;
- evaluation of the proposed approach in terms of accuracy of the *top-N* recommendations on real data from MovieLens and Last.fm.

The remainder of this work is structured as follows. In Section 2 we discuss related work. We present our approach for *top-N* recommendation in Section 3. The experimental evaluation is carried out in Section 4. Conclusion closes the paper.

2. RELATED WORK

Several approaches have been proposed to incorporate ontological knowledge in recommender systems. In the following we review some of them and more recent literature on LOD-based approaches. In addition, since we propose an ontological *top-N* recommendation algorithm for implicit feedback, we present related work in the same area.

Ontological RSs. In [15] *Quickstep* and *Foxtrot* are presented, two ontological recommender systems that make use of semantic user profiles to compute collaborative recommendations. A hybrid recommendation system is proposed in [5] where user preferences and item features are described by semantic concepts to obtain users' clusters corresponding to implicit *Communities of Interest*. In [16] the authors introduce the so called *semantically enhanced collaborative filtering* where structured semantic knowledge about items is used in conjunction with user-item ratings to create a combined similarity measure for item comparisons. In [2] an approach is presented that integrates user rating vectors with an item ontology. In all of these works, the experiments prove an accuracy improvement over collaborative approaches especially in presence of sparse datasets.

LOD-based RSs. Most of the works described so far have been produced before the LOD initiative was officially launched. In [8, 9] a model-based approach and a memory-based one to compute content-based recommendations are presented leveraging LOD datasets. In [10] the authors present a knowledge-based framework leveraging DBpedia for computing cross-domain recommendations.

Top-N RSs with implicit feedback. The rating prediction task is the main focus of all the ontological approaches presented so far. Instead, referring to the most recent *top-N* recommendation problem in the context of collaborative filtering, several works have been proposed in the last few years. *SLIM* [17] adopts a *Sparse Linear* method for learning a sparse aggregation coefficient matrix that is used for computing *top-N* recommendations. In [18] the authors propose an extension of SLIM to incorporate both users and side information about items thus showing an improvement of the performance associated to the usage of such information.

Other works represent the *top-N* recommendation task as a ranking problem using learning to rank. In [22] *CLiMF* the authors present a collaborative-filtering algorithm able to directly optimize the Mean Reciprocal Rank. The authors of [20] propose a *Bayesian Personalized Ranking* (BPR) criterion for optimizing a ranking loss. Following this, in [12] a hybrid extension of BPR is presented that learns a linear mapping on the user/item features from the factorization and auxiliary user/item-attribute matrix. This extension of BPR is able to compute useful recommendations in cold-start scenarios. All these approaches deal with binary relevance data or only positive implicit feedback.

3. SPRANK: SEMANTIC PATH-BASED RANKING

The main idea behind SPrank is exploring *paths* in a *semantic* graph in order to find items that are related to the ones the user is interested in. From the analysis of these paths we extract *path-based* features and apply a learning to rank algorithm for getting a ranking function able to recommend the most relevant items to the user. However, applying learning to rank to hybrid recommender systems is not as straightforward as in Information Retrieval for document ranking since we need to conciliate content-based and collaborative features in the same feature space. In the following we detail the data model and the formulation of the recommendation problem, the path-based feature extraction and the algorithm for learning the ranking function.

3.1 Data Model

The standard language to semantically describe resources in the Web of Data – and in the Semantic Web – is RDF. The RDF data model is a labeled directed graph where nodes correspond to entities and edges are properties connecting them. The semantics of such properties is explicitly modeled by means of an ontological schema represented in RDFS[3] or OWL[4]. Indeed, LOD datasets can be seen as semantic graphs where the knowledge related to an entity, e.g., a movie, a song or an artist, is encoded by linking different nodes/entities with each other via semantic-enabled edges. Semantic datasets can be used as the input for content-based recommender systems. In fact, given a node representing an item, we can use the knowledge associated to the corresponding entity to discover similar items available in the graph.

Also the data model behind collaborative filtering problems

[2]http://dbpedia.org

[3]http://www.w3.org/TR/rdf-schema/

[4]http://www.w3.org/TR/owl2-overview/

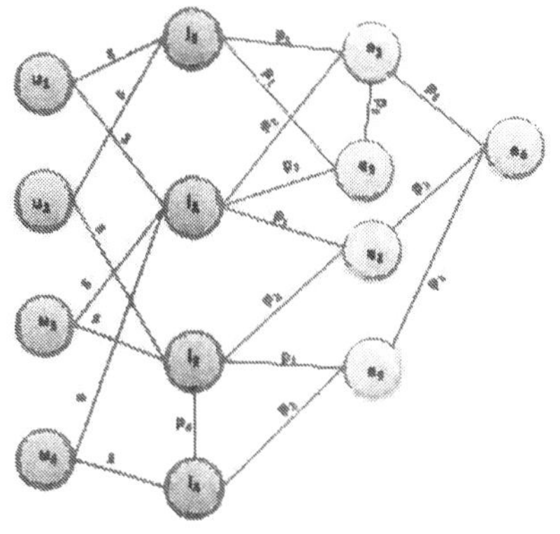

Figure 1: Graph-based representation of the data model.

can be seen as a graph as well – in this case a bipartite graph – where users and items are the nodes and users' feedback are the links.

The common graph-based nature of the data models for the two problems – content-based exploiting LOD and collaborative filtering – suggests interesting ways to model a hybrid recommendation engine. We can merge these two graphs obtaining a new graph $G = (V, R)$ as shown in Figure 1, where V denotes the set of vertices and R the set of relationships. Due to the nature of the problem we identify three relevant subsets of V: U, I and E representing *users*, *items* and *entities*, respectively. Moreover, in our model the two following relations hold: $I \subseteq E$ and $V = U \cup E$. Similarly, R contains two categories of relationships. In fact, we have $R = S \cup P$ where $S = U \times I$ and $P \subseteq E \times E$. More precisely, an edge $s \in S$ links a user $u \in U$ to his/her relevant items $i \in I$ while an edge $p \in P$ connects either an item i to another entity $e \in E$ in the graph or an entity $e_j \in E \setminus I$ to another entity $e_k \in E$. In the rest of the paper we will use u, i, e and v to represent a node belonging to U, I, E and V, respectively. Analogously, we will denote with s, p and r the edges in S, P and R. Thanks to this graph-based formulation of the problem we consider both collaborative and content aspects in a unified representation and hence a unified feature space. The purpose is recommending relevant items i to users u leveraging the knowledge encoded in the graph G. In the rest of the paper, in our data model we will always consider G as undirected.

3.2 Problem Formulation

Following the notation introduced by [20] for implicit feedback scenarios, let $\hat{S}$ be the matrix of implicit feedback, where $\hat{s}_{ui} = 1$ if item i is relevant for user u (i.e., there is an edge of type s between u and i), 0 otherwise. Looking at the graph in Figure 1, for user u_1 we have $\hat{s}_{u_1 i_1} = 1$, $\hat{s}_{u_1 i_2} = 1$ while $\hat{s}_{u_1 i_3} = 0$, $\hat{s}_{u_1 i_4} = 0$.

Starting from $\hat{S}$ we define $I_u^+ = \{i \in I | \hat{s}_{ui} = 1\}$ as the set of relevant items for u and $I_u^- = \{i \in I | \hat{s}_{ui} = 0\}$ as the set of unknown items for u. We call I_u^+ the *user profile* of u. In Figure 1, with reference to user u_1, we have $I_{u_1}^+ = \{i_1, i_2\}$ and $I_{u_1}^- = \{i_3, i_4\}$.

The main assumptions behind our approach are the following two: *(I)* only binary data of the user's interactions can be observed through implicit feedback such as purchases, friendships, clicks, etc.; *(II)* most of the items in I_u^- (items with no observed interactions) are irrelevant, but some of them could actually be relevant. The unobserved items are exactly the items that have to be ranked. The ultimate goal of the system is to rank in the *top-N* positions items likely to be relevant for the user.

We formulate the problem of computing the *top-N* recommendations in a learning to rank fashion similar to the document ranking problem adopted in Web search [14]. In particular we adopt a regression based point-wise method.

For each user-item pair (u, i) , we encode the features able to characterize the interaction between user u and item i in the vector $\mathbf{x_{ui}} \in \mathbb{R}^D$ where D is the dimension of the feature space. Each component in $\mathbf{x_{ui}}$ represents the relevance score between user u and item i with respect to a specific feature[5]. For each user u we assume to have information on the set of relevant items I_u^+, the set of unknown items I_u^-, the implicit binary feedback $\hat{s}_{ui}$ and the feature vector $\mathbf{x_{ui}}$. Finally, we introduce $I_u^{-*} \subseteq I_u^-$ computed by sampling, with a uniform probability distribution, a fixed number of unobserved items from I_u^- equal to K times the size of I_u^+, being K a constant. In other words, I_u^{-*} is the set of the $K \cdot | I_u^+ |$ uniformly sampled items from I_u^-. In Section 4.3.1 we will motivate the choice of K by means of experimental results.

Now we have all the elements to formally define the training set TR as:

$$TR = \bigcup_u \{(\mathbf{x_{ui}}, \hat{s}_{ui}) | i \in (I_u^+ \cup I_u^{-*})\}$$

Given the training set TR, computing the *top-N* recommendations for user u can be formulated as the task of generating a ranking function $f : \mathbb{R}^D \rightarrow \mathbb{R}$ such that $f(\mathbf{x_{ui}}) \approx \hat{s}_{ui}$. Eventually, we use $f(\cdot)$ to rank the items in I_u^- and getting the *top-N* recommendation list for u.

3.3 Path-based features

Given a graph G as the one represented in Figure 1, we want to extract features able to characterize the interactions between users, items and entities capturing the complex relationships between them. The aim is to recommend items exploiting their underlying properties and attributes expressed in the semantic graph. The basic idea is to consider all the paths that connect the user to an item in order to have a relevance score for that item. The more paths between user and item, the more the item is relevant for the user. However, in this formulation of the problem there are several types of paths and not all of them have the same relevance. Moreover, some paths that involve useless properties can be noisy for the purpose of recommendation. Based on these assumptions, we leverage a supervised approach and we delegate to the learning to rank algorithm the task of finding what paths are most relevant for computing *top-N* recommendations. In the previous section we introduced the feature vector $\mathbf{x_{ui}}$ encoding the interest of the user u in the item i. In the following we detail how the vector values are computed.

Given an undirected graph G as defined in Section 3.1, we define a path as the acylic sequence of edges of the form $(s, \ldots, r_l, \ldots, r_L)$ where $s = (u, i)$ and $r_L = (v, i')$ with

[5]In SPrank we rely on *path-based* features as we will detail in Section 3.3.

$i \neq i'$. We also define the *length of a path* as the number of edges contained within such path. We consider paths having length greater than 1 and less than or equal than a given L. We collect all the possible paths in G to build a *Path* index. $Path(j)$ represents the j-th component in the index and it corresponds to a specific sequence of edge labels (i.e., to a path disregarding the actual nodes). Considering a user-item pair (u, i), we denote $\#path_{ui}(j)$ as the number of paths between u and i corresponding to the specific $Path(j)$ entry in the index. In other words, it represents how many paths of type $Path(j)$ connect u and i. This aggregate information corresponds to the frequency of $Path(j)$ in the sub-graph composed by all paths between u and i. We are now ready to define the path-based features. We define the j-th component in the feature vector $\mathbf{x_{ui}}$ as:

$$\mathbf{x_{ui}}(j) = \frac{\#path_{ui}(j)}{\sum_{d=1}^{D} \#path_{ui}(d)} \quad (1)$$

Equation (1) represents the importance of the specific sequence of edge labels $Path(j)$ between u and i in the sub-graph constituted by all the associations between these two nodes. Specifically, it is the frequency of the specific path $Path(j)$ normalized with respect to the frequencies of all the existing paths between u and i.

In order to clarify how to compute the feature vector $\mathbf{x_{ui}}$ we show an example with reference to the graph in Figure 1. For $L = 4$ we have the following paths: (s, s, s), (s, p_1, p_2), (s, p_2, p_1), (s, p_1, p_3, p_2), (s, p_2, p_3, p_1), (s, p_4, s, s), (s, p_4), (s, s, s, p_4), (s, p_1, p_2, p_4), (s, p_4, p_2, p_1). We call them, respectively: $path_1, \cdots, path_{10}$ and build the index $Path = \{path_1, \ldots, path_{10}\}$ such that $Path(1)$ corresponds to $path_1$ and so on. Between user u_3 and item i_1, there are only paths $Path(1)$, $Path(3)$ and $Path(5)$. In particular, $\#path_{u_3 i_1}(j) = 0$ for $j = 2, 4, 6, 7, 8, 9, 10$, and $\#path_{u_3 i_1}(1) = 2$, $\#path_{u_3 i_1}(3) = 2$ and $\#path_{u_3 i_1}(5) = 1$. We can now compute the feature vector $\mathbf{x_{u_3 i_1}}$ for the pair (u_3, i_1). Following Equation (1), at the denominator we have the sum of the number of all the paths connecting u_3 and i_1. This sum is equal to 5. Then, $\mathbf{x_{u_3 i_1}} = (2/5, 0, 2/5, 0, 1/5, 0, 0, 0, 0, 0)$.

Path types. Depending on the type of links composing a path there are different types of paths. In particular, such paths can be: (I) *collaborative* if only links in S are involved as for (s, s, s); (II) *content-based* if there are only $r_l \notin S$ with $l = 2, \ldots, L$ as for (s, p_1, p_2) or (s, p_4, p_2, p_1); (III) *hybrid* if there is more than one link in S and at least one link in P as for (s, p_4, s, s) or (s, s, s, p_4). In Figure 2 we represent several examples of path types, referring to the music domain. In particular, musical artists are items (red nodes) to be recommended to users (blue nodes). The green nodes are the entities, coming from `DBpedia`. Artists and entities are connected via `DBpedia` properties. In these paths there are user feedback edges (`likes`) and content-based `RDF` properties (`dcterm:subject`, `skos:broader`, `dbprop:writer`, `dbprop:title`). In Figure 2, the paths connect the user `Andrew` to the artist `Craig David`[6] through the singer `Adele`[7], liked by `Andrew`. Given that `Andrew` has shown interest for `Adele`, the task of the recommender system is to find other artists that are related to `Adele`. In this case we want to know if `Craig David` is a good candidate to be recommended to `Andrew`. A possible way for doing this is by exploiting the tastes of the crowd to find if users who like `Adele` also like `Craig David`. The path *(a)* of Figure 2 is an example of collaborative path because it shows that there is another user (`Alex`) who likes both `Adele` and `Craig David`. We can also have longer chains of people with similar tastes, as shown in path *(b)*. Another way of recommending artists to `Andrew` is to find singers with similar characteristics to `Adele` (e.g., the genre of her songs, the prizes she won). These are content-based paths, as represented in Figure 2 by the paths *(c)*, *(d)*, *(e)*. We note that the usage of a `LOD` knowledge base such as `DBpedia` gives us the advantage of leveraging a valuable source of structured information. In fact, we can catch fine grained and not obvious relationships that in a non-ontological system we would otherwise miss. The last type of path is the hybrid one and it is shown in Figure 2 by path *(f)*. In this case both collaborative and content-based information is combined.

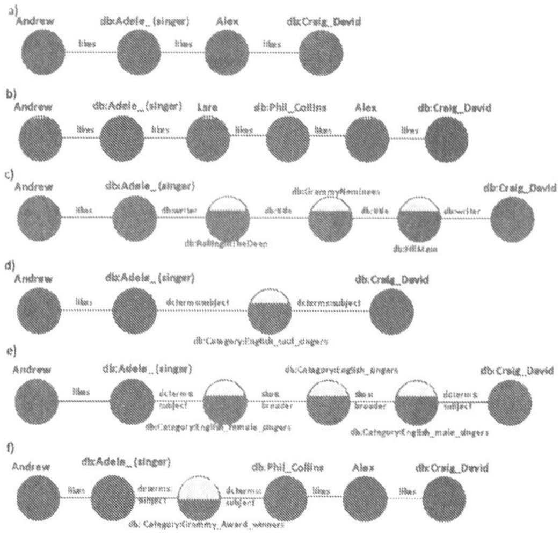

Figure 2: Various examples of content, collaborative and hybrid paths.

3.4 Learning the ranking function

In order to predict the ranking and form the *top-N* recommendation lists we deal with the learning to rank problem by adopting a *point-wise* approach. Point-wise methods have shown to be very effective in Web search ranking [14]. There are two point-wise algorithms that have proven particularly successful: *Random Forests* [4] and *Gradient Boosted Regression Trees* [11]. In fact, all of the top placed teams in the recent *Yahoo! Learning to Rank Challenge* used variants of these two algorithms coping with regression trees [6].

The fundamental concept underlying Random Forests is *bagging*. Bagging – or bootstrap aggregation – is a technique for reducing the variance of an estimated prediction function. It works especially well for high-variance, low-bias procedures, such as trees. The idea behind this technique is to apply multiple times the same learning algorithm to bootstrap sampled versions of the training set. At the end, all the resulting models are averaged to reduce overfitting. Random Forest is essentially bagging applied to *Classification And Regression Trees* (*CART*) with full depth, where at each split only a subset of features is uniformly chosen

[6]`http://dbpedia.org/resource/Craig_David`
[7]`http://dbpedia.org/resource/Adele_(singer)`

and evaluated to find the best splitting point.
Similar to Random Forests, *Gradient Boosted Regression Trees* (*GBRT*) is a state-of-the-art regression model, which is a combination of regression trees constructed using the boosting approach. Instead of training many full high variance trees and average them to avoid overfitting, GBRT sequentially adds small trees (weak learners), each of them with high bias. During each iteration, the new tree to be added focuses explicitly on the data points that are responsible for the current remaining regression error.
We formulate the learning to rank problem as a combination of both Random Forest and GBRT following the idea of *BagBoo* introduced by [19]. BagBoo combines the high accuracy of gradient boosting with resistance to overfitting and variance reduction of random forests. The basic idea is replacing simple tree models that are at the base of random forests with powerful and accurate gradient boosted trees. For a better understanding of BagBoo let us discuss the pseudo-code listed in Algorithm 1. The input of the learning algorithm is the training data TR as defined in Section 3.2, on which learning the ranking function. Q, T, B are the parameters of the algorithm. Q specifies the number of features to be considered for each node in order to find the best split in the CART used in GBRT. T is the number of bags used in Random Forests and B is the number of iterations required by GBRT. The final model f returned by the algorithm is basically a Random forests of $T \cdot B$ trees. We have T GBRTs each one composed by B regression trees. These T GBRTs are learned in the for-loop at line 1. At line 2 TR_t is sub-sampled with replacement from TR. At line 3 the f_t GBRT is learned. At the end all the GBRTs learned in the loop are combined in the forest to form our final ranking function f.

Algorithm 1: BagBoo

```
  Input: training set TR
  Output: ranking function f
  /* Q is the number of uniformly chosen features, T is
     the number of bags, B is the number of boosting
     iterations                                        */
1 for t = 1 to T do
    /* Sample with replacement                         */
2   set TR_t ⊆ TR;
    /* Build GBRT with TR_t using Q randomly chosen
       features and B boosting iterations              */
3   f_t ← GBRT(TR_t, Q, B);
4 end
5 f = 1/T Σ_{t=1}^{T} f_t;
```

4. EXPERIMENTAL EVALUATION

In this section, we detail the results of the experiments accomplished to evaluate the effectiveness of **SPrank** in terms of accuracy for *top-N* recommendations. The evaluation has been carried out on two real world datasets belonging to two different domains: **MovieLens** (movies) and **Last.fm** (music).

4.1 Datasets

The first dataset is a subset of the **MovieLens** 1M dataset[8]. The original dataset contains 1,000,209 ratings for 3,883 movies by 6,040 users. Since our recommendation approach is based on positive implicit feedback, we chose 5-star ratings as relevant for the user and we ignored all the other ratings. Hence, for each user u we set $\hat{s}_{ui} = 1$ iff $rating_{ui} = 5$. In this way we can reasonably assert that I_u^+ contains only items relevant to u [7]. The second dataset comes from recent initiatives on information heterogeneity and fusion in recommender systems[9] [1]. In particular, we used the dataset collected from the **Last.fm** music system[10]. This is an implicit feedback dataset consisting of user-artist listening data, indicating the frequency a user listened to an artist's song. This dataset contains 1,892 users, 17,632 artists and 92,834 relations between a user and a listened artist together with their corresponding listening counts. In this case we chose the users' average listening count as threshold to identify the relevant artists for each user. Then, for each user u we set $\hat{s}_{ui} = 1$ iff $count_{ui} > avg_u$, with the obvious meaning for $count_{ui}$ and avg_u. For the purpose of our experiments in both datasets we removed users with less than twenty relevant items. In the following we will denote the two datasets **MovieLens** and **Last.fm** with ML and LF, respectively. Being our approach based on **LOD** knowledge bases, we need to map items in ML and LF to resources in **LOD**. In this work, the **LOD** knowledge base we leverage is **DBpedia**. It is one of the main projects in the **Linked Open Data** cloud. It currently describes more than 3.77 million things and all this information is stored in **RDF** triples. We can extract sub-graphs related to the movie and the music domain by querying its **SPARQL** endpoint[11]. In the current 3.8 release there are about 71,715 movies and 34,186 artists. In the following we detail the procedure we used to map items in ML and LF to the correspondent **DBpedia** URIs and extract the semantic sub-graphs of interest.

4.1.1 Mapping and Linking datasets with DBpedia

As the initial step for the mapping, we extracted from **DBpedia** the title and the year of production for all the movies in ML, by the following **SPARQL** query:

```
SELECT DISTINCT ?movie ?title ?year WHERE {
  ?movie rdf:type dbpedia-owl:Film.
  ?movie rdfs:label ?title.
  ?movie dcterms:subject ?cat .
  ?cat rdfs:label ?year .
  FILTER langMatches(lang(?title), "EN") .
  FILTER regex(?year, "^[0-9]{4} film", "i")
}
```

We used a similar query to extract music artists from **DBpedia**. Then, we performed a one-to-one mapping between the obtained sets of labels and the name of the movies and artists respectively in ML and LF by using the Levenshtein distance and checking also the year of production in case of ML. For ML we found a positive correspondence for 3,148 out of a total of 3,883 movies. For LF we found a match for 9,490 out of a total of 17,632 artists. The dump of the mappings is available here[12]. At the end of this mapping phase we removed the unmapped items from the two datasets and we replaced the item IDs in the two datasets with the corresponding **DBpedia** URIs.

[8]http://www.grouplens.org/node/73

[9]http://ir.ii.uam.es/hetrec2011/datasets.html

[10]http://www.lastfm.com

[11]http://dbpedia.org/sparql

[12]http://sisinflab.poliba.it/mappingdatasets2dbpedia.zip

4.1.2 *Entity extraction from DBpedia*

For each URI we extracted from DBpedia all the RDF triples containing it. For example the following SPARQL query returns all the triples corresponding to the songs written by Adele:

```
SELECT ?s WHERE
{ ?s dbpedia-owl:writer dbpedia:Adele_(singer). }
```

An example of a returned triple is:
dbpedia:Chasing_Pavements dbpedia-owl:writer dbpedia:Adele_(singer).
This triple states that **Chasing Pavements** has been written by **Adele**. At the end of this step we have an initial version of our graph of interest, consisting of entities directly linked to items. Starting from this set of entities we further query DBpedia to find other entities linked to them. Iteratively, we obtain a graph of increasing size incrementing the distance from the original items. In the queries, we consider the RDF properties belonging to the DBpedia Ontology[13] plus two more properties: **dcterms:subject** and **skos:broader**. The former relates a resource to its categories. They are used in Wikipedia to organize the entire project, and to help users to give a structure to the knowledge base, by grouping together pages on the same subject. The latter models the hierarchical structure of the categories. An example of these two properties is the path *(e)* in Figure 2. We decided to leverage the properties belonging to the DBpedia Ontology, because they represent high-quality, clean and well-structured information. The list of all the properties related to the Film class in the DBpedia ontology is available at **http://mappings.dbpedia.org/server/ontology/classes/Film**. The list related to the Musical Artist class is available at **http://mappings.dbpedia.org/server/ontology/classes/MusicalArtist**. At the end of the process, the final graph for ML contains 3,792 users, 2,795 movies and 104,351 entities (actors, directors, categories, etc.) while the one for LF it contains 852 users, 6,256 artists and 150,925 entities (songs, genres, categories, etc.). We considered entities within paths of length $L = 4$.

4.2 Evaluation Protocol

For the evaluation of our approach we adopted a method similar to the one described in [7]. From the original matrix $\hat{S}$, we built two new matrices: $\hat{S}_{train}$ and $\hat{S}_{test}$. We used the former for producing the sets I_u^+, I_u^- and TR (used for training the model), as detailed in Section 3.2, the latter for evaluating the trained model. To create $\hat{S}_{test}$ we randomly selected ten positive feedback for each user from the initial matrix $\hat{S}$. In order to assess the performance of SPrank in situations affected by different level of data sparsity, we evaluated our algorithm considering different sizes of user profiles as done by [22]. Specifically, for each user we randomly considered at most m positive feedback from the original matrix $\hat{S}$ (denoted with "**given m**" in Tables 1, 2 and 4) to form $\hat{S}_{train}$, and we discarded all the others. We say *at most* m because some users can actually have less than m positive feedback. Different values of m correspond to different matrices $\hat{S}_{train}$, different sets I_u^+, I_u^- and then different training sets TR. In Table 1 we show some statistics about the number of non-zero entries in $\hat{S}_{train}$ (**nnz**), the average number of non-zero entries for each user (**avg nnz**) and the sparseness (**spars**) of $\hat{S}_{train}$ for the different conditions (**given 5**, **given 10**, etc.). For each condition we learned the model on the training set TR and we applied the learned model to predict the unknown values (0-entries) in $\hat{S}_{train}$. We got the full recommendation lists by sorting the predicted values for each user and then we evaluated the accuracy for the *top-N* items. We repeated the procedure 5 times for each condition by randomly drawing new training/test sets in each round and at the end we averaged the results. To evaluate the accuracy of the system we measured the *recall@N*, widely used for evaluating *top-N* recommender systems [7, 17]. The computation of *recall@N* goes through a procedure similar to the one introduced in [7], as detailed in the following.
For each $\hat{s}_{ui}$ in $\hat{S}_{test}$, from the full recommendation list computed for u, we randomly selected 100 items appearing neither in the test set related to that user nor in the user profile. We got a ranked list consisting of these 101 items. The *top-N* recommendation list is obtained by considering just the first N items ($N = 5, 10, 20$) in this ranked list. Being *pos* the position of the test item i within the ranked list, we have a hit if $pos \leq N$, otherwise we have a miss. We note that for any single test case, we have just one relevant item (i.e., the tested item i). The recall for a single test case is either 0 (in case of a miss) or 1 (in case of a hit). The overall recall on all users is defined by averaging over all test cases:

$$recall@N = \frac{\#hits}{|\hat{S}_{test}|} \qquad (2)$$

The formula for *precision@N* differs from Equation 2 just by a multiplicative term N appearing at the denominator [7]. For this reason, in our results we do not report it.

	MovieLens			LastFM		
given	nnz	avg-nnz	spars	nnz	avg-nnz	spars
5	18960	5.00	99.82%	4260	5.00	99.92%
10	36650	9.66	99.65%	8146	9.56	99.84%
20	64137	16.91	99.39%	13542	15.89	99.74%
30	84301	22.23	99.2%	-	-	-
50	111001	29.27	98.95%	-	-	-
All	157194	41.45	98.51%	17783	20.87	99.66%

Table 1: Statistics of the ML and LF training matrices under different conditions of user profile size.

4.3 Evaluation and results discussion

In the following, we present the results of the experiments that have been carried out to answer to the following questions:

1. *Is the chosen learning to rank algorithm effective?*
2. *Does the proposed approach improve, in situations affected by different degree of data sparsity, the recommendation accuracy with respect to existing state-of-the-art ranking-oriented approaches for positive implicit feedback?*

4.3.1 *Effectiveness of the learning to rank algorithm*

To answer the first question we compared *BagBoo*, the learning to rank algorithm used in **SPrank**, with two other algorithms: *Sum* and *GBRT*. In *Sum*, the ranking function $f(\mathbf{x}_{ui})$ is the arithmetic sum of all the path-based feature values. On the one side, the comparison with *Sum* gives us a baseline for semantic-based recommendation algorithm where all associations are equally considered.This allows us to evaluate our learning to rank algorithm against a basic

[13] **http://wiki.dbpedia.org/Downloads38#dbpedia-ontology**

not ranking-oriented semantic recommender. On the other side, the comparison with *GBRT* is useful to prove the effectiveness of combining bagging and boosting. We recall that *BagBoo* is an extension of *GBRT* as it is an ensemble of gradient boosting regression trees.

Table 2 summarizes the accuracy results obtained on the two datasets. For the ML dataset we observe that *BagBoo* outperforms both *GBRT* and *Sum* in all the different conditions of sparsity degree, even when there are few positive examples for each user. For example, if we analyze the *recall@5*, the improvement of *BagBoo* over *Sum* goes from +6.6% to +11% respectively for the two limit conditions (`given 5` and `given All`). We also see that for the condition `given 5` the improvement with respect to *GBRT* is very marked (+15.8%), but it decreases with the increasing of positive examples (+2% for `given 30` and +3.2% for `given All`). For this dataset we observe that when there are only a few positive training examples for each user, *GBRT* is not able to learn an effective ranking function. This is not the case for the bagging of several *GBRT*s. Looking at the results for LF we observe again *BagBoo* outperforms the other algorithms but for the condition `given 5`.

From the results on the two datasets we can draw the following conclusions: `SPrank` benefits from learning to rank, both *GBRT* and *BagBoo* show substantial improvements with respect to the *Sum* baseline, particularly when the number of positive examples, and then the training data, increases; due to bagging, *BagBoo* outperforms *GBRT* in all the analyzed situations. Hence, *BagBoo* is a valid candidate for learning the ranking function in `SPrank`.

	MovieLens			LastFM		
Alg.	r@5	r@10	r@20	r@5	r@10	r@20
			given 5			
BagBoo	**0.420**	**0.578**	**0.745**	**0.349**	0.457	0.551
GBRT	0.262	0.405	0.572	0.323	0.442	0.572
Sum	0.354	0.560	0.541	0.319	**0.482**	**0.593**
			given 10			
BagBoo	**0.462**	**0.623**	**0.786**	**0.423**	**0.541**	0.636
GBRT	0.427	0.603	0.771	0.371	0.510	0.615
Sum	0.382	0.581	0.565	0.349	0.517	**0.668**
			given 20			
BagBoo	**0.496**	**0.661**	**0.816**	**0.496**	**0.618**	**0.721**
GBRT	0.475	0.653	0.810	0.452	0.592	0.689
Sum	0.396	0.599	0.587	0.385	0.533	0.693
			given 30			
BagBoo	**0.515**	**0.679**	**0.831**	-	-	-
GBRT	0.495	0.669	0.824	-	-	-
Sum	0.417	0.610	0.595	-	-	-
			given 50			
BagBoo	**0.524**	**0.691**	**0.841**	-	-	-
GBRT	0.497	0.668	0.825	-	-	-
Sum	0.423	0.618	0.613	-	-	-
			given All			
BagBoo	**0.539**	**0.699**	**0.846**	**0.543**	**0.657**	**0.752**
GBRT	0.507	0.679	0.837	0.448	0.587	0.708
Sum	0.429	0.633	0.632	0.399	0.546	0.702

Table 2: Results for *BagBoo*, *GBRT* and *Sum* given different user profile size.

Impact of irrelevant item sampling. In Table 3 we show how different values of K, that is the factor that influences the size of I_u^{-*} (cf. Section 3.2), affects the accuracy of `SPrank`. We can observe that increasing K and hence the number of unknown examples in the training data, the accuracy does not increase. An evident advantage in selecting a small K is the reduction of the training set size and consequently of the time required to build the model. Based on these observations, we chose $K = 2$ in all our experiments.

	MovieLens			LastFM		
K	r@5	r@10	r@20	r@5	r@10	r@20
1	0.529	0.691	0.84	0.541	0.643	0.737
2	0.539	0.699	0.846	0.543	0.657	0.752
5	0.531	0.690	0.841	0.544	0.658	0.749
10	0.525	0.691	0.839	0.530	0.639	0.736
25	0.525	0.689	0.838	0.537	0.642	0.737

Table 3: Accuracy results for different values of K (used to create I_u^{-*}).

4.3.2 Comparison with other Algorithms

In order to evaluate `SPrank` we compared it both with a hybrid algorithm proposed to address cold-start scenarios and with ranking oriented collaborative filtering algorithms. All of these approaches are state-of-the-art methods for positive implicit feedback scenarios. *BPRLinearMap* (*BPRLin*), *BPRMF* and *SLIM* have been presented in Section 2. For *BPRLinearMap* we built the item-attribute matrix using the same content data used for `SPrank`. *SoftMarginRankingMF* (*SMRMF*) is a matrix factorization model for item prediction optimized for a soft margin ranking loss using stochastic gradient descent inspired by [23] [20].The computation of the recommendations for all these comparative algorithms has been done with the publicly available software library *MyMediaLite* [13].

Results discussion. Table 4 shows the results obtained for `SPrank` and all the other comparative methods on both ML and LF. We observe that on the ML dataset our algorithm outperforms the others under all the different user profile conditions but `given All` where *BPRMF* achieves the best recall values, and `SPrank` gets the second best place. We can note that `SPrank` outperforms significantly the other methods when $\hat{S}$ is very sparse. Referring to the *SLIM* method, for the conditions `given 5` and `given 10`, the improvements in terms of *recall@5* are respectively +20.2% and +23.3%.

For the LF dataset, which is slightly sparser than ML, `SPrank` is always the best performing algorithm. In this case, *BPRLin* – the most suited approach for dealing with data sparsity – is the second best performing. Also in this case the improvements are substantial especially for the conditions of higher sparseness.

From these experimental results, we can conclude that `SPrank` is able to compute accurate *top-N* recommendations even when there are few positive feedback where instead collaborative filtering algorithms have showed lower accuracy. On both datasets `SPrank` has also outperformed *BPRLin*, the other hybrid recommendation method proposed to address cold start and sparsity problems.

5. CONCLUSION

In this paper we have presented `SPrank`, a novel hybrid *top-N* item recommendation algorithm from implicit feedback able to exploit `LOD` knowledge bases to compute accurate recommendations. In `SPrank`, positive implicit feedback and semantic item descriptions are merged in a unique graph-based representation that allows us to extract *path-based* features describing complex relationships between items preferred by the user and items to be recommended. Then,

Alg.	MovieLens r@5	MovieLens r@10	MovieLens r@20	LastFM r@5	LastFM r@10	LastFM r@20
given 5						
SPrank	**0.420**	**0.578**	**0.745**	**0.349**	**0.457**	**0.551**
BPRMF	0.353	0.502	0.672	0.213	0.308	0.413
SLIM	0.218	0.363	0.552	0.077	0.152	0.287
BPRLin	0.218	0.314	0.442	0.289	0.381	0.440
SMRMF	0.216	0.354	0.526	0.111	0.181	0.280
given 10						
SPrank	**0.462**	**0.623**	**0.786**	**0.423**	**0.541**	**0.636**
BPRMF	0.383	0.533	0.704	0.278	0.386	0.503
SLIM	0.229	0.377	0.569	0.128	0.217	0.350
BPRLin	0.279	0.384	0.510	0.407	0.495	0.567
SMRMF	0.263	0.423	0.614	0.178	0.261	0.372
given 20						
SPrank	**0.496**	**0.661**	**0.816**	**0.496**	**0.618**	**0.721**
BPRMF	0.429	0.589	0.756	0.335	0.451	0.570
SLIM	0.320	0.437	0.614	0.182	0.278	0.427
BPRLin	0.348	0.464	0.592	0.486	0.577	0.643
SMRMF	0.360	0.505	0.698	0.236	0.343	0.470
given 30						
SPrank	**0.515**	**0.679**	**0.831**	-	-	-
BPRMF	0.486	0.648	0.802	-	-	-
SLIM	0.388	0.495	0.652	-	-	-
BPRLin	0.377	0.497	0.621	-	-	-
SMRMF	0.387	0.563	0.752	-	-	-
given 50						
SPrank	**0.524**	**0.691**	**0.841**	-	-	-
BPRMF	0.519	0.682	0.834	-	-	-
SLIM	0.453	0.566	0.688	-	-	-
BPRLin	0.392	0.513	0.639	-	-	-
SMRMF	0.416	0.596	0.783	-	-	-
given All						
SPrank	0.539	0.699	0.846	**0.543**	**0.657**	**0.752**
BPRMF	**0.564**	**0.727**	**0.865**	0.373	0.495	0.615
SLIM	0.513	0.651	0.761	0.228	0.323	0.470
BPRLin	0.414	0.535	0.658	0.527	0.616	0.679
SMRMF	0.471	0.651	0.818	0.266	0.383	0.510

Table 4: Comparison of SPrank with other approaches under different conditions of the user profile size.

the recommendation problem is cast in a learning to rank fashion to compute *top-N* recommendations.
We have demonstrated in our experiments that **SPrank** outperforms several state-of-the-art approaches for implicit feedback in two datasets belonging to two different domains: MovieLens for movie and Last.fm for music. The experiments have been conducted varying the sparseness of the implicit feedback matrix for analyzing how **SPrank** deals with sparse data with respect to other competitive approaches. We have observed significant improvements over collaborative filtering methods especially in case of high sparsity.

6. REFERENCES

[1] Hetrec '11: Proceedings of the 2nd international workshop on information heterogeneity and fusion in recommender systems. ACM, 2011.

[2] S. S. Anand, P. Kearney, and M. Shapcott. Generating semantically enriched user profiles for web personalization. *ACM Trans. Internet Technol.*, 7(4), 2007.

[3] C. Bizer, T. Heath, and T. Berners-Lee. Linked data - the story so far. *Int. J. Sem. Web Inf. Syst*, 5(3):1–22, 2009.

[4] L. Breiman. Random forests. *Machine Learning*, 45(1):5–32, 2001.

[5] I. Cantador, A. Bellogín, and P. Castells. A multilayer ontology-based hybrid recommendation model. *AI Commun.*, 21(2-3):203–210, 2008.

[6] O. Chapelle and Y. Chang. Yahoo! learning to rank challenge overview. *Journal of Machine Learning Research - Proceedings Track*, 14:1–24, 2011.

[7] P. Cremonesi, Y. Koren, and R. Turrin. Performance of recommender algorithms on top-n recommendation tasks. In *Proceedings of the fourth ACM conference on Recommender systems*, pages 39–46. ACM, 2010.

[8] T. Di Noia, R. Mirizzi, V. C. Ostuni, and D. Romito. Exploiting the web of data in model-based recommender systems. In *Proceedings of the sixth ACM conference on Recommender systems*, pages 253–256. ACM, 2012.

[9] T. Di Noia, R. Mirizzi, V. C. Ostuni, D. Romito, and M. Zanker. Linked open data to support content-based recommender systems. In *Proceedings of the 8th International Conference on Semantic Systems*, I-SEMANTICS '12, pages 1–8. ACM, 2012.

[10] I. Fernández-Tobías, I. Cantador, M. Kaminskas, and F. Ricci. A generic semantic-based framework for cross-domain recommendation. In *Proc. of the 2nd Int. Workshop on Information Heterogeneity and Fusion in Recommender Systems*, HetRec '11, pages 25–32. ACM, 2011.

[11] J. H. Friedman. Greedy function approximation: A gradient boosting machine. *Annals of Statistics*, 29:1189–1232, 2000.

[12] Z. Gantner, L. Drumond, C. Freudenthaler, S. Rendle, and L. Schmidt-Thieme. Learning attribute-to-feature mappings for cold-start recommendations. In *Proceedings of the 2010 IEEE International Conference on Data Mining*, ICDM '10, pages 176–185. IEEE Computer Society, 2010.

[13] Z. Gantner, S. Rendle, C. Freudenthaler, and L. Schmidt-Thieme. Mymedialite: a free recommender system library. In *Proceedings of the fifth ACM conference on Recommender systems*, RecSys '11, pages 305–308. ACM, 2011.

[14] T.-Y. Liu. Learning to rank for information retrieval. *Found. Trends Inf. Retr.*, 3(3):225–331, 2009.

[15] S. E. Middleton, D. D. Roure, and N. R. Shadbolt. Ontology-based recommender systems. *Handbook on Ontologies*, 32(6):779–796, 2009.

[16] B. Mobasher, X. Jin, and Y. Zhou. Semantically enhanced collaborative filtering on the web. In B. Berendt, A. Hotho, D. Mladenic, M. Someren, M. Spiliopoulou, and G. Stumme, editors, *Web Mining: From Web to Semantic Web*, volume 3209 of *LNCS*, pages 57–76. Springer Berlin Heidelberg, 2004.

[17] X. Ning and G. Karypis. Slim: Sparse linear methods for top-n recommender systems. In *Proceedings of the 2011 IEEE 11th International Conference on Data Mining*, ICDM '11, pages 497–506. IEEE Computer Society, 2011.

[18] X. Ning and G. Karypis. Sparse linear methods with side information for top-n recommendations. In *Proceedings of the sixth ACM conference on Recommender systems*, RecSys '12, pages 155–162. ACM, 2012.

[19] D. Y. Pavlov, A. Gorodilov, and C. A. Brunk. Bagboo: a scalable hybrid bagging-the-boosting model. In *Proc. of the 19th ACM int. conference on Information and knowledge management*, CIKM '10, pages 1897–1900. ACM, 2010.

[20] S. Rendle, C. Freudenthaler, Z. Gantner, and L. Schmidt-Thieme. Bpr: Bayesian personalized ranking from implicit feedback. In *Proceedings of the Twenty-Fifth Conference on Uncertainty in Artificial Intelligence*, UAI '09, pages 452–461. AUAI Press, 2009.

[21] G. Semeraro, P. Lops, P. Basile, and M. de Gemmis. Knowledge infusion into content-based recommender systems. In *Proceedings of the third ACM conference on Recommender systems*, pages 301–304. ACM, 2009.

[22] Y. Shi, A. Karatzoglou, L. Baltrunas, M. Larson, N. Oliver, and A. Hanjalic. Climf: learning to maximize reciprocal rank with collaborative less-is-more filtering. In *Proceedings of the sixth ACM conference on Recommender systems*, RecSys '12, pages 139–146. ACM, 2012.

[23] M. Weimer, A. Karatzoglou, Q. V. Le, and A. J. Smola. Cofi rank - maximum margin matrix factorization for collaborative ranking. In *Proceedings of the Twenty-First Annual Conference on Neural Information Processing Systems*, 2007.

Exploring Temporal Effects for Location Recommendation on Location-Based Social Networks

Huiji Gao, Jiliang Tang, Xia Hu, and Huan Liu
Computer Science and Engineering, Arizona State University, Tempe, AZ, USA
{huiji.gao, jiliang.tang, xia.hu, huan.liu}@asu.edu

ABSTRACT

Location-based social networks (LBSNs) have attracted an inordinate number of users and greatly enriched the urban experience in recent years. The availability of spatial, temporal and social information in online LBSNs offers an unprecedented opportunity to study various aspects of human behavior, and enable a variety of location-based services such as location recommendation. Previous work studied spatial and social influences on location recommendation in LBSNs. Due to the strong correlations between a user's check-in time and the corresponding check-in location, recommender systems designed for location recommendation inevitably need to consider temporal effects. In this paper, we introduce a novel location recommendation framework, based on the temporal properties of user movement observed from a real-world LBSN dataset. The experimental results exhibit the significance of temporal patterns in explaining user behavior, and demonstrate their power to improve location recommendation performance.

Categories and Subject Descriptors

H.4 [**Information Systems Applications**]: Miscellaneous; D.2.8 [**Software Engineering**]: Metrics—*complexity measures, performance measures*

Keywords

Location Recommendation, Location-Based Social Networks, Temporal Effects

1. INTRODUCTION

The rapid growth of location-based social networks (LBSNs) has attracted billions of users, promoting our urban experience to a new stage [30]. Typical location-based social networking sites (e.g., Foursquare[1] and Facebook Places[2]) allow a user to "check in" at a location of interest with her smartphone, which informs her friends, along with creating the opportunity to make new friends or receive better recommendations. To benefit LBSN users and advance location-based marketing, location recommendation on LBSNs has become an essential task [24, 25], aiming to recommend *new* POIs (Points of Interest) to a user according to his personal preferences and facilitate his exploration of new areas of the city.

Location-based social networks present unprecedented large-scale check-in data to describe a user's mobile behavior in spatial, temporal, and social aspects. In previous work researchers explored users' personal static check-in preferences through geographical check-ins for location recommendation [28, 1, 29, 26]. Inspired by social influence theories that social friends tend to have similar check-in behavior, researches started to investigate the explicit social friendships on LBSNs [5, 9, 8] and leverage their power for improving location recommendation services [23, 3, 25]. Among existing work, the temporal patterns of a user's check-in actions have not been explored in depth.

As suggested in [22, 4, 16], human geographical movement exhibits significant temporal patterns on LBSNs and is highly relevant to the location property, while the daily pattern (hours of the day) is one of the most fundamental patterns that reflects a user's mobile behavior. For example, a user may regularly arrive to the office around 9:00 am, go to a restaurant for lunch at 12:00 pm, and watch movies at night around 10:00 pm. Therefore, investigating the features embedded in daily patterns enables us to better understand human mobile behavior, providing a potential opportunity to design more advanced location recommender systems on LBSNs.

Previous work reports that a user's preferences change continuously over time [21, 10], indicating two temporal properties of a user's daily check-in preferences: (1) **non-uniformness**: a user exhibits distinct check-in preferences at different hours of the day; and (2) **consecutiveness**: a user tends to have more similar check-in preferences in consecutive hours than in non-consecutive hours. In Section 5 we validate these properties experimentally on a real-world dataset. Figure 1 plots an illustrative example of a user's aggregated check-in activities on his top 5 most visited locations over 24 hours on a real-world LBSN. Each cell represents the total number of check-in activities happened at a specific location during the corresponding hour, colored from black (least active) to white (most active). The user's check-in behavior presents a different check-in location distribution at each hour, which changes continually over time.

The non-uniformness and consecutiveness properties suggest strong correlations between a user's check-in time and the corresponding check-in preferences. However, these properties have not been exploited for location recommendation on LBSNs. In this paper, we aim to leverage them for location recommendation. To the best of our knowledge, this is the first work of modeling temporal ef-

[1] `http://foursquare.com/`
[2] `http://www.facebook.com/about/location/`

RecSys'13, October 12–16, 2013, Hong Kong, China.

http://dx.doi.org/10.1145/2507157.2507182.

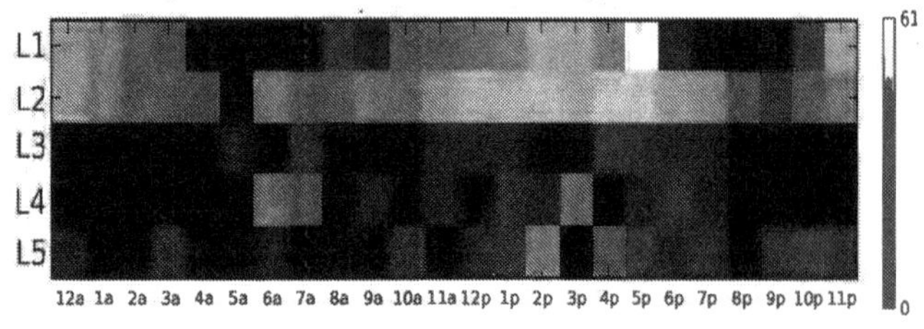

Figure 1: Daily Check-in Activities on LBSN

fects on location-based social networks for location recommendation. The contributions of this paper are summarized below:

- We propose a location recommendation framework with temporal effects based on observed temporal properties.
- We introduce four temporal aggregation strategies to integrate a user's check-in preferences of different temporal states.
- We evaluate the temporal effects for location recommendation; the results exhibit its good recommendation performance, and demonstrate the advantage of considering time-dependent check-in preferences over static check-in preferences.

The remainder of this paper is organized as follows. We first give a brief review of some related work in Section 2, then introduce a basic location recommendation model and discuss the modeling of temporal properties in Section 3. Next we introduce our location recommendation framework **LRT** with temporal effects in terms of temporal regularization and temporal aggregation in Section 4, followed by the discussion of experimental design and results on a real-world LBSN dataset in Section 5. We conclude this work with future work in Section 6.

2. RELATED WORK

The properties of location-based social networks has been widely studied w.r.t. the geographical and social aspects. Cheng et al. [4] investigated the "Lèvy Flight" property of human check-in patterns, and discovered that social status is affected by geographic constraints. In [19, 18], the authors investigated the spatial properties of the social networks on main popular LBSNs. They observed strong heterogeneity across users with different characteristic geographic scales of interactions across social ties. Efforts have also been made to utilize the geo and social properties for improving location-based social services. Gao et al. [9] studied geo-social correlations on LBSNs to solve the "cold start" location prediction problem. Zhang et al. [27] proposed a unified influence metric to evaluate the geo-social influence among users in LBSNs.

Ye et al. [24] introduced location recommendation into location-based social networks. Specifically, the authors investigated the geographical influence [25] and social influence [23] for location recommendation, and discovered that user preference plays a more important role in contributing to the recommendation than social and geographical influence. Berjani et al. [1] proposed a location recommendation system utilizing matrix factorization methods. Cheng [3] investigated the geographical influence through a multi-center Gaussian model, together with matrix factorization and social influence for location recommendation. Zhou et al. [29] studied the location recommendation problem on location-based social networks with various collaborative filtering approaches. Ying et al. [26] proposed a set of features related to social factor, individual preference, and location popularity, and utilized a regression-tree model to recommend POIs. Most recently, Yang et al. [7] introduced sentiment information into location recommendation system, and reported its good performance over state-of-the-art approaches.

Among the current work in LBSNs, temporal information has not been explored for location recommendation. Temporal information has been studied for other location-based social services such as location prediction and location classification. Liu et al. [14] analyzed the daily temporal distribution of check-ins and leveraged them to infer the types of locations. Cho et al. [5] proposed a Periodic & Social Mobility Model for location prediction with two temporal states ("home" and "work") affected by social effects and non-social effects. Chang et al. [2] proposed a logistic regression model with observed temporal patterns as one type of feature, and found that hourly patterns have a small but significant effect, while weekly patterns are not predictive.

3. MODELING TEMPORAL EFFECTS FOR LOCATION RECOMMENDATION

The large-scale check-in data on LBSNs is usually very sparse due to the user-driven check-in property [19, 17, 8]. To solve large-scale recommendation problems, matrix factorization is state-of-the-art technology that has been proven to be successful in the Netflix Competition [11, 12], and is being used for item recommendation and trust prediction on product review sites like Epinions and Ciao for research purposes [15, 20, 21]. Therefore, in this paper, we leverage the temporal properties on LBSNs with low-rank matrix factorization for location recommendation.

3.1 Location Recommendation without Temporal Effects

We first introduce a basic location recommendation model based on low-rank matrix factorization without considering temporal effects. Let $\mathbf{u} = \{u_1, u_2, ..., u_m\}$ be the set of users, and $\mathbf{l} = \{l_1, l_2, ..., l_n\}$ be the set of locations, where m and n denote the number of users and locations, respectively. $\mathbf{C} \in \mathbb{R}^{m\times n}$ is a user-location matrix with each element $\mathbf{C}_{ij}$ representing the number of check-ins made by user u_i at location l_j. Let $\mathbf{U} \in \mathbb{R}^{m\times d}$ be the user check-in preferences and $\mathbf{L} \in \mathbb{R}^{n\times d}$ be the location characteristics, with $d \ll min(m, n)$ being the number of latent preference factors. The basic location recommendation model approximates u_i's check-in preference on an unvisited l_j via solving the following optimization problem:

$$\min_{\mathbf{U}_i\geq 0, \mathbf{L}_j\geq 0} \sum_{i}^{m}\sum_{j}^{n} \mathbf{Y}_{ij}(\mathbf{C}_{ij} - \mathbf{U}_i\mathbf{L}_j^\top)^2, \quad (1)$$

where $\mathbf{Y} \in \mathbb{R}^{m\times n}$ is a check-in indicator matrix, $\mathbf{Y}_{ij} = 1$ indicating that u_i has checked in at l_j, $\mathbf{Y}_{ij} = 0$ otherwise.

After obtaining $\mathbf{U}_i$ and $\mathbf{L}_j$, the missing value in $\mathbf{C}$, represented as $\widetilde{\mathbf{C}}_{ij}$, indicating the preference of a user u_i at an unvisited location l_j, is then approximated by $\mathbf{U}_i\mathbf{L}_j^\top$. To avoid over-fitting, two smoothness regularizations are added on $\mathbf{U}_i$ and $\mathbf{L}_j$ respectively. Eq.(1) can then be represented in matrix format as

$$\min_{\mathbf{U}\geq 0, \mathbf{L}\geq 0} \|\mathbf{Y} \odot (\mathbf{C} - \mathbf{U}\mathbf{L}^\top)\|_F^2 + \alpha\|\mathbf{U}\|_F^2 + \beta\|\mathbf{L}\|_F^2, \quad (2)$$

where α and β are non-negative parameters to control the capability of $\mathbf{U}$ and $\mathbf{L}$. $\odot$ is the Hadamard product operator, where $(A \odot B)_{i,j} = A_{i,j} \times B_{i,j}$. $\|\cdot\|_F$ is the Frobenius norm of a matrix.

3.2 Modeling Temporal Non-Uniformness for Location Recommendation

According to the temporal property of non-uniformness as described above, users exhibit distinct check-in preferences at different hours of the day. This inspires us to consider a user's check-in behavior as a set of time-dependent check-in preferences, with each preference corresponding to an hour of the day. To model this property, we first introduce temporal state $t \in [1, T]$ to represent the hour of the day, where $T = 24$ is the total number of temporal states. For example, $t = 1$ for check-in time at "2012-10-24 00:30:00pm", indicating the check-in happens during hour 0 to 1.

We then define $\mathbf{U}_t \in \mathbb{R}^{m \times d}$ as the time-dependent user check-in preferences under temporal state t. As observed in [22], location characteristics are inherent properties that do not change much as time goes by. Therefore, we define location characteristics to be time-independent, denoted as $\mathbf{L} \in \mathbb{R}^{n \times d}$. By approximating the check-in activities at each temporal state t and minimizing their aggregation, we obtain time-dependent user check-in preferences via the following optimization problem:

$$\min_{\mathbf{U}_t \geq 0, \mathbf{L} \geq 0} \sum_{t=1}^{T} ||\mathbf{Y}_t \odot (\mathbf{C}_t - \mathbf{U}_t \mathbf{L}^\top)||_F^2 + \alpha \sum_{t=1}^{T} ||\mathbf{U}_t||_F^2 + \beta ||\mathbf{L}||_F^2, \quad (3)$$

where $\mathbf{C}_t \in \mathbb{R}^{m \times n}$ contains the check-in activities at temporal state t, and $\mathbf{Y}_t$ is the corresponding indicator matrix.

3.3 Modeling Temporal Consecutiveness with Temporal Regularization

Inspired by the temporal consecutiveness property, which implies that users on LBSNs tend to have closer check-in preferences on consecutive temporal state, we propose a temporal regularization to minimize the following terms:

$$\min \sum_{t=1}^{T} \sum_{i=1}^{m} \psi_i(t, t-1) ||\mathbf{U}_t(i,:) - \mathbf{U}_{t-1}(i,:)||_2^2, \quad (4)$$

where $\psi_i(t, t-1) \in [0, 1]$ is defined as a temporal coefficient that measures the temporal closeness of u_i's check-in preferences between temporal state t and $t-1$. The larger $\psi_i(t, t-1)$ is, the closer u_i's check-in preferences between t and $t-1$. We use cosine similarity to measure $\psi_i(t, t-1)$, defined as

$$\psi_i(t, t-1) = \frac{\mathbf{C}_t(i,:) \cdot \mathbf{C}_{t-1}(i,:)}{\sqrt{\sum_j \mathbf{C}_t^2(i,j)} \sqrt{\sum_j \mathbf{C}_{t-1}^2(i,j)}}. \quad (5)$$

Note that we consider the temporal state $t-1$ as T when $t = 1$, e.g., $U_{t-1} = U_T$ when $t = 1$. After some derivations, we can get the matrix form of temporal regularization,

$$\begin{aligned}
&\sum_{t=1}^{T} \sum_{i=1}^{m} \psi_i(t, t-1) ||\mathbf{U}_t(i,:) - \mathbf{U}_{t-1}(i,:)||_2^2 \\
&= \sum_{t=1}^{T} \sum_{i=1}^{m} \psi_i(t, t-1) (\mathbf{U}_t - \mathbf{U}_{t-1})^\top (i,:) (\mathbf{U}_t - \mathbf{U}_{t-1})(i,:) \\
&= \sum_{t=1}^{T} \sum_{i=1}^{m} (\mathbf{U}_t - \mathbf{U}_{t-1})^\top (i,:) \psi_i(t, t-1) (\mathbf{U}_t - \mathbf{U}_{t-1})(i,:) \\
&= \sum_{t=1}^{T} Tr((\mathbf{U}_t - \mathbf{U}_{t-1})^\top \Sigma_t (\mathbf{U}_t - \mathbf{U}_{t-1})), \quad (6)
\end{aligned}$$

where Σ_t is the diagonal temporal coefficient matrix among m users, defined as

$$\Sigma_t = \begin{bmatrix} \psi_1(t, t-1) & 0 & \cdots & 0 \\ 0 & \psi_2(t, t-1) & \cdots & 0 \\ \vdots & \vdots & \ddots & \vdots \\ 0 & 0 & \cdots & \psi_m(t, t-1) \end{bmatrix}. \quad (7)$$

4. LRT: LOCATION RECOMMENDATION FRAMEWORK WITH TEMPORAL EFFECTS

In this section, we formally introduce our location recommendation framework **LRT**. Figure 2 illustrates the working flow of our location recommendation framework. "x" denotes the observed check-in frequency by the user on the corresponding location, and "?" represents the user's check-in preferences on an unvisited location that the framework is going to infer. The whole framework consists of three steps: temporal division, temporal factorization, and temporal aggregation. Firstly, the original user-location matrix $\mathbf{C}$ is divided into T sub-matrices according to the T temporal states, with each sub-matrix only containing check-in actions that happened at the corresponding temporal state. Secondly, each $\mathbf{C}_t$ is factorized into the user check-in preference $\mathbf{U}_t$ and the location characteristics $\mathbf{L}$ based on the model presented in Section 3, while $\mathbf{L}$ is shared by all of $\mathbf{U}_t$. Finally, the corresponding low-rank approximation $\widetilde{\mathbf{C}}_t$ is constructed and aggregated into $\widetilde{\mathbf{C}}$, representing the user check-in preferences of each location.

Since the temporal division is straightforward to implement, in the following, we will describe in details the second and third steps, i.e., learning user temporal check-in preferences at each temporal state and aggregating temporal check-in preferences for location recommendation.

4.1 Learning Temporal Check-in Preferences

Based on the discussion of modeling temporal non-uniformness and consecutiveness properties in the above sections, the user temporal check-in preferences can be obtained by solving the following optimization problem:

$$\begin{aligned}
\min_{\mathbf{U}_t \geq 0, \mathbf{L} \geq 0} &\sum_{t=1}^{T} ||\mathbf{Y}_t \odot (\mathbf{C}_t - \mathbf{U}_t \mathbf{L}^\top)||_F^2 + \alpha \sum_{t=1}^{T} ||\mathbf{U}_t||_F^2 + \beta ||\mathbf{L}||_F^2 \\
&+ \lambda \sum_{t=1}^{T} Tr((\mathbf{U}_t - \mathbf{U}_{t-1})^\top \Sigma_t (\mathbf{U}_t - \mathbf{U}_{t-1})), \quad (8)
\end{aligned}$$

where λ is a non-negative parameter to control the temporal regularization. The corresponding objective function $\mathcal{J}$ is

$$\begin{aligned}
\mathcal{J} = &\sum_{t=1}^{T} Tr((\mathbf{Y}_t^\top \odot \mathbf{C}_t^\top)(\mathbf{Y}_t \odot \mathbf{C}_t) - (\mathbf{Y}_t^\top \odot \mathbf{C}_t^\top)(\mathbf{Y}_t \odot \mathbf{U}_t \mathbf{L}^\top) \\
&- (\mathbf{Y}_t \odot \mathbf{C}_t)(\mathbf{Y}_t^\top \odot \mathbf{L}\mathbf{U}_t^\top) + (\mathbf{Y}_t^\top \odot \mathbf{L}\mathbf{U}_t^\top)(\mathbf{Y}_t \odot \mathbf{U}_t \mathbf{L}^\top)) \\
&+ \lambda \sum_{t=1}^{T} Tr((\mathbf{U}_t - \mathbf{U}_{t-1})^\top \Sigma_t (\mathbf{U}_t - \mathbf{U}_{t-1})) \\
&+ \alpha \sum_{t=1}^{T} Tr(\mathbf{U}_t^\top \mathbf{U}_t) + \beta Tr(\mathbf{L}^\top \mathbf{L}) \\
&- \sum_{t=1}^{T} Tr(\Gamma_{\mathbf{U}_t} \mathbf{U}_t^\top) - Tr(\Gamma_{\mathbf{L}} \mathbf{L}^\top), \quad (9)
\end{aligned}$$

where $\Gamma_{\mathbf{U}_t}$ and $\Gamma_{\mathbf{L}}$ are Lagrangian multipliers for non-negativity of $\mathbf{U}_t$ and $\mathbf{L}$, respectively. By taking the derivation of $\mathcal{J}$ with respect to $\mathbf{U}_t$ and $\mathbf{L}$, we obtain

$$\frac{\partial \mathcal{J}}{\partial \mathbf{U}_t} = -2(\mathbf{Y}_t \odot \mathbf{C}_t)\mathbf{L} + 2(\mathbf{Y}_t \odot \mathbf{U}_t\mathbf{L}^\top)\mathbf{L} + 2\lambda\Sigma_t(\mathbf{U}_t - \mathbf{U}_{t-1}) + 2\alpha\mathbf{U}_t - \Gamma_{\mathbf{U}_t},$$

$$\frac{\partial \mathcal{J}}{\partial \mathbf{L}} = -2\sum_{t=1}^{T}(\mathbf{Y}_t \odot \mathbf{C}_t)^\top\mathbf{U}_t + 2\sum_{t=1}^{T}(\mathbf{Y}_t \odot \mathbf{U}_t\mathbf{L}^\top)^\top\mathbf{U}_t + 2\beta\mathbf{L} - \Gamma_{\mathbf{L}}. \quad (10)$$

Let $\frac{\partial \mathcal{J}}{\partial \mathbf{U}_t} = 0$ and $\frac{\partial \mathcal{J}}{\partial \mathbf{L}} = 0$, we obtain

$$\Gamma_{\mathbf{U}_t} = -2(\mathbf{Y}_t \odot \mathbf{C}_t)\mathbf{L} + 2(\mathbf{Y}_t \odot \mathbf{U}_t\mathbf{L}^\top)\mathbf{L} + 2\lambda\Sigma_t(\mathbf{U}_t - \mathbf{U}_{t-1}) + 2\alpha_t\mathbf{U}_t,$$

$$\Gamma_{\mathbf{V}} = -2\sum_{t=1}^{T}(\mathbf{Y}_t \odot \mathbf{C}_t)^\top\mathbf{U}_t + 2\sum_{t=1}^{T}(\mathbf{Y}_t \odot \mathbf{U}_t\mathbf{L}^\top)^\top\mathbf{U}_t + 2\beta\mathbf{V}. \quad (11)$$

According to the Karush-Kuhn-Tucker condition,

$$\mathbf{U}_t(i,k)\Gamma_{\mathbf{U}_t}(i,k) = 0, \forall i \in [1,m], k \in [1,d], t \in [1,T]$$
$$\mathbf{L}(i,k)\Gamma_{\mathbf{L}}(i,k) = 0, \forall i \in [1,n], k \in [1,d]. \quad (12)$$

We obtain the following updating formula of $\mathbf{U}_t$ and $\mathbf{L}$ with a similar derivation process in [6]

$$\mathbf{U}_t(i,k) \leftarrow \mathbf{U}_t(i,k)\sqrt{\frac{[(\mathbf{Y}_t \odot \mathbf{C}_t)\mathbf{L} + \lambda\Sigma_t\mathbf{U}_{t-1}](i,k)}{[(\mathbf{Y}_t \odot \mathbf{U}_t\mathbf{L}^\top)\mathbf{L} + \lambda\Sigma_t\mathbf{U}_t + \alpha\mathbf{U}_t](i,k)}}$$

$$\mathbf{L}(i,k) \leftarrow \mathbf{L}(i,k)\sqrt{\frac{[\sum_{t=1}^{T}(\mathbf{Y}_t \odot \mathbf{C}_t)^\top\mathbf{U}_t](i,k)}{[\sum_{t=1}^{T}(\mathbf{Y}_t \odot \mathbf{U}_t\mathbf{L}^\top)^\top\mathbf{U}_t + \beta\mathbf{L}](i,k)}}. \quad (13)$$

4.2 Temporal Aggregation for Location Recommendation

By solving the above optimization problem, the user check-in preferences $\widetilde{\mathbf{C}}_t(i,j)$ at each temporal state can be computed through $\mathbf{U}_t(i,:)\mathbf{L}(j,:)^\top$. To recommend locations to a user w.r.t. each $\widetilde{\mathbf{C}}_t(i,j)$, we define an aggregation function $f(\cdot)$ to compute the final user check-in preferences $\widetilde{\mathbf{C}}(i,j)$.

$$\widetilde{\mathbf{C}}(i,j) = f(\widetilde{\mathbf{C}}_1(i,j), \widetilde{\mathbf{C}}_2(i,j), ..., \widetilde{\mathbf{C}}_T(i,j)). \quad (14)$$

In this paper, we propose four aggregation strategies for $f(\cdot)$, defined below:

- **Sum**: we consider a user's check-in preferences at a location as the sum of his check-in preferences from each temporal state, i.e., $\widetilde{\mathbf{C}}(i,j) = \sum_{t=1}^{T}\widetilde{\mathbf{C}}_t(i,j)$.
- **Mean**: we consider a user's check-in preferences at a location as the average non-zero preferences from each temporal state, i.e., $\widetilde{\mathbf{C}}(i,j) = \frac{\sum_{t=1}^{T}\widetilde{\mathbf{C}}_t(i,j)}{\|\{\widetilde{\mathbf{C}}_t(i,j)|\widetilde{\mathbf{C}}_t(i,j)\neq 0\}\|}$.
- **Maximum**: we consider a user's check-in preferences at a location as his maximum temporal check-in preferences, i.e., $\widetilde{\mathbf{C}}(i,j) = max(\widetilde{\mathbf{C}}_1(i,j), ..., \widetilde{\mathbf{C}}_T(i,j))$.
- **Voting**: Each $\widetilde{\mathbf{C}}_t(i,j)$ acts as a recommender, and nominates top n locations to a user. The final recommended locations are those locations that have been nominated by most $\widetilde{\mathbf{C}}_t(i,j)$.

The location recommendation will then be performed based on the final user check-in preference $\widetilde{\mathbf{C}}(i,j)$.

4.3 Algorithm Analysis and Time Complexity

Algorithm 1 presents the detailed procedures of the proposed framework. Compared to the temporal division of C and temporal aggregation of $\widetilde{\mathbf{C}}$, the updating rules for $\mathbf{U}_t$ and L in each iteration corresponds to the major cost of Algorithm 1. Therefore, we next analyze the time complexity of updating $\mathbf{U}_t$ and L. For the updating rule of $\mathbf{U}_t$, $(\mathbf{Y}_t \odot \mathbf{C}_t)\mathbf{L}$ takes $O(md^2)$ operations due to the sparsity of $\mathbf{Y}_t$ and $\mathbf{C}_t$. Since Σ_t is a diagonal matrix, the time complexity of $\lambda\Sigma_t\mathbf{U}_{t-1}$ is $O(md)$. $(\mathbf{Y}_t \odot \mathbf{U}_t\mathbf{L}^\top)\mathbf{L}$ takes $O(mnd)$ operations, while the time complexity of $\lambda\Sigma_t\mathbf{U}_t$ and $\alpha\mathbf{U}_t$ is $O(md)$. Therefore, it takes $O(mndT)$ operations to update all of $\mathbf{U}_t$. Similarly, the time complexity of $\sum_{t=1}^{T}(\mathbf{Y}_t \odot \mathbf{C}_t)^\top\mathbf{U}_t$ for updating $\mathbf{L}$ is $O(md^2T)$. $\sum_{t=1}^{T}(\mathbf{Y}_t \odot \mathbf{U}_t\mathbf{L}^\top)^\top\mathbf{U}_t$ takes $O(mndT)$ operations and $\beta\mathbf{L}$ takes $O(nd)$ operations, resulting in the time complexity of updating $\mathbf{L}$ as $O(mndT)$. Since T is usually a constant of small value, in sum, the time complexity of Algorithm 1 is $O(mnd)$.

Algorithm 1 Location Recommendation with Temporal Effects

Input: user-location check-in matrix $\mathbf{C}$, α, β, possible temporal states $\{1, 2, ..., T\}$
Output: approximated user-location preference matrix $\widetilde{\mathbf{C}}$

```
Divide C into {C_1, C_2,..., C_T} according to T
Generate {Y_1, Y_2,..., Y_T} based on {C_1, C_2,..., C_T}
Construct {Σ_1, Σ_2, ..., Σ_T} based on {C_1, C_2,..., C_T}
Initialize {U_1, U_2,..., U_T} and L randomly
while Not Convergent do
  for t = 1 to T do
    for i = 1 to m do
      for k = 1 to d do
        U_t(i,k) ← U_t(i,k) sqrt( [(Y_t⊙C_t)L+λΣ_tU_{t-1}](i,k) / [(Y_t⊙U_tL^T)L+λΣ_tU_t+αU_t](i,k) )
      end for
    end for
  end for
  for i = 1 to n do
    for k = 1 to d do
      L(i,k) ← L(i,k) sqrt( [Σ_{t=1}^T (Y_t⊙C_t)^T U_t](i,k) / [Σ_{t=1}^T (Y_t⊙U_tL^T)^T U_t+βL](i,k) )
    end for
  end for
end while
for t = 1 to T do
  Set C̃_t = U_t L^T
end for
for i = 1 to m do
  for j = 1 to n do
    Set C̃(i,j) = f(C̃_1(i,j), C̃_2(i,j), ..., C̃_T(i,j))
  end for
end for
return C̃
```

5. EXPERIMENTS

In this section, we evaluate the performance of our framework **LRT** for location recommendation. In particular, we evaluate the following: (1) how the proposed framework fares in comparison with state-of-the-art models that capture static check-in preferences; (2) how the proposed framework recommends locations with various temporal aggregation strategies; and (3) whether other temporal patterns could be leveraged for location recommendation with the proposed framework. Before we delve into experiment details, we first discuss an LBSN dataset and evaluation metrics.

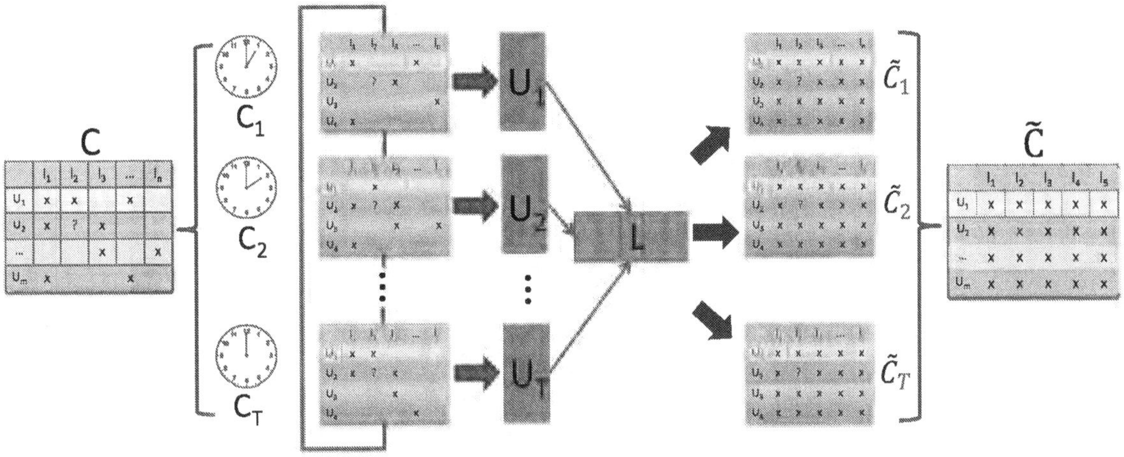

Figure 2: Location Recommendation Framework with Temporal Effects

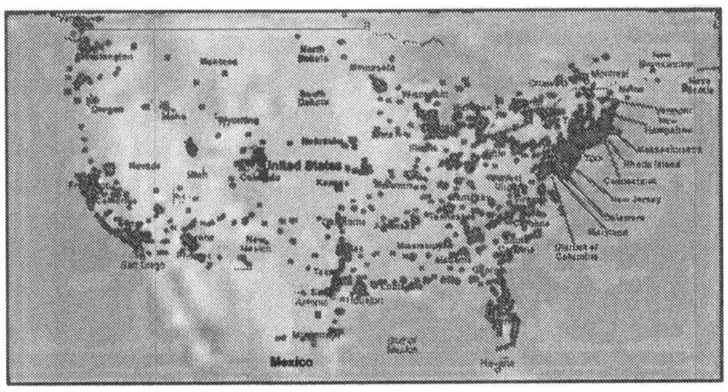

Figure 3: The Check-in Distribution over the U.S.

5.1 Dataset and Experiment Setup

We crawled the experimental dataset from Foursquare and obtained check-ins for three months (Jan 2011 - Mar 2011) to evaluate our proposed framework. The dataset is publicly available from the first author's homepage[3]. Foursquare allows a user to check in at a physical location via his cellphone, and then let his online friends know where he is by publishing such check-in action online. We select check-in locations which have been visited by at least two distinct users, and users who have checked in at least 10 distinct locations. The statistics of the final dataset are shown in Table 1. The majority of check-ins happened in the U.S.; Figure 3 shows the corresponding check-in distributions in the U.S.

We organize the dataset as a user-location matrix. The check-in density of the matrix is 8.84×10^{-4}. Logistic function $\frac{1}{1+(e^x)^{-1}}$ is commonly used in recommender system [15] to map each matrix element into [0,1]. We notice that in contrast with online item recommendation, where x (the rating of an item) is usually ranging from 1 to 5, in location recommendation, the value of x (check-in frequency of a location) is commonly large, while the function "$(e^x)^{-1}$" would result in very small and indistinguishable values, with x being larger than 7. Therefore, we adjust the mapping function as $\frac{1}{1+x^{-1}}$, with x corresponding to $\tilde{C}(i,j)$ in our data, which works better than the logistic function in our experiment.

[3] http://www.public.asu.edu/~hgao16/dataset.html

Table 1: Statistical Information of the Dataset

duration	Jan 1, 2011-Mar 31, 2011
No. of users	5,269
No. of check-ins	288,079
No. of unique locations	26,381
Average check-ins per user	55
Check-in density	8.84×10^{-4}

For each individual user in the dataset, we randomly mark off 20% and 40% of all locations that he has checked-in for testing. The rest of the user-location pairs are used as training data to infer $\mathbf{U}_t$ and $\mathbf{L}$ for location recommendation. The random selection is conducted 5 times individually, and we report the average results.

To evaluate the recommendation performance, we are interested in: (1) how many previously marked off locations are recommended to the users among the total number of recommended locations, and (2) how many previously marked off locations are recommended to the users among the total number of marked off locations. Thus, we use *precision@N* and *recall@N* as our evaluation metrics, defined as follows:

$$precision@N = \frac{\sum_{u_i \in U} |TopN(u_i) \bigcap L(u_i)|}{\sum_{u_i \in U} |TopN(u_i)|} \quad (15)$$

$$recall@N = \frac{\sum_{u_i \in U} |TopN(u_i) \bigcap L(u_i)|}{\sum_{u_i \in U} |L(u_i)|}, \quad (16)$$

where $TopN(u_i)$ is the set of locations recommended to user u_i that u_i has not visited in the training set. $L(u_i)$ is the set of locations that has been visited by u_i in the testing set. In our experiment, N is set to 5 and 10, respectively.

All the parameters in this paper are set through cross-validation. For the proposed method, the experimental results use d=10 dimensions to represent the latent features, the regularization coefficients α and β are set to 2, and λ is set to 1. As suggested in [23], the effectiveness of recommender systems with sparse datasets (i.e., low-density user-item matrix) is usually not high. For example, the reported top 5 precision is 5% over a dataset with 8.02×10^{-3} density and 3.5% over a dataset with 4.24×10^{-5} density [23, 25]. Therefore, the low precision obtained in our experiment is reasonable. In this paper, we focus on **comparing the relative performance of algorithms instead of comparing their absolute performance**.

5.2 Evaluating Data Properties of Temporal Non-uniformness and Consecutiveness

In this section, we discuss the properties of temporal non-uniformness and temporal consecutiveness in our dataset. The temporal non-uniformness property, which states that a user exhibits distinct check-in preferences at different hours of the day, is straightforward to evaluate with a two-sided hypothesis testing on the check-in behavior of two temporal states for each user. Our experiment shows that this property does hold in our dataset. Due to the space limit, we will ignore its evaluation details and focus on evaluating temporal consecutiveness. We firstly define the check-in similarity of a user between two temporal states t_i and t_j:

$$sim_u(t_i, t_j) = \frac{\mathbf{C}_{t_i}(u, :) \cdot \mathbf{C}_{t_j}(u, :)}{|\mathbf{C}_{t_i}(u, :)|_2 \times |\mathbf{C}_{t_j}(u, :)|_2}, \tag{17}$$

where $\mathbf{C}_t(u, :)$ is the check-in vector of user u at temporal state t. $| \bullet |_2$ is the 2-norm of a vector.

To evaluate temporal consecutiveness, we calculate two similarities for each user u: consecutive similarity $\mathbf{S}_c(u)$ and non-consecutive similarity $\mathbf{S}_n(u)$. $\mathbf{S}_c(u)$ is the average similarity of all $sim_u(t_i, t_j)$, where t_i and t_j are consecutive temporal states. Note that T temporal states have T consecutive temporal similarities in total, i.e., $sim_u(t_1, t_2)$, $sim_u(t_2, t_3)$,..., $sim_u(T-1, T)$, and $sim_u(T, 1)$. Similarly, $\mathbf{S}_n(u)$ is the average similarity of all $sim_u(t_i, t_j)$, where t_i and t_j are non-consecutive temporal states. For fair comparison, we randomly sample T non-consecutive temporal similarities $sim_u(t_i, t_j)$ to ensure that both $\mathbf{S}_c(u)$ and $\mathbf{S}_n(u)$ have the same sample size and then take the average to calculate $\mathbf{S}_n(u)$.

We conduct a two-sample t-test on the vectors $\mathbf{S}_c$ and $\mathbf{S}_n$. The null hypothesis is H_0: $\mathbf{S}_c \le \mathbf{S}_n$, i.e., check-ins between consecutive temporal states are less or equally similar than that between non-consecutive temporal states. The alternative hypothesis is H_1: $\mathbf{S}_c > \mathbf{S}_n$. In our experiment, the null hypothesis is rejected at significant level $\alpha = 0.001$ with p-value of $5.6e$-191, i.e., a user's check-ins in two consecutive temporal states have a higher similarity than those in non-consecutive temporal states.

5.3 Comparison of Various Recommendation Models

In this section, we compare our proposed location recommendation framework **LRT** with various recommendation models. Three baseline methods are introduced w.r.t. time-dependent and static check-in preferences, as defined below:

- **User-Based Collaborative Filtering (CF)**
  User-based collaborative filtering is a state-of-the-art approach for recommender systems. We adopt the user-based recommender [29] for location recommendation. It computes a user's interest in a location based on other users' interests in that location. Temporal information is not considered in this approach.

- **Non-negative Matrix Factorization (NMF)**
  Non-negative Matrix Factorization (NMF) [13] computes non-negative user check-in preferences under the whole user-location matrix, which is our basic location recommendation model, as defined in Eq. (2), without temporal effects.

- **Random LRT (R-LRT)**
  We randomly divide the original user-location matrix $\mathbf{C}$ into 24 pieces $\mathbf{C}_t$ without considering the temporal state, and then apply the same recommendation process in Figure 2.

Figure 4 reports the comparison results of **LRT** with the proposed baseline methods. The aggregation strategy is selected as voting due to its superior performance (more details on the comparison of aggregation strategies will be discussed in the next subsection). The results precipitate several observations, which we summarize below:

- CF performs the worst among all the approaches. The data sparseness could be one reason to explain this performance. Due to the low density of the user-location matrix, the collaborative filtering approach fails to accurately recommend locations and performs worse than matrix factorization approaches, which leverage the low-rank approximation of user check-in preferences.

- Both NMF and R-LRT perform better than CF, demonstrating their ability in dealing with sparse data for location recommendation. Furthermore, the better performance of **LRT** than NMF suggests that time-dependent check-in preference capture user mobile behavior better than static check-in preferences.

- **LRT** performs better than R-LRT, suggesting that the division strategy is important. Our model, with the consideration of temporal effects, is able to improve location recommendation performance, while without an appropriate temporal division the matrix divide-aggregation strategy could result in a bad performance.

LRT performs the best among all the baseline methods. It considers time-dependent check-in preferences and outperforms approaches that capture static check-in preferences. The standard deviation of the performance from each method is less than 2×10^{-4}, confirming the reliability of our comparison results. As we mentioned before, **the recommendation effectiveness is usually low due to the sparseness of data with low density**. Therefore, the absolute performance on precision and recall of **LRT** seems to be small but is still reasonable and significant compared to other baseline methods.

To further evaluate the significance of our framework, we launch a random recommendation [24]. For each user, we randomly select 5/10 locations from the total 26,381 locations (excluding locations that have been previously visited by the user), and recommend them to the user. The recommendation performance with this strategy is shown in Table 2. Compared to the random recommendation, our proposed framework is, on average, 73.27 times better than the random performance, demonstrating the power of temporal effects for improving location recommendation performance.

Table 2: Performance of Random Recommendation

Testing	Metrics	@5	@10
20%	Precision	0.0152%	0.0190%
	Recall	0.0177%	0.0442%
40%	Precision	0.0266%	0.0361%
	Recall	0.0149%	0.0403%

5.4 Location Recommendation with Various Aggregation Strategies

In this subsection, we discuss the performance of various aggregation strategies. We compare the recommendation performance

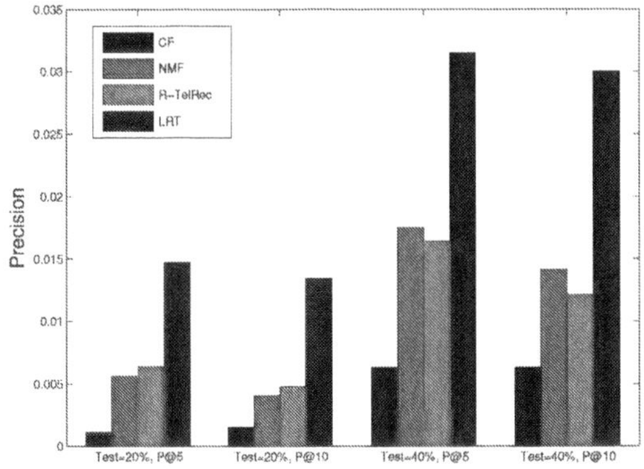

(a) Recommendation Performance (Precision)

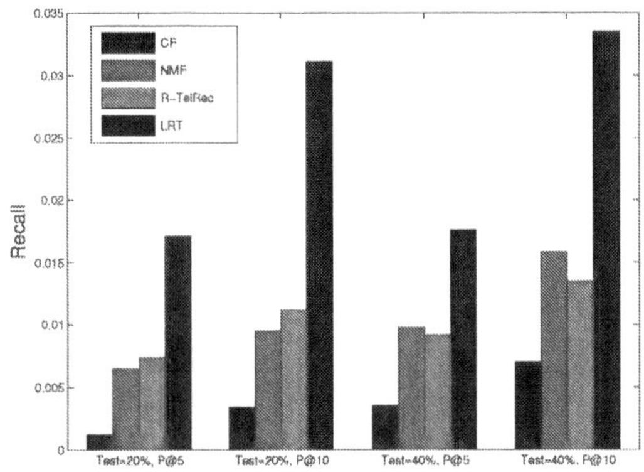

(b) Recommendation Performance (Recall)

Figure 4: Performance of Location Recommendation Models

of four aggregation strategies and list the results in Table 3 and Table 4. We summarize the essential observations below:

- The **mean** performs the worst among all the aggregation strategies. This is because taking the average of all the temporal preferences degrades the preference variance and makes the personal preferences indistinguishable. It validates the fact that a user's check-in preferences are highly dependent on the temporal state, approaches regardless of this may fail in recommending the right locations.

- The **maximum** has similar performance to the **sum**, suggesting that if a user's check-in preferences are strongly indicated by one temporal state, there is a high probability it indicates the true preferences of the user. This is also consistent with the observation reported by [10] that a user's check-in behavior presents Gaussian distribution over hours of the day, in which a user mostly checks-in at a location during a specific period of time and rarely visits during other time periods.

- The **voting** performs the best among all the aggregation strategies. Compared to the **sum**, it filters controversial location candidates at each temporal state, and reduces the uncertainty brought by the noisy location candidates, demonstrating its robustness in dealing with noisy data.

Table 3: Comparison of Aggregation Strategies (Precision)

Testing	Metrics	Sum	Mean	Max	Voting
20%	P@5	1.37%	0.03%	1.35%	1.47%
	P@10	1.31%	0.03%	1.30%	1.34%
40%	P@5	3.08%	0.46%	3.10%	3.20%
	P@10	2.95%	0.44%	2.95%	3.00%

Table 4: Comparison of Aggregation Strategies (Recall)

Testing	Metrics	Sum	Mean	Max	Voting
20%	R@5	1.60%	0.03%	1.57%	1.71%
	R@10	3.05%	0.08%	3.03%	3.11%
40%	R@5	1.73%	0.03%	1.74%	1.79%
	R@10	3.25%	0.05%	3.30%	3.35%

5.5 Exploring Various Temporal Patterns

LRT is designed to recommend locations to a user by taking advantage of temporal patterns. So far, we have evaluated its recommendation performance with daily patterns, while its recommendation ability is not limited to one specific temporal pattern. By taking different definitions of temporal state, many other temporal patterns can be used for location recommendation with **LRT**, as long as they contain the non-uniformness and consecutiveness properties. For example, we could define the temporal state as t=[1,T], with T=7 for weekly (day of the week) patterns, T=2 for weekday/weekend patterns, and T=12 for monthly (month of the year) patterns, etc. The only change is to divide the original user-location matrix **C** into a set of $\mathbf{C}_t$ according to the corresponding temporal state. Table 5 shows the recommendation results of **LRT** with weekly patterns and weekday/weekend patterns. Due to the space limit, we only present the results on testing size = 40%. The results indicate that weekly patterns and weekday/weekend patterns can also capture users' temporal check-in preferences and improve the location recommendation performance.

Table 5: Comparison of Temporal Patterns

Temporal Patterns	Metrics	@5	@10
Day of the Week	Precision	2.32%	2.18%
	Recall	1.30%	2.45%
Weekday/Weekend	Precision	2.23%	2.04%
	Recall	1.21%	2.28%

6. CONCLUSION AND FUTURE WORK

In this paper, we investigated the temporal properties of user check-in behavior on location-based social networks, and leveraged them to generate a location recommendation framework with temporal effects. The experimental results exhibit the power of temporal effects for capturing a user's mobile behavior, and demonstrate their potential ability in improving location recommendation performance. Considering the various types of temporal patterns, investigating other patterns (e.g., monthly/ yearly patterns) could provide the model with potential power to predict the future. On the other hand, how to integrate these patterns for location recommendation could also be an interesting direction for future work. Furthermore, it would be interesting to study the complementary effects of temporal patterns with social and geographical information on LBSNs, and leverage multiple resources to generate a spatial-temporal-social framework for location recommendation.

7. ACKNOWLEDGMENTS

This work is supported, in part, by ONR (N000141010091).

8. REFERENCES

[1] B. Berjani and T. Strufe. A recommendation system for spots in location-based online social networks. In *Proceedings of the 4th Workshop on Social Network Systems*, pages 1–6. ACM, 2011.

[2] J. Chang and E. Sun. Location 3: How users share and respond to location-based data on social networking sites. *Proceedings of the Fifth International AAAI Conference on Weblogs and Social Media*, 2011.

[3] C. Cheng, H. Yang, I. King, and M. Lyu. Fused matrix factorization with geographical and social influence in location-based social networks. *AAAI, Toronto, Canada*, 2012.

[4] Z. Cheng, J. Caverlee, K. Lee, and D. Sui. Exploring millions of footprints in location sharing services. In *Proceedings of the Fifth International Conference on Weblogs and Social Media*, 2011.

[5] E. Cho, S. Myers, and J. Leskovec. Friendship and mobility: user movement in location-based social networks. In *Proceedings of the 17th ACM SIGKDD International Conference on Knowledge Discovery and Data Mining*, pages 1082–1090. ACM, 2011.

[6] C. Ding, T. Li, and M. Jordan. Nonnegative matrix factorization for combinatorial optimization: Spectral clustering, graph matching, and clique finding. In *Data Mining, 2008. ICDM'08. Eighth IEEE International Conference on*, pages 183–192. IEEE, 2008.

[7] Z. Y. Dingqi Yang, Daqing Zhang and Z. Wang. A sentiment-enhanced personalized location recommendation system. *ACM Hypertext*, 2013.

[8] H. Gao, J. Tang, and H. Liu. Exploring social-historical ties on location-based social networks. In *Proceedings of the Sixth International Conference on Weblogs and Social Media*, 2012.

[9] H. Gao, J. Tang, and H. Liu. gSCorr: Modeling geo-social correlations for new check-ins on location-based social networks. *21st ACM International Conference on Information and Knowledge Management*, 2012.

[10] H. Gao, J. Tang, and H. Liu. Mobile location prediction in spatio-temporal context. *Nokia Mobile Data Challenge Workshop*, 2012.

[11] Y. Koren. Factorization meets the neighborhood: a multifaceted collaborative filtering model. In *Proceeding of the 14th ACM SIGKDD international conference on Knowledge discovery and data mining*, pages 426–434. ACM, 2008.

[12] Y. Koren, R. Bell, and C. Volinsky. Matrix factorization techniques for recommender systems. *Computer*, 42(8):30–37, 2009.

[13] D. Lee, H. Seung, et al. Learning the parts of objects by non-negative matrix factorization. *Nature*, 401(6755):788–791, 1999.

[14] H. Liu, B. Luo, and D. Lee. Location type classification using tweet content. In *Machine Learning and Applications (ICMLA), 2012 11th International Conference on*, volume 1, pages 232–237. IEEE, 2012.

[15] H. Ma, H. Yang, M. Lyu, and I. King. Sorec: social recommendation using probabilistic matrix factorization. In *Proceedings of the 17th ACM conference on Information and knowledge management*, pages 931–940. ACM, 2008.

[16] E. Malmi, T. Do, and D. Gatica-Perez. Checking in or checked in: Comparing large-scale manual and automatic location disclosure patterns. *The 11th International Conference on Mobile and Ubiquitous Multimedia (MUM 2012)*, 2012.

[17] A. Noulas, S. Scellato, C. Mascolo, and M. Pontil. An empirical study of geographic user activity patterns in foursquare. *Proceeding of the 5th International AAAI Conference on Weblogs and Social Media*, 2011.

[18] S. Scellato, C. Mascolo, M. Musolesi, and V. Latora. Distance matters: Geo-social metrics for online social networks. In *Proceedings of the 3rd conference on online social networks*, pages 8–8. USENIX Association, 2010.

[19] S. Scellato, A. Noulas, R. Lambiotte, and C. Mascolo. Socio-spatial properties of online location-based social networks. *Proceeding of the 5th International AAAI Conference on Weblogs and Social Media*, 11, 2011.

[20] J. Tang, H. Gao, and H. Liu. mTrust: Discerning multi-faceted trust in a connected world. In *the 5th ACM International Conference on Web Search and Data Mining*, 2012.

[21] J. Tang, H. Gao, H. Liu, and A. D. Sarma. eTrust: Understanding trust evolution in an online world. In *KDD*, 2012.

[22] M. Ye, K. Janowicz, C. Mülligann, and W. Lee. What you are is when you are: the temporal dimension of feature types in location-based social networks. In *Proceedings of the 19th ACM SIGSPATIAL International Conference on Advances in Geographic Information Systems*, pages 102–111. ACM, 2011.

[23] M. Ye, X. Liu, and W. Lee. Exploring social influence for recommendation - a probabilistic generative approach. In *Annual International ACM SIGIR Conference on Research and Development in Information Retrieval*, pages 325–334, 2012.

[24] M. Ye, P. Yin, and W. Lee. Location recommendation for location-based social networks. In *Proceedings of the 18th SIGSPATIAL International Conference on Advances in Geographic Information Systems*, pages 458–461, 2010.

[25] M. Ye, P. Yin, W. Lee, and D. Lee. Exploiting geographical influence for collaborative point-of-interest recommendation. In *Annual International ACM SIGIR Conference on Research and Development in Information Retrieval*, pages 325–334, 2011.

[26] J. Ying, E. Lu, W. Kuo, and V. Tseng. Urban point-of-interest recommendation by mining user check-in behaviors. In *Proceedings of the ACM SIGKDD International Workshop on Urban Computing*, pages 63–70. ACM, 2012.

[27] C. Zhang, L. Shou, K. Chen, G. Chen, and Y. Bei. Evaluating geo-social influence in location-based social networks. In *Proceedings of the 21st ACM international conference on Information and knowledge management*, pages 1442–1451. ACM, 2012.

[28] Y. Zheng, L. Zhang, Z. Ma, X. Xie, and W. Ma. Recommending friends and locations based on individual location history. *ACM Transactions on the Web (TWEB)*, 5(1):5, 2011.

[29] D. Zhou, B. Wang, S. Rahimi, and X. Wang. A study of recommending locations on location-based social network by collaborative filtering. *Advances in Artificial Intelligence*, pages 255–266, 2012.

[30] K. Zickuhr. Three-quarters of smartphone owners use location-based services. *Pew Internet & American Life Project*, 2012.

The Curated Web: A Recommendation Challenge

Zurina Saaya[1], Rachael Rafter[2], Markus Schaal[1] and Barry Smyth[2]
[1]CLARITY: Centre for Sensor Web Technologies, University College Dublin, Ireland
[2]INSIGHT: Centre for Data Analytics, University College Dublin, Ireland
{firstname.lastname}@ucd.ie

ABSTRACT

In this paper we consider the application of content-based recommendation techniques to web curation services which allow users to curate and share topical collections of content (e.g. images, news, web pages etc.). Curation services like Pinterest are now a mainstay of the modern web and present a range of interesting recommendation challenges. In this paper we consider the task of recommending collections to users and evaluate a range of different content-based techniques across a variety of content signals. We present the results of a large-scale evaluation using data from the Scoop.it[1] web page curation service.

Categories and Subject Descriptors

H.3.3 [**Information Search and Retrieval**]: Information Filtering; H.3.5 [**Online Information Services**]: Web-based Services

Keywords

content-based recommendation, social web, curation

1. INTRODUCTION

Recently there has been a shift in web usage from content consumption to content production and a pattern of *content curation* has emerged through sites and services like Pinterest, Tumblr, Storify, and Scoop.it. These curation sites allow users to curate collections of content (e.g. images, news, web pages etc.) on topics that matter to them and to share these collections with others.

In this paper we consider some of the recommendation challenges that exist within such curation services using Scoop.it (a web page curation site) as an evaluation case-study. Specifically, we consider the challenge of matching users with collections. We look at different ways to profile the interests of users and the contents of collections in order to develop a content-based recommendation framework to suggest relevant collections to users based on their current collections/topics/interests. We evaluate the efficacy of different types of content signals during user profiling and collection indexing, from high-level collection descriptions to detailed information about the contents of individual pages within a collection. We do this to better understand the relationship between these different types of signals and recommendation performance, and describe the results of a large-scale evaluation based on Scoop.it user and collection data.

Social curation is a relatively new trend and has received little attention to date. In previous work we examined how to assist curators during the content curation phase, using machine learning to identify the correct target collection for new content the user wishes to gather [7]. In [5] the authors look at recommending curators, identifying the important users that form the community around a news story on Twitter using network analysis. Others focus on how users curate tweets, and how to recommend new tweets to them [4]. The work in [2] also studies content recommendation on Twitter, using both content and social signals.

2. WEB CURATION USING SCOOP.IT

Scoop.it is a web-based curation tool that provides a platform for users to curate all of their favorite resources on a given topic for sharing with interested parties. Users can create their own collections (or *topics* in the Scoop.it parlance) and the service provides a range of tools to help users identify and filter content for their collections. Creating a collection or topic is a simple matter of providing a name, a short description, and a set of suitable keywords.

For instance, a curator may create a new *JQuery for Web Dev* topic (or collection) as a place to curate all things related to web development using *jquery* (see Fig. 1(a)). For each topic, the user can specify a title and short description of the topic, and every page added to the topic is associated with a page title and short summary. Furthermore, curators can annotate the pages that they include in their topic with their insights, and others can comment on the pages included. In addition to curating their own topics, users can also follow the topics of others that interest them, (see Fig. 1(b)). This can be a useful way for users to maintain and improve their own topics, by keeping up-to-date with what others are curating in similar topics. Scoop.it provides a handy *rescoop* functionality, allowing users to conveniently incorporate content from other topics into their own.

[1]http://www.scoop.it

RecSys'13, October 12–16, 2013, Hong Kong, China.

http://dx.doi.org/10.1145/2507157.2507216.

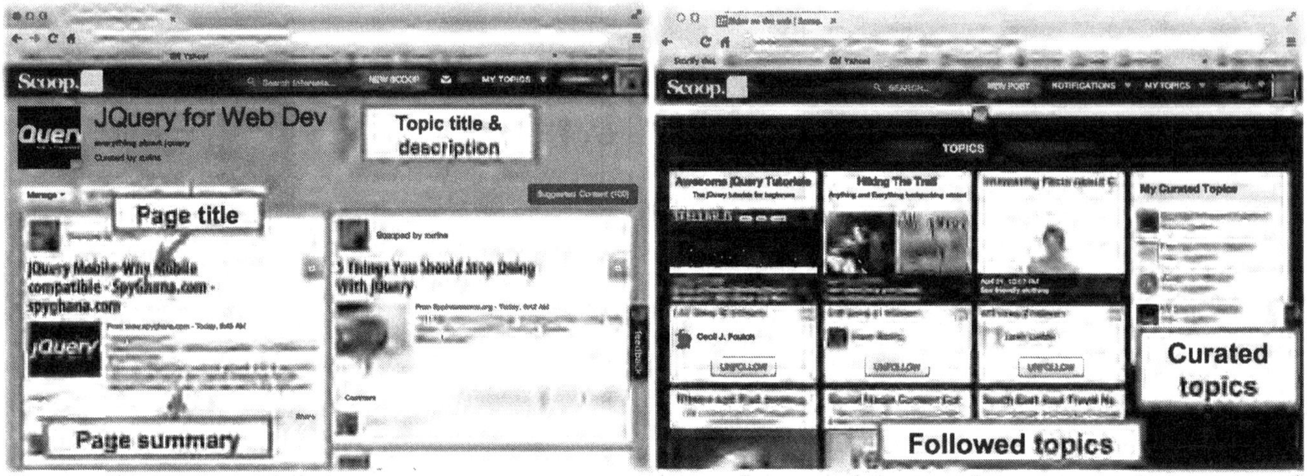

(a) Topic page (b) Topics dashboard

Figure 1: Scoop.it in action

3. RECOMMENDER FRAMEWORK

We describe a content-based recommendation framework that explores the relative benefits of different sources of data for modelling curated collections and user profiles.

3.1 Representing Topics for Querying and Indexing

In Scoop.it each topic is a collection of curated pages and has an associated topic title and description. Each page in a topic has a URL, a title, and a summary (snippet) description. In addition we can also extract a set of content terms from the page directly. This means that we can represent and index topics at different levels of granularity:

1. *TopicTitleDesc* - The terms in the topic's title and description elements.
2. *PageTitleSumm* -The combination of terms from the page titles and summary descriptions of all pages in the topic.
3. *PageContent* - The combination of the top-N terms taken from the full content of each page in the topic.

In addition to representing topics with raw terms as above we also produce *feature-based* descriptions by applying LDA [1] and LSI [3] to both page-level and content-level terms to produce *LSIPageTitleSumm*, *LSIPageContent*, *LDAPageTitleSumm*, *LDAPageContent* representations.

This produces 7 different content *types* that can be used as the basis of collection indexing and user profiling. In the case of the former we use a standard indexing approach in which each topic is represented as a document vector based on the different content types. So in the case of *TopicTitleDesc* each topic (t_i) is represented as a vector of the topic's title and description terms; we refer to this as $I(t_i, TopicTitleDesc)$.

Users in Scoop.it are associated with the topics they curate (create) and other topics they choose to follow. Therefore we can profile a user u_i based on her curated topics ct^{u_i}, or her followed topics ft^{u_i}, or both $ctft^{u_i}$; we refer to these as the *source* of the profile data. And then we can represent each of these profile types using one of the 7 different approaches above. In other words, if we profile u_j from her curated topics using *LSIPageContent* then the profile will be made up of the LSI features extracted from the page content terms of all pages in the user's curated topics only; we refer to this as $P_{ct}(u_j, LSIPageContent)$.

3.2 Recommending New Topics

We adopt a simple retrieval-based content recommendation approach, treating user profiles as queries against the topic index to recommend the n most similar topics. In fact, we take a weighted retrieval approach using Lucene's TF-IDF weighting metric during retrieval [6]; for a given user u_j, we score a topic t_i based on those terms/features it shares with the user's profile $P = P_{src}(u_j, type_u)$, in proportion to their frequency in u_j's profile and inversely proportional to their frequency in the topic index $I = \bigcup_{t_i} I(t_i, type_I)$ as a whole.

$$Score(u_j, t_i, src, type_u, type_I) = \sum_{e \in t_i \cap u_j} tf(e, P) \times idf(e, I)$$

Once again it is worth stressing that our aim here is not to propose a novel recommendation technique but rather establish an approach that facilitates a *like-for-like* comparison between different types of profile/index representation and profile source. The above combinations of profile representation and source, and indexing data, accommodate many different combinations of recommendation techniques: 3 sources of profiling data, 7 types of profile, and 7 types of index for a total of 147 recommendation configurations.

4. EVALUATION

The purpose of this evaluation is to consider how the different types of indexing data and profiling sources impact overall recommendation quality when it comes to suggesting new topics to users. To do this we ran an offline, training-test style recommendation study over Scoop.it data scraped from their API during October-November 2012. This data include 22,000 unique topics covering more than 2 million

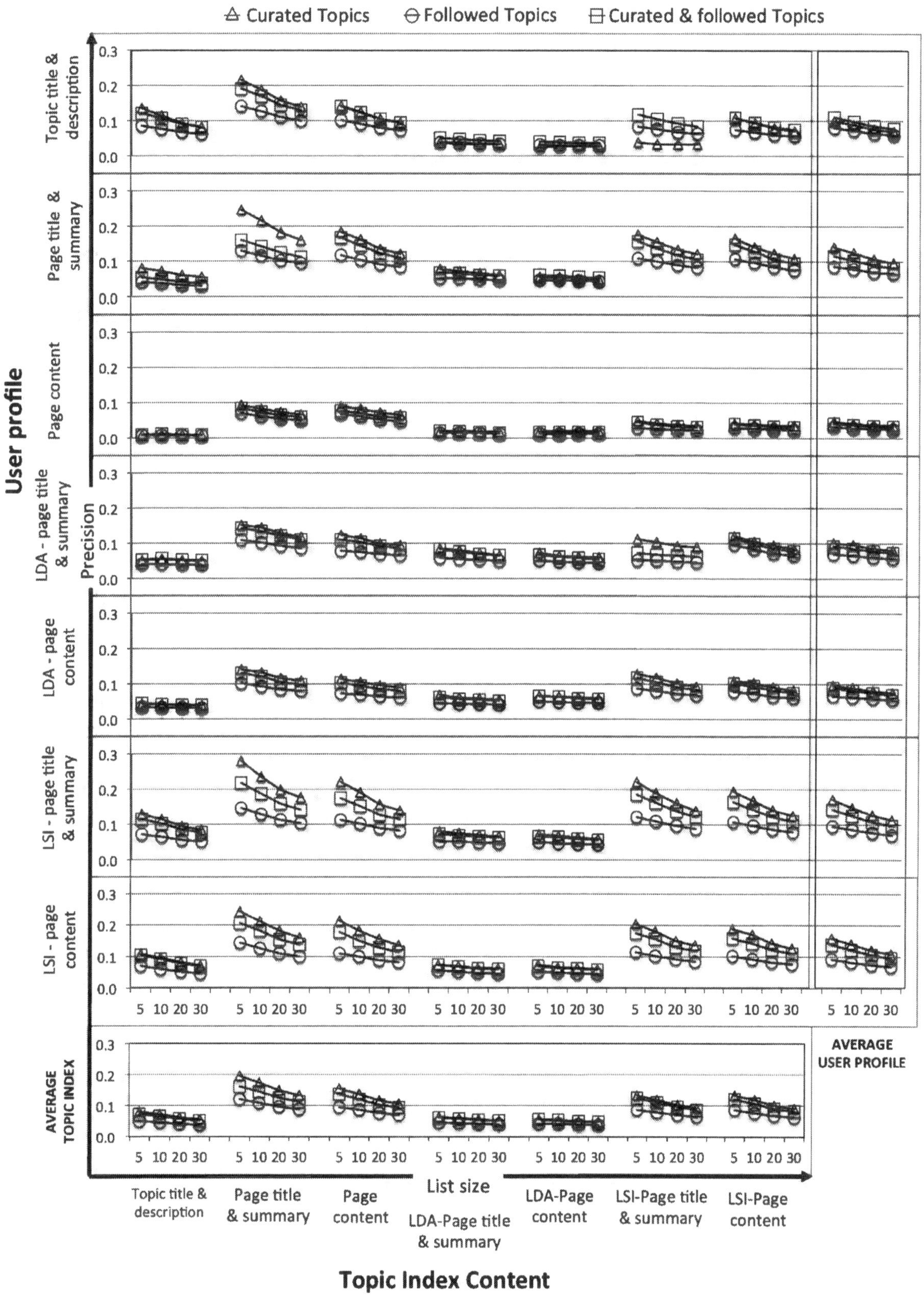

Figure 2: Average precision for different user profile configurations (rows) across various topic index configurations (columns). The rightmost graphs show summary precision data for user profile configurations (averaged across topic index configurations); similarly, graphs in the bottom row show summary precision data for topic index configurations (averaged across profile configurations).

pages and we focus on a subset of 845 active users who follow at least 20 topics; on average these users follow 90 topics and have created 5 topics of their own, each of which contains at least 100 pages. In this study the *training* instances are made up of user profiles containing all of the user's created topics plus random selections of 10% of their followed topics. The remaining followed topics serve as *test* instances. We do this 10 times to select different sets of followed topics for training and average our results across these folds.

For each set of training-test data we create all possible configuration combinations (7 x 7 x 3) of profile and recommendation index as described above. For each user a set of n (n = 5, 10, 20, 30) recommendations is made, and compared to the *followed* topics in the test profile in order to compute the average *precision*. Of course there are other standard measures we could apply here such as *recall*, *F1-measure* or *normalised discounted cumulative gain (NDCG)*; due to limited space however, we only consider precision at this point. The results are presented in Figure 2; the rows represent different types of profile data and the columns different types of index data. There are actually 3 sets of graphs presented in this figure: (1) the main *core* of 7 x 7 graphs shows the individual results of each of the (7 x 7 x 3) configurations that represent our recommendation design space; (2) the bottom row of 7 graphs (*average topic index*) represent summary precision data, for a given index configuration, averaged across the profile configurations (the average of the columns); and (3) the rightmost column (*average user profile*) shows a similar averaging across the rows, each profile configuration averaged across the index configurations.

There is a lot of result data presented but a number of interesting patterns can be observed. Focusing on the core graphs we can see that there is considerable precision variation across the different profiling and indexing configurations; precision results vary from <10% to almost 30%. And so the choice of profiling and indexing data matters. Generally speaking better results are observed when using curated topics versus followed or curated plus followed topics. Even though a given profile is only made up of a small fraction of curated topics this information provides a much clearer recommendation signal. For example, the results when using *page title* and *summary* information for profiling show a clear benefit for curated topics with precision ranging from about 0.25 to 0.15 (as n increases) compared to 0.2 - 0.1 for the followed and curated plus followed source configuration. Interestingly, this result aligns with the findings in [2] which show that the content in a user's own tweets (on Twitter) are a better signal of her information seeking preferences, than the content in the tweets of the people she follows.

The row and column averages help us to draw some general conclusions. We can see that extracting LDA features rarely helps, at least not as much as using LSI. And generally speaking basing recommendations on topic-level information from the *topic title* and *description* produces limited precision results. At the same time, using detailed *page content* (i.e. extracting actual term-content from pages) performs similarly poorly when used as the profile query but performs well when used to index topics; compare the *page content* configurations in the *average user profile* summary column to the *average topic index* summary row. Generally speaking it appears that page-level content, in the form of *page title & summary* configurations (using terms and LSI derived features) provides the right level of representational clarity to deliver the best performing recommendations. Specifically building a term-based index from *page title & summary* data and using LSI to extract *page title & summary* profiles gives the best overall recommendation results.

5. DISCUSSION

Our evaluation using Scoop.it data covered a comprehensive design space of recommendation configurations from which some general conclusions can be drawn. First and foremost, we demonstrated that relevant recommendations can be delivered even when evaluated against a traditionally conservative precision metric that focuses on those topics/collections only already followed by users. We often achieve precision scores up to 0.3 indicating that 30% of the recommended topics were found to be relevant in the sense that the user already followed them. Generally speaking, curated topics (those topics the user has created themselves) provided a strong recommendation signal than those they followed and delivered better precision, despite their relative sparsity compared to followed topics. And finally, the representational granularity offered by the intermediate *page title & summary* data provided superior precision results, although indexing (but not profiling) using detailed *page content* information also performed well.

Acknowledgments

This work is supported by Science Foundation Ireland under grant number 07/CE/I1147, Ministry of Education Malaysia and Universiti Teknikal Malaysia Melaka. The INSIGHT Centre for Data Analytics is supported by Science Foundation Ireland under Grant Number SFI/12/RC/2289.

6. REFERENCES

[1] D. M. Blei, A. Y. Ng, and M. I. Jordan. Latent dirichlet allocation. *the Journal of machine Learning research*, 3:993–1022, 2003.

[2] J. Chen, R. Nairn, L. Nelson, M. Bernstein, and E. Chi. Short and tweet: experiments on recommending content from information streams. In *Proceedings of the 28th international conference on Human factors in computing systems*, pages 1185–1194. ACM, 2010.

[3] S. Deerwester, S. T. Dumais, G. W. Furnas, T. K. Landauer, and R. Harshman. Indexing by latent semantic analysis. *Journal of the American society for information science*, 41(6):391–407, 1990.

[4] K. Duh, T. Hirao, A. Kimura, K. Ishiguro, T. Iwata, and C. Yeung. Creating stories: Social curation of twitter messages. In *Sixth International AAAI Conference on Weblogs and Social Media*, pages 447–450, 2012.

[5] D. Greene, F. Reid, G. Sheridan, and P. Cunningham. Supporting the curation of twitter user lists. In *NIPS 2011 Workshop on Computational Social Science and the Wisdom of Crowds*, Sierra Nevada, Spain, December 2011.

[6] E. Hatcher and O. Gospodnetic. *Lucene in action*. Manning Publications, 2004.

[7] Z. Saaya, M. Schaal, R. Rafter, and B. Smyth. Recommending topics for web curation. In *User Modeling, Adaptation, and Personalization*, pages 242–253. Springer, 2013.

Personalized News Recommendation with Context Trees

Florent Garcin Christos Dimitrakakis Boi Faltings

Artificial Intelligence Lab
Ecole Polytechnique Fédérale de Lausanne
Switzerland
firstname.lastname@epfl.ch

ABSTRACT

The proliferation of online news creates a need for filtering interesting articles. Compared to other products, however, recommending news has specific challenges: news preferences are subject to trends, users do not want to see multiple articles with similar content, and frequently we have insufficient information to profile the reader.

In this paper, we introduce a class of news recommendation systems based on context trees. They can provide high-quality news recommendations to anonymous visitors based on present browsing behaviour. Using an unbiased testing methodology, we show that they make accurate and novel recommendations, and that they are sufficiently flexible for the challenges of news recommendation.

Categories and Subject Descriptors

H.3.3 [**Information Storage and Retrieval**]: Information Search and Retrieval—*Information filtering*

Keywords

online recommender system, personalization, news

1. INTRODUCTION

The first recommender systems were originally designed for news forums. Since then, they have been used with considerable success for products such as books and movies, but have found surprisingly little application in recommending news articles, due to the unique challenges of the area.

When users are identifiable as regular visitors to a news website, techniques from product recommendation can be adapted [8, 11]. However, most websites operated by individual newspapers do not have a strong base of electronic subscribers. Visitors to these websites are casual users, often accessing them through a search engine, and little is known about them except what can be gathered through an ephemeral browsing history.

RecSys'13, October 12–16, 2013, Hong Kong, China.
Copyright 2013 ACM 978-1-4503-2409-0/13/10 ...$15.00.
http://dx.doi.org/10.1145/2507157.2507166.

Figure 1: A story with dynamic recommendations on the right side, and manually-generated recommendations on the bottom left (red-dashed areas).

The main page of a news website is already a set of recommended articles, which simultaneously addresses the needs of many users (Fig. 1). More specific recommendations are sometimes available to readers of individual articles. There are two shortcomings to this strategy: first, recommendations are usually edited manually, and second, they only consider the last article read. Our goal is to construct recommendations automatically and use the complete browsing history as a basis for giving personalized recommendations.

In principle, common recommender techniques such as collaborative filtering could be applied to such a task, and have been adapted to temporal sequences [28, 24, 19]. However, they face several challenges specific to news. First, news are rapidly evolving: new stories and topics appear and disappear quickly, and old news are no longer interesting. Second, recommendations should provide added value, and not just consist of the most popular stories that the reader would have already seen on the front page.

To address these issues, we propose a class of *online* recommendation algorithms based on *Context Trees (CT)*, which provide recommendations and are updated fully incrementally. A CT defines a *partition tree* organised in a hierarchy of increasingly precise partitions of a space of contexts. We consider as context the sequence of articles, the sequence of topics, or the distribution of topics. Each node in the tree is called *context* and corresponds to a set of sequences or topic distributions within a partition. The main idea is to give context-dependent recommendations, with contexts becoming progressively finer-grained deeper in the tree.

To make actual recommendations, we associate a set of prediction models, called *experts*, with each context. Their predictions are combined to make recommendations. We tailor our expert models to specifically take into account the idiosyncrasies of news. In particular, our expert models take into account the *popularity* and *freshness* of news items.

Using an unbiased testing methodology, emulating the process involved in implementing a system on a real website, we show that CT recommendations have state-of-the-art performance both with respect to prediction accuracy and to recommendation novelty, which is crucial for news articles since users want to read stories they do not know.

2. RELATED WORK

In general, there are two classes of recommender systems: collaborative filtering [25], which use similar users' preferences to make recommendations, and content-based systems [16], which use content similarity of news items.

The Grouplens project is the earliest example of collaborative filtering for news recommendation, applied to newsgroups [21]. News aggregation systems such as Google News [8] also implement such algorithms. Google News uses the probabilistic latent semantic indexing and MinHash for clustering news items, and item covisitation for recommendation. Their system builds a graph where the nodes are the stories and the edges represent the number of covisitations. Each of the approaches generates a score for a given news, aggregated into a single score using a linear combination.

Content-based recommendation is more common for news personalization [5, 1, 11]. NewsWeeder [12] is probably the first content-based approach for recommendations, but applied to newsgroups. NewsDude [5] and more recently YourNews [1] implemented a content-based system.

It is possible to combine the two types in a hybrid system [7, 14, 13]. For example, Liu et al. [14] extend the Google News study by looking at the user click behaviour in order to create accurate user profiles. They propose a Bayesian model to recommend news based on the user's interests and the news trend of a group of users. They combine this approach with the one by Das et al. [8] to generate personalized recommendations. Li et al. [13] introduce an algorithm based on a contextual bandit which learns to recommend by selecting news stories to serve users based on contextual information about the users and stories. At the same time, the algorithm adapts its selection strategy based on user-click feedback to maximize the total user clicks.

We focus on a class of recommender systems based on context trees. Usually, these trees are used to estimate Variable-order Markov Models (VMM). VMMs have been originally applied to lossless data compression, in which a long sequence of symbols is represented as a set of contexts and statistics about symbols are combined into a predictive model [22]. VMMs have many other applications [2].

Closely related, variable-order hidden Markov models [26], hidden Markov models [17] and Markov models [18, 23, 9] have been extensively studied for the related problem of click prediction. These models suffer from high state complexity. Although techniques [27] exist to decrease this complexity, multiple models have to be maintained, making these approaches not scalable and not suitable for online learning.

Few works [28, 24, 19] apply such Markov models to recommender systems. Zimdars et al. [28] describe a sequential model with a fixed history. Predictions are made by learning a forest of decision trees, one for each item. When the number of items is big, this approach does not scale. Shani et al. [24] consider a finite mixture of Markov models with fixed weights. They need to maintain a reward function in order to solve a Markov decision process for generating recommendations. As future work, they suggest the use of a context-specific mixture of weights to improve prediction accuracy. In this work, we follow such an approach. Rendle et al. [19] combine matrix factorization and a Markov chain model for baskets recommendation. The idea of factoring Markov chains is interesting and could be complementary to our approach. Their limitation is that they consider only first-order Markov chains. A bigger order is not tractable because the states are baskets which contain many items.

3. PRELIMINARIES

Because of the sequential nature of news reading, it is intuitive to model news browsing as a k-order Markov process [24]. The user's state can be summarised by the last k items visited, and predictions can be based only on this information. Unfortunately, it is not clear how to select the order k. A *variable-order Markov model* (VMM) alleviates this problem by using a context-dependent order. In fact, VMM is a special type of context-tree model [2].

There are two key ideas behind a CT recommender system. First, it creates a hierarchy of contexts, arranged in a tree such that a child node completely contains the context of its parents. In this work, a context can be the set of sequences of news items, sequence of topics, or a set of topic distributions. As new articles are added, more contexts are created. Contexts corresponding to old articles are removed as soon as they disappear from the current article pool.

The second key idea is to assign a local prediction model to each context, called an expert. For instance, a particular expert gives predictions only for users who have read a particular sequence of stories, or users who have read an article that was sufficiently close to a particular topic distribution.

In the following, we first introduce the notion of context tree. Then, we describe various prediction models, how to associate them with the context tree and combine them in order to make recommendations.

3.1 Sequence Context Tree

When a user browses a news website, we track the sequence of articles read.

Definition 1. A *sequence* $\mathbf{s} = \langle n_1, \ldots, n_l \rangle$ is an ordered list of articles $n_i \in \mathcal{N}$ read by a user, and we denote $\mathbf{s}_t$ the sequence of articles read until time t. We write the set of all sequences by $\mathcal{S}$.

Note that a sequence can also be a sequence of topics of articles.

A context tree is built based on these sequences and their corresponding suffixes.

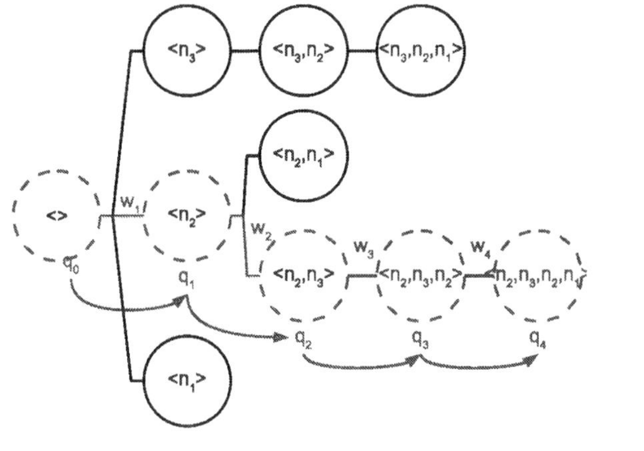

Figure 2: VMM context tree for the sequence $\mathbf{s} = \langle n_1, n_2, n_3, n_2 \rangle$. Nodes in red-dashed are active experts $\mu \in A(\mathbf{s})$.

Definition 2. A k-length sequence ξ of is a *suffix* of a l-length sequence $\mathbf{s}$, if $k \leq l$, and the last elements of $\mathbf{s}$ are equal to ξ, and we write $\xi \prec \mathbf{s}$ when ξ is a suffix of $\mathbf{s}$.

For instance, one suffix ξ of the sequence $\mathbf{s} = \langle n_1, n_2, n_3, n_4 \rangle$ is given by $\xi = \langle n_3, n_4 \rangle$.

If two sequences have similar context, the next article a user wants to read should also be similar.

Definition 3. A *context* $S = \{\mathbf{s} \in \mathcal{S} : \xi \prec \mathbf{s}\}$, $S \subset \mathcal{S}$ is the set of all possible sequences $\mathcal{S}$ ending with the suffix ξ.

We can now give a formal definition of a context tree.

Definition 4. A *context tree* $\mathcal{T} = (\mathcal{V}, \mathcal{E})$ with nodes $\mathcal{V}$ and edges $\mathcal{E}$ is a partition tree over the contexts $\mathcal{S}$. It has the following properties: (a) *The set of contexts at a given depth forms a partition*: If $\mathcal{V}_k$ are the nodes at depth k of the tree, then $S_i \cap S_j = \emptyset \; \forall i, j \in \mathcal{V}_k$, while $\bigcup_{i \in \mathcal{V}_k} S_i = \mathcal{S}$ (b) *Successive refinement*: If node i is the parent of j then $S_j \subset S_i$.

Thus, each node $i \in \mathcal{V}$ in the context tree corresponds to a context S_i. Initially the context tree $\mathcal{T}$ only contains a root node with context $S_0 = \mathcal{S}$. Every time a new article n_t is read, the active leaf node is split in a number of subsets, which then become nodes in the tree. This construction results in a variable-order Markov model, illustrated in Fig. 2.

The main difference between news articles and products is that articles continuously appear and disappear, and the system thus maintains a current article pool that is always changing. The model for recommendation changes along with the article pool, using a dynamically evolving context tree. As new articles are added, new branches are created corresponding to sequences or topic distributions. At the same time, nodes corresponding to old articles are removed as soon as they disappear from the current pool.

3.2 Topic Distribution Context Tree

Because of the large number of news items relative to topics, a context tree on topics might make better predictions. In particular, stories that have not been read by anyone can be recommended thanks to topic similarity. In this type of tree, each context represents a subset of the possible *topic distributions* of the last read article. The structure of the tree is slightly different and is modelled via a k-d tree.

A k-d tree is a binary tree that iteratively partitions a k-dimensional space $\mathcal{S}$ into smaller sets [4]. The i-th node corresponds to a hyper-rectangle $S_i \subset \mathcal{S}$ and has two children j, j' such that $S_j \cup S_{j'} = S_i$ and $S_j \cap S_{j'} = \emptyset$. In particular, the two children are always defined via a hyperplane splitting S_i in half, through the center of S_i, and which is perpendicular to one principal axis. In practice, we simply associate each node to one of the k axes based on the depth such that we cycle through all possible axes: $a = depth \bmod k$. The set $\mathcal{S}$ is $[0,1]^k$, the set of k-dimensional multinomial distributions on the possible topics.

In analogy to the sequence CT, a context is a hyper-rectangle S_i and a suffix is the center θ of S_i in a topic distribution CT.

For instance, consider a node i with center $\theta \in S_i$ and associated axis a. Its two children correspond to two sets of topic distributions: Its left child j contains the distributions $\theta' \in S_i$ with $\theta'_a < \theta_a$, while its right child j' is the set on the other side of the hyperplane: $S_{j'} = \{\theta' \in S_i : \theta'_a \geq \theta_a\}$. When the system observes a new topic distribution θ, the distribution is added to the tree, and possibly the tree expands.

3.3 Experts

We assign a local prediction model called *expert* to each context (node) in the tree. More formally,

Definition 5. An *expert* μ_i is a function associated with a specific context S_i that computes an estimated probability of the next article n_{t+1} given that context, i.e. $\mathbb{P}_i(n_{t+1} \mid \mathbf{s}_t)$.

The user's browsing history $\mathbf{s}_t$ is matched to the context tree and identifies a path of nodes (see Fig. 2). All experts associated with these nodes are called *active* and are responsible for the recommendation.

Definition 6. The set of *active* experts $\mathcal{A}(\mathbf{s}_t) = \{\mu_i : \xi_i \prec \mathbf{s}_t\}$ is the set of experts μ_i associated to contexts $S_i = \{\mathbf{s} : \xi_i \prec \mathbf{s}_t\}$ such that ξ_i are suffix of $\mathbf{s}_t$.

3.4 Combining Experts into Predictions

The active experts $\mathcal{A}(\mathbf{s}_t)$ are combined by marginalizing to obtain a mixture of probabilities of all active experts:

$$\mathbb{P}(n_{t+1} = x \mid \mathbf{s}_t) = \sum_{i \in \mathcal{A}(\mathbf{s}_t)} u_i(\mathbf{s}_t) \, \mathbb{P}_i(n_{t+1} = x \mid \mathbf{s}_t), \quad (1)$$

with $u_i(\mathbf{s}_t) = \mathbb{P}(i|\mathbf{s}_t)$ being the probability of the i-th expert relevant for this context. These probabilities are derived as follows.

With each node i in the context tree we associate a weight $w_i \in [0,1]$ that represents the usefulness of the corresponding expert. Given a path in the context tree, we consider experts in the order of the most specific to the most general context, i.e. along the path from the most specific node to the root. In this process, with probability equal to the weight w_i we stop at a node without considering the more general experts. Thus, we take into account the relative usefulness of the experts.

Letting w_j be the probability of stopping at j given that we have not stopped yet, we thus obtain the probability u_i that the i-th expert is considered as $u_i(\mathbf{s}_t) = w_i \prod_{j : S_j \subset S_i} (1 - w_j)$ if $\mathbf{s}_t \in S_i$ and 0 otherwise.

The calculation of the total probability can be made efficiently via the recursion $q_k = w_k \mathbb{P}_k(n_{t+1} = x|\mathbf{s}_t) + (1 -$

$w_k)q_{k-1}$, where q_k is the combined prediction of the first k experts. In Figure 2, the prediction of the root expert for the next item x is q_0, while q_4 is the complete prediction by the model for this sequence.

The weights are updated by taking into account the success of a recommendation. When a user reads a new article x, we update the weights of the active experts corresponding to the suffixes ending before x according to the probability $q_k(x)$ of predicting x sequentially via Bayes' theorem [10]:

$$w'_k = \frac{w_k \mathbb{P}_k(n_{t+1} = x \mid \mathbf{s}_t)}{q_k(x)}. \tag{2}$$

No other weights are updated[1]. Finally, we also update the local models of the active experts (see Section 3.5).

3.5 Expert Models

Recommending news articles depends on multiple factors: the popularity of the news item, the freshness of the story, the sequence of news items or topics that the user has seen so far. Thus, each expert is decomposed into a set of *local models*, each modelling one of these properties. The first model ignores the temporal dynamics of the process. The second model assumes that users are mainly looking at popular items, and the last model that they are interested in fresh items (i.e. breaking news).

3.5.1 Standard model

A naïve approach for estimating the multinomial probability distribution over the news items is to use a Dirichlet-multinomial prior for each expert μ_i. The probability of reading a particular news item x depends only on the number of times α_x it has been read when the expert is active.

$$\mathbb{P}_i^{std}(n_{t+1} = x|\mathbf{s}_t) = \frac{\alpha_x + \alpha_0}{\sum_{j\in\mathcal{N}}(\alpha_j + \alpha_0)}, \tag{3}$$

where α_0 is the initial count of the Dirichlet prior.

The dynamic of news items is more complex. A news item provides new content and therefore has been seen by few users. News is subject to trends and frequent variations of preferences. We improve this simple model by augmenting it with models for *popular* or *fresh* news items.

3.5.2 Popularity model

A news item $x \in \mathcal{P}$ is in the set of popular items $\mathcal{P}$ when it has been read at least once among the last $|\mathcal{P}|$ read news items. We compute the probability of a news item x given that x is *popular* as:

$$\mathbb{P}_i^{pop}(n_{t+1} = x|\mathbf{s}_t) = \frac{c_x + \alpha_0}{\sum_{j\in\mathcal{N}}(c_j + \alpha_0)}, \tag{4}$$

where c_x is the total number of clicks received for news item x. Note that c_x is not equal to α_x (Eq. 3). α_x is the number of clicks for news item x when the expert is *active*, while c_x is the number of clicks received by news item x in *total* whether the expert is active or not.

The number of popular items $|\mathcal{P}|$ is important because it is unique for each news website. When $|\mathcal{P}|$ is small, the expert considers only the most recent read news. It is important to tune this parameter appropriately.

[1] $w_0 = 1$ since we must always stop at the root node.

3.5.3 Freshness model

A news item $x \in \mathcal{F}$ is in the set of fresh items $\mathcal{F}$ when it has not been read by anyone but is among the next $|\mathcal{F}|$ news items to be published on the website, i.e. a breaking news. We compute the probability of news item x given that x is *fresh* as:

$$\mathbb{P}_i^{fresh}(n_{t+1} = x|\mathbf{s}_t) = \begin{cases} \frac{1}{|\mathcal{F}|+1}, & \text{if } x \in \mathcal{F} \\ \frac{1}{(|\mathcal{F}|+1)(|\mathcal{N}|-|\mathcal{F}|)}, & \text{if } x \notin \mathcal{F}. \end{cases} \tag{5}$$

The number of fresh items $|\mathcal{F}|$ influences the prediction made by this expert, and is unique for each news website.

3.5.4 Mixing the expert models

We combine the three expert models using this mixture:

$$\mathbb{P}_i(n_{t+1} = x|\mathbf{s}_t) = \sum_{\tau\in\{std,pop,fresh\}} \mathbb{P}_i^{\tau}(n_{t+1} = x|\mathbf{s}_t)p_i^{\tau}. \tag{6}$$

There are two ways to compute the probabilities p_i^{τ}: either by using a Dirichlet prior that ignores the expert prediction or by a Bayesian update to calculate the posterior probability of each expert according to their accuracy.

For the first approach, the probability of the next news item being *popular* is:

$$\begin{aligned} p_i^{pop} = \mathbb{P}_i(n_{t+1} \in \mathcal{P}) &= \frac{\alpha_{pop} + \alpha_0}{(\alpha_{pop} + \alpha_0) + (\alpha_{notpop} + \alpha_0)} \\ &= \frac{\alpha_{pop} + \alpha_0}{2\alpha_0 + \sum_j \alpha_j}, \end{aligned} \tag{7}$$

where $\sum_j \alpha_j$ represents the number of times the expert μ_i has been active, α_{pop} and α_{notpop} the number of read news items which were respectively popular and not popular when the expert μ_i was active.

Similarly, the probability of the next news item being *fresh* is given by:

$$p_i^{fresh} = \mathbb{P}_i(n_{t+1} \in \mathcal{F}) = \frac{\alpha_{fresh} + \alpha_0}{2\alpha_0 + \sum_j \alpha_j}, \tag{8}$$

where α_{fresh} is the number of read news items which were fresh when the expert μ_i was active.

Noting that $\mathcal{P} \cap \mathcal{F} = \emptyset$, the probability of the next news item being neither popular nor fresh is:

$$p_i^{std} = \mathbb{P}_i(n_{t+1} \notin \mathcal{P}\cup\mathcal{F}) = 1 - \mathbb{P}_i(n_{t+1} \in \mathcal{P}) - \mathbb{P}_i(n_{t+1} \in \mathcal{F}). \tag{9}$$

It might happen that by using the Dirichlet priors, predictions are mainly made by only one expert model. To overcome this issue, we compute the probabilities p_i^{τ}, $\tau \in \{std, pop, fresh\}$ via a Bayesian update, which adapts them based on the performance of each expert model:

$$p_i^{\tau} \leftarrow \frac{\mathbb{P}_i^{\tau}(n_{t+1} = x|\mathbf{s}_t)p_i^{\tau}}{\mathbb{P}_i(n_{t+1} = x|\mathbf{s}_t)}. \tag{10}$$

4. CONTEXT-TREE RECOMMENDERS

We describe here the general algorithm to generate recommendations for the class of context-tree recommender systems. This algorithm can be applied to domains other than news in which timeliness and concept drift are of concern. We then focus on the news domain and describe in more details three VMM-based recommender systems and one based on the k-d context tree.

4.1 General Algorithm

Algorithm 1 presents a sketch of the CT recommender algorithm. For simplicity, we split our system in two procedures: *learn* and *recommend*. Both are executed for each read article x of a user with browsing history $\mathbf{s}$ in an online algorithm such as [20, 15], without any further offline computation. The candidate pool $\mathcal{C}$ is always changing and contains the popular $\mathcal{P}$ and fresh $\mathcal{F}$ stories. The system estimates the probability of each candidate and recommends the news items with the highest probability. In order to estimate the probability of a candidate item, the system *1)* selects the active experts $\mathcal{A}(\mathbf{s})$ which correspond to a path in the context tree from the most general to the most specific context, *2)* propagates q from the root down to the leaf, i.e the most specific context. q at the leaf expert is the estimated probability of the recommender system for the candidate item x, i.e. $\mathbb{P}(n_{t+1} = x|\mathbf{s}_t)$ (see Eq. 1).

Algorithm 1 CT recommender system

procedure LEARN($x, \mathbf{s}$, context set Ξ)
  $q \leftarrow 0$ and $t \leftarrow |\mathcal{A}(\mathbf{s})|$
// loop from most general expert μ_0 to most specific expert μ_t
  for $i \leftarrow 0, t$ **do**
    $p_i \leftarrow \mathbb{P}_i(n_{t+1} = x|\mathbf{s})$ // ith expert prediction
    $q \leftarrow w_i p_i + (1 - w_i)q$ // combined prediction
    $w_i \leftarrow \frac{w_i p_i}{q}$ // weight update
    update $p_i^{std}, p_i^{pop}, p_i^{fresh}$ (Eq. 7-9 or Eq. 10)
  if $x \circ \mathbf{s} \notin \Xi$ **then** // is the context in the tree?
    $\Xi = \Xi \bigcup \{x \circ \mathbf{s}\}$ // add a new leaf.
end procedure
procedure RECOMMEND($\mathbf{s}$)
  for all candidate $n \in \mathcal{C}$ **do**
    $q^{(n)} \leftarrow 0$ and $t \leftarrow |\mathcal{A}(\mathbf{s})|$
// loop from most general expert μ_0 to most specific expert μ_t
  for $i \leftarrow 0, t$ **do**
    $q^{(n)} \leftarrow w_i \mathbb{P}_i(n|\mathbf{s}) + (1 - w_i)q^{(n)}$
  $\mathcal{R} \leftarrow$ sort all $n \in \mathcal{C}$ by $q^{(n)}$ in descending order
  return first k elements of $\mathcal{R}$
end procedure

4.2 Recommender Systems

We consider three VMM variants of recommender systems, and one based on the k-d context tree.

4.2.1 VMM Recsys

The standard VMM recommender builds a context tree on the sequences of news items. That is $\mathbf{s}_t = \langle n_1, \ldots, n_t \rangle$ is a sequence of news items, and each active expert predicts n_{t+1}, the next news item.

4.2.2 Content-based VMM (CVMM) Recsys

In order to build a CT on topic sequences, we find a set of topics for each story, and assign the most probable topic to the news item. We then perform predictions on *topics*.

More precisely, we use the Latent Dirichlet Allocation (LDA) [6] as a probabilistic topic model. After concatenating the title, summary and content of the news item together, we tokenize the words and remove stopwords. We then apply LDA to all the news stories in the dataset, and obtain a topic distribution vector $\theta^{(n)}$ for each news item n.

We now define a context tree as follows. Let z_t be the most probable topic of the t-th news item. Then the *topic sequence* is $\mathbf{s}_t = \langle z_1, ..., z_t \rangle$ and ξ is a suffix of topic sequences. The context tree generates a topic probability distribution $\mathbb{P}(z_{t+1} = j|\mathbf{s}_t)$, while the LDA model provides us with a topic distribution $\mathbb{P}(z = j|n)$ for each news item n. These are then combined into the following score:

$$score(n \mid \mathbf{s}_t) = \max_j \{\mathbb{P}(z_{t+1} = j \mid \mathbf{s}_t) \cdot \mathbb{P}(z = j \mid n)\}. \quad (11)$$

The system recommends the articles with the highest scores.

4.2.3 Hybrid VMM (HVMM) Recsys

We combine the standard VMM with the content-based system into a hybrid version. The context tree is built on *topics*, similarly to the CVMM system, but the experts make predictions about *news items*, like the VMM system.

HVMM system builds a tree in the space of *topic sequences*. Each suffix ξ of size k is a sequence of most probable topics $\langle z_1, z_2, ..., z_k \rangle$. However, all predictive probabilities (Eq. 1 and later) are defined on the space of news items.

4.2.4 k-d Context-Tree (k-CT) Recsys

The CVMM and HVMM structures make predictions on the basis of the sequence of most probable topics. Instead, we consider a model that takes advantage of the complete topic distribution of the last news item. We use a k-d tree to build a context model in the space of *topic distributions*.

4.2.5 Baselines

In addition, we have the following baselines:

Z-k is a fixed k-order Markov chain recommender similar to the ones by Zimdars et al. [28].

MinHash is the minhash system used in Google News [8].

MostPopular recommends a set of stories with the highest number of clicks among the last read news items.

5. EVALUATION AND COMPARISON

We investigate whether the class of CT recommender systems has an advantage over standard methods and if so, what is the best combination of partition and expert model.

We measure performance both with respect to accuracy and novelty of recommendations. Novelty is essential because it exposes the reader to relevant news items that she would not have seen by herself. Obvious but accurate recommendations of most-popular items are of little use.

We evaluate our systems on two datasets described below. We examine on the first dataset the sensitivity of the CT models to hyperparameters. The second dataset is used to perform an unbiased comparison between the different models. We select the optimal hyperparameters on the first dataset, and then measure the performance on the second dataset. This methodology [3] mirrors the approach that would be followed by a practitioner who wants to implement a recommender system on a newspaper website.

5.1 Datasets

We collected data from the websites of two daily Swiss-French newspapers called *Tribune de Genève* (TDG) and *24 Heures* (24H)[2]. Their websites contain news stories ranging

[2]www.tdg.ch and www.24heures.ch

	News stories	Visits	Clicks
TDG	10'400	600'256	1'069'131
24H	8'613	249'099	509'978

Table 1: Datasets after filtering.

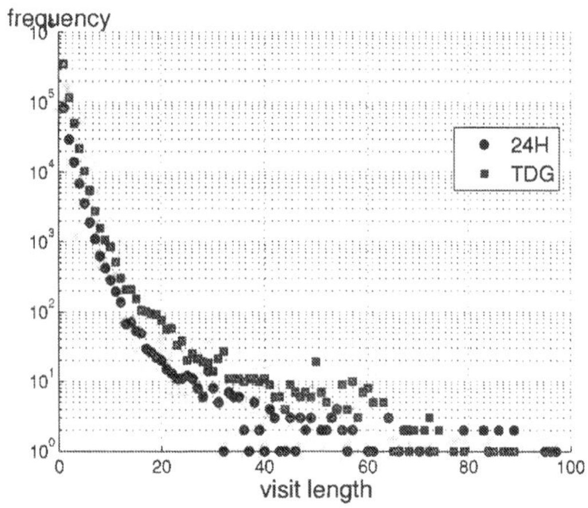

Figure 3: Distribution of the length of visits.

from local news, national and international events, sports to culture and entertainment.

The datasets span from Nov. 2008 until May 2009. They contain all the news stories displayed, and all the visits by anonymous users within the time period. Note that a new visit is created every time a user browses the website, even if she browsed the website before. The raw data has a lot of noise due to, for instance, crawling bots from search engines or browsing on mobile devices with unreliable internet connections. Table 1 shows the dataset statistics after filtering out this noise, and Figure 3 illustrates the distribution of visit length for each dataset.

5.2 Evaluation Metrics

We evaluate how good the systems are in predicting the future news a user is going to read. Specifically, we consider sequences of news items $\mathbf{s} = \langle n_1, n_2, ..., n_l \rangle$, $n_i \in \mathcal{N}, \mathbf{s} \in \mathcal{S}$ read by anonymous users. The sequences and the news items in each sequence are sorted by increasing order of visit time. When an anonymous user starts to read a news item n_1, the system generates 5 recommendations. As soon as the user reads another news item n_2, the system updates its model with the past observations n_1 and n_2, and generates a new set of recommendations. Hence the training set and the testing set are split based on the current time: at time t, the training set contains all news items accessed before t, and the testing set has items accessed after t.

We consider three metrics. The first is the **Success@5** (s@5). For a given sequence $\mathbf{s} = \langle n_1, n_2, ..., n_t, ..., n_l \rangle$, a current news item n_t in this sequence, and a set of recommended news items $\mathcal{R}$, s@5 is equal to 1 if $n_{t+1} \in \mathcal{R}$, 0 otherwise.

The second metric is **personalized s@5**, where we remove the popular items $\mathcal{R}_\mathcal{T}$ from the set $\mathcal{R}$, to get a reduced set $\mathcal{R}_P = \mathcal{R} \backslash \mathcal{R}_\mathcal{T}$. This metric is important because it filters out the bias due the fact that data is collected from websites which recommend the most popular items by default.

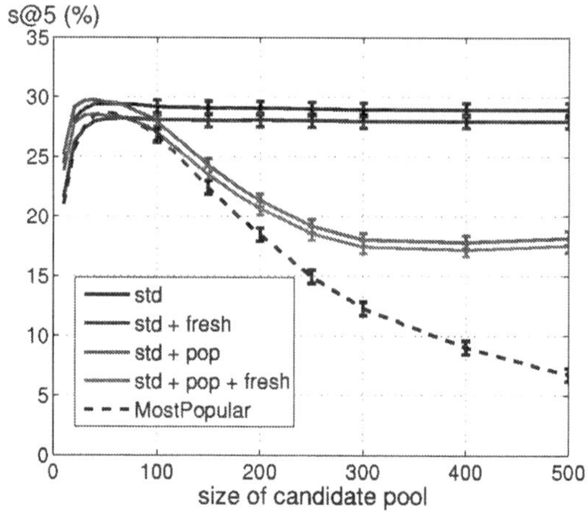

Figure 4: VMM recommender system: different mixtures of experts (Bayesian update, $|\mathcal{F}| = 10$).

The final metric is **novelty**, defined by the ratio of unseen and recommended items over the recommended items: $novelty = |\mathcal{R} \cap \mathcal{F}| / |\mathcal{R}|$. This metric is essential because users want to read about something they do not already know.

5.3 Sensitivity Evaluation

For all systems, we use a prior $\alpha_0 = 1/|\mathcal{N}|$ for the Dirichlet models, and the initial weights for the experts as $w_k = 2^{-k}$, where k is the depth of the node. We evaluated experimentally the optimal number of topics in the range of 30 to 500, and found that 50 topics bring the best accuracy. We varied the size of candidate pool: number of popular items $|\mathcal{P}|$ from 10 to 500, and fresh items $|\mathcal{F}|$ from 10 to 100. When the candidate set is small, the experts consider only the most recent read stories. We report averages over all recommendations with confidence intervals at 95%. We omit figures for the TDG dataset because we witnessed the same behaviours.

Although naïve, the approach of recommending the most popular stories is actually used very often on newspaper websites. This strategy does not pay off when the size of candidate pool increases. "Good" recommendations are drowned in popular items. This can also be seen by the fact that mixture of expert models integrating the popularity model are very sensitive to the number of popular items while others are more robust (e.g. Fig. 4 for VMM recsys).

We noticed that, when using the Dirichlet priors to update the mixture probabilities, the prediction was mostly made by the popularity model, resulting in the same behaviour as the most-popular recommender system as the size of candidate pool increases. However, as the Bayesian update (Eq. 10) adapts the probabilities based on the performance of each expert model, it is more robust when we increase the candidate set. We also observed that as the number of fresh items increased, CT models were getting slightly better.

When we look at the general accuracy of CT recommender systems (Fig. 5(a)), their performance is close to the existing techniques. However when we consider only personalized items (Fig. 5(b)), CT recommender systems outperform current techniques, showing that the order of the model is important. Indeed, we observed that the weights of the experts are well distributed over the space even for long sequences. If the sequence is not important, the weights of the experts

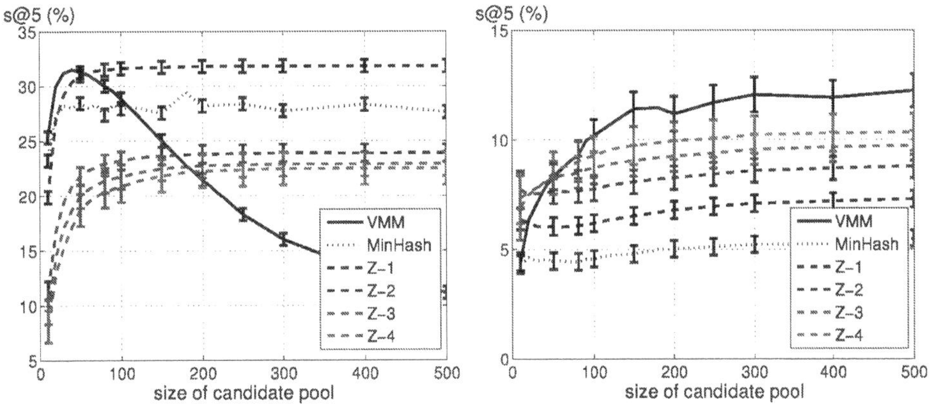

(a) Non-personalized news items

(b) Personalized news items

Figure 5: Accuracy for personalized and non-personalized news items.

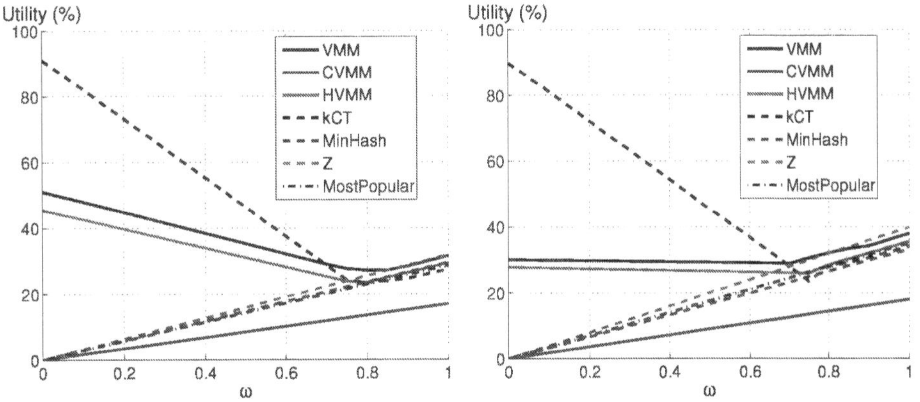

(a) Tuning: 24H dataset

(b) Testing: TDG dataset with optimal parameters from 24H dataset.

Figure 6: Expected performance curves: accuracy and novelty trade-off.

would have been 0 except for the root expert, resulting in a performance similar to Z-1.

We have seen that recommending popular news is easy and relatively accurate. However, a recommender system with a high accuracy on an offline evaluation does not imply that in practice it will give useful recommendations to the users. In the context of news, novelty plays a crucial role, and the users expect both personalized and novel recommendations. In the next section, we study this trade-off.

5.4 Comparison

In practice, we may be interested in some particular mix of accuracy and novelty. We formalize this by defining a utility function: $U(\omega|D, A) = \omega * s@5 + (1 - \omega) * \mathit{novelty}$, where ω specifies the trade-off between accuracy and novelty, D is the dataset (24H or TDG) and A is an assignment of parameters. For CT systems, the parameters are the number of popular $|\mathcal{P}|$ and fresh $|\mathcal{F}|$ items, whether the probabilities are computed via a Bayesian update or not, the mixture of experts (standard, popularity and/or freshness). It might be the case that different parameters are optimal for different utilities. The same holds for the parameters of the other methods we compare against.

To perform the comparison, we simulate the process of a designer who is going to tune each system on a small dataset (24H), before deploying the recommender online (on the TDG dataset). For any value of ω, we find the best parameters for the 24H dataset, and then measure the performance on the other dataset. This gives the Expected Performance Curve (EPC) [3], which provides an unbiased evaluation of the performance obtained by different methods.

Figure 6 illustrates the EPCs for 24H and TDG datasets. Fig. 6(a) shows the optimal utility $U(\omega|D, A^*(\omega, D))$ with $A^*(\omega, D) = \arg\max_A U(\omega|D, A)$ for D = 24H dataset. Figure 6(b) shows the corresponding utility $U(\omega|D', A^*(\omega, D))$ achieved on the test dataset D' = TDG using the parameters found for the tuning dataset. First, we observe that all methods are robust in that they have similar performance in the testing dataset. Second, we observe that the purely content-based method (CVMM) performs poorly both with respect to novelty and accuracy. The hybrid approach (HVMM) is significantly better. Third, the approaches that disregard the content (VMM and Z) perform similarly in terms of accuracy, but only the VMM has a reasonable novelty. Finally, the k-d tree approach (kCT) has a much higher novelty than anything else. Thus, if one were to select a method based on performance on the tuning set, one should choose kCT for smaller values of ω and VMM for larger values.

6. CONCLUSION

News recommendation is challenging due to the rapid evolution of topics and preferences. We introduced a class of recommender systems based on context trees that accommodate a dynamically changing model. We considered context trees in the space of sequences of news, sequences of topics, and in the space of topic distributions. We defined expert models which consider the popularity and freshness of news items, and examined ways to combine them into a single model. We proposed an incremental algorithm that adapts the models continuously, and is thus better suited to such a dynamic domain as the context tree evolves over time and adapts itself to current trends and reader preferences. Our approach requires only one tree (the context tree), and thus scales very well. Our work is not restricted to the history of logged-in users, but considers a one-time session for recommendation, where users do not log in. Surprisingly, we do not know of any existing research that considers context-tree models for recommender systems.

Each proposed variant has its strengths and weaknesses. To evaluate them, we used the expected performance curve methodology, whereby each method is tuned in a training set according to a parametrized utility metric. In doing so, we showed that if we are interested in accuracy in a static dataset, a context tree that implements a variable-order Markov model is ideal, while novelty is best served with a k-d tree on the space of topics. In addition, we showed that a large order is mainly important when we are not interested in recommending highly popular items. An open question is whether the results we obtained on a static trace will be qualitatively similar in an actual recommender system. In future work, we aim to perform an online test of the system on a real news website.

7. REFERENCES

[1] J. Ahn, P. Brusilovsky, J. Grady, and D. He. Open user profiles for adaptive news systems: help or harm? In *Conf. on WWW*, pages 11–20, 2007.

[2] R. Begleiter, R. El-Yaniv, and G. Yona. On prediction using variable order markov models. *J. of AIR*, pages 385–421, 2004.

[3] S. Bengio, J. Mariethoz, and K. M. The expected performance curve. In *ICML*, pages 9–16, 2005.

[4] J. Bentley. Multidimensional binary search trees used for associative searching. *Com. ACM*, 1975.

[5] D. Billsus and M. Pazzani. A hybrid user model for news story classification. In *Conf. on User Modeling*, pages 99–108, 1999.

[6] D. Blei, A. Ng, and M. Jordan. Latent dirichlet allocation. *J. of MLR*, 3:993–1022, 2003.

[7] R. Burke. Hybrid recommender systems: Survey and experiments. *User Modeling and User-Adapted Interaction*, 12:331–370, November 2002.

[8] A. Das, M. Datar, A. Garg, and S. Rajaram. Google news personalization: scalable online collaborative filtering. In *Conf. on WWW*, pages 271–280, 2007.

[9] M. Deshpande and G. Karypis. Selective markov models for predicting web page accesses. *ACM Trans. Internet Technol.*, 4(2):163–184, 2004.

[10] C. Dimitrakakis. Bayesian Variable Order Markov Models. In *Proc. of AIStat*, pages 161–168, 2010.

[11] W. IJntema, F. Goossen, F. Frasincar, and F. Hogenboom. Ontology-based news recommendation. In *W. on Data Semantics*, 2010.

[12] K. Lang. Newsweeder: Learning to filter netnews. In *ICML*, pages 331–339, 1995.

[13] L. Li, W. Chu, J. Langford, and R. Schapire. A contextual-bandit approach to personalized news article recommendation. In *Conf. on WWW*, 2010.

[14] J. Liu, P. Dolan, and E. Pedersen. Personalized news recommendation based on click behavior. In *Proc. of IUI*, pages 31–40, 2010.

[15] N. Liu, M. Zhao, E. Xiang, and Q. Yang. Online evolutionary collaborative filtering. In *Conference on Recommender systems*, pages 95–102, 2010.

[16] P. Lops, M. Gemmis, and G. Semeraro. Content-based recommender systems: State of the art and trends. In *Recommender Systems Handbook*, pages 73–105. Springer, 2011.

[17] A. Montgomery, S. Li, K. Srinivasan, and J. Liechty. Modeling online browsing and path analysis using clickstream data. *Marketing Sci.*, 23(4):579–595, 2004.

[18] J. Pitkow and P. Pirolli. Mining longest repeating subsequences to predict world wide web surfing. In *Proc. of USITS*, page 13, 1999.

[19] S. Rendle, C. Freudenthaler, and L. Schmidt-Thieme. Factorizing personalized markov chains for next-basket recommendation. In *Conf. on WWW*, pages 811–820, 2010.

[20] S. Rendle and L. Schmidt-Thieme. Online-updating regularized kernel matrix factorization models for large-scale recommender systems. In *Conference on Recommender systems*, pages 251–258, 2008.

[21] P. Resnick, N. Iacovou, M. Suchak, P. Bergstrom, and J. Riedl. Grouplens: an open architecture for collaborative filtering of netnews. In *Proc. of CSCW*, pages 175–186, 1994.

[22] J. Rissanen. A universal data compression system. *Trans. Info. Th.*, pages 656–664, 1983.

[23] R. Sarukkai. Link prediction and path analysis using markov chains. *Computer and Telecommunications Networking*, 33(1-6):377–386, 2000.

[24] G. Shani, D. Heckerman, and R. Brafman. An mdp-based recommender system. *J. of MLR*, 6:1265–1295, December 2005.

[25] X. Su and T. Khoshgoftaar. A survey of collaborative filtering techniques. *Adv. in Artif. Intell.*, pages 4:2–4:2, January 2009.

[26] Y. Wang, L. Zhou, J. Feng, J. Wang, and Z. Liu. Mining complex time-series data by learning markovian models. In *Proc. of ICDM*, pages 1136–1140, 2006.

[27] M. Zaki, C. Carothers, and B. Szymanski. Vogue: A variable order hidden markov model with duration based on frequent sequence mining. *Trans. KDD*, 4:1–31, 2010.

[28] A. Zimdars, D. Chickering, and C. Meek. Using temporal data for making recommendations. In *Conf. on UAI*, pages 580–588, 2001.

What to Read Next?: Making Personalized Book Recommendations for K-12 Users

Maria Soledad Pera
Computer Science Department
Brigham Young University
Provo, Utah, U.S.A.
mpera@cs.byu.edu

Yiu-Kai Ng
Computer Science Department
Brigham Young University
Provo, Utah, U.S.A.
ng@compsci.byu.edu

ABSTRACT

Finding books that children/teenagers are interested in these days is a non-trivial task due to the diversity of topics covered in huge volumes of books with varied readability levels. Even though K-12 readers can turn to book recommenders to look for books, the recommended books may not satisfy their personal needs, since they could be beyond/below their readability levels or fail to match their topics of interest. To address these problems, we introduce BReK12, a book recommender that makes personalized suggestions tailored to each K-12 user U based on books available on a social bookmarking site that (i) are *similar in content* to the ones that are known to be of interest to U, (ii) have been bookmarked by users with *reading patterns* similar to U's, and (iii) can be *comprehended* by U. BReK12 is an asset to its users, since it suggests books that are appealing to its users and at grade levels that they can cope with, which can increase their reading selection choices and motivate them to read. We have also developed ReLAT, the readability analysis tool employed by BReK12 to determine the grade level of books. ReLAT is novel, compared with existing readability formulas, since it can predict the grade level of a book even if an excerpt of the book is not available. We have conducted empirical studies which have verified the accuracy of ReLAT in predicting the grade level of a book and the effectiveness of BReK12 over existing baseline recommendation systems.

Categories and Subject Descriptors

H.3.3 [**Information Search and Retrieval**]: Information Filtering, Retrieval Models, Selection Process

Keywords

Book recommendation system, readability, K-12

1. INTRODUCTION

Reading, an essential skill required for acquiring knowledge, is an integral part of the educational system. It is imperative to encourage K-12 students to read, since research studies have confirmed the enormous influence of reading on students' development as learners and members of society, especially at an early age. Finding books that K-12 readers are interested in, however, is a difficult task due to the diversity of topics covered in the huge volume of books that target readers of different backgrounds and age groups. Recommender systems, which have been developed to suggest items of interest to their users, are supposed to alleviate the book-finding problem. However, existing recommenders employed at well-known book-affiliated websites, such as Novelist (www.ebscohost.com/novelist) and Amazon.com, adopt a "one-size-fits-all" strategy, which makes the same suggestions to different users on a given book without considering their individual preferences [14]. On the contrary, recommenders that offer personalized book suggestions overlook the readability levels of their users, since they are conceived with a general audience in mind. As a result, even if a book recommended to a user U matches U's interests, the book might include complex (simple, respectively) content that is beyond (below, respectively) the readability level of U, which fails to sustain the mission of matching users' reading abilities with the suggested literature [1]. Moreover, these recommenders rely heavily on the existence of *personal ratings* [26] assigned to books by users, which are rarely provided by K-12 users of the existing social bookmarking sites established for them.

To address the aforementioned design problems of book recommendation systems, we have developed BReK12, a book recommender that makes personalized suggestions for K-12 users. To locate books for a user U based on U's reading ability and interests, BReK12, which is designed to be integrated into a social bookmarking site on books, analyzes U's profile, i.e., books that have been bookmarked by U on the site. If U is a new user, BReK12 treats a book provided by U as U's profile. In doing so, BReK12 bypasses the *cold-start* problem often encountered by recommenders [24]. BReK12 first infers U's readability level by analyzing the grade levels of books in his/her profile, which are determined using ReLAT, a robust readability level analysis tool that we have developed. Hereafter, BReK12 identifies a set of candidate books, among the ones archived at the site, with grade levels compatible to the inferred readability level of U. For each candidate book, BReK12 determines its *content similarity* and *readership similarity* with books in the profile of U based on the brief *descriptions* of books that are publicly available online and users' *bookmarking patterns* on the site, respectively. An aggregation strategy [3] is adopted

RecSys'13, October 12–16, 2013, Hong Kong, China.
Copyright 2013 ACM 978-1-4503-2409-0/13/10 ...$15.00.
http://dx.doi.org/10.1145/2507157.2507181.

so that the top-10 candidate books, with grade levels appropriate for U and with the highest combined content- and readership-similarity scores, are recommended to U.

BReK12 is unique, since its design goal is to suggest books to K-12 users that simultaneously match their *interests* and *reading abilities*, which in turn can motivate them to read. Unlike state-of-the-art recommenders [24], BReK12 simply employs *readily available* data, i.e., user bookmarks and brief descriptions of books, accessible from the social bookmarking sites where BReK12 is installed and book-affiliated websites, respectively to make recommendations. Moreover, BReK12 applies similarity, besides exact, matching on words to recommend books that are *similar* in content to users' bookmarks, which otherwise could be ignored.

BReK12 relies on ReLAT to determine the grade level of a book B based on the *subject areas* addressed in B, the readability level of the intended audience of books written by the *author* of B, *subject headings* assigned to B, and the *grammatical/sentence structures* in (an excerpt of) B, if any is available. Unlike existing readability formulas/tools, such as Lexile Analyzer and Flesch-Kincaid, ReLAT can predict the readability level of a book even if (a sample of) the text of the book is unavailable, which is its novelty.

Besides serving social bookmarking site users, BReK12 can also recommend books for each K-12 patron of a school/public library, assuming that the list of books of interest provided by the library patron and the book catalog used by the library are given. In addition, BReK12 can be adapted to make recommendations for users of any book-affiliated website based on books searched by the users on the site.

The remaining of this paper is organized as follows. In Section 2, we discuss existing readability formulas and book recommenders. In Sections 3 and 4, we introduce ReLAT and BReK12, respectively. In Section 5, we present the results of the empirical studies conducted to (i) assess the performance of ReLAT and BReK12 and (ii) compare their performances with existing approaches. In Section 6, we give a concluding remark and directions for future work.

2. RELATED WORK

In this section, we present a number of widely-used readability formulas/analysis tools and book recommenders and compare them with ReLAT and BReK12, respectively.

2.1 Readability Formulas/Analysis Tools

For almost a century, hundreds of readability formulas have been developed for predicting the readability level of a text [4, 7]. Traditional readability formulas, such as Flesch-Kincaid and Coleman-Liau, rely on shallow features, which include word frequency and sentence length, to compute the grade level of a text. These formulas, however, often provide a rough estimation of text difficulty, which "(may) judge a nonsense passage as *quite readable* if the text's jumbled words are frequent, short, and organized into brief sentences" [4]. Recently-developed formulas are based on (i) *linguistic* features, such as the ones introduced by Feng et al. [9] and Collins-Thompson and Callan [7], (ii) *pre-defined word lists*, such as Lexile and Revised Dale-Chall formula, (iii) *enhanced shallow features*, such as the *Advantage-TASA Open Standard for Readability* (ATOS) formula, and (iv) *non-textual features*, such as SVM-Ranker [15], which examines images on books to predict their grade levels, and ReadAid [22], which considers information about the authors of a book and US Curriculum topics addressed in the book in addition to exploring the lexicographical and syntactical structures of the book. While most of these formulas are widely-used and popular, none of them can predict the readability level of a book if (a sample of) its text is not available, which can be achieved by ReLAT. (See [4] for an in-depth discussion of existing readability formulas.)

2.2 Book Recommenders

A number of book recommenders [14, 20, 26] have been proposed in the past. Amazon's recommender [14] suggests books based on the purchase patterns of its users. Yang et al. [26] analyze users' access logs to infer their preferences and apply the traditional collaborative-filtering (CF) strategy, along with a ranking method, to make book suggestions. Givon and Lavrenko [10] combine the CF strategy and social tags to capture the content of books. Similar to the recommenders in [10, 26], the one in [25] adopts the standard user-based CF framework and uses a domain ontology to determine the users' topics of interest. The recommenders in [10, 25, 26] overcome the problem that arises due to the lack of initial information to perform the recommendation task, i.e., the cold-start problem. However, unlike BReK12, they are constrained by requiring historical data in the form of *ratings* to make recommendations, which may not always be available. Moreover, the recommender in [25] relies on the existence of a book ontology, which can be labor-intensive and time-consuming to construct. In making recommendations, Park and Chang [20] analyze individual/group behaviors, such as clicks and shopping habits, and features describing books, such as their library classification, whereas *PReF* [21] suggests books bookmarked by connections of a LibraryThing user. Similar to BReK12, *PReF* adopts a similarity-matching strategy, which differs from the exact-matching constraint imposed in [20] and a number of content-based recommenders [11, 18]. However, neither *PReF* nor any of the aforementioned recommenders considers the readability level of their users as part of their recommendation strategies. While BReK12 is not a recommender system for learning [24] per se, its design goal is to aid children/teenagers in developing good reading habits so that they can succeed at school and in the living of a good life. With that in mind, BReK12 is designed as an educational enrichment tool. (An in-depth discussion of existing recommender systems in the educational domain can be found in [16].)

3. A GRADE LEVEL PREDICTION TOOL

As previously stated, existing readability formulas/analysis tools rely on at least a sample of a text to compute its readability level, which is a severe constraint, since text in a book is not always freely accessible due to the copyright laws. To alleviate the text constraint, we have developed *ReLAT*, which determines the grade level of any book using *metadata* on books publicly accessible from reputable online sources, in addition to sample texts of books only if they are available. Analyzing a book using multiple perspectives, ReLAT can predict its grade level even if an excerpt on the book is missing. Furthermore, ReLAT *instantly* produces the grade level of a book, which is not always possible using commercial readability analysis tools. For example, Lexile offers scores for only approximately 150,000 out of the millions of books published worldwide in English, and requires

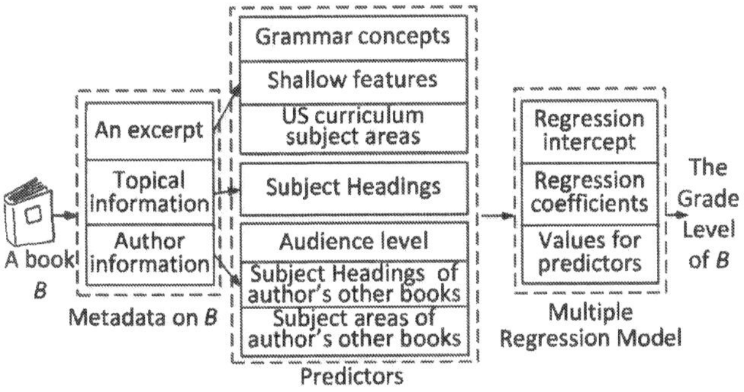

Figure 1: The grade-level prediction process of ReLAT, our proposed readability level analysis tool

direct involvement of its developers to generate the readability level of any book which has not yet been analyzed [4].

Figure 1 depicts the grade level prediction process of ReLAT. To determine the grade level of a book B, ReLAT takes as an input a unique identifier of B, which can be its ISBN number or its title and author. Thereafter, ReLAT extracts from reputable online sources, such as WorldCat.org and OpenLibrary.org, (i) an excerpt of B, (ii) topical information of B, and (iii) information about the author[1] of B, whatever is available. Based on the extracted data on B, ReLAT examines up to *fifty-nine predictors* to determine the grade level of B. The predictors are treated as *contributing factors*, i.e., evidences, which are used in analyzing the grade level of B. Due to the space constraint, we do not define each predictor[2]. Instead, we present the nature of predictors in each category (as shown in Figure 1) below.

(I) Predictors based on an *excerpt* of B examine

- *Grammar Concepts.* ReLAT analyzes the complexity of the grammar usage in B by counting the occurrences of various grammatical concepts in its sentences, which are present perfect, modal verbs, past progressive tense, parts of speech, phrases, suffixes, prefixes, and key vocabulary words.

- *Shallow Features.* ReLAT considers a number of well-established textual features commonly used by traditional readability formulas: the average number of syllables per word, average sentence length, percentage of words with at least three syllables, average number of characters per word, and absolute number of words.

- *Subject Areas.* The US Curriculum dictates which subject areas should be taught at each K-12 grade level. For example, *multiplication* is taught at the 3rd grade while *trigonometry* at the 12th grade. ReLAT relies on a Latent Dirichlet Allocation (LDA) model [5] to identify a set of *representative keywords* that best describes the content of B. Thereafter, ReLAT calculates the resemblance (using word-correlation factors [12]) between these keywords and each of the pre-defined subject areas established by the US Curriculum. The subject area SA with the highest degree of resemblance is treated as the subject area of B and the grade level associated with SA is used for predicting the grade level of B.

(II) Predictors based on *topical information* of B analyze its Subject Headings, e.g., "Biography", which are short phrases that capture the topics covered in books and are used by the US Library of Congress to categorize books. Based on a mapping between Subject Headings and grade levels (that we have already determined using Subject Headings assigned to books with a known grade level), ReLAT identifies the grade levels that correspond to each of the Subject Headings of B. These grade levels are taken into account by ReLAT to determine the grade level of B.

(III) Predictors that consider *author information* of B are based on the fact that, in general, K-12 authors write for a particular group of readers at a certain grade level. For this reason, ReLAT treats the *audience level* metric of an author defined by WorldCat, which captures the "intellectual level of the audience for which the item is intended," in addition to the topical information and subject areas of the author's other books (as introduced in I and II, respectively) as additional predictors that determine the overall grade level of B.

Since the information required to compute the value of a predictor can be missing, it may not be possible to use all the predictors for predicting the grade level of B. ReLAT considers various combinations of the 59 predictor coefficients and applies multiple linear regression analysis [17] (given below) on predictors applicable to B to predict its grade level.

$$c_0 + c_1x_1 + c_2x_2 + ... + c_nx_n = y \qquad (1)$$

where c_0 is the *intercept* term, c_i ($1 \leq i \leq n$) is the *regression coefficient* of predictor x_i, and y is the predicted grade level.

Prior to applying Equation 1 to predict the grade level of a book, the *intercept* and *coefficients* associated with each applicable predictor are computed through a one-time training process using the *ordinary least squares* estimation method [17] on a training set of 8,737 K-12 books written by different authors that cover diverse topics and were extracted from various publishers' websites and the Children's Literature Comprehensive Database (CLCD.com). Each training instance consists of the (values of) predictors that apply to a book B and the grade level of B determined by its publisher. Since publishers usually suggest a *range* of readability levels for each of their published books, ReLAT considers the *average* grade level of the range defined for B as its grade level during the training process. In doing so, ReLAT avoids any bias that might occur by assigning books their lower/upper grade bound during the regression training.

Example 1. Consider the book "Five Little Kittens" by Nancy Geller Jewell, which is a 32-page picture book with some long sentences. As stated in [23], unlike existing readability formulas that often overstate the difficulty of books for emergent readers, Accelerated Reader (AR) is a decent measure on the readability levels of books. Even though "Five Little Kittens" is appropriate for grades K-3, as suggested by its publisher, its Flesch-Kincaid grade level is 4.6 and its Lexile score is 970 (which corresponds to grades 6-7). The AR grade level for the book is 2.6, which matches the target audience for the book. The AR score, however, sug-

[1]We have empirically verified that by considering only the *first* author of a book B, the processing time of ReLAT is minimized without affecting its accuracy in predicting the grade level of B. This is expected, since less than 10% of the hundreds of thousands of K-12 books we examined at ARbookfind.com and Scholastic.com are written by co-authors.

[2]The list of all the predictors and the categories to which they belong can be found in tinyurl.com/dyp6ysl.

gests that children should be at least in the 2nd grade to read "Five Little Kittens," whereas the grade level predicted by ReLAT, which is 0.9, indicates that Kindergartners can read the book, providing a grade level more compatible (than AR's) with the book publisher's. (See Section 5.3 for the performance analysis of ReLAT.) □

4. THE BOOK RECOMMENDER

In this section, we present the design of BReK12. Given the profile P of a user U, BReK12 selects a set of candidate books, which are compatible with the readability level of U (determined in Section 4.1). Hereafter, BReK12 assigns a *ranking* score to each candidate book B, which is computed using an aggregation strategy (introduced in Section 4.4) on the *content* and *readership similarity* of B with respect to the books in P (defined in Sections 4.2 and 4.3, respectively).

4.1 Identifying Candidate Books

BReK12 recognizes that "reading for understanding cannot take place unless the words in the text are accurately and efficiently decoded" [19] and only recommends books with readability levels appropriate to its users.

BReK12 applies Equation 2 to estimate the readability level of a user U, denoted $RL(U)$, based on the grade level of each book P_B in U's profile predicted by ReLAT, denoted ReLAT(P_B). Note that only books bookmarked in a user's profile during the most recent academic year are considered, since it is anticipated that the grade levels of books bookmarked by users gradually increase as the users enhance their reading comprehension skills over time.

$$RL(U) = \frac{\sum_{P_B \in P} ReLAT(P_B)}{|P|} \quad (2)$$

where $|P|$ denotes the number of books in U's profile and *average* is employed to capture the *central tendency* on the grade levels of books bookmarked by U.

Having established U's readability level, BReK12 creates *CandBks*, the subset of books archived at the bookmarking site that are within-one-grade-level range from U's. By considering books within *one* grade level above/below U's mean readability level, BReK12 recommends books with an appropriate level of complexity for U and grade levels approximate to the grade levels of books that have been read by U (as of the most recent academic year).

EXAMPLE 2. Consider a BiblioNasium.com user U who has bookmarked a number of books from Dav Pilkey's "Captain Underpants" series. Based on the grade levels predicted by ReLAT for the books archived at BiblioNasium (see a sample of BiblioNasium books in Table 1) and U's readability level, which is 4, BReK12 does not include Bk_1 or Bk_3 in *CandBks*, since their grade levels are below/beyond the range deemed appropriate for U. □

4.2 Content Similarity Measure

BReK12 depends on the profile P of U to infer U's interests/preferences. To determine the degree to which the content of a book B in *CandBks* appeals to U, BReK12 computes the *content similarity* between B and each book P_B in P, denoted $CSim(B, P)$ as defined in Equation 3, using a "bag-of-words" representation on the *brief descriptions* of B and P_B obtained from book-affiliated websites, such

Table 1: A number of BiblioNasium books

ID	Book Title	Grade Level
Bk_1	Mummies in the Morning	2.9
Bk_2	Captain Underpants and the Big, Bad Battle of the Bionic Booger Boy	4.7
Bk_3	The Hidden Boy	5.6
Bk_4	Dragon's Halloween	3.1
Bk_5	Junie B. Jones Smells Something Fishy	3.0
...	...	...

Table 2: TF-IDF weighting scheme used in the enhanced cosine similarity measure in Equation 3

Condition	Weight Assignment
$B_i \in B$ and $P_{B_i} \in P_B$	$V_{B_i} = tf_{B_i,B} \times idf_{B_i}$ and $V_{P_{B_i}} = tf_{P_{B_i},P_B} \times idf_{P_{B_i}}$
$B_i \in B$ and $P_{B_i} \notin P_B$	$V_{B_i} = tf_{B_i,B} \times idf_{B_i}$ and $V_{P_{B_i}} = \frac{\sum_{c \in HS_{B_i}} tf_{c,P_B} \times idf_c}{\lvert HS_{B_i} \rvert}$
$B_i \notin B$ and $P_{B_i} \in P_B$	$V_{B_i} = \frac{\sum_{c \in HS_{P_{B_i}}} tf_{c,B} \times idf_c}{\lvert HS_{P_{B_i}} \rvert}$ and $V_{P_{B_i}} = tf_{P_{B_i},P_B} \times idf_{P_{B_i}}$

as Amazon. To compute $CSim(B, P)$, BReK12 employs an enhanced version of the *cosine similarity measure* based on word-correlation factors [12], which relaxes the exact-matching constraint imposed by the cosine measure and explores words in the description of B that are *analogous* to, besides the *same* as, words in the description of P_B.

Word-correlation factors in the correlation matrix introduced in [12] reflect the degree of similarity between any two words according to their (i) frequencies of co-occurrence and (ii) relative distances in Wikipedia(.org) documents. Approximately 880,000 documents covering a wide range of topics and written by more than 89,000 authors with varied writing styles were used to construct the matrix. Compared with synonyms/related words compiled by WordNet (wordnet.princeton.edu) in which pairs of words are not assigned similarity weights, word-correlation factors offer a more sophisticated measure of word similarity. In addition, word-correlation factors have been successfully employed to solve a number of content-similarity problems [21, 22].

$$CSim(B, P) = \max_{P_B \in P} \frac{\sum_{i=1}^{n} VB_i \times VP_{B_i}}{\sqrt{\sum_{i=1}^{n} VB_i^2} \times \sqrt{\sum_{i=1}^{n} VP_{B_i}^2}} \quad (3)$$

where B and P_B are represented as n-dimensional vectors $VB = <VB_1, ..., VB_n>$ and $VP_B = <VP_{B_1}, ..., VP_{B_n}>$, respectively, n is the number of distinct words in the descriptions of B and P_B, and VB_i (VP_{B_i}, respectively), which is the *weight* assigned to word B_i (P_{B_i}, respectively), is calculated as shown in the equations in Table 2.

HS_w in Table 2 is the set of words that are *highly similar*[3] to, but not the *same* as, a given word w in the description of a book Bk, which is either B or P_B, $|HS_w|$ is the size of HS_w, $tf_{w,Bk} = \frac{f_{w,Bk}}{\sum_{w \in Bk} f_{w,Bk}}$ is the normalized *term fre-*

[3]Two words are *highly similar* if their correlation factor is included in a reduced version of the aforementioned word-correlation matrix which contains 13% of the most frequently-occurring words in the Wikipedia documents.

quency of w in Bk, and $idf_w = log\frac{N}{n_w}$ is the *inverse document frequency* for w in the collection of books N archived at a social bookmarking site, where n_w is the number of books in N that include w in their descriptions. Relying on the *tf-idf* weighting scheme, BReK12 prioritizes discriminating words that capture the content of its respective book.

The *max* function in Equation 3 emulates the "most pleasure" strategy (commonly applied in game theory and group profiling [24]). Applying this strategy, BReK12 selects the *highest* possible score among the ones computed for each P_B in P and B. The *larger* the number of exact-matched or highly-similar words in the descriptions of both B and P_B is, the *more likely* B is a relevant recommendation for U. Moreover, BReK12 adopts the widely-used cosine measure, which has been effectively applied to determine the degree of resemblance between any two items in content-based recommenders [18]. While content-similarity is computed by BReK12 using book descriptions, other textual information on books, such as their tag representations, can be used. Tags, however, are not always publicly available.

EXAMPLE 3. To illustrate the merit of using the enhanced cosine similarity measure in Equation 3 to compute $CSim(B, P)$, consider the profile P of user U in Example 2 and two of the books, Bk_2 and Bk_4 as shown in Table 1. Using the *traditional* cosine measure, Bk_2 and Bk_4 yield the same content similarity score with respect to P. However, employing the *enhanced* cosine similarity measure, BReK12 obtains a more accurate content-similarity score for each book, since $CSim(Bk_2, P) = 0.57$ and $CSim(Bk_4, P) = 0.39$. These scores reflect that U is likely more interested in books similar to the ones in the "Captain Underpants" series (by Dav Pilkey) than books about "dragons," which we have verified by manually examining the profile of U. □

4.3 Readership Similarity Measure

$CSim$ locates books that are similar in content, to a certain degree, to the ones users have read in the past. This measure, however, does not consider books that are dissimilar in content but match users' specific preferences/interests. Hence, BReK12 explores another dimension of resemblance between each book B in *CandBks* and books in U's profile P by using the Lennon similarity measure [13] to perform co-readership analysis on users' bookmarks on a social bookmarking site. This *readership similarity* measure (as defined in Equation 4) is based on the popular item-item similarity approach employed by collaborative-filtering recommenders to examine *patterns of co-occurrence* of items bookmarked by users to make recommendations [6].

$$RSim(B,P) = \max_{P_B \in P}\left(1 - \frac{min(|S_B - S_\cap|, |S_{P_B} - S_\cap|)}{min(|S_B - S_\cap|, |S_{P_B} - S_\cap|) + |S_\cap|}\right) \quad (4)$$

where S_B (S_{P_B}, respectively) is the set of users who bookmarked B (P_B, respectively), $S_\cap = S_B \cap S_{P_B}$, $|S_\cap|$ is the number of users who bookmarked both B and P_B, $|S_B - S_\cap|$ ($|S_{P_B} - S_\cap|$, respectively) is the number of users who bookmarked B, but not P_B (P_B, but not B, respectively) at a social bookmarking site, and the use of the *max* function was discussed in Section 4.2.

In Equation 4, the *min*(imum) of the two differences between $|S_B - S_\cap|$ and $|S_{P_B} - S_\cap|$ is chosen, since by using the *smaller* of the two differences, we can *more accurately* capture the similarity between B and P_B. As a *difference* reflects the number of users who bookmark B, but not P_B (or vice versa), a *smaller* difference signifies that proportionally a *larger* number of users who bookmark one book also prefer the other book, which is a *better* indication of the degree of readership similarity between the two books.

EXAMPLE 4. To illustrate the usefulness of readership similarity measure for making recommendations, consider Bk_5 in Table 1 and the book "The Adventures of Captain Underpants" by Dav Pilkey, denoted P_B, which is a book in the profile of user U introduced in Example 2. The contents of the books differ, since P_B is about the adventures of two fourth graders and a superhero, whereas Bk_5 details the events that occur when Junie, the main character in the book, takes her pet to school. The books, however, share some *common thread* of interest to a group of BiblioNasium users who have bookmarked both, since the books include characters of *similar age*, written in *similar literary styles*, and share the *same genre*. Relying partially on the readership similarity between Bk_5 and P, which is 0.67, BReK12 retains Bk_5 as one of the top-10 recommendations for U, which otherwise would have been ignored due to the lack of related content between the two books. □

4.4 Rank Aggregation

Using the computed *content-* and *readership*-similarity scores of each book B (with a readability level appropriate for U) in *CandBks*, BReK12 applies the *Borda Count voting scheme* [3] to determine the *ranking* score for B. The Borda Count voting scheme is a positional-scoring procedure such that given k (≥ 1) candidates, each voter casts a vote for each candidate according to his/her preference. A candidate that is given a first-place vote receives k-1 points, a second-ranked candidate k-2 points, and so on up till the last candidate, who is awarded no points. Hereafter, the points assigned to each candidate across all the voters are added up and the candidate with the *most* points *wins*.

The Borda Count strategy, which has been successfully applied to different information retrieval tasks [3], is employed by BReK12 to generate a single ranking score for B, denoted $Borda(B)$ as defined in Equation 5, that regards the content- and readership-similarity scores as equally important in determining the degree to which a user is interested in B. Using Equation 5, BReK12 assigns (i) $k = |CandBks|$, which is the number of candidate books selected for a user U, and (ii) $C = 2$, which is the number of voters, i.e., the two ranked lists of similarity scores on books computed in Sections 4.2 and 4.3, respectively. Candidate books with the top-10 Borda scores are recommended to U.

$$Borda(B) = \sum_{c=1}^{C}(k - S_c^B) \quad (5)$$

where S_c^B is the position on the ranking of B based on the cth ranked list to be fused.

BReK12 adopts Borda as an *aggregation strategy*, since (i) its combination algorithm is *simple* and *efficient*, which requires neither training nor compatible relevance scores that may not be available and (ii) its performance is competitive with other existing combination strategies [3].

5. EXPERIMENTAL RESULTS

In this section, we first introduce the datasets, metrics, and evaluation protocol used for assessing the performance

Table 3: The BookGL dataset

Online Sources	No. of Books	Online Sources	No. of Books
CLCD.com	663	Penguin Group	498
Simon & Schuster	388	YABC	699

of ReLAT and BReK12 (in Sections 5.1 and 5.2, respectively). Hereafter, we present the results of the empirical studies conducted for evaluating the effectiveness of ReLAT and BReK12 (in Sections 5.3 and 5.4, respectively).

5.1 The Datasets

To the best of our knowledge, there is no benchmark dataset that can be used for evaluating readability-level prediction tools on books. Thus, to evaluate ReLAT we constructed BookGL[4], using data extracted from CLCD.com, a website established to assist teachers, parents, and librarians in choosing appropriate books for K-12 readers, the Young Adults Book Central (YAbookscentral.com), and reputable publishers' websites. BookGL consists of 2,248 books distributed among the K-12 grade levels with the grade level (range) of each book assigned by its publisher. (See Table 3 for the source websites and their number of books in BookGL.) Due to the lack of consensus among researchers on the accuracy of existing readability prediction tools [4], we consider publisher-provided grade levels as the "gold-standard," since they are defined by human experts.

Even though the BookCrossing dataset (informatik.uni-freiburg.de/~cziegler/BX) has been employed to evaluate book recommenders tailored to a general audience, it is not specifically designed for assessing the performance of book recommenders for K-12 users. Hence, we used data provided by BiblioNasium, which is a safe and secure social networking site on books developed exclusively for children and teenagers, to evaluate BReK12. The dataset consists of the profile of, i.e., books that have been bookmarked by, each of the 297 BiblioNasium users who joined the site within its first month of being launched. As the design methodology of BReK12 relies on brief descriptions and predicted grade levels of books, we extracted the former from Amazon.com and predicted the latter using ReLAT.

5.2 Metrics and Evaluation Protocol

To assess the performance of ReLAT, we apply the *(absolute) error rate* (ER) [8], which is the absolute difference between an *expected* and a *predicted* grade level for a book B.

$$ER = \frac{1}{|BookGL|} \sum_{B \in BookGL} |PR(B) - GL(B)| \quad (6)$$

where $|BookGL|$ is the total number of books in BookGL, $GL(B)$ is the predicted grade level of B by a readability formula/analysis tool, and $PR(B)$ is either the lower or upper bound of the grade level range of B determined by its publisher, whichever is closest to $GL(B)$. (Recall that publishers often assign a grade range, not a level, to a book.)

We evaluate BReK12 using *Precision@10, Mean Reciprocal Rank* (MRR), and *Normalized Discounted Cumulative Gain* (nDCG) [8]. Precision@10 measures the fraction of the top-10 ranked recommendations that are *relevant*, whereas MRR computes the average ranking position of the *first* relevant recommended book. nDCG determines the *overall* ranking performance of BReK12 and *penalizes* relevant books ranked *lower* in the recommendation list. The penalization is based on a reduction, which is logarithmically proportional to the position of each relevant book in a ranked list.

We adopt the popular five-fold cross validation strategy to evaluate BReK12 (and recommender systems considered for the comparison purpose). In each of the five repetitions, 80% of the books bookmarked by a user U in the BiblioNasium dataset are used to create U's profile and the remaining 20% are reserved for the testing purpose. A recommended book B is treated as *relevant* to U if it is included in the 20% of the books withheld for the testing purpose, and is *non-relevant* otherwise, which is a commonly-employed protocol for assessing the performance of recommendation systems [11]. Since only withheld books are considered *relevant*, it is not possible to account for potentially relevant books a user has not bookmarked, which is a well-known limitation of this evaluation protocol. As the limitation affects all the recommenders evaluated in the conducted empirical studies, the results are consistent for the comparative purpose.

5.3 Performance Evaluation of ReLAT

Using the 127 books in BookGL with excerpts, we compared the grade-level prediction accuracy of ReLAT with a number of well-known readability formulas: Coleman-Liau, Flesch-Kincaid, Rix, and Spache, which we have implemented. (See detailed discussion on these readability formulas in [4].) Figure 2(a) shows that (i) on the average the grade level predicted by ReLAT for a book with text (in BookGL) is about *half* a grade from the grade (range) determined by its publisher and (ii) ReLAT's error rate is *at least* 33% lower than the error rate created by its counterparts.

We also evaluated the performance of ReLAT in predicting the grade level of books for which their excerpts cannot be obtained online. Among the 2,121 books in BookGL without sample text, the 0.82 error rate generated by ReLAT is *less than one* grade level off the ranges specified by the publishers of the books. This low error rate is not only an accomplishment of ReLAT, but also it cannot be achieved by *any* of the existing readability formulas/analysis tools, since *none* of them can predict the grade level of books without excerpts. The overall error rate of ReLAT on BookGL, in which 94% of the books are without text, is 0.81, which is within one grade level of the targeted grade level.

We further compare the performance of ReLAT with two popular readability analysis tools widely-accepted by grade schools and reading programs in the USA: Accelerated Reader (AR) and Lexile. Recall that the algorithms developed to compute AR and Lexile scores are not publicly accessible, but we were able to find 897 books with AR scores and 314 books with Lexile scores among the books in BookGL at ARbookfind.com and Lexile.com, respectively. As shown in Figure 2(b), ReLAT outperforms AR and is significantly more accurate than Lexile in predicting the grade level of the analyzed books (in BookGL).

5.4 Performance Evaluation of BReK12

In this section, we verify the correctness of the design methodology of BReK12 and compare its performance with a number of existing recommendation strategies.

[4]BookGL and the set of books used to train ReLAT's multiple regression predictor (discussed in Section 3) are disjoint.

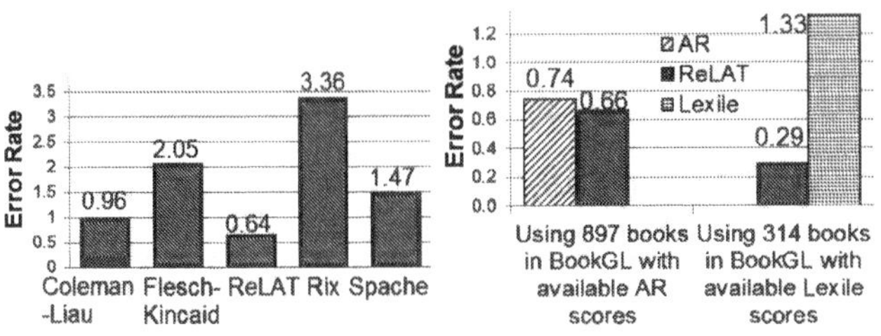

(a) Readability Formulas (b) Analysis Tools

Figure 2: Performance evaluation of ReLAT

5.4.1 Effectiveness of BReK12

The results of the study conducted to validate the methodologies applied by BReK12 for *selecting* and *ranking* books to be recommended for K-12 users are presented as follows:

- The Enhanced Cosine (EC) measure employed by BReK12 to perform content-similarity matching outperforms the Traditional Cosine measure (as shown in Figure 3), which has been verified based on the improvements in Precision@10, MRR, and nDCG that are statistically significant as determined by using the Wilcoxon signed-rank test [8] (with $p < 0.05$).
- We have observed statistically significant improvement ($p < 0.05$) when books with unsuitable readability levels for the respective BiblioNasium users are excluded prior to applying the content-similarity matching on potential book recommendations. (See EC versus EC + ReLAT Filtering in Figure 3.)
- The statistically significant improvements ($p < 0.01$) on various performance metrics achieved by EC + Readership over EC indicate that examining both the content and readership similarity of candidate books with respect to books in the profile of each BiblioNasium user increases the accuracy of the recommendations.
- We have verified (based on the results of a conducted empirical study) that recommending books that match users' reading abilities without considering their individual preferences is not beneficial. This is anticipated, since users might not find particular topics addressed in books appealing even if the books are suitable to their readability levels.
- When books beyond/below users' readability levels are not chosen as candidate books by BReK12, its overall effectiveness increases, according to the statistically significant improvements ($p < 0.01$) achieved by BReK12 over EC + Readership. This comparison validates the correctness of BReK12's design methodology, i.e., to recommend books of interest to individual users that they can read and understand.

5.4.2 Comparing BReK12 with Other Recommenders

As previously stated, no other personalized book recommender explicitly considers the reading abilities of its users. Thus, we have compared the performance of BReK12 with a number of recommenders developed for a general audience. *Tag Vector Similarity* (TVS) [11], *L-Cosine* (L-Cos) [18], and *Item-Based Collaborative Filtering* (IICF) [6] were employed for comparison purposes, as opposed to other state-of-the-art book recommenders introduced in Section 2, since the latter require *personal ratings* on (K-12) books provided by individual users or *social connections* established by social bookmarking site (K-12) users, neither of which are archived by BiblioNasium. To determine which books should be recommended to a user, TVS applies the *cosine similarity measure* on *TF-IDF* tag vector representations of books[5], whereas L-Cos considers the *weighted frequency* of each keyword in the description or title of a book. IICF, on the other hand, calculates the *degree of similarity* between any two books based on the number of users who have bookmarked both books on a social bookmarking site, which is a variation of the popular *collaborative filtering* strategy commonly adopted for making recommendations.

As shown in Figure 3, BReK12 outperforms its counterparts based on the evaluation metrics introduced in Section 5.2. The improvements achieved by BReK12 over the others are statistically significant (with $p < 0.01$). According to the computed MRR, on the average BReK12 users are required to browse through about one ($\cong \frac{1}{0.60} = 1.67$) recommended book before locating a relevant one, whereas users of TVS, L-Cos, and IICF are required to scan through at least 4 ($\cong \frac{1}{0.23} = 4.3$ and $\cong \frac{1}{0.21} = 4.8$) or 2 ($\cong \frac{1}{0.45} = 2.2$) recommended books, respectively. The Precision@10 values reflect that, in general, close to 8 (out of 10) books suggested by BReK12 are relevant, as opposed to close to 4, 2, and 6 relevant books recommended by TVS, L-Cos, and IICF, respectively. The nDCG scores indicate the superiority of BReK12 over TVS, L-Cos, and IICF in ranking relevant books to be recommended *higher* in the list of suggested books.

While TVS, L-Cos, and IICF consider only textual descriptions of books or bookmaking patterns of users on a social site, BReK12 examines *multiple* contributing factors to identify potential recommendations, which increases the number of relevant reading selections for the users.

6. CONCLUSIONS AND FUTURE WORK

We have introduced BReK12, a unique recommender tailored to K-12 readers, which makes *personalized* suggestions on books that satisfy both the *preferences* and *reading abilities* of its users. Unlike current state-of-the-art recommenders that rely on the existence of users' historical data in the form of *ratings*, which are missing among the K-12 users, BReK12 simply considers readily available *brief descriptions* on books, *patterns* of *co-occurrence* among books bookmarked on a social bookmarking site on which BReK12 is installed, and *grade levels* of books computed using our newly-developed ReLAT. ReLAT is novel, since it can determine the grade level of any book (even if a sample of the text of a book is unavailable) by analyzing the Subject Headings of books, US Curriculum subject areas identified in books, and information about the authors of books. As children continue to read more books if they can *choose* what to read [2], a significant contribution of BReK12 is to provide K-12 readers a selection of suitable books to choose from that are not only appealing to them, but can be comprehended

[5]Tag descriptions on books can be extracted from the INEX 2012 Social Book Search Track dataset (inex.mmci.uni-saarland.de/tracks/books/).

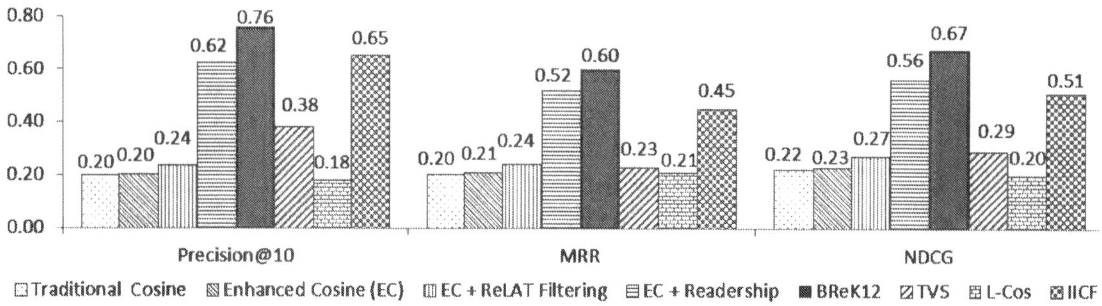

Figure 3: Performance evaluation of TVS, L-Cos, IICF, and BReK12 using the BiblioNasium dataset

by them. The conducted experiments demonstrate (i) the accuracy of ReLAT and its superiority over existing readability formulas/analysis tools, and (ii) the effectiveness of BReK12, which outperforms baseline recommenders in suggesting books for K-12 users.

As part of our future work, we plan to extend BReK12 so that it can suggest reading materials for struggling readers, i.e., readers with learning disabilities and those who learn English as a second language, for whom the grade level of a recommended book is an important factor to be considered.

7. REFERENCES

[1] R. Allington. *What Really Matters for Struggling Readers: Designing Research-Based Programs, 3rd Edition.* Pearsons, 2011.

[2] R. Allington and E. Gabriel. Every Child, Every Day. *Reading: The Core Skill*, 69(6):10–15, 2012.

[3] J. Aslam and M. Montague. Models for Metasearch. In *ACM SIGIR*, pages 267–276, 1997.

[4] R. Benjamin. Reconstructing Readability: Recent Developments and Recommendations in the Analysis of Text Difficulty. *Educational Psychology Review*, 24:63–88, 2012.

[5] D. Blei, A. Ng, and M. Jordan. Latent Dirichlet Allocation. *JMLR*, 3:993–1022, 2003.

[6] T. Bogers and A. van den Bosch. Fusing Recommendations for Social Bookmarking Websites. *IJEC*, 15(3):33–75, 2011.

[7] K. Collins-Thompson and J. Callan. A Language Modeling Approach to Predicting Reading Difficulty. In *HLT/NAACL*, pages 193–200, 2004.

[8] W. Croft, D. Metzler, and T. Strohman. *Search Engines: Information Retrieval in Practice.* Addison Wesley, 2010.

[9] L. Feng, N. Elhadad, and M. Huenerfauth. Cognitively Motivated Features for Readability Assessment. In *EACL*, pages 229–237, 2009.

[10] S. Givon and V. Lavrenko. Predicting Social-Tags for Cold Start Book Recommendations. In *ACM RecSys*, pages 333–336, 2009.

[11] Z. Guan, C. Wang, J. Bu, C. Chen, K. Yang, D. Cai, and X. He. Document Recommendation in Social Tagging Services. In *WWW*, pages 391–400, 2010.

[12] J. Koberstein and Y.-K. Ng. Using Word Clusters to Detect Similar Web Documents. In *KSEM*, pages 215–228, 2006.

[13] J. Lennon, P. Koleff, J. Greenwood, and K. Gaston. The Geographical Structure of British Bird Distributions: Diversity, Spatial Turnover and Scale. *Journal of Animal Ecology*, 70:966–979, 2001.

[14] G. Linden, B. Smith, and J. York. Amazon.com Recommendations: Item-to-Item Collaborative Filtering. *IEEE Internet Computing*, 7(1):76–80, 2003.

[15] Y. Ma, E. Fosler-Lussier, and R. Lofthus. Ranking-based Readability Assessment for Early Primary Children's Literature. In *HLT/NAACL*, pages 548–552, 2012.

[16] N. Manouselis, H. Drachsler, K. Verbert, and E. Duval. *Recommender Systems for Learning.* Springer Briefs in Electrical and Computer Engineering, 2013.

[17] R. Myers. *Classical and Modern Regression with Applications.* Duxbury Press Belmont, 1990.

[18] C. Nascimento, A. Laender, A. da Silva, and M. Goncalves. A Source Independent Framework for Research Paper Recommendation. In *ACM/IEEE JCDL*, pages 297–306, 2011.

[19] J. Oakhill and K. Cain. The Precursors of Reading Ability in Young Readers: Evidence From a Four-Year Longitudinal Study. *SSR*, 16(2):91–121, 2012.

[20] Y. Park and K. Chang. Individual and Group Behavior-based Customer Profile Model for Personalized Product Recommendation. *Expert Systems with Applications*, 36(2):1932–1939, 2009.

[21] M. Pera and Y.-K. Ng. With a Little Help From My Friends: Generating Personalized Book Recommendations Using Data Extracted from a Social Website. In *IEEE/WIC/ACM WI*, pages 96–99, 2011.

[22] R. Qumsiyeh and Y.-K. Ng. ReadAid: A Robust and Fully-Automated Readability Assessment Tool. In *IEEE ICTAI*, pages 539–546, 2011.

[23] Renaissance Learning. ATOS vs. Lexile Which Readability Formula is Best? Available at kmnet.renlearn.com/Library/R003520002GE7114.pdf, 2006.

[24] F. Ricci, L. Rokach, B. Shapira, and P. Kantor. *Recommender Systems Handbook.* Springer, 2011.

[25] A. Sieg, B. Mobasher, and R. Burke. Improving the Effectiveness of Collaborative Recommendation with Ontology-based User Profiles. In *ACM HetRec*, pages 39–46, 2010.

[26] C. Yang, B. Wei, J. Wu, Y. Zhang, and L. Zhang. CARES: a Ranking-oriented CADAL Recommender System. In *ACM/IEEE JCDL*, pages 203–212, 2009.

Movie Recommender System for Profit Maximization

Amos Azaria, Avinatan Hassidim and Sarit Kraus
Dep. of Computer Science, Bar-Ilan University
Ramat Gan 52900, Israel
{azariaa1,avinatan,sarit}@cs.biu.ac.il

Adi Eshkol, Ofer Weintraub and Irit Netanely
Viaccess-Orca,
22 Zarhin Street, Ra'anana 43662, Israel
{adi.eshkol, ofer.weintraub,irit.netanely}@viaccess-orca.com

ABSTRACT

Traditional recommender systems minimize prediction error with respect to users' choices. Recent studies have shown that recommender systems have a positive effect on the provider's revenue.

In this paper we show that by providing a set of recommendations different than the one perceived best according to user acceptance rate, the recommendation system can further increase the business' utility (e.g. revenue), without any significant drop in user satisfaction. Indeed, the recommendation system designer should have in mind both the user, whose taste we need to reveal, and the business, which wants to promote specific content.

We performed a large body of experiments comparing a commercial state-of-the-art recommendation engine with a modified recommendation list, which takes into account the utility (or revenue) which the business obtains from each suggestion that is accepted by the user. We show that the modified recommendation list is more desirable for the business, as the end result gives the business a higher utility (or revenue). To study possible reduce in satisfaction by providing the user worse suggestions, we asked the users how they perceive the list of recommendation that they received. Differences in user satisfaction between the lists is negligible, and not statistically significant.

We also uncover a phenomenon where movie consumers prefer watching and even paying for movies that they have already seen in the past than movies that are new to them.

Categories and Subject Descriptors

I.2.m [**Computing Methodologies**]: ARTIFICIAL INTELLIGENCE—*General*

Keywords

Human Modeling, Movies, Recommender Systems

1. INTRODUCTION

The main goal in designing recommender systems is usually to predict the user's wish list and to supply her with the best list of recommendations. This trend is prevalent whether we consider a social network recommending friends [2], consumer goods [14] or movies [11].

However, in most cases, the engineers that design the recommender system are hired by the business which provides the suggestions (in some cases the web-site buys a recommendation engine from a third party - but also in these cases the site is paying for the recommendations). The business' end goal is usually to increase sales, revenues, user engagement, or some other metric. In that sense, the user is not the end customer of the recommendation system, although she sees the recommendations [13]. Still, one could argue that it is better for the business to give the user the best possible recommendations, as it will also maximize the business' profit, either in the short run (no point in giving recommendations which are not followed by the users) or at least in the long run (good recommendations make users happy).

In this paper, we provide evidence that a business may gain significantly by providing users with recommendations that may not be best from the users point of view but serve the business' needs. We provide an algorithm which uses a general recommender system as a black-box and increases the utility of the business. We perform extensive experiments with it in various cases. In particular, we consider two settings:

1. The *Hidden Agenda* setting: In this setting, the business has items that it wants to promote, in a way which is opaque to the user. For example, a movie supplier which provides movies on a monthly fee basis but has different costs for different movies, or a social network which wants to connect users who are less engaged to more engaged ones. Netflix, for instance, set a filter to avoid recommending new releases which have high costs to them [24].

2. The *Revenue Maximizing* setting: In this case the goal of the recommender system is to maximize the expected revenue, e.g. by recommending expensive items. In this setting, there is an inherent conflict between the user and the business.

To study these settings, we conducted experiments on Amazon Mechanical Turk (AMT) in which subjects were asked to choose a set of favorite movies, and then were given recommendations for another set of movies. For each recommendation, the subjects were asked if they would or would not watch the movie[1]. Finally, in order to test possible reduce in satisfaction cased by tuning the recommendations to the business' needs, we asked each subject how good she feels about the recommendations she received.

[1]In the Revenue Maximization setting each recommended movie also came with a price tag. We describe the experiments later in the experiments section.

RecSys'13, October 12–16, 2013, Hong Kong, China.

http://dx.doi.org/10.1145/2507157.2507162.

This form of experimentation makes two assumptions. First, we simulate long term effects by asking users about their satisfaction from the list. Second, we assume that asking users if they are willing to pay for a movie is the same as actually taking their money and showing them the movie. Both assumptions are common in the literature (for a comparison between hypothetical and real scenarios see [18]). We hope to integrate the algorithm in a real world system to circumvent the assumptions.

Manipulating the recommender system in order to increase revenue (or to satisfy some other hidden agenda) raises some ethical concerns. If users believe that a particular algorithm is being used (e.g. collaborative filtering), then they could be irritated if they find out that recommendations are being edited in some way. However, most businesses do not provide the specification of their recommender system (treating it as a "secret sauce"), which diminishes this concern. Furthermore, several companies (including Netflix, Walmart and Amazon) admitted human intervention in their recommender system [17], so it may well be that different companies are already tweaking their recommender systems for their own good. In this sense, an important lesson to take away from this work is "users beware". We show that businesses garner a large gain by manipulating the system, and many companies could be tempted by this increase in revenue. In this paper we proposes a method which allows businesses to mount their existing recommender system in order to increase their revenue.

An interesting phenomenon that we uncover is that subjects are more willing to pay for movies that they've already seen. While a similar phenomena is known for other types of consumer goods, coming across it with regards to movies is new and somewhat counter-intuitive. Interestingly, in movie watching, two opposite effects come into play: 1. Variety seeking: users want new experiences (see the survey [15] for a model of variety seeking customers). 2. Loyalty: users are loyal to brands that they know and used. It is usually assumed that in movies the former effect is far more dominant [12, 7]. Although we supply some explanation for this phenomenon, further research is required in order to fully understand it. We note that this phenomena has implications to the design of recommender systems – some systems take care not to recommend a movie which was previously watched. Instead, one may be better off recommending movies that the user saw in the past as well.

To summarize, the main contribution of this paper is twofold:

- Providing an algorithm for utility maximization of a movie supplier service, in two different settings, one with prices and the other without. This algorithm is provided along with an extensive experiment demonstrating its performance.
- Uncovering the interesting behavior of movie consumers, who prefer watching and paying for movies that they have already seen in the past (to watching and paying for movies which are new to them).

These findings have major consequences for design of recommendation systems for movie providers..

2. RELATED WORK

Models for predicting users' ratings have been proposed that are used by recommendation systems to advise their users (See Ricci et al. [19] for a recent review). It has been shown that recommender systems, in general, are beneficial for the providing business [22]. However, most works in this realm do not explicitly try to maximize the system's revenue, but only consider the utility of the user. The works that do try to directly increase the system's revenue usually take a more holistic approach, changing the pricing and using the inner workings of the recommendation system. As far as we know, this is the first work which treats the recommender system as a black box, does not change the pricing and tries to increase the revenue directly.

Pathak et al. [17] study the cross effects between sales, pricing and recommendations on Amazon books. They show that recommendation systems increase sales and cause price changes. However, the recommendation systems that they consider are price independent, and the effect on prices is indirect - items which are recommended more are bought more, which affects their price (the pricing procedure used in their data takes popularity into account). They do not consider having the price as an input to the system, and do not try to design new recommendation systems.

Chen et al. [4] develop a recommender system which tries to maximize product profitability. Chen et al. assume the usage of a collaborative filtering recommender system which, as part of its construction, provides a theoretically-based probability that a user will purchase each item. They multiply this probability by the revenue from each item and recommend the items which yield the highest expected revenue. However, in practice, many recommender systems do not rely only upon collaborative filtering (which can't be applied to new items or when the data is sparse), but also rely on different engines (such as popularity, semantic similarity, etc.). Even a business using a pure collaborative filtering engine may not necessarily have access to (or may not want to access) the internal workings of their own recommender system. Therefore, we assume a generic recommender system which is treated as a black-box component, and dedicate most of our work to building a human model in order to predict the acceptance rate of a given item using a generic recommender system.

Das et al. [5] provide a mathematical approach for maximizing business revenue using recommender systems. However, they assume that as long as the recommendations are similar enough to the customer's own ratings, the customer is likely to follow the recommendations. Therefore, Das et al. do not model the actual drop in user acceptance rate as the item becomes less relevant or as the item price increases, as is done in this work. Similarly, Hosanagar et al. [9] use a mathematical approach to study the conflict which a business confront when using recommender systems. On one hand the business would like to recommend items with higher revenue (margins), but on the other hand it would like to recommend items which the users are more likely to buy. Hosanagar et al. show that in order to increase its total revenue, the business must balance between these two factors. Unfortunately, neither paper provides any actual experimental evaluation with people, as is provided in this paper.

Shani et al. [23] use a discrete-state MDP model to maximize the system's utility function, taking into account the future interactions with their users. In their work, the system may, for example, decide to recommend a game console, since, if purchased, the user is likely to purchase many games for it in the future. This approach is not applicable to our domain as we consider a single-shot recommendation. Furthermore, in the movie recommendation domain, most movies have very little impact on each other, and watching a certain movie doesn't usually increase or decrease the probability that the user will watch a different movie. In [1] we model the long-term affect of advice given by a self-interested system on the users in route selection problems. In order for the system to maximize its long term expected revenue, we suggest that it uses what we term the "social utility" approach. However, in [1] we assume that the user must select his action among a limited number of options and the system merely recommends a certain action. Therefore the system does not act as a classic recommender system, which recommends a limited number of items from a very large corpus. Still, both of the above works may be found useful if combined with the approach given in this paper, when considering repeated interactions scenarios.

We now turn to discuss related work to the phenomenon where movie consumers prefer watching movies that they have already seen. The marketing literature contains many examples in which an individual experiencing one type of event is more likely to experience it again. Such examples include unemployment, accidents and buying a specific product (or brand). Heckman [8] discusses two possible explanations: either the first experience changes the individual and makes the second one more likely (e.g. the individual bought a brand and liked it), or that this specific individual is more likely to have this experience (e.g. a careless driver has a higher probability of being involved in a car accident). Kamakura and Russell [10] show how to segment a market into loyal and non-loyal customers, where the loyal customers are less price sensitive and keep buying the same brand (see the works of [6] and [20] who show that even a very short purchase history data can have a huge impact, and that of [16] which shows that consuming one product from a particular company increases the probability of consuming another product from the same company).

Russel and Levy [21] interviewed 23 subjects regarding repeated experiences. They describe several benefits people might have from rereading a book, re-watching a movie etc. For example, when rereading a book, the person can pay more attention to the language and the expressions used. Since people's memory is imperfect, when re-watching a movie, people reconstruct their memory, and this reconstruction may tack back and forth between the actual memory and new knowledge acquired since. The reconstructive experience may add levels of complexity and depth.

3. PUMA

In this section we present the Profit and Utility Maximizer Algorithm (PUMA). PUMA mounts a black-boxed recommender system which supplies a ranked list of movies. This recommender system is assumed to be personalized to the users, even though this is not a requirement for PUMA.

3.1 Algorithm for Hidden Agenda Setting

In the hidden agenda setting, the movie system supplier wants to promote certain movies. Movies aren't assigned a price. We assume that each movie is assigned a promotion value, $v(m)$, which is in $V = \{0.1, 0.2, ..., 1\}$. The promotion value is hidden from the user. The movie system supplier wants to maximize the sum of movie promotions which are watched by the users, i.e. if a user watches a movie, m, the movie supplier gains $v(m)$; otherwise it gains nothing.

The first phase in PUMA's construction is to collect data on the impact of the movie rank ($r(m)$) in the original recommender system on the likelihood of the users to watch a movie ($p(m)$). To this end we provide recommendations, using the original recommender system, ranked in leaps of a given k (i.e. each subject is provided with the recommendations which are ranked: $\{1, k, ..., (n-1) \cdot k + 1\}$ for the given subject in the original recommender system). We cluster the data according to the movie rank and, using least squared regression, we find a function that best explains the data as a function of the movie rank. We consider the following possible functions: linear, exponent, log and power (see Table 1 for function forms). We do not consider functions which allow maximum points (global or local) which aren't at the edges, as we assume that the acceptance rate of the users should be highest for the top rank and then gradually decrease. Since these functions intend to predict the probability of the acceptance rate, they must return a value between 0 and 1, therefore a negative value returned must be set to 0 (this may only happen with the linear and log functions - however, in practice, we did not encounter this need).

Table 1: Function forms for considered functions. α and β are non-negative parameters and $r(m)$ is the movie rank.

function	function form
linear (decay)	$\alpha - \beta \cdot r(m)$
exponent (exponential decay)	$\alpha \cdot e^{-\beta \cdot r(m)}$
log (logarithmic decay)	$\alpha - \beta \cdot \ln(r(m))$
power (decay)	$\alpha \cdot r(m)^{-\beta}$

Among the functions that we tested, the linear function turned out to provide the best fit to the data in the hidden agenda setting (it resulted with the greatest coefficient of determination (R^2)). Therefore, the probability that a user will want to watch a movie as a function of its rank (to the specific user) takes the form of (where α and β are constants):

$$p(m|r(m)) = \alpha - \beta \cdot r(m) \quad (1)$$

Given a new user, PUMA sorts the list of movies which is outputted by the original recommender system according to its expected promotion value, which is given by:

$$p(m|r(m)) \cdot v(m) \quad (2)$$

and provides the top n movies as its recommendation.

3.2 Algorithm for Revenue Maximizing

In this setting, every movie is assigned a fixed price (different movies have different prices). Each movie is also assumed to have a cost to the vendor. PUMA intends to maximize the revenue obtained by the vendor, which is the sum of all movies purchased by the users minus the sum of all costs to the vendor.

PUMA's variant for the Revenue Maximizing settings confronts a much more complex problem than the PUMA's variant for the hidden agenda for the following two reasons: 1. There is a direct conflict between the system and the users. 2. PUMA must model the likelihood that the users will watch a movie as a function of both the movie rank *and* the movie price.

Building a model by learning a function of both the movie rank and the movie price together is unfeasible as it requires too many data points. Furthermore, in such a learning phase the movie supplier intentionally provides sub-optimal recommendation, which may result in a great loss. Instead, we assume that the two variables are independent, i.e. if the movie rank drops, the likelihood of the user buying the movie drops similarly for any price group. This assumption was used since we found no correlation between the prices of movies in Amazon and their popularity in IMBD.

In order to learn the impact of the price on the likelihood of the users buying a movie, we use the recommender system as is, providing recommendations from 1 to n. We cluster the data into pricing sets where each price (fee f) is associated with the fraction of users who want to buy a movie (m) for that price. Using least squares regression we find a function that best explains the data as a function of the price. We tested the same functions described above (see Table 1 - replace movie rank with movie fee), and the log function resulted with a nearly perfect fit to the data. Therefore, the probability that a user will be willing to pay in order to watch a movie as a function of its fee takes the form of (where α and β are constants):

$$p(m|f(m)) = \alpha_1 - \beta_1 \cdot ln(f(m)) \tag{3}$$

In order to learn the impact of the movie rank (r) in the recommender system on the likelihood of the users buying a movie, we removed all prices from the movies and asked the subjects if they were willing to pay to watch the movie (without mentioning its price). As in the hidden agenda settings, we provided recommendations in leaps of k' (i.e. recommendations are in the group $\{1, k'+1, ..., (n-1) \cdot k' + 1\}$). We clustered the data according to the movie rank and once again using least squared regression we found a function that best explains the data as a function of the movie rank. Among the functions that we tested (see Table 1), the log function turned out to provide the best fit to the data for the movie rank as well (resulting with the greatest coefficient of determination (R^2)). Using the log function (which is a convex function) implies that the drop in user acceptance rate between movies in the top rankings is larger than the drop in user acceptance rate within the bottom rankings. The difference in the function which best fits the data between the hidden agenda setting and the revenue maximizing setting is sensible, since, when people must pay for movies they are more keen that the movies be closer to their exact taste, therefore the acceptance rate drops more drastically. The probability that a user will be willing to pay in order to watch a movie as a function of its rank takes the form of:

$$p(m|r(m)) = \alpha_2 - \beta_2 \cdot ln(r(m)) \tag{4}$$

A human model for predicting the human willingness to pay to watch a movie, $p(m|r(m), f(m))$, requires combining Equations 3 and 4; however this task is non-trivial. Taking $p(m|r(m)f(m)$ to be $p(m|r(m)) \cdot p(m|f(m))$ does not make sense: for example if both signals say that the probability of watching is 0.5 then the output should be 0.5 and not 0.25. Using this intuition, we assume that Equation 3 is exact for the average rank it was trained upon which is $\frac{n}{2} + 1$. Therefore, by adding a correction term, $\gamma(m)$, to Equation 4 we require that Equation 4 gives the same viewing probability as Equation 3 on $\frac{n}{2} + 1$:

$$\alpha_2 + \gamma(f(m)) - \beta_2 \cdot ln(\frac{n}{2} + 1) = \alpha_1 - \beta_1 \cdot ln(f(m)) \tag{5}$$

Isolating $\gamma(m)$ we get:

$$\gamma(f(m)) = (\alpha_1 - \alpha_2) + \beta_2 \cdot ln(\frac{n}{2} + 1) - \beta_1 \cdot ln(f(m)) \tag{6}$$

Therefore, our human model for predicting the fraction of users who will buy a movie, m, given the movie price, $f(m)$, and the movie rank, $r(m)$ (obtained from the recommender system) is:

$$p(m|r(m), f(m)) = \alpha_2 + ((\alpha_1 - \alpha_2) + \beta_2 \cdot ln(\frac{n}{2} + 1) - \beta_1 \cdot ln(f(m))) - \beta_2 \cdot ln(r(m)) \tag{7}$$

and after simple mathematical manipulations:

$$p(m|r(m), f(m)) = \alpha_1 - \beta_2 \cdot ln(\frac{r(m)}{\frac{n}{2} + 1}) - \beta_1 \cdot ln(f(m))$$

Once a human model is obtained, PUMA calculates the expected revenue from each movie simply by multiplying the movie revenue with the probability that the user will be willing to pay to watch it (obtained from the model) and returns the movies with the highest expected revenues. The revenue is simply the movie price ($f(m)$) minus the movie cost to the vendor ($c(m)$). I.e. given a human model, PUMA recommends the top n movies which maximize:

$$(f(m) - c(m)) \cdot p(m|r(m), f(m)) \tag{8}$$

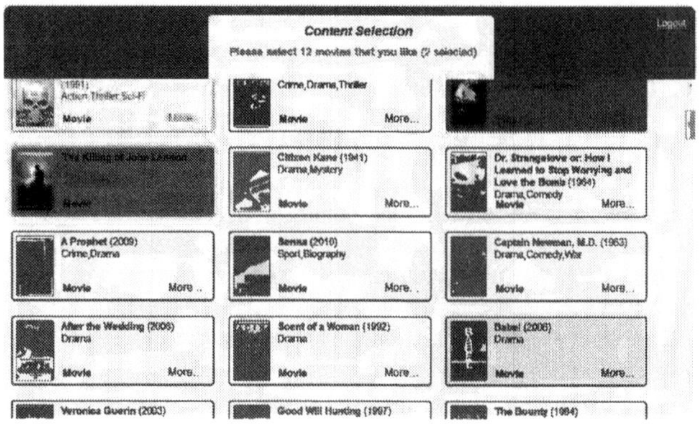

Figure 1: A screen-shot of a subject selecting movies he liked

4. EXPERIMENTS

All of our experiments were performed using Amazon's Mechanical Turk service (AMT). Participation in all experiments consisted of a total of 245 subjects from the USA, of which 50.6% were females and 49.4% were males, with an average age of 31.5. The subjects were paid 25 cents for participating in the study and a bonus of additional 25 cents after completing it. We ensured that every subject would participate only once (even when considering different experiments). The movie corpus included 16,327 movies. The original movie recommender system receives a list of 12 preferred movies for each user and returns a ranked list of movies that have a semantically similar description to the input movies, have a similar genre and also considers the released year and the popularity of the movies (a personalized non-collaborative filtering-based recommender system). We set $n = 10$, i.e., each subject was recommended 10 movies.

After collecting demographic data, the subjects were asked to choose 12 movies which they enjoyed most among a list of 120 popular movies (see Figure 1 for a screen-shot). Then, depending on the experiment, the subjects were divided into different treatment groups and received different recommendations.

The list of recommendations included a description of each of the movies (see Figure 2 for an example). The subjects were shown the price of each movie, when relevant, and then according to their treatment group were asked if they would like to pay in order to watch it, or simply if they would like to watch the movie. In order to assure truthful responses, the subjects were also required to explain their choice ("Please explain why (mandatory)"). After receiving the list of recommendations and specifying for each movie if they would like to buy it (watch it), the subjects were shown another page including the exact same movies. This time they were asked whether they have seen each of the movies ("Did you ever watch *movie name*?"), whether they think that a given movie is a good recommendation ("Is this a good recommendation?") and rated the full list ("How would you rate the full list of recommendations?") on a scale from 1 to 5. These questions were intentionally asked on a different page in order to avoid framing [25] and to ensure that the users return their true preferences[2].

[2]We conducted additional experiments where the subjects were first asked whether they watched each movie and then according

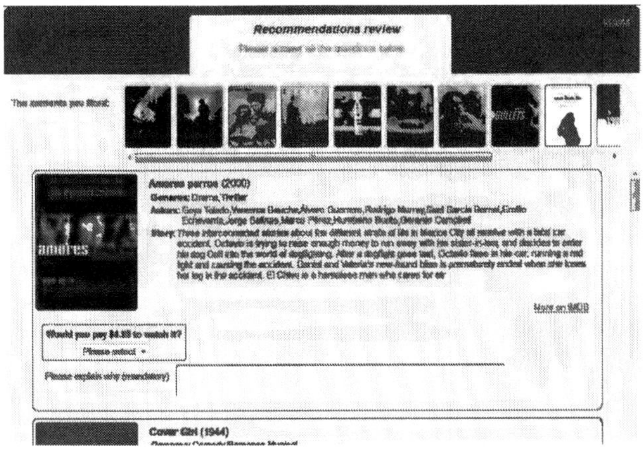

Figure 2: Recommendation page screen-shot

Table 2: Demographic statistics for the hidden agenda setting

treatment group	number of subjects	fraction of females	average age
Rec-HA	31	58.1%	32.3
PUMA-HA	30	50.0%	32.6%
Learn-HA	30	53.3%	29.4%

4.1 Hidden Agenda Setting

In the hidden agenda setting we assume that the subjects have a subscription and therefore they were simply asked if they would like to watch each movie ("Would you watch it?"). The hidden agenda setting experiment was composed of three different treatment groups. Subjects in the *Rec-HA* group received the top 10 movies returned by the original recommender system. Subjects in the *PUMA-HA* group received the movies chosen by PUMA. Subjects in the *Learn-HA* group were used for data collection in order to learn PUMA's human model. Table 2 presents some demographic statistics on the subjects in these three treatment groups.

For the data collection on the movie rank phase (Learn-HA) we had to select a value for k (which determines the movie ranks on which we collect data; see Section 3.1). The lower the k is, the more accurate the human model is for the better (lower) rankings. However, on the other hand, the higher k is, the more rankings the human model may cover. In the extreme case where the ranking has a minor effect on the human acceptance rate, the vendor may want to recommend only movies with a promotion value of 1. Even in that extreme case, the highest movie rank, on average, should not exceed $|V| \cdot n$, which is 100. Therefore, we set $k = 10$, which allows us to collect data on movies ranked: $\{1, 11, 21, 31, 41, 51, 61, 71, 81, 91\}$.

Unfortunately, the data collected in the Learn-HA group was very noisy, as the movies in the 11th rank resulted with a much higher acceptance rate than those in the 1st rank. Furthermore, the movies in the 71st rank resulted in a much lower acceptance rate than those in the 81st rank. Therefore the coefficient of determination (R^2) was only 0.31. Still, the tendency of the data was clear (the correlation between the movie rank and the acceptance rate

to their answer, were asked whether they would pay for watching it (again). We obtained similar results to those presented in Section 4.3, regarding peoples preference to movies that they have already seen. However, we do not include these results, since they may have been contaminated by the framing effect.

Table 3: Coefficient of determination for functions tested for the hidden agenda setting

function	R^2
linear	**0.31**
exponent	0.29
log	0.21
power	0.21

Table 4: The fraction of subjects who wanted to watch each movie, average promotion gain, overall satisfaction and fraction of movies who were marked as good recommendations

treatment group	want to watch	average promotion	overall satisfaction
Rec-HA	76.8%	0.436	4.13
PUMA-HA	69.8%	**0.684**	3.83
Learn-HA	62.0%	-	3.77

was negative 0.56, which implies that the original recommender system performed well), and additional data would have probably yielded a better coefficient of determination. Nevertheless, the fit-to-data reached was definitely good enough, as can be seen by the performance results. Table 3 lists coefficient of determination for all functions tested.

The specific human model obtained, which was used by PUMA (in the hidden agenda settings) is simply:

$$p(m|r(m)) = 0.6965 - 0.0017 \cdot r(m) \quad (9)$$

As for the results: PUMA significantly ($p < 0.001$ using student t-test) outperformed the original recommender system by increasing its promotion value by 57% with an average of 0.684 per movie for PUMA-HA versus an average of only 0.436 per movie for the Rec-HA group. No statistically significant differences were observed between the two groups from the average satisfaction for each of the movies or in the user satisfaction from the full list. It is likely that using more data, one could get a statistically significant drop in user satisfaction. Our best estimate is a 3% drop in the fraction of good recommendations (from 71% rated as good recommendations in the Rec-HA group vs. 69% in the PUMA-HA group), and a 7% loss in the satisfaction from the entire list. See Table 4 for additional details.

4.2 Revenue Maximizing Setting

For the revenue maximizing settings, all movies were randomly assigned a price which was in $F = \{\$0.99, \$2.99, \$4.99, \$6.99, \$8.99\}$. [3] We assumed that the vendor's cost doesn't depend on the number of movies sold and therefore set $c(m) = 0$ for all movies. The subjects were asked if they would pay the movie price in order to watch the movie ("would you pay $*movie price* to watch it?"). As in the hidden agenda setting, subjects were divided into three treatment groups. Subjects in the *Rec-RM* group received the top 10 movies returned by the original recommender system. Subjects in the *PUMA-RM* group received the movies chosen by PUMA. Subjects in the *Learn-RM* group were used in order to obtain data about the decay of interest in movies as a function of the movie rank (as explained in Section 3.2). The subjects in this group were asked if they were willing to pay for a movie, but were not told its

[3] We used random pricing since we didn't find correlation between Amazon's movie price and features such as popularity of the movie in IMDB, release year, parental rating and country production.

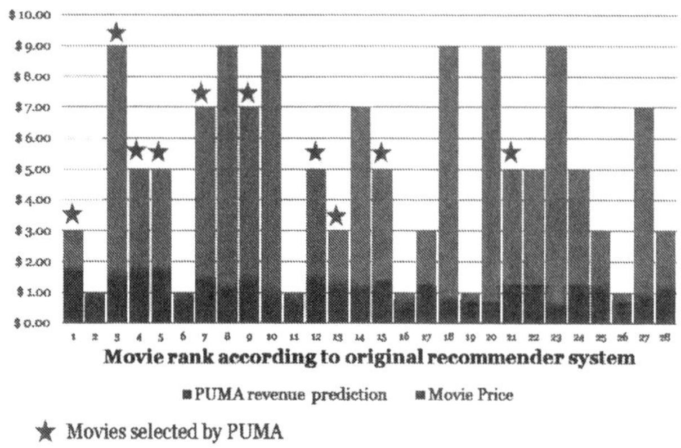

Figure 3: An example of PUMA's selection process

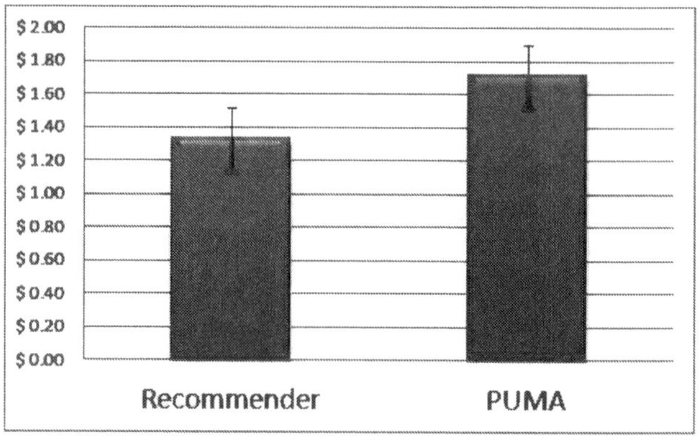

Figure 4: Average revenue for system (in dollars)

Table 5: Demographic stats. for the revenue maximizing setting

treatment group	number of subjects	fraction of females	average age
Rec-RM	31	41.9%	32.1
PUMA-RM	28	67.8%	29.7
Learn-RM	30	40.0%	33.9

Table 7: the fraction of subjects who wanted to pay for a movie, average revenue and overall satisfaction.

treatment group	want to buy	average revenue	overall satisfaction
Rec-RM	39.1%	$1.33	4.13
PUMA-RM	37.1%	**$1.71**	4.04
Learn-RM	56%	–	4.03

price ("Would you pay to watch it?"). Table 5 presents some demographic statistics on the subjects in these three treatment groups.

In the movie rank learning phase, we set $k' = 5$, i.e., recommendations were in the group $\{1, 6, 11, 16, 21, 26, 31, 36, 41, 46\}$. Once again, this is because $k' \cdot n = |F| \cdot n$ (even if the movie ranking has minor impact on the probability that the user will watch the movie, and therefore PUMA would stick to a certain price; still, on average, it is not likely that PUMA will provide movies which exceed rank $|F| \cdot n$, and therefore no data is needed on those high rankings). The coefficient of determination value using the log function on the learning data was 0.60, as can be seen in Table 6.

The specific human model obtained, which was used by PUMA (in the revenue maximizing settings), is:

$$p(m|r(m), f(m)) = 0.82 - 0.05 \cdot ln(\frac{r(m)}{6}) - 0.31 \cdot ln(f(m))$$

As can be seen in Figure 4, PUMA significantly ($p < 0.05$ using student t-test) outperformed Rec-RM, yielding an average revenue of $1.71, as opposed to only $1.33 obtained by Rec-RM. No significance was obtained when testing the overall satisfaction level from the list: 4.13 vs. 4.04 in favor of the Rec-RM group. However, more data could probably give a statistically significant difference. Our best estimate for this loss would be about 2.2%. While the average movie price was also similar in both groups, with an average movie price of $5.18 for Rec-RM and an average movie price of $5.27 for PUMA-RM, the standard deviation was quite different: 2.84 for the Rec-RM group, and only 1.95 for PUMA-RM, in which 64.6% of the movies were either priced at $2.99 or $4.99.

Table 6: Coefficient of determination for the functions tested for the revenue maximizing setting.

function	R^2
linear	0.43
exponent	0.39
log	**0.60**
power	0.54

Figure 3 demonstrates the selection process performed by PUMA for a specific user. After calculating the expected revenue using the human model, PUMA selects movies #1, #3, #4, #5, #7, #9, #12, #13, #15 and #21, which yield the highest expected profit. In this example, when comparing PUMA's recommendation's expected revenue to the expected revenue from the first 10 movies (which would have been selected by the original recommender system), the expected revenue increases from $1.34 to $1.52 (13%).

4.3 Subject-Preference for Movies that Have Been Watched Before

We discovered that in all three groups in the revenue maximizing setting, many subjects were willing to pay for movies that they have already watched before. As we discussed in the related work section, marketing literature deals both with the variety effect (buyers who want to enrich their experiences) and with loyalty (or the mere-exposure effect). However, movies are considered to be a prominent example of a variety product, in which customers want to have new experiences, and therefore this result is surprising.

Furthermore, subjects were willing to pay for movies that they have already watched more often than movies which were new to them (although only in the Learn-RM group, where no price was present, these differences reached statistical significance with $p < 0.001$ using Fisher's exact test). Similar behavior was also observed in the hidden agenda setting, where the subjects in all three groups were simply asked if they would like to watch each movie (and neither the word 'buy' nor a price was present). In the hidden agenda settings the subjects significantly ($p < 0.001$) preferred watching a movie again to watching a movie that was new to them. We therefore set out to test whether this behavior will reoccur when the movies are cheap and have a fee of $0.99, $1.99 or $2.99 - the *Cheap* group (see demographic details in Table 8).

This pattern was indeed repeated in the cheap group when prices were mentioned and with statistical significance ($p < 0.001$ using

Table 8: Demographic statistics on the Cheap treatment group

treatment group	number of subjects	fraction of females	average age
Cheap	35	34.3%	29.3

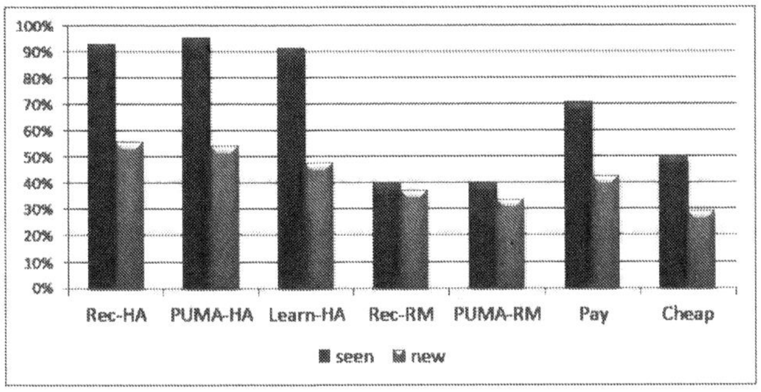

Figure 5: Comparison between the fraction of subjects who wanted to watch/pay for movies they have already seen and movies that were new to them.

Fisher's exact test). Figure 5 compares the fraction of subjects who chose to pay or watch a movie that they hadn't watched before to those who chose to pay or watch a movie that they had watched before (see Table 9 for the exact values). We term this phenomenon the WAnt To See Again (WATSA) phenomenon. On average 53.8% of the movies recommended were already seen in the past by the subjects. One should not be concerned about the differences in the column heights in Figure 5 across the different treatment groups as, obviously, more subjects wanted to watch the movies for free (in the hidden agenda), where no specific price was mentioned (Learn-RM), and when the movies were cheap than when the movies were more expensive (Rec-RM and PUMA-RM).

In practice, when a recommender system is present, many times the users are instructed to simply choose a (fixed size) set of movies which they would like to watch. We therefore conducted an additional treatment group (*Choose-3*) in which the original experimental settings were slightly modified. In this treatment group the subjects were instructed to choose the movies which they would like to watch ("Assume you are entitled to watch three of the recommended movies listed below, which movies would you choose?"). Please refer to Table 8 for demographic details on the choose-3 treatment group.

As we hypothesized, in the choose-3 treatment group, subjects were significantly ($p < 0.001$) more likely to select movies which they have already seen in the past more than movies which were new to them. While only 8.4% of the movies which were new to the subjects were chosen - 45.0% of the movies that have already

Table 9: The fraction of subjects who wanted to watch/pay for movies they had already seen and movies that were new to them

treatment group	seen movies	new movies	delta
Rec-HA	92.2%	55.4%	36.8%
PUMA-HA	94.7%	53.7%	41,0%
Learn-HA	91.1%	47.2%	43.9%
Rec-RM	39.1%	36.6%	2.5%
PUMA-RM	39.5%	33.3%	6.2%
Learn-RM	70.1%	42.5%	27.6%
Cheap	49.8%	28.5%	21.3%

Table 10: Demographic statistics on the Choose-3 group

treatment group	number of subjects	fraction of females	average age
Choose-3	30	60.0%	33.1

been watched were chosen by the subjects. (In total, 59% of the movies have already been watched by the subjects.)

All these findings may be very relevant to designers of recommender systems for movies. Today, most systems take great care not to recommend movies that the user has already seen, while instead perhaps one should try to recommend movies that the user has both seen and liked.

5. DISCUSSION AND FUTURE WORK

One may be concerned about PUMA's performance in the long run, when it is required to interact with the same person many times. Although this hasn't been explicitly tested, we believe that PUMA's advantage over the recommendation system will not degrade; as the overall satisfaction from PUMA's recommendations and the average movie fee for PUMA's recommendations (in the revenue maximization setting) are both very close to that of the original recommender system. An interesting property of PUMA is that it allows online learning, as it may collect additional statistics on-the-fly and use it to refine its human model. In the revenue maximization setting, there is a clear conflict between the business and the user: recommending movies that the advertiser prefers (expensive ones) is bound to reduce the probability that suggestions are accepted. In the hidden agenda setting, all movies are a-priori the same for the user, and hence the only loss in showing a recommendation that the business likes to promote is that it's lower on the user's list. Due to this, there is an even greater gain in changing the list of recommendations, and we see a larger gap between PUMA and the recommendation engine in the hidden agenda setting.

The WATSA phenomenon is heavily linked to the mere-exposure effect [26]. It is well known that people prefer to consume products from brands they know, or to consume the same product several times [3]. However, seeing this phenomenon in movies is surprising. Movies are often believed to be novelty driven, and watching the same movie more than once may eliminate many properties upon which movie enjoyment relies heavily (such as the element of surprise, punch lines etc.). We assume that WATSA is also linked to risk aversion, in which people prefer to watch or even pay for movies that they have seen in the past since they have already enjoyed them and are therefore less likely to regret watching them again. This may be a result of people not fully trusting the movie recommender system. A different reason might be that people truly enjoy watching movies that they have seen in the past, more than new movies. This might be due to the fact that most people watch movies that they expect to enjoy, and therefore people are more likely to enjoy movies that they have already seen. An interesting future experiment would be to have subjects watch a set of movies returned by a recommender system. Upon completion, the subjects would be asked how much they enjoyed each movie and then to compare the average enjoyment from already seen movies to new movies. Such an experiment will reveal whether people's preference for watching movies that they have already seen is not justified and may only be superfluous risk aversion, or a true preference that is linked to people's enjoyment from watching movies that have already been seen. Further research is also required here in order to see if there is a difference between movies which were seen recently and ones which were seen a long time ago, how many times a user is likely to want to watch a movie, whether there is a dependency on the genre, culture, etc. It is also very likely that the WATSA phenomenon is a unique property of personalized recommender systems, which supply good recommendations. We leave all these question for future work.

An interesting property of the WATSA phenomenon may be implied from Table 9: the cheaper the movies are, the greater the WATSA phenomenon. When the prices are the highest (in the Rec-RM and PUMA-RM groups), the difference between the fraction of subjects willing to pay for movies that they have seen and the fraction of subjects willing to pay for new movies is only $2.5\% - 6.2\%$. When the movies are cheap, this difference leaps to 21.3%, when no price is mentioned it reaches 27.6%, and when the subjects are just asked whether they would like to watch the movies, this difference shoots up to $36.8\% - 43.9\%$! Such behavior may be explained by the fact that people might be willing to pay large amounts only for new movies that they are sure that they would enjoy, and they are willing to pay small amounts for movies that they have enjoyed in the past as they see it as a risk-less investment. However, when testing the prices within the Rec-RM, PUMA-RM and Cheap groups, the WATSA phenomenon clearly increased as the prices decreased only in the PUMA-RM group. In the other two groups (Rec-RM and Cheap), the WATSA phenomenon remained quite steady among the different price groups. This may imply that the average cost has greater impact on the WATSA phenomenon than the specific price of each movie. Therefore this property still requires additional study.

6. CONCLUSIONS

In this paper we introduce PUMA, an algorithm which mounts a given black-boxed movie recommender system and selects movies which it expects will maximize the system's revenue. PUMA builds a human model which tries to predict the probability that a user will pay for a movie, given its price (if applicable) and its rank in the original recommender system. We consider two different environments, one in which the movies are associates with different prices and the other in which no prices are present. We empirically demonstrate PUMA's high performance.

Another important contribution of the paper is the uncovering of a phenomenon in which people prefer watching and even paying for movies which they have already seen (when suggested by a recommender system) to movies which are new to them. This phenomenon was tested and found statistically significant in an extensive experimental study as well.

7. REFERENCES

[1] A. Azaria, Z. Rabinovich, S. Kraus, C. V. Goldman, and Y. Gal. Strategic advice provision in repeated human-agent interactions. In *AAAI*, 2012.

[2] L. Backstrom and J. Leskovec. Supervised random walks: predicting and recommending links in social networks. In *Proceedings of the fourth ACM international conference on Web search and data mining*, pages 635–644. ACM, 2011.

[3] Robert F Bornstein, Paul R D'Agostino, et al. Stimulus recognition and the mere exposure effect. *Journal of personality and social psychology*, 63:545–545, 1992.

[4] LS. Chen, FH. Hsu, MC. Chen, and YC. Hsu. Developing recommender systems with the consideration of product profitability for sellers. *Information Sciences*, 178(4):1032–1048, 2008.

[5] A. Das, C. Mathieu, and D. Ricketts. Maximizing profit using recommender systems. *ArXiv e-prints*, August 2009.

[6] F. Gönül and K. Srinivasan. Modeling multiple sources of heterogeneity in multinomial logit models: Methodological and managerial issues. *Marketing Science*, 12(3):213–229, 1993.

[7] John R Hauser and Julian Marewski Dzyabura. Consideration-set heuristics. *Journal of Business Research,(forthcoming)*, 2010.

[8] J. Heckman. Heterogeneity and state dependence. In *Studies in labor markets*, pages 91–140. University of Chicago Press, 1981.

[9] K. Hosanagar, R. Krishnan, and L. Ma. Recomended for you: The impact of profit incentives on the relevance of online recommendations. 2008.

[10] W. A. Kamakura and G. J. Russell. A probabilistic choice model for market segmentation and elasticity structure. *Journal of Marketing Research*, pages 379–390, 1989.

[11] Yehuda Koren, Robert Bell, and Chris Volinsky. Matrix factorization techniques for recommender systems. *Computer*, 42(8):30–37, 2009.

[12] James M Lattin. A model of balanced choice behavior. *Marketing Science*, 6(1):48–65, 1987.

[13] Andrew Lewis. If you are not paying for it, you're not the customer; you're the product being sold. *Metafilter*, 2010.

[14] Greg Linden, Brent Smith, and Jeremy York. Amazon. com recommendations: Item-to-item collaborative filtering. *Internet Computing, IEEE*, 7(1):76–80, 2003.

[15] Leigh McAlister and Edgar Pessemier. Variety seeking behavior: An interdisciplinary review. *Journal of Consumer research*, pages 311–322, 1982.

[16] N. V. Moshkin and R. Shachar. The asymmetric information model of state dependence. *Marketing Science*, 21(4):435–454, 2002.

[17] Bhavik Pathak, Robert Garfinkel, Ram D Gopal, Rajkumar Venkatesan, and Fang Yin. Empirical analysis of the impact of recommender systems on sales. *Journal of Management Information Systems*, 27(2):159–188, 2010.

[18] Daniel Read. Monetary incentives, what are they good for? *Journal of Economic Methodology*, 12(2):265–276, 2005.

[19] F. Ricci, L. Rokach, B. Shapira, and P.B. Kantor, editors. *Recommender Systems Handbook*. Springer, 2011.

[20] Peter E Rossi, Robert E McCulloch, and Greg M Allenby. The value of purchase history data in target marketing. *Marketing Science*, 15(4):321–340, 1996.

[21] C. A. Russell and S. J. Levy. The temporal and focal dynamics of volitional reconsumption: A phenomenological investigation of repeated hedonic experiences. *Journal of Consumer Research*, 39(2):341–359, 2012.

[22] J Ben Schafer, Joseph Konstan, and John Riedi. Recommender systems in e-commerce. In *Proceedings of the 1st ACM conference on Electronic commerce*, pages 158–166. ACM, 1999.

[23] Guy Shani, David Heckerman, and Ronen I. Brafman. An MDP-based recommender system. *J. Mach. Learn. Res.*, 6:1265–1295, 2005.

[24] W. Shih, S. Kaufman, and D. Spinola. Netflix. *Harvard Business School Case*, 9:607–138, 2007.

[25] A. Tversky and D. Kahneman. The framing of decisions and the psychology of choice. *Science*, 211(4481):453–458, 1981.

[26] Robert B Zajonc. Attitudinal effects of mere exposure. 1. *Pers. Soc. Psycho*, 9(2 pt 2), 1968.

Xbox Movies Recommendations: Variational Bayes Matrix Factorization with Embedded Feature Selection

Noam Koenigstein
Microsoft R&D
Israel
noamko@microsoft.com

Ulrich Paquet
Microsoft Research
Cambridge, UK
ulripa@microsoft.com

ABSTRACT

We present a matrix factorization model inspired by challenges we encountered while working on the Xbox movies recommendation system. The item catalog in a recommender system is typically equipped with meta-data features in the form of labels. However, only part of these features are informative or useful with regard to collaborative filtering. By incorporating a novel sparsity prior on feature parameters, the model automatically discerns and utilizes informative features while simultaneously pruning non-informative features.

The model is designed for binary feedback, which is common in many real-world systems where numeric rating data is scarce or non-existent. However, the overall framework is applicable to any likelihood function. Model parameters are estimated with a Variational Bayes inference algorithm, which is robust to over-fitting and does not require cross-validation and fine tuning of regularization coefficients. The efficacy of our method is illustrated on a sample from the Xbox movies dataset as well as on the publicly available MovieLens dataset. In both cases, the proposed solution provides superior predictive accuracy, especially for long-tail items. We then demonstrate the feature selection capabilities and compare against the common case of simple Gaussian priors. Finally, we show that even without features, our model performs better than a baseline model trained with the popular stochastic gradient descent approach.

Categories and Subject Descriptors

H.3.3 [**Information Search and Retrieval**]: Information Filtering

General Terms

Recommender System, Feature Selection

1. INTRODUCTION

The item catalog in a recommender system is often equipped with many meta-data features in the form of labels, tags, or a "bag-of-words". These features consist of a word or a short phrase describing the item. For example, for movies we may have features such as *Funny*, *Martial Arts*, and *Oscar Winner*. Some of these features are highly informative with regard to the recommendation task, but many others are redundant or irrelevant. We therefore present a matrix factorization (MF) model with an embedded feature selection mechanism which on the one hand identifies and utilizes informative features, and on the other hand ignores and suppresses non-informative features. This approach is successfully used to enhance movies recommendations in the Xbox marketplace, serving more than 50 million users [11, 15].

Feature selection algorithms typically belong to one of three categories: *wrapper* methods, *filter* methods, or *embedded* methods. Wrapper methods evaluate subsets of features by training a model with each subset and scoring on a held-out set. This approach is independent of the prediction algorithm in use, but scales poorly for large commercial systems with many features. Filter methods use heuristic measures such as *Mutual Information* or *Pearson Correlation* to score features based on their informative power with regard to the prediction target (e.g. in the context of recommendation system see [19]). These methods are more scalable than wrapper methods as they do not require training many models. However, they are highly dependent on the specific heuristic metric used to score the features, and there is no structured approach or clear guidelines for preferring one metric over the other. The proposed solution in this work belongs to the last category – embedded methods. These are a family of algorithms in which feature selection is performed during model construction. Embedded methods are not based on cross-validation and therefore scale well with data size. The features are chosen based on their relative usefulness and informative power with regard to the prediction task at hand (not based on some external heuristic).

In this paper we present *MF-EFS – Matrix Factorization with Embedded Feature Selection.* MF-EFS is a matrix factorization model aided by item features in the form of labels. The features are notably used to improve accuracy by mitigating the "cold-start" problem in items[1]. As explained next, not all features are informative in a recommendation task. MF-EFS automatically discerns and utilizes the informative features while "ignoring" the non-informative ones by encouraging sparsity and setting non-relevant parameters to near zero values. In this paper we do not assume the presence of numeric ratings; it is a setting shared by most real-world recommender systems. MF-EFS is a binary

[1] User features can be introduced in an equivalent way.

RecSys'13, October 12–16, 2013, Hong Kong, China.
ACM 978-1-4503-2409-0/13/10.
http://dx.doi.org/10.1145/2507157.2508221.

model based only on *like / dislike* observations, or implicit usage patters such as *watch / didn't watch* or *buy / didn't buy*. However, its feature selection framework is general and can be extended to numeric ratings as well as other types of data.

This paper makes several contributions: Firstly, we propose a novel model that can utilize features to improve long-tail accuracy. It is especially effective in systems with a large catalog, many long-tail items and many features. The algorithm is unique in its sparsity encouraging property and can easily cope with many non-informative features. Secondly, the training is based on Variational Bayes inference that is less prone to over-fitting and does not require cross-validation [10]. While we are not first to present a Variational Bayes MF model [13, 16, 17], MF-EFS is different than these previous works. Variational Bayes inference techniques are still relatively new in our field, and we hope the reader will benefit from the discussion and comparison to more traditional training methods. Finally, we highlight real-world challenges that arose while working on the Xbox recommender system. We present "working" solutions that may benefit applied scientists and academics who are designing similar systems.

1.1 Related Work

Many previous studies dealt with combining content data with collaborative-filtering (CF) data. A substantial body of work deals with *hybrid* models and the reader is referred to [5] for a survey of these methods. Notably, Basilico et al. proposed a unified approach that integrates user-item ratings as well as content-based data into a single feature domain [2]. A different direction was taken by [6], where the items' taxonomy was used to improve accuracy in predicting music ratings. Our solution differs from these approaches in its embedded feature selection, its Variational Bayes inference, its use of binary data, and its real world application and scale.

The "bag-of-words" representation for item meta-data was studied by [1] and later in [22]. Both works combine an MF model with a Latent Dirichlet Allocation (LDA) model. In essence, these are multi-task models where the LDA component learns a structure on the item-to-feature relations by assigning latent topics to each of the items. Common parameters are used to explain both the user-to-item patterns as well as the item-to-feature patterns. In general, this approach can improve accuracy in the long-tail. However, it is a delicate practice that may eventually hurt the overall accuracy, as the multi-task nature of the model forces the common parameters to find a fine balance between the two goals of the system.

This work is dedicated to improving a CF based recommender; the modeling of features is therefore merely a means to an end. Another key difference from [1] and [22] is that we assume a small number of features per item that may not suffice for learning topic mixtures on the items. Furthermore, we assume that the features are noisy and many are non-informative with regard to the CF task. Our model therefore needs to be robust to these features, and still take full advantage of the few informative features.

Notation.

We reserve special indexing for distinguishing users from items: for users m, and for items n. We assume a model with

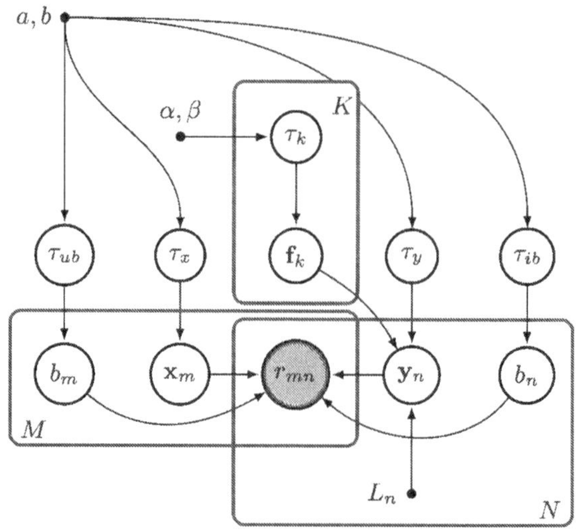

Figure 1: A graphical model of MF-EFS with N users, M items and K features.

M users and N items, and binary observations (e.g. *'like'*, *'dislike'*). We denote by $r_{mn} = 1$ the fact that user m liked item n, and by $r_{mn} = 0$ otherwise. We denote by $\mathcal{D} \stackrel{\text{def}}{=} \{r_{mn}\}$ a dataset of such ratings, and use $\Omega(m) \stackrel{\text{def}}{=} \{n : r_{mn} \in \mathcal{D}\}$ to index a user's rated items, and similarly $\Pi(n) \stackrel{\text{def}}{=} \{m : r_{mn} \in \mathcal{D}\}$ to index an item's raters (users).

We distinguish vectors and matrices from scalars by using bold letters. We capitalize when denoting matrices and use minuscule letters for vectors, e.g. $\mathbf{X}$ is a matrix, $\mathbf{x}$ is a vector and x and X are scalars. As explained above, every item in our model is associated with a set of features in the form of descriptive labels. We assume a dictionary of $k = 1 \ldots K$ labels and denote by L_n the set of labels describing item n, and by $|L_n|$ the size of the set L_n. We denote by $\mathcal{L} = \{L_n\}_{n=1}^{N}$ all items' label sets. Finally, we denote by $\langle f \rangle_q$ the expectation of f over some distribution q.

2. MODEL DESCRIPTION

Many MF models strive to optimize some specific objective function like the root mean squared error (RMSE) [12], hinge loss [18], or ranking-based objective functions [21]. This is often the best approach in competitions such as the Netflix Prize [3], where algorithms are evaluated on a single metric like RMSE. At Xbox, however, we are additionally interested in gaining a broader understanding of users' tastes when watching movies on their Xbox consoles. We therefore turn to probabilistic generative models which model the data while striving to explain it.

We assume that user m's rating of item n is generated by the linear combination of latent user and item trait vectors. The latent user and item vectors are denoted by $\mathbf{x}_m \in \mathbb{R}^D$ and $\mathbf{y}_n \in \mathbb{R}^D$ respectively, with D being the dimensionality of the model. We additionally assume that the user and the item have latent biases, $b_m \in \mathbb{R}$ and $b_n \in \mathbb{R}$. The odds of a user liking or disliking an item is modeled by

$$p(r \,|\, \mathbf{x}, \mathbf{y}, b) = \sigma(\mathbf{x}^\top \mathbf{y} + b)^r \Big[1 - \sigma(\mathbf{x}^\top \mathbf{y} + b)\Big]^{1-r}, \quad (1)$$

where subscripts m and n are dropped as they are clear

from the context, b denotes the sum of both of the biases $b = b_m + b_n$, and the function σ denotes the logistic sigmoid $\sigma(a) = 1/(1 + e^{-a})$.

Each item n has a set of feature labels L_n. We believe *a priori* that some (but not necessarily all) of an item's features $k \in L_n$ are informative in determining its latent vector $\mathbf{y}_n$, and their effect is modeled by letting $\mathbf{y}_n$ depend on them *hierarchically*. We therefore assume a latent vector $\mathbf{f}_k \in \mathbb{R}^D$ for each feature label $k = 1, \ldots, K$, and place a hierarchical Gaussian prior on each $\mathbf{y}_n$ with

$$p(\mathbf{y}_n | \{\mathbf{f}_k\}, L_n, \tau_y) = \mathcal{N}\left(\mathbf{y}_n \,;\, \frac{1}{\sqrt{|L_n|}} \sum_{k \in L_n} \mathbf{f}_k,\, \tau_y^{-1}\mathbf{I}\right) ,$$

where τ_y is a precision parameter. The division by $\sqrt{|L_n|}$ ensures that the prior variance of $p(\mathbf{y}_n|\tau_y)$, when marginalized over $\{\mathbf{f}_k\}_{k \in L_n}$, does not grow or shrink with $|L_n|$; namely, we do not have different degrees of certainty about $\mathbf{y}_n$ on the basis of it being tagged with more or less features.

The generative model is shown in Figure 1, and requires additional priors for the user vectors and for the biases. We let these be centered Gaussian distributions: $p(\mathbf{x}_m) = \mathcal{N}(\mathbf{x}_m \,;\, \mathbf{0},\, \tau_x^{-1}\mathbf{I})$ and $p(b_m) = \mathcal{N}(b_m \,;\, 0,\, \tau_{ub}^{-1})$ for each user m, and $p(b_n) = \mathcal{N}(b_n \,;\, 0,\, \tau_{ib}^{-1})$ for each item n. The precisions of the Gaussian distributions are governed by parameters τ_x, τ_{ub}, and τ_{ib} for the user trait vectors and biases, and the item biases respectively. To infer the various precision parameters τ, we place a conjugate Gamma hyperprior on each of $\tau_x, \tau_y, \tau_{ib}, \tau_{ub}$. For example, for τ_x we have:

$$p(\tau_x | a, b) = \mathcal{G}(\tau_x ; a, b) \stackrel{\text{def}}{=} b^a / \Gamma(a) \cdot \tau_x^{a-1} e^{-b\tau_x} .$$

The rate and shape parameters of the hyperprior were set to $a = b = 0.1$, giving a hyperprior on the τ 's with mean 1 and a variance of 10.

2.1 Embedded Feature Selection

The prior density on each feature vector $\mathbf{f}_k$ is governed by its own precision parameter τ_k. Namely, for each vector $\mathbf{f}_k$ we have:

$$p(\mathbf{f}_k|\tau_k) = \mathcal{N}(\mathbf{f}_k \,;\, \mathbf{0},\, \tau_k^{-1}\mathbf{I}) \quad \text{and} \quad p(\tau_k|\alpha, \beta) = \mathcal{G}(\tau_k \,;\, \alpha,\, \beta) .$$

There are therefore K precision parameters τ_k, each takes its own conjugate Gamma hyperprior $\mathcal{G}(\tau_k \,;\, \alpha,\, \beta)$.

This particular setting is designed to give raise to a sparsity prior on the features that encourages the model to discern informative features from non-informative ones. When we marginalize out τ_k, we obtain the *effective* prior distribution for features $p(\mathbf{f}_k|\alpha,\, \beta)$. It is a multivariate t-distribution:

$$\begin{aligned} p(\mathbf{f}_k|\alpha,\, \beta) &= \int p(\mathbf{f}_k|\tau_k)\, p(\tau_k|\alpha,\, \beta)\, d\tau_k \\ &= \frac{\Gamma\left(\frac{\nu+D}{2}\right)}{\Gamma\left(\frac{\nu}{2}\right) (\nu\pi)^{\frac{D}{2}} |\boldsymbol{\Sigma}|^{\frac{1}{2}}} \left[1 + \frac{\alpha}{\beta\nu} \mathbf{f}_k^{\top} \mathbf{f}_k\right]^{-\frac{\nu+D}{2}} , \end{aligned} \quad (2)$$

where the D-dimensional t-distribution has a zero mean, $\nu = 2\alpha$ degrees of freedom, and a scale matrix $\boldsymbol{\Sigma} = \frac{\beta}{\alpha}\mathbf{I}$. The marginalization in (2) is explained in the Appendix.

The multivariate t-distribution is a generalization of the well known univariate Student's t-distribution. It serves as an effective prior on the $\mathbf{f}_k$ vectors; the effective prior mean remains zero, and the $\mathbf{f}_k$ vectors are still regularized based on their norms $\mathbf{f}_k^{\top}\mathbf{f}_k$. However, for small degrees of freedom ν this distribution exhibits very heavy tails (compared to a Gaussian). The density in (2) is isotropic, but with heavy tails. However, unlike a product of Gaussians, the product of these densities doesn't have spherical contours, and the resulting probability mass is not isotropically spread. Hence, the product $p(\{\mathbf{f}_k\}|\alpha, \beta) = \prod_{k=1}^{K} p(\mathbf{f}_k|\alpha,\, \beta)$ favors variables that are axis-aligned, i.e. where $\|\mathbf{f}_k\|$ is around zero for many feature indexes k (see Figure 2).

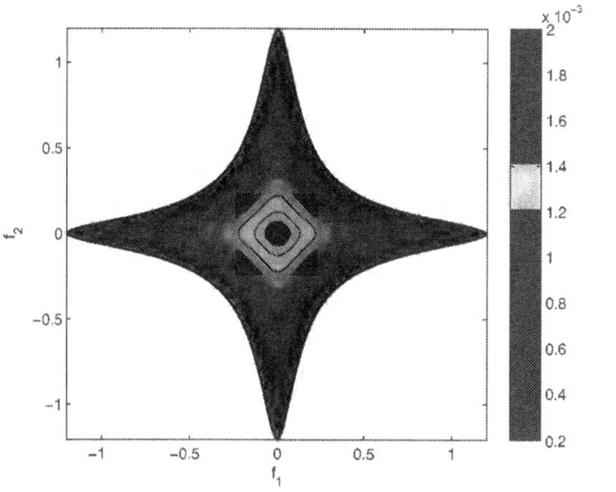

Figure 2: Contours of the probability mass of the *effective* prior for two feature vectors ($\mathbf{f}_1$ and $\mathbf{f}_2$): $p(f_1, f_2|\alpha = 0.01, \beta = 0.01)$. For the sake of the visualization, the feature vectors here are one-dimensional ($D = 1$). The heavy tails originating from the underlaying t-distributions are clearly seen along the axes. As the number of features is higher, this effect results in a concentration of probability mass along the corners which encourages sparse solutions.

This effect is similar to L_1 regularization, albeit on a Bayesian hierarchical probabilistic model. The rate parameter α of the features hyperprior determines the degrees of freedom of the t-distribution. In MF-EFS, we set α and the shape parameter β to $\alpha = \beta = 0.01$, giving a hyperprior on the τ_k's with mean 1 and variance of 100.

2.2 The Posterior Distribution

We collectively denote the model's parameters by

$$\boldsymbol{\theta} = \Big\{\{\mathbf{x}_m, b_m\}, \{\mathbf{y}_n, b_n\}, \{\mathbf{f}_k, \tau_k\}, \tau_x, \tau_y, \tau_{ib}, \tau_{ub}\Big\} ,$$

and hyperparameters by $\mathcal{H} = \{a, b, \alpha, \beta\}$. The joint density of an observed dataset $\mathcal{D}$, given the hyperprior parameters $\mathcal{H}$ and item feature sets $\mathcal{L}$ is

$$\begin{aligned} & p(\boldsymbol{\theta}, \mathcal{D}|\mathcal{L}, \mathcal{H}) = \\ & \prod_{r_{mn} \in \mathcal{D}} \sigma\Big(\mathbf{x}_m^{\top}\mathbf{y}_n + b_m + b_n\Big)^{r_{nm}} \Big[1 - \sigma\Big(\mathbf{x}_m^{\top}\mathbf{y}_n + b_m + b_n\Big)\Big]^{1 - r_{nm}} \\ & \cdot \prod_{m=1}^{M} \mathcal{N}(\mathbf{x}_m \,;\, \mathbf{0},\, \tau_x^{-1}\mathbf{I})\, \mathcal{N}(b_m \,;\, 0,\, \tau_{ub}^{-1}) \\ & \cdot \prod_{n=1}^{N} \mathcal{N}\left(\mathbf{y}_n \,;\, \frac{1}{\sqrt{|L_n|}} \sum_{k \in L_n} \mathbf{f}_k,\, \tau_y^{-1}\mathbf{I}\right) \mathcal{N}(b_n \,;\, 0,\, \tau_{ib}^{-1}) \\ & \cdot \prod_{k=1}^{K} \mathcal{N}(\mathbf{f}_k \,;\, \mathbf{0},\, \tau_k^{-1}\mathbf{I})\, \mathcal{G}(\tau_k \,;\, \alpha,\, \beta) \\ & \cdot \mathcal{G}(\tau_x; a, b)\, \mathcal{G}(\tau_y; a, b)\, \mathcal{G}(\tau_{ub}; a, b)\, \mathcal{G}(\tau_{ib}; a, b) . \end{aligned} \quad (3)$$

We note that the MF-EFS model presented here can be trivially extended to also incorporate user features, but these are omitted for clarity.

We now appeal to Bayes' theorem to infer the posterior density of $\boldsymbol{\theta}$,

$$p(\boldsymbol{\theta}|\mathcal{D},\mathcal{L},\mathcal{H}) = \frac{p(\mathcal{D}|\boldsymbol{\theta})\, p(\boldsymbol{\theta}|\mathcal{L},\mathcal{H})}{p(\mathcal{D}|\mathcal{L},\mathcal{H})} \ , \tag{4}$$

A direct computation of this posterior distribution is hard. Hence, in the following section we approximate $p(\boldsymbol{\theta}|\mathcal{D},\mathcal{F},\mathcal{H})$ with a surrogate distribution $q(\boldsymbol{\theta})$ from a simpler family.

3. VARIATIONAL INFERENCE

We seek a distribution $q(\boldsymbol{\theta})$ that will minimize the Kullback-Leibler divergence from the true posterior to $q(\boldsymbol{\theta})$:

$$\mathbb{D}_{\mathrm{KL}}\left(q(\boldsymbol{\theta})\middle\|p(\boldsymbol{\theta}|\mathcal{D},\mathcal{L},\mathcal{H})\right) \stackrel{\text{def}}{=} \int q(\boldsymbol{\theta}) \log \frac{q(\boldsymbol{\theta})}{p(\boldsymbol{\theta}|\mathcal{D},\mathcal{L},\mathcal{H})} \mathrm{d}\boldsymbol{\theta} \ . \tag{5}$$

This divergence can be rewritten in terms of the model's log likelihood and the variational free energy $\mathcal{F}[q(\boldsymbol{\theta})]$ (see [4]),

$$\mathbb{D}_{\mathrm{KL}}\left(q(\boldsymbol{\theta})\middle\|p(\boldsymbol{\theta}|\mathcal{D},\mathcal{L},\mathcal{H})\right) + \mathcal{F}[q(\boldsymbol{\theta})] = \log p(\mathcal{D}|\mathcal{L},\mathcal{H}) \ , \tag{6}$$

where $\mathcal{F}[q(\boldsymbol{\theta})] \stackrel{\text{def}}{=} \int q(\boldsymbol{\theta}) \log \frac{p(\boldsymbol{\theta},\mathcal{D}|\mathcal{L},\mathcal{H})}{q(\boldsymbol{\theta})} \mathrm{d}\boldsymbol{\theta}$.

From the expression in (6) and the non-negativity of the Kullback-Leibler divergence, we concur two things: we can minimize (5) by *maximizing* $\mathcal{F}[q(\boldsymbol{\theta})]$ with respect to our choice of q, and $\mathcal{F}$ additionally serves as a *lower bound* to the model's log marginal likelihood.

3.1 Logistic Bound

The joint density in (3) includes Gaussian priors which are not conjugate with respect to the sigmoid link function used in our likelihood (1). In order to facilitate approximate inference, the sigmoids are replaced by a "squared exponential" form, which is conjugate to a Gaussian prior. Hence we *lower-bound* the sigmoids in (3) by employing the logistic or Jaakkola-Jordan bound [9]. We introduce an additional variational parameter ξ_{mn} on each observation r_{mn} and bound the sigmoids in (3) as follows (dropping subscripts m and n, and using $h \stackrel{\text{def}}{=} \mathbf{x}^{\top}\mathbf{y} + b$):

$$\sigma(h)^{r}[1-\sigma(h)]^{1-r} \geq \mathrm{e}^{rh}\left[\sigma(\xi)\,\mathrm{e}^{-\frac{1}{2}(h+\xi)-\lambda(\xi)(h^2-\xi^2)}\right] \ , \tag{7}$$

where $\lambda(\xi) \stackrel{\text{def}}{=} \frac{1}{2\xi}[\sigma(\xi) - \frac{1}{2}]$. Using (7), we substitute the sigmoid functions in $p(\boldsymbol{\theta},\mathcal{D}|\mathcal{L},\mathcal{H})$ to get $p_{\boldsymbol{\xi}}(\boldsymbol{\theta},\mathcal{D}|\mathcal{L},\mathcal{H})$. Hence, we now have

$$\begin{aligned}\log p(\mathcal{D}|\mathcal{L},\mathcal{H}) &\geq \mathcal{F}[q(\boldsymbol{\theta})] \\ &\geq \mathcal{F}_{\boldsymbol{\xi}}[q(\boldsymbol{\theta})] \stackrel{\text{def}}{=} \int q(\boldsymbol{\theta}) \log \frac{p_{\boldsymbol{\xi}}(\boldsymbol{\theta},\mathcal{D}|\mathcal{L},\mathcal{H})}{q(\boldsymbol{\theta})} \mathrm{d}\boldsymbol{\theta} \ ,\end{aligned}$$

where $\mathcal{F}_{\boldsymbol{\xi}}[q(\boldsymbol{\theta})]$ is our new objective to be maximized. We note that the above bound now additionally relies on the variational parameters $\boldsymbol{\xi} = \{\xi_{mn}\}$, which are adjusted along with $q(\boldsymbol{\theta})$ to maximize $\mathcal{F}_{\boldsymbol{\xi}}[q(\boldsymbol{\theta})]$. The following section discusses the approximating family $q(\boldsymbol{\theta})$, and the maximization of $\mathcal{F}_{\boldsymbol{\xi}}$.

3.2 Optimization Procedure

We estimate each component of $\mathbf{x}$, $\mathbf{y}$, and $\mathbf{f}$, as well as the biases with Gaussian densities. As an example, $q(x_{md}) = \mathcal{N}(x_{md}; \langle x_{md}\rangle, \mathsf{var}(x_{md}))$. We further approximate the τ's with Gamma densities, and let $q(\boldsymbol{\theta})$ fully factorize with:

$$\begin{aligned} q(\boldsymbol{\theta}) = &\prod_{m=1}^{M} q(b_m) \prod_{d=1}^{D} q(x_{md}) \cdot \prod_{n=1}^{N} q(b_n) \prod_{d=1}^{D} q(y_{nd}) \\ &\cdot \prod_{k=1}^{K} q(\tau_k) \prod_{d=1}^{D} q(f_{kd}) \cdot q(\tau_x)\, q(\tau_y)\, q(\tau_{ub})\, q(\tau_{ib}) \ . \end{aligned} \tag{8}$$

One might also choose $q(\mathbf{x}_m)$ as a full multivariate Gaussian, instead of a diagonal one; it gives a richer approximating family, but requires that a $D \times D$ covariance be kept in memory for each user (or item).

Optimization of $\mathcal{F}_{\boldsymbol{\xi}}$ proceeds by coordinate ascent in the function space of the variational distributions. Namely, we compute functional derivatives $\partial\mathcal{F}_{\boldsymbol{\xi}}/\partial q$ with respect to each distribution q in (8). Equating the derivatives to zero, together with a Lagrange multiplier constraint to make q integrate to one, we get the update steps for each q in (8). We iteratively update the q's, where each update increases our objective $\mathcal{F}_{\boldsymbol{\xi}}$. As $\mathcal{F}_{\boldsymbol{\xi}}$ is bounded, the optimization is guaranteed to converge. In what follows, we describe these update steps in terms of the sufficient statistics of each distribution.

3.2.1 *Updating* $q(x_{md})$

Before describing the update of $q(x_{md})$ for $d = 1, \ldots, D$, an update is given if the factor was a richer, *full covariance Gaussian* $\tilde{q}(\mathbf{x}_m)$, instead of a fully factorized one. Equating $\partial\mathcal{F}_{\boldsymbol{\xi}}/\partial\tilde{q}(\mathbf{x}_m)$ to zero gives a multivariate $\tilde{q}(\mathbf{x}_m)$ with precision matrix $\mathbf{P}_m$ and mean-times-precision vector $\boldsymbol{\mu}_m\mathbf{P}_m$ of

$$\begin{aligned}\mathbf{P}_m &= \sum_{n\in\Omega(m)} 2\lambda(\xi_{mn}) \left\langle \mathbf{y}_n\mathbf{y}_n^{\top}\right\rangle_q + \langle\tau_u\rangle\,\mathbf{I} \\ \boldsymbol{\mu}_m\mathbf{P}_m &= \sum_{n\in\Omega(m)} \left[r_{mn} - \frac{1}{2} - 2\lambda(\xi_{mn})\,\langle b_m + b_n\rangle_q\right] \langle\mathbf{y}_n\rangle_q \ .\end{aligned} \tag{9}$$

These define the natural parameters in terms of their sufficient statistics. Note that (9) has no dependence on other user parameters $\mathbf{x}_{m'}$, and updating all user parameters is an embarrassingly parallel computation.

For the fully factorized case, single-variable updates like (9) would have to be repeated D times, once for each $q(x_{md})$. This involves D loops over $n \in \Omega(m)$. Instead, a simpler technique allows us to estimate all $q(x_{md})$ in bulk by using $\tilde{q}(\mathbf{x}_m) = \mathcal{N}(\mathbf{x}_m; \boldsymbol{\mu}_m, \mathbf{P}_m^{-1})$ in (9) as an *intermediate* computation: Each of the $q(x_{md})$'s are recovered from the minimizer of $\mathbb{D}_{\mathrm{KL}}(\prod_{d=1}^{D} q(x_{md})\|\tilde{q}(\mathbf{x}_m))$. Thus, the sufficient statistics of $q(x_{md})$ based on $\boldsymbol{\mu}_m$ and $\mathbf{P}_m$ are

$$\langle x_{md}\rangle = \mu_{md} \quad \text{and} \quad \mathsf{var}(x_{md})^{-1} = [\mathbf{P}_m]_{dd} \ .$$

The following sections only present the updates for (intermediate) full Gaussian factors, after which the above procedure can be employed to efficiently find the factorized parameters.

3.2.2 *Updating* $q(y_{nd})$

The natural parameters of $\tilde{q}(\mathbf{y}_n)$, from which each $q(y_{nd})$

is recovered, are

$$\mathbf{P}_n = \sum_{m\in\Pi(n)} 2\lambda(\xi_{mn}) \left\langle \mathbf{x}_m\mathbf{x}_m^\top \right\rangle_q + \langle\tau_y\rangle_q \mathbf{I}$$

$$\boldsymbol{\mu}_n\mathbf{P}_n = \sum_{m\in\Pi(n)} \left[r_{mn} - \frac{1}{2} - 2\lambda(\xi_{mn}) \langle b_m + b_n\rangle_q \right] \langle\mathbf{x}_m\rangle_q$$

$$\cdots + \frac{\langle\tau_y\rangle_q}{\sqrt{|L_n|}} \sum_{k\in L_n} \langle\mathbf{f}_k\rangle_q \,, \tag{10}$$

where $\mathbf{P}_n$ and $\boldsymbol{\mu}_n\mathbf{P}_n$ indicate its precision matrix and mean-times-precision vector.

The mean vector therefore has two contributions, statistics from the relevant user vectors $\mathbf{x}_m$, and a sum of the relevant feature vectors $\mathbf{f}_k$. Even if $\Pi(n)$ is empty, cold items with no usage still have non-trivial solutions based on their features. Again, updating all the item vectors is an embarrassingly parallel operation.

3.2.3 Updating $q(f_{kd})$

The natural parameters of $\tilde{q}(\mathbf{f}_k)$, from which each $q(f_{kd})$ is recovered, are

$$\mathbf{P}_k = \left(\langle\tau_k\rangle_q + \langle\tau_y\rangle_q \sum_{n\in Y_k} \frac{1}{|L_n|} \right) \mathbf{I}$$

$$\boldsymbol{\mu}_k\mathbf{P}_k = \langle\tau_y\rangle \sum_{n\in Y_k} \left(\frac{1}{\sqrt{|L_n|}} \langle\mathbf{y}_n\rangle_q - \frac{1}{|L_n|} \sum_{i\in L_n/k} \langle\mathbf{f}_i\rangle_q \right) ,$$

where $\mathbf{P}_k$ and $\boldsymbol{\mu}_k\mathbf{P}_k$ again indicate its precision matrix and mean-times-precision vector. Here, Y_k denotes the set of all items having feature k, and L_n/k are all the features in L_n except k.

3.2.4 Updating $q(b_m)$ and $q(b_n)$

Both $q(b_m)$ and $q(b_n)$ are Gaussian distributions, and as their update steps are symmetric, only the sufficient statistics of $q(b_m)$ are given. They are

$$\sigma_{b_m}^{-2} = \sum_{n\in\Omega(m)} 2\lambda(\xi_{mn}) + \langle\tau_{ub}\rangle_q$$

$$\frac{\mu_{b_m}}{\sigma_{b_m}^2} = \sum_{n\in\Omega(m)} \left[r_{mn} - \frac{1}{2} - 2\lambda(\xi_{mn}) \left\langle \mathbf{x}_m^\top\mathbf{y}_n + b_n \right\rangle_q \right] ,$$

with μ_{b_m} and $\sigma_{b_m}^2$ denoting the mean and variance of $q(b_m)$.

3.2.5 Updating $q(\tau_k)$, $q(\tau_x)$, $q(\tau_y)$, $q(\tau_{ub})$, $q(\tau_{ib})$

The precision hyperpriors are all approximated with Gamma distributions. For the sake of brevity only the update step of $q(\tau_k) = \mathcal{G}(\tau_k; \phi_k, \varphi_k)$ is presented. Its shape parameter is $\phi_k = \frac{D}{2} + \alpha$, and its rate parameter is $\varphi_k = \frac{1}{2}\left\langle \mathbf{f}_k^\top\mathbf{f}_k \right\rangle_q + \beta$.

3.2.6 Finding ξ_{mn}

The updates in (9) and (10) rely on the variational parameters ξ_{mn}. The current maximum of $\mathcal{F}_{\boldsymbol{\xi}}$ with respect to them are computed and discarded as needed, with

$$\xi_{mn} = \left\langle (\mathbf{x}_m^\top\mathbf{y}_n + b_m + b_n)^2 \right\rangle_q^{1/2} .$$

We refer the reader to [4, 9] for a deeper discussion of the Jaakkola-Jordan bound.

4. RESULTS

Unlike more familiar algorithms that compute a point estimate of some objective function, the advantage of Variational Bayesian inference is in its posterior approximation, which aims to approximate the whole posterior density. In this framework, when making predictions we take an expectation over all possible parameter values which often leads to better overall accuracy. This is especially true when not aiming to optimize any one single metric (such as root mean squared error), or when the metric is too complex to be optimized directly. The posterior distribution models parameter uncertainty, which makes Variational Bayes less prone to under-fitting and over-fitting without the need for an exhaustive cross-validation process.

When predicting whether a user will like an item, we average over the posterior density with $p(r = 1|\mathcal{D},\mathcal{L},\mathcal{H}) = \int p(r = 1|\boldsymbol{\theta})\, p(\boldsymbol{\theta}|\mathcal{D},\mathcal{L},\mathcal{H})\, \mathrm{d}\boldsymbol{\theta}$. This is made tractable by approximating the true marginal density with an average over $q(\boldsymbol{\theta})$, where $p(r = 1|\mathcal{D},\mathcal{L},\mathcal{H}) \approx \int p(r = 1|\boldsymbol{\theta})\, q(\boldsymbol{\theta})\, \mathrm{d}\boldsymbol{\theta}$. In other words,

$$p(r_{mn} = 1|\mathcal{D},\mathcal{L},\mathcal{H}) \approx \left\langle \sigma(\mathbf{x}_m^\top\mathbf{y}_n + b_m + b_n) \right\rangle_q$$

$$\approx \int \sigma(h)\, \mathcal{N}(h;\, \mu_h, \sigma_h^2)\, \mathrm{d}h \,, \tag{11}$$

where the random variable $h \stackrel{\text{def}}{=} \mathbf{x}_m^\top\mathbf{y}_n + b_m + b_n$ is approximated with a Gaussian based on its first two moments under q, i.e.

$$\mu_h \stackrel{\text{def}}{=} \left\langle \mathbf{x}_m^\top\mathbf{y}_n + b_m + b_n \right\rangle_q$$

$$\sigma_h^2 \stackrel{\text{def}}{=} \left\langle (\mathbf{x}_m^\top\mathbf{y}_n + b_m + b_n - \mu_h)^2 \right\rangle_q .$$

Finally, the logistic Gaussian integral in (11) is approximated with

$$\int \sigma(h)\, \mathcal{N}(h;\, \mu_h, \sigma_h^2)\, \mathrm{d}h \approx \sigma\left(\mu_h \Big/ \sqrt{1 + \pi\sigma_h^2/8} \right) ,$$

which follows from MacKay [14].

4.1 Datasets

We evaluate using two different datasets. The first is a sample taken from Xbox movies[2] containing approximately 100 million binary ratings to more than 15K movies made by 5.8 million users. The binary ratings come from a processed dataset based on a mixture of explicit and implicit user inputs such as movies purchases, explicit ratings, the *not interested* button, etc. Each movie is associated with a list of 20-30 labels (features) from a dictionary of 1,000 labels. These labels describe movie attributes such as genre, plot, time-period, praise, etc.

The second dataset is based on the publicly available MovieLens 10M dataset[3]. We used it to construct a binary *like / dislike* dataset as follows: First, we took only positive ratings of 4 stars or higher. After filtering we were left with 5,005,684 ratings by 69,878 users to 10,677 movies. We than added fictitious negative ratings by sampling items and adding them to the dataset. For every user we sampled the same number of negative ratings as the number of positive

[2] `http://marketplace.xbox.com/en-US/Movies`

[3] `http://www.grouplens.org/node/73`

	SGD	NoFeatures	MF-EFS
Xbox Movies	0.0941	0.0884	**0.0881**
MovieLens	0.153	0.147	**0.139**

Table 1: Mean Percentile Rank (MPR) of the proposed model with features (*MF-EFS*) and without features (*NoFeatures*) against a baseline trained with Stochastic Gradient Descent (*SGD*).

ratings she already had. The items for the negative ratings were sampled in proportion to their popularity. This dataset construction process follows from KDD Cup'11 [7]. The popularity sampling was chosen to discourage trivial solutions where biases are learned instead of personalization patterns. The movies in the MovieLens 10M dataset are associated with 3-5 labels from a dictionary of 20 genre labels.

4.2 Evaluation

In both datasets, we created test-sets by randomly selecting and hiding 10% of the *positive* ratings. These ratings come from items the user liked or consumed. We measure performance in terms of *Mean Percentile Rank* (MPR), a common metric in studies of implicit feedback datasets [8, 20]. For every user item pair (m, n) in the test-set, we rank all items not in m's history and compute the percentile rank PR_{mn} of item n using this ranking:

$$PR_{mn} \stackrel{\text{def}}{=} \frac{1}{N - |\Omega(m)|} \sum_{n':n' \notin \Omega(m)} \mathbb{I}\Big[p_{mn} < p_{mn'}\Big],$$

where $\mathbb{I}[\cdot]$ is the indicator function, $\Omega(m)$ are the items in m's history, and p_{mn} is the probability that user m likes item n according to (11). The MPR metric is computed by averaging the percentile ranks (PR_{mn}) over all test examples. Accordingly, MPR values closer to zero indicate better rankings.

We compared against a regression MF baseline utilizing Stochastic Gradient Descent (SGD) such as in [12]. In the following analysis, we dub this baseline *SGD*. In order to isolate the contribution of the features in MF-EFS, we trained two versions of our model – one with ratings and features data and one with ratings only (without the features). We dubbed these two variants *MF-EFS* and *NoFeatures* respectively. Effectively, the *NoFeatures* variant amounts to a simple MF model similar to the *SGD* model but with Variational Bayes inference instead of stochastic gradient descent. All the models are trained with $D = 50$.

Table 1 summarizes the results of our evaluation. On both datasets *MF-EFS* performed best. Notably, the two variants of our algorithm are better than the *SGD* baseline. The difference between the *NoFeatures* model and the *SGD* model is attributed to the Variational Bayes inference which is more accurate than the point estimates of the SGD algorithm. The difference between *MF-EFS* and *NoFeatures* is attributed to the ability of the proposed model to utilize the informative content of the features.

In Figure 3, we further investigate these results by plotting MPR vs. the item support (the number of ratings per item). The advantage of *MF-EFS* over *NoFeatures* is clearly evident for items with low item-support ("cold-items"). We attribute this advantage to the features data that is utilized only in *MF-EFS*. The two variants seem to perform equally on items with higher support.

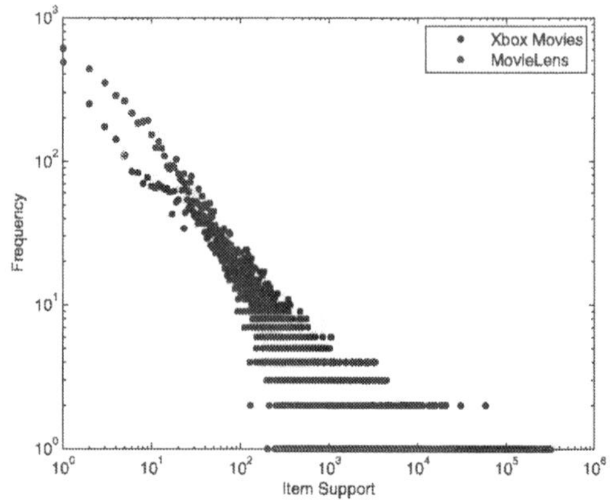

Figure 4: Item support distribution of Xbox Movies and MovieLens datasets. The Xbox Movies dataset is larger and its distribution is more skewed.

The Xbox Movies dataset is much larger than the MovieLens dataset and the item support distribution is more skewed (see Figure 4). It is therefore more susceptible to underfitting and over-fitting by the *SGD* model. As discussed above, Variational Bayes algorithms are more robust to these effects. This explains the relative advantage of both variants of our model over *SGD* in the Xbox Movies dataset for items with high support. It also explains the relative advantage of *NoFeatures* over *SGD* for cold items in that dataset.

4.3 Feature Selection

In order to investigate the feature selection mechanism of *MF-EFS* we trained another variant of the model in which the traits' precision parameters (the τ_k's) are held fixed and not updated. This model therefore lacks the sparsity encouraging property of the multivariate t-distribution in *MF-EFS*. Instead it employs simple Gaussian priors on the feature vectors which are the probabilistic equivalent to the common L_2 regularization. In the following, we dub this variant *GaussianPrior*.

As explained in Section 2.1, the sparsity constraint is held on the feature vector norms. Figure 5, depicts the histograms of the mean feature-vector norms in the Xbox Movies dataset. The sparsity in *MF-EFS* compared to *GaussianPrior* is eminent in the general shift of the histogram towards mean zero norms, as well as in the larger number of high norm features (the two rightmost bins).

Figure 6 depicts an insightful visualization of the mean feature vectors in an *MF-EFS* model trained with dimensionality $D = 2$. A small number of features have a high norm vector, while the vast majority of the features have near zero norms. This is a direct result of the feature selection mechanism of our algorithm. The high norm features are the "informative" features as found by *MF-EFS*. We added text labels to these features. The most informative feature according to the algorithm is the label *Kids*. This is expected, as this label encodes clear information on the audience that may like the movie.

The vectors in an MF model span a latent space in which the angular direction of a vector encodes information on the "taste". Item vectors and feature vectors in the same direction belong to items that fit a similar type of users. Indeed,

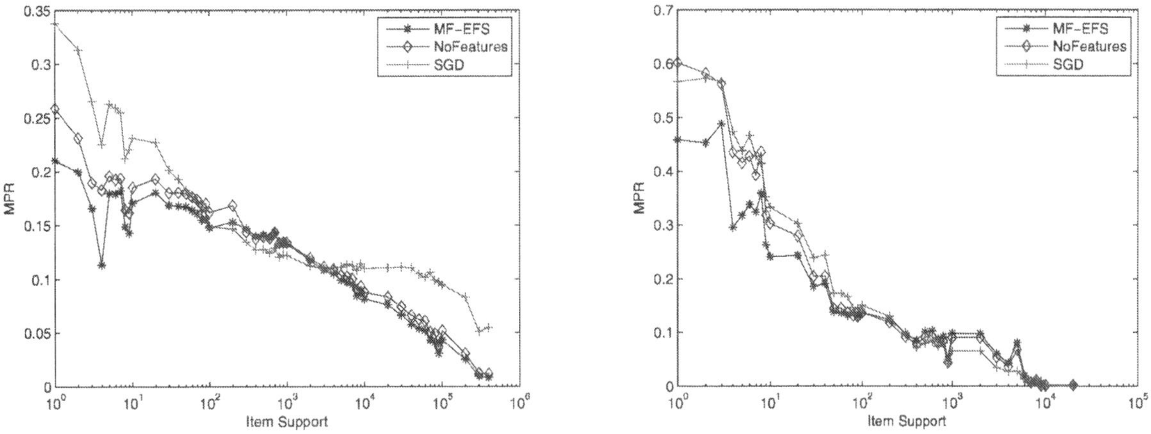

(a) Xbox Movies (b) MovieLens

Figure 3: Mean Percentile Rank (MPR) vs. Item Support (lower is better). The contribution of the features in *MF-EFS* is clearly evident in improving cold-items recommendations.

we see in the same direction of the *Kids* vector other vectors that indicate children's content, e.g. *Pets*, *Semi-Fantastic*, *Adventures*, etc. Interestingly, in the opposite direction we find features that indicate adult content such as *Profanity*, *Drugs/Alcohol*, *Erotic*, etc. We therefore identify a meaningful axis in this latent space which roughly spans between the upper right corner and lower left corner – the upper right direction indicates children movies and the opposite direction indicates adult movies.

Another meaningful axis in Figure 6 roughly spans orthogonal to the first one – between the lower right corner and towards the upper left corner. The lower right direction indicates more "sophisticated" taste with features such as *Foreign*, *Experimental* and *New Wave*. To the opposite of these features we see features belonging to the Horror genre such as *Horror*, *Scary* and *Serial Killer*. The fact that these two groups are placed opposite to each other indicates a negative correlation between the audiences of these two types of movies.

5. CONCLUSION

We presented a novel probabilistic Matrix Factorization model with Embedded Feature Selection (MF-EFS) for Xbox Movies. The model utilizes items' meta-data in the form of label features to enhance accuracy in the long tail. We assume that only a subset of these features is informative with regard to collaborative-filtering. Our model therefore performs embedded feature selection that ignores non-informative features while fully utilizing informative features. We compared against a traditional baseline trained by minimizing root mean squared error and demonstrate superior results for Xbox Movies as well as on the publicly available MevieLens dataset. Finally, we note that MF-EFS can be trivially extended to incorporate also user features.

6. ACKNOWLEDGMENTS

The authors thank Nir Nice and the rest of Xbox Recommendations for their invaluable input, management, and stellar engineering skills.

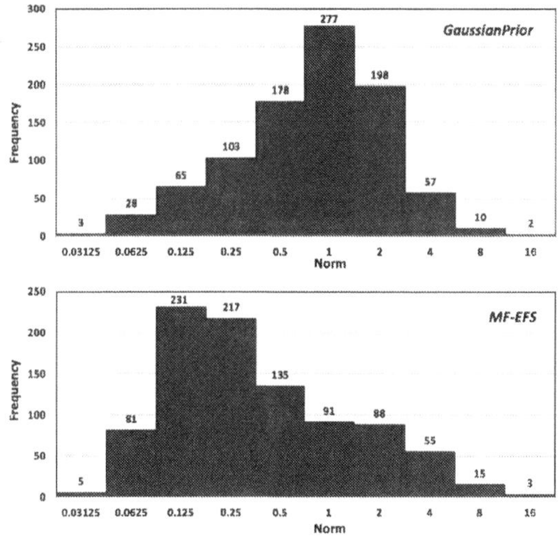

Figure 5: A histogram of the feature-vector norms. The x-axis depicts the mean feature vector norm, and the y-axis is the frequency. The sparsity encouraging effect of the *MF-EFS* model over the *GaussianPrior* model is eminent in the general shift towards mean zero norms, as well as in the larger number of high norm features (the two rightmost bins).

7. REFERENCES

[1] D. Agarwal and B.-C. Chen. fLDA: matrix factorization through Latent Dirichlet Allocation. In *WSDM*, pages 91–100, 2010.

[2] J. Basilico and T. Hofmann. Unifying collaborative and content-based filtering. In *Proceedings of the twenty-first international conference on Machine learning*, ICML '04, 2004.

[3] J. Bennett and S. Lanning. The netflix prize. In *Proc. KDD Cup and Workshop*, 2007.

[4] C. M. Bishop. *Pattern Recognition and Machine Learning (Information Science and Statistics)*.

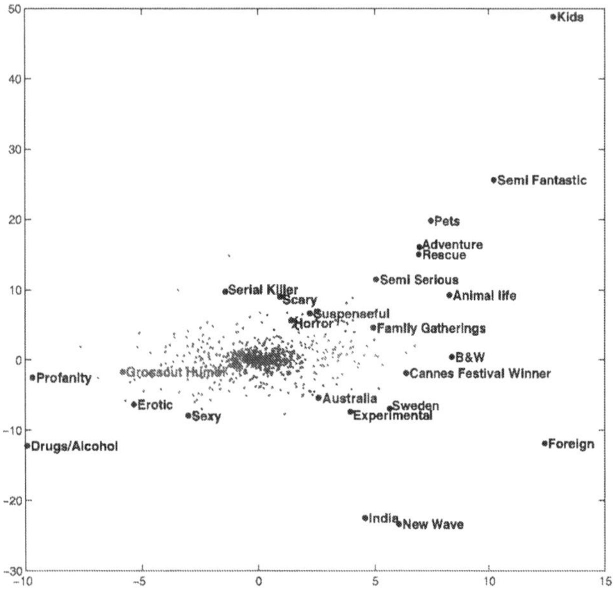

Figure 6: A visualization of the mean feature-vectors in Xbox Movies trained with a $D = 2$ dimensional *MF-EFS* model. The sparsity is evident by the concentration of near zero feature vector norms. We added text labels to the smaller number of "informative" features – those with a high norm.

Springer-Verlag New York, Inc., 2006.

[5] R. D. Burke. Hybrid recommender systems: Survey and experiments. *User Model. User-Adapt. Interact.*, 12(4):331–370, 2002.

[6] G. Dror, N. Koenigstein, and Y. Koren. Yahoo! music recommendations: Modeling music ratings with temporal dynamics and item taxonomy. In *Proc. 5th ACM Conference on Recommender Systems*, 2011.

[7] G. Dror, N. Koenigstein, Y. Koren, and M. Weimer. The Yahoo! music dataset and KDD-Cup'11. *Journal Of Machine Learning Research*, 18:3–18, 2012.

[8] Y. F. Hu, Y. Koren, and C. Volinsky. Collaborative filtering for implicit feedback datasets. In *IEEE International Conference on Data Mining*, 2008.

[9] T. Jaakkola and M. Jordan. A variational approach to Bayesian logistic regression problems and their extensions. In *Artificial Intelligence and Statistics*, 1996.

[10] M. Jordan, Z. Ghahramani, T. Jaakkola, and L. Saul. An introduction to variational methods for graphical models. *Machine Learning*, 37:183–233, 1999.

[11] N. Koenigstein, N. Nice, U. Paquet, and N. Schleyen. The Xbox recommender system. In *Proc. 6th ACM Conference on Recommender Systems*, 2012.

[12] Y. Koren, R. M. Bell, and C. Volinsky. Matrix factorization techniques for recommender systems. *IEEE Computer*, 42(8):30–37, 2009.

[13] Y. J. Lim and Y. W. Teh. Variational Bayesian approach to movie rating prediction. In *Proceedings of KDD Cup and Workshop*, 2007.

[14] D. J. C. MacKay. The evidence framework applied to classification networks. *Neural Computation*, 4(5):698–714, 1992.

[15] N. Nice et al. Feature embedding in matrix factorization. In *Microsoft Patent MS# 337667.01.*

[16] U. Paquet and N. Koenigstein. One-class collaborative filtering with random graphs. In *Proceedings of the 22nd international conference on World Wide Web*, WWW '13, pages 999–1008, 2013.

[17] U. Paquet, B. Thomson, and O. Winther. A hierarchical model for ordinal matrix factorization. *Statistics and Computing*, 22(4):945–957, 2012.

[18] J. D. M. Rennie and N. Srebro. Fast maximum margin matrix factorization for collaborative prediction. In *Proceedings of the 22nd international conference on Machine learning*, ICML '05, pages 713–719, 2005.

[19] R. Ronen, N. Koenigstein, E. Ziklik, and N. Nice. Selecting content-based features for collaborative filtering recommenders. In *Proc. 7th ACM Conference on Recommender Systems*, 2013.

[20] H. Steck. Training and testing of recommender systems on data missing not at random. In *KDD*, pages 713–722, 2010.

[21] G. Takács and D. Tikk. Alternating least squares for personalized ranking. In *Proceedings of the sixth ACM conference on Recommender systems*, RecSys '12, pages 83–90, 2012.

[22] C. Wang and D. M. Blei. Collaborative topic modeling for recommending scientific articles. In *Proceedings of the 17th ACM SIGKDD international conference on Knowledge discovery and data mining*, KDD '11, pages 448–456, 2011.

APPENDIX

We marginalized over τ_k and get $p(\mathbf{f}_k|\alpha, \beta)$ as follows:

$$p(\mathbf{f}_k|\alpha,\beta) = \int p(\mathbf{f}_k|\tau_k)p(\tau_k|\alpha,\beta)\mathrm{d}\tau_k$$

$$= \int \left(\frac{\tau_k}{2\pi}\right)^{\frac{D}{2}} \exp\left\{-\frac{\tau_k}{2}\mathbf{f}_k^\top\mathbf{f}_k\right\} \cdot \frac{1}{\Gamma[\alpha]}\beta^\alpha\tau_k^{\alpha-1}\exp\{-\beta\tau_k\}\,\mathrm{d}\tau_k$$

$$= \frac{\beta^\alpha}{\Gamma[\alpha](2\pi)^{\frac{D}{2}}}\int (\tau_k)^{\frac{D}{2}+\alpha-1}\exp\left\{-\left(\frac{\mathbf{f}_k^\top\mathbf{f}_k}{2}+\beta\right)\tau_k\right\}\mathrm{d}\tau_k.$$

We employ the substitution $t = \left(\frac{\mathbf{f}_k^\top\mathbf{f}_k}{2}+\beta\right)\tau_k$ to get:

$$p(\mathbf{f}_k|\alpha,\beta) = \frac{\beta^\alpha}{\Gamma[\alpha](2\pi)^{\frac{D}{2}}\left(\frac{\mathbf{f}_k^\top\mathbf{f}_k}{2}+\beta\right)^{\frac{D}{2}+\alpha}}\int t^{\frac{D}{2}+\alpha-1}e^{-t}\mathrm{d}t$$

$$= \frac{\beta^\alpha\,\Gamma\left[\frac{D}{2}+\alpha\right]}{\Gamma[\alpha](2\pi)^{\frac{D}{2}}}\left[\frac{\mathbf{f}_k^\top\mathbf{f}_k}{2}+\beta\right]^{-\left(\frac{D}{2}+\alpha\right)}$$

$$= \frac{\Gamma\left[\frac{\nu+D}{2}\right]}{\Gamma\left[\frac{\nu}{2}\right](\nu\pi)^{\frac{D}{2}}|\boldsymbol{\Sigma}|^{\frac{1}{2}}}\left[1+\frac{1}{\nu}(\mathbf{f}_k-\boldsymbol{\mu})^\top\boldsymbol{\Sigma}^{-1}(\mathbf{f}_k-\boldsymbol{\mu})\right]^{-\frac{\nu+D}{2}}.$$

where

$$\nu = 2\alpha \qquad \boldsymbol{\Sigma} = \mathbf{I}\frac{\beta}{\alpha} \qquad \boldsymbol{\mu} = \mathbf{0}.$$

Hence, $p(\mathbf{f}_k|\alpha,\beta) = \text{Multi-t}_\nu(\mathbf{f}_k|\boldsymbol{\mu},\boldsymbol{\Sigma})$ is a D dimensional t-distribution with location vector $\boldsymbol{\mu}$, scale matrix $\boldsymbol{\Sigma}$ and ν degrees of freedom.

Personalized Next-song Recommendation in Online Karaokes

Xiang Wu[1], Qi Liu[1], Enhong Chen[1], Liang He[1] Jingsong Lv[2], Can Cao[2], Guoping Hu[2]
[1]School of Computer Science and Technology University of Science and Technology of China
[2]Anhui USTC iFLYTEK Co., Ltd., China
wux@mail.ustc.edu.cn, {qiliuql,cheneh}@ustc.edu.cn
hshl05@mail.ustc.edu.cn {jslv, cancao, gphu}@iflytek.com

ABSTRACT

In this paper, we propose Personalized Markov Embedding (PME), a next-song recommendation strategy for online karaoke users. By modeling the sequential singing behavior, we first embed songs and users into a Euclidean space in which distances between songs and users reflect the strength of their relationships. Then, given each user's last song, we can generate personalized recommendations by ranking the candidate songs according to the embedding. Moreover, PME can be trained without any requirement of content information. Finally, we perform an experimental evaluation on a real world data set provided by ihou.com which is an online karaoke website launched by iFLYTEK, and the results clearly demonstrate the effectiveness of PME.

Categories and Subject Descriptors

H.3.3 **[Information Storage and Retrieval]**: Information Search and Retrieval—*Information filtering*

Keywords

Music Recommendation; Personalization; Markov Embedding

1. INTRODUCTION

Advances in the Internet and mobile technologies have exposed people to the massive amount of online multimedia entertainment. Among them, online karaoke has attracted significant attention, since everybody can sing along with the recorded music anytime and anywhere, or even with a music video like a professional singer. As a trend, much more music are becoming available, and thus the demand for intelligent karaoke services, i.e., personalized song recommendation, is expected to increase dramatically.

Actually, music recommendations have been widely studied and applied in the literature. For instance, since music is rich in both textual and acoustic information (e.g., artists, genres and pitches), several recommendation algorithms[4, 8, 12, 15] exploited it and modeled users or user behaviours based on extracted features. However, content information cannot be easily extracted in many cases. Thus, collaborative filterings have become the most popular music recommendation techniques. Methods such as neighborhood based methods[14], matrix factorization[9] and Markov model[5] are commonly adopted. These technical achievements further secured the success of many music station websites, such as Pandora[1] and douban.fm[2]. In summary, most of the existing works try to predict the possible ratings from a given user to each song (or other multimedia items such as videos and movies), and then generate the candidate songs (or videos) for users to listen to (or to watch). However, the above strategies cannot be directly applied to the next-song recommendation for karaoke users due to the domain and technical challenges.

Figure 1: A screenshot of ihou.com, where a user is singing.

To illustrate the first challenge, we will take ihou.com[3] as an example. ihou.com is a famous online karaoke website launched by iFLYTEK[4], the leading provider of Chinese speech and language technology. Figure 1 is a screenshot of ihou.com, where a user is singing a Chinese song and just got an 80 out of 100 for the latest performed sentence. Thus, different from traditional online entertainment (e.g., music listening and movie watching[10]) where users passively experience items and give ratings to the items and systems, the users in karaoke systems like ihou.com are usually being evaluated by the system, based on their singing performances. This leads to the challenge that we cannot refer to the explicit user ratings for representing user preferences. However, we could assume that every choice of a song indicates a strong interest of the karaoke user in that music, since the user has to spend minutes performing himself and meanwhile take the risk of being judged.

The second challenge lies in the sequential behavior of users's singing[11]. Similar to web searches[3], where user's preceding queries can help to capture his/her search intents, the recent choices of karaoke users also reflect their current moods and interests[2]. For instance, it is not likely for you to sing *"My Heart Will Go On"*,

[1]http://www.pandora.com
[2]http://douban.fm
[3]http://www.ihou.com/
[4]http://www.iflytek.com/english/

RecSys'13, October 12–16, 2013, Hong Kong, China.
Copyright 2013 ACM 978-1-4503-2409-0/13/10 ...$15.00.
http://dx.doi.org/10.1145/2507157.2507215.

when the cheerful *"Uptown Girl"* is just sung, even if you do like these two songs. Thus, besides capturing the general (long-term) preference of each user, it is also important to model the sequential nature of singing lists for the user's contextual (short-term) preference[13] when making personalized next-song recommendations.

To address the above challenges, in this paper, we extend the existing Logistic Markov Embedding (LME)[5] algorithm and propose Personalized Markov Embedding (PME), a next-song recommendation strategy for online karaoke users. Specifically, we first embed songs and users into a Euclidean space in which distances between songs and users reflect the strength of their relationships. This embedding could efficiently combine users' long-term and short-term preferences together. Then, given each user's last song, we can generate recommendations by ranking the candidate songs according to the embedding. Moreover, our PME can be trained without any content information of songs, namely just with the interaction history of users' singing. Finally, we perform an experimental evaluation on a real world data set, and the results demonstrate that the PME algorithm outperforms several state-of-the-arts, including the non-personalized LME algorithm.

2. NEXT-SONG RECOMMENDATION

2.1 Problem Formalization

Given the songs that have been performed previously by each karaoke user, our goal is to recommend a ranked list of songs to a given user for the current context (the last song). We formalize this problem as follows. Let $S = \{s_1, s_2, \cdots, s_{|S|}\}$ be the song set and $U = \{u_1, u_2, \cdots, u_{|U|}\}$ be the user set. The neighbouring song records, which are usually similar, performed by the same user during short time intervals form a session. For instance, the j-th session of user u is represented by $p_{u,j} = \left(p_{u,j}^{(1)}, p_{u,j}^{(2)}, \cdots, p_{u,j}^{(|p_{u,j}|)}\right)$ where $p_{u,j}^{(k)}$ is the k-th song in session $p_{u,j}$. All sessions produced by user u is $p_u = \left(p_{u,1}, p_{u,2}, \cdots, p_{u,|p_u|}\right)$. Thus, the entire data set can be represented as $D = \{(u, p_u) | u \in U\}$. In other words, given D, the current user u and the last song s performed by user u, we want to train a model to generate a candidate song list for user u to choose from for his/her next performance. Along this line, we should estimate the transition probabilities between songs for each user (session) by measuring user preferences.

2.2 Personalized Markov Embedding

In this subsection, we describe the way to simultaneously measure users' long-term and short-term preferences and the relationships between users and songs by PME. Thus, the next-song recommendation list can be generated naturally.

To this end, we map songs and users into points in a $\mathbb{R}^d$ space, and use vector $\mathbf{x}(s)$ and vector $\mathbf{y}(u)$ to denote song s's and user u's coordinates in this space, respectively. The Euclidean distance between two points reflects the relation between corresponding users/songs. If two songs stay apart from each other, it is not likely that they will show up in the same session. Also, if a user stays close to a song, he/she may often sing it. Worth noting that the relations are asymmetric, and this can be inferred from the later illustration.

First, we assume the probability $Pr(s_b|s_a, u)$ of a transition from song s_a to song s_b made by user u is related to the Euclidean distances $\|\mathbf{x}(s_a) - \mathbf{x}(s_b)\|_2$ and $\|\mathbf{y}(u) - \mathbf{x}(s_b)\|_2$, which can be viewed as user u's short-term and long-term preferences. Straightforwardly, it can be described as:

$$Pr(s_b|s_a, u) \propto e^{-\|\mathbf{x}(s_a)-\mathbf{x}(s_b)\|_2^2 - \|\mathbf{y}(u)-\mathbf{x}(s_b)\|_2^2} \tag{1}$$

Note that $Pr(s_b|s_a)$ is proportional to $e^{-\|\mathbf{x}(s_a)-\mathbf{x}(s_b)\|_2^2}$ in LME[5]. Thus, the user information is ignored by LME, while being considered by our PME.

Since $\sum_{b=1}^{|S|} Pr(s_b|s_a, u) = 1$, we add a denominator to the exponential value for normalization, and Equation (1) becomes:

$$Pr(s_b|s_a, u) = \frac{e^{-\|\mathbf{x}(s_a)-\mathbf{x}(s_b)\|_2^2 - \|\mathbf{y}(u)-\mathbf{x}(s_b)\|_2^2}}{\sum_{s\in S} e^{-\|\mathbf{x}(s_a)-\mathbf{x}(s)\|_2^2 - \|\mathbf{y}(u)-\mathbf{x}(s)\|_2^2}} \tag{2}$$

And now, we can get the coordinate mappings through a likelihood maximization approach:

$$(\mathbf{X}, \mathbf{Y}) = \arg\max_{\mathbf{X},\mathbf{Y}} \prod_{(u,p_u)\in D} \prod_{j=1}^{|p_u|} \prod_{k=2}^{|p_{u,j}|} Pr\left(p_{u,j}^{(k)} \middle| p_{u,j}^{(k-1)}, u\right) \tag{3}$$

where the song-mapping matrix $\mathbf{X} = [\mathbf{x}(s_1), \mathbf{x}(s_2), \cdots, \mathbf{x}(s_{|S|})]$ and the user-mapping matrix $\mathbf{Y} = [\mathbf{y}(u_1), \mathbf{y}(u_2), \cdots, \mathbf{y}(u_{|U|})]$.

Then, we could transform Equation (3) into its equivalent form by applying the ln function:

$$\begin{aligned}
(\mathbf{X}, \mathbf{Y}) &= \arg\max_{\mathbf{X},\mathbf{Y}} \sum_{(u,p_u)\in D} \sum_{j=1}^{|p_u|} \sum_{k=2}^{|p_{u,j}|} \ln Pr\left(p_{u,j}^{(k)} \middle| p_{u,j}^{(k-1)}, u\right) \\
&= \arg\max_{\mathbf{X},\mathbf{Y}} \sum_{u\in U} \sum_{s_a\in S} \sum_{s_b\in S} c_{u,s_a,s_b} \ln Pr(s_b|s_a, u) \\
&= \arg\max_{\mathbf{X},\mathbf{Y}} \sum_{u\in U} \sum_{s_a\in S} \sum_{s_b\in S} c_{u,s_a,s_b} \Bigg[-\|\mathbf{x}(s_a) - \mathbf{x}(s_b)\|_2^2 \\
&\quad - \|\mathbf{y}(u) - \mathbf{x}(s_b)\|_2^2 - \ln \sum_{s\in S} e^{-\|\mathbf{x}(s_a)-\mathbf{x}(s)\|_2^2 - \|\mathbf{y}(u)-\mathbf{x}(s)\|_2^2} \Bigg] \\
&\stackrel{\text{def}}{=} \arg\max_{\mathbf{X},\mathbf{Y}} L_1(D|\mathbf{X}, \mathbf{Y})
\end{aligned} \tag{4}$$

where c_{u,s_a,s_b} is the number of occurrence of song s_b after song s_a by user u in the whole data set D. While both $\frac{\partial L_1(D|\mathbf{X},\mathbf{Y})}{\partial \mathbf{x}(i)}$ and $\frac{\partial L_1(D|\mathbf{X},\mathbf{Y})}{\partial \mathbf{y}(i)}$ are non-convex, we find that gradient descent algorithm can still find proper solutions. However, both of the partial derivatives are so complex that the time complexity of a single iteration is as high as $O\left(|U||S|^2\right)$ even after optimization.

Then, to overcome the time-consuming problem, we propose Equation (5) to simulate Equation (2). In this way, the two types of Euclidean distances can be decoupled:

$$Pr(s_b|s_a) Pr(s_b|u) = \frac{e^{-\|\mathbf{x}(s_a)-\mathbf{x}(s_b)\|_2^2}}{\sum_{s\in S} e^{-\|\mathbf{x}(s_a)-\mathbf{x}(s)\|_2^2}} \frac{e^{-\|\mathbf{y}(u)-\mathbf{x}(s_b)\|_2^2}}{\sum_{s\in S} e^{-\|\mathbf{y}(u)-\mathbf{x}(s)\|_2^2}} \tag{5}$$

where $Pr(s_b|s_a)$ is the transition probability from song s_a to song s_b and $Pr(s_b|u)$ is the probability of user u singing song s_b. Note that Equation (5) is not simply an assembled model, since all parameters will be trained simultaneously.

Following a similar process of Equation (3) and Equation (4), we could get:

$$\begin{aligned}
(\mathbf{X}, \mathbf{Y}) &= \arg\max_{\mathbf{X},\mathbf{Y}} \sum_{u\in U} \sum_{s_a\in S} \sum_{s_b\in S} c_{u,s_a,s_b} \ln Pr(s_b|s_a) Pr(s_b|u) \\
&= \arg\max_{\mathbf{X},\mathbf{Y}} \sum_{u\in U} \sum_{s_a\in S} \sum_{s_b\in S} c_{u,s_a,s_b} \Bigg[-\|\mathbf{x}(s_a) - \mathbf{x}(s_b)\|_2^2 \\
&\quad - \ln \sum_{s\in S} e^{-\|\mathbf{x}(s_a)-\mathbf{x}(s)\|_2^2} - \|\mathbf{y}(u) - \mathbf{x}(s_b)\|_2^2 \\
&\quad - \ln \sum_{s\in S} e^{-\|\mathbf{y}(u)-\mathbf{x}(s)\|_2^2} \Bigg] \\
&\stackrel{\text{def}}{=} \arg\max_{\mathbf{X},\mathbf{Y}} L_2(D|\mathbf{X}, \mathbf{Y})
\end{aligned} \tag{6}$$

It can be found that the time complexity of one iteration has decreased to $O(|U||S|)$, if $\sum_{s\in S} e^{-\|\mathbf{x}(s_a)-\mathbf{x}(s)\|_2^2}$ and $\sum_{s\in S} e^{-\|\mathbf{y}(u)-\mathbf{x}(s)\|_2^2}$ are cached for approximate calculation.

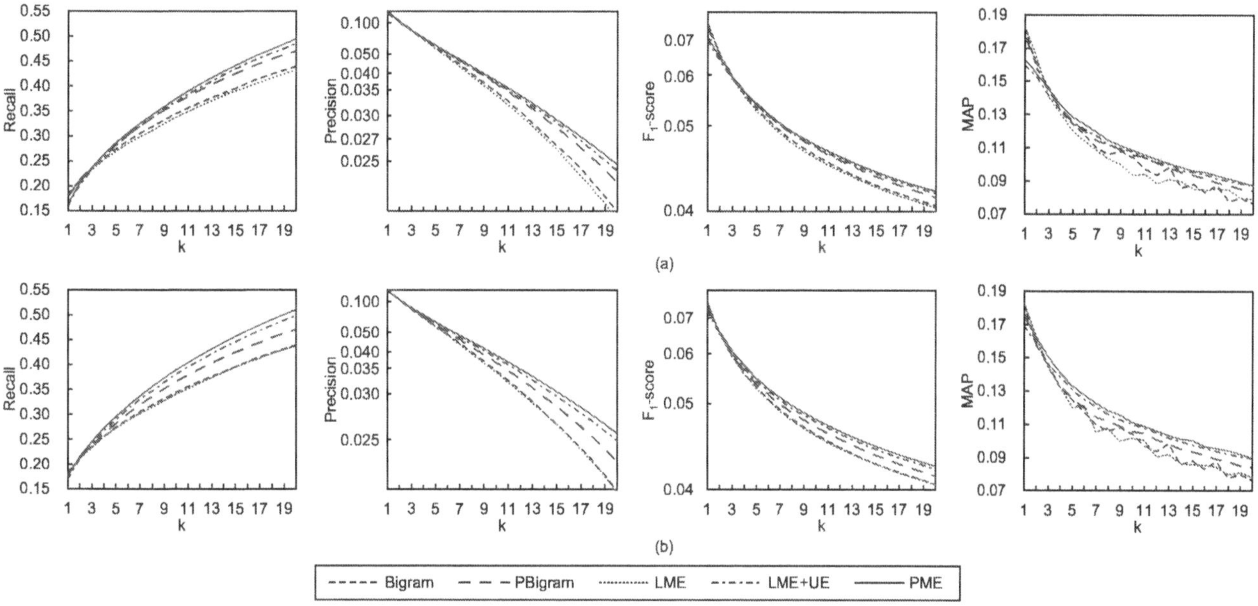

Figure 2: Top-k comparisons of Bigram, PBigram, LME, LME+UE and our PME in $\mathbb{R}^{20}$ (a) and $\mathbb{R}^{50}$ (b) with $k \in [1, 20]$.

Further, we apply regularization of Frobenius norm to Equation (6), and our target becomes:

$$(\mathbf{X}, \mathbf{Y}) = \arg\max_{\mathbf{X},\mathbf{Y}} \left[L_2\left(D \,|\mathbf{X}, \mathbf{Y}\right) - \lambda \|\mathbf{X}\|^2_{Frob} - \lambda \|\mathbf{Y}\|^2_{Frob} \right] \quad (7)$$

where λ is the regularization coefficient, and we can get the updating rules through partial derivations:

$$\mathbf{x}(s) \leftarrow \mathbf{x}(s) + \frac{\tau}{n} \left[\frac{\partial L_2\left(D \,|\mathbf{X}, \mathbf{Y}\right)}{\partial \mathbf{x}(s)} - \frac{\partial \lambda \|\mathbf{X}\|^2_{Frob}}{\partial \mathbf{x}(s)} \right] \quad (8)$$

$$\mathbf{y}(u) \leftarrow \mathbf{y}(u) + \frac{\tau}{n} \left[\frac{\partial L_2\left(D \,|\mathbf{X}, \mathbf{Y}\right)}{\partial \mathbf{y}(u)} - \frac{\partial \lambda \|\mathbf{Y}\|^2_{Frob}}{\partial \mathbf{y}(u)} \right] \quad (9)$$

where τ is the learning rate and n is the total number of song transitions in data set D.

Finally, after the embedding, given the current user u and his/her last song s_a, we could generate the next-song recommendation by ranking the candidate songs based on Equation (5). Meanwhile, we can figure out why $Pr(s_b|s_a, u)$ and $Pr(s_a|s_b, u)$ are not symmetric.

3. EXPERIMENTAL RESULTS

Table 1: Statistics of the data set.

#Users	#Items	#Sessions	#Training Transitions	#Test Transitions
13,452	943	105,743	332,640	58,687

In this section, we evaluate PME on the real world karaoke data provided by ihou.com from July 2011 to April 2012. To reduce noise, we only consider the users who have sung more than 10 different songs and the songs which have been sung by more than 3 different users. For the singing session segmentation, we let the songs to be in the same session, if the user's inactive intervals between adjacent songs are less than 1 hour. We put the last transition of songs from each session into the test set, the rest for training, and ensure that every test song exists in the training set. The statistical information of the final data can be found in Table 1.

Evaluation Metrics. To measure the ranking accuracy, we adopt Precision, Recall, F_1-score and Mean Average Precision (MAP) as our evaluation metrics[7]. These metrics pay more attention to the first several candidates in the ranked list, and try to characterize the recommendation results from different perspectives.

Baselines. We choose the following four baseline methods:

- **Bigram Model (Bigram)**[1] is a first-order Markov model which considers the probability of the appearance of songs separately for different preceding songs, in other words, it calculate $Pr(s_b|s_a)$ based on statistics. We adopt Witten-Bell discounting [6] for smoothing.
- **Personalized Bigram Model (PBigram)** is an assembled algorithm which combines two bigrams $Pr(s_b|s_a)$ and $Pr(s_b|u)$ together by multiplying their results, and Witten-Bell discounting is also used.
- **Logistic Markov Embedding (LME)**[5] is similar to PME. However, it outputs the same $Pr(s_b|s_a)$ for all users.
- **LME with User Embedding (LME+UE)** includes personalization into LME by a two-phased training approach, where song-embeddings are first trained and fixed before the training of user-embeddings are conducted.

All of the aforementioned four baselines can be seen as the related methods for PME. Worth noting that similar to bigram model, uniform model and unigram model [5] are also popular models for Natural Language Processing. However, their performances are no better than the selected baselines.

Performance Comparison. Parameters such as τ and λ in certain methods are determined experimentally, and all iterative methods are run until convergence. The performances under different dimensionalities are tested for LME, LME+UE and PME. For instance, the results of models trained in $\mathbb{R}^{20}$ and $\mathbb{R}^{50}$ are shown in Figure 2. From both Figure 2(a) and Figure 2(b), we could observe that our personalized methods (PBigram, LME+UE and PME) are better than their corresponding benchmark methods (Bigram and LME). More importantly, PME performs best in all cases. Another interesting observation is that LME performs very similarly to Bigram under the ranking metrics, which is different from that in [5] where the likelihood metric is adopted.

Also, we compare the efficiency difference between LME and PME. For instance, under the same platform, when the dimensionality equals to 50, it takes 1.3s for LME and 16.5s for PME to run a single iteration, whose time complexities are $O\left(|S|^2\right)$ and $O(|U|\,|S|)$, respectively.

Deep Understanding. For comparing the performance of the algorithms under different sparsity, we conduct another experiment.

Specifically, we first separate transitions in the test set into 5 different splits according to their occurrence time in the training data, with each split having roughly the same amount of transitions. For instance, the transitions in the test set that didn't occur or occurred only once in the training set and transitions in the test set that occurred 2 to 5 times are evaluated separately. We calculate the Recall value on Top-10 recommendations of three typical algorithms (Bigram, LME and PME) for all 5 splits in $\mathbb{R}^{50}$, and the final results are shown in Figure 3.

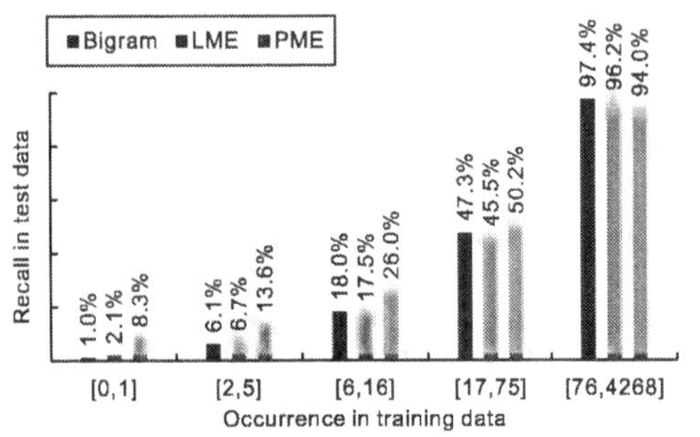

Figure 3: Comparisons of the Recall value on Top-10 recommendations of Bigram, LME and PME with different splits.

From Figure 3 we can see that for the transitions that don't occur many times (less than 17) in the training set, PME performs much better than Bigram and LME. However, the advantage of PME becomes smaller with the increase of the occurrence. Specifically, PME achieves an average lead of 7.6% over the first three ranges, which take up about 60% percent of the test data, and Bigram is slightly better than PME only on the last range. Since most of the transitions have comparably low occurrence rate, PME could outperforms LME and Bigram in real applications, i.e., PME is better at predicting the unseen and sparse data.

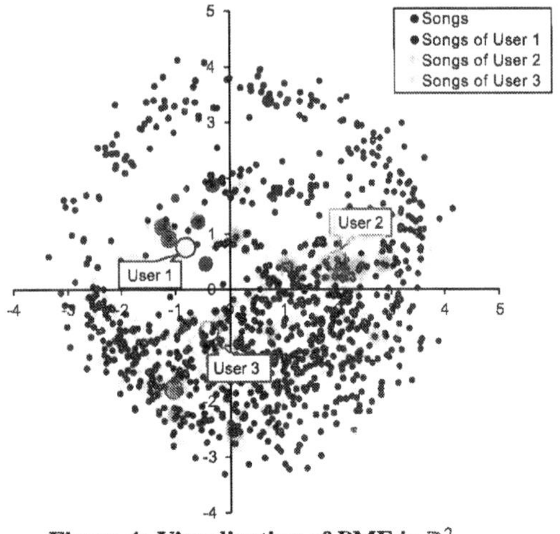

Figure 4: Visualization of PME in $\mathbb{R}^2$.

Case Study. Figure 4 is a visualization of the trained PME model in $\mathbb{R}^2$ where all songs are represented by blue dots and 3 randomly picked users are represented by circles with different colors. We find out the songs sung by these 3 users in the training set, and then highlight them by semitransparent circles with their sizes proportional to the singing frequency of the corresponding user.

It shows that PME can successfully extract user preferences, since the embedding position of each user is near to his/her previous actions. In the stage of recommendation, the songs that are close to the given user, or in other words close to the songs which the given user have sung, are more likely to be recommended to this user according to Equation (5).

4. CONCLUSIONS

In this paper, we presented Personalized Markov Embedding, a next-song recommendation strategy for online karaoke users. We first proposed to embed the songs and users into a Euclidean space in which distances between songs and users reflect the strength of their relationships. We also used a simulation to ensure that the embedding process can converge in time. In this way, the short-term and long-term preferences of each user can be captured without requiring any content information. Then, the next-song recommendations are conducted according to the embedding. Finally, the performance of the proposed PME are evaluated on a real world data set, and the experimental study delivers encouraging results.

5. ACKNOWLEDGEMENTS

The work was supported by grants from Natural Science Foundation of China (Grant No. 61073110), the Key Program of National Natural Science Foundation of China (Grant No. 60933013), Research Fund for the Doctoral Program of Higher Education of China (20113402110024), and the National Major Special Science and Technology Project (Grant No. 2011ZX04016-071).

6. REFERENCES

[1] P. F. Brown, P. V. Desouza, R. L. Mercer, V. J. D. Pietra, and J. C. Lai. Class-based n-gram models of natural language. *Computational Linguistics*, 18(4):467–479, 1992.

[2] R. Cai, C. Zhang, C. Wang, L. Zhang, and W.-Y. Ma. Musicsense: contextual music recommendation using emotional allocation modeling. In *Proc. of MM'07*, pages 553–556. ACM, 2007.

[3] H. Cao, D. Jiang, J. Pei, Q. He, Z. Liao, E. Chen, and H. Li. Context-aware query suggestion by mining click-through and session data. In *Proc. of KDD'08*, pages 875–883. ACM, 2008.

[4] H.-C. Chen and A. L. Chen. A music recommendation system based on music data grouping and user interests. In *Proc. of CIKM'01*, volume 5, pages 231–238, 2001.

[5] S. Chen, J. L. Moore, D. Turnbull, and T. Joachims. Playlist prediction via metric embedding. In *Proc. of KDD'12*, pages 714–722. ACM, 2012.

[6] S. F. Chen and J. Goodman. An empirical study of smoothing techniques for language modeling. *Computer Speech and Language*, 13(4):359–393, 1999.

[7] J. L. Herlocker, J. A. Konstan, L. G. Terveen, and J. T. Riedl. Evaluating collaborative filtering recommender systems. *ACM TOIS*, 22(1):5–53, 2004.

[8] K. Hoashi, K. Matsumoto, and N. Inoue. Personalization of user profiles for content-based music retrieval based on relevance feedback. In *Proc. of MM'03*, pages 110–119. ACM, 2003.

[9] N. Koenigstein, G. Dror, and Y. Koren. Yahoo! music recommendations: modeling music ratings with temporal dynamics and item taxonomy. In *Proc. of RecSys'11*, pages 165–172. ACM, 2011.

[10] Q. Liu, E. Chen, H. Xiong, C. H. Ding, and J. Chen. Enhancing collaborative filtering by user interest expansion via personalized ranking. *IEEE TSMC-B*, 42(1):218–233, 2012.

[11] K. Oku, S. Nakajima, J. Miyazaki, S. Uemura, and H. Kato. A recommendation method considering users' time series contexts. In *Proc. of ICUIMC'09*, pages 465–470. ACM, 2009.

[12] E. Pampalk. *Computational models of music similarity and their application in music information retrieval.* 2006.

[13] S. Rendle, C. Freudenthaler, and L. Schmidt-Thieme. Factorizing personalized markov chains for next-basket recommendation. In *Proc. of WWW'10*, pages 811–820. ACM, 2010.

[14] P. Resnick, N. Iacovou, M. Suchak, P. Bergstrom, and J. Riedl. Grouplens: an open architecture for collaborative filtering of netnews. In *Proc. of CSCW'94*, pages 175–186. ACM, 1994.

[15] M. Tiemann and S. Pauws. Towards ensemble learning for hybrid music recommendation. In *Proc. of RecSys'07*, pages 177–178. ACM, 2007.

Topic Diversity in Tag Recommendation*

Fabiano M. Belém, Rodrygo L. T. Santos, Jussara M. Almeida, Marcos A. Gonçalves
Computer Science Department
Universidade Federal de Minas Gerais, Brazil
{fmuniz, rodrygo, jussara, mgoncalv}@dcc.ufmg.br

ABSTRACT

Tag recommendation approaches have historically focused on maximizing the relevance of the recommended tags for a given object, such as a movie or a song. Nevertheless, different users may be interested in the same object for different reasons—for instance, the Star Wars movies may appeal to both adventure as well as to fantasy movie fans. In this situation, a sensible strategy is to provide a user with diverse recommendations of how to tag the object. In this paper, we address the problem of recommending relevant and diverse tags as a ranking problem. In particular, we propose a novel tag recommendation approach that explicitly takes into account the possible topics (e.g., categories) underlying an object in order to promote tags with high coverage and low redundancy with respect to these topics. We thoroughly evaluate our proposed approach using data collected from two popular Web 2.0 applications, namely, LastFM and MovieLens. Our experimental results attest the effectiveness of our approach at promoting more relevant and diverse tags in contrast to state-of-the-art relevance-based methods as well as a recently proposed method that takes both relevance and diversity into account.

Categories and Subject Descriptors

H.3.1 [**Information Storage and Retrieval**]: Content Analysis and Indexing; H.3.5 [**Information Storage and Retrieval**]: Online Information Services

General Terms

Algorithms, Experimentation

Keywords

Tag Recommendation, Relevance, Diversity

*This work is supported by the INWeb (grant 57.3871/2008-6) and by the authors grants from CNPq and FAPEMIG.

RecSys'13, October 12–16, 2013, Hong Kong, China.

http://dx.doi.org/10.1145/2507157.2507184.

1. INTRODUCTION

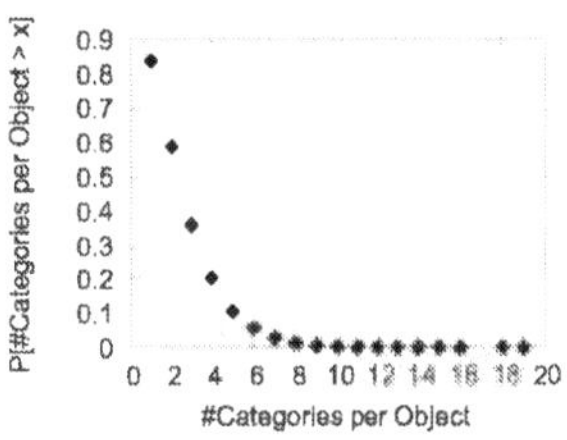

(a) Artist styles in AllMusic

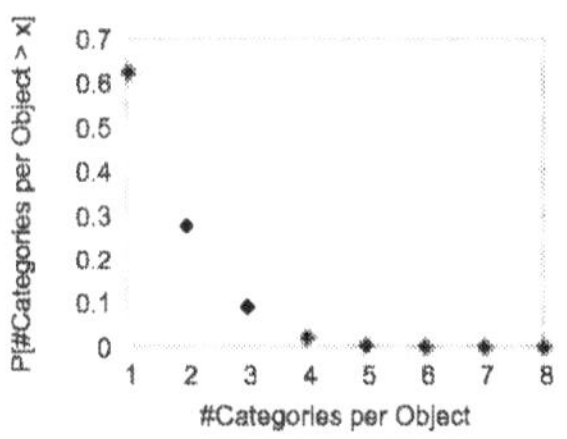

(b) Genres in MovieLens

Figure 1: Complementary cumulative distribution of the number of categories per object.

The Web 2.0 is characterized by an unprecedented amount of user-generated content. This content usually comprises a main *object* (e.g., a video) and several sources of data associated with it, referred to as its *features*. The *textual features* of an object are well-defined blocks of text such as title, tags, description and user comments, used to describe the object's content [5]. Among all textual features, tags have attracted special attention as they offer an effective data source for Information Retrieval (IR) services such as search [17] and classification [13], and may capture user interests reasonably well [17]. In this context, there is a large interest in developing strategies to recommend tags to users, providing *relevant* and *useful* tag suggestions for a target object, and improving the quality of the generated tags and, indirectly, of the IR services that rely on them.

Tag recommendation methods have historically focused mostly on maximizing the *relevance* of the recommended tags [5, 18, 27]. When recommending tags for a target object, relevance refers to how well the recommended tags describe the contents of the target object. However, relevance by itself may not be enough to guarantee recommendation usefulness and effectiveness [4, 25]. For example, a list of synonyms that well describe the object's content is arguably relevant, but also redundant and less useful than a more diversified list covering more aspects related to the object. As argued in [4], objects on the Web 2.0 may be *multifaceted*, being related to various aspects and topics.

We illustrate this point by showing, in Figure 1, the distributions of the number of styles for different music artists and the number of genres for different movies, computed over datasets collected from AllMusic and MovieLens[1], re-

[1] http://www.allmusic.com and http://MovieLens.umn.edu

spectively. According to Figure 1, 84% of the artists and 63% of the movies are associated with *more* than one category (style or genre). Take for instance the movie "Sister Act", starring Whoopi Goldberg. Its main genre is Comedy, but it also presents elements from the Action and Musical genres. Arguably, it would be appropriate to recommend tags related to all these genres for this movie. According to Figure 1, the distribution is even more biased towards larger numbers of categories for music artists.

While *diversity* is an important aspect in tag recommendation, our previous work [4] is, to our knowledge, the only one to address aspects other than relevance for tag recommendation. In [4], we defined the diversity of a list of recommended tags *implicitly*, as the average *semantic distance* [4, 13, 19] between each pair of tags in the list, such that a set of synonyms or semantically similar words has low diversity. However, this approach has the disadvantage of being more subject to data sparsity, because the estimates of the semantic similarities are based on tag co-occurrences [4].

We here propose an alternative approach to address diversity in tag recommendation. We define diversity *explicitly*, in terms of the capacity of the recommended tags to cover different aspects or topics of the target object, an approach inspired by diversification algorithms proposed in the context of search [22]. To this end, we exploit an explicit taxonomy represented by categories, commonly available in Web 2.0 applications, as topics for objects.

In order to recommend relevant and diverse tags, we model tag recommendation as a ranking problem. That is, we aim to produce a ranking function f that assigns scores to candidate tags based on: (1) relevance estimates generated by a baseline state-of-the-art tag recommendation strategy, and (2) our diversification approach, which rescores candidate tags such that they better cover the topics of the target object. This allows us to sort candidate tags according to their joint relevance and diversity estimates.

Our method is a re-ranking strategy, and thus can be applied over the recommendations produced by any relevance-based strategy. In particular, we apply it over a state-of-the-art Genetic Programming (GP) based tag recommender [5], here referred to as GP_r, and over a novel strategy that uses *Random Forests* (*RF*), a learning-to-rank technique [6] that has not been applied to tag recommendation yet. Our approach, called explicit Tag Recommendation Diversifier or *xTReD*, modifies the original scores produced by GP_r (or by *RF*), bringing tags that better contribute to covering the topics of the target object to higher positions of the ranking.

We evaluate our method on datasets collected from 2 popular applications - LastFM and MovieLens - comparing it against GP_r and GP_{rnd} [4], which extends GP_r to include metrics of diversity and novelty. Our goals are: (1) assessing to which extent we can improve diversity without harming relevance, and (2) comparing our explicit diversification strategy against the implicit GP_{rnd} method. Our results show that our method outperforms the best relevance-based strategy on which it is based by up to 45% in diversity without harming relevance. It also outperforms GP_{rnd} by up to 54% in diversity and 10% in relevance, with the best results produced when xTReD is applied jointly with RF. Moreover, among the two relevance-driven strategies, the new RF-based recommender outperforms the state-of-the-art GP_r by up to 7% in relevance.

In sum, the main contributions of this paper are: (1) an alternative definition of diversity for tag recommendation that explicitly captures the multifaceted nature of many Web 2.0 objects; (2) a novel strategy to diversify tag recommendations that leads to significant gains in diversity, with no harm to relevance, over state-of-the-art strategies; (3) an analysis of Random Forests as an alternative learning-to-rank strategy for recommending relevant tags, and (4) an extensive evaluation of all strategies in large real datasets.

The rest of this paper is organized as follows. Section 2 discusses related work. Section 3 formally states the problem we tackle. Section 4 introduces the tag recommendation methods analyzed here. Our experimental methodology and results are discussed in Sections 5 and 6, while Section 7 offers conclusions and directions for future work.

2. RELATED WORK

The tag recommendation literature is rich in techniques exploiting co-occurrence patterns computed over a history of tag assignments [5, 4, 27], words extracted from multiple textual features of the target object [18], as well as metrics of tag relevance to filter out irrelevant terms or give more importance to the relevant ones [5, 18]. In [5], we proposed several heuristic methods that jointly exploit these three dimensions, and showed that they outperform previous approaches in various datasets. We, as well as other authors [7, 27], also exploited learning-to-rank (L2R) techniques, such as RankSVM [5, 7], RankBoost [27] and Genetic Programming (GP) [5], to "learn" a model that ranks tags based on a set of relevance metrics. Other dimensions of the problem, such as personalization, have also been tackled, often using the user's history of tag assignments [20].

In common, all these previous efforts focus on tag relevance as the single criterion of tag *quality*. However, other aspects such as diversity may also be important. Indeed, result diversification is a problem that has been addressed in other contexts, particularly web search [11]. In this context, two main families of diversification approaches have emerged to tackle query ambiguity [23]. *Implicit approaches* seek to promote diversity by scoring a given search result proportionally to its difference to the results ranked ahead of it, e.g., in terms of these results' textual dissimilarity [8] or the divergence of their language models [28]. In contrast, explicit approaches seek to diversify the search results on the basis of their coverage of some property of the user's query, such as multiple query categories [1] or multiple query reformulations [22]. Explicit approaches represent the current state-of-the-art [23], and provide the basis for our approach.

In the general context of (item) recommendation, previous work mostly focused on implicit approaches. Celma *et al.* [9] and Vargas *et al.* [25] evaluated novelty and diversity in terms of popularity and dissimilarity of items, based on the idea that novel and diverse items must be different from all items that have been seen or consumed. Ribeiro *et al.* [21] exploited a multi-objective pareto optimization algorithm to jointly address relevance, novelty and (implicit) diversity. Wartena and Wibbels [26] improve item recommendation by detecting different topics of interest in the user profile and then generating recommendations for each of these topics.

We are aware of only one previous attempt to explore result diversification in the specific context of tag recommendation. Very recently, we extended our previous GP-based method [5] to include metrics related to both diversity and novelty [4]. However, inspired by [25], we previously adopted an *implicit* definition of diversity, which captures the semantic distance between different tags in a recommendation list. In contrast, building from recent search result diversification efforts [22, 23], we here adopt an alternative definition by *explicitly* representing the multiple topics associated with an object, as discussed in Section 3.

The original GP-based solution proposed in [5] and its recent extension [4] are here taken as baselines for comparison against our novel approach, being described in Section 4.1. We note that, although we currently do not address personalization, our approach can be easily extended to produce personalized recommendations, by taking into account a topic distribution biased towards each user's interests.

3. PROBLEM STATEMENT

The tag recommendation problem we address here can be stated as: *Given a set of initial tags I_o, priorly assigned to the target object o, and a set of textual features $F_o = \{F_o^1, ..., F_o^n\}$, where F_o^i contains the terms in textual feature i of o, produce a sorted list of candidate tags C_o ($C_o \cap I_o = \emptyset$) so that both relevance and diversity objectives are maximized, and recommend the k candidates in the top positions of C_o.* We focus on recommending tags for a target object, aiming at improving the quality of tags in the objects, and indirectly the effectiveness of services that use tags as a data source. We leave the task of tackling diversity in personalized recommendations to the future.

The main focus of this work is on the diversity of the recommended tags. Diversity can be defined implicitly or explicitly. As an example of the former, Vargas *et al.* [25] defined diversity as the average pairwise difference between the items in the recommendation list. Inspired by them, we have previously defined diversity in the specific context of tag recommendation as the average semantic distance between the recommended tags, such that a list of synonyms or semantically related words present low diversity [4].

An explicit definition of diversity usually exploits a taxonomy, such as a set of categories or topics. In that perspective, a list of recommended items is diverse if it presents items that cover different topics. This approach has been applied in search result diversification [22, 23], being useful to increase the chances that at least one document will satisfy the information need of the target user. This is also the perspective we employ here, thus a diversified list of tags must cover as many topics related to the target object as possible, and as early in the ranking as possible.

Given our focus, we approach the tag recommendation task as a *ranking problem*. That is, we aim at developing a *ranking function* that assigns scores to each candidate tag c, allowing us to sort candidates so that those that represent more relevant and diverse recommendations for the object o appear in higher positions in C_o. This is achieved in two steps: (1) a state-of-the-art relevance-driven tag recommendation strategy is used to produce relevance estimates, and (2) our diversifier approach rescores candidate tags such that they better cover the topics of the target object.

4. TAG RECOMMENDATION METHODS

This section describes the analyzed tag recommendation methods. All approaches employ a learning-to-rank (L2R) technique, for example, Genetic Programming (GP) or Random Forest (RF), to build a ranking function that assigns scores to candidate tags according to some criterion (e.g., probability of relevance). The two state-of-the-art baselines use GP as L2R technique, and are described in Section 4.1. We present our new relevance-driven RF-based strategy as well as our new diversifier approach in Section 4.2. All methods extract candidate tags from (1) co-ocurrence patterns with tags already in the target object o (tags in I_o), and (2) other textual features in o, namely, title and description.

Table 1: Metrics of tag relevance.

Relevance aspect	Metrics
Tag co-occurrences	*Sum*, Sum^+, *Vote*, $Vote^+$ [24]
Discriminative power	Stability (*Stab*) [24], Inverse Feature Frequency (*IFF*) [13]
Descriptive power	Term Spread (*TS*) [13], Term Freq. (*TF*) [2] weighted *TS* (*wTS*), weighted *TF* (*wTF*) [5]
Predictability	*Entropy* [5]

4.1 State-of-the-Art Baselines

Our baseline methods are based on Genetic Programming (GP), a framework inspired by the biological mechanisms of genetic inheritance and evolution of individuals in a population [3]. GP is a non-linear method that has been applied to various IR tasks. We were the first to use it for recommending tags [4, 5], having obtained competitive (or superior) results over other approaches.

GP implements a global search mechanism by evolving a population of individuals over multiple generations. Each individual, representing a possible solution for the target problem, is modeled as a tree composed of terminals (leaves) and functions (inner nodes), related to the target problem. In each generation, each individual is evaluated by a *fitness* function, defined based on quality metrics related to the problem at hand. Only individuals with the highest fitness values are selected, according to some selection method, to evolve the population. An initial randomly generated population is evolved, generation after generation, through *crossover* and *mutation* operations. The individual with the best fitness value, usually part of the last generation, is chosen as the final solution for the problem.

GP directly optimizes a target (fitness) function, and allows for easy extensions to include more problem-related features (terminals) and to address other aspects of the target problem (by, for instance, adapting the fitness function). In particular, as reported in [5], GP outperforms other learning-to-rank techniques (RankSVM) in some scenarios, being statistically tied with it in many others. Thus, GP provides a promising framework to develop effective tag recommendation solutions.

In our first GP-based baseline, here referred to as GP_r [5], an individual is a tag ranking function with a tree representation built from nodes defined as follows. The sum (+), subtraction (−), multiplication (×), division (/) and natural logarithm (*ln*) operations are used as inner nodes. Protected division and logarithm are implemented such that these operations return 0 (default) when their inputs are outside their domains. Terminals are either constants, uniformly distributed between 0 and 1, or variables, selected from a set including (the values of) the metrics listed in Table 1. These metrics capture the following aspects related to the *relevance* of a candidate tag c to a target object o: (1) co-occurrence patterns, whose strengths are expressed by the confidences of association rules between previously assigned tags (tags in I_o) and c, where the rules are extracted from the training set, (2) the power of c to discriminate o from other objects, (3) the power of c to describe o's content, and (4) the predictability of c as a tag in the object collection. For illustration purposes, a tree representation of function $Vote + wTS/0.5$ has operation '+' as root, with variable $Vote$ and operation '/' as its children. The inner node '/' has variable wTS and constant 0.5 as children.

The fitness of an individual represents the quality of the recommendations produced by the corresponding ranking function. It is computed as the Normalized Discounted Cumulative Gain ($NDCG$) [2] of the top-k tags in the recommendation list produced by the function for a sample of objects in a validation set, with k=5.

Only relevance metrics are used by GP_r (as terminals and fitness function). Since our approach diversifies GP_r results, comparing both methods allows us to assess to which extent we can exploit a tradeoff between relevance and diversity.

GP_r was recently extended to include attributes related to the diversity and novelty of a list of tags [4]. This extension, here called GP_{rnd} (our second baseline), adds the Average Distance to other Candidates (ADC) metric to the list of terminals. ADC captures the diversity that a candidate c brings to a recommendation list C_o by the average semantic distance between c and each other candidate tag in C_o. The ADC of c with respect to C_o is defined as $ADC(c, C_o) = \frac{1}{|C_o|} \sum_{t \in C_o, t \neq c} dist(c, t)$, where $dist(c_1, c_2)$ measures the dissimilarity between candidates c_1 and c_2 as the relative difference between the sets of objects O_1 and O_2 in which they appear as tags. That is, $dist(c_1, c_2) = \frac{|O_1 \setminus O_2|}{|O_1 \cup O_2|}$. If both sets are empty, $dist(c_1, c_2)$ is set to 1, the maximum value. GP_{rnd} also adopts a different fitness function, aiming at jointly maximizing relevance, diversity and novelty. For each object o in the validation set, the fitness of a candidate ranking function f is computed as:

$$fitness(C_o) = \alpha \times AIP@k(C_o) + \beta \times AILD@k(C_o) + (1 - \alpha - \beta) \times NDCG@k(C_o), \quad (1)$$

where C_o is the recommendation list produced by f for o, and $0 \leq \alpha \leq 1$ and $0 \leq \beta \leq 1$ are tuning parameters. The fitness function includes $NDCG@k$ to capture the relevance of the recommended tags in C_o, as well as $AIP@k$ and $AILD@k$, which are related to the novelty and the diversity of these tags, respectively.

$AIP@k$, or Average Inverse Popularity over the top k positions of the ranking, was adapted from [25] to be a normalized average of the IFF values of the top-k tags in C_o. IFF, a variation of the traditional IDF metric [2], favors tags that do not occur too often. It was used to estimate the novelty of a tag under the assumption that the lower the popularity of a tag, the higher its novelty [4].

$AILD@k$, or Average IntraList Distance in the top k positions [25], captures the diversity of the tags in C_o. Specifically, given the normalization constant $K' = (k^2 - k)/2$ and $dist(c_i, c_j)$ as defined above, $AILD@k$ of C_o is computed as $AILD(C_o) = \frac{1}{K'} \sum_{i=1}^{k} \sum_{j=i+1}^{k} dist(c_i, c_j)$. Note that both $AILD@k$ and ADC metrics capture the notion of diversity in a list of tags implicitly, by means of the $dist(c_i, c_j)$ function: a list with tags that are more semantically *dissimilar* is considered more diverse.

Although GP_{rnd} captures novelty, in addition to relevance and diversity (our goal), a comparison against our solution is fair since, as noted in [4], a simplified version of the method with the novelty component turned off (α=0) does not outperform the complete solution in any of the three aspects.

4.2 Our New Solutions

We now describe the new tag recommendation strategies proposed here. We start by describing a relevance-driven tag recommender that exploits Random Forests to learn a tag ranking function, being thus an alternative to GP_r (Section 4.2.1). We then introduce our topic diversifier, which can be jointly applied with any relevance-driven strategy to produce relevant and diversified recommendations (Section 4.2.2).

4.2.1 Random Forests Based Tag Recommender

Random Forests (RF) is an ensemble learning method in which n_t decision trees are trained with distinct subsets of the training set (with size n_b), randomly sampled with replacement in order to reduce the correlation among them. The decision tree learning happens in a recursive way: first, the most discriminative feature (according to some measure, such as Information Gain) is selected as a decision node. The selected training samples are split according to a split value (such as the average attribute value), and the process repeats in a top-down fashion. In order to further reduce the correlation between the decision trees, before each split a fraction ϕ of the features is randomly selected to be considered as candidates for splitting, instead of considering the whole set of attributes. The decision rule is given by averaging the n_t predictions of the trained trees. The crucial aspects that make RF a good learner are (i) the reduced correlation between the decision trees composing the ensemble and (ii) the better-than-random-guess predictions of each tree. To achieve strong decision trees (i.e, trees with better prediction performance than random guessing), each decision tree is typically grown to its maximum depth, containing n_l terminal nodes, where n_l is a tuning parameter.

In order to be applied to our context, each tree outputs a relevance score to be assigned to each candidate tag c in a (test) object. The scores given by each tree to c are averaged and used to produce the final ranking of candidates. RF has achieved promising results in other contexts (e.g, document ranking [14]). It is used here as an alternative to GP_r to produce a relevance based ranking of candidate tags. We use the RF implementation available in the RankLib tool[2], and exploit the same attributes used by GP_r (Table 1) to build the trees.

4.2.2 Explicit Tag Recommendation Diversifier

Unlike GP_{rnd}, we propose to address tag diversity in an explicit way, by seeking to directly maximize the set of topics (or categories) covered by the recommended tags. In its general form, maximizing topic coverage is an NP-hard problem [1]. Fortunately, there is a well-known greedy algorithm for this problem, which achieves an approximation factor of $(1-1/e) \approx 0.632$ of the optimal solution [15]. This is also the best possible polynomial-time approximation for the problem, unless NP $\subseteq$ DTIME$(n^{O(\log \log n)})$, where n is the number of items to be diversified [12, 16]. Our method, called explicit Tag Recommendation Diversifier, or $xTReD$, builds upon this greedy approach, as described in Algorithm 1.

[2]http://people.cs.umass.edu/~vdang/ranklib.html

xTReD takes as input an object o and a diversification cut-off τ. In its first step, *xTReD* calls a tag recommendation method rec to produce an initial ranking C_o of recommended tags *based only on relevance* (line 1). Any relevance-driven tag recommender could be used in this step. We here evaluate: (1) GP_r, to make our approach comparable to the GP_{rnd} baseline, and (2) our new relevance-driven method *RF*.

xTReD(o, τ)

1 $C_o^\tau \leftarrow rec(o, \tau)$ // relevance-driven recommendations
2 $C_o^S \leftarrow \emptyset$
3 **while** $|C_o^S| < min(\tau, |C_o|)$ **do**
4 $\quad t^* \leftarrow \arg\max_{t \in C_o^\tau} f(o, t, C_o^S)$
5 $\quad C_o^\tau \leftarrow C_o^\tau \setminus \{t^*\}$
6 $\quad C_o^S \leftarrow C_o^S \cup \{t^*\}$
7 **end while**
8 **return** C_o^S

Algorithm 1: The xTReD algorithm.

Let C_o^τ be the top τ recommendations in C_o. The goal is to produce a permutation of C_o^τ so as to raise the diversity in the top positions of the ranking of recommended tags, given that those tags are often the ones that the user looks at. A complete permutation of C_o (τ=$|C_o|$) could be produced. However, we can reduce τ for efficiency reasons and as a means to restrict the search for more diverse tags among the most relevant ones, avoiding severe relevance penalties.

The permutation C_o^S is initialized as an empty set (line 2), and is iteratively constructed (lines 3-7). The sub-modular objective function $f(o, t, C_o^S)$ scores each yet unselected tag $t \in C_o^\tau \setminus C_o^S$ in light of the object o and the tags already in C_o^S, selected in the previous iterations of the algorithm (line 4). The highest scored tag, t^*, is then removed from C_o^τ (line 5) and added to C_o^S (line 6). Finally, the produced diverse ranking C_o^S is returned (line 8).

To instantiate the objective function $f(o, t, C_o^S)$ in Algorithm 1, we build upon a state-of-the-art framework for diversifying search results, called xQuAD [22]. The xQuAD framework instantiates the aforementioned function in order to score the documents retrieved for a given query proportionally to these documents' coverage and novelty in light of the multiple possible information needs underlying this query [22]. In our adaptation, instead of a ranking of documents for a query, we seek to diversify a ranking of tags for a given object. More precisely, we propose a novel instantiation of the objective function $f(o, t, C_o^S)$, such that:

$$f(o, t, C_o^S) = (1 - \lambda) p(t|o) + \lambda \sum_{z \in Z} p(z|o) p(t|o, z) \prod_{t' \in C_o^S} (1 - p(t'|o, z)), \quad (2)$$

where Z is a set of topics associated with the object o and $0 \leq \lambda \leq 1$ is a tuning parameter used to balance the trade-off between promoting relevance or diversity. The greater the value of λ, the more importance is given to diversity. The idea is to promote tags which are simultaneously highly related to at least one of the topics of the target object and little related to the topics of the tags already selected as recommendation (captured by the product over $t' \in C_o^S$), hence increasing the coverage of topics in the top positions of the list of recommendations. Besides addressing an explicit notion of diversity, our strategy has the advantage of making the weight given to diversity adjustable at recommendation time, unlike GP_{rnd}, which needs to train a new model for each new value of α, and is hence more time-consuming.

When $\lambda = 0$, Equation (2) reduces to $p(t|o)$, which results in a pure relevance-driven tag recommendation, as produced by a non-diversification baseline. In our experiments in Section 6, we define $p(t|o) = 1/r_t$, where r_t is the position of the tag t in the ranking produced by the initial ranker rec. In order to estimate the second half of Equation (2), we infer the distribution $p(z|o)$ of topics $z \in Z$ for an object o from the available training data, as we will discuss in Section 5.2. Finally, to estimate how much a given tag t covers the topic z of the object o, we approximate the probability $p(t|o, z)$ as $p(t|o, z) \approx p(t|o) \times p(z|t)$, where $p(z|t)$ is an estimate of the probability that tag t is related to topic z. In turn, $p(z|t)$ is defined as $p(z|t) = f(t, z)/f(t)$, where $f(t, z)$ is the number of objects in which z appears as a topic and t appears as a tag, and $f(t)$ is the number of objects containing tag t, both in the training set.

5. EXPERIMENTAL SETUP

This section describes the setup used in our experimental evaluation of the tag recommendation methods, including datasets (Section 5.1), evaluation methodology (Section 5.2), and method parameterization (Section 5.3).

5.1 Datasets

Our evaluation is performed using two datasets, containing *title*, *tags*, *description* and *categories* associated with objects from MovieLens and LastFM. The MovieLens dataset[3] contains 100,000 tags applied to 10,000 movies. The genres associated with each movie were used as categories. The LastFM dataset[4] is the same used in [4, 5]. We collected the musical styles associated with 35,975 artists in this dataset from the AllMusic site[5], and used them as artist categories.

We removed *stopwords* and applied the Porter stemming algorithm[6] to avoid trivial recommendations (e.g., plurals and other variations of the same word). We also discarded objects with fewer than 2 tags. Our processed datasets comprise a sample of the textual features of 35,975 LastFM artists and 6,500 MovieLens movies.

5.2 Evaluation Methodology

As in most tag recommendation studies [4, 5, 24, 18], we adopted an automatic evaluation approach: half of the tags, randomly selected from all tags previously assigned to an object, are used as *gold standard*, i.e., as the relevant tags for that object. These tags are *not* used by the tag recommenders, being thus removed from $\mathcal{I}_o$, which is used as input by the recommenders. A manual evaluation of tags is an expensive process in terms of time and human effort, besides being subjective, and thus is left for future work.

As in [5], the experiments were performed using a 5-fold cross-validation. That is, the objects are distributed into five equal-sized portions. Three portions are treated as the training set, used to compute all features exploited by both GP and RF. A fourth portion is used as the validation set,

[3] http://www.grouplens.org/taxonomy/term/14
[4] http://www.vod.dcc.ufmg.br/recc/
[5] http://www.allmusic.com
[6] http://snowball.tartarus.org/algorithms/porter/stemmer.html

which, in turn, is used to "learn" the solutions (i.e., generate the ranking function by both techniques) and to tune parameters of the methods (e.g., λ, GP and RF parameters). The last portion is used for testing.

In order to estimate how related a tag t is to a topic, which is necessary to evaluate topic diversity and used by the diversifier algorithm, we estimate the probability of a topic given a tag using training data. That is, the level of relationship of a tag t to a topic z is given by $p(z|t)$, defined in Section 4.2. The topics correspond to categories obtained from our datasets, as described in Section 5.1.

We evaluate the tag recommendation methods in terms of the relevance and the diversity of their results. We use $NDCG@k$ to assess the relevance of a ranked list of tags. To assess the diversity of this list, we used three metrics traditionally used for evaluating search result diversification methods [10]. Two of them—ERR-IA and α-NDCG—are the primary evaluation metrics used in the diversity task of the TREC Web track [11]. They are cascade metrics that penalize redundancy by modeling the behavior of a user who stops inspecting the ranking once a relevant tag is observed [25]. While ERR-IA measures the *expected retrieval performance* with respect to multiple topics, α-NDCG incorporates a notion of the *expected gain* attained by each ranked tag. We also report (sub)topic recall—*S-Recall* [28], which quantifies the fraction of unique topics associated with the object that are covered by the top ranked tags. All diversity metrics use the probability of a topic z given a tag t, $p(z|t)$, to estimate whether a recommended tag is related to a given topic of the object. They are computed over the top-k tags in the recommendation list, with k=5 as in [4, 5].

Following [4], we evaluate diversity orthogonally to relevance. Thus, a tag considered irrelevant might contribute with higher diversity. Alternatively, we could embed relevance in the diversity metric such that only relevant tags could contribute to raise diversity. We opted for an orthogonal assessment of diversity because, unlike in previous diversification efforts in other contexts [11], our data about tag relevance and object topics is sparse, that is, we do not have a complete sample of all relevant tags spread across the topics they cover for each object. Instead, we estimate how related the tags are to a topic using training data, and use this estimation in the diversity metrics. One might argue that tags considered irrelevant[7] should not contribute to raise diversity, despite being related to a topic of the object. We note however that we tuned all methods to maximize the average diversity across all objects, *without harming relevance* (on average). After this tuning, we observed that a tag considered irrelevant contributed to amplify diversity for only a small fraction of the objects (less than 4%). Thus, we did indeed filter out the vast majority of such cases.

Note that we can evaluate the diversity of recommendations for objects with a single category by verifying if the recommended tags are related to that single topic. However, the redundancy is high when recommending tags from the same topic, which could cause a loss in α-$NDCG$.

5.3 Parameterization

We ran a series of experiments using data from the validation set to determine the best parameters for each method. For both GP_r and GP_{rnd} we fixed the parameters of the evolutionary process at the same values reported in [5]. We set the population size at 200, the maximum tree depth at 8, and the maximum number of generations at 200. We also employed *tournament selection* of individuals to evolve the population, i.e., we randomly select, with replacement, 2 individuals from the population and choose the one with highest fitness. Moreover, crossover and mutation operations were performed at rates 0.6 and 0.1, respectively.

For GP_{rnd}, as in [4], we set α=β, varying both at the same time[8], in the [0,0.6] interval. These parameters capture the tradeoff between relevance and the combination of novelty and diversity. Larger values of α (or β) lead to great losses in relevance. The value that lead to the best diversity[9] without harming relevance is 0.25 and 0.1 for LastFM and MovieLens, respectively.

According to validation experiments, our RF-based tag recommender is very insensitive to parameterization. The results obtained with different numbers of trees (n_t=1, 5, 50) are statistically tied (with 95% confidence). We chose n_t=1 due to the lower cost. We also fixed the fraction of attributes selected in each node as ϕ=0.3, after verifying that other values (e.g., 0.25, 0.5 and 0.75) lead to the same results. Different sizes for the bootstrap sample n_b also led to the same results, and we set n_b=300. The only parameter that (slightly) impacts results is the number of leaves n_l: the best result is obtained with the largest value tested (n_l=1000).

For our diversifier $xTReD$, we set the number of positions of the ranking to be diversified τ=25, for efficiency reasons and because the tags in the top positions are much more likely to be selected (and visualized by the user) than lower ranked tags. Our objective with $xTReD$ is also to maximize diversity without harming relevance. Thus, we performed a grid search to find the best values for λ, the trade-off between relevance and diversity, as will be discussed in Section 6.1.

6. EXPERIMENTAL RESULTS

We now discuss the results of the analyzed tag recommendation methods, namely, the baselines GP_r and GP_{rnd}, and our new strategies RF and $xTReD$. Whenever necessary, we refer to our diversifier as $xTReD_{rec}$, where rec is the initial ranker used (GP_r or RF) All results are averages of 25 executions (5 folds, 5 random seeds). Our goal is to answer the following key research questions:

1. Can we effectively diversify tag recommendations without harming relevance? We explore the tradeoff between relevance and diversity in Section 6.1.
2. Is our explicit diversifier effective in contrast to a state-of-the-art implicit approach? In Section 6.2, we compare $xTReD$ against GP_{rnd} and against the relevance-driven strategies it builds upon (either GP_r or RF).
3. Is Random Forests an effective learning-to-rank technique when applied to tag recommendation? In Section 6.2, we also compare our new RF-based method against the state-of-the-art GR_r recommender.

6.1 The Relevance and Diversity Tradeoff

We here analyze the sensitivity of our method to its key parameter λ, by searching for the best parameter value in

[7]Note that a tag may be relevant even if it is not in the gold standard.

[8]The results obtained following this approach are not worse than the best results when we set α=0 (thus removing the novelty component AIP) and varied only β.

[9]The best results were chosen in terms of α-$NDCG$, but the best parameter values are the same for the other metrics.

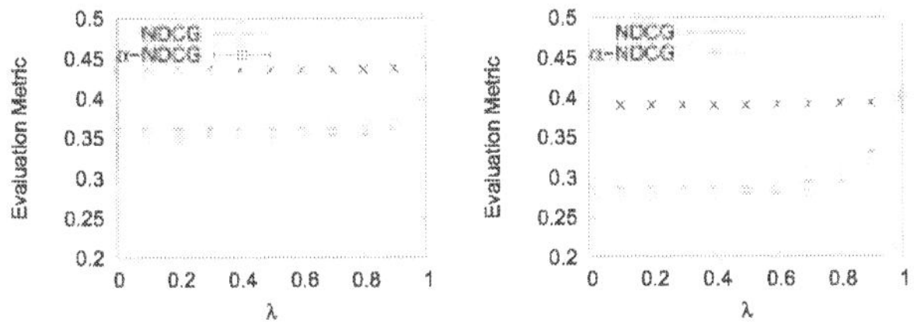

(a) LastFM (b) MovieLens

Figure 2: Impact of parameter λ in $xTReD$ effectiveness.

the *validation set*. Figure 2 shows average $NDCG$ and α-$NDCG$ results for $xTReD_{GP_r}$, along with 95% confidence intervals[10], as functions of λ. Results for $xTReD_{RF}$ and for other diversity evaluation metrics are similar (omitted).

When λ=0, $xTReD$ outputs the same recommendation list as the baseline it uses as initial ranker (GP_r or RF). The closer λ gets to 1, the more the baseline's recommendation list is rearranged, favoring diversity, which reaches its maximum at λ=1, for both datasets. The gains of $xTReD_{GP_r}$ in α-$NDCG$ over the results for λ=0 (i.e., GP_r) reach 39% in LastFM and 44% in MovieLens for λ=1. Corresponding gains for $xTReD_{RF}$ over RF are 46% and 40%.

Such impressive gains in diversity come with no statistically significant loss in relevance (NDCG). Thus, for both initial rankers, the maximum diversification level (λ=1) does not hurt relevance. This is possibly due to: (1) tags promoted by $xTReD$ may present high relevance as they tend to be related to the topics (categories) of the object, and (2) $xTReD$ promotes relevant tags even if λ=1, due to the probability $p(t|o,z) \approx p(t|o) \times p(z|t)$. Indeed, recall that $p(t|o,z)$ is part of the diversity component of Equation (2), representing the probability that tag t is related to *both* topic z and object o. Thus, the diversifier also promotes tags with high chance of being related to the object. In contrast, the benefits introduced by GP_{rnd} are much more modest (if any), as discussed in the next section.

Thus, recalling our first research question, we found that it is possible to significantly increase diversity without harming relevance with our xTReD method by adjusting its parameter λ. Best results are obtained with λ=1.

6.2 Test Results

We now turn to our second and third research questions, on the effectiveness[11] of our explicit diversification approach and of the RF relevance-driven method. Towards answering them, we perform a series of experiments with objects in the *test set*, comparing our $xTReD$ approach (with both RF and GP_r as initial rankers), the state-of-the-art GP_{rnd} implicit diversifier, and the two relevance-driven methods (GP_r and RF). All methods are parameterized with the best parameter values found in the validation set.

In the following, we fix the maximum allowed degradation in relevance at 3%, and assess the gains in diversity, in terms of all metrics, achieved by $xTReD$ and GP_{rnd} over the relevance-driven method they build upon. We choose the 3% threshold to favor the GP_{rnd} baseline since this threshold leads to the best tradeoff between relevance and diversity for that method. We note however that our $xTReD$ methods produce statistically tied relevance results even if we allow maximum diversification (as discussed in Section 6.1).

[10]The intervals are not visible in some points as they are smaller than the symbols used.

[11]Regarding the efficiency (execution time) of our methods, the training stage of the L2R-based methods (GP_r and RF) represents the only significant additional cost, but this stage can be performed entirely offline [5], thus not impacting the recommendation time.

Table 2: Results of the analyzed methods in test set. Best results (and their statistical ties) in bold.

	Method	NDCG	α-NDCG	ERR-IA	S-Recall
LastFM	GP_r	0.436	0.357	0.329	0.499
	GP_{rnd}	0.423 ▽	0.369 ∘	0.339 ∘	0.511 ∘
	$xTReD_{GP_r}$	0.439 ∘△	0.498 △△	0.458 △△	0.643 △△
	RF	**0.466** △△	0.391 △△	0.353 △△	0.563 △△
	$xTReD_{RF}$	**0.464** △△	**0.567** △△	**0.517** △△	**0.717** △△
MovieLens	GP_r	0.389	0.280	0.235	0.462
	GP_{rnd}	0.387 ∘	0.282 ∘	0.238 ∘	0.459 ∘
	$xTReD_{GP_r}$	0.389 ∘∘	0.406 △△	0.339 △△	0.633 △△
	RF	**0.404** △△	0.302 △△	0.250 △△	0.509 △△
	$xTReD_{RF}$	**0.402** △△	**0.424** △△	**0.353** △△	**0.656** △△

Table 2 shows average $NDCG$, α-$NDCG$, ERR-IA and *S-Recall* results for all methods, for both datasets. It also shows statistical significance indicators (according to a two-sided t-test with $p < 0.05$): the first indicator symbol refers to the comparison of the corresponding method against GP_r, while the second refers to the comparison against GP_{rnd}. Symbols △, ▽ and ∘ indicate significant improvement, decrease and statistical tie, respectively, with 95% confidence.

We start by comparing the state-of-the-art baselines. We find that GP_{rnd} produces only small improvements, on average, in explicit diversity (up to 3.4% in α-$NDCG$, 3.1% in ERR-IA and 2.5% in *S-Recall*). These average results are consistent with [4], which reports similar gains in terms of implicit diversity, captured by the $AILD$ metric (Section 4.1). However, due to higher variability, the average gains of GP_{rnd} in the explicit diversity metrics adopted are *not* statistically significant, as they are tied with GP_r results with 95% confidence. This is because $AILD$ promotes infrequent tags, which tend to be more dissimilar to any tag since there is little information about their co-occurrence (the source of information for $AILD$ to estimate the semantic differences between tags). On the other hand, infrequent tags also carry little information about their related topics, being less appropriate to cover the object's topics.

We now turn to our diversifier $xTReD$. Following the discussion in Section 6.1 (which was based on results of the validation set), we find that $xTReD_{GP_r}$ greatly outperforms GP_r, achieving gains of up to 45%, 44% and 37%, on average, in α-$NDCG$, ERR-IA and *S-Recall*, respectively, in the test sets. The corresponding gains of $xTReD_{RF}$ over RF reach 45%, 47% and 29%, respectively. Such gains in diversity come with no statistically significant losses in relevance in neither dataset. One might argue that our diversity improvements are expected because the diversifier exploits the same source of topics used to evaluate diversity. However, this is a valid approach because this information is commonly available in objects in the form of categories. The surprising aspect is the possibility of obtaining very large gains with no loss in relevance, as discussed in Section 6.1.

We next compare our $xTReD$ methods against the state-of-the-art GP_{rnd} baseline, which provides implicit diversification. We find that $xTReD_{GP_r}$ outperforms GP_{rnd} by as much as 44%, 43% and 38% in average α-$NDCG$, ERR-IA and *S-Recall*, respectively. The gains are larger in MovieLens, but are also quite impressive in LastFM, ranging from 26% to 35%. In terms of relevance, $xTReD_{GP_r}$ produces results with average $NDCG$ at least as good as those of GP_{rnd}, with even some modest gains (3%) in LastFM. Comparing $xTReD_{RF}$ against GP_{rnd}, we find that the former provides even further improvements in all diversity and relevance metrics, with average gains in *α-NDCG*, *ERR-IA* and *S-Recall* and *NDCG* reaching 54%, 53%, 43% and 10%, respectively. In sum, answering our second question, our explicit *xTReD* diversifier, particularly when using *RF* as the initial ranker, is much more effective than the alternative GP_{rnd} method in improving the diversity of recommendations produced by the relevance-driven strategies.

Finally, tackling our third research question, we find that our new *RF* method outperforms the state-of-the-art GP_r strategy, with statistically significant gains in all (relevance and diversity) metrics, in both datasets. The average improvements in *NDCG*, *α-NDCG*, *ERR-IA* and *S-Recall* reach 7%, 10%, 7% and 13%, respectively. Thus, the use of *RF* is a competitive alternative to GP_r, producing gains in terms not only of relevance but also diversity, even though both strategies are focused on relevance only and exploit the same set of attributes. This happens because since *RF* recommends more relevant tags in higher positions of the ranking (higher *NDCG*), these recommended tags have higher probability of being related to the topics of the target object, thus presenting a higher topic diversity. This also impacts the effectiveness of our diversifier, which is higher when *RF* is exploited as initial ranker, as discussed above.

In sum, we found that: (1) although relevance and diversity of recommendations may seem conflicting objectives, it is possible to effectively increase diversity without harming relevance with our *xTReD* diversifier, which also has the advantage of being flexible (adjustable) at recommendation time, (2) our explicit diversifier is much more effective at reducing redundancy and covering different topics of the target object than the state-of-the-art GP_{rnd} baseline, the only previous tag recommender that exploits diversity (implicitly), and (3) our new relevance-driven *RF* tag recommender outperforms the alternative, state-of-the-art GP_r in terms of not only relevance but also diversity.

7. CONCLUSIONS AND FUTURE WORK

We have addressed the problem of recommending tags for Web 2.0 objects, which are usually multifaceted, by proposing two new methods: a diversification approach (*xTReD*), which exploits an explicit taxonomy to decrease redundancy and increase the number of topics of the target object covered by the recommended tags, and a relevance-driven Random Forests (RF) based tag recommender. Our evaluation of the methods on two datasets showed that it is possible to increase the average diversity of a list of recommended tags in up to 45% with no significant impact on relevance. We also found that our explicit diversifier is much more effective than GP_{rnd}, a state-of-the-art implicit diversification strategy and the only alternative to *xTReD* in the literature, reaching gains in both diversity and relevance of 54% and 10%, respectively. Our approach also has the advantage of being adjustable at recommendation time, unlike GP_{rnd}, which requires the user to choose the weight given to the relevance/diversity tradeoff at model training time. Finally, we also found that our new RF-based recommender outperforms a state-of-the-art relevance driven Genetic Programming based method not only in terms of relevance (gains of up to 7%) but also diversity (gains of up to 10%).

As future work, we intend to deal with other aspects of the problem, such as personalization and the novelty of recommendations in the perspective of specific users. We also plan to employ multi-clustering strategies as an alternative to infer the object topics, which can be useful when no category information is available.

8. REFERENCES

[1] R. Agrawal, S. Gollapudi, A. Halverson, and S. Ieong. Diversifying search results. In *WSDM*, pages 5–14, 2009.

[2] R. Baeza-Yates and B. Ribeiro-Neto. *Modern Information Retrieval*. Addison-Wesley, 1999.

[3] W. Banzhaf, P. Nordin, R. E. Keller, and F. D. Francone. *Genetic Programming – An Introduction On The Automatic Evolution Of Computer Programs And Its Applications*. Morgan Kaufmann, 1998.

[4] F. Belém, E. Martins, J. Almeida, and M. Gonçalves. Exploiting relevance, novelty and diversity in tag recommendation. In *ECIR*, pages 380–391, 2013.

[5] F. Belém, E. Martins, T. Pontes, J. Almeida, and M. Gonçalves. Associative tag recommendation exploiting multiple textual features. In *SIGIR*, pages 1033–1042, 2011.

[6] L. Breiman. Random forests. *Machine Learning*, 45:5–32, 2001.

[7] H. Cao, M. Xie, L. Xue, C. Liu, F. Teng, and Y. Huang. Social tag prediction based on supervised ranking model. In *ECML PKDD*, pages 35–48, 2009.

[8] J. Carbonell and J. Goldstein. The use of MMR, diversity-based reranking for reordering documents and producing summaries. In *SIGIR*, pages 335–336, 1998.

[9] O. Celma and P. Herrera. A new approach to evaluating novel recommendations. In *RecSys*, pages 179–186, 2008.

[10] C. L. Clarke, N. Craswell, I. Soboroff, and A. Ashkan. A comparative analysis of cascade measures for novelty and diversity. In *WSDM*, pages 75–84, 2011.

[11] C. L. A. Clarke, N. Craswell, and E. M. Voorhees. Overview of the TREC 2012 Web track. In *TREC*, 2012.

[12] U. Feige. A threshold of $\ln(n)$ for approximating set cover. *J. ACM*, 45:634–652, 1998.

[13] F. Figueiredo, F. Belém, H. Pinto, J. Almeida, and M. Gonçalves. Assessing the quality of textual features in social media. *IP&M*, pages 222–247, 2012.

[14] P. Geurts and G. Louppe. Learning to rank with extremely randomized trees. *JMLR*, 14:49–61, 2011.

[15] D. S. Hochbaum, editor. *Approximation algorithms for NP-hard problems*. PWS Publishing Co., 1997.

[16] S. Khuller, A. Moss, and J. S. Naor. The budgeted maximum coverage problem. *Inf. Proc. Lett.*, 70:39–45, 1999.

[17] X. Li, L. Guo, and Y. E. Zhao. Tag-based social interest discovery. In *WWW*, 2008.

[18] M. Lipczak and E. Milios. Efficient tag recommendation for real-life data. *TIST*, 3(1):2:1–2:21, Oct. 2011.

[19] B. Markines, C. Cattuto, F. Menczer, D. Benz, A. Hotho, and G. Stumme. Evaluating similarity measures for emergent semantics of social tagging. In *WWW*, pages 641–650, 2009.

[20] S. Rendle and L. Schmidt-Thie. Pairwise interaction tensor factorization for personalized tag recommendation. In *WSDM*, pages 81–90, 2010.

[21] M. T. Ribeiro, A. Lacerda, A. Veloso, and N. Ziviani. Pareto-efficient hybridization for multi-objective recommender systems. In *RecSys*, pages 19–26, 2012.

[22] R. L. T. Santos, C. Macdonald, and I. Ounis. Exploiting query reformulations for web search result diversification. In *WWW*, pages 881–890, 2010.

[23] R. L. T. Santos, C. Macdonald, and I. Ounis. On the role of novelty for search result diversification. *Inf. Retr.*, 15(5):478–502, 2012.

[24] B. Sigurbjörnsson and R. Zwol. Flickr tag recommendation based on collective knowledge. In *WWW*, pages 327–336, 2008.

[25] S. Vargas and P. Castells. Rank and relevance in novelty and diversity metrics for recommender systems. In *RecSys*, pages 109–116, 2011.

[26] C. Wartena and M. Wibbels. Improving tag-based recommendation by topic diversification. In *ECIR*, pages 43–54, 2011.

[27] L. Wu, L. Yang, N. Yu, and X. Hua. Learning to tag. In *WWW*, pages 361–370, 2009.

[28] C. Zhai, W. W. Cohen, and J. Lafferty. Beyond independent relevance: Methods and evaluation metrics for subtopic retrieval. In *SIGIR*, pages 10–17, 2003.

Rating Support Interfaces to Improve User Experience and Recommender Accuracy

Tien T. Nguyen[1] Daniel Kluver[1] Ting-Yu Wang[1] Pik-Mai Hui[1]
Michael D. Ekstrand[1] Martijn C. Willemsen[2] John Riedl[1]

[1]GroupLens Research
Computer Science and Engineering
University of Minnesota
Minneapolis, MN 55455
{tien,kluver,twang,hui,ekstrand,riedl}@cs.umn.edu

[2]Human-Technology Interaction Group
School of Innovation Sciences
Eindhoven University of Technology
m.c.willemsen@tue.nl

ABSTRACT

One of the challenges for recommender systems is that users struggle to accurately map their internal preferences to external measures of quality such as ratings. We study two methods for supporting the mapping process: (i) reminding the user of characteristics of items by providing personalized tags and (ii) relating rating decisions to prior rating decisions using exemplars. In our study, we introduce interfaces that provide these methods of support. We also present a set of methodologies to evaluate the efficacy of the new interfaces via a user experiment. Our results suggest that presenting exemplars during the rating process helps users rate more consistently, and increases the quality of the data.

Categories and Subject Descriptors

H.1.2 [**Information Systems**]: User/Machine Systems—*Human information processing*; H.5.2 [**Information interfaces and presentation**]: User Interfaces—*Evaluation / methodology*

Keywords

preference elicitation; user experience; human factors; interface design; experimentation; cognitive load; recommendation accuracy

1. INTRODUCTION

Herlocker et al. coined the term *magic barrier* to refer to the supposition that there may be a lower bound on the minimum error that can be achieved by any ratings-based recommender system [9]. The idea is that user ratings include some level of noise, as evidenced by inconsistencies observed when asking users to rerate previously rated items [10]. One interpretation of the magic barrier is that it is unlikely that new algorithms can produce large decreases in recommender error. Another interpretation, and the one that motivates this research, is that if we can understand the cognitive processes that drive the magic barrier then perhaps we can create new ways for users to rate items, reducing the minimum achievable error in our systems.

Psychological research on preference construction and expression provides insight into how users go about rating items. This research suggests that most users do not form a rating at the time of consumption and store that rating in their memory [7]. Rather, they store a complex set of thoughts, feelings, perspectives and insights, and map those complex stored values into a rating when they are asked to provide one. This process is labeled preference construction [15]. There are many ways this process can go poorly, potentially increasing the noise, and raising the magic barrier.

In this work we address two likely sources of errors in the rating process. The first is that users may not clearly remember items, especially if the users experience these items a long time prior to rating them. The second is that users may struggle to accurately and consistently map their constructed preferences to the rating scale.

It seems plausible that modifying the rating interface may mitigate these problems. To that end, we study four interfaces inspired by these two key methods of support: one that is a baseline, one to help users *remember movies*, one to help users *understand their personal rating scale*, and one combined interface to help *with both* simultaneously.

We explore a novel set of methodologies to examine the effectiveness of the interfaces by performing a re-rating experiment involving 386 users and 38,586 ratings in MovieLens. We apply the information theoretic framework developed in our previous work [13], and the magic barrier framework developed by Said et al. [21] to measure the effect of our interfaces on the consistency of, and noise in, a user's ratings. Furthermore, we investigate the impact of these interfaces on cognitive load and user satisfaction via a user survey.

Noise in user rating is one of the main challenges in recommender systems. We argue that we can improve the quality of rating data by implementing interfaces that help users map their constructed preference to the rating scales better. With this in mind, our contributions are novel interface designs to collect user data with less noise, and a set of methodologies to evaluate the effectiveness of these interfaces.

RecSys'13, October 12–16, 2013, Hong Kong, China.

http://dx.doi.org/10.1145/2507157.2507188.

2. BACKGROUND

There is noise in user ratings. Such noise can occur because of inconsistencies in ratings over time [10]. There are two reasons for these inconsistencies. First, user preferences are unstable and therefore vulnerable to external influences such as anchoring effects [1] or manipulated predictions [5]. Second, users may have difficulty mapping their preferences into provided rating scales. Mapping their preferences accurately to the rating scales can be demanding for users, resulting in inconsistencies [20].

To address the noise and to increase the prediction quality, several researchers investigate the mapping process. From the algorithm perspective, reducing noise and improving predictions is possible using multiple ratings on the same user item-pair. [2]. From the interface design perspective, changing to more granular rating-scales can help recommender systems collect and produce more information about user preference [13]. However, it has been shown that more granular rating scales demand more cognitive effort from users [23], and that gaining more accurate user models sometimes can lead to decrease in user experience and user loyalty [16].

Preference elicitation research.

To inspire our interface design we turn to research of preference construction and elicitation. The field of decision making shows an 'emerging consensus' [22] towards the idea that decision makers do not have well defined preferences [3, 7]. Preferences are not easily retrieved from some master list in memory, but rather are constructed while making a decision [15] and depend strongly on the situational context and task characteristics. Researchers have recently linked these phenomena to memory processes [27]. When a person is asked to evaluate an item, a memory query will be activated to recall information that is needed for the evaluation. This query will activate knowledge and associations of the particular item that will be used to form a preference of that item. In other words the evaluation of the item will depend on how the preference for that item is (re)constructed from memory and from information provided in the interface.

One cause of rating noise is in the memory processes involved in recalling the item. As our memory is reconstructive, different aspects will come to mind at different times and in different situations [27], resulting in different constructed preferences. Our memories might also become less detailed and precise over time, and the importance of certain aspects might change, leading to our ratings' changes over time [4]. System designers help users form consistent and useful preferences by helping the user recall the item. They do this by presenting descriptions and attributes of the item that will help the user remember the item. We call these features 'memory support' as they help users remember the item.

For memory support to be helpful, we argue that it should be tailored to the user as much as possible. If we are able to predict which aspects are most important for a user, we can use these aspects to provide more effective personalized memory support than general background information. Therefore we will compare memory support interfaces using personalized tags against a minimal support interface.

Noise in ratings can also be caused by difficulty in mapping a formed preference to a rating. Past research shows strong impact of anchors [24] and task characteristics [11, 25] on rating responses, when a user lacks a good internal representation of the rating scale. While it is intuitive that three stars means less preference than four stars, it can be difficult for a user to decide (in an absolute sense) whether to rate an item three or four stars. System designers help users represent their preference by making the rating scale more intuitive. A common way to do this is by providing community guidelines mapping each rating to a simple description such as: (4 stars = 'I liked it'). We call these features 'rating support' as they help convert a preference to a formal rating. However, simple labels won't be sufficient to solve the mapping problem. Tailored rating support is needed to help the user express the evaluation in a consistent way.

Prior work on rating interface design [19] has suggested using the users' past ratings to help them make future ratings. In particular they suggest an interface in which rating options are annotated with past ratings will help people make ratings that are ordered consistently. Indeed, research on preference elicitation has investigated the differences between comparing items on their own (single evaluation) and comparing items against each other (joint evaluation) [11]. When items are evaluated in isolation, the evaluation is absolute and will be predominantly based on aspects that are easy to evaluate. Using joint evaluation allows users to be more sensitive to dimensions on which items vary. We will support joint evaluation in our interface by showing exemplars for each point on the rating scale. These exemplars will be other similar items rated in the past that serve as personalized anchors on the scale, e.g.: 'you previously rated this item 3 stars'. Research on comparative evaluation [17] suggests these exemplars should be similar to serve as good anchors otherwise it might be hard to make any comparison (or even contrast effects can occur). We will compare this interface with exemplars (supporting joint evaluation) to an interface without exemplars (single evaluation).

3. INTERFACE DESIGN

To answer the research questions, we develop four interfaces: one with minimalistic support that serves as the baseline, one that shows tags, one that provides exemplars, and another that combines the previous two features (figures 1).

Figure 1a presents the baseline design allowing users to map their internal preferences into ratings. To assist our users in the rating process, we provide basic information such as posters and titles. However, posters and titles might not provide sufficient memory support. Therefore, we design the tag interface that provides personalized memory support.

3.1 The Tag Interface

In our design process, we look for a personalizable form of memory support that easily triggers the recall process. While some users remember a movie because it is funny, others remember the movie because it is visually appealing. To provide personalized information about the movie, we use the tag genome [26] combined with users' previous ratings. The tag genome is a tag-movie relevance matrix, inferred from user-supplied tags, ratings, and external textual sources. The relevance of a tag t to a movie m determined by the tag genome is a value between 0 and 1 denoted as $rel(t, m)$. We remove two classes of tags from the genome prior to rendering our interfaces. The first is tags such as 'excellent' and 'great' that indicate a general quality judgement of the movie; these are redundant with ratings and do not provide any information about the movie. The second is binary metadata tags such as directors, actors, 'based on a book', etc. These tags

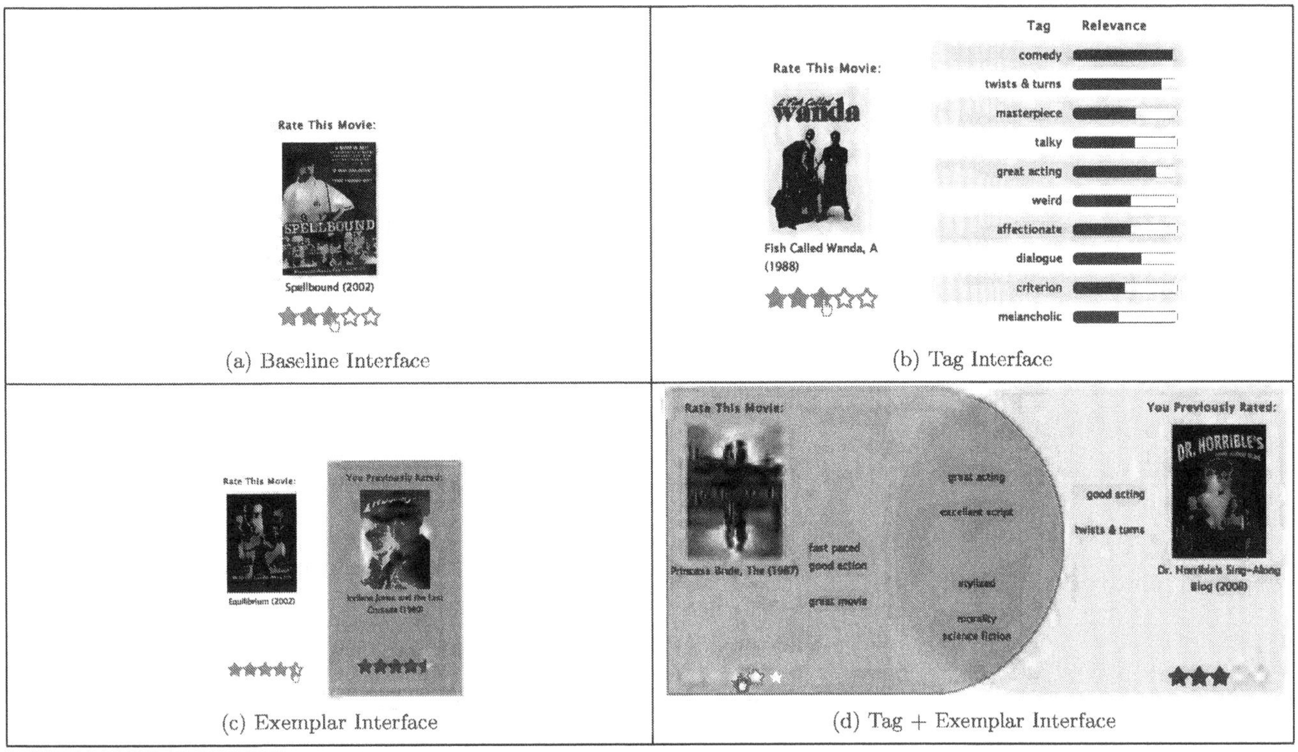

Figure 1: Our four interface designs to provide memory-support, rating support and joint-evaluation support.

describe properties that are objectively verifiable and either true or false; it is incorrect to infer them when they are not explicitly added to the item. Future work should build a way to incorporate such metadata tags, but for now we restrict our use of the tag genome to tags for which inference makes sense. Figure 1b shows the tag interface.

To personalize the interface, we select tags that best help users reconstruct their memory about the movies. Due to the limited space on the interface, only a set of 10 personalized tags from 1574 candidates can be displayed. To address this problem, we use Nguyen et al.'s approach [18] to compute how much information about user u's preference a tag t can tell, denoted as $pMI(t, u)$. We hypothesize that the more information a tag can tell about user u's preference, the more likely it is helpful to the user. Moreover, a useful tag must be sufficiently relevant to the movie. Therefore, we require that any selected tag must have a minimum relevance of 0.25.

Similar tags, such as 'political' and 'world politics', diminish the effectiveness of memory support if they are displayed together. To address this challenge, we place a similarity constraint on the tag selection algorithm. Our prototyping suggests that mutual information between tags works well. Formally, let $P(t_1)$ be the probability that tag t_1 is applied to a random movie, $P(t_1, t_2)$ be the joint-probability that tags t_1 and t_2 are both applied to a random movie. Hence, the tag similarity, denoted as $dTagsim(t_1, t_2)$, is defined as $dTagSim(t_1, t_2) = \frac{I(t_1,t_2)}{H(t_2)}$, where $I(t_1, t_2)$ is the mutual information of the two tags, and $H(t_2)$ is the entropy of tag t_2. Note that dTagSim, or directed tag similarity, is asymmetric, i.e. $dTagSim(t_1, t_2) \neq dTagSim(t_2, t_1)$. After several trials, we find that 1% (0.01)to be a reasonable cut-off.

With these concepts laid out, our tag selection approach is a constrained optimization problem described as follow:

$$\begin{aligned} &\underset{T^\star}{\text{argmax}} \sum_{t \in T^\star} rel(t,i) \times pMI(t,u) \\ &\text{subject to } \mid T^\star \mid = 10 \\ &\qquad dTagSim(t_i, t_j) < 1\% \;\; \forall\, t_i, t_j \in T^\star,\ i \neq j \\ &\qquad rel(t,i) > 0.25 \;\; \forall\, t \in T^\star \end{aligned}$$

Since finding sets of perfect personalized tags is computationally expensive, we implement a greedy algorithm to find an approximate solution. Starting with an empty set of tags, the algorithm iteratively selects the tag with the highest $rel(t, i) \times pMI(t, u)$ such that when added to the result the constraints are still satisfied.

3.2 The Exemplar Interface

The exemplar interface improves upon the baseline by showing exemplars. An exemplar for a rating-movie pair is a movie that the user previously gave the same rating. Figure 1c shows the design of the exemplar interface. To support the joint evaluation, we provide anchoring points by annotating rating options with the exemplars. Each exemplar at a specific rating option is the most similar movie to the movie to rate based on the cosine similarity of the movie rating vectors. At any star on the rating scale, if the user has not rated any movie, a blank image is shown.

3.3 The Tag + Exemplar Interface

To investigate the effect of combining 'memory support' and 'rating support', we develop the fourth interface as seen in figure 1d. In this interface, users make use of personalized tags to compare their rated movies to the movie to rate. When users hover over a star, an exemplar is shown. Each tag then moves either flush left, or flush right to denote which movie the tag is more relevant to (the movie to rate or the exemplar respectively). The tag will move to the center if the tag is equally relevant to both movies (relevance values within 0.1 of each other). To help the users understand the movement of the tags a Venn diagram is shown in the background of the interface. This diagram reinforces the idea that tags on one side or the other best describe the associated movie, and tags in the center describe both movies equally well.

The tag + exemplar interface uses the same exemplar selection strategy as the exemplar interface. Selecting tags, however, is more complicated in this interface. We want tags that not only are relevant to the user and movie, but also may help the user compare between movies. We measure this in two ways. First, for each tag t we measure $\sigma(t)$ the standard deviation of the relevance values of each chosen exemplar to that tag. If a tag's relevance varies greatly between the exemplars then it can help serve to differentiate them.

Secondly, we measure how well a tag splits between being more relevant to the movie to rate, or the exemplars. If a tag is always more relevant to the movie to rate, or always more relevant to the exemplars, then the tag does not help the user compare the different rating choices. To measure this we define $Z(i,t) = \frac{\max(M_t, L_t)}{\min(M_t, L_t)}$, where M_t is the number of exemplars to which tag t has higher relevance than to the movies to rate, and L_t is the number of exemplars to which tag t has lower relevances than to the movies to rate. When the tag would appear with the exemplar as often as with the movie to rate then $Z(i,t) = 1$, as the balance becomes less equal $Z(i,t)$ becomes larger.

Our algorithm for this tag + exemplar interface is also a constraint optimization problem described as follow:

$$\begin{aligned} &\underset{T^\star}{\operatorname{argmax}} \sum_{t \in T^\star} rel(t,i) \times pMI(t,u) \times \sigma(t) \div Z(i,t) \\ &\text{subject to } \mid T^\star \mid = 10 \\ &\qquad dTagSim(t_i, t_j) < 1\% \ \forall\, t_i, t_j, \in T^\star,\ i \neq j \end{aligned}$$

Since finding sets of perfect personalized tags is computationally expensive, we implement a greedy algorithm to find an approximate solution. Starting with an empty set of tags, the algorithm iteratively selects the tag with the highest $rel(t,i) \times pMI(t,u) \times \sigma(t) \div Z(i,t)$ such that when added to the result the constraints are still satisfied.

4. EXPERIMENTAL DESIGN

To compare the our interfaces, we ask users to rate 50 movies, and re-rate these movies after at least two weeks. Users are asked to answer 22 survey questions after finishing the second round. To help users understand the interfaces, we provide a tutorial for each interface explaining the interface and walking users through the interface step by step. Our analyses are based on techniques described as below.

4.1 Efficacy Metrics

RMSE.

One of the hopes in improving rating quality is to reduce the magic barrier of a recommendation system. One easy to measure consequence of reducing the magic barrier is to reduce the RMSE of a recommendation system. To measure this effect we estimate the minimum RMSE possible over the ratings using the technique introduced by Said et al. [21]. Said et al. argue that the average variance of ratings (measured at each user item pair) gives an estimate of the minimum possible RMSE over these ratings. If any of our interfaces lower the magic barrier we should see a lower minimum RMSE. To confirm our findings with this method we also build simple item-item recommenders for each interface and compare the RMSE on these interfaces directly.

Although the RMSE quality metrics can suggest that we have lowered the magic barrier, these metrics do not capture the whole picture of rating quality. For example, RMSE can trivially be reduced by influencing users to use a smaller range of the rating scale, which would lead to overall less informative ratings. An absolute measure of the information and noise contained in ratings could be a more useful tool in evaluating the efficacy of the interfaces. Therefore, in the next two sub-sections, we propose approaches to measuring the amount of noise and information about user preferences in ratings collected from each interface.

Preference Bits per Rating.

In prior work [13] we showed how to measure the preference bits of ratings from an interface. This framework can be used to estimate the total amount of information ratings contain about user preferences. An increase in preference bits from any interface would indicate that ratings on that interface tell us more about users' preferences.

We measure preference bits by gathering two ratings for each user-item pair and computing the mutual information between the two sets of ratings. This measures how much the first round of ratings reduces our uncertainty about ratings in the second round, providing a lower bound for the information that one rating contains about the preference that caused it. If ratings on one interface give us more information about user preferences than ratings on another interface, we say that the interface is more effective at eliciting preference.

Rating Noise.

It is possible for ratings from different interfaces to contain the same amount of information with different amounts of noise. Therefore, even if our interfaces yield the same amount of preference information, we may still prefer one with less noise. Information theory gives us a clear way of measuring the amount of noise contained in our ratings.

Let π and R be random variables representing the user's true preference for, and rating on, an item respectively. The total randomness in ratings is measured by the entropy of the ratings $H(R)$. Relative to any other random variable X, the entropy of R can be split into two parts, the mutual information $I(R;X)$ measuring the amount of information R contains about X, and the conditional entropy of R given X, $H(R|X)$. Taking this decomposition with respect to the user's true preference π we get the following identity.

$$H(R) = I(R;\pi) + H(R|\pi) \tag{1}$$

Based on equation 1, we will measure the amount of noise contained in ratings by the conditional entropy of a rating given the user's preference, $H(R|\pi)$. Because true preference π cannot be measured we will have to estimate the true rating noise. In our previous work [13] we showed that we can estimate the true preference bits using two ratings for the same user-item pair taken at different times R_1, R_2,. We prove a similar result about the rating noise. Formally in previous work we showed:

$$I(R;\pi) < I(R_1;R_2) \tag{2}$$

Using equations 1 and 2 we have the following:

$$H(R|\pi) = H(R) - I(R;\pi) < H(R_1) - I(R_1;R_2) = H(R_1|R_2)$$

The conditional entropy between two ratings is therefore an upper limit to the true rating noise. We will use this metric as an estimate of the true rating noise of our interfaces. Because recommendation algorithms are likely sensitive to noise in the ratings, we hypothesize that we can learn better from ratings with less total noise.

4.2 User Experience Metrics

Objective User Experience (Cognitive Load).

Harper et al. [8] investigate motivations behind user rating behaviors in a recommender system domain, and find that users perceive rating-time costs when they provided ratings. Harper et al. also point out that the users keep providing ratings when they perceive that the benefits outweigh the costs they pay. Sparling et al. [23] investigate further to estimate the mental cost and benefits on different rating scales. Since accurately measuring user mental costs is hard, we follow Sparling et al.'s approach to use rating time to estimate cognitive load. We use this metric, as well the user experience metric below, to evaluate the trade-offs between getting more information about user preference and overloading users.

Subjective User Experience (Self-report).

To learn how users perceive the usefulness and difficulty of the four interfaces, we conclude our experiment with a survey. We then follow Knijnenburg et al.'s [14] evaluation framework for user experience. The framework models how objective system aspects such as the user interface influence users' subjective perceptions and experience, controlling for other factors such as situational characteristics and personal characteristics. Particularly, we measure how usefulness of the system (experience) is influenced by the perceived difficulty of the system (subjective system aspect), and how each of these are affected differently by the 4 different interfaces, controlling for the self-reported expertise as a personal characteristic. The survey consists of 22 7-likert-scale statements, ranging from 'Strongly disagree' to 'Strongly agree', that query the theoretical constructs of interest: usefulness of the interface, difficulty of the interface and self-reported movie expertise. Some questions are inverted to check users responses for coherence and lack of effort. Participants have to answer all questions. They can change their answers before submission. Participants can provide extra feedback in a text-box. We also ask (but not require) participants' age and gender.

4.3 Design

We conduct our study with users of MovieLens,[1] an online collaborative filtering-based movie recommender system. In order to make our algorithms work on these interfaces, we select only users who have rated at least 100 movies that have both tag genome and Netflix title data available. We also require that the 100 ratings be provided since MovieLens changed to its current half-star rating scales [2]. Finally, we require that users have logged in at least once during the last four years. After preparing data for the experiment (2013-03-01), we randomly invited 3829 users via email invitations. The users were randomly assigned to one of the four interfaces.

Our participants are asked to rate 50 movies in the first round, and re-rate these 50 movies in the second round. To simulate the real rating experience, the participants are asked to rate the most recent 50 movies that they rated prior to the study. To avoid users recalling recently rated movies, we wait at least 14 days after data preparation before inviting users to participate in our study (round 1). This guarantees that at least two weeks have passed since the user last rated the selected movies in MovieLens. For the same reason, we also wait 14 days before starting round 2. After finishing the second round, participants are asked to complete a survey asking their experience with the interfaces as well as the rating process. For each 20 participants, a randomly selected one receives a $50 Amazon Gift card.

5. RESULTS

Our experiment ran from March 21st 2013 until April 25th 2013, collecting 38,586 [4] ratings from 386 users, of which 103 users were assigned the baseline interface, 100 to the exemplar interface, 98 to the tags interface, and 85 to the tags + exemplars interface. 352 provided information about age (mean: 36, min: 18, max: 81, σ : 11). 304 were male, 72 female, and 10 did not report. Our analyses don't reveal significant differences between the two genders.

5.1 Efficacy Metrics

RMSE.

We follow the procedure described in [21] to estimate the minimum RMSE for each interface. The estimated minimum RMSE for our interfaces are given in table 1. To test these differences for statistical significance we compute an estimated minimum RMSE for each user. Using an ANOVA on the per user minimum RMSE estimates we find marginal significance that the average per-user minimum RMSE differs between interfaces ($p = 0.0574$). Using a TukeyHSD we find marginal evidence that the exemplar interface has a lower average minimum RMSE than the tag and baseline interfaces (adjusted $p = 0.0689$, 0.098 respectively).

To control for possible error in the ANOVA due to violations of the normality assumption we confirm these results with a pairwise Wilcoxon rank sum test over the per user minimum RMSE using the Holm method to correct for multiple comparisons. We find that the minimum RMSE is significantly different between the exemplar interface and baseline($p < 0.005$), however, we find only minimal support for the conclusion that the exemplar interface differs significantly from the tag interface ($p = 0.208$). Therefore we conservatively conclude that the only significant pairwise difference in our minimum RMSE estimates is between exemplar and baseline.

To compare these results against actual predictive accuracy we use the LensKit toolkit [6] to train and evaluate an item-item collaborative filtering recommender over the ratings from the four interfaces. We use 10-fold cross validation with a 10 item holdout set for each test user. Table 1 shows the per-user RMSE of each condition for each round. The exemplar interface has the lowest RMSE in both rounds. The measured RMSEs are significantly different ($p < 0.001$ using ANOVA on the user RMSEs); the exemplar had lower RMSE than the baseline in round 1 ($p < 0.001$ using Tukey HSD

[1]http://www.movielens.org/

[2]We estimate that MovieLens switched to a five-rating-star with half-star increment on 2003-02-12

[4]Due to network issues, we had 14 incomplete ratings which were removed from all of the analyses.

Interface	Minimum RMSE	RMSE (round 1)	RMSE (round 2)	Preference Bits per Rating [3]	Rating Noise	Mean Rating Time	Median Rating Time
Baseline	0.232	1.13	1.12	1.26	1.71	4.26	3.71
Exemplar	0.209	0.95	0.95	1.22	1.62	5.53	4.60
Tag	0.237	1.03	1.10	1.22	1.72	4.49	4.07
Tag + Exemplar	0.227	1.04	1.01	1.25	1.70	6.70	5.60

Table 1: Our quantitative results for four interfaces

post-hoc test), and both the baseline and tag interfaces differ significantly in round 2 ($p < 0.05$).

Preference Bits per Rating.

We estimate preference bits using the technique described in [13]. The results are summarized in table 1.

To our knowledge significance testing on information theoretic values is not a widely studied field. Therefore, to test for significance in our measured mutual information differences we use a resampling based strategy to test each pairwise difference. Under the null hypothesis ratings from any two interfaces are drawn from the same distribution (and therefore have the same true mutual information). To test for differences between any two conditions we randomly permute the assignments of users to conditions. It is important to permute interface labels over users rather than ratings to control for outlier users who rate with significantly more or less information or noise than the average user. For each permutation we compute the difference in means of measured mutual information between the two conditions. We reject our null hypothesis if fewer than 5% of our random trials have differences of means as large or larger than observed. We perform this test using 10000 permutations and find that no pairwise difference in mutual information is statistically significant. Therefore we do not have sufficient evidence to conclude that our interface modifications had a significant effect on the amount of preference information extracted.

Rating Noise.

The preference noise of an interface is estimated by the conditional entropy of the first rating given the second rating in a rerating dataset. The conditional entropy estimates for each interface can be seen in table 1. The rating noise metric generally agrees with the RMSE based metrics, especially in measuring the exemplar interface as having the least noise. To test these measurements for differences we use the same resampling strategy discussed above. Using 10000 random permutations we find that no pairwise difference in conditional entropies is significant. Therefore we do not have sufficient evidence to conclude that our interface modifications had a significant effect on rating noise.

It is interesting to note that while we are not able to conclude that our interfaces have an effect on rating noise, we are still able to conclude effects on the RMSE of the ratings. This result is contrary to our belief that noise in user ratings is a primary cause of the magic barrier. We expect this finding is largely due to differences in power between our statistical tests for rating noise, and the RMSE based metrics. Because statistics on information theoretic measures is a not-well explored field of statistics, it is possible that analysis with a more powerful technique would allow us to find significance in our rating noise metric that match the results found in the RMSE section. Nonetheless we feel that the rating noise metric is a better metric for future use because it directly measures the noise in ratings, rather than measuring a consequence of this noise.

5.2 User Experience Metrics

Objective User Experience (Cognitive Load).

Cognitive load is estimated by measuring the time it takes users to rate a movie. We assume that it will take users time to process the information when using interfaces. A good interface could decrease the cognitive load and time required.

Before analyzing the rating times, we first exclude long rating times that occur because users are distracted during rating or take a break. Such long times introduce bias in our analysis since these rating times do not reflect real users' cognitive loads. We exclude the top 1% of the data points for each interface, resulting in cut-off points of 41 seconds for the baseline interface, 43 seconds for the tag interface, 55 seconds for the exemplar interface, and 79 seconds for the tag + exemplar interface.

As users made 50 ratings in each round, we take the average rating time per round as an estimated measure of cognitive load. Table 1 shows the statistics of rating time per interface aggregated over both rounds. Our ANOVA analyses suggest that the required cognitive load for the baseline and tags interfaces be the smallest among the four ($p < 0.01$). The difference between the two interfaces is not significant ($p = 0.29$). This suggests that users do not take advantage of the memory support provided by the tags interface. Participants spent the most time on the tag + exemplar interface, followed by the exemplar interface (The difference is significant, $p < 0.0001$). All other pairwise comparison are also significant ($p < 0.0001$). This suggests that users utilize the supports provided by the two exemplar empowered interfaces [5].

Subjective User Experience (Self-report).

Our questionnaire was designed to measure user experience of usefulness and difficulty of the interface and participant's expertise. The items in the questionnaires were submitted to a confirmatory factor analysis (CFA). The CFA used ordinal dependent variables and a weighted least squares estimator, estimating 3 factors. Items with low factor loadings, high cross-loadings, or high residual correlations were removed from the analysis. Factor loadings of included items are shown in table 2, as well as Cronbach's alpha and average variance extracted (AVE) for each factor. The values of AVE and Cronbach's alpha are good, indicating convergent validity. The square roots of the AVEs are higher than any of the factor correlations, indicating good discriminant validity.

The subjective constructs from the CFA (table 2) were organized into a path model using a confirmatory structural equation modeling (SEM) approach with ordinal dependent variables and a weighted least squares estimator. In the resulting model, the subjective constructs are structurally

[5] we also perform multilevel linear regression analysis with random intercepts that also take into account the 50 repeated observations per round, with similar results. We also apply separate ANOVA analyses for two rounds, and observe that in the second round, there is a marginal significant difference between the two exemplar empowered interfaces $p = 0.068$)

Considered Aspects	Items	Factor Loading
Usefulness Alpha: 0.83 AVE: 0.546	MovieLens should use this interface	0.89
	The interface helped me think carefully about how much I liked the movie	0.70
	The interface helped me express my ratings consistently	0.66
	The interface did not make rating easier compared to the usual MovieLens rating interface	-0.71
	Rating movies with this interface was fun	0.71
	The interface helped me to remember what I like and dislike about movies	
	I found the interface helpful in relating a movie to other movies I have seen	
	The interface did not motivate me to think carefully about my ratings	
	I know of other sites with rating interfaces I would rather use than this one	
	I would recommend this interface to other users	
Difficulty Alpha: 0.84 AVE: 0.71	I found the interface confusing	0.86
	The interface was easy to understand	-0.86
	I found the interface difficult to use	-0.82
	Rating with this interface was fast	
	Rating with this interface was easy	
Movie Expertise Alpha: 0.68 AVE: 0.55	I'm a movie lover	0.75
	Compared to people I know, I read a lot about movies	0.85
	Compared to people I know, I'm not an expert on movies	-0.61
	I mostly like popular movies	
	I get very excited about some upcoming movies	
	I know why I like the movies I like	
	I often like to compare a new movie to others I've seen	

Table 2: Items presented in the questionnaires. Items without a factor loading were excluded from the analysis.

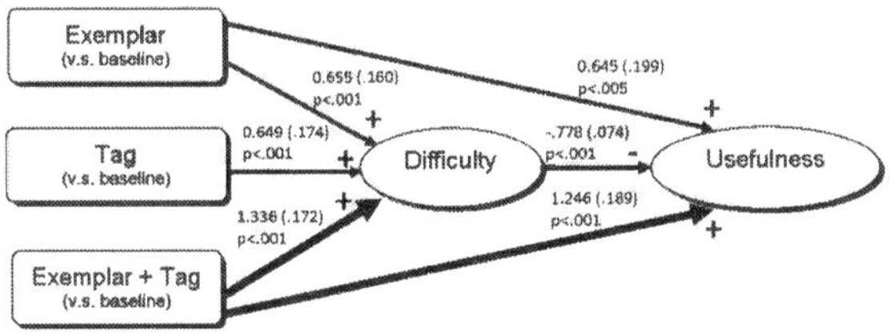

Figure 2: The structural equation model fitted on the Subject constructs difficulty and usefulness and their relations to the 4 interfaces

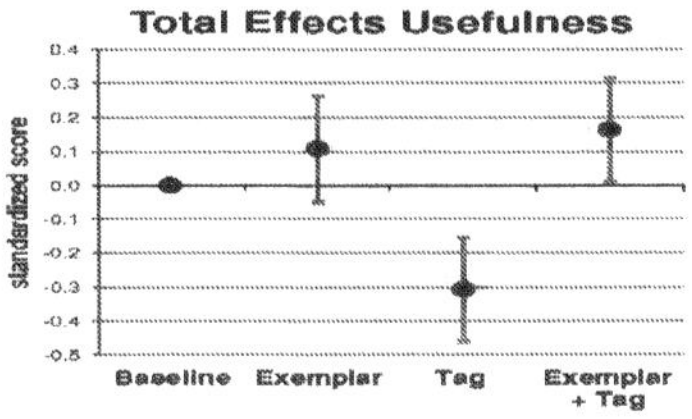

Figure 3: Total effects of the interfaces on usefulness: error bars are 1 standard error of the mean. Comparisons are made against the baseline interface.

related to each other and to the 4 interface types. In the final model, the expertise factor did not relate to any other variable, and was therefore removed from the analysis. The final model had a good model fit [6] ($\chi^2(52) = 3408$, $p < .001$, CFI = 0.979, TLI = 0.971, RMSEA = .070, 90% CI: [.054, .085]). Figure 2 displays the effects found in this model. Factor scores in the final model are standardized; the numbers on the arrows ($A \to B$) denote the estimated mean difference in B, measured in standard deviations, between participants that differ one standard deviation in A. The number in parentheses denotes the standard error of this estimate, and the p-value below these two numbers denotes the statistical significance of the effect. As per convention, we exclude effects with $p >= .05$. The three interfaces are compared to the baseline interface. The SEM model shows that all three interfaces are seen as more difficult than the baseline condition, with the exemplar + tag interface having roughly twice the impact (1.336) as the exemplar (0.655) and tag (0.649) interfaces. Both interfaces with exemplars are perceived more useful than the baseline interface, with the exemplar + tag interface almost twice as useful than the baseline as the exemplar interface. The tag interface is not more useful than the baseline (no significant loading). Reviewing the total structure of the model we observe that difficulty loads negatively on usefulness: the interfaces that are more difficult are also perceived as less useful. We should therefore inspect the total effects on usefulness, which are plotted in figure 3. Compared to the baseline interface the two exemplar-powered interfaces are only slightly more useful (differences not significant) because their difficulty stands in the way of a much better user experience. This suggests that one could increase the user experience of these interfaces by making them less difficult (i.e less confusing, easier to understand), which should increase their perceived usefulness. Note that the total effect on usefulness suggests that the tag interface is actually perceived to be less useful than the baseline ($p<.05$) mainly because it is more difficult than the baseline. Thus the tag interface is seen as worse than the baseline interface.

[6]Hu and Bentler [12] propose cut-off values for the fit indices to be: CFI > .96, TLI > .95, and RMSEA < .05, with the upper bound of its 90% CI falling below 0.10

6. DISCUSSION

Our user survey reveals that in general providing rating support, as in the exemplar interface, helps users rate more consistently. Although our participants felt that the interfaces providing rating support are more difficult than our baseline interface, they liked these interfaces because they perceived the interfaces to be more useful. Several participants requested to see these interfaces implemented on MovieLens. This is consistent with our quantitative analyses. Between the two interfaces providing rating support, the exemplar one appears to have the lowest RMSE, the lowest minimum RMSE, and the least amount of natural noise.

Our quantitative analyses, however, show that reminding users of movie features in personalized fashion, as in the tag interface, did not help to improve the rating quality or the perceived usefulness of the interface. Our participants perceived the tag-interface as more difficult than the baseline. One potential reason for this is our tag selection algorithm. It is possible that an improved algorithm would select tags that have a more positive effect on the user.

The SEM analysis shows that the perceived usefulness and difficulty of our interfaces is related. This correlation is what led to having only small gains in total usefulness. While our interfaces had a positive effect on usefulness, they also had an opposite effect by being more perceived difficult. This leads us to believe that efforts simplifying our interfaces could significantly improve the user experience.

One of the contributions of this work is an exploration of a set of methodologies to evaluate rating interfaces. It is important that we have techniques for comparing novel recommender interfaces. Future work should continue exploring methodologies for comparing interfaces. Many of our metrics required a large amount of data to give statistically significant results, and metrics such as RMSE should be suspect when too few ratings are used. Likewise, while we feel the information theoretic metrics can be very informative, more work is still needed to develop robust techniques for comparing information theoretic values.

Improving prediction accuracy is one of the main interests in recommender system research, both in academia and in industry. For example, Netflix awarded \$ 1 million dollars to a research team for the 10% of improvement in prediction accuracy[7]. Our efforts modifying recommender interfaces to gather high quality data with less noise complement the efforts to improve prediction accuracy. Overall we see the results of this work, and feedback from our participants, as promising. We believe that future work building upon our interfaces, algorithms, and methodologies can help us improve recommender systems.

7. ACKNOWLEDGEMENT

This work is supported by the NSF grants IIS 09-68483, IIS 08-08692, and IIS 10-17697. We also thank Professor Joseph A. Konstan for his helps during the revision.

8. REFERENCES

[1] G. Adomavicius, J. Bockstedt, S. Curley, and J. Zhang. Recommender systems, consumer preferences, and anchoring effects. In *Decisions@RecSys Workshop*, pages 35–42, Chicago, 2011.

[2] X. Amatriain, J. M. Pujol, N. Tintarev, and N. Oliver. Rate it again: increasing recommendation accuracy by user re-rating. In *In Proc. of RecSys '09*, pages 173 – 180, New York, NY, USA, 2009. ACM.

[3] J. R. Bettman, M. F. Luce, and J. W. Payne. Constructive consumer choice processes. *Journal of Consumer Research*, 25(3):187 – 217, Dec. 1998. ArticleType: research-article / Full publication date: December 1998 / Copyright ©1998 Journal of Consumer Research Inc.

[4] D. Bollen, M. Graus, and M. C. Willemsen. Remembering the stars?: effect of time on preference retrieval from memory. In *In Proc. of RecSys '12*, pages 217 – 220, New York, NY, USA, 2012. ACM.

[5] D. Cosley, S. K. Lam, I. Albert, J. A. Konstan, and J. Riedl. Is seeing believing?: how recommender system interfaces affect users' opinions. In *In Proc. of CHI '03*, pages 585–592, New York, NY, USA, 2003. ACM.

[6] M. D. Ekstrand, M. Ludwig, J. A. Konstan, and J. T. Riedl. Rethinking the recommender research ecosystem: reproducibility, openness, and LensKit. In *In Proc. of RecSys '11*, pages 133 – 140, New York, NY, USA, 2011. ACM.

[7] B. Fischhoff. Value elicitation: Is there anything in there? *American Psychologist*, 46(8):835–847, 1991.

[8] F. M. Harper, X. Li, Y. Chen, and J. A. Konstan. An economic model of user rating in an online recommender system. In *User Modeling 2005*, pages 307–316. Springer, 2005.

[9] J. L. Herlocker, J. A. Konstan, L. G. Terveen, and J. T. Riedl. Evaluating collaborative filtering recommender systems. *ACM Transactions on Information Systems*, 22(1):5–53, 2010.

[10] W. Hill, L. Stead, M. Rosenstein, and G. Furnas. Recommending and evaluating choices in a virtual community of use. In *In Proc. of CHI '95*, pages 194–201, New York, NY, USA, 1995.

[11] C. K. Hsee. The evaluability hypothesis: An explanation for preference reversals between joint and separate evaluations of alternatives. *Organizational Behavior and Human Decision Processes*, 67(3):247–257, Sept. 1996.

[12] L.-t. Hu and P. Bentler. Cutoff criteria for fit indexes in covariance structure analysis: Conventional criteria versus new alternatives. *Structural Equation Modeling: A Multidisciplinary Journal*, 6(1):1–55, 1999.

[13] D. Kluver, T. T. Nguyen, M. Ekstrand, S. Sen, and J. Riedl. How many bits per rating? In *In Proc. of RecSys '12*, pages 99 – 106, New York, NY, USA, 2012. ACM.

[14] B. P. Knijnenburg, M. C. Willemsen, Z. Gantner, H. Soncu, and C. Newell. Explaining the user experience of recommender systems. *User Modeling and User-Adapted Interaction*, 22(4-5):441–504, Mar. 2012.

[15] S. Lichtenstein and P. Slovic. *The Construction of Preference*. Cambridge University Press, Sept. 2006.

[16] S. M. McNee, S. K. Lam, J. A. Konstan, and J. Riedl. Interfaces for eliciting new user preferences in recommender systems. In P. Brusilovsky, A. Corbett, and F. d. Rosis, editors, *User Modeling 2003*, number 2702 in Lecture Notes in Computer Science, pages 178–187. Springer Berlin Heidelberg, Jan. 2003.

[17] T. Mussweiler. Comparison processes in social judgment: Mechanisms and consequences. *Psychological Review*, 110(3):472–489, 2003.

[18] T. T. Nguyen and J. Riedl. Predicting users' preference from tag relevance. *User Modeling, Adaptation, and Personalization, UMAP 2013*, pages 274–280, 2013.

[19] S. Nobarany, L. Oram, V. K. Rajendran, C.-H. Chen, J. McGrenere, and T. Munzner. The design space of opinion measurement interfaces: exploring recall support for rating and ranking. In *In Proc. of CHI '12*, pages 2035 – 2044, New York, NY, USA, 2012. ACM.

[20] M. P. O'Mahony, N. J. Hurley, and G. C. Silvestre. Detecting noise in recommender system databases. In *Proceedings of the 11th international conference on Intelligent user interfaces*, IUI '06, pages 109 – 115, New York, NY, USA, 2006. ACM.

[21] A. Said, B. J. Jain, S. Narr, and T. Plumbaum. Users and noise: The magic barrier of recommender systems. In *UMAP 2012*, pages 237–248. Springer, 2012.

[22] I. Simonson. Determinants of customers' responses to customized offers: Conceptual framework and research propositions. *Journal of Marketing*, 69(1):32–45, Jan. 2005.

[23] E. I. Sparling and S. Sen. Rating: how difficult is it? In *In Proc. of RecSys '11*, pages 149 – 156, New York, NY, USA, 2011. ACM.

[24] A. Tversky and D. Kahneman. Judgment under uncertainty: Heuristics and biases. *Science*, 185(4157):1124–1131, Sept. 1974.

[25] A. Tversky, S. Sattath, and P. Slovic. Contingent weighting in judgment and choice. *Psychological Review*, 95(3):371–384, 1988.

[26] J. Vig, S. Sen, and J. Riedl. The tag genome: Encoding community knowledge to support novel interaction. *ACM Trans. Interact. Intell. Syst.*, 2(3):13:1 – 13:44, Sept. 2012.

[27] E. U. Weber and E. J. Johnson. Mindful judgment and decision making. In *Annual Review of Psychology*, volume 60, pages 53–85. Annual Reviews, Palo Alto, 2009.

[7] http://www.netflixprize.com

ReComment: Towards Critiquing-based Recommendation with Speech Interaction

Peter Grasch
Institute for Software Technology
Graz University of Technology
Inffeldgasse 16b/II
8010 Graz, Austria
peter.grasch@ist.tugraz.at

Alexander Felfernig
Institute for Software Technology
Graz University of Technology
Inffeldgasse 16b/II
8010 Graz, Austria
afelfern@ist.tugraz.at

Florian Reinfrank
Institute for Software Technology
Graz University of Technology
Inffeldgasse 16b/II
8010 Graz, Austria
freinfra@ist.tugraz.at

ABSTRACT

In contrast to search-based approaches, critiquing-based recommender systems provide a navigation-based interface where users are enabled to critique displayed recommendations as a means of preference elicitation. In this paper we present RECOMMENT, our approach to natural language based unit critiquing. We discuss the developed prototype and present the corresponding user interface. In order to show the applicability of our concepts, we present the results of a user study. This study shows that speech interfaces have the potential to improve the perceived ease of use as well as the overall quality of recommendations.

Categories and Subject Descriptors

H.4.2 [**Information System Applications**]: Types of System – Decision support; H.5.2 [**Information Interfaces and Presentation**]: User Interfaces – Evaluation/methodology, Interaction styles, Natural language, Voice I/O

Keywords

Knowledge-based recommender systems; critiquing-based recommendation; speech interfaces; applied speech recognition

1. INTRODUCTION

Critiquing-based recommender systems are a form of conversational recommender systems that employ user-articulated critiques on the currently recommended item as a means of preference elicitation. Over the last decade these systems have attracted a significant amount of academic interest and have repeatedly shown to provide high quality recommendations while requiring relatively little effort from the user [7, 16, 18].

A multitude of different approaches to critiquing-based recommendation have been proposed over the years. Unit critiquing based recommenders use a single, directional critique of the recommended item to improve their recommendations [4]. For example, the unit critique 'less' on the attribute 'price' would cause the recommender system to search for a cheaper product [6, 13]. So-called compound critiques may be used to critique multiple attributes in the course of a single feedback cycle [14]. Different approaches of finding the optimal set of compound critiques to present to the user have been explored with the apriori method outlined in [14], and especially the application of multi-attribute utility theory described in [25] being particularly notable. Orthogonally to the used critiquing method, valuable information may also be extracted from the users evolving preferences over the course of a recommendation session by maintaining a user preference model. For example, incremental critiquing systems keep track of recent critiques in a recommendation session and try to find products that not only fit the current- but also previously articulated critiques [21]. More recently, an experience-based critiquing approach has been introduced that uses the final, accepted product of similar critiquing sessions (of different users) as the next recommendation [15]. This approach has since been improved upon with the introduction of nearest neighbor compatibility critiquing that selects the product of a comparable critiquing session that best fits the current users preference model as the next recommendation [12].

Clearly, a substantial body of research has been dedicated to help improve critiquing-based recommenders by employing intelligent prediction algorithms. The major motivation of this work is to reduce the number of interaction (critiquing) cycles needed to identify an item of relevance for the user. With the same goal but a different approach we introduce a natural language interface for unit critiquing based recommenders.

Natural language interfaces have remained largely unexplored in existing recommender systems that instead support user interactions through mouse, keyboard, and touch devices. While natural language processing remains a hard task in general, its complexity in severely limited domains is manageable [2]. Some fundamentals of applied dialog systems for recommender systems are discussed in [1] and a prototype of a natural language speech-based recommender system, the Adaptive Place Advisor, was presented in [24]. The latter proved to be promising, but user feedback was limited to providing specific attribute values which may be unsuitable for more complex domains where users are less aware of the problem space and preferences are subject to incompleteness or rapid change [22]. Recently, a speech-based natural language recommender system was mentioned as a promising future research direction in [8].

The major contributions of this paper are the following. We present RECOMMENT[1], a speech-based unit critiquing-based recommender system that demonstrates how speech recognition can

RecSys'13, October 12–16, 2013, Hong Kong, China.

ACM 978-1-4503-2409-0/13/09 ...$15.00.
http://dx.doi.org/10.1145/2507157.2507161.

[1]Portmanteau of "Recommend" and "Comment".

enable natural language communication with conversational recommender systems. We discuss the implementation of a prototype for the domain of digital compact cameras and report the results of an empirical study that compares the performance of RECOMMENT with standard unit critiquing approaches. We show that our novel user interface significantly reduces the number of required critiquing cycles and demonstrate how natural language understanding can help to improve future recommender systems.

The remainder of this paper is organized as follows. In Section 2 we discuss related research to position our work in relation to the state of the art in critiquing-based recommendation. Section 3 presents the algorithms and components of the developed prototype in detail. The conducted empirical study to analyze the impact of RECOMMENT is discussed in Section 4. The results of this study are reported in Section 5. We conclude the paper with Section 6.

2. RELATED WORK

The RECOMMENT implementation of unit critiquing is largely based on the original ideas of the FindMe systems developed by Burke et. al. [6]. An initial product is presented and unit critiques can be articulated by the user. After each critique, a new best-matching product is suggested, completing the feedback cycle. An example critique for the digital camera domain would be "More optical zoom", introducing a 'smaller than the value of the currently shown product'-constraint on the optical zoom attribute [6, 21].

As mentioned earlier, compound critiques are often used in critiquing recommender systems to reduce the number of required interaction cycles [14]. Compound critiques impose multiple constraints in a single feedback cycle (e.g., "More optical zoom but less weight"). The inclusion of such critiques in RECOMMENT was considered but they were ultimately omitted because their selection criteria reveals implicit information of the problem domain that is hard to represent equivalently in both interfaces, thus possibly skewing the results of the study. For example, showing the compound critique "Larger sensor size but more expensive" as an option in the traditional interface (control group) not only provides the user with another critiquing option but also exposes a correlation between sensor size and price that might otherwise be unknown to the user [20]. However, mentioning the same proposed critique (as text) in the speech-based interface would certainly guide the user's choice of words not just in this critiquing cycle but from then on, because the sentence also contains the information that "larger sensor size" and "less weight" are understood commands. In an effort to make the different interfaces more comparable, support for compound critiques was therefore not included[2].

A user preference model consisting of recently added critiques is tracked across several feedback cycles in a manner very similar to the incremental critiquing approach presented in [21]. However, RECOMMENT does not permanently remove recommended products from the search space, but instead temporarily biases the recommender against them to avoid the problem of diminishing choices [17].

RECOMMENT uses the current sales rank of a popular online retailer to add a prior probability to the products in its database. In a sense this could be compared to experience-based critiquing as described in [15] in that it also harnesses information from other users' buying decisions. However, instead of detailed critiquing information, only the accepted products influence current recommendations.

[2]The speech-based input accepts more than one condition during a feedback cycle but it treats them as a collection of unit critiques.

RECOMMENT starts directly with the most popular product in the domain instead of first requiring an initial query (see, e.g., [6]). To ensure quick adaption to a user's preferences, the traditional unit critiquing recommendation algorithm was relaxed to not enforce similarity with the current recommendation. This property is however naturally re-introduced through the maintained user preference model as returned products will become more and more similar once the user's requirements have been sufficiently determined to codify underlying intentions. Additionally, a special utility function discourages large jumps through the search space for critiqued attributes (see Section 3.1.3).

Finally, it is interesting to note that Burke et. al. already presented natural language queries in their seminal paper on the FindMe systems [6] as examples of how a critique might be formulated. On the subject of renting a movie, the authors refer to a possible user thinking "That would be good, but it's too violent for my kids." leading to a new critique on the "level of violence" attribute. Had the user in their example actually articulated this thought, a system like RECOMMENT could have extracted the contained critiquing information automatically.

3. SYSTEM DESCRIPTION

This section outlines the developed RECOMMENT prototype.

3.1 Recommender

RECOMMENT is based on a unit critiquing algorithm that exploits iteratively added, user-defined critiques. The final recommendation in each step is ensured to fulfill at least the last given critique. From this subspace, the item with the overall highest utility rating in regards to the user preference model is selected (see Subsection 3.1.1 for more information about the maintained user preference model and Subsection 3.1.3 for details about the calculation of the utility value of a single critique). Unfulfillable critiques are rejected. For example, if the user requests a less expensive product than the cheapest one, a warning message will be shown briefly, telling the user that there are no such products. This basic algorithm is outlined in Algorithm 1.

Input: known products P, list of critiques C, current recommendation r_{old}
Output: next recommendation r_{new}
$P' \leftarrow \{p \in P | p\ satisfies\ last\ given\ critique\}$
if P' *is empty* **then**
  show warning and return r_{old}
end
$maxUtility \leftarrow -\infty$
$bestOffer \leftarrow r_{old}$
for $p \in P'$ **do**
  $thisUtility \leftarrow \infty$
  for $c \in C$ **do**
    $thisUtility \leftarrow thisUtility + (1 - \frac{c.age}{MaxAge}) * c.utility(p)$
  end
  if $thisUtility > maxUtility$ **then**
    $maxUtility \leftarrow thisUtility$
    $bestOffer \leftarrow p$
  end
end
return $bestOffer$

Algorithm 1: Selecting the next recommendation.

3.1.1 *User preference model*

Over the course of a recommendation session, a user preference model is maintained. It contains the 15 most recent critiques, linearly weighted based on their age.

Each new critique is checked against the preference model. Critiques that contradict or refine existing constraints replace their older equivalents [21]. If a feedback cycle is undone by the user (by selecting the "Back" button or giving an equivalent voice command, depending on the interface; see Section 3.3), any newly added constraints from this cycle are removed and any replaced critiques are restored, essentially restoring the system state before the last given critique.

In order to curb the problem of unreachable products that are "overshadowed" by numerically better matching but potentially less appealing ones, each feedback cycle also adds a $product \neq current$ critique as suggested in [16]. Because this constraint is subject to the same aging process and eventual removal, RECOMMENT does not suffer from diminishing choices [17].

3.1.2 Prior probability

The 100 most frequently sold compact digital cameras were retrieved from the popular online retailer Amazon[3] and their sales rank was added to the domain database to act as a prior probability for the selection process. Because of this additional information, the first suggested product presented to a new user is the most popular product of the domain based on recent sales.

3.1.3 Rate of change

In order to be able to represent critiques such as "much cheaper" or "a little bit cheaper", the base utility expressed by each critiqued numerical attribute is not just a binary measure ("cheaper") but rather represents the *distance* of an implicitly expressed goal. The measure of distance between two numerical values is shown in Formula 1 (for non-numerical attributes the distance is either 0, for equal values, or 1 otherwise). The algorithm to calculate the utility value from this calculated distance is outlined in Algorithm 2.

$$distance(a,b) = \begin{cases} -distance(b,a) & if\ a < b \\ a & if\ b = 0 \\ \frac{a}{b} - 1 & else \end{cases} \quad (1)$$

The utility function has been designed such that it tries to avoid large jumps in the product space based on a single critique and instead tries to stay within a certain acceptance region from the last shown product. A piecewise function was selected that has the following properties. If the critique is violated, the utility value will be negative, otherwise positive. Attribute values that are very different or too close to the current recommendation are assigned lower utility values than products closer to the deduced implicit goal. Given symmetric relations and both lower and upper bounds specified for one attribute, traditional, linear (triangular) acceptance functions would theoretically create an optimal region between those bounds, therefore having the combined utility function only depend on the age (weight) of the individual critiques. In contrast, the non-linear approach outlined in Formula 1 provides what we believe to be a better representation of the user's goal (see Figure 2 for an example). The implicit goal can be influenced with what we call a "modifier factor". The modifier factor is extracted from adjectives to the critique (e.g., "much cheaper") and defaults to 1.0, representing a desired 50 % change of the attribute value[4]. A selection of sample adjectives influencing the modifier factor can be found in Table 1.

For example, a critique of "larger than 50" for a given attribute would result in RECOMMENT trying to find a product with an attribute value of around 100 (modifier factor: 1.0; refer to Figure 1 for a plot of the utility function). A subsequent critique of "smaller" (from the new position of 100) would result in the recommender trying to find a product with a value of around 75[5] for the given attribute (refer to Figure 2 for a plot of the utility function of a combination of both critiques). Had the second critique instead been "a little bit smaller", the expressed implicit goal would have instead been a value of around 95 (see Figure 2).

Sample adjectives	Modifier factor	Deduced desired change
"slightly"	0.2	10 %
"very"	2.0	100 %
"not"	-1.0	-50 %

Table 1: Sample adjectives that affect the modifier factor.

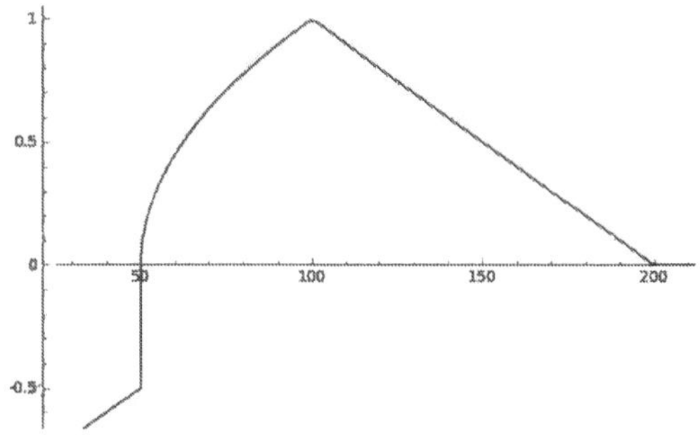

Figure 1: Utility function of the critique $x > 50$.

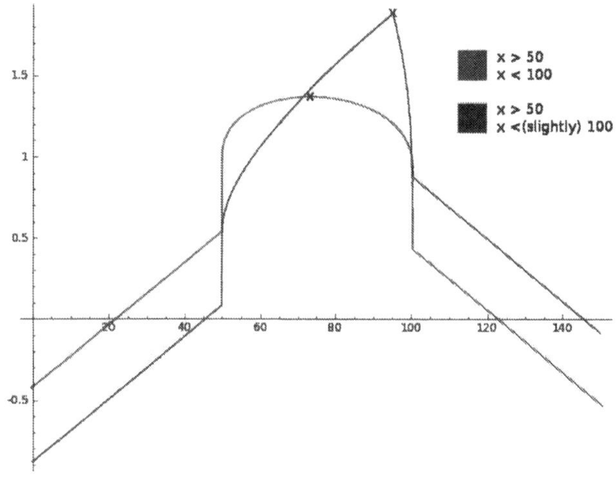

Figure 2: Utility function of the subsequent critiques $x > 50$ and $x < 100$ as well as $x > 50$ and $x <_{slightly} 100$.

Traditional interfaces, including the mouse-based interface developed for RECOMMENT, have not been expressive enough to capture such nuances in a user's critiquing input. To the best of the authors' knowledge, this feature of the speech-based interface is therefore a novel approach for critiquing recommender systems and presents one of the main advantages of natural language interfaces for recommender systems.

[3]http://www.amazon.com

[4]In order to make "smaller than" and "larger than" relationships symmetric, the percentage is always calculated from the larger value to the smaller value.

[5]In practice, this value would be around 73 as the older critique would have already aged once and thus would have reduced influence on the overall utility of the product.

Input: product p, relationship r, attribute a, modifier factor m
Output: utility u
$distance = distance(a.value, p[a.id].value) * r.direction$
$perfectDistance = m * 0.5$
if *critiqueViolated* **then**
  return $-abs(distance - perfectDistance)$
else
  if $distance < perfectDistance$ **then**
    return $\sqrt{\frac{distance}{perfectDistance}}$
  else
    return $max(perfectDistance - distance + 1, 0.0001)$
  end
end

Algorithm 2: Schematic utility calculation.

3.2 Speech recognition

Any speech-based natural language interface needs to address a number of challenges that arise when processing spontaneous speech: Speech disfluencies like filler words, repetitions, and false starts (self-interruption) are common [23]. Additionally, dialectal speech, emotive speech patterns and even occasional laughs or angry snorts exacerbate the situation for speech models that are usually trained on manually cleaned utterances articulated in a neutral, sometimes almost clinical tone.

A sufficiently well performing speech recognizer is an essential component of any successful speech-based user interface. Therefore, a custom, domain specific solution for Austrian German[6] and the domain of digital cameras was developed using the Simon[7] system and the CMU SPHINX speech recognition framework[8].

3.2.1 Speech model

The speech model represents the target language and can be broken into the following parts. (1) the dictionary, containing the set of recognized words as well as their phonetic transcriptions; (2) a (context-infused) word probability model (N-Gram) that forms the language model (LM) and (3) a learned representation of how the individual phones that make up the spoken words are pronounced, stored in the acoustic model (AM).

λ	**Base corpus**
0.5	Critiquing sentence fragments
0.4	Sentence fragments for explicit value elicitation
0.1	Standard, written German

Table 2: Selected LM mixtures.

For the purpose of our digital camera project, a custom 3-gram language model was developed based on the accepted sentence fragments of the parser (refer to Section 3.2.2). The training corpus itself was split into three parts. (1) the basic sentence fragments expected during critiquing ("cheaper", "a bit smaller", etc.), (2) a training corpus for explicit value elicitation ("more than 5 megapixel", etc.) and (3) the base corpus modeling standard German[9]. Separate 3-grams of these three components were built and mixed into a final language model heavily focusing on expected, domain specific sentence fragments. Based on experimentation on recordings from pilot testers of early prototypes, the mixture weights shown in Table 2 were selected. These mixture weights (lambdas) govern the influence of the individual N-Grams on the resulting language model. A higher value of λ represents more influence ($\sum \lambda_i = 1$).

An existing acoustic model built from various data sources such as Voxforge[10], LibriVox[11] and supplemental data from professional speakers from the spoken language corpus of the ADABA database[12] was adapted with a small speech corpus recorded from the interactions of pilot testers with early prototypes using the maximum a posteriori probability speaker adaption [10].

3.2.2 Parser

To interpret the output of the speech recognition system, a custom parser was developed. It identifies attributes (mapping to properties of the products of the problem space), pre- and post-binding relationships (which may be conditioned on certain attribute types), as well as modifier factors ("a bit", "not") and commands ("cheaper").

The system supports regular expressions with optionally provided arguments. For example, the post-binding relationship "more than" and the attribute "(\d+) Euro"[13] matches the recognition result "more than 100 Euro" and creates a corresponding critique. Commands without explicit values ("more expensive") are interpreted to relate to the currently shown product.

Default relationship targets enable RECOMMENT to understand "larger" as referring to object size while also interpreting "larger sensor size" correctly.

Compound critiques (e.g., "Can you show me a smaller Canon?") are broken into their individual relationships and added as separate, equally prioritized unit critiques. RECOMMENT guarantees that at least one of these constraints will be fulfilled by the next recommended product but will of course prefer products that are closer to all the constraints in the current user model with the just added constraints naturally receiving the highest priority (see Section 3.1.1).

The language description itself is stored in an easily extendable XML file. The final NLP rules used for the empirical study recognize more than 300 different command fragments which can be combined to form millions of different sentences.

3.3 User interface

Simple, unit critiquing-based user interfaces were developed for both the mouse- and the speech-based interaction methods.

Instead of an initial query, the user starts immediately with the "best matching" product. In lieu of critiquing information, the prior probability dominates the selection process resulting in the most sold product being shown initially (see Subsection 3.1.2).

Both interfaces use auditory cues to inform the user of any of the following three events: 'new recommendation generated', 'failed to find a matching product' and 'stopped recording' (after the user releases the PTT switch; only triggered in the speech-based interface). The first two mark both possible outcomes of the end of a critiquing cycle.

[6] Example sentences used in this paper are translated from German.
[7] http://simon.kde.org
[8] http://cmusphinx.sourceforge.net/
[9] Created from a recent dump of the German Wikipedia.
[10] http://voxforge.org
[11] http://librivox.org
[12] http://www-oedt.kfunigraz.ac.at/ADABA/
[13] In Perl Regular expressions, "\d+" match one or more digits whereas the surrounding parenthesis mark the subexpression that RECOMMENT will treat as the extracted attribute value.

3.4 Mouse-based user interface

The traditional, mouse-based user interface shown in Figure 3[14] is very similar to other unit critiquing interfaces such as the FindMe systems and, except for the lack of compound critiques, especially the Qwikshop system [5, 21].

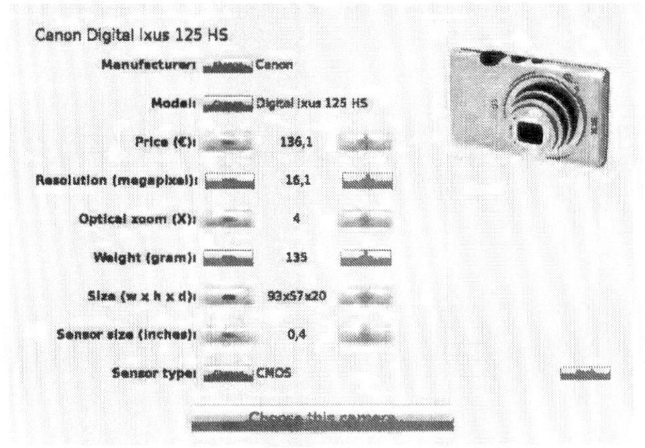

Figure 3: RECOMMENT: Mouse-based user interface.

Next to the unit critiquing controls themselves, the interface also provides a "Back" button to remove critiques from the user preference model. This was added to encourage users to browse for even better matching products after finding an acceptable one without fearing to be unable to return to the current recommendation.

3.5 Speech-based user interface

The speech-based interface is depicted in Figure 4[14].

A simple, energy-based automatic voice activity detection was implemented, but was ultimately deactivated in an effort to make users' speech more focused on the task at hand and to avoid possible accidental recognition results brought on by, e.g., talking with the person conducting the study. Instead, RECOMMENT uses a "push to talk" (PTT) methodology similar to a walkie-talkie, requiring users to press and hold a button while giving voice commands.

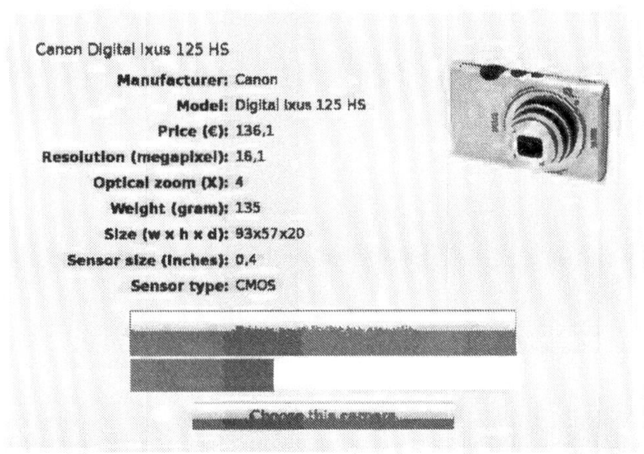

Figure 4: RECOMMENT: Speech-based user interface.

[14]The original interface is in German, the screenshots show a translated version.

The measured noise level is shown in the user interface at all times as a moving bar under the PTT button (VU meter). This was included to instill a sense of an actively listening system, especially for users who had not used speech-based interfaces before.

Because study participants were not informed about what kind of sentences would be interpreted correctly (see Section 4), the system instead showed correction hints as needed. These sparse instructions were displayed only in case of multiple successive recognition errors or when a sentence was already partially recognized (in which case the instructions referred specifically to this partial match). A state diagram of this process, including some examples, is shown in Figure 5. Correction hints, just like correct recognition results, are shown inside the VU meter control element discussed above and automatically hidden after 3.5 seconds. Again, these measures were taken to encourage free articulation by minimizing guidance as much as possible without compromising learnability.

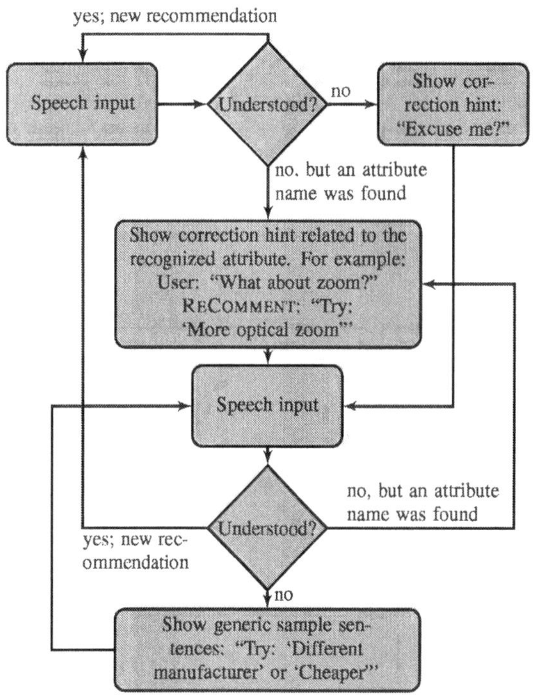

Figure 5: Guiding user input.

4. STUDY DESIGN

To examine the hypothesis that speech-based recommender systems can outperform traditional interfaces, we conducted an empirical study.

4.1 Test demography

The test group, consisting primarily of undergraduate and postgraduate students, was split into two groups, each consisting of 40 users for a total of 80 participants. One group, henceforth referred to as group A, used the speech-controlled interface whereas the other group, group B, used the mouse-based interface.

A more detailed breakdown of both groups can be found in Table 3.

4.2 Task definition

Each participant was instructed to imagine buying a new digital compact camera. To this end, users were told to try to think about

Characteristics	Group A	Group B
Male	35	33
Female	5	7
Total	40	40
Median age	24	22
Personally own camera	67.5 %	60 %
Seeked help when buying this camera	19.4 %	26.7 %

Table 3: Demography of the test groups of the empirical study.

a camera that best fits their personal needs and use RECOMMENT to find such a product. Participants were asked to ignore product dimensions that were not included in the recommendation interface (e.g. display size, shutter speed, etc.).

Both groups received purposefully minimal instructions regarding the actual user interface. The group using the mouse-based interface was simply told to 'use the buttons' to find products that matched their requirements whereas the instructions for the speech-based interface were limited to an equivalent sentence and a small note explaining the PTT system (see Section 3.3).
Specifically, the group testing the developed natural language interface did *not* receive any kind of tutorial or list of supported voice commands but was instead told to 'try it out' in an effort to encourage users to use their own words when interacting with the system.

4.3 Evaluation

Direct feedback was collected with a questionnaire that was filled out by each participant immediately after completion of the assigned task. This questionnaire included questions about the participant's knowledge of the domain, the quality of the last given recommendation, questions about the general usability as well as questions designed to gauge the user's personal impression of the used interaction method.

The standard usability survey scale presented in [3] was used but had to be slightly adapted to better fit the tested system. Specifically, questions related to the "various functions" or the "inconsistency" potentially introduced by a rich feature set were not applicable to RECOMMENT and were thus removed. Additionally, the question about the user "frequently using" the presented system was reworded to instead ask if the user could see themselves using the system when purchasing his or her next digital compact camera. In order to maintain the same scale of 0 to 100 as the original SUS, the final multiplier of the calculation formula was increased, giving the remaining questions more, equally distributed, weight.

4.4 Case Base

To evaluate RECOMMENT, a database of currently available, compact digital cameras was assembled. Product data, images, and recent pricing information for a total of more than 600 distinct models was collected from various online retailers and compiled into a single database.

The following feature set was collected: Model*, Manufacturer*, Price (€)*, Resolution (Megapixel)*, Sensor size (inches)*, Sensor type*, Size (wxhxd)*, Weight (gram)*, Internal memory (megabyte), Digital zoom (times), Optical zoom (times)*, External storage. Features marked with a * were selected for inclusion in the final interface after receiving feedback from early pilot testers. The 100 most popular cameras were additionally tagged with their current product sales rank (see 3.1.2).

5. RESULTS

In this section we will present the results obtained from the conducted empirical study.

5.1 Recognition performance

An adequately performing speech recognition component is a necessary prerequisite for the potential success of any speech-based user interface. To determine the recognizers' performance we will look at both the perceived and the actual recognition accuracy. To judge participants' impressions, they were asked to rate the performance of the speech recognition as part of the questionnaire. The generally very positive result can be seen in Figure 6[15].

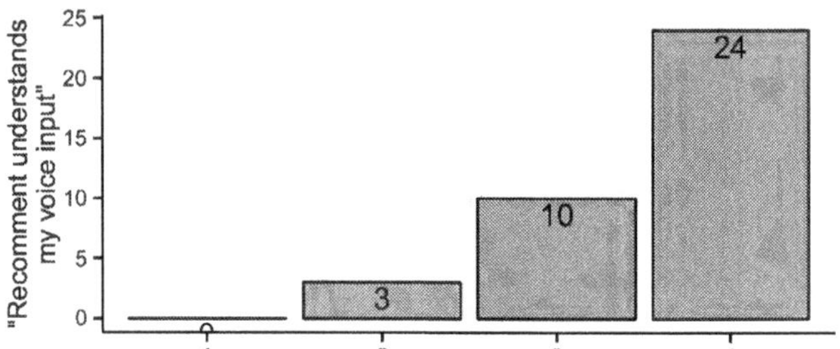

Figure 6: Participants' perception of the speech-recognition accuracy ($[1, 4]$, higher is better).

For the purposes of our evaluation, all recorded dialogs were manually transcribed after the completion of the study. To accurately evaluate the acoustic model and the recognizer itself, we compared the resulting (parsed) critiques (from the recognition results) with the critiques extracted from the manually transcribed reference set. In this context, sentences such as "cheaper, please" and, e.g., "cheaper, pepper" are therefore treated as equal because their difference does not impact RECOMMENT's performance. Sentences consisting of more than one command or including modifying adjectives (see Section 3.1.3) where the system only captured part of the intention, are treated as partial errors. To establish a frame of reference, Google's speech recognition web service[16] was used to transcribe the samples recorded during the course of the study. The results of the comparison of both recognition systems can be seen in Figure 7. As can be seen, our custom recognition component based on Simon and PocketSPHINX manages to significantly outperform the off-the-shelf online service for our limited domain and proved to be sufficiently accurate for the purposes of this study.

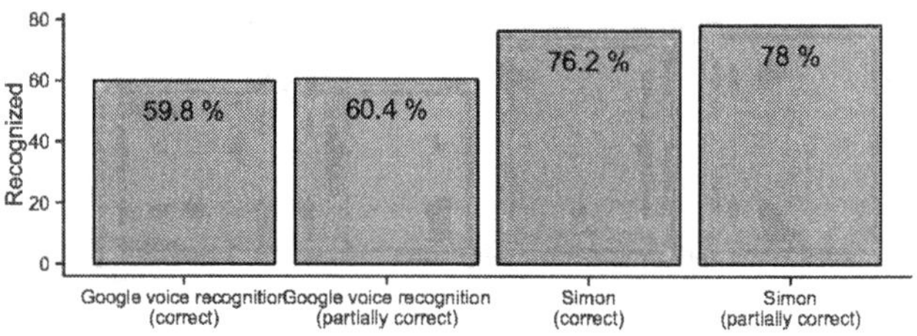

Figure 7: Comparison of the developed recognizer in comparison with a state of the art, off-the-shelf online service.

[15]The results were verified with a counter question. Questionnaires where either both questions were answered positively or both negatively have been removed before interpreting the results
[16]http://www.google.com/speech-api/v1/recognize?lang=de

The natural language parser was evaluated by manually reviewing spoken commands of utterances and comparing them with the system's interpretation. Out of 384 sentences collected as part of the study, only 21 sentences (5.5 %) failed to parse correctly (in part or completely). Most of these errors were due to unexpected constructs like "7 optical zoom" with notable exceptions being semantically complex commands like "credit card size" or "highest resolution for 120 Euro" or commands referencing earlier critiques like "even more". The majority of sentences referred to a single attribute, i.e., unit critiques were the predominant interaction mode (used in 85.7% of the cases) whereas compound critiques were rarely used. 74 sentences included references to explicit values and 12 used modifier factors (see Section 3.1.3). Table 4 shows an overview of the recognized sentences and Table 5 shows the beginning of a sample recommendation session.

Category	Count
Discarded	49 (12.8%)
Unit critique	329 (85.7%)
Compound critique (2 attributes)	3 (0.8%)
Compound critique (3 attributes)	2 (0.5%)
Compound critique (5 attributes)	1 (0.3%)

Table 4: Types of used commands.

Sentence
I am looking for a camera with 12 megapixel and a weight of around 200 gram.
This camera with the same properties just smaller.
An even smaller camera.
Optical zoom of 14 times would be better.
More optical zoom.
[...]

Table 5: Sample user interactions with ReComment.

5.2 Usability

To determine the usability of our created interfaces, we included a slightly modified version of the standard usability scale in the questionnaire (see Section 4.3). We compared the resulting SUS scores of the participants using the mouse-based interface (group B) with those using the speech-based interface (group A). Additionally, for comparison purposes, we also present the reported usability of those 24 users that reported that the recognizer understood them well as a separate group. All three results are shown in Figure 8.

While the increase in perceived usability between group A and B is not entirely conclusive ($p = 0.13$), the users that reported to be well understood by ReComment clearly preferred the speech-based interface over the traditional one ($p < 0.02$). Moreover, participants of group A answered more favorably 'yes' on the question asking if they would use ReComment before next purchasing a digital camera than the control group, suggesting increased user satisfaction (mean of group A: 3.1, group B: 2.7; $p < 0.5$).

5.3 Recommendation quality

Despite using the same basic recommender algorithm, the reported recommendation quality and efficiency differed substantially. Participants using the speech-based user interface reported to like the last presented product better than those using the traditional user interface ($p < 0.05$). A more detailed breakdown of their

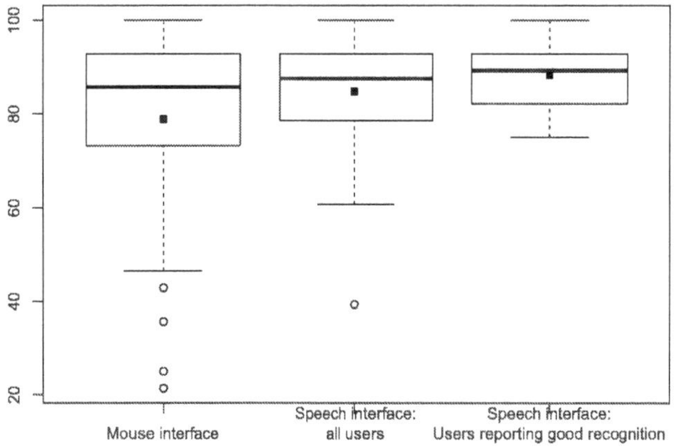

Figure 8: Usability evaluation (adapted SUS scores).

answer to the related question on the questionnaire can be found in Figure 9.

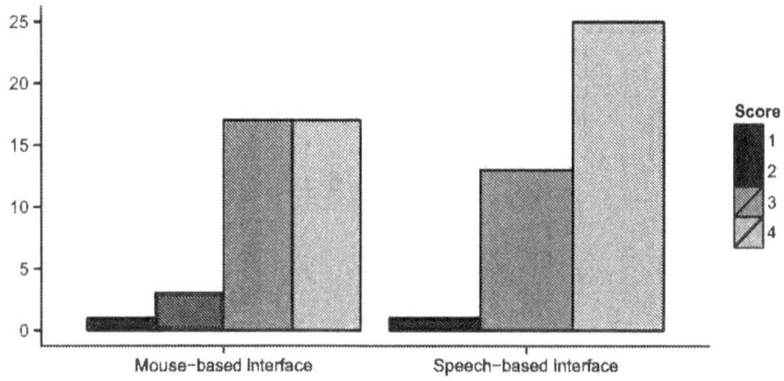

Figure 9: User score of last recommended item ([1, 4], higher is better).

Furthermore, users of the speech-based interface used considerably fewer interaction cycles before arriving at the desired product (see Figure 10). However, although the sessions were not timed, it is worth mentioning that this may not directly translate into significantly shorter overall session length (seconds) because articulating preferences by voice is obviously more time consuming than clicking a button.

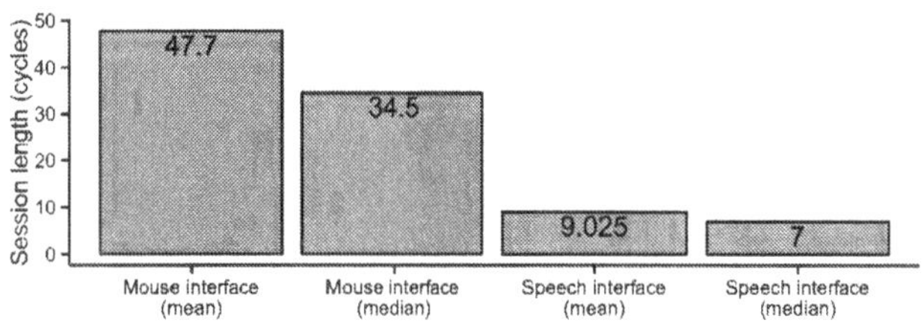

Figure 10: Session length (lower is better).

6. CONCLUSION AND FURTHER WORK

In this paper we presented ReComment, a new approach to critiquing-based recommender systems using a speech-controlled natural language interface. We compared the speech-based interface with a traditional, mouse-based user interface in an empirical study. The results show that users of the speech-based interface found overall more satisfactory products, required less interaction cycles and were more likely to want to use the system again.

Without further research, it is hard to draw definitive conclusions as to why users reliably reached better fitting products with the speech-based interface, but it may be argued that users spent less time exploring the product space and instead concentrated on their actual needs, likely because of the increased effort required to formulate a voice command. This and other theories should be further explored in future work.

The speech recognition and natural language parsing components used in RECOMMENT, while sufficient for basic functionality, certainly leave much room for improvement, including support for other languages than German. The surprisingly low amount of compound critiques in natural interaction should also be investigated further. Monitored user sessions with a voice controlled, compound critiquing system could also yield valuable insight into hidden correlation between attributes by detecting patterns of frequently co-occurring attributes in user input.

Moreover, future works should also compare and contrast the performance of speech-based interfaces for alternate recommender approaches (e.g., constraint-based recommenders [11]).

Some users also had trouble to adjust to talking to what essentially still looked like a traditional computer program. Integration of speech output and an avatar to talk to has been shown to lower this entry barrier [19]. Moreover, human conversational speech also includes other, subtle emotional cues that can be extracted by an appropriate system [9]. Future systems could integrate this additional information to influence (e.g., the weight of) the deduced constraints to potentially improve recommendation quality even further.

7. ACKNOWLEDGMENTS

The work presented in this paper has been partially funded by the Austrian Research Promotion Agency (Casa Vecchia, 825889)

8. REFERENCES

[1] D. Bridge. Towards conversational recommender systems: A dialogue grammar approach. In *Proceedings of the Workshop in Mixed-Initiative Case-Based Reasoning, Workshop Prog. at the 6th Europ. Conf. in CBR*, pages 9–22, 2002.

[2] E. Brill and R. J. Mooney. An overview of empirical natural language processing. *AI magazine*, 18(4):13, 1997.

[3] J. Brooke. Sus-a quick and dirty usability scale. *Usability evaluation in industry*, 189:194, 1996.

[4] R. Burke. Knowledge-based recommender systems. In *Encyclopedia of Library and Information Systems*. Marcel Dekker, 2000.

[5] R. D. Burke, K. J. Hammond, and B. Yound. The findme approach to assisted browsing. *IEEE Expert*, 12(4):32–40, 1997.

[6] R. D. Burke, K. J. Hammond, and B. C. Young. Knowledge-based navigation of complex information spaces. In *Proceedings of the national conference on artificial intelligence*, volume 462, page 468, 1996.

[7] L. Chen and P. Pu. Evaluating critiquing-based recommender agents. In *Proceedings of the National Conference on Artificial Intelligence*, volume 21, page 157. Menlo Park, CA; Cambridge, MA; London; AAAI Press; MIT Press; 1999, 2006.

[8] L. Chen and P. Pu. Critiquing-based recommenders: survey and emerging trends. *User Modeling and User-Adapted Interaction*, 22(1-2):125–150, 2012.

[9] R. Cowie, E. Douglas-Cowie, N. Tsapatsoulis, G. Votsis, S. Kollias, W. Fellenz, and J. G. Taylor. Emotion recognition in human-computer interaction. *Signal Processing Magazine, IEEE*, 18(1):32–80, 2001.

[10] S.-J. Doh. *Enhancements to transformation-based speaker adaptation: principal component and inter-class maximum likelihood linear regression*. PhD thesis, Carnegie Mellon University, 2000.

[11] A. Felfernig and R. Burke. Constraint-based recommender systems: technologies and research issues. In *Proceedings of the 10th international conference on Electronic commerce*, page 3. ACM, 2008.

[12] M. Mandl and A. Felfernig. Improving the performance of unit critiquing. In *User Modeling, Adaptation, and Personalization*, pages 176–187. Springer, 2012.

[13] K. McCarthy, L. McGinty, and B. Smyth. Dynamic critiquing: An analysis of cognitive load. In *Proceedings of the 16th Irish Conference on Artificial Intelligence and Cognitive Science*, pages 19–28, 2005.

[14] K. McCarthy, J. Reilly, L. McGinty, and B. Smyth. On the dynamic generation of compound critiques in conversational recommender systems. In *Adaptive Hypermedia and Adaptive Web-Based Systems*, pages 176–184. Springer, 2004.

[15] K. McCarthy, Y. Salem, and B. Smyth. Experience-based critiquing: reusing critiquing experiences to improve conversational recommendation. In *Case-Based Reasoning. Research and Development*, pages 480–494. Springer, 2010.

[16] L. McGinty and J. Reilly. On the evolution of critiquing recommenders. In *Recommender Systems Handbook*, pages 419–453. Springer, 2011.

[17] D. McSherry and D. W. Aha. The ins and outs of critiquing. In *IJCAI*, pages 962–967, 2007.

[18] P. H. Z. Pu and P. Kumar. Evaluating example-based search tools. In *Proceedings of the 5th ACM conference on Electronic commerce*, pages 208–217. ACM, 2004.

[19] L. Qiu and I. Benbasat. An investigation into the effects of text-to-speech voice and 3d avatars on the perception of presence and flow of live help in electronic commerce. *ACM Trans. Comput.-Hum. Interact.*, 12(4):329–355, 2005.

[20] J. Reilly, K. McCarthy, L. McGinty, and B. Smyth. Explaining compound critiques. *Artificial Intelligence Review*, 24(2):199–220, 2005.

[21] J. Reilly, K. McCarthy, L. McGinty, and B. Smyth. Incremental critiquing. *Knowledge-Based Systems*, 18(4):143–151, 2005.

[22] J. Reilly, J. Zhang, L. McGinty, P. Pu, and B. Smyth. Evaluating compound critiquing recommenders: a real-user study. In *Proceedings of the 8th ACM conference on Electronic commerce*, pages 114–123. ACM, 2007.

[23] E. Shriberg. Toerrrr'is human: ecology and acoustics of speech disfluencies. *Journal of the International Phonetic Association*, 31(1):153–169, 2001.

[24] C. A. Thompson, M. H. Goeker, and P. Langley. A personalized system for conversational recommendations. *J. Artif. Intell. Res. (JAIR)*, 21:393–428, 2004.

[25] J. Zhang and P. Pu. A comparative study of compound critique generation in conversational recommender systems. In *Adaptive Hypermedia and Adaptive Web-Based Systems*, pages 234–243. Springer, 2006.

Hidden Factors and Hidden Topics: Understanding Rating Dimensions with Review Text

Julian McAuley
Stanford University
jmcauley@cs.stanford.edu

Jure Leskovec
Stanford University
jure@cs.stanford.edu

ABSTRACT

In order to recommend products to users we must ultimately predict how a user will respond to a new product. To do so we must uncover the implicit tastes of each user as well as the properties of each product. For example, in order to predict whether a user will enjoy *Harry Potter*, it helps to identify that the book is about wizards, as well as the user's level of interest in wizardry. *User feedback* is required to discover these latent product and user dimensions. Such feedback often comes in the form of a numeric rating accompanied by review text. However, traditional methods often discard review text, which makes user and product latent dimensions difficult to interpret, since they ignore the very text that *justifies* a user's rating. In this paper, we aim to combine latent *rating* dimensions (such as those of latent-factor recommender systems) with latent review *topics* (such as those learned by topic models like LDA). Our approach has several advantages. Firstly, we obtain highly interpretable textual labels for latent rating dimensions, which helps us to 'justify' ratings with text. Secondly, our approach more accurately predicts product ratings by harnessing the information present in review text; this is especially true for new products and users, who may have too few ratings to model their latent factors, yet may still provide substantial information from the text of even a single review. Thirdly, our discovered topics can be used to facilitate other tasks such as automated genre discovery, and to identify useful and representative reviews.

Categories and Subject Descriptors

H.3.3 [**Information Search and Retrieval**]: Information Search and Retrieval

Keywords

recommender systems, topic models

1. INTRODUCTION

Recommender systems have transformed the way users discover and evaluate products on the web. Whenever users assess products, there is a need to model *how* they made their assessment, either to suggest new products they might enjoy [19], to summarize the important points in their reviews [13], or to identify other users who may share similar opinions [24]. Such tasks have been studied across a variety of domains, from hotel reviews [6] to beer [21].

To model how users evaluate products, we must understand the hidden dimensions, or facets, of their opinions. For example, to understand why two users agree when reviewing the movie *Seven Samurai*, yet disagree when reviewing *Casablanca*, it helps to know that these films belong to different genres; these users may have similar preferences toward action movies, but opposite preferences for romantic dramas.

Modeling these hidden factors is key to obtaining state-of-the-art performance on product recommendation tasks [2]. Crucially, recommender systems rely on *human feedback*, which typically comes in the form of a plain-text review and a numeric score (such as a star rating). This type of feedback is used to train machine learning algorithms, whose goal is to predict the scores that users will give to items that they have not yet reviewed [12].

In spite of the wealth of research on modeling *ratings*, the other form of feedback present on review websites—namely, the reviews themselves—is typically ignored. In our opinion, ignoring this rich source of information is a major shortcoming of existing work on recommender systems. Indeed, if our goal is to *understand* (rather than merely predict) how users rate products, we ought to rely on reviews, whose very purpose is for users to explain *why* they rated a product the way they did. As we show later, 'understanding' these factors helps us to justify users' reviews, and can aid us in tasks like genre discovery and identification of informative reviews.

Thus our goal in this paper is to develop statistical models that combine latent dimensions in rating data with topics in review text. This leads to natural interpretations of rating dimensions, for instance we automatically discover that movie ratings are divided along topics like genre, while beer ratings are divided along topics like beer style. Rather than performing *post-hoc* analysis to make this determination, we discover both rating dimensions and review topics in a single learning stage, using an objective that combines the accuracy of rating prediction (in terms of the mean squared error) with the likelihood of the review corpus (using a topic model). We do this using a transform that aligns latent rating and review terms, so that both are determined by a single parameter. Essentially, the text likelihood acts as a 'regulariser' for rating prediction, ensuring that parameters that are good at predicting ratings are also likely in terms of the review text.

Not only does our model help us to 'explain' users' review scores by better understanding rating dimensions, but it also leads to better predictions of the ratings themselves. Traditional models (based on ratings alone) are difficult to apply to new users and products, that have too few ratings to model their many latent dimensions or

RecSys'13, October 12–16, 2013, Hong Kong, China.

ACM 978-1-4503-2409-0/13/10 ...$15.00.
http://dx.doi.org/10.1145/2507157.2507163.

factors [14]. In contrast, our model allows us to accurately uncover such factors from even a single review.

Furthermore, by understanding how hidden *rating* dimensions relate to hidden *review* dimensions, our models facilitate a variety of novel tasks. For instance, we apply our models to automatically discover product categories, or 'genres', that explain the variation present in both ratings and reviews. We also apply our models to find 'informative' reviews, whose text is good at explaining the factors that contributed to a user's rating.

1.1 Contributions and Findings

Our main contribution is to develop statistical models that combine latent dimensions in rating data with topics in review text. In practice, we claim the following benefits over existing approaches.

Firstly, the topics we obtain readily explain the variation present in ratings and reviews. For example, we discover that beer style (e.g. light versus dark) explains the variation present in beer rating and review data; platform (e.g. console versus PC) explains the variation present in video game data; country (e.g. Italian versus Mexican) explains the variation present in restaurant data, etc.

Secondly, combining ratings with review text allows us to predict ratings more accurately than approaches that consider either of the two sources of data in isolation. This is especially true for 'new' products: product factors cannot be fit from only a few *ratings*, though we can accurately model them from only a few *reviews*. We improve upon state-of-the-art models based on matrix factorization and LDA by 5-10% in terms of the mean squared error.

Thirdly, we can use our models to facilitate novel tasks. We apply our models to the task of automatic genre discovery, where they are an order of magnitude more accurate than methods based on ratings or reviews alone. We also apply our models to the task of identifying informative reviews; we discover that those reviews whose text best 'explains' the hidden factors of a product are rated as being 'useful' by human annotators on sites like *yelp.com*.

Last, we apply our models to novel corpora consisting of over forty million reviews, from nine million users and three million products. To our knowledge, this is the largest-scale study of public review data conducted to date. Our methods readily scale to datasets of this size.

1.2 Further Related Work

Although many works have studied ratings and review text in isolation, few works attempt to combine the two sources of information. The most similar line of work is perhaps that of *aspect discovery* [6, 25, 29]. Aspects generally refer to *features* that are relevant to all products. Individual users may assign such aspects different weights when determining their overall score; for example a spendthrift hotel reviewer might assign a low weight to 'price' but a high weight to 'service', thus explaining why their overall rating differs from a miserly reviewer who is only interested in price [6].

Though our work shares similarities with such studies, the topics we discover are not similar to aspects. 'Aspects' explain dimensions along which ratings and reviews vary, which is also our goal. Yet while aspects are dimensions common to every individual review, they may not explain the variation present across entire review corpora. For instance, although one may learn that individual users assign different weights to 'smell' and 'taste' when reviewing beers [21], this fails to explain why one user may love the smell of a beer, while another believes the *same* beer smells terrible.

An early work that combines review text and ratings is [6]. They observe that reviews often discuss multiple aspects, and that a user's rating will depend on the importance that they ascribe to each aspect. They find that these dimensions can be recovered from review

Symbol	Description
$r_{u,i}$	rating of item i by user u
$d_{u,i}$	review ('document') of item i by user u
$rec(u,i)$	prediction of the rating for item i by user u
α	global offset term
β_u	bias parameter for user u
β_i	bias parameter for item i
γ_u	K-dimensional latent features for user u
γ_i	K-dimensional latent features for item i
K	number of latent dimensions/topics
θ_i	K-dimensional topic distribution for item i
ϕ_k	word distribution for topic k
ψ_k	unnormalized word distribution for topic k
$w_{u,i,j}$	j^{th} word of user u's review of item i
$z_{u,i,j}$	topic for the jth word of user u's review of item i
N_d	number of words in document d

Table 1: Notation.

text, and that this information can be harnessed for rating prediction. However, their method differs from ours in that their 'aspects' are provided by human annotators (e.g. they use domain knowledge to determine that the 'aspects' of a restaurant are price, service, etc.) for each of which a sentiment classifier must be trained.

We briefly mention works where aspects are *explicit*, i.e., where users rate individual features of a product in addition to their overall rating [1, 9, 17, 25], though this work differs from ours in that it requires *multiple* ratings per review. We also briefly mention orthogonal work that studies 'interpretations' of ratings using sources other than reviews, e.g. information from a user's social network [24].

A few works have considered the task of automatically identifying review dimensions. Early works discover such dimensions based on frequently occurring noun phrases [7], or more sophisticated grammatical rules [23]. More recent works attempt to address this problem in an unsupervised manner [5, 26, 30], however these sophisticated methods are limited to datasets with only a few thousand reviews. Furthermore, although related to our work, the goal of such studies is typically summarization [5, 13, 18], or feature discovery [23], rather than rating prediction *per se*.

Beyond product reviews, modeling the dimensions of free-text is an expansive topic. The goal of Latent Dirichlet Allocation (LDA) [4], like ours, is to discover hidden dimensions in text. Such models have been applied in recommendation settings, e.g. to recommend scientific articles in citation networks [28]. Although related, such approaches differ from ours in that the dimensions they discover are not necessarily correlated with ratings. Variants of LDA have been proposed whose dimensions *are* related to output variables (such as ratings), for example supervised topic models [3]. This is but one of a broad class of works on *sentiment analysis* [10, 15], whose goal is to model numeric scores from text.

In spite of the similarity between our work and sentiment analysis, there is one critical difference: the goal of such methods—at test time—is to predict sentiment from text. In contrast, in recommendation settings such as our own, our goal at test time is to predict ratings of products that users have *not* reviewed.

2. MODELS OF RATINGS AND REVIEWS

We begin by briefly describing the 'standard' models for latent factor recommender systems and Latent Dirichlet Allocation, before defining our own model. The notation we shall use throughout the paper is defined in Table 1.

Latent-Factor Recommender Systems

The 'standard' latent-factor model [11] predicts ratings $r_{u,i}$ for a user u and item i according to

$$rec(u,i) = \alpha + \beta_u + \beta_i + \gamma_u \cdot \gamma_i, \quad (1)$$

where α is an offset parameter, β_u and β_i are user and item biases, and γ_u and γ_i are K-dimensional user and item factors (respectively). Intuitively, γ_i can be thought of as the 'properties' of the product i, while γ_u can be thought of as a user's 'preferences' towards those properties. Given a training corpus of ratings $\mathcal{T}$, the parameters $\Theta = \{\alpha, \beta_u, \beta_i, \gamma_u, \gamma_i\}$ are typically chosen so as to minimize the Mean Squared Error (MSE), i.e.,

$$\hat{\Theta} = \underset{\Theta}{\operatorname{argmin}} \frac{1}{|\mathcal{T}|} \sum_{r_{u,i} \in \mathcal{T}} (rec(u,i) - r_{u,i})^2 + \lambda \Omega(\Theta), \quad (2)$$

where $\Omega(\Theta)$ is a regulariser that penalizes 'complex' models, for example the ℓ_2 norm $\|\gamma\|_2^2$. A variety of methods exist to optimize (eq. 1), for instance alternating least-squares, and gradient-based methods [11].

Latent Dirichlet Allocation

Unlike latent factor models, which uncover hidden dimensions in review *ratings*, Latent Dirichlet Allocation (LDA) uncovers hidden dimensions in review *text*. LDA associates each document $d \in \mathcal{D}$ with a K-dimensional topic distribution θ_d (i.e., a stochastic vector), which encodes the fraction of words in d that discuss each of the K topics. That is, words in the document d discuss topic k with probability $\theta_{d,k}$.

Each topic k also has an associated word distribution, ϕ_k, which encodes the probability that a particular word is used for that topic. Finally, the topic distributions themselves (θ_d) are assumed to be drawn from a Dirichlet distribution.

The final model includes word distributions for each topic ϕ_k, topic distributions for each document θ_d, and topic assignments for each word $z_{d,j}$. Parameters $\Phi = \{\theta, \phi\}$ and topic assignments z are traditionally updated via sampling [4]. The likelihood of a particular text corpus $\mathcal{T}$ (given the word distribution ϕ and topic assignments for each word) is then

$$p(\mathcal{T}|\theta, \phi, z) = \prod_{d \in \mathcal{T}} \prod_{j=1}^{N_d} \theta_{z_{d,j}} \phi_{z_{d,j}, w_{d,j}}, \quad (3)$$

where we are multiplying over all documents in the corpus, and all words in each document. The two terms in the product are the likelihood of seeing these particular topics ($\theta_{z_{d,j}}$), and the likelihood of seeing these particular words for this topic ($\phi_{z_{d,j}, w_{d,j}}$).

2.1 The HFT Model

Our model, which we title 'Hidden Factors as Topics', or HFT for short, attempts to combine these two ideas. Unlike supervised topic models (for example), that learn topics that are correlated with an output variable [3], HFT discovers topics that are correlated with the 'hidden factors' of products and users, γ_i and γ_u.

Topic models operate on *documents*, so first we must define the concept of a 'document' in HFT. We shall derive documents from review text, so an obvious choice is to define each review as a document $d_{u,i}$ (for user u and item i). Alternately, we could define a document d_i as the set of all reviews of an item i, or d_u as the set of all reviews by a user u.

Although we will later consider other alternatives, for the moment, let us consider the set of all reviews of a particular item i as a document d_i. Our reasoning is that when users review products, they tend to discuss properties of the product more than they discuss their own personal preferences; as we see in Section 4, modeling documents in this way leads to the best performance in practice.

With documents defined in this way, for each item i we learn a topic distribution θ_i (a stochastic vector, i.e., $\theta_i \in \Delta^K$). This vector encodes the extent to which each of K topics is discussed across all reviews for that product. Note that we implicitly assume that the number of rating factors is the same as the number of review topics.

Given our motivation, we do not wish to learn *rating* parameters γ_i and *review* parameters θ_i independently. Rather, we want the two to be linked. Intuitively, rating 'factors' γ_i can be thought of as properties that a product possesses; users will then give the product a high rating if they 'like' these properties according to γ_u. On the other hand, 'topics' θ_i define particular distributions of words that appear in reviews of a product. By linking the two, we hope that if a product exhibits a certain property (high $\gamma_{i,k}$), this will correspond to a particular topic being discussed (high $\theta_{i,k}$).

However, such a transformation is non-trivial, for example, we cannot simply define the two to be equal. Critically, θ_i is a stochastic vector, i.e., each of its entries describes a *probability* that a topic is discussed, while rating factors γ_i can take any value in $\mathbb{R}^K$.

If we simply enforced that γ_i was also stochastic, we would lose expressive power in our rating model, yet if we relaxed the requirement that θ_i was stochastic, we would lose the probabilistic interpretation of review topics (which is crucial for sampling). In short, we desire a transform that allows arbitrary $\gamma_i \in \mathbb{R}^K$, while enforcing $\theta_i \in \Delta^K$ (i.e., $\sum_k \theta_{ik} = 1$). We also desire a transform that is *monotonic*, i.e., it should preserve orderings so that the largest values of γ_i should also be the largest values of θ_i. Therefore to link the two we define the transformation

$$\theta_{i,k} = \frac{\exp(\kappa \gamma_{i,k})}{\sum_{k'} \exp(\kappa \gamma_{i,k'})}. \quad (4)$$

Here the exponent in the denominator enforces that each $\theta_{i,k}$ is positive, and the numerator enforces that $\sum_k \theta_{i,k} = 1$. In this way γ_i acts as a natural parameter for the multinomial defined by θ_i [27]. We introduce the parameter κ (which we fit during learning) to control the 'peakiness' of the transformation. As $\kappa \to \infty$, θ_i will approach a unit vector that takes the value 1 only for the largest index of γ_i; as $\kappa \to 0$, θ_i approaches a uniform distribution. Intuitively, large κ means that users only discuss the *most important* topic, while small κ means that users discuss all topics evenly.

Note that in practice, we do not fit both γ and θ, since one uniquely defines the other (in practice we fit only γ). For convenience, we shall still use γ_i when referring to rating parameters, and θ_i when referring to topics.

Our final model is based on the idea that the factors γ_i should accurately model users' ratings (as in eq. 1), but also that the review corpus should be 'likely' when these factors are transformed into topics (as in eq. 3). To achieve this, we define the objective of a corpus $\mathcal{T}$ (ratings and reviews) as

$$f(\mathcal{T}|\Theta, \Phi, \kappa, z) = \sum_{r_{u,i} \in \mathcal{T}} \underbrace{(rec(u,i) - r_{u,i})^2}_{\text{rating error}} - \mu \underbrace{l(\mathcal{T}|\theta, \phi, z)}_{\text{corpus likelihood}}. \quad (5)$$

Recall that Θ and Φ are rating and topic parameters (respectively), κ controls the transform (eq. 4), and z is the set of topic assignments for each word in the corpus $\mathcal{T}$. The first part of this equation is the error of the predicted ratings as in (eq. 1), while the second part is the (log) likelihood of the review corpus as in (eq. 3). μ is a hyperparameter that trades-off the importance of these two effects.

Note that the presence of the corpus likelihood in (eq. 5) is critical, even if our ultimate goal is only to predict ratings. Essentially, the corpus likelihood acts as a regulariser for the rating prediction model, replacing the regulariser Ω from (eq. 1). When few ratings are available for a product i (or user u), the regulariser Ω of (eq. 1) has the effect of pushing γ_i and γ_u toward zero. What this means in practice is that the standard model of (eq. 1) reduces to an offset and bias term for products and users that have few ratings.

Alternately, HFT can accurately predict product factors γ_i even for items with only a few reviews; or, for users with few reviews if we model documents at the level of users. In essence, a small number of *reviews* tells us much more about a product or a user than we can possibly glean from the same number of *ratings*.

In the next section, we describe in detail how we fit the parameters Θ and Φ of the HFT model.

3. FITTING THE HFT MODEL

Our goal is to simultaneously optimize the parameters associated with ratings $\Theta = \{\alpha, \beta_u, \beta_i, \gamma_u, \gamma_i\}$ and the parameters associated with topics $\Phi = \{\theta, \phi\}$. That is, given our review and rating corpus $\mathcal{T}$ our objective is to find

$$\operatorname*{argmin}_{\Theta,\Phi,\kappa,z} f(\mathcal{T}|\Theta, \Phi, \kappa, z). \quad (6)$$

Recall that θ and γ are linked through (eq. 4), so that both Θ and Φ depend on γ. So, a change in γ modifies *both* the rating error *and* the corpus likelihood in (eq. 5). Thus we cannot optimize Θ and Φ independently.

Typically, recommender parameters like those in (eq. 1) are fit by gradient descent, while those of (eq. 3) would be found by Gibbs sampling [4]. Since HFT consists of a combination of these two parts, we use a procedure that alternates between the two steps.

We define a stochastic optimization procedure consisting of the following two steps, which we describe in more detail below:

$$\text{update } \Theta^{(t)}, \Phi^{(t)}, \kappa^{(t)} = \operatorname*{argmin}_{\Theta,\Phi,\kappa} f(\mathcal{T}|\Theta, \Phi, \kappa, z^{(t-1)}) \quad (7)$$

$$\text{sample } z_{d,j}^{(t)} \text{ with probability } p(z_{d,j}^{(t)} = k) = \phi_{k,w_{d,j}}^{(t)}. \quad (8)$$

In the first of these steps (eq. 7) topic assignments for each word (our latent variable z) are fixed. We then fit the remaining terms, Θ, Φ, and κ, via gradient descent. We use L-BFGS, a quasi-Newton method for non-linear optimization of problems with many variables [22]. This is similar to 'standard' gradient-based methods [11], but for the presence of the additional terms arising from (eqs. 3 and 4), whose gradients are easily computed.

The second step (eq. 8) iterates through all documents d and all word positions j and updates their topic assignments. As with LDA, we assign each word to a topic (an integer between 1 and K) randomly, with probability proportional to the likelihood of that topic occurring with that word. Recalling that each item i has a K-dimensional topic distribution θ_i, for each word $w_{u,i,j}$ (in user u's review of item i), we set $z_{u,i,j} = k$ with probability proportional to $\theta_{i,k}\phi_{k,w_{u,i,j}}$. This expression is the probability of the topic k being used for this product ($\theta_{i,k}$), multiplied by the probability of the particular word $w_{u,i,j}$ being used for the topic k ($\phi_{k,w_{u,i,j}}$).

To ensure that ϕ_k (the word distribution for topic k) is a stochastic vector ($\sum_w \phi_{k,w} = 1$), we introduce an additional variable ψ and define

$$\phi_{k,w} = \frac{\exp(\psi_{k,w})}{\sum_{w'} \exp(\psi_{k,w'})}. \quad (9)$$

As with (eq. 4), we can then optimize $\psi_k \in \mathbb{R}^D$ to determine $\phi_k \in \Delta^D$ (where D is the size of the dictionary, i.e., the number of unique words in the corpus). That is, $\psi_k \in \mathbb{R}^D$ acts as a natural parameter for the multinomial $\phi_k \in \Delta^D$.

The above procedure (eq. 8) is analogous to updating topic assignments using LDA. The critical difference is that in HFT, topic proportions θ are not sampled from a Dirichlet distribution, but instead are determined based on the value of Θ^t found during the previous step, via (eq. 4). What this means in practice is that only a single pass through the corpus is required to update z. We only sample new topic assignments z once Θ^t has been updated by (eq. 7).

Finally, the two steps (eqs. 7 and 8) are repeated until convergence, i.e., until the change in Θ and Φ between iterations is sufficiently small. Although our objective (like other 'standard' recommender system objectives) is certainly non-convex [12] and subject to local minima, in our experience it yields similar topics (though possibly permuted) when restarting with different initial conditions.

4. EXPERIMENTS

In this section, we show that:

1. Our model leads to more accurate predictions (in terms of the MSE) on standard recommendation tasks (Sec. 4.4)
2. HFT allows us to address the 'cold-start' problem. HFT's ability to fuse review text and rating information allows for more accurate recommendations for products with few ratings (Sec. 4.5)
3. HFT allows us to automatically discover product categories or 'genres' (Sec. 4.7)
4. HFT can be used to automatically identify representative reviews, which are considered 'useful' by human annotators (Sec. 4.8)

4.1 Datasets

We collect review data from a variety of public sources. Our primary source of data is *Amazon*, from which we obtain approximately 35 million reviews. To obtain this data, we started with a list of 75 million asin-like strings (Amazon product identifiers) obtained from the Internet Archive;[1] around 2.5 million of them had at least one review. We further divide this dataset into 26 parts based on the top-level category of each product (e.g. books, movies). This dataset is a superset of existing publicly-available Amazon datasets, such as those used in [8, 16, 19] and [21].

We also consider 6 million beer and wine reviews previously studied in [19, 21], though in addition we include *pub* data from *ratebeer.com*, and we consider restaurant data from *citysearch.com*, previously used in [6]. Finally, we include 220 thousand reviews from the recently proposed *Yelp Dataset Challenge*.[2]

A summary of the data we obtain is shown in Table 2. In total, we obtain 42 million reviews, from 10 million users and 3 million items. Our datasets span a period of 18 years and contain a total of 5.1 billion words. Data and code are available online.[3]

4.2 Baselines

We compare HFT to the following baselines:

(a) Offset only: Here we simply fit an offset term (α in eq. 1), by taking the average across all training ratings. In terms of the MSE, this is the best possible constant predictor.

(b) Latent factor recommender system: This is the 'standard' latent factor model, i.e., the model of (eq. 1). We fit all parameters using L-BFGS [22].

---

[1] http://archive.org/details/asin_listing/
[2] https://www.yelp.com/dataset_challenge/
[3] http://snap.stanford.edu/data/

dataset	#users	#items	#reviews	#words	av. words	since
Amazon (total)	9,505,488	2,490,432	35,276,583	4.63B	90.90	Jun. 1995
Pubs (Ratebeer)	13,957	22,418	140,359	9.89M	70.52	Jan. 2004
Beer (Ratebeer)	29,265	110,369	2,924,163	154.01M	52.67	Apr. 2000
Pubs (Beeradvocate)	15,268	16,112	112,184	21.85M	194.79	Mar. 2002
Beer (Beeradvocate)	33,388	66,055	1,586,614	195.31M	123.09	Aug. 1996
Wine (Cellartracker)	35,235	412,666	1,569,655	60.02M	38.24	
Citysearch	5,529	32,365	53,122	3.94M	74.18	May. 2002
Yelp Phoenix	45,981	11,537	229,907	29.88M	129.98	Mar. 2005
Total	9,684,111	3,161,954	41,892,587	5.10B		

Table 2: Dataset statistics (number of users; number of items; number of reviews; total number of words; average number of words per review, time of oldest review).

dataset	(a) offset	(b) +lat. factors	(c) LDA	(d) HFT ($\theta \sim \gamma_u$)	(e) HFT ($\theta \sim \gamma_i$)	improvement e vs. b	e vs. c
Amazon (average)	1.774 (0.00)	1.423 (0.00)	1.410 (0.00)	1.329 (0.00)	1.325 (0.00)*	6.89%	6.03%
Pubs (Ratebeer)	0.699 (0.01)	0.477 (0.00)	0.483 (0.01)	0.456 (0.00)*	0.457 (0.00)	4.13%	5.44%
Beer (Ratebeer)	0.701 (0.00)	0.306 (0.00)	0.306 (0.00)	0.301 (0.00)*	0.302 (0.00)	1.18%	1.24%
Pubs (Beeradvocate)	0.440 (0.00)	0.331 (0.00)	0.332 (0.00)	0.311 (0.00)*	0.311 (0.00)	6.16%	6.31%
Beer (Beeradvocate)	0.521 (0.00)	0.371 (0.00)	0.372 (0.00)	0.367 (0.00)	0.366 (0.00)*	1.50%	1.61%
Wine (Cellartracker)	0.043 (0.00)	0.029 (0.00)	0.029 (0.00)	0.028 (0.00)	0.027 (0.00)*	4.84%	4.03%
Citysearch	2.022 (0.04)	1.873 (0.03)	1.875 (0.03)	1.728 (0.03)*	1.731 (0.03)	7.56%	7.66%
Yelp Phoenix	1.488 (0.01)	1.272 (0.01)	1.282 (0.01)	1.225 (0.01)	1.224 (0.01)*	3.78%	4.53%
Average MSE	1.577	1.262	1.253	1.181	1.178	6.70%	5.98%
Average MSE with $K = 10$	1.577	1.260	1.253	1.180	1.176	6.64%	6.11%

Table 3: Results in terms of the Mean Squared Error for $K = 5$ (the best performing model on each dataset is starred; the standard error is shown in parentheses). Due to the large size of our datasets, all reported improvements are significant at the 1% level or better. HFT is shown with topics tied to user parameters (column d), and with topics tied to product parameters (column e)

(c) **Product topics learned using LDA:** Finally, as a baseline that combines text with product features, we consider Latent Dirichlet Allocation [4]. By itself, LDA learns a set of topics and topic proportions (stochastic vectors) for each document. By treating each 'document' as the set of reviews for a particular product, LDA generates a stochastic vector per product (θ_i), which we use to set γ_i. With γ_i fixed, we then fit α, β_u, β_i, and γ_u using L-BFGS. In other words, we fit a 'standard' recommender system, except that γ_i is set using the per-document topic scores produced by LDA. Like HFT, this baseline benefits from review text at training time, but unlike HFT its topics are not chosen so as to explain variation in ratings.

We compare these baselines to two versions of HFT:

(d) **HFT, user topics** In this version of HFT, topics in review text are associated with *user* parameters γ_u.

(e) **HFT, item topics** In this version of HFT, topics in review text are associated with *item* parameters γ_i.

4.3 Evaluation Procedure

We randomly subdivide each of the datasets in Table 2 into training, validation, and test sets. We use 80% of each dataset for training, up to a maximum of 2 million reviews. The remaining data is evenly split between validation and test sets. Offset and bias terms α, β_u, and β_i are initialized by averaging ratings and residuals; other parameters are initialized uniformly at random. Parameters for all models are fit using L-BFGS, which we run for 2,500 iterations. After every 50 iterations, topic assignments are updated (for HFT), and the Mean Squared Error (MSE) is computed. We report the MSE (on the test set) for the model whose error on the validation set is lowest.

Experiments were run on commodity machines with 32 cores and 64gb of memory. Our largest dataset fits on a single machine, and our update equations (eqs. 7 and 8) are naïvely parallelizable. Using L-BFGS on *Beeradvocate* data (for example), our algorithm required 30 minutes to fit, compared to 11 minutes for a 'standard' latent-factor recommender system. Our largest model (Amazon books) required around one day to fit. Although our optimization procedure yields local optima, we observed less than 3% deviation in MSE and energy across ten random initializations.

4.4 Rating Prediction

Results in terms of the Mean Squared Error are shown in Table 3. HFT achieves the best performance on 30 of the 33 datasets we consider (columns d and e). Due to space constraints, we only show average results across the 26 Amazon product categories.[4]

On average, across all datasets with $K = 5$ topics, a latent factor model achieves an MSE of 1.262; latent dirichlet allocation achieves a similar MSE of 1.253. HFT (with item topics) achieves on average an MSE of 1.178. Increasing the number of topics to $K = 10$ improves the performance of all models by a small amount, to 1.262 (latent factor model), 1.253 (LDA), and 1.176 (HFT). With $K = 10$ HFT achieves the best performance on 32 out of 33 datasets.

On several categories, such as 'clothing' and 'shoes', we gain improvements of up to 20% over state-of-the-art methods. Arguably, these categories where HFT is the best performing are the most 'subjective'; for example, if a user dislikes the style of a shirt, or the size of a shoe, they are arguably revealing as much about

[4]Refer to our extended version for complete tables [20].

themselves as they are about the product. By using review text, HFT is better able to 'tease apart' the objective qualities of a product and the subjective opinion of the reviewer.

It is worth briefly addressing the fact that we obtain only small benefits with $K > 10$ topics, contrary to established wisdom that traditional latent-factor models often use many more [12]. We note that while there may be many factors that influence a user's rating, only a few of these factors may be *discussed* in a typical review. A natural extension of HFT would be to augment it with additional latent factors, some of which are *not* constrained to be related to review text.

Modeling User Features with Text

We have primarily focused on how HFT can be used to align product features γ_i with review topics θ_i. However, it can also discover topics associated with *users*. This simply means treating the set of all reviews by a particular user u as a document, with an associated topic vector θ_u; HFT then associates γ_u with θ_u as in (eq. 4).

Results for HFT, trained to model user features with text, are shown in Table 3 (column d). Both models exhibit similar performance; their MSEs differ by less than 1%. A few individual datasets show greater variation, e.g. item features are more informative in the 'music' category, while user features are more informative in the 'office' category (see our extended version [20]).

This high level of similarity indicates that there is not a substantial difference between user and product topics. This seems surprising in light of the fact that our product topics tend to correspond with product categories (as we show later); we would not necessarily expect *product* categories to be similar to *user* categories. However a simple explanation is as follows: users do not review all products with the same likelihood, but rather they have a preference towards certain categories. Thus, while a 'dark beer' topic emerges from reviews of dark beers, a 'dark beer' topic *also* emerges from users who preferentially review dark beers. In both cases, the topics we discover are qualitatively similar.

4.5 Recommending New Products

The 'cold-start' problem is a common issue in recommender system. In particular, when a product or a user is new and one does not have enough rating data available, it is very hard to train a recommender system and make predictions.

In particular, with latent factor recommender systems, as with HFT, each user and product is associated with $K + 1$ parameters (K-dimensional latent factors and a bias term). As a consequence, when given only a few ratings for a particular user u or product i (e.g. fewer than K ratings), a latent factor recommender system cannot possibly estimate γ_u or γ_i accurately due to lack of data. The presence of the regulariser $\Omega(\Theta)$ in (eq. 1) pushes γ_u and γ_i towards zero in such cases, meaning that such users and products are modeled using only their bias terms.

However, *review text* provides significant additional information and our hope is that by including review text the relationship between products and ratings can be more accurately modeled. Even a single review can tell us many of a product's properties, such as its genre. Our hypothesis is that when training data for a product is scarce (e.g. when a new product appears in the corpus), the benefit gained from using review text will be greatest.

In Figure 1 we compare the amount of training data (i.e., the number of training reviews available for a particular product, x-axis) to the improvement gained by using HFT (y-axis). Specifically, we report the MSE of a latent-factor recommender system minus the MSE of HFT; thus a positive value indicates that HFT has better performance. Results are shown for $K = 5$ on our three largest datasets (Amazon books, movies, and music). Figure 1 (left) shows the absolute improvement in MSE when using HFT compared to a latent factor recommender system. Notice that our model gains significant improvement when training data is particularly scarce. The improvement on movie data is the largest, while for books the 'standard' model is on par with HFT once ratings are abundant. Similar results are obtained for new *users*.

4.6 Qualitative Analysis

Some of the topics discovered by HFT are shown in Table 4. Topics are shown with $K = 5$ for beer, musical instruments, video game, and clothing data, and for $K = 10$ for Yelp data. We find that the most common words (in all topics) are stop words ('the'/'and'/'it' etc.), so to visualize each topic, we first compute averages across all topics for each word w: $b_w = \frac{1}{K}\sum_k \psi_{k,w}$. This generates a 'background' distribution that includes words that are common to all topics. Subtracting this value from $\psi_{k,w}$ gives us topics with common words and stop words removed. These values (i.e., $\psi_{k,w} - b_w$) are shown in Table 4. Note that we show *all* K topics, i.e., none are hand-selected or excluded.

The topics we discover are clean and easy to interpret. Discovered topics are similar to genres, or categories of products. For instance, beer topics include pale ales, lambics (sour Belgian beers), dark beers, and wheat beers, with an additional topic describing spices. From a modeling perspective, there is a simple explanation as to why HFT discovers 'genre-like' topics. Firstly, users are likely to rate products of the same genre similarly, so separating products into genres explains much of the variation in rating data. Secondly, different language is used to describe products from different genres, so genres also explain much of the variation in review data. As we see in the next section, if our goal is to *discover* genres, combining these two sources of data (ratings and reviews) leads to much better performance than using either in isolation.

4.7 Genre Discovery

We noted that the 'topics' discovered by HFT are similar to product 'categories', or 'genres'. Now, we confirm this quantitatively, and investigate the possibility of using HFT to automatically discover such categories. For brevity we focus on the Yelp Phoenix dataset, which contains detailed product category information.

Each of the models compared in the previous section outputs a K-dimensional vector per product, where K is the number of latent product/user dimensions (θ_i in the case of LDA, γ_i in the case of the latent factor model and HFT). We define the category of a product, which we denote c_i, to be the latent dimension with the highest weight, i.e.,

$$c_i = \operatorname*{argmax}_k \gamma_{i,k} \tag{10}$$

(or $\operatorname{argmax}_k \theta_{i,k}$ for LDA). Thus each product has a 'category' between 1 and K. We then compute the best alignment between these K categories and the K most popular (i.e., most frequently occurring) categories in the Yelp dataset. We denote by C_k the set of products whose predicted category is k (i.e., $\{i | c_i = k\}$), and by C^*_k the set of products whose *true* category is k. The score of the optimal correspondence is then

$$\min_f \frac{1}{K} \sum_{k=1}^{K} F_1(C_k, C^*_{f(k)}), \tag{11}$$

where $f(\cdot)$ is a one-to-one correspondence (computed by linear assignment) between predicted product categories k and ground-truth categories $f(k)$; (eq. 11) is then the average F_1 score between the predicted and the true product categories.

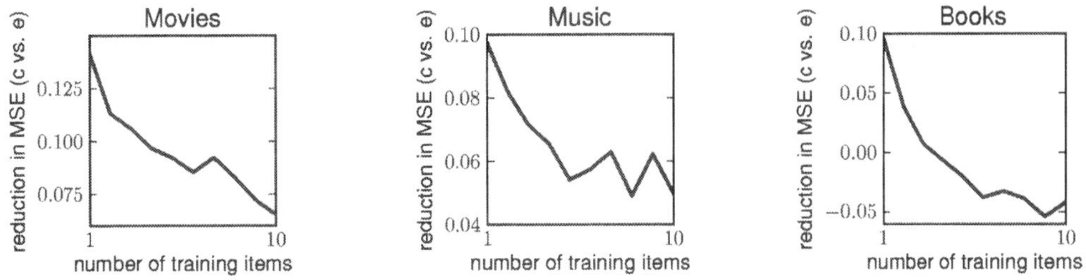

Figure 1: When training data is scarce, the benefit gained from modeling review text is the greatest. Improvement in MSE compared to a latent factor model on three Amazon datasets.

Beer (Beeradvocate)				
pale ales	lambics	dark beers	spices	wheat beer
ipa	funk	chocolate	pumpkin	wheat
pine	brett	coffee	nutmeg	yellow
grapefruit	saison	black	corn	straw
citrus	vinegar	dark	cinnamon	pilsner
ipas	raspberry	roasted	pie	summer
piney	lambic	stout	cheap	pale
citrusy	barnyard	bourbon	bud	lager
floral	funky	tan	water	banana
hoppy	tart	porter	macro	coriander
dipa	raspberries	vanilla	adjunct	pils

Musical instruments (Amazon)				
drums	strings	wind	microphones	software
cartridge	guitar	reeds	mic	software
sticks	violin	harmonica	microphone	interface
strings	strap	cream	stand	midi
snare	neck	reed	mics	windows
stylus	capo	harp	wireless	drivers
cymbals	tune	fog	microphones	inputs
mute	guitars	mouthpiece	condenser	usb
heads	picks	bruce	battery	computer
these	bridge	harmonicas	filter	mp3
daddario	tuner	harps	stands	program

Video games (Amazon)				
fantasy	nintendo	windows	ea/sports	accessories
fantasy	mario	sims	drm	cable
rpg	ds	flight	ea	controller
battle	nintendo	windows	spore	cables
tomb	psp	xp	creature	ps3
raider	wii	install	nba	batteries
final	gamecube	expansion	football	sonic
battles	memory	program	nhl	headset
starcraft	wrestling	software	basketball	wireless
characters	metroid	mac	madden	controllers
ff	smackdown	sim	hockey	component

Clothing (Amazon)				
bags	winter	formal	pants	bras
backpack	vest	scarf	pants	bra
bag	jacket	cards	jeans	bras
jansport	fleece	shirt	pair	support
costume	warm	shirts	dickies	cup
books	columbia	suit	these	cups
hat	coat	silk	levis	underwire
laptop	sweatshirt	wallet	waist	supportive
bags	russell	belt	pairs	breasts
backpacks	gloves	leather	socks	sports
halloween	sweater	tie	they	breast

Yelp Phoenix									
theaters	spas	mexican	vietnamese	snacks	italian	medical	donuts	coffee	seafood
theater	massage	mexican	pho	cupcakes	pizza	dr	donuts	coffee	sushi
movie	spa	salsa	vietnamese	cupcake	crust	stadium	donut	starbucks	dish
harkins	yoga	tacos	yogurt	hotel	pizzas	dentist	museum	books	restaurant
theaters	classes	chicken	brisket	resort	italian	doctor	target	latte	rolls
theatre	pedicure	burrito	beer	rooms	bianco	insurance	subs	bowling	server
movies	trail	beans	peaks	dog	pizzeria	doctors	sub	lux	shrimp
dance	studio	taco	mojo	dogs	wings	dental	dunkin	library	dishes
popcorn	gym	burger	shoes	frosting	pasta	appointment	frys	espresso	menu
tickets	hike	carne	froyo	bagel	mozzarella	exam	tour	stores	waiter
flight	nails	food	zoo	bagels	pepperoni	prescription	bike	gelato	crab

Table 4: Top ten words from each of $K = 5$ topics from five of our datasets (and with $K = 10$ from Yelp). Each column is labeled with an 'interpretation' of that topic. Note we display all the topics (and not only the 'interpretable' ones). All topics are clean and easily interpretable.

	(b)	(c)	(e)	improvement	
K	lat. factors	LDA	HFT	e vs. b	e vs. c
5	0.166	0.205	0.412*	148.15%	100.23%
10	0.097	0.169	0.256*	163.54%	51.16%
20	0.066	0.091	0.165*	151.34%	81.82%
50	0.042	0.047	0.199*	369.14%	317.58%

Table 5: Genre discovery (on Yelp data). Values shown are average F_1 score between the predicted and the ground-truth product categories (higher is better).

This score is shown in Table 5 for different values of K. Neither latent factor models nor LDA produce latent dimensions that are similar to genres, while HFT recovers these genres accurately; with 50 genres HFT outperforms latent factor models and LDA by over 300%. It is worth noting that $K = 50$ is far larger than what we found beneficial when predicting ratings in Section 4.4. We note that when K is small, 'similar' genres tend to be combined in a single topic, e.g. 'yoga' and 'massage' in Table 4. Pleasingly, this implies that even after further topics no longer improve rating prediction accuracy, HFT continues to generate meaningful topics.

4.8 Identifying Useful Reviews

In addition to modeling how users rate products, HFT can identify reviews that users are likely to find 'useful'. As we have shown, for each product i, HFT generates a topic vector θ_i, which determines the distribution of topics, and consequently the distribution of *words*, that are likely to be used when describing that product.

We use this topic distribution to identify 'representative' reviews. Specifically, we identify reviews $r_{u,i}$ whose language matches the topic distribution θ_i closely. Recall that in HFT, 'topics' are learned in order to explain the variation present in product ratings. Thus, in order for a reviewer to adequately explain their rating, they ought to discuss each of these topics in proportion to their importance.

Recall that for each word $w_{u,i,j}$ (j^{th} word in user u's review of item i), HFT estimates a topic assignment $z_{u,i,j}$ for that word (i.e., each word belongs to a topic from 1 to K). Given the full set of words in a review $d_{u,i}$, we can then compute the proportion of each topic in that review. Specifically, we compute

$$\vartheta_{u,i,k} = \frac{1}{N_{d_{u,i}}} \sum_{j=1}^{N_{d_{u,i}}} \delta(z_{u,i,j} = k). \qquad (12)$$

Here we are simply counting the number of times each topic k occurs in a review $d_{u,i}$, and normalizing so that the entries of $\vartheta_{u,i}$

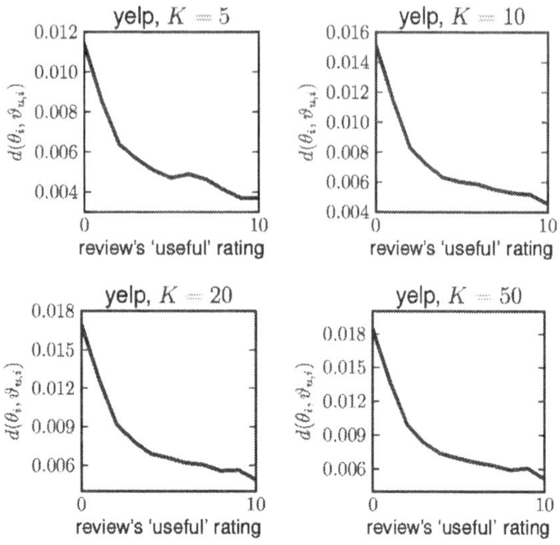

Figure 2: Reviews that are 'useful' (according to Yelp users) are those whose choice of language matches the topic distribution learned by HFT.

sum to 1. In this way, we have a topic distribution for each product, θ_i, and a topic distribution for each individual review, $\vartheta_{u,i}$ (both of which are stochastic vectors).

Our definition of a 'representative' review is one for which $\vartheta_{u,i}$ is similar to θ_i, i.e., a review that discusses those topics that explain the variation in product i's ratings. We identify this by computing the distance

$$d(\theta_i, \vartheta_{u,i}) = \|\theta_i - \vartheta_{u,i}\|_2^2. \tag{13}$$

We hypothesize that reviews with small $d(\theta_i, \vartheta_{u,i})$ will be 'representative' of the product i. We evaluate this quantitatively by comparing $d(\theta_i, \vartheta_{u,i})$ to 'usefulness' ratings on Yelp.

In Figure 2 we compare Yelp 'useful' ratings (non-negative integers) to $d(\theta_j, \vartheta_{u,i})$. Results are shown for $K \in \{5, 10, 20, 50\}$. We observe a clear relationship between the two quantities. When $K = 5$ (for example), reviews with even two useful votes are *half* the distance from θ_i compared to reviews with no useful votes; reviews with 10 useful votes are *one third* the distance from θ_i. This experiment suggests that in addition to predicting ratings, HFT can also be used to identify 'useful', or 'representative' reviews.

5. CONCLUSION

We have presented HFT, a model that combines ratings with review text for product recommendations. HFT works by aligning hidden factors in product *ratings* with hidden topics in product *reviews*. Essentially, these topics act as regularisers for latent user and product parameters. This allows us to accurately fit user and product parameters with only a few *reviews*, which existing models cannot do using only a few *ratings*. We evaluated HFT on large, novel corpora consisting of over forty million product reviews. In addition to more accurately predicting product ratings, HFT discovers highly interpretable product topics, that can be used to facilitate tasks such as genre discovery and to suggest informative reviews.

Acknowledgements

Thanks to David Blei for comments on an initial draft of this paper, and to Dan Jurafsky for discussions. This research has been supported in part by NSF IIS-1016909, CNS-1010921, CAREER IIS-1149837, IIS-1159679, ARO MURI, DARPA SMISC, the Okawa Foundation, Docomo, Boeing, Allyes, Volkswagen, Intel, as well as the Alfred P. Sloan and the Microsoft Faculty Fellowships.

6. REFERENCES

[1] S. Baccianella, A. Esuli, and F. Sebastiani. Multi-facet rating of product reviews. In *ECIR*, 2009.
[2] J. Bennett and S. Lanning. The Netflix prize. In *KDD Cup and Workshop*, 2007.
[3] D. Blei and J. McAuliffe. Supervised topic models. In *NIPS*, 2007.
[4] D. Blei, A. Ng, and M. Jordan. Latent dirichlet allocation. *JMLR*, 2003.
[5] S. Brody and N. Elhadad. An unsupervised aspect-sentiment model for online reviews. In *ACL*, 2010.
[6] G. Ganu, N. Elhadad, and A. Marian. Beyond the stars: Improving rating predictions using review text content. In *WebDB*, 2009.
[7] M. Hu and B. Liu. Mining and summarizing customer reviews. In *KDD*, 2004.
[8] N. Jindal and B. Liu. Opinion spam and analysis. In *WSDM*, 2008.
[9] Y. Jo and A. Oh. Aspect and sentiment unification model for online review analysis. In *WSDM*, 2011.
[10] S.-M. Kim and E. Hovy. Determining the sentiment of opinions. In *COLING*, 2004.
[11] Y. Koren and R. Bell. Advances in collaborative filtering. In *Recommender Systems Handbook*. Springer, 2011.
[12] Y. Koren, R. Bell, and C. Volinsky. Matrix factorization techniques for recommender systems. *Computer*, 2009.
[13] K. Lerman, S. Blair-Goldensohn, and R. McDonald. Sentiment summarization: evaluating and learning user preferences. In *EACL*, 2009.
[14] A. Levi, O. Mokryn, C. Diot, and N. Taft. Finding a needle in a haystack of reviews: cold start context-based hotel recommender system. In *RecSys*, 2012.
[15] C. Lin and Y. He. Joint sentiment/topic model for sentiment analysis. In *CIKM*, 2009.
[16] G. Linden, B. Smith, and J. York. Amazon.com recommendations: Item-to-item collaborative filtering. *IEEE Internet Computing*, 2003.
[17] B. Lu, M. Ott, C. Cardie, and B. Tsou. Multi-aspect sentiment analysis with topic models. In *Workshop on SENTIRE*, 2011.
[18] Y. Lu, C. Zhai, and N. Sundaresan. Rated aspect summarization of short comments. In *WWW*, 2009.
[19] J. McAuley and J. Leskovec. From amateurs to connoisseurs: modeling the evolution of user expertise through online reviews. In *WWW*, 2013.
[20] J. McAuley and J. Leskovec. Hidden Factors and Hidden Topics: Understanding Rating Dimensions with Review Text. Extended version `http://i.stanford.edu/~julian/pdfs/recsys_extended.pdf`
[21] J. McAuley, J. Leskovec, and D. Jurafsky. Learning attitudes and attributes from multi-aspect reviews. In *ICDM*, 2012.
[22] J. Nocedal. Updating quasi-newton matrices with limited storage. *Mathematics of Computation*, 1980.
[23] A. Popescu and O. Etzioni. Extracting product features and opinions from reviews. In *HLT*, 2005.
[24] A. Sharma and D. Cosley. Do social explanations work? Studying and modeling the effects of social explanations in recommender systems. In *WWW*, 2013.
[25] I. Titov and R. McDonald. A joint model of text and aspect ratings for sentiment summarization. In *ACL*, 2008.
[26] I. Titov and R. McDonald. Modeling online reviews with multi-grain topic models. In *WWW*, 2008.
[27] M. Wainwright and M. Jordan. Graphical models, exponential families, and variational inference. *Foundations and Trends in Machine Learning*, 2008.
[28] C. Wang and D. Blei. Collaborative topic modeling for recommending scientific articles. In *KDD*, 2011.
[29] H. Wang, Y. Lu, and C. Zhai. Latent aspect rating analysis on review text data: a rating regression approach. In *KDD*, 2010.
[30] W. Zhao, J. Jiang, H. Yan, and X. Li. Jointly modeling aspects and opinions with a MaxEnt-LDA hybrid. In *EMNLP*, 2010.

Improving Augmented Reality Using Recommender Systems

Zhuo Zhang, Shang Shang, Sanjeev R. Kulkarni
Department of Electrical Engineering
Princeton University
Princeton, NJ
USA
{zhuoz,sshang,kulkarni}@princeton.edu

Pan Hui
CSE Department
The Hong Kong University of Science and Technology
Hong Kong
panhui@cse.ust.hk

ABSTRACT

With the rapid development of smart devices and wireless communication, especially with the pre-launch of Google Glass, augmented reality (AR) has received enormous attention recently. AR adds virtual objects into a user's real-world environment enabling live interaction in three dimensions. Limited by the small display of AR devices, content selection is one of the key issues to improve user experience. In this paper, we present an aggregated random walk algorithm incorporating personal preferences, location information, and temporal information in a layered graph. By adaptively changing the graph edge weight and computing the rank score, the proposed AR recommender system predicts users' preferences and provides the most relevant recommendations with aggregated information.

Categories and Subject Descriptors

H.4 [**Information Systems Applications**]: Miscellaneous

Keywords

Augmented Reality, Recommender System, Random Walk, PageRank, Graph, High-dimensional

1. INTRODUCTION

Augmented reality (AR) is an emerging technology that embraces cutting-edge developments in sensing and smart devices, wireless communication, pervasive computing and intelligent environments. It augments users' experiences by adding virtual objects and allowing users to interact in real time and space [4]. Current AR systems are mainly based on smart devices such as Google Glass and iPhone, with limited screen size. Content displayed on a small screen can be difficult and frustrating for end-users, thus high performance recommender systems are desired in AR systems [8]. Although recommendation algorithms, especially collaborative filtering techniques, have been intensively studied during the past decade, we cannot trivially adapt and deploy traditional recommender in AR systems, because they differ in the following respects:

- Location: Nearby recommendations are usually more interesting than a place in a remote location.
- Timing: Short-term or in-time preferences have high priority. For example, at Sunday 11am, a user is more likely looking for a restaurant for brunch rather than a night club.
- Cold start: New users are sensitive to application user experience but sparse data may lead to inaccurate recommendations.
- Immediate feedback: AR recommender systems have to react quickly based on users' behaviors. Users may click interesting items immediately after a recommendation is made. Recommendation lists are then updated accordingly.

Currently most AR applications use distance-based filtering and visibility-based filtering. Some advanced techniques include a spatial model, e.g., [6], which uses focus and nimbus to determine the importance of objects. Alternatively, model-based filtering with prior knowledge of human motivation has been applied in AR recommendation [9]. Popular AR applications such as Wikitude and Layar also use this recommendation. Individual preference can be captured quite well, though they fail to combine historical information and other users' data for the recommendation.

In this paper, we propose a random walk algorithm for AR recommendation, incorporating user preference, behavior patterns, history records, and social network information. We construct a layered graph consisting of users, places and labels as nodes, and we incorporate temporal and location information into the edge weight. We simulate the user decision making process as a biased random walk on the graph. The stationary distribution of the random walk represents the ranking score, inspired by the PageRank algorithm[7]. The rest of the paper is organized as follows: We formulate the AR recommendation problem in Section 2. We propose the random walk based algorithm in Section 3, followed by preliminary experimental results in Section 4. Conclusion and further work are discussed in Section 5.

*This research was supported in part by the Center for Science of Information (CSoI), an NSF Science and Technology Center, under grant agreement CCF-0939370, and by support from Deutsche Telekom T-Labs.

RecSys'13, October 12–16, 2013, Hong Kong, China.
Copyright 2013 ACM 978-1-4503-2409-0/13/10 ...$15.00.
http://dx.doi.org/10.1145/2507157.2507211.

2. PROBLEM FORMULATION

In recommender systems, there are lists of both users and items. Each user provides scores or linguistic terms such as "like" or "dislike" to rate a subset of all possible items. Recommender systems such as Netflix and Amazon are designed to help select useful and relevant information for a specific user. It can be formulated as a matrix completion problem for the user-item rating matrix [2]. However, in some cases, extra information may help improve recommendation quality, such as temporal information, location information and social network information [12, 10]. One possible approach for incorporating this additional information is multi-dimensional collaborative filtering. [11] and [1] used a reduction-based algorithm and applied classic 2D collaborative filtering algorithms to produce a final recommendation. This approach has limitations. For example, when we extend available ratings into high dimension, the data will become extremely sparse and many existing algorithms will lose their effectiveness. Also, when multiple dimensions are decoupled as pairs of dimensions, relationships among more than two dimensions are likely to be lost. Therefore in this paper, we propose a layered graph to aggregate high dimensional information and use a random walk algorithm to make recommendations. The problem is formally formulated as below.

Assume that there is a set of users $U = \{u_1, ..., u_m\}$ and a set of places $I = \{i_1, ..., i_n\}$. Traditionally, a two dimensional rating matrix $U \times I \to R$ can be constructed. Each element $r_{u,i}$ in R denotes user u's rating of place i. The ratings can be either explicit, for example, on a 1-5 scale as in TripAdvisor, or implicit such as "visited" or "not visited". The rating data typically specifies only a small number of the elements of R. We further assume binary label and user social information is given. Let $L = \{l_1, ..., l_k\}$ be the set of label information of items. For example, for places, L can be restaurants, shopping malls, bus stops, etc. $L_i \in \{0,1\}^k$ denote the features of place i, where k is the total number of labels. Correspondingly, let $S = (U, \varepsilon)$ contain social network information, represented by an undirected or directed graph, where U is a set of nodes while ε is a set of edges. $\forall u, v \in U$, $(u,v) \in \varepsilon$ if v is a friend of u. We further denote set of times as T and location set as P. Then the multidimensional rating matrix will be formulated as $R = U \times I \times L \times T \times P$. Given the target user u, the current time t and current location p, our ultimate goal is to find the optimal place defined below.

$$\forall u \in U, t \in T, p \in P, i_{u,t,p} = \arg\max_i R(u, l, i, t, p) \quad (1)$$

In the following part, we will address the questions mentioned above with a proposed random walk algorithm.

3. RANDOM WALK IN AR RECOMMENDER SYSTEMS

Several random walk algorithms [12, 10] have been proposed for the traditional recommender systems but they fail to handle with the characteristics of AR systems. In this section, we will describe our random walk algorithm in detail, and discuss how to deal with specific issues in multidimensional AR recommender systems.

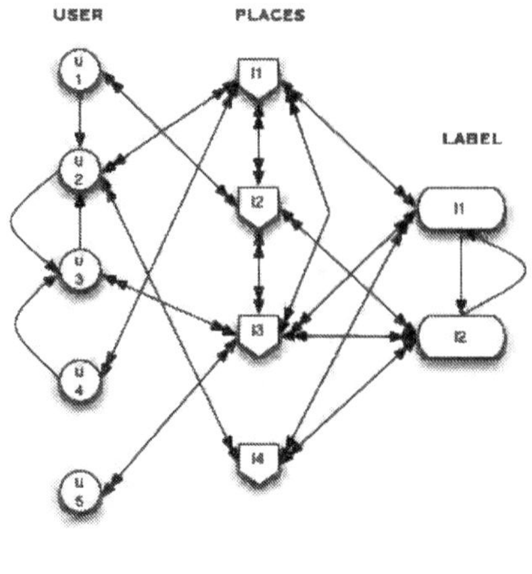

Figure 1: An example of recommendation graph

3.1 Model Construction

3.1.1 Graph Formulation

Let $G = \{V, E\}$ be a directed graph model for AR recommender systems, as shown in Fig.1. We construct the graph by the following rules. 1) Nodes V represent constant attributes such as users, places and labels; for each entity all the nodes stay in the same layer; 2) Edges/Weighted edges E represent variables such as locations or time, or relationships, e.g. social network information.

In this recommender system, the nodes $V = U \cup I \cup L$ form three layers, which consist of users, places and labels. The edges E are classified as the following five classes based on the layers that the nodes belong to. Higher weight means higher chance to transition from one node to another. We incorporate personal records, location information, and label information into the graph. Note that we use the inverse exponential distribution to model a human's mobility [3]. Let d denote the distance between current location and the target place. Then the human's mobility is modeled by the distribution $\frac{1}{Z}\exp(-\alpha d)$ where $\alpha \geq 0$ is a decay parameter and Z is a normalization factor. α is a tunable factor set by users. For example, if $\alpha = 0$, distance to the current location would not affect recommendation results. In contrast, if α is large, only nearby places will be recommended. Experimental results in Section 4 show the effect of α on average distance between local position and recommendation.

- For $u \in U, i \in I, (u,i) \in E$ and $(i,u) \in E$ if and only if user u has visited i (assume only implicit ratings are available) and the weight $w_{u,i} = \exp(-\alpha(d(i,p))$, $w_{i,u} = 1$ where $d(:,:)$ is the distance between two places, p is the current location.

- For $i \in I, l \in L, (i,l) \in E$ and $(l,i) \in E$ if and only if $L_i^l \neq 0$, i.e., the place i belongs to label l and the weight $w_{i,l} = w_{l,i} = 1$.

- For $u_1, u_2 \in U, (u_1, u_2) \in E$ if and only if $(u_1, u_2) \in \varepsilon$, which means u_2 is a friend of u_1. Note that the relationship in social networks is not necessarily mutual such as "follow" in Twitter.

- For $i_1, i_2 \in I, (i_1, i_2) \in E$ and $(i_2, i_1) \in E$ if and only if $i_1 \neq i_2$. Define $w_{i_1,i_2} = \exp(-\alpha(d(i_1, i_2))$.

- For $l_1, l_2 \in L, (l_1, l_2) \in E$ if and only if the transition probability from label l_1 to l_2 is greater than 0, which we will get from the training data set.

3.1.2 Transition Probability

Assume that a random walk with an initial distribution is applied in such a weighted graph. The path is a sequence of random variables $X_1, ..X_t, ...$, which form a Markov chain and the future state only depends on the current state. We need to further normalize the weight to make it a transition probability.

Let $Y_1, Y_2, ..., Y_s$ denote s layers in the graph. We first define the transition probability T_{ij} between different layers Y_i, Y_j.

$$T_{ij} := \sum_{n_1 \in Y_i, n_2 \in Y_j} P(X_{t+1} = n_2 | X_t = n_1). \quad (2)$$

Specifically in this case, we have 3 layers U, I, L and we define $T_{ij} = \frac{1}{3}, \forall i, j \in \{1, 2, 3\}$.

We further define the transition probability between different nodes $n_i \in Y_x, n_j \in Y_y$. It is normalized by all weights to the layer Y_y times a layer transition probability T_{xy}.

$$P_{ij} := P(X_{t+1} = n_j | X_t = n_i) = \frac{w_{n_i, n_j} T_{xy}}{\sum_{n \in Out_i \cap n \in Y_y} w_{n_i, n}}, \quad (3)$$

where $Out_i = \{n | (n_i, n_j) \in E\}$.

3.1.3 Temporal Information

Another important factor in the AR recommender system is the temporal information. For example, users at noon may look for restaurants rather than nightclubs, while at around 3pm they might prefer coffee or ice cream rather than fine food. Accordingly, we will calculate the probability $P_u(t)$ of every label activities within each time slot, say half an hour or an hour. Here $P_u(t)$ is a $k \times 1$ histogram distribution vector to denote the probability that a specific user u looks for some places related to label l at time slot t.

3.2 Score Computation

3.2.1 Random Walk

For the recommendation graph $G = (V, E)$, let the $|V| \times 1$ vector θ denote the customized probability vector. We will illustrate how to set θ based on a customized request in the following. We define another parameter $\beta \in [0, 1]$, called the damping factor. With probability β, the random walk will continue its path in G. Otherwise, it will go back to the customized probability distribution θ. Let the $|V| \times |V|$ matrix M denote the Markov transition matrix, in which $M_{ij} = P_{ji}$ in Eqn.(3). We further define γ as the stationary distribution for this random process. It satisfies the following equations:

$$\gamma = \beta M \gamma + (1 - \beta)\theta \quad (4)$$

Therefore, we can transform Eqn.(4) into

$$\gamma = (\beta M + (1 - \beta)\theta 1^T)\gamma, \quad (5)$$

where 1^T is a $|V| \times 1$ vector and $1^T \gamma = |\gamma|_1 = 1$.

We define $A = \beta M + (1 - \beta)\theta 1^T$ and the rank score γ would be the eigenvector of A. In the following section we will assign suitable θ for different purposes. Based on Eqn.(5), we can calculate the rank score γ.

3.2.2 Temporal Information

For a specific time t and a target user u at a location p, we aggregate the user information and location information into the graph. In order to combine $P_u(t)$ and γ to make an effective recommendation, we let Q be the $|V| \times k$ label matrix where Q_{ij} denote whether v_i belongs to label l_j. $Q_{ij} = 1$ if and only if v_i is a place node (i.e., in the place layer) and v_i belongs to label l_j. Otherwise $Q_{ij} = 0$. Then our final recommendation score will be

$$\gamma(t) = \gamma \cdot (Q \times P_u(t)), \quad (6)$$

where $\cdot$ is the dot product between two vectors.

3.3 Personalized Recommendation through θ

Now the only challenge for this random walk algorithm is how to set θ to meet each user's personal requirement in AR systems.

3.3.1 Regular Case

We set $\theta = e_u$ where e_u is the $|V| \times 1$ unit vector, and get the rank score γ. We sort all the nodes in V based on γ and select the top n places for the top n recommendations.

3.3.2 Cold Start Case

The cold start problem has been one of the most important issues in recommender system for years. For AR recommender systems, it is crucial since new users will not tolerate a bad user experience for a long time. In other words, if the AR recommender systems cannot give good predictions for the first several attempts, the new user may quite possibly delete the application forever. However sparse data may lead to inaccurate personal rank score γ for new users. Averages based on relatively low support (small values of $|I_u|$, i.e. the number of places that user u has visited) can generally be improved by shrinkage towards a common mean $\bar{\gamma}$ [5]. Set $\theta = \frac{1}{|U|}\mathbb{1}_{\{v \in U\}}$ and we can compute the rank score $\bar{\gamma}$ for overall users. Therefore we can further define the rank score for cold start users as follows.

$$\gamma_{cold} = \frac{|I_u|\gamma + \tau\bar{\gamma}}{|I_u| + \tau}, \quad (7)$$

where the parameter τ controls the extent of the shrinkage.

3.3.3 Interaction/Update Case

Users will interact with an AR system in real time. When several selected places are shown in the AR system, users will use their finger to click on the item, denoted as i, which they are interested in. Here we propose two methods for further updates, listed below.

- Label-driven Update: This method is fast and focuses on the label behind the place i only. Every time user u selects place i among all the available items the recommender system provides, we regard u's purpose to be the label set to which i belongs. We then replace all the top n recommendations by the top n places that belongs to these labels.

- Place-driven Update: This method is relatively slow and needs to recompute the rank score. Basically, we will set $\theta = e_i$ to compute the rank score γ for the recommendations.

Table 1: Average Percentile of Recommendations

α	0	0.1	0.5	1
Percentile(%)	93.5	76.3	57.4	50.1

Table 2: Recall of Top Recommendations

Recall (%)	$\alpha = 0$	$\alpha = 0.1$	$\alpha = 0.5$	$\alpha = 1$
Top 10	83.3	32.1	26.6	24.5
Top 30	95.2	75.1	47.1	30.1
Top 50	100.0	81.0	65.3	43.0

Table 3: Average Distance of Top Recommendations

Distance (km)	$\alpha = 0$	$\alpha = 0.1$	$\alpha = 0.5$	$\alpha = 1$
Top 10	18.46	7.52	5.82	3.65
Top 30	20.01	9.30	7.63	6.34
Top 50	22.85	13.32	10.90	9.60

4. PRELIMINARY EXPERIMENTAL RESULT

We downloaded the Gowalla dataset[1], which contains 19,183 users, 30,367 places in NYC and 357,753 check-ins in each of which records a specific place a user has visited. We randomly select 100 users, 100 most popular places and 831 corresponding check-ins to construct the transition graph. Due to the incomplete data, in this experiment the layered graph only contains users, locations and check-in information. Then a target user is randomly picked and the current location is randomly generated. We use the proposed algorithm to recommend places to the target user and calculate three measures of the top recommendation list. *Percentile* is the average position (in percentage) of the actual visited places out of the whole set of places, where 99% denotes the top 1%. *Recall* is the number of hits (i.e., the visited places) of the top n recommendations divided by the total number of visited places. These two measures can evaluate the effectiveness of recommendations. The *average distance* of the top recommendations can evaluate whether the location factor is taken into account in the recommendations. In the experiment, we set $\beta = 0.85$ and vary α to see the different performance of the algorithm. Note that when $\alpha = 0$, the algorithm will become the traditional random walk without location information. We compare the average percentile, recall, and average distance with different α. We repeatedly generate target user and current location 500 times. The average results are reported in Table 1, 2 and 3.

The results show that incorporating location indeed improves AR applications by reducing the average distance of top recommendations. When α becomes larger, the average distance decreases while the percentile and recall decrease as well. Therefore the value of α can deal with the trade-off between recommendation accuracy and average distance. Larger α means higher priority of distance and lower weight on personal tastes.

5. CONCLUSION AND FUTURE WORK

In this paper, we have proposed using recommender systems to improve AR, specifically by applying a random walk algorithm to AR recommender systems. We incorporate location information into the weight of edge in the graph and incorporate temporal statistics as well into the rank score. Therefore we aggregate the user's personal preference, location information and temporal information into the biased random walk to recommend places for AR device users. We have also proposed the recommendation list updating methods when users take actions. Preliminary results show that location is indeed incorporated into the layered graph.

For future work, it may be interesting to find more comprehensive datasets with complete information on history record, location and temporal preference. Parameter tuning is another key issue to handle the tradeoff between different factors. Furthermore, user feedback can help provide a true evaluation of the effectiveness of AR recommender systems.

[1] http://code.google.com/p/locrec/downloads/list

6. REFERENCES

[1] G. Adomavicius, R. Sankaranarayanan, S. Sen, and A. Tuzhilin. Incorporating contextual information in recommender systems using a multidimensional approach. *ACM Transactions on Information Systems*, 23(1):103–145, 2005.

[2] G. Adomavicius and A. Tuzhilin. Toward the next generation of recommender systems: A survey of the state-of-the-art and possible extensions. *IEEE Transactions on Knowledge and Data Engineering*, 17(6):734–749, 2005.

[3] M. Allamanis, S. Scellato, and C. Mascolo. Evolution of a location-based online social network: analysis and models. In *Proceedings of the 2012 ACM Internet Measurement Conference*, pages 145–158. ACM, 2012.

[4] R. T. Azuma et al. A survey of augmented reality. *Presence-Teleoperators and Virtual Environments*, 6(4):355–385, 1997.

[5] R. M. Bell and Y. Koren. Improved neighborhood-based collaborative filtering. In *KDD Cup and Workshop at the 13th ACM SIGKDD*, 2007.

[6] S. Benford and L. Fahlén. A spatial model of interaction in large virtual environments. In *Proceedings of the 3rd Conference on European Conference on Computer-Supported Cooperative Work*, pages 109–124. Kluwer Academic Publishers, 1993.

[7] S. Brin and L. Page. The anatomy of a large-scale hypertextual web search engine. *Computer Networks and ISDN Systems*, 30(1):107–117, 1998.

[8] F. Ricci. Mobile recommender systems. *Information Technology & Tourism*, 12(3):205–231, 2010.

[9] F. Ricci and Q. N. Nguyen. Acquiring and revising preferences in a critique-based mobile recommender system. *Intelligent Systems*, 22(3):22–29, 2007.

[10] S. Shang, S. R. Kulkarni, P. W. Cuff, and P. Hui. A random walk based model incorporating social information for recommendations. In *2012 International Workshop on Machine Learning and Signal Processing*, pages 1–6. IEEE, 2012.

[11] K. H. Tso-Sutter, L. B. Marinho, and L. Schmidt-Thieme. Tag-aware recommender systems by fusion of collaborative filtering algorithms. In *Proceedings of the 2008 ACM Symposium on Applied computing*, pages 1995–1999. ACM, 2008.

[12] L. Xiang, Q. Yuan, S. Zhao, L. Chen, X. Zhang, Q. Yang, and J. Sun. Temporal recommendation on graphs via long-and short-term preference fusion. In *Proceedings of the 16th ACM SIGKDD*, pages 723–732. ACM, 2010.

Exploiting Non-content Preference Attributes through Hybrid Recommendation Method*

Fernando Mourão[1], Leonardo Rocha[2], Joseph Konstan[3], Wagner Meira Jr.[1]

[1]Universidade Federal de Minas Gerais
Computer Science
Belo Horizonte, MG, Brazil
{fhmourao,meira}@dcc.ufmg.br

[2]Universidade Federal de São João Del Rey
Computer Science
São João Del Rey, MG, Brazil
lcrocha@ufsj.edu.br

[3]University of Minnesota
Computer Science and Engineering
Minneapolis, MN, USA
konstan@cs.umn.edu

ABSTRACT

This paper explores a method for incorporating into a recommender system explicit representations of user's preferences over non-content attributes such as popularity, recency, and similarity of recommended items. We show how such attributes can be modeled as a preference vector that can be used in a vector-space content-based recommender, and how that content-based recommender can be integrated with various collaborative f ltering techniques through re-weighting of Top-M recommendations. We evaluate this approach on several recommender systems datasets and collaborative f ltering methods, and f nd that incorporating the three preference attributes can lead to a substantial increase in Top-50 precision while also enhancing diversity and novelty.

Categories and Subject Descriptors

H.4.m [**Information System Applications**]: Miscellaneous; H.m [**Information System**]: Miscellaneous

Keywords

Recommendation; User Modeling; Hybrid Methods

1. INTRODUCTION

One common thread in recommender systems research is to combine recommendation methods as a strategy to improve performance [7]. Existing recommendation methods have strengths and weaknesses, and researchers proposed a large number of combination strategies. In most cases, Collaborative Filtering (CF) methods, which correlate user ratings with items, are combined to Content-based (CB) methods, which correlate user ratings with item attributes [1, 8]. While CF methods assume that users with similar consumption history would share common interests, CB methods conjecture that each user exhibits a systematic preference correlated with some item attributes [18]. Such preferences may stem from usual content-related data, such as genres or movie actors, but they may also come from metadata or consumption attributes that are not usually handled as "content", such as popularity, recency, or similarity to other consumed items.

This work evaluates whether those non-content preference attributes are properly captured by CF methods, and, wherever they are not exploited, how they may be incorporated into CB models to produce better hybrid recommenders. First, aiming to evaluate to what extent a non-content preference attribute is captured by CF models, we def ne the *preference mismatching* metric that quantif es how the recommendations provided by a given CF match the user previous consumptions w.r.t. the values along such attribute. Further, we present a characterization methodology to evaluate the preference mismatching metric for any CF method in real domains. Finally, we implement a method to build CB models by using non-content attribute information and combine these new models with existing CF methods to produce better recommendations.

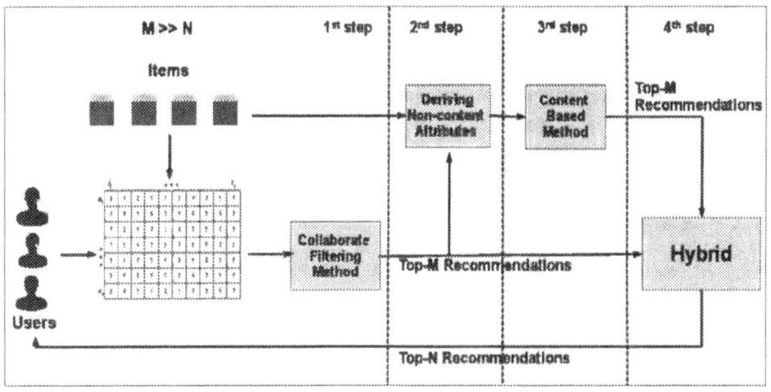

Figure 1: Our hybrid method

Figure 1 depicts our four-step hybrid method for the Top-N recommendation task. In the f rst step, we execute a given CF method, providing an ordered recommendation list L of size $M \gg N$. We then derive, in the second step, item attributes based on non-content attributes such as popularity, recency, and similarity. These derived attributes conform a vector space V where each item from L is represented. In the third step, we build a CB model for each user u considering attribute space V and determine a new score for each item from L, based on the preference mismatching metric. Finally, in the fourth step, we combine the CF score with the CB score, re-ranking the recommendation list L, and issue the N best ranked items as a recommendation to user u. It is worth emphasizing that our method differs from previous efforts by considering attribute data different from content ones, specif cally data related to aggregate consumption (popularity), metadata (recency), and data based on individual consumption (similarity) as attributes that are mod-

*This work was partially supported by CNPq, CAPES, Fapemig, and INWEB.

RecSys'13, October 12–16, 2013, Hong Kong, China.
http://dx.doi.org/10.1145/2507157.2507179.

eled and exploited from a CB perspective and integrated into a hybrid recommender.

We employ a somewhat unusual approach to compute our CB scores, designed to ref ect the fact that CF recommendations may or may not adequately represent user's preferences in the dimensions we model. Instead of directly computing a CB score, and then the hybrid recommender mix the CF and CB scores, we compute a CB delta score, a CB score that already has built into it a ref ection of the degree to which the CF recommendation ref ects the modeled user preference. Hence, if a highly-ranked item already ref ects the user's preferences in non-content attributes, the CB delta will leave this item where it is in the recommendation list. But if an item is over or under recommended relative to the preference dimensions, the CB recommendation may move it down or up as is appropriate.

We evaluate our method in real domains as follows. We f rst derive three non-content preference attributes that span various domains: popularity, similarity and recency. Popularity refers to the percentage of distinct users who have consumed each item. Similarity is a measurement of how similar the items consumed by the users are, measured using the pairwise cosine distance of the item consumption vectors. Finally, recency refers to how long an item has been consumed in a domain. Then, we instantiate the hybrid method, modeling the non-content preference of users through a multivariate Gaussian and linear function that combines CF and CB scores. We evaluate it experimentally using f ve distinct real data collections derived from *Netf ix*, *LastFm*, *MovieLens* and *Echo Nest* systems and six well known representative CF techniques implemented and distributed by the MyMediaLite project[9]. Besides demonstrating the existence of signif cant preference mismatching in all experimental conf gurations (data collections and techniques), the results also evince that major gains, regarding precision, novelty and diversity simultaneously, are achieved by exploiting non-content preference attributes. We observe improvements that range from 15% to 100% on all datasets. Further, we found that our hybrid method is able to improve the recommendations for more than 40% of the users who have room for improvement in a Top-500 CF recommendation.

In summary, we highlight as a main contribution of this work the modeling and the use of information that, so far, has not been completely exploited by RSs. Our results indicate a new and relevant research direction in recommender systems, through which signif cant enhancements may be achieved. Finally, to the best of our knowledge, our work is the f rst effort that effectively exploits non-content preference attributes in RSs.

2. RELATED WORK

The accurate modeling of the user's preferences is a core task for recommender systems (RSs) [18, 16]. Despite the number of efforts on this direction, it still represents a complex task due to distinct challenges [1, 11]. First, individual user's preferences do not follow strict and easily predictable patterns. Second, different users exhibit distinct preferences. Finally, we could mention the lack of enough information about user consumption in several domains [10]. Aiming to overcome individual limitations of RSs for addressing these challenges, an increasing number of researches combine existing methods in order to provide more robust and effective models, def ning the so-called hybrid methods.

In most of the cases, the Collaborative Filtering (CF) methods are combined with Content-based (CB) ones [1]. CF methods model dependencies between user ratings and items by using consumption information, assuming that users with similar consumption history share common interests for sake of recommendation [8]. Many of these methods are inspired by machine learning algorithms, such as nearest neighbors [19], neural network classif ers [5], induction rule learning [3], Bayesian networks [6] and latent factor models [12], among others. On the other hand, CB methods model dependencies between user ratings and item attributes, assuming that each user exhibits a systematic preference related to one or more content attributes from the item, such as price, author or genre of books, for instance [18]. As these methods often come from information retrieval and f ltering, many of them are based on traditional approaches of this area [14]. By combining CF with CB, hybrid methods are able to attenuate the weaknesses of both while exploiting simultaneously their strengths for recommendation. In this sense, for instance, [13] presents a hybrid approach that incorporates multidimensional clustering into collaborative f ltering recommendation models. Also, in [17] it was employed an evolutionary search for hybrid models following the Strength Pareto approach, which identif es hybrid models that are in the Pareto frontier. Burke [7] presents a broad survey on hybrid methods.

Despite all advances in RSs, mainly on hybrid methods, we believe that there are improvement opportunities to be exploited, since even state-of-the-art methods are not able to provide good recommendations in different real scenarios [10]. This work aims to exploit one of these opportunities. We assume that systematic preferences of users may also be correlated to non-content attributes that refer to metadata or consumption. As such correlation is not modeled explicitly by CFs, we believe that they are under captured in practice. Thus, we model explicitly these correlations through CB models that are combined with traditional CFs, def ning a new hybrid method that exploits complementary information available in the consumption data. Indeed, results related to our method demonstrate the usefulness of this information for enhancing recommendation. Further, we did not identify in the literature efforts on explicitly modeling and exploiting non-content attributes as we do.

3. NON-CONTENT PREFERENCE MISMATCHING

3.1 Non-Content Preference Attributes

A formal description of the Preference Mismatching requires, f rst, to def ne non-content preference attributes. A non-content preference attribute is derived from previous consumption data and quantif es a criterion by which an item might have been chosen previously. For instance, how long an item has been consumed in a domain or the item's popularity are non-content preference attributes available in almost all domains. Specif cally, such attributes fulf ll three requirements:

1. The consumption data are enough for allowing the computation of the attribute values;
2. There is a function that maps the represented criterion to a numeric spectrum of values, so that it is possible to assign a value to each item in the population;
3. The per user consumption must be related to a short range of values along the spectrum. In practice, we focus on attributes that may be exploited for sake of prediction. For instance, the last moment in which an item was consumed in a domain would not be relevant whether the user consumption disregards this information.

3.2 Preference Mismatching

Aiming to measure how well a specif c non-content preference attribute is captured by RSs, we describe each item by D non-content attributes and def ne the statistical measure *Expected Value*

$(E(D_i))$ for any subset of items along each attribute D_i. In practice, such expected value can be approximated by the mean value observed in training data. Thus, we mathematically define user's preference in recommendation domains through Definition 1.

DEFINITION 1. *The **user's preference** is a D-dimensional vector that quantifies, for each attribute D_i, the relative difference between the expected value $E(D_i|S)$, given the subset S of items consumed by a specific user, and the expected value $E(D_i|I)$ given the entire item set I.*

More formally, let C_{u_k} be the set of items consumed by user u_k, during a given period of time. Also, let $E(D_i|C_{u_k})$ be the expected value of the set C_{u_k} for each $D_i \in D$. Thus, the preference $Preference[u_k, D_i]$ is given by Equation 1.

$$Preference[u_k, D_i] = \begin{cases} \frac{E(D_i|C_{u_k}) - E(D_i)}{E(D_i)}, & \text{if } E(D_i) \neq 0 \\ \lim\limits_{E(D_i) \to 0} \frac{E(D_i|C_{u_k})}{E(D_i)}, & \text{otherwise} \end{cases} \quad (1)$$

We assume that consumption is not random and users present a systematic preference about items from a specific range of values for distinct non-content attributes. Therefore, explicitly considering such non-content preference allows us to refine the identification of user interests. For instance, the information that a specific user's preference is towards old and unpopular items allows selecting a subset of items that better suit his/her interests.

Analogously, we define the per user recommendation's non-content description as the relative difference between the expected value $E(D_i|R)$ observed in the subset R of items recommended to a specific user and the expected value $E(D_i|I)$ of the entire item set I. Let R_{a_n,u_k} be the set of items recommended by a method a_n to a specific user u_k. Further, let $E(D_i|R_{a_n,u_k})$ be the expected value of R_{a_n,u_k} along each $D_i \in D$. Thus, the description $Desc[a_n(u_k), D_i]$ of R_{a_n,u_k} is given by Equation 2.

$$Desc[a_n(u_k), D_i] = \begin{cases} \frac{E(D_i|R_{a_n,u_k}) - E(D_i)}{E(D_i)}, & \text{if } E(D_i) \neq 0 \\ \lim\limits_{E(D_i) \to 0} \frac{E(D_i|R_{a_n,u_k})}{E(D_i)}, & \text{otherwise} \end{cases} \quad (2)$$

Such as expected for users, we assume that recommenders prioritize a specific range of values for each non-content attribute, since they are based on inductive premises that make some assertions about items or users. Thus, from this perspective, a relevant question concerns the match between user non-content preference and recommendation non-content attributes. Aiming to evaluate such match, we define a metric named **Preference Mismatching** that measures the difference between our mathematical definition of user's preference and the recommendation's non-content description. We assume that this difference can be calculated using different approaches and it is significant when its absolute value is higher than a minimum positive value ϵ that determines whether a recommendation description is similar to a user preference in a given domain. Therefore, a relevant hypothesis to be assessed is whether Preference Mismatching is usually significant in real domains.

4. ASSESSING PREFERENCE MISMATCHING EXISTENCE

Aiming to verify the existence of non-content preference mismatching in real domains, we present a characterization methodology that answers some crucial questions:

1. Is the user consumption associated with a short range of values for each attribute D_i?
2. What is the user's preference w.r.t. each attribute D_i?
3. Does the user consumption present high variability w.r.t. his/her individual preference for each attribute D_i?
4. What is the recommendation's non-content description w.r.t. each attribute D_i?
5. What is the preference mismatching w.r.t. each attribute D_i?

We conduct analyses related to each of these questions on a set of transactions T, which comprises the transactional history of users in a domain. Further, we divide T into two disjoint sets, a training set T_a and a test set T_e, such that $T = T_a \cup T_e$. In all steps, only the test set T_e is used for calculating the expected values and all other measures related to each non-content attribute. In turn, the training set T_a is used for assigning the values, for each attribute D_i, to each test item. For instance, the popularity inherent to each test item is defined as its prior popularity on T_a.

We evaluate the correlation between the user consumption and a given non-content attribute D_i through the *Normalized Standard Deviation* (NSD) defined for each user u_k, as described in Equation 3, where $\sigma(D_i|C_{u_k})$ denotes the standard deviation of values of D_i in the set of consumed items C_{u_k}. This metric assumes that a non-content attribute provides predictive relationship w.r.t user consumptions whether the dispersion of values observed for the consumed items is significantly smaller than the dispersion observed in the whole spectrum of values. Thus, the smaller the NSD, the more the user consumption is correlated to a subset of values.

$$NSD(u_k) = \frac{\sigma(D_i|C_{u_k})}{|max(D_i) - min(D_i)|} \quad (3)$$

Considering the assessments of non-content preference in real domains, we measure, for each user u_k, his/her $Preference[u_k, D_i]$ for each attribute D_i, as described by Equation 1. Besides preference, the consumption variability exhibited by each user is also relevant. Predicting consumption of attributes that present small variability w.r.t. its values tends to be easier, since the consumption becomes similar to the user preference. Conversely, when this variability is more pronounced, information about expected values becomes less useful and predicting future consumption becomes more challenging. We measure the contribution of each attribute D_i to the user consumption variability through the *Relative Standard Deviation* (RSD) defined for each user u_k, as presented in Equation 4. The higher the RSD, the higher the variability that D_i brings to u_k consumption.

$$RSD(u_k) = \frac{\sigma(D_i|C_{u_k})}{E(D_i|C_{u_k})} \quad (4)$$

Similarly to the measurements of user preferences, the per user recommendation's non-content description is measured through the $Desc[a_n(u_k), D_i]$, described by Equation 2. Finally, we evaluate the Preference Mismatching for each user u_k as the difference between $Desc[a_n(u_k), D_i]$ and $Preference[u_k, D_i]$. Thus, we can verify whether CF models fail to incorporate accurate information about non-content preferences. The relevance of such analysis is that whenever the per user recommendation's non-content description differs significantly from the user consumption, the user interests are not satisfied, affecting the quality of the recommendations.

5. EXPLOITING PREFERENCE MISMATCHING ON RECOMMENDERS

In this section, we present our hybrid recommendation method for the Top-N recommendation task that combines rating information, assigned by traditional CF models to items, with the score defined by CB models that represent how well an item matches the user non-content preference. In this sense, we assume that the smaller the preference mismatching value, the better an item matches the user non-content preference. Therefore, explicitly approximating the recommendation non-content description to the user preference should mean a significant recommendation improvement. From this perspective, an item should be recommended to a specific user whenever, besides exhibiting a high rating, it has a high probability of matching this user non-content preference for a set of selected attributes.

Our method consists of four main steps. First, we execute a given CF method, such as *Matrix Factorization*, in order to obtain an initial list of M items deemed as relevant by the CF model, such that $M \gg N$. In the second step, we derive non-content attribute values and define a vector attribute space composed of these derived attributes. Then, we represent each item present in the CF recommendation list within this space by computing the item value along each attribute. In this paper we derive three attributes: **popularity**, **similarity** and **recency**. We selected these attributes based on some economic and social theories currently employed in RSs [2], which suggest that similarity, recency and popularity may be related to the user's taste. Further, previous studies have pointed out evidences of systematic trends along these attributes, reinforcing their relevance for this study. For instance, in [21], the authors argue that RSs are more apt to recommend popular items, while recommending unpopular ones remains a challenge.

We now define more formally each non-content attribute. Popularity refers to the receptivity of items in a domain, with respect to the desire of consumption. We measure its values as the percentage of distinct users who have consumed each item, regardless when, in a data sample. Similarity measures to what extent the items consumed by the user are similar to each other, using the pairwise cosine distance of the item consumption vectors. A user's preference for similarity is then computed as the average of the similarity scores of each consumed item with all other items consumed for that user. When assessing an item that is candidate for recommendation, its similarity score is the average of the similarity scores of that item with all already-consumed items for that user. Finally, recency refers to how long an item is available in a domain. We measure its values as the difference between a reference timestamp and the timestamp when the item was first consumed in a domain. By these definitions, it is straightforward that the selected non-content attributes fulfill the two first requirements discussed in Section 3.1. Since the third requirement is domain dependent, we evaluate it in the case study section.

In the third step, we define a CB model for preference on the vector space using a multivariate Gaussian due to its computational simplicity and the lack of evidences for adopting a more specific model. Thus, the non-content preference of each user u_k is a function $\mathcal{N}(\mu, \sigma^2)_{u_k}$ derived from the user non-content preference information. We define the average of the values, along each attribute, of all items already consumed by u_k as the mean μ, and the covariance matrix σ^2 is derived from u_k consumption history. Then, for each item t_j issued by the CF method in the first step, we define a new score that quantifies the preference mismatching between the item representation and the user preference model. In this case, such score is simply the probability defined by the function $\mathcal{N}(\mu, \sigma^2)_{u_k}$ at the point defined by the vector that represents t_j. The adoption of a probabilistic perspective for measuring the preference mismatching in this case stems from the need of models to take into account distinct attributes simultaneously and to capture both the user non-content preference and the variability around this preference. Differently from the characterization methodology, where we calculate the preference mismatching through an Euclidean perspective due to the goal of just measuring individually the mismatching along each attribute, we used a more robust perspective of analysis.

The last step combines the rating information provided by the CF method with this probabilistic score, generating a final score used for re-rank the recommendations. Among the possible combination strategies, we choose a simple linear combination between ratings and probabilities for defining the final score of each item t_j, such as presented in Equation 5.

$$Score(u_k, t_j) = \alpha \cdot \frac{R_{a_n,u_k}(t_j)}{\max R_{a_n,u_k}(*)} + (1-\alpha) \cdot \frac{G_{u_k}(t_j)}{\max G_{u_k}(*)} \quad (5)$$

where $R_{a_n,u_k}(t_j)$ denotes the rating assigned by a_n to t_j considering the target user u_k; G_{u_k} refers to the Gaussian distribution that models the user non-content preference and variabilities in the training set and α represents a weighting factor in the linear combination. In this work we just perform an exhaustive evaluation of several α values between 0 and 1, aiming to evaluate the relevance of the non-content preference information on this combination. Also, given the complexity of evaluating individual α values for each user, we adopted a single global α for all users, although it is expected that distinct users require different combination weights. Furthermore, we normalize each rating $R_{a_n,u_k}(t_j)$ and probability $G_{u_k}(t_j)$, since they vary on distinct scale of values.

Finally, we highlight that such hybrid method can be easily incorporated to the traditional recommendation process, regardless the domain or adopted CF. Whenever it is possible to identify any significant non-content attribute that users follow, we have an approach to incorporate it explicitly into the recommendations. Also, we can apply distinct strategies for building preference models, calculating preference mismatching and combining CF and CB scores.

6. CASE STUDIES

In this section, we assess the existence of the non-content preference mismatching and practical usefulness for recommendation in real domains. We start by presenting the data collections used in our experiments. Next, we briefly describe the evaluated CF methods. Then, we discuss the results related to our characterization methodology. Finally, we present the results related to the hybrid method that exploits the non-content preference.

6.1 Datasets

We perform the empirical evaluations considering five distinct real data collections. The first one is the well-known Netflix dataset from the movie domain. *Netflix* (http://www.netflix.com) is an online rental movie service that made available, for research purposes on recommendation, a database with information about its movies and users. As the second collection, we employ a sample from the *Last.fm* system (http://www.last.fm/), which is a UK-based Internet radio and music community website. This sample was collected through an API provided by *Last.fm* (http://www.last.fm/api). Our third and fourth datasets (ML-1M and ML-10M) comprise rating data samples from MovieLens (http://movielens.umn.edu), gathered and made available for research purposes by GroupLens Research. Finally, as the fifth collection, we choose a random sample from the Million Song Dataset (http://labrosa.ee.columbia.edu/millionsong/tasteprofile) [4], made available recently for research purposes on recommendation. Table 1 summarizes the main features of each evaluated dataset. All selected non-content attributes were evaluated in these five datasets, except the recency attribute that could not be evaluated in the Million dataset, since it does not provide temporal information about user actions. Also, we should mention that, for the calculation of each non-content attribute, rating based datasets were transformed into consumption data simply by considering all ratings as consumptions, disregarding the rating.

Table 1: Dataset information.

	Netf ix	LastFm	ML-1M	ML-10M	Million
# Users	480,189	35,000	6,000	72,000	200,000
# Items	17,770	4 million	4,000	10,000	348,360
# Actions	100 million	85 million	1 million	10 million	19 million
# Time	310 weeks	281 weeks	149 weeks	671 weeks	-
Type	rating	play count	rating	rating	play count
Domain	movies	songs	movies	movies	songs

6.2 Evaluated CF Methods

Our analyses also take into account six representative CF techniques, both memory-based and model-based, for the Top-N recommending task. Specif cally, the set A of evaluated methods comprises the algorithms *Matrix Factorization* (MF), *Latent Feature Log Linear Model* (LF), *Biased Matrix Factorization* (BMF), *SVD-PlusPlus* (SVD) implemented and distributed by the MyMediaLite project [9]. For simplicity of analysis, we use the default parameters of each algorithm in the library on all evaluations. Furthermore, since the memory-based implementations of MyMediaLite are not able to handle the analyzed datasets, we implemented our versions of the traditional algorithms *UserKNN* and *ItemKNN* using the Cosine measure as similarity function, such as presented in [1]. Also, for both algorithms, we incorporate the sample bias regularization with the original parameters used in MyMediaLite and 80 as the maximum number of neighbors. Our experiments were performed in octa-core machines with 96 *GB* of RAM. However, we should mention that these machines were not able to run LF, SVD and ItemKNN methods on LastFm and LF method on our MillionSongs data sample, due the inability of these methods to scale to huge volumes of data.

6.3 Assessments of Preference Mismatching Existence

Starting our analyses by the measurements of consumption correlation, we plot a *Complementary Cumulative Distribution Function* (*CCDF*) of the NSD values found for each user. This distribution shows that, in general, users consume items belonging to a restricted range of values along each attribute. In all datasets, we observe that more than 80% of the users exhibit a normalized standard deviation smaller than 25%, 30% and 15% for popularity, recency and similarity, respectively. It means that the variability of consumption exhibited by each user usually relies on a range of values smaller than one quarter of the whole spectrum. Hence, despite not being suff cient for determining accurate preferences for each user, values in each of these non-content attributes may help to f lter out irrelevant items.

By taking into account the user preference analysis, we plotted a *CCDF* of the $Preference[u_k, D_i]$ values found for each user in our data collections, such as presented by Figure 2. We observe that users exhibit distinct preference for each attribute. Further, the absence of gaps in these plots evinces that there is no predominant preference in the evaluated attributes. We observe low probabilities related even to zero, marked as dashed lines in the plots, although there is a concentration of preferences in a range near to zero (-0.5 and 0.5) in almost all cases. Basically, it means that user non-content preferences mostly deviate from a single and global expected value $E(H)$ half of the $E(H)$ value, for each attribute. Therefore, a single expected value is not enough for describing accurately all users. Finally, we point out that users exhibit a slightly higher interest towards more popular, similar and recent items than the expected in almost all datasets, since the probability of positive preference values along popularity and similarity is 60% and negative preference values along recency is 65%.

By plotting a *CCDF* of the RSD values found for each user, we evince large variabilities in all evaluated datasets, for the three selected attributes, as shown by Figure 3. Through these plots we observe that variability values higher than 50% are very likely in almost all datasets and attributes. That is, the length of the total variability observed for each user is larger than the expected value estimated from his/her consumption history. Thus, besides presenting distinct preference values, we observe that users also consume a range of items with different characteristics w.r.t. each attribute. Based on these results, we conclude that users are not strongly tied to their individual preference, presenting high variability of consumption in all evaluated collections.

In order to assess the recommendation non-content description values in the evaluated datasets, we plot a *CCDF* of $Desc[a_n(u_k), D_i]$ for each user u_k. Similarly to users, we observe that RSs provide distinct non-content descriptions, which also vary according to each dataset. Starting by recency, despite presenting distinct descriptions, we observe almost consensual behaviors among the six evaluated RSs. Most of them prioritize recent items, presenting over than 60% of probability for negative description values. For popularity and similarity, we observe a more diversif ed scenario. The same methods exhibit distinct behaviors on different datasets. For instance, whereas LF and SVD present positive popularity and similarity description values in ML-1M and ML-10, they exhibit negative ones in Netf ix. Further, most of these non-content description values lie between -0.5 and 1.0 for both attributes, demonstrating a high diversity of descriptions. Also, the results show an unexpected behavior for UserKNN and ItemKNN w.r.t. popularity and similarity. Differently from previously stated [15], KNN-based methods prioritize items less popular and similar than those usually consumed by each user, exhibiting negative popularity and similarity description values. Such divergence stems from the fact that the consolidation of neighborhoods is heavily based on more popular and similar items, since similarity is usually def ned over a consumption intersection between user transactions. However, the items actually recommended, which are outside of this intersection, tend to be less popular and similar.

Finally, analyses on the preference mismatching demonstrate that all evaluated methods provide recommendations that systematically deviate from the user preferences. Figure 4 shows a *CCDF* of the difference $Desc[a_n(u_k), D_i]-Preference[u_k, D_i]$ def ned for each user u_k. We observe a high concentration of difference values near to zero within ranges of ±1, ±0.5 and ±0.05 for popularity, similarity and recency, respectively. Thus, an ϵ value of 0.33, for instance, would be enough for def ning a signif cant preference mismatching along similarity for more than half of users in almost all datasets, methods and attributes. Indeed, these are expressive differences when we take into account the expected values. For example, for a user who exhibits a similarity preference of 0.30, such difference means that RSs usually recommend items with non-content description from 0.20 to 0.40. Considering each attribute individually, through recency we observe that, besides presenting description values towards recent items (i.e., negative values), most RSs present recommendation descriptions stronger than the user preferences, recommending to them items more recent than they usually consume. For popularity and similarity, RSs present diversif ed behaviors. Whereas positive description values are observed in some datasets, negative ones, related to the same RSs, are observed in other datasets. We believe that these behaviors result from inherent characteristics of each dataset and a deeper analysis in this direction would be required.

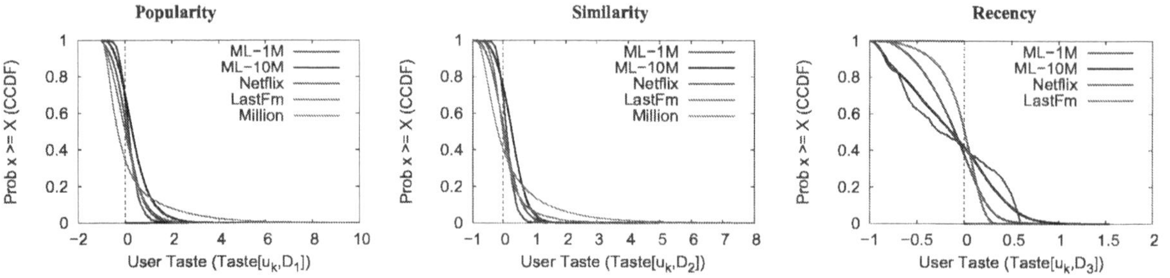

Figure 2: Analysis of user preferences.

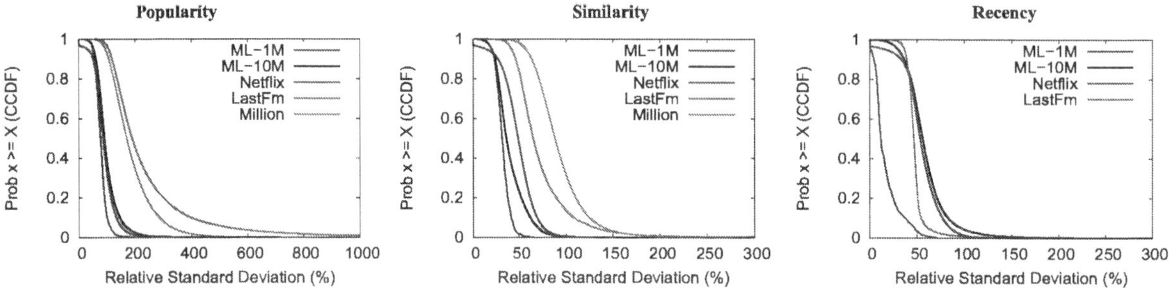

Figure 3: Distributions of relative standard deviations of user consumptions.

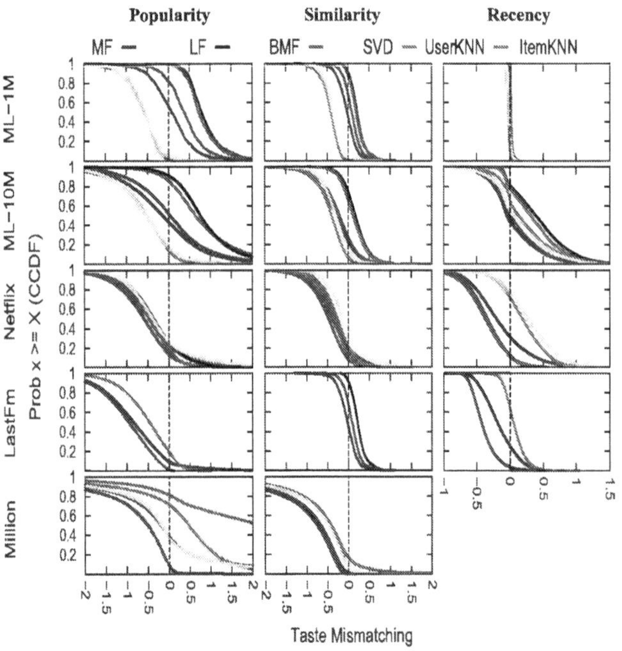

Figure 4: Analysis of preference mismatching.

6.4 Assessments of Preference Mismatching Exploitation

Besides demonstrating the existence of signif cant non-content preference mismatching in real domains, it is of paramount relevance verifying the utility of reducing this mismatching towards better recommendations. In this sense, we evaluate our hybrid method. Since a proper *n-fold cross validation* design would require a careful design in temporally ordered data and demand huge execution time for the evaluated datasets and algorithms, the following analyses employs a traditional training (70%) / test (30%) partition. Further, aiming at a broader notion of quality in recommendation, our analyses take into account three distinct quality dimensions for a Top-50 recommendation task: accuracy, novelty and diversity. Assessments on accuracy are based on the classical $Precision@50$ and precision is measured by counting the number of distinct items of the Top-50 recommendation that appears in the per user test set. We measure novelty and diversity through a formal framework of analysis presented in [20]. More specif cally, we use the EPC_rank, and the EILD for measuring novelty and diversity, respectively, considering in both cases the discount function ($disc(K)$) equals to 0.85^{k-1}, Pearson correlation as similarity distance measure and relevance aware recommendations [20]. Also, we set the parameter M given as input for our hybrid method to 500, aiming to exploit signif cantly larger lists of items than the f nal recommendation list (ten times larger in this case) while keeping computationally feasible the experimentation. Finally, we point out that our strategy of analysis is based on contrasting the results of each original CF method a_n against the results of our hybrid model when performed with a_n. Our primary goal is to identify the relevant of non-content preference attributes for improving traditional CFs, rather than contrasting it against other hybrid methods.

We start our analyses by investigating the individual usefulness of each selected non-content attribute, for providing better recommendations. Figure 5 shows the gains and loses of $Precision@50$ when building a probabilistic model for each attribute individually and using distinct combination weights. We observe expressive gains when exploiting the popularity attribute in MF, BMF, UserKNN and ItemKNN in all datasets. However, the methods LF and SVD, which exhibited the highest popularity preference mismatching values in Figure 4, could not be improved through this attribute. As they exhibit such a strong deviation towards popular items, reducing preference mismatching among the 500 recommended items was not enough to improve the results. Taking into account similarity and recency, we could not improve the CF results in most of the cases. In summary, it shows that our hybrid method is not able to effectively exploit alone each of these attributes in order to improve recommendations.

An immediate question is what happens when we take into account the three selected attributes simultaneously. Figure 6 answers this question regarding accuracy, novelty and diversity. We observe that, besides even higher gains in terms of accuracy in almost all CF algorithms and datasets, we also achieve simultaneous gains w.r.t. novelty and diversity. In general, the most expressive gains

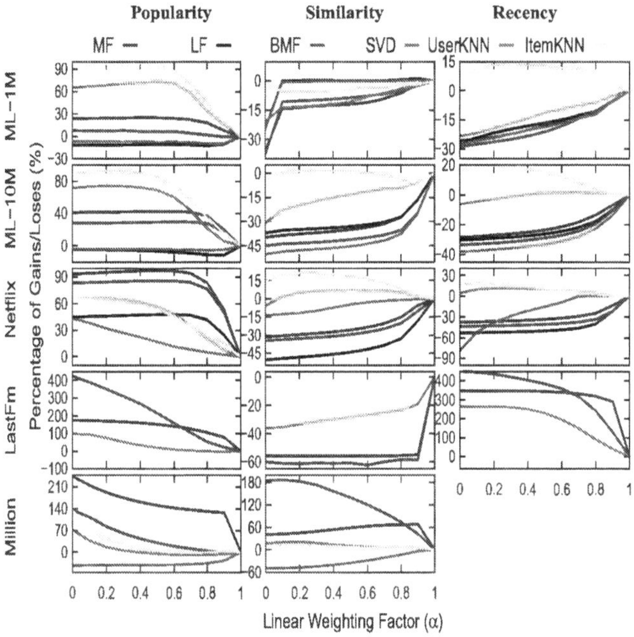

Figure 5: Analysis of $Precision@50$ gains|loses by exploiting, individually, popularity, similarity and recency.

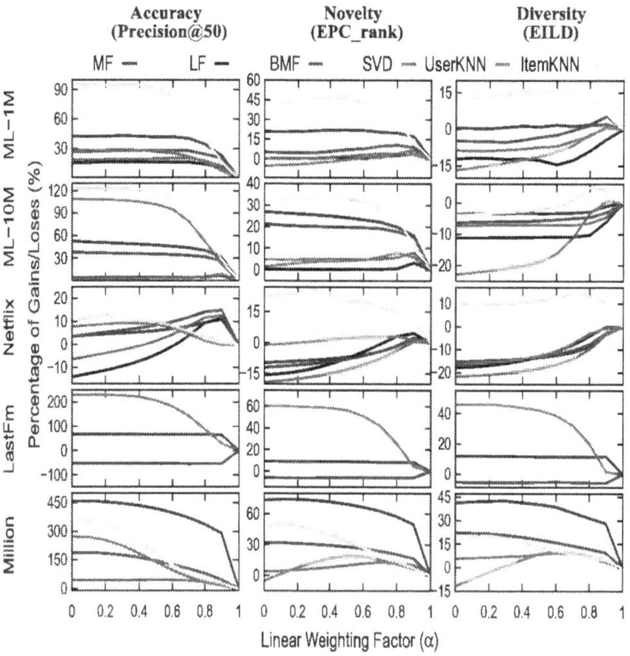

Figure 6: Analysis of quality gains|loses by exploiting, simultaneously, popularity, similarity and recency.

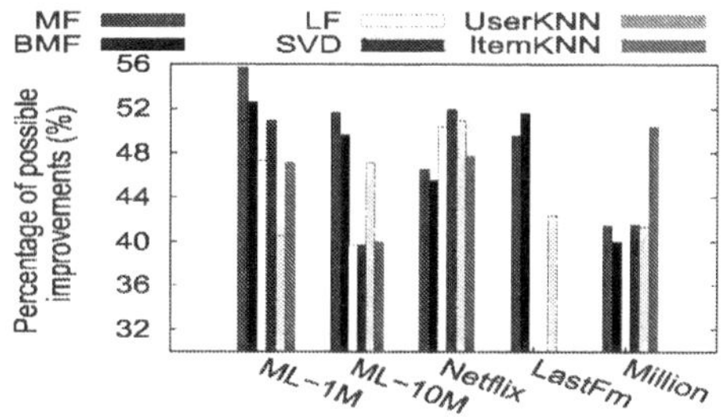

Figure 7: Percentage of users for whom the non-content preference information produced any improvement.

were observed in CFs with the worse performance in each dataset. For instance, we observed gains over 200% on LastFm and Million datasets. In these cases, the original CF results were actually not signif cant. However, among the Top-500, the CFs were able to rescue several relevant items for each user and the non-content preference information was enough for identifying these items. On the other hand, gains around 10% were consistently related to CFs focused on suggesting items more popular, similar and older than the user expected interest (i.e., LF and SVD). Therefore, although they could achieve high accuracy rates, several recommended items not necessarily suit the user non-content preference. This fact explains why the gains in these cases are not as expressive as for the other methods. As the lists provided by such CF exhibit non-content description far from the non-content preference of each user, the suggested items do not necessarily present characteristics close to the user interests. Thus, items closer to the user preference in the Top-500 are still far from the actual user non-content preference.

Besides verifying the strength of the improvements provided by exploiting non-content preference in RSs, it is also important to investigate how often these gains happen. That is, we also evaluated the percentage of users in each database for whom our hybrid method was able to produce any improvement in a Top-N recommendation, in terms of accuracy. As our method processes a prior recommendation list of size $M \gg N$ provided by a CF method for each user, such percentage is limited by the percentage of these prior lists that have more relevant items than those present among its N f rst items. Figure 7 presents the percentage of possible improvements as the number of distinct users for whom our hybrid method enhances, divided by the number of users for whom the recommendation list provided by each CF could be improved. Our method, even adopting a global linear combination weight, is able to improve recommendation for more than 40% of these users in most of the cases. Further, the percentage of user for whom our method produced losses was at most 10% in all datasets.

In summary, our hybrid method allowed us to verify the relevance of the user non-content preference in practical scenarios. Through this information, we are able to provide expressive gains in terms of accuracy, novelty and diversity in six major current CFs in the Top-50 recommendation task. We explain these gains by the fact that non-content preference information is able to f lter out items that seem to suit the user preferences, but mismatch non-content characteristics from the items consumed by each user. Aiming to evince the existence of such mismatch items among the sorted Top-N list originally recommended by each CF, we calculate the non-content preference mismatching, such as performed in our methodology, but considering now each rank in this list. For sake of brevity, we show the mean of this deviation per rank among all users for one dataset (ML), such as presented in Figure 8, although the same behavior was observed in all other collections. We observe that the preference mismatching varies signif cantly among the ranks, not presenting any monotonic behavior. It reinforces that CF recommendations do not capture the systematic preference existing along each non-content attribute.

Additionally, we evaluate to what extent Gaussian functions are appropriate for modeling the user non-content preferences for the selected attributes. By plotting the probability distribution of the mean expected value of all users, along each attribute, and its standard deviation, we found that, indeed, the global behavior in our domains present a Gaussian shape. However, these distributions point out two main issues. First, users exhibit behavior signif cantly distinct from each other, demonstrated by high standard deviations in all points. Hence, distinct users would require, besides different parameters, different model functions. For instance, while a set of

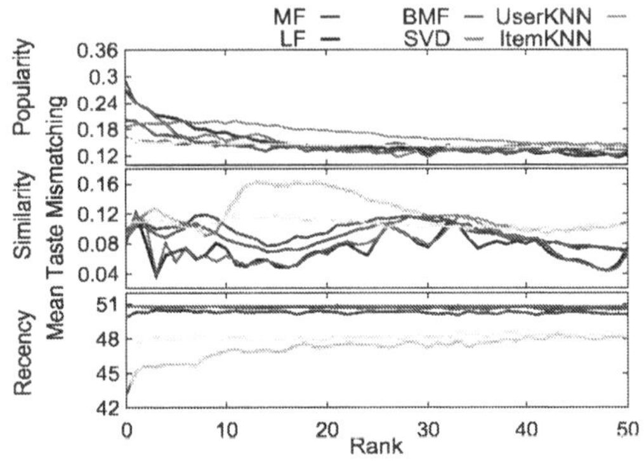

Figure 8: Analysis of mean preference mismatching per rank in CF recommendation lists.

users exhibit a Gaussian-like behavior w.r.t. the preference, others would present a power law like. In this case, non-parametric solutions should be applied. Second, we observe that the evaluated attributes do not vary in the same way, requiring distinct models. While recency seems much more an exponential function, popularity and similarity present a Gaussian shape. Therefore, besides all gains achieved by our simple method, these issues point out a room for even more improvements.

7. CONCLUSIONS AND FUTURE WORK

This work evaluates the use of attributes thought of as "non-content" towards better recommendations. We def ne as non-content attributes those related to metadata or consumption information. Specif cally, we evaluate the attributes of popularity, similarity and recency derived for each item from consumption data. Besides demonstrating that recommendations issued by current CF methods do not capture properly the user preference along these attributes in real domains, through a characterization methodology, we implement a hybrid method that exploits such attributes in practice. Our method def nes a CB model for user non-content preferences through a multivariate Gaussian function. We use this model for def ning a score for each item, previously issued by a CF method, which represents how well this item matches the user non-content preference model. Finally, we combine the original CF score with the CB score, re-ranking the CF recommendation list.

Empirical evaluations conducted on f ve distinct real datasets and six representative CFs allowed us to verify the relevance of the user non-content preference in practical scenarios. Indeed, we achieved expressive gains regarding accuracy, novelty and diversity simultaneously in a Top-50 recommendation task, which range from 15% to 100%. Further, we found that this simple method was able to improve the recommendations for more than 40% of the users who have room for improvements in a Top-500 CF recommendation.

Besides signif cant enhancements over CFs, the exploitation of non-content attributes brings many questions not answered by this work yet. For instance, we are not able to make strong claims about the best approach for minimizing the preference mismatching or even the necessary conditions on which the implemented method provides gains. Further, we are aware of some weaknesses related to implementation and evaluation decisions. An immediate future step is conducting a comparative analysis of our method against other hybrid ones. Designing more robust experiments that balance time demanding and statistical robustness of analysis is also desirable. In addition, our gains are limited by the Top-500 recommendation lists provided by each CF. Whether the items recommended by a given CF do not cover those with characteristics similar to the user non-content interests, our method will not be able to bring improvements. Finally, simplistic implementation decisions, such as a single global linear combination weight α, should be ref ned to handle the actual conditions of recommendation domains.

8. REFERENCES

[1] G. Adomavicius and A. Tuzhilin. Toward the next generation of recommender systems: A survey of the state-of-the-art and possible extensions. *IEEE TKDE*, 17(6):734–749, 2005.
[2] C. Anderson. *The long tail.* Gramedia Pustaka Utama, 2006.
[3] C. Basu, H. Hirsh, and W. Cohen. Recommendation as classif cation: Using social and content-based information in recommendation. In *Proc. of the NCAI*, 1998.
[4] T. Bertin-Mahieux, D. P. Ellis, B. Whitman, and P. Lamere. The million song dataset. In *Proc. of the 12th ISMIR*, 2011.
[5] D. Billsus and M. Pazzani. Learning collaborative information f lters. In *Proc. of the 15th ICML*, volume 54, page 48, 1998.
[6] J. Breese, D. Heckerman, and C. Kadie. Empirical analysis of predictive algorithms for collaborative f ltering. *Learning*, 9:309–347, 1992.
[7] R. Burke. Hybrid web recommender systems. *The adaptive web*, pages 377–408, 2007.
[8] M. Ekstrand, J. Riedl, and J. Konstan. *Collaborative f ltering recommender systems*. Now Publishers Inc, 2011.
[9] Z. Gantner, S. Rendle, C. Freudenthaler, and L. Schmidt-Thieme. Mymedialite: a free recommender system library. In *Proc. of the 5th ACM RecSys*, 2011.
[10] J. L. Herlocker, J. A. Konstan, L. G. Terveen, and J. T. Riedl. Evaluating collaborative f ltering recommender systems. *ACM Trans. Inf. Syst.*, 22(1):5–53, Jan. 2004.
[11] D. Jannach, M. Zanker, A. Felfernig, and G. Friedrich. *Recommender systems: an introduction*. Cambridge University Press, 2010.
[12] Y. Koren. Factorization meets the neighborhood: a multifaceted collaborative f ltering model. In *Proc. of the 14th SIGKDD*, pages 426–434, NY, USA, 2008. ACM.
[13] X. Li and T. Murata. Multidimensional clustering based collaborative f ltering approach for diversif ed recommendation. In *Proc. of the 7th IEEE ICCSE*, 2012.
[14] P. Lops, M. Gemmis, and G. Semeraro. Content-based recommender systems: State of the art and trends. *Recommender Systems Handbook*, pages 73–105, 2011.
[15] R. Rafter, M. O'Mahony, N. Hurley, and B. Smyth. What have the neighbours ever done for us? a collaborative f ltering perspective. *17th UMAP*, pages 355–360, 2009.
[16] P. Resnick and H. Varian. Recommender systems. *Communications of the ACM*, 40(3):56–58, 1997.
[17] M. Ribeiro, A. Lacerda, A. Veloso, and N. Ziviani. Pareto-eff cient hybridization for multi-objective recommender systems. In *6th ACM RecSys*, 2012.
[18] F. Ricci, L. Rokach, and B. Shapira. Introduction to recommender systems handbook. *Recommender Systems Handbook*, pages 1–35, 2011.
[19] J. Schafer, J. Konstan, and J. Riedi. Recommender systems in e-commerce. In *1st ACM EC*, pages 158–166. ACM, 1999.
[20] S. Vargas and P. Castells. Rank and relevance in novelty and diversity metrics for recommender systems. In *Proc. of the 5th ACM RecSys*, pages 109–116. ACM, 2011.
[21] H. Yin, B. Cui, J. Li, J. Yao, and C. Chen. Challenging the long tail recommendation. *VLDB Endowment*, 2012.

Hybrid Event Recommendation using Linked Data and User Diversity

Houda Khrouf
Eurecom
Biot, France
houda.khrouf@eurecom.fr

Raphaël Troncy
Eurecom
Biot, France
raphael.troncy@eurecom.fr

ABSTRACT

An ever increasing number of social services offer thousands of diverse events per day. Users tend to be overwhelmed by the massive amount of information available, especially with limited browsing options perceived in many event web services. To alleviate this information overload, a recommender system becomes a vital component for assisting users selecting relevant events. However, such system faces a number of challenges owed to the the inherent complex nature of an event. In this paper, we propose a novel hybrid approach built on top of Semantic Web. On the one hand, we use a content-based system enriched with Linked Data to overcome the data sparsity, a problem induced by the transiency of events. On the other hand, we incorporate a collaborative filtering to involve the social aspect, an influential feature in decision making. This hybrid system is enhanced by the integration of a user diversity model designed to detect user propensity towards specific topics. We show how the hybridization of CB+CF systems and the integration of interest diversity features are important to improve predictions. Experimental results demonstrate the effectiveness of our approach using precision and recall measures.

Categories and Subject Descriptors

H.3.3 [**Information Search and Retrieval**]: Information filtering

General Terms

Algorithms, Experimentation

Keywords

Event recommendation, Linked Data, LODE ontology, user diversity

1. INTRODUCTION

Recommendation in online social services have gained momentum over the past years as a key factor to deliver personalized content and enhance the user experience. Reducing the information overload and assisting customers to make decision become part of primary concerns in the e-service area. In this sense, recommender systems attempt to provide efficient filters that decode the users' interests, and optimize accordingly the information perceived. To help these systems predict items of interest, various clues are available, ranging from a user profile, explicit ratings, to past activities and social interactions. More specifically, integrating such systems in an event-based web service is a key advantage to attract people for attending diverse events, and to promote face-to-face social interactions. Indeed, the event recommendation can draw on different information sources such as the user preferences (ratings, likes, etc.), the attended events (visited places, involved artists), or even the social co-participation. Broadly speaking, the decision making upon attending events depends on some restrictions such as time, location, category, popularity and which friend will attend. However, the existing collaborative and content-based techniques cannot cope at all with this complex inherent nature of such decision. In addition, attended events are often topically diverse inducing a significant variety of topics in the user profile. This diversity will obviously affect the similarity between the new events and the prior ones, which can decrease the accuracy of content-based recommendation.

To tackle these issues, we propose a hybrid event recommender system by means of Semantic Web technologies. Our belief is that a structured event model presents one solution to cope with the complexity of event-specific characteristics. This modeling will ensure a more straightforward way to explore and reason over the data. It makes possible to ask complex queries, for example, to retrieve events involving the same artist within a specific geographical area. In addition, the semantic model empowers the enrichment of event descriptions with additional information from Linked Data [1], a set of connected and distributed RDF datasets. Such enrichment could potentially provide valuable inputs for the content-based recommender system [5].

In the second step of our approach, we propose to quantify the user interests based on topic modeling technique. This model detects the user propensity towards specific topics. It will be integrated in the recommender system to control the impact caused by the diversity of a user profile. Finally, we exploit the collaborative participation assuming that the social information about "which friend will attend an event" plays an important role in decision making. In this paper, we mainly investigate the influence degree that could have the data enrichment, the social information and the user

RecSys'13, October 12 - 16, 2013, Hong Kong, China.

diversity to improve the system performance.

The remainder of this paper is organized as follows: Section 2 describes our event model and details how to build a recommender system using semantic metadata from Linked Data. Section 3 outlines our hybrid method for event recommendation. In Section 4 and 5, we describe some based techniques to train the system and we evaluate the proposed approach. We review related work in Section 6, and we conclude in Section 7.

2. LINKED DATA FOR CONTENT-BASED RECOMMENDATION

The principle of the content-based recommender system is to suggest new items similar to those a user liked in the past. The similarity between items is computed using the internal structure of the item profile by means of a variety of distance measures such as Cosine similarity, Pearson correlation or Latent Semantic Analysis. The most common representation of the item profile is the keyword-based model, in which attributes are represented by weighted vectors of keywords usually computed using TF-IDF scheme (term frequency/inverse frequency). To build such a profile from unstructured data, feature extraction techniques are needed to shift the item description from the original representation to a structured form suitable for next processing (e.g. keyword vectors). This task becomes straightforward by the use of Semantic Web technologies thanks to data structuring into ontologies known as machine understandable format. In fact, one principle of Semantic Web is to use common vocabularies for the integration of fragmentary information into a logically coherent knowledge. This huge and distributed knowledge, also called Linked Data, contains growing set of public and linked RDF datasets, covering diverse domains such as government, media, geography or more generally encyclopedic data. A content-based recommender system can greatly benefit from the ease of ontology-enabled feature extraction, and the availability of connected data in different domains to enrich the item profile. In order to fully leverage the assets of Linked data, we published in a previous work a RDF dataset of events and linked it with relevant open datasets [10]. In the following, we provide an overview of our RDF dataset of events and we explain how to compute the similarities between items based on Linked Data.

2.1 RDF Dataset of Events

In their daily life, people naturally organize their personal data according to occurring events: wedding, birthday party, concert, etc. In this paper, the events considered are a natural way for referring to any observable occurrence grouping persons, places, times and activities. To represent the events as structured data, we use LODE ontology[1], a minimal model that encapsulates the most useful properties. The goal of this ontology is to enable an interoperable modeling of the "factual" aspects of events, where these can be characterized in terms of the four Ws: What happened, Where did it happen, When did it happen, and Who was involved. Figure 1 depicts the metadata attached to the event identified by `1380633` on Last.FM[2]. More precisely, it indicates that this concert has been given on the `21th of May 2012 at 12:45 PM` in the `The Paramount Theatre` featuring the

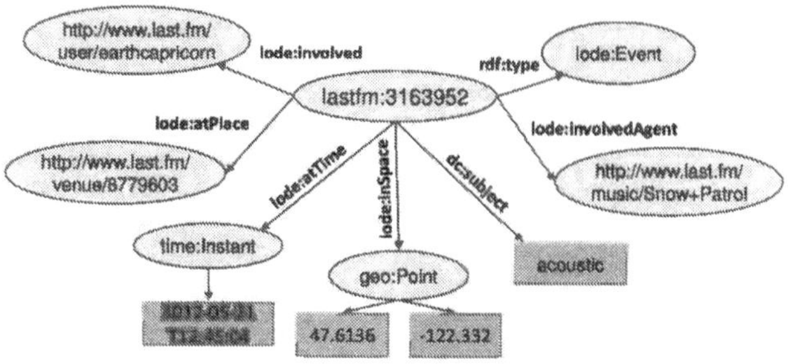

Figure 1: The *Snow Patrol Concert* described with LODE ontology

`Snow Patrol` rock band, and attended by the user `earthcapricor`.

The dataset was collected from three large event web directories (Eventful, Last.FM and Upcoming) and published in the Linked Data Cloud[3]. Using our SPARQL (RDF query language) endpoint[4], we can easily retrieve meaningful and semantic relationships about users. For instance, the following query extracts the list of attendees co-participating with a specific user along with the number of common events. A set of filters can simply be incorporated to target a specific geographical area or a period of time.

```
PREFIX UserURI:<http://data.linkedevents.org/user/6e150c44-
d5f3-4dfc-97f1-1c593d9cc4a2>
SELECT ?coattendee COUNT(DISTINCT ?event) as ?NB
WHERE {
    ?event  lode:involved UserURI: .
    ?event  lode:involved ?coattendee .
    ?event  lode:atPlace ?place .
    ?place  vcard:adr ?address .
    ?address vcard:locality "London" .
    FILTER(?coattendee!=UserURI:)
} ORDER BY DESC (?NB)
```

2.2 Linked Data as Tensor Space Model

In order to compute the similarity between items from Linked Data, we decided to apply the approach proposed by Di Noia et al [5]. The inceptive idea is that semantically similar items from RDF graph are the subject of two RDF triples having the same property and the same object (where a triple=<subject,property,object>). This approach is based on an adaptation of the classic Vector Space Model (VSM) [16], a well known technique in information retrieval. In this model, similarity between documents and queries is computed between their representative t-dimensional weighted vectors assigned to index discriminating terms. The application of VSM to RDF graph projects the Linked Data to 3-dimensional tensor, where each of its slices represents an adjacency matrix for one ontology property. In fact, the Semantic Web graph can be defined as a graph $G = (V, E)$, where V is a set of RDF resources and E is the set of properties between resources in V. For each existing property p in E, the adjacency matrix models the linkage between subjects (on the rows) and objects (on the columns) from V by this property p. Hence, a non null weight is assigned to each entry

[1] `http://linkedevents.org/ontology/`

[2] `http://www.last.fm`

[3] `http://linkeddata.org/`

[4] `http://eventmedia.eurecom.fr/sparql`

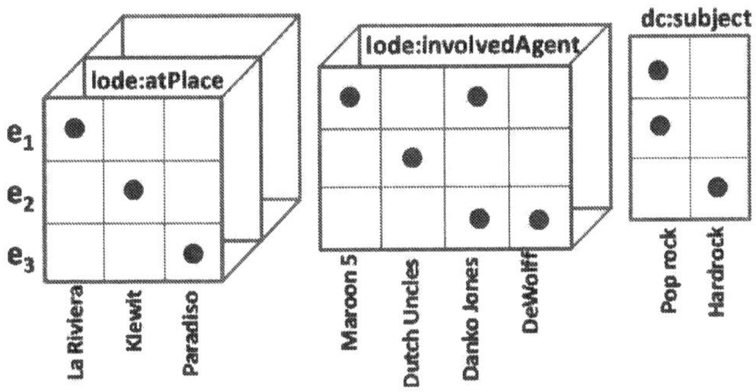

Figure 2: Tensor slices of some event properties

X_{ijp} in the tensor for each existing triple `<i-th subject, p-th property, j-th object>`. Figure 2 shows a small example of tensor slices related to some properties, namely: `lode:atPlace`, `lode:involvedAgent` and `dc:subject`.

Considering the data sparsity and the independent properties, we would be able to apply the approach above and compute the similarity between events with respect to each property separately. The representation of an event e_i according to the property p is a t-dimensional vector indexing the terms/resources related to e_i via p. The TF-IDF weight of each resource r is computed as:

$$w_{r,i,p} = f_{r,i,p} \; * \; log \left(\frac{N}{m_{r,p}} \right) \tag{1}$$

where $f_{r,i,p} = 1$ if a link exists between the node e_i to the resource r via the property p, otherwise $f_{r,i,p} = 0$. N is the total number of events in the dataset. $m_{r,p}$ is the number of events linked to the resource r via the property p. Then, the similarity between two events e_i and e_j with respect to the property p is calculated using Cosine distance between their representative vectors as following:

$$sim^p(e_i, e_j) = \frac{\sum_{r=1}^{t} w_{r,i,p} * w_{r,j,p}}{\sqrt{\sum_{r=1}^{t} w_{r,i,p}^2} * \sqrt{\sum_{r=1}^{t} w_{r,j,p}^2}} \tag{2}$$

The approach described above can be simply applied to detect similarity between subjects or objects of RDF triples. It has been successfully used to recommend movies and to improve the quality of content-based system [5]. Nevertheless, it is still limited when the adjacency matrix is very sparse such as the case of matrices associated with `lode:atPlace` and `lode:involvedAgent` properties. In fact, such predicates are considered as discriminant properties in RDF, which are characterized by the diversity of its object values. For instance, the t-dimensional vector related to `lode:atPlace` property has only one non null weight since an event always takes place in one venue.

2.3 Similarity-based Interpolation

In order to mitigate the sparsity of the adjacency matrix, we decided to interpolate fictitious values based on the similarity between objects. First, we introduce a discriminability metric [17] to gain insights into the properties concerned by the similarity-based interpolation. The metric is defined via the following formula:

$$Discriminability(p) = \frac{\mid \{o \mid t =< s, p, o > \in G\} \mid}{\mid t =< s, p, o > \in G \mid} \tag{3}$$

where G is the RDF graph, t is the triple representing the link between the subject s and the object o via the property p. From this formula, it is trivial to see that having high discriminability means that many instances have different object values on this property. For instance, from a set of 1700 events (related to 10,323 agents, 627 places and 5,758 subjects), we found a discriminability score of 0.64 for the `lode:involvedAgent`, and 0.45 for the `lode:atPlace`, while it is only 0.10 for the `dc:subject` predicate. This is also reflected by the sparsity measures of the related adjacency matrices. Moreover, we intuitively know that similar events are not necessary occurred in the same venue or featuring the same performers. As a solution for such typical items, we propose to interpolate the similarity scores between objects in the adjacency matrix. More precisely, if the resource r_k is similar to the resource r_h, and both $f_{r_h,i,p} = 1$ and $f_{r_k,i,p} = 0$, then $f_{r_k,i,p} = sim(r_k, r_h)$. Note that $f_{r_k,i,p}$ reflects the strength of the fictitious link which associates event e_i with the resource r_k via the property p. If r_k is similar to more than one resource originally linked with e_i via the property p, the weight $f_{r_k,i,p}$ will be equal to the highest similarity score. For each resource r_k, the equation 1 becomes more generally:

$$w_{r_k,i,p} = \max_{r_h \in H} sim(r_k, r_h) \; * \; log \left(\frac{N}{m_{r_k,p}} \right) \tag{4}$$

where H is the set of objects originally linked with the event e_i. In this context, we do not pay attention to how similarity between objects is computed. In fact, this measure depends on the structure of the object itself and there exist several existing distances that can be used. In our case, we have been based on the similarity scores between agents provided by third party services such as Last.FM, and we computed the normalized geographical distance between venues. A key advantage of the similarity-based interpolation is that the discriminability and the sparsity rates are 3 times reduced. Finally, the similarity between two events e_i and e_j is a normalized combination of their similarities according to each property p.

3. EVENT RECOMMENDATION

Different from a classic item, events occur at a specific place and during a period of time to become worthless for recommendation. Moreover, while the classic items continuously receive useful feedbacks, the user ratings about events are very sparse due to their transiency. In our dataset, these ratings are represented by the binary user-event attendance matrix with 98% sparsity rate (a set of users only attend a very limited number of all the available events). As a solution, one can address event recommendation using content-based algorithm relating event metadata to user preferences. This perfectly complies with the constraints a person considers to decide whether or not to attend an event. Metadata such as distance, time, topics and performers are important and influential factors in such decision. Nevertheless, the content-based recommendation might suggest items with a limited diversity, and it does not consider the social information that answers to the question: "which friend is going?".

To fill this gap, we first analyze the pure content-based recommendation where a weight value is assigned to each of metadata fields. We attempt to improve its performance by enriching descriptions from Linked Data. Then, we incorporate the social dimension (collaborative-filtering) and the topical user diversity by means of weighted hybrid recommendation.

3.1 Content-based Recommendation

The underlying principle of content-based system is to recommend future events similar to ones a user has attended in the past. We assume that there is a sufficiently number of past attended events to avoid the cold-start problem, which is out of the scope of the present work. Similarity values between events are then used to obtain a ranked list of recommended items, as following:

$$rank_{cb}(u, e_i) = \frac{\sum_{e_j \in E_u} \sum_{p \in P} \alpha_p \ sim^p(e_i, e_j)}{\mid P \mid \ * \mid E_u \mid} \tag{5}$$

where e_i is the event to recommend, P is the set of properties shared between two events, E_u is the set of past events attended by the user u, and α_p is the weight assigned to each property reflecting its contribution to respect the user profile. In the next section we describe some methods how to learn these weights α. The selected properties to compute the similarity between events are those which are related to the location, subjects (tags) and involved agents (artists). Note that we do not deal with the temporal property at the moment. We mainly focus our analysis on the topic enrichment, the social factor and the user diversity. We believe that temporal property could be harnessed to index only recent and future events in a specific period of time. This will reduce the computational processing time and increase the scalability. However, as this method reduces the knowledge about the user past ratings, there is a need to investigate its impact on the recommendation accuracy, an analysis left for further studies.

Geographic Closeness. Roughly speaking, users tend to attend nearby social events, thus the location is always considered as a valuable feature in event recommendation [15]. In our approach, to measure the similarity between events according to the `lode:atPlace` property, we need to normalize it according to a specific threshold θ. Since the location of the user home is missing in our data, we analyzed the distance between attended events for each user and we reported results for all users in Figure 3. Note that the attendance rate becomes extremely low from $\theta = 80$ Km. This value is considered as the threshold from which the similarity between events equals to zero according to the location property.

Enrichment with Linked Data. One method to enrich the item profile from Linked Data lies in the exploitation of DBpedia, the RDF version of Wikipedia. The key advantage of this dataset is the availability of semantically rich information in various domains. In a previous study [9], we have automatically interlinked our dataset with DBpedia. As a result, a significant number of high quality mappings has been obtained between the artists of both datasets. Consequently, we decided to enrich the topics of an event using the DBpedia topics of the involved artists. More precisely,

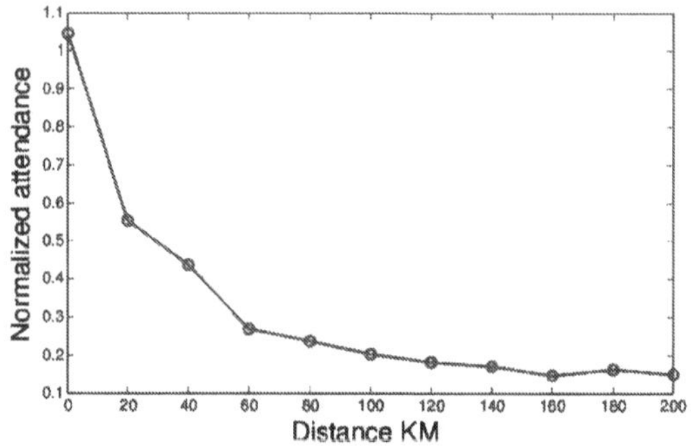

Figure 3: Normalized average attendance rates per distance KM

we retrieve the categories associated with the property `dcterms:subject` of artists by simply querying the DBpedia SPARQL endpoint[5]. The reason behind our interest in DBpedia categories is their classification into a well defined hierarchical structure with highly consistent labeling.

3.2 Topical User Diversity

In the recommender system, one fundamental goal is to suggest items in compliance with the user interests. This aim is particularly difficult to achieve in event recommendation due to the presence of topically diverse events. In fact, the real-world social events can be classified into large set of categories, ranging from large festivals and conferences to small concerts and social gatherings. When attending an event, the user might be interested in a specific show or artist, or might have broad interests. In consequence, relying on events similarity in content-based recommendation can be influenced by the topical diversity of past attended events. To alleviate this impact, we decided to put an emphasis on the role of interesting events to predict the unknown ratings. This means that we assign different weights to the events included in the peaks of interest, and to those which are out of these peaks (equation 8). These weights β are then estimated using training methods. The formula 5 becomes:

$$rank_{cb++}(u, e_i) = \frac{\sum_{e_j \in E_u} \sum_{p \in P} \alpha_p \ \beta_p \ sim^p(e_i, e_j)}{\mid P \mid \ * \mid E_u \mid} \tag{6}$$

where $\beta_p = 1$ if the property p is different from `dc:subject`, otherwise the $\beta_{subject}$ is an estimated value depending on whether the event e_j corresponds to a peak of interest or not. In order to detect these peaks of interest, we propose to quantify the interest diversity using Latent Dirichlet Allocation (LDA) [2], a topic modeling technique based on the co-occurrence of terms. Inspired by the method in [19], we consider that the interest diversity of each user is reflected by the previously attended events, where each event is considered as a document represented by a set of terms. For each event e_i, LDA generates a T-dimensional vector of topic proportions $\Theta_i = [\theta_i^1, \theta_i^2, ...\theta_i^T]$, where T is the number of topics. Then, we calculate the variance of each topic dimension t of all the events E attended by a user $\Theta^t = [\theta_1^t, \theta_2^t, ...\theta_E^t]$. The diversity score of a user is the mean of the variances of all topics dimensions (mean of $\Theta^1, \Theta^2 ... \Theta^T$). The normalized

[5]`http://dbpedia.org/sparql`

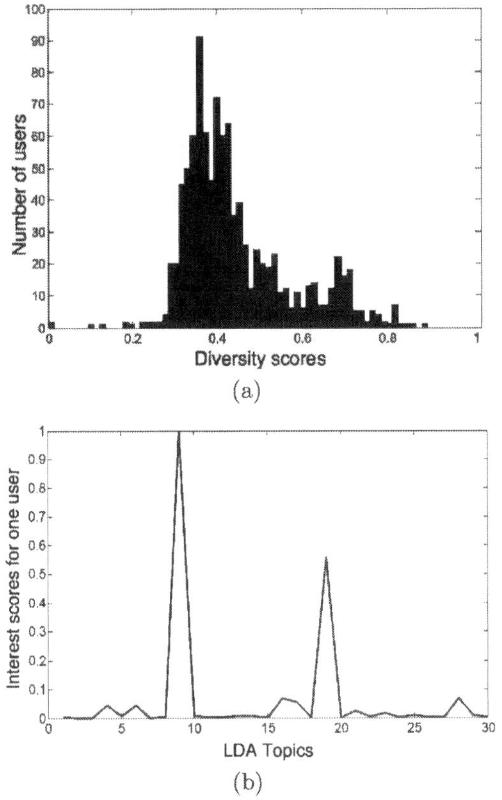

Figure 4: Distribution of topical diversity scores with T = 30: (a) for all the users; (b) for one specific user.

scores obtained from a sample of 1,000 Last.fm users are depicted in Figure 4. From the histogram, it is shown that most of diversity scores range from 0.3 to 0.5 indicating users with relatively high interest in specific topics. The diversity scores near to 1 represent a very strong interest in some topics such as the user plotted in Figure 4(b) having a strong bias towards topic 9. Finally, the diversity score of zero represents the users associated with few attended events (the cold-start problem).

3.3 Collaborative filtering

A form of social interaction is the collaborative participation such as co-authoring a paper or co-attending an event. In [12], Liu et al. highlight the existence of an offline social network built by means of co-attending the social events. Such network seems cohesive but still less denser than an online social network. Accordingly, we consider that two users involved in the same event can potentially have a stronger tie than others users. The involvement could be offline by directly attending the event, or online by sharing media and comments about it. This let us assume that the more events in which the users involve, the more strongly their tie is. Thus, the sufficiently similar consumptions could probably provide information at first glance about which "friends" will attend an event. Since our dataset contains users intentions upon attending upcoming events, we exploit them to predict unknown ratings. However, unlike the traditional user-based collaborative filtering (CF), we would like in our approach to not only consider the similarity between users, but also the contribution of a group of friends. We define the following formula as the prediction that a user u_i will attend an event e based on the intentions of his co-attendees (users who have attended past events with the user u_i):

$$rank_{cf}(u_i, e) = \frac{\sum_{j \in C} a_{i,j}}{\mid C \mid} * \frac{\mid E_i \cap (\cup_{j \in C} E_j) \mid}{\mid E_i \mid} \quad (7)$$

where C is the set of co-attendees of the user u_i that will attend the event e, E_i is the set of attended events by the user u_i, and $a_{i,j}$ represents the fraction of common events between the users u_i and u_j by the cardinality of E_j. Note that the weight $a_{i,j}$ reflects whether the most of events which are attended by the user u_j are also attended by the user u_i. The rationale behind this formula is two-fold: (1) in the first part, the contribution of each co-attendee is considered individually; (2) in the second part, we consider the co-attendees as a group of friends, and we assume that the more events they attended together with the user u_i, the more strongly is their relationship.

3.4 Hybrid Recommendation

To combine the features of both content-based and collaborative filtering algorithms, we propose a weighted hybridization using a linear combination of recommendation scores. Taking into account the user diversity and combining the equations (6) and (7), we propose the following rank function:

$$rank(u, e) = rank_{cb++}(u, e) + \alpha_{cf}\ rank_{cf}(u, e) \quad (8)$$

where α_{cf} is the weight of collaborative filtering feature, estimated in conjunction with the weights of content-based features using different approaches to train the system.

4. LEARNING RANK WEIGHTS

To learn the weights of our prediction function, we first test the linear regression with gradient descent that minimizes the least-squares cost function. Then, we use two evolutionary computation methods motivated by their success in a wide range of tasks. Results are reported in Section 5.

4.1 Genetic Algorithm

Genetic Algorithms (GAs) [20] are stochastic methods inspired from the mechanism of natural evolution and genetic inheritance. They have been applied to various domains including information retrieval, image processing and machine learning. In GAs, a population is a set of chromosomes (candidate solutions) and each chromosome denotes a set of genes. A fitness criterion is a function which provides an estimation of the quality of each solution. An initial population of candidate solutions (chromosomes) are evaluated using the fitness function. The solutions having higher fitness values than others are stochastically selected, recombined and randomly mutated to produce a new population for the next generation. The algorithm stops iterating when the optimal solution is produced or a maximal number of iterations is reached. To apply GA in our approach, a chromosome is represented by a vector of the coefficients α (the genes). Each chromosome is then evaluated using a fitness function that maximizes the precision@N on the training data. We set the following GA parameters: population size=30, iterations=80, crossover rate=0.9 and mutation rate=0.01.

4.2 Particle Swarm Optimization

Particle Swarm Optimization (PSO) [7] is a population based stochastic optimization technique inspired by the social behavior of bird flocking or fish schooling. The algorithm initializes a population of random solutions called swarms (particles), and searches for optima of a fitness function by updating generations. Compared with GA, PSO is easy to implement with few parameters to adjust, and has no evolution operators such as crossover and mutation. In each generation, each particle accelerates in the direction of its own personal best solution found so far, as well as in the direction of the global best position discovered so far by any of the particles in the swarm. Each particle i in the swarm has the following attributes: a current position x_i, a current velocity v_i, and a personal best position p_i in the search space, and the global best position p_{gbest} among all the p_i. In each iteration, the velocity and the position of each particle is updated as following:

$$v_i(t+1) = w.v_i(t) + c_1 r_1 (p_i - x_i(t)) + c_2 r_2 (p_{gbest} - x_i(t))$$
$$x_i(t+1) = x_i(t) + v_i(t+1)$$

where c_1 and c_2 are the acceleration coefficients, r_1 and r_2 are random numbers uniformly distributed within [0,1], and w is the inertia weight. The velocity and acceleration are responsible for changing the position of the particle to explore the space of all possible solutions, instead of using existing solutions to reproduce. The personal and the global best positions are the optima of a fitness function respectively in each iteration and for all past iterations. Following the same setting in GAs, a particle is represented by a vector of the weights α, and the fitness function aims at maximizing the precision results. We set the following PSO parameters: population size=30, iterations=80, c_1=1.494, c_2=1.494 and w=0.729 (more details in [7]).

5. EVALUATION

We carried out a set of experiments measuring the precision and recall metrics to assess the contribution of each step and the quality of our recommendation compared with existing approaches.

5.1 Real World Dataset

As described in Section 2, our RDF dataset is obtained from three large public event directories (Last.fm, Eventful and Upcoming). In particular, we have been interested in Last.fm directory containing a large number of active users, that explicitly announce their participation to future events. Using SPARQL, we collected 2,436 events, 481 active users whose the attendance rates are within [15,50] generating 12,729 distinct consumptions. This set of events are related to 14,748 different artists, 897 different locations and 4265 distinct tags (music domain). For evaluation purpose, we used a test set containing the most recent 30% of the consumptions and a training test with the remaining 70% consumptions. Then, we calculated two metrics used in top-N recommendation task: Precision is the ratio of correctly recommended items and the length of the recommendation N; Recall is the ratio of correctly recommended items and the total number of future consumptions. Precision and recall were computed at different N values.

Task	location	agent	subject
(1)	0.9942	0.9174	0.3175
(2)	0.6854	0.7392	0.2843

Table 1: Sparsity rates of the similarity matrix for each property before (1) and after the similarity-based interpolation and linked data enrichment (2)

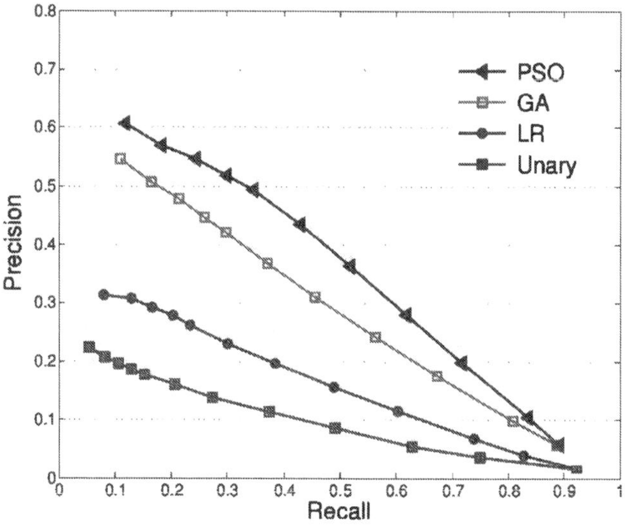

Figure 5: Recall and Precision based on different approaches to estimate the vector α

5.2 Experiment

To highlight the importance of the similarity-based interpolation and linked data enrichment, we report the sparsity rates in Table 1. We see that our method succeed to discover latent similarities between items attributes especially for discriminant properties. This similarity was not considered in keyword-based recommender system, and its interpolation becomes straightforward thanks to the ontology-based modeling.

As a second step of our evaluation, we assess the performance of the training methods to learn the coefficients α in the hybrid recommendation algorithm. Note that, for this experiment, we do not include the user diversity and set the $\beta_{subject} = 1$ since our aim is rather to compare the behavior of our training methods. Figure 5 shows the Precision and Recall curves computed using different approaches. It is evident that setting all the coefficients equal to 1 achieves the worst performance because no adaptive optimization was considered. Moreover, it is shown that precision optimization methods (GA and PSO) deliver considerably better top-N results compared with error (RMSE) minimization method (LR). This also confirms recent works [4] showing that methodologies based on error metrics do not necessarily improve the accuracy of top-N recommendation task. One given explanation is that the RMSE-oriented methods account only for known ratings to train the system, and do not consider the unrated items. Finally, Figure 5 highlights the better performance of PSO compared with GA algorithm. We observed a faster convergence to the optimal solution in PSO compared with GA which may need more iterations. This owed to the inherent behavior of PSO where the evolu-

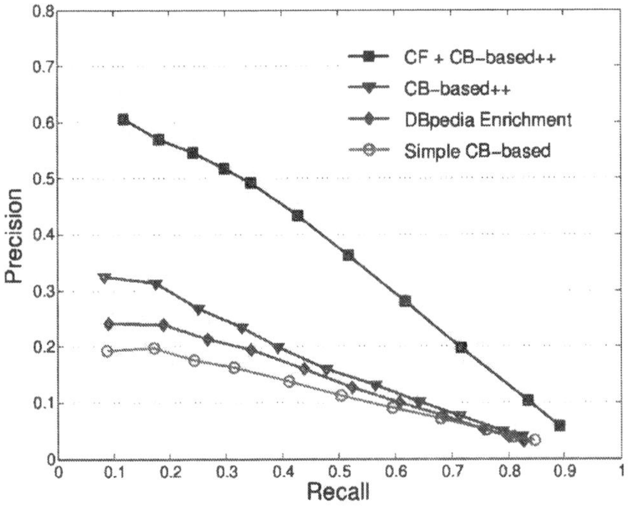

Figure 6: Evolution of the recommendation accuracy by incorporating the DBpedia enrichment, user diversity (CB-based++) and collaborative filtering (CF)

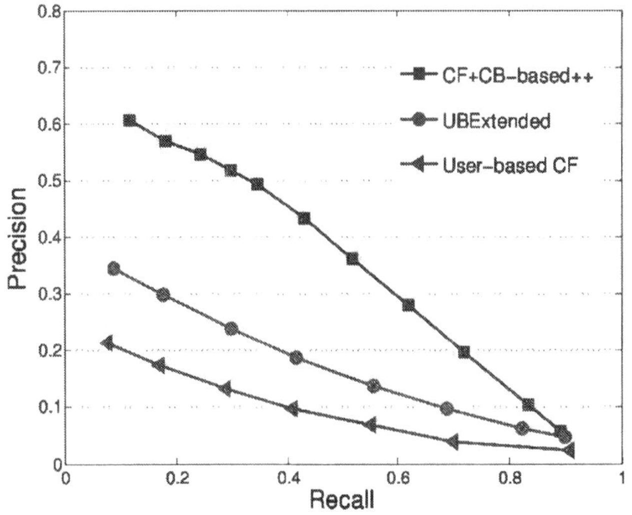

Figure 7: Comparison of hybrid event recommendation with pure CF algorithms

tion is only guided by the best particle, while it is guided by a group of solutions in GA (in which even weak candidates continue to survive after some iterations). In the following, we rely on PSO algorithm to compute the coefficients α and the weight $\beta_{subject}$.

To gain insights into the influence of the different steps in our recommendation, we decided to examine the evolution of the system performance by adding in each experiment (by order) the Linked Data enrichment, the user diversity and the collaborative filtering. Results are illustrated in Figure 6. We can observe that enriching data with DBpedia categories slightly improves both precision and recall. Indeed, introducing more coherent and qualitative data is one solution to reduce the noise that can be found in the collective knowledge of crowd tagging. Then, the integration of the user diversity model also enhances the system performance. For this experiment, we fixed the coefficients α obtained with PSO, and trained the system to compute the coefficient $\beta_{subject}$ which depends on the peaks of the user interests. We obtained $\beta_{subject}$=0.4 when the past event is not included in an interest peak, and $\beta_{subject}$=1.6 (4 times more) otherwise. This confirms the importance to account for the peaks of interest when recommending items, especially for the users who have strong propensity towards specific topics and when items are topically diverse. Finally, combining these results with the collaborative filtering notably increases the recommendation accuracy. We believe that this improvement is perfectly tangible with the use of a real world dataset. Indeed, according to the user-centric study in [18], social aspects such as people and friends who are attending an event have strong priority and influence on decision making.

In the last part of our evaluation, we assess to which extent a hybrid event recommendation outperforms the existing pure collaborative filtering. We compared our algorithm with the traditional user-based CF and the Probability based Extended Profile Filtering (UBExtended) proposed for event recommendation in [14]. This method employs a cascade of user-based CF systems attempting to recommend popular (most consumed) events among the users. The rationale behind is that the probability to consume an event is proportional to the current popularity of the event, an important aspect that will be considered in a future study. The comparison results are depicted in Figure 7. It is shown that the UBExtended improves the outcome of the system compared with the pure user-based CF algorithm. We can also observe that our hybrid algorithm exhibits the best accuracy in terms of precision and recall. This owed to the benefits of hybridization technique which have been extensively highlighted in several recommender systems.

6. RELATED WORK

In the research area of recommender systems, many approaches have been proposed to recommend movies, but few are the studies that deal with event recommendation. Considered as one-and-only items, events are particularly hard to recommend due to their short life time and the system often suffers from highly sparse data. Some works have been proposed to overcome these issues and improve the recommendation accuracy. Cornelis et al. [3] build a hybrid approach within a fuzzy relational framework which allows to reflect the uncertain information in the domain. The rationale behind is to recommend future events if they are similar to past ones that similar users have liked. However, this framework was not evaluated and there is no clear insight about its performance especially for large scale dataset. Minkov et al. [13] follow the same rationale and propose a low rank collaborative method to predict the ratings of future events. They highlight the performance of the collaborative filtering over the pure content based system. Nevertheless, their approach has mainly focused on the recommendation of scientific talks in the same building, and there is no consideration of the user location. Some other systems have been also developed such as "Pittcult" [11] and "Eventer" [8] which position the user within a social network and leverage the trustworthiness between users, a valuable information that is not available in many systems. Finally, a user-centric evaluation [6] showed that the straightforward combination of CF and CB recommendations outperforms both individual algorithms on almost qualitative metrics such as accuracy, novelty, diversity, satisfaction and trust.

Another innovative direction also interesting in our research is the recent studies proposed to harness Linked Data in recommender systems. In [5], Di Noia et al. use the Linked Data as the only background knowledge to recommend movies. They highlight the performance of the system compared to the keyword-based methods. However, there is no deep exploitation of latent similarities that may exist between movies attributes. In event recommendation and to the best of our knowledge, our system is one of the first initiative that combines the benefits of the hybrid algorithms and Linked Data.

7. CONCLUSION

In this paper, we have presented an event recommendation approach which combines the CB and CF methods, and utilizes Linked Data to enrich the item profile. We have also employed a statistical model of user interests to overcome the topical diversity of rated items and improve the system performance. The evaluation particularly highlights the importance of social information and the user diversity model to improve the event recommendation. In the future, we plan to involve other significant features such as event popularity and temporal indexing of recent consumptions to enhance the scalability. Moreover, we want to utilize some advanced similarity techniques such as tensor factorization in Linked Data, which has shown excellent performance in sparse and high dimensional domains.

Acknowledgments

This work was supported by the project AAL-2009-2-049 "Adaptable Ambient Living Assistant" (ALIAS) and the project "Social Annotations and eXperiences" (S-MAX).

8. REFERENCES

[1] C. Bizer, T. Heath, K. Idehen, and T. Berners-Lee. Linked data on the web. In *LDOW, 1st Workshop on Linked Data on the Web*, Beijing, China, 2008.

[2] D. M. Blei, A. Y. Ng, and M. I. Jordan. Latent dirichlet allocation. *Journal of Machine Learning Research*, 3:993–1022, 2003.

[3] C. Cornelis, X. Guo, J. Lu, and G. Zhang. A fuzzy relational approach to event recommendation. In *2nd Indian International Conference on Artificial Intelligence*, Pune, India, 2005.

[4] P. Cremonesi, Y. Koren, and R. Turrin. Performance of recommender algorithms on top-n recommendation tasks. In *ACM Conference on Recommender Systems (RecSys'10)*, Barcelona, Spain, 2010.

[5] T. Di Noia, R. Mirizzi, V. C. Ostuni, D. Romito, and M. Zanker. Linked open data to support content-based recommender systems. In *8th International Conference on Semantic Systems, I-SEMANTICS*, Graz, Austria, 2012.

[6] S. Dooms, T. D. Pessemier, and L. Martens. A user-centric evaluation of recommender algorithms for an event recommendation system. In *Workshop on Human Decision Making in RecSys'11*, Chicago, IL, USA, 2011.

[7] R. C. Eberhart and Y. Shi. Particle swarm optimization: developments, applications and resources. In *IEEE Congress on Evolutionary Computation*, volume 1, pages 81–86, 2001.

[8] M. Kayaalp, T. Özyer, and S. T. Özyer. A collaborative and content based event recommendation system integrated with data collection scrapers and services at a social networking site. In *International Conference on Advances in Social Networks Analysis and Mining*, Athens, Greece, 2009.

[9] H. Khrouf, V. Milicic, and R. Troncy. Eventmedia live: Exploring events connections in real-time to enhance content. In *Semantic Web Challenge at 11th International Semantic Web Conference*, Boston, USA, 2012.

[10] H. Khrouf and R. Troncy. Eventmedia: a LOD dataset of events illustrated with media. *Semantic Web Journal, Special Issue on Linked Dataset descriptions*, 2012.

[11] D. H. Lee. Pittcult: trust-based cultural event recommender. In *ACM Conference on Recommender Systems (RecSys'08)*, Lausanne, Switzerland, 2008.

[12] X. Liu, Q. He, Y. Tian, W.-C. Lee, J. McPherson, and J. Han. Event-based social networks: Linking the online and offline social worlds. In *18th ACM SIGKDD conference on Knowledge Discovery and Data Mining*, KDD'12, Beijing, China, 2012.

[13] E. Minkov, B. Charrow, J. Ledlie, S. J. Teller, and T. Jaakkola. Collaborative future event recommendation. In *19th ACM Conference on Information and Knowledge Management*, Toronto, Ontario, Canada, 2010.

[14] T. D. Pessemier, S. Coppens, K. Geebelen, C. Vleugels, S. Bannier, E. Mannens, K. Vanhecke, and L. Martens. Collaborative recommendations with content-based filters for cultural activities via a scalable event distribution platform. *Multimedia Tools Appl.*, 58(1):167–213, 2012.

[15] D. Quercia, N. Lathia, F. Calabrese, G. Di Lorenzo, and J. Crowcroft. Recommending social events from mobile phone location data. In *10th IEEE International Conference on Data Mining*, Sydney, Australia, 2010.

[16] G. Salton, A. Wong, and C. S. Yang. A vector space model for automatic indexing. *Communications of The ACM*, 18:613–620, November 1975.

[17] D. Song and J. Heflin. Automatically generating data linkages using a domain-independent candidate selection approach. In *10th International Semantic Web Conference (ISWC'11)*, Bonn, Germany, 2011.

[18] R. Troncy, A. T. S. Fialho, L. Hardman, and C. Saathoff. Experiencing events through user-generated media. In *1st International Workshop on Consuming Linked Data*, Shanghai, China, 2010.

[19] H. Wu, V. Sorathia, and V. Prasanna. When diversity meets speciality: Friend recommendation in online social networks. *ASE Human Journal*, 1(1):52–60, 2012.

[20] J. yuan Yeh, J. yi Lin, H. ren Ke, and W. pang Yang. Learning to rank for information retrieval using genetic programming. In *SIGIR Workshop on Learning to rank for Information Retrieval*, 2007.

Pairwise Learning in Recommendation: Experiments with Community Recommendation on LinkedIn

Amit Sharma
Dept. of Computer Science
Cornell University
Ithaca, NY 14853 USA
asharma@cs.cornell.edu

Baoshi Yan
LinkedIn Corp.
Mountain View, CA 94043 USA
byan@linkedin.com

ABSTRACT

Many online systems present a list of recommendations and infer user interests implicitly from clicks or other contextual actions. For modeling user feedback in such settings, a common approach is to consider items acted upon to be relevant to the user, and irrelevant otherwise. However, clicking some but not others conveys an implicit ordering of the presented items. Pairwise learning, which leverages such implicit ordering between a pair of items, has been successful in areas such as search ranking [12, 14]. In this work, we study whether pairwise learning can improve community recommendation. We first present two novel pairwise models adapted from logistic regression. Both offline and online experiments in a large real-world setting show that incorporating pairwise learning improves the recommendation performance. However, the improvement is only slight. We find that users' preferences regarding the kinds of communities they like can differ greatly, which adversely affect the effectiveness of features derived from pairwise comparisons. We therefore propose a probabilistic latent semantic indexing model for pairwise learning (Pairwise PLSI), which assumes a set of users' latent preferences between pairs of items. Our experiments show favorable results for the Pairwise PLSI model and point to the potential of using pairwise learning for community recommendation.

Categories and Subject Descriptors

H.3.3 [**Information Search and Retrieval**]: Information filtering; H.3.5 [**Online Information Services**]: Web-based services

Keywords

pairwise learning, community recommendation

1. INTRODUCTION

An increasing number of recommendation systems on the web depend on implicit binary feedback – the presence or absence of a user action on an item. Examples of binary user actions include liking an item, following a person, joining a community or clicking through a news story. In such systems, user feedback differs from traditional rating-based systems in two important ways–feedback is only partial (negative ratings are implicit), and always binary. The presence of only positive feedback creates a challenge in learning user preferences.

One intuitive approach is to consider items with positive feedback as relevant, and consider all the other items as irrelevant. This is a common approach in collaborative filtering, and is an effective way of understanding user feedback [4, 7]. However, collaborative filtering algorithms work best when given ratings across the good-bad spectrum, and even typical classification algorithms rely on a comparable number of positive and negative examples. To counter for the positive bias in feedback, another approach in literature has been to consider the problem as a special case of one-class classification and develop algorithms to generate artificial negative data [16, 15].

The above approaches, however, lose the relative nature of the information conveyed by the items that are shown to a user, but are not acted upon. Assuming a user sees all the recommendations and acts only on some of them, her inaction on certain items does not directly convey an absolute rejection of those items. Instead, we argue that it conveys an implicit negative feedback for those items, relative to the ones she acted upon. Thus, we can reasonably assume that clicked items are more relevant for the user than unclicked ones, though we cannot be sure about the absolute quality of unclicked items. This is the basis of pairwise learning, a popular approach for relevance feedback in search [3].

Past experiments with pairwise learning in collaborative recommendation systems have shown promising results [20, 17]. In this paper, we explore how a pairwise approach for preference learning can be used in a content-based recommender. In particular, we study the problem of recommending communities to users, where a community is a social unit consisting of people with certain common characteristics or interests, for example, a LinkedIn group for RecSys 2013, a LinkedIn group for Cornell alumni, or a Facebook page for RecSys. Our findings are three-fold. First, we present general pairwise adaptations for content-based recommendation based on logistic regression, and show that pairwise models are comparable and in general slightly better than the non-pairwise model. Second, we show that a direct pairwise adaptation might not yield significant improvement for community recommendation, due to users' vast different commu-

RecSys'13, October 12–16, 2013, Hong Kong, China.
Copyright 2013 ACM 978-1-4503-2409-0/13/10 ...$15.00.
http://dx.doi.org/10.1145/2507157.2507175.

Figure 1: Group recommendation interface on linkedin.com

nity preferences which make pairwise comparison less meaningful. Third, we present a probabilistic latent semantic indexing model for pairwise learning, which models latent user preferences and significantly outperforms the direct pairwise adaptation models and the non-pairwise model.

Application domain. We choose community recommendation on LinkedIn.com as a domain for evaluating our recommendation models. LinkedIn is the world's largest professional network in which members create profiles and connect with other individuals. In addition, members are free to create and join communities (or *groups* [1]) of their liking (subject to admin approval, in certain cases). Members may add themselves to a group when they see it on another member's profile, through search or when they get recommendations. At present, there are more than 2 million groups on LinkedIn. The recommendation problem is to select a set of top-k groups to join for each user.

Figure 1 shows a typical recommendation interface. A user is presented with a list of k recommendations. A user conveys positive feedback by either clicking the link corresponding to a group, and/or choosing to join the group. However, the interface does not allow negative feedback, which provides a motivation for using pairwise learning.

2. RELATED WORK

We first discuss pairwise learning, and its relevance for recommendation systems. In the second part of this section, we present previous work on community recommendation.

2.1 Pairwise learning

Understanding implicit feedback has been an active problem for search engines. Joachims [9] was the first to show how information retrieval can be improved by considering user feedback in pairs of items. He assumed that users are more likely to see items ranked higher in the list (position bias [6]). Thus, between a clicked item and an unclicked item ranked higher than that item, we can infer safely that the clicked item is more relevant than unclicked one. These clicked and unclicked items in search logs are clubbed together to form pairs, which convey a relative ordering between their constituent items. Encoding user actions into pairwise preferences converts the problem into a classification problem on pairs, instead of classifying relevance for individual items. This approach was shown to improve retrieval results, and is now a popular method of relevance feedback in search engines [12, 14].

In principle, one could construct triplets, or even arbitrary lists [3] to encode relative preference. However, in a recent paper, Radinsky and Ailon [18] demonstrate that triplets do not give any more information than pairs in terms of the statistical significance of preference. Further, in a user study, Joachims et al. [10] provided empirical support for the pairwise approach by showing that people are more consistent at making comparisons between items than evaluating on an absolute scale of relevance or quality. The use of pairs is also consistent with an axiom in decision theory, which states that the relative attractiveness of two choices does not depend upon other choices available (Independence of Irrelevant alternatives [19]).

Apart from using click logs, pairs can also be constructed in other ways to convey relative preference of users. For example, Balakrishnan and Chopra [1] have proposed an adaptive scheme in which users are explicitly asked for their relative preference between a pair of items. Thus, users give pairwise feedback to the underlying algorithm, which updates user parameters as it receives more responses. Instead of pairs of items, one may also ask users to order a set of items [11]. Though it may provide an accurate measure of a user's preference, explicitly asking users for their preference may not be feasible for large numbers of users or items, or desirable as a design strategy in certain cases.

To the extent that recommendations are shown as an ordered list, the problem of recommendation quality is similar to that of relevance in search engines. Just as relevance in search depends on the information need, quality in recommendation depends on the user preference and context. For matrix factorization and kNN models, recommendation performance on movies has been shown to improve by incorporating pairwise preferences from recommendation feedback logs [20]. A pairwise strategy may also be applied to explicit ratings, where pairs are generated by comparing Likert-scale ratings of a user [13, 17]. In the present work, we focus on problem domains where such rich ratings are not present, using content-based recommendation models. As in [9], we use system logs of clicked recommendations to construct pairs.

2.2 Community Recommendation

We now present a brief overview of previous work on community recommendation. In one of the first papers on community recommendation, Spertus et al. [21] used similarity measures to recommend communities in Orkut which are similar to a particular community. Chen et al. [4] extended the work on Orkut communities and compared two different algorithms, Association Rule Mining and Latent Dirichlet Allocation for the purposes of community recommendation. In [5], Chen et al. describe a latent model that conditions a user joining based on the hidden topics that a community represents. In another domain (Flickr), different memory-based and model-based approaches have been compared in terms of top-k recommendation, and tags were found to be helpful [22].

Owing to the rich profile data (education, career, skills, interests, publications etc.) available for each user on LinkedIn, we adopt a content-based approach to recommendation. This

[1]We use the term community recommendation to disambiguate against the more common use of the term group recommendation to mean recommendation *for* groups.

is not unlike many other online social networks, where users self-create an elaborate personal profile. For example, Facebook hosts a profile for each user which spans a user's interests. LinkedIn groups, especially, is an example of a recommendation domain where we have rich data about a user as well as the group. We build on previous work by adapting a similarity-based algorithm (logistic) and a latent model (PLSI) with pairwise feedback and comparing their performance to non-pairwise models.

3. MODEL PRELIMINARIES

For clarity, let us first formally define the problem. Given a user u, the recommendation task is to suggest communities that may be of interest, from a set of candidate communities Y. Suppose there are $|U| = m$ users and $|Y| = n$ communities. Each observed preference is in the form of a tuple (u, y), where u is a user, y is a community, and $u \in \{1, 2, 3...m\}$, $y \in \{1, 2, 3...n\}$. We assume that we are given a set of known (u, y) and the task is to predict a set $R(u)$ for each user which denotes recommendations for a user u.

For our problem, we specify another variable s which denotes the impression list, or the communities that are shown together to a user. For example, in Figure 1, the three communities presented will belong to the same impression list. Thus each observation is given as a (u, y, s).

Current system. There are three main components: feature generation, model learning, and computation of the results from the learned model. Although continual feature generation and free-text standardization over millions of members is a complex problem in itself, here we provide a brief overview. Features for members are largely profile-driven, such as skills, industry, past positions, education etc. Similarly, a group is represented by features such as group summary and category. In addition, a group's features are also constructed in aggregate from the features of its constituent members. Elements of these two feature sets are matched to each other, to determine similarity between a user and a group. In the limiting case, the number of matchings can be quadratic in the number of features. Thus, individual features are matched only when semantically relevant. For example, it may be useful to match the group description with "interests" feature for a user, but not with the "connection counts" feature. For every user and group, a dot product of matched user-group features $(u.y)$ gives us a similarity score. In addition, we introduce social features that reflect user-group interactions, for instance, whether and how many friends of a user have joined a group. The final similarity vector conveys the degree of similarity between a user and a group. All models described utilize the similarity feature vector, thus constructed.

We now describe the current model in production on LinkedIn (as of May 2012), starting from some basic definitions. Given a similarity vector for each pair of user and item, a simple recommendation model can be described as:

$$R(u) = \{y \in Y : Sim(f_u, f_y) > \epsilon\}$$

for some $\epsilon > 0$, where $Sim(f_u, f_g)$ is the similarity vector for user u and group y feature vectors. If the similarity function is just a dot product of the vectors, we get:

$$Sim(f_u, f_y) = \sum_{i=1}^{n} w_i * f_u^{(i)} * f_y^{(i)}$$

where w_i represents the relative importance of different similarity features. Using the sigmoid function for similarity and setting $\epsilon = 0.5$, we can represent the problem in the form of standard logistic regression.

$$R(u) = \{y \in Y : \frac{1}{1 + e^{-Sim(f_u, f_y)}} > 0.5\} \quad (1)$$

Given this model, we precompute the similarity between a users and all items. For each user, the most similar items can be chosen for recommendation. This is the baseline model implementation for our experiments.

Pairwise approach. We now turn to the preliminaries for using pairwise approach for recommendation. We first discuss how pairs are created from group-join data.

The first step is to access the group-join log as well as the recommendation impressions log. To connect a group-join with a recommendation impression, we choose the latest impression for each user-item pair and select all group-joins which occured within 10 minutes of the impression (a recommendation is not shown after a user joins a group). This is a conservative assumption, considering that the join may still happen on account of the impression or otherwise. But for the purposes of this study, a hard stance of 10 minutes is taken. We now have a a set of ranked impression lists. Each element of the ranked list contains an item and an indicator of whether it led to a group-join or not. From these lists, we create item pairs by the following rule (see [9]):

$$\begin{aligned} rank(I_{y_2}) > rank(I_{y_1}) \ and \ join(y_2) \ and \ !join(y_1) \\ \Rightarrow pair(y_1, y_2) \end{aligned} \quad (2)$$

where I_{y_2} and I_{y_1} represent impressions in the same list for $y2$ and $y1$. Once we have the pairs, we define a variable t for each user and a pair of items (y_1, y_2), such that the learning problem translates to a classification problem on t.

$$t_u(y_i, y_j) = \begin{cases} 1 & \text{if } y_j \text{ is preferred over } y_i \\ 0 & \text{otherwise} \end{cases}$$

given a user u and two items y_1 and y_2.

Note that our above strategy for creating pairs will lead to pairs where the first group in the pair is always higher in preference ($t = 1$) than the second group. To ensure equal number of positive and negative examples for classification, we randomly invert all pairs with probability 0.5.

Any classification algorithm can be used to learn preferences on pairs, thus constructed. However, an important requirement is to have a fast way of ranking individual items, once we have a learnt a model for classifying pairs. For a naive implementation, ranking k items will require constructing $O(k^2)$ pairs, which will be too computation intensive. For the best performance, the ranking function should be independent of the pairs. In the next two sections, we discuss how we can derive fast ranking functions for logistic regression and PLSI-based pairwise models.

4. LOGISTIC PAIRWISE MODELS

We now describe two pairwise models derived from logistic regression. We assume that we are given a list of M known pairwise preferences $t_u(y_i, y_j)$. Let us define an item ranking function $h_\theta(y)$, which has the following property (as in [9]):

$$h_\theta(y_i) > h_\theta(y_j) \Leftrightarrow y_i \ is \ preferred \ over \ y_j$$

Then our task is to learn such a function h_θ from the available pairwise preferences. We make a simplifying assumption that pairwise preferences are independent of each other, drawing on the Independence of Irrelevant Alternatives assumption from decision theory literature [19]. Thus, our task can be set-up as a likelihood maximization problem:

$$maximize\ \Pi_{k=1}^{M} P(t|y_i, y_j, u; \theta)$$

If we redefine t in terms of h,

$$t_u(y_i, y_j) = \begin{cases} 1 & \text{if } h_\theta(y_j) \geq h_\theta(y_i) \\ 0 & \text{otherwise} \end{cases}$$

then we can write the equivalent maximization problem.

$$maximize\ \Pi_{k=1}^{M} P[h_\theta(y_j) \geq h_\theta(y_i)]^t P[h_\theta(y_j) < h_\theta(y_i)]^{(1-t)}$$

$$maximize\ \Pi_{k=1}^{M} P[h_\theta(y_j) \geq h_\theta(y_i)]^t (1 - P[h_\theta(y_j) \geq h_\theta(y_i)])^{(1-t)}$$

Based on how we model $h_\theta(y)$, the above formulation gives rise to two novel pairwise models.

4.1 Feature Difference Model

In the special case that $h_\theta(y)$ is a linear function, we have $h_\theta(y) = \theta^T y$. Then the problem reduces to:

$$max\ \Pi_{k=1}^{M} P[\theta^T(y_j - y_i) \geq 0]^t (1 - P[\theta^T(y_j - y_i) \geq 0])^{(1-t)}$$

Taking $y_{ji} = y_j - y_i$, this formulation is the same as standard logistic regression with features y_{ji}. Hence if we assume that the ranking function is linear, we can simply learn a logistic model on the difference of features of the items.

To rank the items, we use the linearity property again. We can see that $h_\theta(y_j) \geq h_\theta(y_i) \Leftrightarrow y_j \geq y_i$. Thus, it is sufficient to calculate $\theta^{*T} y_i$ for each item to rank the items.

4.2 Logistic Loss Model

The feature difference model lends itself well to a standard learning framework, but makes a strong assumption about the ranking function. We now propose a model for any general ranking function. We define:

$$g_\theta(y_i, y_j) = h_\theta(y_j) - h_\theta(y_i)$$

as the difference in ranking scores for two items y_i and y_j. Then, we can write $P(t|y_i, y_j)$ as (where t is as before):

$$P(t = 1|y_i, y_j; \theta) = \frac{g_\theta(y_i, y_j) + 1}{2}$$

Since $h_\theta(y) \in [0, 1]$, we add the additional constants to ensure that the $P(t|y_i, y_j) \in [0, 1]$. This formulation is based on the intuition that difference in ranking scores for two items is proportional to the probability of one being more preferred than the other.

We can now frame this as a maximum likelihood estimation problem.

$$max\ \Pi_{k=1}^{M} \left(\frac{g_\theta(y_i, y_j) + 1}{2}\right)^t \left(1 - \frac{g_\theta(y_i, y_j) + 1}{2}\right)^{1-t}$$

$$l(\theta) = max \sum_{k=1}^{M} t \log[g(y_i, y_j) + 1] + (1 - t) \log(1 - g(y_i, y_j))$$

Using gradient descent,

$$\frac{\partial l(\theta)}{\partial \theta_n} = \sum_i \left(\frac{2t - g(y_i, y_j) - 1}{1 - g(y_i, y_j)^2}\right) \frac{\partial g(y_i, y_j)}{\partial \theta_n}$$

We can use any ranking function h_θ in the above equation. For our experiments, we choose the logistic function because it is used as the base for LinkedIn recommendation platform. Setting $h_\theta(y) = \frac{1}{1+\exp(-\theta^T y)}$, we get the gradient in Equation 3 (Figure 2).

The likelihood can be optimized using any of the gradient methods. We use L-BFGS [2] in our implementation. For generating top recommendations, we have to order items by $h_{\theta*}(y)$. Since logistic is an increasing function, this reduces to ranking items based on their $\theta^{*T} y$ scores, as in the Feature Difference model.

5. PAIRWISE PLSI MODEL

Given the success of pairwise learning in domains such as information retrieval, it is natural to expect similar improvement in recommendation. However, as that will be shown later in Section 6, the two pairwise models described above only slightly outperform a baseline non-pairwise model.

One of the major reasons for the limited improvement is the heterogeneity in communities and users' vast different preferences for the communities they want to join, which make features derived from pairwise comparison less effective. For example, a user might look to expand her network. Thus even though a relevant interest-based group (e.g, a machine learning group) is recommended, the user might choose an alumni group instead, which as a result of pairwise comparison would penalize the feature representing user interest and reward the feature representing user's education history. When presented with a similar list of recommendations, however, another user might choose an interest group over an alumni group, thus producing the opposite impact on the two features. In the extreme case that an equal number of users make the opposite choices, the two features representing interest and education would not serve as discriminative features as we would have expected.

We now present a pairwise model that also accounts for variation in users' preferences towards different features, by treating a user as a mixture of some latent preferences. Our model is based on probabilistic latent semantic indexing [8]. The intuition is that users may have different reasons for joining a group, such as networking, learning skills or for social support [3]. Each user may also value these reasons differently. Assuming the possible reasons people join groups are consistent across users, we can think of each user's decision to join a group as a combination of these reasons, or *core preferences.*

Figure 3 shows the plate notation for our proposed model. We assume that each user can be described by a set of Z core latent preferences. We also assume that given a core preference z and two items y_i and y_j, the preference value t for the two items is independent of the user. Thus, when presented with a pair of communities (y_1,y_2), a user's decision is computed from the mixture of core preferences, weighted by the relative importance of each core preference to the user.

[2]http://www.chokkan.org/software/liblbfgs/

[3]We verified this intuition by considering different types of groups on LinkedIn (networking, professional, alumni, philanthropy, corporate and conference) as proxies for reasons to join. Using a random sample of 1M users, we found that most users join groups of more than one type; mean number of group types per user is 3.1 and median is 3.

$$\frac{\partial l(\theta)}{\partial \theta_n} = \sum_i \frac{2t - g(y_i, y_j) - 1}{1 - g(y_i, y_j)^2} (h_\theta(y_j)(1 - h_\theta(y_j))y_{jn} - h_\theta(y_i)(1 - h_\theta(y_i))y_{in}) \tag{3}$$

$$\textbf{E Step: } Q_k(z) = \frac{(h_{\theta_z}(y_j) - h_{\theta_z}(y_i) + 1)^t (1 - (h_{\theta_z}(y_j) - h_{\theta_z}(y_i))^{1-t} \exp(w_z^T u^{(k)})}{\sum_{z'} (h_{\theta_{z'}}(y_j) - h_{\theta_{z'}}(y_i) + 1)^t (1 - (h_{\theta_{z'}}(y_j) - h_{\theta_{z'}}(y_i))^{1-t} \exp(w_{z'}^T u^{(k)})} \tag{4}$$

$$\textbf{M Step: } \begin{aligned} & maximize_{\theta,w} \sum_k \sum_z Q_k(z)[w_z^T u^{(k)} - \log(\sum_{z'} \exp(w_{z'}^T u^{(k)}))+ \sum_{k\{t=1\}} \sum_z Q_k(z) \log(\frac{h_{\theta_z}(y_j^{(k)}) - h_{\theta_z}(y_i^{(k)}) + 1}{2}) \\ & + \sum_{k\{t=0\}} \sum_z Q_k(z) \log(\frac{1 - (h_{\theta_z}(y_j^{(k)}) - h_{\theta_z}(y_i^{(k)}))}{2}) \end{aligned} \tag{5}$$

$$\begin{aligned} \frac{\partial l(\theta, w)}{\partial \theta_{zk}} = & \sum_{k\{t=1\}} Q_k(z) \frac{h_{\theta_z}(y_j^{(k)})(1 - h_{\theta_z}(y_j^{(k)})y_{jk} - h_{\theta_z}(y_i^{(k)})(1 - h_{\theta_z}(y_i^{(k)})y_{ik}}{h_{\theta_z}(y_j^{(k)}) - h_{\theta_z}(y_i^{(k)}) + 1} \\ & - \sum_{k\{t=0\}} Q_k(z) \frac{h_{\theta_z}(y_j^{(k)})(1 - h_{\theta_z}(y_j^{(k)})y_{jk} + h_{\theta_z}(y_i^{(k)})(1 - h_{\theta_z}(y_i^{(k)})y_{ik}}{1 - (h_{\theta_z}(y_j^{(k)}) - h_{\theta_z}(y_i^{(k)}))} \end{aligned} \tag{6}$$

$$\frac{\partial l(\theta, w)}{\partial w_{zk}} = \sum_k Q_k(z) u_j^{(k)} - \sum_k \frac{\exp(w_z^T u^{(k)})}{\sum_{z'} \exp(w_{z'}^T u^{(k)})} u_j^{(k)} \tag{7}$$

Figure 2: E and M steps for the Pairwise PLSI algorithm. Here $h_\theta(y)$ is the logistic function.

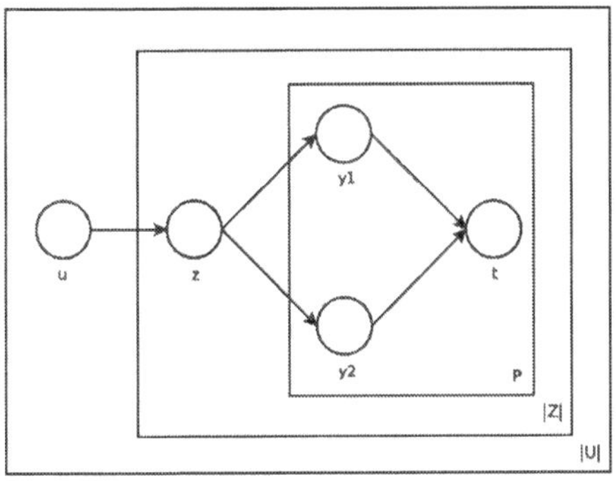

Figure 3: Graphical model describing the relationship between user's pairwise preferences and his/her latent core preferences. Here P is the number of item pairs, $|Z|$ is the number of latent preferences and $|U|$ is the number of users.

In accordance with the above assumptions:

$$P(t|y_i, y_j, u) = \sum_{z \in Z} P(t|y_i, y_j, z) P(z|u)$$

where t is as before, and z is a latent variable representing core preference. Then, for all training pairs, using maximum likelihood estimation,

$$maximize \sum_{k=1}^{M} \log(\sum_z P(t^{(k)}|z, y_i^{(k)}, y_j^{(k)}) P(z|u^{(k)}))$$

We discuss modeling choices first, and then describe learning and inference for the model.

5.1 Number of core preferences

The parameter Z controls how much personalized the model is – a Z value of $|U|$ effectively creates a different core preference for each user. There is a tradeoff between accurately modeling a user's preference and model size. A paper describing Google news recommendation [7] followed a comparable approach by assigning a different probability for each user. In the present case, however, that would result in a lot of parameters to learn since the number of parameters in the model is linear in the number of latent preferences. Hence, we consider $|Z|$ to be a small positive number (≤ 8 for our experiments).

5.2 Choosing probability models

We have two model choices to make, $P(t|y_i, y_j, z)$ and $P(z|u)$. For the first, we may use any of the user-agnostic models (latent preferences do not change across users). In the following analysis, we use Logistic Loss as our base model.

$$P(t|y_i, y_j, z; \theta_z) = \frac{h_{\theta_z}(y_j) - h_{\theta_z}(y_i) + 1}{2} \tag{8}$$

$P(z|u)$ represents the relative propensity of users to associate with different latent preferences. We use a softmax-based multinomial function to represent this probability.

$$P(z|u) = \frac{\exp(w_z^T u)}{\sum_{z'} exp(w_{z'}^T u)}$$

5.3 Model fitting

We use Expectation-Maximization to fit the parameters to the model, assuming z as the hidden random variable. Thus, we maximize the likelihood:

$$maximize \sum_{k=1}^{m} \log(P(t|y_i, y_j, u))$$

$$maximize \sum_{k=1}^{m} \log(\sum_z P(t, z|y_i, y_j, u))$$

Let Q_z be an arbitrary distribution over z, for each kth training example $< u, y_i, y_j >$. Then, the E step yields:

$$Q_k(z) = \frac{P(t^{(k)}|y_i^{(k)}, y_j^{(k)}, z)P(z|u^{(k)})}{\sum_{z'} P(t^{(k)}|y_i^{(k)}, y_j^{(k)}, z')P(z'|u^{(k)})}$$

And the M-step becomes:

$$\theta := argmax_\theta \sum_k \sum_{z^{(k)}} Q_k(z^{(k)}) \log(\frac{P(t^{(k)}, z^{(k)}; \theta|y_i, y_j, u)}{Q_k(z^{(k)})})$$

$$\theta := argmax_\theta \sum_k \sum_{z^{(k)}} Q_k(z^{(k)}) \log(P(t^{(k)}; \theta|y_i, y_j, z^{(k)})P(z^{(k)}|u))$$

Substituting the Logistic Loss and the multinomial models, we get the equivalent equations shown in Figure 2. Unlike [8], for the pairwise case, we do not get a closed form expression in the M-step. Hence, we use gradient descent to compute the maximization in each M-step, as shown in Figure 2.

5.4 Inference

Once we have fitted the parameters, we can compute the output class of a pair as follows:

$$P(t|y_i, y_j, u) = \sum_{z \in Z} P(t|y_i, y_j, z)P(z|u)$$

To generate recommendations, we would need a way to rank the communities for a user. It turns out that we get a simple metric for the logistic loss base model, that can be used to rank the recommendations. This becomes possible due to a special property of the logistic and multinomial functions. We present it next.

THEOREM 1. *Let $P(t|u, y_i, y_j)$ be the probability that y_j is preferred over y_i, given by*

$$P(t|y_i, y_j, u) = \sum_{z \in Z} P(t|y_i, y_j, z)P(z|u)$$

where $P(t|y_i, y_j)$ is a logistic function, and $P(z|u)$ is a multinomial distribution. Then $A_{y_k} = \sum_z h_{\theta_z}(y_k)P(z|u)$ is a valid ranking function.

PROOF. Let us assume there exist two items y_i, y_j for which $P(t|u, y_i, y_j)$ is computed. We further assume that y_j is preferred over y_i iff $P(t|u, y_i, y_j) > 0.5$. Define two function values A_1 and A_2, of A_y function.

$$A_1 = \sum_z h_{\theta_z}(y_i)P(z|u), A_2 = \sum_z h_{\theta_z}(y_j)P(z|u)$$

We will proceed to show that $A_2 > A_1 \Leftrightarrow P(t|u, y_i, y_j) > 0.5$ by showing $A_2 - A_1 = 2P(t|u, y_i, y_j) - 1$. Consider

$$A_2 - A_1 = \sum_z h_{\theta_z}(y_j)P(z|u) - \sum_z h_{\theta_z}(y_i)P(z|u)$$
$$= \sum_z P(z|u)(h_{\theta_z}(y_j) - h_{\theta_z}(y_i))$$

Using Equation 8,

$$A_2 - A_1 = \sum_z P(z|u)(2P(t|y_i, y_j, z) - 1)$$
$$= 2(\sum_z P(z|u)P(t|y_i, y_j, z)) - 1$$
$$= 2P(t|u, y_i, y_j) - 1$$

Hence proved. □

6. EVALUATION

We now turn to the evaluation of our proposed models. We first compare the time complexity and scalability of the algorithms, followed by offline evaluation, and finally an online evaluation on linkedin.com.

6.1 Complexity and scalability

We analyze the time complexity for two major operations – model learning (offline), and recommendation computation (online). In a typical scenario, a learned model is used to recompute recommendations frequently for all the users, to utilize new user feedback. But because model learning is not done so frequently, a model with low online complexity and reasonable offline complexity is acceptable.

If L is the size of the recommendation list shown to a user, and J is the total number of group joins, then the number of pairs P generated is $O(L * J)$. For both pairwise models, one step of the gradient descent takes $O(F * P)$, where F is the number of features. In contrast, Pairwise PLSI model is slower to learn, since learning is based on EM iterations. Each E step takes $O(Z * P)$ time, and each M-step consists of another minimization using gradient descent, which is $O(Z * P^2)$.

For non-latent pairwise models, it takes constant time ($O(F)$) to compute ranking score for each user and item. For Pairwise PLSI model, the corresponding time complexity is $O(Z * F)$, where F is the number of features. Thus, ranking for each item is fast in all three algorithms, provided Z is small (2-8).

The parametric models also lend themselves to parallelized rank computation. Given the same model file, different nodes can compute recommendation lists for different users independently. Thus, we can easily scale recommendation computation for millions of users.

6.2 Offline evaluation

We collected log data for group recommendation over the summer of 2012. The log entries were converted to pairs as described in Section 3. Table 1 shows some statistics for the data. The number of group-pairs are 13 per user on average. For prediction, the test data was selected from logs beginning from a later date than the training data. We chose a relatively small train dataset to speed up model fitting as the learning gains from a bigger dataset were not substantial.

The baseline is a logistic regression model that does not use pairs for learning, as represented in Equation 1. We compare the two base pairwise models, Feature Difference and Logistic Loss, and three versions of the Pairwise PLSI model, with $Z \in \{2, 4, 8\}$.

	Train	Test
Number of users	262K	11.2M
Number of group-pairs	3.4M	NA
Number of group-joins	NA	31.6M

Table 1: Summary statistics for the data collected. Since our ranking function does not require pairs (learning does), we do not compute group-pairs for the test set.

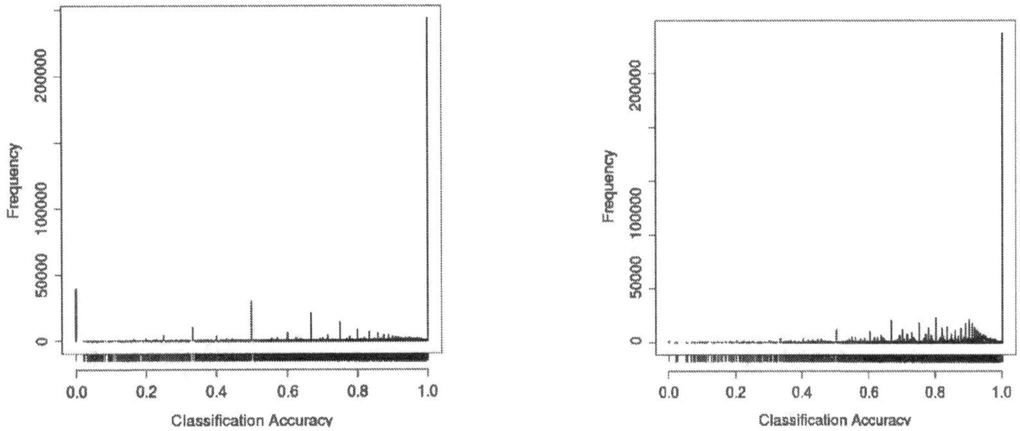

(a) Feature Difference

(b) Pairwise PLSI (z=2)

Figure 4: Per User Accuracy for the best performing non-latent model, and the Pairwise PLSI preferences model (z=2). Pairwise PLSI leads to higher number of users with PUA >0.5. Note the large number of 1's in both algorithms is due to the fact that a lot of users had only 1-2 group joins in the dataset.

Algorithm	Accuracy
Baseline	74.5
Feature Difference	79.4
Logistic Loss	75.4
Pairwise PLSI ($Z = 2$)	83.2
Pairwise PLSI ($Z = 4$)	87.1
Pairwise PLSI ($Z = 8$)	88.6

Table 2: Accuracy on the pair classification task. All pairwise models perform better than the baseline. Latent Preference models deliver a higher accuracy overall.

Learning pairwise preferences. We first evaluate how well the models learn user preference within a pair of groups, by framing it as a classification task. For each pair of groups (y_1, y_2) in the dataset, we classify the pair as positive (1) if y_2 is more preferred than y_1, and zero (0) otherwise. For all models, 5-fold cross validation is used during training. We report accuracies of different models on the pair classification task and compare them in Table 2.

Among non-latent models, Feature Difference delivers the highest accuracy for pair classification, but both pairwise models beat the baseline. Latent models perform better than the other algorithms. Performance of Pairwise PLSI increases with the number of latent preferences, although the relative boost decreases with z. We next see how the accuracy varies for different users.

Per user accuracy. One of the goals of recommendation is user satisfaction, and hence we desire a model that delivers "good" recommendation to all users. For our purposes, we define "good" to be the fraction of group-pairs for a user in the test set that are correctly classified. More precisely,

$$PUA_u = \frac{\textit{Correctly Classified Pairs for user } u}{\textit{Total test pairs for user } u}$$

Figure 4 shows frequency plots of the per user accuracy of the algorithm in the group-pair classification task, for Feature Difference and Pairwise PLSI($Z = 2$). We see that the number of users with non-zero correct classification increase with the Pairwise PLSI model. Also, the number of users with $PUA > 0.5$ is higher for Pairwise PLSI. This suggests that the Pairwise PLSI gives an overall better recommendation experience per user.

Algorithm	Top-5	Top-10	Top-25
Baseline	17.32	25.21	35.72
Feature Difference	17.81	26.25	37.78
Logistic Loss	17.39	25.56	37.81
Pairwise PLSI ($Z = 2$)	18.93	27.82	39.83
Pairwise PLSI ($Z = 4$)	20.04	28.91	41.82

(a) Test set: All groups

Algorithm	Top-5	Top-10	Top-25
Baseline	5.45	8.01	11.25
Feature Difference	5.48	8.03	10.87
Logistic Loss	5.06	7.39	10.54
Pairwise PLSI ($Z = 2$)	5.80	8.40	11.26
Pairwise PLSI ($Z = 4$)	5.99	8.75	11.66

(b) Test set: Groups that have never been recommended to the user during the training period

Table 3: Number of top-k recommendations that were also joined by users during the test period, compared for different models and under two versions of the test set. All reported numbers are in millions. Pairwise PLSI model retrieves more accurate top-k results for both test sets (15% and 10% boost over the baseline for the top-5 metric). For non-latent pairwise models, Feature Difference performs slightly better than the baseline for both test sets, Logistic Loss only for case (a).

Top-k recommendation. We now evaluate the algorithms on the list of groups returned as recommendation. We choose top-k metric for comparing the different models, with $k \in \{5, 10, 25\}$. For any k, the top-k metric is defined as the number of groups among the highest ranked k recommendations that are also joined by the user in the test data. $k = 5$ and $k = 10$ represent the number of group recommendations

Algorithm	Avg. CTR
Baseline	0.0204
Feature Difference	0.0214 (5%)
Logistic Loss	0.0210 (3%)

Table 4: Comparative performance of non-latent models, when deployed on the LinkedIn website. Numbers in parenthesis denote relative improvement over the baseline. Feature Difference delivers a 5% higher click-through-rate (CTR) than the baseline algorithm in production.

typically shown on the homepage, and on the groups page of LinkedIn respectively.

Generating a test set for evaluation is non-trivial due to presentation bias [2]. Since the baseline algorithm also generated recommendations for the users during the test period, there might be a bias in the groups that a user gets exposed to for joining. In one scenario, we could collect all group joins and label them as positive examples. In an alternative overcompensatory scenario, we remove all group joins that happened because of a recommendation and consider the rest as the examples to test on. These are groups that are joined by 'organic' traversal of the website, and hence are a closer estimate of user's preference. We use both types of test sets for evaluation.

Tables 3a and 3b show the top-k metric for the models, under the two versions of the test set. As expected, the number of correctly retrieved groups increases with the increase in k for all models. We observe that Feature Difference again performs better than Logistic Loss among the base pairwise models, but the difference is only slight. The Pairwise PLSI model outperforms all the others, offering a more than 10% boost over the baseline top-5 metric for both test scenarios.

6.3 Online Evaluation

To test whether offline evaluation translates to on-site performance too, we compare the performances of pairwise models after deploying them on the LinkedIn website. We ran the logistic loss and feature difference models to a 5% subset of total LinkedIn users respectively, in addition to the current baseline model, for a period of 2 weeks. We evaluate the click-through-rate (CTR) of the recommendations. The pairwise models perform slightly better, as predicted by the offline analysis. In particular, Feature Difference reports a lift of 5% on the CTR metric (Table 4).

Thus, our results suggest that there is value in learning from pairwise feedback. Although the performance boost using only base pairwise algorithms is slight, Pairwise PLSI model performs better on both top-k and classification metrics. However, the tradeoff is in the learning time of the model, which is considerably higher for Pairwise PLSI.

7. CONCLUSION

As users interact with online recommender systems more and more, understanding user feedback has become important for recommendation quality. We presented our results of applying pairwise learning to community recommendation. Our experiment results show that pairwise models directly adapted from a baseline recommendation model perform better than the baseline non-pairwise model, although only slightly. We argue that the nature of community recommendation does not lend itself well to pairwise comparision due to vast different user preferences towards communities. To that end we proposed a probabilistic latent preference model (Pairwise PLSI) which assumes a set of inherent preferences within each user. Offline evaluation shows that the Pairwise PLSI model significantly outperforms other models.

Acknowledgments The authors would like to thank Dan Cosley, for feedback on initial drafts of the paper, and LinkedIn for providing the data used in the experiments.

8. REFERENCES

[1] S. Balakrishnan and S. Chopra. Two of a kind or the ratings game? Adaptive pairwise preferences and latent factor models. In *Proc. ICDM*, 2010.

[2] J. Bar-Ilan, K. Keenoy, M. Levene, and E. Yaari. Presentation bias is significant in determining user preference for search results-A user study. *American Soc. for Inf. Science and Tech.*, 2009.

[3] Z. Cao, T. Qin, T.-Y. Liu, M.-F. Tsai, and H. Li. Learning to rank: from pairwise approach to listwise approach. In *Proc. ICML*, 2007.

[4] W.-Y. Chen, J.-C. Chu, J. Luan, H. Bai, Y. Wang, and E. Y. Chang. Collaborative filtering for orkut communities: discovery of user latent behavior. In *Proc. WWW*, 2009.

[5] W.-Y. Chen, D. Zhang, and E. Y. Chang. Combinational collaborative filtering for personalized community recommendation. In *Proc. KDD*, 2008.

[6] N. Craswell, O. Zoeter, M. Taylor, and B. Ramsey. An experimental comparison of click position-bias models. In *Proc. WSDM*, 2008.

[7] A. S. Das, M. Datar, A. Garg, and S. Rajaram. Google news personalization: scalable online collaborative filtering. In *Proc. WWW*, 2007.

[8] T. Hofmann. Latent semantic models for collaborative filtering. *ACM Trans. Inf. Syst.*, 2004.

[9] T. Joachims. Optimizing search engines using clickthrough data. In *Proc. KDD*, 2002.

[10] T. Joachims, L. Granka, B. Pan, H. Hembrooke, F. Radlinski, and G. Gay. Evaluating the accuracy of implicit feedback from clicks and query reformulations in web search. *ACM Trans. Inf. Syst.*, 2007.

[11] T. Kamishima. Nantonac collaborative filtering: recommendation based on order responses. In *Proc. KDD*, 2003.

[12] H. Li. Learning to rank for information retrieval and natural language processing. *Synthesis Lectures on Human Language Tech.*, 2011.

[13] N. N. Liu, M. Zhao, and Q. Yang. Probabilistic latent preference analysis for collaborative filtering. In *Proc. CIKM*, 2009.

[14] T.-Y. Liu. *Learning to rank for information retrieval.* Springerverlag Berlin, 2011.

[15] R. Pan and M. Scholz. Mind the gaps: weighting the unknown in large-scale one-class collaborative filtering. In *Proc. KDD*, 2009.

[16] R. Pan, Y. Zhou, B. Cao, N. N. Liu, R. Lukose, M. Scholz, and Q. Yang. One-class collaborative filtering. In *Proc. ICDM*, 2008.

[17] J.-F. Pessiot, T.-V. Truong, N. Usunier, M.-R. Amini, and P. Gallinari. Learning to rank for collaborative filtering. In *ICEIS (2)'07*, 2007.

[18] K. Radinsky and N. Ailon. Ranking from pairs and triplets: information quality, evaluation methods and query complexity. In *Proc. WSDM*, 2011.

[19] P. Ray. Independence of irrelevant alternatives. *Econometrica: Journal of the Econometric Soc.*, 1973.

[20] S. Rendle, C. Freudenthaler, Z. Gantner, and L. Schmidt-Thieme. Bpr: Bayesian personalized ranking from implicit feedback. In *Proc. UAI*, 2009.

[21] E. Spertus, M. Sahami, and O. Buyukkokten. Evaluating similarity measures: a large-scale study in the orkut social network. In *Proc. KDD*, 2005.

[22] N. Zheng, Q. Li, S. Liao, and L. Zhang. Which photo groups should i choose? a comparative study of recommendation algorithms in flickr. *J. Inf. Sci.*, 2010.

Which App Will You Use Next? Collaborative Filtering with Interactional Context

Nagarajan Natarajan*
naga86@cs.utexas.edu
Dept. of Computer Science
University of Texas at Austin

Donghyuk Shin*
dshin@cs.utexas.edu
Dept. of Computer Science
University of Texas at Austin

Inderjit S. Dhillon
inderjit@cs.utexas.edu
Dept. of Computer Science
University of Texas at Austin

ABSTRACT

The application a smart phone user will launch next intuitively depends on the sequence of apps used *recently*. More generally, when users interact with systems such as shopping websites or online radio, they click on items that are of interest in the *current* context. We call the sequence of clicks made in the current session *interactional context*. It is desirable for a recommender system to use the context set by the user to update recommendations. Most current context-aware recommender systems focus on a relatively less dynamic *representational* context defined by attributes such as season, location and tastes. In this paper, we study the problem of collaborative filtering with interactional context, where the goal is to make personalized and dynamic recommendations to a user engaged in a session. To this end, we propose the iConRank algorithm that works in two stages. First, users are clustered by their transition behavior (one-step Markov transition probabilities between items), and cluster-level Markov models are computed. Then personalized PageRank is computed for a given user on the corresponding cluster Markov graph, with a personalization vector derived from the current context. We give an interpretation of the second stage of the algorithm as adding an appropriate *context bias*, in addition to *click bias* (or rating bias), to a classical neighborhood-based collaborative filtering model, where the neighborhood is determined from a Markov graph. Experimental results on two real-life datasets demonstrate the superior performance of our algorithm, where we achieve at least 20% (up to 37%) improvement over competitive methods in the recall level at top-20.

Categories and Subject Descriptors

H.2.8 [**Database Management**]: Database Applications—*Data mining*; H.3.3 [**Information Storage and Retrieval**]: Information Search and Retrieval—*Information filtering*

*Equal contribution to the work.

RecSys'13, October 12–16, 2013, Hong Kong, China.

ACM 978-1-4503-2409-0/13/10 ...$15.00.
http://dx.doi.org/10.1145/2507157.2507186.

Keywords

Collaborative Filtering, Interactional Context, Markov Model, Personalized PageRank, Context-Aware

1. INTRODUCTION

The problem of recommending an item to a user given a sequence of items that the user *recently* interacted with arises in many systems. The problem is best understood by considering a smart phone user navigating through various applications (apps) on the mobile device. Mobile apps are often used in conjunction with other relevant apps. For example, if a user launches the 'contacts' app, the next app is likely to be the 'mail' or the 'messages' app. The current context of the user can be characterized from recently launched apps. Recommending the "right" app to use next based on the context of the user's actions would improve user experience and multitasking efficiency.

Based on the classification presented in [8], we call the context that arises from user's activity within a session *interactional* context. In contrast, most of the existing context-aware recommender systems focus on *representational* context, usually defined *before* the user interacts and provided as attributes such as location, weather and interests [1].

The problem differs from traditional collaborative filtering settings, such as the Netflix rating prediction problem, in many respects. First, user interaction with items such as apps is *brief* and *repetitive* in nature, whereas items like movies are usually watched/rated once. Second, the user feedback is inherently implicit in the form of item clicks, as opposed to explicit feedback like ratings or comments. Additionally, we have a temporal ordering of clicks within user sessions. Third, recommendations must be made available *dynamically* as the user interacts with the system. That is, recommendations should be updated each time a user clicks an item. Finally, we have the notion of interactional context defined by the session in progress, to which the recommendations are targeted. It is desirable for a recommender system to use the context set by the user to update its recommendations. It might be tempting to relate the aspect to that of online collaborative filtering systems [7], where systems could use newly available ratings to recompute predictions. However, there is a subtle difference. The interactional context should help better zero in on the apps that the user would launch next while she interacts with the system. It is therefore necessary to treat the current session differently from past sessions.

The problem is applicable in any setting where items are generally used repeatedly, such as listening to tracks from online music streaming services or browsing products in shopping websites. If a user has been listening to a series of rock music, she is more likely to prefer other rock music than tracks from a different genre. Note that in such general settings, the system should be able to recommend *new* or *unseen* items to the user. In the next app prediction setting, one could restrict the recommended apps to those that are already installed in the user device, or even recommend new apps that other users have used in similar context.[1] A less obvious but tangible benefit of predicting the next app is that the predicted apps can be pre-loaded to reduce both app launch latency and energy consumption [19].

In this paper, we propose a novel method, iConRank, for collaborative filtering with interactional context. The fundamental observation is that we do not want to treat the sequence of item clicks as raw counts, but as ordered transitions. We model users' transition behavior between items as a Markov chain, where transition probabilities are empirically estimated. A single global Markov model would fall short of capturing diverse transition patterns. On the other hand, a fully personalized Markov model would suffer from extreme sparsity of observed transitions. So, we seek cluster-level Markov models, where the clusters themselves are *behavioral*. That is, we cluster users by their sparse one-step item transition probabilities and compute a representative Markov model per behavioral cluster. We develop our method by introducing a *context bias* to a classical neighborhood-based collaborative filtering model. Our formulation essentially leads to a personalized PageRank [10] on a particular Markov graph, where the so-called "personalization" vector is derived from interactional context.

Our contributions are as follows:

- The problem of incorporating interactional context in collaborative filtering is relatively unexplored (See Section 2). Though the setting is motivated from app launch patterns of smart phone users, it is applicable in many click-based interactive systems.
- We propose iConRank that makes personalized and dynamic recommendations given the current session. Recommendations are updated as the user interacts with the system. We show that the quality of recommendations made by our algorithm is superior to those of competitive methods on two real-life datasets.
- Behavioral clustering of users allows the system to make recommendations using past item transitions of a given user as well as transitions from users with similar navigational patterns.
- Our method is scalable and can handle large problems efficiently. The clustering stage of our algorithm is done offline. Personalized PageRank can be computed in a scalable manner, as detailed in Section 4.3, which enables implementation on devices with limited processing power.

The remainder of the paper is organized as follows. In Section 2, we review some closely related work. We present a formal description of the problem setting in Section 3. In Section 4, we discuss important aspects of the problem that need to be addressed, and develop our algorithm iConRank. Experimental results on two real-life datasets are reported in Section 5. We conclude in Section 6.

[1]This choice is made when the recommender system is deployed. In experiments, we evaluate with the latter option.

2. RELATED WORK

Traditional collaborative filtering techniques use a history of item preferences by a set of users in order to recommend items of interest to a given user. Commonly used classes of methods are neighborhood-based and latent factor models. Neighborhood-based methods involve computing a measure of similarity between pairs of users or items, and obtaining predictions by taking a weighted average of ratings of similar users or items [17, 4]. Another family of model-based collaborative filtering algorithms is based on latent factor models [12, 16], where user preferences are modeled as interactions between unobserved user and item factors.

Previous research has shown that contextual information can enhance the performance of recommender systems in various applications. Based on the classification of context introduced in [8], context can be distinguished into two types: *representational* and *interactional*. The majority of context-aware recommender systems have investigated the use of representational context, such as time, location and weather [1]. Some context-aware neighborhood-based models [5, 13] incorporate such contextual information in the similarity measure between users. Another approach described in [3] introduces item splitting, where item ratings are split into two virtual items based on a given contextual condition. The virtual items are used instead of the original ones in different collaborative filtering algorithms and a rating is predicted for the virtual item corresponding to the current user's context. The context-aware latent factor model in [2] includes attribute-based context variables as biases to appropriately learn the model parameters. In the tensor factorization method proposed in [15], additional dimension for contextual information is added to the standard user-item ratings matrix.

There has been limited work on recommender systems that incorporate interactional context. Hariri, et. al [9] also consider the problem of recommending the next track given a sequence of tracks recently played. Each sequence of tracks in a hand-compiled playlist database is first represented as a sequence of latent topics (using topic modeling). Frequent patterns of topics are discovered from the topic sequences using a pattern-mining algorithm. These sequential patterns are then used to predict relevant topics given a user session. The predicted topics are used to post-filter an initial ranking produced by a traditional recommendation algorithm. The method is applicable only when the number of topics is small or the maximum length of a session is short. Enumerating all possible sequences can be computationally infeasible otherwise. Moreover, recommendations are not personalized as sequential patterns are mined from the entire population. In the domain of mobile application, recent work on predicting app launch [19] uses both representational (location, time) and interactional (app launch) context information to engineer features. However, the approach in [19] uses only the first app in a given session, which is considered as the trigger. In contrast, our approach considers all apps launched in the current session.

3. PROBLEM SETTING

Our problem setting is motivated by smart phone users who exhibit patterns of interaction with the device through mobile apps. The sequence of apps launched by a user defines the *interactional* context of the user's actions. Interactional context arises from the user's activity within a session and is dynamic. The setting is applicable to any click-based recommender system, where recommendations are updated as the users *click* on an item (Youtube, Spotify, etc).

We refer to the sequence of items accessed by a user over a certain contiguous period as a *session*. In practice, sessions are defined based on the type of activity (e.g. articles read by an online user when she is signed in). Note that we do not consider any temporal aspects of the session, other than the ordering of clicks. Existing context-aware recommender systems focus on attribute-based representational context that is less dynamic and often fixed *before* the start of a session. A given user may have specified a set of preferences globally, but it is often the case that user preferences change between sessions. The goal of this paper is to present recommendations to a given user based on her past sessions, sessions of other users in the system *and* the current session *in progress*. The key aspects of our problem setting are:

1. There are no explicit "likes" or "dislikes" of an item, unlike the case of Netflix ratings. We want to come up with a ranking of items that the user will click next in the current session. Following the recommender systems literature, our setting relies on *implicit feedback* as against the Netflix prize setting that uses *explicit feedback*.
2. Users may be interested in multiple categories of items, but given the sequence of clicks made in the current session, there is an added *context bias* that needs to be accounted for. In general recommender systems, user bias and item bias are accounted for whereas context bias is either ignored or is not applicable.

We would like to emphasize here that though the first aspect in isolation is well-known in the recommender systems community [14, 20], the second aspect has received little attention [9].

3.1 The problem statement

The item recommendation problem in the *Collaborative Filtering with Interactional Context* setting is formally stated as follows. Given a history of sessions $\mathcal{S}$ of users $\mathcal{U} = \{u_1, u_2, \ldots, u_{|\mathcal{U}|}\}$ over a set of items $\mathcal{I} = \{a_1, a_2, \ldots, a_{|\mathcal{I}|}\}$, and a specific user $u \in \mathcal{U}$ with session *in progress* $s = \langle a_{i_1}, a_{i_2}, \ldots, a_{i_t}\rangle$, for some $t \geq 1$, we want to recommend the best candidate item $a_{i_{t+1}} \in \mathcal{I}$. Note that we want the recommendations to be (a) *personalized* to the user u, and (b) relevant to the context of the session s. The classical collaborative filtering systems (with implicit feedback) consider a specific case of the problem where the current session is ignored and the goal is to come up with a set of recommendations based on the click history.

4. PROPOSED METHOD

In our problem setting, we work with implicit feedback in the form of click sequences. A widely-used collaborative filtering approach for implicit feedback data is to simply form a user-item count matrix, where an entry represents the number of times[2] a user has clicked on an item in the past. Any of the collaborative filtering approaches for explicit feedback such as matrix factorization or similarity-based methods can then be applied on the count matrix. However, such a naive approach is not appropriate for reasons manyfold. Most importantly, we do not want to predict any exact rating — we just need a ranking of relevant items. It is inherently hard to gauge user preferences with clicks — lack of an established scale like star ratings makes it tricky to compute similarities between users or items. For a detailed discussion of what prevents a direct use of algorithms designed for explicit feedback, see [14]. We will see later in the experiments (Section 5) that collaborative filtering methods on the count matrix perform poorly.

Some latent factor models for ratings data include biases due to attribute-based context variables such as location to appropriately learn the model parameters [2]. Other than the absence of explicit feedback, such context-aware models pose another immediate challenge — they rely on rating instances for different settings of context variables to learn the appropriate biases. In the case of interactional context, it is not obvious how to succinctly define context variables and obtain associated training examples. Also, it must be efficient to *update* model parameters as the current session progresses in order to provide dynamic recommendations.

In this section, we first describe how we model history in the form of click sequences. Then, we derive our PageRank-based method by incorporating interactional context in an existing collaborative filtering framework. Finally, we present our algorithm iConRank.

4.1 Modeling Implicit Feedback

The fundamental observation is that we do not want to treat the session history as counts but as sequences instead. A simple and effective way to model sequences is to use Markov models. Ideally, we would want to know the probability of user clicking on an item given the current session. To this end, we model the users as Markov. The set of items $\mathcal{I}$ corresponds to the state space of the Markov model, and the state transition probability M_{ij} is the probability that item j is clicked immediately after item i. From the sessions data, we can estimate M_{ij} as the fraction of times item j appears immediately after item i, whenever i appears.

Typically, a given user does not have enough training data to estimate $|\mathcal{I}| \times |\mathcal{I}|$ parameters of the Markov model. On the other hand, we do not need to determine a personalized Markov model for each user. The basic idea of collaborative filtering is to combine preferences from "similar" users in order to make recommendations for a given user. One naive way to combine preferences in our setting is to use session data of *all* users to determine a single *global* Markov model. While the training data may be rich enough to estimate a global model, it is less likely to be a good characterization of the diverse transition behavior of users. The aforementioned fully personalized and fully global models fall short, and our approach is to use cluster-level Markov models. It is reasonable to suppose that there are different clusters of users exhibiting a common navigational pattern. To discover behavioral clusters using session data, we need to find a good representation of users, where users who have similar transition patterns are "close" to each other than those that are not.

4.1.1 Behavioral clustering

First, we note that the user-item count matrix itself cannot be used for clustering — we want the clusters to indicate *how* users click and not *what* users click. In particular, we want a feature map Φ_u that encodes the fraction of times a particular transition was made, rather than the number of transitions. Let $\Phi : \mathcal{U} \to \mathcal{M}$, where $\mathcal{M}$ denotes the set of row-stochastic matrices, i.e. $\mathcal{M} = \{M \in \mathbb{R}^{|\mathcal{I}|\times|\mathcal{I}|} : M_{ij} \geq$

[2]Or a monotonic function such as log of the count.

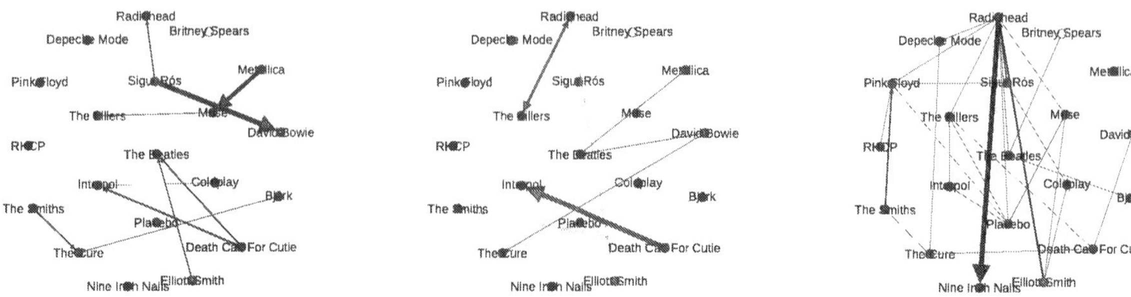

(a) Cluster 1. (b) Cluster 2. (c) Cluster 3.

Figure 1: Behavioral clusters in `lastfm` dataset (see Section 5.1.2). We see how different clusters of users move between the top-20 artists with the highest play counts in the training data. Thicker edges represent higher transition probabilities. Cluster 1 users predominantly move between *Muse, Metallica, David Bowie* and *Sigur Rós*. Cluster 2 users move between *Radiohead* and *The Killers*, and *Interpol* and *Death Cab For Cutie*. Cluster 3 users are marked by transitions to *Nine Inch Nails, Radiohead* and *Placebo*.

$0, \sum_j M_{ij} = 1\}$. In particular, $\Phi(u) = M^{(u)}$ where $M^{(u)}$ denotes the one-step Markov transition probability matrix estimated from the session history of user u. Now, we need a distance measure to cluster users in the space of transition probability matrices. An appropriate measure of distance between two probability distributions is the KL-divergence or the relative entropy. The KL-divergence $d_{KL}(x, y)$ between two p-dimensional probability distributions x and y is defined as:

$$d_{KL}(x, y) = \sum_{i=1}^{p} x_i \log_2 \left(\frac{x_i}{y_i}\right) .$$

The distance between two users u and v is in turn defined as:

$$d(u, v) = \frac{1}{|\mathcal{I}|} \sum_{i=1}^{|\mathcal{I}|} d_{KL}(M_{i\cdot}^{(u)}, M_{i\cdot}^{(v)}) . \quad (1)$$

We have[3] $d(u, v) \geq 0$ since $d_{KL}(.,.) \geq 0$ and $d(u, v) = 0 \iff M^{(u)} = M^{(v)}$. For the actual clustering step, we optimize the k-means objective. The centroid of the cluster π_k is computed as

$$M_k = \frac{1}{|\pi_k|} \sum_{u \in \pi_k} M^{(u)}, \quad (2)$$

where $|\pi_k|$ denotes the number of users assigned to cluster k. Note that $M_k \in \mathcal{M}$ and we use M_k as the Markov model for the kth cluster.

In Figure 1, we show[4] three behavioral clusters discovered in one of our experimental datasets consisting of logs of artists played by users of an online radio station (see Section 5.1.2). The clusters are computed using k-means with the KL-divergence measure (1). Observe that different clusters of users exhibit distinct navigational patterns among the top-20 artists.

4.2 Incorporating interactional context

We motivate our approach from a classical memory-based collaborative filtering model. Memory-based algorithms predict ratings for a given user based on past ratings of the user and other users in the system [17, 4]. The neighborhood models are a classical example, where the predicted rating of an item by a user is given by a weighted combination of "k-nearest neighbor" items (or users). The weights are proportional to the "similarity" between items, which is represented by the vector of observed user ratings. The Pearson correlation coefficient and cosine similarity are two commonly used similarity measures. The similarities between all item pairs are computed offline, and the predicted rating $\hat{r}_{u,i}$ for a user u and an item i is given by

$$\hat{r}_{u,i} = b_{u,i} + \sum_{j \in \mathcal{N}(i)} w(i, j)(r_{u,j} - b_{u,j}) \quad (3)$$

where $\mathcal{N}(i)$ denotes the "neighborhood" set of item i. For example, in the cosine similarity case, the top-k items with highest cosine similarity with item i constitute $\mathcal{N}(i)$. Typically, a rating bias term $b_{u,i}$ is included to account for the user bias (some users are predisposed to rate higher in general) and item bias (some movies get higher ratings than others). The weights are usually normalized for rating prediction tasks.

Let us focus on the item recommendation problem in the interactional context setting, where the knowledge of the current session is available. First, we want to use the cluster Markov models computed using (2) to learn a ranking of items given the user u and the current session s. Second, we want to incorporate interactional context in (3). In particular, we want to introduce a *context bias* term $c_{u,i}$ in addition to the rating bias $b_{u,i}$. In the implicit feedback setting, we interpret $b_{u,i}$ as accounting for *click bias* rather than rating bias. To this end, we want a scoring function $f_{u,i}$ using both past sessions and current session s for the user u. Suitably modifying (3), we have,

$$f_{u,i} = b_{u,i} + \alpha \sum_{j \in \mathcal{N}(i)} w(i, j)(f_{u,j} - b_{u,j}) + (1 - \alpha)c_{u,i} \quad (4)$$

where the nonnegative weight α controls the tradeoff between the current context and information from the past sessions. Notice the recurrence nature of the above equation — we want to estimate all user-item scores *as the session progresses*, as against the context-aware model suggested in [2] based on attribute-based context variables.

Define $z_{u,i} = f_{u,i} - b_{u,i}$ for all $u \in \mathcal{U}$ and $i \in \mathcal{I}$, so that we can remove the click bias from the equation resulting in a simpler model:

$$z_{u,i} = \alpha \sum_{j \in \mathcal{N}(i)} w(i, j) z_{u,j} + (1 - \alpha)c_{u,i}. \quad (5)$$

[3]In practice, many of M_{ij}'s are 0, and to have a well-defined $d_{KL}(.,.)$ we add a relatively tiny value to all the entries of the transition matrices.

[4]For clarity, we only show the top-20 artists with the highest play counts in the training data and omit edges whose transition probability is lower than a certain threshold.

From the graph corresponding to the Markov model with transition probability matrix M, we set $w(i,j) = M_{ji}$. This gives an intuitive interpretation that items that tend to transition to i more often should receive higher similarity than items that do not. Given the choice of $w(i,j)$, $\mathcal{N}(i)$ corresponds to items that are adjacent to i in the Markov graph. Estimating $c_{u,i}$ using the click sequences can be hard and expensive. However, it is easy to specify what items appear in the current session s. We let $c_{u,i} = 1$ if the item a_i appears in s or 0 otherwise. Let $\mathbf{c}_u$ denote the indicator vector with ith entry equal to $c_{u,i}$, and let the vector of item scores for a given user u be $\mathbf{z}_u$. Rewriting (5) in matrix form:

$$\mathbf{z}_u = \alpha M^T \mathbf{z}_u + (1-\alpha)\mathbf{c}_u$$

Letting $\mathbf{1}$ denote vector of all ones, and normalizing $\mathbf{z}_u$ to sum to 1, the above equation can be rewritten as:

$$\mathbf{z}_u = (\alpha M + (1-\alpha)\mathbf{1}\mathbf{c}_u^T)^T \mathbf{z}_u \tag{6}$$

The quantity $\mathbf{z}_u$ is nothing but the personalized PageRank vector for user u, using the graph M and personalization vector $\mathbf{c}_u$. Thus we have an efficient way to estimate $z_{u,i}$. Recall that the click bias $b_{u,i}$ was obviated to compute $\mathbf{c}_u$. So, the final score is given by $f_{u,i} = z_{u,i} + b_{u,i}$. A standard way to estimate click bias is to average the launch count of item a_i over users.[5] However, a better choice would be to use transition probabilities of item a_{i_t} to other items, where i_t is the index of the last item in s, since we focus on item transitions. We find in our experiments that $M^{(u)}_{i_t,i}$ is an effective choice for click bias. The final score for the user-item pair (u,i), given the current session $s = \langle a_{i_1}, a_{i_2}, \ldots, a_{i_t}\rangle$ is:

$$f_{u,i} = z_{u,i} + M^{(u)}_{i_t,i}, \tag{7}$$

where $z_{u,i}$ is the solution to (6).

4.3 iConRank Algorithm

We are now ready to give our algorithm iConRank for recommending items in the collaborative filtering with interactional context setting. Given a current session $s = \langle a_{i_1}, a_{i_2}, \ldots, a_{i_t}\rangle$ executed by a given user u, history of sessions $\mathcal{S}$ for all users in $\mathcal{U}$, and number of behavioral clusters K, the iConRank algorithm is specified as follows:

1. (**Offline step**) Cluster $\mathcal{U}$ using the sessions history $\mathcal{S}$ into K clusters by first forming the per-user transition matrices and then using the k-means algorithm as described in Section 4.1.1. Compute the corresponding Markov transition probabilities M_k for each cluster $k \in [K]$ using (2).
2. Let $\pi(u)$ denote the cluster to which user u belongs. Set $\mathbf{c}_u$ to be the normalized indicator vector of items appearing in s. Compute the personalized PageRank $\mathbf{z}_u$ by (6) with $M = M_{\pi(u)}$ and current $\mathbf{c}_u$.
3. Compute scores $f_{u,i}$, for all $i \neq i_t$ using (7).
4. Rank the items using the computed scores, and return the top-N items as recommendations for $a_{i_{t+1}}$.

A few remarks on iConRank algorithm are in order:

Efficiency: Note that the clustering step is done offline as it is independent of current session s. Steps 2 through 4 are executed *every time* the user clicks, i.e. as session s progresses, so that the recommendations can be updated. Computing the personalized PageRank in Step 2 can be expensive if $|\mathcal{I}|$ is of the order of tens of thousands, even if the matrices M_k are sparse. Scalability is even more of a concern if the algorithm is to be implemented in real-time systems with small processing capabilities like mobile phones. The linearity property of personalized PageRank [10] stated below can be exploited to implement Step 2 in a scalable way. Let $\mathbf{z}_u(\mathbf{v})$ denote the solution to (6) computed with the personalization vector $\mathbf{c}_u = \mathbf{v}$. Then:

$$\mathbf{z}_u(\beta\mathbf{v}_1 + (1-\beta)\mathbf{v}_2) = \beta\mathbf{z}_u(\mathbf{v}_1) + (1-\beta)\mathbf{z}_u(\mathbf{v}_2)$$

for nonnegative β and distributions $\mathbf{v}_1$ and $\mathbf{v}_2$. We can precompute $\mathbf{z}_u(\mathbf{e}_i)$ for $i = 1, 2, \ldots, |\mathcal{I}|$, where $\mathbf{e}_i$ denotes the ith column of the identity matrix. Then, for a given session $s = \langle a_{i_1}, a_{i_2}, \ldots, a_{i_t}\rangle$, and chosen $\mathbf{c}_u = \mathbf{v}$ we can compute $\mathbf{z}_u$ efficiently as:

$$\mathbf{z_u}(\mathbf{v}) = \sum_{j=1}^{t} v_{i_j} \cdot \mathbf{z_u}(\mathbf{e}_{i_j})$$

It is easy to see why the above equality holds: Our choice of $\mathbf{c}_u = \mathbf{v}$ is such that it is non-zero only in the positions corresponding to items that appear in s, and is normalized to sum to 1.

Cold-start: The algorithm can seamlessly deal with new users. In particular, we can choose $\mathbf{c}_u$ to be the uniform distribution over items and use the global Markov model instead of $M_{\pi(u)}$.

5. EXPERIMENTAL EVALUATION

In this section we present experimental results of our proposed algorithm, iConRank, on two real-life datasets: Apps and LastFM. We first give a detailed description of the two datasets and the experimental setting. Next we compare the recommendation performance of iConRank to a number of other successful methods. We also evaluate the methods on recommending existing and new items and study how performance is influenced by current session length.

For testing, we measure the accuracy of recommending the next item $a_{i_{t+1}}$, given the current session $s = \langle a_{i_1}, a_{i_2}, \ldots, a_{i_t}\rangle$ of a user. Thus, there is only one correct item for each test case. A user is usually presented with a small list of recommended items. Therefore, we measure *recall at top-N* (Recall@N) for $N = 5, 10, 15, 20$. For the sake of completeness, we also report the *ROC curve* (recall vs. precision plot up to $N = 1,000$), which is the standard measure for comparing the recommendation qualities of different methods for recommender systems. Recall and precision are measured in the standard way for top-N recommendation tasks [6].

5.1 Dataset Description

The datasets used in this study consist of user event logs with timestamps, where the events are launching mobile apps or streaming tracks of an artist. Sessions are formed from the user logs. We note that consecutive uses of the same item are considered as a single interaction for methods using sequences, including ours. However, launch counts are retained for use by methods based on the user-item matrix.

Statistic	Apps	LastFM
# of users	17,062	941
# of items (apps/artists)	9,583	98,412
# of training sessions	1,167,171	644,001
# of testing sessions	459,899	95,038
Average session length	6.53	18.33
Median session length	3	7

Table 1: Statistics of Apps and LastFM datasets.

[5]Note that user bias need not be added, as we only need to rank items.

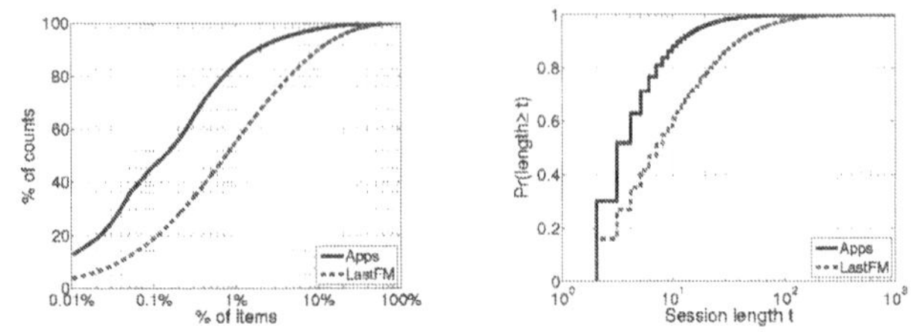

(a) Item count distribution (most frequent item on the left).

(b) CDF of the length of sessions.

Figure 2: Item count and session length distributions for LastFM and Apps datasets.

Training data consists of all sessions before a chosen date.[6] Table 1 shows relevant statistics of each dataset.

5.1.1 *Apps Dataset*

The **Apps** dataset is a proprietary dataset obtained from a manufacturer of mobile devices. It consists of mobile app usage patterns of smart phone users.[7] The dataset spans over a one year period and each log record consists of user, timestamp information and one of the two events, app launch and screen on/off. The screen on/off event is used as an indicator of a new session, i.e., a new session is started when the screen is on and the current session is ended when the screen is off *and* at least one minute has elapsed.[8] Figure 2(a) plots the distribution of item count, which corresponds to launch count of apps. Apps in the horizontal axis are ordered by their launch counts, with the most frequently launched app on the left. We can see in Figure 2(a) that top 1% of the most frequently launched apps cover about 85% of total launch counts. Figure 2(b) shows the CDF of the length of sessions. About 87% of sessions have at most length 10. Our statistics align with the findings in [18] that interactions with smart phones are mostly brief.

5.1.2 *LastFM Dataset*

The **LastFM** (**last.fm**) dataset consists of listening habits of about 1,000 users, where each log contains user, track, artist and timestamp. It has been used in many studies [11, 20]. Here, the task is to recommend the next artist to listen to. Unlike the **Apps** dataset, the **LastFM** dataset lacks any explicit indication of start or end of a session. So, we mark sessions by periods of inactivity. We end a session if there is no other artist streamed within an hour from the last artist and start a new one with the next artist.[8] Listening to music is a more time consuming activity than using a smart phone. Furthermore, preference over artists is more diverse than the apps case, where pre-installed apps are more commonly used. These differences show up in Figure 2. Sessions in **LastFM** tend to be longer and more diverse — about 50% of sessions have at least length 10 and top 1% of the most frequent artists cover only about 55% of total counts.

5.2 Results

We first analyze the behavioral clusters obtained. Then we compare the performance of iConRank to baseline and other context-aware collaborative filtering methods.

[6]Date was chosen to maximize the number of users appearing in both training and testing sets.

[7]We emphasize that the data provided to us was highly anonymized and contained only generic identifiers that cannot be correlated or traced back to actual users.

[8]Time lapses were tuned to achieve the most meaningful session statistics.

Dataset	Cluster	Users	nnz(M_k)	Session Length	
				Avg.	Median
Apps	1	4,695	68,967	6.37	3
	2	5,711	73,121	6.32	3
	3	6,656	78,963	6.83	3
LastFM	1	327	1,733,056	19.15	7
	2	320	1,500,913	18.55	7
	3	294	1,227,933	17.01	7

Table 2: Statistics of clusters in Apps and LastFM datasets.

Cluster1	Cluster2	Cluster3
(contacts,phone)	(phone,dialer)	(phone,dialer)
(message,contacts)	(*search,browser*)	(1,phone)
(contacts,dialer)	(*mail,browser*)	(phone,2)
(*settings,phone*)	(message,mail)	(phone,3)
(*data,settings*)	(*calendar,mail*)	(4,phone)
(*camera,photo*)	(*browser,video*)	(5,phone)
(*contacts,settings*)	(*phone,browser*)	(message,mail)

Table 3: Most frequent app transitions of each cluster. (Some apps in the dataset do not have names, so we refer to them by numbers.)

5.2.1 *Discovered clusters*

We cluster the users as described in Section 4.1.1. In our experiments, we set the number of clusters $k = 3$. We note that there was no significant difference in terms of performance with larger k. To help characterize each cluster, we summarize some statistics of each cluster in Table 2. For the **Apps** dataset, the first cluster is smaller than the other two, but has longer sessions than the second cluster. The third cluster has the largest nnz(M_k), i.e., number of nonzeros in M_k or the number of unique transitions. For the **LastFM** dataset, the clusters are of similar sizes, but the number of unique transitions is relatively distinct.

For the **Apps** dataset, we report the most frequent transitions of each cluster in Table 3. As expected, transitions occur between related apps, such as contacts and phones, browser and search, etc., and it is apparent from Table 3 that each cluster represents a distinct type of app transition behavior. For example, users in the first cluster can be viewed as power users who transition between apps like 'settings', 'data' and 'camera'. In contrast, the second cluster has shorter sessions as reported in Table 2, and transitions are concentrated on basic apps such as 'browser', 'search' and 'calendar'. For the **LastFM** dataset, we visualize behavioral patterns for each cluster in Figure 1 (see Section 4.1.1).

5.2.2 *Performance Comparison*

We compare iConRank to the following collaborative filtering methods:

- NNCosNgbr: Non-Normalized Cosine Neighborhood [6] is a neighborhood-based model using cosine similarity between items (represented as vectors of launch counts). The score for item a_i for a given user is calculated as a weighted average of the k-nearest neighbor items of a_i as in (3), where we set $k = 5$ and use cosine similarity as the weights.
- SVD(r): The scores are computed as $\hat{R} = U\Sigma V^T \approx A$, where $A \in \mathbb{R}^{|\mathcal{U}|\times|\mathcal{I}|}$ is the user-item count matrix, r is the number of latent factors, $U \in \mathbb{R}^{|\mathcal{U}|\times r}$, $V \in \mathbb{R}^{|\mathcal{I}|\times r}$ are orthonormal matrices and $\Sigma \in \mathbb{R}^{r\times r}$ is a diagonal matrix of the top r singular values. Missing values of A are typically set to zero. The method has been shown

(a) Apps dataset.

Method	Recall@N			
	$N=5$	$N=10$	$N=15$	$N=20$
NNCosNgbr	0.4301	0.5478	0.6167	0.6636
SVD	0.4574	0.5853	0.6480	0.6851
Markov	0.4592	0.5744	0.6370	0.6754
ContextNgbr	0.5266	0.6248	0.6739	0.7045
SeqPattern	0.5517	0.6451	0.6899	0.7223
iConRank	**0.6701**	**0.7927**	**0.8386**	**0.8632**

(b) LastFM dataset.

Method	Recall@N			
	$N=5$	$N=10$	$N=15$	$N=20$
NNCosNgbr	0.0691	0.1044	0.1328	0.1560
SVD	0.0810	0.1286	0.1633	0.1922
Markov	0.0631	0.0905	0.1113	0.1285
ContextNgbr	0.0597	0.0775	0.0884	0.0971
SeqPattern	0.0371	0.0536	0.0656	0.0748
iConRank	**0.1277**	**0.1882**	**0.2304**	**0.2633**

Table 4: Recall@N results on Apps and LastFM datasets for $N = 5, 10, 15, 20$. iConRank outperforms the other methods in all cases, achieving 20% and 37% improvement in Recall@20 over the next best method on Apps and LastFM datasets, respectively.

to achieve good performance in top-N recommendation tasks [6].

- Markov: The recommended item a_{t^*} depends on the last item a_t in the current session via the global Markov model. Formally, $t^* = \text{argmax}_j M_{tj}$, where M is the global transition probability matrix estimated from the sessions of all users.
- ContextNgbr: Identical to NNCosNgbr except that the k-nearest neighbors are computed from the set of items in the current session. We use $k = 5$ (include all items in the current session if its length is less than k).
- SeqPattern: Sequence mining algorithm used in [9].[9] We use the last 10 items as the user's active session.

The last three methods are context-aware approaches that consider user's current session. We note that ranking items by popularity (i.e. number of times an item is accessed in the training phase), which is known to perform reasonably well in recommendation tasks, does significantly worse in our setting than the methods we compare here.

Table 4 reports the Recall@N of the methods on both datasets for $N = 5, 10, 15, 20$. Our algorithm, iConRank, significantly outperforms all other methods with impressive recall rates. It achieves the highest recall of 0.8632 for the Apps dataset, which means the app $a_{i_{t+1}}$ that a user will use has a probability of about 86% to be ranked in the top-20 results returned by iConRank. The next best performing method for the Apps dataset is SeqPattern followed by ContextNgbr, both of which use current context. However, they are the two worst performing methods for the LastFM dataset. This can be expected as the number of items is much larger than in the Apps dataset. SeqPattern suffers from the sheer diversity of artists and lack of adequate representative patterns in the training data. Among the two collaborative filtering based techniques, SVD performs better than NNCosNgbr in both the datasets confirming the findings of [6].[10] Surprisingly, the simple Markov model performs better than collaborative filtering based methods for the Apps dataset, but fails in the LastFM dataset conforming to our intuition that a single global Markov model is not enough. In evaluating the methods on the Apps dataset, the recommended candidate apps for a given user can contain apps that are *not* installed in the user's device, which is consistent with the evaluation on the LastFM dataset.[11]

[9] [9] applies sequence mining on latent topics discovered from playlists, but we mine sequence of items directly as we don't have item features.

[10] We tested SVD with various ranks r, and chose $r = 200$ for the Apps dataset and $r = 300$ for the LastFM dataset. Higher ranks yielded only marginal performance improvements.

[11] The Apps dataset did not contain information about which apps are installed in the user device.

The ROC curve (up to top-1,000 recommendations) is given in Figure 3. iConRank generally achieves the highest precision for any given recall. One exception is SeqPattern which achieves slightly better recall (about 0.05 higher) at top-1 for the Apps dataset. However, it immediately starts to degrade in performance falling below iConRank for $N > 1$. We further study the performance in different categories: existing and new items. Specifically, evaluation is restricted to items that appeared at least once in the training data ("existing") or those that were not seen in the training data ("new") for each user. The results are presented in Figure 4. We can see that iConRank not only performs well on existing items, but is also capable of recommending new items to users significantly better than the rest.

A desirable property of our algorithm is that it is able to make more accurate recommendations as more items are observed in a given session. We examine how iConRank per-

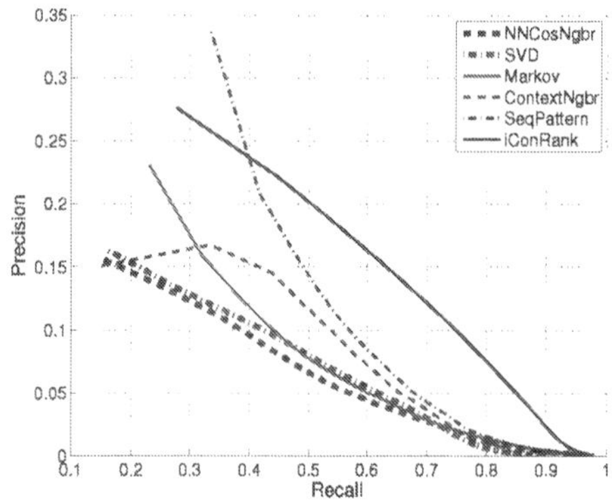

(a) Apps dataset.

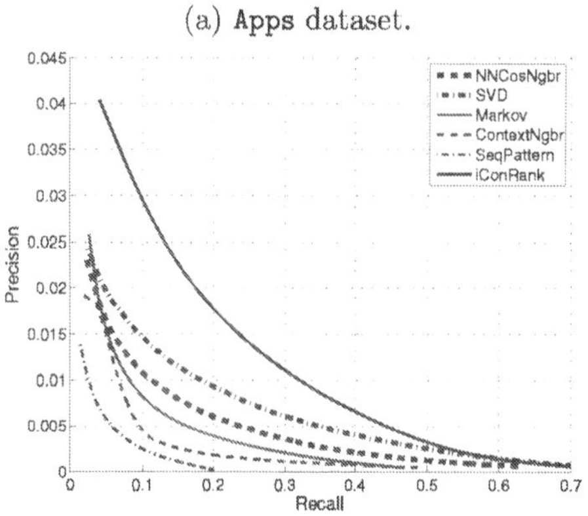

(b) LastFM dataset.

Figure 3: ROC curve for Apps and LastFM datasets up to top-1,000 recommendations. iConRank achieves highest precision-recall rates.

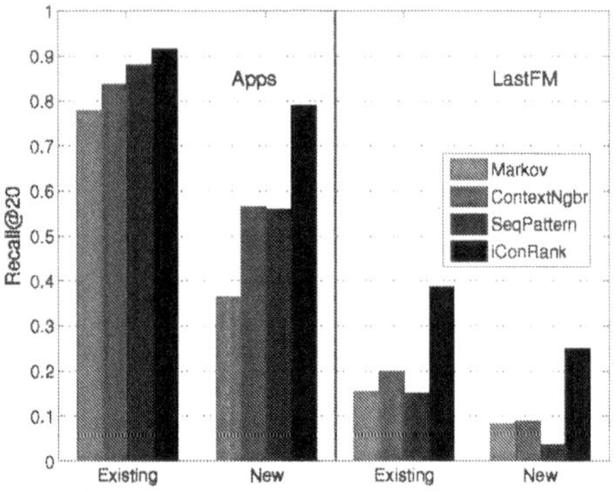

Figure 4: Recall@20 for existing and new items. iConRank performs the best in all cases.

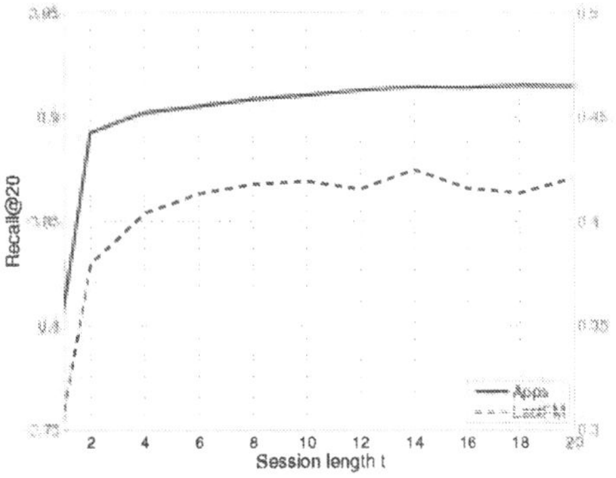

Figure 5: Recall@20 of different session lengths. Performance increases as the session length increases showing that iConRank effectively captures the current context.

forms as more of the current session is revealed. In particular, we measure Recall@20 when t (length of s) varies as shown in Figure 5. As the session length increases, Recall@20 also increases for both datasets, illustrating that iConRank effectively captures the current context of the session. Especially, the performance greatly increases after observing just two items in a given session. However, we also find that recall rates can drop when t becomes very large (not shown in the figure) — the personalization vector tends to a uniform distribution and context ceases to have relevance. In practice, most of the sessions are short as shown in Figure 2(b).

6. CONCLUSIONS

In this paper we have considered the problem of collaborative filtering with interactional context to recommend potential items of interest to a user already engaged in a session, using past sessions of the user and of other users. We are given implicit feedback in the form of clicks and a session that establishes the current context of a user. Our problem setting differs from the traditional setting of collaborative filtering in crucial respects. We propose iConRank, a novel method that is motivated by introducing 'context bias' in the neighborhood-based model. Our formulation essentially leads to the personalized PageRank, where context is captured by the personalization vector. Experimental results on real-life datasets demonstrate that our algorithm achieves superior recommendation performance illustrating its ability to capture the context of a given session.

As part of future work, we plan to study how to combine both interactional context and representational context such as location and time. Exploring other collaborative and content filtering methods to incorporate interactional context are promising research directions.

7. ACKNOWLEDGMENTS

This research was supported by NSF grant CCF-1117055.

8. REFERENCES

[1] L. Baltrunas. *Context-aware collaborative filtering recommender systems.* PhD thesis, Free University of Bozen-Bolzano, 2011.

[2] L. Baltrunas, B. Ludwig, and F. Ricci. Matrix factorization techniques for context aware recommendation. In *ACM RecSys*, pages 301–304, 2011.

[3] L. Baltrunas and F. Ricci. Context-based splitting of item ratings in collaborative filtering. In *ACM RecSys*, pages 245–248, 2009.

[4] R. M. Bell and Y. Koren. Scalable collaborative filtering with jointly derived neighborhood interpolation weights. In *ICDM*, pages 43–52, 2007.

[5] A. Chen. Context-aware collaborative filtering system: predicting the user's preferences in ubiquitous computing. In *CHI EA*, pages 1110–1111, 2005.

[6] P. Cremonesi, Y. Koren, and R. Turrin. Performance of recommender algorithms on top-N recommendation tasks. In *ACM RecSys*, pages 39–46, 2010.

[7] E. Diaz-Aviles, L. Drumond, L. Schmidt-Thieme, and W. Nejdl. Real-time top-N recommendation in social streams. In *ACM RecSys*, pages 59–66, 2012.

[8] P. Dourish. What we talk about when we talk about context. *Personal and Ubiquitous Computing*, 8(1):19–30, 2004.

[9] N. Hariri, B. Mobasher, and R. Burke. Context-aware music recommendation based on latent topic sequential patterns. In *ACM RecSys*, pages 131–138, 2012.

[10] T. H. Haveliwala. Topic-sensitive PageRank: a context-sensitive ranking algorithm for web search. *IEEE Trans. on Knowl. and Data Eng.*, 15(4):784–796, 2003.

[11] B. Hidasi and D. Tikk. Fast ALS-based tensor factorization for context-aware recommendation from implicit feedback. In *ECML PKDD*, pages 67–82, 2012.

[12] T. Hofmann and J. Puzicha. Latent class models for collaborative filtering. In *IJCAI*, pages 688–693, 1999.

[13] R. Hu, W. Dou, and J. Liu. A context-aware collaborative filtering approach for service recommendation. In *CSC*, pages 148–155, 2012.

[14] Y. Hu, Y. Koren, and C. Volinsky. Collaborative filtering for implicit feedback datasets. In *ICDM*, pages 263–272, 2008.

[15] A. Karatzoglou, X. Amatriain, L. Baltrunas, and N. Oliver. Multiverse recommendation: N-dimensional tensor factorization for context-aware collaborative filtering. In *ACM RecSys*, pages 79–86, 2010.

[16] Y. Koren, R. M. Bell, and C. Volinsky. Matrix factorization techniques for recommender systems. *Computer*, 42(8):30–37, 2009.

[17] B. Sarwar, G. Karypis, J. Konstan, and J. Riedl. Item-based collaborative filtering recommendation algorithms. In *WWW*, pages 285–295, 2001.

[18] C. Shepard, A. Rahmati, C. Tossell, L. Zhong, and P. Kortum. LiveLab: measuring wireless networks and smartphone users in the field. *SIGMETRICS Performance Evaluation Review*, 38(3):15–20, 2011.

[19] T. Yan, D. Chu, D. Ganesan, A. Kansal, and J. Liu. Fast app launching for mobile devices using predictive user context. In *MobiSys*, pages 113–126, 2012.

[20] D. Yang, T. Chen, W. Zhang, Q. Lu, and Y. Yu. Local implicit feedback mining for music recommendation. In *ACM RecSys*, pages 91–98, 2012.

A Food Recommender for Patients in a Care Facility

Toon De Pessemier
iMinds-WiCa-Ghent University
G. Crommenlaan 8 box 201
B-9050 Ghent, Belgium
toon.depessemier@ugent.be

Simon Dooms
iMinds-WiCa-Ghent University
G. Crommenlaan 8 box 201
B-9050 Ghent, Belgium
simon.dooms@ugent.be

Luc Martens
iMinds-WiCa-Ghent University
G. Crommenlaan 8 box 201
B-9050 Ghent, Belgium
luc1.martens@ugent.be

ABSTRACT

In this research, a food recommendation strategy for patients in a care facility is proposed. Since many of these patients cannot express their personal preferences, a recommender system can assist the caregivers in the selection of the menu items that match the patients' preferences. Recommendations are generated based on three information sources: explicit ratings for menu items, implicit feedback based on the patient's eating behavior and the amount of food that was eaten, and inferred preferences for the ingredients of the menu items. In addition, monitoring the amount of food that was eaten by each patient can provide insights into the optimal amount of each menu item that has to be served to each patient. Furthermore, monitoring food consumption allows to detect irregularities in the eating behavior of the patient, which can be a symptom of illness.

Categories and Subject Descriptors

H.4 [**Information Systems Applications**]: Miscellaneous

Keywords

recommender system; food; implicit feedback

1. INTRODUCTION

Three times a day, patients in care facilities receive a prepared meal tailored to their personal needs and health condition. For each meal, various menu options are available for the patients to choose. Some of these menu options themselves can be tailored according to the preferences of the patients, such as the filling of a sandwich, the presence of sauce or not, or the accompanying beverage. However, due to illness or age, many patients of the care facility are unable to express their personal preferences for the meal options they receive. E.g., some patients cannot speak anymore or are unintelligible and patients suffering from dementia might not be able to link the name of a dish to the actual food.

RecSys'13, October 12–16, 2013, Hong Kong, China.

ACM 978-1-4503-2409-0/13/10 ...$15.00.
http://dx.doi.org/10.1145/2507157.2507198.

Until now, if patients are unable to express their choice, the caregivers make the decision instead of the patients. Since caregivers have many different patients, and a patient can receive meals from different caregivers, caregivers are not able to optimally estimate the food preferences of patients. Therefore, the selection of meal options made by the caregivers can be alternating (e.g., Monday option 1, Tuesday option 2, etc.) or even be random.

The goal of this research was to develop a recommender system that provides food recommendations for patients who are unable to make or express their own choices. By using this recommender, caregivers can offer patients a meal that is more tailored to the patients' personal preferences.

2. RELATED WORK

In the past years, various systems have been developed to assist people in the kitchen or to provide personal suggestions for (healthy) meals. Meals can be suggested by providing the user with the recipe, explaining how to prepare the food. However, the lack of competence and confidence is a common barrier towards the preparation of a (new) dish [8]. Therefore, the cooking competence is an important factor to take into account while recommending recipes. This cooking competence can be estimated by tracking the user's activities in the kitchen by means of sensors in the kitchen utensils [8]. The number of ingredients and activities involved in preparing a meal is an indication for the difficulty of preparing the meal. If users have no experience with preparing difficult meals, the recommender system can take this knowledge into account and avoid complicated recipes. Moreover, this knowledge can be used to assist people to gradually increase their cooking competence [5].

Besides the cooking competence, various other factors, both context and content related, influence the user's preferences for meals and ratings for recipes. The most common reasons for a negative evaluation of a recipe are that the recipe contains a particular disliked ingredient, the combination of ingredients, or the recipe would take too long to prepare and cook. The most common reasons for appreciating a recipe (and providing positive feedback) are the ease and quickness of preparation, the user's own preference for the recipe or an ingredient, and the type of dish or recipe being novel or interesting [4]. So in the context of food recommendations, research has pointed to the highly significant influence of the individual tastes of the user and the content of the recipes in terms of ingredients [4].

Based on these insights, ratings for a meal can be broken down into ratings for its ingredients or component foods, and ratings for ingredients or component foods can be composed into ratings for meals [4]. Using these inferred ratings for ingredients, a fine-grained food item strategy can take into account the various ingredients of a meal during the recommendation process. Research has shown that more accurate food recommendations can be made when calculations are based on implied user ratings on ingredients rather than on recipes [4].

In some circumstances, the food recommendations are not intended for assisting individuals in the food selection process, but rather as suggestions for groups of people, for example in a family context. This raises the need to uncover the most appropriate group recommendations, taking into account the preferences of all group members in the recommendation process. In the context of recipe recommendations, two strategies to generate group recommendations have been compared: a strategy that aggregates the individual user preferences into a model representing the group preferences and then calculates group recommendations based on this model, and a strategy that calculates recommendations for each individual member of the group and then aggregates the recommendations of the individual members into group recommendations [2].

The specific use case of food recommendations for patients in a care facility has some direct consequences on the factors that have to be taken into account in the recommendation process. E.g., since meals are prepared by professional cooks, the cooking competences of the end-users (i.e., the patients) are irrelevant. The personal preferences of the patients are an important influencing factor as well as diet or medical restrictions such as diabetes, lactose intolerant, allergies, etc. Since food choices can be made on an individual basis, no group recommendation strategy has to be used.

3. RECOMMENDATION STRATEGY

In order to enable personal recommendations for menu items in the context of a care facility, a framework was developed to store data about the preferences, activities, and behavior of the patients regarding the meals. This framework stores explicit personal ratings of the patient for the menu items (if available), the ingredients of each menu item, and for each meal, details about the amounts of food that each patient received from the caregivers, the amounts of food that were eaten by each patient, and the choices regarding menu items that each patient (or the caregiver) made.

Explicit ratings can be used to specify the patient's favorite meals or his/her aversion for menu items or ingredients. These explicit preferences can be specified by the patient (in an early stage of the disease), the caregivers, or even by family members who visit the patient.

The amount of food that was eaten by the patient is considered as implicit feedback for the item. Menu items that are completely eaten receive positive feedback, whereas menu items that are not eaten receive negative feedback, thereby relying on the assumption that patients eat more if they like the food. This feedback is acquired by means of a mobile application, available on the smartphones and tablets used by caregivers to register the activities and behavior of the patients as well as special situations.

All this information is used by a hybrid recommendation algorithm, which combines content-based [7] and collaborative filtering techniques [3] in order to generate personal recommendations for the patients. For each menu choice, (i.e., for each food option that patients have), the recommendation algorithm calculates a *preference score* that estimates how much the patient will like the food option. Subsequently, the menu item(s) with the highest preference score will be recommended to the patient (if no restrictions apply). During the calculation of this preference score for a menu item, the following three different cases are considered in the recommendation algorithm.

1. An explicit rating for the item is available.
2. No explicit rating is available, but implicit feedback for the item is available
3. No explicit rating and no implicit feedback are available. The ingredients of the menu item are the only available information.

3.1 Prediction Based on Explicit Ratings

For the food recommendations, the explicit ratings are considered as an important information source for estimating the patient's preferences. So if the patient has specified an explicit rating for a menu item, this will strongly influence the patient's preference score for this item.

In order to take into account the possible changes in the preferences of patients, the implicit feedback for the item is also considered in the calculation process in addition to the explicit ratings, which might not be updated frequently. Moreover, the implicit feedback, which reflects the eating behavior of the patient, may refine the preferences inferred from the explicit ratings.

As a result, the *Explicit Prediction* of the patient's preference of an item consists of a weighted average of the patient's explicit rating and a prediction of the patient's preference based on his/her implicit feedback for the item, which is referred to as *Implicit Prediction*.

$$\begin{aligned} ExplicitPrediction &= \alpha \cdot ExplicitRating \\ &\quad + (1-\alpha) \cdot ImplicitPrediction \end{aligned} \tag{1}$$

In this formula, α is a weighting factor that has a value ranging from 0 to 1 if an explicit rating for the menu item is available, and that is 0 if no explicit rating is available. The explicit prediction is used as input for the *AlreadyKnown* recommendation algorithm of the Duine recommender framework [7]. This recommendation algorithm generates a preference score for the menu item, thereby taking into account the fact that the user has already provided feedback for that item.

3.2 Prediction Based on Implicit Feedback

If the patient (or someone who knows the patient's preferences) has not specified an explicit rating for the menu item, the patient's preference for the menu item is estimated based on his/her eating behavior (enthusiastically or reluctantly) and the amount of food that the patient has eaten. The eating behavior and the amount of food (i.e., the implicit feedback for the item) is registered by the caregivers using their mobile device as part of the monitoring process of the patients.

However, this implicit feedback is not always a perfect predictor of the patient's preferences, since the patient's eating behavior and the amount of food that was eaten can be influenced by other factors besides the patient's preference for the item. Unpredictable factors, such as the current appetite of the patient or illness, have also a significant impact on the eating behavior and the amount of food that was eaten. Consequently, the implicit feedback for an item can deviate from the true preferences of the patient.

Therefore, a prediction of the patient's preference for the item, based on the patient's preferences for the ingredients of the item, is added to the calculation process. So, the *Implicit Prediction* is calculated by means of a weighted average of the implicit feedback for the item, and a prediction based on the ingredients of the item, i.e., *Ingredient Prediction.*

$$\begin{aligned} ImplicitPrediction &= \beta \cdot ImplicitFeedback \\ &+ (1-\beta) \cdot IngredientPrediction \end{aligned} \tag{2}$$

In this formula, β is a weighting factor that has a value ranging from 0 to 1 if implicit feedback for the menu item is available, and that is 0 if no implicit feedback is available. The implicit prediction is used as input for the *Already-Known* recommendation algorithm, in order to calculate a preference score, which estimates how much the patient will like the menu item.

3.3 Prediction Based on Ingredients

For new menu items that never have been served to the patient, explicit ratings or implicit feedback may not be available. Therefore, the preference of the patient for a new menu item is estimated based on the ingredients of the menu item and the patient's preferences for these ingredients.

As an alternative for a reasoning based on the ingredients, a standard collaborative filtering approach could be used to predict the patient's preferences for menu items. Nevertheless, research has shown that the menu breakdown into ingredients with reasoning on the ingredients provides more accurate recommendations than a collaborative filtering algorithm reasoning on the menu items [4].

First, the menu item is decomposed into high-level ingredients. E.g., the menu item "macaroni" is split into "cheese", "ham", and "pasta". Next, the patient's preferences for these ingredients are inferred. Similar to the approach of Freyne and Berkovsky [4], ratings for menu items are transferred to the ingredients of these menu items. In other words, the ingredients (e.g., cheese, ham, and pasta) get the same rating as the item that contains the ingredients (e.g., macaroni). Hereby, cooking processes and combinations effects are ignored, and all ingredients are considered to be equally weighted in a menu item.

For an ingredient that is new for the patient, i.e., the patient has not yet (implicitly or explicitly) evaluated a menu item containing that ingredient, ingredient preferences cannot be inferred from the item preferences of the patient. If the patient's historical data provide no clue about his/her preferences for some ingredients, preferences have to be inferred by using the *collaborative filtering* implementation of the Duine framework [7].

Through collaborative filtering, personal preferences for new ingredients are inferred from the preferences of neighboring patients, i.e., patients with similar preferences. Research has shown that more accurate neighbor determination and food prediction occurs when neighbors are based on implied user ratings for ingredients rather than on ratings for menu items [4]. So in our developed recommender system, neighboring patients are determined by calculating the Pearson similarity between the patients' inferred preferences for the ingredients of the menu items.

To summarize, the patient's preferences for ingredients are inferred from his/her ratings and implicit feedback for menu items that contain these ingredients. If the patient has never (implicitly or explicitly) evaluated a menu item containing a specific ingredient, his/her preference for this ingredient is calculated using collaborating filtering. The *Ingredient Prediction* for an item is calculated by averaging the patient's preferences for the n ingredients of the item.

$$IngredientPrediction = \frac{1}{n}\sum_{i=1}^{n} IngredientPreference_i \tag{3}$$

However, (the taste of) some ingredients can be predominant in a menu, so that if these ingredient are disliked, the entire menu will be disliked, irrespective of other likable ingredients in the same menu item. If more information about the (relative importance of) ingredients becomes available, the compensatory approach of the average function can be replaced by a more informed aggregation method such as a weighted average in which the weights reflect the importance of the ingredients in the menu. Finally, the patient's preference for a menu item (i.e., the preference score) is estimated by the *content-based* recommender of the Duine framework [7], which reasons on the user's preferences for the ingredients of the item.

3.4 Rule-Based Restrictions

The main goal of the recommender system is to generate accurate recommendations by suggesting menu items that match the patient's (inferred) preferences. However being accurate is not enough for a recommender system [6]; also other characteristics like diversity are essential for a valuable list of suggestions. Especially for a food recommender, diversity is an important quality aspect. Without diversity, patients risk to get recommended their favorite dish every day. Therefore, caregivers can specify how often a menu item can be recommended to a patient. Last but not least, diet or medical restrictions can be specified for specific menu items or in terms of the ingredients of the menu items. The restrictions of each patient are taken into account during the recommendation process, thereby also considering the previous meals. E.g., some patients can only eat a limited amount of sugar each day, so the choice of the breakfast influences the options for the lunch. Menu items or ingredients not fulfilling these personal requirements are eliminated from the patient's recommendations.

4. ANALYZING THE EATING BEHAVIOR

4.1 Predicting the Optimal Amount of Food

Besides assisting the patients in the food selection process by providing personal recommendations, the system analyzes the gathered data in order to provide insights into the eating habits of the patients. This data analysis is performed by the monitoring engine of the system, which operates in parallel with the recommendation engine. To facilitate the usage of the system, the monitoring engine is self-learning without the need for configuration of rules.

By analyzing the amount of food eaten by every patient over a long period of time, the monitoring engine can make a prediction about the amount of food that will be eaten by a patient in the future. For each menu item that is served to a patient, the system can make such a prediction. Predicting the amounts of food that patients will eat, can be useful for determining the size of the food portions as well as for food ordering and stock management of the care facility.

The optimal amount of a specific menu item for a patient is predicted by using a standard regression analysis based on the knowledge available in the system (independent variables): the menu item and its ingredients, the amounts of the menu item that were eaten by the patient in the past, and the general appetite of the patient, which is measured by the amounts of other menu items that were eaten by the patient during the past meals. To reflect the recent changes in the eating behavior of patients, the most-recently acquired data, i.e., data about the meals of the past week, are analyzed separately from the formerly acquired data.

4.2 Detecting Irregularities

Another task of the monitoring engine is to detect irregularities in the eating behavior of the patients. The system can detect abrupt and unexpected increases or decreases in the amount of food eaten by a patient. A sudden decrease can for example be an indication of illness. Although the monitoring engine passes no judgment about the cause of such a change in eating behavior, detecting these changes can be helpful for the caregivers in order to monitor the health condition of the patients. Data regarding the eating behavior of a patient is analyzed using regression analysis to calculate the variations in the amount of food eaten by the patient, and to determine if these variations are statistically significant. Exceptional small (or large) amounts of food or drinks consumed by the patient are detected using the outlier detection mechanisms of the ELKI framework [1]. Statistically significant trends or exceptional cases in the eating behavior are automatically reported to the caregivers via their mobile device, so that they can intervene if the health of the patient might be in danger.

However, a health problem is not the only possible cause of a variation in the amount of food that patients eat. Significant variations might be caused by external conditions such as the temperature in the dining room. E.g., if the temperature rises a few degrees in the summer, one might expect an increased consumption of water by the patients in the care facility. Information about the environment is retrieved at regular time intervals by means of sensors installed in the care facility. This way, the system can calculate the correlation between the increase or decrease of the amount of consumed food and the environmental conditions such as the temperature or humidity in the room. Moreover, the environmental conditions are used as independent variables in the regression analysis to explain trends. The results of the regression analysis and the correlation values are reported to the caregivers, together with a visual presentation of the variations in the food consumption, to enable them to make a more informed decision.

5. CONCLUSIONS

This paper proposes a hybrid recommendation algorithm for suggesting menu items to patients in a care facility. In the context of food recommendations, suggesting already-consumed items again is desirable if the user liked the item in the past. As a result, feedback for the potential recommendation might already be available as an additional information source during the calculation process. In contrast, for many traditional application domains, such as recommenders for online shops or movies, users generally prefer not to buy or watch the same item twice. Future work will focus on the evaluation of the proposed recommender system. Therefore, the recommender will be integrated into the central data system of two care facilities in order to evaluate the food suggestions and the analysis of eating behavior. Subsequently, a qualitative evaluation consisting of interviews with patients and caregivers will provide insight into the usefulness of the system.

6. ACKNOWLEDGMENTS

This work was supported by the iMinds aToM (A Touch of Memory) project. This is a project co-funded by iMinds (Interdisciplinary institute for Technology) a research institute founded by the Flemish Government.

7. REFERENCES

[1] ELKI: Environment for Developing KDD-Applications Supported by Index-Structures, 2012. Online available at `http://elki.dbs.ifi.lmu.de/`.

[2] S. Berkovsky and J. Freyne. Group-based recipe recommendations: analysis of data aggregation strategies. In *Proceedings of the fourth ACM conference on Recommender systems*, RecSys '10, pages 111–118, New York, NY, USA, 2010. ACM.

[3] J. S. Breese, D. Heckerman, and C. Kadie. Empirical analysis of predictive algorithms for collaborative filtering. In *Proceedings of the Fourteenth conference on Uncertainty in artificial intelligence*, UAI'98, pages 43–52, San Francisco, CA, USA, 1998. Morgan Kaufmann Publishers Inc.

[4] J. Freyne and S. Berkovsky. Intelligent food planning: personalized recipe recommendation. In *Proceedings of the 15th international conference on Intelligent user interfaces*, IUI '10, pages 321–324, New York, NY, USA, 2010. ACM.

[5] M. Harvey, B. Ludwig, and D. Elsweiler. Learning user tastes: a first step to generating healthy meal plans? In *First International Workshop on Recommendation Technologies for Lifestyle Change (LIFESTYLE 2012)*, page 18, 2012.

[6] S. M. McNee, J. Riedl, and J. A. Konstan. Being accurate is not enough: how accuracy metrics have hurt recommender systems. In *CHI '06 extended abstracts on Human factors in computing systems*, CHI EA '06, pages 1097–1101, New York, NY, USA, 2006. ACM.

[7] Telematica Instituut / Novay. Duine Framework, 2009. Online available at `http://duineframework.org/`.

[8] J. Wagner, G. Geleijnse, and A. van Halteren. Guidance and support for healthy food preparation in an augmented kitchen. In *Proceedings of the 2011 Workshop on Context-awareness in Retrieval and Recommendation*, CaRR '11, pages 47–50, New York, NY, USA, 2011. ACM.

Evaluation of Recommendations: Rating-Prediction and Ranking

Harald Steck*
Netflix Inc.
Los Gatos, California
hsteck@netflix.com

ABSTRACT

The literature on recommender systems distinguishes typically between two broad categories of measuring recommendation accuracy: *rating prediction*, often quantified in terms of the root mean square error (RMSE), and *ranking*, measured in terms of metrics like precision and recall, among others. In this paper, we examine both approaches in detail, and find that the dominating difference lies *instead* in the training and test data considered: rating prediction is concerned with *only the observed ratings*, while ranking typically accounts for *all items in the collection*, whether the user has rated them or not. Furthermore, we show that predicting observed ratings, while popular in the literature, only solves a (small) part of the rating prediction task for *any* item in the collection, which is a common real-world problem. The reasons are selection bias in the data, combined with data sparsity. We show that the latter rating-prediction task involves the prediction task *'Who rated What'* as a sub-problem, which can be cast as a classification or ranking problem. This suggests that solving the ranking problem is not only valuable by itself, but also for predicting the rating value of *any* item.

Categories and Subject Descriptors

H.2.8 [**Database Management**]: Database Applications—*Data Mining*

Keywords

Recommender Systems; Selection Bias; Rating Prediction; Ranking

1. INTRODUCTION

The idea of recommender systems (RS) is to automatically suggest items to each user that s/he may find appealing, e.g., see [2] for an overview. Prior to a user study or deployment, offline testing on historical data provides a time and cost efficient initial assessment of an RS. A meaningful offline test ideally provides a good approximation to the utility function to be optimized by the deployed system (e.g., user satisfaction, increase in sales). Recommendation accuracy is an important part of such an offline metric.

The literature on recommender systems typically distinguishes between two ways of measuring recommendation accuracy: *rating prediction*, often measured in terms of the root mean square error (RMSE); and *ranking*, which is measured in terms of metrics like precision and recall, among others. In this paper, we examine both kinds of accuracy measures in detail and identify different variants.

Concerning rating prediction, the literature has focused mainly on predicting the rating values for those items that a user has *deliberately chosen to rate*. This kind of data can be collected easily, and is hence readily available for offline training and testing of recommender systems. Moreover, the root mean square error (RMSE), the most popular accuracy metric in the recommender literature, can easily be evaluated on the user-item pairs that actually have a rating value in the data.

The objective of common real-world rating prediction tasks, however, is often different from this scenario: typically, the goal is to predict the rating value for *any* item in the collection, independent of the fact if a user rates it or not. The reason for the difference is that the ratings are missing not at random (MNAR) in the data sets typically collected [14, 13, 22, 23, 17]. For instance, on the Netflix web site, a personalized rating value is predicted for *any* video in the collection, as to provide the user with an indication of enjoyment if s/he watches it.

These two variants of *rating prediction* motivated us to examine it in more detail. In the first part of this paper, we identify *three* variants of rating prediction, and show how they differ from each other in terms of answers they provide to the recommendation problem and in terms of the degree of difficulty to solve them. Moreover, we show that many real-world rating prediction tasks require an additional sub-problem to be solved: as to which user deliberately chooses to assign a rating to which item in the collection (also known as *'Who rated What'* [1]). This sub-problem may be cast as a *classification* or *ranking* problem.

In the second part of this paper, we focus on ranking for solving real-world recommendation tasks. As just motivated, ranking may not only be an important sub-problem of many real-world rating-prediction tasks, but ranking is a

*Part of this work was done while at Bell-Labs, Alcatel-Lucent, Murray Hill, New Jersey.

RecSys'13, October 12–16, 2013, Hong Kong, China.
ACM 978-1-4503-2409-0/13/10.
http://dx.doi.org/10.1145/2507157.2507160.

relevant approach on its own—for instance, when the objective is to select a small subset of items from the entire collection (top N recommendations). We examine three variants of ranking: ranking of all items in the collection, ranking of only those items that the user has not rated yet, and ranking of only those items that the user has already rated. Our experiments provide strong empirical evidence that the difference in ranking accuracy due to these variants is considerably larger than the difference due to different ranking metrics. This suggests that the appropriate choice of training and testing *protocol*, e.g., which user-item pairs to consider, may be more important than the ranking *metric* for solving a given real-world ranking problem.

The main contributions of this paper can be summarized as follows:

1. we identify three variants of rating prediction. We show that the variant that is the main focus in the literature solves only a part of many real-world rating-prediction problems. This suggests further research is needed to develop rating prediction approaches for the (various) real-world tasks.

2. concerning ranking, we find that in practice the choice of an appropriate training and testing protocol makes a bigger difference than the choice of ranking metric.

3. when comparing rating prediction with ranking, we find that their *main* difference is *not* caused by the different metrics (e.g., RMSE vs. ranking metrics). Instead, it is due to the user-item pairs that are taken into account: only the subset of user-item pairs where a rating is *observed* in the data (e.g., for RMSE), vs. *all* user-item pairs—whether the user deliberately chose to assign a rating value to an item or not. As main causes, we identify selection bias in the data combined with data sparsity.

This paper is organized into two main parts: first, we examine rating prediction, which we model as a two-stage problem: the user's deliberate choice as to which item to rate, and which rating value to assign (Section 2.1). This leads immediately to three variants of rating prediction (Section 2.2), and we derive their general relationships and differences in Section 2.3. In Section 2.4, we discuss general implications on modeling the two-stage rating process, while Section 2.5 justifies a particular model approach. In the second part of this paper (Section 3), we outline three variants of ranking protocols (Section 3.1), which is analogous to the variants for rating prediction. In Section 3.2, we briefly review various ranking metrics, so that we are ready to compare the effects of ranking protocols and ranking metrics in our experiments in Section 3.3. We finish with our Conclusions.

2. RATING PREDICTION

The root mean square error (RMSE) is by far the most popular accuracy measure in the recommender literature. It is commonly associated with the objective of *rating prediction*, i.e., predicting the rating value that a user would assign to an item which s/he has not rated yet. In this section, we examine this objective in detail, and identify three variants with important differences.

2.1 Modeling the Decision to Rate

There has been recent work on the fact that ratings are *missing not at random (MNAR)* in the data typically collected in recommender system applications [14, 13, 22, 23, 17]. The main reason for this selection bias in the observed data is that the users are free to deliberately choose which items to rate.

This motivates us to model the rating-prediction task as shown in Figure 1 (left): In this graphical model, U denotes the random variable concerning users, and takes values u, where $u \in \{1, ..., n\}$ denotes user IDs, and n is the number of users. Similarly, I is the random variable concerning items, taking values $i \in \{1, ..., m\}$, where m is the number of items in the collection. The decision if a user u deliberately chooses to rate item i is represented by the random variable C, which takes values $c \in \{c_+, c_-\}$, where c_+ denotes that the user chooses to rate the item, while c_- means that the user does *not* deliberately choose to rate the item. Finally, R is the random variable regarding rating values, taking values r. For instance, $r \in \{1, ..., 5\}$ in case of ratings on a scale from 1 to 5 stars like in the Netflix Prize competition [3] or MovieLens data [5].

Note that C depends on the user and the item, such that this model is able to capture any reason that depends on u and i for choosing to give a rating (e.g., the item's popularity [23, 17]). This is more general than the approaches presented in [13], where this decision does not depend on the user-item pair directly, but only on the rating value itself. The dependence on the rating value as a decision-criteria whether to provide a rating is included as a special case in the model in Figure 1: using theory on graphical models, the graph in Figure 1 is *Markov-equivalent* to the graph where the orientation of the edge between C and R is reversed. Markov-equivalence means that both graphical models represent the same probability distribution (even though the graphs look different). The reason why the edge can be reversed is that both nodes C and R in the graph have the same parents, namely U and I. This is a key difference to the graphs used in [13], where C is not connected to the user or item.

Given that all random variables U, I, C, and R are discrete, we assume the most general probability distribution, the multinomial distribution. Note that this may be too general a model assumption as to learn a "good" model in practice, but in the first part of this paper, we are concerned with general insights that we can obtain without resorting to a more specific model.

2.2 Rating-Prediction Variants

Rating prediction is concerned with predicting the *rating value* r that a user u assigns to an item i. It can be cast as predicting the probability of each rating value r that user u assigns to each item i, denoted by $p(r_{u,i}) = p(r|u, i)$. Based on the graphical model in Figure 1, this can be decomposed as follows:

$$\underbrace{p(r|u,i)}_{(1)} = \underbrace{p(r|c_+,u,i)}_{(2)} p(c_+|u,i) + \underbrace{p(r|c_-,u,i)}_{(3)} p(c_-|u,i) \tag{1}$$

This equation shows that there are *three* variants of rating prediction, i.e., three probabilities concerning rating value r. Additionally, Eq. 1 also shows that these terms are linked via *two* terms regarding the probability that the user de-

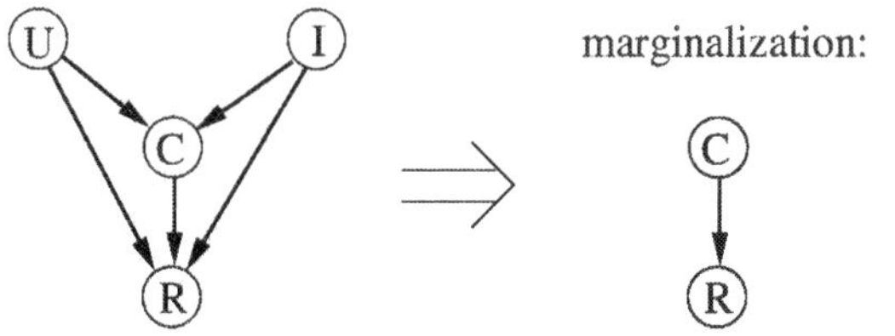

Figure 1: When a user (node U) provides a rating value (node R) for an item (node I), the user typically has the freedom to deliberately choose *which* item(s) to rate. The user's implicit decision as to whether rate an item or not, is represented by node C in the graphical model. The graph on the right hand side is obtained by marginalizing out U and I.

liberately chooses to rate an item (*'Who rated What'* [1]), which is discussed at the end of this sub-section. We first discuss the three variants of rating prediction:

1. $p(r|u,i)$: This is the probability that user u assigns rating value r to item i in the collection. It is important that there is no restriction on which item i it is; it can be *any* item in the collection. The ability to make an accurate rating prediction for any item i is extremely useful in practical applications, as it allows one to find the items with the highest (predicted) enjoyment value from the *entire collection*.

2. $p(r|c_+,u,i)$: This is the probability that user u assigns rating value r to item i under the condition that the user deliberately chooses to rate this item. This condition may not hold for any item i in the collection. In fact, due to data sparsity, it may apply to *only a (small) subset of items*, as shown in the next section. For instance, it is commonly observed in practice that users tend to assign ratings mainly to items they like or know [14, 13, 22, 23, 17]. The reason is that the observed data is collected by allowing users to choose which items to rate. As a consequence, this conditional probability is learned when optimizing RMSE or MAE on the *observed* data.

3. $p(r|c_-,u,i)$: This is the probability that user u would assign rating value r to item i under the condition that the user would not deliberately choose to rate this item. In practice, this rating value could be elicited, for instance, by providing the user with some reward for completing this task. These ratings are typically costly to elicit, and burdensome for the user to provide. For this reason, ratings under this condition are typically not available, which obviously makes it difficult to estimate this probability distribution accurately. Due to data sparsity, this distribution applies to the vast majority of user-item pairs, as discussed in more detail in the next section. In the rare case that they were collected, for instance in the Yahoo!Music data [13], it becomes obvious that this conditional distribution of rating values can be very different from the rating distribution under the condition that the user deliberately chose an item to rate. For instance, compare Figures 2(a) and (b) in [13], or Figure 1 in [17].

The decomposition in Eq. 1 also shows that, in addition, the two *conditional* probabilities $p(r|c_+,u,i)$ and $p(r|c_-,u,i)$ have to be estimated as to obtain valid rating predictions for *any* item in the collection. These probabilities capture whether user u deliberately chooses to rate item i or not. This shows their importance for rating prediction of *any* item, and motivates further research beyond the few works conducted so far, like the KDD Cup 2007, titled *'Who rated What'* [1]; there, one of the insights was that it was difficult to make accurate predictions as to which user deliberately chooses to rate which items.

2.3 Relationship of the three Variants

This section presents our main results concerning rating prediction, i.e., a general relationship between the three variants of rating prediction.

2.3.1 Marginal Probabilities

A necessary condition for accurate *personalized* rating prediction is that the *average* (and hence unpersonalized) rating predictions have to be accurate on average as well. This is outlined in detail in the following. To this end, let us consider $p(r)$, which is the probability of rating value r averaged over all users u and items i. Based on our graphical model in Figure 1, this can be derived by marginalizing over u and i in Eq. 1:

$$
\begin{aligned}
p(r) &= \sum_{c,u,i} p(r|c,u,i) \cdot p(c|u,i) \cdot p(u) \cdot p(i) && (2)\\
&= \sum_{c} p(r|c) \cdot p(c) && (3)\\
&= p(r|c_+) \cdot p(c_+) + p(r|c_-) \cdot p(c_-) && (4)\\
&= p(r|c_-) + p(c_+)\,\{p(r|c_+) - p(r|c_-)\} && (5)\\
&\approx p(r|c_-) && (6)
\end{aligned}
$$

The line-by-line comments are as follows: equality (2) in the first line follows from the definition of $p(r)$ in terms of the graphical model in Figure 1. In equality (3), the random variables U and I are marginalized out from the probability distribution, so that we obtain the marginal distribution over C and R, which is also represented in Figure 1 (right). This is valid [11] because the class of graphical models representing probability distributions from the exponential family, like the multinomial distribution used here, is closed when marginalizing out over a variable that is connected with all its edges to the same clique[1] in the graph, which is obviously the case in Figure 1. Equality (4) re-states the previous line, using $c \in \{c_+, c_-\}$, and equality (5) uses $p(c_-) = 1 - p(c_+)$. The interesting approximation in the last line is accurate due the *sparsity of the data*, which is typical for recommender applications: based on the graph, we have

$$p(c_+) = \sum_{u,i} p(c_+|u,i) \cdot p(u) \cdot p(i). \qquad (7)$$

Any accurate prediction for $p(c_+)$ has to be close to the empirical estimate $\hat{p}(c_+)$, which is given by

$$\hat{p}(c_+) = \frac{\#ratings}{|U| \cdot |I|} = \text{data sparsity}$$

[1]A clique is a completely connected sub-graph.

where $\#ratings$ is the number of ratings in the data; $|U| = n$ and $|I| = m$ denote the number of users and items, respectively. Hence, $p(c_+)$ equals the data sparsity. In typical applications the data sparsity is in the single-digit percent range, and often even one or more orders of magnitudes lower. For instance, it was about 1% in the Netflix Prize data [3], which may be considered a relatively dense data set compared to other recommender applications. Hence, the approximation in Eq. 6 is accurate up to a few percent in general. This is orders of magnitudes more accurate than any real-world rating-prediction accuracy, e.g., see RMSE for the Netflix Prize data [3] or MovieLens data [5]. We hence arrive at

Conclusion 1: *Due to data sparsity, the rating prediction variants 1. and 3., as outlined in Section 2.2, have to be closely related. In contrast, variant 2. is not required to be similar to variants 1. or 3.*

This suggests that there is a difference between the main focus of the literature (variant 2.), and many real-world rating-prediction problems (variants 1. and 3.).

2.3.2 Average Ratings

The *average* of the predicted rating values of a recommender system has an important impact on its accuracy in terms of RMSE (and similarly for MAE). This is outlined in the following.

Analogous to Eq. (2) - (6), one obtains for the average rating value:

$$
\begin{aligned}
\mathrm{E}[R] &= \sum_{r,c,u,i} r \cdot p(r|c,u,i) \cdot p(c|u,i) \cdot p(u) \cdot p(i) \quad (8) \\
&= \mathrm{E}[R|c_-] + p(c_+)\left\{\mathrm{E}[R|c_+] - \mathrm{E}[R|c_-]\right\} \quad (9) \\
&\approx \mathrm{E}[R|c_-] \quad (10)
\end{aligned}
$$

where $\mathrm{E}[\cdot]$ denotes the (conditional) expectation/average of the random variable R, i.e., the rating values. Not surprisingly, this confirms the previous relationships among the three variants of rating prediction: the average rating value of variants 1. and 3. has to be approximately the same due to data sparsity, while the average rating of variant 2. is not required to be similar.

In fact, there is strong empirical evidence, for instance, provided by the Yahoo! Music data[2] [13], suggesting that these average rating values can actually be very different: Figures 2 (a) and (b) in [13] show that, on a rating scale from 1 to 5, we have:

- $\mathrm{E}[R|c_-] \approx \mathrm{E}[R] \approx 1.8$: this is the average rating when users where asked to rate songs that were *randomly* selected by Yahoo! (instead of selected by the users). These rating data may hence be considered as (approximately) fulfilling the *missing at random* condition [18, 12], such that its rating distribution provides an unbiased estimate of the (unknown) true distribution.

- $\mathrm{E}[R|c_+] \approx 2.9$: this is the average rating when users were free to deliberately choose which items to rate. Evidently, this value is significantly larger than 1.8, suggesting a strong selection bias.

[2]The actual Yahoo! Music data set was not available to us, so that we had to resort to the histograms published in [13].

This difference in the average rating is extremely large when compared to typical improvements in terms of RMSE, as outlined in the following. In the Netflix Prize data, the winning approach achieved $RMSE \approx 0.86$, which was so difficult to achieve that it required about three years of research work. In comparison, when simply predicting the average rating for all users and all items, one achieves $RMSE \approx 1.0$. This shows that an improvement in RMSE of 0.14 (on a rating scale of 1 to 5) may look small, but is actually very large. The numbers for MovieLens data are slightly different, but also here, the improvement of a sophisticated approach over a simple approach in terms of RMSE is much less than 1.

This shows that a difference in the average predicted rating of about 1 can easily dominate over the improvement of a more accurate recommender system. This becomes clear from the following thought experiment: Let us assume we train a recommender system on available rating data where the users were free to choose which items to rate. This is the typical scenario for collecting data. Let its RMSE (on a test set) be given by $RMSE_0$; its average predicted rating value will be close to the average rating value in the training data, $\mathrm{E}[R|c_+]$. This recommender system will hence be accurate for variant 2. Now, let us consider the common real-world task of rating-prediction for *any/each* item in the collection (variant 1): in this case, the (unknown) true average rating is $\mathrm{E}[R]$; now, the previously trained recommender system has a bias $b = \mathrm{E}[R|c_+] - \mathrm{E}[R]$. This results in a degraded RMSE: $RMSE_1 = \sqrt{RMSE_0^2 + b^2}$. Using the numerical values from above, this suggests that $RMSE_1 \gg 1$. Interestingly, this is worse than RMSE$\approx$ 1, which can be achieved by an (unpersonalized) recommender system that predicts the average rating $\mathrm{E}[R]$. Even though the value $\mathrm{E}[R]$ may be unknown in many practical applications, it may also be possible to determine its value with some additional efforts, for instance, by running a truly randomized experiment with a small subset of the users. This leads us to the following conclusion:

Conclusion 2: *A recommender system with a low RMSE concerning the rating-prediction variant 2, is not guaranteed to achieve a low RMSE regarding rating-prediction tasks 1 or 3.*

Among these three variants, variant 1 refers to a common real-world rating-prediction task, like e.g., on the Netflix web site, which provides a personalized rating prediction for any video on its website. While many excellent solutions have been developed for variant 2 in the literature, this conclusion suggests that additional research is needed as to develop accurate prediction models for variant 1.

2.4 Implications for Modeling

Conclusions 1 and 2 above show that a key challenge in building real-world recommender systems is that rating distributions $p(R|U,I)$ (variant 1) or $p(R|c_-,U,I)$ (variant 3) are relevant for the user experience in many real-world applications; in contrast, the data that are readily available in large quantities follow the distribution $p(R|c_+,U,I)$ (i.e., variant 2). Given the practical importance of variants 1 and 3, it is crucial to build recommender systems that account for the items (and their ratings) that a user has *not* rated. Developing solutions for these new objectives of rating-prediction is an interesting area for future work.

In the following, we outline a Bayesian approach that uses an informative prior distribution that incorporates the rating distributions of the items that were *not* rated by a user. There are different ways of defining this prior distribution. First, one may run an experiment and elicit ratings for random items from users, like in the Yahoo! Music data. This provides a good estimate of the ratings concerning items that a user would not have rated otherwise. But it is also a costly experiment, and puts a burden onto users. Especially, if the items to rate are movies, it would be very time-consuming for users to watch random movies as they might not enjoy them.

Second, one may use a prior distribution with a small number of free parameters, which can be then tuned to achieve the desired result, e.g., by cross-validation. Such an approach was outlined in [22] for rating data, and a probabilistic version with prior distributions in [25]. The latter paper also shows that several rating values assigned to the same item i by a user u, i.e., a *distribution* of rating values $p(R|u,i)$, is equivalent to using the *average* rating $\bar{r}_{u,i} = \mathrm{E}[R|u,i] = \sum_r r \cdot p(r|u,i)$ when *optimizing* the least squares objective function.[3] This allows one to parameterize the prior distribution in terms of its mean. In [22], a single mean rating value is used for all users and items. It is an interesting result that, when this mean rating value is optimized as to achieve the best ranking[4] performance on the Netflix test set, a mean rating value of about 2 is found. This appears like a reasonable value for approximating the (unknown) mean rating value for the items that a user did not rate, as it agrees well with the results found for the Yahoo! Music data. Hence, this approach may provide a way for approximating relevant parameters of the (otherwise unknown) rating distribution concerning the items that a user did *not* rate. The approach in [22] is summarized in the following section; it will also be used in our experiments later in this paper.

2.5 Model and Training

In this section, we briefly review the low-rank matrix-factorization (MF) model named *AllRank* in [22], which was introduced as a point-wise ranking approach that accounts for all (unrated) items for each user. However, one can also view it from the perspective of rating prediction: the observed ratings in the data (i.e., $p(r|c_+,u,i)$), are complemented by imputed ratings with low values (as to approximate the unknown $p(r|c_-,u,i)$). As a result, an approximation to $p(r|u,i)$ is achieved, which applies to *any* item in the collection. For comparison, also the standard MF approach of minimizing RMSE on the *observed* ratings is discussed, and denoted by MF-RMSE.

The matrix of predicted ratings $\hat{R} \in \mathbb{R}^{m \times n}$, where m denotes the number of items, and n the number of users, is modeled as

$$\hat{R} = r_0 + PQ^\top, \tag{11}$$

with matrices $P \in \mathbb{R}^{m \times j_0}$ and $Q \in \mathbb{R}^{n \times j_0}$, where the rank $j_0 \ll m, n$; and $r_0 \in \mathbb{R}$ is a (global) offset.

[3]Note that this holds only for optimization/maximum-a-posteriori estimates, but does not apply for estimating the full posterior distribution, e.g., by means of Markov Chain Monte Carlo.

[4]Note that, in contrast to RMSE, (some) ranking measures can be applied to the entire collection of items, and hence account for both items with and without ratings assigned by the user.

For computationally efficient training, the square error (with the usual L2-norm regularization) is optimized:

$$\sum_{\text{all } u} \sum_{\text{all } i} W_{i,u} \cdot \left\{ \left(R^{\text{o\&i}}_{i,u} - \hat{R}_{i,u} \right)^2 + \lambda \left(\sum_{j=1}^{j_0} P^2_{i,j} + Q^2_{u,j} \right) \right\}, \tag{12}$$

where $\hat{R}_{i,u}$ denotes the ratings predicted by the model in Eq. 11; and $R^{\text{o\&i}}_{i,u}$ equals the actual rating value in the training data if observed for item i and user u; otherwise the value $R^{\text{o\&i}}_{i,u} = r_0 \in \mathbb{R}$ is imputed. The key is in the training weights,

$$W_{i,u} = \begin{cases} 1 & \text{if } R^{\text{obs}}_{i,u} \text{ observed} \\ w_0 & \text{otherwise} \end{cases}. \tag{13}$$

In *AllRank* [22], the weight assigned to the imputed ratings is *positive*, i.e., $w_0 > 0$ [22], and the imputed rating value is *lower* than the observed average rating in the data. This captures the fact that the (unknown) probability $p(r|c_-,u,i)$ is larger for lower rating values, compared to the observed probabilities $p(r|c_+,u,i)$. In contrast, *MF-RMSE* is obtained for $w_0 = 0$. This seemingly small difference has the important effect that AllRank is trained on a combination of both distributions, $p(r|c_-,u,i)$ and $p(r|c_+,u,i)$, geared towards approximating $p(r|u,i)$. In contrast, MF-RMSE is optimized towards $p(r|c_+,u,i)$. Due to this difference, in [22] AllRank was found to achieve a considerably larger top-N hit-rate or recall when ranking *all* items in the collection, compared to various state-of-the-art approaches optimized on the observed ratings only, see results in [22] and compare to [10, 4].

Alternating least squares can be used for computationally efficient training of AllRank [22] and MF-RMSE. We found the following values for the tuning parameters in Eq. 12 for the Netflix data (see also [22]) to yield the best results: $r_0 = 2$, $w_0 = 0.005$ and $\lambda = 0.04$ for AllRank; and $\lambda = 0.07$ for MF-RMSE (and $w_0 = 0$); we use rank $j_o = 50$ for both approaches.

While there are several state-of-the-art approaches, e.g., [6, 9, 10, 16, 19], that achieve a lower RMSE on *observed* ratings than MF-RMSE does, note that their test performances on *all* (unrated) items is quite similar to each other, e.g., see [10, 4]. This is interesting, as some of these approaches, like [16, 19, 10, 20], actually account in some sense for the MNAR nature of the data–but in the context of *observed* ratings (minimizing RMSE). Note that AllRank does not only apply to explicit feedback data, but can also be used for implicit feedback data, similar to [8, 15].

3. RANKING

In this section, we examine *ranking* as a means for assessing recommendation accuracy. Ranking is a useful approach when the recommendation task is, for each user, to pick a *small* number, say N, of items from among *all available* items in the collection. We divide the ranking task into two parts in this section: ranking protocols and ranking metrics, as outlined and compared to each other in the following.

3.1 Ranking Protocols

With ranking protocols, we refer to the fact as to which items are ranked. One may distinguish between two slightly different variants: (a) all items are eligible for recommendation, including the items that have been rated by the user in the past (this assumes that a user may consume an item possibly several times, e.g., listen to a song on the on-line radio); (b) only all those items are eligible for recommendation that have not been rated by the user in the past (this assumes that a user consumes each item at most once, e.g., purchase of a movie DVD). This immediately suggests the corresponding ranking protocols:

- *all items:* for each user, all items are considered, whether rated or not by the user (in the training or test set).
- *rated test-items:* for each user, only those items are considered that have been rated by the user in the test set. Note that the ratings for those items follow the same distribution $p(r|c_+, u, i)$ as in the training data, as in both cases the user has deliberately chosen to rate these items.
- *all unrated items:* for each user, only those items are considered that have not yet been rated by the user in the training set. Note that this contains items with and without ratings in the test data.

Before we are ready to present experimental results, we briefly review various ranking metrics.

3.2 Ranking Metrics

There is a multitude of performance measures discussed in the RS literature, e.g., see [7, 21] for an overview. Here, we only have space to briefly review the ranking metrics used in our experiments in Table 1.

Information retrieval and ranking measures may be divided into ones that require *binary* feedback/rating values, and ones that can account for multiple values (e.g., ratings 1,...,5).

The binary measures can be applied naturally to binary feedback data (e.g., purchases, clicks), while explicit feedback data (e.g., rating values 1,...,5) have to be discretized into two values: *relevant* and not relevant to a user. For instance, in our experiments with Netflix data, we consider 5-star ratings as relevant to a user (i.e., the user definitely likes these movies),[5] while we consider all items with other or no rating values as not relevant.

Precision is defined as $\text{P@}N = m^{+,N}/N$, where $m^{+,N}$ is the number of relevant items among the top N items; N is chosen by the researcher. Obviously, if only a small fraction of all relevant items is observed, then P@N underestimates the 'true' precision on the (unknown) complete data. For this reason, the absolute value of P@N on observed data has little meaning, as the fraction of missing relevant items is typically unknown, and the 'true' precision on the complete data cannot be determined. However, P@N on available data may still be useful for relative comparisons, as to determine the best among competing models. Relevant items being missing are a main reason for the low precision values in Table 1.

While P@N captures only the number of relevant items in the top-N items, **Mean Average Precision** also accounts for the ranking within the top-N items. It is defined as $\text{MAP@}N = \frac{1}{m^+}\sum_i^N \frac{i}{\text{Rank}^{+,N}_{\text{sort},i}}$, where $\text{Rank}^{+,N}_{\text{sort},i}$ is the ith element of the sorted ranks (in ascending order, i.e., the highest ranked item has the smallest rank value) of the relevant items in the top N (all relevant and not relevant items are ranked together). The total number of relevant items is denoted by m^+. Like precision, when computed from the observed relevant ratings only, it underestimates the 'true' MAP@N value on the unknown complete data. This follows immediately from its definition, and is also reflected by the small values in Table 1. We define MAP = MAP@m, where m is the number of *all* items. It is well known that MAP may also be viewed as the area under the precision recall curve.

Recall is defined as $\text{R@}k = m^{+,N}/m^+$, where $m^{+,N}$ is the number of relevant items among the top N items, and m^+ is the number of all relevant items. While many researchers may prefer precision over recall, recall has interesting properties in the context of missing ratings: if we assume that *relevant* ratings are missing at random (while allowing all other rating values to be missing not at random), then R@N can be estimated without bias from observed MNAR data [22]. This is very desirable, as its absolute value then has a meaning in the sense that it provides information on the expected performance of the recommender system regarding the unknown complete data (i.e., all items), which exactly is what is experienced by the user.

The **Area under the Recall curve (ATOP)** is related to recall via $\text{ATOP} = \frac{1}{m}\sum_{N=1}^{m}\text{R@}N$, as defined in [22]. Note that ATOP can also be expressed in terms of the average rank of the relevant items, and it is also a leading order approximation of the area under the ROC curve (AUC) if $m^+ \ll m$ [22].

An example of a *multiple-value ranking measure* is **normalized Discounted Cumulative Gain (nDCG)**. When some rating values are missing in the test data, however, it cannot be readily evaluated. One approach is to ignore missing ratings, and to use only observed ratings [24], like in the case of RMSE. The user-experience depends, however, on the ranking of *all* items, as outlined above. To this end, we amend nDCG as to account for missing ratings as well. We take the simple approach of imputing (the same) value Y_0 for each missing rating. Then nDCG is defined w.r.t. *all* items, and can be evaluated in the usual way, as outlined in the following. The permutation/ordering π of rating values Y_i on the entire list of items i in the test data results in the ordered list or ratings $Y_{\pi,i}$. In particular, we are interested in the permutation that sorts according to the predicted scores of the various items: $Y_{\text{sort},i}$ denotes the list or ratings in descending order of the predicted scores of the items (highest ranked item is first in list). Moreover, the best and worst possible permutations are also of interest. As the maximum value of DCG may vary across different data sets, the normalized version is typically defined as

$$\text{nDCG@}N = \frac{\text{DCG}_{\text{sort}}\text{@}N}{\max_\pi \text{DCG}_\pi\text{@}N},$$

where

$$\text{DCG}_\pi\text{@}N = \sum_{i=1}^{N} \frac{2^{Y_{\pi,i}} - 1}{\log(i+1)}.$$

Given that most ratings are missing and we impute Y_0, the absolute value of DCG is notably affected by the im-

[5]When we considered both 4 and 5 star ratings as relevant, we obtained qualitatively identical results/conclusions.

Table 1: Test results of two different RS approaches (MF-RMSE and AllRank) regarding various accuracy measures and three different item sets on the Netflix data. Obviously, AllRank considerably outperforms MF-RMSE when tested on all (unrated) items (tables a1 and a2), while the opposite holds true when tested on observed ratings (table b). The difference due to the various accuracy measures is small in comparison.

measure	(a) observed and missing ratings in test data				
		(a1) all items		(a2) all unrated items	
	worst case	MF-RMSE	AllRank	MF-RMSE	AllRank
RMSE	-	-	-	-	-
MAE	-	-	-	-	-
P@20	0.0000 ±0.0000	0.0205 ±0.0001	**0.0352** ±0.0001	0.0218 ±0.0001	**0.0382** ±0.0001
MAP	0.0000 ±0.0000	0.1136 ±0.0004	**0.2146** ±0.0006	0.1298 ±0.0007	**0.2810** ±0.0010
R@20	0.0000 ±0.0000	0.3680 ±0.0019	**0.6319** ±0.0017	0.3927 ±0.0022	**0.6864** ±0.0024
ATOP	0.0000 ±0.0000	0.8962 ±0.0007	**0.9596** ±0.0006	0.9018 ±0.0008	**0.9646** ±0.0007
nDCG @20	0.6405 ±0.0006	0.6856 ±0.0007	**0.7335** ±0.0006	0.6906 ±0.0006	**0.7518** ±0.0006
nDCG	0.9649 ±0.0001	0.9704 ±0.0001	**0.9745** ±0.0001	0.9709 ±0.0001	**0.9763** ±0.0001

measure	(b) only observed ratings in test data		
	worst case	MF-RMSE	AllRank
RMSE	-	**0.9224** ±0.0006	1.0731 ±0.0022
MAE	-	**0.7215** ±0.0006	0.8612 ±0.0016
P@2	0.0000 ±0.0000	**0.5989** ±0.0016	0.5935 ±0.0016
MAP	0.0000 ±0.0000	**0.7098** ±0.0007	0.7013 ±0.0006
R@2	0.0000 ±0.0000	**0.4412** ±0.0014	0.4358 ±0.0006
ATOP	0.0000 ±0.0000	**0.7412** ±0.0006	0.7305 ±0.0005
nDCG @2	0.1939 ±0.0003	0.8049 ±0.0009	0.8041 ±0.0009
nDCG	0.6742 ±0.0003	**0.9208** ±0.0003	0.9195 ±0.0003

puted value. In particular, the minimum value of DCG may be markedly larger than 0, see Table 1. While its absolute value does not provide information on the user experience, nDCG may still be useful for comparing different recommender systems with each other.

When a measure refers only to the top N items of the ranked list of items, this is denoted by '@N'; otherwise it refers to the entire list. While smaller values of RMSE and MAE indicate better accuracy, larger values of the (binary and multi-level) ranking measures are better. While all the above measures apply to each user, their average over all users is reported in our experiments, where each user is weighted by the number of relevant ratings (i.e., more active users have a larger weight). We also considered uniform weights among the users, and found that the obtained results for the accuracy measures were almost unchanged.

3.3 Experiments

This section outlines our results on the Netflix data [3]. Note that we obtained qualitatively identical experimental results/conclusions on the MovieLens data [5]. The Netflix Prize data [3] contains 17,770 movies and almost half a million users. About 100 million ratings are available. Ratings are observed for about 1% of all possible movie-user pairs. The ratings take integer values from 1 (worst) to 5 (best). The provided data are already split into a training and a probe set. We removed the probe set from the provided training set as to split these data into a training set and a disjoint test set.

Table 1 summarizes our comparison of the various offline tests for two different RS approaches: MF-RMSE and AllRank (see Section 2.5 for their definitions). Note that we used the usual split of the Netflix data for training and testing, except for evaluating the ranking measures in table (b): there we only considered users with at least 20 ratings, randomly assigned 10 ratings to the test set (so that we have a fair number of items to rank), and the remaining ones to the training set (on this data, RMSE=0.88 and 0.96 for MF-RMSE and AllRank, respectively). Hence, the top-2 items represent the top 20% of items in table (b), while in table (a) the top-20 items correspond to 2% (for each user, we used a random subset of 1,000 items without a rating, besides the rated items in the test set, as to allow for a direct comparison to the results in [10, 22, 4]). We further split the test set randomly into five sets of about equal size as to obtain an estimate of the standard deviation regarding each measure. We also report the worst values, which are obtained by ranking the items in the test data in the worst possible order, as this value can be quite large (especially when we impute a value for the missing ratings for nDCG in table (a)).

The results in Table 1 concerning each individual measure are discussed in Section 3.2, together with the measures' definitions.

Overall, the most striking observation in Table 1 is the clear difference between testing on (a) all (unrated) items vs. (b) only the observed ratings in the test set: AllRank is found best in (a), and MF-RMSE in (b). In comparison, the difference due to the various accuracy measures is very small. This dominating difference due to the ranking protocol may be explained by the fact that the ratings are missing not at random (MNAR) in the available data [14, 13, 22]. Note that an offline test on all (unrated) items intuitively reflects much better the situation in many real-world recommendation tasks (Table 1 (a1) and (a2)); and it evidently is very different from testing on observed ratings (Table 1(b))–whether using RMSE (like in, e.g., [6, 9, 10, 16, 19]) or a ranking metric (like in, e.g., [24]).

While RMSE and MAE can only be applied to observed ratings, other measures may be applied either to all items or to only the observed ratings. For instance, as shown in Table

1, the model with the highest recall on the *observed* ratings may not be the model with the highest recall on *all* items. This suggests that it is not sufficient to test a recommender system on various accuracy measures. Instead it is more important whether it is tested on all items, or on observed ratings only–i.e., the ranking protocol appears to be crucial.

As expected, the accuracy when testing on (a1) all items is lower than on (a2) all unrated items in Table 1, but only slightly due to data sparsity.

Conclusions

In the literature, the assessment of recommendation accuracy is typically divided into (1) *rating prediction* and (2) *ranking*. In this paper, we examined their details, and found that the crucial difference between these two methods lies *instead* in the distribution of the rating values considered: (a) rating-values of items that the user deliberately chooses to rate vs. (b) rating-values of all the items in the catalog (whether the user deliberately chooses to rate them or not). In the vast majority of the literature, (1) goes implicitly with (a), as RMSE naturally can only be measured with respect to observed ratings in the data; and (2) implicitly goes with (b), as there exist ranking metrics that can be applied to all items in the catalog.

Like for ranking, also for rating prediction, many *real-world* problems are concerned with *all* items in the catalog, i.e., *variant (b)*. As we have shown, the popular rating-prediction variant (1)(a) is very different from the common real-world scenario (1)(b). Interestingly, as to solve (1)(b), a classification or ranking problem has to be solved as well, namely the *'Who rated What'* problem. The common real-world rating-prediction problem (1)(b) is hence more involved to solve than the ranking problem. For this reason, practical applications may benefit from first solving the ranking problem, as top N recommendations by themselves are already very useful.

4. REFERENCES

[1] KDD Cup 2007. Task 1: Who rated what, 2007. `http://www.cs.uic.edu/ liub/KDD-cup-2007/proceedings.html`.

[2] G. Adomavicius and A. Tuzhilin. Toward the next generation of recommender systems: A survey of the state-of-the-art and possible extensions. *IEEE Transactions on Knowledge and Data Engineering*, 17:734–49, 2005.

[3] J. Bennet and S. Lanning. The Netflix Prize. In *Workshop at SIGKDD-07, ACM Conference on Knowledge Discovery and Data Mining*, 2007.

[4] P. Cremonesi, Y. Koren, and R. Turrin. Performance of recommender algorithms on top-N recommendation tasks. In *ACM Conference on Recommender Systems*, pages 39–46, 2010.

[5] MovieLens data. homepage: `http://www.grouplens.org/node/73`, 2006.

[6] S. Funk. Netflix update: Try this at home, 2006. `http://sifter.org/simon/journal/20061211.html`.

[7] A. Gunawardana and G. Shani. A survey of accuracy evaluation metrics of recommendation tasks. *Journal of Machine Learning Research*, 10:2935–62, 2009.

[8] Y. Hu, Y. Koren, and C. Volinsky. Collaborative filtering for implicit feedback datasets. In *IEEE International Conference on Data Mining (ICDM)*, pages 263–72, 2008.

[9] R. Keshavan, A. Montanari, and S. Oh. Matrix completion from noisy entries. *Journal of Machine Learning Research*, 11:2057–78, 2010.

[10] Y. Koren. Factorization meets the neighborhood: a multifaceted collaborative filtering model. In *ACM Conference on Knowledge Discovery and Data Mining*, pages 426–34, 2008.

[11] S. L. Lauritzen. *Graphical Models*. Oxford University Press, 1996.

[12] R. Little and D. B. Rubin. *Statistical Analysis with missing data*. Wiley, 1986.

[13] B. Marlin and R. Zemel. Collaborative prediction and ranking with non-random missing data. In *ACM Conference on Recommender Systems (RecSys)*, pages 5–12, 2009.

[14] B. Marlin, R. Zemel, S. Roweis, and M. Slaney. Collaborative filtering and the missing at random assumption. In *Conference on Uncertainty in Artificial Intelligence (UAI)*, pages 267–75, 2007.

[15] R. Pan, Y. Zhou, B. Cao, N. Liu, R. Lukose, M. Scholz, and Q. Yang. One-class collaborative filtering. In *IEEE International Conference on Data Mining (ICDM)*, pages 502–11, 2008.

[16] A. Paterek. Improving regularized singular value decomposition for collaborative filtering. In *KDDCup*, 2007.

[17] B. Pradel, N. Usunier, and P. Gallinari. Ranking with non-random missing ratings: influence of popularity and positivity on evaluation metrics. In *ACM Conference on Recommender Systems (RecSys)*, pages 147–54, 2012.

[18] D. B. Rubin. Inference and missing data. *Biometrika*, 63:581–92, 1976.

[19] R. Salakhutdinov, A. Mnih, and G. Hinton. Restricted Boltzmann machines for collaborative filtering. In *International Conference on Machine Learning (ICML)*, pages 791–8, 2007.

[20] R. Salakhutdinov and N. Srebro. Collaborative filtering in a non-uniform world: Learning with the weighted trace norm. In *Advances in Neural Information Processing Systems 24 (NIPS)*, 2010.

[21] G. Shani and A. Gunawardana. Evaluating recommendation systems. In *Recommender Systems Handbook*, pages 257–97. Springer, 2011.

[22] H. Steck. Training and testing of recommender systems on data missing not at random. In *ACM Conference on Knowledge Discovery and Data Mining*, pages 713–22, 2010.

[23] H. Steck. Item popularity and recommendation accuracy. In *ACM Conference on Recommender Systems (RecSys)*, pages 125–32, 2011.

[24] M. Weimer, A. Karatzoglou, Q. Le, and A. Smola. Cofi rank - maximum margin matrix factorization for collaborative ranking. In *Advances in Neural Information Processing Systems (NIPS)*, 2008.

[25] Y. Xin and H. Steck. Multi-value probabilistic matrix factorization for IP-TV recommendations. In *ACM Conference on Recommender Systems (RecSys)*, pages 221–8, 2011.

You Are What You Consume: A Bayesian Method for Personalized Recommendations

Konstantinos Babas
Electronic and Computer Engineering
Technical University of Crete
Chania, Greece
kbabas@isc.tuc.gr

Georgios Chalkiadakis
Electronic and Computer Engineering
Technical University of Crete
Chania, Greece
gchalkiadakis@isc.tuc.gr

Evangelos Tripolitakis
Electronic and Computer Engineering
Technical University of Crete
Chania, Greece
vtripolitakis@isc.tuc.gr

ABSTRACT

In this paper, we propose a novel Bayesian approach for personalized recommendations. In our approach, we model *both* user preferences *and* items under recommendation as *multivariate Gaussian* distributions; and make use of *Normal-Inverse Wishart* priors to model the recommendation agent beliefs about user types. We employ a lightweight agent-user interaction process, during which the user is presented with and asked to rate a small number of items. We then interpret these ratings in an innovative way, using them to guide a Bayesian updating process that helps us both capture a user's current mood, and maintain her overall user type. We produced several variants of our approach, and applied them in the movie recommendations domain, evaluating them on data from the MovieLens dataset. Our algorithms are shown to be competitive against a state-of-the-art method, which nevertheless requires a minimum set of ratings from various users to provide recommendations—unlike our entirely personalized approach.

Categories and Subject Descriptors

H.3.3 [**Information Storage and Retrieval**]: Information Search and Retrieval—*Information Filtering*

Keywords

Bayesian methods; personalized recommendations

1. INTRODUCTION AND RELATED WORK

Making decisions on what movie to see, what kind of music to listen to, or what book to read can be a hard problem when one is presented with a multitude of choices. Research in recommendation systems attempts to understand a user's needs, preferences and mood, and help her make a decision. Typically, however, most recommendation methods require pre-training on data gathered from many users, who are classified according to their inferred similarity in preferences. Moreover, many approaches require much user involvement in a potentially cumbersome, lengthy interaction with the system. This can impose serious limitations to the usability of a recommendation system, especially when a user wishes to make a fast decision that is also dependent on her current mood.

In more detail, most established recommendation systems exploit user ratings over a large number of items via the use of *collaborative filtering (CF)*, *content-based* methods, or a combination thereof. *Content-based methods* usually make recommendations by analyzing the content of textual information about an item. On the other hand, *collaborative filtering* is based on the assumption that, if two users rate n items similarly, they will probably rate other items similarly as well. So, collaborative filtering techniques use ratings from a specific user on some items (e.g., movies), and combine them with ratings of other users on a set of items in order to infer about the ratings of that user on unrated items.

Some examples of CF and content-based systems are those of [2, 18, 9, 25]. Many such systems find application in the movie recommendations domain. For instance, *Content-Boosted Collaborating Filtering* [18] uses a content-based predictor, enhanced with CF, to provide personalized movie recommendations; Debnath *et al.* [9] use a *collaborative social network graph* to assign weights on attributes of content-based recommendations, depending on their perceived importance; while Barbieri *et al.* [2] intertwine Bayesian methods with CF, in order to group users into "communities" based on their rating patterns. Another interesting application of CF methods is introduced in [25], which presents an interactive story generation system that employs *probabilistic principle component analysis* and *non-negative matrix factorization*, in order to compose a personalized story according to user storytelling preferences.

Now, utility theory-inspired *preference elicitation (PE)* techniques have also been tried out in various recommendation domains (see, e.g., [6, 23]). PE tries to collect user preferences in order to construct the user's *utility function*. To do so, most Preference Elicitation techniques set queries to the user asking her to evaluate, order, or constrain potential system outcomes; while others attempt to translate a user's interaction with the system to preferences. There also exist systems which use *semantics* and *social choice* or *voting theory* for making recommendations [24, 19, 12, 17]. For instance, Szomszor *et al.* [24] use movies *folksonomy* to enrich the current knowledge with descriptions of movies and interests of users; while [12] presents a website which uses *trust* in *social networks* for making movie recommendations. The website generates predictive personalized ratings based on a *trust inference algorithm*, which employs "trusted users" ratings in order to calculate the rating of a user for that movie. Others employ *WWW questionnaires* and *Bayesian networks* to model the collected data [22].

The work most relevant to ours is perhaps that of [16] and [26], which model users and items using a common representation. Both approaches use vectors for modelling purposes. In some detail, Langseth and Nielsen [16] propose a CF technique which uses a

RecSys '13, October 12 - 16 2013, Hong Kong, China
Copyright 2013 ACM 978-1-4503-2409-0/13/09 ... $15.00.
http://dx.doi.org/10.1145/2507157.2507158.

Bayesian network to support the inference procedure. They model items using *feature vectors*, and users using vectors which describe user's liking for each item feature. These vectors are incorporated in the Bayesian network in order to predict user's ratings about unrated items using her previous ratings on other items. On the other hand, Zhang and Koren [26] introduce a Bayesian hierarchical model for content-based recommendations. They model each user as a *k-dimensional vector* sampled randomly from a Gaussian distribution, and items as k-dimensional *feature vectors*. They then incorporate data *from all users* in the hierarchical model in order *to predict a label-rating* of an item for a specific user.

The recommendation technique we present in this paper differs to all aforementioned approaches in many ways. First of all, we neither set questions to the user, nor use textual information regarding an item so as to elicit user preferences. Moreover, we do not rely on any kind of user classification or other users' inferred preferences, but attempt to fine-tune recommendations over time for each specific individual. That is, we progressively build a user type for each individual, which gradually converges to the real one. In contrast to most social networks, social choice-inspired, and CF approaches, we *do not* attempt to estimate user ratings; but just recommend the item which matches the user preferences more closely.

Approach Overview and Contributions.

Indeed, in this paper we design and evaluate a *Bayesian recommendation agent,* based on a *simple, fast,* and *easy-to-use* elicitation and modelling process; and apply it in the movie recommendations domain. By means of this process, our agent is able to recommend a user items (e.g., movies) that best fit *both* her long-time preferences and current mood. To achieve its objective, the agent maintains *item types* (summarizing item characteristics); and *user types* (corresponding to modeled user preferences). Crucially, these are *both* represented as *multivariate Gaussian distributions* over ranges of values (ratings), describing the degree to which an item is composed of certain attributes (e.g., movie genres); and the degree to which a user likes the particular attributes, respectively. This allows for the establishment of a correspondence between user and item types: *intuitively, a user model is viewed by the agent as being an amalgamation of items this user likes.* We term this the *"you are what you consume"* idea. The employment of *Normal-Inverse Wishart (NIW)* conjugate priors to model agent beliefs about types guarantees that these beliefs can be readily updated.

Now, to learn about a specific user's current mood, we first *only* ask her to rate a small number of *demonstrative items* (*"demos"* for short; e.g., movie trailers), also represented by multivariate Gaussians (just like other items), and which are selected based on the current agent beliefs about user type. Each rating is treated as a unit, that is, we do not ask the user to rate different item attributes. We then employ these ratings in an innovative way, interpreting them as an indication of the *number of samples* to take from the corresponding demo type; i.e., to indicate a demo's "weight", or, to put otherwise, the "degree of correspondence" that the specific demo has with user preferences and current mood. This is reasonable, as a user's rating of, e.g., trailers, intuitively reflects her current mood—which is, nevertheless, not independent of her long-term tastes. The agent takes this into account: each demo presented was already selected according to perceived *user type*—thus, long-term user preferences *are* incorporated in the choice of demos.

The samples thus collected are then utilized by a Bayesian updating process that infers a *temporary demo-based user type,* given demo ratings. Having the demo-based type, we can then search for the best possible match (employing a *KL-divergence* metric) with an *item* to actually recommend—and which is *not* necessarily one of the demos shown earlier. The selected item is then presented to the user, who *rates* it, leading to an update of her overall *user type.*

The overall recommendation process effectively corresponds to a *Bayesian exploration* approach in this domain—since, when selecting demos or items to present to the user, our method optimises with respect to Bayes-updated beliefs, rather than taking explicit "exploration" actions. Moreover, intuitively our method allows for a better user experience, and implicitly helps the user "discover" more about her own real preferences, as it does not rigidly disallow suggestion possibilities or prune vast parts of the search space (as methods relying on explicit user statements about their preferences or ratings probably would), but only makes suggestions given its probabilistic beliefs regarding user preferences. For interest, we devised and tested certain additional *variants* of our approach, which employ alternative (Bayesian and non-Bayesian) exploration methods when selecting a demo or item to present to the user. One of these variants most probably constitutes the first adaptation of the well-known *Value of Perfect Information* Bayesian exploration heuristic [8, 7] in the recommendations domain.

Though to some extent conceptually straightforward, to the best of our knowledge an approach such as ours has not been used before in the literature. It is a *simple* yet *generic* approach that combines elements from various techniques. The idea of modelling the types of *both* the user and the object under recommendation *by a probability distribution of the same form* is a novel one. Representing users and items as *complete probability distributions* over a collection of features, instead of as, e.g., vectors of point-values corresponding to specific features' weights, enables the implicit inference of *latent* features, or *hidden and otherwise unrepresentable feature mixtures, combinations, and interconnections.* Moreover, our translation of "demo" ratings into weights for guiding the sampling process used during Bayesian updating is innovative, and allows us to build a *temporary user type* that captures both current user mood and long-time preferences simultaneously.

We evaluated our approach in the movie recommendations domain. As a note, the use of Multivariate Gaussians and Normal-Inverse Wishart distributions to model types and corresponding beliefs in this particular domain is novel, as is the use of "trailer" ratings for inference purposes. Our experimental results are highly encouraging, demonstrating as they do that the agent quickly learns to recommend movies that receive high user ratings. In particular, our agent manages to exhibit performance that is comparable to that of a popular, state-of-the-art, collaborative filtering-based method for movie recommendations. Importantly, it does so without the need of looking at pre-gathered/pre-processed data involving the current user or her peers. As such, the ever-present "cold start" problem, a constant challenge to CF methods due to ratings scarcity (see, e.g., [3] for a discussion), does not apply to our personalized method—since it does not employ any ratings of other users whatsoever, and does not aggregate past ratings to predict future ones.

2. BACKGROUND: BAYESIAN UPDATING

A key component of our agent is performing probabilistic inference regarding the types of the system's users, by means of *Bayesian updating*. In many cases, there exists the need of estimating the parameters of an unknown probability distribution—a *model*; and Bayesian updating can be employed to this end. Key to a computationally feasible application of Bayesian updating, is the use of *Bayes rule*, in conjunction with proper *conjugate priors* describing our beliefs about the model [10].

In some detail, in the face of new data (observations) regarding the unknown model, Bayes rule takes into account a *prior* distribution (reflecting our belief on the values of the model's parameters), a *likelihood function*, and a marginal probability, in order to derive a *posterior*. The likelihood function brings together the prior and the observations and follows the form of the model. The posterior represents an updated *belief* about the prior, taking into account the new data. One can then use these posterior beliefs to derive new estimates of the parameters of the unknown distribution.

Both prior and posterior distributions must be of the same family–i.e., they must have the same algebraic form. If that is the case, they are termed *conjugate distributions*. Additionally, the family of the *likelihood function* gives rise to the choice of the prior's family. If the prior is appropriately selected to be *conjugate* for the *likelihood*, then the posterior will be of the same family as the prior [11]. *Conjugacy* offers a closed form for the posterior, allowing for the easy update of the prior—via straightforward manipulations of the prior's *hyperparameters* in the face of new evidence.

In our case, the data provided to the agent is in the form of a multivariate Gaussian, corresponding to *demo* or *item types*. We also need to maintain the *demo-based user type* or the overall *user type*, which will also be multivariate Gaussians. Since we are not aware of the underlying type parameters—determining its *mean* and *covariance matrix*—we can model the *conjugate prior* as a *Normal-Inverse Wishart* distribution *(NIW)* [20, 1]. We can then readily update the *prior* hyperparameters using samples drawn from the data[1] to get the *posterior* ones:

$$\mu_n = \frac{\kappa_0}{\kappa_0 + n}\mu_0 + \frac{n}{\kappa_0 + n}\overline{x} \quad (1)$$

$$\kappa_n = \kappa_0 + n \quad (2)$$

$$\nu_n = \nu_0 + n \quad (3)$$

$$\Lambda_n = \Lambda_0 + S + \frac{\kappa_0 n}{\kappa_0 + n}(\overline{x} - \mu_0)(\overline{x} - \mu_0)^T \quad (4)$$

$$S = \sum_{i=1}^{n}(x_i - \overline{x})(x_i - \overline{x})^T \quad (5)$$

where $\overline{x}$ is the sample mean, *n* is the number of the samples and x_i are the samples from the data. Also, $\mu_0, \kappa_0, \nu_0, \Lambda_0$ are the known hyperparameters of the prior NIW distribution. Specifically, ν_0 represents its *degrees of freedom*, while μ_0 (the *mean vector*) and Λ_0 (the *precision matrix*) are the hyperparameters that specify the multivariate Gaussian component of the prior; and *S* is a *scatter matrix*, a statistic characterizing the model's covariance matrix and intuitively providing a measure of the samples' dispersion. Finally, the model's parameters, *mean* (μ) and *covariance matrix* (Σ), can be calculated ("integrated-out") given the updated beliefs, using an *Inverse Wishart* and a *Gaussian* as follows.

$$\Sigma \sim IW(\Lambda_n, \nu_n) \quad (6)$$

$$\mu \mid \Sigma \sim N(\mu_n, \Sigma/\kappa_n) \quad (7)$$

3. RECOMMENDATION PROCESS

We have already described the main intuitions and key ideas of our approach in Section 1 above. Here, we provide a more detailed picture of our system's architecture and overall recommendation process, also summarized in Figure 1(a).

When a user enters the system, she is shown and asked to rate a number of 5 demos.[2] The agent decides which demos to show based on its knowledge about the user—i.e., the stored *user type*. Thus, it presents demos that most closely match her preferences, as these have been embodied in the *user type* so far. In the case of *a new user*, the agent again shows 5 demos, but now those have few common features, since they are—out of necessity—selected randomly (as the long-term *user type* is first constructed after the user rates some *item*). Then, the user provides a rating for each demo, and a *Bayesian updating* process is used to create the *demo-based user type* from rated demo items.

Bayesian updating actually takes place two times during the recommendation process, firstly to infer a *temporary, demo-based user type*; and, secondly, to update the overall *user type*. The process takes into account user ratings regarding demos or items shown to the user, and, given the ratings, samples the respective *demo* or *item types* the appropriate number of times; and uses these samples to come up with an (updated) system-inferred type regarding the user. This can be done given the fact that the user type ("demo-based" or not) *is of the same form as the items' type*, and via the proper use of conjugate NIW priors. The intuition is that, in the absence of *explicit* data regarding the *user type* (which is the model whose parameters we need to infer), we utilize user ratings as an *implicit* way to indicate the extent to which a user "associates" herself with the demo or item she is shown. Thus, we can then sample the model this item (e.g., a trailer or a movie) originates from a number of times (proportional to the degree of the user's liking of that item), and treat these samples as new evidence for the Bayesian updating process. It is important to note that, to ensure the efficiency of the update, the number of samples must be high enough. To achieve this, we multiply the *rating* with 100, thus guaranteeing that hundreds of samples are used during an update.[3]

In more detail, the user observes and rates the first demo item (e.g., watches and rates the first trailer). Then, the system takes *rating*×100 samples from the *demo type* distribution of that demo item, and updates the posterior's *hyperparameters* based on those *samples* and the *hyperparameters* of the *demo-based user type* prior (which has to be an *uninformative* one [20]). Subsequently, the user watches and rates the second demo and the system samples that *demo type* and updates the *hyperparameters*, in the same way as for the first one—but now the posterior of the first step has become the *informative* prior of the second step. After all such steps, the *hyperparameters* of the NIW distribution can be used to estimate the parameters (μ, Σ) of the multivariate Gaussian, which models the *demo-based user type*. Figure 1(b) summarizes this process.

Now, when the system has the final estimate of the *demo-based user type*, it has to recommend a specific item to the user. To do so, it must search the database to find the item matching that *demo-based user type* best. To this end, it uses the *Kullback-Leibler (KL) Divergence* criterion. The *KL-divergence* between a Gaussian t (modelling, e.g., a demo-based user type), and a Gaussian i (corresponding to some item), of dimension d each, is given by:

$$KL(t \parallel i) = \frac{1}{2}\log \mid S_t^{-1}S_i \mid + \frac{1}{2}tr((S_t^{-1}S_i)^{-1}) - \frac{d}{2} + \frac{1}{2}(m_t - m_i)^T S_i^{-1}(m_t - m_i) \quad (8)$$

[1] In our case, we will be utilizing user ratings to determine the number of samples to draw from different data distributions.

[2] The number of projected trailers (demos) used in our experiments is "5", as a tradeoff between receiving enough information for accurate inference of user preferences, and avoiding user distraction and frustration [14, 15]. Of course, when testing the agent with actual human subjects in real time, the number of trailers shown and their length will definitely have to be adjusted according to the users' reaction and perceived frustration levels. However, our main objective here is to evaluate the potential of our novel Bayesian user modelling method. Thus, while adjusting for specific real-time usage concerns in a given domain is important, current parameter choices are adequate for confirming the soundness of this approach.

[3] Taking a *rating*×100 number of samples ensures that each *given* demo or item type is *represented* accurately enough to be combined with prior information regarding the user (who is also represented as a Gaussian) to estimate a user type via Bayesian updating. This is not an attempt to "estimate" a demo or item type via sampling.

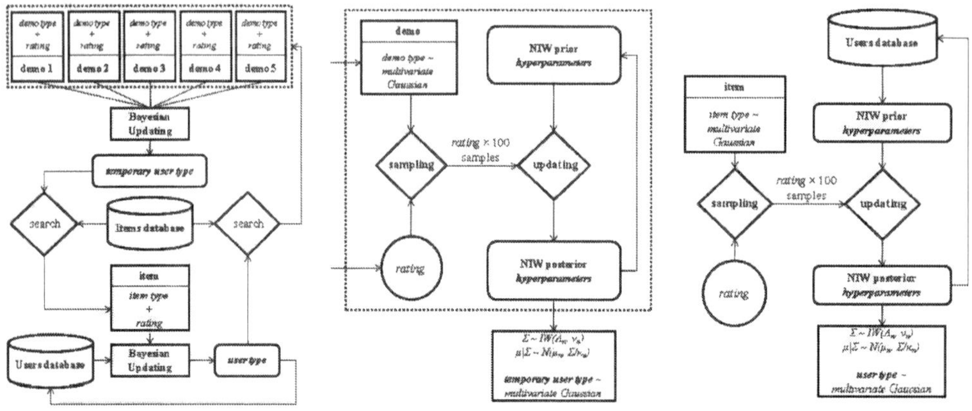

(a) (b) (c)

Figure 1: (a) The overall recommendation process. (b) Deriving the *demo-based user type*. (c) Deriving the *user type*.

where S_t, m_t, S_i and m_i are the distributions' parameters, and $tr(\cdot)$ is the *trace* of the corresponding matrix [21]. The lower the *KL-divergence* between two Gaussian types, the greater their proximity. This is the item (e.g., the movie) recommended to the user. Notice that this *might not* be one of the demos shown to the user before recommendation. This effectively corresponds to a *Bayesian* rather than a heuristic exploration approach in this domain: the system employs its probabilistic beliefs regarding (long-term) *user type* and (short-term) *temporary user type* to come up with a recommendation; and makes recommendations based on beliefs given sampled evidence, rather than, e.g., greedily matching a demo.

Subsequently, the user puts a rating on the item (after, e.g., watching the movie). Then, the system performs another Bayesian update, resulting to a new *user type* estimate. The Bayesian updating of the *user type* is similar to the *demo-based* one; but now the *rating*$\times 100$ samples collected are drawn from the distribution corresponding to the item the user was finally recommended and rated *only* (Figure 1(c)). Note that *user type* and corresponding beliefs are stored for future use, unlike the *demo-based user type* which lasts only for the current session. Thus, in the case of a future system use by a known user, the hyperparameters of the posterior from which the previous *user type* was inferred, will be the hyperparameters of the *(informative)* prior for deriving the next *user type*. Moreover, as stated, the updated and stored *user type* serves as a prior to guide the system to select demos. This is also done via using the *KL-divergence* minimization criterion.

3.1 Alternative action selection methods

The "basic" Bayesian method described above behaves "greedily" wrt. beliefs when selecting a demo or item: it just picks the one with minimum KL-divergence from the Bayes-updated user type. We also devised alternative *action exploration* techniques, to assess whether these would lead to improved recommendation decisions.

3.1.1 VPI-based selection of demos or items

The first of these techniques attempts to account for the expected *value of perfect information (VPI)* [7] characterizing the various "agent actions"—i.e., in this domain, potential recommendation choices. The rationale behind this technique is that a choice has a value not only because of its immediate benefit to the user, but also because of the information it relays with respect to user preferences. Intuitively, if a recommendation and observed user reaction leads to a reassessment of what the user really prefers, then this recommendation action carries a high information value. Thus, the *VPI exploration* technique, adapted for the recommendation domain, attempts to "simulate" various *alternative* user type reactions to future recommendations; calculates the value of information gained from these reactions when compared to the thus far modeled user type's expected behaviour; and averages out these results to come up with an *information gain estimate* that is used to "boost the desirability" of the recommendations to be made.

In more detail, let us suppose that the reward that some user derives from a specific item is $reward = f(KL\,divergence) = M - \lfloor KL\,divergence/M \rfloor$, where M is the maximum rating the user can give to a movie (e.g., $M = 10$). We define as i_1 the item with the highest reward r_1 for the user (given the model built for her so far), and as i_2 the second best with reward r_2. Consider now an item i selected for recommendation to a user type j (possibly different to the type modeled for the user so far), and assume that this in fact represents the "actual" type for the user—therefore, presenting this user type j with an item will lead to "perfect information" regarding the value of this item to the user. (Of course, this is just an assumption the method makes, but allows it to compute a value of information estimate, via "sampling" user types and averaging out their behaviour.) Assume that this recommendation results to a user reward of r_i for item i. We distinguish the following two cases (in all other cases, the gain due to perfect information is 0):

1. if i coincides with the item considered best for the user so far ($i = i_1$), then the *gain* from presenting the user with this item is either: *(a)* $\text{gain}_i^j = 0$, for $r_i > r_1$ (since we derived no new information from presenting the user with this item: the "perfect" information we got by fixing the user type to the assumed "actual" user type j coincides with what we had already estimated—i.e., that i_1 is the "best" item for the user); or *(b)* $\text{gain}_i^j = r_2 - r_i$, for $r_i < r_2$ (since we "learned" that the item i is actually worth less to the user than the item considered so far to be only second-best).

2. if i does not coincide with i_1, then the *gain* from presenting j with i is *(a)* $\text{gain}_i^j = 0$, for $r_i < r_1$ (since we only observed i to be sub-optimal, as expected); or *(b)* $gain_i^j = r_i - r_1$, for $r_i > r_1$ (since we now "learned" that i was actually better than the item considered best so far).

Given this, our *VPI exploration* method works as follows: We estimate the modeled-so-far *user type*[4] by "integrating out" our NIW

[4]This can be a long-term or a short-term user type, depending on whether we are attempting to select demos or actual items.

prior, as described in Section 2 (Eqs 6 & 7). Subsequently, for this integrated-out user type, we discover the i_1 item with the highest reward, and the second-best item i_2. We then sample from our NIW prior a number of s Gaussians, which represent "alternative" user types. (In our experiments, we set s=10.) After that, we calculate for each j user type (corresponding to one of the s sampled Gaussians), the rewards from presenting it with every i item, and compute the corresponding gain_i^j values, as outlined above.

The next step is the calculation of the *average gain*, $\overline{\text{gain}_i}$, for presenting an item i to our user; this is computed by averaging out, over all s samples (i.e., over all user types j sampled), the gain_i^j gains estimated for this item. Finally, the *VPI* method selects (and presents) the item I that maximizes the sum of the integrated-out user type's reward and the corresponding gain from selecting I:

$$I = \arg\max_i \{V_i = reward_i + \overline{\text{gain}_i}\} \quad (9)$$

3.1.2 Boltzmann selection

We also tried the well-known *Boltzmann exploration* [5] method to select the appropriate demo or item. At each time step t, it assigns a selection probability to all available i actions:

$$Pr(i) = \frac{e^{U_i/T}}{\Sigma_{j=1}^{n} e^{U_i/T}} \quad (10)$$

where $T = c \cdot \alpha^t$, with c a constant and $\alpha < 1$. An action i is chosen with probability proportional to its utility U_i; and with T decreasing over time, exploration is progressively reduced.

We tried Boltzmann selection with two different utility functions in our experiments. The first of these methods, simply called *Boltzmann*, employs a U function equal to the KL-divergence between the user type and the items. The second one uses as U the metric of the VPI method described above, i.e., sets $U_i = V_i$, where V_i is the quantity in Eq. 9. We call this method *Boltzmann-VPI*.

4. APPLICATION TO THE MOVIES DOMAIN

We chose to apply our method to movie recommendations, an important domain that has inspired much research in recommendation systems. Here, *items* correspond to *movies*; *demos* correspond to *movie trailers*; and we use the term *trailer-based user type* to refer to a *demo-based user type*.

Each *movie type* is modeled as a *multivariate Gaussian*, with each of its variables corresponding to a movie genre. The probabilities are distributed over ratings, which are provided in some scale of choice (e.g., $1-10$ or $1-5$). To create these multivariate Gaussians, we were inspired from the *MovieLens* (http://www.grouplens.org) datasets, which are actually used in our experiments below. These datasets comprise of ratings provided by thousands of users on thousands of movies. In the *MovieLens* dataset containing 1 *million* ratings, movies are characterized by 18 specific genres. We therefore define *movie types* to be *k-dimensional Gaussians*, with $k = 18$ in our experiments involving real MovieLens ratings.

Let us now describe the exact form (and attribute values) of such a Gaussian representing a movie or a trailer. The *mean* is essentially determined by the overall rating of that movie, so it is a $1 \times k$ vector which, on each dimension, contains values equal to that movie's rating—under the assumption that the movie rating corresponds to every genre available. Of course, one cannot be certain about the rating of a genre not associated with the movie, but this is taken care of by the way we construct the covariance matrix. Specifically, a movie's $k \times k$ covariance matrix is constructed as a *diagonal covariance matrix* [4], assuming that the movie genres are independent of each other. Each element on the diagonal is associated to a genre, and the element's value depends on whether the movie is characterized by that genre or not. We assume that the uncertainty about the rating of the actual genres of the movie is small, and thus set the values of the corresponding elements to $\sigma^2 = 1$. In contrast, uncertainty about those genres *not* associated to the movie is naturally *high*, and thus we assign a σ^2=20 (an empirically chosen value that is high enough so as to not "disturb" the distribution) to those diagonal elements. As an example, consider the movie 'Movie' with an overall rating of 7, whose genres are *action, sci-fi, thriller*. Its type is the following. The mean vector's entries all carry a value of 7; while its covariance matrix is a diagonal one, with diagonal entries corresponding to the *action, sci-fi and thriller* variables having a value of 1, and all other (diagonal) entries having the value of 20. The Gaussians for the *user* and *trailer-based user* types have the same form as that of movies (i.e., k-dimensional Gaussians).

In addition, the agent needs to store and update beliefs about user's types (*trailer-based* and overall). As mentioned, these beliefs take the form of Normal-Inverse Wishart priors, which can be easily manipulated to infer the corresponding types as k-dimensional Gaussians, and match them to movies as required by the system.

5. EXPERIMENTS

We ran several sets of experiments to validate our algorithm, which we call *BayesYouLikeIt*, and its variants, with very encouraging results. In all experiments, the *hyperparameters* of an uninformative NIW prior take the following values: $\kappa_0 = 0, \nu_0 = -1, |\Lambda_0| = 0$. Thus, the *updated hyperparameters* of the NIW posterior after observing n samples become: $\mu_n = \overline{x}, \kappa_n = n, \nu_n = n-1, \Lambda_n = S = \sum_{i=1}^{n}(x_i - \overline{x})(x_i - \overline{x})^T$.

Now, to test the scalability of our technique, we initially ran experiments with *simulated* users on databases with *10,000*, *20,000*, and *40,000* randomly generated movies. Simulated movies' representation and ratings were based on those of the popular *IMDB* website (http://www.imdb.com). Specifically, we defined *movie types* to be 16-dimensional Gaussians, corresponding to the 16 most common genres available in *IMDB*. Also, we generated 50 simulated users that interact with the system. Each simulated user is characterized by its *real user type*, a 16-dimensional Gaussian distribution with a random mean in the range of $[1-10]$ on each dimension, corresponding to *IMDB* ratings, and a covariance matrix which is *spherical*, assuming that the *real user type* is confident regarding the degree to which it likes each genre [4].

To avoid the exhaustive search for trailers and movies within these large databases, we apply clustering methods on the set of stored movies. This reduces the number of comparisons between a *user type* and stored *movie types*. In our experiments, the movies were clustered in clusters with 1,000 movies each, on average (e.g., 20,000 movies clustered into 20 clusters), based on their similarity using the *Kullback-Leibler hard k-means*, a variation of the *Bregman hard k-means* clustering [21].[5] We also had to create a *rating function*, to be used by the simulated users to assign ratings. The function exploits the *KL divergence* between the *real user type* and each *trailer type* or *movie type* of movies in our system—the less the divergence, the higher the rating: $rating = f(KL\,divergence) = 10 - \lfloor KL\,divergence/10 \rfloor$ (where $0 < KL\,divergence < 100$).

In Figure 2, we can see that *BayesYouLikeIt* recommends movies that constantly receive high ($> 8/10$) ratings, when tested on the *20,000* simulated movies database. The experimental results for the *10,000* and *40,000* movie databases are of the same quality. We

[5]Note that after a few hundreds of recommendations leading to movies being removed from their clusters, the need for reclustering arises. This is not a problem, as it can be executed off-line.

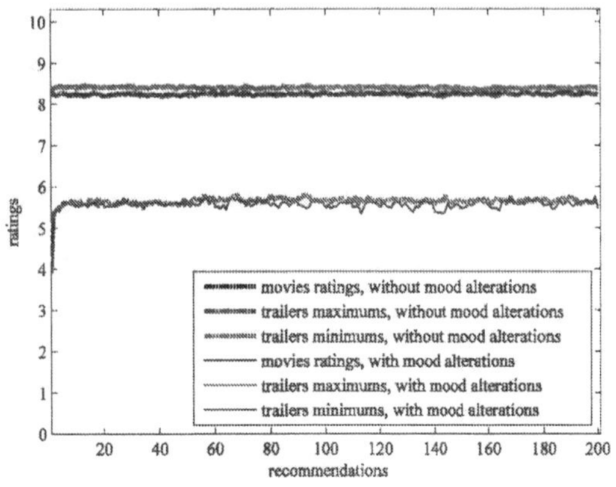

Figure 2: Comparison of *average per iteration ratings* from 50 *simulated* users on 200 movies for 10 runs, and *average range of corresponding trailer ratings*, with and without mood alterations simulation.

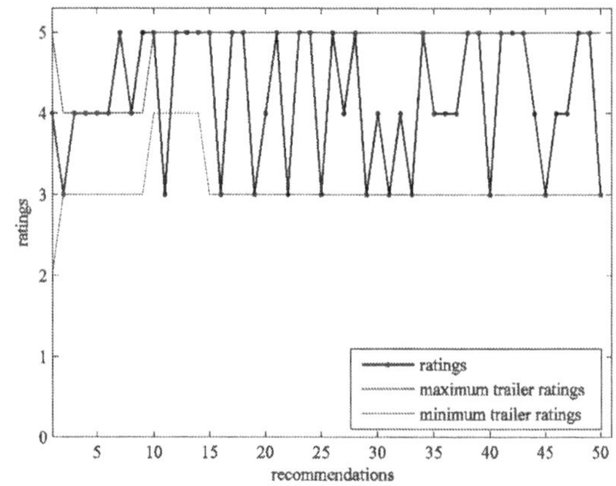

Figure 3: Typical run ratings of a *single, real* user on 50 movies, and *range* of corresponding trailer ratings.

also observe that, in an average iteration, the user is shown trailers whose ratings range is about 3 degrees wide; and whose average *maximum* rating is *almost always* higher than the (average) rating received for the movie shown during that iteration. This is because Bayesian exploration: *(1)* does not *necessarily* return a movie that matches the best trailer shown in an iteration; while, at any given iteration, there are still on average many "good" movies whose trailer the method can show; and *(2)* enables the system to actually project trailers of *movies already shown* at any iteration, and thus trailers of "preferred" movies might be shown to a user again—since these are just used to detect the *current mood* of the user. At no point is a *movie* already shown to the user actually recommended again; however, *BayesYouLikeIt* might re-use *trailers* derived from the "believed" user type to infer the *temporary* user type (though in practice this will occur only rarely in a large database).

We also evaluated the ability of our agent to capture temporary changes of a user's *mood*. We simulate such mood changes by periodically changing the mean values of the *"real user type"*'s multivariate Gaussian distribution (which represent the preferences of the assumed "real" user). Specifically, after every 10 recommendations, we randomly change the mean of each variable of the corresponding Gaussian (via sampling a normal distribution over the range of $[1-10]$). The "mood changes" last only for 5 recommendations, and then the real user type returns to its original form. Figure 2 confirms that our method is able to successfully capture the user's mood, since it constantly recommends movies that are subsequently rated highly. Indeed, our method's performance appears to be robust, and is not negatively affected by mood changes.

Following that, we ran experiments to test our agent on data coming from *real users*, that reflect actual human preferences and behaviour. This kind of data also offer an ideal testbed for comparison with other well known techniques. We used the *MovieLens* dataset with *1 million ratings* from *6,040* users on *3,952* movies. Thus, there is no longer a need to generate simulated users and ratings: we can now have a user's rating on a movie (or trailer) by just referring to the real-world dataset.[6] No clustering was used in these experiments. The movies inside the system's database are modeled as in Section 4, with a movie's *mean* being the average rating it has in the MovieLens dataset. Ratings are integers in $[1-5]$.

We executed different sets of experiments with *200 recommendations each*, using all aforementioned *variants* for trailer/movie selection. For each such experiment, we employed *5 sets* of *100 users* each, consisting of real users with *200 or more* ratings in the MovieLens dataset. In some detail, we took the histogram of the number of ratings per user in the MovieLens dataset, and sampled 100 different users for each experimental user set in accordance to that distribution. This ensures there is no bias in the ratings used as input in the experiments. Also, each experiment involving a specific user set was executed for *10 independent runs*. We then sequentially produced 200 recommendations to each individual user; and calculated the *average per iteration (true) ratings* assigned by the real users, across all user sets and experimental runs.

Now, as explained in Section 3, *BayesYouLikeIt* progressively builds the *user type*, and recommends the movie that best matches the *trailer-based user type* at each iteration—or the one selected according to some variant exploration criterion. Indeed, in addition to the "basic" *BayesYouLikeIt (BYLI)* algorithm, we ran experiments exploiting the VPI and Boltzmann exploration methods described in Section 3.1. We used these criteria in two different ways. First, we employed them only during the trailer selection phase of the algorithm; and second, during both the trailers and the movie selection phases. Boltzmann exploration parameters were set to: $c = 1, \alpha = 0.5$ and $t \leq 3$, with $t_0 = 0$ and $t_{i+1} = t_i + 1$.

We compare our algorithm with an established recommender engine, built on the *Apache Mahout* machine learning library, adapted to yield the *Myrrix* software.[7] The algorithm used by the engine is the *large, sparse matrix factorization (LSMF)* method [13, 27], implemented using a modified version of the *alternating least squares (ALS)* algorithm. LSMF requires a number of ratings to be entered in the system, so that matrix factorization can be performed.

Figure 3 helps us gain further insights in *BayesYouLikeIt* behaviour when recommending movies to a single (real) user. We can see in the figure that, while learning, *BayesYouLikeIt* might occasionally recommend a movie which the user ranks *lower* than the trailers projected to her during that iteration; however, some times the algorithm might also recommend a movie that the user prefers to all trailers shown to her during that iteration. Over time, *BayesYouLikeIt* returns movies that receive consistently good ratings.

[6] We remark that since we care about best "online" user experience and *do not* predict ratings, the use of comparison metrics like *Root Mean Square Error (RMSE)* is not very meaningful here. Instead, we compare the methods wrt. average per recommendation ratings.

[7] http://mahout.apache.org; http://www.myrrix.com/design

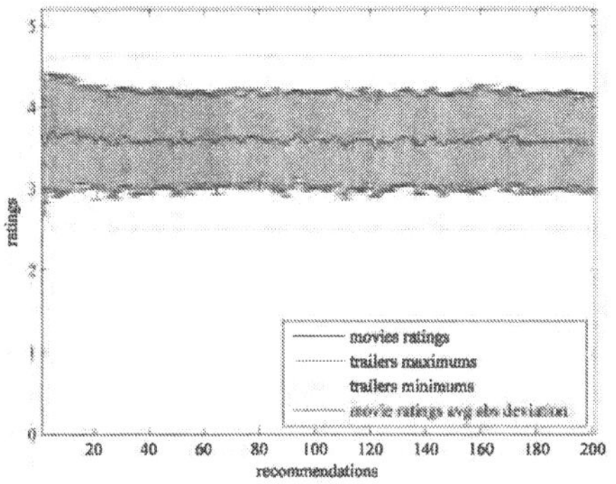

Figure 4: *Average per iteration ratings*, *average range* of corresponding trailer ratings and *movie ratings average mean absolute deviation* for *BYLI - Boltzmann-VPI on trailers & movies*.

Methods	Average ratings
LSMF - pretrained	3.6848
LSMF - untrained	3.6540
BayesYouLikeIt (BYLI)	3.6112
BYLI - VPI on trailers	3.5968
BYLI - VPI on trailers & movies	3.5911
BYLI - Boltzmann-VPI on trailers	3.5968
BYLI - Boltzmann-VPI on trailers & movies	3.5911
BYLI - Boltzmann on trailers	3.5920
BYLI - Boltzmann on trailers & movies	3.5592

Table 1: Comparison of average ratings of all methods (across all user sets, iterations and experimental runs).

This fact is confirmed by the *average per iteration ratings* results of Figs. 4 and 5. Fig. 4 shows that *BayesYouLikeIt* manages to recommend movies that are on average highly rated by the users.[8] Moreover, average ratings deviation can be observed to decrease over time, demonstrating an ability to "learn" and progressively become more confident on its assessment of users' preferences. We note that the over time decrease in ratings average absolute deviation is a bit sharper for the variants using *VPI* (or *Boltzmann-VPI*) on both trailers and movies. This figure also shows the (average) maximum and minimum trailer ratings received by users (per iteration). Maximum trailer ratings are consistently higher than ratings received for movies recommended, for the same reasons as in the experiments with simulated users above.

In Fig. 5(a), we observe that the VPI and Boltzmann exploration methods (and their combinations) are successfully intertwined with our "basic" Bayesian algorithm, since all *BYLI* variants return recommendations that receive consistently high ratings from the users. Average ratings across all iterations, depicted in Table 1, confirm that all *BYLI* variants perform very similarly, with the "pure" *BYLI* method achieving a slightly better average score than the rest. However, *BYLI - VPI on trailers* provides an advantage when it comes to sequential behavior (notice that on average it provides better recommendations at the initial steps). When Boltzmann is combined with VPI, VPI is the defining component, and thus *Boltzmann-VPI* and *VPI* exhibit identical behavior.

Fig. 5(b) then compares our method to *LSMF*. Note that *LSMF* was tested under two assumptions in these experiments. First, on the assumption that it is completely unaware of *any* user preferences at system start (this is marked as *"LSMF-untrained"* in the figures); and on the assumption that the system is *pre-trained* on ratings data from all other (i.e., the $6,040 - 100 = 5,940$ non-picked) users in the database (*"LSMF-pretrained"*). These results clearly demonstrate that *(a)* the average user ratings value of *BayesYouLikeIt*-recommendations is about $3.5 - 3.7$ (out of 5); and *(b)* although our method does not depend on other users' ratings in order to recommend movies to a user, ratings received are almost indistinguishable in average quality to those received when using the *LSMF* technique. Moreover, we can observe that, *LSMF* being a CF method, it has to first collect a small number of ratings from users in order to be able to return good recommendations, and thus cannot respond to a user request in a meaningful manner during the very first iteration. This is clearly visible in Fig. 5(c). In contrast, our personalised method can *immediately* suggest a good movie to a user. After the very first iterations, *LSMF* is able to exploit knowledge of "similar" users ratings and performs strongly—but as the number of "preferred" movies drops (since our dataset contains a "closed set" of movies), its performance drops (Fig. 5(b)). *BayesYouLikeIt* does not start as strong, but due to progressively converging to real user types, its performance is quite *stable* throughout all recommendations. As a final remark, running on MATLAB on a 2.20 GHz / 4 GB RAM PC, it takes a *BayesYouLikeIt* agent only about 0.3 sec on average to recommend a movie to a user.

6. CONCLUSIONS AND FUTURE WORK

In this paper, we presented a novel approach for making entirely personalized recommendations, and applied it in the movie recommendations domain. Our approach uses Bayesian updating to infer a *user model*, which is *a distribution of the same form* with the models of the items under recommendation. This is, we believe, key to enabling the implicit inference of an individual's latent or otherwise unrepresentable, complicated preferences; and enables us to devise and employ a kind of *Bayesian exploration* in this domain. We presented and tested several variants of our method, and evaluated their performance, with very promising results. In a sense, what we exploit in this work is the fact that modern-world data sets contain much "annotated" information regarding the nature of contained data (e.g., in the form of "genre"-specifying labels). This information allows us to properly define the dimensions of multivariate Gaussians representing users (according to our "you are what you consume" idea), without relying on the tastes of others—and without attempting to explicitly predict user ratings.

We remark that our method is generic, and not "fine-tuned" for movie recommendations. Nonetheless, our *personalized* method's performance almost matches that of a state-of-the-art movie recommendations method, which is able to exploit preference data originating from thousands of users. As our method proves to be competitive against algorithms that do have this "advantage", it is most probably especially well-suited for environments where user preferences data is scarse. In sparse datasets, our approach is expected to perform better than methods which require other users' ratings. Therefore, it could be used as a "bootstrapping" tool, generating recommendations until more data is available; moreover, it can be readily employed as a "training" component used during a more sophisticated system's initial operation period.

Regarding future work, we plan to conduct a user satisfaction survey, based on a number of users testing our system. We also intend to run experiments on larger movie datasets, and perform a more thorough evaluation of the *BayesYouLikeIt* variants. It is also worth testing our approach in other domains—e.g., use it for recommending scientific papers; studying nutritional habits; or em-

[8]Fig. 4 depicts the *BYLI-Boltzmann-VPI on trailers and movies* variant; results are similar for other *BayesYouLikeIt* variants.

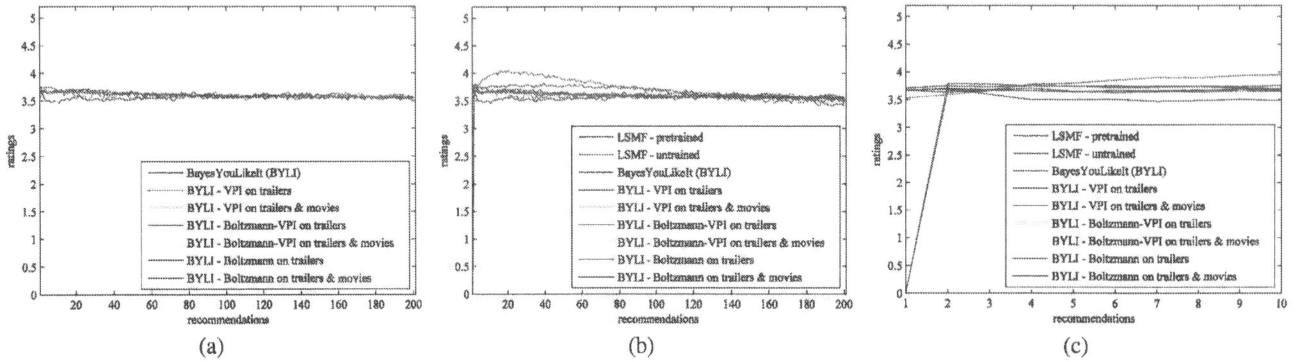

Figure 5: (a) Behaviour of *BayesYouLikeIt* and its variants. (b) Comparison between *LSMF* and *BYLI*. (c) Methods behaviour during the first 10 recommendations. All subfigures depict *average per iteration ratings* across all user sets and experimental runs.

ploy it in story-telling environments. Finally, we aim to incorporate multiagent systems techniques in our model, allowing us to exploit user-specific information coming from other types of online agents.

7. REFERENCES

[1] T. Anderson. *An introduction to multivariate statistical analysis.* John Wiley and Sons, 2003.

[2] N. Barbieri, G. Costa, G. Manco, and R. Ortale. Modeling Item Selection and Relevance for Accurate Recommendations: a Bayesian Approach. In *Proceedings of the 5th ACM Conference on Recommender systems*, RecSys '11, 2011.

[3] S. Berkovsky, T. Kuflik, and F. Ricci. Distributed Collaborative Filtering with Domain Specialization. In *Proceedings of the 1st ACM Conference on Recommender systems*, RecSys '07, 2007.

[4] C. M. Bishop. *Pattern Recognition and Machine Learning.* Springer, Corr. 2nd printing edition, October 2007.

[5] D. Carmel and S. Markovitch. Exploration strategies for model-based learning in multiagent systems. *Autonomous Agents and Multi-agent Systems*, 2(2):141–172, 1999.

[6] U. Chajewska, D. Koller, and R. Parr. Making rational decisions using adaptive utility elicitation. In *Proceedings of AAAI-2000*, 2000.

[7] G. Chalkiadakis and C. Boutilier. Coordination in multiagent reinforcement learning: a bayesian approach. In *Proceedings of the 2nd International Joint Conference on Autonomous Agents and Multiagent Systems*, AAMAS '03, 2003.

[8] R. Dearden, N. Friedman, and D. Andre. Model based Bayesian Exploration. In *Proceedings of Fifteenth Conference on Uncertainty in Artificial Intelligence*, pages 150–159, 1999.

[9] S. Debnath, N. Ganguly, and P. Mitra. Feature Weighting in Content Based Recommendation System Using Social Network Analysis. *WWW 2008*, April 2008.

[10] M. DeGroot and J. Schervish. *Probability and Statistics.* 2002.

[11] D. Fink. A Compendium of Conjugate Priors. Technical report, 1997.

[12] J. Golbeck. Generating Predictive Movie Recommendations from Trust in Social Networks. In *iTrust-2006*, pages 93–104, 2006.

[13] Y. Hu, Y. Koren, and C. Volinsky. Collaborative filtering for implicit feedback datasets. In *Proceedings of the 2008 IEEE International Conference on Data Mining*, ICDM '08, pages 263–272, Washington, DC, USA, 2008. IEEE Computer Society.

[14] K. E. Kendall and J. E. Kendall. *Systems Analysis and Design.* 2011.

[15] G. Kurtenbach, A. Sellen, and W. Buxton. Some Articulatory and Cognitive Aspects of "Marking Menus": An Empirical Study. *Journal of Human-Computer Interaction*, July 1991.

[16] H. Langseth and T. D. Nielsen. A latent model for collaborative filtering. *Int. J. Approx. Reasoning*, 53(4):447–466, June 2012.

[17] A. Liu, Y. Zhang, and J. Li. Personalized Movie Recommendation. In *Proc. of the 17th Intern. Conf. on Multimedia 2009*, October 2009.

[18] P. Melville, R. J. Mooney, and R. Nagarajan. Content-Boosted Collaborative Filtering for Improved Recommendations. *In Proceedings of AAAI-2002*, pages 187–192, July 2002.

[19] R. Mukherjee, P. S. Dutta, and S. Sen. MOVIES2GO - A new approach to online movie recommendation. *In the IJCAI Workshop on Intelligent Techniques for Web Personalization*, 2001.

[20] K. P. Murphy. Conjugate bayesian analysis of the gaussian distribution. Technical report, University of British Columbia, 2007.

[21] F. Nielsen and R. Nock. Clustering Multivariate Normal Distributions. *ETVC 2008, LNCS 5416*, pages 164–174, 2009.

[22] C. Ono, M. Kurokawa, Y. Motomura, and H. Asoh. A Context-Aware Movie Preference Model Using a Bayesian Network for Recommendation and Promotion. *UM 2007, LNAI 4511*, 2007.

[23] S. Shearin and H. Lieberman. Intelligent Profiling by Example. *In Proc. of the 2001 ACM Conference on Intelligent User Interfaces (IUI-2001)*, Santa Fe, NM, January 2001.

[24] M. Szomszor, C. Cattuto, H. Alani, K. O'Hara, A. Baldassarri, V. Loreto, and V. D. Servedio. Folksonomies, the semantic web, and movie recommendation. In *4th European Semantic Web Conf.*, 2007.

[25] H. Yu and M. O. Riedl. A Sequential Recommendation Approach for Interactive Personalized Story Generation. *In Proceedings of AAMAS 2012*, pages 71–78, 2012.

[26] Y. Zhang and J. Koren. Efficient bayesian hierarchical user modeling for recommendation system. In *Proceedings of the 30th Annual intern. ACM SIGIR Conf. on Research and Development in Information Retrieval*, pages 47–54. ACM, 2007.

[27] Y. Zhou, D. Wilkinson, R. Schreiber, and R. Pan. Large-scale parallel collaborative filtering for the netflix prize. In *Proc. 4th Int. Conf. on Algor. Aspects in Information and Management, LNCS 5034*, pages 337–348. Springer, 2008.

To Personalize or Not: A Risk Management Perspective

Weinan Zhang, Jun Wang, Bowei Chen, Xiaoxue Zhao
Department of Computer Science, University College London
Malet Place, London, WC1E 6BT, UK
{w.zhang, j.wang, bowei.chen, x.zhao}@cs.ucl.ac.uk

ABSTRACT

Personalization techniques have been widely adopted in many recommender systems. However, experiments on real-world datasets show that for some users in certain contexts, personalized recommendations do not necessarily perform better than recommendations that rely purely on popularity. Broadly, this can be interpreted by the fact that the parameters of a personalization model are usually estimated from sparse data; the resulting personalized prediction, despite of its low bias, is often volatile. In this paper, we study the problem further by investigating into the ranking of recommendation lists. From a risk management and portfolio retrieval perspective, there is no difference between the popularity-based and the personalized ranking as both of the recommendation outputs can be represented as the trade-off between expected relevance (reward) and associated uncertainty (risk). Through our analysis, we discover common scenarios and provide a technique to predict whether personalization will fail. Besides the theoretical understanding, our experimental results show that the resulting *switch* algorithm, which decides whether or not to personalize, outperforms the mainstream recommendation algorithms.

Categories and Subject Descriptors

H.3.3 [**Information Systems**]: Information Search and Retrieval—*Information Filtering*

Keywords

Personalization; Collaborative Filtering; Recommender Systems; Portfolio Theory

1. INTRODUCTION

Personalization techniques have been widely adopted in many recommender systems. Personalized recommendations are generally derived by distinguishing individuals and their contexts. Example applications such as Amazon [17] and YouTube [7] show personalized recommendations have been well acknowledged and implemented by some of the most successful recommender systems. In particular, Collaborative Filtering (CF) techniques, which make use of the aggregated user preference data to make personalized interest predictions, have proven to be both efficient and effective, as evidenced by a series of recommendation algorithm competitions [1, 10].

Nevertheless, it is somewhat unclear as to whether personalization will *always* outperform the non-personalized. The fact is, in some cases non-personalized recommendations are able to provide more relevant (or interesting) items, while in other cases the personalized may fail to catch the users' current personal interest and result in low quality recommendations. The work in [5] found surprisingly good performance from popularity-based recommendations. Furthermore, Figure 1 illustrates a performance comparison between the Bayesian personalized ranking (BPR) [22], a state-of-the-art ranking-based CF algorithm, and the popularity-based (non-personalized) algorithm on the MovieLens dataset. It illustrates that, although the personalized algorithm works better overall, on each evaluation measure, there are a large proportion of cases where the popularity-based recommendation outperforms the Bayesian personalized ranking.

From a machine learning perspective, the personalized recommendation can reduce the bias but may increase the variance of prediction for user's preference [9]. More importantly, such bias and variance are different across different users and in different recommendation contexts. Therefore, compared with non-personalized recommendation, the overall performance of the personalized recommendation is usually higher but it does not guarantee to be better in each of the cases. In some research work, regularization and cross validation are adopted for model selection and the bias-variance balance of the model [12]. Thus, it is of great interest to study in what situations the personalization fails and develop a *switch* to judge which model should be adopted to provide recommendations to the target user.

In this paper, we analyze different characteristics of personalized and non-personalized recommendations. As a by-product, we provide effective switch algorithms in order to decide whether *to personalize or not* for each user. Specifically, we introduce the concept of *risk* borrowed from finance [15] into the preference prediction model. We then leverage modern portfolio theory [11] to optimize the expected reward and risk of the recommendations from both of the personalized and non-personalized algorithms. Finally, a series of switch algorithms are proposed both by heuristics and learning-based methods. As an empirical study, we conduct our experiments on two collaborative filtering benchmark datasets: MovieLens and Netflix. The experimental results support our idea of introducing risk into the preference estimation and our proposed *mean-variance-aware switch algorithms*.

The rest of this paper is organized as follows. Related work is discussed in Section 2. Next, we introduce the concepts and methods of risk management in item recommendation, and provide an analysis on whether to personalize

RecSys'13, October 12–16, 2013, Hong Kong, China.

http://dx.doi.org/10.1145/2507157.2507167.

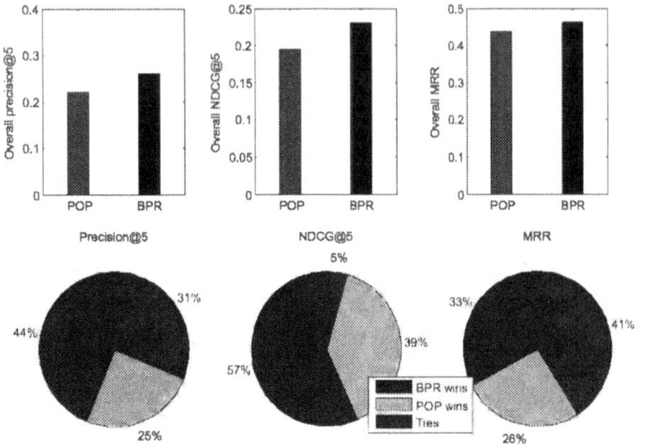

Figure 1: Performance comparison of personalized and non-personalized recommendations.

or not in a risk management perspective. Motivated by our analysis, we propose our methodology in Section 4. The experiments are described in Section 5, and finally, this paper is concluded in Section 6.

2. RELATED WORK

Collaborative Filtering has been widely applied and researched [23, 26]. It refines user-specific profiles by analyzing the historic behavior from a large corpus of users and makes the recommendation based on that. There are two major catergories for CF algorithms: the memory-based methods explicitly figure out the user or item similarities [13, 8] or combine them together [30] and make recommendations directly based on the target user's past behavior. The model-based methods learn a "model" of each user's behavior and use it to provide recommendations. The latent factor models [14] implemented by matrix factorization [16, 25, 21] have become quite popular during recent years. Today both the memory and model-based methods are widely used in commercial personalized recommender systems [7, 6].

While many research efforts focus on the personalization algorithms for recommender systems, there are, to the best of our knowledge, very few work that investigates which situations the users need personalized recommendation or not. Such idea has been proposed in Web search scenario [29], where the variation of user search intent is modelled by characterizing the queries with a variety of features and the search results. Even that work is still essentially different from our scenario where there is no any query and the recommender system needs to judge the user's preference on whether to personalize at each recommendation request. Another work [28] studies the relationship between recommendation accuracy and the item popularity but it does not address the problem of whether to personalize or not.

Risk management and modelling are a significant component for financial institutions, where the companies need to evaluate the risk (i.e, the possibility of failing) for each new candidate investment and how it fits in their previous portfolio [15]. Recently, this idea has been introduced to the information retrieval area: risk-sensitive models are proposed to measure the uncertainty of document ranking performance [34, 33]; optimization algorithms are introduced to improve the robustness of ranking models [2, 33]; the modern portfolio theory is applied to the ranking model (as a document recombination process) to reduce the risk [31]. In addition, a risk-sensitive retrieval task is added in TREC Web track 2013 to maintain the good robustness of IR models [3]. For recommender systems, the risk of delivering an item or a list of items is actually much significant. However, quite few work explicitly models the risk to improve the performance of recommender systems. In [27], the idea of portfolio theory for ranking documents is borrowed to collaborative filtering to adaptively diversify the recommended items. Compared with our work, it mainly focuses diversification of recommended items instead of carefully modelling the individual item risk and the decision making of whether to personalize.

3. RECOMMENDATION RISK ANALYSIS

In this section, we make use of the concepts of portfolio retrieval [31, 20] to conduct our analysis. To make this paper self-contained, we first present the basic concepts of portfolio retrieval in the preliminaries section, and the details are referred to [31, 20]. We then analyze the (non-) personalized item portfolios using the expected reward and its associated risk and study their relationships in the risk-reward diagram.

3.1 Preliminaries

Definition 1 (Item Portfolio). *An item portfolio p is a collection of n items with a weight w_i assigned to each item i:*

$$p = \{(i, w_i)\}_{i=1...n}, \; where \sum_i w_i = 1. \tag{1}$$

As will be detailed later, the weight is relevant to the importance of each item, which will finally determine the ranking of it. In our proposal, the weight w_i can be any positive or negative value in $\mathbb{R}$, and the larger the weight the more important the item is. Such setting is different from [31] but this is a more general case of portfolio weight, just as the asset short-selling in finance [18]. Without loss of generality, we assume the portfolio includes n items with indices $i = 1 \dots n$. Suppose the user u's preference on item i is a random variable, denoted as $r_{u,i}$, and its mean and variance are $\mu_{u,i}$ and $\sigma^2_{u,i}$ respectively, then the user u's preference for an item portfolio p, denoted as $R_{u,p}$, is calculated as a linear function over the item weights:

$$R_{u,p} = \sum_{i=1}^{n} w_i r_{u,i}. \tag{2}$$

The expected reward and variance of $R_{u,p}$ are

$$\mu_{u,p} \equiv E[R_{u,p}] = \sum_{i=1}^{n} w_i E[r_{u,i}] = \boldsymbol{w}^T \boldsymbol{\mu}, \tag{3}$$

$$\sigma^2_{u,p} \equiv Var[R_{u,p}] = \sum_{i=1}^{n}\sum_{j=1}^{n} w_i w_j Cov(i,j) = \boldsymbol{w}^T \boldsymbol{\Sigma} \boldsymbol{w}, \tag{4}$$

where we have already used vector representations with $\boldsymbol{w}$ as weight vector for the items; $\boldsymbol{\mu} = (\mu_{u,1} \dots \mu_{u,n})^T$; $\boldsymbol{\Sigma}$ as the covariance matrix about the user's preference on items in p. The element of $\boldsymbol{\Sigma}$ is $\boldsymbol{\Sigma}_{ij} = \rho_{ij}\sigma_{u,i}\sigma_{u,j}$ [18, 31], where ρ_{ij} is the correlation between item i and j. With the above definition and the calculation of the mean and variance of the user's preference on an item portfolio, Figure 2(a) gives an illustration of the mean and standard deviation of three individual items, as well as the different portfolios based on these items.

Definition 2 (Item Portfolio Domination). *For a user u, an item portfolio p_1 is said to dominate another item portfolio p_2, denoted as $p_1 \rhd p_2$, if and only if it satisfies*

$$\mu_{u,p_1} > \mu_{u,p_2} \quad \textit{(larger expected reward), and} \tag{5}$$

$$\sigma^2_{u,p_1} < \sigma^2_{u,p_2} \quad \textit{(smaller uncertainty).} \tag{6}$$

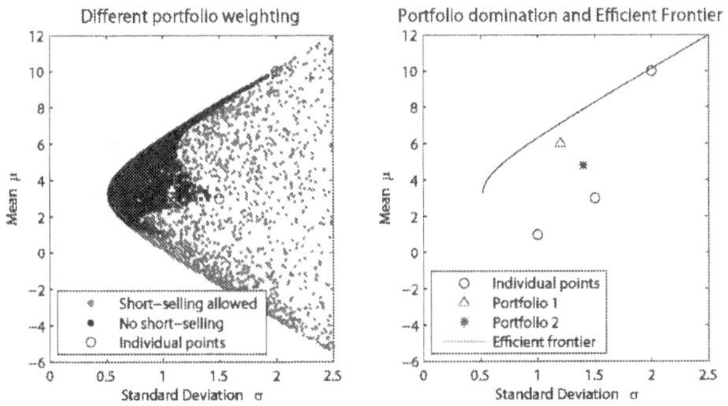

(a) (b)

Figure 2: An example of portfolio mean-variance, domination and efficient frontier.

An example of item portfolio domination is given in Figure 2(b) where portfolio 1 dominates portfolio 2. Obviously, in the μ-σ plot, left-upper points dominate the right-lower ones as the former is with larger expectation and smaller standard deviation than that of the latter.

Definition 3 (Efficient Frontier). *Given a set of items with their individual means, variances, and correlations, the efficient frontier is a set of item portfolios, each of which is dominated by none of other possible item portfolios.*

Given an expected relevance μ_p, the corresponding point on the efficient frontier can be calculated by minimizing the risk; examples include the well-known Markowitz's Objective [18]. Its variant for web search diversification was also proposed in [20]. More specifically, we have

$$\begin{aligned} \min_{\boldsymbol{w}} \quad & \boldsymbol{w}^T \boldsymbol{\Sigma} \boldsymbol{w} \\ s.t. \quad & \boldsymbol{w}^T \mathbf{1} = 1 \\ & \boldsymbol{w}^T \boldsymbol{\mu} = \mu_p. \end{aligned} \tag{7}$$

The closed form solution of Eq. (7) is

$$\boldsymbol{w}_M = \frac{\begin{vmatrix} 1 & \mathbf{1}^T\boldsymbol{\Sigma}^{-1}\boldsymbol{\mu} \\ \mu_p & \boldsymbol{\mu}^T\boldsymbol{\Sigma}^{-1}\boldsymbol{\mu} \end{vmatrix} \boldsymbol{\Sigma}^{-1}\mathbf{1} + \begin{vmatrix} \mathbf{1}^T\boldsymbol{\Sigma}^{-1}\mathbf{1} & 1 \\ \boldsymbol{\mu}^T\boldsymbol{\Sigma}^{-1}\mathbf{1} & \mu_p \end{vmatrix} \boldsymbol{\Sigma}^{-1}\boldsymbol{\mu}}{\begin{vmatrix} \mathbf{1}^T\boldsymbol{\Sigma}^{-1}\mathbf{1} & \mathbf{1}^T\boldsymbol{\Sigma}^{-1}\boldsymbol{\mu} \\ \boldsymbol{\mu}^T\boldsymbol{\Sigma}^{-1}\mathbf{1} & \boldsymbol{\mu}^T\boldsymbol{\Sigma}^{-1}\boldsymbol{\mu} \end{vmatrix}}. \tag{8}$$

With such setting of μ_p and $\boldsymbol{w}_M$, the variance of p is

$$\sigma_p^2 = \boldsymbol{w}_M^T \boldsymbol{\Sigma} \boldsymbol{w}_M, \tag{9}$$

which is a quadratic polynomial of μ_p

$$\sigma_p^2 = \theta_1 \mu_p^2 + \theta_2 \mu_p + \theta_3, \tag{10}$$

where

$$\begin{aligned} \theta_1 &= \frac{(x\boldsymbol{\mu} - y\mathbf{1})^T \boldsymbol{\Sigma}^{-1} (x\boldsymbol{\mu} - y\mathbf{1})}{(xz - y^2)^2}, \\ \theta_2 &= \frac{2(x\boldsymbol{\mu} - y\mathbf{1})^T \boldsymbol{\Sigma}^{-1} (z\mathbf{1} - y\boldsymbol{\mu})}{(xz - y^2)^2}, \\ \theta_3 &= \frac{(z\mathbf{1} - y\boldsymbol{\mu})^T \boldsymbol{\Sigma}^{-1} (z\mathbf{1} - y\boldsymbol{\mu})}{(xz - y^2)^2}, \end{aligned} \tag{11}$$

and $x = \mathbf{1}^T\boldsymbol{\Sigma}^{-1}\mathbf{1}$, $y = \mathbf{1}^T\boldsymbol{\Sigma}^{-1}\boldsymbol{\mu} = \boldsymbol{\mu}^T\boldsymbol{\Sigma}^{-1}\mathbf{1}$, and $z = \boldsymbol{\mu}^T\boldsymbol{\Sigma}^{-1}\boldsymbol{\mu}$. From Eq. (10) we can see σ_p is a squared root of a quadratic polynomial of μ_p and it forms part of a hyperbola in the μ-σ plot. Figure 2(b) gives an illustration of the corresponding frontier curve.

Up to this point, we have introduced the basic building blocks of portfolio theory for recommendation tasks, such as item portfolio, item portfolio domination and efficient frontier. The detailed information on such concepts in finance can be found in [11, 15]. Next, we shall introduce our initial risk analysis of two recommendation portfolios.

3.2 Risk Analysis of Two Rec. Portfolios

We are now ready to analyze the expected reward and its risk on two item portfolios (one from the personalized and one from the non-personalized). Without loss of generality, in this paper we consider two well-known recommendations algorithms. For the personalized recommendation algorithm, we consider Bayesian personalized ranking (BPR) [22], one of the state-of-the-art ranking-based CF algorithms. And for the non-personalized recommendation algorithm, we consider the popularity-based recommendation (POP), which simply recommends the items with the highest number of positive feedbacks.

The relationship between the personalized recommendation and non-personalized recommendation can be illustrated by four typical cases in the risk-reward diagram, as shown in Figure 3. For each case, the three bar diagrams show the actual ranking performance comparison between BPR and POP after portfolio optimization, which picks an optimal point on the efficient frontier. The right μ-σ plot gives the mean (expected reward) and the standard deviation (risk) for two sets of individual items, two efficient frontiers, and two optimized item portfolios. In this section, we focus the analysis on whether to personalize or not, given these two item portfolios optimized independently. The detailed discussion of estimating the individual item mean and standard deviation and optimizing the item portfolio for reranking will be presented in the following sections.

Figure 3(a) and 3(b) show two cases that one item portfolio dominates the other. We can see the dominating one always obtains higher ranking performance than the dominated one. In both cases, the selection (switch) criterion is straightforward: given two item portfolios, the one with higher expected reward and lower risk (i.e., the dominating portfolio) will be chosen.

Figure 3(c) and 3(d) present another two cases of no direct dominance, where one portfolio has higher expected reward while the other has lower risk. The item portfolio cannot be easily selected as the cases of direct dominance. For example, as shown in Figure 3(c), the portfolio with lower risk fails to outperform the one with higher expected reward. A different result is exhibited in Figure 3(d), where the item portfolio with higher expected reward is outperformed by the one with lower risk. In such situations, a switch algorithm that considers how to select an optimal portfolio from those of no direct dominance is needed.

Based on previous analysis, given two recommended item lists from personalized and non-personalized recommendation algorithms, what we need to do is threefold:

Item Level - Estimate the expected reward and risk for each individual item. That is to obtain the individual item points on μ-σ plots in Figure 2 and 3. In our paper, we leverage Bayesian linear regression based on latent factor model to estimate the mean and variance of the preference value of user u on each candidate item i, which will be briefly discussed in Section 4.1.

Portfolio Level - Given the mean and variance of each item and their correlations, find the optimal weighting combination of them. That is to obtain the optimal weighting points on the efficient frontiers in Figure 3. We propose our portfolio optimization algorithm in Section 4.2.

Two-Portfolio Level - Given the two optimized item port-

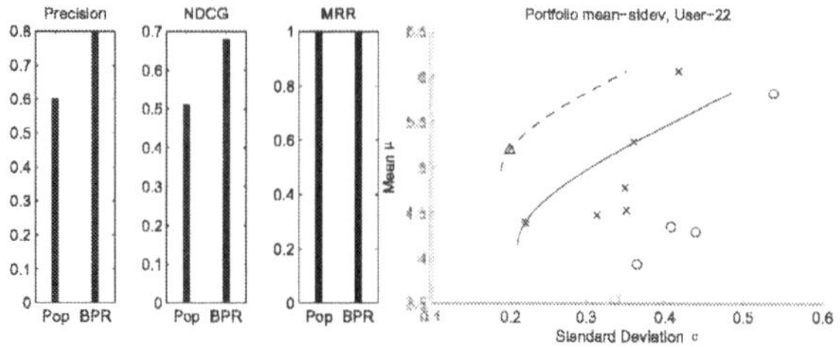

(a) Personalize dominantes

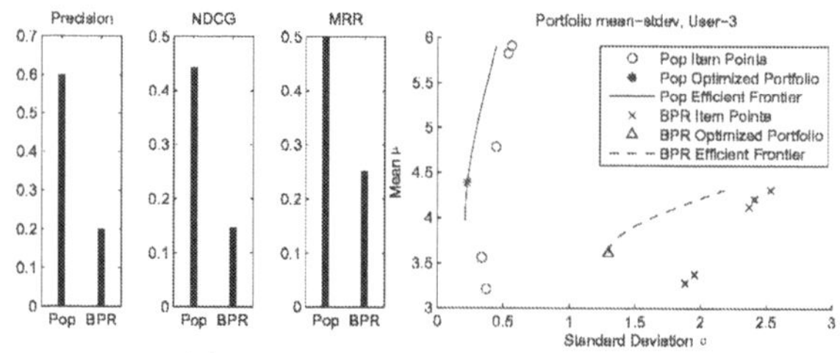

(b) Non-personalize dominantes

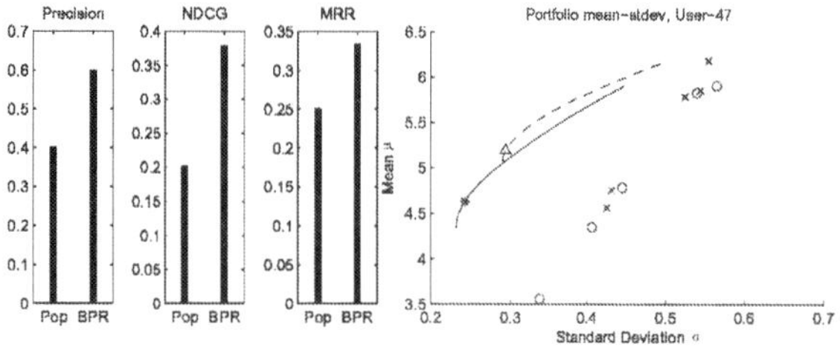

(c) No dominance, Personalize wins

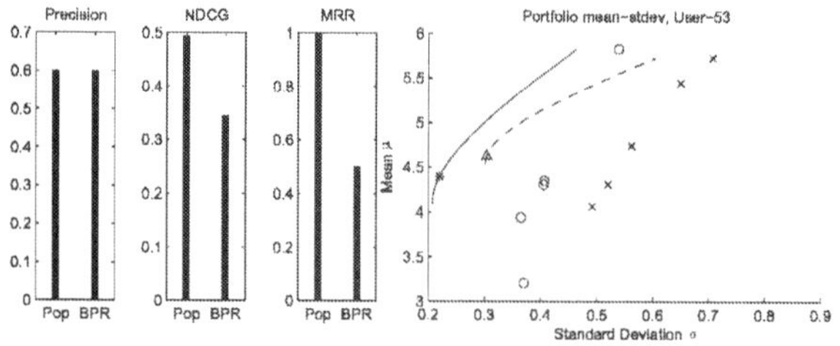

(d) No dominance, non-personalize wins

Figure 3: Typical cases for the expected reward and risk analysis of the personalized and non-personalized portfolios. Data source: MovieLens.

folios from personalized and non-personalized recommendations respectively, design the mean-variance-aware switch algorithms to choose whether to personalize or not. We propose a series of switch algorithms in Section 4.3.

4. THE ALGORITHM

4.1 Individual Item Estimation

On the item level, we focus on the estimation of $\mu_{u,i}$, $\sigma_{u,i}$ for each item. Here we leverage the Bayesian latent factor model to estimate them, inspired by [25, 12][1]. Latent factor model is a typical well-known personalized recommendation algorithm. Considering the probability distribution of the user's rating, we can use the probabilistic matrix factorization (PMF) [25] to model, that is

$$p(r_{u,i}|\boldsymbol{U}_u, \boldsymbol{V}_i, \sigma^2) = \mathcal{N}(r_{u,i}|\boldsymbol{U}_u^T\boldsymbol{V}_i, \sigma^2). \quad (12)$$

PMF suggests to provide prior distributions for $\boldsymbol{U}$ and $\boldsymbol{V}$ and then the *maximum a posteriori* (MAP) solutions for $\boldsymbol{U}$ and $\boldsymbol{V}$ for the given rating data can be directly obtained. Here we relate the uncertainty in the user-item rating $r_{u,i}$ with the uncertainty from the user factors [27], while taking the item factors as learnt and fixed. Therefore, here we fix the item latent factors $\boldsymbol{V}$ from this MAP solution [25], and the distribution of $\boldsymbol{U}$ in a form of Bayesian inference in linear regression can be obtained.

Denote the user u's behavior observation as $\boldsymbol{D}_u$, where each row is the latent factor $\boldsymbol{V}_i^T$ of the item i that he/she has rated, and denote the corresponding rating vector as $\boldsymbol{r}_u$. Suppose the prior distribution of u's latent factor $\boldsymbol{U}_u$ is a Gaussian $p(\boldsymbol{U}_u) = \mathcal{N}(\boldsymbol{U}_u|\boldsymbol{U}_0, \boldsymbol{\Sigma}_0)$. Then its posterior distribution is still a Gaussian

$$p(\hat{\boldsymbol{U}}_u) = \mathcal{N}(\boldsymbol{U}_u|E[\hat{\boldsymbol{U}}_u], Var[\hat{\boldsymbol{U}}_u]), \quad (13)$$

where

$$E[\hat{\boldsymbol{U}}_u] = (\boldsymbol{\Sigma}_0^{-1} + \sigma^{-2}\boldsymbol{D}_u^T\boldsymbol{D}_u)^{-1}(\boldsymbol{\Sigma}_0^{-1}U_0 + \sigma^{-2}\boldsymbol{D}_u^T\boldsymbol{r}_u),$$
$$Var[\hat{\boldsymbol{U}}_u] = (\boldsymbol{\Sigma}_0^{-1} + \sigma^{-2}\boldsymbol{D}_u^T\boldsymbol{D}_u)^{-1}. \quad (14)$$

[1]Note that other alternatives to estimate these parameters can also be adopted [24, 35].

Therefore, the Gaussian distribution of the rating $r_{u,i}$ can be written as

$$p(r_{u,i}) = \mathcal{N}(r_{u,i}|\mu_{u,i}, \sigma_{u,i}^2), \quad (15)$$

where the mean and variance are

$$\mu_{u,i} = E[\hat{\boldsymbol{U}}_u]^T\boldsymbol{V}_i, \quad \sigma_{u,i}^2 = \boldsymbol{V}_i^T Var[\hat{\boldsymbol{U}}_u]\boldsymbol{V}_i. \quad (16)$$

We also need to estimate the mean values and variances of the items from a non-personalized perspective. To do this, we assume an "average user" who has an averaged rating behavior across the whole user set. The posterior distribution of latent factors of the "average user" is calculated by taking average across the parameters of the posterior distributions of all users. Then the mean and variance of individual items are estimated by Eq. (16)[2].

In addition, for the item correlation $\rho_{i,j}$, a routine solution is to leverage the item-item rating similarity in item-based kNN algorithms [8]. Note that the Pearson correlation of item latent factors can also be adopted here.

4.2 Item Portfolio Optimization

In this section, we focus on the item portfolio weighting optimization analysis. Investors in finance always adjust their shares in an investment portfolio in order to have better expected reward as well as to reduce risk [15], here in the recommendation scenario, it is preferred to provide highly relevant items while the risk of the user dissatisfaction being controlled. This target can be achieved by refining the item ranking list according to the weights of the items.

4.2.1 *Objective and Solution*

In [31], Wang et al. provided a general form of the objective function in practice of information retrieval.

$$\max_{\boldsymbol{w}} \ \boldsymbol{w}^T\boldsymbol{\mu} - b\boldsymbol{w}^T\boldsymbol{\Sigma}\boldsymbol{w} \quad (17)$$
$$s.t. \ \boldsymbol{w}^T\boldsymbol{1} = 1$$

Here the parameter b indicates the risk-averse level of the user. Thus the contour line of objective function forms a

[2]Due to the rating prediction model of PMF, mean values of some items are possibly higher than 5 (rating upper bound), as shown in Figure 3.

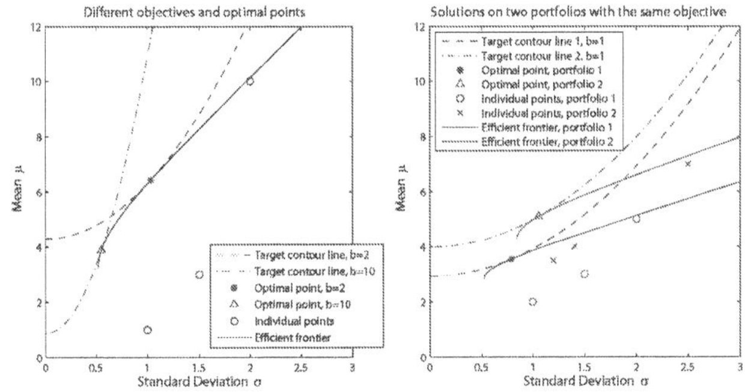

(a) (b)

Figure 4: Contour lines of objective functions and the different optimal solution for different objective functions.

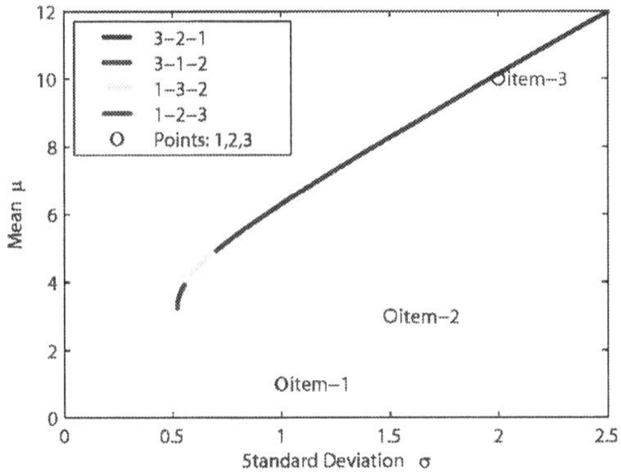

Figure 5: An example of rankings and their corresponding regions on the efficient frontier. The covariances are $cov(1,2) = -0.5$, $cov(1,3) = -0.7$, $cov(2,3) = -0.4$.

quadratic curve on the μ-σ plot. To illustrate, the left panel of Figure 4 shows the efficient frontier of three individual items, and two contour lines with two different risk-averse levels ($b = 2$ and $b = 10$). The right panel of the figure shows two portfolios and two contour lines with the same risk-averse level tangent with them.

The optimal weight point is the point of tangency between the objective quadratic curve and the efficient frontier. The solution can be obtained by the following equations:

$$\begin{aligned} \mu_p &= t + b\sigma_p^2, \\ \sigma_p^2 &= \theta_1\mu_p^2 + \theta_2\mu_p + \theta_3, \\ \frac{\partial\sigma_p}{\partial\mu_p} &= \frac{1}{2(b\mu_p - bt)^{\frac{1}{2}}} = \frac{2\theta_1\mu_p + \theta_2}{2(\theta_1\mu_p^2 + \theta_2\mu_p + \theta_3)^{\frac{1}{2}}}, \end{aligned} \tag{18}$$

where the intercept t of the contour line $\mu_p = t + b\sigma_p^2$ is the objective value in Eq. (17), θ_i's are the same as in Eq. (11). The solution of μ_p is

$$\mu_p = \frac{1 - b\theta_2}{2b\theta_1}, \tag{19}$$

and the analytic solution for the optimal weight w^* can be further obtained by Eq. (8).

4.2.2 *Item Reranking via Portfolio Optimization*

Compared to the portfolio weighting in finance, here the weight w_i for each item indicates how much attention the recommender system wants the target user to pay on the item i. Therefore, according to the position bias [4], the final delivered items should be ranked by the descending order of their weights.

Figure 5 gives an illustration of the relationship between item rankings and their corresponding regions on the efficient frontier. We can see not all possible item rankings necessarily occur on the efficient frontier (no 2-1-3 and 2-3-1). Specifically, the mean is more emphasized in the portfolios with ranking 3-2-1 while the variance is more emphasized in the portfolios with ranking 1-2-3. The other two rankings try to strike a balance between mean and variance.

4.3 Proposed Switch Algorithms

From previous sections, we can now use the proposed risk management model to calculate the expected reward and risk for any item portfolio to the target user, and then find the optimal portfolio weighting strategy to rerank the recommended items. Now we aim to propose switch algorithms, which make decisions between personalized and non-personalized recommendation portfolios to get the highest utility, based on the expected reward and risk.

4.3.1 *Switch Problem Statement*

Choosing whether to personalize or not in recommendation is essentially a switch decision problem. Given the information of two item portfolios (from personalized and non-personalized recommendation respectively), the switch policy π chooses one to deliver, denoted as $\pi(u, p_1, p_2)$.

Suppose there is a utility function $r(u, p)$ which estimates the utility of recommending an item portfolio p to user u. Then the corresponding optimal policy can be defined according to the utility as follows:

$$\pi^* = \arg\max_{\pi} \sum_{(u,p_1,p_2)} r(u, \pi(u, p_1, p_2)). \tag{20}$$

4.3.2 *Switch Algorithms*

Here we propose some heuristic and learning-based switch algorithms.

Mean prior (Mean) - Select the portfolio with higher expected reward.

$$\pi(u, p_1, p_2) = \arg\max_{p\in\{p_1,p_2\}} \mu_{u,p}. \tag{21}$$

Variance prior (Var) - Select the portfolio with lower risk.

$$\pi(u, p_1, p_2) = \arg\min_{p\in\{p_1,p_2\}} \sigma_{u,p}. \tag{22}$$

Linear risk target (Lin) - Select the portfolio with higher $\mu - b\sigma$ value.

$$\pi(u, p_1, p_2) = \arg\max_{p\in\{p_1,p_2\}} \mu_{u,p} - b\sigma_{u,p}. \tag{23}$$

Quadratic risk target (Quad) - Select the portfolio with higher $\mu - b\sigma^2$ value.

$$\pi(u, p_1, p_2) = \arg\max_{p\in\{p_1,p_2\}} \mu_{u,p} - b\sigma_{u,p}^2. \tag{24}$$

Dominance motivated (Dom) - Select the personalized portfolio by default, unless it is dominated by the non-personalized one.

$$\pi(u, p_1, p_2) = p_2 \rhd p_1 \ ?\ p_2 \ :\ p_1. \tag{25}$$

Golden Switch (Golden) - In order to check the potential of these switch algorithms, here we provide an upper bound algorithm, which exactly switches to the better one.

Adaptive risk parameter (X-A)[3]- Different users have different risk-averse levels. For example, some users expect the recommender system could provide some serendipitous items for them to discover new interest, while some users may just need the recommendations to be consistent with their previous interest. This risk-averse level parameter is indeed the b in Eq. (17), denoted as b_u here.

In order to adaptively learn this parameter for each individual user, we conduct a cross validation on the training data to empirically tune the parameter b_u for each user u and pick the optimal value. Then during the portfolio optimization for each user u, we adopt this adaptive parameter b_u. And during the latter switch decision process, for the Lin and Quad algorithm, we also adopt b_u to make decision.

Note that the calculations on item level, portfolio level, and two-portfolio level are all independent from (non-) personalized recommendation algorithms, which indicates that our work can be seamlessly generalized on other (non-) personalized recommendation algorithms.

5. EXPERIMENT

In this section, we intend to answer the following questions from the experiments: (i) Will the portfolio optimization models improve the ranking performance in both personalized and non-personalized cases? (ii) Given the two optimized ranking lists, which switch algorithm works the best and why?

5.1 Experiment Setup

Datasets - We base our experiments on the two popular datasets MovieLens-100k[4] and Netflix. MovieLens contains 100K ratings from 943 users and 1,682 items, while Netflix contains 100M ratings from 480,189 users and 17,770 items. Following the experimental setting of [19] we pick the 4 or 5-star ratings as positive feedbacks and give a 4:1 random splitting for the training and test data.

Compared Algorithms - We compare the portfolio-based reranking algorithms and switch algorithms to the base recommendation algorithms. Also, we explore and discuss the combination of the three types of algorithms.

Base recommendation algorithms retrieve top-N items for each target user. Here we choose BPR and POP as the personalized and non-personalized algorithms respectively.

Portfolio-based reranking algorithms take the retrieved top-N items (from based recommendation algorithms) and the target user u's profile as inputs. It evaluates the expected reward and risk for each item and then performs the portfolio optimization to obtain the optimal weighting for the combination of items, which finally will determine the ranking of the items. Specifically, we propose to directly solve out the optimal weighting solution (denoted as Opt) as in Section 4.2.1 and then rerank the items by the descending order of the optimal weighting. Furthermore, the Bayesian latent factor model discussed in Section 4.1 is leveraged to estimate the individual item expected reward and risk. For comparison, a portfolio-based greedy ranking algorithm proposed in [31, 27] is used (denoted as Greedy) which sequentially chooses the item to maximize the incremental target in Eq. (17), and the expected reward and risk are calculated accordingly [27].

Switch algorithms take the expected reward and risk of the two optimized item portfolios (Opt-BPR and Opt-POP) along with the user's risk-averse level parameter b as inputs, and choose between the two portfolios and finally return the

[3]Here X is one of the previously introduced algorithms.

[4]This small dataset is chosen because of its convenience of providing case illustrations.

Table 1: Item reranking performance on MovieLens

Algorithm	P@3	P@5	NDCG@3	NDCG@5	MRR
BPR	**0.2865**	**0.2623**	0.2465	0.2289	0.4393
Greedy-BPR			0.2580	0.2312	0.4547
Opt-BPR			0.2496	0.2342	0.4640
Opt-BPR-A			**0.2593**	**0.2409**	**0.4863**
POP	0.2485	0.2202	0.2127	0.1955	0.4378
Greedy-POP			0.2237	0.2034	0.4772
Opt-POP			0.2193	0.2036	0.4760
Opt-POP-A			0.2223	0.2064	0.4847
Improvement	-	-	5.19%	5.24%	10.70%*

Table 2: Item reranking performance on Netflix

Algorithm	P@3	P@5	NDCG@3	NDCG@5	MRR
BPR	**0.1177**	**0.1142**	0.1198	0.1168	0.2069
Greedy-BPR			0.1286	0.1296	0.2472
Opt-BPR			0.1308	0.1317	0.2544
Opt-BPR-A			**0.1329**	**0.1328**	**0.2580**
POP	0.0887	0.0907	0.0881	0.0895	0.1642
Greedy-POP			0.0915	0.0969	0.1902
Opt-POP			0.0917	0.0970	0.1905
Opt-POP-A			0.0983	0.0999	0.2000
Improvement	-	-	10.93%*	13.70%*	24.70%*

corresponding item ranking list as the output. The compared switch algorithms are listed in Section 4.3, denoted as Mean, Var, Lin, Quad, Dom, and Golden respectively. Note that "-A" denotes that the algorithm is based on the adaptive risk parameter setting, such as Opt-BPR-A and Opt-Mean-A.

Evaluation Measures - Three ranking measures are used in our experiments: precision (P@n), normalized discounted cumulative gain (NDCG@n) and mean reciprocal rank (MRR). Besides the absolute performance values, the improvement of the best algorithm against the baseline algorithm is also calculated. In addition, Wilcoxon signed-rank tests are conducted and statistically significant improvements are marked with *.

5.2 Results and Analysis

In this section, we first compare portfolio-based reranking algorithms and then we test the effectiveness of different switch algorithms. Finally, we provide case studies to further illustrate the effectiveness of our models.

5.2.1 Item Reranking via Portfolio Optimization

We present the performance for the two portfolio-based reranking algorithms (Opt and Greedy) based on the two base recommendation algorithms (BPR and POP). In addition, we add the algorithms with adaptive risk parameter (Opt-X-A) into the comparison. The overall results on MovieLens and Netflix datasets are shown in Table 1 and 2 respectively. The improvement is calculated between the best algorithm and the baseline BPR.

From the overall results we can have the following observations. (i) On all evaluation measures, the two portfolio-based reranking algorithms Greedy and Opt bring improvement on both of the output of base recommendation algorithms BPR and POP. (ii) Compared with Greedy, Opt brings a higher improvement, which verifies the effectiveness of our method that tries to find the optimal portfolio weighting for items and ranks them by the weight. (iii) Furthermore, Opt-X-A with the setting of adaptive learning on parameter b_u for each target user leads a further high improvement. This indicates different users have different risk-averse levels, which can be traced through analyzing each user's history data. (iv) Among the three evaluation measures, the improvements on MRR are the most significant, which is consistent with the findings in [31, 32] that reciprocal ranking metric is optimized when diversifying the ranking list.

To see the impact of the risk-averse level parameter b, we trace the performance of Opt-BPR and Greedy-BPR against b in comparison with non-b BPR and adaptively tuned-b Opt-

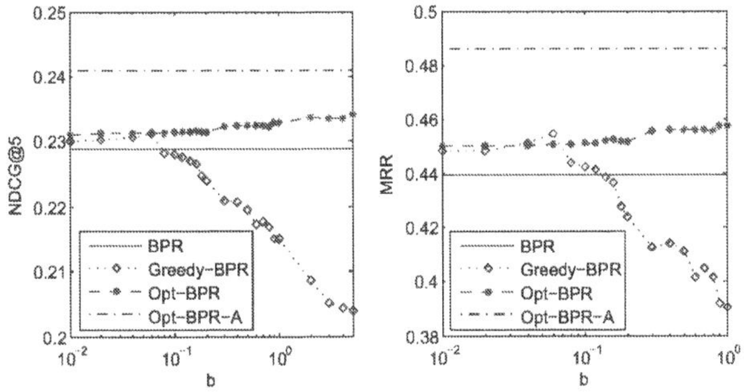

Figure 6: Performance of different item reranking algorithms against b - MovieLens.

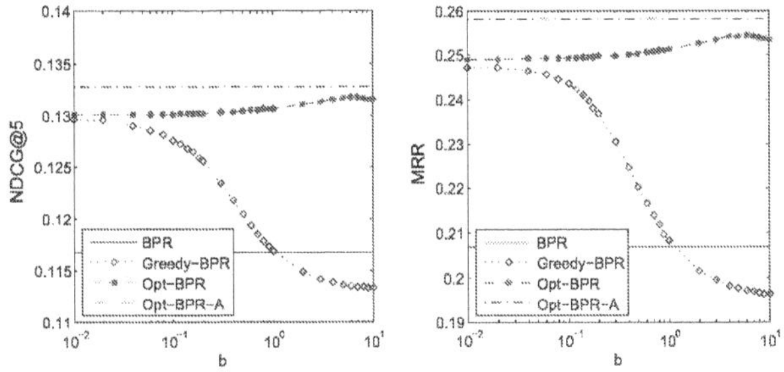

Figure 7: Performance of different item reranking algorithms against b - Netflix.

BPR-A. The results are shown in Figure 6 and 7. The corresponding results on POP are much similar. We can see that the performance of Greedy is much sensitive against b and will drop even lower than the original BPR when b gets larger than some value. This is mainly caused by the myopic picking strategy of Greedy. On the other hand, as has been shown in Figure 5, as the risk parameter b changes, the item ranking from Opt will not change frequently which is consistent with the results in Figure 6 and 7.

5.2.2 *Switch Algorithms*

Based on the portfolio-based reranking algorithm, for each user, consider there are two item recommendation lists (portfolios), from Opt-BPR (or Opt-BPR-A) and Opt-POP (or Opt-POP-A), the switch algorithm chooses one list (portfolio) to recommend. The results on two datasets are presented in Table 3 and 4 respectively. The switch/total improvements are calculated between the best algorithm and BPR-Opt-A/BPR, respectively.

From the results we can observe: (i) the baseline switch algorithm Mean usually results in a performance drop from Opt-BPR, which means that purely selecting a list by the higher expected reward is not sufficiently effective. (ii) The risk-aware baseline switch algorithm Var leads to improvement on MovieLens while bringing some decreases of NDCG and MRR on Netflix. Given the item lists from portfolio-based reranking algorithms, choosing the list with less risk is somewhat reasonable but the performance drop on Netflix indicates the instability of this algorithm across different datasets. (iii) Compared with Mean and Var, the mean-variance-aware algorithms Lin and Quad bring improvement of all the measures on two datasets, exhibiting the stable effectiveness of such switch algorithms. Compared with each other, there is no obvious difference of the performance between Lin and Quad. (iv) The dominance-based switch algorithm Dom, although not as effective as Lin or Quad, still improves the performance. Hence the dominating portfolio should always be selected whenever it exists. (v) Equipped with the adaptive risk parameter setting, all the switch algorithms bring further improvements. On MovieLens, Opt-Lin-A obtains the best performance, while on Netflix, the best performance is brought by Opt-Quad-A in Precision and NDCG, and Opt-Lin-A in MRR.

Table 3: Switch performance on MovieLens

Algorithm	P@3	P@5	NDCG@3	NDCG@5	MRR
Opt-BPR	0.2865	0.2623	0.2496	0.2342	0.4640
Opt-POP	0.2485	0.2202	0.2193	0.2036	0.4760
Opt-Mean	0.2873	0.2500	0.2493	0.2242	0.4841
Opt-Var	0.3070	0.2789	0.2622	0.2454	0.5047
Opt-Lin	0.3048	0.2741	0.2609	0.2432	0.4981
Opt-Quad	0.3034	0.2693	0.2598	0.2390	0.4954
Opt-Dom	0.3056	0.2781	0.2617	0.2443	0.4883
Opt-Golden	0.3494	0.3101	0.3070	0.2749	0.5636
Opt-BPR-A	0.2865	0.2623	0.2593	0.2409	0.4863
Opt-POP-A	0.2485	0.2202	0.2223	0.2064	0.4847
Opt-Mean-A	0.2712	0.2456	0.2395	0.2253	0.4890
Opt-Var-A	0.3048	0.2671	0.2714	0.2430	**0.5085**
Opt-Lin-A	**0.3085**	**0.2728**	**0.2745**	0.2458	0.5057
Opt-Quad-A	0.3019	0.2662	0.2705	0.2436	0.5046
Opt-Dom-A	0.2990	0.2715	0.2661	**0.2483**	0.5051
Opt-Golden-A	0.3494	0.3101	0.3131	0.2805	0.5802
Switch Imprv.	7.68%*	4.00%	5.86%	3.07%	4.57%
Total Imprv.	7.68%*	4.00%	11.36%*	8.48%*	15.75%*

Table 4: Switch performance on Netflix

Algorithm	P@3	P@5	NDCG@3	NDCG@5	MRR
Opt-BPR	0.1177	0.1142	0.1308	0.1317	0.2544
Opt-POP	0.0887	0.0907	0.0918	0.0970	0.1905
Opt-Mean	0.1194	0.1186	0.1302	0.1319	0.2510
Opt-Var	0.1231	0.1180	0.1295	0.1211	0.2309
Opt-Lin	0.1241	0.1187	0.1335	0.1267	0.2493
Opt-Quad	0.1241	0.1188	0.1335	0.1319	0.2492
Opt-Dom	0.1188	0.1159	0.1311	0.1318	0.2522
Opt-Golden	0.1578	0.1393	0.1724	0.1578	0.3090
Opt-BPR-A	0.1177	0.1142	0.1329	0.1328	0.2580
Opt-POP-A	0.0887	0.0907	0.0983	0.0999	0.2000
Opt-Mean-A	0.1259	0.1145	0.1469	0.1351	0.2730
Opt-Var-A	0.0876	0.0913	0.0929	0.0993	0.1882
Opt-Lin-A	0.1289	**0.1206**	0.1483	**0.1391**	**0.2776**
Opt-Quad-A	**0.1291**	**0.1206**	**0.1486**	**0.1391**	0.2771
Opt-Dom-A	0.1178	0.1151	0.1329	0.1333	0.2586
Opt-Golden-A	0.1578	0.1393	0.1792	0.1605	0.3173
Switch Imprv.	9.69%*	5.60%*	11.81%*	4.74%	7.60%*
Total Imprv.	9.69%*	5.60%*	24.04%*	19.09%*	34.17%*

5.2.3 *Case Studies*

Figure 8 provides two typical MovieLens cases with the users' historic item information, mean-variance-aware analysis for (non-) personalized recommendations, and their ranking performances.

User-82 is a 50 years old male programmer. He has rated 86 movies, most of which are of relatively low popularity. It is typical that the mainstream movies do not match the interest of people of such an age. On the other hand, the 86 movies he has rated provide sufficient information for the recommender system to learn his profile and to catch his personal interest. In the mean-variance-aware analysis, the portfolio of the three recommended movies from personalized algorithm dominates that from non-personalized algorithm. Thus all the switch algorithms will choose the personalized recommendation. And the final ranking performances support such analysis.

User-247 is a 28 years old male engineer. Compared to User-82, he has only 15 feedbacks, most of which are popular ones. It is yet another common case as young people tend to find their interests in the mainstream movies. Also the relatively low number of feedbacks do not support a sufficiently learned preference profile for him. In the mean-variance-aware analysis, it shows the dominance of the non-personalized portfolio on the personalized one. Therefore, the non-personalized recommendation should be chosen for him. Again, the ranking performances are consistent with the analysis.

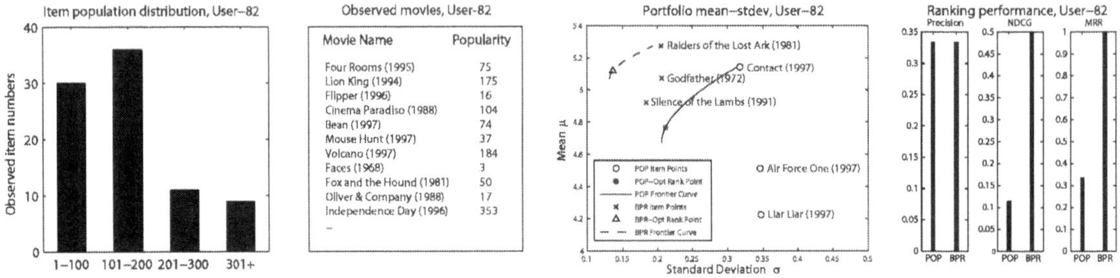

(a) Case study for User-82: a 50-year old male programmer.

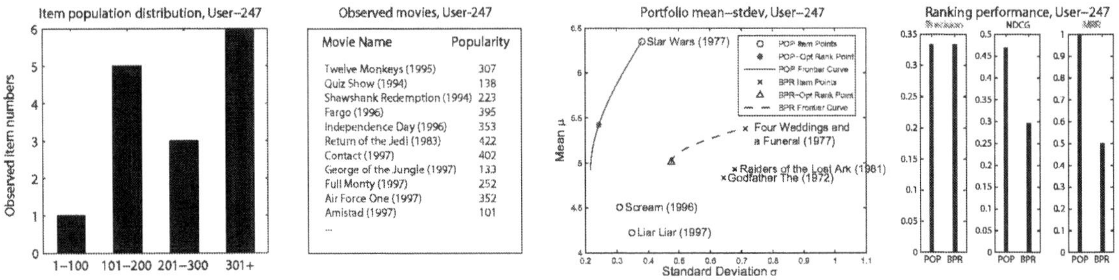

(b) Case study for User-247: a 28-year old male engineer.

Figure 8: Examples of the user history, mean-variance-aware analysis, and the performance.

6. CONCLUSION AND FUTURE WORK

In this paper, the portfolio retrieval theory [31, 20] is used to study the relationships between personalized and non-personalized recommendations. Under a single risk-reward diagram, we studied the efficient frontiers for both recommendation solutions. In either case, diversifying a ranking list would reduce the risk of a recommended item list. We found that the personalized recommendation does not always dominate the non-personalized one. For each target user, we developed several strategies to determine whether or not to personalize the recommendation. The experimental results demostrated the effectiveness of the proposed portfolio-based reranking algorithms and the switch algorithms. For the future work, we plan to generalize the study in this paper and deal with the blending of two or multiple item lists from different (non-) personalized recommendation algorithms.

7. REFERENCES

[1] J. Bennett and S. Lanning. The netflix prize. In *KDD Cup*, 2007.

[2] K. Collins-Thompson. Reducing the risk of query expansion via robust constrained optimization. In *CIKM*, 2009.

[3] K. Collins-Thompson, P. Bennett, and F. Diaz. Trec 2013 web track proposal. 2013.

[4] N. Craswell, O. Zoeter, M. Taylor, and B. Ramsey. An experimental comparison of click position-bias models. In *WSDM*, 2008.

[5] P. Cremonesi, Y. Koren, and R. Turrin. Performance of recommender algorithms on top-n recommendation tasks. In *RecSys*, 2010.

[6] A. S. Das, M. Datar, A. Garg, and S. Rajaram. Google news personalization: scalable online collaborative filtering. In *WWW*, 2007.

[7] J. Davidson et al. The youtube video recommendation system. In *RecSys*, 2010.

[8] M. Deshpande and G. Karypis. Item-based top-N recommendation algorithms. *ACM Trans. Inf. Syst.*, 2004.

[9] P. Domingos. A unified bias-variance decomposition. In *ICML*, 2000.

[10] G. Dror, N. Koenigstein, Y. Koren, and M. Weimer. The yahoo! music dataset and kdd-cup'11. In *KDD Cup*, 2011.

[11] E. J. Elton, M. J. Gruber, S. J. Brown, and W. N. Goetzmann. *Modern portfolio theory and investment analysis.* John Wiley & Sons, 2009.

[12] T. Hastie, R. Tibshirani, J. Friedman, and J. Franklin. The elements of statistical learning: data mining, inference and prediction. *The Mathematical Intelligencer*, 27(2):83–85, 2005.

[13] J. L. Herlocker, J. A. Konstan, A. Borchers, and J. Riedl. An algorithmic framework for performing collaborative filtering. In *SIGIR*, 1999.

[14] T. Hofmann and J. Puzicha. Latent class models for collaborative filtering. In *Proc. of IJCAI*, 1999.

[15] J. Hull. *Risk Management and Financial Institutions,+ Web Site*, volume 733. Wiley, 2012.

[16] Y. Koren, R. Bell, and C. Volinsky. Matrix factorization techniques for recommender systems. *Computer*, 2009.

[17] G. Linden, B. Smith, and J. York. Amazon. com recommendations: Item-to-item collaborative filtering. *Internet Computing, IEEE*, 7(1):76–80, 2003.

[18] H. Markowitz. Portfolio selection*. *The journal of finance*, 7(1):77–91, 1952.

[19] U. Paquet and N. Koenigstein. One-class collaborative filtering with random graphs. 2013.

[20] D. Rafiei, K. Bharat, and A. Shukla. Diversifying web search results. In *WWW*. ACM, 2010.

[21] S. Rendle. Factorization machines. In *ICDM*, 2010.

[22] S. Rendle, C. Freudenthaler, Z. Gantner, and L. Schmidt-Thieme. Bpr: Bayesian personalized ranking from implicit feedback. In *UAI*, 2009.

[23] P. Resnick and H. R. Varian. Recommender systems. *Communications of the ACM*, 40(3):56–58, 1997.

[24] R. Salakhutdinov and A. Mnih. Bayesian probabilistic matrix factorization using markov chain monte carlo. In *ICML*, 2008.

[25] R. Salakhutdinov and A. Mnih. Probabilistic matrix factorization. *NIPS*, 2008.

[26] B. Sarwar, G. Karypis, J. Konstan, and J. Riedl. Analysis of recommendation algorithms for e-commerce. In *EC*, 2000.

[27] Y. Shi, X. Zhao, J. Wang, M. Larson, and A. Hanjalic. Adaptive diversification of recommendation results via latent factor portfolio. In *SIGIR*, 2012.

[28] H. Steck. Item popularity and recommendation accuracy. In *RecSys*, 2011.

[29] J. Teevan, S. T. Dumais, and D. J. Liebling. To personalize or not to personalize: modeling queries with variation in user intent. In *SIGIR*, 2008.

[30] J. Wang, A. P. de Vries, and M. J. T. Reinders. Unifying user-based and item-based collaborative filtering approaches by similarity fusion. In *SIGIR*, 2006.

[31] J. Wang and J. Zhu. Portfolio theory of information retrieval. In *SIGIR*, 2009.

[32] J. Wang and J. Zhu. On statistical analysis and optimization of information retrieval effectiveness metrics. In *SIGIR*, 2010.

[33] L. Wang, P. N. Bennett, and K. Collins-Thompson. Robust ranking models via risk-sensitive optimization. In *SIGIR*, 2012.

[34] J. Zhu, J. Wang, I. J. Cox, and M. J. Taylor. Risky business: modeling and exploiting uncertainty in information retrieval. In *SIGIR*, 2009.

[35] Y.-X. Zhu, W. Zeng, and Q.-M. Zhang. The effect of rating variance on personalized recommendation. In *CCSE*, 2010.

Online Multi-Task Collaborative Filtering for On-the-Fly Recommender Systems

Jialei Wang*, Steven C.H. Hoi*, Peilin Zhao*, Zhi-Yong Liu†
*School of Computer Engineering, Nanyang Technological University, Singapore 639798
†State Key Lab of Management and Control for Complex System, Chinese Academy of Sciences, China
{jl.wang,chhoi,peilinzhao}@ntu.edu.sg, zhiyong.liu@ia.ac.cn

ABSTRACT

Traditional batch model-based Collaborative Filtering (CF) approaches typically assume a collection of users' rating data is given a priori for training the model. They suffer from a common yet critical drawback, i.e., the model has to be re-trained completely from scratch whenever new training data arrives, which is clearly non-scalable for large real recommender systems where users' rating data often arrives sequentially and frequently. In this paper, we investigate a novel efficient and scalable online collaborative filtering technique for on-the-fly recommender systems, which is able to effectively online update the recommendation model from a sequence of rating observations. Specifically, we propose a family of online multi-task collaborative filtering (OMTCF) algorithms, which tackle the online collaborative filtering task by exploiting the similar principle as online multitask learning. Encouraging empirical results on large-scale datasets showed that the proposed technique is significantly more effective than the state-of-the-art algorithms.

Categories and Subject Descriptors

H.3.3 [**Information Storage and Retrieval**]: Information Filtering; I.2.6 [**Artificial Intelligence**]: Learning

Keywords

Recommender systems, Collaborative Filtering, Online learning, Multi-task Learning

1. INTRODUCTION

Collaborative filtering (CF) aims to make accurate predictions ("filtering") about the preferences of a user by learning/leveraging from a collection of preferences from many other users ("collaborative"). It is a core learning technique widely used in real-world recommender systems [30]. In literature, a variety of CF algorithms have been proposed, which can be generally grouped into two schools: (i) memory based methods [26, 20, 16, 11, 32, 13], and (ii) model based methods [27, 15, 31, 29, 23]. The model-based methods, typically powered by machine learning techniques, are more desired than the memory-based methods, especially when the amount of rating observations is relatively limited or sparse, which is common for real recommender systems.

Most existing model-based CF approaches assume a collection of users' rating data is given a priori to train the model in a batch learning fashion. Typically, the model has to be re-trained whenever there is new training data. Such approaches are impractical for real-world recommender systems where training data often arrive sequentially as new users are being added daily or even hourly, and new products/items are being offered dynamically. As a result, traditional batch learning methods are non-scalable due to their highly expensive re-training cost. This calls for an urgent need of efficient and scalable CF techniques for learning the model on-the-fly for real-world recommender systems.

To this end, we investigate Online Collaborative Filtering (OCF) techniques for on-the-fly recommender systems in this paper. The state-of-the-art OCF approach is based on the online low-rank matrix approximation algorithm [1, 17] by applying the simple online gradient descent (OGD) algorithms to solve the matrix factorization task, which thus avoids the highly expensive re-training cost of traditional batch matrix factorization algorithms. Despite their merit of high efficiency, their naive gradient descent approaches may not be very effective since they completely neglect the underlying structure of the collaborative filtering task.

To overcome the limitation of the existing OCF approaches, we propose a novel framework of Online Multi-Task Collaborative Filtering (OMTCF) by exploiting the close relationship between collaborative filtering and multi-task learning [22]. The key idea of OMTCF is to not only update the weight vectors of the user (task) related to the current observed data, but also the weight vectors of some other users (tasks) according to a user interaction matrix. As a result, OMTCF is able to learn the model more accurately than the existing OCF algorithms, with the only disadvantage of being slightly less efficient due to the cost of multi-task learning. In this paper, we propose a family of OMTCF algorithms to trade off between efficacy and efficiency, and extensively examine their performance for on-the-fly recommender systems on various large benchmark data sets.

The rest of the paper is organized as follows. Section 2 introduce the background and related work, Section 3 proposes the framework of Online Multi-Task Collaborative Filtering. Section 4 discusses our experimental results, and Section 5 sets out the conclusion of our work.

RecSys'13, October 12–16, 2013, Hong Kong, China.
Copyright 2013 ACM 978-1-4503-2409-0/13/10 ...$15.00.
http://dx.doi.org/10.1145/2507157.2507176 .

2. BACKGROUND AND RELATED WORK

This section briefly reviews the background of some major groups of related work, including batch collaborative filtering, online collaborative filtering, and multi-task learning.

One of the state-of-the-art methods for regular CF tasks is the latent factor or matrix factorization method [31, 23], which is one of the major techniques used by the Netflix prize winner's algorithms [14]. The key idea of latent factor model assumes that the similarity between users and items is simultaneously induced by some hidden lower-dimension structure in the data. For example, the rating that a user gives to a movie might depend on a few implicit factors such as the user's taste across various movie genres. Beyond this direction, some probabilistic and Bayesian matrix factorization for collaborative filtering methods have also been proposed [25, 19]. For a more comprehensive survey on regular CF techniques, please refer to the survey paper [30]. Although the batch algorithms for matrix factorization have shown great successes, they generally suffer from high time complexity and memory cost, which thus are non-scalable for building on-the-fly recommender systems.

Online collaborative filtering has received emerging attention recently. The work in [10] is perhaps one of early work, in which OCF is cast as an online ranking problem [8]. This algorithm is however not very practical because it assumes all the users' preferences can be known for each training instance, which is not always true. The related work most relevant to our study is the online collaborative filtering by stochastic gradient descent [1, 2] and another improved work in [17], which attempted to optimize the objective function of matrix factorization based formulation for collaborative filtering in online learning fashion. Their naive gradient descent strategy simply neglects the underlying structure of CF tasks which thus limits their learning efficacy. Our work is partially motivated to overcome their limitation. Besides, our work is also somewhat related to the online evolutionary collaborative filtering work in [18] which assigns larger weights to the new rating and incrementally updates the users' and items' similarities, but differs in two major aspects: (i) to be more precise from an online learning perspective, [18] is essentially a mini-batch or incremental algorithm that does not update the model upon a single observation; and (ii) [18] generally belongs to a simple memory-based approach, which is usually less effective as compared to the state-of-the-art matrix factorization approaches. Finally, our work is very different from the work [9] which tried to improve scalability of batch CF methods by exploring practical tricks, such as the MapReduce framework.

Our work is also inspired in part by some related work in Multi-task learning (MTL) [3], which is a machine learning method where multiple tasks are jointly learnt such that each of them benefits from each other. A popular framework for MTL is multi-task feature learning [4], which assumes that all tasks share a common yet latent feature representation. Similarly, although MTL has many advantages, it also suffers some disadvantages, e.g., low efficiency. Recently, online multi-task learning [7, 24] has been proposed to extend traditional MTL in online learning setting. The online multi-task learner proceeds in rounds by observing a sequence of examples, each belonging to some task from a pre-defined set tasks. The basic idea of the online multi-task learning in [7] is that instead of only updating the weight vector of the task related to the current instance, it online updates weight vectors of multiple tasks based on a task interaction matrix. Furthermore, instead of using a fixed task interaction matrix, [24] proposed to update the task relationship matrix during the online learning process.

Although both online collaborative filtering and online multi-task learning have been actively studied in different research communities separately, to the best of our knowledge, no existing work has attempted to tackle online collaborative filtering by exploiting the idea of online multi-task learning for building on-the-fly recommender systems.

3. ONLINE MULTI-TASK COLLABORATIVE FILTERING

3.1 Problem Setting and Formulation

In this section, we present the proposed framework for Online Multi-Task Collaborative Filtering (OMTCF) for building on-the-fly recommender systems. We emphasize that an essential difference between online CF and traditional batch CF tasks is that batch CF assumes the entire collection of training data is given a prior before the learning task, while online CF learns the model on-the-fly from a sequence of training data. In the following, we will firstly introduce the problem setting and then present a family of OMTCF algorithms for addressing a variety of practical issues.

First of all, we introduce the problem of a regular collaborative filtering task. In a collaborative filtering task, some users from a total of n users rated some products (items) from a total of m products, and these ratings form an incomplete matrix $\mathrm{R} \in \mathbb{R}^{n\times m}$, where r_{ij} is the rating on the j-th item given by the i-th user. The goal of collaborative filtering is to predict the unknown ratings based on the known ones. For collaborative filtering, one of the well-known approach is the matrix factorization algorithm, which learns the latent structure by factorizing the rating matrix to a user matrix $\mathrm{U} \in \mathbb{R}^{n\times k}$ and an item matrix $\mathrm{V} \in \mathbb{R}^{m\times k}$ through the following optimization problem:

$$\arg\min_{\mathrm{U}\in\mathbb{R}^{n\times k},\mathrm{V}\in\mathbb{R}^{m\times k}} \|\mathrm{R} - \mathrm{U}\mathrm{V}^\top\|_F^2, \quad (1)$$

where $\|\mathrm{R}\|_F$ is the Frobenius norm of the matrix R. If the rating matrix R is fully observable, then this problem can be reduced to a Singular Value Decomposition (SVD) problem. However, the matrix for collaborative filtering is only partially observed, which results in an ill-posed problem for the above formulation. To tackle the challenge, we can apply the low-rank matrix approximation technique to re-formulate this problem. Specifically, let U_a be the a-th row of U, and V_b be the b-th row of V, then given a partial collection of observed pairs $\mathcal{C} = \{(a, b)\}$, let $|\mathcal{C}|$ denote the number of observed ratings, the collaborative filtering problem can be re-formulated as the regularized optimization task for low-rank matrix factorization:

$$\arg\min_{\mathrm{U}\in\mathbb{R}^{n\times k},\mathrm{V}\in\mathbb{R}^{m\times k}} \sum_{\forall(a,b)\in\mathcal{C}} \ell(U_a, V_b, r_{a,b}) + \lambda(\|\mathrm{U}\|_F^2 + \|\mathrm{V}\|_F^2) \quad (2)$$

where $\lambda > 0$ is a regularization parameter, and $\ell(U_a, V_b, r_{a,b})$ is a loss function that defines the loss between the true $r_{a,b}$ and the prediction $U_a V_b^\top$.

However, this new problem is a non-convex optimization which cannot be solved directly using a standard SVD algorithm. Since the optimization problem (2) is non-convex, [28] proposed to replace the Frobenius norm regularization by a trace norm regularization in order to relax it to a convex optimization problem, which can be solved by Semi-definite Programming (SDP) using the following property of trace norm regularization:

$$\|R\|_\Sigma = \inf_{R=UV^\top} \frac{1}{2}(\|U\|_F^2 + \|V\|_F^2). \quad (3)$$

However, the heavy cost of solving a sparse SDP task makes it infeasible for real datasets with millions of observations.

To overcome this limitation of regular collaborative filtering, [1] proposed the online collaborative filtering based on a simple gradient descent approach. In particular, given a single prediction problem of user a on item b, the algorithm first makes a prediction of rating $\hat{r}_{a,b} = U_a V_b^\top$; after the true rating $r_{a,b}$ is revealed, the algorithm suffers a loss $\ell(U_a, V_b, r_{a,b})$; finally, the OCF algorithm makes updates on their model U and V based on the gradient descent approach:

$$U_a = (1 - 2\tau\lambda)U_a - \tau\frac{\partial \ell(U_a, V_b, r_{a,b})}{\partial U_a}, \quad (4)$$

$$V_b = (1 - 2\tau\lambda)V_b - \tau\frac{\partial \ell(U_a, V_b, r_{a,b})}{\partial V_b}. \quad (5)$$

where τ is the learning rate parameter. In general, one can define different type of loss function for different purposes. For example, to optimize the Root Mean Square Error (RMSE), i.e., RMSE $= \sqrt{\frac{1}{|C|}\sum_{(a,b)\in C}(r_{a,b} - \hat{r}_{a,b})^2}$, we can define the loss by the square error function as:

$$\ell_1(U_a, V_b, r_{a,b}) = (r_{a,b} - U_a V_b^\top)^2 \quad (6)$$

Similarly, if one aims to optimize the Mean Absolute Error (MAE), i.e., MAE $= \frac{1}{|C|}\sum_{(a,b)\in C}|r_{a,b} - \hat{r}_{a,b}|$, we can define the absolute loss function as:

$$\ell_2(U_a, V_b, r_{a,b}) = |r_{a,b} - U_a V_b^\top| \quad (7)$$

3.2 A Family of OMTCF Algorithms

The proposed OMTCF method is generally inspired by noticing the equivalence between multi-task learning and collaborative filtering formulations. To illustrate this clearly, we rewrite the formulation of the optimization task of collaborative filtering as follows:

$$\arg\min_{U\in\mathbb{R}^{n\times k}, V\in\mathbb{R}^{m\times k}} \sum_{i=1}^{n}\sum_{\forall(i,b)\in C} \ell(U_i, V_b, r_{i,b}) + \lambda(\|U\|_F^2 + \|V\|_F^2) \quad (8)$$

By treating each user i as an individual task, each U_i as the task model, V as the features of items and $r_{i,b}$ as the prediction output of model i for item b, it is not difficult to see that the above formulation is essentially equivalent to the formulation of a multi-task learning that optimizes the models of multiple tasks simultaneously. The equivalence between collaborative filtering and multi-task learning has also been shown by some previous studies in literature [22, 21], which partially inspire our study in this paper.

Motivated by the above equivalence fact, our approach is to exploit the idea of online multi-task learning [7] to tackle the online collaborative filtering task. For online multi-task learning, one important step is to define a task interaction matrix $A \in \mathbb{R}^{n\times n}$, which essentially indicates the similarity or interaction degree between tasks. Following the similar idea, we can define a user interaction matrix $A \in \mathbb{R}^{n\times n}$ such as a large value $A_{i,j}$ indicates a close interaction should be imposed between user i and user j. In general, matrix A can be computed if prior knowledge about the users is available. If however such prior knowledge is not available, one can define some constant matrix. For example, one simple approach used by the previous study is to define A as follows:

$$A_{fixed} = \begin{bmatrix} 1 & \frac{1}{2} & \cdots & \frac{1}{2} \\ \frac{1}{2} & 1 & \cdots & \frac{1}{2} \\ \cdots & \cdots & \cdots & \cdots \\ \frac{1}{2} & \frac{1}{2} & \cdots & 1 \end{bmatrix}. \quad (9)$$

where the above matrix indicates that we should make a full update ($A_{ii} = 1$) of the user's model when the instance belongs to, and make a half update ($A_{ij} = \frac{1}{2}\forall i \neq j$) of other users' models otherwise.

Unlike the existing OCF approach where only one user is updated for every observed rating, the proposed online multi-task collaborative filtering (OMTCF) approach will update multiple users for each observed rating. More formally, given an incoming rating $r_{a,b}$ with respect to user a and item b, the algorithm will update the models of multiple users (i.e., multiple rows of U) according to the user interaction matrix A. Specifically, we have the following functions for updating the models of multiple users:

$$U_i = (1 - 2\tau\lambda)U_i - \tau A(a,i)\frac{\partial \ell(U_a, V_b, r_{a,b})}{\partial U_a}, \quad (10)$$

$$V_b = (1 - 2\tau\lambda)V_b - \tau\frac{\partial \ell(U_a, V_b, r_{a,b})}{\partial V_b}, \quad (11)$$

where $i = 1, \ldots, n$, τ is the learning rate and $\ell(U_a, V_b, r_{a,b})$ is a loss function which is defined based on either Eq. (6) for RMSE or Eq. (7) for MAE. In the above, a larger value of $A(a,i)$ will result in a stronger update on U_i eventually. With respect to the two kinds of loss functions, we derive the detailed online updating rules by gradient descent associated with the interaction matrix in the following propositions.

PROPOSITION 1. *In an OMTCF task, given an observed rating pair (a, b), the updating rule with respect to the loss function ℓ_1 defined in Eq. (6) can be expressed as follows:*

$$U_i = (1 - 2\tau\lambda)U_i + 2\tau A_t(a,i)(V_b(r_{a,b} - U_a V_b^\top)) \quad (12)$$

$$V_b = (1 - 2\tau\lambda)V_b + 2\tau U_a(r_{a,b} - U_a V_b^\top) \quad (13)$$

where $i = 1, \ldots, n$.

PROPOSITION 2. *In an OMTCF task, given an observed rating pair (a, b), the updating rule with respect to the loss function ℓ_2 defined in Eq. (7) can be expressed as follows:*

$$U_i = (1 - 2\tau\lambda)U_i + 2\tau A_t(a,i)(V_b \cdot sign(r_{a,b} - U_a V_b^\top)) \quad (14)$$

$$V_b = (1 - 2\tau\lambda)V_b + 2\tau U_a \cdot sign(r_{a,b} - U_a V_b^\top) \quad (15)$$

where $i = 1, \ldots, n$.

In the proposed OMTCF algorithms, one key issue is how to determine an appropriate user interaction matrix A. The following will discuss this issue in detail.

3.3 Online Updating User Interaction Matrix

Instead of choosing a constant user interaction matrix A as shown in Eqn (9), another possible approach is to calculate a (sparse) matrix A from prior knowledge of user information when available:

$$A(i,j) = \text{similarity}(i,j) \quad (16)$$

where similarity(i,j) is a function of defining the similarity between two users according to the prior knowledge. For example, if we only have the age information about users, we can probably set the similarity value for the users who belongs to the same age group as 1, and 0 otherwise.

The above approaches are generally limited in that they either require the prior knowledge which is not always available or often fix the user interaction matrix as a constant matrix, which may somewhat restrict the power of the proposed algorithm for achieving faster convergence. To overcome these limitations, we also propose to learn the user interaction matrix A automatically during the online learning process. In particular, we can choose the user interaction matrix by using the covariance matrix of user matrix U that is updated sequentially as follows:

$$A = cov(U), \tag{17}$$

which is somewhat inspired by the Gaussian Process based multi-task learning [5], where the task relatedness is measured by the Gaussian Process covariance function.

Although the above suggested matrices are fairly reasonable, in a real-world scenario, they are only an approximation of the user similarity, which may not exactly reflect the true user interaction. In addition, online multi-task learning often converges much faster than online single task learning at the beginning of the online learning process, but the advantage of performing multi-task updates will become less significant as time goes by as the models become more and more accurate. To address these issues, we propose to define the following attenuation coefficient function over the user relationship matrix:

$$\theta_t(i,j) = (\frac{1}{t})^{\frac{1}{3}}\mathbb{I}_{i\neq j} + \mathbb{I}_{i=j} \tag{18}$$

where $\mathbb{I}_x$ is an indicator function that outputs 1 when x is true and 0 otherwise. This attenuation function weakens the effect of updating the multiple users as time goes. Thus, the final true user interaction matrix used in OMTCF will be the user interaction matrix multiplied by the attenuation coefficient as:

$$A_t = \theta_t \odot A, \tag{19}$$

where $\odot$ is the element-wise produce, i.e., $A_t(i,j) = \theta_t(i,j) * A(i,j)$. Finally, Algorithm 1 summarizes the framework of the proposed OMTCF algorithms. It is not difficult to see that the proposed algorithms are efficient and scalable with linear time and space complexity.

Algorithm 1 OMTCF — Framework of Online Multi-Task Collaborative Filtering algorithms

Input: a sequence of rating pairs $\{(a_t, b_t), t = 1, \ldots, M\}$
Initialization: Initialize a random matrix for user matrix U and item matrix V, and initialize user relationship matrix A_0 as an identity matrix I
for $t = 1, 2, \ldots, M$ **do**
  receive rating prediction request of user a_t on item b_t
  make prediction $\hat{r}_{a_t,b_t} = U_{a_t}V_{b_t}^\top$
  the true rating r_{a_t,b_t} is revealed
  the algorithm suffers a loss $\ell(U_a, V_b, r_{a,b})$
  update U and V_{b_t} by Proposition 1(RMSE) or 2(MAE)
  update the user interaction matrix A_t as follows:

$$A_t = \theta_t \odot \begin{cases} A_{fixed} & \text{(OMTCF-I)} \\ A_{\text{similarity}} & \text{(OMTCF-II)} \\ cov(U) & \text{(OMTCF-III)} \end{cases}$$

end for

3.4 Efficient Hybrid Algorithm for OMTCF

Although the proposed OMTCF algorithms achieve significantly faster convergence rate than the traditional OCF approach, this advantage is paid by higher computation cost of performing the multi-task updates. Specifically, because OMTCF needs to update the models of multiple users during the online learning step, the running time cost would be much higher than OCF. In this part, we would propose a hybrid algorithm to trade off between efficiency and efficacy.

The proposed algorithm follows the similar framework as the OMTCF-I algorithm. In the online learning process, we monitor the amount of prediction change (in either RMSE or MAE) over a past certain period (defined by a window size T) $\Delta(t,T)$ defined as follows:

$$\Delta(t,T) = \begin{cases} \text{RMSE}(t-T) - \text{RMSE}(t) & \text{(RMSE)} \\ \text{MAE}(t-T) - \text{MAE}(t) & \text{(MAE)} \end{cases}$$

We then introduce a threshold ζ to indicate whether the learning process has converged sufficiently. If the change $\Delta(t,T)$ is smaller than ζ, the algorithm will then switch to a single-task update, i.e.,

$$A_t = \begin{cases} \theta_t \odot A_{fixed} & \Delta(t,T) \geq \zeta \\ I & \text{otherwise} \end{cases}$$

We denote this hybrid algorithm as "OMTCF-IV" for short.

3.5 OMTCF for Novel User/Item Extension

The above OMTCF algorithms follow a formal online learning setting, but they make an implicit assumption, i.e., both the number of users and the number of items are fixed and they are both known beforehand. In a real-world online application, this is not realistic. In this part, we aim to extend OMTCF algorithms to handle the situation where an incoming rating observation is related to a novel user or a novel item. The key idea of the proposed algorithm here is that we will try to expand the user/item matrix by adding one user/item vector whenever a new user/item appears. We assume the user interaction matrix is fixed as Eq.(9), which is the same as "OMTCF-I" (we could also consider other type of interaction matrix). We keep a multi-task cumulative updated user vector and update it at each iteration. This multi-task cumulative updated user vector will be applied to initialize the new user vector whenever a new user is added. This strategy is able to guarantee the algorithm achieves the same performance as the "OMTCF-I" without considering the difference caused by different random initializations. We denote this algorithm for handling novel sample extension as "OMTCF-V" for short. The details are summarized in Algorithm 2.

3.6 Practical Online Multi-task Collaborative Filtering for Large-Scale Datasets

As we can see, algorithm "OMTCF-V" can build the user and item matrix from scratch and online extended the user and item matrix based on the data observed, which could save the memory and make the algorithm more efficient. The algorithm "OMTCF-IV" can avoid unnecessary multiple updates when the online learning process has converged well. In fact, we can adopt the two improvements over original online multi-task collaborative filtering algorithm simultaneously into a single new algorithm, which is able to make online multi-task learning strategy for collaborative filtering more practical and efficient for large-scale datasets. We

Algorithm 2 OMTCF-V: The proposed OMTCF algorithm for handling novel sample extension

Input: a sequence of rating pairs $\{(a_t, b_t), t = 1, \ldots, M\}$, window size T (e.g. T=1000), convergence threshold ζ
Initialization: $\mathrm{U} = \mathrm{V} = \mathrm{A} = []$ and randomize U_{ini}.
for $t = 1, 2, \ldots, M$ **do**
  receive rating prediction request of user a_t on item b_t
  if user a_t is new **then**
    initialize $U_{a_t} = U_{ini}$
    expand the user matrix U as $\mathrm{U} = [\mathrm{U}; U_{a_t}]$
    expand the user interaction matrix as:
    $\mathrm{A}_{t-1} \leftarrow [\mathrm{A}_{t-1}, \frac{1}{2}(\frac{1}{t})^{\frac{1}{3}}\mathbf{1}; \frac{1}{2}(\frac{1}{t})^{\frac{1}{3}}\mathbf{1}, 1]$, where $\mathbf{1}$ is a vector of all elements equal to 1
  end if
  if item b_t is new **then**
    initialize V_{b_t} as a random vector.
    expand the item matrix V as $\mathrm{V} = [\mathrm{V}; V_{b_t}]$
  end if
  make prediction $\hat{r}_{a_t,b_t} = U_{a_t} V_{b_t}^{\top}$
  the true rating r_{a_t,b_t} is revealed
  the algorithm suffers a loss $\ell(U_a, V_b, r_{a,b})$
  update U and V_{b_t} by Proposition 1(RMSE) or 2(MAE)
  calculate U_{ini} as

$$\begin{cases} (1 - 2\tau\lambda)U_{ini} + \tau(\frac{1}{t})^{\frac{1}{3}}(V_b(r_{a,b} - U_a V_b^{\top})) & \text{(RMSE)} \\ (1 - 2\tau\lambda)U_{ini} + \tau(\frac{1}{t})^{\frac{1}{3}}(V_b sign(r_{a,b} - U_a V_b^{\top})) & \text{(MAE)} \end{cases}$$

  update A_t by $\mathrm{A}_t = \theta_t \odot \mathrm{A}_{fixed}$
end for

name the new algorithm as "OMTCF-VI", which is a combination of OMTCF-IV and OMTCF-V. We omit the detailed algorithm due to space limitation.

Remarks on Parallelization. One important advantage of online CF over batch CF is that online algorithms only need to process one rating at a time, making the updating efficient and scalable. Although our OMTCF algorithms are generally more computationally expensive than the simple OCF algorithm in [1], this disadvantage can be somewhat compensated by exploring the advantages of parallel computing techniques, which can be easily deployed by the proposed OMTCF algorithms. In particular, in contrast to the OCF algorithm, our OMTCF algorithms update multiple users simultaneously and the updates of these users do not affect each other at each learning round, making them to be easily parallelized by a trivial implementation.

4. EXPERIMENTAL RESULTS

In this section, we evaluate the empirical performance of the proposed OMTCF algorithms for online collaborative filtering tasks. It is important to note that we do not compare the proposed algorithms with other existing batch collaborative filtering algorithms since the performance evaluation protocol and settings between online and batch learning algorithms are very different, making them unfair and meaningless to be compared directly.

4.1 Compared Algorithms

We compare the proposed OMTCF algorithms with the emerging online collaborative filtering algorithm. Specifically, the compared algorithms in our experiments include:

- "OCF": the Online Collaborative Filtering algorithm by online gradient descent method described in [1];
- "DA-OCF" the Dual-Averaging method for online collaborative filtering proposed in [17];
- "OMTCF-I": the proposed OMTCF in Algorithm 1 where the user-interaction matrix is set as Eq.(9) as suggested in [7];
- "OMTCF-II": the proposed OMTCF algorithm with one sparse user interaction matrix is computed using prior user information in Eq.(16);
- "OMTCF-III": the proposed OMTCF algorithm with the task covariance matrix in Eq.(17);
- "OMTCF-IV": the proposed Hybrid OMTCF algorithm;
- "OMTCF-V": the proposed OMTCF for new sample extension algorithm, as shown in Algorithm 2.
- "OMTCF-VI": our practical OMTCF algorithm.

4.2 Experimental Testbed and Setup

To extensively examine the empirical performance, we conduct the experiments on a variety of publicly available datasets widely used for benchmark evaluation of CF in literature. The first two relatively smaller datasets include: (i) the "MovieLens 100k" dataset collected by the Grouplens Research Project from the MovieLens web site [1], where users can freely give their ratings on various movies and receive movie recommendations; it consists of 100,000 ratings from 943 users on 1682 movies, and also provides additional user info, such as their genders, and ages, etc; (ii) the "HetRec 2011 MovieLens" dataset, which links the movies of MovieLens with their corresponding web pages at IMDb and Rotten Tomatoes movie review systems; this dataset consists of 855,598 ratings from 2113 users on 10197 movies; it however does not contain any user info. We also test on other four large-scale data sets which will be introduced later.

To make fair comparisons, all the algorithms adopt the same experimental setup. Firstly, for the proposed "OMTCF-II" algorithm, we set the similarity between a pair of users as 1 when they are from the same gender and in the same age period, while the similarities of others pairs as 0. Note that two users are considered as in the same age period if the difference of their ages is less than 5 years. Considering the fact that only the "MovieLens 100k" dataset consists of the user information, the algorithm "OMTCF-II" is only tested on this dataset. Secondly, for the proposed "OMTCF-III" algorithm, we use the gaussian kernel for the users vectors to compute the user similarity, where the kernel width σ is set as 1. To make a fair comparison, the learning rate γ of all algorithms is set to 0.005, and the regularization parameter is set to 3^{-6}, the λ parameter in DA-OCF algorithm was set to 0.006, which was suggested to achieve the best performance according to [17]. The rank parameter k of matrix U and V is set to two cases: 5 and 10, respectively. After the parameters are chosen, all the experiments were conducted over 20 runs of different random permutations for each dataset. All the experimental results were reported by averaging over these 20 runs. For performance metric, we evaluate the performance of online collaborative filtering algorithms by measuring their scores of online Root Mean Square Error (RMSE) and online Mean Absolute Error (MAE) on the test set.

4.3 Evaluation on Two Smaller Datasets

Table 1 summarizes the average performance of the compared algorithms over the two datasets. From the experimental results, several observations can be drawn as follows.

[1] `http://movielens.umn.edu`

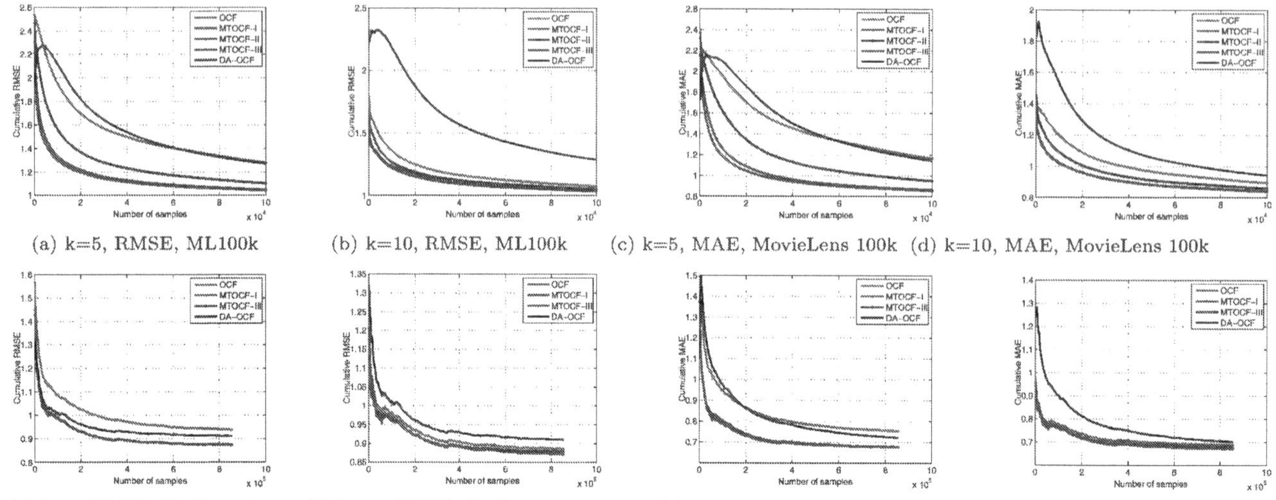

(a) k=5, RMSE, ML100k (b) k=10, RMSE, ML100k (c) k=5, MAE, MovieLens 100k (d) k=10, MAE, MovieLens 100k

(e) k=5, RMSE, HetRec 2011 (f) k=10, RMSE, HetRec 2011 (g) k=5, MAE, HetRec 2011 (h) k=10, MAE, HetRec 2011

Figure 1: Online cumulative predictive performance of different online collaborative filtering algorithms for on-the-fly recommendation (best viewed in color).

Table 1: Evaluation of online CF algorithms, where k is the rank parameter for matrix U and V. The bold element indicates the best performance for each setting. Note that OMTCF-II is not applicable to the second dataset as user info is unavailable.

MovieLens 100k	k=5 RMSE	k=5 MAE	k=10 RMSE	k=10 MAE
OCF	1.2808	1.1685	1.0781	0.8970
DA-OCF	1.2722	1.1438	1.2898	0.9369
OMTCF-I	1.0509	0.8665	1.0506	0.8434
OMTCF-II	1.1057	0.9527	1.0543	0.8614
OMTCF-III	**1.0429**	**0.8564**	**1.0359**	**0.8393**
HetRec 2011 MovieLens	**k=5 RMSE**	**k=5 MAE**	**k=10 RMSE**	**k=10 MAE**
OCF	0.9386	0.7540	0.8859	0.6887
DA-OCF	0.9114	0.7273	0.9098	0.7018
OMTCF-I	0.8750	**0.6777**	0.8784	0.6786
OMTCF-III	**0.8734**	**0.6777**	**0.8715**	**0.6716**

First, compared with the previous OCF and DA-OCF approach, we observe that all the proposed OMTCF algorithms achieve significantly better performance of smaller RMSE/MSE values for all the cases. This shows that the proposed learning strategy is more effective than the existing naive gradient descent approach in improving the online prediction performance of collaborative filtering tasks.

Second, we found that, when the dimensionality is relatively lower (i.e., k=5), the gap between the OMTCF and OCF tends to be more significant. This shows that OMTCF is more suitable to learn an effective low-rank matrix factorization for collaborative filtering tasks. DA-OCF seems dose not benefit much as the dimensionality increases.

Third, by comparing the performance between several variants of OMTCF algorithms using different user interaction matrices, we found that OMTCF-III performs the best among all the proposed algorithms. This validates the efficacy of learning the user interaction matrix in online collaborative filtering learning tasks. Further, OMTCF-II tends to perform worse than the other OMTCF algorithms, which indicates that it should be careful to exploit the user information for user interaction matrix, especially when such user information is noisy or incomplete in real applications. For such situations, a simple user interaction matrix, e.g., defined in Eq.(9), might be even better than some complicated user interaction matrix which may be corrupted with noise.

Besides, in order to inspect the details of online collaborative filtering performance, we also show the online performance convergence of all the compared algorithms in the entire online learning process in Figure 1. Similar to the above observations, the experimental results in the figure again verify the efficacy of the proposed OMTCF algorithms, which consistently outperform the previous OCF algorithm. Specifically, we observe that the OMTCF algorithms in general converge much faster than OCF in the beginning of the learning process, which is very important and beneficial to many recommender systems as a fast convergence performance makes the online recommendation solution being able to effectively adapt the fast changes in a real online recommendation environment.

4.4 Efficiency and New Sample Extension

Although the OMTCF algorithms are able to significantly improve the online RMSE/MAE performance, they generally suffer high time complexity. The time efficiency of an online collaborative filtering algorithm is also very important for large-scale applications. To overcome this limitation of the previous OMTCF algorithms, we also evaluate the efficient hybrid algorithm, which aims to achieve a trade off between efficacy and efficiency. In particular, it will reduce to a single-task updating algorithm when the online RMSE or MAE performance is no longer improved significantly. In addition to improving the efficiency issue of OMTCF, we also propose OMTCF-V to tackle the new sample extension issue, which is also evaluated in the following.

Specifically, we compare all the OMTCF algorithms with OCF in terms of both predictive performance (RMSE/MAE) and time efficiency. For OMTCF-I,II,III algorithms, the parameters are set as the same as the previous experiment. For OMTCF-IV, the parameters are set the same as OMTCF-I, except that ζ is set to 5×10^{-2} for RMSE and set to 3×10^{-2} for MAE, the rank parameter k is set to 5 for all algorithms.

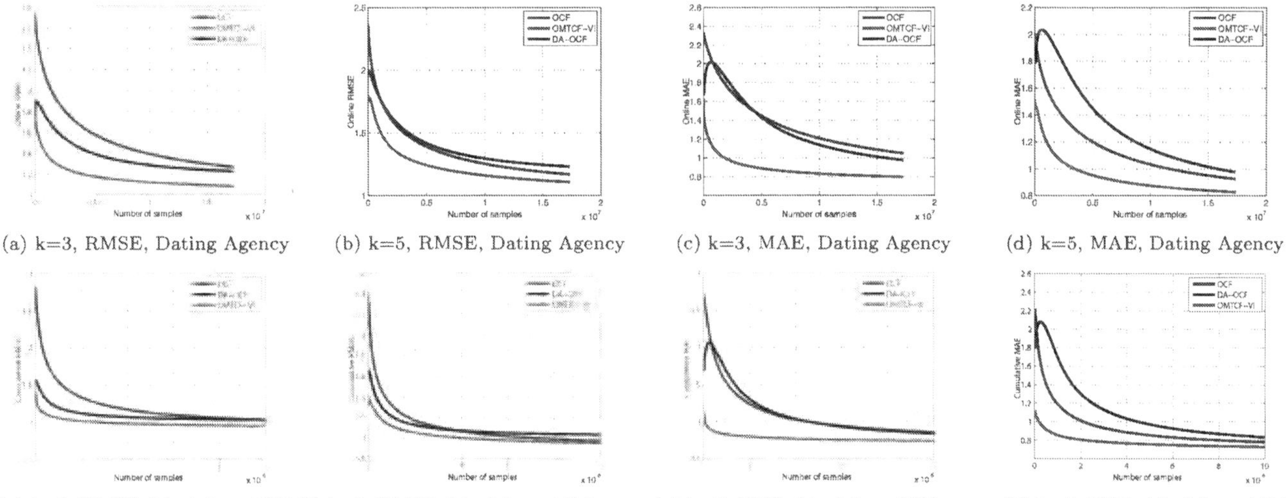

(a) k=3, RMSE, Dating Agency (b) k=5, RMSE, Dating Agency (c) k=3, MAE, Dating Agency (d) k=5, MAE, Dating Agency

(e) k=3, RMSE, MovieLens 10M (f) k=5, RMSE, MovieLens 10M (g) k=3, MAE, MovieLens 10M (h) k=5, MAE, MovieLens 10M

Figure 2: Online cumulative predictive performance of three online algorithms for on-the-fly recommendation on large-scale datasets (best viewed in color). We can only show two largest datasets due to space limitation.

Table 2: Evaluation of Efficacy and Time Cost

MovieLens 100k	RMSE		MAE	
	RMSE	TIME(s)	MAE	TIME(s)
OCF	1.2779	0.76	1.1890	0.68
DA-OCF	1.2722	2.01	1.1438	2.06
OMTCF-I	1.0534	102.41	0.8644	104.08
OMTCF-II	1.1103	23.81	0.9514	24.03
OMTCF-III	1.0443	5883.83	0.8514	5732.84
OMTCF-IV	1.0607	2.19	0.8967	2.99
OMTCF-V	1.0532	88.61	0.8648	91.66
OMTCF-VI	1.0521	1.34	0.8625	1.96
HetRec 2011 MovieLens	RMSE		MAE	
	RMSE	TIME(s)	MAE	TIME(s)
OCF	0.9408	7.79	0.7560	5.99
DA-OCF	0.9114	17.08	0.7273	16.93
OMTCF-I	0.8757	1964.89	0.6786	1992.89
OMTCF-III	0.8719	2.3×10^6	0.6785	2.3×10^6
OMTCF-IV	0.8794	22.27	0.6818	33.85
OMTCF-V	0.8767	1126.62	0.6779	1159.84
OMTCF-VI	0.8757	12.78	0.6713	16.57

The parameters for OMTCF-V is the same as OMTCF-IV. After choosing the parameters, all the experiments were conducted over 20 runs of different random permutations for each dataset. All the experimental results were reported by averaging over these 20 runs. The performance evaluations are summarized in Table 2.

Several observations can be drawn from the results. First, we found that OMTCF-III, though achieving the best RMSE and MAE performance, runs significantly slower than the other algorithms, indicating the importance of improving efficiency of the proposed algorithms. Further, we can see that OMTCF-IV achieves significantly smaller values of both RMSE and MAE than OCF, which demonstrates the strategy of the proposed OMTCF-IV algorithm is significantly more effective than the state-of-the-art OCF algorithm. In addition, the OMTCF-IV algorithm is slightly worse than the OMTCF-I algorithm in terms of RMSE and MAE values, but the difference is very small. In addition, according to the time evaluation results, OMTCF-IV runs slightly slower than the OCF algorithm, but significantly faster than OMTCF-I. From these promising results, we can conclude that the proposed OMTCF-IV algorithm empirically achieves fairly comparable RMSE/MAE performance as OMTCF-I, and shares quite similar empirical time complexity as OCF, which indicates the OMTCF-IV algorithm in general achieves a good trade-off between efficacy and efficiency.

Finally, we examine the efficacy of the proposed OMTCF-V algorithm for handling new sample extension issue. In particular, by inspecting the performance of the OMTCF-V algorithm, we observe that OMTCF-V achieves almost identical values of RMSE and MAE as compared with the OMTCF-I algorithm (the marginal differences should be caused by different randomization for the user and item vectors), but save much time cost than the OMTCF-I algorithm, which demonstrates that the proposed OMTCF-V algorithm is not only capable of handling the new sample extension issue perfectly, but also runs more efficiently than the previous OMTCF algorithms. Among all the OMTCF algorithms, OMTCF-VI is the most efficient one and has comparable RMSE/MAE performance with other algorithms, making it more applicable for large-scale applications.

4.5 Evaluation on Large-Scale Datasets

We now evaluate the practical OMTCF-VI algorithm on four large-scale datasets: (i) **Dating Agency [6]:** The Dating Agency dataset[2], which contains 17,359,346 anonymous ratings of 168,791 profiles made by 135,359 LibimSeTi users; (ii) **Jester Joke:** this dataset from online Joke recommendation system[3] contains 1,761,439 ratings of 150 jokes from 63,974 users; (iii)**Movielens 1M:** this Movie rating dataset[4] contains 1,000,209 ratings of 3,900 movies by 6,040 users; and (iv) **Movielens 10M:** this Movie rating dataset[5] contains 10,000,054 ratings of 10,681 movies by 71,567 users.

Table 3 and Figure 2 summarize the empirical results of our evaluation. We can observe that OMTCF-VI performs significantly better than the OCF algorithm in terms of both RMSE and MAE metrics. In terms of the time efficiency, the online algorithms (OCF and OMTCF-VI) are generally fairly efficient, which typically took several hundreds sec-

[2] `http://www.occamslab.com/petricek/data/`
[3] `http://goldberg.berkeley.edu/jester-data/`
[4] `http://movielens.umn.edu`
[5] `http://movielens.umn.edu`

onds to run on a dataset with 10,000,000 ratings. Finally, among all the online algorithms, the proposed OMTCF-VI algorithm is on average just 2-3 times slower than the OCF algorithm, and slightly slower than or sometimes comparable to the DA-OCF algorithm.

Table 3: Evaluation on Large-scale datasets.

Dating Agency	RMSE, k = 3		RMSE, k = 5	
	RMSE	TIME(s)	RMSE	TIME(s)
OCF	1.2684	183.85	1.1700	189.86
DA-OCF	1.2269	342.15	1.2324	340.18
OMTCF-VI	**1.0823**	583.21	**1.1094**	563.54
Dating Agency	**MAE, k = 3**		**MAE, k = 5**	
	MAE	TIME(s)	MAE	TIME(s)
OCF	1.0494	189.69	0.9265	192.68
DA-OCF	0.9757	393.43	0.9767	405.70
OMTCF-VI	**0.7986**	520.34	**0.8263**	626.79
Jester Joke	**RMSE, k = 3**		**RMSE, k = 5**	
	RMSE	TIME(s)	RMSE	TIME(s)
OCF	1.1243	18.56	1.1287	18.50
DA-OCF	1.1305	34.77	1.1279	34.82
OMTCF-VI	**1.1195**	30.10	**1.1261**	29.33
Jester Joke	**MAE, k = 3**		**MAE, k = 5**	
	MAE	TIME(s)	MAE	TIME(s)
OCF	0.8866	18.64	0.8896	18.81
DA-OCF	0.8977	34.54	0.8962	35.16
OMTCF-VI	**0.8530**	30.68	**0.8708**	30.88
MovieLens 1M	**RMSE, k = 3**		**RMSE, k = 5**	
	RMSE	TIME(s)	RMSE	TIME(s)
OCF	1.1070	10.29	1.0441	10.57
DA-OCF	1.0636	19.76	1.0644	19.98
OMTCF-VI	**0.9766**	19.90	**0.9738**	18.07
MovieLens 1M	**MAE, k = 3**		**MAE, k = 5**	
	MAE	TIME(s)	MAE	TIME(s)
OCF	0.9773	10.70	0.8770	10.53
DA-OCF	0.8800	19.50	0.8833	19.54
OMTCF-VI	**0.7737**	22.19	**0.7719**	22.12
MovieLens 10M	**RMSE, k = 3**		**RMSE, k = 5**	
	RMSE	TIME(s)	RMSE	TIME(s)
OCF	1.0226	104.17	0.9700	105.35
DA-OCF	1.0262	194.67	1.0285	196.29
OMTCF-VI	**0.9515**	331.39	**0.9565**	333.38
MovieLens 10M	**MAE, k = 3**		**MAE, k = 5**	
	MAE	TIME(s)	MAE	TIME(s)
OCF	0.8494	107.24	0.7822	109.09
DA-OCF	0.8284	192.78	0.8328	195.55
OMTCF-VI	**0.7370**	380.13	**0.7425**	347.20

5. CONCLUSIONS

This paper proposed a novel framework of Online Multi-Task Collaborative Filtering (OMTCF) for on-the-fly recommender systems, in which a family of novel OMTCF algorithms were proposed. We conducted an extensive set of experiments by comparing several variants of the proposed algorithms with the existing online algorithms. Our promising empirical results showed that (i) online algorithms are very efficient and highly scalable which can run on large datasets with 10-million ratings in several minutes using a regular machine; and (ii) the proposed online technique is considerably more effective than the existing online algorithms. Future work will address the theoretical analysis of the proposed algorithms and explore new algorithms. For example, our current algorithms treat users as tasks and update the models of multiple users simultaneously. One can also treat items as tasks and update the models of multiple items simultaneously. Our technique may also be extended to tackle some open challenges in CF, e.g., tracking temporal dynamics [12], for which online algorithms potentially could be a natural and perhaps better solution.

Acknowledgements

This work was supported by MOE tier-1 grant (RG33/11).

References

[1] J. Abernethy, K. Canini, J. Langford, and A. Simma. Online collaborative filtering. *UC Berkeley, Tech. Rep.*, 2011.

[2] M. Ali, C. C. Johnson, and A. K. Tang. Parallel collaborative filtering for streaming data. *UT Austin, Tech. Rep.*, 2011.

[3] R. K. Ando and T. Zhang. A framework for learning predictive structures from multiple tasks and unlabeled data. *Journal of Machine Learning Research*, 6:1817–1853, 2005.

[4] A. Argyriou, T. Evgeniou, and M. Pontil. Multi-task feature learning. In *NIPS*, pages 41–48, 2006.

[5] E. V. Bonilla, K. M. A. Chai, and C. K. I. Williams. Multi-task gaussian process prediction. In *NIPS*, 2007.

[6] L. Brozovsky and V. Petricek. Recommender system for online dating service. *arXiv preprint cs/0703042*, 2007.

[7] G. Cavallanti, N. Cesa-Bianchi, and C. Gentile. Linear algorithms for online multitask classification. *Journal of Machine Learning Research*, 11:2901–2934, 2010.

[8] K. Crammer and Y. Singer. Pranking with ranking. In *NIPS*, pages 641–647, 2001.

[9] A. Das, M. Datar, A. Garg, and S. Rajaram. Google news personalization: scalable online collaborative filtering. In *WWW*, pages 271–280, 2007.

[10] E. F. Harrington. Online ranking/collaborative filtering using the perceptron algorithm. In *ICML*, pages 250–257, 2003.

[11] J. L. Herlocker, J. A. Konstan, L. G. Terveen, and J. Riedl. Evaluating collaborative filtering recommender systems. *ACM Trans. Inf. Syst.*, 22(1):5–53, 2004.

[12] Y. Koren. Collaborative filtering with temporal dynamics. In *KDD*, pages 447–456, 2009.

[13] Y. Koren. Factor in the neighbors: Scalable and accurate collaborative filtering. *ACM Trans. KDD*, 4(1):1:1–1:24, 2010.

[14] Y. Koren, R. M. Bell, and C. Volinsky. Matrix factorization techniques for recommender systems. *IEEE Computer*, 42(8):30–37, 2009.

[15] D. Lemire and A. Maclachlan. Slope one predictors for online rating-based collaborative filtering. In *SDM*, 2005.

[16] G. Linden, B. Smith, and J. York. Amazon.com recommendations: Item-to-item collaborative filtering. *IEEE Internet Computing*, 7(1):76–80, 2003.

[17] G. Ling, H. Yang, I. King, and M. R. Lyu. Online learning for collaborative filtering. In *IJCNN*, pages 1–8, 2012.

[18] N. N. Liu, M. Zhao, E. W. Xiang, and Q. Yang. Online evolutionary collaborative filtering. In *RecSys*, pages 95–102, 2010.

[19] L. W. Mackey, D. Weiss, and M. I. Jordan. Mixed membership matrix factorization. In *ICML*, pages 711–718, 2010.

[20] P. Melville, R. J. Mooney, and R. Nagarajan. Content-boosted collaborative filtering for improved recommendations. In *AAAI/IAAI*, pages 187–192, 2002.

[21] X. Ning and G. Karypis. Multi-task learning for recommender system. *JMLR - Proceedings Track*, 13:269–284, 2010.

[22] N. D. Phuong and T. M. Phuong. Collaborative filtering by multi-task learning. In *RIVF*, pages 227–232, 2008.

[23] J. D. M. Rennie and N. Srebro. Fast maximum margin matrix factorization for collaborative prediction. In *ICML'05*, pages 713–719, Bonn, Germany, 2005.

[24] A. Saha, P. Rai, H. D. III, and S. Venkatasubramanian. Online learning of multiple tasks and their relationships. In *AISTATS*, 2011.

[25] R. Salakhutdinov and A. Mnih. Probabilistic matrix factorization. In *NIPS*, 2007.

[26] B. M. Sarwar, G. Karypis, J. A. Konstan, and J. Riedl. Item-based collaborative filtering recommendation algorithms. In *WWW*, pages 285–295, 2001.

[27] L. Si and R. Jin. Flexible mixture model for collaborative filtering. In *ICML*, pages 704–711, 2003.

[28] N. Srebro, J. D. M. Rennie, and T. Jaakkola. Maximum-margin matrix factorization. In *NIPS*, 2004.

[29] D. H. Stern, R. Herbrich, and T. Graepel. Matchbox: large scale online bayesian recommendations. In *WWW'09*, pages 111–120, Madrid, Spain, 2009.

[30] X. Su and T. M. Khoshgoftaar. A survey of collaborative filtering techniques. *Adv. Artificial Intellegence*, 2009, 2009.

[31] M. Weimer, A. Karatzoglou, Q. V. Le, and A. J. Smola. Cofi rank - maximum margin matrix factorization for collaborative ranking. In *NIPS*, 2007.

[32] G.-R. Xue, C. Lin, Q. Yang, W. Xi, H.-J. Zeng, Y. Yu, and Z. Chen. Scalable collaborative filtering using cluster-based smoothing. In *SIGIR*, pages 114–121, Salvador, Brazil, 2005.

Learning to Rank Recommendations with the k-Order Statistic Loss

[Extended Abstract]

Jason Weston
Google Inc.
76 9th Avenue, New York
New York, NY 10011 USA
jweston@google.com

Hector Yee
Google Inc.
901 Cherry Avenue,
San Bruno, CA 94066 USA
hyee@google.com

Ron J. Weiss
Google Inc.
76 9th Avenue, New York
New York, NY 10011 USA
ronw@google.com

ABSTRACT

Making recommendations by learning to rank is becoming an increasingly studied area. Approaches that use stochastic gradient descent scale well to large collaborative filtering datasets, and it has been shown how to approximately optimize the mean rank, or more recently the top of the ranked list. In this work we present a family of loss functions, the k-order statistic loss, that includes these previous approaches as special cases, and also derives new ones that we show to be useful. In particular, we present (i) a new variant that more accurately optimizes precision at k, and (ii) a novel procedure of optimizing the mean maximum rank, which we hypothesize is useful to more accurately cover all of the user's tastes. The general approach works by sampling N positive items, ordering them by the score assigned by the model, and then weighting the example as a function of this ordered set. Our approach is studied in two real-world systems, Google Music and YouTube video recommendations, where we obtain improvements for computable metrics, and in the YouTube case, increased user click through and watch duration when deployed live on www.youtube.com.

Categories and Subject Descriptors

H.4 [**Information Systems Applications**]: Miscellaneous

Keywords

learning to rank, loss functions, stochastic gradient, collaborative filtering, matrix factorization

1. INTRODUCTION

While low-rank factorizations have been a standard tool for recommendation for a number of years [2] optimizing them using a ranking criterion is a relatively recent and increasingly popular trend amongst researchers and practicioners alike. Methods like CofiRank [7], CLiMF [5], or Wsabie [9] all learn, in some manner, to rank items that a user prefers at the top of the ranked list of items. Such loss functions are natural because the end product of such systems is usually to suggest a few recommendations to the user by choosing the top scoring (top ranked) items that the model predicts. However, in contrast to methods like SVD, where the user-item rating matrix is factorized in a least-squares sense, the optimization is not always straightforward. For example, it is difficult to optimize a metric like precision@k directly by gradient descent due to the discontinuities introduced by ranking. That is, when two items at the top of the list switch rank, the objective function score can change drastically. On the other hand, when two items at the bottom of the list switch rank there is no change in the objective at all. Researchers have found many approximations to the ranking functions they would like to optimize that are amenable to gradient descent. Note that several methods in the information retrieval domain have been proposed, e.g. [10, 11], but they have mostly focused on linear models rather than factor models. Those methods are not often applicable to recommendation tasks which typically involve thousands or millions of users and thousands or millions of items to rank, thus direct modeling of the full rank user-item matrix is infeasible. Hence, factored ranking models are desirable.

Due to the size of recommendation datasets learning via stochastic gradient descent (SGD) training is an attractive option, however again not all loss functions are easily optimized in this manner. For example the ListNet [10], SVM$_{map}$ [11] or OWPC (ordered weighted pairwise classification) [6] objectives involve computing the rank of positive examples which is too slow in an SGD step when there are hundreds of thousands or millions of items. Two choices of ranking loss that can be trained via SGD are the AUC (area under the curve) [4, 3] and WARP (weighted approximately ranked pairwise) [8] losses. However, both methods ignore the fact that there are multiple positive items per user and treat those items independently, clearly an incorrect assumption.

In this work we propose a new class of loss functions, the k-order statistic loss, which generalizes the existing AUC and WARP methods, as well as providing novel choices of loss, by taking into account the *set* of positive examples during the gradient steps. In particular, it can more accuratel optimize precision at k than the WARP loss, which WARP was designed for. Secondly, it can optimize novel metrics like maximum mean rank which we believe are useful for accurately covering all of the user's tastes when recommending

RecSys'13, October 12–16, 2013, Hong Kong, China.

http://dx.doi.org/10.1145/2507157.2507210 .

items. Experiments on real-world datasets indicate the usefulness of our approach.

2. K-ORDER STATISTIC LOSS

We consider the general recommendation task of ranking a set of items $\mathcal{D}$ for a given user, the returned list should have the most relevant items at the top. To solve this task, we are given a training set of users $\mathcal{U}$ each with a set of known ratings. We consider the case where each user has purchased / watched / liked a set of items, which are considered as positive ratings. No negative ratings are given. All non-positive rated items are thus considered as having an unknown rating[1]. We define the set $\mathcal{D}_u$ to be the positive items for user u. We consider factorized models of the form

$$f_d(u) = \frac{1}{|\mathcal{D}_u|} \sum_{i \in \mathcal{D}_u} V_i^\top V_d,$$

where V, which is an $m \times |\mathcal{D}|$ matrix, one vector for each item, contains the parameters to be learnt. We can further define $f(u)$ to be the vector of all item scores $1, \ldots, |\mathcal{D}|$ for the user u. To learn f one typically minimizes an objective function of the following form:

$$\sum_{u=1}^{|\mathcal{U}|} L(f(u), \mathcal{D}_u)$$

where L is the loss function, which measures the discrepency between the known ratings $\mathcal{D}_u$ and the predictions for user u. The well-known AUC loss (sometimes known as the margin ranking loss) [4, 3] is defined as:

$$L_{AUC}(f(u), \mathcal{D}_u) = \sum_{d \in \mathcal{D}_u} \sum_{\bar{d} \in \mathcal{D} \setminus \mathcal{D}_u} \max\Big(0, 1 - f_d(u) + f_{\bar{d}}(u)\Big).$$

To optimize it by stochastic gradient descent, one selects a user, a positive item and a negative item at random, and makes a gradient step, corresponding to one term in the double sum of the equation above. Repeated updates gradually visit all the terms.

The AUC loss is known to not optimize well the top of the rank list. Another set of loss functions called the OWPC loss [6] and its SGD counterpart, WARP loss [8], attempt to focus on the top of the list. The loss is defined as:

$$L_{WARP}(f(u), \mathcal{D}_u)) = \sum_{d \in \mathcal{D}_u} \Phi\Big(rank_d(f(u))\Big) \qquad (1)$$

where $\Phi(\eta)$ converts the rank of a positive item d to a weight. Here, the rank of d is defined as

$$rank_d(u) = \sum_{\bar{d} \notin \mathcal{D}_u} I\Big(f_d(u) \geq 1 + f_{\bar{d}}(u)\Big), \qquad (2)$$

where I is the indicator function.

Choosing $\Phi(\eta) = C\eta$ for any positive constant C is equivalent to the AUC loss. However, a weighting such as $\Phi(\eta) = \sum_{i=1}^{\eta} 1/i$ pays more attention to optimizing the top of the ranked list. Unfortunately, training such an objective by SGD directly is not tractable as eq. 2 sums over all items, which is too slow to compute per gradient update. The

[1]The binary rating case described is rather common in many real world recommendation tasks, especially for those where ratings are harvested from implicit feeback.

Algorithm 1 K-OS algorithm for picking a positive item.

We are given a probability distribution P of drawing the ith position in a list of size K. This defines the choice of loss function.
Pick a user u at random from the training set.
Pick $i = 1, \ldots, K$ positive items $d_i \in \mathcal{D}_u$.
Compute $f_{d_i}(u)$ for each i.
Sort the scores by descending order, let $o(j)$ be the index into d that is in position j in the list.
Pick a position $k \in 1, \ldots, K$ using the distribution P.
Perform a learning step using the positive item $d_{o(k)}$.

Algorithm 2 K-OS WARP loss

Initialize model parameters (mean 0, std. deviation $\frac{1}{\sqrt{m}}$).
repeat
  Pick a positive item d using Algorithm 1.
  Set $N = 0$.
  repeat
    Pick a random item $\bar{d} \in \mathcal{D} \setminus \mathcal{D}_u$.
    $N = N + 1$.
  until $f_{\bar{d}}(u) > f_d(u) - 1$ or $N \geq |\mathcal{D} \setminus \mathcal{D}_u|$
  if $f_{\bar{d}}(y) > f_d(u) - 1$ **then**
    Make a gradient step to minimize:
      $\Phi(\frac{|\mathcal{D} \setminus \mathcal{D}_u|}{N}) \max(0, 1 + f_{\bar{d}}(u) - f_d(u))$.
    Project weights to enforce constraints, e.g. if $||V_i|| > C$ then set $V_i \leftarrow (CV_i)/||V_i||$.
  end if
until validation error does not improve.

Algorithm 3 K-OS AUC loss

Initialize model parameters (mean 0, std. deviation $\frac{1}{\sqrt{m}}$).
repeat
  Pick a positive item d using Algorithm 1.
  Pick a random item $\bar{d} \in \mathcal{D} \setminus \mathcal{D}_u$.
  if $f_{\bar{d}}(u) > f_d(u) - 1$ **then**
    Make a gradient step to minimize:
      $\max(0, 1 + f_{\bar{d}}(u) - f_d(u))$.
    Project weights to enforce constraints, e.g. if $||V_i|| > C$ then set $V_i \leftarrow (CV_i)/||V_i||$.
  end if
until validation error does not improve.

WARP loss [8] was proposed to solve this problem. Using WARP, the $rank_d(u)$ is replaced with a sampled approximation: sample N items $\bar{d}$ until a violation is found, i.e. $f_u(d) < 1 + f_{\bar{d}}(u)$ and then approximate the rank with $|\mathcal{D} \setminus \mathcal{D}_u|/N$.

While OWPC/WARP provides a generalized class of loss functions including AUC as a special case, note that it still treats each positive item independently via the sum in eq. 1. In contrast, many evaluation metrics that we are interested in do not treat positive examples in this way. For example, precision at 1 only cares if one of the positives is at the top of the ranked list, and does not care about the position of the others. We thus generalize the above loss functions by proposing the k-Order Statistic (k-OS) loss as follows. For a given user u, let o be the vector of indices indicating the order of the positive examples in the ranked list:

$$f_{\mathcal{D}_{U o_1}}(u) > f_{\mathcal{D}_{U o_2}}(u) > \cdots > f_{\mathcal{D}_{U o_{|s|}}}(u).$$

The k-OS loss is then defined as:

$$L_{K\text{-OS}}(f(u),\mathcal{D}_u)) = \frac{1}{Z}\sum_{i=1}^{|\mathcal{D}_u|} P\Big(\frac{i}{|\mathcal{D}_u|}\Big)\Phi\Big(rank_{\mathcal{D}_{u_{o_i}}}(f(u))\Big)$$

where $Z = \sum_i P\Big(\frac{i}{|\mathcal{D}_u|}\Big)$ normalizes the weights induced by P. $P(\frac{j}{100})$ is the weight assigned to the jth percentile of the ordered positive items. Different choices of P result in different loss functions. $P(j) = C$ for all j and any positive constant C results in the original WARP or AUC formulations. Choices where $P(i) > P(j)$ for $i < j$ result in paying more attention to positive items that are at the top of the ranked list, and tends to ignore the lower ranked positives. This should have the effect of improving precision and recall at the top whilst sacrificing some of the user's taste preferences. Conversely, choosing $P(i) < P(j)$ for $i < j$ should focus more on improving the worst ranked positives in the user's rating set. We hypothesize that this may more accurately cover all of the user's tastes, and try to measure this in our experiments using the mean maximum rank metric.

To optimize k-OS easily via SGD we make the following simplification. During each SGD step we draw, for a random user, K random positives and order them by $f(u)$. Then the P distribution only takes on K possible values. The overall method is detailed in Algorithms 1, 2 and 3, for both AUC and WARP generalizations. In the majority of our experiments we use $P(j) = 1$ if $j = k/N$, and 0 otherwise, and leave k as a hyperparemater. That is, we simply always select the positive in the kth position in the list.

3. EXPERIMENTS

We conducted experiments on three large scale, real world tasks: artist recommendation and track recommendation using proprietary data from Google Play Music (`http://music.google.com`), and video recommendation from YouTube (`http://www.youtube.com`). In all cases, the datasets consist of a large set of anonymized users, where for each user there is a set of associated items based on their watch/listen history. The user-item matrix is hence a sparse binary matrix. The approximate dataset sizes are given in Table 1.

To construct evaluation data, we randomly selected 5 items for testing per user, and kept them apart from training. At prediction time for the set of test users we then ranked all unrated items (i.e. items that they have not watched/listened to that are present in the training set) and observe where the 5 test items are in the ranked list of recommendations. We then evaluate the following metrics: mean rank (the position in the ranked list, averaged over all test items and users), mean maximum rank (the position of the lowest ranked item out of the 5 test items, i.e. the furthest from the top, averaged over all test users), precision at 1 and 10 (P@1 and P@10), and recall at 1 and 10 (R@1 and R@10).

Hyperparameters (C, learning rate) were chosen using a portion of the training set for validation, although for memory and speed reasons we limited the embedding dimension to be $m = 64$. As we trained our model, K-os, with a ranking criteria which includes the WARP loss and AUC losses as special cases, we consider those as our baselines, and report relative changes in metrics compared to them. For K-os in all cases we used $K = 5$ in Algorithm 1, i.e we sample 5 positive items. After ordering them by score, we then select the item in the kth position. We report results for different

Table 1: Recommendation Datasets

Dataset	Music: Artists	Music: Tracks	YouTube
Number of Items	≈75k	≈700k	≈500k
Train Users	Millions		
Test Users	Tens of Thousands		

Table 2: Google Music Artist Recommendation. The baseline model is AUC. Mean/Max Rank, P@N and R@N metrics are given relative to it. Decreases in rank and increases in R@N and P@N indicate improvements. K-os uses AUC via Algorithm 3.

Method	Mean Rank	Max Rank	P@1	P@10	R@1	R@10
SVD	+254%	+284%	+1.6%	-2.5%	+0.72%	-2.1%
WARP	+23%	+26%	+25%	+14%	+25%	+13%
AUC	-	-	-	-	-	-
K-os k=1	+159%	+194%	+1.3%	-5%	-0.1%	-5.6%
K-os k=2	+65%	+80%	+9%	+0.3%	+7%	-0.4%
K-os k=3	+15%	+20%	+10%	+3.9%	+9%	+3.6%
K-os k=4	-2.7%	-1.6%	+6%	+3%	+5.9%	+2.7%
K-os k=5	-2.2%	-3.7%	-25%	-8%	-24%	-8%

Table 3: Google Music Artist Recommendation with WARP baseline. K-os uses WARP via Algorithm 2.

Method	Mean Rank	Max Rank	P@1	P@10	R@1	R@10
SVD	+187%	+205%	-19%	-14%	-19%	-14%
WARP	-	-	-	-	-	-
K-os k=1	+195%	+224%	-1.3%	-5.2%	-1.8%	-5.6%
K-os k=2	+88%	+110%	+1%	-0.4%	+0.7%	-0.6%
K-os k=3	+23%	+32%	-1%	-0.4%	-1.6%	-0.4%
K-os k=4	-7.7%	-6.4%	-3%	-2%	-4%	-2%
K-os k=5	-16%	-18%	-14%	-7%	-14%	-7%

Table 4: Google Music Track Recommendation

Method	Mean Rank	Max Rank	P@1	P@10	R@1	R@10
WARP	-	-	-	-	-	-
K-os k=1	+323%	+271%	+16%	+3.3%	+17%	+4.3%
K-os k=2	+209%	+199%	+22%	+14%	+23%	+15%
K-os k=3	+50.7%	+61%	+22%	+19%	+22%	+20%
K-os k=4	-44.1%	-40.9%	+9.1%	+15%	+12%	+16%
K-os k=5	-54.7%	-54.8%	-50%	-32%	-50%	-33%

Table 5: YouTube Video Recommendation

Method	Mean Rank	Max Rank	P@1	P@10	R@1	R@10
SVD	+56%	+45.3%	-54%	-57%	-54%	-96%
WARP	-	-	-	-	-	-
K-os k=1	+119%	+101%	+14%	+6.5%	+12%	+3.5%
K-os k=2	+55%	+71%	+7%	+6%	+5.8%	+4.8%
K-os k=3	+10%	+19%	-1.4%	+1.3%	-1.2%	+2.1%
K-os k=4	-10%	-13%	-10%	-6.4%	-8%	-3.8%
K-os k=5	-14%	-23%	-36%	-32%	-34%	-30%
K-os k<2	+119%	+101%	+14%	+6.5%	+12%	+3.5%
K-os k<3	+76%	+84%	+10%	+6.7%	+10%	+4.7%
K-os k<4	+39%	+54%	+6.1%	+5.6%	+6%	+5.1%
K-os k<5	+16%	+24%	+2.6%	+1%	+2.7%	+0.4%
K-os k>1	-4.3%	-5.8%	-12%	-10%	-12%	-9.9%
K-os k>2	-6.4%	-10%	-28%	-25%	-28%	-25%
K-os k>3	-18%	-26%	-23%	-23%	-20%	-20%
K-os k>4	-14%	-23.1%	-36%	-32%	-34%	-30%

values of k to show its effect. On YouTube and the Google Music artist recommendation task we also compare to SVD (factorization for the complete matrix with log-odds weighting on the columns which downweights the popular features as that worked better than uniform weights). Results on the three datasets are given in Tables 2, 3, 4 and 5.

For the first dataset, Google Music artist recommendation, we report two sets of results. Table 2 gives performance of K-OS using AUC (Algorithm 3) relative to standard AUC training. Table 3 gives performance of K-OS using WARP (Algorithm 2) relative to standard WARP training. We also compare to SVD, which is outperformed by both AUC and WARP ranking losses, presumably because they are better at optimizing these ranking metrics as has been observed before [9]. Note that a strongly performing model has a small mean/max rank, and large values of precision/recall, hence we are looking for negative percentage changes in rank but positive changes in the other metrics. In both the AUC and WARP cases the choice of k in K-OS gives clear control over the loss function. Small values of k tend to optimize precision and recall metrics as they focus on the top ranked positives in the set. Larger values of k tend to optimize mean maximum rank as they focus on the bottom ranked positives in the set. For example, the choice of $k = 5$ in Table 2 gives improved rank metrics over the AUC baseline, at the expense of decreases in precision and recall. Conversely, choices of $k \leq 4$ give improved precision and recall metrics over the AUC baseline at the expense of larger rank metrics. Note that $k = 1$ does not give the best precision improvements as you might at first expect ($k = 2$ is better). We hypothesize that this is because concentrating too much on only the top ranked positive makes the overall model suffer from not seeing enough training data with varying labels. (The same effect appears in the next dataset too.)

The second dataset, Google Music track recommendation, is comprised of the same set of anonymized users, but with items represented at the track rather than the artist level. That means there are more items to rank ($\approx$700k rather than $\approx$75k) so one could expect bigger differences between the methods as the task is more difficult. Table 4 shows larger improvements over the WARP baseline both in rank metrics ($k \geq 4$) and precision and recall metrics ($k \leq 4$). In this case $k = 4$ is actually a sweet spot which gives improvements in all metrics compared to the baseline.

The third dataset, YouTube video recommendation, also shows improvements in metrics for various choices of k. Again, we see smooth transitions from optimizing max or mean rank metrics versus precision or recall at the top as we vary k. In these experiments as well as showing results for single values of k we also report distributions P where we sample uniformly at random different values of k. For example, K-OS $k < 4$ in the table means that we select uniformly at random one of the top 3 positives after ordering the 5 sampled positives. The conclusions are similar to those of the experiments in the previous datasets.

YouTube Live Experiment.

We next tried our method using the K-OS loss (using WARP and $k = 5$, $N = 5$) in the live YouTube video recommendation system where we attempted to improve an already strong baseline machine learning system [1]. In our experiments above we measured rank, precision and recall. However, all these metrics are merely a proxy for the online metrics that matter more, such as video click through rate and duration of watch. When evaluating our method in the real-world system, it gave statistically signicant increases in both click through rate and watch duration (approximately 1%) compared to using the standard WARP loss, which in turn was superior to the AUC loss.

4. CONCLUSIONS

In this paper we have introduced a general class of ranking loss functions for training large-scale factorized recommendation models. This class generalizes several well known loss functions such as AUC and WARP and also provides new choices of objective function. In particular, by focusing the training on more highly ranked items one can obtain better precision and recall metrics compared to those existing approaches. Alternatively, by focusing the training on lower ranked items one can obtain better mean or maximum rank metrics. Depending on the overall goal, both of these approaches may be useful. We hypothesize that the latter improves the overall diversity of the recommendations which in live YouTube experiments resulted in more engaged users. Future work could try to understand further the impact of these loss function choices on such end goals.

5. REFERENCES

[1] J. Davidson, B. Liebald, J. Liu, P. Nandy, T. Van Vleet, U. Gargi, S. Gupta, Y. He, M. Lambert, B. Livingston, et al. The youtube video recommendation system. In *Proceedings of the fourth ACM conference on Recommender systems*, pages 293–296. ACM, 2010.

[2] K. Goldberg, T. Roeder, D. Gupta, and C. Perkins. Eigentaste: A constant time collaborative filtering algorithm. *Information Retrieval*, 4(2):133–151, 2001.

[3] D. Grangier and S. Bengio. A discriminative kernel-based model to rank images from text queries. *PAMI*, 30:1371–1384, 2008.

[4] R. Herbrich, T. Graepel, and K. Obermayer. Large margin rank boundaries for ordinal regression. *NIPS*, pages 115–132, 1999.

[5] Y. Shi, A. Karatzoglou, L. Baltrunas, M. Larson, N. Oliver, and A. Hanjalic. Climf: learning to maximize reciprocal rank with collaborative less-is-more filtering. In *Proceedings of the sixth ACM conference on Recommender systems*, pages 139–146. ACM, 2012.

[6] N. Usunier, D. Buffoni, and P. Gallinari. Ranking with ordered weighted pairwise classification. *ICML*, 2009.

[7] M. Weimer, A. Karatzoglou, Q. Le, A. Smola, et al. Cofirank-maximum margin matrix factorization for collaborative ranking. *NIPS*, 2007.

[8] J. Weston, S. Bengio, and N. Usunier. Wsabie: Scaling up to large vocabulary image annotation. In *IJCAI*, pages 2764–2770, 2011.

[9] J. Weston, C. Wang, R. Weiss, and A. Berenzweig. Latent collaborative retrieval. *ICML*, 2012.

[10] F. Xia, T.-Y. Liu, J. Wang, W. Zhang, and H. Li. Listwise approach to learning to rank: theory and algorithm. In *ICML*, 2008.

[11] Y. Yue, T. Finley, F. Radlinski, and T. Joachims. A support vector method for optimizing average precision. In *SIGIR*, pages 271–278, 2007.

A Fast Parallel SGD for Matrix Factorization in Shared Memory Systems

Yong Zhuang, Wei-Sheng Chin, Yu-Chin Juan, and Chih-Jen Lin
Dept. of Computer Science, National Taiwan University
Taipei 106, Taiwan
{r01922139, d01944006, r01922136, cjlin}@csie.ntu.edu.tw

ABSTRACT

Matrix factorization is known to be an effective method for recommender systems that are given only the ratings from users to items. Currently, stochastic gradient descent (SGD) is one of the most popular algorithms for matrix factorization. However, as a sequential approach, SGD is difficult to be parallelized for handling web-scale problems. In this paper, we develop a fast parallel SGD method, FPSGD, for shared memory systems. By dramatically reducing the cache-miss rate and carefully addressing the load balance of threads, FPSGD is more efficient than state-of-the-art parallel algorithms for matrix factorization.

Categories and Subject Descriptors

G.4 [**Mathematics of Computing**]: Mathematical Software—*Parallel and vector implementations*

Keywords

Recommender system, Matrix factorization, Stochastic gradient descent, Parallel computing, Shared memory algorithm

1. INTRODUCTION

Many customers are overwhelmed with the choices of products in the e-commerce activities. For example, Yahoo! Music and GrooveShark provide a huge number of songs for on-line audiences. An important problem is how to let users efficiently find items meeting their needs. Recommender systems have been constructed for such a purpose. As demonstrated in KDD Cup 2011 [3] and Netflix competition [1], a collaborative filter using latent factors has been considered as one of the best models for recommender systems. This approach maps both users and items into a latent feature space. A latent factor, though not directly measurable, often contains some useful abstract information. The affinity between a user and an item is defined by the inner product of their latent-factor vectors. More specifically, given m users, n items, and a rating matrix R that encodes the preference of the uth user on the vth item at the (u,v) entry, $r_{u,v}$, matrix factorization [7] is a technique to find two dense factor matrices $P \in \mathbb{R}^{k\times m}$ and $Q \in \mathbb{R}^{k\times n}$ such that $r_{u,v} \simeq \mathbf{p}_u^T\mathbf{q}_v$, where $\mathbf{p}_u \in \mathbb{R}^k$ and $\mathbf{q}_v \in \mathbb{R}^k$ are respectively the uth column of P and the vth column of Q. The optimization problem is

$$\min_{P\in\mathbb{R}^{k\times m},Q\in\mathbb{R}^{k\times n}} \sum_{(u,v)\in R} (r_{u,v}-\mathbf{p}_u^T\mathbf{q}_v)^2+\lambda_P \|P\|_F^2+\lambda_Q \|Q\|_F^2, \tag{1}$$

where k is the pre-specified number of latent factors, $\|\cdot\|_F$ is the Frobenius norm, $(u,v) \in R$ indicates that rating $r_{u,v}$ is available, λ_P and λ_Q are regularization coefficients for avoiding over-fitting. Because $\sum_{(u,v)\in R}\left(r_{u,v} - \mathbf{p}_u^T\mathbf{q}_v\right)^2$ is a non-convex function of P and Q, (1) is a difficult optimization problem. Many past studies have proposed optimization methods to solve (1), e.g. [7] [14] [11]. Among them, stochastic gradient descent (SGD) is popularly used. For example, all of the top three teams in KDD Cup 2011 (track 1) employed SGD in their winning approaches.

The basic idea of SGD is that, instead of expensively calculating the gradient of (1), it randomly selects a (u,v) entry from the summation and calculates the corresponding gradient [12] [6]. Once $r_{u,v}$ is chosen, the objective function in (1) is reduced to

$$\left(r_{u,v} - \mathbf{p}_u^T\mathbf{q}_v\right)^2 + \lambda_P\mathbf{p}_u^T\mathbf{p}_u + \lambda_Q\mathbf{q}_v^T\mathbf{q}_v.$$

After calculating the sub-gradient over $\mathbf{p}_u$ and $\mathbf{q}_v$, variables are updated by the following rules

$$\mathbf{p}_u \leftarrow \mathbf{p}_u + \gamma\left(e_{u,v}\mathbf{q}_v - \lambda_P\mathbf{p}_u\right), \tag{2}$$

$$\mathbf{q}_v \leftarrow \mathbf{q}_v + \gamma\left(e_{u,v}\mathbf{p}_u - \lambda_Q\mathbf{q}_v\right), \tag{3}$$

where

$$e_{u,v} = r_{u,v} - \mathbf{p}_u^T\mathbf{q}_v$$

is the error between the real and predicted ratings for the (u,v) entry, and γ is the learning rate. The overall procedure of SGD is to iteratively select an instance $r_{u,v}$, apply update rules (2)-(3), and may adjust the learning rate.

Although SGD has been successfully applied to matrix factorization, it is not applicable to handle large-scale data. The iterative process of applying (2)-(3) is inherently sequential, so it is difficult to parallelize SGD under advanced architectures such as GPU, multi-core CPU or distributed clusters. Several parallel SGD approaches have been proposed (e.g., [15] [9] [8] [5] [4] [10]), although their focuses may be on other machine learning techniques rather than matrix factorization. In this work, we aim at developing an

RecSys'13, October 12–16, 2013, Hong Kong, China.

effective parallel SGD method for matrix factorization in a shared memory environment. Although for huge data a distributed system must be used, in many situations running SGD on a data set that can fit in memory is still very time consuming. For example, the data set of KDD Cup 2011 is less than 4GB and can be easily stored in the memory of one computer, but a single SGD iteration of implementing (2)-(3) takes more than 30 seconds. The overall SGD procedure can take hours. Therefore, an efficient parallel SGD to fully take the power of multi-core CPU can be very useful in practice.

Among existing parallel-SGD methods for matrix factorization, some are directly designed or can be adapted for shared-memory systems. We briefly discuss two state-of-the-art methods because our method will improve upon them. HogWild [10] randomly selects a subset of $r_{u,v}$ instances and apply rules (2)-(3) in all available threads simultaneously without synchronization between threads. The reason why they can drop the synchronization is that their algorithm guarantees the convergence when factorizing a highly sparse matrix with the rare existence of the over-writing problem where different threads access the same data or variables such as $r_{u,v}$, $\mathbf{p}_u$ and $\mathbf{q}_v$ at the same time. That is, one thread is allowed to over-write another's work. DSGD [4] is another popular parallel SGD approach although it is mainly designed for cluster environments. Given s computation nodes and a rating matrix R, DSGD uniformly grids R into s by s blocks first. Then DSGD assigns s different blocks to the s nodes. On each node, DSGD performs (2)-(3) on all ratings of the block in a random order. As expected, DSGD can be adapted for shared-memory systems if we replace a computational node with a thread.

In this paper, we point out that existing parallel SGD methods may suffer from the following issues when they are applied in a shared-memory system.

- Data discontinuity: the algorithm may randomly access data or variables so that a high cache-miss rate is endured.
- Block imbalance: for approaches that split data to blocks and utilize them in parallel, cores/CPUs for sparser blocks (i.e., a block contains fewer ratings) must wait for those assigned to denser blocks.

Our main contribution is to design an effective method to alleviate these issues. This paper is organized as follows. We give details of HogWild and DSGD in Section 2, and then Section 3 discusses difficulties in parallel SGD for matrix factorization. Our proposed method is introduced in Section 4. We compare our method with state-of-the-art algorithms using root mean square error (RMSE) as the evaluation measure in Section 5. RMSE is defined as

$$\sqrt{\frac{1}{\text{number of ratings}} \sum_{(u,v)\in R} (r_{u,v} - \hat{r}_{u,v})^2}, \qquad (4)$$

where R is the rating matrix of the test set and $\hat{r}_{u,v}$ is the predicted rating value. Finally, Section 6 summarizes our work and gives future directions.

2. EXISTING PARALLELIZED STOCHASTIC GRADIENT DESCENT ALGORITHMS

Following the discussion in Section 1, in this section, we present two parallel SGD methods, HogWild [10] and DSGD [4], in detail.

Algorithm 1 HogWild's Algorithm

Require: number of threads s, R, P, and Q
for each thread i parallelly **do**
  while true **do**
    randomly select an instance $r_{u,v}$ from R
    update corresponding $\mathbf{p}_u$ and $\mathbf{q}_v$ using (2)-(3), respectively
  end while
end for

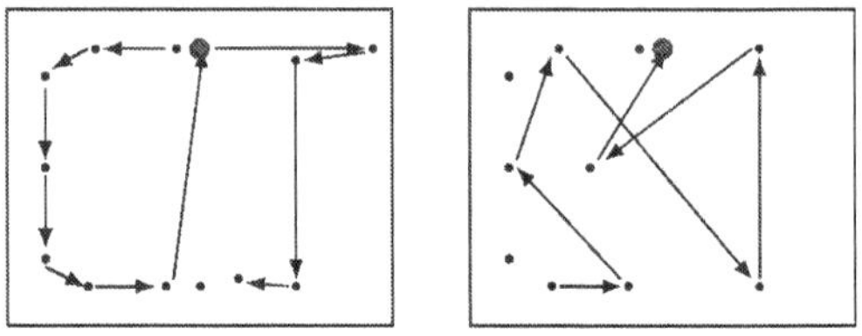

Figure 1: An example shows updating sequences of two threads in HogWild

2.1 HogWild

HogWild [10] assumes that the rating matrix is highly sparse and deduces that for two randomly sampled ratings, the two serial updates via (2)-(3) are likely to be independent. The reason is that the selected ratings to be updated almost never share the same user identity and item identity. That is to say, iterations of SGD, (2)-(3), can be in parallel executed in different threads. HogWild drops the synchronization that prevents concurrent variable access via atomic operations, each of which is a series of CPU instructions that can not be interrupted. Even through the potential over-writing may occur, they prove the convergence under some assumptions such as the rating matrix is very sparse.

Algorithm 1 shows the whole process of HogWild. We use Figure 1 to illustrate how two threads run SGD updates simultaneously. The left matrix and the right matrix are the updating sequences of two threads, where black dots are ratings randomly selected by a thread and arrows indicate the order of processed ratings. The red dot, which is simultaneously accessed by two threads in their last iterations in Figure 1, indicates the occurrence of the over-writing problem. That is, two threads conduct SGD updates using the same rating value $r_{i,j}$. From Algorithm 1, the operations include

- reading $r_{i,j}$, $\mathbf{p}_i$ and $\mathbf{q}_j$,
- evaluating the right-hand sides of (2)-(3), and
- assigning values to the left-hand sides of (2)-(3)

The second operation does not change shared variables because it is a series of arithmetic operations on local variables $r_{i,j}$, $\mathbf{p}_i$ and $\mathbf{q}_j$. However, for the first and the last operations, we use atomic instructions that are executed without considering the situation of other threads. All available threads would continuously execute the above-mentioned procedure until achieving the user-defined number of iterations.

2.2 DSGD

Although SGD is a sequential process, DSGD takes the property that some blocks of the rating matrix are mutually independent and their corresponding variables can be updated in parallel [4]. DSGD uniformly grids the rating matrix R into many sub-matrices (also called blocks), and

Algorithm 2 DSGD's Algorithm

Require: number of threads s, maximum iterations T, R, P, and Q

1: grid R into $s \times s$ blocks B and generate s patterns covering all blocks
2: **for** $t = \{1, \ldots, T\}$ **do**
3: Decide the order of s patterns sequentially or by random permutation
4: **for each** pattern of s independent blocks of B **do**
5: assign s selected blocks to s threads
6: **for** $b = \{1, \ldots, s\}$ parallellly **do**
7: randomly sample ratings from block b
8: apply (2)-(3) on all sampled ratings
9: **end for**
10: **end for**
11: **end for**

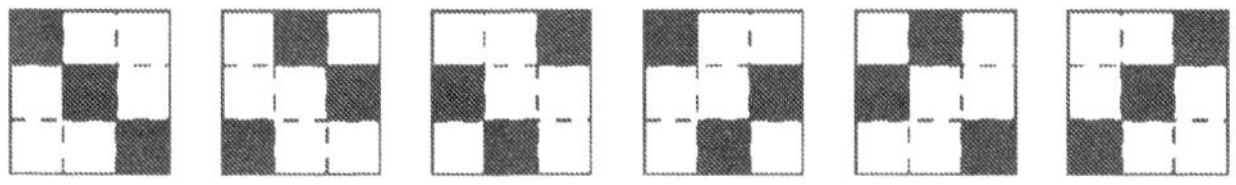

Figure 2: Patterns of independent blocks for a 3 by 3 grided matrix

applies SGD to some independent blocks simultaneously. In the following discussion, we say two blocks are independent to each other if they share neither any common column nor any common row of the rating matrix. For example, in Figure 2, the six patterns of gray blocks in R cover all possible patterns of independent blocks. Note that [4] restricts the number of blocks in each patten to be s, the number of available computational nodes, for reducing the data communication in distributed systems; see also the explanation below.

The overall algorithm of DSGD is shown in Algorithm 2, where T is the maximal number of iterations. In line 2, R is grided into $s \times s$ uniform blocks, and the intermediate for-loop continuously assigns s independent blocks to computation nodes until all blocks in R have been processed once. The bth iteration of the innermost for-loop updates P and Q by performing SGD on ratings in the block b. Given a 4-by-4 divided rating matrix and 4 threads as an example in Figure 3a, we show two consecutive iterations of the innermost for-loop in Figure 3b. The left iteration assigns 4 diagonal blocks to 4 nodes (i_0, i_1, i_2, i_3); node i_0 updates p_0 and q_0, node i_1 updates p_1 and q_1, and so on. In the next (right) iteration, each node updates the same segment of P, but for Q, q_1, q_2, q_3 and q_0 are respectively updated by nodes i_0, i_1, i_2 and i_3. This example shows that we can keep p_k in node i_k to avoid the communication of P. However, nodes must exchange their segments of Q, which are alternatively updated by different nodes in different iterations. For example, from Figure 3a to Figure 3b, node i_0 must send node i_3 the segment q_0 after finishing its computation. Consequently, the total amount of data transferred in one iteration of the intermediate loop is the size of Q because each of s nodes sends $|Q|/s$ and receives $|Q|/s$ entries of Q from another node, where $|Q|$ is the total number of entries in Q.

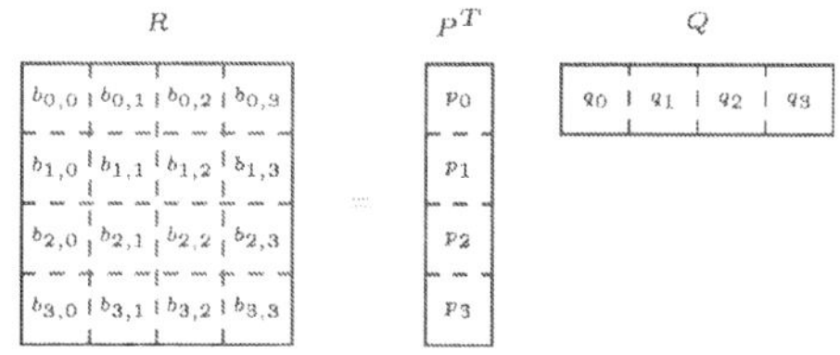

(a) 4 by 4 grided rating matrix R and corresponding segments of P and Q. Note that p_i is the ith segment of P and q_j is the jth segment of Q.

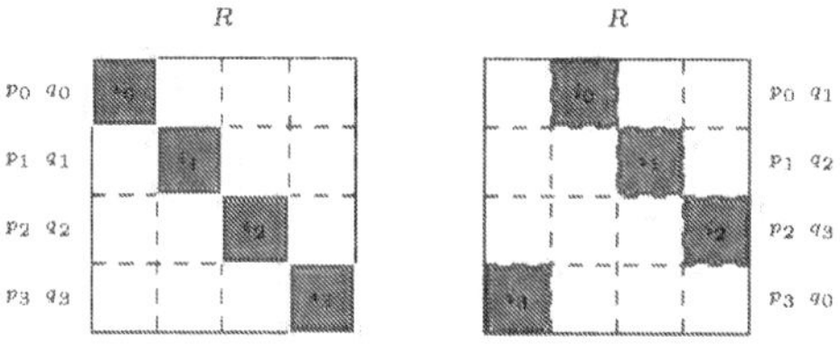

(b) An example of two consecutive iterations (the left is before the right) of the innermost for-loop of Algorithm 2. Each iteration considers a set of 4 independent blocks.

Figure 3: An illustration of the DSGD algorithm

3. PROBLEMS IN PARALLEL SGD METHODS FOR MATRIX FACTORIZATION

In this section, we point out that parallel SGD methods discussed in Section 2 may suffer some problems when they are applied in a shared-memory environment. These problems are *locking problem* and *memory discontinuity*. We introduce what these problems are, and explain how they result in performance degradation.

3.1 Locking Problem

For a parallel algorithm, to maximize the performance, keeping all threads busy is important. The *locking problem* occurs if a thread idles because of waiting for other threads. In DSGD, if s threads are used, then according to Algorithm 2, s independent blocks are updated in a batch. However, if the running time for each block varies, then a thread that finishes its job earlier may need to wait for other threads.

The locking problem may be more serious if R is unbalanced. That is, available ratings are not uniformly distributed across all positions in R. In such a case, the thread updating a block with fewer ratings may need to wait for other threads. For example, in Figure 4, after all ratings in block $b_{1,1}$ have been processed, only one third of ratings in block $b_{0,0}$ have been handled. Hence the thread updating $b_{1,1}$ idles most of the time.

A simple method to make R more balanced is *random shuffling*, which randomly permutes user identities and item identities before processing. However, the amount of ratings in each block may still not be exactly the same. Further, even if each block contains the same amount of ratings, the computing time of each code can still be slightly different. Therefore, other techniques are needed to address the locking problem.

Interestingly, DSGD has a reason to ensure that s blocks are processed before moving to the next s. As mentioned in Section 2.2, it is designed for distributed systems, so minimizing the communication cost between computing nodes may be more important than reducing the idle time of nodes.

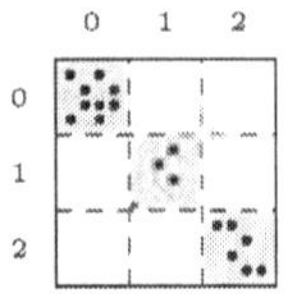

Figure 4: An example of the locking problem in DSGD. Each dot represents a rating; gray blocks indicate a set of independent blocks. Ratings in white blocks are not shown.

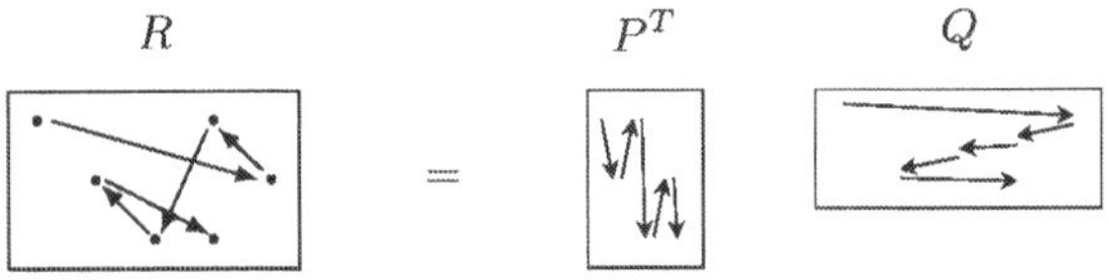

Figure 5: Random method to select rating instances for update.

However, in shared memory systems the locking problem becomes an important issue.

3.2 Memory Discontinuity

When a program accesses data in memory discontinuously, it suffers from a high cache-miss rate and performance degradation. Most SGD solvers for matrix factorization including HogWild and DSGD randomly pick instances from R (or from a block of R) for update. We call this setting as the *random method*, which is illustrated in Figure 5. Though the random method generally enjoys good convergence, it suffers from the memory discontinuity seriously. The reason is that not only are rating instances randomly accessed, but also user/item identities become discontinuous.

The seriousness of the memory discontinuity varies in different methods. In HogWild, each thread randomly picks instances among R independently, so it suffers from memory discontinuity in R, P, and Q. In contrast, for DSGD, though ratings in a block are randomly selected, as we will see in Section 4.2, we can easily change the update order to mitigate the memory discontinuity.

4. OUR APPROACHES

In this paper, we propose two techniques, *lock-free scheduling* and *partial random method*, to respectively solve the locking problem mentioned in Section 3.1 and the memory discontinuity mentioned in Section 3.2. We name the new parallel SGD method as *fast parallel SGD* (FPSGD). In Section 4.1, we discuss how FPSGD flexibly assigns blocks to threads to avoid the locking problem. In Section 4.2, we observe that a comprehensive random selection may not be necessary, and show that randomization can be applied only among blocks instead of within blocks to maintain both the memory continuity and the fast convergence. In Section 4.3, we overview the complete design of FPSGD. Finally, in Section 4.4, we introduce our implementation techniques to accelerate the computation.

4.1 Lock-Free Scheduling

We follow DSGD to grid R into blocks and design a scheduler to keep s threads busy in running a set of independent blocks. For a block $b_{i,j}$, if it is independent from all blocks being processed, then we call it as a *free* block. Otherwise, it is a *non-free* block. When a thread finishes processing a block, the scheduler assigns a new block that meets the following two criteria:

1. It is a free block.
2. Its number of past updates is the smallest among all free blocks.

The number of updates of a block indicates how many times it has been processed. The second criterion is applied because we want to keep a similar number of updates for each block. If two or more blocks meet the above two criteria, then we randomly select one. Given s threads, we show that FPSGD should grid R into at least $(s+1) \times (s+1)$ blocks. Take two threads as an example. Let T_1 be a thread that is updating certain block and T_2 be a thread that just finished updating a block and is getting a new job from the scheduler. If we grid R into 2×2 blocks shown in Figure 6a, then T_2 has only one choice: the block it just processed. A similar situation happens when T_1 gets its new job. Because T_1 and T_2 always process the same block, the remaining two blocks are never processed. In contrast, if we grid R into 3×3 blocks like Figure 6b, T_2 has three choices: $b_{1,1}$, $b_{1,2}$ and $b_{2,1}$, when getting a new block.

As discussed above, because we can always assign a free block to a thread when it finishes updating the previous one, our scheduler does not suffer from the locking problem. However, for extremely unbalanced data sets, where most available ratings are in certain blocks, our scheduler is unable to keep the number of updates in all blocks balanced. In such a case blocks with many ratings are updated only very few times. A simple remedy is the random shuffling technique introduced in Section 3.1. In our experience, after random shuffling, the number of ratings in the heaviest block is smaller than twice of the lightest block. We then experimentally check how serious the imbalance problem is after random shuffling. Here we define *degree of imbalance* (DoI) to check the number of updates in all blocks. Let $\mathrm{UT}_M(t)$ and $\mathrm{UT}_m(t)$ be the maximal and the minimal numbers of updates in all blocks, respectively, where t is the iteration index. (FPSGD does not have the concept of iterations. Here we call every cycle of processing $(s+1)^2$ blocks as an iteration.) DoI is defined as

$$\mathrm{DoI} = \frac{\mathrm{UT}_M(t) - \mathrm{UT}_m(t)}{t}.$$

A small DoI indicates that the number of updates is similar across all blocks. In Figure 7, we show DoI for three different data sets. We can see that our scheduler reduces DoI to be close to zero in just a few iterations. For details of the data set used in Figure 7, please refer to Section 5.1.

(a) 2×2 blocks (b) 3×3 blocks

Figure 6: An illustration of how the split of R to blocks affects the job scheduling. T_1 is the thread that is updating block $b_{0,0}$. T_2 is the thread that is getting a new block from the scheduler. Blocks with "x" are dependent on block $b_{0,0}$, so they cannot be updated by T_2.

(a) MovieLens (b) Netflix (c) Yahoo!Music

Figure 7: DoI on three data sets. Eight threads are used, and R is grided into 9×9 blocks after being randomly shuffled.

4.2 Partial Random Method

To achieve memory continuity, in contrast to the random method, we can consider an *ordered method* to sequentially select rating instances by user identities or item identities. Figure 8 gives an example of following the order of users. Then matrix P can be accessed continuously. Alternatively, if we follow the order of items, then the continuous access of Q can be achieved. For R, if the order of selecting rating instances is fixed, we can store R into memory with the same order to ensure its continuous access.

Although the ordered method can access data in a more continuous manner, empirically we find that it is not very stable. Figure 9 gives an example showing that under two slightly different learning rates for SGD, the ordered method can be either much faster or much slower than the random method.

The above experiment indicates that a random access of data/variables may be useful for the convergence. This property has been observed in related optimization techniques. For example, in coordinate descent methods to solve some optimization problems, [2] shows that a random rather than a sequential order to update variables significantly improves the convergence speed. To compromise between data continuity and convergence speed, in FPSGD, we propose a *partial random method*, which selects ratings in a block orderly but randomizes the selection of blocks. Although our scheduling is close to deterministic by choosing blocks with the smallest numbers of accesses, the randomness can be enhanced by griding R into more blocks. Then at any time point, some blocks have been processed by the same number of times, so the scheduler can randomly select one of them. Figure 10 illustrates how the partial random method works. The overall update sequence is neither user-by-user nor item-by-item, so some randomness is achieved. Figure 11 extends the running time comparison in Figure 9 to include FPSGD. We can see that FPSGD enjoys both fast convergence and excellent RMSE.

Some related methods have been investigated in [4], although they showed that the convergence on the ordered method in terms of training loss is worse than the random method. Their observation is opposite to our experimental results. A possible reason is that we consider RMSE on the testing set while they consider the training loss.

Some subtle implementation details must be noted. We discussed in Section 4.1 that FPSGD applies random shuffling to avoid the unbalanced number of updates of each block. However, after applying the random shuffling and griding R in to blocks, the ratings in each block are not sorted by user (or item) identities. To apply the partial random method we must sort user (or item) identities before processing each block because an ordered method is applied within the block.

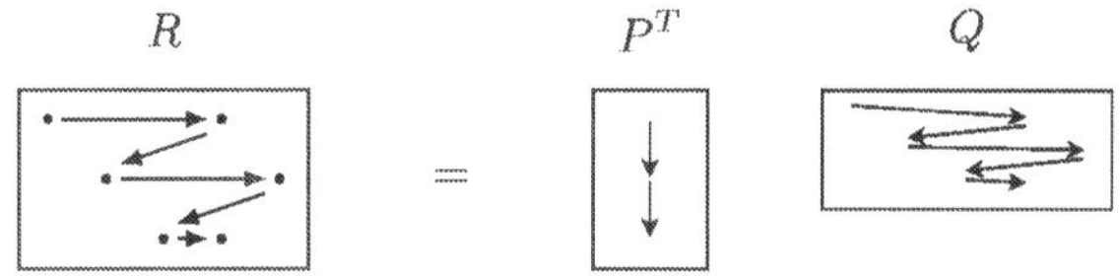

Figure 8: Ordered method to select rating instances for update.

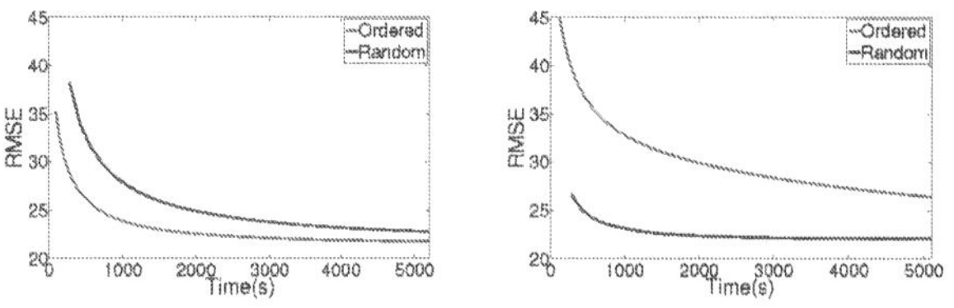

(a) $\gamma = 0.0001$ (b) $\gamma = 0.0005$

Figure 9: A comparison between the random method and the ordered method using the Yahoo!Music data set. Here one thread is used.

4.3 Overview of FPSGD

Algorithm 3 gives the overall procedure of FPSGD. It first randomly shuffles R to avoid data imbalance as we mentioned in Section 4.1. Then it grids R into at least $(s+1) \times (s+1)$ blocks and sorts each block by user (or item) identities so that the partial random method discussed in Section 4.2 can be applied. Finally it constructs a scheduler and launches s working threads. After the required number of iterations is reached, it notifies the scheduler to stop all working threads.

The pseudo code of the scheduler and each working thread are shown in Algorithm 4 and Algorithm 5, respectively. Each working thread continuously gets a block from the scheduler by invoking `get_job`, and the scheduler returns a block that meets criteria mentioned in Section 4.1. After a working thread gets a new block, it processes ratings in the block in an ordered manner (see Section 4.2). In the end, the thread invokes `put_job` of the scheduler to update the number of times that the block has been processed.

4.4 Implementation Issues

FPSGD is implemented in C++. For the data set Yahoo!Music of about 250M ratings, using a typical machine (details specified in Section 5.1), FPSGD finishes processing all ratings once in 6 seconds and takes only about 8 minutes to converge to a reasonable RMSE. Here we describe some techniques employed in our implementation. First, empirically we find that using single-precision floating-point computation does not suffer from numerical error accumulation. For the data set Yahoo!Music, using single precision runs 1.1 times faster then using double precision. Second, modern CPU provides SSE instructions that can concurrently run floating-point multiplications and additions. We apply SSE instructions for vector inner products and additions. For Yahoo!Music data set, the speed up is 2.4 times. Figure 12 shows the speedup after these techniques are applied in two data sets.

5. EXPERIMENTS

In this section, we compare FPSGD with other parallel

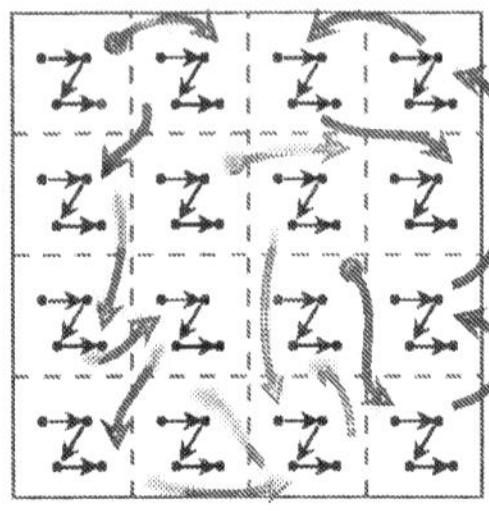

Figure 10: An illustration of the partial random method. Different colors indicate different threads. Each colored dot represents the initial block of a thread.

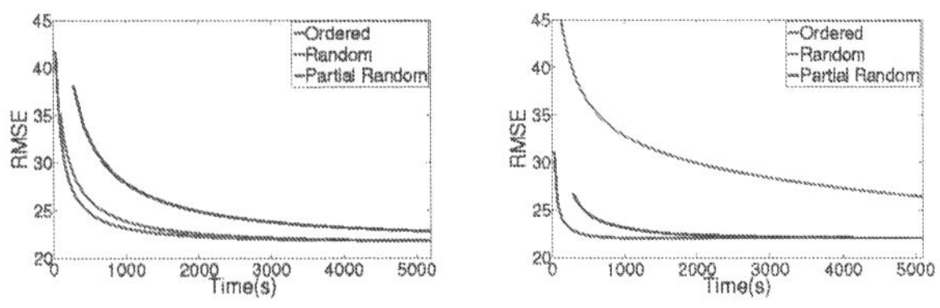

(a) $\gamma = 0.0001$ (b) $\gamma = 0.0005$

Figure 11: A comparison between the ordered method, the random method, and the partial random method on the set Yahoo!Music. One thread is used.

SGD methods mentioned in Section 2. Besides, we also compared with CCD++ [13], which is a parallel coordinate descent method for matrix factorization. It considers a feature-wise update sequence based on coordinate descent. At each iteration, one row of P and the corresponding row of Q are selected for update. Their parallelization relies on splitting the update of one row to several independent sub-tasks. CCD++ is currently considered the best parallel implementation in a shared-memory environment.

5.1 Settings

Data Sets: Three data sets, MovieLens,[1] Netflix and Yahoo!Music, are used for the experiments. For reproducibility, we consider the original training/test sets in our experiments (as for MovieLens, we use Part B of the original data set generated by the official script). Because the test set of Yahoo!Music is not available, we consider the last four ratings of each user for testing, while the remaining ratings for training set. The statistics of each data set is in Table 1.

Platform: We use a server with two Intel Xeon E5620 2.4GHz processors and 64GB memory. There are four cores in each processor.

Parameters: Table 1 lists the parameters used for each data set. We let $\lambda_P = \lambda_Q$ and follow the parameters chosen in [13] for Netflix and Yahoo!Music. For MovieLens, we set $\lambda_P = \lambda_Q = 0.05$. The learning rate is determined by an ad hoc parameter selection. Because we focus on the running speed rather than RMSE in this paper, we do not apply an adaptive learning rate. From empirical experiences, the influence of the initial value of P and Q cannot be ignored, so we carefully set these values to be identical to [13].

In our platform, 8 physical cores are available, so we use 8 threads in all experiments. For FPSGD, Section 4 shows that $(s+1) \times (s+1)$ blocks are already enough for s threads,

[1] http://www.grouplens.org/node/73

Algorithm 3 The overall procedure of FPSGD

```
randomly shuffle R
grid R into a set B with at least (s+1) × (s+1) blocks
sort each block by user (or item) identities
construct a scheduler
launch s working threads
wait until the total number of updates reaches a user-
  defined value
```

Algorithm 4 Scheduler of FPSGD

```
procedure GET_JOB
    b_x = NULL
    for all b in B do
        if b is non-free then
            continue
        else if b.ut ≤ b_x.ut then        ▷ ut: number of
  updates
            b_x=b
        end if
    end for
    return b_x
end procedure
procedure PUT_JOB(b)
    b.ut = b.ut + 1
end procedure
```

we use more blocks to ensure the randomness of blocks that are simultaneously processed. For Yahoo!Music and Movielens, R is grided into 32×32 blocks; for Netflix, R is grided into 16×16 blocks because the number of items is smaller.

Evaluation: As most recommender systems do, the metric adopted as our evaluation is RMSE on the test set, which is disjoint with the training set; see Eq. (4). In addition, the time in each figure refers to the training time.

Implementations: Among methods included for comparison, HogWild[2] and CCD++[3] are publicly available. We reimplement HogWild under the same framework of our FPSGD and DSGD implementations for a fairer comparison. In the official HogWild package, the formulation includes the average value of training ratings. After trying different settings, the program still fails to converge. Therefore, we present only results of our HogWild implementation in the experiment.

5.2 Results

We first illustrate the effectiveness of our solutions for data imbalance and memory discontinuity. Then, we compare parallel matrix factorization methods including DSGD, CCD++, HogWild and our FPSGD.

5.2.1 The effectiveness to address the locking problem

In Section 3.1, we mentioned that updating several blocks in a batch may suffer from the locking problem if the data is unbalanced. To verify the effectiveness of FPSGD, we compare it with a modification where the scheduler processes a batch of independent blocks as DSGD (Algorithm 2) does. We call the modified algorithm as FPSGD**.

[2] http://hazy.cs.wisc.edu/hazy/victor/
[3] http://www.cs.utexas.edu/~rofuyu/libpmf/

Algorithm 5 Working thread of FPSGD

```
while true do
    get a block b from scheduler->get_job()
    process elements orderly in this block
    scheduler->put_job(b)
end while
```

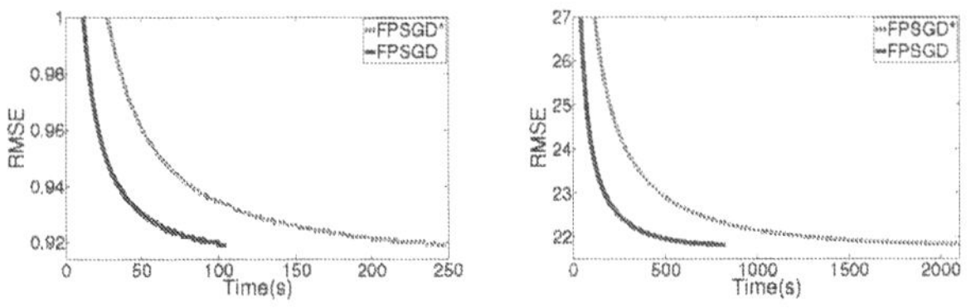

(a) Netflix (b) Yahoo!Music

Figure 12: A comparison between two implementations of FPSGD in Netflix and Yahoo!Music. FPSGD implements the two techniques discussed in Section 4.4, while FPSGD* does not.

In Figure 13a, we compare the running time of FPSGD and FPSGD** on three data sets. As we can see, FPSGD runs much faster than FPSGD** because it does not suffer from the locking problem. In Table 2, we find that FPSGD runs 1.9 times, 1.3 times, and 1.6 times faster than FPSGD** on MovieLens, Netflix, and Yahoo!Music, respectively.

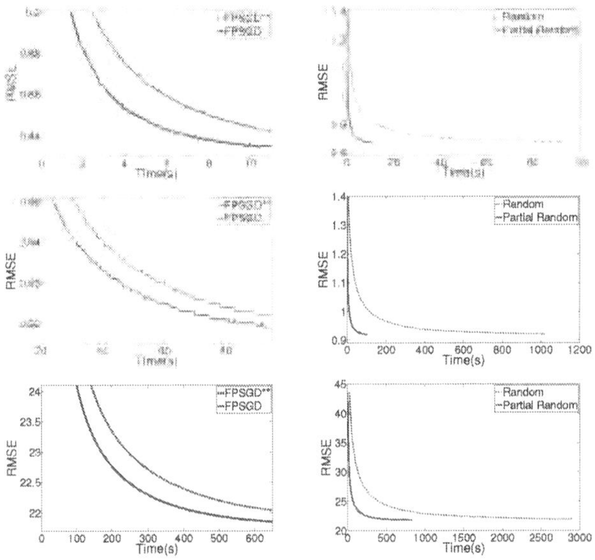

(a) (b)

Figure 13: (a) A comparison between FPSGD** and FPSGD. (b) A comparison between the partial random method and the random method. The data set from top to bottom are: MovieLens, Netflix, and Yahoo!Music.

5.2.2 *The effectiveness for discontinuous memory access*

We conduct experiments to investigate if the proposed partial random method can not only avoid memory discontinuity, but also keep good convergence.

Data Set	MovieLens	Netflix	Yahoo!Music
m	71,567	2,649,429	1,000,990
n	65,133	17,770	624,961
#Training	9,301,274	99,072,112	252,800,275
#Test	698,780	1,408,395	4,003,960
k	40	40	100
λ_P	0.05	0.05	1
λ_Q	0.05	0.05	1
γ	0.003	0.002	0.0001

Table 1: The statistics and parameters for each data set

Data Set	Method	Time (s)	RMSE
MovieLens	FPSGD**	18.71	0.835
	FPSGD	9.72	0.835
Netflix	FPSGD**	116.60	0.919
	FPSGD	90.37	0.919
Yahoo!Music	FPSGD**	728.23	21.985
	FPSGD	462.55	21.985

Table 2: A comparison between FPSGD** and FPSGD. See Section 5.2.1 for the details of FPSGD**.

In Figure 13b, we select rating instances in each block orderly (the partial random method) or randomly (the random method). Both methods converge to a similar RMSE. However, the training time of the partial random method is obviously faster then the random method.

5.2.3 *Comparison with the state-of-the-art methods*

Figure 14 presents the test RMSE and training time of various parallel matrix factorization methods.

Among the three parallel SGD methods, FPSGD is faster than DSGD and HogWild. We believe that this result is because FPSGD is designed to effectively address issues mentioned in Section 3. However, we must note that for DSGD, it is also easy to incorporate similar techniques (e.g., the partial random method) to improve the performance.

From Figure 14, CCD++ is the fastest in the beginning, but becomes slower than FPSGD. Because the optimization problem of matrix factorization is non-convex and CCD++ is a more greedy setting than SGD by accurately minimizing the objective function over certain variables at each step, we suspect that CCD++ may converge to some local minimum pre-maturely. On the contrary, SGD-based methods may be able to escape from a local minimum because of the randomness.

6. CONCLUSIONS AND FUTURE WORKS

To provide a better SGD solver for recommender systems, we will extend our algorithm to solve variants of matrix-factorization problems. To further reduce the cache-miss rate, we plan to investigate non-uniform splits of the rating matrix or other permutation methods such as Cuthill-McKee ordering.

In conclusion, we point out some computational bottlenecks in existing parallel SGD methods for shared-memory systems. We propose FPSGD to address these issues and confirm its effectiveness by experiments. The comparison shows that FPSGD is more efficient than state-of-the-art methods.

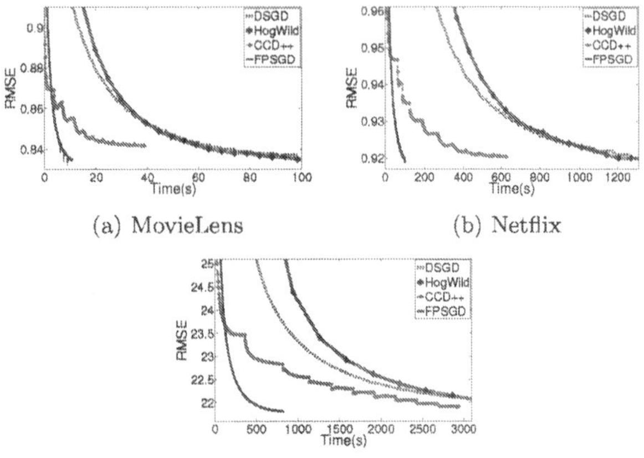

(a) MovieLens (b) Netflix

(c) Yahoo!Music

Figure 14: A comparison among the state-of-the-art parallel matrix factorization methods.

Based on this study, we develop the papckage `LIBMF`. It is available at `http://www.csie.ntu.edu.tw/~cjlin/libmf`

7. REFERENCES

[1] R. M. Bell and Y. Koren. Lessons from the Netflix prize challenge. *ACM SIGKDD Explorations Newsletter*, 9(2):75–79, 2007.

[2] K.-W. Chang, C.-J. Hsieh, and C.-J. Lin. Coordinate descent method for large-scale L2-loss linear SVM. *Journal of Machine Learning Research*, 9:1369–1398, 2008.

[3] G. Dror, N. Koenigstein, Y. Koren, and M. Weimer. The Yahoo! music dataset and KDD-Cup 11. In *JMLR Workshop and Conference Proceedings: Proceedings of KDD Cup 2011*, volume 18, pages 3–18, 2012.

[4] R. Gemulla, E. Nijkamp, P. J. Haas, and Y. Sismanis. Large-scale matrix factorization with distributed stochastic gradient descent. In *Proceedings of the 17th ACM SIGKDD international conference on Knowledge discovery and data mining*, KDD '11, pages 69–77, New York, NY, USA, 2011. ACM.

[5] K. B. Hall, S. Gilpin, and G. Mann. MapReduce/Bigtable for distributed optimization. In *Neural Information Processing Systems Workshop on Leaning on Cores, Clusters, and Clouds*, 2010.

[6] J. Kiefer and J. Wolfowitz. Stochastic estimation of the maximum of a regression function. *The Annals of Mathematical Statistics*, 23(3):462–466, 1952.

[7] Y. Koren, R. M. Bell, and C. Volinsky. Matrix factorization techniques for recommender systems. *Computer*, 42(8):30–37, 2009.

[8] G. Mann, R. McDonald, M. Mohri, N. Silberman, and D. Walker. Efficient large-scale distributed training of conditional maximum entropy models. In Y. Bengio, D. Schuurmans, J. Lafferty, C. K. I. Williams, and A. Culotta, editors, *Advances in Neural Information Processing Systems 22*, pages 1231–1239. 2009.

[9] R. McDonald, K. Hall, and G. Mann. Distributed training strategies for the structured perceptron. In *Proceedings of the 48th Annual Meeting of the Association of Computational Linguistics (ACL)*, pages 456–464, 2010.

[10] F. Niu, B. Recht, C. Ré, and S. J. Wright. HOGWILD!: A lock-free approach to parallelizing stochastic gradient descent. In J. Shawe-Taylor, R. Zemel, P. Bartlett, F. Pereira, and K. Weinberger, editors, *Advances in Neural Information Processing Systems 24*, pages 693–701, 2011.

[11] I. Pilászy, D. Zibriczky, and D. Tikk. Fast ALS-based matrix factorization for explicit and implicit feedback datasets. In *Proceedings of the Fourth ACM Conference on Recommender Systems*, pages 71–78, 2010.

[12] H. Robbins and S. Monro. A stochastic approximation method. *The Annals of Mathematical Statistics*, 22(3):400–407, 1951.

[13] H.-F. Yu, C.-J. Hsieh, S. Si, and I. S. Dhillon. Scalable coordinate descent approaches to parallel matrix factorization for recommender systems. In *Proceedings of the IEEE International Conference on Data Mining*, pages 765–774, 2012.

[14] Y. Zhou, D. Wilkinson, R. Schreiber, and R. Pan. Large-scale parallel collaborative filtering for the Netflix prize. In *Proceedings of the Fourth International Conference on Algorithmic Aspects in Information and Management*, pages 337–348, 2008.

[15] M. Zinkevich, M. Weimer, A. Smola, and L. Li. Parallelized stochastic gradient descent. In J. Lafferty, C. K. I. Williams, J. Shawe-Taylor, R. Zemel, and A. Culotta, editors, *Advances in Neural Information Processing Systems 23*, pages 2595–2603. 2010.

DrunkardMob: Billions of Random Walks on Just a PC

Aapo Kyrola
Carnegie Mellon University
5000 Forbes Avenue
Pittsburgh, PA, USA
akyrola@cs.cmu.edu

ABSTRACT

Random walks on graphs are a staple of many ranking and recommendation algorithms. Simulating random walks on a graph which fits in memory is trivial, but massive graphs pose a problem: the latency of following walks across network in a cluster or loading nodes from disk on-demand renders basic random walk simulation unbearably inefficient. In this work we propose DrunkardMob[1], a new algorithm for simulating hundreds of millions, or even billions, of random walks on massive graphs, on just a single PC or laptop. Instead of simulating one walk a time it processes millions of them in parallel, in a batch. Based on DrunkardMob and GraphChi [19], we further propose a framework for easily expressing scalable algorithms based on graph walks.

Categories and Subject Descriptors

H.3.3 [**Information Storage and Retrieval**]: Information Search and Retrieval–*Information Filtering*

General Terms

Graph computation, Recommendations, Random walks

Keywords

recommender systems, random walks, graph computation

1. INTRODUCTION

Many popular algorithms for ranking and recommending nodes in graphs are based on random walk models. Most notably, the PageRank algorithm [26] and its personalized adaption the Personalized PageRank (PPR) compute ranking for webpages based on the probability that a "random web surfer" (we will use the term *random walker*) ends up on the page by following random links from web pages. The same model can be used for ranking users in social networks or graphs of other entities.

To compute the global PageRank, we can compute the stationary distribution of the random process by iterated multiplications of an initial ranking vector by the transition matrix (the *power method*). However, for computing all PPR vectors [26], the direct methods are too expensive, with complexity of $O(V^2)$ [16]. Fortunately, Fogaras et. al. [10] proved that by simulating a modest number of short random walk segments from each node, we can efficiently obtain a good approximation of the PPR vector for each user.

In this work, we show how to simulate hundreds of millions, or even billions, of number of short (random) walks on extremely large graphs, on just a single computer. We propose a new algorithm, DrunkardMob, which processes the graph from disk but maintains the current state of each random walk in memory. A typical modern PC or laptop has several gigabytes of memory and can scale up to several hundred million parallel walks. On high-end servers with large RAMs, we simulate billions of walks in parallel. Because the graph is processed efficiently from disk, we can process even the biggest social graphs on just a laptop. Our solution is generic, not limited to the basic PageRank algorithm, and is as easy to program as the basic in-memory random walk procedure. We implement DrunkardMob on GraphChi [19], a general graph computation system that allows us to naturally combine the walk simulator with other recommendation algorithms such as matrix factorization.

Outline: after reviewing related work and preliminaries in Section 2 and 3, Section 4 presents the DrunkardMob algorithm and discusses its implementation.We present a case study on implementing Twitter's Who-to-Follow algorithm using our system in Section 5. Evaluation of the system follows in Section 6, after which we conclude and discuss future research.

Summary of our contributions:

- DrunkardMob, an algorithm for simulating billions of walks on just a single computer.
- Generic architecture for representing graph walk -based computation in the *vertex-centric* computational model.
- Implementation of DrunkardMob on top of GraphChi and an evaluation of its performance and scalability.

DrunkardMob is available in the open-source at **https://github.com/GraphChi/**.

[1]Random walks are often called "drunkards' walks", thus our algorithm, which simulates many of such walks simultaneously is appropriately called DrunkardMob.

ACM RecSys'13 October 12 - 16 2013, Hong Kong, Hong Kong
Copyright 2013 ACM 978-1-4503-2409-0/13/09 ...$15.00.
http://dx.doi.org/10.1145/2507157.2507173 .

2. RELATED WORK

Random walks and recommender systems: Models based on random walks on a graph are popular in the recommender system research due to their scalability. This work was initially motivated by the problem of recommending friends or connections in a social network, called the *link prediction* problem [23]. Perhaps the most common approach is to return the top k ranked nodes of the Personalized Pagerank [26] vector for the user in question. Recently [12] describe an extensions to this technique used at the microblogging service Twitter (`http://www.twitter.com`). We implement their method in our case study (Section 5).

Random walk -based models are also used in other contexts: FolkRank [13] is an adapted version of PageRank for ranking in *folksonomies* (graphs of users, tags, and resources). TrustWalker [15] improves item-based recommendation by modeling trust between users in a social network, approximated by simulating random walks on the graph. Finally, [20] proposes a ranking of entities in an entity graph using random walks. In a closely related field, random walks have been successfully used for inference and learning in a large knowledge base [?]. Previous work has been evaluated on relatively small datasets, and we believe our toolkit will help researchers to tackle problems of much larger scale.

Scaling Personalized PageRank: As most work on link prediction and personalized web search has focused on Personalized PageRank (PPR), its scalability has also been object of intensive research, which we briefly review here. The seminal work by Jeh and Widom [16] proposed how PPR can be approximated by computing the rank vectors to a smaller set of hub nodes and using linear algebraic relations of the PPR vectors. However, to allow good accuracy for full personalization, the hub set would need to be very large.

Another important work by Fogaras et. al. [10] proposed using short random walk segments, *fingerprints*, to approximate the PPR vectors. They propose an external memory (disk-based) algorithm to efficiently simulate a very large number of walks from all vertices at once. Our work is closely related to their work but is more general and utilizes the memory of the computer to keep track of very large number of walks. To our knowledge, there is no available implementation of the algorithm of [10].

Related algorithm to compute PageRank on graphs streamed from disk was proposed by Das Sarma et. al. [7], but their approach is to sample the vertices and edges of the graph and simulate a small number of hops on the sampled graph to produce a large number of short walks. Their method requires a rather complicated scheme to stitch small walk segments and handle special cases, while our method and that of Fogaras can simulate the walks on the full graph and thus are not limited to PageRank. Bahmani et. al. [4] study how to efficiently update a database of random walk segments when new edges are inserted into the graph. Their method could be combined with DrunkardMob.

Finally, [3] proposes a method to compute PPR efficiently on the popular MapReduce [8] parallel data processing framework. Their method is a generalization of the method by Das Sarma et. al. [7]. While MapReduce provides impressive scalability with very large clusters, our method can process extremely large graphs on just a single computer.

3. PRELIMINARIES

Our objective is to simulate walks (not necessarily random) on a graph $G = (V, E)$, where V denotes the set of vertices (nodes) $v \in \mathbb{Z}$, and $E = \{(u,v) \mid u, v \in V\}$ the set of *directed* edges connecting the vertices. We call edge $e = (a, b)$ *out-edge* of vertex a and *in-edge* of vertex b. We generally assume the graph to be sparse, i.e that most vertices do not have an edge between them. In addition, each edge can be associated a value, typically a real valued *weight*. Let *out-degree* $D_o(v)$ be the number of out-edges of vertex v.

A **walk** $w_s^t = [s, v^1, v^2, ..., v^t]$, $s, v^j \in V$ on a graph is an ordered sequence of t visits to vertices (called *hops*), with **source vertex** (the origin of the walk) s. We denote $w^t(i)$ the i'th visit of the walk. Random variable W_s^t represents a walk where each visit $W_s^t(j+1)$ is chosen randomly according to some transition probability $\mathbf{P}(v \mid W^t(j) = v')$ based on the previous hop.

Example (global PageRank): For the global PageRank [26] model, the probability of moving from vertex v to v' is:

$$\mathbf{P}(v \mid W_s^t(j) = v') := \begin{cases} d/|V| & \text{if } (v', v) \notin E \\ d/|V| + \frac{1-d}{D_o(v')} & \text{if } (v', v) \in E \end{cases}$$

Above, d is the damping factor, which represents the probability of the random walk to *reset* and "teleport" to a random node in the graph.

Example (Personalized PageRank): The Personalized PageRank [26] model is used for estimating the ranking of nodes "personalized" to a source vertex s. The only difference to global PageRank is that when a walk resets, it will always return to the source:

$$\mathbf{P}(v \mid W_s^t(j) = v') := \begin{cases} 0 & \text{if } (v', v) \notin E \text{ and } v \neq s \\ d & \text{if } v = s \\ \frac{1-d}{D_o(v')} & \text{if } (v', v) \in E \end{cases}$$

The probabilities above are for unweighted PageRank, but are easily modified to use edge weights for bias.

In the context of this work, we do not require a walk to be random, or even follow a well-defined transition model. Computationally, walks are simulated by defining a **walk-update function**:

```
update := (G, vertex, walk-info) → (vertex, walk-info)
```

Above, `vertex` denotes the current visit of the walk, and type `walk-info` is an application dependent structure that stores information about the walk. For example to simulate Personalized PageRank, it is used to store the source vertex of the walk. In addition, it can also contain information about the current hop-number of the walk or an unique walk identifier. In general, we use as few bits as possible to represent `walk-info` in order to store as many walks in memory as possible. Walk-update function returns the next visit of the walk and the `walk-info` value, which it can modify. Walk-update functions are general and may utilize any information about the graph and it is straight-forward to define specialized walks that follow only, for example, certain types of edges.

3.1 Large Graphs

If the graph fits into main memory (RAM), simulating walks on a graph is trivial, using the Algorithm 1. On line 6 we have added a call to `recordHop()` function, which is used to keep track of the visits made by the walk (not described). The algorithm can be easily made parallel by executing several walks simultaneously. This simple algorithm is able to execute millions of hops in second on a typical PC.

Algorithm 1: In-memory walk on a graph

```
SimulateWalk(G, src, upFun) begin
    walkInfo ← initializeWalk(src)
    curvertex ← src
    for i = 1...t do
        (curvertex, walkinfo) ← upFun(G, src, walkInfo)
        recordHop(src, walkInfo, curvertex)
    end
end
```

If the graph does not fit into RAM, it needs to be accessed from disk (parts of the graph may reside in RAM) or the graph must be partitioned and distributed across a cluster of computers. Unfortunately, in both cases the simple algorithm 1 is extremely inefficient.

If the graph resides on disk, each hop requires loading the next vertex from disk. Even if the graph is partially in memory, on typical real-world graphs [22, 19] a large portion of the hops would require accessing vertices stored on disk. On a typical rotational hard drive, random seek costs a few milliseconds, limiting us to some hundreds of hops per second. Flash-based Solid-State Drives (SSD) have much better performance, but even they provide several orders of magnitude slower random access performance than DRAM.

In the distributed setting, the graph is partitioned across a cluster. Now each hop with the simple algorithm moves the walk to a partition owned either by the node owning the current vertex, or to another partition. If the hop requires changing partition, this will incur a cost equivalent to the network latency. With 1Gb Ethernet the typical latency is in the order of 0.1 milliseconds, allowing maximum of tens of thousands of walks per second.

In both cases, the inefficiency arises from increased latency between hops. In this work, we propose to solve this problem by simulating a very large number walks in parallel. Instead of executing one walk a time, we instead consider each vertex in turn and add one hop to each walk currently at the given vertex. Similar idea was first proposed in the external memory setting by [10], but we instead use the available RAM to keep track of walks while efficiently processing the graph from disk.

4. DRUNKARDMOB

We now describe the main contribution of this paper, the DrunkardMob algorithm.

4.1 High-level description

Instead of simulating one walk a time, DrunkardMob reverses the execution and instead simulates a massive number of walks in parallel, possibly from a large number of source vertices, and processes one *vertex* a time: at each vertex, all walks currently visiting that vertex are processed and moved forward. The graph is streamed from disk, thus all memory can be utilized for storing the walk states. The performance relies on compact representation of walks in memory, which we discuss in the next section.

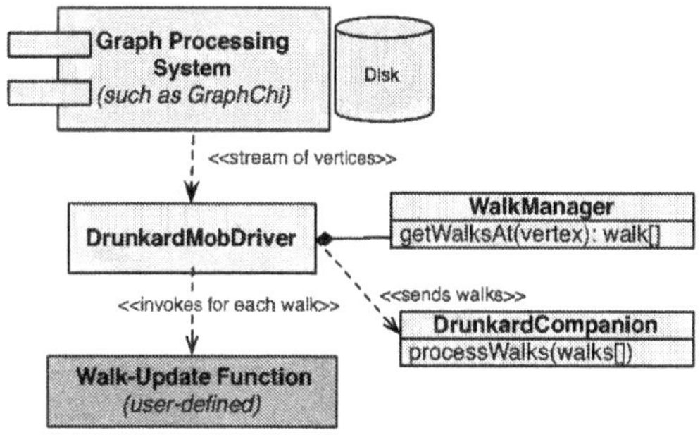

Figure 1: DrunkardMob: Class diagram.

The high-level object-oriented class diagram of the algorithm is shown in Figure 1. We assume that the graph is loaded efficiently from disk by some graph processing system, which provides a stream of vertices with their incident edges to the `DrunkardMobDriver`. `WalkManager` is a container that keeps track of the current vertex each walk is visiting (its interface is similar to an associated map from vertex ids to lists of walk-items). For each vertex it receives from the graph processor, `DrunkardMobDriver` queries `WalkManager` for the set of walks currently at that vertex. For each walk in the list, it invokes the user-defined walk-update function that returns new destination for the walk and possibly updates the meta-data associated with the walk. In addition, `WalkManager` provides the list of walks at the vertex to `DrunkardCompanion`, which is a component that keeps track of the visit frequencies (discussed in Sec. 4.3). Finally, `DrunkardMobDriver` provides the updated walks to the `WalkManager`. This cycle is repeated over all vertices in the graph for a predefined number of *iterations*. The number of hops for each walk is equal to the number of iterations.

Algorithm 2: Batched operation of DrunkardMob

```
DrunkardMobDriverCallback(vertexArray) begin
    walksForSet ←
    walkManager.allWalksAt(vertexArray)
    updatedWalks ← []
    foreach vertex ∈ vertices do
        foreach w ∈ walksForSet[vertex] do
            w' ← walkUpdateFunc(vertex, w)
            updatedWalks.add(w')
        end
    end
    walkManager.insert(updatedWalks)
end
```

For improved performance, DrunkardMob handles vertices in batched manner, i.e instead of processing one vertex a time, it handles vertices in large chunks. This allows `DrunkardMobDriver` to query walks from the `WalkManager` for many vertices at once, enabling more efficient data structures in the `WalkManager` (see below). The pseudocode for the batched operation is shown in Algorithm 2.

4.2 Efficient data structures

DrunkardMob assumes that the states of all walks is held in memory. To maximize the throughput (number of walks

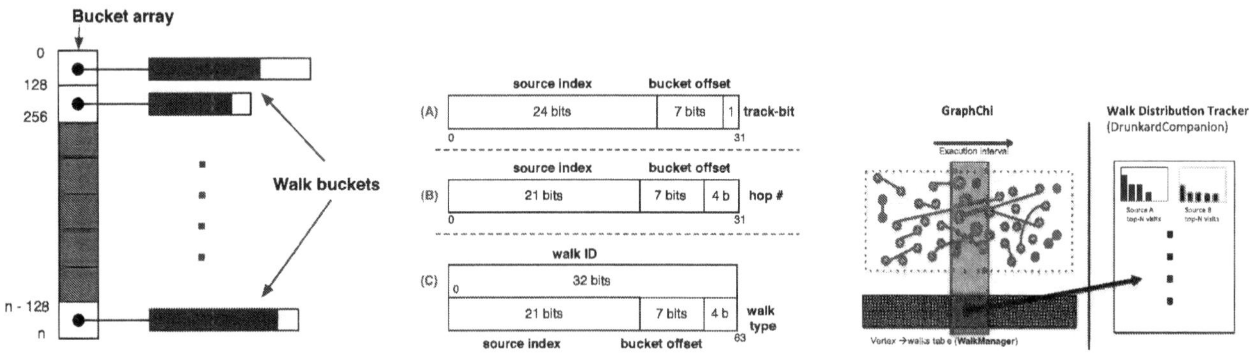

(a) WalkManager buckets (b) Walk encoding (c) DrunkardMob + GraphChi

Figure 2: (a) WalkManager bucket data structure; (b) Examples of walk encodings. A and B use 32 bits to represent a walk. B uses 4 bits to encode the hop-count of the walk, thus allowing less different source vertices then A. Example C allows keeping track of each walk separately and uses 64 bits to represent each walk. (c) Schematic diagram showing the DrunkardMob algorithm implemented on GraphChi.

simulated in time), it is important to minimize the memory footprint of each walk. We will first discuss the mapping of vertices to walks and then describe how the walks themselves are encoded.

`WalkManager` continuously manages a mapping from vertices to walks: for each vertex, it knows the walks whose last hop is in that vertex. Simplest choice would be to define an array A of lists, where $A[i]$ contains a linked list or array-buffer of walk objects (alternatively, we could store the vertex-list pairs in an associative map). Unfortunately, as we are interested in working with very large graphs with potentially hundreds of millions or a few billion vertices, the memory required to store pointers to the lists for each vertex quickly becomes a dominating cost. Moreover, with high-level languages such as Java, each individual list object can take tens of bytes of memory [14]. Instead we divide the range of vertices $[0, n-1]$ to sufficiently long sub-intervals (such as 128). For each sub-interval we associate a *bucket*, which is implemented as a buffered array, see Figure 2(a). When `DrunkardMobDriver` retrieves walks for a range of vertices, the walks from the corresponding buckets (whose intervals intersect the query interval) are sorted by the vertex. Thus, each walk object needs to be associated with the *offset* from the first vertex of the bucket. If the bucket intervals have length 128, the offset requires in 7 bits (Figure 2(b)).

The walk objects themselves are also represented compactly, typically as 32-bit words. Figure 2(b) shows three examples of how to encode information into 32-bit or 64-bit walk objects. Typically they encode the source vertex by using 24 bits to represent the index of the source vertex in the source vertex array. That is, this allows us to simulate walks from a maximum of $2^{24} = 16,777,216$ distinct source vertices. The sources thus need to be registered to `WalkManager` before the start of the simulation. Each walk needs to also encode a bucket offset to store the current position of the walk. Rest of the bits can be used to encode meta-data of the walk. For example, one bit can be used for a "track-bit" to set whether the walk should be counted in the visit frequency statistics (for example, we might not want to include the immediate connections of a vertex in the statistics).

The compact encoding of walks allows us to run up to 0.5 billion walks on a typical laptop with 8 gigabytes in memory using Java. With C/C++, we could probably execute significantly more walks due to lower runtime overheads.

4.3 Keeping track of walk visit frequencies

The next challenge is to keep track of the visit frequencies for the walks, for each source vertex separately. As shown In the class diagram (Figure 1), this is done by component `DrunkardCompanion`, of which we have two different versions:

- *Log each hop of the walk to a file or database* (files can be partitioned by sources) and analyze these log files separately. For PPR and related algorithms, this is efficient because each hop only requires storing the source vertex and current vertex identifier. The final analysis is done off-line.
- *Continuous in-memory tracking.* In this model we keep track of visit frequencies in-memory as they happen. The tracking can be done either locally in the same address space as the DrunkardMob simulation or remotely on a separate machine. Since walks are processed in batches, the walks can be efficiently sent over network in big packets.

In this paper, we concentrate in the in-memory tracking of walks. The main challenge is how to keep track of visit frequencies (for each source vertex separately), if the memory is limited. Formally, we want to keep track of the empirical distribution $\#\{v_i = w(i) \mid w \in \mathbb{W}_s, \forall i\}$, where $\mathbb{W}_s$ is the set of all simulated walks from source s. Alternatively, we might only be interested in the top k vertices visited by the walks for each source (not the actual frequencies).

In worst case, each hop visits a separate vertex and we need $O(\text{num-of-walks} \times \text{num-of-hops})$ of memory to store the visit frequencies. This problem is similar to the classic problem in data streams: estimating the top-K frequent items with limited memory. In our case, we can consider the stream of hops for walks from a given source s as a single data stream. For each source we maintain a vertex $\times$ visits mapping for some maximum of K elements. To limit the number of vertices in the map to K in principled manner we use the FREQUENT algorithm described in [5], which was originally proposed by [25]. The idea is simple: when we record a new visit to vertex v, as long as the number of distinct vertices in the map is less than K, we either insert $(v, 1)$ into the mapping or increase the count for v by one if it already was being tracked. If the size of the map is already K and we were to insert a new value $(v, 1)$, we decrease the count of each vertex by one and remove all values that have a zero count. The intuition is that if the map contains a long tail, i.e many vertices with a count of one, the long tail will be "cut" when the capacity limit of K is exceeded.

Theoretical guarantees for this algorithm are given in [5]. In practice a sufficiently skewed distribution (such as Zipfian) of the visits is required to maintain good approximation. In many real-world graphs, the in-degree distribution of nodes is highly skewed, follows the power-law degree [9], and thus also the visits frequencies of walks concentrate to a small number of vertices. However, this may not be true for walks from all sources: some vertices may be less connected to the "hot" nodes than average nodes or reside in distinct subgraphs outside the core of the graph [22]. We leave further study of this issue as future work.

Our architecture allows programmers to easily plug in different implementations of **DrunkardCompanion** which could support different trade-offs in approximation quality than our solution.

4.3.1 Long random walks as many short ones

To advance each walk by one hop, we need to do a full pass over the graph. Since we assume the graphs to be very large, also full pass is expected to be rather expensive. DrunkardMob is therefore suited only for walks that are relatively short. However, the definition of PageRank [26] and its variations is based on an infinitely long random walk with resets (i.e jump to a random vertex or the source vertex in Personalized PageRank). Therefore it would be natural to simulate as long walk as possible to approximate the model. But because of the resets, a random walk $W_s^t \rightarrow W_s^\tau$ can be decomposed into a sequence of τ short walks ω_s^i with the same source vertex s (note, that τ is a random variable):

$$W_s^\tau = s \circ \omega_s^1 \circ \omega_s^2 \circ \cdots \circ \omega_s^\tau$$

The short ω_s^i walks have length $|\omega_s^i| \sim Geom(d)$ where d is the reset-probability (damping factor). The expected length of the short walk is $\frac{1}{d}$ hops and the expected fraction of short walks longer than k is $(1-d)^k$. For example, with the usual choice of $d = 0.15$, the expected length is approximately 6.7 hops. For a more detailed analysis, see Fogaras et. al. [10].

It therefore appears that a large number of short walks could approximate the PageRank and related models well. In the context of recommender systems, it may make sense to bias towards shorter walks[2]: on typical social networks and other natural graphs, the number of nodes in a k−hop radius increases extremely fast as the expected distance between any two nodes is very small [1], even less than the famous "six degrees of separation" result by Milgram [24]. For computing sensible recommendations, it thus makes sense to concentrate the graph exploration using random walks to a smaller radius of the source vertex.

[2]Our implementation of Personalized PageRank actually continues the short walk after a reset, from the source vertex, causing a large number very short walks to be simulated.

4.4 Implementation on GraphChi

GraphChi [19] is a recently proposed very efficient disk based graph processing system. It is able to execute *vertex-centric* graph computation algorithms on graphs with billions of edges on just a commodity PC or laptop. GraphChi's performance is based on a "Parallel Sliding Windows" technique [19] : The edges of the graph are partitioned into a set of P *shards* by their destination vertex, each shard representing a contiguous *interval* of vertex IDs, and then sorted by their source vertex. Now to load a subgraph corresponding to one interval of vertices, only the associated shard (in-edges) and $P-1$ contiguous blocks from the other shards (out-edges) are loaded from disk. Updating the values of edges to disk is symmetric. GraphChi can execute a full pass over the graph by doing only a $O(P^2)$ non-sequential disk accesses, enabling it to perform well on both hard drives and SSDs.

We chose to implement DrunkardMob on GraphChi, because its method of processing vertices in large contiguous intervals matches perfectly the batched operation of DrunkardMob (Algorithm 2). In principle, DrunkardMob does not require many of the features of GraphChi, and a simple procedure to load the graph one vertex a time from disk (in adjacency list format) would have sufficed. However, in addition to saving us development time, the benefit of using GraphChi is that DrunkardMob could work alongside any other graph algorithm.

Figure 2(c) shows the high level operation of DrunkardMob as implemented on GraphChi. GraphChi provides a batch of vertices (corresponding to the vertex intervals that define the shards) a time, and calls **DrunkardMobEngine** which is implemented as a standard GraphChi **update-function** [19]. When receiving a **beginSubInterval()** call from GraphChi, **DrunkardMobEngine** requests the walks currently visiting the vertices in the interval from **WalkManager**. This batch of walks is also sent to the **DrunkardCompanion**, which can be a local or remote component. Subsequently, GraphChi invokes the **DrunkardMobEngine** for each of the vertices in the interval separately: **DrunkardMobEngine** selects the walks for the given vertex and calls the user-defined **walk-update function** for each of the walks as shown in Algorithm 2. DrunkardMob uses efficiently all available processor cores because different vertices can be processed in parallel. Figure 3 shows the actual Java-code for the walk-update function for Personalized PageRank.

For improved performance, DrunkardMob utilizes the *selective scheduling* feature of GraphChi. Each vertex is associated a bit which is set if the vertex has any walks currently visiting it. This allows GraphChi to save memory and avoid loading inactive vertices from disk.

5. CASE STUDY: TWITTER'S WHO-TO-FOLLOW

To demonstrate the viability of DrunkardMob to large-scale applications, we implemented a complete recommendation engine for the microblogging service Twitter following the description in recently published paper by Gupta et. al. [12]. The Twitter folllow-graph is a directed graph where users are represented by vertices and an edge (u, v) exists if user u *follows* user v's postings. The purpose of Who-to-Follow (WTF) service is to compute for each user a set

```
public void PPWalkUpdate(int[] walks,
    ChiVertex vertex, DrunkardContext drunkardCtx) {
    for(int walk : walks) {
        if (rand.nextDouble() < RESET_PROBABILITY) {
            drunkardCtx.resetWalk(walk, false);
        } else {
            int next = vertex.getOutEdgeId(
                    rand.nextInt(vertex.numOutEdges()));
            drunkardCtx.forwardWalkTo(walk, next, true);
        }
    }
}
```

Figure 3: Walk-update function for Personalized PageRank for DrunkardMob's Java implementation.

of recommendations for other users she could follow. The algorithm presented in [12] works in three steps.

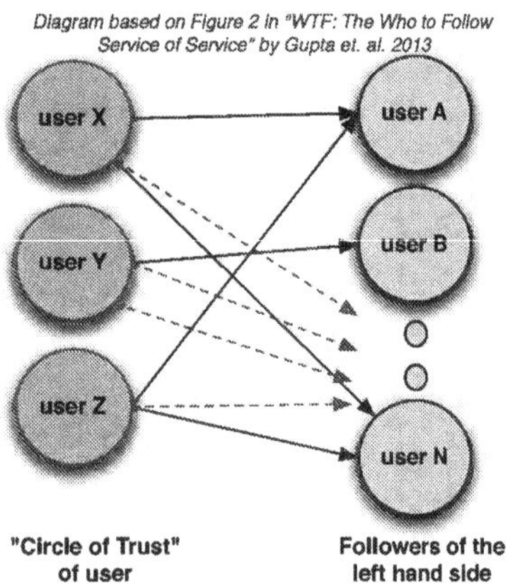

Figure 4: Bipartite graph used for computing recommendations for a Twitter user using the SALSA algorithm [21]. Diagram is based on Figure 2 in [12].

For each user: **(1)** Simulate an egocentric random walk and pick N most frequently visited vertices as the "Circle-of-Trust" (CoT) for the user. **(2)** Construct a bipartite graph by placing CoT vertices on the left side and a subset of the users they follow on the right side (see Figure 4a). **(3)** Compute SALSA algorithm on this graph and choose the top K scored nodes on the right side as recommendations for the user.

All details are not given in [12], so our algorithm might differ slightly from theirs. First step is equivalent to approximating the Personalized PageRank [26] and choosing the top ranked vertices. In our experiments, we chose $N = 200$ top vertices as the CoT for each user. Using DrunkardMob we simulate the egocentric random walks for a large number of users in parallel, using DrunkardMob. For the second step, we query the followers for each user in the CoT and count the number of common followings among CoT and eliminate all that have less than four common followers (this somewhat arbitrary filtering was done to improve performance). We can query followers efficiently by imposing a sparse index over the GraphChi shard files and finding followers for many users simultaneously. It is out of scope of this paper to describe the graph query functionality of GraphChi in more detail. Finally, in the third step we execute SALSA [21] algorithm in-memory on the constructed bipartite graph. Steps 2 and 3 are done for each user separately, but we use multi-threading to compute several recommendations in parallel.

Experiment: We run the Twitter recommendation algorithm on the *twitter_rv* graph, which is the almost complete Twitter graph from year 2010[3], using a Mac Mini (8GB, SSD, two cores) and a MacBook Pro laptop (8GB, SSD, 4 cores). On the Mac Mini we computed recommendations for 60,000 users a time, with average time of 2 hours and 52 minutes for a batch. For the MacBook Pro we computed 100,000 recommendations with mean time of 1 hour and 50 minutes. In both cases over 85% of the time was spent in steps 2 and 3.

6. EXPERIMENTS

All experiments were done on DrunkardMob implemented on top of Java-version of GraphChi. The graphs we used for the experiments are listed in Table 1.

Graph name	Vertices	Edges
live-journal [2]	4.8M	69M
domain [27]	26M	370M
twitter_rv[18]	65M	1.5B
uk-2007-05 [6]	106M	3.7B
yahoo-web [27]	1.4B	6.6B
Twitter follow-graph (Sep 2012)	-	>20B

Table 1: Experiment graphs. The exact size of Twitter's follow graph cannot be disclosed.

6.1 Large-scale experiments

We run DrunkardMob to compute estimate of Personalized PageRank for almost 15 million users on Twitter's full follow-graph in Sept 2012[4]. The exact size of the graph is not public information, but we can disclose that it had more than 20 billion follower-edges. For each source we started 900 walks and run six iterations. The total number of walks was approximately 13.1 billion.

The experiment was run using two server machines with 144GB of RAM, an SSD and 24-core Intel Xeon 2.4GHz CPUs. One server executed DrunkardMob on GraphChi, while the other one was used to run **DrunkardCompanion**.

Approximate running times of our results are provided in Table 2. The times have been scaled as-if the graph would have 20 billion edges. It is interesting to note that the algorithm runs much faster when the source vertices are the first 15 million vertices than when vertices from the middle of the ID range are chosen. This skew is probably explained by the fact that Twitter issues user IDs in order: the early Twitter users have smaller IDs than users who have registered later. Also, many of the celebrities are early users of Twitter, and simply have had more time to collect followers than later users. Based on this, we postulate random walks started from early users concentrate faster around the popular nodes, allowing DrunkardMob to operate on smaller set of active vertices. Unfortunately, we did not have opportunity to study this phenomenon further.

[3]Unfortunately, we did not have access to the complete Twitter follow-graph for this experiment.

[4]This experiment was conducted during author's internship at Twitter Inc in Fall 2012

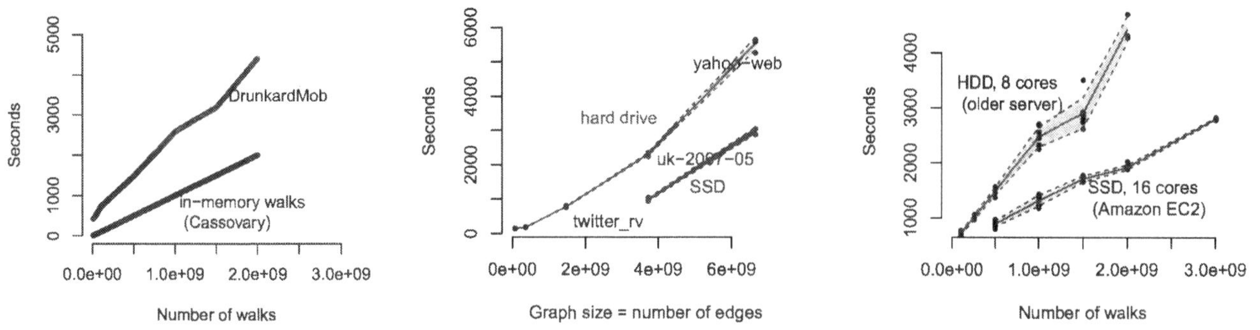

(a) Comparison to in-memory walks (b) Running time / graph size (c) Running time / number of walks

Figure 5: (a) Running time of DrunkardMob and in-memory graph walks with Cassovary. Both experiments were made on a server with hard drive, 32 gigabytes of memory and 8 cores. Cassovary's timings are extrapolated for clarity. (b) Running time of six iterations of DrunkardMob for 200 million walks on various graphs (Mac Mini, hard drive and SSD). (c) Running time on the `twitter_rv` graph when the number of walks is varied. Upper line is for a server with a normal hard drive, while lower is for a high-performance server with an SSD. Time increases approximately linearly with the number of walks and the graph size. Shaded areas show the standard deviation.

Source vertex IDs	Type	Runtime (1 iter.)
0 - 14.6M	unweighted	47 min
14.6M - 29.2M	unweighted	100 min
0 - 14.6M	weighted	55 min
14.6M - 29.2M	weighted	98 min
100M - 114.6M	weighted	91 min
50M - 64.6M	weighted	97 min
200M - 214.6M	weighted	88 min

Table 2: Running time of DrunkardMob on the full Twitter follow-graph. The numbers have been scaled to approximate results on a graph with 20B edges. For each source, 900 walks were issued.

Interestingly weighted and unweighted versions of DrunkardMob have approximately the same running times. For fast weighted sampling of edges we used the alias method by Kronmal and Peterson [17]. It is plausible that the weighted sampling causes the walks to concentrate faster on popular nodes, accelerating the DrunkardMob operations and hiding the increased cost of weighted sampling.

This experiment shows that DrunkardMob with GraphChi can scale to one of the biggest graphs in the industry, on just a single machine. We also run DrunkardMob on the full Twitter graph on a MacBook Pro laptop with SSD and 8 gigabytes of RAM, and could execute half a billion walks simultaneously in approximately one hour / iteration (these experiments were run without a DrunkardCompanion, and are thus not comparable with the results in Table 2).

6.2 Scalability and Performance

Comparison to in-memory walks: We compared DrunkardMob with Cassovary[5], a high-performance in-memory graph library by Twitter which is able to load relative large graphs into memory. Cassovary is implemented in Java/Scala, similarly to ours, allowing a fair comparison. In our experiments, we found Cassovary to be roughly 30% faster in simulating walks than DrunkardMob on a small graph (`live-journal`) and 2 times faster on the larger `twitter_rv.net` graph. Timings for the latter are shown in Fig. 5a.

Scalability: Figure 5 shows the running time of DrunkardMob when the graph size or number of walks is varied. in Fig. 5b we plot the running time as function of graph size. The experiments was conducted on a Mac Mini with 8 GB of memory and an SSD. For each experiment we simulated a total of 200 million walks. In Figure 5c we used the `twitter_rv.net` graph and varied the number of sources and the number of walks simulated from each source. The higher curve is on an old (from year 2008) 8-core Intel Xeon 3.4GHz server with 32GB RAM and a hard drive; lower curve is for a high performance Amazon *hi1.4xlarge* instance with 16 virtual cores, 64GB of RAM and an SSD drive. The latter is faster, but both show close to linear scalability as the number of walks increases. We found that the overhead of Java's garbage collection becomes the main bottleneck when the the number of walks is very large.

On sufficiently large problems, the performance is close to linear in both the graph size and the number of walks being simulated. Based on these experiments, we can conclude that DrunkardMob can simulate random walks in similar time as an in-memory algorithm, but can process much bigger graphs, as it is not limited by the amount of RAM.

7. CONCLUSIONS AND FUTURE WORK

We presented DrunkardMob and demonstrated how it could be used to simulate very large scale random walk simulations on some of the biggest graphs available, on just a single computer. Compared to previous work which have used similar approaches, DrunkardMob on GraphChi provides a generic platform for implementing algorithms based on walks (not necessarily random) on graphs. Programming walks for DrunkardMob is as easy as it is for an in-memory

[5]`https://github.com/twitter/cassovary`

graph: programmer provides a simple walk-update function and the system takes care of the rest.

There are several remaining challenges for future work: First, could DrunkardMob be implemented on top of a distributed graph system such as GraphLab [11]? We also would like to study whether we could increase the scalability of DrunkardMob by utilizing the disk also to store the walk status array. Finally, we would like to extend the DrunkardMob to naturally support evolving graphs in a principled manner, by implementing the incremental technique proposed in [4].

Acknowledgments

This work was initiated during author's internship at Twitter Inc during Fall 2012. Author is advised by Carlos Guestrin and Guy Blelloch. We thank Pankaj Gupta, Matthew Gardner and Mayank Mohta for helpful feedback and encouragement. Funded by ISTC Cloud Computing and NSF IIS-1258741

8. REFERENCES

[1] L. Backstrom, P. Boldi, M. Rosa, J. Ugander, and S. Vigna. Four degrees of separation. In *Proceedings of the 3rd Annual ACM Web Science Conference*, pages 33–42. ACM, 2012.

[2] L. Backstrom, D. Huttenlocher, J. Kleinberg, and X. Lan. Group formation in large social networks: membership, growth, and evolution. The 12th ACM SIGKDD International Conference on Knowledge Discovery and Data Mining, KDD'06. ACM, 2006.

[3] B. Bahmani, K. Chakrabarti, and D. Xin. Fast personalized pagerank on mapreduce. In *SIGMOD Conference*, pages 973–984, 2011.

[4] B. Bahmani, A. Chowdhury, and A. Goel. Fast incremental and personalized pagerank. *Proceedings of the VLDB Endowment*, 4(3):173–184, 2010.

[5] R. Berinde, P. Indyk, G. Cormode, and M. J. Strauss. Space-optimal heavy hitters with strong error bounds. *ACM Transactions on Database Systems (TODS)*, 35(4):26, 2010.

[6] P. Boldi, M. Santini, and S. Vigna. A large time-aware graph. *SIGIR Forum*, 42(2):33–38, 2008.

[7] A. Das Sarma, S. Gollapudi, and R. Panigrahy. Estimating pagerank on graph streams. In *Proceedings of the twenty-seventh ACM SIGMOD-SIGACT-SIGART symposium on Principles of database systems*, pages 69–78. ACM, 2008.

[8] J. Dean and S. Ghemawat. Mapreduce: simplified data processing on large clusters. In *Proc. of the 6th USENIX conference on Operating systems design and implementation*, OSDI'04, pages 10–10, San Francisco, CA, 2004. USENIX.

[9] M. Faloutsos, P. Faloutsos, and C. Faloutsos. On power-law relationships of the internet topology. In *ACM SIGCOMM Computer Communication Review*, volume 29, pages 251–262. ACM, 1999.

[10] D. Fogaras, B. Rácz, K. Csalogány, and T. Sarlós. Towards scaling fully personalized pagerank: Algorithms, lower bounds, and experiments. *Internet Mathematics*, 2(3):333–358, 2005.

[11] J. Gonzalez, Y. Low, H. Gu, D. Bickson, and C. Guestrin. PowerGraph: Distributed graph-parallel computation on natural graphs. OSDI'12, Hollywood, CA, 2012.

[12] P. Gupta, A. Goel, J. Lin, A. Sharma, D. Wang, and R. Zadeh. Wtf: The who to follow service at twitter.

[13] A. Hotho, R. Jäschke, C. Schmitz, and G. Stumme. Folkrank: A ranking algorithm for folksonomies. *Proc. FGIR*, 2006, 2006.

[14] IBM. http://www.ibm.com/developerworks/java/library/j-codetoheap/.

[15] M. Jamali and M. Ester. Trustwalker: a random walk model for combining trust-based and item-based recommendation. In *Proceedings of the 15th ACM SIGKDD international conference on Knowledge discovery and data mining*, pages 397–406. ACM, 2009.

[16] G. Jeh and J. Widom. Scaling personalized web search. In *Proceedings of the 12th international conference on World Wide Web*, pages 271–279. ACM, 2003.

[17] R. A. Kronmal and A. V. Peterson Jr. On the alias method for generating random variables from a discrete distribution. *The American Statistician*, 33(4):214–218, 1979.

[18] H. Kwak, C. Lee, H. Park, and S. Moon. What is Twitter, a social network or a news media? In *Proc. of the 19th international conference on World wide web*, pages 591–600. ACM, 2010.

[19] A. Kyrola, G. Blelloch, and C. Guestrin. Graphchi: Large-scale graph computation on just a pc. In *Proceedings of the 10th USENIX Symposium on Operating Systems Design and Implementation (OSDI '12)*, Hollywood, October 2012.

[20] S. Lee, S.-i. Song, M. Kahng, D. Lee, and S.-g. Lee. Random walk based entity ranking on graph for multidimensional recommendation. In *Proceedings of the fifth ACM conference on Recommender systems*, pages 93–100. ACM, 2011.

[21] R. Lempel and S. Moran. Salsa: the stochastic approach for link-structure analysis. *ACM Transactions on Information Systems (TOIS)*, 19(2):131–160, 2001.

[22] J. Leskovec, K. J. Lang, A. Dasgupta, and M. W. Mahoney. Statistical properties of community structure in large social and information networks. In *Proceedings of the 17th international conference on World Wide Web*, pages 695–704. ACM, 2008.

[23] D. Liben-Nowell and J. Kleinberg. The link-prediction problem for social networks. *Journal of the American society for information science and technology*, 58(7):1019–1031, 2007.

[24] S. Milgram. The small world problem. *Psychology today*, 2(1):60–67, 1967.

[25] J. Misra and D. Gries. Finding repeated elements. *Science of computer programming*, 2(2):143–152, 1982.

[26] L. Page, S. Brin, R. Motwani, and T. Winograd. The pagerank citation ranking: Bringing order to the web. Technical Report 1999-66, Stanford InfoLab, 1999.

[27] Yahoo WebScope. Yahoo! altavista web page hyperlink connectivity graph, circa 2002, 2012. `http://webscope.sandbox.yahoo.com/`.

Using Maximum Coverage to Optimize Recommendation Systems in E-Commerce*

Mikael Hammar
Apptus Technologies
Trollebergsvägen 5
SE-222 29 Lund, Sweden
mikael.hammar@apptus.com

Robin Karlsson
Apptus Technologies
Trollebergsvägen 5
SE-222 29 Lund, Sweden
robin.karlsson@apptus.com

Bengt J. Nilsson
Dept. of Computer Science
Malmö University
SE-205 06 Malmö, Sweden
bengt.nilsson.TS@mah.se

ABSTRACT

We study the problem of optimizing recommendation systems for e-commerce sites. We consider in particular a combinatorial solution to this optimization based on the well known *Maximum Coverage* problem that asks for the k sets (products) that cover the most elements from a ground set (consumers). This formulation provides an abstract model for what k products should be recommended to maximize the probability of consumer purchase. Unfortunately, Maximum Coverage is NP-complete but an efficient approximation algorithm exists based on the Greedy methodology.

We exhibit test results from the Greedy method on real data sets showing 3–8% increase in sales using the Maximum Coverage optimization method in comparison to the standard best-seller list. A secondary effect that our Greedy algorithm exhibits on the tested data is increased *diversification* in presented products over the best-seller list.

Categories and Subject Descriptors

H.3.3 [**Information Storage and Retrieval**]: Information Search and Retrieval—*Information filtering, Retrieval models, Search process*

Keywords

Recommendation systems; e-Commerce; Optimization; Maximum Coverage

1. INTRODUCTION

Consider an e-commerce site selling products to potential customers. The aim of the e-commerce marketer is to maximize the profit of the site. From the consumer's perspective, the process of purchasing a product on a site can consist of a general search on a search engine to find the site, followed by further searches and browsing on the site to find the product and conclude the purchase.

In fact, we consider searches to be just one aspect of more general searching schemes, denoted *navigation*. Navigation strategies where the customers probe the site to try to reach a loosely specified goal in several steps are called *associative searches*. A solution to associative search needs to let the customers explore the site to achieve a possibly undefined search goal. In contrast, a *deterministic search* is performed to reach a specific search goal, a purchase, already known to the customer. We therefore differentiate between customers doing associative search and deterministic search and call them *associative customers* and *deterministic customers* respectively.

The associative customer is a potential but uncertain buying customer, and it is the marketer's responsibility to ensure that the customer buys something. A common strategy is to provide recommendations based on the customer's navigation history and knowledge about the sales history of the site. The navigation history provides a selection of the product catalogue but this may still be much too large to be presented to the customer. Therefore, a small number of products, we denote this number k, have to be selected to be presented to the customer. In reality, many e-commerce sites present the k most popular products, i.e., the products with the highest sales, possibly weighted with profit margin or product type, the so-called *best-seller list*. The best-seller list is a natural choice for recommendations. The underlying assumption is that, in the short term, the sales history of the site is an accurate model for the future sales distribution.

Our main insight is that, instead of optimizing on popularity, one should maximize the probability that a customer makes a purchase. We show that this, together with some natural design changes to the e-commerce site, will increase total sales. For a marketer, it is important to make the customer purchase something as early as possible. The customer life-time value is optimized by other means, such as product recommendations or targeted campaigns once more information about the customer is available. This strategy leads to presenting a different set of products than the best-seller list. Just presenting the most popular products is not the best strategy since several of the products on the best-seller list may be products that are commonly purchased together. In this case, it is beneficial to present other prod-

*This research is part of the project "Self Learning Optimization Systems for Electronic Commerce" funded by a grant from the Swedish VINNOVA innovation agency; see http://www.vinnova.se/en/.

RecSys'13, October 12–16, 2013, Hong Kong, China.

ACM 978-1-4503-2409-0/13/10 ...$15.00.
http://dx.doi.org/10.1145/2507157.2507169

ucts that have lower sales but attract more varied consumer groups.

The problem of finding the k items from a product list that maximizes the probability of a purchase is a well-known computational problem called *Maximum k-Coverage*, a variant of the famous *Set Cover* problem [9, 14]. A greedy algorithm can be used to efficiently approximate a solution [5, 13, 19].

We can make additional recommendations to the customer using data associated to each product that was listed. We call such recommendations *product associated recommendations*. In marketing terms they are known as "Those who bought this also bought..." or "Those who viewed this bought...". Product associated recommendations can be implemented efficiently using common graph algorithms [6].

Our aim is to illustrate how the *maximum coverage* list in conjunction with product associated recommendations improves on the standard practice to use the best-seller list, even if these are taken together with product associated recommendations. We perform several experiments on real e-commerce data to show that the greedy algorithm together with product associated recommendations significantly outperforms the best-seller list, even with product associated recommendations.

The implication of our research is that the e-commerce site needs to 1) apply the maximum coverage algorithm while the user is interacting with the site, and 2) apply product recommendations as easily and naturally as possible during the user's interaction with the site. The first implication means that every interaction with the site should be optimized towards converting the customer rather than selling a particular product. This view is customer centric rather than product centered. The second implication is the key towards what we call *natural browsing*. A site that applies this recommendation methodology makes sure that recommendations are available on every page, not just hidden on product pages.

The paper is organized as follows. In the next section, we present the details of our experimental setup. Section 3 shows empirically that the Greedy algorithm produces the optimal maximum coverage list in almost every case and, in the few cases that it does not, it produces a list that covers 99% of the optimal list, thus significantly beating the guaranteed approximation ratio of 63%. Section 4 presents the results from our experiments and in Section 5, we show that the maximum coverage list also improves on the diversification of the presented products in relation to the best-seller list. In Section 6 we discuss the significance of our results. In Section 7, we give a suggestion of how to adjust a site to exploit our results to further improve the sales figures. In Section 8, we discuss future research and possible extensions.

2. METHOD

2.1 Best-Seller and Maximum Coverage Lists

Let us look at the first step of the sales process separately, to maximize the probability that a customer makes a purchase. We assume that the marketer has data about previous sales. Given the current navigation selection, what choice of products should the marketer present on the site? The most common method is to present the currently most popular products, often in a *best-seller list* displaying the k products with the highest number of purchases. The ambition with this scheme is to attract future customers to the products of the site. This method is easy to understand and simple to compute, even dynamically, in $O(kn)$ time, where n is the number of products in the current product selection. We call it the *B-list* (short for *best-seller list*).

However, this tentative solution does not take into account that several best-selling products can appeal to the same group of customers. The marketer can be better off presenting products that sell slightly less than those in the B-list but spread across larger groups of customers. To achieve this, we want our list to appeal to as many different types of customers as possible. We look at recent sales data as a probability distribution of sales over the product selection and find, for an arbitrary customer, the k products maximizing the probability that the customer makes a purchase from these k products. With knowledge of what previous customers have bought, we have additional information about dependencies between products and we can make use of this knowledge. Let us formalize this and let $U = \{u_1, \ldots, u_m\}$, be the customers that previously have bought products and let $F = \{S_1, \ldots, S_n\}$ denote the products in the product selection. If we associate the customers that have purchased product S_i, we can view S_i as a *set* of those customers. The family F represents the products, where u_j is in S_i if and only if customer u_j has bought product S_i. Our objective now is to establish the k sets $F^* = \{S_{i_1}, \ldots, S_{i_k}\}$ that together contain as many different customers u_j as possible. This is a well-known problem from Combinatorial Optimization denoted the Maximum k-Coverage problem and is formally defined as follows:

> **Name:** MAXIMUM k-COVERAGE
>
> **Instance:** A universe of elements $U = \{u_1, \ldots, u_m\}$, an integer value k and a family of sets $F = \{S_1, \ldots, S_n\}$, where each set S_i is a subset of U.
>
> **Objective:** Find a subfamily $F^* \subseteq F$ such that $|F^*| \leq k$ and the number of covered elements $|\bigcup_{S \in F^*} S|$ is maximised, i.e. using up to k sets, cover as many elements as possible.

The maximum coverage problem is a variant of the set cover problem and these problems are well researched [2, 3, 5, 11, 12, 13, 18, 19, 20]. Unfortunately, these are NP-hard problems [9, 14], and thus we cannot expect to optimally solve them efficiently. However, using a simple greedy algorithm (as shown in Algorithm 1), we can achieve an approximate solution for maximum coverage that is guaranteed to have an approximation ratio of $(e-1)/e \approx 0.6321$, where e is the base of the natural logarithm, so the greedy algorithm will always cover at least 63% of the maximum possible number of customers that can be covered, and it can be shown that this is essentially as good as can be achieved with a polynomial time approximation algorithm [7]. This algorithm can be implemented to run in $O(k \cdot \sum_{S \in F} |S|) \subseteq O(knm)$ time. We denote the list of k products produced by the greedy algorithm, the *M-list* (short for *Maximum Coverage list*).

2.2 Ageing

One very important aspect to consider is how to deal with older sales in relation to newer ones. Since recent sales data

Algorithm 1 GREEDY-MAX-COVERAGE(U, k, F)

$R \leftarrow U$
$F^* \leftarrow \emptyset$
for i from 1 to k **do**
  $S \leftarrow \max_{S \in (F \setminus F^*)} |S \cap R|$
  $F^* \leftarrow F^* \cup \{S\}$
  $R \leftarrow R \setminus S$
  if $|R| = 0$ **then break**
return F^*

will say more about what products are popular at the moment than old data, some kind of *ageing model* is needed to make older sales have less impact than more recent ones. A time-based window, that forgets sales data as they turn older than some time t, is perhaps the easiest and most intuitive kind of model. Another approach is the session-based window, that always keeps the same number of sessions in the sales data. This window will keep the amount of data constant even if the rate of sales on the site changes. More advanced models can gradually decrease the importance of sales with time [17]. No matter what model is used, a long window is slow to catch on to trends and tends to show products that are less trend sensitive. A short window catches trends faster but is more sensitive to noise due to lack of data. One such kind of noise is customers that purchase several copies of the same product. This spike in sales could push an otherwise unremarkable product to the top of the B-list. An easy way to avoid this unwanted effect is to order products by the number of customers that have bought the product, rather than the product's total number of sales.

2.3 Product Associated Recommendations

When the customer reaches the product page on the way to make a purchase, it is customary to show some kind of recommendations based on the product viewed (and sometimes also based on knowledge about the customer). Popular methods are "Those who bought this also bought..." (denoted BB) and "Those who viewed this bought..." (denoted VB) or variations thereof. In many cases, such recommendations can also be presented in earlier phases of the navigation and not only when the customer reaches the product page. We denote recommendations that depend on given products (and possibly other information) *product associated recommendations* or PARs and in the second step of our strategy, we use PARs to further enhance the total recommendations of the e-commerce site.

PARs can be implemented efficiently using common graph algorithms [6]. We maintain a weighted graph where each product in the product catalogue is a node and whenever two products are purchased together (in the case of BB), we increase the weight between the corresponding nodes. For other variants of PAR methods, similar strategies can be implemented.

2.4 Motivation

As we will see, (BB) PARs complement Maximum Coverage as a product S that has sold well but is not on the M-list is very likely to be picked as a PAR for something else on the M-list. The reason for this is that the M-list contains a product S' that is likely to be bought in conjunction with S, and hence, S is a PAR of S'.

In contrast, PARs do not complement the B-list as well. The reason for this is that if a product S' is in the B-list, and has an associated PAR S that has sold well, it is likely that S will also be in the best-seller list. Thus, the products on the best-seller list will, in many cases, be in each other's recommendations.

The M-list effectively presents the products that maximize the probability of a purchase, whereas the B-list simply presents the most popular products. Our experiments will show that by presenting the M-list instead of the B-list during browsing, and, in the same context, present related just-in-time product recommendations, the user is confronted with all the benefits of the M-list but also with the most popular products of the B-list available via recommendations. Hence, product associated recommendations together with the M-list give us the best of both maximizing the probability of sales and also showing the most popular products.

2.5 The Experiments

We make two types of experiments on data from two real e-commerce sites. The two sites are a book store and a hardware store (selling DIY material). The first experiment compares the greedy method to the optimal solution to the maximum coverage problem on data from our sites. The results of this experiment are presented in Section 3.

The second and main type of experiment aims to compare the effect on sales between the M-list and the B-list, together with PARs. This can be done with live evaluations such as A/B tests, where the users would be split in two groups and each group is shown a different alternative. However, live testing requires control over what is shown on a website and can be costly if one strategy performs significantly worse than the other strategy. Instead, we evaluate the two strategies using logged sales data. This problem of evaluating a new behavior, or *policy*, using only observations collected during the execution of another policy is known as *policy evaluation* [15].

To simplify our experiments, we compare the M-list and B-list with PARs as they would appear on the sites' top pages but we are confident that our method works equally well under the general situation that the customer navigates through the site, dynamically changing the part of the product catalogue currently considered by the recommendation system.

The data available for the experiments is a sequence of sessions where each session contains a time, a customer ID and a list of purchased products. The data contains the complete sales information of the book store (116 000 sessions) and the hardware store (28 000 sessions) during 60 days. We use the data from the first 30 days as "warm-up" data to stabilize the results of the algorithms. The result we present are from runs of the algorithms on the last 30 days, as follows:

- Data A: 30 days of sales data from a book store.
- Data B: 30 days of sales data from a hardware store.

Our evaluation method is to go through the recorded sales data in chronological order and update the different lists according to the data seen so far. Then the different lists are scored as follows:

- For each session, give a list one *product point* for each product sold that is in the list at the time of the transaction.
- For each session, give a list one *session point* if the list shows any of the products purchased in the session at the time of the transaction.

These two different scores correspond to the two different types of lists we want to evaluate. Essentially, the B-list tries to optimize product points and the M-list tries to optimize session points.

In order to measure the effect of PARs on a list we also construct an associated set of PARs in the following way: For each product in the list take the top three BB PARs for the product and put them in a PAR set. As two products could both recommend the same product any duplicates are removed, also any product in the original list is removed from the PAR set. We keep the number of PARs considered for each product low since, in reality, a large number of product associated recommendations would not be considered by a customer.

Our way of measuring using session points gives a value that relates to the effective probability that the user makes a purchase from either list (also accounting for purchases from the PARs). We know that the measure (under weak assumptions) is a linear factor from the probability of sale for a consumer, which is the aspect we want to emphasize. Product points, on the other hand, relate to the probability of sale for a product.

In addition, we maintain session-based ageing windows from 50 to 50 000 sessions on the bookstore and from 50 to 20 000 sessions on the hardware store. The book store's web site actually maintains a list of the ten most popular books (excluding paperbacks) on its top page, updated each day based on the sales from the previous day. This provides us with a base line for our comparisons and also specifies a reasonable value for k ($k = 10$) for our experiments. We call this list the *A-list* (short for *Actual list*). Note that the hardware store's web site does not maintain an A-list as the top page here presents marketer chosen recommendations.

As a measure of optimality, we use the knowledge about the data of future sales to construct a list that will match what is purchased as well as possible. We call this list a *clairvoyant list*, or *C-list* for short. This list maintains the list of $k = 10$ best-selling products for the next day.

3. APPROXIMATING THE M-LIST

We would like to know how close the solution that the greedy algorithm produces is to the optimal solution. In theory, to compute the optimal solution, we would have to run a brute-force algorithm for the maximum coverage problem with thousands of sets and thousands of elements, which would be utterly intractable. However, we can take advantage of the known structure in our data to reduce the running time significantly.

The product sales exhibit what is known as a *long tail effect*, i.e., a large number of products have only been bought a few times and a relatively small amount of products are responsible for a large proportion of all sales. The customers exhibit a similar, albeit less pronounced, long tail effect. We can take advantage of these combined long tail effects to reduce the number of *interesting* sets and elements significantly. The interesting sets are those products that have been purchased by at least two customers, and the interesting elements are those customers that have bought at least two products. This means that the brute-force algorithm can produce the optimal maximum coverage list for $k = 10$ products in a few seconds.

Table 1: Results from comparing the greedy and optimal maximum coverage algorithms.

	Data 1	Data 2
Number of non-optimal solutions	5 / 60	2 / 60
Average % of optimal covered	99.98	99.98
Minimum % of optimal covered	99.37	99.16

In this experiment, we have 60 days of sales data from the book store and the hardware store (this is a different set of sales data from the one used in Section 4) that we call *Data 1* and *Data 2* respectively. We make runs through the data sets and compare the results from greedy with optimal solutions using a session based ageing window with a size of 5 000 sessions. For each day in the data set we calculate an optimal M-list and an approximate M-list and compare the number of customers covered. Table 1 shows the number of times the greedy algorithm found a non-optimal solution and the total number of days in the first row, an average of the number of customers covered by the greedy solution compared to the number of customers covered by the optimal solution in percent in the second row, and how close to the optimum the greedy algorithm is, in the worst case in percent in the third row.

As we can see in Table 1, the greedy algorithm finds an optimal solution most of the times for our data. On the few cases where it does not, it is still almost optimal. Our experiments show that we can use the greedy solution as an accurate and practical solution to the maximum coverage problem.

4. RESULTS

In this section we show results from the evaluation described in Section 2.5. All lists contain $k = 10$ products and they are all updated once per day (at midnight).

4.1 Data A — The Book Store

Figure 1 presents the experimental results from our tests on the book store. In both plots, we display in order from the top, the C-list in magenta, the M-list in red, the B-list in blue and the A-list in green. The dashed curves below are points given for recommendations associated to the list of the same color. For each list we count the total number of product (left) and session (right) points accumulated during

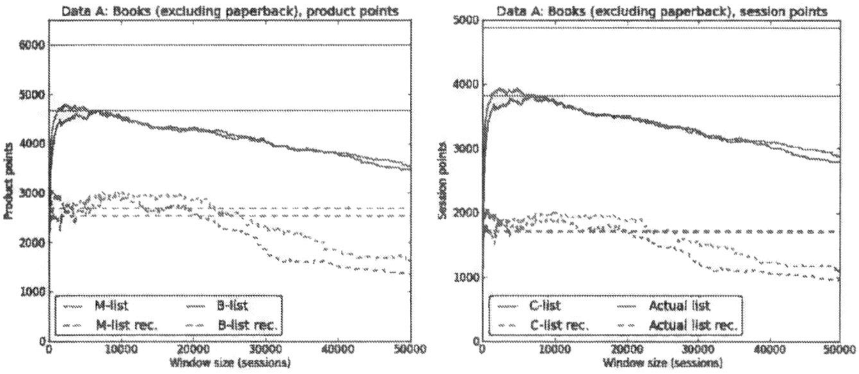

Figure 1: Plots over product points (left plot) and session points (right plot) for Data A for M-list (red) and B-list (blue) for different window sizes and lines for C-list (magenta) and the A-list (green). Dashed lines are points for the recommendations.

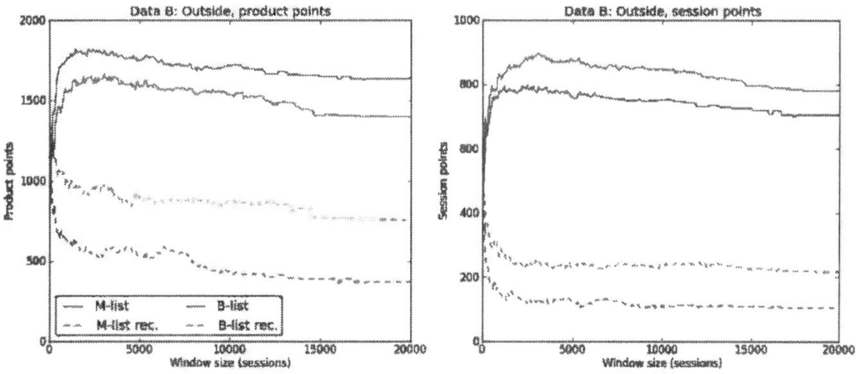

Figure 2: Plots over product points (left plot) and session points (right plot) for Data B for M-list (red) and B-list (blue) for different window sizes. Dashed lines are points for the recommendations.

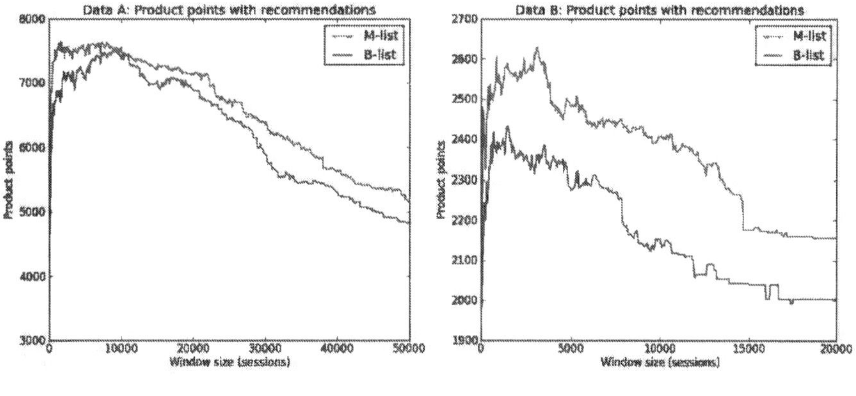

Figure 3: Plots over total product points (including points for recommendations) for M-list (red) and B-list (blue), for Data A (left plot) and Data B (right plot). Note the different axes.

the 30 day period. Note that the horizontal axis shows the size of the ageing window. In the left plot, the B-list obtains its maximum product points of 4680 points for a window size of 6500. The M-list obtains its maximum of 4702 points for a window size of 1750, i.e., for a significantly shorter window. The A-list counts 4669 product points and the C-list counts 5988 product points. In the right plot, the B-list obtains its maximum session points of 3834 points for a window size of 6500 and the M-list obtains its maximum of 3947 points for a window size of 2300. Counting either the maximum product or session points, the M-list is actually better than the A-list in both cases even without taking PARs into account. The A-list counts 3828 product points and the C-list counts 4885 product points.

In the left plot of Figure 3, we display the sum of product points for the B-list and its PARs in blue and similarly for the M-list in red. This sum maximizes at 7400 with a window size of 6500 for the accumulated B-list. The accumulated M-list maximizes at 7639 with a window size of 1750. This gives us a ratio between the accumulated maxima of 1.032, hence, a 3% improvement in sales in comparison to the B-list. The accumulated A-list in turn, counts 7214 product points, giving us a ratio of 1.058, hence almost a 6% improvement.

4.2 Data B — The Hardware Store

The results for the hardware store are similar but with even more pronounced differences between the two lists.

In Figure 2, the results for the hardware store are shown. Here we only display the B-list in blue and the M-list in red together with their associated recommendation points as dashed curves. For each list we count the total number of product (left) and session (right) points accumulated during the 30 day period. Again, the horizontal axis shows the size of the ageing window. In the left plot, the B-list obtains its maximum product points of 1820 points for a window size of 1500. The M-list obtains its maximum of 1645 points for a window size of 3100. In the right plot, the B-list obtains its maximum session points of 799 points for a window size of 2450 and the M-list obtains its maximum of 896 points for a window size of 3100.

In the right plot of Figure 3, we again display the sum of product points for the B-list and its PARs in blue and similarly for the M-list in red. This sum maximizes at 2432 with a window size of 1400 for the accumulated B-list. The accumulated M-list maximizes at 2629 with a window size of 3100. This gives us a ratio between the accumulated maxima of 1.081, hence, an 8% improvement in sales.

4.3 Effect of PARs

To include the effect of product recommendations in the comparison between the M-list and the B-list we use a linear model where the effect of a list X is calculated as $P_X + wR_X$, where P_X and R_X are the product points for the X-list and its recommendations respectively. The factor w denotes the probability that a customer takes notice of the PARs, the *PAR probability*. In Section 7 we discuss some ways to design a site to achieve a high w. In Figure 3 we show the results for product points for both data sets with $w = 1$. In Table 2 we show ratios of M-list points and B-list points for different w. A fixed window size is used per row, chosen to optimize the list in the "Opt." column. A ratio larger than 1 means that the M-list is better. For both data sets we establish that the M-list is better than the B-list for all w above 0.58. In other words, the M-list approach is proven better than the B-list if customers take notice of product recommendations at least 58% of the times.

Table 2: Ratios between the M-list and the B-list that take PARs into account.

Data	Opt.	w				
		0	0.25	0.5	0.75	1
A	B-list	0.990	1.000	1.007	1.013	1.018
A	M-list	1.079	1.089	1.097	1.103	1.108
B	B-list	0.891	0.943	0.988	1.028	1.062
B	M-list	0.914	0.977	1.031	1.078	1.120

4.4 Window Time Span Distributions

Since the window size is measured in sessions, the time span of the window varies with the session rate. As can be seen in Figure 4, the time span increase is essentially linear with the increase in window size, with slight "waves" due to the cyclic nature of the session rate, with both daily and weekly cycles. The reason for the atypical behavior in the right plot in Figure 4 is that for large window sizes there is not enough data to "fill up" the window before evaluation starts as there is only about a month of "warm up" data.

5. DIVERSIFICATION

A product list should be both relevant and reflect several aspects of interest. An item in the list, although relevant, might be too similar to a better item in the list and should therefore be replaced by a different item. There exist many methods to achieve such *diversification* [4, 10, 21, 22]. Our optimization criterion for the M-list tries to diversify users, so we also expect some sort of diversification effect over the products in the M-list in our experiments.

Modifications of classical information retrieval metrics have been used to measure both relevance and diversification [1], but they require predefined manual relevance judgments. Since relevance is covered in Section 4, we now focus on measuring diversification. Most products in our data have one or more associated categories. Typically, products from different categories are not similar. We therefore look at product categories to measure diversification.

As we want to be able to compare products, and each product may be associated with a set of categories, we apply a distance measure between sets of categories. The most common measure used for sets is the Jaccard distance. The distance J between two sets C_i and C_j, is defined as:

$$J(C_i, C_j) = 1 - \frac{|C_i \cap C_j|}{|C_i \cup C_j|}.$$

In our case, C_i and C_j represents the set of categories related to product S_i and S_j respectively. With some modifications to handle products with no categories, the measure gives values between 0 and 1, where 0 means that the two products have identical categories and 1 means that the products share no categories.

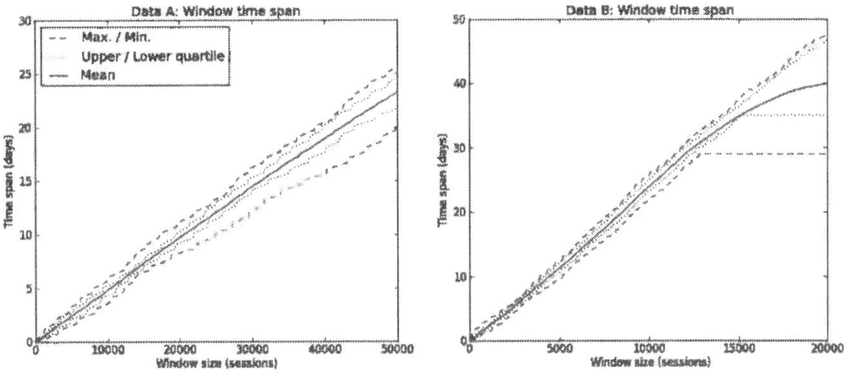

Figure 4: Plots over window time span for Data A (left plot) and Data B (right plot). Dashed lines are minimum/maximum values, dotted lines are upper and lower quartiles and solid lines are averages. Note the different axes.

For a list of products, L, we define the function $D(L)$ as the average distance between all pairs of sets in L using the Jaccard measure J, or

$$D(L) = \frac{\sum_{S_i \in L} \sum_{S_j \in (L \setminus \{S_i\})} J(C_i, C_j)}{|L|(|L| - 1)}.$$

This function can be used to get a value from 0 (all products have the same categories) to 1 (all products have unique categories) as a measure of the diversity of a list.

Table 3: Diversification results. Average, standard deviation and a five-number summary for D-values on lists updated at midnight each day. A session-based window of size 5000 was used.

	Data A		Data B	
	M-list	B-list	M-list	B-list
Average	0.862	0.847	0.870	0.728
Standard deviation	0.033	0.065	0.021	0.038
Minimum	0.800	0.644	0.848	0.667
Lower quartile	0.844	0.822	0.848	0.712
Median	0.856	0.856	0.864	0.742
Upper quartile	0.889	0.900	0.894	0.758
Maximum	0.922	0.956	0.909	0.803

Table 3 shows the diversification results between the presented products in the two lists when only the top level categories associated to each product for both data sets are used. For Data A, this gives 26 categories for 41 951 products. (6.83% of these are uncategorized, i.e., they have Jaccard distance 1 to all other products.) For Data B we have 16 top level categories and here each of the 4 093 products belongs to at most one category. (1.69% are uncategorized in this set.) The table would change only slightly if we made measurements using the full category trees for the data sets.

On average, the M-list achieves a higher diversification value than the B-list for both Data A and Data B. Note, however, that the M-list has lower upper quartile and lower maximum values than the B-list for Data A. Together with the lower standard deviation this indicates that the M-list gives a more consistent diversification although not necessarily higher in all cases. For Data B, the B-list has relatively low diversification and therefore there is more room for improvement. The results for the M-list are diversification values comparable to the M-list results for Data A but with even smaller standard deviation. Also note that the improvement for Data B is so large that the minimum value for the M-list is larger than the maximum value for the B-list.

It is important to note that the improved diversification on the presented products is a side-effect of the maximum coverage algorithm. We make no claims on the diversification on sales, although it is a natural assumption that increased diversification in recommendations will also lead to increased diversification in sales [8].

6. ANALYSIS

Our experiment show that our maximum coverage method is consistently better than the best-seller by 3% for the Data A and 8% for the Data B; see Figure 3.

It can be argued that our experiments are not truly valid since we rely on recorded data to express potential sales on future data. In fact, the A-list presented on the book site may not be the same as the B-list computed, hence, the impact that A-list has on sales does not adequately reflect the impact that either the B-list or the M-list would have had on the sales. However, there is no doubt that the B-list approximates the behavior of the A-list. Hence, if the M-list can beat the B-list already in our experiments then it makes a strong case in favor of the new algorithm. This is due to so called *false negatives*. These are cases when customers would have bought a product if we showed it to them. Since we cannot discern the positive effect of showing such products by looking only at historical data, we fail to give the new algorithm points it would have scored if run on a live experiment.

7. FROM THEORY TO PRACTICE

How can we use the insights given from our research on actual e-commerce sites? If we want to optimize for profit, we need to design the site in accordance with our findings. Below we go through the steps necessary to accomplish this.

Our main conclusion is that e-commerce sites place product recommendations too deep into the site structure (typically on product pages) to be efficiently used while browsing the site. The probability that a customer follows a recommendation link located on a product page, while browsing the site is far too small. Instead, we suggest that recommendation links are added to product list items, for example as a badge on the product picture with the text "More like this". The "More like this" toggle shows a set of product recommendations as the user hovers over a product. This is especially efficient on landing pages such as the start page, since we know that such pages contribute to a large part of the sales. It is as if we have increased the number of products visible on the page and we rely on what we call natural navigation to make sure that all hidden products are readily obtainable through intuitive product associations, PARs.

Natural navigation is navigation through the site following recommendations. Since PARs normally are of the type "Those who bought this also bought..." there is an increased risk of cyclic navigation patterns if they are used together with the B-list, especially if the product list contains products related to each other. Once a customer has entered such a cycle, natural navigation cannot exit from it. To avoid such cycles and to make sure that the number of products spanned by each page is as large as possible, the e-commerce ranking system should include the maximum coverage algorithm.

Our experiments have been restricted to recommendations from the complete product catalogue. As a customer browses a site, he restricts the product selection, but the recommendation problem remains the same. The maximum coverage algorithm can thus be applied to any product list on the site.

8. CONCLUSIONS

We observe that to optimize sales on an e-commerce site, the first step is to optimize the number of converting customers, and then do up-sales on them. This suggests that all marketing lists should be optimized with this in mind. However, today's sites normally sort their product listings on popularity, which as we have shown is not optimal. We demonstrate a new approach based on the maximum coverage algorithm that better optimizes sales, with an improvement of 3–8%. A secondary effect that our algorithm exhibits on the tested data is measurably increased diversification in presented products.

An extension of maximum coverage is to use it to optimize entire pages. This extension would also make optimizations between different lists displayed on a page, making the lists aware of each other. One benefit of this optimization method is to avoid showing duplicate information on multiple lists.

9. REFERENCES

[1] R. Agrawal, S. Gollapudi, A. Halverson, and S. Ieong. Diversifying search results. In *Proceedings of WSDM'09*, pages 5–14, 2009.

[2] N. Alon, B. Awerbuch, and Y. Azar. The online set cover problem. In *Proceedings of STOC'03*, pages 100–105, 2003.

[3] N. Buchbinder and J. Naor. The design of competitive online algorithms via a primal-dual approach. *Foundations and Trends in Theoretical Computer Science*, 3(2–3):93–263, 2009.

[4] H. Chen and D.R. Karger. Less is more: probabilistic models for retrieving fewer relevant documents. In *Proceedings of ACM SIGIR'06*, pages 429–436, 2006.

[5] V. Chvatal. A greedy heuristic for the set-covering problem. *Mathematics of Operations Research*, 4(3):233–235, 1979.

[6] T.H Cormen, C. Stein, R.L. Rivest, and C.E. Leiserson. *Introduction to algorithms.* McGraw-Hill Higher Education, 2nd edition, 2001.

[7] U. Feige. A threshold of $\ln n$ for approximating set cover. *Journal of the ACM*, 45(4):634–652, 1998.

[8] D.M. Fleder, K. Hosanagar and A. Buja. Recommender systems and their effects on consumers: the fragmentation debate. In *Proceedings of EC'10*, pages 229–230, 2010.

[9] M.R. Garey and D.S. Johnson. *Computers and intractability: a guide to the theory of NP-completeness.* W.H. Freeman and Company, 1979.

[10] S. Gollapudi and A. Sharma. An axiomatic approach for result diversification. In *Proceedings of WWW'09*, pages 381–390, 2009.

[11] D.S. Hochbaum. Approximation algorithms for the weighted set covering and node cover problems. *SIAM Journal of Computing*, 11(3):555–556, 1982.

[12] D.S. Hochbaum, editor. *Approximation algorithms for NP-hard problems.* PWS Publishing Company, 1997.

[13] D.S. Johnson. Approximation algorithms for combinatorial problems. *Journal of Computer and System Sciences*, 9:256–278, 1974.

[14] R.M. Karp. Reducibility among combinatorial problems. In R.E. Miller and J.W. Thatcher, editors, *Complexity of Computer Computations*, pages 85–103. Plenum Press, 1972.

[15] J. Langford, A. Strehl, and J. Wortman. Exploration scavenging. In *Proceedings of ICML'08*, pages 528–535, 2008.

[16] A. Lipkus. A proof of the triangle inequality for the Tanimoto distance. *Journal of Mathematical Chemistry*, 26(1):263–265, oct 1999.

[17] T. Malmer. Time-dependent predictions of user purchases on e-commerce sites. Master's thesis, Lund University, 2011.

[18] B. Saha and L. Getoor. On maximum coverage in the streaming model & application to multitopic blog-watch. In *Proceedings of SIAM SDM'09*, pages 697–708, 2009.

[19] S.K. Stein. Two combinatorial covering theorems. *Journal of Combinatorial Theory, Series A*, 16(3):391–397, 1974.

[20] V.V. Vazirani. *Approximation algorithms.* Springer-Verlag, 2001.

[21] M.R. Vieira, H.L. Razente, M.C. Barioni, M. Hadjieleftheriou, D. Srivastava, C. Traina, and V.J. Tsotras. On query result diversification. In *Proceedings of ICDE'11*, pages 1163–1174, 2011.

[22] C. Yu, L. Lakshmanan, and S. Amer-Yahia. It takes variety to make a world: Diversification in recommender systems. In *Proceedings of EDBT'09*, pages 368–378, 2009.

Efficient Top-N Recommendation for Very Large Scale Binary Rated Datasets

Fabio Aiolli
University of Padova, Italy
aiolli@math.unipd.it

ABSTRACT

We present a simple and scalable algorithm for top-N recommendation able to deal with very large datasets and (binary rated) implicit feedback. We focus on memory-based collaborative filtering algorithms similar to the well known neighboor based technique for explicit feedback. The major difference, that makes the algorithm particularly scalable, is that it uses positive feedback only and no explicit computation of the complete (user-by-user or item-by-item) similarity matrix needs to be performed.

The study of the proposed algorithm has been conducted on data from the Million Songs Dataset (MSD) challenge whose task was to suggest a set of songs (out of more than 380k available songs) to more than 100k users given half of the user listening history and complete listening history of other 1 million people.

In particular, we investigate on the entire recommendation pipeline, starting from the definition of suitable similarity and scoring functions and suggestions on how to aggregate multiple ranking strategies to define the overall recommendation. The technique we are proposing extends and improves the one that already won the MSD challenge last year.

Categories and Subject Descriptors

H.4 **[Information Systems Applications]**: Miscellaneous; H.3.3 **[Information Storage and Retrieval]**: Information Search and Retrieval

General Terms

Algorithms

Keywords

Collaborative Filtering, Top-N Recommendation, Implicit Feedback, Million Song Dataset Challenge

1. INTRODUCTION

Recommender systems are common tools to improve customer experience in e-commerce applications. These systems typically use the history of their interaction with the users to improve future recommendations. Different kinds of interactions can be tracked. For example, users can be required to leave an *explicit feedback* (a vote, a rate, or any degree of satisfaction) for the available items. In contrast, the system can autonomously keep track of user behaviors, for instance by keeping the history of user purchases, browsing activity of the users, etc. This second case is usually referred to as *implicit feedback*. Web Retrieval literature is plenty of works dealing with the implicit feedback problem while less effort has been devoted so far to recommendation settings (see [7, 15, 11]).

The Million Song Dataset Challenge [10] was a large scale, music recommendation challenge, where the task is to predict which songs a user will listen to, provided the listening history of a user. The challenge was based on the Million Song Dataset (MSD), a freely-available collection of meta data for one million of contemporary songs (e.g. song titles, artists, year of publication, and much more) [4]. About one hundred and fifty teams participated to the challenge. The subset of data actually used in the challenge was the so called Taste Profile Subset that consists of more than 48 million triplets *(user,song,count)* gathered from user listening histories. Data consists of about 1.2 million users and covers more than 380,000 songs in MSD. The user-item matrix is very sparse as the fraction of non-zero entries (a.k.a. density) is only 0.01%.

The task of the challenge was to recommend the most appropriate songs for a user given half of her listening history and the complete history of another 1 million users. Thus, the challenge focused on the ordering of the songs on the basis of the relevance for a given user (top-N recommendation), and this makes the particular problem different from the more classical problem of predicting rates a user will give to unseen items [6, 13]. For example, popular tasks like Netflix [3] and Movielens fall in this last case. A second important characteristic of the MSD problem is that we do not have explicit or direct feedback about what users like and how much they like it (implicit feedback). In fact, we only have information of the form "user u listened to song i" without any knowledge about whether user u actually liked song i or not. A third important aspect of the MSD data is the presence of meta data concerning songs including title, artist, year of publication, etc. An interesting open question then was whether this additional information could help or not. Finally, given the huge size of the datasets involved, time and memory efficiency of the method used turned out to be another very important issue in the challenge.

The most popular technique adopted in recommender systems is Collaborative Filtering (CF) where the matrix of rates users have previously assigned to the items is used to discover other users with similar behaviors as the active user (i.e. the user for which we want

RecSys'13, October 12–16, 2013, Hong Kong, China.

http://dx.doi.org/10.1145/2507157.2507189

to make the prediction). Current CF approaches can be grouped in the two classes of neighborhood and model-based methods.

The main intuition in neighborhood-based methods is that, if other users, similar to the active user, already purchased a certain item, then it is likely that the active user will like that item as well. Similarly, knowing that a set of items are often purchased together (they are similar in some sense), then, if the active user has bought one of them, probably he/she will be interested to the other too. Both views have been effectively adopted in recent literature for explicit feedback settings.

In this paper, we demonstrate that the choice of the right prediction technique or similarity measure is not all that we need to obtain a good recommender. Here, we propose a flexible pipeline of steps each one with its own (small) set of parameters to tune for the specific domain. Moreover, we show that, although the item-based view has turned out more useful to win the MSD competition, the user-based view also brings useful and diverse information that can be aggregated to boost the performance of the recommendation.

In Section 2, collaborative filtering is described and proposed as a first approach to solve the problem of MSD. In particular, we briefly discuss the most popular state-of-the-art techniques: model based and memory based CF methods. In Section 3, we propose the *asymmetric cosine* similarity, a parameterized similarity function that can be adapted to different applicative domains. Furthermore, the notion of locality is taken in account. In Section 4 a new memory based CF approach is presented which is particularly suitable to tasks with implicit feedback. Finally, in Section 5, empirical results of the proposed techniques are presented and discussed.

2. CF AND THE MILLION SONG DATASET

Collaborative Filtering (CF) techniques use a database in the form of a user-item matrix R of preferences. A typical CF setting consists of a set $\mathcal{U}$ of n users, a set $\mathcal{I}$ of m items, and a user-item matrix $R = \{r_{ui}\} \in \mathbb{R}^{n \times m}$ represents how much user u likes item i. In this paper, we assume binary ratings $r_{ui} \in \{0, 1\}$ as this was the setting of the MSD challenge[1]. In the MSD setting, an entry $r_{ui} = 1$ represents the fact that user u have listened to the song i. In the following, we refer to terms item or song interchangeably. The MSD challenge task can be properly described as a *top-N recommendation* task, that is, for any *active user* u, we want to identify a list of N ($N = 500$ in the challenge) items $I_u \subseteq \mathcal{I}$ she/he will like the most. Clearly, this set must be disjoint with the set of items already rated (purchased, or listened to) by the active user.

2.1 Model-based Collaborative Filtering

Model-based CF techniques construct a model of the information contained in the matrix R. There are many proposed techniques of this type, including Bayesian models, Clustering models, Latent Factor models, and Classification/Regression models, just to name a few.

In more recent literature about CF, Matrix Factorization (MF) techniques [9] have become a very popular and effective choice to implement the CF idea. In this kind of models one tries to learn an embedding of both users and items into a smaller dimensional space.

[1]Note that in this definition we are neglecting the information given by the *count* attribute of the triplets indicating how many times the song has been listened to by a user. However, the organizers of the challenge have warned us on the fact that this attribute is likely to be unreliable and absolutely not correlated with likings.

More formally, one needs to find two matrices $X \in \mathbb{R}^{k \times n}$ and $Y \in \mathbb{R}^{k \times m}$ such that $R \approx X^\top Y$, in such a way to minimize a loss over training data. A common choice for this loss is the root mean square error (RMSE).

Despite MF is recognized to be a state-of-the-art technique in CF, we note that it has some drawbacks that made it impractical and unsuccessful for the MSD task. First of all, training the corresponding model is computationally honerous and this fact is crucial when the size of the matrix R is very large as in the MSD case. Second, since MF is tipically modelled as a regression problem, then it seems unsuitable for implicit feedback tasks and some modifications to the original technique are needed [7]. In the MSD, for example, we have binary values of relevance and the value 0 cannot properly be considered as unrelevant since the no-action on an item can be due to many other reasons beyond not liking it (the user can be unaware of the existence of the song, for example). Third, MF techniques typically solve the associated minimization problem by using gradient descent algorithms which do not guarantee the convergence to a global minimum and, it is well known, the rate of convergence is quite low when near to local minima. Finally, matrix factorization based baselines provided by the organizers at the beginning of the challenge, and final results by other team entries, have confirmed quite poor results of MF based algorithms for this particular task, thus supporting our previous claims.

2.2 Memory-based Collaborative Filtering

In Memory-based Collaborative Filtering (MBCF) the entire user-item matrix is used to generate a prediction. In this case, there is not a real training of the model. Instead, a priori knowledge about typical behaviours of a user is exploited to some extent. Given a new user for which we want to obtain the prediction, the set of items to suggest are computed looking at "similar" users. This strategy is typically referred to as *user-based recommendation*. Alternatively, in the *item-based recommendation* strategy, one computes the most similar items for the items that have been already rated by the active user, and then prefer those items to form the final recommendation. There are many different proposal on how to combine the information provided by similar users/items (see [13] for a good survey). However, most of them are tailored to classical recommendation systems and they are not promptly compliant with the implicit feedback setting. More importantly, computing the neirest neighbors requires the computation of similarities for every pair of users or songs. This is simply infeasible in our domain given the huge size of the datasets involved.

In principle, the MBCF strategy can be used to do prediction for the implicit feedback setting as well and this can be done in the following very general ways.

In the *user-based* type of recommendation, the scoring function, on the basis of which the recommendation is made, is computed by

$$\hat{r}^U_{ui} = \sum_{v \in \mathcal{U}} w_{uv} r_{vi} = \sum_{v \in \mathcal{U}(i)} w_{uv}, \qquad (1)$$

that is, the score obtained on an item for a target user is proportional to the similarities between the target user u and other users v that have rated before the item i ($v \in \mathcal{U}(i)$). This score will be higher for items which are often rated by similar users.

On the other hand, within a *item-based* type of recommendation [5, 12], the target item i is associated with a score

$$\hat{r}^I_{ui} = \sum_{j \in \mathcal{I}} w_{ij} r_{uj} = \sum_{j \in \mathcal{I}(u)} w_{ij}, \quad (2)$$

and hence, the score is proportional to the similarities between item i and other items already purchased by the user u ($j \in \mathcal{I}(u)$).

2.3 MF and MBCF unified

We end the section by noticing that, in both user-based and item-based MBCF, the user and item contributions are decomposed, that is, we can write

$$\hat{r}^U_{ui} = \mathbf{x}_u^\top \mathbf{y}_i, \text{ with } \mathbf{x}_u, \mathbf{y}_i \in \mathbb{R}^n,$$

and

$$\hat{r}^I_{ui} = \mathbf{x}_u^\top \mathbf{y}_i, \text{ with } \mathbf{x}_u, \mathbf{y}_i \in \mathbb{R}^m.$$

In other words, similarly to the MF case, we are implicitly defining an embedding for users and items. This embedding is performed onto an n-dimensional space in user based recommendation systems ($k = n$) or performed onto an m-dimensional space in item based recommendation systems ($k = m$).

3. SIMILARITIES FOR CF

The cosine similarity is undoubtely the most popular measure of correlation between two vectors. An important characteristic of this similarity measure is that it is symmetric and this feature can be important for certain applications. However, in our opinion, there are cases where the simmetry of the similarity measure does not match exactly the features of a domain. As we will see in the following, asymmetries are very common in CF applications. Now, we generalize the cosine similarity and suggest a nice probabilistic interpretation for binary valued vectors.

3.1 Asymmetric Cosine (asymC) Similarity

Consider three sets $\mathcal{A}, \mathcal{B}, \mathcal{C}$ such that $|\mathcal{C}| = q$ and assume two relations exist, namely $\mathcal{R}_\mathcal{A} \subset \mathcal{A} \times \mathcal{C}$, and $\mathcal{R}_\mathcal{B} \subset \mathcal{B} \times \mathcal{C}$. Now, let $a \in \mathcal{A}$ and $b \in \mathcal{B}$, we can define binary q-dimensional vector representations ($\mathbf{a} \in \{0,1\}^q, \mathbf{b} \in \{0,1\}^q$), for a and b respectively, on the basis of the corresponding relation. Specifically, each position in $\mathbf{a}$ and $\mathbf{b}$ corresponds to a specific element $c \in \mathcal{C}$ and it is set to 1 whenever $(a, c) \in \mathcal{R}_\mathcal{A}$, and $(b, c) \in \mathcal{R}_\mathcal{B}$, respectively.

Now, we can formally define the conditional probabilities $P(a|b)$, that is, the probability that given $c \in \mathcal{C}$ such that $(b, c) \in \mathcal{R}_\mathcal{B}$, then $(a, c) \in \mathcal{R}_\mathcal{A}$ also holds. Similarly, we can define $P(b|a)$. These probabilities can be computed with simple vector operations:

$$P(a|b) = \frac{\mathbf{a}^\top \mathbf{b}}{\mathbf{b}^\top \mathbf{b}} \text{ and } P(b|a) = \frac{\mathbf{a}^\top \mathbf{b}}{\mathbf{a}^\top \mathbf{a}}$$

where $\mathbf{a}^\top \mathbf{b}$ computes the number of times $(a, c) \in \mathcal{R}_\mathcal{A}$ and $(b, c) \in \mathcal{R}_\mathcal{B}$ co-occur. Similarly, $\mathbf{a}^\top \mathbf{a} = ||\mathbf{a}||^2$ and $\mathbf{b}^\top \mathbf{b} = ||\mathbf{b}||^2$ computes the number of times $(a, c) \in \mathcal{R}_\mathcal{A}$ occurs, and the number of times $(b, c) \in \mathcal{R}_\mathcal{B}$ occurs, respectively.

Nicely, with the definition above, the cosine similarity function can be seen as a product of the square roots of the two conditional probabilities:

$$S_{1/2}(a, b) := \cos(\mathbf{a}, \mathbf{b}) = \frac{\mathbf{a}^\top \mathbf{b}}{||\mathbf{a}|| \cdot ||\mathbf{b}||} = P(a|b)^{\frac{1}{2}} P(b|a)^{\frac{1}{2}} \quad (3)$$

The idea behind the asymmetric cosine similarity is to give asymmetric weights to the conditional probabilities in the formula above:

$$S_\alpha(a, b) = P(a|b)^\alpha P(b|a)^{1-\alpha} = \frac{\mathbf{a}^\top \mathbf{b}}{||\mathbf{a}||^{2\alpha} ||\mathbf{b}||^{2(1-\alpha)}}$$

where $0 \leq \alpha \leq 1$.

Using the notation of sets, and setting $\mathcal{R}(x) = \{c \in \mathcal{C} | (x, c) \in \mathcal{R}\}$, then we can simply write:

$$S_\alpha(a, b) = \frac{|\mathcal{R}_\mathcal{A}(a) \cap \mathcal{R}_\mathcal{B}(b)|}{|\mathcal{R}_\mathcal{A}(a)|^\alpha |\mathcal{R}_\mathcal{B}(b)|^{1-\alpha}}$$

Finally, note that eq. (3) still holds for real valued (non binary) vector representations. Clearly, in this case, the strict probabilistic interpretation cannot be applied but we can still consider $P(a|b)$ as a function indicating how much information we can get from knowing $(b, c) \in \mathcal{R}_\mathcal{B}$ in order to predict whether $(a, c) \in \mathcal{R}_\mathcal{A}$.

3.2 User-based and Song-based similarity

Cosine and Pearson's are standard measures of correlation in CF applications. To the best of our knowledge not much has been done until now to adapt these similarities to given problems. Our opinion is that it cannot exist a single similarity measure that can fit all possible domains where collaborative filtering is used. To bridge this gap and try to fit different problems, we consider a parametric family of similarities obtained by instanciating the asymmetric cosine both for the user-based and item-based setting.

MSD data have not relevance grades since the ratings are binary values. This is a first simplification that, as we have seen, we can exploit in the definition of the similarity functions. In the case of binary rates the cosine similarity can be computed as in the following. Let $\mathcal{I}(u)$ be the set of items rated by a generic user u, then the cosine similarity between two users u, v is defined by

$$w_{uv} = S_{1/2}(u, v) = \frac{|\mathcal{I}(u) \cap \mathcal{I}(v)|}{|\mathcal{I}(u)|^{\frac{1}{2}} |\mathcal{I}(v)|^{\frac{1}{2}}}$$

and, similarly for items, by setting $\mathcal{U}(i)$ the set of users which have rated item i, we obtain:

$$w_{ij} = S_{1/2}(i, j) = \frac{|\mathcal{U}(i) \cap \mathcal{U}(j)|}{|\mathcal{U}(i)|^{\frac{1}{2}} |\mathcal{U}(j)|^{\frac{1}{2}}}.$$

Note that, especially for the item case, we are more interested in computing how likely it is that an item will be appreciated by a user when we *already* know that the same user likes another item. It is clear that this definition is not symmetric. For example, say we know that a user already listened to the U2's song "Party Girl" which we know is not so popular. Then, probably that user is a fan of U2 and we can easily predict that she/he would also like something far more popular by U2, like "Sunday Bloody Sunday" for instance. Clearly, the opposite is not true.

As an extreme alternative to the cosine similarity, we can resort to the conditional probability measure which can be estimated with the following formulas:

$$w_{uv} = S_1(u, v) = P(u|v) = \frac{|\mathcal{I}(u) \cap \mathcal{I}(v)|}{|\mathcal{I}(v)|}$$

and

$$w_{ij} = S_1(i, j) = P(i|j) = \frac{|\mathcal{U}(i) \cap \mathcal{U}(j)|}{|\mathcal{U}(j)|}$$

Previous works (see [8] for example) pointed out that the conditional probability measure of similarity, $P(i|j)$, has the limitation that items which are purchased frequently tend to have higher values not because of their co-occurrence frequency but instead because of their popularity. As we have seen, this might not always be a limitation in a recommendation setting like ours. Experimental results in this paper will confirm that, emphasizing asymmetrically one of the conditionals, will help in general.

In the following of the paper we will use the parametric generalization of the above similarity measures called asymmetric cosine similarity. The parametrization on α permits ad-hoc optimizations of the similarity function for the domain of interest. In our case, this is done by validating on available data.

Summarizing, we have:

$$w_{uv} = S_\alpha(u,v) = \frac{|\mathcal{I}(u) \cap \mathcal{I}(v)|}{|\mathcal{I}(u)|^\alpha |\mathcal{I}(v)|^{1-\alpha}} \quad (4)$$

$$w_{ij} = S_\alpha(i,j) = \frac{|\mathcal{U}(i) \cap \mathcal{U}(j)|}{|\mathcal{U}(i)|^\alpha |\mathcal{U}(j)|^{1-\alpha}} \quad (5)$$

where $\alpha \in [0,1]$ is a parameter to tune.

Note that, this similarity function generalizes the one given in [5] where a similar parameterization is also proposed for the item-based case with strictly empirical motivations. Here, we give a formal justification of the rescaling factor they used by defining the similarity as an asymmetric product of conditional probabilities.

3.3 Locality of the Scoring Function

In Section 2.2 we have seen how the final recommendation is computed by a scoring function that combines the scores obtained using individual users or items. So, it is important to determine how much each individual scoring component influences the overall scoring. MBCF algorithms typically approach this problem by restricting the computation to neirest neighbors. Alternatively, we propose to use a monothonic not decreasing function $f(w)$ on the weights to emphasize/deemphasize similarity contributions in such a way to adjust the *locality* of the scoring function, that is how many, and how much of, nearest users/items really matter in the computation. As we will see, a correct setting of this function turned out to be very useful with the challenge data.

In particular, we use the exponential family of functions, that is $f(w) = w^q$ where $q \in \mathbb{N}$. The effect of this exponentiation in both the eq. (1) and eq. (2) is the following: when q is high, smaller weights drop to zero while higher ones are (relatively) emphasized; at the other extreme, when $q = 0$, the aggregation is performed by simply adding up the ratings. We can note that, in the user-based type of scoring function, this corresponds to take the popularity of an item as its score, while, in the case of item-based type of scoring function, this would turn out in a constant for all items (the number of ratings made by the active user).

4. RECOMMENDATION

In this section, we describe a novel recommendation technique based on the asymmetric cosine combination between user and item embeddings. Furthermore, we describe additional techniques, like calibration and aggregation, to improve the final recommendation.

4.1 Asymmetric Cosine based CF

In Section 2.3 it is shown how the scoring function of a memory-based model can be formulated as $\hat{r}_{ui} = \mathbf{x}_u^\top \mathbf{y}_i$, where $\mathbf{x}_u$ and $\mathbf{y}_i$ are appropriate representations of users and items, respectively. To increase the flexibility of the prediction further we can resort again to the asymmetric cosine similarity defined in Section 3.1 and replace the scoring function with the following:

$$\hat{r}_{ui} = S_\beta(u,i) = \frac{\mathbf{x}_u^\top \mathbf{y}_i}{||\mathbf{x}_u||^{2\beta} ||\mathbf{y}_i||^{2(1-\beta)}} \quad (6)$$

One can easily note that, when $\beta = 1$, the order induced by this scoring function over different songs is the same as the one induced by the standard scoring function because the two scoring functions are basically the same up to a (positive) constant. Since we are focusing on top-N recommendation and we are only interested to the ranking among songs, then we can consider that above as a generalization of the standard memory-based CF scoring function.

Now, we can analyze a little more in depth this new scoring function for the user-based and item-based prediction cases.

User-based prediction. In this case, the embedding is performed in $\mathbb{R}^n$, the space of users, according to:

$$\mathbf{x}_u^{(v)} = w_{uv} \quad \text{and} \quad ||\mathbf{x}_u||^2 = ||\mathbf{w}_u||^2$$

$$\mathbf{y}_i^{(v)} = r_{vi} \quad \text{and} \quad ||\mathbf{y}_i||^2 = |\mathcal{U}(i)|$$

and the user-based scoring function consists of:

$$\hat{r}_{ui} = \frac{\sum_{v \in \mathcal{U}(i)} w_{uv}}{||\mathbf{w}_u||^{2\beta} |\mathcal{U}(i)|^{(1-\beta)}} \propto \frac{\sum_{v \in \mathcal{U}(i)} w_{uv}}{|\mathcal{U}(i)|^{(1-\beta)}}$$

Item-based prediction. In this case, the embedding is performed in $\mathbb{R}^m$, the space of items, according to:

$$\mathbf{x}_u^{(j)} = r_{uj} \quad \text{and} \quad ||\mathbf{x}_u||^2 = |\mathcal{I}(u)|$$

$$\mathbf{y}_i^{(j)} = w_{ij} \quad \text{and} \quad ||\mathbf{y}_i||^2 = ||\mathbf{w}_i||^2$$

and the item-based scoring function consists of:

$$\hat{r}_{ui} = \frac{\sum_{j \in \mathcal{I}(u)} w_{ij}}{|\mathcal{I}(u)|^{\beta} ||\mathbf{w}_i||^{2(1-\beta)}} \propto \frac{\sum_{j \in \mathcal{I}(u)} w_{ij}}{||\mathbf{w}_i||^{2(1-\beta)}}$$

Note that, in the item case, the normalization is defined in terms of the weight norms whose computation requires the computation of the weights w_{ij} for every $j \in \mathcal{I}$ and this is quite inefficient. Then, a further step of preprocessing where this norm is estimated for each item i is needed in this case. In our implementation, this step is implemented by drawing items j from a subsample of items.

4.2 Calibration

The focus of the present work is on very large datasets. For this, until now, we have proposed memory and time efficient algorithms that avoid any time and space consuming model training. However, simple statistics from a dataset can still be estimated efficiently and can potentially result useful for recommending.

In this section, we present a simple technique to learn a basic model for songs. The model is trained using positive feedback only hence resulting quite efficient given the sparsity of data. Basically, the idea is to calibrate the obtained scores for each item by comparing them to the average score on positive user-item pairs.

For each song the mean, and maximum, value of the scoring function obtained for positive pairs is estimated from data. More formally, let $\mathcal{R}$ the relation for which we want to compute the statistics. Then, we define the positive feedback mean and positive feedback maximum as in the following:

$$m_i \approx \mathbb{E}_{(u,i)\in\mathcal{R}}[\hat{r}_{ui}] \quad \text{and} \quad M_i \approx \max_{(u,i)\in\mathcal{R}}[\hat{r}_{ui}]$$

For the MSD data, for example, these statistics are estimated by taking $\hat{r}_{ui}$ values for a sample of training users such that $i \in \mathcal{I}(u)$. So, we need to estimate the average value of the scoring obtained by the same song for user that listened to it.

Now, let be given $0 < \theta < 1$, then the calibrated scoring function is defined as a simple piece-wise linear function:

$$\hat{r}'_{ui} = C(\hat{r}_{ui}) = \begin{cases} \frac{\hat{r}_{ui}}{m_i}\theta & \text{if } \hat{r}_{ui} \leq m_i \\ \theta + \frac{\hat{r}_{ui}-m_i}{M_i-m_i}(1-\theta) & \text{if } m_i < \hat{r}_{ui} \leq M_i \\ 1 & \text{otherwise} \end{cases}$$

In our experiments we used $\theta = 0.5$.

4.3 Aggregation

There are many sources of information available regarding songs. For example, it could be useful to consider the additional metadata which are also available and to construct alternative rankings based on that. In the following, we propose three simple strategies. We assume we have a distribution of probability p_k, such that $\sum_k p_k = 1$ that determines the weight to give to the predictor k to form the aggregated prediction. In our approach the best p_k values are simply determined by validation on training data.

4.3.1 Stochastic Aggregation

Different recommendation strategies are usually individually *precision oriented*, meaning that each strategy is able to correctly recommend a few of the correct songs with high confidence but, other songs which the user likes, cannot be suggested by that particular ranker. Hopefully, if the rankers are diverse, then the rankers can recommend different songs. If this is the case, a possible solution is to predict a final recommendation that contains all the songs for which the single strategies are more confident. The stochastic aggregation strategy used in the challenge can be described in the following way. We assume we are provided with the list of songs, not yet rated by the active user, given in order of confidence, for all the basic strategies. On each step, the recommender randomly choose one of the lists according to a probability distribution p_k over the predictors and recommends the best scored item of the list which has not yet been inserted in the current recommendation.

4.3.2 Linear Aggregation

Another very simple aggregation rule is here presented were the scores given by different predictors are simply averaged. Clearly, in this case, the scores should be comparable. When they are not, we can assume the scores $\hat{r}^{(k)}_{ui}$ are proportional to the probability of observing item i given the user u as estimated by the k-th predictor. In this case, item scores of each predictor can be normalized in such a way that $||\hat{r}^{(k)}_u||_1 = \sum_i \hat{r}^{(k)}_{ui} = 1$.

Data Statistics	min	max	ave	median
users per song	0	110479	125.794	13
songs per user	10	4400	47.45681	27

4.3.3 Borda Aggregation

The last aggregation method we propose is a slight variant of the well known Borda Count method. In this case, each item i gets a score $\sum_k p_k * (|\mathcal{I}| - q_k(i) + 1)$ where $q_k(i) \in [1, |\mathcal{I}|]$ is the position of item i in the list produced by ranker k.

4.4 Optimizations

The computational complexity of the technique proposed mainly depends on the number of weight computations. In the item-based strategy, for each test user, the number of weights to compute is proportional to $\bar{I}|\mathcal{I}|$ where $\bar{I} = \mathbb{E}_u[|\mathcal{I}(u)|]$ where the expectation is taken over visible songs of test users.

In the user-based strategy, for each test user, the number of weights to compute is proportional to $\bar{U}|\mathcal{I}|$ where $\bar{U} = \mathbb{E}_i[|\mathcal{U}(i)|]$ where the expectation is taken over available songs. However, in this second case, we can compute all the $|\mathcal{U}|$ weights for a user u and, the contribution of each weight w_{uv} accumulated on the item scores when the item is in $\mathcal{I}(v)$. This strategy empirically reduced the time required by a factor of 12 on MSD data.

5. EXPERIMENTS AND RESULTS

In the MSD challenge we have: *i)* the full listening history for about 1M users, *ii)* half of the listening history for 110K users (10K validation set, 100K test set), and we have to predict the missing half. We use a "home-made" random validation subset (*HV*) of the original training data of about 900K users of training (*HVtr*, with full listening history). The remaining 100K user's histories has been split in two halves (*HVvi* the visible one, *HVhi* the hidden one).

The experiments presented in this section are based on this *HV* data and compare different similarities and different approaches. The baseline is represented by the simple popularity based method which recommends the most popular songs not yet listened to by the user. Besides the baseline, we report experiments on both the user-based and song-based scoring functions, and an example of the application of ranking aggregation. Given the size of the datasets involved we do not stress on the significance of the presented results. This is confirmed by the fact that the presented results do not differ significantly from the results obtained over the indipendent set of users used as the test set in the challenge.

In the following results, when not explicitely indicated, we assume $\beta = 1$ in eq. (6) thus obtaining the standard scoring function for memory-based CF.

5.1 Taste Profile Subset Stats

For completeness we report some statistics about the original challenge training data. In particular, the following table shows the minimum, maximum, and average, number of users per song and songs per user. The median value is also reported.

We can see that the large majority of songs have only few users which have listened to it (less than 13 users for half of the songs) and the large majority of users have listened to few songs (less than 27 for half of the users). These characteristics of the dataset make the top-N recommendation task quite challenging.

5.2 Truncated Mean Average Precision

Conformingly to the challenge, we used the truncated mAP (mean average precision) as the evaluation metric [10]. Let y denote a ranking over items, where $y(p) = i$ means that item i is ranked at position p. The mAP metric emphasizes the top recommendations. For any $k \leq N$, the *precision at k* (π_k) is defined as the proportion of correct recommendations within the top-k of the predicted ranking (assuming the ranking y does not contain the visible songs),

$$\pi_k(u, y) = \frac{1}{k} \sum_{p=1}^{k} r_{uy(p)}$$

For each user the (truncated) average precision is the average precision at each recall point:

$$AP(u, y) = \frac{1}{N_u} \sum_{p=1}^{N} \pi_k(u, y) r_{uy(p)}$$

where N_u is the smaller between N and the number of user u's positively associated songs. Finally, the average of $AP(u, y_u)$'s over all users gives the mean average precision (mAP).

5.3 Results on MSD data

The result obtained on the HV data with the baseline (recommendation by popularity) is presented in Table 1(a). With this strategy, each song i simply gets a score proportional to the number of users $|\mathcal{U}(i)|$ which have listened to it.

Effect of locality (q). In Table 1, we report on experiments that show the effect of the locality parameter q for different strategies: item based and user based, using conditional probability ($\alpha = 0$) and the cosine version ($\alpha = 0.5$). As we can see, beside the case IS with cosine similarity (Table 1c), a correct setting of the parameter q drammatically improves the effectiveness on HV data. We can clearly see that the best performance is reached with the conditional probability on an item based strategy (Table 1b).

Effect of using Asymmetric Cosine (α). In Figure 1, results obtained fixing the parameter q and varying the parameter α for both user and item-based recommendation strategies are given. In the item-based case, the results improve when setting a non-trivial α. In fact, the best result has been obtained for $\alpha = 0.15$.

Effect of Asymmetric Prediction (β). In Table 2 we report the results of user-based AsymC memory-based collaborative filtering algorithm of Section 4.1 with $\alpha = 0.5$. Interestingly, as we can see from the table, the best parameter β always improves (sometimes dramatically) the baseline ($\beta = 1$, results in Table 1(e)).

Effect of Calibration. To test the effect of calibration in item-based recommandation we started with the best parameter setting for uncalibrated recommendation ($\alpha = 0.15, q = 3, mAP@500 = 0.177322$) and calibrated using the technique depicted in Section 4.2. The calibration in fact improve the result, obtaining an interesting $mAP@500 = \mathbf{0.181084}$ (the best result obtained for this dataset so far).

Concerning the effect of calibration on user-based recommendation we started again with the best setting for uncalibrated user-based recommendation ($\alpha = 0.5, q = 4, \beta = 0.7, mAP@500 =$

Baseline	mAP@500
Recommendation by Popularity	0.02262

(a)

IS ($\alpha = 0$)	mAP@500
q=1	0.12224
q=2	0.16581
q=3	**0.17144**
q=4	0.17004
q=5	0.16830

(b)

IS ($\alpha = \frac{1}{2}$)	mAP@500
q=1	**0.16439**
q=2	0.16214
q=3	0.15587
q=4	0.15021
q=5	0.14621

(c)

US ($\alpha = 0$)	mAP@500
q=1	0.08030
q=2	0.10747
q=3	0.12479
q=4	0.13298
q=5	**0.13400**
q=6	0.13187
q=7	0.12878

(d)

US ($\alpha = \frac{1}{2}$)	mAP@500
q=1	0.07679
q=2	0.10436
q=3	0.12532
q=4	0.13779
q=5	0.14355
q=6	**0.14487**
q=7	0.14352

(e)

Table 1: Results obtained by the baseline, item-based (IS) and user-based (US) CF methods varying the locality parameter (exponent q) of the similarity function.

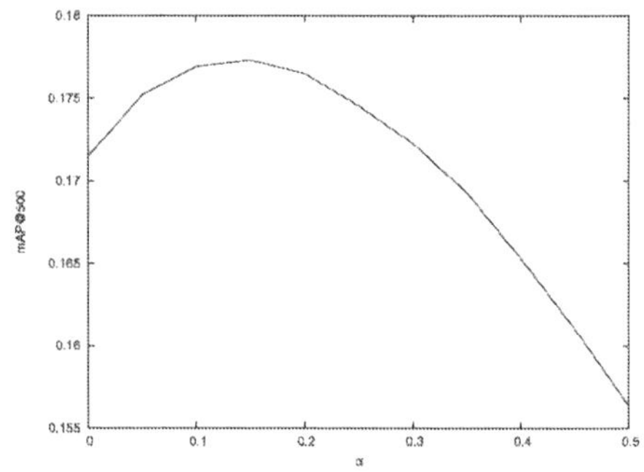

(a) IS with $0 \leq \alpha \leq 0.5$, $q = 3$, best-mAP@500: $0.177322 (\alpha = 0.15)$

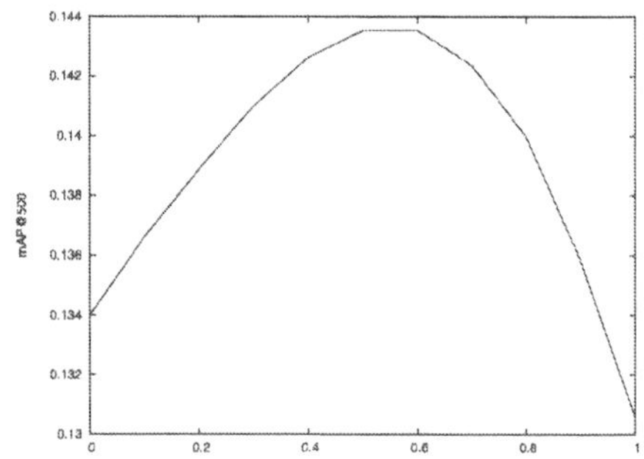

(b) US with $0 \leq \alpha \leq 1$, $q = 5$, best-mAP@500: $0.143551 (\alpha = 0.6)$

Figure 1: Results obtained by item-based (IS) and user-based (US) CF methods varying the α parameter.

US ($\alpha = \frac{1}{2}$)	Best β	mAP@500
q=1	0.3	0.14890
q=2	0.5	0.15801
q=3	0.6	0.16132
q=4	0.7	**0.16229**
q=5	0.8	0.16152
q=6	0.9	0.15975
q=7	0.9	0.15658

(a)

Table 2: User-based AsymC MBCF ($\alpha = 0.5$). Results obtained varying the parameter q and selecting the best parameter β.

(IS, $\alpha = 0.15, q = 3$)	(US, $\alpha = 0.3, q = 5$)	mAP@500
0.0	1.0	0.14098
0.1	0.9	0.14813
0.2	0.8	0.15559
0.3	0.7	0.16248
0.4	0.6	0.16859
0.5	0.5	0.17362
0.6	0.4	0.17684
0.7	0.3	0.17870
0.8	0.2	**0.17896**
0.9	0.1	0.17813
1.0	0.0	0.17732

(a)

Table 3: Results obtained aggregating the rankings of two different strategies, item-based (IS, $\alpha = 0.15$, $q = 3$) and user-based (US, $\alpha = 0.3$, $q = 5$), by Stochastic Aggregation as discussed in Section 5.3, with different combinations. The $(0.8, 0.2)$ combination corresponds exactly to the winning configuration used in the MSD challenge (see Figure 2).

IS($\alpha = 0.15, q = 3$)	US($\alpha = 0.5, q = 4, \beta = 0.7$)	mAP@500
0.5	0.5	0.18014
0.6	0.4	0.18042
0.7	0.3	0.18074
0.8	0.2	**0.18092**
0.9	0.1	0.17853
1.0	0.0	0.17732

(a)

Table 4: Results obtained aggregating the rankings of two different strategies, item-based (IS, $\alpha = 0.15$, $q = 3$) and user-based (US, $\alpha = 0.3$, $q = 5$) AsymC MBCF ($\beta = 0.7$), with different combinations.

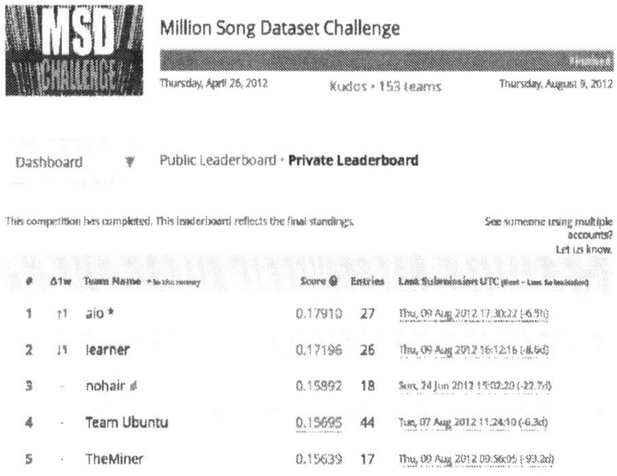

Figure 2: Screenshot of the final MSD challenge leaderboard.

0.16229) and calibrated using the technique described in Section 4.2 obtaining a $mAP@500 = 0.16487$.

Stochastic Aggregation. Concerning the stochastic aggregation we report results obtained using the exact configuration that allowed us to win the MSD challenge (see Figure 2). In particular, in Table 3, two rankers are combined, and their recommendation aggregated, by using the stochastic algorithm described in Section 4.3.1. In order to maximize the diversity of the two rankers, we aggregated an item-based ranker and a user-based ranker. We can see that the combination improves the performance with respect to the individual rankers on validation data.

Linear Aggregation. In Table 4 we report on results obtained by linearly combining the best performing uncalibrated item-based ranker ($\alpha = 0.15$, $q = 3$, $\beta = 1$) with the best performing uncalibrated user-based ranker ($\alpha = 0.5$, $q = 4$, $\beta = 0.7$) varying the combination parameters. The aggregation is performed according to the algorithm given in Section 4.3.2.

5.4 Comparison with other approaches

We end this section by comparing our with other approaches that have been used in the challenge. Best ranked teams all used variants of memory based CF, besides the 5-th ranked team that used the Absorption algorithm by YouTube [2] which is a graph based method that performs a random walk on the rating graph to propagate preferences information over the graph. The team placed second used an approach similar to ours to get 17 user-item joint features to use in a learning-to-rank method (RankNet) [14]. On the other side, matrix factorization based techniques showed a very poor performance on this task and people working on that faced serious memory and time efficiency problems. Finally, some teams tried to inject meta data information in the prediction process with scarse results. In our opinion, this can be due to the fact that there is a lot of implicit information contained in the user's history and this is much more than explicit information one can get from metadata. We conclude that meta data information can be more effectively used in a *cold start* setting.

5.5 Results on MovieLens Data

To demonstrate the generality of the approach, we present results on a different dataset, MovieLens1M[2]. This dataset originally consists of more than 1 million of ratings for $3,883$ movies and $6,040$ users. The dataset has been made suitable to implicit feedback by considering the $226,310$ 5-stars ratings as positive feedback and ignoring all the other available ratings, thus obtaining a density of 0.01. Similarly to the MSD dataset, data have been split in a 90% training users and 10% test users. Test user histories has been split again in two halves (visible and hidden). Finally, the task consists on predicting 5-stars movies in the hidden half using 5-stars movies in the visible half and complete history of training users.

[2]http://www.grouplens.org/node/73

Baseline	Best Parameters	mAP@500
User-based kNN	$k = 100$	0.18318

(a)

No	Ranker	Best Parameters	mAP@500
1	IS	$\alpha = 0.6, q = 1$	0.18146
2	IS ($\beta = 0.8$)	$\alpha = 0.55, q = 1$	0.18297
3	US	$\alpha = 0.6, q = 6$	0.18549
4	US ($\beta = 0.8$)	$\alpha = 0.55, q = 5$	**0.18984**

(b)

Aggregated	Best (p_i, p_u)	mAP@500
1 + 3 (Borda)	(0.4,0.6)	0.19008
2 + 4 (Borda)	(0.2,0.8)	**0.19554**
1 + 3 (Stochastic)	(0.5,0.5)	0.19015
2 + 4 (Stochastic)	(0.1,0.9)	0.19052

(c)

Table 5: MovieLens1M results. (a) Best results obtained with the kNN baseline, (b) best results obtained with single rankers (not aggregated), (c) best results obtained with aggregated rankers

Results are presented in Table 5. Specifically, in Table 5(a) the best result obtained with the user-based kNN baseline is reported. In this case, the score of an user-item pair (u, i) is

$$\hat{r}_{ui} = \frac{\sum_{v \in \mathcal{N}_u} w_{uv} r_{vi}}{\sum_{v \in \mathcal{N}_u} w_{uv}}$$

where $\mathcal{N}_u$ is the set of k nearest neighbors of user u according to the similarity w_{uv}. Note that, in this case, differently from the proposed approach, the similarity has to be computed for the entire set of users. This clearly requires far more computational efforts and would be unfeasible for the MSD task. In Table 5(b) the results obtained using symmetric and asymmetric, item and user-based scoring functions are reported. From the table it is clear that user-based rankers are better than item-based ones and asymmetric scoring is beneficial in both the cases. Finally, in Table 5(c) results obtained by aggregation are presented confirming that aggregating item-based and user-based rankers always improves significantly the recommendation performance.

6. CONCLUSION

In this paper we have presented an efficient memory-based CF technique suitable for very large recommendation problems with implicit feedback. The proposed technique extends the one we used to win the MSD challenge [3] (see also [1]). The main contributions of the paper are: a novel scoring function for memory based CF that results particularly effective (and efficient) on implicit rating settings and a new asymmetric similarity measure that can be adapted to the problem at hand that seems to work very well for CF problems. In the near future we want to investigate on the possibility of using metadata information to boost the performance and in a more solid way to aggregate multiple predictions. Finally, it would be interesting to generalize the method to other types of recommendation, including explicit feedback and non binary ratings.

[3]The MSD challenge has been organized by the Computer Audition Lab at UC San Diego and LabROSA at Columbia University, and hosted at www.kaggle.com

7. ACKNOWLEDGMENTS

This work was supported by the Italian Ministry of Education, University, and Research (MIUR) under Project PRIN 2009LNP494_005. Many thanks to Marta Aduasio for helping us with the experiments.

8. REFERENCES

[1] F. Aiolli. A preliminary study on a recommender system for the million songs dataset challenge. In *IIR*, pages 73–83, 2013.

[2] S. Baluja, R. Seth, D. Sivakumar, Y. Jing, J. Yagnik, S. Kumar, D. Ravichandran, and M. Aly. Video suggestion and discovery for youtube: taking random walks through the view graph. In *Proceedings of the 17th international conference on World Wide Web*, WWW '08, pages 895–904, New York, NY, USA, 2008. ACM.

[3] J. Bennett, S. Lanning, and N. Netflix. The netflix prize. In *In KDD Cup and Workshop in conjunction with KDD*, 2007.

[4] T. Bertin-Mahieux, D. P. Ellis, B. Whitman, and P. Lamere. The million song dataset. In *Proceedings of the 12th International Conference on Music Information Retrieval (ISMIR 2011)*, 2011.

[5] M. Deshpande and G. Karypis. Item-based top-*n* recommendation algorithms. *ACM Trans. Inf. Syst.*, 22(1):143–177, 2004.

[6] C. Desrosiers and G. Karypis. A comprehensive survey of neighborhood-based recommendation methods. In *Recommender Systems Handbook*, pages 107–144. 2011.

[7] Y. Hu, Y. Koren, and C. Volinsky. Collaborative filtering for implicit feedback datasets. In *ICDM*, pages 263–272, 2008.

[8] G. Karypis. Evaluation of item-based top-n recommendation algorithms. In *CIKM*, pages 247–254, 2001.

[9] Y. Koren and R. M. Bell. Advances in collaborative filtering. In *Recommender Systems Handbook*, pages 145–186. 2011.

[10] B. McFee, T. Bertin-Mahieux, D. P. Ellis, and G. R. Lanckriet. The million song dataset challenge. In *Proceedings of the 21st international conference companion on World Wide Web*, WWW '12 Companion, pages 909–916, New York, NY, USA, 2012. ACM.

[11] V. C. Ostuni, T. Di Noia, E. Di Sciascio, and R. Mirizzi. Top-n recommendations from implicit feedback leveraging linked open data. In *7th ACM Conference on Recommender Systems (RecSys 2013)*. ACM, ACM Press, 2013.

[12] B. M. Sarwar, G. Karypis, J. A. Konstan, and J. Riedl. Item-based collaborative filtering recommendation algorithms. In *WWW*, pages 285–295, 2001.

[13] X. Su and T. M. Khoshgoftaar. A survey of collaborative filtering techniques. *Advances in Artificial Intelligence*, Jan. 2009.

[14] M. Volkovs and R. Zemel. Collaborative ranking with 17 parameters. In P. Bartlett, F. Pereira, C. Burges, L. Bottou, and K. Weinberger, editors, *Advances in Neural Information Processing Systems 25*, pages 2303–2311. 2012.

[15] J. Wang, A. P. de Vries, and M. J. T. Reinders. A user-item relevance model for log-based collaborative filtering. In M. Lalmas, A. MacFarlane, S. M. RÃijger, A. Tombros, T. Tsikrika, and A. Yavlinsky, editors, *ECIR*, volume 3936 of *Lecture Notes in Computer Science*, pages 37–48. Springer, 2006.

Distributed Matrix Factorization with MapReduce using a series of Broadcast-Joins

Sebastian Schelter Christoph Boden Martin Schenck
Alexander Alexandrov Volker Markl

Technische Universität Berlin, Germany
firstname.lastname@tu-berlin.de

ABSTRACT

The efficient, distributed factorization of large matrices on clusters of commodity machines is crucial to applying latent factor models in industrial-scale recommender systems. We propose an efficient, data-parallel low-rank matrix factorization with Alternating Least Squares which uses a series of broadcast-joins that can be efficiently executed with MapReduce.

We empirically show that the performance of our solution is suitable for real-world use cases. We present experiments on two publicly available datasets and on a synthetic dataset termed *Bigflix*, generated from the Netflix dataset. Bigflix contains 25 million users and more than 5 billion ratings, mimicking data sizes recently reported as Netflix' production workload. We demonstrate that our approach is able to run an iteration of Alternating Least Squares in six minutes on this dataset. Our implementation has been contributed to the open source machine learning library Apache Mahout.

Categories and Subject Descriptors

H.4 [**Information Systems Applications**]: Miscellaneous

Keywords

Scalable Collaborative Filtering, MapReduce

1. INTRODUCTION

Today's information overload has triggered the development of recommender systems: intelligent filters that learn about the users' preferences and find the information most relevant to them.

On the technical side, the processing efficiency and scalability of the systems becomes a major concern in light of rapidly growing data sizes [2]. In a production environment, the offline computations necessary to run a recommender system must be periodically executed as part of larger analytical workflows and thus have to adhere to strict time and resource constraints. Additionally, computations must be executed repeatedly and in parallel to find good model parameters via cross-validation. For economic and operational reasons it is often undesirable to execute such offline computations on a single machine: this machine might fail and with growing data sizes, constant hardware upgrades might be necessary to improve the machine's performance to meet the time constraints. Due to these disadvantages, a single machine solution can quickly become expensive and hard to operate. Running data-intensive, analytical computations in a parallel and fault-tolerant manner on a cluster of commodity machines [9, 14] poses a solution to this problem. The computation becomes independent of single machine failures and performance can be increased by simply adding more machines to the cluster.

In recent research, we showed how to efficiently apply neighborhood methods in such a scenario [18]. When we apply advanced techniques such as latent factor models [13] in a distributed manner, we face a problematic situation: The algorithms used to solve latent factor models are of iterative nature. The execution of iterative programs imposes serious overhead when carried out with established paradigms such as MapReduce [9, 14], where every iteration is scheduled as a separate job and has to re-scan all iteration-invariant data. Although recently proposed specialized systems [15, 22] provide superior performance for iterative algorithms, they have the drawback that they are difficult to employ in production settings, where the existing analytics infrastructure is very often built on top of the open source MapReduce implementation Hadoop [3] and its ecosystem. Integrating specialized systems into such an environment requires heterogeneous analytics pipelines where e.g. preprocessing is done by a MapReduce system and model training is conducted by a specialized machine learning system. Such pipelines are undesirable because they are complex to setup and have high maintenance cost [14].

In this paper, we show that the low-rank matrix factorization of commonly used datasets in recommendation mining is a corner case that can be efficiently computed with MapReduce although the underlying computation is iterative. The performance of our proposed solution is suitable for production settings and at the same time, our approach is easy to integrate into existing analytics infrastructures, as it runs on Hadoop. We describe how to execute the underlying computation using only a series of broadcast-joins [7], which are efficiently executable in MapReduce and avoid a lot of the common drawbacks of the Hadoop framework.

For evaluation, we conduct experiments on two publicly available datasets consisting of several hundred million movie and song ratings. To test our approach on industrial-scale, we run experiments on a synthetic dataset with 25 million users and more than 5 billion ratings, mimicking real-world data sizes recently reported by Netflix [2].

The contributions of this paper are the following: (1) We show how to efficiently execute an iterative low-rank matrix factorization algorithm with MapReduce in a scalable manner. (2) We provide

RecSys'13, October 12–16, 2013, Hong Kong, China.

ACM 978-1-4503-2409-0/13/10 ...$15.00.
http://dx.doi.org/10.1145/2507157.2507195.

an experimental evaluation on two real-world datasets and on a synthetic industrial-scale dataset with more than 5 billion ratings.

The rest of the paper is organized as follows. Section 2 briefly introduces MapReduce and latent factor models. Section 3 in detail discusses our proposed approach. Section 4 describes related work. Section 5 gives the results we obtain from our experimental evaluation, whereas Section 6 concludes and discusses future work.

2. PRELIMINARIES

2.1 MapReduce and its limitations

MapReduce [9] is a functional paradigm for data-intensive parallel processing on shared-nothing clusters running a distributed filesystem (DFS). Under this paradigm, the user has to express algorithms as first-order functions supplied to the second-order functions *map* and *reduce*. The framework then automatically parallelizes the program and takes care of details such as scheduling the program's execution on the cluster, managing the inter-machine communication as well as coping with machine failures. Hadoop [3] is a popular and widely deployed open source implementation of MapReduce. In Hadoop, jobs are executed as a pipeline *map-shuffle-reduce*, where the map function is invoked on the input data in the DFS in parallel, the output tuples are grouped by their key and then sent to the reducer machines in the shuffle phase. The receiving machines merge the tuples, invoke the reduce function on all tuples sharing the same key and finally write the output to the DFS . The shuffle phase is typically the most costly operation as the mappers' output is spilled to disk at first and each reducer downloads its assigned data from every mapper afterwards.

In general, such a framework is a poor fit for iterative algorithms, as each iteration has to be scheduled as a single MapReduce job with a high startup cost (potentially up to tens of seconds). Further, the system creates a lot of unnecessary I/O and network traffic as all static, iteration-invariant data has to be re-read from disk and re-processed during each iteration and the intermediary result of each iteration has to be materialized in the DFS.

2.2 Collaborative Filtering

Collaborative Filtering (CF) is a popular approach in recommender systems which analyzes the historical interactions between a user and an arbitrary kind of item. Based on patterns found in the historical data, a CF algorithm recommends new, potentially high-preferred items to the users. Let A be a $|C| \times |P|$ matrix holding all known interactions between a set of users C and a set of items P. If a user i interacted with an item j, then a_{ij} holds a numeric value representing the strength of the interaction.

During the much-noticed Netflix prize [6], "latent factor models", approaches to CF that leverage a low-rank matrix factorization of the interaction data, became very popular [13]. The idea is to approximately factor the sparse $|C| \times |P|$ matrix A into the product of two rank r feature matrices U and M such that $A \approx UM$. The $|C| \times r$ matrix U models the latent features of the users, (the rows of A), while the $r \times |P|$ matrix M models the latent features of the items (the columns of A). A prediction for the strength of the relation between a user and an item (e.g., the preference of a user towards a movie) is given by the dot product $u_i^\top m_j$ of the vectors for user i and item j in the low-dimensional feature space. A popular technique to compute such a factorization is Stochastic Gradient Descent (SGD) [11,13,20], which randomly loops through all observed interactions a_{ij}, computes the error of the prediction $u_i^\top m_j$ for each interaction and modifies the model parameters in the opposite direction of the gradient. Another technique is Alternating Least Squares (ALS) [12,23], which repeatedly keeps one of the unknown matrices (either U or M) fixed, so that the other one can be optimally re-computed. ALS then rotates between re-computing the rows of U in one step and the columns of M in the subsequent step. Note that such alternating convex optimization techniques can also be applied to CF approaches that learn a ranking function [21].

3. APPROACH

3.1 Parallelization

For single machine implementations, SGD is the preferred technique to compute a low-rank matrix factorization [4, 10]. SGD is easy to implement and computationally less expensive than ALS, where every iteration runs in $O((|C| + |P|) * r^3)$, as $|C| + |P|$ linear systems have to be solved. Unfortunately, SGD is inherently sequential, because it updates the model parameters after each processed interaction. Techniques for parallel SGD have been proposed, yet they are either hard to implement, exhibit slow convergence or require shared-memory [11,16,20].

Following this rationale, we chose ALS for our parallel implementation. Although it is computationally more expensive than SGD, it naturally amends itself to parallelization. When we re-compute the user feature matrix U for example, u_i, the i-th row of U, can be re-computed by solving a least squares problem only including a_i, the i-th row of A, which holds user i's interactions, and all the columns m_j of M that correspond to non-zero entries in a_i. This re-computation of u_i is independent from the re-computation of all other rows of U and therefore, the re-computation of U is easy to parallelize if we manage to guarantee efficient data access to the rows of A and the corresponding columns from M. In the following we refer to the sequence of re-computing of U followed by re-computing M as a single iteration in ALS.

From a data processing perspective, this means that we have to conduct a parallel join between the interaction data A and M (the item features) in order to re-compute the rows of U. Analogously, we have to conduct a parallel join between A and U (the user features) to re-compute M. Finding an efficient execution strategy for these joins is crucial to the performance of our proposed parallel solution.

3.2 Execution with MapReduce

When executing joins in a shared-nothing environment, minimizing the required amount of inter-machine communication is decisive for the performance of the execution, as network bandwidth is the most scarce resource in a cluster. For matrix factorization with ALS, we have to alternatingly join A with M and U. In both cases, the interaction matrix A is usually much larger than any of the feature matrices. We limit our approach to use-cases where neither U nor M need to be partitioned (which means they individually fit into the memory of a single machine of the cluster). A rough estimate of the required memory for the re-computation steps in ALS is $\max(|C|, |P|) * r * 8$ byte, as alternatingly, a single dense double-precision representation of the matrices U or M has to be stored in memory on each machine. Even for 10 million users or items and a rank of 100, the estimated required memory would be less than 8 gigabyte, which can easily be handled by today's commodity hardware. Our experiments in Section 5 show that, despite this limitation, we can handle datasets with billions of data points.

In such a setting, an efficient way to implement the necessary joins for ALS in MapReduce is to use a parallel broadcast-join [7]. The smaller dataset (U or M) is replicated to every machine of the cluster. Each machine already holds a local partition of A which is stored in the DFS. Then the join between the local partition of A and the replicated copy of M (and analogously between the local partition of A and U) can be executed by a map operator. This operator can additionally implement the logic to re-compute the feature vectors from the join result, which means that we can execute a whole re-computation of U or M with a single map operator.

Figure 1 exemplarily illustrates the parallel join for re-computing U using three machines. We broadcast M to all participating machines, which create a hashtable for its contents, the item feature vectors. A is stored in the DFS partitioned by its rows and forms the input for the map operator (cf. Figure 1, where e.g., $A(1)$ refers to partition 1 of A). The map operator reads a row a_i of A (the interaction history of user i) and selects all the item feature vectors m_j from the hashtable holding M that correspond to non-zero entries j in a_i. Next, the map operator solves a linear system created from the interactions and item feature vectors and writes back its result, the re-computed feature vector u_i for user i. The re-computation of M works analogously, with the only difference that we need to broadcast U and store A partitioned by its columns (the interactions per item) in the DFS.

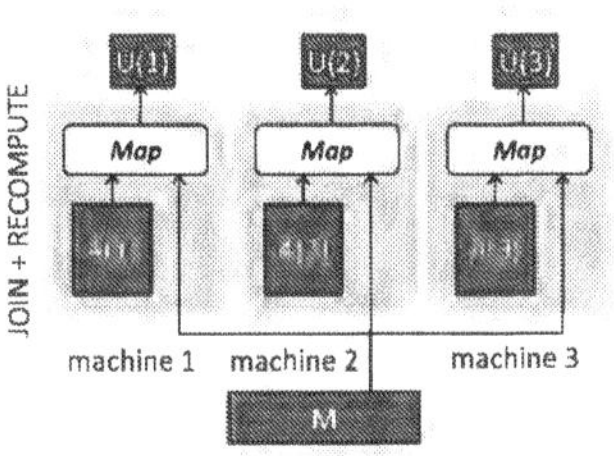

Figure 1: Parallel re-computation of user features by a broadcast-join.

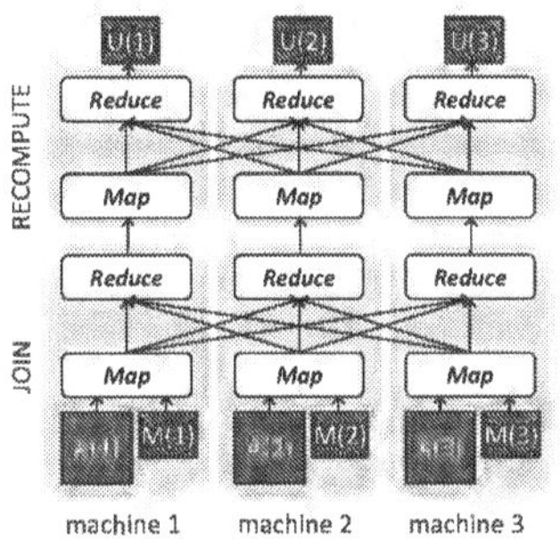

Figure 2: Parallel re-computation of user features by a repartition-join.

The proposed approach is able to avoid some of the drawbacks of MapReduce and the Hadoop implementation described in Section 2.1. It uses only map jobs that are easier to schedule than jobs containing map and reduce operators. Additionally, the costly shuffle-phase is avoided, in which all data would be sorted and sent over the network. As we can execute the join and the re-computation using a single job, we also spare to materialize the join result in the DFS. Our implementation contains multithreaded mappers that leverage all cores of the worker machines for the re-computation of the feature matrices and uses JBlas [5] for solving the dense linear systems present in ALS. The broadcast of the feature matrix is conducted via Hadoop's distributed cache in the initialization phase of each re-computation. Furthermore, we configure Hadoop to reuse the VMs on the worker machines and cache the feature matrices in memory to avoid that later scheduled mappers have to reread the data. The main drawback of a broadcast approach is that every additional machine in the cluster requires another copy of the feature matrix to be sent over the network. An alternative would be to use a repartition join [7] with constant network traffic and linear scale-out (cf., Figure 2). However, this technique has an enormous constant overhead. Let n_i denote the number of interactions, n_m the number of machines in the cluster, n_r the replication factor of the DFS and n_e the number of users or items[1]. If we employ a repartition-join we need two map-reduce jobs per re-computation then. In the first job, we conduct the join which sends the interaction matrix A and either U or M over the network, accounting to $n_i * 4 + n_e * r * 8$ bytes of network traffic. The result must be materialized in the DFS, which requires another $(n_i * 4 + n_e * r * 8) * n_r$ bytes of traffic. The re-computation of the feature matrix must be conducted via a second map-reduce job that sends all the ratings and corresponding feature vectors per user or item over the network, accounting for an additional $n_i * r * 8$ bytes. On the contrary, the traffic for our proposed broadcast-join technique depends on the number of machines and accounts to $n_e * r * n_m * 8$ bytes. Applying these estimations to the datasets used for our experiments, the cluster size would have to exceed several hundred machines to have our broadcast-join technique cause more network traffic than a computation via repartition-join. Further, this argumentation only looks at the required network traffic and does not account for the fact that the computation via repartition-join would also need to sort and materialize the intermediate data in each step. We conclude that our approach with a series of broadcast-joins is to be preferred for common production scenarios.

[1] we assume that rating values are stored with single precision

4. RELATED WORK

Zhou et. al. describe a distributed implementation using Matlab, which is only suitable for running scientific experiments as it offers no fault tolerance [23]. GraphLab [15] is a specialized system for parallel machine learning, where programs operate on a graph expressing the computational dependencies of the data. It provides an asynchronous implementation of ALS. Gemulla et. al presented a parallel matrix factorization using Stochastic Gradient Descent [11], which leverages an intelligent partitioning to avoid conflicting updates. They switched their implementation to MPI [20] due to the overhead incurred by Hadoop. SystemML [19] is a proprietary library for machine learning on MapReduce which allows the declarative specification of matrix factorization algorithms. The recommender system of Google News [8] uses a MapReduce implementation of probabilistic latent semantic indexing. As Google uses a proprietary implementation of MapReduce, it is hard to assess the technical details of this approach.

5. EVALUATION

In this section, we experimentally show that our approach is suitable for real-world production settings where an approach has to be compatible to the Hadoop ecosystem and has to run in a few hours to be integratable into analytical workflows. We solely focus on measuring the runtime of computing a factorization, as the prediction quality of the ALS approach is well studied [11,12,23]. We use a formulation of ALS that is aimed at rating prediction [23].

Setup: The cluster for our experiments consists of 26 machines running Java 7 and Hadoop 1.0.4 [3]. Each machine has two 8-core Opteron CPUs, 32 GB memory and four 1 TB disk drives.

Datasets:[2] We use two publicly available datasets for our experiments: A set of 100,480,507 ratings given to 17,770 movies by 480,189 users from the Netflix prize [6] and another set comprised of 717,872,016 ratings given to 136,736 songs by 1,823,179 users of the Yahoo! Music community[3]. For tests at industrial-scale, we generate a synthetic dataset termed Bigflix using the Myriad data generation toolkit [1]. From the training set of the Netflix prize, we extract the probability of rating each item and increase the item space by a factor of six to gain more than 100,000 movies. Next, we extract the distribution of ratings per user. We configure Myriad to create data for 25 million users by the following process: For each user, Myriad samples a corresponding number of ratings from the extracted distribution of ratings per user. Then, Myriad samples

[2] Details about our experiments can be found at http://goo.gl/YXj9B

[3] http://webscope.sandbox.yahoo.com/catalog.php?datatype=r

an item from the item probability distribution for each rating. The corresponding rating value is simply chosen from a uniform distribution, as we do not interpret the result anyways, but only want to look at the performance of computing the factorization. Bigflix contains 5,231,536,647 interactions and mimicks the 25 million subscribers and 5 billion ratings, which Netflix recently reported as its current production workload [2].

Experimental results: We start by measuring the average runtime per individual re-computation of U and M for different feature space sizes on the Netflix dataset and on the Yahoo Songs dataset (cf., Figure 3) using 26 machines. For Netflix, the average runtime per re-computation always lies between 35 and 60 seconds regardless of the feature space size. This is a clear indication that for this small dataset the runtime is dominated by the scheduling overhead of Hadoop. For the larger Yahoo Songs dataset we see the same behavior for small feature space sizes and observe that the computation becomes dominated by the time to broadcast one feature matrix and re-compute the other one for larger feature space sizes of 50 and 100. We notice that re-computing M is much more costly then re-computing U. This happens because in this dataset, the number of users is nearly twenty times as large as the number of items, which means that it takes much longer to broadcast U. The experiments show that we can run 37 to 47 iterations per hour on Netflix and 15 to 38 iterations per hour on the Yahoo Songs dataset (e.g., ALS typically needs about 15 iterations to converge on Netflix [23]). This shows that our approach is easily able to compute factorizations of datasets with hundreds of millions of interactions repeatedly per day.

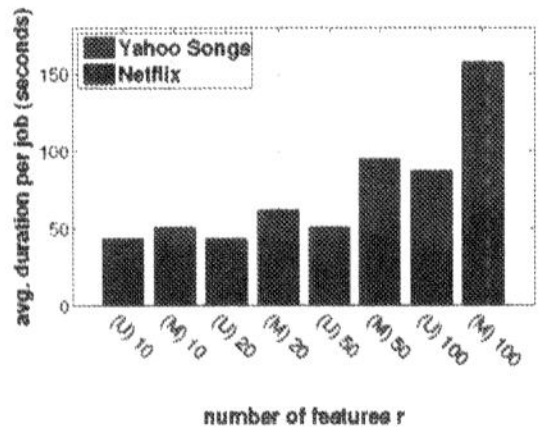

Figure 3: Runtimes on Netflix and Yahoo Songs with different feature space sizes.

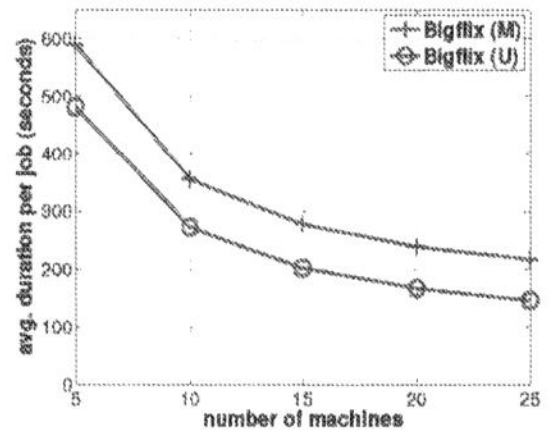

Figure 4: Runtimes on Bigflix with different cluster sizes.

Finally we run scale-out tests on Bigflix: we measure the average runtime per re-computation of U and M during five iterations of ALS on this dataset on clusters of 5, 10, 15, 20 and 25 machines (cf., Figure 4) conducting a factorization of rank ten. With 5 machines, an iteration takes about 19 minutes and with 25 machines, we are able to bring this down to 6 minutes. We observe that the computation speedup does not linearly scale with the number of machines. This behavior is expected because of the broadcast-join we employ, where every additional machine causes another copy of the feature matrix to be sent over the network. As discussed in Section 3.2, on clusters with less than several hundred machines, our chosen approach is much more performant than a repartition-join, although the latter is linearly scaling. With 25 machines, we can run about 9 to 10 iterations per hour, which allows us to obtain a factorization in a few hours, a timeframe completely suitable for a production setting.

6. SUMMARY

We presented an efficient scalable approach for a data-parallel low-rank matrix factorization using Alternating Least Squares on a cluster of commodity machines. We explained our choice of ALS as algorithm and described how to implement it on MapReduce with a series of broadcast-joins, which can be efficiently executed using only map jobs. We experimentally validated our approach on two large datasets commonly used in research and on a synthetic dataset with more than 5 billion datapoints, which mimicks an industry usecase. Furthermore, our code has partially been contributed to the open source machine learning library Apache Mahout [4]. In future work we would like to compare our approach to implementations in specialized systems [15, 22] and see if we can incorporate approximate solutions for ALS [17].

7. ACKNOWLEDGMENTS

We thank Zeno Gantner for early comments on the paper. The research is funded by the European Union (EU) under grants no. 25789 'ROBUST' and no. 270137 'SCAPE', the BMBF under grant no. 01ISI2033 'RADAR' and the European Institute of Innovation and Technology (EIT). We used data provided by 'Yahoo! Academic Relations'.

8. REFERENCES

[1] A. Alexandrov, K. Tzoumas, and V. Markl. Myriad: scalable and expressive data generation. *VLDB*, 2012.

[2] X. Amatriain. Building industrial-scale real-world recommender systems. *RecSys*, 2012, http://goo.gl/cqKAi.

[3] Apache Hadoop, http://hadoop.apache.org.

[4] Apache Mahout, http://mahout.apache.org.

[5] JBlas, http://jblas.org.

[6] J. Bennett and S. Lanning. The netflix prize. 2007.

[7] S. Blanas, J. M. Patel, V. Ercegovac, J. Rao, E. J. Shekita, and Y. Tian. A comparison of join algorithms for log processing in mapreduce. *SIGMOD*, 2010.

[8] A. S. Das, M. Datar, A. Garg, and S. Rajaram. Google news personalization: scalable online collaborative filtering. *WWW*, 2007.

[9] J. Dean and S. Ghemawat. Mapreduce: simplified data processing on large clusters. *Commun. ACM*, 2008.

[10] Z. Gantner, S. Rendle, C. Freudenthaler, and L. Schmidt-Thieme. Mymedialite: a free recommender system library. *RecSys*, 2011.

[11] R. Gemulla, E. Nijkamp, P. J. Haas, and Y. Sismanis. Large-scale matrix factorization with distributed stochastic gradient descent. *KDD*, 2011.

[12] Y. Hu, Y. Koren, and C. Volinsky. Collaborative filtering for implicit feedback datasets. *ICDM*, 2008.

[13] Y. Koren, R. Bell, and C. Volinsky. Matrix factorization techniques for recommender systems. *Computer*, 2009.

[14] J. Lin. MapReduce is Good Enough? If All You Have is a Hammer, Throw Away Everything That's Not a Nail! *CoRR*, 2012

[15] Y. Low, J. Gonzalez, A. Kyrola, D. Bickson, C. Guestrin, and J. Hellerstein. Distributed graphlab: A framework for machine learning in the cloud. *PVLDB*, 2012.

[16] F. Niu, B. Recht, C. Ré, and S. Wright. Hogwild!: A lock-free approach to parallelizing stochastic gradient descent. *NIPS*, 2011.

[17] I. Pilászy, D. Zibriczky and D. Tikk. Fast als-based matrix factorization for explicit and implicit feedback datasets. *RecSys*, 2010.

[18] S. Schelter, C. Boden, and V. Markl. Scalable Similarity-Based Neighborhood Methods with MapReduce. *RecSys*, 2012.

[19] A. Ghoting, R. Krishnamurthy, E. Pednault, B. Reinwald, V. Sindhwani, S. Tatikonda, T. Yuanyuan and S. Vaithyanathan. SystemML: Declarative machine learning on MapReduce. *ICDE*, 2011.

[20] C. Teflioudi, F. Makari, and R. Gemulla. Distributed matrix completion. *ICDM*, 2012.

[21] M. Weimer, A. Karatzoglou, Q. Viet Le and A. Smola. CofiRank - Maximum Margin Matrix Factorization for Collaborative Ranking. *NIPS*, 2007.

[22] M. Zaharia, M. Chowdhury, M. J. Franklin, S. Shenker, and I. Stoica. Spark: cluster computing with working sets. *HotCloud*, 2010.

[23] Y. Zhou, D. Wilkinson, R. Schreiber, and R. Pan. Large-scale parallel collaborative filtering for the netflix prize. *AAIM*, 2008.

Catch-up TV Recommendations: Show Old Favourites and Find New Ones

Mengxi Xu
University of Sydney and NICTA
Cynthia.Xu@nicta.com.au

Shlomo Berkovsky, Sebastien Ardon
Sipat Triukose, Anirban Mahanti
NICTA
firstname.lastname@nicta.com.au

Irena Koprinska
University of Sydney
irena@it.usyd.edu.au

ABSTRACT

Web-based catch-up TV has revolutionised watching habits as it provides users the opportunity to watch programs at their preferred time and place, using a variety of devices. With the increasing offer of TV content, there is an emergent need for personalised recommendation solutions, which help users to select programs of interest. In this work, we study the watching patterns of users of an Australian nationwide catch-up TV service provider and develop a suite of approaches for a catch-up recommendation scenario. We evaluate these approaches using a new large-scale dataset gathered by the Web-based catch-up portal deployed by the provider. The evaluation allows us to compare the performance of several recommenders that address the discovery of both TV programs already watched by users and new programs that users may find relevant.

Categories and Subject Descriptors

H.3.4 [**Information Storage and Retrieval**]: Systems and Software—*distributed systems, user profile and alert services*; H.5.m [**Information Interfaces and Presentation**]: Miscellaneous

General Terms

Algorithms, Design, Experimentation.

Keywords

Recommender Systems; Catch-up TV; Grouped Video Content Recommendations; Large-Scale Evaluation.

1. INTRODUCTION

Catch-up TV refers to a TV content delivery paradigm where already broadcast programs are uploaded to a dedicated portal, so that users can watch these programs later at their own convenience. Several TV networks, such as the ABC and SBS in Australia, and the BBC in the UK, offer catch-up TV services to their viewers, and this content delivery model is fast evolving as a new approach for engaging users and combating piracy within the TV broadcasting industry. Recent marketing studies found that users tend to watch stored TV programs in addition to live broadcast, and frequently combine the two delivery modes.

With the flexibility of watching any TV program at any time and place, users often face information overload when selecting a program to watch. This challenge becomes particularly acute considering the entertainment context of TV watching, where users prefer to lay-back and relax rather than actively search for a suitable program [6]. Consequently, there is an emergent need for personalised solutions and recommender systems capable of selecting programs on behalf of their users.

The practical challenge of generating accurate recommendations is, however, arduous for several reasons. First, due to privacy restrictions, TV content providers often can only use partial user data they possess. Second, user logs are often noisy and inaccurate, often for technical reasons, i.e. due to lack of a single sign-on. Third, some users may use multiple devices to watch programs and, vice versa, some devices may be used by multiple users. Finally, users' TV content consumption may be strongly affected by external contextual factors, which cannot be captured.

In this work, we partner with a leading Australian national TV network, and study and evaluate a number of recommendation approaches that leverage observed real-life user interactions and viewing logs, to generate personalised TV program recommendations. Specifically, we consider the recommendation for catch-up TV services with *grouped* content. Grouped content refers to multiple programs bound by the same plot or theme (e.g., TV series and football games), or to programs shown at fixed days or certain time slots (e.g., daily news and weekly talk shows). For the sake of simplicity, we denote the groups of content as series and the individual programs belonging to these series as episodes. We disregard in this work standalone individual programs such as movies.

The recommendation engine consists of two components, each responsible for selecting a different type of program. The first component, which we refer to as the *subscribed* series recommender, identifies content regularly watched by a user and recommends unwatched programs that belong to this content. For the sake of simplicity, these recommendations can be considered as recommendations for new episodes of shows the user has been regularly watching. The subscribed recommendation component is implemented as a rule-based recommender aimed to maximise the consump-

RecSys'13, October 12–16, 2013, Hong Kong, China.
Copyright 2013 ACM 978-1-4503-2409-0/13/10 ...$15.00.
http://dx.doi.org/10.1145/2507157.2507204.

tion of the subscribed content. The second component, which we refer to as the *new* series recommender, recommends content that a user is unfamiliar with, i.e., new programs. This component capitalises on the preferences of the entire community of users and builds upon well established collaborative recommendation methods. The goal of this recommender is to expand the users' horizons and expose users to new TV content. Finally, the recommendations generated by the two components are combined using the mixed hybridisation technique [7].

We present an extensive offline evaluation of the aforementioned recommendation components using a dataset gathered by our partner catch-up TV service provider. The dataset contains six months of Australia-wide usage logs that encompass nearly 20 million views by more than 2 million unique users, who collectively watched more than 11,000 unique programs. We evaluate and compare the performance of several recommendation approaches and assess their ability to recommend subscribed content of interest, as well as new unwatched content. Our evaluation shows that we can recommend subscribed content with a high degree of accuracy such that around 75% of the recommended programs are watched by users. The task of recommending new TV content is, however, much more challenging as the ground truth regarding new content that users watch in the catch-up scenario is less reliable. Accordingly, the performance of the new recommender is poorer than of the subscribed recommender. We evaluate several methods for the new recommender, but they reach at best the 12% accuracy level. To summarise, the main contribution of this paper is a thorough evaluation, with a new real-life catch-up TV dataset, of a suite of recommendation approaches for catch-up TV services.

The remainder of this paper is structured as follows. Section 2 presents background on catch-up TV services. Section 3 discusses data collection and presents a high-level characterisation of the dataset used in the evaluation. Section 4 describes the user modelling and recommendation approaches we apply, while Section 5 presents the experimental evaluation and the obtained results. Related work is discussed in Section 6. Finally, Section 7 summarises the work and outlines future research directions.

2. BACKGROUND

Catch-up TV is a video-on-demand service that allows users to watch at their preferred time recently broadcast TV programs that they missed. Catch-up TV services are usually provided via a Web portal and accessible through a variety of devices, such as PCs, tablets, smartphones, and gaming consoles. Catch-up TV differs from traditional video-on-demand services in that the content is typically accessible for a limited time period following the program broadcast. Often, the availability period depends on the licensing terms negotiated between the catch-up service providers and content right holders.

The popularity of catch-up TV has recently sky-rocketed and its consumption figures are approaching those of the traditional TV [9]. Similarly to other video-on-demand services, catch-up TV service providers are looking to maximise user satisfaction, increase user engagement, and increase content consumption. To achieve this, many catch-up TV providers are interested in personalisation and recommendation approaches that allow to have the programs presented to users tailored to their interest and watching preferences.

For this work, we partner with a leading national TV broadcaster in Australia. Each program shown on the TV channels of the broadcaster is made available through its Web-based catch-up portal, typically on the day following the broadcast. Programs remain typically available in the catch-up portal for a period of one, two, or four weeks. However, there are some exceptions; e.g., news and trailers remain available for two days only. The catch-up portal can be accessed through a variety of devices and platforms, e.g., Apple iOS, smart TVs, and Web browsers.

The main user interface of the portal is currently non-personalised. It offers to viewers three lists of programs: two time-based lists ordered by popularity ('just added' and 'about to expire'), and an editorially-curated list ('featured'). It should be highlighted that the selection of programs in these lists is done manually by domain experts in a generic manner, and no personalisation is applied. In addition to the main interface, users can access the programs through several search interfaces. The programs are mapped by domain experts into 12 categories: arts, children (aged 6 to 15), comedy, documentaries, drama, education, lifestyle, news, panel, preschool (children aged under 6), shop, and sport. Users can browse the tree of categories and programs, search for programs through channels on which they were broadcast, or alternatively use a free-text search.

Once a user finds a program of interest and clicks on its thumbnail, a detailed program information is shown. This information includes the program title, category, textual description, broadcast data, publication date (when it was uploaded to the portal), expiry date (when it will be removed from the portal), parental rating, duration, and availability of captions. If the program belongs to the grouped content, other available episodes of the same series are also displayed. The user can then invoke the player and watch the program, share it via online social networks, or email the link to the program. The service allows deep-linking of videos, so that they can be accessed directly from a link on a news article, blog, or social network post, without going through the main or search interface of the portal.

3. OVERVIEW OF DATASET

3.1 Data Collection

As already mentioned, the data used in this work originates from the catch-up TV service of a leading Australian broadcaster that runs a number of national free-to-air channels. It is a popular network, offering both local and international programs. We obtained the complete Australia-wide portal logs for a period of 184 days (26 weeks), from March to August 2012. As shown in Table 1, the dataset includes nearly 20 million views of more than 2 million unique users, who collectively watched 11,699 unique programs.

Time span	184 days
View count	19.8 millions
Unique videos viewed/available	9,114/27,621
Unique cookie	2.02 millions

Table 1: **Dataset high-level description.**

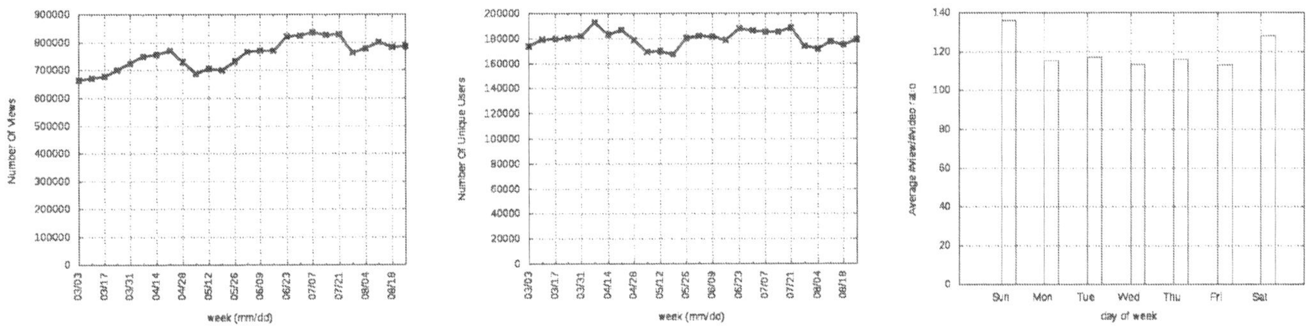

(a) (b) (c)

Figure 1: High-level characterisation: (a) number of videos watched per week; (b) number of unique users per week; (c) average number of views per video as a function of day-of-the-week.

The gathered data includes very little information about the users, as the catch-up service does not include a user sign-on identification. As the service uses HTTP cookies for audience measurement purposes, we use these cookie IDs as a proxy for user IDs. We admit that this mapping of cookie IDs to users is clearly imprecise, as multiple users may use a single device to access the catch-up portal (and have the same cookie ID) and, vice versa, a single user may use multiple devices or browsers (and have multiple cookie IDs). Moreover, users can clear cookies at any time, in which case a new user is created next time they use the service. Alternatively, users can just block cookies, in which case no records of that user are available. It is important to note that this may be one of the key sources of inaccuracy for the recommender. However, these limitations are those typically faced by the industry when deploying catch-up TV services, as requiring users to sign-on before watching TV content may impair user experience. Thus, the gathered logs characterise the real-life usage data accessible by a commercial catch-up TV portal.

For each video that was accessed via the portal, the logs contain a cookie ID, the access date (with no time stamp), and the video ID. No information about the portion of the video that was actually watched is available. In addition, the service provider partially exposed the content meta-data, which was collected on a daily basis. For each video, the meta-data contains a unique video ID, a series ID, the video title, duration, publication date, expiry date, a category tag (chosen from the above 12 categories), and the size of the video file. The logs contain only the observed watching events and do not include any evidence of searches, information accesses, social media posts, and so on.

3.2 High-Level Characterisation

In this section, we present a high-level characterisation of the dataset. Figure 1 (a) shows the number of video accesses per week observed during the data collection period. We observe a slow, but steady, increase in the video access rate over time, with the number of requests increasing from under 700,000 requests/week at the beginning to about 800,000 requests/week at the end. Figure 1 (b) shows the number of unique users, counted using the cookie IDs, seen each week, which steadily hovers around the 180,000 users/week mark. We also study whether there are changes in the the average number of requests per video between weekdays and weekends. Figure 1 (c) shows the average number of video accesses as a function of the day-of-the-week. It can be clearly seen that the average request rate for videos on the weekends is higher than on the weekdays.

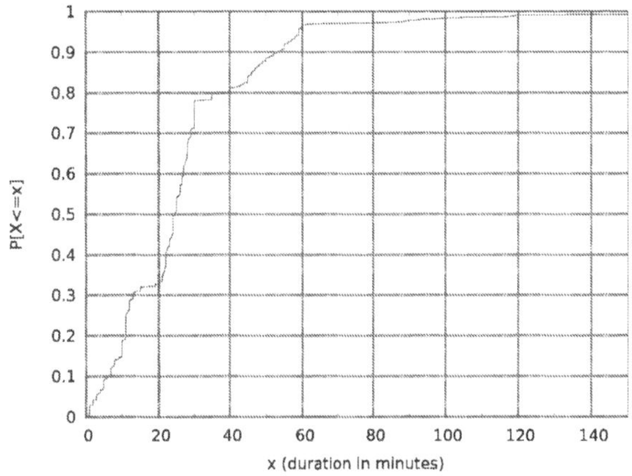

Figure 2: Distribution of video durations (minutes).

Figure 2 shows the empirical cumulative distribution of the duration of the available videos. It can be seen that more than 30% of videos are shorter than 20 minutes, about 45% are between 20 and 30 minutes in length, and only 2% are longer than 60 minutes. The bulk of the content is between 20 and 30 minutes long, corresponding to the typical length of TV programs shown by the broadcaster. The shorter programs in the dataset primarily include news and program trailers.

Next, we measure how the number of views per video changes as a function of their age, where the age is measured as the number of days since the publication date. Earlier, we noted that the portal typically made videos available for a period of one, two, or four weeks. Figure 3 considers these three catch-up availability windows, and shows for these three groups how the average viewing rate varies as a function of the video age. For all three groups considered, the average viewing rate decreases exponentially with the video age, showing that most of the requests are made when the videos are only a few days old. This is likely a function of both the viewing behaviour of the users and the organisation of the portal interface of the catch-up portal interface,

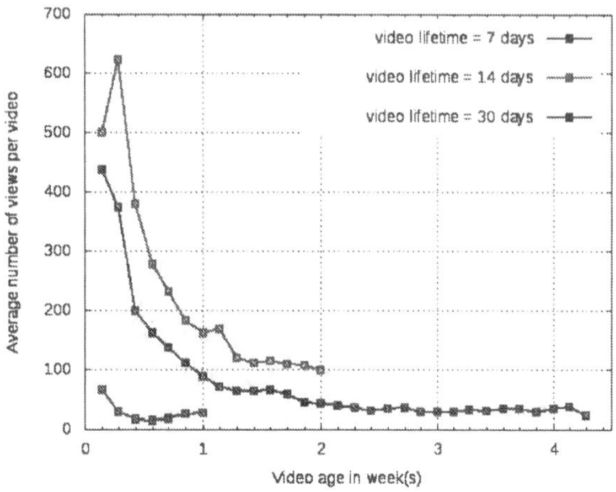

Figure 3: Average viewing rate as a function of video age.

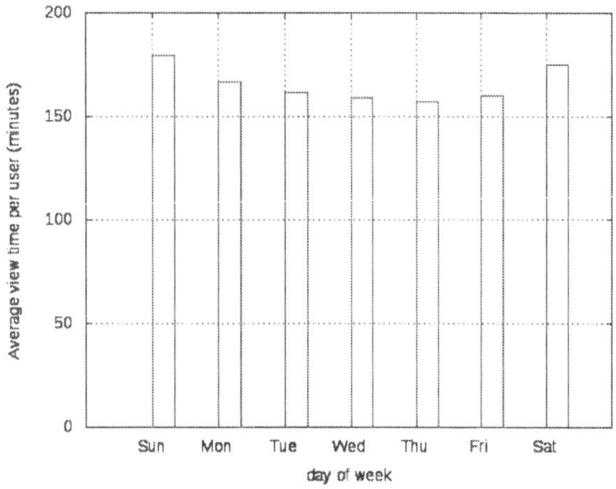

Figure 4: Average viewing time of users as a function of day-of-the-week.

which prominently displays recently uploaded videos. This suggests that most users catch-up on the missed TV content as closely as possible to the content broadcast.

Figure 4 shows, for each day-of-the-week, an upper bound on the average time spent by users watching catch-up TV. Recall that our dataset only includes information on video accesses and does not contain information on the duration of each video playback by the users. This computations assume that each video accessed was watched in its entirety, and, hence, it is an upper bound for the viewing time. Nonetheless, we observe that, on average, users watched content between 150 and 180 minutes per day, with watching time increasing on weekends compared to weekdays. Given that a typical video is 20 to 30 minutes long, this represents an engagement of 5 to 6 videos per day. Note that on any day the catch-up TV portal offers to users between 1000 and 1200 videos. This result highlights the content discovery problem: users are faced with finding 5 to 6 programs from this overwhelming volume of video content.

Related to the above analysis is the typical user stickiness, i.e., the frequency with which users return to the portal. Among the unique users (identified through cookie IDs) seen each week, Figure 5 shows the breakdown of total views into

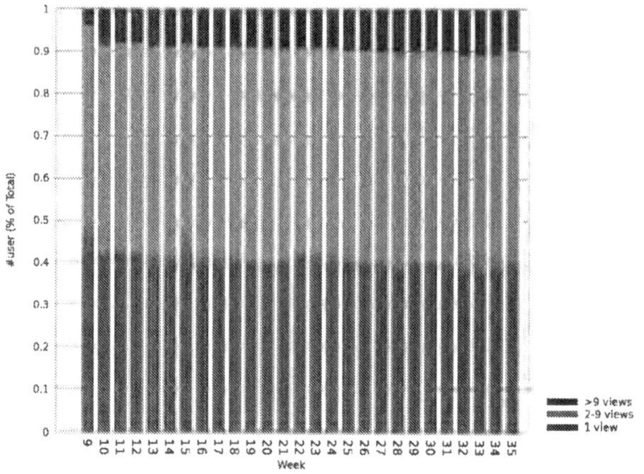

Figure 5: Number of k-time users as a function of time.

those made by users that requested only one video, between two and nice videos, and ten videos or more. The analysis shows that approximately 40% of users are one-timers, who view only one video and do not return to the portal any more. We also observe that only 10% of users are active enough to view ten videos or more over the course of the logs. It appears that a large fraction of users are accessing the portal as it was conceived, i.e., to catch-up on programs they missed broadcast on TV. A small number of users are frequent visitors, who rely on the catch-up TV service for their viewing needs. In the rest of this paper, we present a recommender focusing on the frequent users.

4. RECOMMENDATION APPROACHES

We outline a number of recommendation approaches that are evaluated with the gathered dataset. Since the TV content is grouped, the problem is reduced from recommending individual programs to recommending series. The task is further split into two sub-tasks: recommending subscribed series that a user has been regularly watching and recommending new series that a user has not watched yet.

4.1 User Data

We start with defining the data used by the recommenders. Raw logs of from the catch-up portal encapsulate binary viewing ratings $r_{u,i}$:

$$r_{u,i} = \begin{cases} 1 & u \text{ watched } i \\ 0 & \text{otherwise} \end{cases}$$

As discussed in Section 3, the number of available programs is much greater than the average number of programs watched by a user on a given day. Thus, the ratings matrix corresponding to raw viewing logs is sparse. Collapsing episodes into series reduces the dimensionality of the problem and increases the density of the data [5].

Let us denote by S the set of series available at the catch-up portal and by U the set of the portal users. The collapsed rating matrix R is built by computing the implicit $score_{u,s}$ of all users $u \in U$ for all series $s \in S$. This is computed as

$$score_{u,s} = \frac{n_{u,s}}{avail_{u,s}}$$

where $n_{u,s} = \sum_{i \in s} r_{u,i}$ denotes the number of episodes of s that u watched and $avail_{u,s}$ denotes the number of episodes of s that were available since u had joined. The joining date for u is approximated by the the earliest view logged for them. In essence, $score_{u,s}$ reflects the degree of interest of u in s. Then, the user profile P_u represents the ordered set of scores of u for all $s \in S$ series, $P_u = \{score_{u,s}\}$, and the resulting rating matrix $R_{|U| \times |S|}$ represents the collection of all the available user profiles.

We also introduce the binary notion of user subscription to a series, denoted by $sub_{u,s}$, which is computed as

$$sub_{u,s} = \begin{cases} 1 & score_{u,s} \geqslant \alpha \ \wedge \ n_{u,s} \geqslant \beta \\ 0 & \text{otherwise} \end{cases}$$

If the implicit score $score_{u,s}$ of u for s is greater than α and u watched more than β episodes of s, then u is considered *subcribed* to s. The relative threshold α corresponds the implicit score for the series as a proxy for the level of user's interest. The absolute threshold β corresponds to the minimal required number of watched episodes and is useful for long running series that may have a large number of episodes. We define the subscription list SL_u as the set of series to which u is subscribed, $SL_u = \{s \in S \mid sub_{u,s} = 1\}$.

4.2 Subscribed Series Recommender

The goal of the subscribed recommender is to select series that a user regularly watches, but have yet unwatched episodes that the user is likely to watch. In other words, the output of the recommender is restricted to series $s \in SL_u$. Note that this cardinally differs from a typical recommendation scenario, where recommendable items have not been experienced by users, such that their score is unknown and it is predicted by the recommender. On the contrary, in our case the goal is to recommend regularly watched series, the score of which is known at the recommendation time.

Hence, we do not apply any of the state-of-the-art recommendation approaches, but rather two personalised rule-based approaches that use the subscription data to recommend series. The first one, *preference-based subscribed* recommender, selects n series with the highest implicit $score_{u,s}$ from the the subscription list SL_u of the target user u and recommends these. The second, *random subscribed* recommender, selects the n recommended series from SL_u at random rather than according to their scores.

In addition to the two rule-based recommenders, we use two non-personalised recommenders, which consider neither the profile P_u nor the subscription list SL_u when generating recommendations, as baselines for comparison. The first, *most popular*, recommends n series with the highest aggregated score across the entire community. The aggregated score for a series s is computed by averaging $score_{u,s}$ of all the users subcribed to s. The second, *random* recommender, picks at random n series amongst all the series S available in the system and recommends these to u.

4.3 New Series Recommender

Recommending series that a user already watches inherently limits the discovery of new content, as series outside a user's subscription list cannot be recommended. Hence, we use four personalised algorithms (user-to-user collaborative filtering, cluster-based, matrix factorisation, and slope one) to recommend new series. They all predict the score $pred_{u,s}$ for unsubscribed series $s \notin SL_u$ and recommend n series with the highest predicted scores. We briefly overview the four new series recommendation algorithms.

User-to-User Collaborative Filtering. User-to-user CF assumes that users will like items that were liked by similar users [10]. Hence, CF initially computes the degree of similarity between the target user u and all other users. Then, for every series s yet unwatched by u, the recommender selects a set of k most similar users who are already subscribed to s, and computes the predicted score of u for s as a weighted average of the scores of these users. The relative weight of users reflects the degree of their similarity to the target user. Finally, n series with the highest scores are recommended to u.

Cluster-Based Recommender. This recommender is similar to user-to-user CF in the sense that the predicted score $pred_{u,s}$ is also computed as a weighted average of the scores of other users. The users are first partitioned into a discrete set of clusters based on their rating patterns, as described in [17]. The scores of all users belonging to the cluster of the target user u are then taken into account, such that no user-to-user similarity computation is needed. Upon the computation of the $pred_{u,s}$ scores, n top-scoring series are recommended.

Slope-One Recommender. Slope-one recommender is a simplified version of item-to-item CF that does not weigh items according to their similarity [13]. It assumes that a linear relationship between the series scores can be identified. The algorithm computes the average difference between the scores of all pairs of series s_a and s_b using the scores of the entire community of users. It then computes the predicted score $pred_{u,s}$ for user u and series s by adding the computed average difference to all the known $score_{u,s_a}$ of u and averaging the results across all the known scores. Finally, n series with the highest predicted scores are recommended.

Matrix Factorisation. MF recommenders represent a family of model-based recommenders that apply dimensionality reduction techniques to the rating matrix R [12]. The algorithm factorises R into a product of two latent matrices: user matrix p and series matrix q, using the alternative least squares approach (latent matrices p and q are iteratively optimised individually rather than in parallel). Upon the completion of the factorisation process, the latent matrices are multiplied to predict the score $pred_{u,s}$ for yet unwatched series. Again, n series with the highest score are finally recommended to u.

For the new series recommendation task we also evaluate two non-personalised baselines: *most popular* and *random*. These are similar to their non-personalised subscribed recommendation counterparts, but pick the recommended series from the set of series to which u is not subscribed.

4.4 Combining Recommendations

We revisit the different purposes of the subscribed and new series recommenders. The former suggests to users series that they regularly watch and there are new episodes that they are likely to watch. The latter, on the contrary, suggests new series that users are likely to find interesting. Hence, the outputs of both recommenders are of relevance, and should be combined and presented to users. This combination fits the *mixed* hybridisation method [7], where "recommendations from several recommenders are presented at the same time".

5. EXPERIMENTAL EVALUATION

We conducted an offline evaluation of the two recommendation components using the gathered dataset. In this section, we first outline the evaluation setting and then present, analyse, and discuss the obtained results.

5.1 Evaluation Setting and Metrics

We split all the available data into the training set and test set. The recommenders are trained on the training set data and their performance is evaluated on the withheld test set data. In our case, the training set includes the data ranging for the first 136 days of the portal logs and the test set includes three immediately following days.

The training period data consists of 14.9 million views. As discussed earlier, many users had too few views to generate personalised recommendations. Hence, we exclude from the evaluation all the users, who watched less than 30 programs during the training period. The remaining training data contains 11.9 million views of almost 125,000 unique users and about 9,000 programs. On average, every user watched 95.1 programs and every program was watched by 14.1 users. During the three day test period, more than 430,000 views were logged for these users.

Since no explicit ratings for the watched programs are available, we cannot use predictive accuracy and use the classification accuracy metrics of precision and recall [16]. Precision quantifies the ability of the recommender to select the watched and filter out the unwatched programs. Recall quantifies the ability of the recommender to select as many watched programs as possible. Given a user u, who was recommended a set of programs Rec and watched a set of programs $Viewed$ over the course of the test period, precision and recall for u are computed as

$$prec_u = \frac{|Viewed \cap Rec|}{|Rec|} \qquad recall_u = \frac{|Viewed \cap Rec|}{|Viewed|}$$

Finally, we compute the average precision, $\overline{prec}$, and average recall, $\overline{recall}$, across all the users.

We also measure the coverage of the recommendations, which communicates the ability of the system to generate recommendations, regardless of their accuracy. Specifically, we apply user-based coverage, $cover_u = |Rec|/n$ (n is the number of recommendations that the systems needs to generate), and average it across all the users to compute $\overline{cover}$.

5.2 Subscribed Series Recommender

In this section, we present the evaluation of the subscribed series recommender aimed at recommending programs regularly watched by users. Since we conduct an offline evaluation, the important metric for subscribed recommendations is the precision. That is, we assess the portion of the recommended programs that were watched by the users.

We evaluate two personalised (preference-based and random profile) and two non-personalised (most popular and random) subscribed recommenders. We set the series subscription thresholds to $\alpha = 0.3$ and $\beta = 3$. These were determined by cross-validation experiments that are not reported due to space limitations. We included in the test set all the users, who watched ten programs or more during the three day test period. We found 9120 users satisfying this criterion. The number of recommendations n was gradually increased from 1 to 10. For each value of n, we averaged $\overline{prec}$ across the 9120 test users.

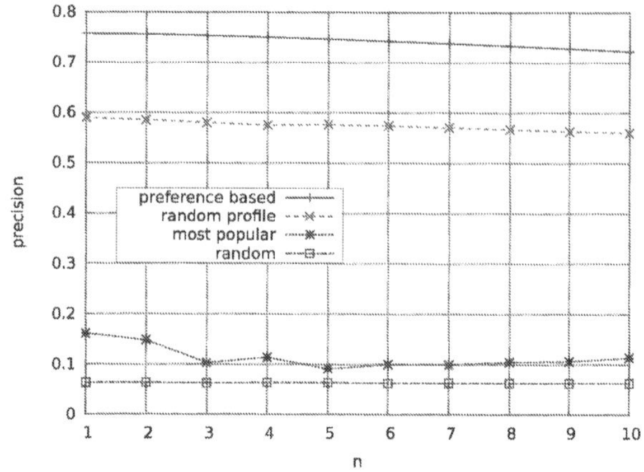

Figure 6: Precision vs. number of recommended series.

Figure 6 shows the average precision for various values of n. As expected, two personalised recommenders clearly outperform the baseline non-personalised ones. We also observe that preference-based recommender is superior to the random profile recommender: the former achieves precision of 0.75, whereas the latter hovers around the 0.55 – 0.6 mark. Note that the obtained precision scores only slightly decrease with n, e.g., preference-based recommender drops from 0.75 for $n = 1$ to 0.72 for $n = 10$. That is, the two simple rule-based recommenders reliably generate accurate recommendations and obtain a high precision, and their performance is stable despite the growth of the recommendation list.

5.2.1 User Profile Temporal Span

One of the key questions in converting the observed viewing logs into user profiles refers to the time span of data considered by the conversion. On the one hand, taking all the available logs into account may lead to reliable profiles and recommendations. On the other hand, outdated logs may lead to imprecise profiles and hamper the accuracy of the recommendations. In this experiment we investigate the temporal aspect of the user profiling.

We evaluate two user profiling methods. The first is denoted as the *complete* profiling and it incorporates all the available user data. The second is the *4-week* profiling and it considers only the four weeks immediately preceding the test period. In both cases, we apply threshold values similar to those used in previous experiments in order determine user subscription to series. Then, we use the preference-based algorithm to generate subscribed series recommendations.

Figure 7 shows the precision and coverage of the recommendations for an increasing from $n = 1$ to $n = 10$ set of recommendations. We observe that precision of recommendations based on the 4-week profiles is superior to the precision of those based on the complete profiles. This is reasonable given that the 4-week profiles are centred on the recent user logs reflecting preferences in a time span close to the test period. However, the improvement in precision comes on the account of coverage. As the 4-week profiles are smaller and contain less subscribed series than the complete profiles, the system struggles to generate as many recommendations as with the complete profiles, and the coverage drops. In both cases, the coverage decreases with n, since

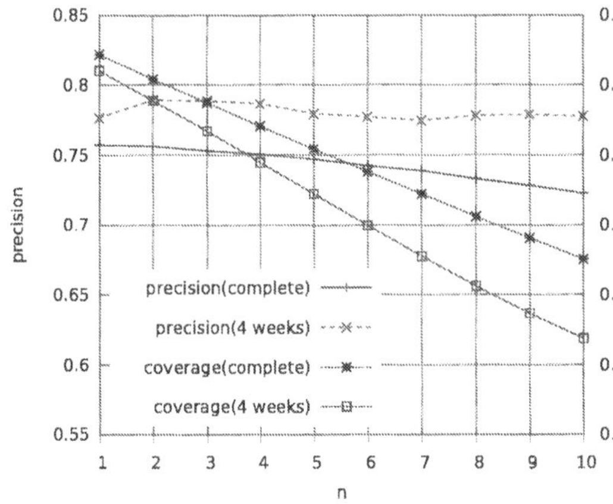

Figure 7: Precision and coverage (complete and 4-week profiles) vs. number of recommended series.

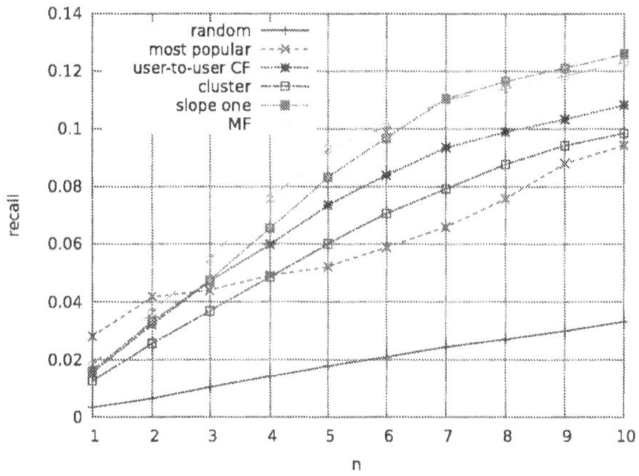

Figure 8: Recall vs. number of recommended series.

the task of generating the required number of recommendations aggravates as the recommendation list grows.

5.3 New Series Recommender

In this section, we present the evaluation of the new series recommender aimed at exposing users to new not yet watched series and virtually subscribing them to new content. Therefore, the evaluation methodology of new series recommender is fairly different. Treating one-off watching events of the recommended series as success indicators may yield a noisy ground truth. Instead, we treat a new subscription to a recommended series as a success. We use the information available beyond the test period to determine "future" subscriptions and measure the ability of the recommender to forecast new subscriptions made in the three day test period. The metric that is measured is recall, i.e., we are interested to assess the portion of new subscriptions that were suggested by the recommender.

We evaluate four personalised (user-to-user CF, cluster-based, slope one, and MF) and two non-personalised (most popular and random) unsubscribed series recommenders. The subscription thresholds are set to $\alpha = 0.3$ and $\beta = 3$, like in previous experiments. The number of similar users is set to $k = 500$ and Pearson's correlation is applied for the user-to-user CF. Clusters used by the clustering recommender are those identified in [17]. Slope one recommender weighs all the items uniformly. Finally, the learning and regularisation parameters of MF were optimised using cross-validation that are not reported due to space limitations.

We included in the test set all the users who subscribed to three new series or more during the three day test period, i.e., users who surpassed the subscription threshold of at least three series during the test period and kept watching these series later on. We found 2803 users satisfying this criterion. The number of recommendations was gradually increased from $n = 1$ to $n = 10$. For each value of n, we averaged $\overline{recall}$ across the 2803 test users.

Figure 8 shows the recall of the six recommenders for various values of n. We observe that from $n = 3$ to $n = 7$, the highest recall is achieved by the MF recommender. This is in line with other works that position MF as the state-of-the-art recommendation technique [12]. Note the high recall achieved by the slope one recommender, which is close to MF and even outperforms it for $n \geq 8$. This supports the findings of [8], which observed that the accuracy of slope one is comparable to that of more complex recommenders, despite its algorithmic simplicity.

The next two algorithms are, respectively, user-to-user CF and cluster-based recommenders. These two are memory-based algorithms and their accuracy is normally lower than of the model-based MF algorithm. Moreover, cluster-based recommender does not use user-to-user similarity scores and this explains its inferiority with respect to user-to-user CF. The lowest recall is achieved by the two non-personalised recommenders. Surprisingly, the top performer for $n \leqslant 2$ is the most popular recommender. This is due to the observed popularity surge of a single series, which attracted during the test period twice the number of views of the second most popular series, and accounted alone for more than 5% of new subscriptions. The most popular recommender identifies the surge and obtains high recall for low values of n.

Overall, the obtained recall scores were low, with the top algorithms achieving $\overline{prec} = 0.12$ for $n = 10$. This is in line with [19], which found that the accuracy of a recommender decreases substantially, if aiming to deliver novel or serendipitous recommendations. Recommendations for not yet subscribed series clearly fall into this category.

5.4 Hybrid Recommender

Finally, we evaluate the overall performance of a hybrid recommender encapsulating the two recommendation components. For each component, we deploy the best performing approach: preference-based for the subscribed and MF for the new recommendations. All the thresholds and parameters are set identically to the standalone experiments. Since we use mixed hybridisation and combine the outputs of the recommenders, each produces five recommendations to generate the final list of $n = 10$ recommendations.

We included in the test set all the users, who satisfy the two criteria of the standalone experiments. That is, the test set contains users, who watched ten programs or more and subscribed to three new series or more during the test period. We found 1907 users satisfying these two criteria. The evaluation metrics we use in this experiment are precision, recall, and coverage. Overall, we obtained $\overline{prec} = 0.221$, $\overline{recall} = 0.227$, and $\overline{cover} = 0.888$. To analyse the performance of the recommender across various users, we sort the

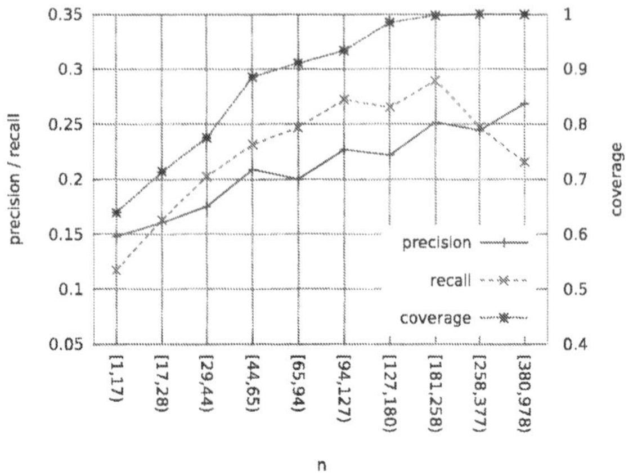

Figure 9: Recall, Precision, and Coverage vs. number of watched programs.

1907 users according to the number of programs watched during the training period (which strongly correlated with the number of programs watched during the test period) and split them into 10 equal-size buckets. We computed the $\overline{prec}$, $\overline{recall}$, and $\overline{cover}$ scores for each bucket.

Figure 9 shows the obtained $\overline{prec}$, $\overline{recall}$, and $\overline{cover}$. We observe that the precision increases with the number of programs watched. This is due to the fact that every watched program improves the accuracy of the user profiles, and, in turn, of the recommendations. An increase in recall is observed for the first eight buckets due to the same reason. However, the recall drops for the last two buckets. We posit that this happens due to the high number of programs watched by users in these buckets. As the number of recommended programs is fixed at 10 and the number of watched programs increases, the recall drops despite the improvement in the accuracy of the user profiles. The coverage of the recommender steadily increases with the number of watched programs, as the list of subscribed series grows and this alleviates the recommendation task.

5.5 Summary

We reported on the evaluation of several approaches for recommending subscribed and new series. Out of the subscribed series recommenders, the one that considers implicit user scores for the subscribed series was found to outperform others. Even a simple rule-based recommender achieved a high precision of 75%. As one may expect, recommending unsubscribed series was harder. We evaluated six recommendation approaches, including the state-of-the-art MF recommender, which achieved the highest recall of 12%. We hybridised the two recommenders and were able to achieve overall average precision and recall scores of around 22%, with a high average user-based coverage of 89%.

It is important to revisit the limitations of the gathered dataset. Note that we have neither reliable indication of the extent of viewing following a program playback nor explicit user feedback for the program. Clearly, obtaining feedback on user experience with the portal is pivotal for the success of catch-up TV recommendations. Finally, it is important to acknowledge the offline nature of our evaluation. In a live system, recommendations can inherently influence user choice, and some programs may receive additional eyeballs only due to the increased exposure through recommendations. Hence, the obtained results underestimate potential uptake of the recommendations, such that results of an online study may surpass those of our offline evaluation.

6. RELATED WORK

We briefly discuss related work pertaining to personalisation and recommendations in the TV domain. These can be grouped into three directions: TV viewer modelling, TV personalisation systems, and group personalisation.

Ardissono et al. [1] investigated the use of hybrid user modelling in the TV domain. Explicit and stereotypical models were combined to capture user preferences for programs. The evaluation showed that enriching the models using community preferences achieved better performance than traditional user modelling. Bellekens et al. [4] introduced the *iFanzy* system with advanced Semantic Web based user modelling capabilities. There, information was extracted from social networks, which resolved the cold start problem and improved the accuracy of the models of new users. Hopfgartner investigated the capture of long-term user interests in the news domain [11]. News items were categorised through their textual content and semantic context, which improved the accuracy of the user models.

O'Sullivan et al. [15] studied the business value of TV personalisation. The *PTVPlus* recommender system they developed applied association rule mining and case-based reasoning methods, and outperformed traditional collaborative filtering recommenders. Zimmerman et al. [20] developed the *Touch and Drag* system, which combined a TV recommender with a usable interface. A user study that was conducted demonstrated the effectiveness of the recommender system. More recent work by Bambini et al. [3] presented a recommender system for *Fastweb*, one of the largest European IPTV providers. The implemented recommender exploited content-based and collaborative filtering techniques and it was observed that up to 30% of recommendations led to the purchasing behaviour.

Masthoff studied how one could cater to the needs of a group of TV viewers [14]. Three different aspects of aggregation of user preferences and the impact of intra-group relationships were investigated. It was shown that aggregated user profiles yielded the highest satisfaction and that users valued the fairness factor. Besides, it was shown that group opinion on a program might fluctuate over time and be affected by other watched programs. Finally, Zhang et al proposed an approach for identifying individual TV viewers behind composite group profiles using subspace clustering [18]. As the number of users behind a composite profile and their preferences were identified, the accuracy of the generated recommendations increased.

Although prior works studied user modelling and personalisation in the TV domain, to the best of our knowledge, none have focussed on the catch-up TV application. Catch-up TV services are still new and a robust catch-up TV recommender requires a dedicated investigation. The fact that in our case the TV programs are grouped, offers an additional domain knowledge that can be incorporated into the recommendation process and differentiates our work from earlier works. To the best of our knowledge, our paper presents the first practical investigation and comparison of recommendation approaches for a catch-up TV.

7. CONCLUSIONS

The convergence of the Social Web and IPTV has exposed users to enormous volumes of content, aggravating the discovery of content of interest. We analysed real-life Australia-wide six month logs of a national catch-up TV provider, which showed the overwhelming volume of the available video content and the choice problem faced by the users. This motivated our work on personalised recommendations that can help the users discover content.

In this work, we evaluated a recommender system for catch-up TV. The recommender, which uses past user interactions to generate TV program recommendations, includes two components. The first recommends subscribed content that the users regularly watch, whereas the second recommends new content that is likely to be of interest for them. We conducted an offline evaluation of several recommendation algorithms and were able to select the best performing algorithms for the two components.

One of the shortcomings of the gathered dataset lies in the unreliable user identification. It is not uncommon for a group of users, e.g., a family, to use the same device to acess the catch-up portal, or, alternatively, for one user to use multiple devices, e.g., computer and tablet. In the future, we aim to develop approaches for identifying composite and duplicate user profiles and evaluate their impact on the accuracy of the generated recommendations.

We will also investigate recommendations for groups of users. TV watching often occurs in groups, e.g., with family or friends, and the recommender should cater for the preferences of the group as a whole and deliver group-based recommendations. Finally, we will investigate various machine learning approaches that can improve the accuracy of the recommendations, and, particularly, of recommendations for new unsubscribed content. We aim to deploy the resulting recommender system into the service offered by our partner broadcaster and their Web-based catch-up portal, and evaluate the performance of the recommender in a longitudinal large scale user study [2].

8. REFERENCES

[1] L. Ardissono, C. Gena, P. Torasso, F. Bellifemine, A. Difino, and B. Negro. User modeling and recommendation techniques for personalized electronic program guides. In *Personalized Digital Television*, pages 3–26. Springer, 2004.

[2] S. Ardon, S. Bensiali, H. Cinis, J. Wang, and S. Berkovsky. Next-generation social TV content discovery. In *International Conference on User Modeling, Adaptation, and Personalization*, 2012.

[3] R. Bambini, P. Cremonesi, and R. Turrin. A recommender system for an IPTV service provider: a real large-scale production environment. In *Recommender Systems Handbook*, pages 299–331. Springer, 2011.

[4] P. Bellekens, G. Houben, L. Aroyo, K. Schaap, and A. Kaptein. User model elicitation and enrichment for context-sensitive personalization in a multiplatform TV environment. In *Proceedings of the European Conference on Interactive TV*, pages 119–128, 2009.

[5] S. Berkovsky. Decentralized mediation of user models for a better personalization. In *Adaptive Hypermedia and Adaptive Web-Based Systems*, pages 404–408. Springer, 2006.

[6] R. Bernhaupt, M. Boutonnet, B. Gatellier, Y. Gimenez, C. Pouchepanadin, and L. Souiba. A set of recommendations for the control of IPTV-systems via smart phones based on the understanding of users practices and needs. In *Proceedings of the European Conference on Interactive TV*, pages 143–152, 2012.

[7] R. Burke. Hybrid recommender systems: survey and experiments. *User modeling and user-adapted interaction*, 12(4):331–370, 2002.

[8] F. Cacheda, V. Carneiro, D. Fernandez, and V. Formoso. Comparison of collaborative filtering algorithms: limitations of current techniques and proposals for scalable, high- performance recommender systems. *ACM Transcactions on Web*, 5(1):2, 2011.

[9] A. Erlandsson, N. Ronblom, and A. Ericson. TV and video 2011 consumer trends, global version. Technical report, Ericsson ConsumerLab, 2011.

[10] J. L. Herlocker, J. A. Konstan, A. Borchers, and J. Riedl. An algorithmic framework for performing collaborative filtering. In *Proceedings of the SIGIR Conference on Research and Development in Information Retrieval*, pages 230–237, 1999.

[11] F. Hopfgartner. Capturing long-term user interests in online television news programs. *TV Content Analysis: Techniques and Applications*, page 309, 2012.

[12] Y. Koren, R. M. Bell, and C. Volinsky. Matrix factorization techniques for recommender systems. *IEEE Computer*, 42(8):30–37, 2009.

[13] D. Lemire and A. Maclachlan. Slope one predictors for online rating-based collaborative filtering. *Society for Industrial Mathematics*, 5:471–480, 2005.

[14] J. Masthoff. Group modeling: Selecting a sequence of television items to suit a group of viewers. *User Modeling and User-Adapted Interaction*, 14(1):37–85, Feb. 2004.

[15] D. O'Sullivan, B. Smyth, D. Wilson, K. Mc Donald, and A. Smeaton. Interactive television personalization. In *Personalized Digital Television*, pages 73–91. Springer, 2004.

[16] G. Shani and A. Gunawardana. Evaluating recommendation systems. *Recommender Systems Handbook*, pages 257–297, 2011.

[17] M. Xu, S. Berkovsky, I. Koprinska, S. Ardon, and K. Yacef. Time dependency in TV viewer clustering. In *TVM2P Workshop, International Conference on User Modeling, Adaptation, and Personalization*, 2012.

[18] A. Zhang, N. Fawaz, S. Ioannidis, and A. Montanari. Guess who rated this movie: identifying users through subspace clustering. In *Proceedings of the International Conference on Uncertainty in Artificial Intelligence*, pages 944–953, 2012.

[19] Y. C. Zhang, D. O. Séaghdha, D. Quercia, and T. Jambor. Auralist: introducing serendipity into music recommendation. In *Proceedings of the International Conference on Web Search and Data Mining*, pages 13–22, 2012.

[20] J. Zimmerman, K. Kauapati, A. Buczak, D. Schaffer, S. Gutta, and J. Martino. TV personalization system. In *Personalized Digital Television*, pages 27–51. Springer, 2004.

Generating Supplemental Content Information Using Virtual Profiles

Haishan Liu
LinkedIn Corporation
2029 Stierlin Court
Mountain View, CA, 94043
haliu@linkedin.com

Mohammad Amin
LinkedIn Corporation
2029 Stierlin Court
Mountain View, CA, 94043
mamin@linkedin.com

Baoshi Yan
LinkedIn Corporation
2029 Stierlin Court
Mountain View, CA, 94043
byan@linkedin.com

Anmol Bhasin
LinkedIn Corporation
2029 Stierlin Court
Mountain View, CA, 94043
abhasin@linkedin.com

ABSTRACT

We describe a hybrid recommendation system at LinkedIn that seeks to optimally extract relevant information pertaining to items to be recommended. By extending the notion of an item profile, we propose the concept of a "virtual profile" that augments the content of the item with rich set of features inherited from members who have already shown explicit interest in it. Unlike item-based collaborative filtering, we focus on discovering the characteristic descriptors that underlie the item-user association. Such information is used as supplemental features in a content-based filtering system. The main objective of virtual profiles is to provide a means to tap into rich-content information from one type of entity and propagate features extracted from which to other affiliated entities that may suffer from relative data scarcity. We empirically evaluate the proposed method on a real-world community recommendation problem at LinkedIn. The result shows that the virtual profiles outperform a collaborative filtering based approach (user who likes this also likes that). In particular, the improvement is more significant for new users with only limited connections, demonstrating the capability of the method to address the cold-start problem in pure collaborative filtering systems.

Categories and Subject Descriptors

H.2.8 [**Database Management**]: Data Mining

Keywords

hybrid recommender systems; feature generation and extraction; model-based recommendation; virtural profiles

http://dx.doi.org/10.1145/2507157.2507213.

1. INTRODUCTION

Large scale recommender systems, in the era of internet scale data deluge, contribute significantly to mitigating information overload by unveiling relevant and interesting objects to users. Rather than hoping for serendipitous encounters, recommender systems bring forth the notion of personalized information discovery by presenting to the user a smaller pool of relevant objects. Collaborative filtering, a popular mechanism for recommendation, is vulnerable to "cold start problems," which has led to the exploration of hybrid recommenders. Hybrid recommenders combine information obtained from different sources and techniques to achieve better outcome. Typically a hybrid recommender system incorporates information from a myriad of sources e.g., content meta data, global popularity, social network and social interaction information, and so on. Each of these information sources offers different level of relevance guarantee at varying computation overhead. Hence, how these information sources are computed and how they are combined play a vital role in the final outcome.

As of today LinkedIn has more than 225 million users. As the largest and most popular professional networking site, LinkedIn presents some unique opportunities and challenges for content discovery and recommendation. It is imperative for the members to be able to discover and subscribe to companies and groups (referred to as community henceforth) that might be relevant to them from a professional context.

In this paper, we describe a hybrid community recommendation system at LinkedIn that optimally combines information from multiple sources. In order to extract more relevant information pertaining to the community to be recommended, i.e., to further extend the notion of content meta data, we have proposed the concept of a "virtual profile" that augments the content meta data with rich set of features inherited from the set of members who have already shown explicit interest in it. In general the notion of virtual profile answers: "What are the most dominant features pertaining to the members who have shown interest in a particular community?" This question essentially maps an object into the same feature space as that of the subscribers'. Content meta data, extended with this inferred information provides additional warranty against cold start problem. LinkedIn data presents a unique opportunity to extend the content features with extracted features since there is no dearth of rich set of information about the subscribers in the data set, which essentially renders the synergy immensely valuable.

The contributions presented in this paper are as follows:

1. A generic content meta data extension method i.e., the virtual profile generation process.
2. A scalable and generic recommendation computation platform that powers multiple real-time recommendation products at LinkedIn.
3. A seamless integration of multiple, heterogeneous data sources to compute the optimal outcome.

The rest or the paper is organized as follows. In Section 2 we briefly review previous effort in hybrid recommender systems where multiple sources of information are utilized. In Section 3 we describe details of the virtual profile generation process and the way it is interfaced with a generic recommender system at LinkedIn. In Section 4 we present experiment results from both online and offline evaluations. The utility of virtual profiles are demonstrated by comparing its performance with various baseline and alternatives. Finally, we conclude the paper in Section 5 and discuss possible future directions.

2. RELATED WORK

There has been a flurry of research in the domain of recommender systems with the objective of improving personalization [1]. Most traditional recommenders are powered by collaborative filtering [10, 21], content-based predictors [9, 18] and knowledge based filtering techniques [13]. Each individual techniques have their own strengths and weaknesses e.g. while collaborative filtering techniques suffer from data sparsity and cold start problems [19], content-based techniques are prone to skewed recommendation [18]. Hybrid recommenders combine the best of both worlds, making the recommenders more robust in practice. Much work has been done to combine multiple recommenders in an effective way to outperform any single one. In [6] Burke depicts a taxonomy of recommender systems, where multiple recommenders are arranged to allow execution in a parallel or cascaded topology. A system described in [5] combines multiple collaborative filtering approaches using a linear combination of static weights learned via linear regression. STREAM [3], which combines multi-tier predictors, uses dynamically generated metrics to learn the next level of predictors. In [15], a hybrid movie recommender system is proposed that uses content based predictors to boost user data which drives the ensuing collaborative filtering based recommendation. The content information is obtained from IMDB and a Naive Bayes classifier is used for building user item profiles. Finally a user-based collaborative filtering is employed to obtain the final recommendation. However, this approach suffers from scalability issues. Pazzani [17] proposed a hybrid recommender system where the content based user profiles are used to group similar users which is subsequently used to predict user preferences.

Previous work has explored ways to propagate information to users from communities they belong to. The intuition is that users with common attributes are more likely to be friends and often form dense communities. For instance, systems described in [16, 14, 2] propose methods to infer incomplete/undisclosed user attributes from their contacts or communities in social networks. These methods work better in cases where more information is available for recommended item than for users. On the other hand, for applications with rich information available about users, we advocate that items to be recommended can be augmented with features from users who have had interaction with them. In other words, these items can be represented as an objects in the same feature space as that of the users. These representations could be thought of "virtual user profiles" or "virtual profiles." This could potentially add another layer of information source to guide the recommendation process. In our approach, we describe a large scale recommender system that combines data from heterogeneous sources including virtual profiles and social network information to serve real time recommendation requests.

3. METHOD

3.1 System Overview

We adhere to building a hybrid recommender system on top of content-based filtering since we have an abundant access to rich-content entities, such as user profiles, which enables a straightforward means for feature extraction, indexing and matching. Target entities (those the client wants recommendations of) are feature extracted and put into an inverted index, and source entities (those the client wants recommendations for) are converted into complex queries against the index. This provides a form of content-based recommendation score where the match is determined by the degree of similarity between the source and target entity features, with different fields weighted by a set of parameters determined by an offline learning-to-rank process.

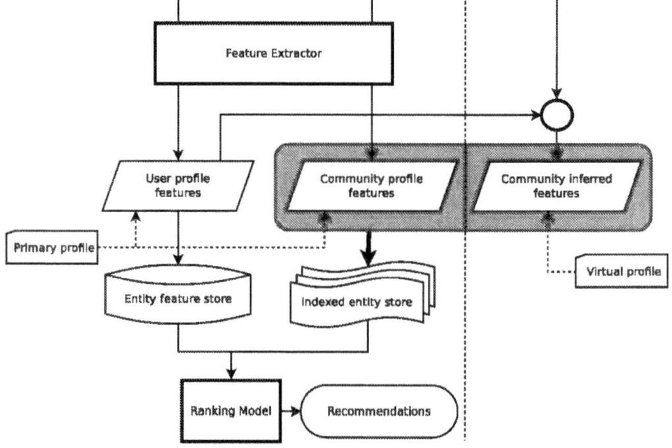

Figure 1: A brief architecture for the recommender system with virtual profiles.

Figure 1 illustrates a brief architecture of the system. On the left side of the dashed line is the core content-based filtering system. The feature space is composed of features extracted from source (e.g., user) and target (e.g., communitiy) entities into standardized fields. Some features are further transformed into pairwise features representing similarity between source and target fields, which are obtained by issuing field-based queries against the inverted index. Extensions to the feature space can be made in the system by including information emanated from various heterogeneous sources, such as virtual profiles (detailed below), network proximity, etc., as additional features to appropriate entities, as is shown on the right side of the figure. These features are fed into an offline regularized logistic regression learning process, and the trained model is subsequently ported online to serve real-time recommendation requests.

We view every entity as being characterized by two set of content features: one extracted from explicit information associated with the entity which we name the "primary profile," and the other inferred from the entity's behavior and association with other entities, which we name the "virtual profile." The main objective of virtual profiles is to provide a means to tap into rich-content information from one type of entity and propagate features extracted from which to other affiliated entities that may suffer from relative data scarcity. Essentially, a virtual profile of an entity is an aggregation of statistically relevant features from primary profiles of affiliated entities, in which way it introduces a collaborative filtering aspect in our content-based filtering system. For example, a virtual profile of a Linkedin group constitutes distinctive features from its participants so that the group can be most effectively distinguished from others.

To first extract features from entities to generate primary profiles, we utilize a feature extractor layer, a standalone service that accumulates underlying entity database change events and identifies various fields in the document. Various types of fields that could be feature extracted include rich text fields, such as job summary, member position summary etc., and specialized fields, such as Geo entities including region, country, city, coordinates, etc.

The presented content-based filtering system can be extended to consider other collaborative filtering aspects, for example, by including network proximity as a feature while computing relevance scores. We describe a method based on the user-community co-affiliation along this line as a comparison in Section 4. As a general platform, every application consuming recommendations from this system can easily build its own logic for reranking/reordering of results based on custom filtering criteria.

3.2 Generating Virtual Profiles

The virtual profile generation process for an entity aims at selecting, from a total of n features of its affiliated entities, a subset with $k < n$ features that is "maximally informative" about the entity. From a classification point of view, the entity that we generate a virtual profile for represents a target class for a set of documents (primary profiles). We need a measure to evaluate the "information content" of each individual feature with regard to the target class. We propose to use mutual information for this purpose. Mutual information measures arbitrary dependencies between random variables. And the fact that the mutual information is independent of the coordinates chosen permits a robust estimation, which makes it suitable for assessing the "information content" of features in complex classification tasks.

In accordance with Shannon's information theory, the uncertainty of a document class C as a random variable can be measured as:

$$H(C) = -\sum_{c \in C} P(c) \log P(c) \,,$$

In this case, a document class is a virtual profile of a target entity, and documents are primary profiles of entities that have or have not been affiliated with the target entity. After knowing the feature vector F, the conditional entropy $H(C|F)$ measures the remaining uncertainty about C:

$$H(C) = -\sum_{f \in F} P(f) \sum_{c \in C} P(c|f) \log P(c|f) \,.$$

And after having observed the feature vector F, the mutual information, i.e., the amount of decreased class uncertainty is defined as:

$$I(C;F) = H(C) - H(C|F) = \sum_{c,f} P(c,f) \log \frac{P(c,f)}{P(c)P(f)} \,,$$

where $P(c, f)$ is the joint probability of class c and feature f.

Therefore, to generate virtual profiles, the goal is to find the optimal feature subset, $S \subseteq F$, such that $I(C;S)$ is maximized. From an information theoretic perspective, selecting features that maximize $I(C;S)$ translates into selecting those features that contain the maximum information about class C. However, locating the optimal subset requires an exhaustive combinatorial search over the feature space, requiring a number of runs equals to $\binom{n}{k}$, where n is the size of the original feature set and k is that of the desired subset. Besides, an exact solution also demands large training sample sizes to estimate the higher order joint probability distribution in $I(C;S)$. For example, Fraser's method [7], a computationally efficient algorithm for calculating the optimal $I(C;S)$, requires for its convergence a number of samples "in the millions" when the number of features in the input vector is larger than 3 or 4.

Given these difficulties, most of the existing approaches approximate $I(C;S)$ based on the assumption of lower-order dependencies between features. For example, a second-order feature dependence assumption is proposed by Battiti [4] to approximate $I(C;S)$ by a greedy incremental selection scheme with a heuristic to account for correlations between features: given a set of already selected features, the algorithm chooses the next feature as the one that maximizes the information about the class corrected by subtracting a quantity proportional to the average mutual information with the selected features.

Unfortunately, the calculation of pairwise feature correlation $I(f, f')$ is impractical in our case because the feature dimension is extremely high given the bag-of-words extracted from textual contents. Therefore, we make a first-order class dependence assumption that each feature independently influences the class variable, which means to select the mth feature, f_m, is independent from the $(m-1)$ already selected features, i.e., $P(f_m|f_1, \ldots, f_{m-1}, C) = P(f_m|C)$. This results in a straightforward greedy algorithm to generate the virtual profile for an entity c, which consists of the following steps: 1) gather features from all primary profiles associated with entities that have an affiliation with c, 2) calculate mutual information, $I(f;c)$, between each feature and c, and 3) select top k features with highest $I(f;c)$ into the virtual profile. More specifically, the mutual information between a specific term (feature value) and target virtual profile, $I(f;c)$, can be calculated as follows.

$$I(f;c) = \sum_{e_f \in \{1,0\}} \sum_{e_c \in \{1,0\}} P(f = e_f, c = e_c) \log \frac{P(f = e_f, c = e_c)}{P(f = e_f)P(c = e_c)}, \quad (1)$$

where f is a random variable that takes values $e_f = 1$ (the entity primary profile contains feature f) and $e_f = 0$ (the entity primary profile does not contain feature f), and c is a random variable that takes values $e_c = 1$ (the entity is affiliated with c) and $e_c = 0$ (the entity is not affiliated with c). The probabilities in Equation 1 can be derived using maximum likelihood estimation.

4. EXPERIMENTS

Our goal is to test if virtual profiles are a useful source of features to improve the recommendation performance. In designing experiments, we want to verify the heuristic assumption that virtual profiles can be made of features greedily selected by mutual information. We also want to compare the performance of virtual profiles with other classic collaborative filtering methods and study their tradeoffs. Furthermore, by experimenting with different parameter settings to generate virtual profiles, we want to provide a general guidance on how virtual profiles can be best implemented in practice.

4.1 Methodologies

We choose a community recommendation problem at LinkedIn as the test application. We gather various feedbacks from the interaction between users and the recommender system. For example, successful recommendations would result in users following certain communities, while users are also presented the choice to opt-out communities at any later point.

We extract three kinds of features from entities (users and communities) in this application domain:

1. content features—features from users' and communities' textual information extracted into predefined standardized fields (e.g., name, industry, description, etc.).
2. virtual profile—as described in Section 3, a set of features selected from a community's followers as supplements to the community's primary profile.
3. co-follows—a collaborative feature representing "users who follow X also follow Y."

The co-follow (CF for short hereafter) feature captures a notion of similarity between communities that is driven by users' preference. To generate CF for a community, from all other communities that it shares followers with, we choose top 50 ones ranked by TF/IDF. And then for each user, we take the closure of communities she has already followed with respect to CF, and select top 50 ones weighted by their TF/IDF scores normalized over the number of communities followed. Communities selected in this way can essentially be seen as recommendations by collaborative filtering. We treat them as an additional feature to be combined with users' content features to generate search queries, which would lead to a larger set of communities to be returned as

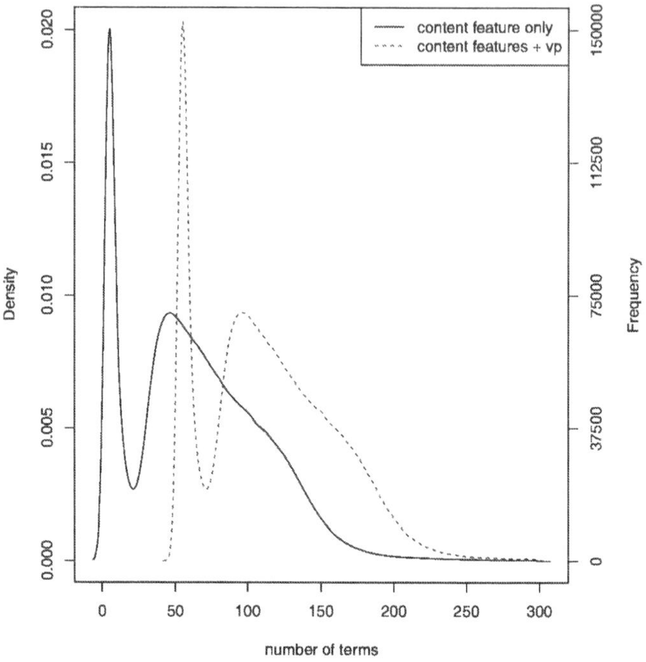

Figure 2: Kernel density of number of selected terms.

matches. And the weight of this feature, similar to others, can be determined in an offline learning process.

The content features extracted for communities contains only three fields (i.e., name, description, and tags). They represent a bare minimum amount of information that is required for a content-based filtering recommender system to function, and are therefore considered as a baseline in the experiment. Co-follows, on the other hand, are designed as an alternative to virtual profiles for comparison, given that they both take into account the interaction among entities.

As for model fitting, we use a training set including 3.4 million positive and 2.2 million negative examples gathered from both explicit and implicit user feedbacks (e.g., follow/unfollow or lack of action to recommendations). We apply an L2-regularized logistic regression with various combination of the above mentioned features. The best model under each configuration is selected by optimizing the area under the ROC curve (AUC-ROC). Performances of different models are evaluated both offline and online. The results are presented in the next sections.

4.2 Results

4.2.1 Offline evaluation

First of all, to qualitatively illustrate the difference from including virtual profiles into content features, Figure 2 shows two kernel densities, comparing the distribution of the number of terms (i.e., feature values that are words extracted from text) for target communites with and without virtual profiles (vp). The size of the virtual profile is capped at 50. It is evident that the original feature space without virtual profiles is a mixture of two underlying distributions: One with a tall spike near zero represents the group of communites that have very limited content information, most

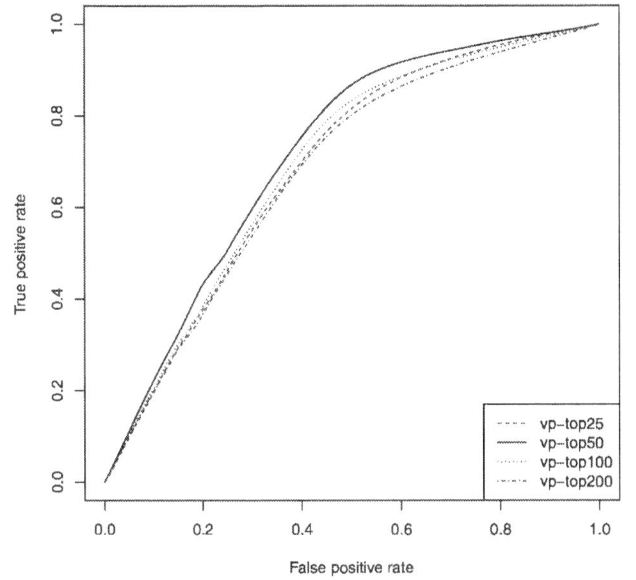

Figure 3: ROC curves for virtual profiles with different number of terms.

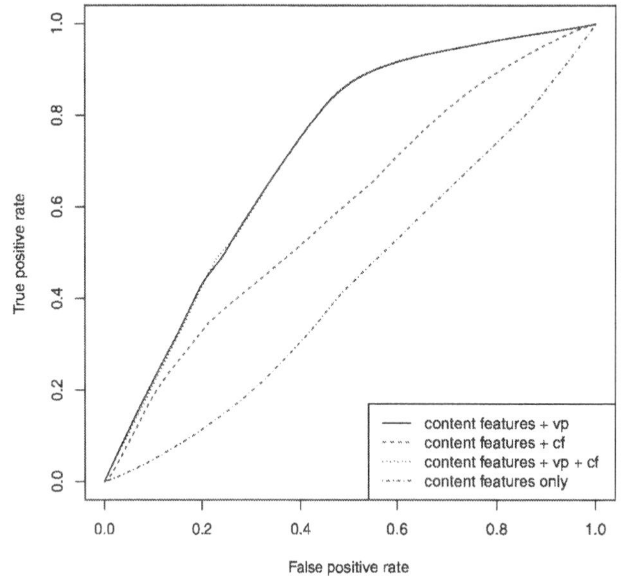

Figure 4: ROC curves for different models.

likely only names available. And the other group are those that have richer content. The effect of adding virtual profiles is shifting the feature number distribution rightwards, increasing the number of terms extracted for both groups by 50 on average. The benefit is especially notable for the first group as they turned from unlikely to be matched to recommendation-worthy with the additional features, as is further demonstrated later in the study of the coverage of recommendations.

Next, we carry out a pilot experiment to empirically determine the optimal size k of virtual profiles. We set k to 25, 50, 100, and 200 and generated virtual profiles accordingly. Figure 3 shows ROC curves of models trained with these various sized virtual profiles. We can see that the trained model performs the best when $k = 50$. This result is inline with a phenomenon known as Hughes effect [12]: As the number of dimensionality increases the predictive power of classifier fails to keep up given a fixed number of training examples. The correlation between features are also part of the reason why including more features does not improve the model performance. We use $k = 50$ for all subsequent experiments discussed below.

Now we proceed to compare models obtained by training with four different feature configurations, namely, (A) content features only, (B) content features plus virtual profiles (vp), (C) content features plus co-follows (cf), and (D) content features plus both vp and cf. It can be seen from Figure 4 that, the ROC curve of model A completely dominates that of model B (with AUCs 0.72 vs. 0.60), and both of them dominate that of model C (AUC 0.44). It can be also seen that the ROC curve of model D is almost identical to that of model C, despite having both the vp and cf features. The same performance pattern is also exhibited in the precision-recall curve, as shown in Figure 5.

Besides classification performance, another important measure that can be evaluated offline is the coverage, which refers to the degree to which recommendations cover the set of available items (item space coverage) [8, 11]. Owing to a distributed algorithm developed at LinkedIn, we are able to calculate recommendations offline for all our 225 million users. Using each of the trained model described above, we calculate a different set of recommendations for each user, with the size of each capped at 50. We counted numbers of times unique communities appeared in recommendations (frequencies) under different models. Figure 6 shows a logarithmic scale of the frequencies sorted in descending order plotted against their ranks.

It is not surprising to see that the baseline curve from the content-features-only model is the lowest since features extracted for communities in this case contains the least amount of information. And the distribution of the recommendation frequency simply reflects the distribution of the amount of textual content of each community (see Figure 2: a large number of communities have only a small number of terms extracted). On the other hand, the curve from the model with the addition of CF visibly bulges outwards from the baseline for about two thirds of points, indicating that those points are getting higher frequencies showing up in recommendations, hence more coverage. Most remarkably, the model with the addition of virtual profiles significantly increased the frequencies for almost all points on the curve except for cases where original baseline frequencies are extremely high or low.

The reason why CF slightly boost the coverage for some communities is because those communities bear little content information yet having followers already. Having follow-

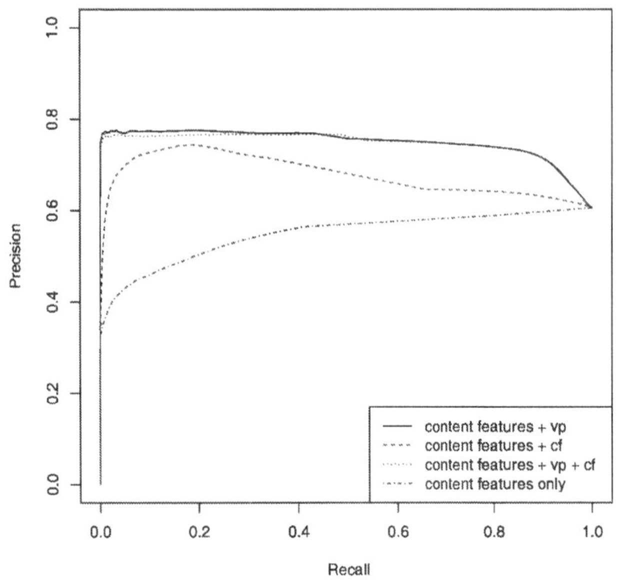

Figure 5: Precision-recall curves for different models.

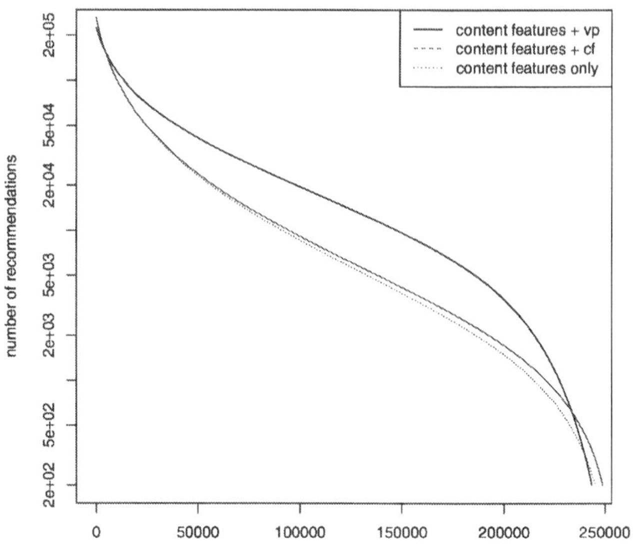

Figure 6: number of recommendations per unique companies.

ers makes them eligible to be potentially included in other communities' CF, and thus leads to a higher chance of being recommended to users. However, for users not having followed any communities at all, CF becomes an empty feature, which is the reason why for about a third of communities, there sees no increase in coverage from CF compared with the baseline. This phenomenon is also illustrated in Figure 7, in which the recommendation frequencies of unique companies are only counted for new users (i.e., users who have not started following communities yet). We observe that the model with CF produces an identical curve to the baseline, while the model with virtual profiles exerts a consistent boost. This shows that CF, as a feature of a collaborative filtering aspect, fails to address cold start, while virtual profiles provides a well-rounded improvement in terms of both coverage and predictive power.

4.2.2 *Online evaluation*

To further evaluate models with various feature configurations (i.e., content features with vp, content features with bm, content features with both vp and bm, and content features only), we deployed them to serve realtime online recommendation requests and compare performances through a bucket test. We assign a distinct bucket of 2.5% randomly selected users from the whole user base to each model. The bucket with the model based only on content features is the control, while others are variants.

The duration of the test is determined according to Wheeler [22], where a conservative estimation of sample size to achieve an 80% power (the probability of correctly rejecting the null hypothesis when it is indeed false) is given by Equation 2.

$$n = (\frac{4r\sigma}{\Delta})^2, \quad (2)$$

where n is the minimum number of samples (impressions to be delivered) for each equal-sized variant, r is the number of variants, σ^2 is the variance of the OEC (Overall Evaluation Criterion [20], a quantitative measure of the experiment's objective), and Δ is the sensitivity, or the desired amount of change. The OEC in this test is the Click-through rate (CTR) of recommendations. Assume each click-through event is a Bernoulli trial with probability $p = ctr_0$ (control CTR, which is estimated from historical data), then $\sigma^2 = p(1-p)$. Applying Equation 2 and knowing the approximate recommendation impressions per day, we derive the length of the test to be 7 days.

Figure 8 presents the results of the test by showing the percentage change in CTR of variant models relative to the control, on each individual day of the test. Overall, the model with virtual profiles outperforms the control by 91.2%. Surprisingly, however, we do not observe any improvement from the model with CF. The model with both virtual profiles and CF increased the CTR by 84.4%. The difference between the two best performing model is not significant (p value 0.062), which is similar to the offline evaluation result. The reason why CF fails to increase overall CTR may be attributed to the fact that only one third of users have followed communities in this particular application, meaning the cold start effect is much pronounced. Virtual profiles, on the other hand, is not vulnerable to this problem since it is content-based and does not rely on pre-existing user-item affiliations, as is demonstrated in this experiment.

5. CONCLUSION AND FUTURE WORK

We presented a generic content meta data extension method called virtual profiles. We also introduced how it is uti-

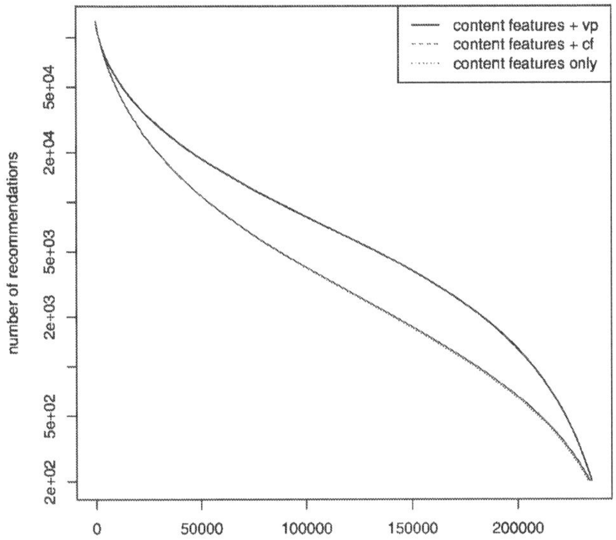

Figure 7: number of recommendations for new users per unique companies.

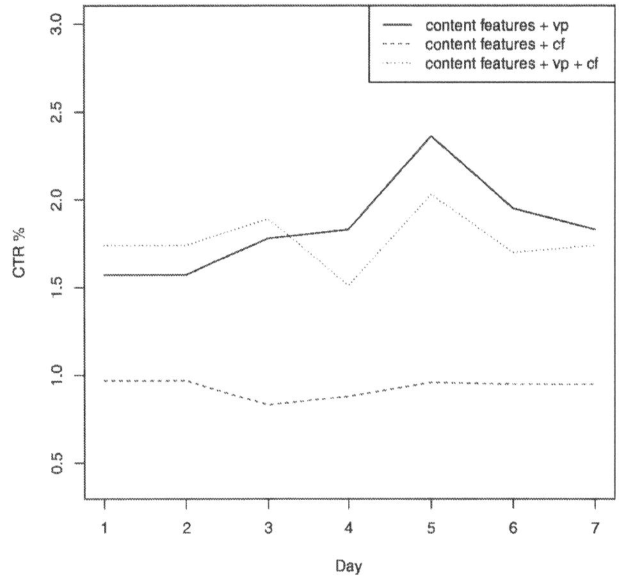

Figure 8: Relative model Click-through rates compared with the baseline.

lized in a scalable and generic content-based hybrid recommender system that powers multiple real-time recommendation products at LinkedIn. The goal of virtual profiles is to provide a means to tap into rich-content information from one type of entity and propagate features extracted from which to other affiliated entities that may suffer from relative data scarcity. It brings a collaborative filtering aspect in the form of a supplement feature to contents in the recommender system. It is shown to outperform a method that directly incorporate network proximity from collaborative filtering.

Experiments supported that our first-order class dependence assumption and the greedy algorithm in calculating the mutual information are reasonable approximations. In future work, we will investigate scalable ways to account for dependencies among features. We plan to explore more term weighting methods besides mutual information, including other classic information theoretic quantities such as the Kullback-Leibler divergence, or TF/IDF. We would also like to experiment with feature transformation techniques to address the feature correlation and dimensionality problems while preserving the capability for field-based search.

6. ACKNOWLEDGEMENTS

We are grateful for the contribution of Christian Posse and Alexis Pribula who have helped in formulating the idea and provided valuable insights.

7. REFERENCES

[1] G. Adomavicius and A. Tuzhilin. Toward the next generation of recommender systems: A survey of the state-of-the-art and possible extensions. *IEEE Transactions on Knowledge and Data Engineering*, 17(6):734–749, 2005.

[2] C. G. Akcora, B. Carminati, and E. Ferrari. Network and profile based measures for user similarities on social networks. In *Information Reuse and Integration (IRI), 2011 IEEE International Conference on*, pages 292–298. IEEE, 2011.

[3] X. Bao, L. Bergman, and R. Thompson. Stacking recommendation engines with additional meta-features. In *Proceedings of the third ACM conference on Recommender systems*, RecSys '09, pages 109–116, 2009.

[4] R. Battiti. Using mutual information for selecting features in supervised neural net learning. *Trans. Neur. Netw.*, 5(4):537–550, July 1994.

[5] R. M. Bell, Y. Koren, and C. Volinsky. The BellKor solution to the Netflix Prize.

[6] R. Burke. Hybrid recommender systems: Survey and experiments. *User Modeling and User-Adapted Interaction*, 12(4):331–370, Nov. 2002.

[7] A. M. Fraser and H. L. Swinney. Independent coordinates for strange attractors from mutual information. *Physical Review A*, 33(2):1134–1140, Feb. 1986.

[8] M. Ge, C. Delgado-Battenfeld, and D. Jannach. Beyond accuracy: evaluating recommender systems by coverage and serendipity. In *Proceedings of the fourth ACM conference on Recommender systems*, RecSys '10, pages 257–260, New York, NY, USA, 2010. ACM.

[9] K. Goldberg, T. Roeder, D. Gupta, and C. Perkins. Eigentaste: A constant time collaborative filtering algorithm. *Inf. Retr.*, 4(2):133–151, July 2001.

[10] J. L. Herlocker, J. A. Konstan, and J. Riedl. Explaining collaborative filtering recommendations. In *Proceedings of the 2000 ACM conference on Computer supported cooperative work*, CSCW '00, pages 241–250, New York, NY, USA, 2000. ACM.

[11] J. L. Herlocker, J. A. Konstan, L. G. Terveen, and J. T. Riedl. Evaluating collaborative filtering recommender systems. *ACM Trans. Inf. Syst.*, 22(1):5–53, Jan. 2004.

[12] G. Hughes. On the mean accuracy of statistical pattern recognizers. *IEEE Trans. Inf. Theor.*, 14(1):55–63, Sept. 2006.

[13] P. B. Kantor. *Recommender systems handbook.* Springer, 2009.

[14] J. Lindamood, R. Heatherly, M. Kantarcioglu, and B. Thuraisingham. Inferring private information using social network data. In *Proceedings of the 18th international conference on World wide web*, pages 1145–1146. ACM, 2009.

[15] P. Melville, R. J. Mooney, and R. Nagarajan. Content-boosted collaborative filtering for improved recommendations. pages 187–192, 2002.

[16] A. Mislove, B. Viswanath, K. P. Gummadi, and P. Druschel. You are who you know: inferring user profiles in online social networks. In *Proceedings of the third ACM international conference on Web search and data mining*, pages 251–260. ACM, 2010.

[17] M. J. Pazzani. A framework for collaborative, content-based and demographic filtering. *Artif. Intell. Rev.*, 13(5-6):393–408, Dec. 1999.

[18] M. J. Pazzani and D. Billsus. The adaptive web. chapter Content-based recommendation systems, pages 325–341. Springer-Verlag, Berlin, Heidelberg, 2007.

[19] P. Resnick, N. Iacovou, M. Suchak, P. Bergstrom, and J. Riedl. Grouplens: an open architecture for collaborative filtering of netnews. In *Proceedings of the 1994 ACM conference on Computer supported cooperative work*, CSCW '94, pages 175–186, New York, NY, USA, 1994. ACM.

[20] R. K. Roy. *Design of experiments using the taguchi approach: 16 steps to product and process improvement.* Wiley, 20011.

[21] B. Sarwar, G. Karypis, J. Konstan, and J. Riedl. Item-based collaborative filtering recommendation algorithms. In *Proceedings of the 10th international conference on World Wide Web*, WWW '01, pages 285–295, 2001.

[22] R. E. Wheller. Portable power. *Technometrics*, 16(2):177–179, 1974.

A People-to-People Content-Based Reciprocal Recommender Using Hidden Markov Models

Ammar Alanazi
King Abdulaziz City for Science and Technology
Computer Research Institute
Riyadh, Saudi Arabia
salanazi@kacst.edu.sa

Michael Bain
The University of New South Wales
Faculty of Engineering
Sydney, Australia
mike@cse.unsw.edu.au

ABSTRACT

Users of online social networks such as dating websites often need help to find successful matches. People-to-people recommender systems can be used in social networks to help users find better matches, which requires solving the problem of *reciprocal* recommendation. However, most existing reciprocal recommenders use either profile similarity or interaction similarity to recommend new matches, without considering *temporal* features. In this paper we introduce a method for temporal reciprocal recommender systems using Hidden Markov Models to generate recommendations. Instead of summarising the whole historical data in one past state, we propose a model that formalises historical data on interactions as a series of successive states changing over time and then tries to find the recommended next state. We have implemented this new approach and the results of testing on industrial-scale data from a real dating website show a noticeable improvement over the previous best-performing recommenders.

Keywords

Recommendation Systems; Content-Based; Hidden Markov Models; People-to-people

Categories and Subject Descriptors

H.3.3 [**Information Search and Retrieval**]: Information filtering; I.5 [**Pattern Recognition**]: Models—*Statistical*; J.4 [**Social and Behavioural Sciences**]: Sociology

1. INTRODUCTION

Most of the existing work on recommender systems is built on the assumption that users' behaviours are static and do not change over time. More recently, this assumption has begun to be relaxed in work on temporal recommendation [9, 10]. However, to the best of our knowledge no work has addressed the problem of temporal *reciprocal* recommendation, such as occurs in the context of online dating, employment websites, and other people-to-people interactions. Reciprocal recommender systems are necessary when the entity recommended to the active user (the one receiving the recommendation) must consent or reciprocate in some way to being the object of the recommendation; typically this "entity" is another user. Analysis of real-world data from a dating website on people-to-people interactions [2] shows that people's behaviour and activity levels do change over time, which leads to the conclusion that we need a dynamic model to generate better recommendations. To capture these temporal changes, in this paper we describe a Hidden Markov Model [8] reciprocal recommender system that captures how each user's behaviour evolves over time and generates recommendations accordingly.

In this research, the main concern is the changes in individuals' behaviours rather than changes in the whole population's behaviour (i.e. trends). Moreover, social networks (including dating websites) are different from typical item-user networks because there is no obvious categorisation of the users in these networks. For example, in article recommender systems, the problem can be abstracted to recommending an article category to minimise the number of classes that the model has to predict. While people can be categorised by age, gender, interests ...etc, minimising the recommendations problem in social networks to recommending a category instead of recommending a specific user does not lead to accurate results. Unlike the classic items recommenders, where the user can just purchase the recommended item, in this type of recommenders the recommendations are people, and these people also have to accept the other party for the interaction to be considered successful.

This paper proposes a Hidden Markov Model to generate recommendations in a people-to-people domain. The model was evaluated using a commercial dataset of a dating website and the results show a significant improvement in success rate. The following section explains how recommendations evolve over a sequence of events. Dataset and model descriptions are in section 3 followed by section 4 that discusses the evaluation of the experiments. Finally, section 5 summarises some of the related literature.

RecSys'13, October 12–16, 2013, Hong Kong, China.
Copyright 2013 ACM 978-1-4503-2409-0/13/10 ...$15.00.
http://dx.doi.org/10.1145/2507157.2507214.

2. GENERATING RECOMMENDATIONS AS A SEQUENCE OF EVENTS

Although research on recommendation systems has been a popular research area in the past few years, there are still some sides to the research problem that have not been studied enough. One of these sides is the temporal aspect of recommendations. Most of the existing recommendations

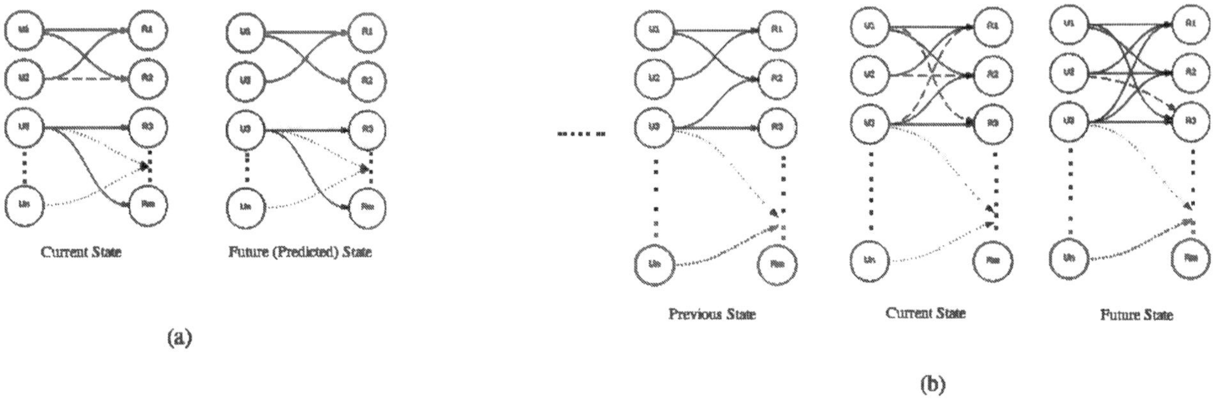

Figure 1: A representation of the recommendations problem as a graph. (a) shows the static representation and (b) shows the dynamic representation of the recommendation system where it is viewed as a graph evolving over time.

algorithms deal with the problem as a two-state problem, in which all historical data is considered one state and the recommendation problem becomes predicting the next state. If the problem was represented as a graph, where vertices are people or items and edges are links between vertices, then the recommendation problem can be minimised to predicting the new links that will appear in the future graph given the links in the present one (figure 1a).

In this paper, we created a model that considers the temporal aspect of the problem and utilises it to better personalise the recommendations. We track the changes of the graph over multiple time periods and observe how it evolves overtime then use this gained knowledge to predict the future graph. This can be extended to predict multiple versions of the graph in the future (i.e. instead of predicting the immediate future state, several successive future states can be predicted, see figure 1b).

3. EXPERIMENTAL DESIGN

3.1 Dataset

The dataset used to test the model is a real-world commercial dataset from a dating website. In the dating domain, there are users who initiate interactions, we call them *senders*, and people who receive interactions, we call them *recipients*. Senders and recipients can overlap which means a user can be a recipient and a sender at the same time. There are different forms of interactions that can be exchanged such as predefined messages, emails and chats. In this research, we use the predefined messages, we call them *messages*, to train and test our model because this is the first method of communication between users in most cases and depending on the success of these messages, users can further their communications and exchange other free text messages.

When a predefined message is sent, the recipient can ignore this message and not reply to it, reply with a positive predefined message or reply with a negative one. We have only considered messages that have replies to them and classify them as positive or negative interactions based on the reply message.

The dataset has over 2 million users and over 20 million interactions exchanged between these users. Therefore, using the whole dataset is not feasible and representative subsets have to be used instead. To generate training and testing data for our model, a time period was randomly selected (e.g. from March 1st to March 15th, 2009) and all active users during this time period were used as the experiment population. Then, for users in the selected population, all their interactions, even interactions outside the selected time period, were obtained and used to build the model. Several populations were generated and average results across these populations will be presented later in this paper.

The average population size is over 158,000 users of which a little over 14,000 were recipients and about 150,000 were senders. These users exchanged just over a million message between them. Each population was divided to 70% training data and 30% testing data.

This dataset was chosen because it is a real-world commercial reciprocal dataset that has temporal dynamics. Although users' life cycles are mostly short in a dating website, there are several lifecycle phases to capture and these changes between phases have their effects on the decision of initiating an interaction and the decision of accepting one.

3.2 Recommendation Using Hidden Markov Models

To capture the concept of recommendations as a sequence of events, we represent each interaction I_k in the model as a sequence of size n as follows:

$I_k = (O_{k-n}, O_{k-n+1}, O_{k-n+2}, ..., O_k)$ if $k \geq n$

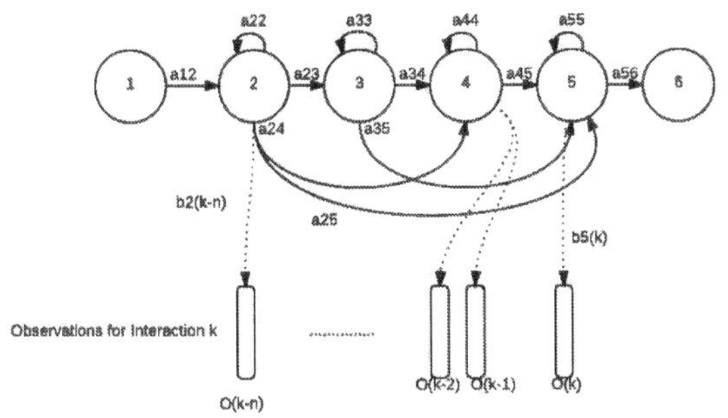

Figure 2: A Hidden Markov Model for people-to-people recommender.

$I_k = (\phi, \phi, ..., O_{k-2}, O_{k-1}, O_k)$ if $k < n$
Where O_k is the k_{th} observation vector. Each observation vector consists of: (1) a selected set of profile data for the sender and the recipient, (2) a set of derived data such as ages of the sender and the recipient and physical distance between them, (3) a set of temporal data such as activity in the past 7 days and activity in the past 28 days. Each interaction is then classified to a successful or a failed interaction. An HMM is then trained using the training data which consists of interactions and their classes and the resulted model is used to predict new interactions. The interactions that are predicted to be successful comprise the generated recommendations. The proposed HMM is shown in Figure 2. We used the Hidden Markov Models Toolkit (HTK) to implement this model.

The model in the top layer is the hidden model that represents the user's behaviour to interactions and the bottom layer shows the observable sequence of interactions. The variable a_{ij} is the transition probability from state i to state j, $b_i(j)$ is the probability of seeing observation vector j in state i and $O(k)$ is the k_{th} observation vector. HMM was the model of choice because it has been reported to work successfully in capturing temporal changes [9] and it has been used in several domains with positive results.

Another factor to consider was to decide whether to implement each observation as a time period (i.e. interactions in a week) or as an event (i.e. a message sent/received). The latter was chosen because a day in an active user's life cycle can be equal to a week or more in a the life cycle of a less active user. This serves as a method of normalisation over the whole population.

Finally, the sequence is built from the perspective of the recipient users because in a reciprocal recommender, the recipient is the one who has to make the final decision.

4. EVALUATION

The proposed model in section 3.2 was evaluated using a dataset obtained from a commercial dating website. Users of the website did not have access to recommendations generated by our model and therefore the model was evaluated using historical data.

4.1 Evaluation Metrics

Two metrics were used to evaluate our model. The first one is the *Success Rate* which is defined as the proportion of generated recommendations that are correct. The other metric used to evaluate the model is *Recall* which is the proportion of successful interactions in the testing set that were predicted by the model. Success rate is equivalent to the standard metric of Precision.

More formally, let R be the set of recommendations generated by the model, R_+ be the subset of R that are correct, I be the set of successful interactions in the testing data and $Size(S)$ is the size of a set S.

$$SuccessRate = \frac{Size(R_+)}{Size(R)}$$

$$Recall = \frac{Size(R_+)}{Size(I)}$$

4.2 Results and Discussion

After training the model with training data, we evaluated the model by asking it to predict whether an interaction will be successful or not. The testing data was different from the training data and it comprise about 30% of the size of the dataset used for the experiment. We have tried different values of n to decide on the one that gives the best results. The predicting accuracy of the system was around 76% but this is for predicting an interaction to be a success or a failure.

The interactions that were predicted to be successful are considered to be the generated recommendations. The success rate in generating these recommendations was 47.1% and recall was 4.9%. The success rate of other collaborative filtering recommendation systems that used the same dataset such as [6] was about 38% with recall 3.6%. Additionally, other content-based recommendation systems that used the same dataset such as [4] have a success rate of about 30% and a recall of about 4%.

In the domain of social networks with the commercial dataset that we have used, it is very difficult to get an improvement in recommendations' success rate and an improvement of about 9% is considered very valuable and significant. Moreover, since the model is content-based, this means that it performs well with new users including users who have no or few interactions [1]. While the results of testing the model on new users who were not included in the training data (table 2) are positive, more specific tests need to be performed to discover the exact figures for each subgroup in the testing population. More precisely, we need to discover what is the success rate of recommendations for users who have not made any interactions yet, for users who have made a few interactions and for people who have made enough number of interactions. More detailed results are shown in table 1 and table 2.

5. RELATED WORK

Although recommender systems have been investigated thoroughly in the literature, there has been little research on temporal aspects of the recommendations problem. Few algorithms [5, 9] were designed recently with temporal aspects and they showed encouraging results. However, all of these algorithms were designed for people-to-item domains.

Another area that has not been researched intensively is the people-to-people recommendation systems. Recent

Table 1: Summary of results using different n values.

n	Success Rate	Recall
2	0.482	0.034
3	0.441	0.043
4	0.436	0.045
5	0.447	0.044
6	0.471	0.049
7	0.466	0.033
8	0.459	0.067

Table 2: Results when testing the model with new users that were not included in the test population.

Number of Users	38000
Number of Interactions	81000
Value of n	6
Success Rate	0.466
Recall	0.169

works [4, 6, 3, 7] on such a domain reported significant improvement in people-to-people recommenders. However, the temporal changes in users' preferences and behaviours are not emphasised in these models due the use of static representation of the recommendation problem.

6. CONCLUSION AND FUTURE WORK

In this paper we presented a model for people-to-people recommendations using HMM that can capture the temporal changes of users' behaviours and generates better personalised recommendations based on this. Evaluating this model using a commercial dataset for a dating website shows a significant improvement in the success rate of recommendations.

The model is built using content-based data only and we believe that extending the model to use some collaborative filtering techniques can improve it. For example, a temporal matrix factorization approach to collaborative filtering [10] would be interesting to extend to reciprocal recommendation. In addition, more testing is required to investigate the success rate and recall for users with no or few interactions. Finally, a method of ranking the generated recommendations and selecting the top-N can improve the success rate.

Acknowledgments

We would like to thank Smart Services Cooperative Research Centre and their industrial partners for providing the datasets.

7. REFERENCES

[1] G. Adomavicius and A. Tuzhilin. Toward the next generation of recommender systems: A survey of the state-of-the-art and possible extensions. *IEEE Transactions on Knowledge and Data Engineering*, 17(6):734–749, June 2005.

[2] A. Alanazi and M. Bain. Ranking interaction-based collaborative filtering recommendations using temporal features in online dating. In *Proceedings of the 18th IBIMA Conference*, May 2012.

[3] Y. S. Kim, A. Mahidadia, P. Compton, X. Cai, M. Bain, A. Krzywicki, and W. Wobcke. People recommendation based on aggregated bidirectional intentions in social network site. In *Knowledge Management and Acquisition for Smart Systems and Services*, pages 247–260. Springer, 2010.

[4] Y. S. Kim, A. Mahidadia, P. Compton, A. Krzywicki, W. Wobcke, X. Cai, and M. Bain. People-to-people recommendation using multiple compatible subgroups. In *AI 2012: Advances in Artificial Intelligence*, pages 61–72. Springer, 2012.

[5] Y. Koren. Collaborative filtering with temporal dynamics. *Communications of the ACM*, 53(4):89–97, April 2010.

[6] A. Krzywicki, W. Wobcke, X. Cai, A. Mahidadia, M. Bain, P. Compton, and Y. Kim. Interaction-based collaborative filtering methods for recommendation in online dating. In L. Chen, P. Triantafillou, and T. Suel, editors, *Web Information Systems Engineering, AI WISE 2010*, volume 6488 of *Lecture Notes in Computer Science*, pages 342–356. Springer Berlin / Heidelberg, 2010.

[7] L. Pizzato, T. Rej, T. Chung, I. Koprinska, and J. Kay. Recon: a reciprocal recommender for online dating. In *Proceedings of the fourth ACM conference on Recommender systems*, pages 207–214. ACM, 2010.

[8] L. Rabiner. A Tutorial on Hidden Markov Models and Selected Applications in Speech Recognition. *Proceedings of IEEE*, 77(2):257–286, 1989.

[9] N. Sahoo, P. Vir Singh, and T. Mukhopadhyay. A hidden markov model for collaborative filtering. *MIS Quarterly-Management Information Systems*, 36(4):1329, 2012.

[10] J. Sun, K. Varshney, and K. Subbian. Dynamic matrix factorization: A state space approach. In *Proc. 2012 IEEE Intl. Conf. on Acoustics, Speech and Signal Processing (ICASSP)*, pages 1897–1900. IEEE, 2012.

Acquiring User Profiles from Implicit Feedback in a Conversational Recommender System

Henry Blanco
Faculty of Computer Science
Free University of Bozen-Bolzano
Bozen-Bolzano, Italy
University of Oriente
Santiago de Cuba, Cuba
Henry.BlancoLores@stud-inf.unibz.it

Francesco Ricci
Faculty of Computer Science
Free University of Bozen-Bolzano
Bozen-Bolzano, Italy
fricci@unibz.it

ABSTRACT

Query revisions in a conversational system can be efficiently computed by assuming that the profiles of the potential users are in a predefined, a priori known and finite set. However, without any additional knowledge of the actual profiles distribution, the system may miss the true profiles of the users, hence deteriorating the system performance. We propose a method for identifying a tailored set of profiles that is acquired by analysing the implicitly shown preferences of the users that interacted with the system. We show that with the proposed method the system can efficiently identify good query revisions.

Categories and Subject Descriptors

H.3.3 [**Information Storage and Retrieval**]: Information Search and Retrieval—*Information filtering*

Keywords

Recommender systems; conversational systems; profile learning; utility function

1. INTRODUCTION

Preference elicitation methods based on implicit feedback are used in Recommender Systems (RS) to deal with users lacking the motivation to completely specify their preferences up front and to help them to unveil preferences that they may not be even aware of [5]. These methods acquire the user model by observing how the user interacts with the RS and are typically implemented in conversational systems. This means that, in a series of user-system interactions, the system acquires and revises the user preferences by monitoring the user reactions to the information or the recommendations shown [5].

We introduced in [2] a conversational technique, which was further improved in [1], aimed at helping users to revise their queries when searching in a product catalog. The products are described by their features and the system suggests query revisions that are likely to retrieve products which maximize the user utility. For example, in our model if the user submits the query "I want a hotel with AC and parking", the system, rather than immediately retrieving the products that satisfy this query, may suggest some query revisions such as: "are you interested also in a sauna; or in a tennis court?". User preferences are then inferred by comparing the query revision chosen by the user, among those that were suggested. For instance, in the above example, the user may additionally request hotels with "sauna" and not "tennis court". The system generated query revisions are those estimated to retrieve products with the largest user's utility, according to the inferred preferences.

In [1] we overcame the computational complexity of finding good query revisions, which is described in [2], by assuming that the users can be modelled with a large but predefined finite set of profiles. Here a profile is a vector of weights which conveys the importance the user assigns to each product feature. The predefined profiles represent the possible users that the system believes it may interact with.

In this paper we reduce the computation time needed to identify the best query revisions by considering a better representative set of profiles: the system iteratively adds to the considered set of profiles those estimated to belong to the users that approached the system. We call this process "acquiring user profiles" because the users will not explicitly reveal their preferences and it is up to the system to conjecture the definition of their profiles by observing their user-system interactions. We show that the proposed method does identify good query revisions and the computation time, compared to the case when the same number of uniformly distributed profiles are used, is reduced.

The paper is organized as follows. Related work is discussed in Section 2. Section 3 describes our models for representing products, queries, user preferences and the unfolding of the user-system interaction. The experiment design and the results are shown in Section 4. Finally the conclusions and future work are described in Section 5.

2. RELATED WORK

In recommendation approaches where items are described by their features, the user profile, which models the user's preferences, is typically a vector of weights measuring the importance assigned by the user to each feature or feature

RecSys'13, October 12–16, 2013, Hong Kong, China.

http://dx.doi.org/10.1145/2507157.2507217.

value. While in content-based approaches the user profile is generally built by mining the users ratings [4] (explicit feedback), in our approach the user profile is constructed by observing a series of user selections among alternative system suggested queries, which is a kind of implicit feedback.

A popular approach where feature-based user preferences are estimated using the user's choices in products comparisons, rather than ratings to items, is Conjoint Analysis [6]. Here the estimation of the user profile depends on several factors: the utility model for each feature (e.g. linear, not linear), the products presented to stimulate the elicitation of the user preferences, the method for estimating the user utility function (e.g., multiple regression analysis).

The major problems are here generated by the large number of products that the user is required to compare and the consequent complex estimation of the true user utility function. In our work we have simplified the preferences elicitation process by iteratively acquiring from the complete user profiles space a small number of profiles compatible with the current user's inferred preferences. This is done only if the system has not yet acquired a profile that is compatible with the current user's (implicitly acquired) preferences.

In Analytic Hierarchy Processing, a popular multi-criteria decision making technique, the feature importance weights are acquired by asking the user to perform pair-wise comparisons between product features [3]. Even in this case the main problem is the large number of pairwise comparisons to be made by the user. Conversely the number of comparisons that the user is required to make in our approach is significantly smaller because only the queries with the largest estimated utility are suggested.

Finally, in the Compound Critiquing approach the importance of the product features (weights) is also used to suggest the best products to the user [7]. Here the feature importance weights are modified according to the user critiques to the selected products. But these profiles are not preserved along the various user-system interactions, making impossible the successive analysis on the users' preferences. Conversely in our approach we maintain this information and we are able to elicit the true preferences' distribution of the users.

3. MODELS AND ALGORITHM

3.1 Queries and Products

A product is modeled by an n-dimensional Boolean vector $p = (p_1, \dots, p_n)$ with n attributes. Boolean product features, such as Air Conditioning, are modeled as Boolean attributes, where $p_i = 1$ ($p_i = 0$) means that the product has (not) the i-th feature. Moreover, using Boolean attributes it is also possible to model discrete features by representing each particular discrete feature value with a single Boolean attribute [1]. A catalogue is a set of products $C = \{p^{(1)}, \dots, p^{(k)}\}$.

Likewise, queries are represented with Boolean vectors $q = (q_1, \dots, q_n)$, where $q_i = 1$ means that the user desires products having the i-th attribute and $q_i = 0$ means that the user has not yet declared her interest on that feature.

A query is *satisfiable* if there exists a product in the catalogue C such that all the features expressed in the query as desired ($q_i = 1$) are present in that product. More details and examples can be found in [1].

3.2 Query Editing Operators

We consider a scenario where the system, with an appropriate GUI, suggests query revisions to the user. These query revisions are generated using application specific editing operators, as those listed here and considered in this study:

- $add_1(q, i)$, $i \in idx0(q)$;
- $trade_{1,2}(q, i, j, k)$, $i \in idx1(q)$ and $j, k \in idx0(q)$;
- $add_2(q, i, j)$, $i, j \in idx0(q)$;
- $trade_{1,3}(q, i, j, k, t)$, $i \in idx1(q)$ and $j, k, t \in idx0(q)$.

$idx0(q)$ and $idx1(q)$ are the sets of indexes corresponding to not requested and requested features in q respectively. The operators add_x extend the query q by adding one or two features not yet requested. Similarly, the operators $trade_{x,y}$ extend the query q by considering two or three not yet requested features in detriment of one already requested. The new queries generated by these operators can be presented to the user, however, the system's goal is not to suggest all the possible query revisions, but only those that retrieve products with the largest utility for the user.

3.3 User Utility Function

A user utility function, or user profile, is defined by a vector of weights $w = (w_1, \dots, w_n)$, $0 \leq w_i \leq 1$. w_i models the importance that the user assigns to the i-th feature of a product: $w_i = 0$ means that the user has no desire for the i-th feature; if $w_i > w_j$ then the i-th feature is more important than the j-th one; and if $w_i \geq w_j$ then the i-th feature is at least as important as the j-th one. If $w_i = w_j$ then the user is indifferent between these two features. The utility of the product $p = (p_1, \dots, p_n)$ is as follows:

$$U_w(p) = \sum_{i=1}^{n} w_i \times f_i(p) \quad (1)$$

where $f_i(p)$ is the value function of the i-th feature of p. Moreover, the utility of the query q for a user with profile w, $U_w(q)$, is defined as the utility $U_w(p)$ of a product p with the same definition as q, i.e., $q = p$.

3.4 User-System Interaction

The considered user-system interaction is described in Figure 1. Here we assume that: 1) the system does not explicitly ask the user about her preferences; 2) the users are rational and prefer products with larger utility; 3) the system contemplates a finite number of predefined profiles P, that is initially small (just 5 in our experiments) and it is expanded anytime the system does not find in P a profile compatible with the current user's implicitly expressed preferences.

A user-system interaction evolves in cycles. At the beginning of a cycle (steps 3 and 4) the user either submits the initial query (first cycle) or selects one query revision in the *AdviseSet* (successive cycles). By observing the user selection the system infers some constraints Φ on the user utility function (step 5). That is, if q_s is the selected query, then the system infers the constraints $U_w(q_s) \geq U_w(q)$, for all the suggested queries $q \in AdviseSet$. Note that here w is unknown. If the set P_Φ of the system's contemplated profiles in P that are compatible with the inferred constraints Φ is not empty then the candidate query revisions are generated by using the query editing operators discussed in Section 3.2 and the queries that are not *satisfiable* are discarded

1. $\Phi = \emptyset$, $P_\Phi = P$ acquired profiles, $AdviceSet = \emptyset$
2. **do** {
3. Present the *AdviceSet* to the user;
4. q_s = initial query or one in the *AdviceSet*;
5. Infer constraints analysing q_s, and add them to Φ;
6. Identify P_Φ, the compatible profiles in P;
7. **if** $P_\Phi \neq \emptyset$
8. Generate satisfiable *CandidateQueries*;
9. $AdviceSet = NotDominated(CandidateQueries)$;
10. $AdviceSet = TopKUtility(AdviseSet)$;
11. **else**
12. Generate compatible profiles and add them to P
13. } **while** ($AdviceSet \neq$ null and user wants advice)

Figure 1: User-System interaction process.

(step 8). In order to suggest the query revisions that are more likely to increase the user utility, the system first discards the queries that are proved to be *dominated* (step 9) and then select the top-K queries with the largest expected utility.

A query $q \in CandidateQueries$ is considered *dominated* if there exists another query $q' \in CandidateQueries$ such that for all the weight vectors $w \in P_\Phi$: $U_w(q') > U_w(q)$. Finally the top K queries (5 in our experiments) with the largest expected utility are identified and included in the *AdviseSet* to the user (step 10). The expected utility of a query is computed as $E[q] = \frac{1}{|P_\Phi|}\sum_{w \in P_\Phi} U_w(q)$.

Otherwise, if there is no profile in P compatible with the inferred constraints in Φ (else statement) then there is a failure point and the system generates a small set of profiles, which are compatible with Φ, and adds them to P (more information on this step is provided in the next section).

This cycle is repeated until the user does not want more advices or there are no more query suggestions. Note that when a new user approaches the system this interaction is repeated and eventually new profiles are added to P, making P larger and larger as needed.

3.5 Acquiring User Profiles

As mentioned in Section 3.4 the absence of compatible profiles is a failure point and prevents the computation of the query revisions for the user. At this point the system conjectures that the current users's profile is missing and adds some profiles that satisfy the inferred constraints. We perform this step by first generating some random profiles $w = (w_1, \ldots, w_n)$ taken from the system conjectured distribution of the user profiles (uniform in our experiments, i.e., $w_i = rand([0,1])$). Then, the generated profiles are added to P, the system considered profiles, if they satisfy the inferred constraints in Φ. In this situation we say that the system has "acquired" the current user profile. These generated compatible profiles update the system knowledge of the users. In our experiments we have considered scenarios where 2, 10 or 20 profiles are generated and acquired when the system does not find in P a compatible profile while interacting with a user. We decided to add more than one single compatible profile to speed up the acquisition process and because these generated profiles represent only hypotheses on the true user's profile.

4. EXPERIMENTS AND RESULTS

In order to validate the proposed user profile acquisition technique and double check that it is not jeopardising the system ability to suggest good query revisions, as shown in [1], we conducted several experiments where 500 virtual users interacted with our system according to the user-system interaction described in Section 3.4.

In order to understand how much difficult it is the profile acquisition task and to identify the best number of profiles that should be included at each interaction failure point, we simulated different scenarios where the users approaching the system were clustered into 1, 5 or 10 groups and where the number of "acquired" profiles at each failure point was 2, 10 or 20. We simulated users in a group with similar preferences by generating their profiles using a normal distribution around a group's prototype profile: for each group, a group's prototype $w^* = (w_1, ..., w_n)$ was randomly set and the other profiles in the group were generated by enforcing that $w = w^* \times \mathcal{N}(1, \sigma)$, where $\mathcal{N}(1, \sigma)$ is the normal distribution with average 1 and standard deviation σ. We used two values for σ, 0.1 and 0.05, to model groups with more or less disperse members. The vectors of weights were then normalized to sum to 1.

We mainly examined the impact of the number of acquired profiles and the quality of the system suggestions, measured with the average utility shortfall. The utility shortfall is the difference in utility between the query selected by the user from the *AdviceSet* and the query that retrieves the products with the largest true user's utility. We used one product database comprising 4056 hotels in "Trentino" (Italy), each of them described by 11 features [1].

We have found that the larger is the number of different user groups the larger is the number of profiles that the system must add to P while interacting with the users in order to provide the same quality of query suggestions, i.e., a utility shortfall smaller than 0.05. This can be observed in columns 4 and 6 of Table 1. In order to achieve this level of performance the system adds more profiles when interacting with more disperse groups of users ($\sigma = 0.1$) compared to when interacting with groups of users with less diverse preferences ($\sigma = 0.05$). Moreover, this conclusion is also supported by the fact that for a given number of acquired profiles (e.g., 45 or 150, as in columns 3 and 5) the quality of query suggestions decreases when interacting with an increasing number of user groups. That is, the task of acquiring the user profiles becomes harder when interacting with more heterogeneous users.

Furthermore, we have discovered that acquiring a larger number of profiles at each failure point (10 or 20) is not effective, especially when there are more groups of diverse users. (see columns 3 and 5 of Table 1). This is better illustrated in Figure 2 that is showing the case when the system interacted with 10 groups of users with dispersion $\sigma = 0.1$. Adding less profiles at each failure point lets the system to converge faster to low utility shortfall values. Furthermore, it is shown that acquiring a selected set of profiles, using the proposed method, compares favourably to an approach where a uniformly distributed set of profiles (of the same cardinality) is used ("no learning").

Finally, the computation time for generating the query suggestions for a user when P contains 100 profiles is around 22 milliseconds. This is roughly 4 times smaller than what is required for computing the query suggestions (86 mil-

Table 1: Utility Shortfall (USh) for different sizes of the acquired profiles set and number of acquired profiles to obtain a desired USh level

		$\sigma = 0.05$		$\sigma = 0.1$	
# of groups	# of profiles acquired at a failure point	USh with 45 added profiles	# profiles for USh ≤ 0.05	USh with 150 added profiles	# profiles for USh ≤ 0.05
1	2	0.050	44	0.050	150
	10	0.052	45	0.076	320
	20	0.054	50	0.116	400
5	2	0.077	66	0.069	170
	10	0.311	140	0.126	280
	20	0.370	220	0.216	460
10	2	0.120	72	0.077	200
	10	0.371	200	0.139	420
	20	0.399	300	0.264	650

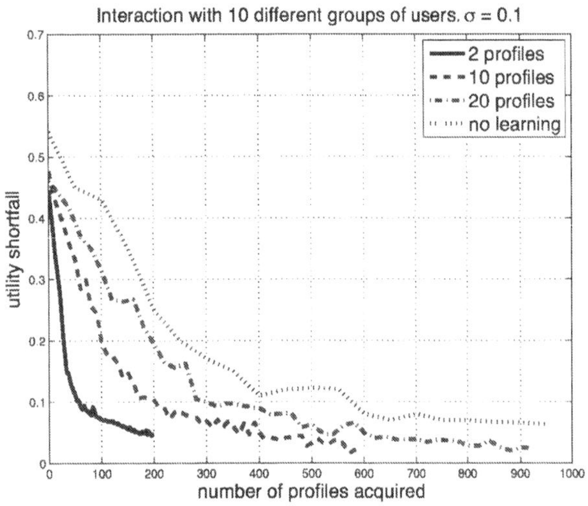

Figure 2: Average utility shortfall in simulated interactions - 10 groups of users, $\sigma = 0.1$.

liseconds) when considering one thousand randomly sampled profiles, which is the number of profiles necessary to achieve the same level of performance of our proposed method with 100 profiles (see Figure 2).

5. CONCLUSIONS AND FUTURE WORK

In this paper we have introduced a method for identifying a tailored set of profiles that represents the users that have interacted and may interact in the future with a conversational system.

We have shown that acquiring this tailored set of profiles is harder when the users are clustered in several groups with a large diversity of their preferences. Additionally, we have shown that acquiring few well selected profiles every time the system fails to generate query suggestions makes the system to converge fast to better performances. We have also shown that the proposed approach substantially improves a simpler method where the profiles are added using the system known a priori distribution of the users preferences. It is worth noting that using the proposed method the system can suggest good query revisions just considering few but tailored profiles and the system response time in multiple and concurrent interactions is in the order of the few seconds per user, making it possible to use it in realistic web scenarios.

Nevertheless, there are some important issues that must be addressed in future work such as initialising the system with a better a priori distribution of user profiles, and devising a solution for removing profiles that may not be anymore suited to represent the users approaching the system, i.e., supporting the dynamic change of the distribution of the users' preferences.

6. REFERENCES

[1] H. Blanco and F. Ricci. Inferring user utility for query revision recommendation. In *Proceedings of the 28th Symposium On Applied Computing*, volume 1, pages 245–252. ACM, 2013.

[2] D. Bridge and F. Ricci. Supporting product selection with query editing recommendations. In *Proceedings of the 2007 ACM conference on Recommender systems*, RecSys '07, pages 65–72. ACM, 2007.

[3] D.-N. Chen, P. J.-H. Hu, Y.-R. Kuo, and T.-P. Liang. A web-based personalized recommendation system for mobile phone selection: Design, implementation, and evaluation. *Expert Syst. Appl.*, 37(12):8201–8210, 2010.

[4] P. Lops, M. de Gemmis, and G. Semeraro. Content-based recommender systems: State of the art and trends. In F. Ricci, L. Rokach, B. Shapira, and P. B. Kantor, editors, *Recommender Systems Handbook*, pages 73–105. Springer Verlag, 2011.

[5] L. McGinty and J. Reilly. On the evolution of critiquing recommenders. In F. Ricci, L. Rokach, B. Shapira, and P. B. Kantor, editors, *Recommender Systems Handbook*, pages 419–453. Springer Verlag, 2011.

[6] M. Scholz. From consumer preferences towards buying decisions. In *21st Bled eConference eCollaboration: Overcoming Boundaries Through Multi-Channel Interaction*, pages 223–235, 2008.

[7] J. Zhang and P. Pu. A comparative study of compound critique generation in conversational recommender systems. In *Procs. of 4th Intl. Conf. on Adaptive Hypermedia & Adaptive Web-Based Systems*, pages 234–243. Springer-Verlag, 2006.

A System for Advice Provision in Multiple Prospect Selection Problems

Amos Azaria[1] and Sarit Kraus[1,2] and Ariella Richardson[3]
[1] Department of Computer Science, Bar-Ilan University, Ramat Gan 52900, Israel
[2] Institute for Advanced Computer Studies University of Maryland, MD 20742
[3] Jerusalem College of Technology, Jerusalem 91160, Israel
{azariaa1,sarit}@cs.biu.ac.il, richards@jct.ac.il

ABSTRACT

When humans face a broad spectrum of topics, where each topic consists of several options, they usually make a decision on each topic separately. Usually, a person will perform better by making a global decision, however, taking all consequences into account is extremely difficult. We present a novel computational method for advice-generation in an environment where people need to decide among multiple selection problems. This method is based on the prospect theory and uses machine learning techniques. We graphically present this advice to the users and compare it with advice which encourages the users to always select the option with a higher expected outcome. We show that our method outperforms the expected outcome approach in terms of user and satisfaction.

Categories and Subject Descriptors

I.2.m [**Computing Methodologies**]: ARTIFICIAL INTELLIGENCE—*Miscellaneous*

Keywords

Advice Provision, Human Modeling, Prospect Theory

1. INTRODUCTION

It is hard to overestimate the importance of decision-making in life. People make decisions on a daily basis; some are trivial such as whether or not to eat ice-cream, while others are important such as which apartment to buy. "Choice Bracketing", termed by Read et al. [7], designates the grouping of individual choices together into sets. "Broadly Bracketing" indicates that the decision-maker takes all choices into account when making his decision, while "Narrow Bracketing" indicates that the decision-maker isolates each choice from all other choices. Of course, in order to bracket several decisions, they must all be converted to a single scale (such as money), where a decision that is a bad choice for one topic may be balanced out by another decision which is a good choice for a different topic.

It has been shown that people tend to use narrow bracketing and usually treat each decision as if in isolation from all other decisions, which in many cases results in a poor choice [10, 7]. Gneezy and Potters [2] have shown that, in investment games, people who are forced into broadly bracketing by viewing their revenue less often become less risk averse and therefore increase their average revenue. Unfortunately, these studies did not test users' satisfaction, only their average total revenue.

In this paper we tackle people's tendency to narrow bracketing using an environment where people need to decide among several independent selection problems, whether they prefer a guaranteed outcome or a higher, but uncertain, outcome. We build an agent which first learns peoples' preferences and generates a general human model. The agent then searches the space of all possible combinations that can be chosen by the user and, based on the human model, advises the user which combination would be most beneficial for him in terms of satisfaction. Evaluating the performance of a system using user satisfaction is a common method in recommender systems [4]. A user is more likely to buy, use and recommend a system with high user satisfaction than without.

Many real life situations resemble our problem. The most obvious example is when building an investment portfolio, where some stocks have a higher risk but also offer an opportunity to receive higher interest and others a lower risk and a lower interest level. Most people combine different stocks and bonds, combining different levels of risk. A similar example might be a manager who wants to market several products, where each product has its own probability for success and failure and its estimated revenue. Another example might be a GPS guiding a driver who can choose between a longer road with a low probability of heavy traffic and a shorter road with a high probability for heavy traffic. Considering the full route may result in greater satisfaction than making a separate decision for each and every junction. We emphasize, that although we focus on advice provision, the agent may utterly replace the decision-maker. For instance, if the GPS is embedded into an autonomous vehicle, it may determine the route on its own.

Our main contributions are: first, we present the algorithmic challenge associated with the human bracketing problem. Second, we developed a multistage procedure for providing humans with a combination of choices in multiple prospect selections aiming at maximizing human satisfaction. The innovation in the preference elicitation of the multistage procedure stems from the use of an off-line learning group. At last, extensive experiments show the success of our proposed method in terms of human satisfaction.

2. RELATED WORK

In a recent work, Azaria et al. [1] propose a method for giving advice to users in an environment where users have several options from which to choose where the decisions are made in sequential order. However, in their work they assume that the users and the agent have different goals and utility functions, while in our work

RecSys'13, October 12–16, 2013, Hong Kong, China.

http://–enter the whole DOI string from rightsreview form confirmation.

the agent's goal is solely to help the user and thus they both have identical utility functions. Sarne et al. [9] attempt to facilitate people's decision-making process by modifying the presentation of the problem in an economic search environment. However, in their work they assume that people want to maximize their expected monetary value. We relax this assumption and assume that people have a non-monetary utility function which they try to maximize. In this paper we base this utility function on the Prospect Theory.

The Prospect Theory was presented by Kahneman and Tversky in [6], and later refined to the Cumulative Prospect Theory in [11]. The Prospect Theory is based on three principles. The first is that people do not take into account their total wealth when accepting or rejecting an uncertain opportunity but rather use their current wealth as a baseline and are happy to win an amount and upset if they lose. The second principle is loss aversion, and the third is that people have a subjective representation of probabilities and do not interpret probabilities fully rationally, but rather use their own decision weights when deciding whether to reject or accept a gamble. Tversky and Kahneman elicited these weights by sequentially asking subjects to choose between a specific lottery and many different guaranteed outcomes. However, these decision weights depend on peoples personality, their wealth, culture and the scope of the payoff in question. Several studies try to estimate parameters for the Prospect Theory [3, 8], however, most studies try to maximize the likelihood of the results obtained by each subject individually. This approach could not be used in our work since we build a model using a group of users and use this model on new users (for whom we have little or no data). We cannot build a model for each and every user - it is impractical and we don't have enough data for that. We build a human model by learning the decision weights which best suit our population and scope of payoff based on machine learning.

3. MULTIPLE PROSPECT SELECTIONS

The term *prospect* comes from Kahneman and Tversky, who refer to a lottery where a player has a chance to win (or lose) a certain amount as a prospect. We only use *simple prospects*, where a player can gain a certain outcome with some probability, and zero otherwise. A *prospect selection problem* $s =< x; p, y >$, is a problem where a player needs to choose between a guaranteed outcome of x and a probability of p to win an outcome y (we use the subscripts s_x, s_p and s_y respectively). We use $c \in \{g, u\}$ to denote the user's choice, where g denotes a choice of the guaranteed value (x), and u denotes the uncertain outcome (the prospect: y with probability p). An important point is that a fully rational player (i.e. one who maximizes expected monetary outcome) would always choose the uncertain outcome if $p \cdot y \geq x$, and the guaranteed outcome otherwise. However, as shown by Tversky and Kahneman [11], people do not act fully rationally not because they cannot do so, but because they use different decision weights.

In our work we consider *multiple prospect selection problems* where a player faces k (different) prospect selection problems. As mentioned in the introduction, people fail to broaden their bracketing and treat each selection problem as if it is isolated from the other selection problems. Therefore, people use their original decision weights, which would imply a lower satisfaction rate for multiple selection problems. Our goal is to build an agent that advises a human player in which of the selection problems to choose the guaranteed outcome and in which to choose the prospect. We denote this advice by $a \in \{g, u\}$. We measure the performance of the agent in terms of human satisfaction from the final result, human satisfaction from the decisions he made, human satisfaction from the advice and the fraction of selection problems where the human followed the advice. We intentionally do not measure success in terms of the raw final stake, since, as mentioned above, people care about how much they have only in context, that is, in comparison to how much they could have had (or lost), and what risks they took or avoided in order to achieve that outcome.

We now present the prospect Selection problem Advice provider for Multiple Problems agent (SAMP). To build this agent we first use machine learning to elicit decision weights which are most appropriate for a given domain and demographic group. Based on these decision weights we build a general human model that can calculate the weighted utility for any combination of choices in a multiple prospect selection problem. On demand, SAMP uses the model to search for the best combination and presents it to the user.

3.1 Decision Weights Elicitation

The first step in building SAMP, is eliciting human decision weights. Since these decision weights will be used to build a *general* human model, we collect data using subjects from a similar culture and using a similar scope of outcome and probabilities. However, we do not collect personal parameters regarding users' preferences (such as risk attitude). This data is collected from subjects who were asked to choose between a guaranteed outcome and a simple prospect (as described earlier). Since this is a very simple choice, we assume that humans can provide their real preferences.

Eliciting these decision weights is not a classification problem, however, we use a classifier, in order to extract its model and then using its model along with mathematical manipulations we obtain a decision weight function. Using the data we build a logistic regression classifier. We feed the classifier for each prospect selection problem with the probability of winning in the prospect, the ratio between the prospect outcome and the guaranteed outcome, and all quadratic combinations of the two, using the the feature vector $v = \{s_p, \frac{s_y}{s_x}, {s_p}^2, (\frac{s_y}{s_x})^2, s_p \cdot \frac{s_y}{s_x}\}$. The classifier needs to classify the data based on the subjects' choices, and is trained on c.

Given a new prospect selection problem feature vector the classifier will output a number between 0 and 1 which, if greater than 0.5, indicates that the user is more likely to choose one option and if smaller than 0.5 indicates that the user is more likely to choose the other. However, since we are interested in learning the decision weights, we would like to know when people are *indifferent* between choosing the guaranteed and the uncertain outcome. We therefore are interested in the cases where the classifier will output exactly 0.5. Since we use a logistic regression classifier, we obtain $\frac{1}{1+e^{-(w^T \cdot v)}} = 0.5$ where w is the vector of weights obtained from the classifier, and v is the feature vector. This implies $(w^T \cdot v) = 0$.

Since we are interested in finding the decision weights for a given probability, we denote: $z = \frac{s_y}{s_x}$ and solve for z. Writing both the feature vector and the weight vector explicitly we obtain:

$$w_0 + w_1 \cdot s_p + w_2 \cdot z + w_3 \cdot s_p^2 + w_4 \cdot z^2 + w_5 \cdot s_p \cdot z = 0$$

and after solving we obtain:

$$z(s_p) = \frac{-w_5 - w_2 \pm \sqrt{(w_5 s_p + w_2)^2 - 4w_4(w_3 {s_p}^2 + w_1 s_p + w_0)}}{2w_4}$$

Given a probability s_p, the actual decision weight $d(s_p)$ is $\frac{1}{z(s_p)}$. Only a single solution is appropriate; in most cases the second solution is either negative or greater than 1. We set $d(1)$ to 1 and $d(0)$ to 0. If in any other case $d(s_p) > 1$ or $d(s_p) < 0$, we set it to 1 or 0 respectively (should not happen with sufficient data).

3.2 Assessing the value of multiple prospects

Using the decision weights obtained above, we can assess a value of a prospect. Given a prospect with a probability s_p of winning an outcome s_y, using the decision weight $d(s_p)$ we obtain that the value of the prospect for the user is simply: $u(s_p, s_y) = d(s_p) \cdot s_y$.

The main challenge which remains is to assess the value of multiple (k) prospects. If we were simply to sum the value of all prospects individually, we would fail by using the exact concept which we are trying to overcome, i.e. narrow bracketing. The first step in assessing the value of multiple prospects is calculating the final probability for each of the possible outcomes. Note that there may be up to $n = 2^k$ possible outcomes and they must be sorted.

Once we obtain the probabilities $\vec{p} = p^1, p^2 \ldots p^n$ ($\sum_{i=1}^{n} p^i = 1$) and outcomes $\vec{y} = y^1, y^2 \ldots y^n$ ($y^1 < \ldots < y^n$), using the Cumulative Prospect Theory [11] we assess the user value.

3.3 Advice Provision

Given a Multiple Prospect Selection Problem, each combination of choices yields different vectors $\vec{p}$ and $\vec{y}$ and therefore using the model above, each combination of choices yields a different user value ($u(\vec{p}, \vec{y})$). SAMP searches for a combination of choices which maximizes this value. This search can be invoked using any search method (such as genetic algorithm or interior-point).

Since human full rationality assumption is broadly used and is a very common assumption, we compare the performance of SAMP to the performance of a *rational agent* which assumes human full rationality (i.e. assumes people want to maximize their expected monetary value). Performance is measured in terms of human satisfaction. In all selection problems the rational agent advises the user to choose the uncertain outcome if $s_p \cdot s_y \geq s_x$, and the guaranteed outcome otherwise. The rational agent's advice does not depend on the number of selection problems k. A user following the rational agent's advice, will maximize his expected outcome.

4. EXPERIMENTAL DESIGN

We ran our experiments using Amazon's Mechanical Turk. We recruited 52 participants for SAMP's learning phase and 202 participants for evaluating SAMP and the fully rational agent.

In the evaluation phase, each subject received a single advice, either from SAMP or from the fully rational agent. In the learning phase the subjects did not receive any advice. Each subject participated only once. 52% of the subjects were males and 48% were females. Subjects' ages ranged from 18 to 75, with a mean of 32.2 and median of 29. All subjects were residents of the USA.

We set $k = 5$, i.e. the subjects had to make their choice regarding five prospect selection problems. This number was chosen to assure that the subjects would find it difficult to bracket on their own. The guaranteed outcome was drawn uniformly between 2 and 10 cents, and the probability to win the uncertain outcome (s_p) was drawn uniformly from $\{0.05, 0.1, 0.15, 0.2, ..., 0.95\}$. Choosing the uncertain outcome yield up to 35% more on the expected utility value of the guaranteed outcome.

Once the subjects selected their preferences, we invoked a lottery on each of the prospect selection problems and paid them according to their preferences. I.e. if a subject chose the guaranteed outcome for a certain selection problem he was paid accordingly, and if he chose the uncertain outcome, the system randomly generated a number r in $[0, 1]$ and paid the subject s_y if $r \leq s_p$. In order to encourage narrow bracketing in the learning phase, the subjects were told to answer each selection problem as if it were standalone, and instead of having the system invoke all the selection problems, the system randomly selected a single selection problem and invoked only that one. The subjects were fully aware of this process.

In the evaluation phase, the system obviously invoked all five prospect selection problems and the subjects were also presented with the agent's advice. Prior to receiving the actual advice, the subjects were told that the advice is provided by a third party agent which is trying to help them. The subjects were shown the consequences of following the advice using a pie chart, which indicated the actual probability of winning each possible outcome.

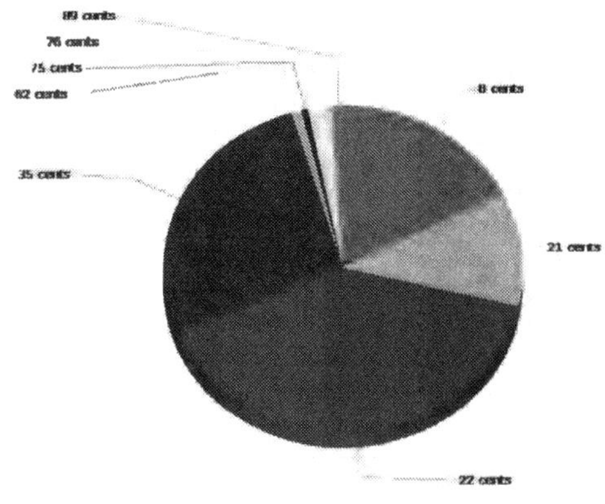

Figure 1: A visualization of the agent's advice

Figure 1 presents an example for a visualization of the agent's advice, where following the exact advice given by the agent, guarantees a win of at least 8 cents, but offers up to 89 cents. The interpretation of the pie chart was explained to the subjects, and their comments indicated that they clearly understood it.

After submitting their choices and told the final results, the subjects were asked the following three questions: 1. Are you happy with the final result? 2. Are you happy with the decisions you made? 3. How good was the advice given to you by the system? The subjects answered these questions on a 1 to 5 scale, where 1 is associated with "not at all" in the first two questions, and "very bad advice" in the third question, 3 is associated with "o.k.", and 5 is associated with "very happy" in the first two questions, and "very good advice" in the third question.

4.1 SAMP construction

Recall that in SAMP construction, after the data is collected a logistic regression classifier is built using this data. This classifier is built in order to find the decision weights, therefore the classifier is trained on all the data. However, in order to evaluate the performance of the classifier we also ran a 10 fold cross validation on the data. We found that the accuracy of the classifier was 67.2% (F-Measure 0.67). These results are satisfying, as we are considering a general human model and people differ in their risk attitudes. Furthermore, this classifier allows us to build a good enough model for people's decision weights. Using other classifiers yield similar results (SVM - 67%, neural networks - 65.6%), however, logistic regression enables the model extraction described in section 3.1.

After extracting the parameters we were able to calculate the decision weights for any given probability. Several decision weights learned by SAMP for some selected probabilities can be found in Table 1. For example the decision weight associated with 0.25 is 0.20. This indicates that people should be indifferent between a prospect that offers a 25% chance to win 10 cents and a guaranteed outcome of 2 cents. Note that the decision weights are lower than the actual probabilities in all cases; this indicates that, in our environment, people were risk averse regardless of the probability.

Using these decision weights SAMP builds a general human model as described in section 3.2. Since we used a small k, we had a small search space and therefore SAMP used an exhaustive search when searching for the best combination to be advised to the users. Figure 1 presents an example of a SAMP's advice, in a scenario

Probability	Decision Weight	Probability	Decision Weight
0.10	0.07	0.25	0.20
0.40	0.32	0.60	0.48
0.75	0.64	0.90	0.85

Table 1: Decision weights for selected probabilities

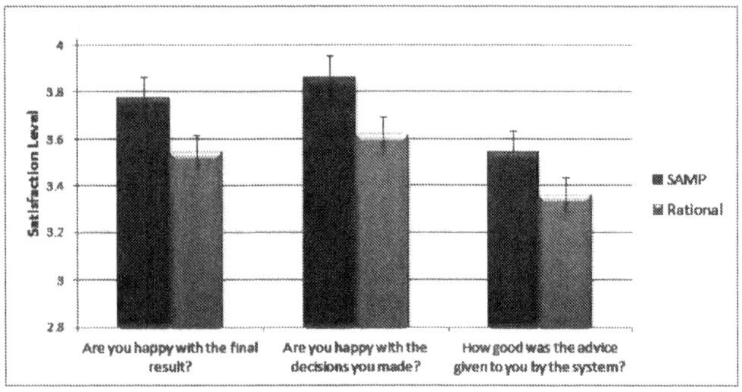

Figure 2: Comparison between user satisfaction levels among subjects who received SAMP's advice and those who received the fully rational agent's advice

where the guaranteed outcome among all selection problems sums up to 21 cents. Following the advice seems preferable to choosing the guaranteed outcome, as the probability of gaining less than the guaranteed outcome by following the advice is less than 14% and the user is very likely to gain more than the guaranteed outcome, with a slight chance of gaining much more. The expected utility from following SAMP's advice is 25.7 cents, however, SAMP evaluated the human value of its advice in 23.4 cents

4.2 Results

Figure 2 presents the final user satisfaction levels for users who received SAMP's advice and users who received the fully rational advice. The higher the satisfaction level the better the result. As can be seen in the figure, in all three questions SAMP outperformed the rational agent. Multi-variant ANOVA test on all three parameters (together) indicates that these results differ significantly ($p < 0.05$). In the first two questions results differ significantly ($p < 0.05$) also using the student's t-test between the two groups, however, results for the third question only came close to the significance level by the student's t-test (with $p = 0.07$). These results indicate that the assumptions used by SAMP are more accurate than assuming full rationality in humans.

The advice given by SAMP for each of the selection problems was followed 76.5% of the time, while the advice given by the rational agent was followed only 70.8% of the time. Therefore, on average, users who received SAMP's advice resulted with a non-statistically significant higher outcome (34.5) than those who received the rational advice (32.2). We attach minor importance to this achievement, as SAMP is destined to increase the users' satisfaction and not expected outcome.

5. CONCLUSIONS AND FUTURE WORK

In this paper we present an agent which advises people in an environment which includes multiple prospect selection problems, where in each selection problem the user must choose between a guaranteed outcome and an uncertain outcome. This agent collects data on humans in the desirable environment and, uses it to build a general human model with prospect theory concepts. Using this model, the agent searches for a combination of selections which is most favorable for humans and recommends it to the user. We present the resulted combination using a pie chart which visualizes the probability of each possible outcome. SAMP significantly outperforms a fully rational agent in terms of user satisfaction.

Reaching such an achievement using a general human model is conspicuous since people differ from each other, and many times advice which might be good for one user may not be as good for another. In this work we have proven the concept of using decision weights, showed how to learn them from data and generalize their use to a combination of multiple prospect selection problems.

Research has shown that people act differently when the stakes are higher, and tend to be more risk-averse [5]. Nonetheless, many users commented that they would act differently if the stakes were higher. Since people tend to reject favorable prospects when the stakes are higher, narrow bracketing will cause them to reject many more favorable prospects than they should. We therefore expect that, when the stakes are higher, our agent will have a larger impact on the user satisfaction. However, in our settings raising the stakes would not allow us to actually pay the subjects and the prospect selection problems would have needed to be hypothetical

In current work, the experiments were based on a single trial. We intend to test a scenario where the user doesn't see all of the selection problems at once, but must make his selections sequentially.

6. ACKNOWLEDGMENTS

This work was supported in part by ERC 267523, MURI W911NF-08-1-0144, ARO W911NF0910206 and W911NF1110344.

7. REFERENCES

[1] A. Azaria, Z. Rabinovich, S. Kraus, C. V. Goldman, and Y. Gal. Strategic advice provision in repeated human-agent interactions. In *AAAI*, 2012.

[2] U. Gneezy and J. Potters. An experiment on risk taking and evaluation periods. *Quarterly Journal of Economics*, pages 631–645, 1997.

[3] G. Harrison and E. RutstrÃűm. Expected utility theory and prospect theory: one wedding and a decent funeral. *Experimental Economics*, 12:133–158.

[4] J. L. Herlocker, J. A. Konstan, L. G. Terveen, and J. T. Riedl. Evaluating collaborative filtering recommender systems. *ACM Transactions on Information Systems (TOIS)*, 22(1):5–53, 2004.

[5] S. J. Kachelmeier and M. Shehata. Examining risk preferences under high monetary incentives: Experimental evidence from the people's republic of china. *American Economic Review*, 82(5):1120–41, December 1992.

[6] D. Kahneman and A. Tversky. Prospect theory: An analysis of decision under risk. *Econometrica*, 47(2):263–291, 1979.

[7] D. Read, G. Loewenstein, and M. Rabin. Choice bracketing. *Journal of Risk and Uncertainty*, 19(1):171–197, Dec. 1999.

[8] J. Rieskamp. The probabilistic nature of preferential choice. *Journal of Experimental Psychology*, 34:1446–1465, 2008.

[9] D. Sarne, A. Elmalech, B. J. Grosz, and M. Geva. Less is more: restructuring decisions to improve agent search. In *Proc. of AAMAS*, pages 431–438, 2011.

[10] A. Tversky and D. Kahneman. The framing of decisions and the psychology of choice. *Science*, 211(4481):453–458, Jan. 1981.

[11] A. Tversky and D. Kahneman. Advances in prospect theory: Cumulative representation of uncertainty. *Journal of Risk and Uncertainty*, 5(4):297–323, Oct. 1992.

Clustering-Based Factorized Collaborative Filtering

Nima Mirbakhsh
Department of Computer Science
Western University, London, ON, Canada
smirbakh@uwo.ca

Charles X. Ling
Department of Computer Science
Western University, London, ON, Canada
cling@csd.uwo.ca *

ABSTRACT

Factorized collaborative models show a promising accuracy and scalability in recommendation systems. They employ the latent collaborative information of users and items to achieve higher accuracy of recommendation. In this paper, we propose a new approach to improve the accuracy of two well-known, highly scalable factorized models: SVD++ and Asymmetric-SVD++. These are cutting-edge factorized models that have played a key role in the Netflix prize winner's solution. We first employ collaborative information to categorize the users and items. We then discover the shared interests between these categories. Including this new information, we extend these cutting-edge models regarding two main goals: 1) to improve their recommendation accuracies; 2) to keep the extended models still scalable. Finally, we evaluate our proposed models on two recommendation datasets: MovieLens100k, and Netflix. Our experiment shows that adding the shared interests among categories into these models improves their accuracy while maintaining scalability.

Categories and Subject Descriptors

H.3 [**Information storage and retrieval**]: Retrieval models, Information filtering, Clustering; H.2 [**Database management**]: Database Applications—*Data mining*

Keywords

Collaborative Filtering, Factorizing, Neighborhood-Aware

1. INTRODUCTION

Between 2007 to 2009, Netflix[1] hold a competition on recommendation systems for the best collaborative filtering algorithm that predicts users' ratings on a collection of its movies. For details of the provided dataset by Netflix, see [4, 1]. The goal of the competition was to achieve a RMSE below 0.8563 (10% improvement from the benchmark). Many models have been tried and proposed by almost 2000 teams who attended in this competition. Finally, a blended model including more than 50 methods has won this competition. SVD++ and Asymmetric-SVD++ [4, 5, 1] were two models that play a central role on improving the accuracy of the winner model. These models effectively include the implicit and explicit information about the users and the items into a factorized model which improves the recommendation accuracy while keeping the model scalable. To the best of our knowledge, these algorithms are still (if not the most) one of the most scalable and accurate collaborative filtering models [1].

In this paper, we employ the collaborative filtering information again to find the categories that these users and items may belong to. We then track how users inside each category rate the other categories containing the items. We expect that adding this novel information will improve the recommendation quality of the current collaborative filtering models including SVD++, and Asymmetric-SVD++. We follow these two main goals: 1) to improve the recommendation accuracy; 2) to keep the extended models scalable. We also evaluate how the quality of the clusters will affect the improvement of the prediction accuracy. Employing clustering to categorize collaborative information, and using these clusters to predict the unknown preferences has been employed before in a number of works [6, 2]. However, to the best of our knowledge there is not any previous works which consider the shared preferences between the categories. Our experiment shows that including this deduced knowledge improves the recommendation accuracy while keeping the model still scalable and practical.

2. PROPOSED MODELS

In a general CF problem, we have a set of users $U = \{u_1, u_2, \dots, u_n\}$ and a set of items $I = \{i_1, i_2, \dots, i_m\}$ that they are companied by a rating matrix $R = [r_{ui}]_{n \times m}$ where r_{ui} represents the rating of user u on item i. Collaborating filtering consists of predicting unknown r_{ij}s based on the known $r_{i'j'}$ s inside the rating matrix R. Matrix Factorization (MF) addresses this problem by decomposing the ratings matrix, R, into two lower dimension matrices Q and P which contain corresponded latent vectors of each user and item in the length of $k \ll m, n$. Such a model is close to the singular value decomposition (SVD) technique for finding latent vectors in information retrieval. Thus, MF and SVD refer to a same concept in this paper. The predictor

*Charles X. Ling is the contact author of this paper.
[1]http://www.netflix.com

RecSys'13, October 12–16, 2013, Hong Kong, China.
Copyright 2013 ACM 978-1-4503-2409-0/13/09 ...$15.00.
http://dx.doi.org/10.1145/2507157.2507233 .

function of a Biased Matrix Factorization (BMF) model is as follows:

$$r_{ui} = q_i^T p_u + b_i + b_u \quad (1)$$

where $q_i \in \mathbb{R}^k$ and $b_i \in \mathbb{R}$ are the corresponded vector and bias value of item i, and $p_u \in \mathbb{R}^k$ and $b_u \in \mathbb{R}$ are the corresponded vector and bias value of user u.

There are two common approaches to include neighborhood information into factorization models: 1) $item - item$ models which consider if user u is interested in item i and its similar items. 2) $user - user$ models that consider if user u and its similar users are interested in item i. However, item-item models are usually preferable as their less space and time complexity. This is because of the typical larger number of users in recommendation systems. Although, both models ignore the neighborhood information of possible categories that items and users may belong to. Thus, we first try to find the possible categories and then apply the shared interests between these categories in a number of CF models.

We first apply BMF on the known ratings to learn the latent vectors of each user and item. Kmeans then is applied on these latent vectors with different selection of K (number of clusters) to find possible categories of items and users. Rating matrices are typically sparse in recommendation systems. Hence, using latent vectors helps to reduce the complexity of clustering these large and sparse datasets. After finding these clusters (categories), we then correspond each a latent vector. We consider the shared ratings between these categories in a new matrix R^*. Lets assume C_u and C_i as the clusters that contain user u and item i. In this new rating matrix, every $r^*_{C_u,C_i}$ reflects the average rating of the users inside the category C_u on the items inside the category C_i. We define $n' < n$ and $m' < m$ as the number of categories for users and items respectively.

2.1 Clustering-Based SVD++

As discussed earlier, neighborhood aware models employ the similarities between users and items to improve the recommendation accuracy. However, they usually need to compute all pairwise similarities between items or users, which its complexity grows quadratically with the input size [5]. Koren [4, 5] solves this limitation by factoring the neighborhood model, which scales both item-item and user-user implementations linearly with the size of the data [5]. Thus, he effectively integrates implicit and explicit neighborhood information about the users and items to extend the pure SVD model (the BMF model in 1). He assumes all the feedbacks from the users no matter what the feedbacks are, as the implicit information, and considers the ratings as the explicit neighborhood information. He defines $N(u)$ and $R(u)$ as the sets of all implicit and explicit feedbacks from user u. However, $N(u)$ is assumed equal to $R(u)$ in his experiment on the Netflix dataset[4]. In SVD++, Koren corresponds each item i with two latent vectors $q_i, y_i \in \mathbb{R}^k$, and models each user with a corresponded latent vector $p_u \in \mathbb{R}^k$ plus the sum of the latent vectors of all the items inside $N(u)$. Thus, he defines the SVD++'s predictor function as follows:

$$r_{ui} = q_i^T (p_u + |N(u)|^{-\frac{1}{2}} \sum_{j \in N(u)} y_j) + b_i + b_u \quad (2)$$

Employing these implicit feedbacks in the SVD model has shown a promising improvement of prediction accuracy in practice[5]. We expect that employing implicit information about the categories that users and items belong to is useful as well. Thus, we assign two latent vectors $q^*_{C_i}, y^*_{C_i} \in \mathbb{R}^k$ to each category of items, and a latent vector $p^*_{C_u} \in \mathbb{R}^k$ to each category of users which reflects their direct and implicit effect on the ratings. To add the effect of the category in this model, we change the equation 2 as follows:

$$r_{ui} = \left((1-\alpha)q_i + \alpha q^*_{C_i}\right)^T \Bigg(\left((1-\alpha)p_u + \alpha p^*_{C_u}\right) + |N(u)|^{-\frac{1}{2}} \sum_{j \in N(u)} \left((1-\alpha)y_j + \alpha y^*_{C_j}\right) \Bigg) + b_i + b_u \quad (3)$$

We call this new model "CB-SVD++" in the experiment section.

2.2 Clustering-Based Asymmetric-SVD++

In the Asymmetric SVD++, Koren employs the explicit feedbacks, $R(u)$, into the SVD++ model and proposed a factorized item-item model as follows:

$$r_{ui} = q_i^T \Bigg(p_u + |N(u)|^{-\frac{1}{2}} \sum_{j \in N(u)} y_j + |R(u)|^{-\frac{1}{2}} \sum_{j \in R(u)} (r_{uj} - b_u - b_j)x_j \Bigg) + b_i + b_u \quad (4)$$

where $x_j \in \mathbb{R}^k$. To apply the shared interest among categories into this model, we assign three latent vectors $q^*_{C_i}, y^*_{C_i}, x^*_{C_i} \in \mathbb{R}^k$ to each category of items, and a latent vector $p^*_{C_u} \in \mathbb{R}^k$ to each category of users which reflect their direct, implicit, and explicit effect on the ratings. The new predictor function is as follows:

$$r_{ui} = \left((1-\alpha)q_i + \alpha q^*_{C_i}\right)^T \Bigg(\left((1-\alpha)p_u + \alpha p^*_{C_u}\right) + |N(u)|^{-\frac{1}{2}} \sum_{j \in N(u)} \left((1-\alpha)y_j + \alpha y^*_{C_j}\right) + |R(u)|^{-\frac{1}{2}} \sum_{j \in R(u)} (r_{uj} - b_u - b_j) \left((1-\alpha)x_j + \alpha x^*_{C_j}\right) \Bigg) + b_i + b_u \quad (5)$$

We call this model "CB-ASVD++" in our experiment. In all the discussed models, the parameters are determined by minimizing the associated regularized squared error function through gradient descent.

3. EXPERIMENT RESULTS

In section 2, we propose a clustering-based approach to improve current CF models. We apply our extending approach on two cutting-edge CF methods with respect to improve their prediction accuracies while keeping their scalability. In this section, we setup our experiment on two well-known recommendation datasets to validate our hypothesis about these extensions[1]. MovieLens100k [3], and Netflix dataset which contains over 100 million ratings from 480189 users who has rated 17770 movies. MovieLens100k contains 100,000 ratings from 943 users on 1682 movies where each user has rated at least 20 movies [3]. The package includes five randomly 80%/20% splits of dataset into training and

[1]The implementation package is publicly accessible at: https://sites.google.com/site/nmirbakhsh/projects/CBSVDpp

test sets. Netflix dataset contains over 100 million ratings from 480189 users who has rated 17770 movies. We run each algorithm 5 times on the datasets to remove the effect of random initialization of latent vectors on the predictions. Thus, our reported RMSE results are the average RMSEs of these 5 runs.

3.1 Categories

We start by applying BMF on both datasets to find their users' and items' latent vectors. These latent vectors (learned on the train sets) then are used for the clustering purpose. Kmeans is applied on the achieved latent vectors to find possible categories of items and categories of users inside the datasets. It is expected that items (users) with similar latent vectors are similar in reality as well. We guess different selection of possible categories by changing in the number of clusters. It usually achieves in 5-10 tries. Finally, by trying different size of clusters on the proposed models, the number of clusters that achieves less RMSE (higher accuracy) on the validation set will be selected as the best choice of m', and n'.

Table 1 shows the movies inside a number of found clusters on the Netflix dataset. As shown, it seems that movies in same genre and almost similar years of production tend to be in same clusters. For instance, 'category 1499' includes different versions of 'Lord of the Rings' and 'Harry Potter'. These movies are both in 'Adventure' and 'Fantasy' genres[2] and also have released between 2001 to 2004. Or, 'category 1028' contains a number of classical movies in the 'Adventure' genre. As no information about the users is provided, so the clusters of users cannot be judged. Lets remind that the movies' names (identities) are not used anywhere in this experiment. These names are only employed for better demonstration of the clusters. On the other hand, the quality of the clusters is effective on the prediction accuracy of the extension models. For instance, the 'CB-SVD++' model results a RMSE of 0.90564 for a random assignment of the clusters ($m' = n' = 100$) on the MovieLens100k dataset. Comparing this value with the achieved RMSE of 0.89928 which is the result of employing the kmeans clusters of the latent vectors, it can be seen that the low quality of clusters will decrease the prediction accuracy of our extensions.

Table 1: The table shows the movies inside a number of formed clusters on the Netflix dataset. As shown, it seems that movies in same genre and almost similar years of production tend to be in same clusters.

Category ID	Movie Name (Production Year)
Category 1499	Harry Potter and the Prisoner of Azkaban(2004), Harry Potter and the Sorcerer's Stone(2001), Lord of the Rings: The Two Towers: Bonus Material(2002), Harry Potter and the Chamber of Secrets(2002), Lord of the Rings: The Fellowship of the Ring: Bonus Material(2001), Lord of the Rings: The Return of the King: Bonus Material(2003)
Category 1028	Treasure Island(1950), Bend of the River(1952), The Far Country(1955), Hondo(1953), Night Passage(1957), Rio Bravo(1959), Sink the Bismarck(1960), Sahara(1943), They Were Expendable(1945), Run Silent(1958), Rio Grande(1950), She Wore a Yellow Ribbon(1949), Destination Tokyo(1943)]

[2]http://www.imdb.com

Table 2: The RMSE results of applying clustering-based extension of a number of factorized CF methods on the Netflix dataset. As the results show, with increasing k the extensions result better improvements.

Models	k=50	k=100	k=200
SVD	0.90658	0.90510	0.90479
SVD++	0.90045	0.89952	0.89910
CB-SVD++	0.89939	0.89852	0.89803
ASVD++	0.89955	0.89907	0.89904
CB-ASVD++	0.89876	0.89770	0.89721

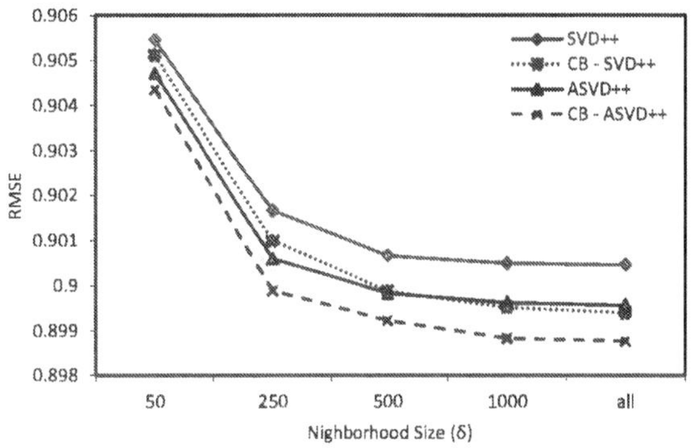

(a) Netflix

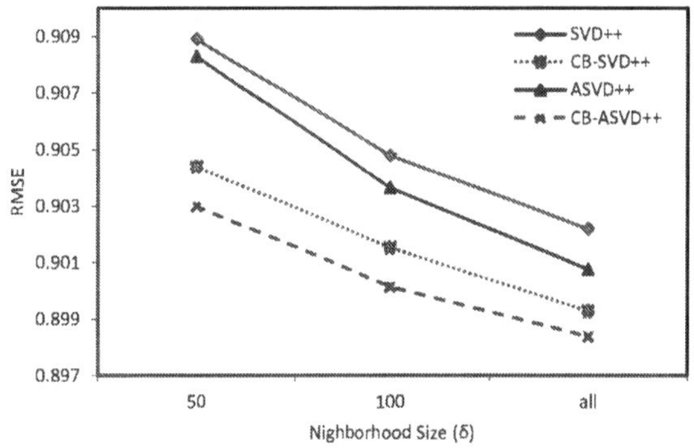

(b) MovieLens100k

Figure 1: The accuracy of the proposed clustering-based models applying on the two datasets. It shows that our proposed extensions outperform both 'SVD++' and 'Asymmetric-SVD++' on these datasets ($k = 50$ is used to achieve these results).

3.2 Comparison

In our all extensions an α value is used to control the balance between direct influence of users and items, and the influence of the categories that they belong to on the prediction function. Figure 2 shows how the accuracy of 'CB-ASVD++' changes with different selection of α. For $\alpha = 0.0$, this model does not consider the effect of the categories so the result RMSE is similar to the 'ASVD++''s accuracy as expected. Also, the shared interests among the categories are too general to be employed lonely for the recommendation purpose. Thus, the accuracy is not improved or even gets worse for very large selection of α. A validation set is used to determine the best selection of α in our experiment.

The Table 2 shows the RMSE results of applying clustering-based extension on a number of factorized CF methods on the Netflix dataset. As the results show, with increasing k the extensions result better improvements. However, another factor which highly affects the accuracy of the neighborhood-aware methods is the neighborhood size that is applied on the model. Lets define the maximum number of employing neighborhood as δ. Figure 1 illustrates how increasing δ results a better prediction accuracy. It also shows that employing the deduced information about the categories that the items and users belong to, is independent from the explicit and implicit feedbacks. Adding the deduced information about the shared interests among the categories improves the prediction quality for any neighborhood size in both datasets. For the MovieLens dataset, the clustering-based extension of 'SVD++' ('CB-SVD++') shows a better prediction accuracy than 'Asymmetric-SVD++' which employs the explicit feedbacks. For employing full set of neighbors, this advantage can be seen on the Netflix dataset too.

The extension models have almost the same complexity as the non-extended models. However, they add a preprocessing complexity in the clustering step. As Table 3 illustrates, the learning time of the extensions is less than twice of the non-extended models on the MovieLens100k dataset. The clustering was also not much time consuming because we perform the clustering on the low dimension latent vectors. For instance, the clustering of the Netflix's users takes less than a hour using the Rapidminer[3] software in our PC with 3.30 GHz CPU. Both extended and non-extended models also take similar number of epochs for converging in the learning time. Thus, the extended models keep the scalability of those models which was our second goal.

4. DISCUSSIONS AND CONCLUSIONS

Because of the disadvantages of the user-user and integrated models, in this paper we only focused on the item-item models. However, we have tried the clustering-based extension method on those models. A similar improvement of prediction results have been observed for those extensions. For the integrated model which is presented in [5], the improvement was even slightly higher. For instance, the basic integrated model achieves a RMSE of 0.89558 on the MovieLens100k dataset. By applying our extension on this model, the RMSE falls to 0.89298. However, the space and time complexity of this model increases dramatically by selecting larger number of δ. It is really difficult to replicate the blended model of the Netflix prize winner's solution. However, based on the central role of SVD++ and Asymmetric-SVD++ in that blended model, we expect that applying our extensions will slightly improve its accuracy.

To summarize, we propose a new approach to improve the accuracy of two well-known highly scalable factorized models: SVD++ and Asymmetric-SVD++. We first employ collaborative information to categorize users and items. We then track how users inside each category rate the other categories containing the items. Including this new information, we extend these cutting-edge models regarding two main goals: 1) to improve their recommendation accuracies. 2) to keep the extended models still scalable. Finally, we evaluate our proposed models on two recommendation systems datasets: MovieLens100k, and Netflix. Our experiment shows that applying the shared interests among the categories into these models improve their accuracies. These extensions also have the same complexity as the non-extended models.

[3]http://www.rapidminer.com

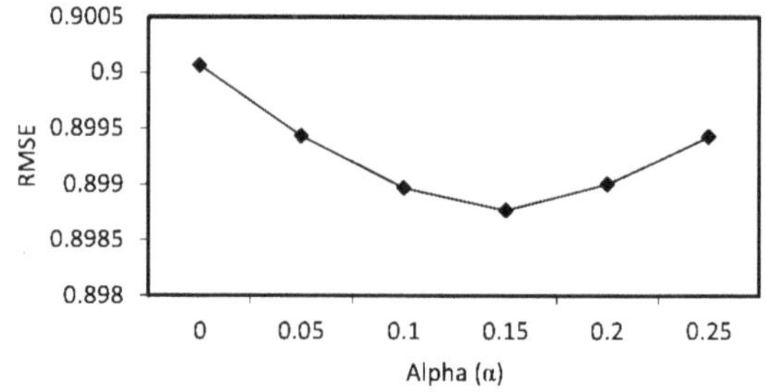

Figure 2: The accuracy of the proposed CB-ASVD++ model applying on the Netflix dataset. It shows how changing α affects the final predictor's accuracy.

Table 3: A comparison between the learning time of the extended and non-extended models on the MovieLens100k dataset (millisecond/epoch). As shown, the extensions increase the learning time to less than twice of the non-extended models' learning times.

SVD++	CB-SVD++	ASVD++	CB-ASVD++
43ms	73ms	54ms	92ms

5. REFERENCES

[1] C. Desrosiers and G. Karypis. A comprehensive survey of neighborhood-based recommendation methods. In F. Ricci, L. Rokach, B. Shapira, and P. B. Kantor, editors, *Recommender Systems Handbook*, pages 107 144. Springer US, 2011.

[2] M. Gueye, T. Abdessalem, and H. Naacke. A cluster-based matrix-factorization for online integration of new ratings. In *Journées de Bases de Données Avancées (BDA)*, pages 1 18, 2011.

[3] J. L. Herlocker, J. A. Konstan, A. Borchers, and J. Riedl. An algorithmic framework for performing collaborative filtering. In *Proceedings of the 22nd annual international ACM SIGIR conference on Research and development in information retrieval*, SIGIR '99, pages 230–237, New York, NY, USA, 1999. ACM.

[4] Y. Koren. Factorization meets the neighborhood: a multifaceted collaborative filtering model. In *Proceedings of the 14th ACM SIGKDD international conference on Knowledge discovery and data mining*, KDD '08, pages 426 434, New York, NY, USA, 2008. ACM.

[5] Y. Koren. Factor in the neighbors: Scalable and accurate collaborative filtering. *ACM Trans. Knowl. Discov. Data*, 4(1):1:1–1:24, Jan. 2010.

[6] B. Xu, J. Bu, C. Chen, and D. Cai. An exploration of improving collaborative recommender systems via user-item subgroups. In *Proceedings of the 21st international conference on World Wide Web*, WWW '12, pages 21–30. New York, NY, USA, 2012. ACM.

Cross Social Networks Interests Predictions Based on Graph Features

Amit Tiroshi[†*], Shlomo Berkovsky[*], Mohamed Ali Kaafar[‡*], Terence Chen[*], Tsvi Kuflik[†]
[†]University of Haifa, Israel [*]National ICT Australia [‡]INRIA, France
[*]firstname.lastname@nicta.com.au [†]{atiroshi,tsvikak}@is.haifa.ac.il

ABSTRACT

The tremendous popularity of Online Social Networks (OSN) has led to situations, where users have their profiles spread across multiple networks. These partial profiles reflect different user characteristics, depending mainly on the nature of the network, e.g., Facebook's social vs. LinkedIn's professional focus. Combining data gathered by multiple networks may benefit individual users, and the community as a whole, as this could facilitate the provision of more accurate services and recommendations. This paper reports on an exploratory study of the process of making such recommendations using a unique multi-network dataset containing user interests across multiple domains, e.g., music, books, and movies. We represent the data using a graph model and generate recommendations using a set of features extracted from and populated by the model. We assess the contribution of various network- and domain-related features to the accuracy of the recommendations and motivate future work into automated feature selection.

Categories and Subject Descriptors

H.3.3 [**Information Storage and Retrieval**]: Information Filtering

Keywords

Social Networks; Graph Model; Interests Prediction

1. INTRODUCTION

The advent of OSNs has revolutionized user-to-user online and offline interactions. Users make a steadily increasing use of a plethora of OSNs, which are fast becoming the place to share and discover news, activities, and content of interest. The use cases notably vary across the networks: some facilitate microblogs, some are a place to share photos, and some serve as a professional playground. Hence, it is not unusual for a user to have accounts and profiles on multiple OSNs. Amalgamating these partial profiles can yield more accurate user models and lead to a better personalization [4].

Several prior works have focused on user modeling and personalization in a multi-OSN and cross-domain setting. In [1], a multi-OSN cross-domain dataset was collected and analysed for profile completeness across networks. The authors reported on the positive effects of the multi-OSN data in alleviating the cold start problem. A similar approach for aggregating data from multiple OSNs was presented in [10], where the dataset was enriched by semantics from external resources, like DBpedia. In [3], data from multiple OSNs was analysed in order to find what information could improve the diversity of recommendations. In [12], the authors investigated the feasibility and effectiveness of using cross-domain data for generating Facebook recommendations.

Our work relies on a rich dataset from multiple OSNs, which contains user interests belonging to multiple domains. We elaborate on prior works into cross-system and cross-domain personalization and aim to investigate what OSNs, domains, and features contribute to the accuracy of personalized interest recommendations. For this, we gather a collection of cross-OSN user profiles, and model this collection as a bipartite bidirectional graph. We engineer a set of user, interest, domain, and network related features and automatically populate these features from the graph model. Then, we apply a Random Forest classifier [6] in order to predict and recommend new topics of interest to users.

We assessed the contribution of data from six OSNs and five application domains. We identified networks and domains that improved the accuracy of the generated recommendations, while some other were neutral or even detrimental for the recommendations. Our results indicate that much attention should be given to the selection of features when aggregating partial user profiles, as the network and domain of origin play an important role and affect the value of information in the features. In summary, our work provides more evidence for the importance of feature selection in cross-system and cross-domain personalization, and calls for more research into automated feature selection.

RecSys'13, October 12–16, 2013, Hong Kong, China.

http://dx.doi.org/10.1145/2507157.2507206.

2. DATASET

The dataset used in this work was collected in [7] and contains user profiles spread across six OSNs: Blogger, Facebook, Lastfm, LinkedIn, LiveJournal (LJ), and Youtube. The linkage of partial profiles across the OSNs was manually done by the users themselves. We extracted the lists of user interests and categorized these into five domains: movies, music, books, TV, and general. The categoriza-

OSN	total	unique	OSN	total	unique
Blogger	27,045	6,587	LJ	30,924	5,198
Facebook	253,217	31,511	Youtube	2,753	1,561
Lastfm	63,952	16,483	overall	425,846	47,314
Linkedin	47,955	6,325			

Table 1: Total and unique interests in each OSN.

domain	total	unique	domain	total	unique
general	154,245	13,053	books	24,404	3,789
movies	54,382	5,190	tv	53,508	4,027
music	139,307	21,255	all	425,846	47,314

Table 2: Total and unique interests in each domain.

tion was explicitly made by the users on Blogger, Facebook, and Youtube; all Lastfm interests were categorized as music; and no categorization was available on LinkedIn and LJ, such that interests listed on these OSNs were treated as general. Users having one interest only in their aggregated profile and interests having one user only associated with them, were removed from the dataset.

The resulting dataset contains closely to 21K users and more than 47K interests, with an average of 19.46 interests listed per user. Table 1 shows the distribution of interests across the OSNs. Notably, almost 60% of the listed interests are coming from Facebook, with Lastfm and LinkedIn jointly providing more than 25% of interests on top of Facebook. Table 2 shows the distribution of interests across the domains. Domain distribution is more even than the OSN-based one, and while general interests accounts for the largest number of listed interests, music has the largest number of unique interests.

Table 3 shows the number of users who have at least one interest and Table 4 shows the average number of interests listed by a user for every domain-OSN combination. General interests and music are the dominant domains on Blogger, followed by movies and books. On Facebook, books is substantially lower than other domains, which are all comparable. The available domains are similar on Youtube, whereas TV interests are absent. As discussed earlier, music and general interests are the only domains on Lastfm and LinkedIn with LJ, respectively. Amongst the original domains (excluding general), movies are listed primarily on Facebook and Blogger, music on Lastfm and Facebook, books on Facebook and Blogger, and TV is listed only on Facebook.

	general	movies	music	books	tv
Blogger	2,716	1,090	1,370	518	–
Facebook	8,391	8,922	10,453	6,565	9,619
Lastfm	–	–	7,042	–	–
LinkedIn	7,755	–	–	–	–
LJ	1,494	–	–	–	–
Youtube	448	484	650	552	–

Table 3: Number of users with one interests listed in each domain and OSN.

	general	movies	music	books	tv
Blogger	5.913	2.976	4.676	2.577	–
Facebook	6.999	5.662	6.509	3.414	5.562
Lastfm	–	–	9.082	–	–
LinkedIn	6.183	–	–	–	–
LJ	20.69	–	–	–	–
Youtube	1.288	1.278	1.395	1.177	–

Table 4: Average number of interests listed by a user in each domain and OSN.

3. METHODOLOGY

In this section we present a classifier designed to predict whether a user would like an interest. We use the Random Forest classifier [6] trained on features extracted both directly from the data (e.g., frequency) and from a graph model representation of the data.

3.1 Graph Model

In order to enrich the original dataset with additional features, we modeled the data using a graph. Consider a bipartite graph G = {U, I, E}, where U = $\{u_i \mid u_i$ is a user$\}$ and I = $\{i_j \mid i_j$ is an interest$\}$ are the vertices. u_i and i_j are connected if the i_j is listed in one of the OSN profiles of u_i, i.e., E = $\{e_{ij} \mid u_i$ listed $i_j\}$. The edge contains labels detailing on which OSNs the interest was listed.

From G, we extract a set of features, which are categorized into two groups: user features U and interest features I. Each of these groups is split into two sub-groups: basic features (IB for interests and UB for users) and graph features (IG and UG). The UB features are: number of OSNs on which the user has profile (UB1), number of interests the user has in each domain (UB2 - books, UB3 - TV, UB4 - movies, UB5 - music, UB6 - general), and total number of interests (UB7). The IB features are: number of users that liked the interest (IB1), number of OSNs on which the interest is listed (IB2), is it listed on each OSN (IB3 - Blogger, IB5 - LinkedIn, IB6 - LastFM, IB7 - LJ, IB8 - Facebook, IB9 - YouTube), and domain of the interest (IB4).

The graph features are similar for users and interests and include: degree centrality (IG1, UG2) [5], node redundancy (IG2, UG1) [9], clustering coeficient (IG3, UG4) [9], average neighbourhood degree (IG4, UG3) [2], and PageRank (IG5, UG1) [11]. Another shared feature is the shortest path length between a user and an interest, denoted by SP.

We also define $IG_{all} = \{\cup IG_i\}$, $UG_{all} = \{\cup UG_i\}$, $IB_{all} = \{\cup IB_i\}$, and $UB_{all} = \{\cup BG_i\}$. Finally, $I_{all} = \{IB_{all} \cup IG_{all}\}$ and $U_{all} = \{UB_{all} \cup UG_{all}\}$.

3.2 Classification

We are interested to explore the effect of various features on the accuracy of predictions for users liking interests. For the predictions, we used the Random Forest classifier [6], which was trained on the user-interest pairs that were augmented with the above mentioned graph features. The classifier was trained using 100 estimators, and 10 folds of the data were used for cross validation. A separate graph model was built for each fold, and the graph features were populated and fed into the classifier.

Random Forest is a binary classifier. As no disliked interests are included in the data, we randomly sampled per user interests not listed as liked ones, and considered these

Feature/Group	Avg Precision	Feature/Group	Avg Precision	Feature/Group	Avg Precision
All	0.6455	IB4	0.5287	UB5	0.4529
IB_All	0.5821	IB5	0.5230	UG1	0.4514
IG1	0.5745	IB6	0.5221	UB6	0.4507
IG2	0.5734	IB7	0.5215	UG_All	0.4465
IG3	0.5691	IB8	0.5206	UG1	0.4442
IB1	0.5687	IB9	0.5205	UG2	0.4430
I_All	0.5642	[illegible]	0.5128	UG3	0.4440
IG_All	0.5599	SP	0.5107	UB7	0.4405
IG4	0.5589	UB1	0.4771	UG4	0.4401
IG5	0.5560	UB2	0.4736	UB_All	0.4391
IB2	0.5482	UB3	0.4646	U_All	0.4376
IB3	0.5307	UB4	0.4632		

Table 5: Average precision across folds for individual features and feature groups

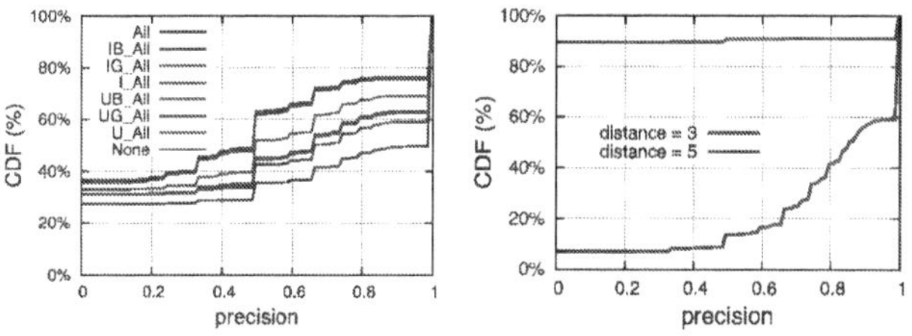

(a) Feature Combinations (b) Shortest Path Feature

Figure 1: Precision CDF (a) feature combinations; (b) two values of the SP feature

as disliked[1]. The number of disliked interests was equal to the number of liked interests for each user.

We used Precision to evaluate the accuracy of the predictions, $P = \frac{TP}{TP+FP}$. Here TP is the number of correct and FP is the number of incorrect 'like' predictions.

4. RESULTS

4.1 Feature Analysis

We examine the average precision values obtained when the classifier is fed with single features, all features, or combinations of these. Table 5 summarises the results. We observe that the average precision scores vary between 0.44 and 0.58. Combining all the available features achieves the highest precision, with 65% of interests being predicted correctly. When no features except for the user-interest pair are embedded in the graph, precision falls closely to 0.5, as expected. This serves as the baseline for comparisons.

Notably, interest features, both individually and in combination, clearly outperform user features. The former score above the baseline (0.52–0.58) and the latter score below (0.44–0.48). Drilling down into specific features, we note that in the majority of cases, graph interest features IG are superior to basic interest features IB, whereas basic user features UB are superior to graph user features UG[2]. This allows us to conclude that interest features contribute valuable information and improve the accuracy of the classifier, whereas user features introduce noise into the model.

We plot in Figure 1(a) the cumulative distribution functions (CDF) of the precision of the combined user/interest features. In similar to Table 5, interest features outperform user features across the board. Consider the I_{All} and U_{All} curves. For I_{All}, precision greater than 0.5 is achieved by 56% of users and greater than 0.75 by 42% of users, while for U_{All}, these figures stand at 36% and 25%, respectively.

Also, we focus on the SP feature denoting the shortest path length between a user and an interest. Figure 1(b) depicts two CDF curves obtained for SP=3 and SP=5. For distant interests with SP=5, only 9% of users achieve precision to close 0.1 and the rest have 0. For interests with SP=3, 86% of users achieve precision greater than 0.5 and 66% of users – greater than 0.75. This shows that predictions for nearby nodes are easier than for distant ones.

[1]A similar approach is used in the Machine Learning community for classification of unary data [8, 13]. This setting reflects common real-life scenarios with only positive labels, e.g., purchase lists, Facebook likes, or browsing logs.

[2]Surprisingly, combining individual features results in an inverse trend. At the group of interest features, IB_{All} achieves precision of 0.58 and IG_{All} – 0.56, and for user features, UG_{All} scores 0.45 and IB_{All} – 0.44.

4.2 OSN and Domain Analysis

We use a combination of all the features and focus on the impact of OSNs and interest sources on the precision. Since the collected interests come from multiple OSNs, we evaluate the precision of the predictions for interests from a particular OSN. Figure 2 exhibits the CDF curves for precision scores for interests on the six OSNs: network=1 when an interest is listed on a network or network=0 otherwise.

As expected, Facebook (Figure 2, top right plot) as the largest source of interest in the dataset, plays a pivotal role in the overall predictions. When an interest is not listed on Facebook, only 30% of users achieve precision greater than 0.5. However, when an interest is listed on Facebook, the precision increases with 87% of users achieving a similar precision score. The gap between the two Facebook curves visually shows the importance of Facebook data; it is clearly wider than for any other OSN. Moreover, Facebook data spans across all the domains and largely overlaps with other OSNs. Hence, the shape and accuracy of the Facebook=1 curve resembles the curves of interests listed on other OSNs.

However, the explanation of this importance does not stem solely from the number of interests in each OSN. For instance, Lastfm (Figure 2, middle left plot) demonstrates a counter-intuitive result. While it provides a high number of music interests – and many of them are unique – being listed on Lastfm has a weaker effect on the predictions than being listed on Facebook. The difference between the two Lastfm curves for precision greater than 0.5 stands at 17% only. Furthermore, Lastfm is the only OSN where Lastfm=0 predictions achieve higher precision scores than Lastfm=1. We posit that these observations are explained by the low overlap between the interests listed on Lastfm[3] and on other OSNs. Hence, predictions for Lastfm-specific music interests are inherently harder than for interests on other OSNs.

We proceed with examining the importance of an interest being listed on more than one OSN. Figure 3(a) shows the precision scores averaged for interests listed on a different number of OSNs, varying from n=1 to n=5. It can be clearly seen that precision increases with n. For example, precision greater than 0.5 is achieved for 96% of interests listed on five OSNs, 70% of interests listed on three OSNs, and 57% of cases listed on one OSN. This suggests that predictions for interests listed on multiple OSNs are easy, as they are based on more reliable data, and these interests could be recommended with high confidence.

[3]Recall that Lastfm's interests belong to music only.

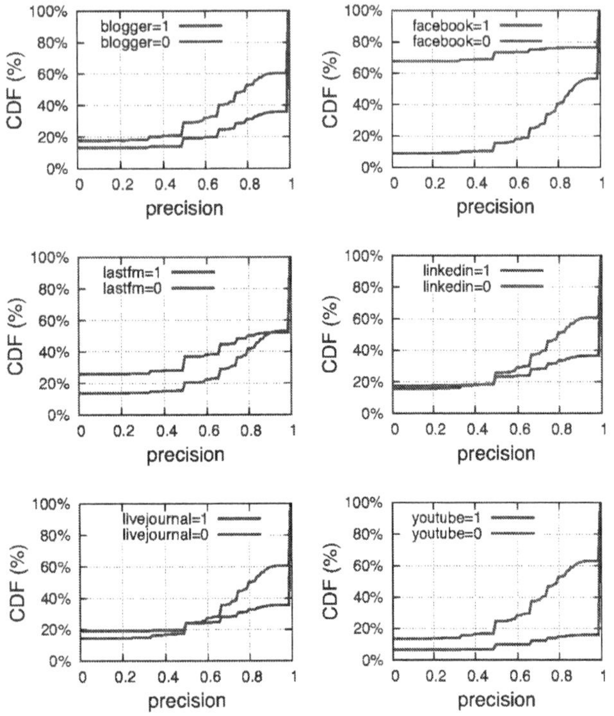

Figure 2: Precision CDF - interests listed on the six OSNs

Finally, we assess the precision scores achieved for interest that belong to various domains. Figure 3(b) show the CDF curve for each domain. We observe that general interests achieve the highest precision, with 73% of interests predicted with precision greater than 0.5. This is followed by music with 64%, TV and movies coming close with 58% and 54%, and books with 40% of interests only. These scores can be explained by the volume and uniqueness of interests within each domain.

General interests include the largest number of interests, while not too many them are unique. Hence, the predictions achieve the highest precision. General interests are followed by music, but the latter have much more unique interests, such that the precision is lower. TV and movies domains have a comparable number of interests, but TV has less unique interests and its precision is slightly higher. Finally, books have the smallest number of interests, and, consequently, achieves the lower precision.

5. CONCLUSIONS

This work follows on previous works on multi-OSN personalization and studies how information gathered from various OSNs can lead to more accurate interest recommendations. Specifically, we investigate the potential of multi-OSN, cross-domain, and graph based features. We showed that the contribution of the gathered data to the accuracy of the predictions varies across the OSNs: it is heavily dependent on the features in use and on the source, domain, popularity, and uniqueness of the interests.

Our work represents the first step towards an aggregated view of user interests, as expressed on social networks. We plan to investigate the ways to obtain the optimal combination of features leading to higher precision rates, and also to conduct a deeper analysis of the impact of data availability on the classification process.

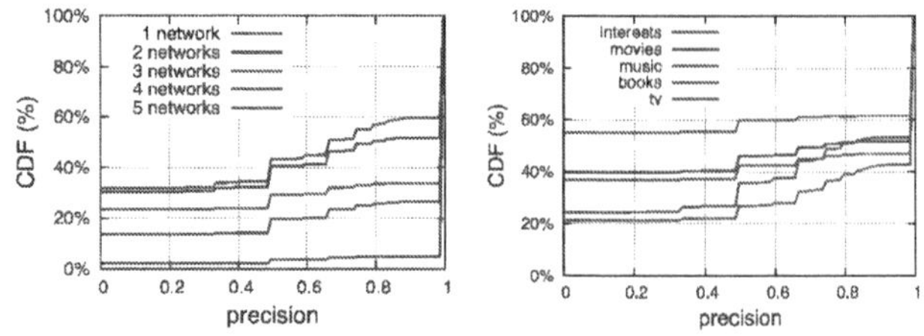

(a) Network Analysis (b) Domain Analysis

Figure 3: Precision CDF (a) interests on multiple OSNs; (b) interests from various domains

6. REFERENCES

[1] F. Abel, E. Herder, G.-J. Houben, N. Henze, and D. Krause. Cross-system User Modeling and Personalization on the Social Web. *User Modeling and User-Adapted Interaction*, 23(2-3):169–209, 2013.

[2] A. Barrat, M. Barthelemy, R. Pastor-Satorras, and A. Vespignani. The Architecture of Complex Weighted Networks. *PNAS*, 2004.

[3] A. Bellogín, I. Cantador, and P. Castells. A Comparative Study of Heterogeneous Item Recommendations in Social Systems. *Information Sciences*, 2012.

[4] S. Berkovsky, T. Kuflik, and F. Ricci. Mediation of User Models for Enhanced Personalization in Recommender Systems. *User Modeling and User-Adapted Interaction*, 18(3):245–286, 2008.

[5] S. P. Borgatti and D. S. Halgin. Analyzing Affiliation Networks. *The Sage handbook of social network analysis*, 2011.

[6] L. Breiman. Random Forests. *Machine learning*, 45(1):5–32, 2001.

[7] T. Chen, M. A. Kaafar, A. Friedman, and R. Boreli. Is More Always Merrier?: A Deep Dive into Online Social Footprints. In *ACM SIGCOMM WOSN*, 2012.

[8] C. Elkan and K. Noto. Learning Classifiers from Only Positive and Unlabeled Data. In *KDD*, 2008.

[9] M. Latapy, C. Magnien, and N. D. Vecchio. Basic Notions for the Analysis of Large Two-Mode Networks. *Social Networks*, 2008.

[10] F. Orlandi, J. Breslin, and A. Passant. Aggregated, Interoperable and Multi-domain User Profiles for the Social Web. In *I-SEMANTICS*. ACM, 2012.

[11] L. Page, S. Brin, R. Motwani, and T. Winograd. The Pagerank Citation Ranking: Bringing Order to the Web. Technical Report, Stanford University, 1999.

[12] B. Shapira, L. Rokach, and S. Freilikhman. Facebook Single and Cross Domain Data for Recommendation Systems. *User Modeling and User-Adapted Interaction*, 23(2-3):211–247, 2013.

[13] J. Xie and T. Xiong. Stochastic Semi-Supervised Learning on Partially Labeled Imbalanced Data. *Active Learning Challenge Challenges in Machine Learning*, 2011.

Differential Data Analysis for Recommender Systems

Richard Chow*
Intel Corporation
richard.chow@intel.com

Hongxia Jin
Samsung Electronics R&D
hongxia.jin@samsung.com

Bart Knijnenburg*
UC Irvine
bart.k@uci.edu

Gokay Saldamli
Samsung Electronics R&D
gokay.s@samsung.com

ABSTRACT

We present techniques to characterize which data contributes most to the accuracy of a recommendation algorithm. Our main technique is called differential data analysis. The name is inspired by other sorts of differential analysis, such as differential power analysis and differential cryptanalysis, where insight comes through analysis of slightly differing inputs. In differential data analysis we chunk the data and compare results in the presence or absence of each chunk. We apply differential data analysis to two datasets and three different attributes. The first attribute is called user hardship. This is a novel attribute, particularly relevant to location datasets, that indicates how burdensome a data point was to achieve. The second and third attributes are more standard: timestamp and user rating. For user rating, we confirm previous work concerning the increased importance to the recommender of high and low user ratings.

Categories and Subject Descriptors

H.3.3 [**Information Storage and Retrieval**]: Information Search and Retrieval—*Information Filtering*

General Terms

Experimentation, Human Factors

Keywords

Recommender Systems

1. INTRODUCTION

Services that use recommender systems have become increasingly common and most of these systems exist by virtue of "big data" stored and used for recommendation and personalization purposes. One example is location recommender systems (e.g., recommending nearby points-of-interest), a large and growing area because of the connection with mobile devices. What part of all this data is really necessary for making good recommendations?

This question is our main motivation for the paper. Our approach starts with techniques to rank data according to usefulness to the recommender system. In essence, we identify attribute values which are associated with usefulness to the recommender. We test the association through what we call *differential data analysis*: we select data according to attribute values and observe the effect of the presence and absence of this data on recommendation accuracy.

Our work has applications to user privacy and data reduction, but due to space considerations we only mention these applications in passing here and defer detailed discussion to the extended version of this paper [1]. One of the main challenges of recommender systems is user privacy, as the data to build a user profile can be potentially sensitive or embarrassing. Adding fake data and suppressing actual data are standard tactics to enhance user privacy, and one consequence of our work is to make these tactics more efficient.

2. DIFFERENTIAL DATA ANALYSIS

Our main experimental technique involves dividing the data into chunks and comparing results in the presence or absence of each chunk. More specifically, suppose a data attribute ranks each user's data in some way, for instance by time or user rating. One can then divide the data into chunks based on this ranking. For convenience, we often divide into 10 chunks, or *deciles*. We can then examine the relative effect of a particular decile on recommendation accuracy as follows. We form a training and test set as usual. We rank each user's training data by the data attribute under examination. We remove the first decile of each user's data from the training set and calculate the recommendation accuracy (using a fixed algorithm). We continue by removing the second decile of each user's data, etc., and we end up with 10 readings for the accuracy, which can then be compared. A relatively high accuracy reading implies the corresponding decile is less important to the recommender; a low accuracy reading implies the corresponding decile is more important.

Note that there are other ways to do the differential data comparison. Rather than removing data deciles from all users simultaneously, an alternative approach would consider each user in isolation. Deciles would be removed from one user at a time, the effect on recommendation accuracy

*Work performed while at Samsung Electronics R&D.

RecSys'13, October 12–16, 2013, Hong Kong, China.
Copyright 2013 ACM 978-1-4503-2409-0/13/10 ...$15.00.
http://dx.doi.org/10.1145/2507157.2507190.

would be measured for that user, and accuracy measurements would be aggregated over all users at the end. For the experiments described in this paper, we used the former approach since it is less computationally intensive.

3. DATA ATTRIBUTES

We study three data attributes in this work. The first attribute we examine is a "user hardship" for each data point, the effort it takes the user to attain the data point. The idea is that data points which are more or less difficult to achieve may be more or less indicative of a user's preferences. This attribute is most intuitively associated with location datasets. To compute the user hardship on our location dataset, a user's location traces can be clustered according to surface-of-the-earth distance, and points are ranked according to their distance to the set of cluster centroids. We call this the KMeans user hardship measure. Points furthest away from the cluster centroids have a higher user hardship score, as these locations are further from a user's usual haunts and require more work to get to. Another way to compute the user hardship is to measure the distance to any other point (rather than the cluster centroid). We call this the Density user hardship measure. We present experimental results in Section 4.1 on user hardship for a location dataset.

The second attribute we investigate is the timestamp of the data, for instance the time of a location checkin or the time a rating is given. We investigate whether certain time periods of the day might correspond to more important data. In Sections 4.1 and 4.3 we present our results on filtering by timestamps for a location dataset and a rating dataset.

Finally, our third attribute has been discussed in previous work: the actual user rating, for instance the number of stars given by a user for a product. Previous work has recognized that data with high and low ratings are more important to the user [5] and to the recommender [3].

4. EXPERIMENTAL RESULTS

We experimented with our techniques using two actual datasets, a location dataset and a movie rating dataset. To measure the effect of various filters on recommendation accuracy, we adopt an application-specific definition of recommendation accuracy, as in [2]. For each dataset, we use standard recommender algorithms and measure the effect of the filters on the output of these algorithms. For example, for movie ratings prediction, we measure the RMSE with and without the filter for the same algorithm.

4.1 Location Dataset

We modeled a location recommender service with a dataset of Gowalla check-ins collected from June to October 2010[1]. We studied mainly Austin, Texas, which was Gowalla headquarters and had the highest amount of activity. We also studied three other cities: Los Angeles, New York, and Dallas (see Table 1).

We considered a simple scheme of each user giving a binary positive rating to each location visited. Locations not visited were considered unrated. We ignored the number of visits. In fact, in our dataset, over 80% of the ratings were the result of a single visit by a user, i.e. checking in multiple times to the same location was less common than checking in once. To give users a realistic chance of checking into any location, we confined ourselves to one city at a time.

City	# Users	# Ratings	# Locations
Austin	4871	245153	9577
Dallas	2991	103569	5473
Los Angeles	2957	61891	10151
New York	3213	106125	16861

Table 1: Gowalla statistics for four cities studied.

We randomly chose 20% of each user's ratings as a held-out test set. We trained a Top-N recommender based on the remaining ratings. The recommender's task is to predict the likelihood of the remaining (user, location)-pairs.

We used the following standard algorithm for computing recommendations, following [7]. We did not try to optimize the algorithm; our goal was not to achieve the best possible accuracy, but to choose a representative algorithm and see the effect on accuracy of various data attribute values. For each user, we form a binary vector $\mathbf{u}$ where $\mathbf{u}[i] = 1$ if the user has visited location i and $\mathbf{u}[i] = 0$ otherwise. From [7], we calculate the cosine similarity between any two users u and v by

$$w_{u,v} = \frac{\mathbf{u} \cdot \mathbf{v}}{\|\mathbf{u}\|\|\mathbf{v}\|}.$$

The normalized similarity measure $c_{\mathbf{u},i}$ of u to location i is given by the fraction of users who checked into location i weighted by similarity:

$$c_{\mathbf{u},i} = \frac{\sum_{\mathbf{v} \in L_i} w_{\mathbf{u},\mathbf{v}}}{\sum_{\mathbf{v}} w_{\mathbf{u},\mathbf{v}}},$$

where L_i are the users who have visited location i.

We took the user's top N predicted locations, as given by our similarity measure, and calculated the number of hits, i.e. the number of locations in the test set in this set of N locations. We measured performance using precision and recall. Precision is the fraction of recommendations that are hits; precision@5 means the precision with 5 recommendations. The recall is the number of hits out of the number of possible hits (i.e., the size of the test set for the user). We use the macro-averaged recall, the average over all users of each user's recall. As explained in [7], low precision and recall numbers are expected with such a Top-N recommender. For Austin, our recommendations are an order of magnitude better than random recommendations: five random recommendations would have a precision of approximately 0.005.

User Hardship. We considered two measures of user hardship. In the first, we used KMeans (with two centroids, modeling home and work/school) to cluster each user's training points. We then ranked each user's training points according to their minimum distance to the centroids. In the second, for every point, we calculated the minimum distance to any of the user's other training points. We call the two user hardship measures "KMeans" and "Density". For each measure, we used differential data analysis to rank a user's training points according to the measure: we divided into deciles, and omitted each decile in turn to see the effect on accuracy.

Figure 1 displays our results. We take precision@5 as our proxy for accuracy. We found that recall and precision behaved very similarly in our experiments. Also similar were

[1]We thank Betim Berjani and Thorsten Strufe for this data.

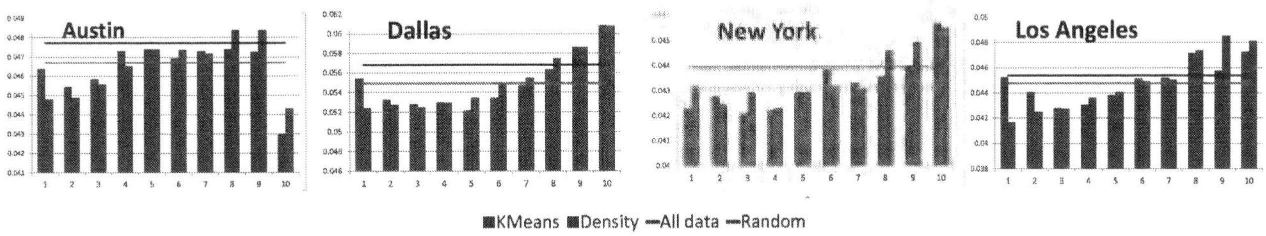

Figure 1: Recommendation accuracy when each decile (measured by user hardship) is omitted from the training set. Two measures of user hardship are shown, using distance to a user's KMeans centroids and using density at the point. Also shown are lines corresponding to accuracy with the entire training set and with random removal of 10% of the data. The figures show that the most useful data for recommendation are generally the first few deciles, i.e. the locations not far from where a user usually spends time.

precision and recall with $N = 10$ and $N = 20$ recommendations.

Observe that user hardship segregates the data well with respect to effect on recommendation accuracy. With the Austin data, we did 20 trials of randomly removing 10% of the training data and computed a mean and standard deviation. The ten sample values of our precision@5 statistic ranged from −3.76 to 2.60 standard deviations away from the mean of the random removals, and only 3 of the 10 sample values were within one standard deviation. In fact, by removing some deciles the accuracy actually became significantly *better* than with all the data, implying these deciles have the effect of noise.

The general trend in the four cities we tried was that the lower hardship deciles (i.e., deciles 2, 3, and 4) were most important for accuracy and higher hardship deciles (i.e., deciles 8, 9, 10) were least important and even could be considered noise. One intuitive explanation is that low- to mid-user hardship is the optimum zone for discovering user preferences. A user would not usually endure high user hardship without other reasons besides just his preferences. Austin is a notable exception for the last decile. The Density user hardship measure generally spreads data points better than KMeans, perhaps owing to the fact that location traces are not defined by only two centroids for many users. We expect the two measures to become closer as the number of KMeans centroids increases.

Timestamp. The Gowalla dataset consists of timestamped checkins, so we also tested whether the timestamp attribute could be used to predict the importance of data for the recommender. These timestamps are in local time of the user. We used our technique of differential data analysis and divided up the day into time intervals so that removal of checkins for each interval corresponds to removing about 10-15% of the data from the training set. We chose this granularity of time interval so one can easily compare with removing 10% of the data randomly or with removing a decile of data using some other attribute. Note that in our experiments we used a binary measure of the user's preference, so removal of a checkin from one time interval does not affect the training set in the case that the user has checked into the same location in a different time interval.

Our results are shown in Figure 2. Overall, timestamp seems less predictive of accuracy than user hardship. The most useful data was around 8 p.m. midnight, and post-2 a.m. data was least useful. In three out of the four cities, the data from 2 a.m. – 4 a.m. seemed to even confuse the recommender and decreased accuracy. There are also notable differences in the cities, perhaps related to culture and geography (at least for Gowalla users). For instance, the more important and less important data for Los Angeles came a few hours later than for the other cities.

4.2 Stability

In this section we examine the stability of our findings, i.e. whether the relative ranking of deciles will change with new data. We used the Austin data (the city with the most data) and the Density user hardship measure. We performed two experiments, one indicating stability with respect to different test and training sets and one indicating stability with respect to different sets of users. We found that using different sets of users was slightly less stable than using different data sets (from the same set of users), but in either case there was consistency in the less important and more important deciles. We did not study stability over time, although that would be another interesting dimension to study.

In our first experiment, we divided the users into four disjoint sets and with any of the user sets, we get a similar qualitative ranking of the deciles: the last and the closer deciles are important, and the middle deciles through Decile 9 are less important (see Figure 3a). In our second experiment, we examined stability with different sets of data. The resulting plots of accuracy versus decile removed all have similar shapes, but appear to be shifted relative to one another due to the differing test sets (see Figure 3b). We note that for all trials, the four most important deciles were always deciles 1 through 3 and 10. The five least important deciles were always contained in deciles 4 through 9.

4.3 Movie Ratings Dataset

We consider movie recommendation as another case study. We used the well-studied MovieLens 1M dataset [6] which contains 1,000,209 anonymous ratings of 3,952 movies made by 6,040 users. Ratings in MovieLens range from one star to five stars. We divided the dataset into a training set and test set by randomly putting 20% of the ratings for each user in a held-out test set. The remainder is the training set.

We used the Biased Stochastic Gradient Descent (SGD) and Alternating Least Squares (ALS) collaborative filtering algorithms to predict user ratings for movies in our dataset, and Root Mean Squared Error (RMSE) and Mean Average Error (MAE) metrics to measure accuracy. For clarity and space, we present only results with the RMSE metric and the Biased SGD algorithm. Results with MAE and ALS were very similar. Biased SGD and ALS are based on a latent factor model found through matrix factorization. We used 20 factors, so users and movies are each summarized by factor

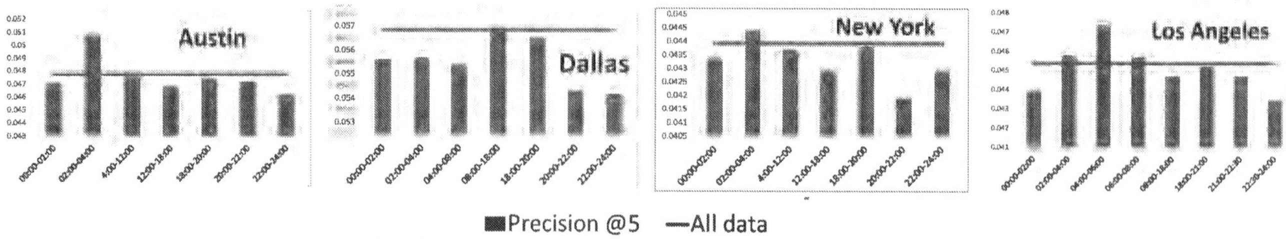

Figure 2: Recommendation accuracy when distinct time intervals are omitted from the Gowalla training set. Each interval corresponds to about 10-15% of all data.

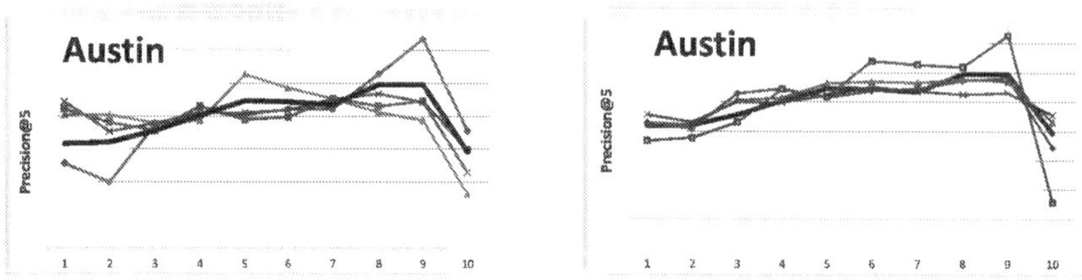

(a) Different user sets

(b) Different test and training sets

Figure 3: Stability of Results. For (a), we randomly divided the Austin data into four sets of users, each containing around 1200 users, and computed accuracy per decile removed for each set. Also shown is the same plot for all users, in bold. Since we were only interested in relative values, we centered by vertically translating each plot. For (b), we randomly divided each Austin user's data into 5 equal pieces and repeated our differential data experiment with the user hardship attribute 5 times, with the test set consisting of one of the pieces from each user and the training set consisting of the remaining four pieces. The original training and test set is in bold.

vectors of length 20. We did not search for optimal algorithms or do extensive parameter selection. Again, our goal was not to reduce error but to see which parts of the data had the most effect on error. We used the implementations from [4].

Berkovsky et al. [3] showed previously that high/low ratings were most important to the recommender. We validated their results using our technique of differential data analysis. We divided each user's ratings into 10 equal deciles according to value, so that Decile 1 contains the user's lowest ratings and Decile 10 contains the users high ratings. Figure 4 shows our results when we remove each decile in turn. We ordered each user's ratings in the training set and examined the effect of removing successive rating deciles. For example, when we removed the 10% lowest ratings from each user, we obtained an RMSE of about 0.89. The figure indicates that high and low ratings are most important for recommendation accuracy and that removing deciles 3 or 4 affect accuracy the least.

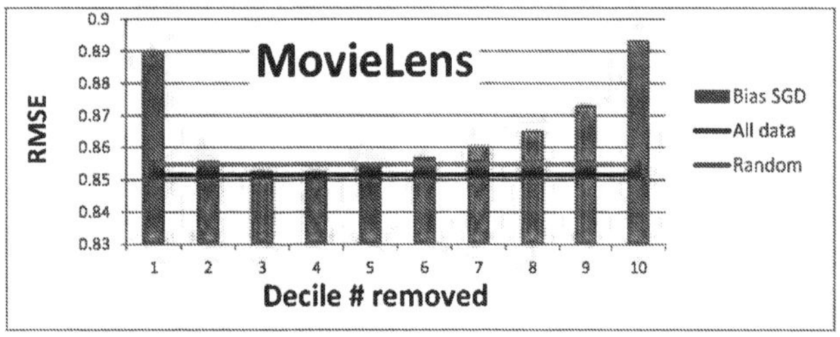

Figure 4: MovieLens Data. Decile 1 contains the user's lowest ratings and Decile 10 contains the user's highest ratings. If necessary, ratings were split randomly across deciles. For example, for a particular user, both decile 1 and decile 2 may contain 1-star ratings; whether a 1-star rating goes in decile 1 or 2 is random. We also show the results with all data (no deciles deleted) and random removal of 10% of the data.

5. CONCLUSION AND FUTURE WORK

We presented a simple technique called differential data analysis. Using a Gowalla checkin dataset and a novel attribute called user hardship, we found that locations closer to a user's usual haunts were most important for recommendation accuracy. It would be interesting to apply the concept of user hardship to other types of data besides location data. For instance, activity data can also be classified according to difficulty or resources required. Using the timestamp attribute, we found that in general very late-night data is least useful and may even confuse the recommender. Interestingly, our results differ from city to city. The root causes for these differences deserve further study. We also applied our techniques to the MovieLens dataset and confirmed previous work that high and low user ratings are most important to the recommender. It would be interesting to explore other data attributes using our technique, for example, to determine which part of the graph for social network data is actually important to the recommender. Finally, our work has applications in user privacy and data reduction; [1] has experiments in this direction, but further study is needed.

6. REFERENCES

[1] Extended version of this paper available on arXiv.org.

[2] R. Agrawal and R. Srikant. Privacy-preserving data mining. In *SIGMOD Conference*, pages 439–450, 2000.

[3] S. Berkovsky, Y. Eytani, T. Kuflik, and F. Ricci. Enhancing privacy and preserving accuracy of a distributed collaborative filtering. RecSys '07, pages 9–16, New York, NY, USA, 2007.

[4] Y. Low, J. Gonzalez, A. Kyrola, D. Bickson, C. Guestrin, and J. M. Hellerstein. Graphlab: A new framework for parallel machine learning. *CoRR*, abs/1006.4990, 2010.

[5] U. Shardanand and P. Maes. Social information filtering: Algorithms for automating "word of mouth". In *CHI*, pages 210–217, 1995.

[6] University of Minnesota. Movielens. http://movielens.umn.edu/.

[7] M. Ye, P. Yin, W.-C. Lee, and D.-L. Lee. Exploiting geographical influence for collaborative point-of-interest recommendation. SIGIR '11, pages 325–334, New York, NY, USA, 2011. ACM.

Effectiveness of the Data Generated on Different Time in Latent Factor Model

Qianru Zheng
Department of Computer Science
City University of Hong Kong
qrzheng2-c@my.cityu.edu.hk

Horace H S IP
Department of Computer Science
City University of Hong Kong
cship@cityu.edu.hk

ABSTRACT

User selection data accumulates as time goes by. Although the recent selections are usually assumed to have higher impact on the recommendation accuracy, empirical studies on this problem are limited. For old data, whether they can contribute to the recommendation accuracy is still to be determined. On one hand, changes in short-term user preference over time may limit their effectiveness in prediction, but on the other hand, one cannot rule out their potential in capturing long term user preferences. The result is important for the system owner to determine which data is useful to make the recommendation accurately. While there have been some related studies on the time dependency of data quality using neighbor-based CF methods (e.g., [4]), its effects remain unverified for other CF methods. In this paper, we study the effect of data generated over different time period on recommendation precision using several popular model-based CF algorithms (latent factor models). Experiment results show that while more recent data expectedly have larger impacts, the usefulness of older data cannot be ignored as long as there are sufficient old samples. However, the addition of insufficient amount of old data seems to have negative impacts.

Categories and Subject Descriptors

H.4 [**Information Systems Applications**]: [Miscellaneous]

Keywords

Data Effectiveness, Latent Factor Model, Recommendation system

1. INTRODUCTION

Recommendation systems generally rely on previous user selections. Intuitively, the more user data is accumulated over time, the higher is the recommendation accuracy. In practice, however, the problem is not as trivial, particularly in cases where less recent data are involved. On one hand, it is reasonable to speculate that inclusion of older data would be ineffective, or would even have negative impacts on prediction of short-term preferences based selections. On the other hand, however, they nevertheless still contribute to the overall improvement in data density, thus should have positive impacts on the learning of long term preference. The overall picture is far from clear, and up to now there are few empirical studies that support or refute either claims.

One related study on the impact of such timeliness of data (and the effect of inclusion of old data in particular) is the work of Pessemier et al. [4]. Their work studied the impact of inclusion of older data on recommendation accuracy in neighbor-based CF algorithms. It was shown that, for certain dataset, old data is indeed useful for improving the resulting accuracy. However, it is still unknown whether similar results will hold if other CF algorithms, such as the model-based approaches, are in place. Moreover, the effectiveness of inclusion of recent user data, although generally believed to be helpful, still needs to be verified. The results would be important for determining the data that are effective in learning user preference, so that the overall recommendation accuracy can be improved. Cremonesi et al.[3] have conducted a research on the effect of data evolution on the accuracy, which concerns how the accuracy changes as more recent data is added. Our work is different from theirs: effectiveness of recent and old data are both considered.

In this paper, we study the effect of inclusion of both old and recent data in model-based collaborative filtering methods. More specifically, we focus on three different latent factor models because of their good performance and that they have recently become more prevalent in recommendation system [2, 7].

The remainder of this paper is organized as follows: Section 2 introduces the latent factor models. Section 3 describes our testing methodology. Section 4 shows the results obtained by three different latent factor models on two representative data sets. Finally, conclusion and discussion of the future work are given in Section 5.

RecSys'13, October 12–16, 2013, Hong Kong, China.

ACM 978-1-4503-2409-0/13/10 ...$15.00.
http://dx.doi.org/10.1145/2507157.2507202 .

2. LATENT FACTOR MODELS

Recently, latent factor models have gained popularity in recommender systems because of their effectiveness in the recommendation accuracy [2]. The majority of latent factor models are based on the factorization of the user-item rating matrix by Singular Value Decomposition (SVD) [7].

The main idea of SVD models is to factorize the user-item rating matrix into three low rank matrices. The idea is illustrated in Eq.1, where U is $n \times k$ orthonormal matrix, Q

is $m \times k$ orthonormal matrix and Σ is $k \times k$ diagonal matrix with the top k singular values. k is the number of latent factors. Alternatively, $\hat{R}$ is represented by $P \cdot Q^T$, see Eq.2. $\hat{R}$ is the estimated rating matrix.

$$\hat{R} = U \cdot \Sigma \cdot Q^T \tag{1}$$

$$\hat{R} = P \cdot Q^T \tag{2}$$

After factorization, each user is associated with a k-d vectors p_u, which represents the user u's preference for k factors. And each item is also associated with a k-d vectors q_i, which describes the item i's importance weight for k factors. In this work, we study three common SVD models, namely, Pure SVD, SVD (bias) and SVDpp [7]. The number of latent factors (k) is 50 for all cases. We first briefly explain the three models as follows. Pure SVD is the basic latent factor models. It measures the association between i (the item) and u (the user) by using the product of user-factor vector p_u and item-factor vector q_i. (Eq.3).

$$\hat{r}_{ui} = p_u \cdot {q_i}^T \tag{3}$$

In the SVD (bias) model, in order to predict the relevance of an item for a given user, a rating bias is also considered. The idea is shown in Eq.4, where b_{ui} is the bias. Refer to [7] for a discussion on the estimation of b_{ui}.

$$\hat{r}_{ui} = b_{ui} + p_u \cdot {q_i}^T \tag{4}$$

SVDpp (also noted as SVD++) is an extension of SVD (bias) by also considering the implicit feedback. The concept is shown in Eq.5, where $R(u)$ denotes the set of items rated by user u and $\sum_{j \in R(u)} y_j$ represents the implicit preference of user u. Interested readers may refer to [7] for more details.

$$\hat{r}_{ui} = b_{ui} + (p_u + |R(u)|^{-\frac{1}{2}} \sum_{j \in R(u)} y_j) \cdot {q_i}^T \tag{5}$$

3. METHODOLOGY

In this paper, we adopt a testing methodology similar to the one adopted in [4]. For each dataset, all user historical selections are chronologically split into a training set and a testing set, with the most recent ones (10%) in testing set while the remaining (90%) as input data (Input data is not equivalent to the training set, as explained later on). To study the usefulness of both old data and recent data, one straightforward approach would be to first divide the data into an old data group and a recent data group, and then compute their recommendation accuracy accordingly. However, the drawback is that there is no objective rule for dividing the data this way. So instead, we divide the input data into 10 chronologically ordered segments, namely $\{D_1, D_2, \ldots, D_{10}\}$. Each segment contains 10% of the total data with D_1 being the oldest and D_{10} being the most recent. Initially, all segments are put into the training set, which is used as the benchmark for comparison. In each subsequent iteration, a new training set is obtained by depleting different number of segments. Recommendation accuracy based on each generated training set is then compared. This way, we can observe the changes in recommendation accuracy and determine which data segment are useful for prediction. The experiment proceeded as follows. To learn the usefulness of recent data, in the rth iteration, the r most recent segments, namely $\{D_{10-r+1}, \ldots, D_{10}\}$, are removed while the remaining segments $\{D_1, \ldots, D_{10-r}\}$ are used as training set. The experiment is then repeated for learning the usefulness of old data. This time, instead of removing the r most recent segments, the r oldest segments are removed in the rth iteration. Regarding evaluation metrics, Root Mean Square Error (RMSE) is a widely used metrics in recommender systems, which measures the difference between predicted rating and the true rating for a given pair of user and item. However, RMSE is not applicable in situations where only 'best bet' items are provided to the user while the predicted ratings are not provided (this is known as the find good items task [5]). So instead, we require a classification metric that measures how frequent the system makes correct or incorrect suggestions [5]. For this purpose, the primary classification metric top n precision is adopted in this work for recommendation accuracy evaluation.

Table 1: Basic statistical information of two employed data sets

	# of users	# of items	# of ratings	Density
Movielens	2,113	10,196	800k	3.976%
Netflix	1,087	1,948	215k	10.18%

3.1 Data Sets

For the dataset selection, we require datasets that are collected over a long period because such datasets contains plenty information for learning the effectiveness of data generated over time (i.e., with both recent data and the data collected long time ago). Two widely used datasets fit this requirements, namely Movielens [1] and Netflix [6]. The Movielens dataset [1] is logged from October 1997 to December 2008. The original Netflix dataset contains more than 480k users and 17K items. For the sake of scalability, a subset of the Netflix dataset is used instead, which was collected over a 2 years period from August 2002 to December 2005. Table 1 shows the basic statistical information of both datasets. The time window of each data segment in Netflix and Movielens is about 2.5 months and 12 months respectively. That is, the most recent data segment in Movielens and Netflix were collected in the last 12 months and last 2.5 months respectively, whereas the oldest data segment in Movielens was collected 10 years before and that of Netflix was collected 2.5 years before.

4. EXPERIMENTAL RESULTS

4.1 Effectiveness of the recent data

We first performed a series of experiments to verify the usefulness of recent data by removing the data segments from the training set starting from the most recent one (as described in Section 2). For instance, in the second iteration, the most recent 10% data (D_{10}) is removed, and in the following iteration, the most recent 20% data ($\{D_9, D_{10}\}$) is removed, and so on. Figure 1 shows the changes in precisions of the three latent factor models as the training data is being reduced in the successive iterations.

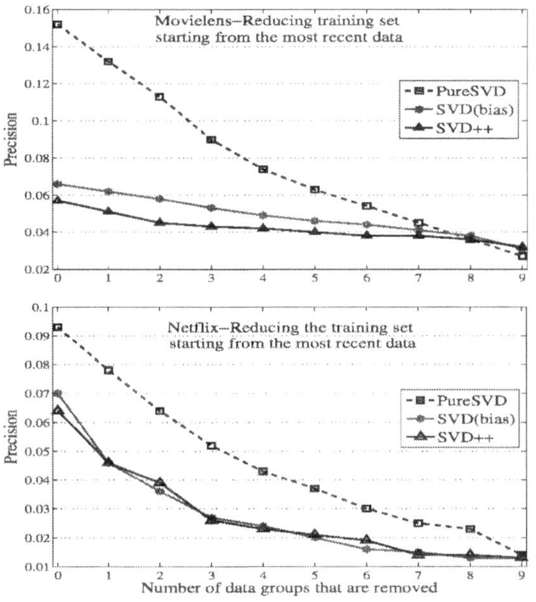

Figure 1: Change of the top n precision by removing the data starting from the most recent one.

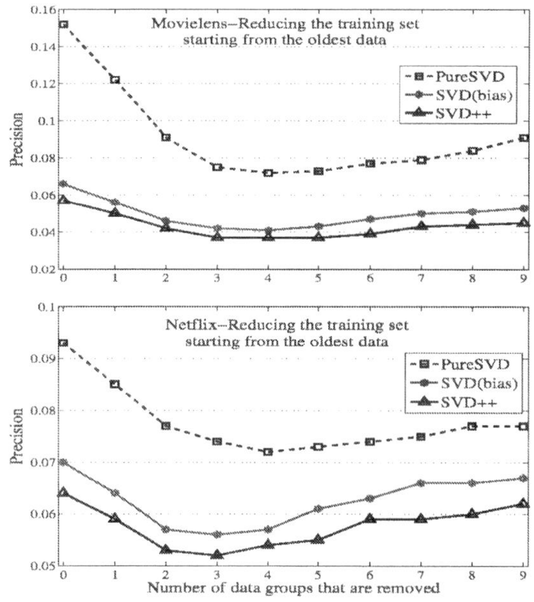

Figure 2: Change of the top n precision by removing the data starting from the oldest one.

As shown in Figure 1, we can observe that in both Movielens and Netflix datasets, the precision of Pure SVD, SVD (bias) and SVDpp decreases linearly as more data (starting from the most recent ones) is eliminated from the training set. The loss of precision may due to that the reduced amount of data leads to lower density of the user-item rating matrix, as a result the recommendation accuracy decreased. For instance, in the first 4 iterations, the precision has decreased no less than 50% after the most recent 40% of the data is removed. For example, in Netflix dataset, precision of PureSVD decreases 53.5% after the most recent 40% of the data is removed from the training set. These results confirm the assumption that the recent data contributes the majority of the recommendation accuracy.

4.2 Effectiveness of the old data

Similarly, another series of experiments were performed to study the effectiveness of the old data by removing the data segments from the training set starting from the oldest one. Experiment results using the three selected latent factor models on the two datasets are shown in Figure 2.

Figure 2 illustrates the decrease in precision of 3 latent factor models when the oldest data segment is removed from the training set. This result confirms the usefulness of oldest data in the recommendation accuracy. But after the oldest 30% of the data are depleted, precision of 3 latent factors model begin to grow. For example, in Movielens dataset, precision of SVD is getting raised after 30% or more percentage of the oldest data is removed. Although the precision increases, it is not as high as the baseline situation. This is an interesting phenomenon that the accuracy increases even though the density of the user-item rating matrix decreases. Compared to Figure 1, precisions decreased linearly without fluctuation. However, in Figure 2, obvious fluctuation can be observed. We try to explain this by two possibilities. One possibility is that some proportion of data is useless to contribute the recommendation accuracy. Hence, by removing this part of data, accuracy gets increased. The second possibility is that some proportion of data is ineffective to improve the accuracy with the absence of other older data. Hence, after this proportion of data is removed, the accuracy begins to increase.

4.3 Discussion

To distinguish the above discussed two possibilities, the effectiveness of the data generated on different time should be investigated respectively to check if there is some proportion of data which is useless for the recommendation accuracy. If such data exists, recommendation accuracy based on it should be zero. Since training set is getting reduced by a data segment, the usefulness of each segment should be verified individually. To fulfill this purpose, recommendations are generated based on each data segment and precisions of different set of recommendations are compared. The results are presented in Figure 3, with the oldest data segment on the left and the most recent one on the right.

From Figure 3, we can see that, data segment generated on different time all contributes to the recommendation accuracy, although the most recent data contributes more on it. Based on this observation, we conclude that each part of data contributes to the recommendation accuracy in latent factor models. Hence, the first possibility which assumes that some proportion of the data is useless to improve the recommendation accuracy is not true. In order to explain the fluctuation of precision in Figure 2, we come to think about the second possibility which relates to the constitution of the training set. Different constitution of data may influence the recommendation accuracy. For example, only the most recent data but without enough older data may lead to inaccurate recommendations.

To further explain this, we introduce the theory of user long-term and short-term preference in [8]. Xiang et al. [8] argued that user selection behavior was affected by long-term and short-term preference. Long-term preference is

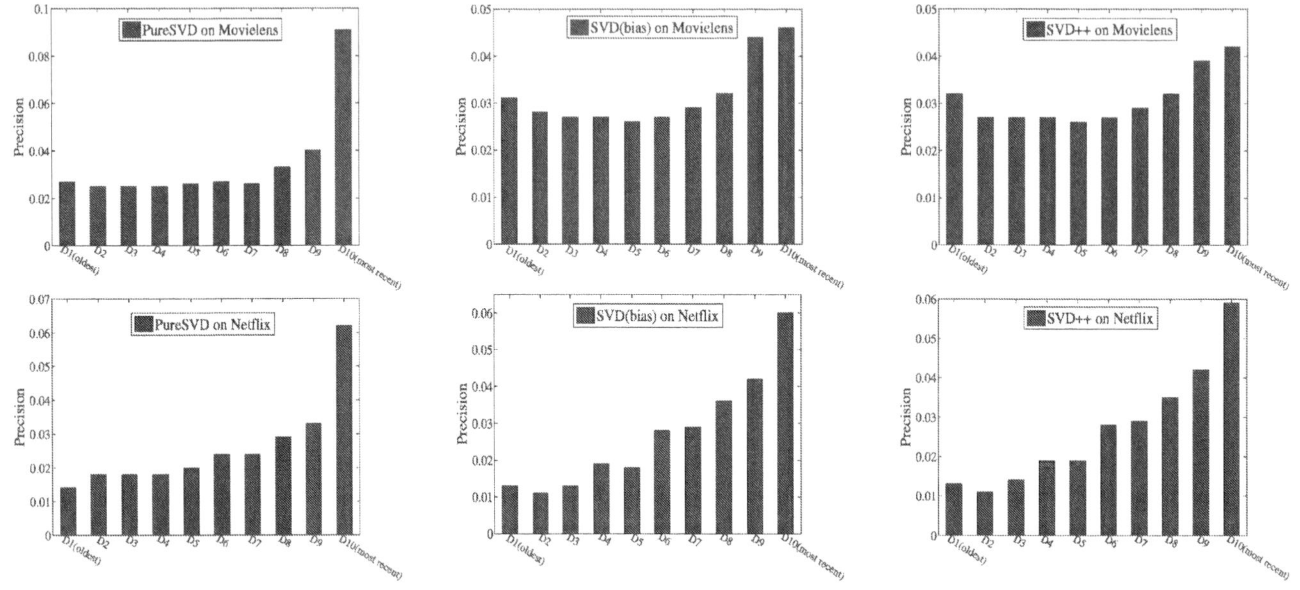

Figure 3: Effectiveness of the data generated on different time in three latent factor models on two datasets

inherent to determine the user behavior all the time, while the short-term preference is triggered by transient events, such as new product releases. Therefore, in order to make recommendation accurately, it is important to study both long-term and short-term preference correctly. According to the characteristics of long-term and short-term preference, short-term preference should be learned from the data generated within a specific time period, while the long-term preference should be learned thoroughly across all the data. Moreover, the long-term preference is time dependent, and hence should be learned starting from the oldest data to the most recent one. If the long-term preference is learned starting from the oldest data, it will be well learned after more selections (recent ones) are put in, as a result recommendation accuracy increased. Results in Figure 1 can illustrate this conclusion. By viewing the results in Figure 1 from right to left (which is equivalent to observe the variation of the precision as the size of the training set gets larger), we can see that recommendation accuracy increased linearly as more data (recent ones) is added in. In contrast, if long-term preference is learned starting from the most recent data but without enough old data, it may be learned incorrectly, as a result, decreasing the recommendation accuracy. Figure 2 can illustrate this conclusion by viewing the results from right to left. In the first several iterations, the recommendation accuracy decreases, mainly due to that based on a small proportion of the most recent data but lack of the older data, estimation of long-term preference is incorrect. In the subsequent iterations, as more data (older ones) is added for training, the long-term preference is well learned, hence the recommendation accuracy increases.

5. CONCLUSIONS

In this paper, we study the usefulness of the recent data and old data in three latent factor models in terms of recommendation accuracy. The experimental results show that data generated on different time all contributes to the recommendation accuracy, although the most recent data has larger contribution on it. Nevertheless, we find that old data is important to learn the user long-term preference. With insufficient old data, user long-term preference will be learned inaccurately, which may reduce the recommendation accuracy. These results are useful for the system owner: in order to make the recommendation accurately, all data should be put into training. Moreover, since the recent data is more effective, system owners can pay more attention on it, such as giving a higher weight to it. In this work, we only verify the usefulness of the old data and recent data in three latent factor models on two datasets. In the future, we hope to verify our conclusion with more datasets and other recommendation algorithms.

6. REFERENCES

[1] I. Cantador, P. Brusilovsky, and T. Kuflik. RecSys, 2011.

[2] P. Cremonesi, Y. Koren, and R. Turrin. Performance of recommender algorithms on top-n recommendation tasks. RecSys, pages 39–46, 2010.

[3] P. Cremonesi and R. Turrin. Time-evolution of iptv recommender systems. EuroITV, pages 105–114, 2010.

[4] T. De Pessemier, S. Dooms, T. Deryckere, and L. Martens. Time dependency of data quality for collaborative filtering algorithms. RecSys, pages 281–284, 2010.

[5] J. L. Herlocker, J. A. Konstan, L. G. Terveen, and J. T. Riedl. Evaluating collaborative filtering recommender systems. *ACM Trans. Inf. Syst.*, 22(1):5–53, 2004.

[6] J.Bennett and S. Lanning. The netflix prize. In *Proceedings of KDD Cup and Workshop*, 2007.

[7] Y. Koren, R. Bell, and C. Volinsky. Matrix factorization techniques for recommender systems. *Computer*, 42(8):30–37, 2009.

[8] L. Xiang, Q. Yuan, S. Zhao, L. Chen, X. Zhang, Q. Yang, and J. Sun. Temporal recommendation on graphs via long- and short-term preference fusion. KDD, pages 723–732, 2010.

Interview Process Learning for Top-N Recommendation

Fangwei Hu, Yong Yu
Dept. of Computer Science and Engineering
Shanghai Jiao Tong University
800 Dongchuan Road, Shanghai China, 200240
{hufangwei,yyu}@apex.sjtu.edu.cn

ABSTRACT

In the field of recommendation system research, a key challenge is how to effectively recommend items for new users, a problem generally known as cold-start recommendation. In order to alleviate cold-start problem, recently systems try to get the users' interests by progressively querying users' preference on predefined items. Constructing the query process via machine learning based techniques becomes an important direction to solve cold-start problem. In this paper, we propose a novel interview process learning algorithm. Different from previous approaches which focus on rate prediction, our model is able to handle wide ranges of loss functions and can be used in collaborative ranking task. Experimental results on three real world recommendation dataset demonstrate that our proposed method outperforms several baseline methods.

Categories and Subject Descriptors

H.3.3 [**Information Search and Retrieval**]: Information filtering; I.2.6 [**Artificial Intelligence**]: Learning

General Terms

Algorithms, Performance, Experimentation

Keywords

Recommender System; Cold-start problem; Ranking; Decision tree; Functional matrix factorization

1. INTRODUCTION

With the development of Internet, recommendation systems have become a significant component in the domain of data mining. However, a key challenge for building an effective recommender system is the well-known cold-start problem, which is to recommend items to new users. While existing collaborative filtering algorithms can obtain high performance under warm-start condition, they will fail to recommend items for fresh users since the recommender system rarely knows the interests of those users. Recently cold-start problem has attracted much attention from researchers, which becomes a hot topic in the field of recommendation.

RecSys'13, October 12–16, 2013, Hong Kong, China.
Copyright 2013 ACM 978-1-4503-2409-0/13/10 ...$15.00.
http://dx.doi.org/10.1145/2507157.2507205.

An intuitive approach to solving the cold-start problem is to model new users' preferences by querying their responses adaptively in an interview process [1, 3, 4]. While there has been researches on the interview process learning, existing literatures focus learning models that optimizing root mean squared error (RMSE) for rate prediction task. While collaborative ranking is equally important as rate prediction, interview process learning for collaborative ranking is not explored.

In this paper, we propose a novel learning algorithm to learn interview questions for collaborative ranking task. The proposed method is based on factorization of the sparse user-item rating matrix, but we define the user latent factor to be the output of a function in the form of a decision tree, whose input is the users' answers to the interview queries. The learning task is effectively carried out with the coordinate descent based update algorithm and a estimation method for general loss function reduction beyond square loss. The contribution of the paper is listed as follows. (1) We propose a general framework of interview decision tree which can handle ranking task. (2) We empirically demonstrate the effectiveness of the proposed method on three real-world datasets.

Outline: In Section 2, we briefly present existing research works for cold-start collaborative filtering. In Section 3, we first introduce basic matrix factorization algorithm for collaborative filtering, then we present our method which models users' preference by constructing the interview process in the form of decision tree. Then, we test our proposed method's performance on three datasets and prove that our model can outperform other baselines in Section 4. Finally we conclude our work and discuss about several future directions in Section 5.

2. ALGORITHM

In this section, we describe our method for cold-start collaborative filtering which incorporate interview process into the matrix factorization model. The key contribution is that we propose a general framework of interview decision tree which can handle ranking task.

2.1 Matrix Factorization

Before describing our method, we first introduce basic matrix factorization algorithm for collaborative filtering. Let r_{ij} denote the rating of user i for item j, where $i = 1, 2, \dots, N$ and $j = 1, 2, \dots M$. We generally use matrix R to present the whole rating matrix. We define observed rating set $O = \{(i,j) | r_{ij} \text{ is observed}\}$. The goal of collaborative filtering is to predict the unknown ratings in R. One method for collaborative filtering is matrix factorization. Specifically, we assign a d-dimension vector $u_i \in \mathbb{R}^d$ for each user i and $v_j \in \mathbb{R}^d$ for each item j. The rating r_{ij} of user i for item j can be estimated by inner production of u_i and v_j, i.e. $\hat{r}_{ij} = u_i^T v_j$.

We can also rewrite the expression above in matrix format, i.e. $\hat{R} = U^T V$. Our object is to estimate the parameters U and V fitting the training data by solving the following optimization problem:

$$\min_{U,V} \mathcal{L}(R, \hat{R}) + Reg(U, V) \quad (1)$$

where $\mathcal{L}$ is a loss function that measuring the difference between the prediction $\hat{R}$ and the target R. $Reg(U, V)$ is the regularization term. For the loss function $\mathcal{L}$, it can be square loss, logistic loss, pairwise rank loss, etc.

2.2 Layer-wise Functional Matrix Factorization

In the basic matrix factorization model described in Section 3.1, the user latent factor u_i is learned by optimizing the loss on the observed data. However, in order to model the new user's latent factor, we propose to search a function which can map the new user's responses into latent space. Specifically, assume we would like to ask users k interview questions, i.e. show k items to users in proper order to ask for their ratings. We also assume an answer to a question can be positive value presenting the rating or zero which means "Unknown". Furthermore, let x_i denote the k-dimension vector representing the answer of user i to the k questions. And we associate x_i with u_i by assuming $u_i = f(x_i)$, where f is a function which maps the answer vector $x_i \in \mathbb{R}^k$ to the user latent vector $u_i \in \mathbb{R}^d$. Then we can rewrite the rating estimation the user i give for item j as $\hat{r}_{ij} = v_j^T f(x_i)$.

Our goal is to learn both f and v_j from the training data. By substituting $u_i = f(x_i)$ into 1, we have the following optimization problem:

$$\min_{f \in \mathcal{F}, V} \mathcal{L}(R, f(X)^T V) + \lambda \|V\|^2 + \lambda \Omega(f) \quad (2)$$

where $f(X) = (f(x_1), \ldots, f(x_N))$ is the matrix of all item latent factors mapped from their response vectors. And $\mathcal{F}$ is the function space from which $f(x)$ is selected and the second term is the regularization term in which $\|\cdot\|$ represent Frobenius norm. $\Omega(f)$ defines the complexity of the function f.

Furthermore, our system should query adaptively, that is follow-up questions should be selected based on the user's response to the previous questions. What's more, since we allow the user to answer "Unknown", our system need to be capable with this situation. Following prior works [2, 4, 5], we use a decision tree to represent function $f(x)$, i.e. the function space $\mathcal{F}$ is decision tree space. Specifically, each node of the decision tree represents an interview question, and it has three branches which mean "higher than threshold", "lower than threshold" and "Unknown", respectively. After the user answer a series of questions, we can obtain a path from the root node to the leaf node according to the user's responses.

We further utilize the decision tree structure to encourage the latent factors of each nodes close to their parents. To achieve this, we assign a preference vector to each node in the decision tree, and define the latent factor of each node to be the sum of all the vectors along the path to the root. This can be formally expressed by following equation

$$f(x_i) = \sum_{s \in path(x_i)} \Delta u_s \quad (3)$$

where $path(x_i)$ gives the node on the path that corresponds to answers x_i in the tree. We use symbol Δu_s to emphasize that each parameter is the difference between current nodes' latent factor to its parent's latent factor. We further define the $\Omega(f)$ as

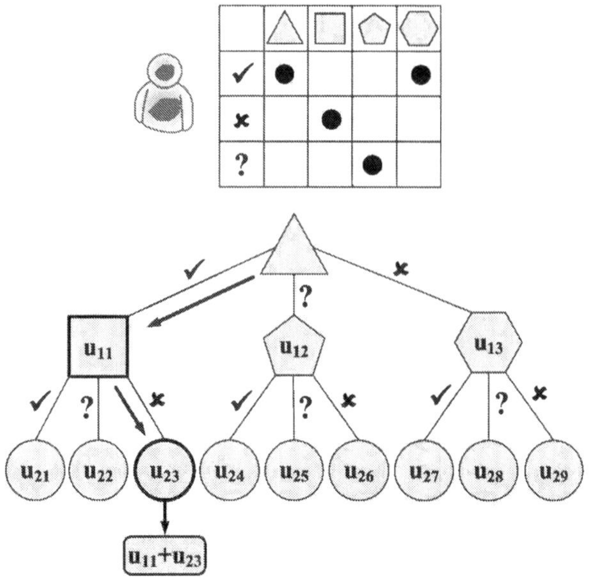

Figure 1: Layer-wise Functional MF

$$\Omega(f) = \sum_s |\Delta u_s|^2 \quad (4)$$

This allows the optimization step to encourage the latent factor of each node to be close to its parent. We call our model layer-wise functional matrix factorization model. Figure (1) gives the outline of our methods.

2.3 Alternating Optimization

The objective function defined in 2 can be optimized through an alternating minimization process. Specifically, we can partition all parameters in Equation (2) into two parts and then optimize them separately between the following two steps:

1. Fix $f(x)$, we can update v_j by regularized coordinate descent. According to the objective function 2, we update one parameter p among all parameters V for each iteration:

$$p = \operatorname*{argmin}_p \mathcal{L}(R, f(X)^T V) + \lambda \|V\|^2 \quad (5)$$

2. Fix v_j, we try to learn a function f formed in decision tree s.t.

$$f = \operatorname*{argmin}_{f \in \mathcal{F}} \mathcal{L}(R, \hat{R}) \quad (6)$$

The most significant problem now is how to find the optimal decision tree from a large function space. Since it is computationally impossible for us to find out the global optimal function, we propose a layer-wise additive update with an efficient greedy update algorithm to find a approximate solution instead.

2.4 Layer-wise Additive Training

In our work, the objective function is defined in Equation (2), and we now describe a greedy algorithm to construct a decision tree which fit the training data approximately best. Specifically, at each node, we select a best interview question(i.e. a best item to rate) and a best rating threshold by optimizing the loss function Equation (2); then the tree will split the user set into three parts. We repeat this procedure recursively until the tree reaches the redefined depth limit. In our experiments, the depth limit is usually set to a small number between 3 and 10.

Formally, starting from the root node, once the interview question q and the rating threshold t are fixed, we can divide the set of users at current node into three disjoint subsets $C_l(q,t)$, $C_r(q,t)$ and $C_m(q,t)$ as mentioned above. For any subset C, we would like to find out the optimal increment on the user factor,

$$\Delta u_{best} = \underset{\Delta u}{\operatorname{argmin}}\, \mathcal{L}(R|C, (u_P+\Delta u, \ldots, u_P+\Delta u)^T V)+\lambda_u\|\Delta u\|^2 \quad (7)$$

Here $R|C$ means that constrain R on the user set C, and $(u_P + \Delta u, \ldots, u_P + \Delta u)$ represents that make $|C|$ copies for the latent factor $u_P + \Delta u$. The vector u_P means the user latent factor obtained by parent node where $C_l \cup C_r \cup C_m$ belongs to. Our method adds a leaf node for each subset, and thus add a Δu to latent factors of each subset.

It is time consuming to directly calculate the Δu_{best} for general loss, we use a more effective approximated solution instead. The first part of the objective function can be approximated by Taylor expansion as:

$$\begin{aligned} & \mathcal{L} \quad (R|C, (u_P + \Delta u, \ldots, u_P + \Delta u)^T V) + \lambda_u\|\Delta u\|^2 \\ \simeq & \mathcal{L} \quad (R|C, (u_P, \ldots, u_P)^T V) + \Delta u^T(\nabla\mathcal{L} + 2\lambda_u\Delta u) \\ + & \frac{1}{2}\Delta u^T(\mathbf{H} + 2\lambda_u)\Delta u \\ = & \widetilde{\mathcal{L}} \quad (\Delta u) \end{aligned}$$

Here $\nabla\mathcal{L}$ means gradient of loss function $\mathcal{L}$ and $\mathbf{H}$ means the Hessian matrix of $\mathcal{L}$ which is formally defined as:

$$\mathbf{H} = \begin{pmatrix} \frac{\partial\mathcal{L}}{\partial\Delta u_1^2} & \frac{\partial\mathcal{L}}{\partial\Delta u_2\Delta u_1} & \cdots \\ \frac{\partial\mathcal{L}}{\partial\Delta u_1\Delta u_2} & \frac{\partial\mathcal{L}}{\partial\Delta u_2^2} & \cdots \\ \vdots & \vdots & \ddots \end{pmatrix} \quad (8)$$

We use $\widetilde{\mathcal{L}}(\Delta u)$ to find the best user latent factor Δu_{best}. Let $g = \nabla\mathcal{L} + 2\lambda_u\Delta u$ and $\widetilde{\mathbf{H}} = \mathbf{H} + 2\lambda_u$, and we can rewrite $\widetilde{\mathcal{L}}$ as:

$$\widetilde{\mathcal{L}}(\Delta u) = \widetilde{\mathcal{L}}(0) + \Delta u^T g + \frac{1}{2}\Delta u^T\widetilde{\mathbf{H}}\Delta u \quad (9)$$

Mathematically, the optimal Δu has a closed-form solution given by $\Delta u_{best} = -\widetilde{\mathbf{H}}^{-1}g$. Substituting the equation into 9, we can get the result that

$$\begin{aligned} \min_{\Delta u}\widetilde{\mathcal{L}}(\Delta u) &= \widetilde{\mathcal{L}}(0) - g^T(\widetilde{\mathbf{H}}^{-1})^T g + \frac{1}{2}g^T(\widetilde{\mathbf{H}}^{-1})^T g \quad (10) \\ &= \widetilde{\mathcal{L}}(0) - \frac{1}{2}g^T(\widetilde{\mathbf{H}}^{-1})^T g \quad (11) \end{aligned}$$

Having above approximate expression for the optimal value of loss function, we can decide which partition strategy is the best one. However, it is also time consuming to calculate the inverse matrix, so we use the diagonal approximation of of $\widetilde{\mathbf{H}}$. Since the inverse matrix of a diagonal matrix is easy to get, we would use the diagonal matrix to estimate Δu_{best}. Denote $\mathbf{D}$ as the diagonal matrix of $\widetilde{\mathbf{H}}$, and Equation (10) can be simplified as

$$\min_{\Delta u}\widetilde{\mathcal{L}}(\Delta u) \simeq \widetilde{\mathcal{L}}(0) - \frac{1}{2}g^T\mathbf{D}^{-1}g \quad (12)$$

We can use Equation (12) to find the optimal interview question q and the best threshold t. Note since there are approximations in the derivations, we only use it to find the interview question. After the question is found, we use coordinate descent to obtain optimal Δu. The update process will enumerate every dimension of Δu_i and fix other dimensions to optimize Δu_i. After the root node is constructed, its children can be constructed in a similar way recursively until the depth of the tree reaches the depth limit.

3. EXPERIMENTS

In this section, we design a set of experiments on three benchmark datasets to make comparison between our method and other baselines.

3.1 Datasets and Experiments Setting

Firstly, we describe our three datasets which are used in experiments.

- The MovieLens 1M dataset contains 6040 users, 3952 movies and about 1 million ratings.
- The Netflix is a large dataset for testing collaborative filtering algorithm. It contains 480189 users, 17770 items and over 100 million ratings.
- The Yahoo! Music KDDCup Track 1 dataset which contains 253 million ratings includes 1 million users and over 624 thousand music from the Yahoo! Music website.

We test the ranking performance in our experiments. The performance of ranking task can be measured by mean average precision (MAP), which is defined as follows

$$MAP = (\frac{1}{|\mathcal{U}|}\sum_{i\in\mathcal{U}}(\frac{1}{|\mathcal{O}_i|}\sum_{j\in\mathcal{O}_i} P@(rank_i(j))) \quad (13)$$

where $\mathcal{U}$ represents the set of all users included in test set, $\mathcal{O}_i$ means the observed item set of user i and $rank_i(j)$ calculates the rank of item j in the ranking list of user i. Furthermore, $P@n$ calculates the fraction of top n recommended items that are positive.

Our experiment setting is as same as that in Zhou et al. [5]. For each dataset, we split the users into two disjoint subsets, the training set and the test set. The ratings of each user in the test set are partitioned into two sets: the first set is used to generate the user responses while the second set is used to evaluate the performance. For ranking task, our experimental setting here is to sample negative instances for training data and test data separately. For test data, to simulate users' rank list, we randomly sample negative items 10 times as positive items for each user as test data.

The algorithms tested in our experiments are summarized as follows,

- **EIP** It is our algorithm which is short for efficient interview process. It can handle various kinds of loss function including rank loss, and it has excellent efficiency. We set λ_u at 10 in our experiments by cross validation.
- **FixQ** It is short for "fixed questions" which represents the method that select top-k popular items as static interview questions, and then use feature based MF to solve the problem by leverage the answers to interview as implicit feedback.
- **Warm-MF** Additionally, we combine training set and answer set together as a new training set to simulate the situation of warm-start matrix factorization.
- **fMF** It is proposed in Zhou et al. [5], in which they use closed-form solution to optimize loss function alternately. Although it cannot handle other loss function but square loss, for completeness, we also conduct experiment on rate prediction and use it as a baseline.

3.2 Results on Ranking

In this section, we test the ranking performance of our algorithm on three datasets.

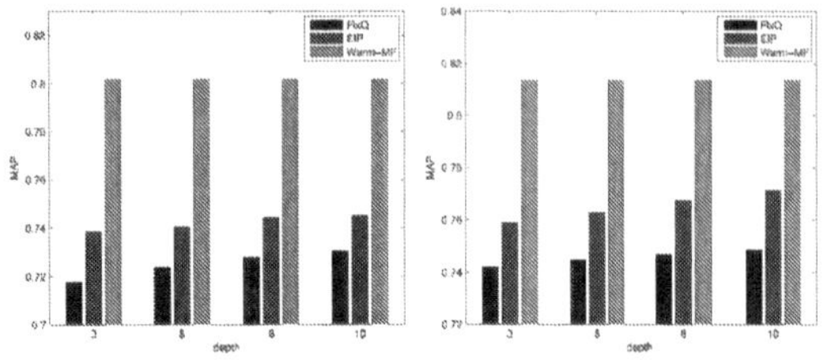

(a) MAP on MovieLens (b) MAP on Netflix

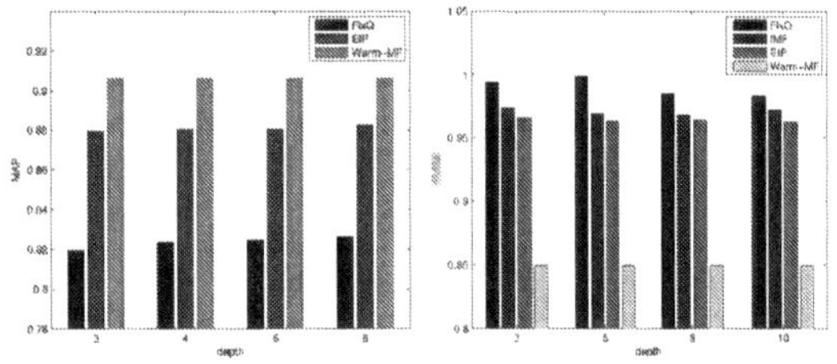

(c) MAP on Yahoo! Music (d) RMSE on MovieLens

Figure 2: Experimental Results

3.2.1 MAP Performance on MovieLens

Firstly, we evaluate the MAP for EIP, FixQ and Warm-MF on MovieLens since fMF cannot handle the logistic loss. We test four sets of results by setting number of interview questions at 3, 5, 8, 10 respectively. The detailed MAP results of three algorithms are shown in Figure (2(a)). From the MAP results of each of the algorithm, we can get some basic observations. Firstly, we find that our proposed approach EIP do outperforms FixQ in this rank task. And MAP of EIP is higher than FixQ by 2% averagely. Secondly, Warm-MF works better than EIP. And the gap between these two algorithm is quite large, which is about 6%. That is, on this dataset, the advantage of warm-start situation is obvious. Finally, the improvement of MAP caused by the increment of the number of interview question is quite notable.

3.2.2 MAP Performance on Netflix

In this section, we report the performance of three algorithms on Netflix. We give the comparison of our method against other two in Figure (2(b)). And here we also set the number of interview questions at 3, 5, 8, 10, which is similar to that in previous sections. It is evident that EIP achieves a significant improvement over FixQ. Here the MAP of EIP is still higher than that of EIP by about 2%. The warm-start situation also has obvious advantage, which outperform EIP by 5% approximately. Furthermore, the effect of the increment of the number of interview questions is still evident here.

3.2.3 MAP Performance on Yahoo! Music

Finally, experiments are conducted on Yahoo! Music dataset, the largest dataset mentioned in this paper. Different from previous sections, we set the number of interview questions at 3, 4, 5, 6 to make the training time shorter because of the scale of the dataset. We present MAP results of three algorithm as Figure (2(c)). Figure (2(c)) gives us an abstract impression that EIP outperform FixQ obviously. The gap between EIP and FixQ reaches about 7% averagely. And another bright spot in Figure (2(c)) is that EIP outperforms Warm-MF by a bit less than 3%, which means our method almost reaches the rank performance of warm-start situation in this dataset. Last but not the least, the improvement caused by the depth of the decision tree is not as evident as above. Even when the depth reaches 6, the MAP begins to decrease, which means our model becomes overfitting.

3.3 Results on Prediction

In this subsection, we show more experimental results of our algorithm on prediction tasks and we use widely used metric RMSE as evaluate the performance of each algorithm.

We compare the prediction performance on MovieLens. We also involve fMF here to make a comparison with other two algorithms. As Figure (2(d)) shows, our method outperforms fMF and FixQ. However, we can also find that the RMSE performance of cold-start algorithms is far worse than that of Warm-MF, which is not similar to MAP performance. Furthermore, when the depth becomes deeper, the results of fMF and EIP show signs of deterioration. We think that this phenomenon is caused by overfitting since the skewness of small dataset.

4. CONCLUSIONS

The main focus of this paper is on the cold-start problem in recommender systems. We have proposed a framework for effectively learning a decision tree to handle different kinds of tasks including ranking task. We can simulate interview process to model the latent factors for new-come users. Furthermore, our framework is able to handle different types of loss function; even they do not have closed form solution of the optimal point. We have established learning algorithm based on alternating optimization. At last, we have demonstrated the effectiveness of our method on real-world recommendation benchmarks and compared our method with other baselines.

The current model make the use of Taylor expansion and some inequality estimation to speed our method up and it may cause the harm to the performance. For future work, we plan to investigate how to make the update rules used in coordinate descent more precise, as well as the expected optimal value of loss function. Moreover, we also plan to apply more kinds of loss function for different tasks.

5. REFERENCES

[1] N. Golbandi, Y. Koren, and R. Lempel. On bootstrapping recommender systems. In *Proceedings of the 19th ACM international conference on Information and knowledge management*, CIKM '10, pages 1805–1808, New York, NY, USA, 2010. ACM.

[2] N. Golbandi, Y. Koren, and R. Lempel. Adaptive bootstrapping of recommender systems using decision trees. In *Proceedings of the fourth ACM international conference on Web search and data mining*, WSDM '11, pages 595–604, New York, NY, USA, 2011. ACM.

[3] A. M. Rashid, I. Albert, D. Cosley, S. K. Lam, S. M. McNee, J. A. Konstan, and J. Riedl. Getting to know you: learning new user preferences in recommender systems. In *Proceedings of the 7th international conference on Intelligent user interfaces*, IUI '02, pages 127–134, New York, NY, USA, 2002. ACM.

[4] A. M. Rashid, G. Karypis, and J. Riedl. Learning preferences of new users in recommender systems: an information theoretic approach. *SIGKDD Explor. Newsl.*, 10(2):90–100, Dec. 2008.

[5] K. Zhou, S.-H. Yang, and H. Zha. Functional matrix factorizations for cold-start recommendation. In *Proceedings of the 34th international ACM SIGIR conference on Research and development in Information Retrieval*, pages 315–324. ACM, 2011.

Escape the Bubble: Guided Exploration of Music Preferences for Serendipity and Novelty

Maria Taramigkou[1] Efthimios Bothos[1] Konstantinos Christidis[1]
Dimitris Apostolou[2] Gregoris Mentzas[1]

[1]Institute of Communication and Computer Systems
National Technical University of Athens
Athens, Greece
{martar, mpthim, kchrist, gmentzas}@mail.ntua.gr

[2]University of Piraeus
Piraeus, Greece
dapost@unipi.gr

ABSTRACT

In order to predict user behaviour recommender systems generate views of the world according to expressed and known user preferences resulting in 'filter bubbles'. This kind of bubbles generally help users to easily identify objects they like. However, it is becoming increasingly difficult for users to escape their personalized world and change their perspectives especially in domains such as music. In this work we present a methodology and related system that allows users to initiate explorations of music genres by taking a gradual path towards the desired genre while viewing the preferences of other users. The proposed methodology is based on identifying 'latent genres' and using user preference graphs for detecting optimal paths towards a selected target latent genre. In this process we generate suggestions of artists a user should listen to, aiming towards serendipitous and novel encounters. We have implemented our approach in a music recommendation system and evaluated it with encouraging results.

Categories and Subject Descriptors

H.3.3 [**Information Search and Retrieval**]: Information filtering, Selection process; H.3.4 [**Systems and Software**]: User profiles and alert servicess

Keywords

Music Recommender Systems, Preference Bubbles, Latent Dirichlet Allocation

1. INTRODUCTION

Recommender systems provide a widely adopted solution to the problem of information overload by helping people to decide where to travel, what to watch, read or listen to by predicting their preferences. Current research in on-line recommender systems focuses mainly on helping users finding items matching their preferences by generating highly personalized suggestions based on one's specific interests. They do so by monitoring users' online behaviour such as search history, cookies stored in browsers and preferences expressed through ratings or other forms of explicit feedback. Hence, most on-line recommender systems do not enable users to experience novelty and serendipity in the provided suggestions. They reinforce the emergence of a phenomenon called 'filter bubbles' [10], where users view content that is aligned only with their personal interests, whereas everything that stands outside the realm of one's personal preferences remains unexplored. Personalized search results of popular search engines and micro-blogging personalized news streams are just few examples of the existence of filter bubbles.

Music is a domain where recommenders are highly useful since the number of music items that the user has to decide upon is enormous. Even though existing methods help users to find items they are interested in, these methods are usually optimized to suggest very similar sets of music items. However, there can be situations where users feel the need to explore the music world under a different perspective, e.g. the perspective of people with different characteristics in order to expand their interests, acquire a more divergent view of music and identify novel or serendipitous content. This is in essence an urge for a state of empathy, an imaginative intellectual and emotional participation in another's experience [2]. Empathy allows individuals to extend beyond their personal views, and experience other perspectives as if it were his or her own. This need is also met in music, where people are often eager to explore alternative music spheres or what other users like to listen to, depending on their mood.

In this paper, we address the music lovers' need for explorations outside their filter bubbles, by empowering them to select what kind of music genres they want to hear and trying to generate a sequence of artists for a guided transition leading to music that best matches the target genre. For this purpose we use topic modelling on user tag collections in order to identify topics of user preferences reflecting music genres. Then we traverse user preference graphs and generate a sequence of artists for a structured transition leading to music that best matches the target genre. Our aim is to provide users a method which will support them to explore preference bubbles and in the process assist them in finding serendipitous and novel items. The proposed methodology

RecSys '13, October 12–16, 2013, Hong Kong, China.
Copyright 2013 ACM 978-1-4503-2409-0/13/10 ...$15.00.
http://dx.doi.org/10.1145/2507157.2507223.

emphasizes more on exploration rather than on the accuracy of the recommended items.

The remainder of this paper is structured as follows. Section 2 presents the proposed methodology and Section 3 describes our evaluation and related results. In Section 4 we review related work on music exploration. We conclude in Section 5 with final remarks and our plan for future research.

2. METHODOLOGY

We aim at providing users a method that can assist them to explore music preferences of others. Figure 1 provides an overview of the proposed methodology. We rely on available content which is comprised of users, who listen and annotate artists using tags. Tags provide a user-defined classification of artists characterizing the genre of the artists' music.

As shown in Figure 1 we distinguish between two phases. The pre-processing phase involves the identification of 'latent music genres' in the dataset by following a topic modelling approach. In real time exploration users select the target latent genre towards which they want to initiate an exploration. This is the intent or purpose of the user and it can be considered as a means to manually establish the context of the exploration. A 'destination user' who is a best match for the selected target latent genre is identified and a search for a path towards that destination user is initiated in the user preferences graph. Using the selected path a predefined number of items - artists in our case - are selected per path node in order to form a sequence of suggestions that are finally presented to the user.

2.1 Pre-processing

The first phase includes a pre-processing of users and items in order to identify latent genres in the available dataset. These genres will provide users a means to understand the preference bubbles which exist in the user-item space. To identify genres, we use Latent Dirichlet Allocation (LDA) [3].

LDA has been proposed as an extension of pLSA that includes prior distributions on the generation of topics and words from a collection of documents. Topic mixture weights are not individually calculated for each document, but are treated as a k-parameter hidden random variable, where k is the number of topics. LDA is a generative method, based on the assumption that a such a model can sufficiently describe a document corpus and can be discovered. The model uses latent topic variables and probabilistic sampling techniques to generate the documents: documents are produced by sampling topics from a distribution of topics over documents and sampling words from a distribution of words over each topic. To fully describe the model these distributions need to be identified. To this end, LDA is trained and distributions converge before the model can be used in applications. In our approach users represent the documents of the LDA model and the tags of the artists listened by users represent the words.

2.2 Graph Search

In order to solve the artist recommendation and music discovery problem, we follow a graph search approach. We consider the user to user similarity matrix S_u as a graph $G = (V, E, W)$ where: each vertex v_i represents a user u_i; each edge e_ij represents a connection between two different users u_i, u_j; the weight $w_ij = sim(u_i, u_j)$ of an edge is

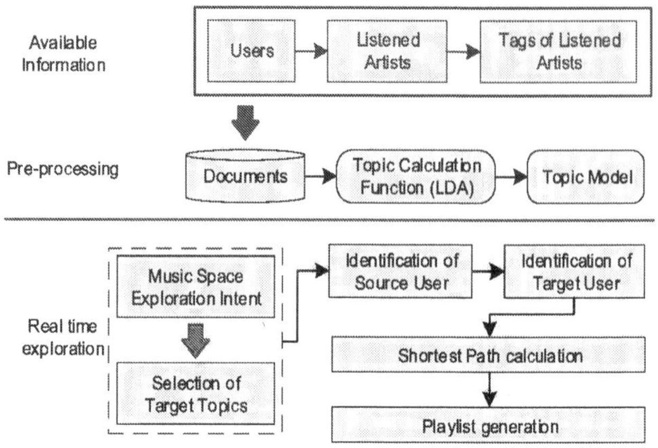

Figure 1: Overview of the proposed approach

based on a similarity metric between two users. Note that we consider an edge between two users to exist if the similarity metric exceeds a threshold value.

Similarity between users is computed as the vector cosine similarity of topic vectors generated for each user by the LDA model:

$$Sim(\vec{i}, \vec{j}) = \frac{\vec{i} \cdot \vec{j}}{\|\vec{i}\| \cdot \|\vec{j}\|} \tag{1}$$

where $\vec{i}, \vec{j}$ are the topic vectors for users i, j.

The path identification is performed using the well known Dijkstra algorithm [6] which solves the single-source shortest path problem for graph with non-negative edge path costs, producing a shortest path tree. But the structure of the preference graph is such that there no connections between every two users. To overcome this situation, we calculate the shortest paths from the source user towards all reachable target users. Then we select as the destination user, the one whose target topic t probability is the highest, i.e. $\arg\max_u f(u) = \{u|f(u) = T_{ut}\}$, where T_u is the topic vector for user u.

2.3 Artist List Generation

For the generation of the suggested artists' list we visit each path node and we select the top n listened artists who match the target latent genre, i.e. the artists whose target topic probabilities are the highest. The list does not have a fixed length and the total displayed items depend on the number of nodes in the path and the number n which is set at deployment time. Our tests showed that the greater the semantic distance of the target topics from the current user's preferences the longest is the path and more items are presented, a result which is in line with our intuition.

3. EVALUATION

Our experimental deployment is based on the Last.fm HetRec 2011 dataset [4]. This dataset has been obtained from the Last.fm online music system and contains (among other information) tagging and music artist listening information from a set of 1892 users. Before building the LDA model we removed tags mentioned less than 4 times in the dataset, users who listen less than 5 artists and artists who have less than 4 distinct tags. After applying the aforementioned filters the dataset resulted to 1790 users, 9880 artists, 2305 tags and 167270 tag assignments by users to artists.

3.1 How the experimental application works

For the purpose of evaluating our approach we implemented a web application which allows the exploration of latent music genres in the Last.fm dataset. The web application uses the LDA model which is trained at a pre-processing phase using all the available information of the dataset. We set the number of topics to 30. This number was selected after several rounds of training with varying LDA parameters and was found to produce topics that make sense and at the same time generate a view of the information structure in the dataset.

In the first screen of the application[1] a display of the top ten words of each topic - latent genre is provided. Note that in our case the words are the tags of the Last.fm dataset. Users can browse the latent genres and the associated tags, and define a 'persona' (i.e. their preferences or the preferences of an imaginary user) by selecting one or more latent genre with the best match. Furthermore users may set a desired proportion of the latent genres associated with the persona (e.g. 60% of topic 1 and 40% of topic 5). Having this information we can match the specified persona to an actual user of the Last.fm dataset. This is the source user in our setting. The same screen offers an option to select target latent genres for exploration. In the second screen users view the assembled sequence of artists. Three artists per node in the identified path are selected.

3.2 Setting

The evaluation involved 25 participants. We explained the concept and the functionalities of our application to each participant and we asked them to explore the music space of the Last.fm dataset by performing at least 3 different queries. As a baseline we provided users with a second list of the most similar artists to target latent genre, i.e. the artists whose target topic probability was high.

Users were asked to listen to a demo song that accompanied each unknown artist they found. At this early stage evaluation we wanted to measure the perceived novelty and serendipitous encounters and overall satisfaction and enjoyment associated our approach compared to the baseline. We asked participants a set of questions, including: "Was the transition from the source genres to the target genre satisfying?" "Did you find new artists you didn't know compared to the baseline list?" (for novelty); "Did you find artists you wouldn't have found easily on your own and which you would like to listen to from now on?" (for serendipity); "Did you find the exploration from a source latent genre to a target latent genre more interesting compared to just listening to popular artists?". "Would you use a similar application in the future?". Furthermore we asked to qualitatively assess the displayed latent genres and provide other comments.

3.3 Results

The qualitative discussion revealed that the majority of latent genres provided by the trained LDA model presented a good overview of the dataset information space e.g. one of the participants stated that "It is a really cool tool that helps you better realize the amazing interconnection between different types of music". Two of the participants though, found the number of genres too high and overlapping. Furthermore, users commented that although most of the artists suggestions were relevant, results that were considered to be out of scope were included in every exploration. The quantitative results (see also Figure 2) revealed that the transition between artists was satisfying and made sense to the users (mean: 4.2, std: 0.5). Both the baseline and the list with our approach provided novel artists so the results with respect to novelty were mixed (mean: 3.6, std: 1.3). With respect to serendipitous encounters (new artists users would like to listen from now on), users tended to agree that they identified more artists with our approach (mean: 3.8, std: 0.8). In more details, users qualitatively reported that the order of the suggestions in our approach was somehow serendipitous while it triggered their interest and urged them to search for more information on new artists: "The presented nodes had a more diverse and therefore unexpected artist result set, containing artists whom I have never before heard of but would listen in the future." Moreover, users found the artists' list generated with our proposed more interesting (mean: 4.3, std: 0.7) and stated that they would use a similar application in the future (mean: 4.5, std: 0.6). Additionally participants commented: "The whole concept is very interesting. I always wanted to explore new music genres but never knew where to start from. I found the step-by-step guidance helpful, easy and helped me encounter artists and music I would never listen to on my own.", "When you select different genres and adjust their proportions the system generates very successful results. Generally it is quite fun! I would definitely use it again".

	Average	Standard Deviation	Mode
Transition from source to target	4,2	0,5	4
Novelty of artists	3,6	1,3	4
Serendipitous encounters	3,8	0,8	4
Interesting list of artists	4,3	0,7	4
Use similar application in the future	4,5	0,6	4

Figure 2: Overview of the evaluation results. The average, standard deviation and mode for our post study questionnaire based on a five point Likert scale from 1, strongly disagree to 5, strongly agree.

4. RELATED WORK

Commonly music exploration is performed through playlist generation and similarities between songs are inferred using audio similarity or song and artist metadata. Ragno et al. [11] take advantage of 'expertly authored' playlists from broadcast music stations and create undirected graphs of tracks that are connected with arcs of specific weights. Markov random walks are subsequently applied in order to find the shortest path from a chosen seed track in order to produce a playlist. Baccigalupo and Plaza [1] describe a recommender system that generates a meaningful sequence

[1]Our application is available at the following url: `http://zeus.epd.ece.ntua.gr/FilterBubbleWeb/topicBrowser.jsp`

of tracks with a case base reasoning process, by analysing information from a repository of existing human compiled playlists. Hariri et al. [8] generate context aware playlists. Similarly to our approach LDA is employed to infer latent topics for songs. Existing human-compiled playlists are then mapped to sequences of topics and frequent sequential patterns are discovered among these topics. Subsequently, the context is determined from a sequence of songs in a user's current interaction and it is used to re-rank the output of traditional recommendation algorithms according to the discovered topic sequential patterns. These approaches focus mainly on satisfying known user preferences and do not focus on novelty or serendipity.

Levy and Bosteels [9] implement a recommender system that considers personal tastes while at the same time recommending novel artists from the long-tail using item-based collaborative filtering based on collections of tags. Zhang et al. [13] try to inject serendipity, novelty and diversity in music recommendations by combining different algorithms. First they use a basic item based recommender that models artists features using LDA. Then they infer artists' diversity with the use of a listener diversity metric. Last they identify users' preference bubbles with the use of artist preference graphs. The different recommendation lists are interpolated to form the final recommendations. These approaches focus on novel recommendations but lack the notion of guided exploration.

Flexer et al. [7] propose a method to produce a playlist given the first and the last songs as well as its length, providing a smooth transition between songs. The approach is based on audio similarity and genre labelling and through the transition it allows users to discover new songs in a music collection. In [12] an affinity propagation clustering technique is used in order to classify artists in music categories and then find a representative artist for each category. Suggested applications of this information include music mentorship, i.e. suggestions of novel music categories not known to the user and artists' lists generation for exploration. Although these approaches support a guided transition to target artists, they do not offer an overview of latent genres hidden in music preferences and do not assist users in formulating their exploration intent.

5. CONCLUSIONS AND FUTURE WORK

We presented an approach and related experimental application that allows users to escape their filter bubble and explore the preferences of others by leveraging recommendation technologies. Our aim is to offer a method that provides a structured and meaningful exploration of the world and assist users in identifying novel content and serendipitous encounters. The use of such a method may not be part of the users' everyday information seeking activities but it can support users in exploration activities when they feel saturated with existing systems that provide somewhat predictable suggestions based on detailed profiles. Our evaluation was based on measuring the perceived novelty of results, serendipitous encounter and overall satisfaction associated our methodology. The preliminary results were encouraging and show that there is potential for improvements and future research. Starting from the method itself, we are going to experiment with alternative settings related to its building blocks. First, a number of graph search algorithms have been proposed and each may provide a modified path leading to different item sequences. Then, the impact of alternative similarity measures and personalization aspects remains to be seen. With respect to the tags, we observed that several are related to personal opinions and are not representative of music genres. To this direction, tags can be filtered using semantic approaches (e.g. [5]). The application area is another issue that deems future research. Currently, our implementation is tailored for the music domain. But other application domains where recommender systems are important, such as news, products, movies and learning content, could benefit from this kind of exploration approaches.

6. ACKNOWLEDGEMENTS

Work reported in this paper has been partially funded by the European Commission in the IST project COLLAGE.

7. REFERENCES

[1] C. Baccigalupo and E. Plaza. Case-based sequential ordering of songs for playlist recommendation. In *Advances in Case-Based Reasoning*, pages 286–300. Springer, 2006.

[2] M. J. Bennett. Overcoming the golden rule: Sympathy and empathy. *Basic concepts of intercultural communication: Selected readings*, 5:191–214, 1998.

[3] D. M. Blei, A. Y. Ng, and M. I. Jordan. Latent dirichlet allocation. *The Journal of Machine Learning Research*, 3:993–1022, 2003.

[4] I. Cantador, P. Brusilovsky, and T. Kuflik. Second workshop on information heterogeneity and fusion in recommender systems (hetrec2011). In *RecSys*, pages 387–388. ACM, 2011.

[5] I. Cantador, I. Konstas, and J. M. Jose. Categorising social tags to improve folksonomy-based recommendations. *Web Semantics: Science, Services and Agents on the World Wide Web*, 9(1):1–15, 2011.

[6] E. W. Dijkstra. A note on two problems in connexion with graphs. *Numerische mathematik*, 1(1):269–271, 1959.

[7] A. Flexer, D. Schnitzer, M. Gasser, and G. Widmer. Playlist generation using start and end songs. In *ISMIR*, pages 173–178, 2008.

[8] N. Hariri, B. Mobasher, and R. Burke. Context-aware music recommendation based on latenttopic sequential patterns. In *RecSys*, pages 131–138. ACM, 2012.

[9] M. Levy and K. Bosteels. Music recommendation and the long tail. In *WOMRAD, ACM RecSys, 2010, Barcelona, Spain*, 2010.

[10] E. Pariser. *The filter bubble: What the Internet is hiding from you.* Penguin, 2011.

[11] R. Ragno, C. J. Burges, and C. Herley. Inferring similarity between music objects with application to playlist generation. In *SIGMM*, pages 73–80. ACM, 2005.

[12] E. Tacchini and E. Damiani. What is a musical world? an affinity propagation approach. In *1st international WS on Music information retrieval with user-centered and multimodal strategies*, pages 57–62. ACM, 2011.

[13] Y. C. Zhang, D. Ó. Séaghdha, D. Quercia, and T. Jambor. Auralist: introducing serendipity into music recommendation. In *WSDM*, pages 13–22. ACM, 2012.

Evaluating Top-N Recommendations "When the Best are Gone"

Paolo Cremonesi, Franca Garzotto, Massimo Quadrana
Politecnico di Milano
Milano – Italy
{paolo.cremonesi, franca.garzotto, massimo.quadrana}@polimi.it

ABSTRACT

In a number of domains of interest for recommender systems, items are characterized by constrained and variable "capacity": the same product or service can be consumed by a limited number of users and the possibility of item consumption depends on contextual circumstances (e.g., time). Our work explores recommenders in the context of these "bounded" domains. We consider online hotel booking as a case study, and investigates if and how "missing" items (hotels that eventually becomes unavailable for users' consumption) affect the quality of recommendations. The paper proposes a technique for defining "missing" items as "best items", and presents an articulated empirical research in which recommendations for hotel online booking are evaluated in different experimental conditions with a user centric approach involving 142 participants.

Categories and Subject Descriptors

H.5.2 [**Information Interfaces and Presentation**]: User Interfaces; H.3.3 [**Information Storage and Retrieval**]: Information Search and Retrieval

General Terms

Design, Experimentation, Human Factors

Keywords

Top-N recommendation task, User-Centric Evaluation, Perceived Quality, Perceived Accuracy, E-tourism, Missing Items

1. INTRODUCTION

An implicit assumption of most existing studies on Recommender System (RS) evaluation is that all items are always available, regardless the number of users who have "consumed" (bought, used) them. In the video-on-demand or e-book business, for example, the electronic format of products allows a potentially infinite number of customers to consume them at any time. Still, in many domains, hereinafter referred to as *bounded domains,* items are characterized by *constrained* and *variable "capacity"*: the same product or service can be consumed by a limited number of users and the possibility for a customer to use or buy it depends on *contextual circumstances,* e.g., varies over time. Examples of items of this type are events and travel services, or tangible products such as clothing.

RecSys '13, October 12 - 16 2013, Hong Kong, China

http://dx.doi.org/10.1145/2507157.2507225

The research interest of bounded domains originates from the observation that, whenever the capacity of an item is emptied, the recommender system should consider that item as "*missing*". Still, *"missing" items of this kind are not missing at random*: as the number of available items decreases, their quality tends to decrease, because *the items that "are gone" are typically the "best ones"*. In e-tourism, for instance, the hotels that are optimal in terms of price/comfort rate are normally booked first and may become unavailable during high season or when the booking time is close to the desired time of usage; what remains available in these circumstances are typically the most expensive accommodations, or the ones that offer low quality services or are in the less attractive locations. Our work investigates how the time-varying capacity of items in bounded domains plays in the recommendation process. Specifically, this paper explores if and how the quality of Top-N recommendations is affected in situations where the "missing items" are those fully consumed and potentially the best ones.

Some prior studies focused on the "missing ratings" problem - a seemingly similar yet very different issue. The missing rating problem is related to the sparsity of user-rating matrixes and if/when missing ratings should be considered as a negative, positive or neutral user feedback when training [6] and evaluating [8] a recommender algorithm. Research in "unbounded" domains – where all items are always available - shows that high-rated items introduce biases in the design and evaluation of recommenders. These are due to the so called popularity effect and positivity effect [8]: the majority of high ratings are condensed in the small fraction of the most popular items, or short-head. The findings of a wide off-line study [3] pinpoint that when the user rating is not taken into account, the accuracy of non-personalized algorithms is comparable to the performance of sophisticated personalized algorithms. When the most popular and widely ranked items in the short head are removed, personalized algorithms are ranked higher than the non-personalized algorithm.

To explore the "missing items" problem arising in bounded domains, our work considers the case-study of hotel on-line booking. We performed a series of experiments that extend a *preliminary* research presented in [4] and are organized in two steps. The first step explores the process through which, in hotel online booking, users select the items they choose to "consume" first, and defines a technique to identify missing items. The second step compares the quality of personalized and non-personalized recommendations in two scenarios – full and limited availability of hotels – using on-line evaluation techniques (142 users). In both steps we exploit a relatively large dataset made available by Venere.com, a subsidiary company of the Expedia group.

Table 1. Dataset used in the study

	Total Venere+TripAdvisor	Venere	TripAdvisor (crawled)
Hotels	3,100	3,100	3,100
Users (reviewers)	210,000	72,000	138,000
Reviews and ratings	246,000	81,000	165,000
Hotel features	481	481	–

2. INSTRUMENTS

For the purpose of our study, we developed *PoliVenus*, a web-based testing framework that can be easily configured to facilitate the execution of controlled empirical studies in on-line booking services. PoliVenus implements the same layout as Venere.com online portal and simulates all Venere.com functionality except payment functions. Users can explore and filter the catalogue of items according to their characteristics (e.g., budget range, stars, accommodation type, city area of hotels). PoliVenus is based on a modular architecture, can operate *with* and *without* recommendations, and can be easily customized to different datasets and 20 different recommendation algorithms. In the baseline configuration (i.e., without recommendations) hotels are presented to the users ordered according to the editor's ranking criteria (e.g., best sellers, marketing strategies). With recommendations, hotels are ordered according to the recommender system ranking.

The user profile required by personalized algorithms to generate recommendations is based on the user's current interaction with the system (*implicit elicitation*). Whenever a user interacts with an object on the interface (e.g., link, button, map, picture, etc.), the system assigns a score to the hotel related to that object. With all these *signals*, PoliVenus builds the user profile for the current user session. The user profile contains implicit hotel ratings, where each rating is computed as a linear combination of all the signals generated for that hotel. The user profile is continuously updated by effect of every new signal and the list of recommended hotels is updated accordingly.

Venere.com has made us available with a catalog of more than 3,000 hotels and 72,000 related users' reviews. Each accommodation is provided with a set of 481 features concerning, among the others: accommodation type (e.g., residence, hotel, hostel, B&B) and service level (number of stars), location (country, region, city, and city area), booking methods, average single-room price, amenities (e.g., spa), and added values (e.g., in-room dining). Users' reviews associated to each accommodation consist of numeric ratings and free-text. We have enriched the original Venere.com dataset with additional reviews extracted from the TripAdvisor.com web site using a web crawling tool. Table 1 reports the detailed statistics of the dataset used in our experiments. The dataset is available by contacting the authors.

3. FIRST STEP: DEFINING "THE BEST"

In the first step of our research, we focused on how to create scenarios of low availability of items that simulate a realistic user experience. The not obvious problem is how to build the missing items set, identifying the items to be removed from the service provider's catalogue during the recommendation process in situations of scarce availability of items. In the hotel online booking domain, experience tells us that the number of hotels that can be reserved decreases during high season, and the best hotels are the first one to be booked and consequently the first ones to become unavailable. Hence we will refer to the missing items situations as the *"the best are gone"* scenario. For our simulation in the empirical study (step 2), we defined a technique to identify *which* are "best" hotels and *how many* of them should be included in the missing items set of the "best are gone" scenario.

To define "best" hotels, we can use two different metrics. According to common sense, the best hotels are the ones with the largest *average rating* $\bar{r}_i$, defined as

$$\bar{r}_i = \frac{\sum_u r_{ui}}{n_i}$$

where r_{ui} is the rating from user u to item i, and n_i is the number of users who rated item i.

As average ratings computed over a larger support n_i are considered more reliable by the user, *popularity* n_i can be used as an alternative metric to define "best" hotels. The two metrics are not necessarily correlated, as low popularity may come along with a high hotel rating and vice versa. To overcome this ambiguity, we adopted the definition of *shrunk average rating* $\bar{\bar{r}}_i$ introduced in [1]

$$\bar{\bar{r}}_i = \frac{\sum_u r_{ui}}{n_i + k}$$

where k is a shrinkage constant that controls the support of the estimate. For $k = 0$ hotels are ranked according to the traditional definition of average rating. For $k \rightarrow \infty$ hotels are ranked according to their popularity. In our experiments we set $k = 10$.

Once hotels are sorted based on their shrunk ratings $\bar{\bar{r}}_i$, the topmost hotels that capture *66%* of ratings are included in the missing items set. In our dataset, the missing set of items comprises 1500 "best" hotels, almost 50% of the 3100 hotels in the complete catalogue of PoliVenus. This value is close to the percentage of fully booked hotel during high season periods in a top level tourism destination in Italy like Rome as reported by *Venere.com*.

It is worth noting that the high season scenario removes from the dataset the short-head items as defined in [3], the only difference being in the notion of popularity (shrunk rating vs. number of ratings). Consequently, the hotels available in the high season scenario are those corresponding to the long-tail, as defined in [3].

4. SECOND STEP: ON-LINE STUDY

We model the quality of recommendations using *subjective* and *objective* variables, among which:

- *choice satisfaction* (subjective): the subjective evaluation of the reserved hotel in terms of quality/value for the user;
- *hotel price* (objective): the cost of one night for the reserved hotel;
- *extent of hotel search* (objective): an indicator of user's effort in terms of number of hotels that have been explored and for which detailed information has been acquired.

Subjective variables are measured using a web based questionnaire (containing 10 questions). Objective variables are assessed by analyzing interaction log data.

The effects of recommendations are explored under different experimental conditions, defined by the combination of two manipulated variables: *hotels availability* and *recommendation algorithm*. Hotels availability can assume two possible values: *low season* (full availability) and *high season* ("when the best are gone"). For algorithms, our study considers three recommendation techniques: *Editorial*, *Hybrid* and *Popular*.

- *Editorial.* We assume as *baseline* "algorithm" the most common approach of online booking systems, which ranks

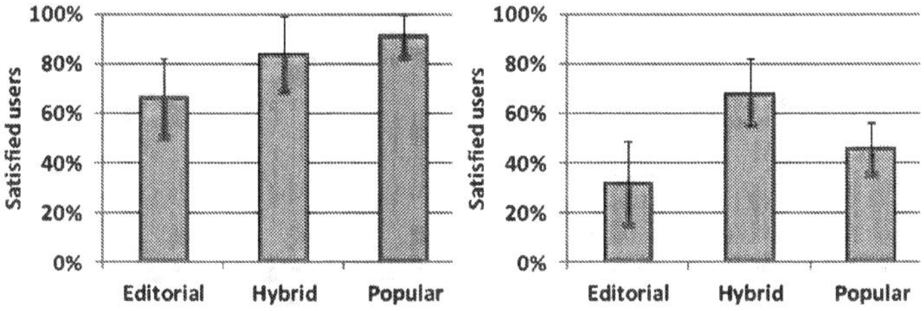

(a) low season (b) high season

Figure 1. Percentage of satisfied users

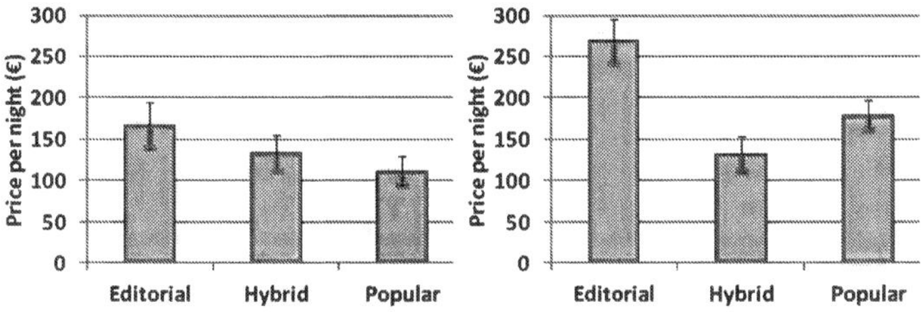

(a) low season (b) high season

Figure 2. Average cost per night

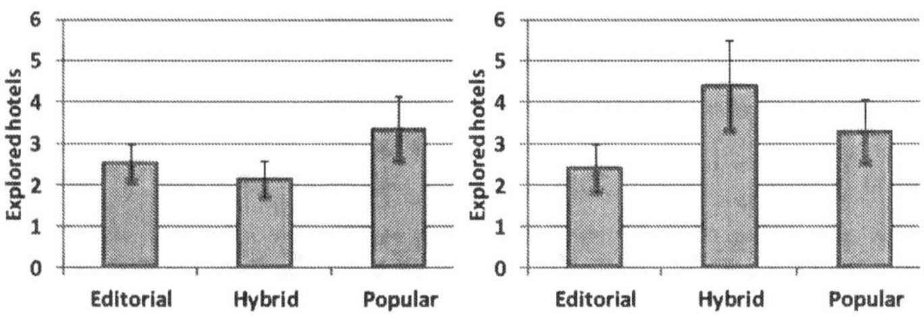

(a) low season (b) high season

Figure 3. Number of explored hotels

hotels based on some marketing strategy. We adopted the default ranking of Venere.com, which is (mainly) based on the number of users who booked a hotel.

- *Hybrid.* This technique generates a list of recommended hotels interleaving the results from *PureSVD* and *DirectContent* algorithms. Interleaving has been proposed in [2] with the name of "mixed hybridization". *PureSVD* is a collaborative algorithm based on matrix-factorization [3]. *DirectContent* recommends hotels whose content is similar to the content of hotels the user has rated [5]. Content analysis takes into account 481 features (e.g., category, price-range, facilities), the free text of the hotel description, and the free text of the hotel reviews. *DirectContent* is a simplified version of the LSA algorithm described in [1].
- *Popular.* This technique generates a ranked list of items based on the shrunk average rating $\bar{\bar{r}}_i$.

Our main research audience is represented by users aged between 20 and 40 who have some familiarity with the use of the web and had never used Venere.com before the study (to control for the potentially confounding factor of biases or misconceptions derived from previous uses of the system). The total number of recruited subjects who completed the task and filled the questionnaire was *142*. They were equally distributed in the 6 experimental conditions. We recruited participants from current students, alumni, and administrative personnel at the School of Engineering and the School of Industrial Design at our university. They were contacted by e-mail, using university mailing lists, and were not informed aware of the true goal of the experiment. To encourage participation and realistic behavior, we used a lottery incentive [7]: a randomly selected person who completed the assigned task and filled the final questionnaire by a given deadline would win a 100€ coupon to be used to stay in the hotel fictitiously reserved using PoliVenus.

All participants were given the following instructions: "*Imagine that you are planning a vacation in Rome and are looking for an accommodation during Easter season; choose a hotel and make a reservation for at most two 2 nights; dates and accommodation characteristics (stars, room type, services, and location) are at your discretion. After confirming the reservation (simulated), please complete the final questionnaire*".

After accessing PoliVenus and agreeing on the study conditions (lottery participation and privacy rules), each participant was automatically redirected to the homepage of the PoliVenus reservation system and randomly assigned to one of the six experimental conditions. After committing the reservation, the user was directed to the questionnaire page.

5. RESULTS

We polished the collected data by removing the ones referring to subjects who showed apparent evidences of gaming with the testing system (e.g., those who interacted with the system for less than 2 minutes) or left too many questions unanswered. In the end, we considered the data referring to *125* participants. They were almost equally distributed in the six experimental conditions, each one involving a number of subjects between *20* and *24*. This section presents the main results, focusing on the comparison between high and low season conditions, i.e., full availability of items vs. when "the best are gone".

Analysis of variance suggests that the six different experimental conditions (type of algorithm and hotel availability) have a significant impact ($p<0.05$) on all variables. We ran multiple pair-wise comparison post-hoc tests using Tukey's method on the mean value of the dependent variables. The results are shown in Figures 1–3, together with the 95% confidence interval.

Figure 1 describes *user satisfaction* in the 6 experimental conditions. In the *low season* scenario (Figure 1.a) more than 90% of the users are happy with top popular recommendations (percentage of "yes" answers to the question about choice satisfaction). In the *high season* scenario users are overall less satisfied than in the low season scenario for all the recommendation strategies. This is not surprising as users may interpret the scarcity of resources in a given period as a weakness of the catalogue of services and ascribe the phenomenon to the service provider rather than an objective contingent situation. For users receiving editorial and top popular recommendations the percentage of satisfied users reduces to half of its value: satisfied users drop from 60% down to 30% in the editorial case, and from 90% down to 45% in the top popular case. In contrast, *users receiving personalized recommendations in the high season situation are now the most satisfied (70%) and their number does not significantly differ from the low season scenario.*

It is interesting to compare these results against an objective variable, the average cost per night of the hotels reserved by users (Figure 2). There is a statistically significant negative correlation between hotel price and satisfaction. In the *low season* scenario (Figure 2.a) users who receive popular recommendations are more satisfied and spend significantly less than users receiving editorial recommendations. In high season, when most hotels are fully booked and the average cost per room is higher, the average price of booked hotels increases by more than 70% in the editorial condition and by approximately 50% in presence of top popular recommendations (Figure 2.b). Still, hotel price it is not significantly different between low and high season scenarios for the users receiving personalized recommendations.

Figure 3 plots the effort measured as *average number of hotels explored* by the users. The diagram confirms the intuition that searching for hotels in the low season period intuitively requires exploring fewer hotels than in the high season period. Less intuitively, in both low and high season conditions, the most satisfied users explore more hotels than the least satisfied users.

6. DISCUSSION

The analysis of three recommendation strategies in the two experimental conditions – low and high season – suggests a number of observations.

In the low season scenario the quality of non-personalized algorithm is comparable to – or even better than – the quality of personalized algorithms. A possible interpretation of this phenomenon is that, when the offer of products abounds, the opinion of the crowd has a stronger persuasion effect than a good match with individual preferences. When a large amount of products potentially satisfy the characteristics that are explicitly specified by the user (e.g., stars, services, location), popularity tends to be the most important attribute of items that drive a user's decision process. Hence in low season conditions the algorithms that are biased by popularity are more appreciated that personalized algorithms where popularity counts less. By their very nature, personalized algorithms rely more on a second order persuasion criterion (personalization), offering recommendations that do not necessarily match the opinion of the crowd (which is evident to the user from the popularity values and ratings of suggested items). In the high season scenario, when available items are in the long tail and have no or few user ratings, all recommended items appear to be "below threshold". They are somehow indistinguishable from one another with respect to persuasive attributes such as average rating and popularity, which become neutral in the decision process; therefore popularity-based algorithms reduce their effectiveness. At this point, other qualities of items become important, such as an acceptable match between item characteristics and personal needs; hence personalized algorithms which are unbiased by popularity increase their persuasion strength as they provide better support to users in discovering novel yet satisfactory alternative solutions.

When the most popular and widely ranked items are removed (i.e., "the best are gone") *the quality of the recommendations for non-personalized algorithms decreases.* In contrast, the effect of missing items is *negligible on the personalized hybrid algorithm.* The robustness of the hybrid algorithm with respect to missing popular items can be explained considering the partial content-based nature of the algorithm itself.

Finally, it is interesting to consider the results of the "price of booked hotels" in the different experimental conditions. It is intuitive that higher levels of choice satisfaction are related to lower price of the chosen hotel. More surprising is that the average cost of reserved hotels in the condition of personalized recommendation is not affected by the scarcity of offer, remaining stable in low and high season. By effect of personalized recommendations, users tend to explore more items, become more conscious of alternative offers, and seem to be more able to discover hotels at reasonable prices.

7. CONCLUSIONS

Our work focuses on business sectors that we call *bounded* domains and are characterized by two features: the *capacity of items*, i.e., the number of users that can consume them, is *limited* and *variable*, i.e., depends on circumstantial factors. We explore the consequences of these characteristics in an exemplar case of bounded domain, hotel online booking. We hypothesize (on the base of common sense and marketing data) that the variable reduced availability of items does not creates "missing data" at random, but it mainly involves "best" items, i.e., those most and highest rated. After defining a technique to calculate missing items and simulate low availability, "best are gone" scenarios, we carried on a series of studies to compare the effects on recommendation quality in two conditions: full availability of items (the implicit assumption underlying most existing research, which works with unbounded domains) and scarcity of items, in which "the best" items are removed from the search space used by the recommendation process.

Our work provides a number of contributions. We pinpoint how bounded domains are a challenge arena for recommender systems research. In addition, we provide empirical evidence that, in the considered case study, the *subtractive effect* resulting from item consumption and removal of missing items may strongly *weaken the performance of non-personalized popularity based recommendations.* In contrast, *personalized recommendations do not exhibit such a negative behavior,* suggesting that their relative quality is stronger in "the best are gone" condition. Finally, we propose a robust technique to define the "missing items" concept, which is needed to realistically simulate "best are gone" scenarios. This method, and the articulated design of our empirical study, can be adopted by other researchers in order to replicate our experiments in different case studies, to test our results using different algorithms, or to explore new research questions in bounded domains.

8. REFERENCES

1. Bell, R., Koren, Y., Scalable Collaborative Filtering with Jointly Derived Neighborhood Interpolation Weights. In *Proc. ICDM '07*. IEEE, pages 43–52, 2009.
2. Burke, R., Hybrid web recommender systems. In *The adaptive web*, Brusilovsky P., Kobsa A, Nejdl W. (Eds.). LNCS Vol. 4321. Springer-Verlag, pages 377–408, 2007.
3. Cremonesi, P., Koren, Y. and Turrin, R., Performance of recommender algorithms on top-n recommendation tasks. In *Proc. RecSys '10.* ACM, pages 39–46, 2010.
4. Cremonesi P., Garzotto F., Smoothly Extending e-Tourism Services with Personalized Recommendations: A Case Study. In *Proc. EC-Web 2013.* Springer, 2013 (to appear)
5. Lops, P., De Gemmis, M., and Semeraro, G., 2011. Content-centric recommender systems: State of the art and trends. In *Recommender Systems Handbook*, F. Ricci, L. Rokach, B. Shapira, P. B. Kantor (Eds). Springer, pages 73–105, 2011.
6. Marlin, B.M. and Zemel, R.S., Collaborative prediction and ranking with non-random missing data. In *Proc. RecSys '09.* ACM, New York, NY, USA, 2009, 5–12.
7. Porter, S. R., and Whitcomb, M. E., The Impact of Lottery Incentives on Survey Response Rates. *Research in Higher Education, 44*(4), 389–407, 2003.
8. Pradel, B., Usunier, N. and Gallinari, P., Ranking with non-random missing ratings: influence of popularity and positivity on evaluation metrics. In *Proc. RecSys '12.* ACM, pages 147–154, 2012.

An Analysis of Tag-Recommender Evaluation Procedures

Stephan Doerfel
University of Kassel
Wilhelmshöher Allee 73
34121 Kassel, Germany
doerfel@cs.uni-kassel.de

Robert Jäschke
L3S Research Center
Appelstraße 4
30167 Hannover, Germany
jaeschke@L3S.de

ABSTRACT

Since the rise of collaborative tagging systems on the web, the *tag recommendation task* – suggesting suitable tags to users of such systems while they add resources to their collection – has been tackled. However, the (offline) evaluation of tag recommendation algorithms usually suffers from difficulties like the sparseness of the data or the cold start problem for new resources or users. Previous studies therefore often used so-called *post-cores* (specific subsets of the original datasets) for their experiments. In this paper, we conduct a large-scale experiment in which we analyze different tag recommendation algorithms on different cores of three real-world datasets. We show, that a recommender's performance depends on the particular core and explore correlations between performances on different cores.

Categories and Subject Descriptors

H.3.3 [**Information Search and Retrieval**]: Information filtering

Keywords

Recommender; Core; Graph; Evaluation

1. INTRODUCTION

Recommender systems often have to deal with sparse data in which only little or nothing is known about many users or items. Alongside works that specifically tackle this task, it is common to focus on a dense subset of the data [12, 5] that contains enough information to produce helpful recommendations. For graph data, a commonly used technique are *generalized cores* [1] which comprise a dense sub-graph in which every vertex fulfills a specific constraint, e.g., the degree of each node is above a certain threshold. The influence of these cores on the performance of different recommendation algorithms has not been analyzed so far.

In this paper, we investigate cores that have been used in the evaluation of *tag recommender systems*. Tag recommenders are useful in *collaborative tagging systems* (whose underlying data structure is called a *folksonomy* – cf. [4] for the model we use) where users post resources and assign arbitrary keywords (*tags*) to them. During the posting process a recommender system typically suggests appropriate tags for annotation. The tag recommendation task is thus to find suitable tags for a given (user, resource) pair. Previously, tag recommender algorithms have often been evaluated on a special *post-core* of the raw dataset using the *LeavePostOut* method: A post is removed from the dataset and the recommended tags are evaluated against the true tags of the post.

We conduct a thorough experimental analysis of tag recommender rankings on three publicly available real-world datasets and critically compare the results on different cores. As post-cores are so-called "generalized cores" [1], we compare the performance of different algorithms on them to the performance on the original *graph-cores* and on the raw data.

This paper is organized as follows: In Section 2, we review related work. In Section 3, we describe the datasets and the experiments, whose results we discuss in Section 4.

RecSys'13, October 12–16, 2013, Hong Kong, China.

ACM 978-1-4503-2409-0/13/10 ...$15.00.
http://dx.doi.org/10.1145/2507157.2507222.

2. RELATED WORK

In many recommendation scenarios, the sparsity of the data is a classical problem which has been tackled either by dealing with the sparseness in particular or by focusing on the dense part of the data (e.g., [12]). Most of the latter approaches are rather ad-hoc, e.g., defining some threshold for the minimal number of ratings an item or user should have. There are few theoretical considerations or experiments that investigate the implications of such thresholds on the performance of different recommender algorithms or the validity of the experiments. One widely applicable methodology to create dense subsets of graphs are the so-called *graph-cores* which were introduced by Seidman [13]. A *graph-core* is a sub-graph in which the degree of each node is above a pre-defined threshold. Upon this work build Batagelj and Zaveršnik [1, 2] who introduce *generalized cores*.

As part of the evaluation of recommender systems, cores have first been used in [5] to focus on the dense part of collaborative tagging systems. Experiments with different tag recommenders were conducted on subsets of such systems, constructed as generalized cores – so-called *post-cores*. A more detailed definition of these cores and extended experiments were presented in [7]. Post-cores were then commonly used in the evaluation of (tag) recommendation algorithms, e.g., in [11] – to compare different PageRank variants on post-cores at levels 5 and 20, in [8] – to evaluate a tag rec-

Table 1: The number of users, tags, resources, tag assignments (tas), and posts of the datasets and the levels l chosen for the experiments.

	#users	#res.	#tags	#tas	#posts	chosen l
publ	4 777	94 427	57 639	397 081	109 984	2, 3, 4, 5, 10
book	4 959	231 907	80 603	1 032 037	268 589	2, 3, 4, 5, 6
deli	75 071	2 999 487	397 028	17 280 065	7 268 305	2, 3, 5, 10, 20

ommendation algorithm based on latent dirichlet allocation on a post-core at level 100 of a dataset from Delicious.

3. EXPERIMENTAL SETUP

In the following, we describe the setup of our experiments to test different evaluation procedures with different cores, levels, and metrics for tag recommender algorithms.

3.1 Datasets

We use three publicly available datasets from two collaborative tagging systems (cf. Table 1): The *BibSonomy*[1] dataset (from 2012-01-01) is based on the regular dumps of the publicly available data.[2] The generation of the dataset is described in [6], including a more in-depth description of the data. BibSonomy supports tagging of both bookmarks and publication metadata, hence we split the data into two parts: book and publ. From *Delicious*[3] we use a dataset (deli) we obtained from July 27 to 30, 2005 [4] which is a subset of the Tagora dataset.[4] As Lipczak et al. [9] pointed out, tags from automatically imported posts are problematic for training and evaluating tag recommenders, since their provenance is unknown. The ability of a recommender to (not) predict such tags does not allow us to draw any conclusion about its performance on predicting user-generated tags. Hence, we applied a similar cleansing strategy as described in [9]: we removed sets of posts that were posted at exactly the same time by the same user. In addition, we cleaned all tags as described in [6], i.e., we ignored tag assignments with the tags *imported*, *public*, *system:imported*, *nn*, *system:unfiled*, converted all tags to lower case, and removed all characters which were neither numbers nor letters.

3.2 Evaluation Methodology

The dimensions of our experiments are the three datasets, the two different core types, the chosen levels (see Table 1), the recommendation algorithms, and the evaluation metrics.

Cores and LeavePostOut.

The construction of the graph-cores and post-cores is described in [7]. The data of a tagging system is modelled as a tripartite hypergraph, which has users, resources and tags as nodes and a hyperedge between a user u, a resource r and a tag t, if the user u assigned the tag t to the resource r. The *graph-core at level* l is the largest possible subgraph of that graph, such that each node (i.e., user, tag, resource) occurs in at least l tag assignments, i.e., has a node degree of at least l. In contrast, the *post-core at level* l is the largest subgraph, such that each node occurs in at least l posts. Since one post can consist of several tag assignments (all with the same user and resource, but with different tags), for users and resources, the condition to be part of the core is stronger in the post-core than in the graph-core.

For the experiments we used – besides the raw datasets (or 'cores at level 1') – both graph-cores and post-cores. For each dataset we chose five levels on which we conducted the experiments (see "chosen l" in Table 1). The difference in choice is due to the different characteristics of the datasets (size, unchanged cores over several levels, etc.).

To evaluate the recommenders we used the variant of the leave-one-out hold-out estimation [3] called *LeavePostOut* [5]. LeavePostOut is a standard approach for offline experiments and has been widely used in the literature. Given a dataset (or a core), for each user u one post p is selected at random. This post is eliminated from the dataset and the remaining data is used for training. The task for the recommender algorithm then is to produce tag recommendations (i.e., to predict the tags of p) given both the user and the resource of p, while the tags of p serve as gold-standard. A score is assigned that measures the prediction quality of the recommendation. The experiment is conducted for every user and the scores are averaged. To ensure statistical validity of the results, we repeated each experiment five times and use the averages of the resulting scores.

Evaluation Metrics.

We determine the quality of a recommender by measuring how successful an algorithm can predict the tags of the left-out post. We use the two common metrics *recall* and *precision* at a given cut-off level k (rec@k and pre@k). For a left-out post p, rec@k is the share of p's tags among the top k positions of a recommender's ranking and pre@k the share of the top k tags in the ranking that belong to p. In the experiments we let k run from 1 through 10. The *mean average precision* (MAP) takes the arithmetic mean of the precision at each new recall-level [10].

Algorithms.

The goal of our investigation is not to find the best tag recommendation algorithm, but rather to evaluate the experimental setups, in which algorithms usually are compared against each other. Therefore, we focus on a subset of well-studied tag recommendation algorithms, namely *most popular tags*, *most popular tags by resource*, *most popular tags by user*, *adapted PageRank*, and *FolkRank* [7].

4. RESULTS

When we compare recommenders' scores on different cores and levels with different metrics we first observe that they tend to yield better scores on the post-cores than on the graph-cores of the same level (in 88.6% of the experiments). The performance of the algorithms on the graph-cores and post-cores, is better than that on the raw datasets in 95.5% and 99.2% of the cases, respectively. This increase of the scores raises the question whether the choice of the core has an influence on the comparison of different algorithms against each other. We will therefore investigate correlations between such rankings on different cores in Section 4.2. Before, we have a look at the performance on different core-levels and particular subsets of the data to find out, whether even using the same core, choosing particular posts can yield better results.

[1] http://www.bibsonomy.org/

[2] http://www.kde.cs.uni-kassel.de/bibsonomy/dumps/

[3] http://www.delicious.com/

[4] http://www.tagora-project.eu/data/#delicious

4.1 Recommendation Performance Depends on Core Type and Level

The most prominent observation is that the performance at different core levels depends both on the dataset and on the algorithm. In Figure 1, we see exemplarily the pre@5 scores for the five algorithms over different levels for the graph-core of the datasets publ and deli. Although most often the scores rise with increasing level, there are exceptions like *most popular tags by user* on publ and *adapted PageRank* on deli with (sometimes) sinking scores. The same plots for book (omitted due to space limitations) are similar to publ. The results for rec@5 are similar to those of pre@5.

Further, we leveraged the property that the graph-core always contains the post-core at the same level: Next to the scores on the graph-cores (×) we plotted the scores of the same experiments with only a slight modification of LeavePostOut's post selection process. Where we usually choose one post per user at random, we now choose posts randomly such that they are also contained in the post-core (+). Comparing the scores on arbitrarily chosen posts to those from the post-core, we see that in particular for low levels it is easier to predict tags for posts from the post-core than for arbitrarily chosen posts. There are however some exceptions, in particular *FolkRank* and *most popular tags by user*. We conclude that focusing on posts from the the dense part of the data often overestimates the performance of recommendation algorithms.

4.2 Recommender Ranking Correlation

Evaluating recommender systems usually has the goal to determine one algorithm that performs best on one or several datasets and therefore several algorithms are ranked according to their performance. Since several setups for experiments are possible – several core types, levels and metrics – the question arises, whether the ranking of recommenders varies depending on the chosen setup. To investigate this question we determine the algorithm rankings, where the algorithms are ranked according to their recommendation quality. A ranking can be computed on the raw datasets, and on each of the two core types at all chosen levels.[5] Between two rankings (on two different setups) we can determine Pearson's correlation coefficient r, as a measure of how likely the score rankings of the recommenders are (linearly) correlated. The coefficient ranges from -1 (anti-correlation) through 0 (no correlation) to 1 (perfect correlation). As Pearson's r takes the particular score values (the value describing one recommender's performance on one setup) of the algorithms into account, we additionally use another metric that only considers the order of the algorithms in a ranking: the *number of discordant pairs* d.[6] Given two rankings, the algorithms A and B are discordant, when in one ranking A performs better than B while in the other ranking B is better than A. Thus in our case of five algorithms, d is between 0 (the rankings agree completely) and 10 (one ranking is the reverse of the other).

Table 2 shows the mean pairwise (averaged over any pair of two different setups) values of r and d together with the standard deviations exemplarily for the metrics pre@5, rec@5, and MAP. We can observe that on no dataset we get

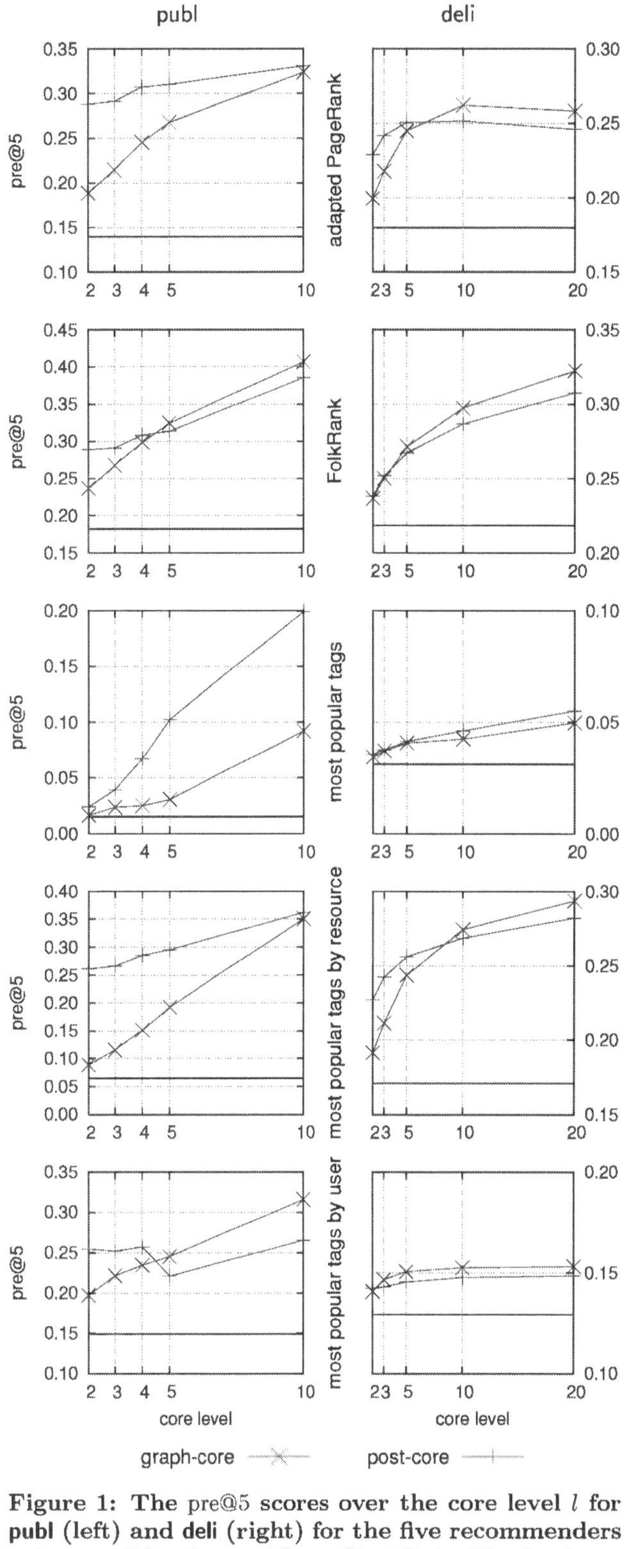

Figure 1: The pre@5 scores over the core level l for publ (left) and deli (right) for the five recommenders using modifications of LeavePostOut. The horizontal line depicts the pre@5 value for the raw dataset.

perfect correlations. Generally, the correlations are rather high, but we clearly see that the rankings are inconsistent. The most stable are the rankings on deli. Here, only in every second pair of setups two recommenders change their

[5] That is, 11 different setups (see Table 1).

[6] This value is closely related to the ranking correlation measure *Kendall's* τ.

Table 2: The mean pairwise Pearson's r, the number of discordant pairs d in the algorithm rankings on different cores, and their standard deviation σ.

dataset	metric	avg. r	σ	avg. d	σ
publ	MAP	0.890	0.093	1.491	1.069
publ	pre@5	0.886	0.101	1.636	1.007
publ	rec@5	0.894	0.099	1.564	1.014
book	MAP	0.899	0.093	1.491	1.069
book	pre@5	0.870	0.116	1.564	1.151
book	rec@5	0.902	0.091	1.455	1.068
deli	MAP	0.989	0.011	0.545	0.503
deli	pre@5	0.987	0.012	0.545	0.503
deli	rec@5	0.988	0.011	0.545	0.503

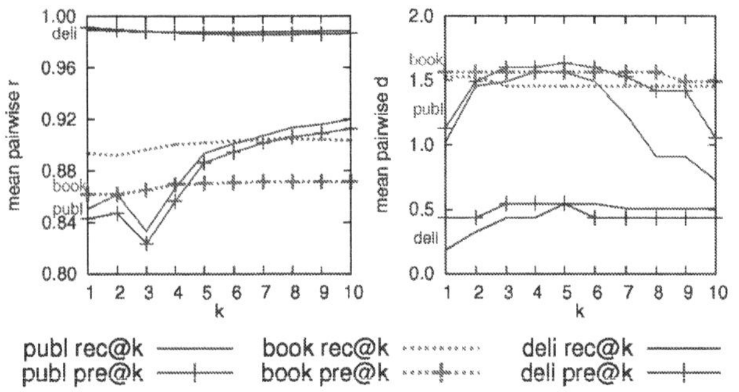

Figure 2: The mean pairwise Pearson's correlation r and number of discordant pairs d over the cut-level k for the metrics rec@k and pre@k.

order. On the two BibSonomy datasets, the values are similar: here, on average, in two rankings one or two pairs of recommenders have different order. Thus it is evident, that different setups lead to different conclusions about the ranking of algorithms. We computed which of the cores yield the ranking that is most consistent with the raw data. For all datasets these are the graph-cores at levels 2 and 3, i.e., the two largest cores.

The consistency of the rankings also depends on the particular metric that is employed. In Figure 2, we see the mean pairwise values of r and d for rec@k and pre@k with k running from 1 through 10. We see that for deli the consistency is quite stable for both metrics precision and recall. However, for the other datasets the values vary and the highest consistency is achieved for $k = 10$.

5. CONCLUSION

We have analyzed the use of cores for the evaluation of tag recommendations. In the experiments, we have shown that using cores for offline evaluation has its pitfalls as recommenders perform differently in different core setups of the same dataset. Focusing on one particular core can produce non-stable results, evaluating the performance of recommenders on another core type or at another core level might yield a different ranking of the algorithms. Thus, we have established, that next to the choice of the dataset(s), the evaluation procedures and measures, the choice of the core is of significance to the outcome of experiments. To minimize this influence, any evaluation should be performed either directly on the raw data or on several core types and levels. On the other hand, we could observe that even cores at higher levels yield correlated results to those of the raw-data. For a preliminary comparison of recommenders it is therefore possible to use several smaller cores to get a quick first impression of their overall performance.

6. ACKNOWLEDGEMENTS

Part of this research was funded by the DFG in the project "Info 2.0 – Informationelle Selbstbestimmung im Web 2.0".

7. REFERENCES

[1] V. Batagelj and M. M. Zaveršnik. Generalized cores. *CoRR*, cs.DS/0202039, 2002.

[2] V. Batagelj and M. Zaveršnik. Fast algorithms for determining (generalized) core groups in social networks. *Advances in Data Analysis and Classification*, 5(2):129–145, 2011.

[3] J. L. Herlocker, J. A. Konstan, L. G. Terveen, and J. T. Riedl. Evaluating collaborative filtering recommender systems. *ACM Trans. Inf. Syst.*, 22(1):5–53, 2004.

[4] A. Hotho, R. Jäschke, C. Schmitz, and G. Stumme. Information retrieval in folksonomies: Search and ranking. In *The Semantic Web: Research and Applications*, volume 4011 of *LNCS*, pages 411–426, Berlin/Heidelberg, 2006. Springer.

[5] R. Jäschke, L. Balby Marinho, A. Hotho, L. Schmidt-Thieme, and G. Stumme. Tag recommendations in folksonomies. In *Proc. 11th European Conf. Principles and Practice of Knowledge Discovery in Databases*, volume 4702 of *LNCS*, pages 506–514, Berlin/Heidelberg, 2007. Springer.

[6] R. Jäschke, A. Hotho, F. Mitzlaff, and G. Stumme. Challenges in tag recommendations for collaborative tagging systems. In *Recommender Systems for the Social Web*, volume 32 of *Intelligent Systems Reference Library*, pages 65–87. Springer, Berlin/Heidelberg, 2012.

[7] R. Jäschke, L. Marinho, A. Hotho, L. Schmidt-Thieme, and G. Stumme. Tag recommendations in social bookmarking systems. *AI Communications*, 21(4):231–247, 2008.

[8] R. Krestel, P. Fankhauser, and W. Nejdl. Latent dirichlet allocation for tag recommendation. In *Proc. 3rd Conf. on Recommender Systems*, pages 61–68, New York, NY, USA, 2009. ACM.

[9] M. Lipczak, Y. Hu, Y. Kollet, and E. Milios. Tag sources for recommendation in collaborative tagging systems. In *ECML PKDD Discovery Challenge*, volume 497 of *CEUR-WS.org*, pages 157–172, 2009.

[10] C. D. Manning, P. Raghavan, and H. Schütze. *Introduction to Information Retrieval*. Cambridge University Press, New York, 2008.

[11] M. Ramezani. Improving graph-based approaches for personalized tag recommendation. *Journal of Emerging Technologies in Web Intelligence*, 3(2), 2011.

[12] B. Sarwar, G. Karypis, J. Konstan, and J. Riedl. Item-based collaborative filtering recommendation algorithms. In *Proc. 10th Int. Conf. World Wide Web*, pages 285–295, New York, NY, USA, 2001. ACM.

[13] S. B. Seidman. Network structure and minimum degree. *Social Networks*, 5(3):269 – 287, 1983.

Recommendation in Heterogeneous Information Networks with Implicit User Feedback*

Xiao Yu† Xiang Ren† Yizhou Sun‡ Bradley Sturt† Urvashi Khandelwal†
Quanquan Gu† Brandon Norick† Jiawei Han†
† University of Illinois at Urbana-Champaign, Urbana, IL
‡ Northeastern Univeristy, Boston, MA
†{xiaoyu1, xren7, sturt1, khndlwl2, qgu3, bnorick, hanj}@illinois.edu
‡yzsun@ccs.neu.edu

ABSTRACT

Recent studies suggest that by using additional user or item relationship information when building hybrid recommender systems, the recommendation quality can be largely improved. However, most such studies only consider a single type of relationship, *e.g.*, social network. Notice that in many applications, the recommendation problem exists in an *attribute-rich heterogeneous information network* environment. In this paper, we study the entity recommendation problem in heterogeneous information networks. We propose to combine various relationship information from the network with user feedback to provide high quality recommendation results.

The major challenge of building recommender systems in heterogeneous information networks is to systematically define features to represent the different types of relationships between entities, and learn the importance of each relationship type. In the proposed framework, we first use meta-path-based latent features to represent the connectivity between users and items along different paths in the related information network. We then define a recommendation model with such latent features and use Bayesian ranking optimization techniques to estimate the model. Empirical studies show that our approach outperforms several widely employed implicit feedback entity recommendation techniques.

Categories and Subject Descriptors

H.3.3 [**Information Search and Retrieval**]: Information Filtering

Keywords

Hybrid Recommender System, Information Network

1. INTRODUCTION

Recommender systems, which provide users with recommendations for products or services (generally referred as *items*), have seen widespread implementation in various domains, *e.g.*, e-commerce, video streaming websites, dating services as well as social network services. Existing recommendation approaches utilize the user-item interaction information and / or content information associated with users and items.

Among different recommendation techniques, hybrid approaches build recommendation models by combining user feedback data with additional information, *e.g.*, user or item attributes and relationships. Previous works show that by utilizing additional user or item relationship, the quality of the recommendation models can be improved. Our proposed method falls in the category of such hybrid recommendation systems. The difference between our work and other relationship based hybrid methods is that most previous works only utilize a single type of relationship, *e.g.*, trust relationship [4], friend relationship [6], and user membership [10]. In many real world applications, the entity recommendation problem exists in a heterogeneous environment with different types of information, entity and link attributes and various relationships between users and items. In this paper, we adopt attribute-rich heterogeneous information networks to represent such heterogeneous entity recommendation environment, and propose to study the well established implicit feedback recommendation problem with such data model.

To take advantage of the heterogeneity of the information network, we first diffuse the observed user preferences along different meta-paths to generate possible recommendation candidates under various user interest semantic assumptions. We then employ matrix factorization techniques on the diffused user preferences to calculate the latent representations for users and items accordingly. Each set of latent features represent one recommendation factor with a specific semantic. We then define a recommendation model by combining these recommendation factors and adopt a Bayesian ranking optimization technique to estimate the model accordingly.

The major contributions of this paper are summarized as follows:

- We propose to build an implicit feedback recommendation framework within an attribute-rich heterogeneous information network, where different types of information and relationships can be used to enhance the quality of the recommender systems.
- We propose a method that can extract latent features to capture different recommendation factors or semantics.
- Empirical studies in two real-world datasets, IMDB-MovieLens-100K and Yelp, demonstrate the power of our methodology.

The remaining of this paper is organized as follows: We discuss the background and preliminaries of this paper in Section 2. We introduce the user preference diffusion based latent features and the global recommendation model in Section 3 and 4. Experiments and

*The work was supported in part by the Army Research Laboratory under Cooperative Agreement Number W911NF-09-2-0053 (NS-CTA), the U.S. Army Research Office W911NF-13-1-0193, NSF CNS-0931975, IIS-1017362, DTRA, and DHS.

RecSys'13, October 12–16, 2013, Hong Kong, China.

ACM 978-1-4503-2409-0/13/10 ...$15.00.

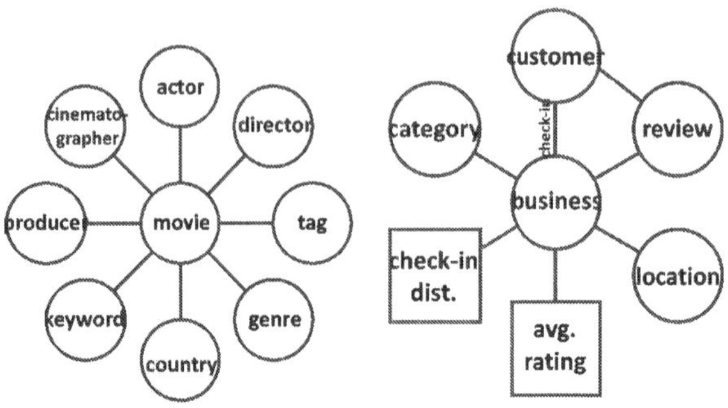

(a) IMDb Network Schema (b) Yelp Network Schema

Figure 1: Information network schemas: circles represent entity types while rectangles represent attribute types

results are presented in Section 5. Conclusions and future works are presented at the end of the paper.

2. BACKGROUND AND PRELIMINARIES

In this section, we present the background and preliminaries of this study.

2.1 Binary User Feedbacks

With m users $\mathcal{U} = \{u_1, ..., u_m\}$ and n items $\mathcal{I} = \{e_1, ..., e_n\}$, we define the binary user feedback matrix $R \in \mathbb{R}^{m\times n}$ as follows:

$$R_{ij} = \begin{cases} 1, & \text{if } (u_i, e_j) \text{ interaction is observed;} \\ 0, & \text{otherwise.} \end{cases}$$

Some previous studies have additional assumptions about the implicit feedback dataset, *e.g.*, user-item interaction frequency. Not to digress from the purpose of this study, we use binary user feedback in its original form as defined above.

2.2 Information Network and Meta-Path

We use the definition of heterogeneous information network (HIN) in [9] and [8], denoted by G. To be consistent with recommender system terminology, we refer entities in the information network being recommended as *items*.

Similar to an entity-relation diagram in a relational database, we use an abstract graph, i.e., *network schema*, to represent the entity and relation type restrictions in HIN, denoted by $G_T = (\mathcal{A}, \mathcal{R})$. Examples of heterogeneous information networks and their network schemas can be found in Figure 1. In a network schema of HIN, two entity types can be connected via different paths, representing relations of different semantic meanings.We use *meta-paths* to represent path types as defined in [8].

[8] and [5] proposed link-based similarity functions to quantify the similarities along different meta-paths in HIN. Given two items e_i and e_j and a meta-path P, such functions can return a similarity scores in $[0, 1]$ to indicate how similar they are under certain similarity semantic (defined by meta-path). By measuring the similarity of all item pairs with one meta-path, we can generate a symmetric similarity matrix, denoted as $S \in \mathbb{R}^{n\times n}$. With L different meta-paths, we can calculate L different similarity matrices with different semantics accordingly, denoted as $S^{(1)}, S^{(2)}, ..., S^{(L)}$.

In empirical study, to further utilize the heterogeneity of the network, besides meta-path based item similarity, we also use attribute-based entity similarities, *e.g.*, geographical similarity.

2.3 Problem Definition

We define the recommendation problem which we study in this paper as follows:

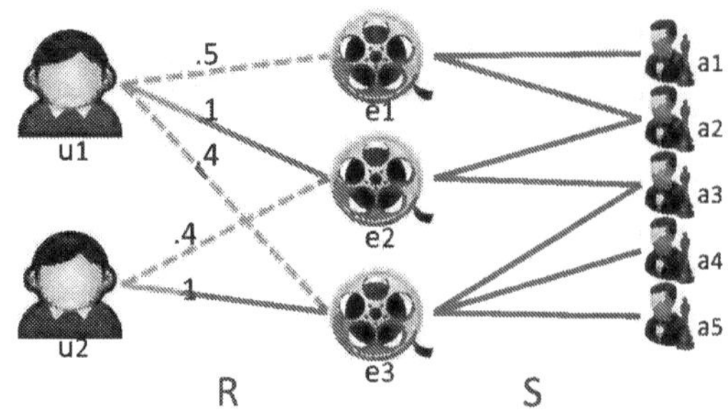

Figure 2: User preference diffusion with meta-path based item similarity matrix (solid red links are observed user preferences while dash links represent diffused preferences)

DEFINITION 1 (PROBLEM DEFINITION). *Given a binary rating matrix R, and a related heterogeneous information network G, for a user $u_i \in \mathcal{U}$, we aim to recommend a ranked list of items $\mathcal{I}_{u_i} \subset \mathcal{I}$ that are of interests to this user.*

3. RECOMMENDATION MODEL

In this section, aiming to alleviate the data sparsity challenge faced by traditional collaborative filtering techniques and utilize the rich yet under-discovered information network, we propose a recommendation approach which combines user feedback and various entity relationship (represented by similarity matrices) derived from the network. We first present a user preference diffusion based feature generation method, and then define a recommendation function with these features. We discuss the recommendation learning algorithm in Section 4.

With the implicit user feedback and item similarity matrices defined in Section 2, we first introduce the diffusion of user preferences based on similarity matrices defined by different meta-paths. Implicit feedback indirectly indicates user preference towards items. Intuitively, if we can find similar items to the ones that the target user was interested in under certain similarity semantic, recommendations to this user could be made by returning the similar items.

More specifically, given a binary user feedback matrix $R \in \mathbb{R}^{m\times n}$ and an item similarity matrix $S^{(q)} \in \mathbb{R}^{n\times n}$, we can diffuse the preference of u_i towards e_j by calculating $\tilde{R}^{(q)}_{ij} = \sum_{t=1}^{n} R_{it} S^{(q)}_{jt}$, which can be rewrite in matrix form for all users as follows:

$$\tilde{R}^{(q)} = RS^{(q)}, \tag{1}$$

where $\tilde{R}^{(q)}$ denotes the diffused user preference matrix. This process propagates user preference along different meta-paths in the item-related HIN and thus is able to find more items a user might be interested in.

We demonstrate the user preference diffusion process with a toy example in Figure 2. In this example, 2 users (u_1 and u_2), 3 movies (e_1, e_2 and e_3), and 5 actors form a small information network. Assume that we observed that u_1 is interested in e_2 and u_2 is interested in e_3 from their previous user log. Under the assumption that users choose movies following meta-path movie-actor-movie, we can claim that u_1 could also be interested in e_1 and e_3 because these two movies are similar to e_2 since they share actors, and u_2 could be interested in e_2 for the same reason. The similarity score between movies along the meta-path movie-actor-movie is calculated with PathSim [8].

With low-rank matrix factorization technique, we derive the low-rank user and item latent features from the diffused matrix $\tilde{R}^{(q)}$ as follows:

$$(\hat{U}^{(q)}, \hat{V}^{(q)}) = \text{argmin}_{U,V} \|\tilde{R}^{(q)} - UV^T\|_F^2 \ \text{ s.t. } U \geq 0,\ V \geq 0, \tag{2}$$

We apply NMF to solve Equation (2), although more advanced factorization techniques can be used instead. By repeating the above process for all L similarity matrices, we can now generate L pairs of representations of users and items $(\hat{U}^{(1)}, \hat{V}^{(1)}, ..., \hat{U}^{(L)}, \hat{V}^{(L)})$. Each low-rank pair represent users and items under a specific similarity semantics due to the user preference diffusion process. Considering that different similarity semantics could have different importance when making recommendations, we define the recommendation model as follows:

$$\hat{r}(u_i, e_j) = \sum_{q=1}^{L} \theta_q \cdot \hat{U}_i^{(q)} \hat{V}_j^{(q)T} \tag{3}$$

where θ_q is the weight for the q-th user and item low-rank representation pair. Based on the meaning and non-negative property of the features, we add $\theta_q \geq 0$ as a constraint.

4. BAYESIAN RANKING OPTIMIZATION

We discuss the learning process for the recommendation model proposed in Section 3 with user implicit feedback data in this section. Implicit feedback data are often noisy and only contain positive instances. The 0 values in user feedback matrix R are a mixture of negative observations and missing values. The common and traditional approach of parameter estimation is to adopt a classification or learning-to-rank objective function and treats all 1 values in R as positives and 0s as negatives. Theoretically, this approach is incorrect and our empirical study in Section 5 also verifies this claim.

Motivated by [7], we employ a different learning approach by considering the correct item pair orders. We define an objective function aiming to generate the correct order of each item pair in R for each user. The assumption behind this approach is that users are more interested in the items with 1 values in R than the rest of the items, which is a weaker and more plausible assumption compared with the traditional approach.

We use $p(e_a > e_b; u_i|\theta)$ to denote the probability that user u_i prefers e_a over e_b. The Bayesian formulation of the optimization criterion is to maximize the posterior probability as follows:

$$p(\Theta|R) \propto p(R|\Theta)p(\Theta), \tag{4}$$

where $\Theta = \{\theta_1, ..., \theta_L\}$ represents the model parameters, and $p(R|\Theta)$ represent the probability that all item pairs can be ranked correctly for all users according to R, *i.e.*, for each user, items with feedback 1 should be ranked before items with feedback 0.

With the assumption that both user preferences and ordering of item pairs are independent, we can expand the likelihood function $p(R|\Theta)$ as follows:

$$p(R|\Theta) = \prod_{u_i \in \mathcal{U}} \prod_{(e_a > e_b) \in R_i} p(e_a > e_b; u_i|\Theta) \tag{5}$$

where $(e_a > e_b) \in R_i$ represent all item pairs with the correct order in the feedback of u_i.

We define $p(e_a > e_b; u_i|\theta)$ as:

$$p(e_a > e_b; u_i|\Theta) = \sigma(\hat{r}(u_i, e_a) - \hat{r}(u_i, e_b)), \tag{6}$$

where σ is the logistic sigmoid function $\sigma(x) = \frac{1}{1+e^{-x}}$.

With probability and likelihood definitions above, we can derive the objective function as follows

$$\min_{\Theta} - \sum_{u_i \in \mathcal{U}} \sum_{(e_a > e_b) \in R_i} \ln \sigma(\hat{r}(u_i, e_a) - \hat{r}(u_i, e_b)) + \frac{\lambda}{2}\|\Theta\|_2^2 \tag{7}$$

where $\frac{\lambda}{2}\|\Theta\|_2^2$ is the L_2 regularization term.

Notice that Equation (7) is differentiable. We can utilize gradient descent based optimization methods or the popular BFGS-B method [2] to learn the parameters. The gradient of Equation (7) with respect to Θ can be found as follows:

$$\frac{\partial O}{\partial \Theta} = - \sum_{u_i \in \mathcal{U}} \sum_{(e_a > e_b) \in R_i} \frac{e^{-\hat{r}_{i,ab}}}{1 + e^{-\hat{r}_{i,ab}}} \frac{\partial}{\partial \Theta} \hat{r}_{i,ab} + \lambda \Theta,$$

where $\hat{r}_{i,ab} = \hat{r}(u_i, e_a) - \hat{r}(u_i, e_b)$.

With the above gradient, we employed stochastic gradient descent (SGD) method [1] to estimate the parameters in our empirical studies. The time complexity of this proposed learning process is $O(mn^2)$ where m is the number of users and n is the number of items. In large dataset this can be overwhelming. With SGD, we only need to sample a small number of training instances (around 10^{-5}) and we can still get good results as reported in Section 5.

Name	#Items	#Users	#Ratings	#Entities	#Links
IM100K	943	1360	89,626	60,905	146,013
Yelp	11,537	43,873	229,907	285,317	570,634

(a) Datasets Description

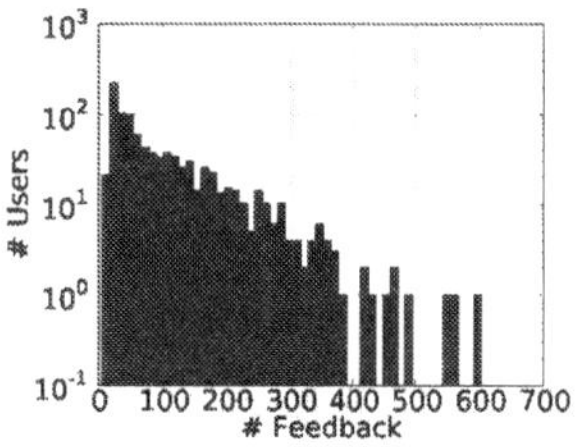

(b) IMDb Feedback Distribution

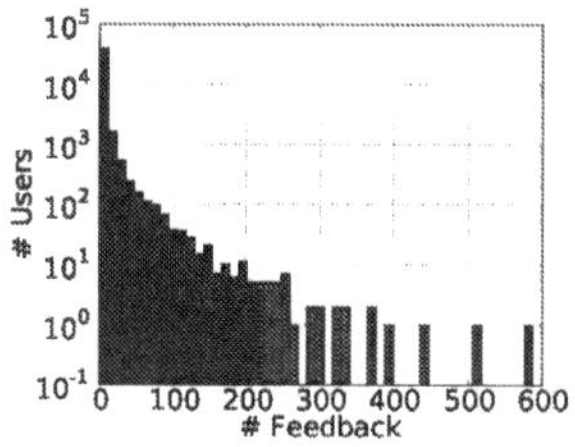

(c) Yelp Feedback Distribution

Figure 3: IM100K and Yelp Datasets

5. EMPIRICAL STUDY

We implemented the proposed recommendation model along with several popularly deployed or state-of-the-art implicit feedback techniques in this section. We apply these methods on two real-world datasets to demonstrate the effectiveness of the proposed approach. We present experimental results with discussion in this section.

5.1 Data

The first dataset is built by combining the popular MovieLens-100K dataset and the corresponding IMDb dataset. We name this dataset IMDb-MovieLens-100K (IM100K). If a user reviewed a certain movie, we set this feedback as 1, otherwise it would be 0. When building this dataset, we mapped two datasets using titles and release date of the movies, which could be erroneous on certain movies so the results we presented below are lower-bound of the actual performance.

The second dataset is the Yelp dataset. When user wrote a review for a restaurant, we set the feedback as 1, otherwise it would be set to 0. Notice that this dataset is much sparser than the IM100K dataset, so the performances of all methods decline accordingly. We summarize these two datasets in Table 3(a). The schema of these two datasets can be found in Figure 1. The distributions of the user feedback can be found in Figure 3.

Both datasets have timestamps with each user item interaction. We split the feedback matrix R of both datasets for each user into training and test based on timestamps, *i.e.*, we use 80% of the "past" feedback to predict 20% of "future" feedback. In Yelp dataset, we filtered out users who have at most 2 reviews since we can not create training and test data for this user.

5.2 Competitors and Evaluation Metrics

We implement several widely deployed recommendation models as follows:

Table 1: Performance Comparison

Method	IM100K				Yelp			
	Prec1	Prec5	Prec10	MRR	Prec1	Prec5	Prec10	MRR
Popularity	0.0731	0.0513	0.0489	0.1923	0.00747	0.00825	0.00780	0.0228
Co-Click	0.0668	0.0558	0.0538	0.2041	0.0147	0.0126	0.01132	0.0371
NMF	0.2064	0.1661	0.1491	0.4938	0.0162	0.0131	0.0110	0.0382
Hybrid-SVM	0.2087	0.1441	0.1241	0.4493	0.0122	0.0121	0.011	0.0337
HeteRec	**0.2094**	**0.1791**	**0.1614**	**0.5249**	**0.0165**	**0.0144**	**0.0129**	**0.0422**

Popularity Recommend the most popular items to users;

Co-Click Estimate conditional probabilities between items and recommend with an aggregated conditional probability calculated with the training data of the target user;

NMF Non-negative matrix factorization on R;

Hybrid-SVM Use SVM based objective function [3] to learn the ranking model, and treat feedback with 1 value as positive and 0 as negative.

We use *HeteRec* to denote the proposed recommendation model. We utilize 9 different item relationships with different similarity semantics in each dataset, *e.g.*, movie-actor-movie, movie-key-movie, biz-user-biz, and biz geographical similarity. Additionally, we add identity matrix as a similarity matrix as well, *i.e.*, items are only similar to themselves. We apply the same feature set in Hybrid-SVM.

For explicit feedback recommendation evaluation, measures like *root mean square error* (RMSE) are the standard evaluation metric. However, these metrics do not suit the definition of implicit feedback problem. In this study, we test all methods as ranking models and use the well-studied information retrieval metrics including precision-at-position and top-10 *mean reciprocal rank* (MRR, Equation (8)) to evaluate and compare the performance of these methods. The MRR metric we used can be found as follows:

$$\text{MRR}_K = \frac{1}{m}\sum_{i=1}^{m}\left(\sum_{e \in test(u_i)} \frac{1}{rank(u_i, e)}\right) \quad (8)$$

5.3 Performance Comparison

The performance of of all 5 methods in the two datasets can be found in Table 1.

Based on Figure 3, user feedback data follow power law distributions, *i.e.*, a very small number of items have interaction with a large number of users. Due to this property, recommending the popular items to users has a decent performance (MRR=0.1923 in IM100K). Co-click method, as one of the most widely deployed technique, achieves MRR = 0.2041 in IM100K and has a similar performance as the NMF method in Yelp (MRR=0.0371).

We implemented the NMF as the CF baseline. We set the dimensionality of the low-rank representations $d = 20$ in IMD100K and $d = 60$ in Yelp. We use the same method and setting when generating features for the proposed approach with Equation (2). With parameter tuning and additional information, NMF may performance better than the results we present in Table 1. However, the same performance improvement can be achieved in our methods accordingly by replacing the NMF solver in Equation (2) with a more advanced technique. As presented in Table 1, NMF outperforms other baselines methods in terms of precision and MRR.

Hybrid-SVM method is a hybrid recommendation approach which uses the same amount of information as our proposed methods. However, if we simply treat all 1 feedback as positive training data and 0 as negative instead of using the objective function proposed in Section 4, the quality of the learned ranking model can be compromised (the overall performance is worse than NMF).

Our proposed HeteRec recommendation model, which takes advantage of both user feedback and the related information network, beats all baseline methods in both datasets. This proves our assumption that adding information network as external knowledge with the proposed approach can alleviate the data sparsity issue and improve the recommendation quality. Moreover, the MRR gain of HeteRec compared with NMF in the relatively dense IM100K dataset is 6.1% while it becomes 10.4% in the sparer Yelp dataset. This observation also fits our intuition that when feedback dataset is sparser, the informative knowledge network can improve the performance even more. When training, we employ a uniform sample rate 10^{-5} in SGD and we apply the same rate to all supervised approaches in this experiment. As discussed in Section 4, although the proposed learning method has a high time complexity, if we evaluate the model with a good sampling rate, we can achieve a good balance of effectiveness and efficiency.

6. CONCLUSION AND FUTURE WORK

In this paper, we study entity recommendation problem in HIN. We propose a recommendation model for implicit feedback by taking advantage of different item similarity semantics in the network. We compared the proposed approaches with several widely employed implicit feedback recommendation techniques, and demonstrate the effectiveness of our methods. Interesting future works include personalized recommendation models, similarity feature selection and on-line recommendation model update.

7. REFERENCES

[1] L. Bottou. Large-scale machine learning with stochastic gradient descent. In *COMPSTAT*. 2010.

[2] R. H. Byrd, P. Lu, J. Nocedal, and C. Zhu. A limited memory algorithm for bound constrained optimization. *SIAM Journal on Scientific Computing*, 16(5):1190–1208, 1995.

[3] R.-E. Fan, K.-W. Chang, C.-J. Hsieh, X.-R. Wang, and C.-J. Lin. LIBLINEAR: A library for large linear classification. *Journal of Machine Learning Research*, 9:1871–1874, 2008.

[4] M. Jamali and M. Ester. A matrix factorization technique with trust propagation for recommendation in social networks. In *SIGKDD*, 2010.

[5] N. Lao and W. W. Cohen. Fast query execution for retrieval models based on path-constrained random walks. In *Proceedings of SIGKDD*, 2010.

[6] H. Ma, H. Yang, M. Lyu, and I. King. Sorec: social recommendation using probabilistic matrix factorization. In *CIKM*, 2008.

[7] S. Rendle, C. Freudenthaler, Z. Gantner, and L. Schmidt-Thieme. Bpr: Bayesian personalized ranking from implicit feedback. In *UAI*, 2009.

[8] Y. Sun, J. Han, X. Yan, S. P. Yu, and T. Wu. PathSim: Meta Path-Based Top-K Similarity Search in Heterogeneous Information Networks. In *VLDB*, 2011.

[9] X. Yu, Q. Gu, M. Zhou, and J. Han. Citation prediction in heterogeneous bibliographic networks. In *SDM*, 2012.

[10] Q. Yuan, L. Chen, and S. Zhao. Factorization vs. regularization: fusing heterogeneous social relationships in top-n recommendation. In *RecSys*, 2011.

Recommendation Opportunities: Improving Item Prediction Using Weighted Percentile Methods in Collaborative Filtering Systems

Panagiotis Adamopoulos
padamopo@stern.nyu.edu

Alexander Tuzhilin
atuzhili@stern.nyu.edu

Department of Information, Operations and Management Sciences
Leonard N. Stern School of Business, New York University

ABSTRACT

This paper proposes a novel method for estimating unknown ratings and *recommendation opportunities* and illustrates the practical implementation of the proposed approach by presenting a certain variation of the classical k-NN method in neighborhood-based collaborative filtering systems using weighted percentiles. We conduct an empirical study showing that the proposed method outperforms the standard user-based collaborative filtering approach by a wide margin in terms of item prediction accuracy and utility-based ranking metrics across various experimental settings. We also demonstrate that this performance improvement is not achieved at the expense of other popular performance measures, such as catalog coverage and aggregate diversity. The proposed approach can also be applied to other popular methods for rating estimation.

Categories and Subject Descriptors

H.4.m [**Information Systems Applications**]: Miscellaneous

Keywords: Weighted Percentiles; Item Accuracy; Collaborative Filtering; Recommendations; Recommender Systems

1. INTRODUCTION

Although there have been many rating estimation methods developed over the last 20 years [6], the classical user-based k-NN collaborative filtering (CF) method still remains one of the most popular and prominent methods used in the recommender systems (RSs) community.

In this paper, we propose a novel method for estimating unknown ratings and *recommendation opportunities* and illustrate the practical implementation of the proposed approach by presenting a certain variation of the classical k-NN method in which the estimation of an unknown rating of the user for an item is based not on the weighted average of the k nearest neighbors but on the weighted percentile of the ratings of these k neighbors. The key intuition behind using this weighted percentiles method, instead of weighted averages, is that high percentiles (such as in the 70% to 90% range) constitute more realistic estimates of how much a targeted user *could* possibly like the candidate item based on the experiences of his/her neighbors. Using such high percentiles is analogous to "shifting the needle" in our rating combining function from the middle of the rating distribution, as in the case of the weighted average, toward the tail on the right side of the distribution, targeting recommendations that the users will like better.

RecSys'13, October 12–16, 2013, Hong Kong, China.

http://dx.doi.org/10.1145/2507157.2507229.

To support this claim, we conducted an empirical study and showed that the proposed percentile method outperforms the standard user-based CF approach by a very wide margin, across various experimental settings, in terms of popular item prediction accuracy and utility-based ranking metrics. Finally, we demonstrate that this performance improvement is not achieved at the expense of some other popular performance measures, such as aggregate diversity.

2. RELATED WORK

In the recommender systems literature, since the first CF systems were proposed in the mid-90's [11], [21], there have been many attempts to improve their performance [20]. For instance, [12] studies variations of rating normalization, similarity weighting and neighbor selection schemes, and [22] calculates similarities using regressions. However, there is still a long way to go in terms of satisfaction of users' actual needs [17] and many approaches that go beyond the rating prediction perspective trying to alleviate the problems pertaining to the narrow rating prediction accuracy-based focus [1] have been gaining significant attention [14].

Moving beyond this narrow focus, in the related field of data mining, [19] discusses the use of combining functions in clustering and [18] utilizes the concept of percentiles, looking for the 80 percent of the conditional spending distribution of customers, in order to identify new sales prospects. Even though this idea of percentiles was applied to clustering techniques in data mining, it has not yet been applied to the RSs problems. In this paper, we apply the concept of percentiles, proposed in the data mining community, to the CF approach and show that this method improves performance on neighborhood models in very significant ways.

3. MODEL

Under a definition of *recommendation opportunity* as how much a user *could* realistically like an item, we are looking for a high percentile (e.g. 80 percent) of the conditional distribution of the rating for the specific target user and candidate item, given all the information we have about them. Utilizing the high percentiles, we aim at recommending items that the users will remarkably like. One of the challenges here is to get a good estimate of the conditional rating percentile for each user and item from the available data. In the next section, we illustrate the practical implementation of the proposed approach in the context of neighborhood models.

3.1 Neighborhood Models

User-based neighborhood recommendation methods predict the rating $r_{u,i}$ of user u for item i using the ratings given to i by users most similar to u, called nearest neighbors and denoted by $\mathcal{N}_i(u)$. Taking into account the fact that the neighbors can have different levels of similarity, $w_{u,v}$, and considering the k users v with the highest similarity to u (i.e. the standard user-based k-NN collaborative filtering approach), the predicted rating is:

$$\hat{r}_{u,i} = \frac{\sum_{v \in \mathcal{N}_i(u)} w_{u,v} r_{v,i}}{\sum_{v \in \mathcal{N}_i(u)} |w_{u,v}|} \quad (1)$$

However, the ratings given to item i by the nearest neighbors of user u can be combined into a single estimation using various combining (or aggregating) functions [6].

In this paper, we propose to use higher weighted percentiles as a combining function. Such a high percentile p (e.g. $70^{\text{th}}, \ldots, 90^{\text{th}}$) of the conditional distribution of the user's rating, given all the information that we have available, characterizes how much the target user u *could* realistically like the candidate item i. Intuitively, using high percentiles is analogous to "shifting the needle" in our rating combining function from the middle of the rating distribution, as is the case with the weighted average, toward the tail on the right side of the distribution targeting recommendations that the users will like better. Formally, the percentile, denoted by $\hat{r}^p_{u,i}$, is defined such that the probability that user u would rate item i with a rating of $\hat{r}^p_{u,i}$ or less is $p\%$. Note that both low and high ratings contribute to the estimation since they affect the rank of the values and, thus, the percentile quantity of interest.

In a typical k-NN collaborative filtering model, the information that we have available in order to estimate an unknown rating, and respectively the quantity $\hat{r}^p_{u,i}$, is the neighbors of user u, denoted by $\mathcal{N}_i(u)$, the similarity levels of these neighbors $w_{\mathcal{N}_i(u)} := (w_{u,v} : v \in \mathcal{N}_i(u))$, and the corresponding ratings $r_{\mathcal{N}(u),i} := (r_{v,i} : v \in \mathcal{N}_i(u))$. As an example of the proposed method and its differences from the classical approaches, consider the neighborhood $\mathcal{N}(u)$ of size 4 with similarity weights $w_{\mathcal{N}(u)} = (0.2, 0.4, 0.3, 0.1)$ and items x and y with ratings $r_{\mathcal{N}(u),x} = (2, 3, 3, 4)$ and $r_{\mathcal{N}(u),y} = (2, 2, 4, 4)$, respectively. Using the standard combining function as in (1), item x would be recommended. However, using, for instance, the weighted 80th percentile of the variable $r_{\mathcal{N}(u),i}$, item y would be recommended since the specific percentile for item y, denoted by $\hat{r}^{p=80}_{u,y}$, corresponds to a higher rating than item x and, thus, there is high potential that user u could realistically like item y more than x; equivalently, the probability of user u assigning a rating greater or equal to 4 is higher for item y than x.

Algorithm 1 summarizes the user-based k-nearest neighbors (k-NN) collaborative filtering approach with a general combining function and Algorithm 2 shows a procedure to estimate a weighted percentile $\hat{r}^p_{u,i}$ (i.e. the proposed combining function), where the values $r_{\mathcal{N}(u),i}$ are the ratings given to candidate item i by neighbors $\mathcal{N}_i(u)$, the k users most similar to target user u, and the weights $w_{\mathcal{N}_i(u)}$ are the corresponding similarity levels of neighbors to user u.

ALGORITHM 1: k-NN Recommendation Algorithm

Input: User-Item Rating matrix R
Output: Recommendation lists of size l

k: Number of users in the neighborhood of user u, $\mathcal{N}_i(u)$

for *each user* u **do**
  Find the k users most similar to user u, $\mathcal{N}_i(u)$;
  for *each item* i **do**
    Combine ratings given to item i by neighbors $\mathcal{N}_i(u)$;
  end
  Recommend to user u the top-l items having the highest predicted rating $\hat{r}_{u,i}$;
end

ALGORITHM 2: Weighted Percentile Estimation

Input: Values $v_1, \ldots, v_n$, Weights $w_1, \ldots, w_n$, and p percentile to be estimated.
Output: p-th weighted percentile of ordered values $v_1, \ldots, v_n$

Order values $v_1, \ldots, v_n$ from least to greatest;
Rearrange weights $w_1, \ldots, w_n$ based on ordered values;
Calculate the percent rank for p based on weights $w_1, \ldots, w_n$;
Use linear interpolation between the two nearest ranks;

4. EXPERIMENTAL SETTINGS

To empirically validate the proposed method and evaluate the generated recommendations, we conduct a large number of experiments on "real-world" data sets and compare our results to the k-NN CF approach, which has been found to perform well also in terms of other performance measures besides the classical accuracy metrics [7], [13], [3, 4].

4.1 Data sets

The data sets that we used are the RecSys HetRec 2011 MovieLens data set [8] and the BookCrossing data set [23].

The RecSys HetRec 2011 MovieLens (ML) data set contains personal ratings and tags about movies and consists of 855,598 ratings from 2,113 users on 10,197 items.

The BookCrossing (BX) data set is described by [23] and gathered from Bookcrossing.com, a social networking site founded to encourage the exchange of books. Following Ziegler et al. [23] and owing to the extreme sparsity of the data, we decided to condense the data set in order to obtain more meaningful results from collaborative filtering algorithms. Hence, we discarded as in [23] all books for which we were not able to find any information, along with all the ratings referring to them. Next, we also removed book titles with fewer than 4 ratings and community members with fewer than 8 ratings each. The dimensions of the resulting data set were considerably more moderate, featuring 8,824 users, 7,818 books, and 107,367 explicit ratings.

4.2 Experimental settings

Using the ML and BX data sets, we conducted a large number of experiments and compared our method against the standard user-based k nearest neighbors collaborative filtering approach. In order to test the proposed approach of weighted percentiles under various experimental settings, we used 2 data sets, 6 different sizes of neighborhoods ($k \in \{30, 40, \ldots, 80\}$), 9 different percentiles as combining functions ($p \in \{10, 20, \ldots, 90\}$), and generated recommendation

Table 1: Item Prediction Accuracy (F_1 score$*10^2$).

Data Set	Method	Recommendation List Size 3	5	10	30	50	100
ML	k-NN	0.0026	0.0039	0.0078	0.0164	0.3575	0.3362
ML	percentile 60th	0.0902	0.1533	0.2975	0.7208	0.8094	0.8611
ML	percentile 70th	0.1784	0.2907	0.5309	1.2440	1.8051	2.3565
ML	percentile 80th	0.0993	0.1575	0.2848	0.6966	0.9525	1.2930
ML	percentile 90th	0.0456	0.0854	0.1848	0.4552	0.6316	0.9344
BX	k-NN	0.1606	0.1876	0.2415	0.2882	0.2899	0.2807
BX	percentile 60th	0.1743	0.2396	0.3149	0.3654	0.3716	0.3526
BX	percentile 70th	0.1864	0.2418	0.3184	0.3751	0.3841	0.3823
BX	percentile 80th	0.2130	0.2590	0.3654	0.4419	0.4361	0.4256
BX	percentile 90th	0.2126	0.3065	0.3772	0.4592	0.4795	0.4728

lists of 13 different sizes ($l \in \{1, 3, 5, 10, 20, \ldots, 100\}$), resulting in 1,404 experiments in total.

For the computation of the weighted percentiles, we used the **gmisclib** [10] scientific library. Besides, we used Pearson correlation to measure similarity. Finally, we used a holdout validation scheme in all of our experiments with 80/20 splits of data to the training/test part in order to avoid overfitting.

5. RESULTS

The aim of this study is to demonstrate that the proposed method is indeed effectively increasing the classical item prediction accuracy measures and performs well in terms of other popular performance measures, such as catalog coverage, by a comparative analysis of our method and the standard k-NN algorithm, in different experimental settings.[1]

5.1 Comparison of Item Prediction

The goal in this section is to compare our method with the standard baseline methods in terms of traditional metrics for *item prediction*, such as precision, recall, and F_1 score. Table 1 presents the results obtained by applying our method to the MovieLens and BookCrossing data sets. The values reported are computed as the average performance over the six neighborhood sizes using the F_1 score for recommendation lists of size $l \in \{3, 5, 10, 30, 50, 100\}$. Respectively, Fig. 1 illustrates the average performance for neighborhoods of size $k \in \{30, 80\}$ and lists of size $l \in \{1, 3, 5, 10, 20, \ldots, 100\}$.

Table 1 and Fig. 1 demonstrate that the proposed method outperforms the k-NN method by a wide margin. In particular, for both data sets, accuracy was improved in all the experiments using high percentiles. Besides, as we can observe, the increase in performance is larger for recommendation lists of larger size. For the ML data set the maximum F_1 score was achieved using the 70th percentile (0.024) whereas for BX the maximum was 0.0048 using the 90th percentile.

To determine statistical significance, we have tested the null hypothesis that the performance of each of the methods is the same using the Friedman test. Based on the results, we reject the null hypothesis with $p < 0.0001$. Performing post hoc analysis on Friedman's Test results, the differences between the *Baseline* k-NN and each one of the experimental settings are statistically significant. Fig. 2 presents the box-

[1]Similar results were also obtained using the k users with the highest similarity to the target user u, $\mathcal{N}(u)$, independently of whether they rated the specific candidate item i. For each metric, only the most interesting dimensions are discussed. Finally, results for low percentiles are not presented, since they constantly underperform the experiments using the high percentiles.

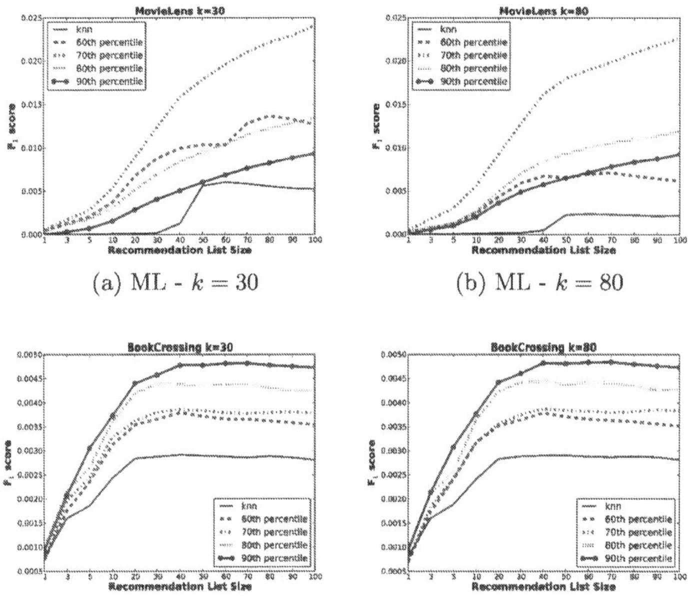

(a) ML - $k = 30$ (b) ML - $k = 80$

(c) BX - $k = 30$ (d) BX - $k = 80$

Figure 1: Prediction Accuracy (F_1 score) for the (a), (b) MovieLens (ML) and (c), (d) BookCrossing (BX) data sets.

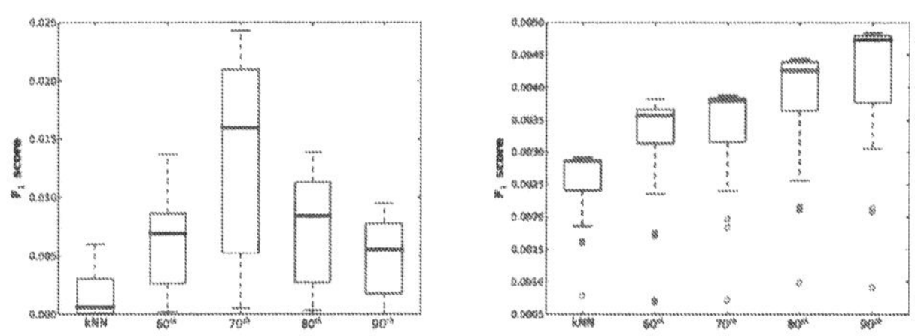

(a) MovieLens data set (b) BookCrossing data set

Figure 2: Post hoc analysis for Friedman's Test of Item Prediction Accuracy (F_1 score) for the both data sets.

and-whisker diagrams displaying the aforementioned differences among the various methods.

Similar results were also obtained using standard utility-based ranking metrics, such as the normalized discounted cumulative gain (nDCG) and mean reciprocal rank (MRR).

5.2 Beyond Accuracy

In this section we investigate the effect of the proposed method on coverage and aggregate diversity, two important metrics for RSs [20], that go beyond the classical perspective of rating prediction accuracy [1]. The results obtained using the *catalog coverage* metric [9] (i.e. the percentage of items in the catalog that are ever recommended to users) are equivalent to those using the *diversity-in-top-N* metric for aggregate diversity [5]; henceforth, only results on coverage are presented. Table 2 presents the results obtained by applying our method to the ML and BX data sets. The values reported are computed as the average catalog coverage over six neighborhood sizes ($k \in \{30, 40, \ldots, 80\}$) for recommendation lists of size $l = \{3, 5, 10, 30, 50, 100\}$.

Table 2 demonstrates that the proposed method performs at least as well as, and is some cases even better than, the

Table 2: Catalog Coverage Performance.

Data Set	Method		Recommendation List Size					
			3	*5*	*10*	*30*	*50*	*100*
ML	*k*-NN		0.50%	0.57%	0.68%	0.92%	2.80%	3.98%
	percentile	**60th**	1.17%	1.29%	1.50%	1.92%	2.30%	3.77%
		70th	2.62%	2.88%	3.24%	3.89%	4.29%	5.28%
		80th	5.99%	6.46%	6.98%	8.08%	8.63%	9.77%
		90th	11.31%	13.29%	15.02%	16.94%	17.93%	19.32%
BX	*k*-NN		45.45%	54.34%	65.52%	84.14%	90.50%	95.36%
	percentile	**60th**	45.44%	54.04%	65.52%	83.85%	90.35%	95.16%
		70th	44.85%	53.34%	64.84%	84.02%	90.13%	95.09%
		80th	46.47%	54.66%	65.90%	84.26%	90.39%	95.16%
		90th	46.33%	54.58%	66.04%	84.28%	90.44%	95.09%

standard user-based *k*-NN method. In particular, for the ML data set, where the *Baseline* *k*-NN results in low coverage, performance is increased on average by 643.77%, with the 90th percentile exhibiting the highest coverage. For the BX data, where the *Baseline* *k*-NN results in high coverage because of the specifics of the particular data set and the larger number of users, the performance is on average the same (+0.00). In terms of statistical significance, using the Friedman test and performing post hoc analysis, for the ML data set the differences among the standard user-based *k*-NN method and all the experimental settings are statistically significant ($p < 0.005$). For the BX data set, only the differences between the 70th percentile and the remaining experimental settings are statistically significant.

The generated recommendation lists can also be evaluated for the inequality across items using the Gini coefficient. In particular, for the ML and BX data sets the Gini coefficient was on average improved by 2.58% and 0.27%, respectively. As we can conclude, in the recommendation lists generated from the proposed method, the number of times an item is recommended is more equally distributed.

In summary, we demonstrated that the proposed method outperforms the standard user-based *k*-NN algorithm by a wide margin in terms of item prediction accuracy and utility-based ranking metrics and performs at least as well as, and in some cases even better than, the standard baseline method in terms of some other popular performance measures.

6. DISCUSSION AND CONCLUSIONS

In this paper, we present a novel method for estimating unknown ratings and *recommendation opportunities* based on weighted percentiles. We illustrate the practical implementation of the proposed approach in the context of neighborhood models adapting the classical *k*-nearest neighbors method. In addition, we conduct an empirical study showing that the proposed method outperforms the standard user-based collaborative filtering approach by a wide margin in terms of item prediction accuracy and utility-based ranking measures, such as the F-measure and normalized discounted cumulative gain, across various experimental settings. We also demonstrate that this performance improvement is not achieved at the expense of some other popular performance measures, such as aggregate diversity.

Moreover, apart from the user-based and item-based *k*-NN collaborative filtering approaches, other popular methods that can be easily extended, with the use of quantile regression, in order to allow us both to build models that predict high percentiles and to evaluate them with regard to the goal of predicting percentiles of estimated ratings, include content-based methods, and Matrix Factorization [16].

Nevertheless, the proposed approach should be tested using various rating normalization and similarity weighting schemes [15] as well as different distance metrics [12].

As a part of the future work, we would like to conduct live experiments with real users in an on-line retail setting as well as in a platform for massive open on-line courses [2]. Also, we will study the impact of the proposed method on novelty, serendipity, and unexpectedness [3, 4] of RSs.

7. REFERENCES

[1] P. Adamopoulos. Beyond Rating Prediction Accuracy: On New Perspectives in Recommender Systems. In *Proceedings of RecSys '13*. ACM, 2013.

[2] P. Adamopoulos. What Makes a Great MOOC? An Interdisciplinary Analysis of Online Course Student Retention. In *Proceedings of ICIS*, 2013.

[3] P. Adamopoulos and A. Tuzhilin. On Unexpectedness in Recommender Systems: Or How to Expect the Unexpected. In *DiveRS 2011*, RecSys '11. ACM, 2011.

[4] P. Adamopoulos and A. Tuzhilin. On Unexpectedness in Recommender Systems: Or How to Better Expect the Unexpected. *Working Paper: CBA-13-03, New York University*, 2013. http://hdl.handle.net/2451/31801.

[5] G. Adomavicius and Y. Kwon. Improving aggregate recommendation diversity using ranking-based techniques. *IEEE Trans. on Knowl. and Data Eng.*, 24(5):896–911, 2012.

[6] G. Adomavicius and A. Tuzhilin. Toward the next generation of Recommender Systems: A Survey of the state-of-the-art and possible extensions. *IEEE Trans. on Knowl. and Data Eng.*, 17(6):734–749, June 2005.

[7] R. Burke. Hybrid recommender systems: Survey and experiments. *User Model. User-Adapt. Interact.*, 12(4), 2002.

[8] I. Cantador, P. Brusilovsky, and T. Kuflik. In *Proceedings of HetRec 2011*, RecSys '11, New York, NY, USA, 2011. ACM.

[9] M. Ge, C. Delgado-Battenfeld, and D. Jannach. Beyond accuracy: evaluating recommender systems by coverage and serendipity. In *Proceedings of RecSys '10*. ACM, 2010.

[10] gmisclib, Scientific Library, 2013. http://kochanski.org/gpk/code/speechresearch/gmisclib/.

[11] D. Goldberg, D. Nichols, B. M. Oki, and D. Terry. Using collaborative filtering to weave an information tapestry. *Communications of the ACM*, 35(12):61–70, 1992.

[12] J. Herlocker, J. A. Konstan, and J. Riedl. An empirical analysis of design choices in neighborhood-based collaborative filtering algorithms. *Information retrieval*, 5(4):287–310, 2002.

[13] D. Jannach, L. Lerche, F. Gedikli, and G. Bonnin. What recommenders recommend–an analysis of accuracy, popularity, and sales diversity effects. In *UMAP '13*. Springer, 2013.

[14] D. Jannach, M. Zanker, A. Felfernig, and G. Friedrich. *Recommender systems: an introduction*. Cambridge University Press, 2010.

[15] R. Jin, J. Y. Chai, and L. Si. An automatic weighting scheme for collaborative filtering. In *Proceedings of SIGIR '04*, 2004.

[16] A. Karatzoglou and M. Weimer. Quantile matrix factorization for collaborative filtering. In *Proceedings of EC-Web '10*, 2010.

[17] J. A. Konstan and J. T. Riedl. Recommender systems: from algorithms to user experience. *User Modeling and User-Adapted Interaction*, 22:101–123, 2012.

[18] R. Lawrence, C. Perlich, S. Rosset, J. Arroyo, Callahan, et al. Analytics-driven solutions for customer targeting and sales-force allocation. *IBM Systems Journal*, 46(4), 2007.

[19] F. Provost and T. Fawcett. *Data Science for Business: What you need to know about data mining and data-analytic thinking*. O'Reilly Media, 2013.

[20] F. Ricci and B. Shapira. *Recommender systems handbook*. Springer, 2011.

[21] E. Rich. User modeling via stereotypes. *Cognitive science*, 3(4):329–354, 1979.

[22] A. Töscher, M. Jahrer, and R. Legenstein. Improved neighborhood-based algorithms for large-scale recommender systems. In *Proceedings of Netflix '08*. ACM, 2008.

[23] C.-N. Ziegler, S. M. McNee, J. A. Konstan, and G. Lausen. Improving recommendation lists through topic diversification. In *Proceedings of WWW '05*. ACM, 2005.

Improving User Profile with Personality Traits Predicted from Social Media Content

Rui Gao
gaorui11@mails.ucas.ac.cn

Bibo Hao
haobibo@gmail.com

Shuotian Bai
baishuotian10@mails.ucas.ac.cn

Lin Li
lilin10@mails.ucas.ac.cn

Ang Li
liang08@mails.ucas.ac.cn

Tingshao Zhu*
tszhu@psych.ac.cn

Institute of Psychology, University of Chinese Academy of Sciences
Beijing 100101, P.R. China

ABSTRACT

Existing studies indicate that there exists strong correlation between personality and personal preference, thus personality could potentially be used to build more personalized recommender system. Personality traits are mainly measured by psychological questionnaires, and it is hard to obtain personality traits of large amount of users in real-world scenes. In this paper, we propose a new approach to automatically identify personality traits with Social Media contents in Chinese language environments. Social Media content features were extracted from 1766 Sina micro blog users, and the predicting model is trained with machine learning algorithms. The experimental results demonstrate that users' personality traits could be predicted from Social Media contents with acceptable Pearson Correlation, which makes it possible to develop user profiles for recommender system. In future, user profiles with predicted personality traits would be used to enhance the performance of existing personalized recommendation systems.

Categories and Subject Descriptors

H.3.1 [**Content Analysis and Indexing**]: Linguistic processing

Keywords

Text Analysis; User profile; Personality; Social Network; Social Media

1. INTRODUCTION

The Internet is growing dramatically and has become part of daily life. Recommender systems using personalized user profiles are widely used in e-commerce sites. Exiting researches about personalized recommendation system enhanced recommendation system performance by taking users' personal preference into consideration when generating user profiles [8]. Some studies have been performed for discovering the correlation between psychological traits(personality) and personal preference [11] [15] [18]. Results of these researches indicate that personality could affect the desire of online purchase, musical taste, etc. Improving user profile with personality traits could probably enhance personalized recommendation system performance. Social Media is one of the most popular kinds of websites, and users are generating large amount of text contents. Sina micro blog is the most popular micro blog in China, which is reported as having 300 million register users and over 100 million micro blog statuses were posted every day [1]. Personalizing Recommendation Systems based on social media usage behavior and content is among the top topics of the overall Internet area in both academia and business. However, user personality traits were mainly measured with psychological questionnaire. It is hardly possible to obtain personality traits of such large amount of users in real-world personalized recommendation system application scenes. In this paper, we propose a new approach to automatically develop user profile (personality traits) with Social Media contents in Chinese language environments. Sogou Cell Lexicons and Simple Chinese dictionaries for LIWC were built for psychological traits analysis in text contents.

Personality is a typical and enduring topic in psychology. The rapid growth of SNS(Social Network Sites) Usage provides a possible approach to automatically determine human personality.

Jon Oberlander found that classifying author personality from web blog text is promising [17]. Golbeck presented a promising method to predict user personality through the information on SNS in English language environment [6] [7].

Nass had demonstrated that personality factors could affect the desire of the users to buy products online [14]. Personality was found to be related to musical taste too [18]. Many other studies have been done for discovering the correlation between personality and personal preference [15]. China will become the biggest market of e-commerce in the world within a few years. Both Chinese SNS and e-commerce websites will significantly benefit from knowing users' personality and provide personalized service.

In this study, a method by which user big five personality traits can be accurately determined through text features extracted from Sina Micro blog status was demonstrated. To

*Author for correspondence.

RecSys'13, October 12–16, 2013, Hong Kong, China.

ACM 978-1-4503-2409-0/13/10 ...$15.00.
http://dx.doi.org/10.1145/2507157.2507219.

the best of our knowledge, this paper may probably make the first attempt to determine personality from micro blog text features in Chinese language environment for recommendation system user profile enhancement.

The rest of the paper is organized as following: Section 2 shows the related work. The method by which data corpus was collected, processed and experiment results will be shown in Section 3. Section 4 concludes this work and indicates an open space for future work.

2. RELATED WORK

2.1 Personality and Personal preferences

Musical tastes are related to personality [14] [19] [18], individuals with similar personality traits prefer to similar types of music. Individual's potential music purchase could be sorted with deals which had been made by other people who share the same personality. People prefer to use graphical user interfaces designed for their personality types [11]. When people review product comments in e-commercial web sites, their desires to buy the product improve significantly if the comments were written by people who have similar personality types [14]. In western, some successful attempts had been made to improving recommendation systems with information getting from social network [14].

Personality could be predicted from micro blog statuses and individuals' preferences are related to personality, providing us a new approach to improve the performances of existing recommendation systems. Otherwise, few study has been conducted in Chinese language environment. China will probably become the biggest market for e-commerce, so research on predicting personality and enhancing recommendation systems in Chinese language environment is essential. In this paper, a new approach was proposed to develop user profile (personality traits) for Recommendation Systems in Chinese language environment.

2.2 Language Usage and Personality

Studies had been done to investigate the relationship between Language Usage and Personality [12] [17] [16]. Linguistic cues in conversation and text were proved to be capable to recognize individuals' personality [12]. Web blog texts generated by individuals could be used for classifying author personality [17] [16], it indicates that text content in the internet environments is related with authors' personality as well as language they use in real world. One study based on the corpus of CRV1 and Enron Email data demonstrates that language features can be used to predict author's gender with accuracy of 85.1 percent [3]. In English language environment, a promising method to predict user personality through their information on SNS was presented by Golbeck [6] [7]. Micro blog status text features of 50 Twitter users' were extracted by LIWC(Linguistic Inquiry and Word Count) software. The correlation ship between text features and personality scores are significant [6]. A model for personality prediction was trained and tested with 279 Facebook users information, and the predicted personality scores and self-reported personality scores were strongly related [7].

All these studies indicate that predicting personality from Sina micro blog text content is feasible, and have potential

3. METHOD

Big five personality model is recently among the most regarded and most widely used personality theory [4] [5] [13]. Big five personality model has been proved effective in different languages [5]. In the Sina Micro blog application, users were invited to complete the 44-question Big Five Inventory [2] [10]. In this inventory, user personality is measured in five dimensions:

- Openness to Experience.
- Conscientiousness: responsible, organized, persevering.
- Extroversion: outgoing, amicable, assertive.
- Agreeableness: cooperative, helpful, nurturing.
- Neuroticism: anxious, insecure, sensitive.

Table 1 shows the score range of each dimension.

3.1 Data Collection

Original status texts of 1766 Sina micro blog users were analyzed in this study. An application was built based on Sina micro blog platform to collect status and administer Big-Five Inventory [8] to users. By calling Sina Application Programming Interface, the basic information (the number of published status, followers and friends) of 99,925,821 users was downloaded in 2012/4/18. These 99,925,821 users were the original user sample set of this text analysis.

Two kinds of users may be inappropriate to be taken into consideration in this text analysis. One kind is the inactive users. They published little original status, so their personality can hardly be reflected by text features of their status. The other kind is entertainment star users or advertisement users. Since almost all this kind of micro blog accounts are used for commercial targets. Thus their status should not be analyzed for personality related research.

All the 99,925,821 users were filtered by the following rules:

1. Users who did not publish any status in the last three months or published less than 512 statuses in total were excluded. In the original user sample set, the number of statuses of each user published is 136.6511 on average with a deviation of 788.8671. Users who published less than 512 (mean + 0.5 * standard deviation) statuses are probably inactive users. All the 99,925,821 users published 2.84 statuses per day in average. Users published less than 2.84 status per day in average were excluded, too.
2. Users who publish more than 40 statuses per day are highly likely to be entertainment star users or advertisement users. They were excluded too.

Then, original status texts of 1,953,485 active users were collected as user sample set for this text analysis. About 30,000 users were randomly picked, they were invited to accomplish widely used O. John's brief 44-item Big-Five Inventory [8] on our application based on Sina micro blog. 1766 volunteers accepted the invitation int the end and accomplished Big-Five Inventory. In this study, these 1766 volunteers' original status texts and Big-Five Inventory result were used as label sample to train predicting model and cross-validation.

3.2 Feature extraction

Text features were extracted from 1766 user's Sina micro blog status, and then all the features vectors were analyzed

Table 1: Big Five Inventory scores range in five dimensions.

Dimension	Openness	Conscientiousness	extroversion	Agreeableness	Neuroticism
Range	[10,50]	[9,45]	[8,40]	[9,45]	[8,40]

to build a predicting model and 10-fold cross-validation with the algorithms Gaussian process, M5'Rules and Pace Regression. One hundred and sixty eight Text features were extracted in six perspectives:

1. Status statistics features (total number of statuses, total number of words in status, etc.);
2. Sentence-based features (average number of Chinese characters per sentence, declarative sentence proportion etc.);
3. Word-based features (number of emotion words, number of greeting words etc.);
4. Character-based features (number of commas, number of colons and number of 23 special characters etc.);
5. Sogou Industry lexicon features. Pinyin input method is the most popular Chinese input method in China, it takes 70% share of the whole Chinese netizens. Sogou Cell Lexicons are optional lexicons users can download from Sogou input method official web site. These lexicons are automatically generated by Sogou search engine or created by netizens. All the cell lexicons are uploaded on the Sogou official web site and rated by all Sogou input method users. Eighty eight official recommended and highest rating cell lexicons were downloaded and merged into 13 industry lexicons, such as, art lexicon, medical lexicon, network popular lexicon, etc. All the weibo statues in the data corpus were processed Chinese word segmentation using the latest version of ICTCLAS(Institute of Computing Technology, Chinese Lexical Analysis System), and word count in each Sogou Industry Lexicons were added up as user text features;
6. LIWC(Linguistic Inquiry and Word Count) features. LIWC is text analysis software widely used by scholars [6] [7] [9]. It can determine the degree of language usage in 88 dimensions. Three versions of Simple Chinese dictionaries for LIWC were generated by master degree candidates, and a final version was developed by manually validating these three dictionaries according to CLIWC dictionary [9]. LIWC software was ran with the final version dictionary to calculate 88 micro blog status text features.

The above features are probably the most related text features to subject information and personality [3]. Chinese text analysis has a challenge: Chinese Word Segmentation. ICTCLAS is one of the most widely used Chinese words parser. Sogou Cell Lexicons and Simplified Chinese dictionaries for LIWC have been both imported into ICTCLAS as user dictionaries to improve recognition rate of parser.

3.3 Model Training and Evaluation

With randomly selected about 90% of 1766 Sina users, M5'Rules, Pace Regression and Gaussian process were applied to build predicting models. These models were used to predict the rest about 10% users' personality traits, and their performances were evaluated by Pearson correlation between predicted personality traits scores and Big-Five Inventory ratings. Pearson correlation is among the most major criteria of correlation ship in psychology, thus it is taken as evaluation criteria to measure the accuracy of the predicting model. It is widely accepted that Pearson correlation between 0.2 to 0.4 indicates weak correlation, 0.4 to 0.6 indicates mid correlation, and above 0.6 indicates strong or extreme correlation.

3.4 Results and Discussion

The results in Table 2 indicate that personality traits could be predicted through text features extracted from original micro blog status. Conscientiousness, Extroversion, and Openness to Experience have more significant correlation than Agreeableness and Neuroticism. That is consistent with many other studies [2] [14] [15]. In psychological point of view, the predicted personality has a bit weaker correlations with self-report personality than expertise observer ratings has [8]. The Pearson correlation between the predicted personality and self-report is about 0.4, which means that they are fairly correlated. Since personality provides some clues to identify new users' preferences, it might be an effective approach to alleviate cold start of recommendation system. Further works could be conducted to improve the correlations between predicted personality and self-reported personality. As predicted personality becomes more and more accurate, it could be used for personalized recommendation systems.

Some correlations between text features and personality dimensions are intuitively sensible. For instance, people using second person pronouns "you"("ni" and "nimen" in Chinese for single and plural) more often are more extraverted, and the more internet popular new words confers higher openness to experience. People with high scores in Neuroticism generated more words about religion and art. Other correlations between features and personality have not been interpreted yet. Exclamation mark usage is highly positively related to conscientiousness and more count of numbers usage and agreeableness are significantly negative related, which leaves an open space for future researches to confirm and explain.

4. CONCLUSIONS

Experimental results demonstrate that Big Five personality traits can be predicted from the users' Sina micro blog status. Personality was proved to be related with personal preferences in music tastes and graphic user interfaces [11] [14] [18]. Recommendation systems accuracy could probably be improved by taking users' personality traits into consideration. This work might provide a promising future to improve user profile with predicted personality traits, which could potentially improve the performances of existing recommendation systems.

On the other hand, while using LIWC2007 to process Chinese content, we found that it might not process Chinese

Table 2: The Evaluation Results on Predicted and Self-report Big Five Scores.

Key Data set	Number of training instances	Number of testing instances	Mean absolute error	Root mean squared error	Relative absolute error	Root relative squared error	Correlation coefficient
A	1590	176	3.7559	4.83402	96.4699	96.26233	0.31079
C	1590	176	3.9956	4.91633	93.0128	92.1287	0.40601
E	1589	177	4.1850	5.16627	93.5224	93.42278	0.40312
N	1589	177	4.4448	5.57428	97.235	95.41558	0.31958
O	1590	176	4.5034	5.49945	94.4791	93.06926	0.37768

properly. We are developing a prototype system TextMind that is optimum for Simplified Chinese analysis. TextMind might could provide an all-in-one solution on Simplified Chinese processing for researchers in the future.

5. ACKNOWLEDGMENTS

The authors gratefully acknowledge the generous support from National High-tech R&D Program of China (2013AA01A606), NSFC (61070115), Institute of Psychology (113000C037), Key Research Program of CAS (KJZD-EW-L04), Strategic Priority Research Program (XDA06030800) and 100-Talent Project (Y2CX093006) from Chinese Academy of Sciences.

6. REFERENCES

[1] Sina weibo has more than 300 million users, over 100 million statuses are posted, 2012. http://news.xinhuanet.com/tech/2012-02/29/c_122769084.htm.

[2] V. Benet-Martinez and O. P. John. Los cinco grandes across cultures and ethnic groups: Multitrait-multimethod analyses of the big five in spanish and english. *Journal of Personality and Social Psychology*, 75(3):729–750, 1998.

[3] N. Cheng, R. Chandramouli, and K. P. Subbalakshmi. Author gender identification from text. *Digital Investigation*, 8(1):78–88, 2011.

[4] P. T. Costa and R. R. *Revised NEO Personality (NEO-PI-R) and NEO Five-Factor Inventory professional manual.* Psychological Assessment Resources, Odessa, FL, 1992.

[5] J. M. Digman. Personality structure: Emergence of the five-factor model. *Annual Review of Psychology*, 41(1):417–440, 1990.

[6] J. Golbeck, M. E. C. R., and K. Turner. Predicting personality from twitter. In *2011 IEEE third international conference on andieee third international conference on social computing (socialcom)*, pages 149–156, Boston, 2011.

[7] J. Golbeck, C. Robles, and K. Turner. Predicting personality with social media. In *CHI '11 Extended Abstracts on Human Factors in Computing Systems*, CHI EA '11, pages 253–262, New York, NY, USA, 2011. ACM.

[8] S. D. Gosling, P. J. Rentfrow, and W. B. S. Jr. A very brief measure of the big-five personality domains. *Journal of Research in Personality*, 37(6):504–528, 2003.

[9] C.-L. Huang, C. K. Chung, N. Hui, Y.-C. Lin, S. Yi-Tai, B. C. P. Lam, W.-C. Chen, M. H. Bond, and J. W. Pennebaker. The development of the chinese linguistic inquiry and word count dictionary. *Chinese Journal of Psychology*, 55:185–201, 2012.

[10] O. P. John, L. P. Naumann, and C. J. Soto. Paradigm shift to the integrative big-five trait taxonomy: History, measurement, and conceptual issues. In O. P. John, R. W. Robins, and L. A. Pervin, editors, *Handbook of personality: Theory and research*, pages 114–158. Guilford Press, New York, NY, 2008.

[11] A. Karsvall. Personality preferences in graphical interface design. In *ACM International Conference Proceeding Series*, pages 217–218, 2002.

[12] F. Mairesse, M. A. Walker, M. R. Mehl, and R. K. Moore. Using Linguistic Cues for the Automatic Recognition of Personality in Conversation and Text. *Journal of Artificial Intelligence Research*, 30:457–500, 2007.

[13] R. R. McCrae and O. P. An introduction to the five-factor model and its application. *Journal of Personality and Social Psychology*, 60(2):175–215, 1992.

[14] C. Nass and K. M. Lee. Does computer-generated speech manifest personality? an experimental test of similarity-attraction. In *Computer Human Interaction*, pages 329–336, 2000.

[15] E. Neustadt, T. Chamorro-Premuzic, and A. Furnham. The relationship between personality traits, self-esteem, and attachment at work. *Journal of Individual Differences*, 27(4):208–217, 2006.

[16] S. Nowson and J. Oberlander. Identifying more bloggers Towards large scale personality classification of personal weblogs. In *International Conference on Weblogs and Social Media*, 2007.

[17] J. Oberlander and S. Nowson. Whose Thumb Is It Anyway? Classifying Author Personality from Weblog Text. In *Meeting of the Association for Computational Linguistics*, 2006.

[18] P. J. Rentfrow and S. D. Gosling. The do re mi's of everyday life: the structure and personality correlates of music preferences. *Journal of personality and social psychology*, 84(6):1236–56, 2003.

[19] J. L. Zhou, Y. Fu, H. Lu, and C. J. Sun. From popularity to personality - a heuristic music recommendation method for niche market. *Journal of Computer Science and Technology*, 26(5):816–822, 2011.

Leveraging the Citation Graph to Recommend Keywords

Ido Blank, Lior Rokach, Guy Shani
Information Systems Engineering &
Deutsche Telekom Innovation Laboratories
Ben Gurion University, Israel
{blank,liorrk,shanigu}@bgu.ac.il

ABSTRACT

Users of scientific papers databases, such as CiteSeer^X, Google Scholar, and Microsoft Academic, often search for papers using a set of keywords. Unfortunately, many authors avoid listing sufficient keywords for their papers. As such, these applications may need to automatically associate good descriptive keywords with papers. This is a well-studied problem given the complete text of the paper, but in many cases, due to copyright privileges, research papers databases do not have the complete text, only metadata, such as the title and abstract. On the other hand, research papers databases typically maintain the citation network of each paper. In this paper we study the problem of predicting which keywords are appropriate for a scientific paper, using only the citation network. We compare our method with predicting keywords using the title and abstract, concluding that the citation network provides much better predictions.

Categories and Subject Descriptors

H.4 [**Information Systems Applications**]: Miscellaneous

Keywords

Keywords Recommendation, Citation Graph, Academic Papers

1. INTRODUCTION

Searching online for scientific papers is a common task for every modern scientist. There are a number of search engines, such as CiteSeer^X, Microsoft Academic, and Google Scholar, that offer services including searching for relevant papers, and viewing the paper metadata — its title, authors names and affiliations, its abstract, and the papers that it cites. The most important part of the paper, its textual content, however, is often unavailable for downloading directly from the search engine due to copyright privileges. In these cases the search engine typically forwards the user to a webpage where the user can download or buy the paper.

When searching for papers in a specific area, keywords can provide a significant advantage in rapidly identifying relevant papers. Such keywords are manually added by the authors of a paper, attempting to encapsulate important aspects of the paper, such as its main research area, the modeling approach that was chosen, the methods that were used, or specific algorithms that were leveraged. There is currently no agreed upon method for choosing keywords, and authors tend to follow different methodologies in choosing them. As such, keywords tend to be highly diverse and noisy, and in many cases contain spelling mistakes. Some authors even misunderstand the essence of the keyword concept. Furthermore, many authors avoid the effort of writing keywords altogether, resulting in papers with no keywords (in the KDD CUP 2013 challenge, about 75% of the papers donated by Microsoft Academic have no keywords).

It is hence advantageous for the search engine to automatically identify keywords for a paper when none exist, or even add additional keywords when number of keywords is insufficient. This task is typically known as keyword recommendation. Most of the work on keyword recommendation for documents in general and scientific papers in particular is to use the document text, perhaps as a bag-of-words, and some technique for identifying important terms within the text, such as the well known TF-IDF approach. In the case of scientific papers, due to the aforementioned copyright problem, the complete text of the paper is unavailable to the search engine. The metadata, i.e., the title, authors, abstract, venue and references, are usually available even though these sections are also protected through copyright. However, practically many publishers (such as ACM or IEEE) provide access to this information without the need to purchase the paper or sign-in.

In this paper we focus on the problem of recommending keywords in the case where the full text of the paper is unavailable. We examine the use of both the matadata and the citation graph in identifying relevant keywords. We show that the upper bound on the value of the information in the citation graph is about twice as much as the upper bound on the information in the title and abstract. Furthermore, we show that simple recommendation techniques that rely on the citation graph provide much better precision-recall curves than using the abstract and title. The proposed method can help search engines to improve their performance and to authors to select the most suitable keywords for their papers.

Our experiments use the huge CiteSeer^X database. We discuss problems with the keywords that were automatically

Source	Method	Corpus	Domain	Predictive Performance	Paper
Full-Text	Supervised Learning	161 papers	Physics	precision@5=55.4%	[3]
Full-Text	Statistical	1 book	Genetics	recall@283=40% and precision@283= 10%	[5]
Full-Text	Statistical	1 book	Genetics	precision@k for k<50 is above 60%	[1]
Full-Text	Statistical	2 books	Varied	NA	[8]
Full-Text	Supervised Learning	332 papers	CS	True-positive of 73%, True-negative of 79%	[11]
Full-Text	Supervised Learning	250 papers	CS	precision@5= 31%, recall@5=10%	[7]
Abstract	Supervised Learning	2000 papers	CS	precision@10=29.7%	[6]
Abstract	Supervised Learning	80 papers	CS	precision@9=23%	[2]

Table 1: Text-based methods for keywords extractions in academic corpus.

extracted from scientific papers by the CiteSeer^X team, and explain the procedure that we ran to clean up the keywords.

2. RELATED WORK

One obvious source for keywords recommendation is the article's text. Shah et al. [10] show that the abstract is the most important section in the text for obtaining qualitative keywords, but analysis of the other sections is required for obtaining a high recall. Several researchers tried to employ text-based methods that analyze the full-text. Specifically, extraction of keyphrases from text is a well-known task that has already been examined in the academic domain. Fewer methods extract keywords merely from the title and the abstract [6, 2].

Although the above mentioned keywords extraction methods can be used for keywords recommendation, no citation-based method for keywords recommendation has been reported in the literature. Most of the methods above have been tested on relatively small corpus containing a few hundreds of papers. The objective of this research is to quantitatively examine the usefulness of citation graph for keywords recommendation on a large corpus. Citation graph analysis has been used in other tasks such as citation recommendation [4] and researchers ranking [9] and have shown to significantly improve the predictive performance. Thus, we hypothesize that citation analysis can also be useful in keywords recommendation

3. SCIENTIFIC PAPERS DATASET

We experiment with the CiteSeer^X dataset, consisting of 1,945,157 papers with metadata, including the paper's title, its abstract, papers that it cites, and its keywords, if they exist. As much of the CiteSeer^X collection process is automated, the dataset contains much noise. We now discuss the clean up process that we used in order to reduce the noise in the dataset. In all the phases below we use standard stemming techniques to compare words.

First, we removed 194,963 papers that did not have a reasonable title (e.g. only two characters). We ignore below the ACM "Terms", which we consider to be too generic to be useful as keywords.

The automated keyword extraction mechanism often fails to properly identify the keywords section, and in many cases the extracted keywords contain obvious parsing noise, such as adding the "Keyword", the name of the keywords section, as a keyword. In many papers the automated extraction also added the words "Abstract", "Terms", "Additional Key Words and Phrases", and so forth. All these were removed from the set of keywords.

We search for prepositions and conjunctions such as "and" or "the", and remove them from the keywords. When a conjunction appears within a keyword, the keyword is split into two. For example, when encountering the keyword "data-mining and clustering", we would split it into two keywords — "data-mining" and "clustering".

A common problem when allowing people to manually add keywords are different terms with the same meaning. Consider for example the terms "learning algorithm", "statistical learning", and "machine learning", all denoting the same meaning. We need to recognize that these terms are all identical. To resolve this problem we use the downloadable Wikipedia database[1], containing a table listing which search terms get redirected to other search terms. Whenever we identify a keyword that Wikipedia redirects to another keyword, we replace this keyword with the redirect target, which we call the keyword's standard form.

Some authors chose long keywords composed of several terms, e.g. "matched multiscale asymptotic analysis". It is unlikely that this keyword would appear more than once or will be searched for in this exact pattern, so it is desierable that the search engine will be able to acknowledge its various parts. We split keywords containing more than 3 words, and appearing less than 5 times in our database using the following technique — we search for popular keywords (keywords that appear more than 50 times in our database) that appear as substrings of the given unpopular keyword, giving priority to longer popular keywords. In addition for popular keywords, we also search for Wikipedia terms that appear as substrings in long keywords. For example, the keyword "matched multiscale asymptotic analysis" will be split into "asymptotic analysis", "multiscale", and "matching". In this process we did not use over-generic keywords such as "algorithm", "data", and "modeling".

Following this process we remain with 470,064 papers with keywords containing 2,075,639 keywords. There are 233,797 distinct keywords and Figure 2 shows the distribution of the number of appearances of keywords.

4. RECOMMENDING KEYWORDS

We now explain two methods for recommending keywords for a given paper, when the complete text of the paper is unavailable. We first present a method based on the citation graph structure, assuming that cited papers have similar keywords. We then present a more standard baseline method, based on the title and the abstract of the paper

4.1 Citation Graph Recommendations

Our first method uses the keywords of papers cited by the current paper (child papers) and by papers that cite at least one paper that the current paper does (sibling papers). We look for keywords that appear in these two sets of papers and construct a list of recommended keywords for the current paper (Figure 1).

[1]`http://wiki.dbpedia.org/Downloads38`

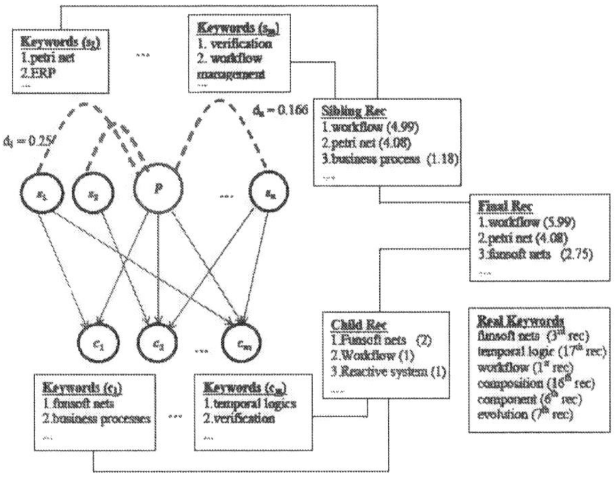

Figure 1: Citation network based example.

Siblings share at least one child with the current paper. We give higher weight to siblings that share more children with the current paper, using the Jaccard similarity: $Jaccard(p_i, p_j) = \frac{citations(p_i) \cap citations(p_j)}{citations(p_i) \cup citations(p_j)}$ where p_i and p_j are papers, and $citations(p)$ are the papers that p cites.

Let $c_{p,k}$ denote the number of times that keyword k appears in a child paper of the current paper p. Let $s_{p,k} = \sum_{p_i \in siblings(p), k \in p_i} Jaccard(p, p_i)$ be the sum of Jaccard weights of siblings of p where k is used as a keyword. We order the keywords that appear in children and siblings of p by decreasing $c_{p,k} + s_{p,k}$.

We use the Wikipedia redirects to identify identical keywords that are written differently in various papers.

4.2 Text-based Recommendation

We now list three more orthodox methods that we used for recommending keywords based on the abstract and title only, which will be used as the baseline for comparison.

TF-IDF: Perhaps the most popular method for finding keywords for a document is to look for terms that appear in the document text. Then, these terms can be ordered in a ranked list, for example by their TF-IDF score. In our case we do not have the full text of the paper, but we still have its title and abstract. We hence implemented a standard TF-IDF algorithm, where the candidate terms are only keywords that appear in our dataset.

In many cases, a keyword can appear as a substring of another keyword. For example, the keyword "clustering algorithm" contains the keyword "algorithm". In such cases, we give priority to longer keywords, and ignore the substring keyword. In addition, when identifying keywords in the text, we use standard stemming techniques, and also use the Wikipedia redirects to search for synonyms of keywords.

Yahoo!: Yahoo! Content Analysis is a free service that can also extract keywords from text, detecting entities/concepts within unstructured content. We used the Yahoo! API, providing the title and the abstract and received a list of detected concepts ranked by their overall relevance and their corresponding pages in Wikipedia if applicable.

Location-based: We implemented a novel algorithm that leverages the location of the keyword in the title and abstract. For each keyword that appears in the title and abstract we give a score based on where it appears.

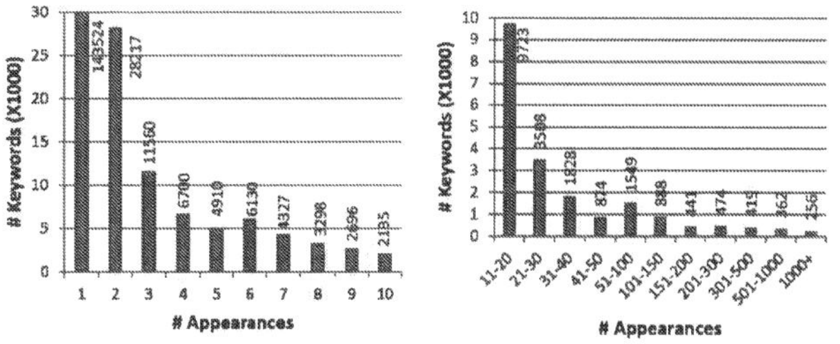

(a) 10 times or less. (b) More than 10 times.

Figure 2: The distribution of keywords appearances in our dataset.

The title generally attempts to define the paper in as little words as possible. Therefore, each keyword that appears in the title gets 1 point. The abstract typically begins with a more general explanation and then becomes more technical. We therefore give higher score to keywords that appear near the beginning of the abstract.

Let $l_{p,k}$ be the location, i.e., the number of characters from the beginning of the abstract of paper p to the first appearance of keyword k, and let $|a_p|$ be the number of characters in the abstract. Let $a_{p,k}$ be the number of times that keyword k appears in the abstract of paper p. The score of k for the abstract of p is: $a_{p,k} \cdot \left(1 - \frac{l_{p,k}}{|a_p|}\right)$. The total score of keyword k for paper p is its abstract score, with an addition of 1 if it also appears in the title.

In our dataset the average length of the title is about 10 words, and the average length of the abstract is 138.7 words.

5. EMPIRICAL EVALUATION

We evaluate the two methods above over the CiteSeer^X datatbase. We follow standard accuracy evaluation by picking a paper with known keywords, computing a list of recommended keywords for it, and comparing the recommended list to the true list of keywords of that paper, computing the precision and recall of the recommendation list.

As we explained above, many of the papers in the database did not have any keywords associated with them, and thus cannot be used in this type of evaluation. Furthermore, our citation-based method requires that not only the paper under evaluation would have keywords, but also that its children and siblings have keywords, further reducing the number of evaluation candidate papers. In our experiments we used only papers where at least 10 of their children have keywords. There were 37,848 such papers.

Figure 3 shows the results of various versions of our algorithms on this datatset. The TF-IDF method over the abstract and title achieved very low results, with maximal precision of 0.05 and maximal recall of 0.07, and was removed from the graph.

As we can see, the citations method, which uses both the children and the siblings of the current paper, achieves the best results. To better understand this performance, we use two auxiliary methods, one that uses only the children, and one that uses only the siblings. Here, the siblings clearly add more value than the children. This is not very surprising, because the number of siblings is much higher than the number of children. A paper typically cites 10-20 papers directly, but can have hundreds of siblings.

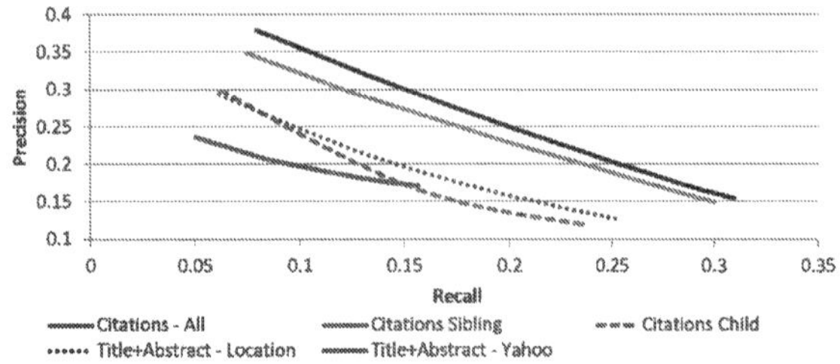

Figure 3: Precision-Recall curves for various keyword recommendation methods, with recommendation lists ranging from 1 to 10. Differences are statistically significant, except for the child citations and the abstract location before the 3rd keyword.

The method that looks at the location of keywords in the abstract and title is doing as well as the children only method, but not as good as the method that uses the siblings or the method that uses both the siblings and the children. This demonstrates the power of using the citation graph over using only the paper metadata for finding good keywords. The location-based method does better than the mature Yahoo! service, which is rather surprising. This can be because the Yahoo! service is generic and designed for any document type, while we leverage several properties specific to scientific papers, such as the structure of the title and abstract.

While the results above seem promising, it may well be that our text-based methods that use the title and abstract are simply not sophisticated enough to provide good results. We hence analyze the paper's keywords appearance in the various sources. In the reduced dataset that was used in the experiments, we find that only 55% of the keywords appear in the abstract and title, while 65% of the keywords appear in the children and the siblings. These numbers provide an upper bound on the possible recall using these two sources. Moreover, almost all keywords that were found in the abstract and title, were also found in the citation graph. This means that if we optimally use the citation graph, there are almost no additional keywords in the abstract and title. Still, the title and abstract may be leveraged to rank the keywords.

6. CONCLUSION

In this paper we explore the problem of recommending keywords for scientific papers using the citation graph. We demonstrate that using simple methods over papers cited by the current paper, and papers that cite the same papers as the current paper, we can get good recommendations in terms of precision and recall, compared with using the title and the abstract of the paper. Obtaining keywords using citation graph can contribute to two aspects. First, previous works show that in order to get reasonable performance using keyword extraction methods, the full-text should be available. The availability of the full-text is not always guaranteed due to many reasons such as copyright restrictions or the author's reluctance to share the text before it is been published. Citation-based method relaxes these restrictions. Moreover, citation-based method can be used in conjunction with text-based methods, to augment the predictive performance of the system.

We also show that there is still much potential in the citation graph for additional improvements, which we will explore in future work. We also intend to combine the citation graph and the abstract and title methods, to better rank the keywords. Another potential extension is in identifying clusters of related keywords, that are interchangeable.

Acknowledgements

We would like to thank Lee Giles and Prasenjit Mitra from The Pennsylvania State University for kindly providing us with the CiteSeerX data used in our research.

7. REFERENCES

[1] C. Carretero-Campos, P. Bernaola-Galván, A. Coronado, and P. Carpena. Improving statistical keyword detection in short texts: Entropic and clustering approaches. *Physica A: Statistical Mechanics and its Applications*, 2012.

[2] Y. HaCohen-Kerner. Automatic extraction of keywords from abstracts. In *Knowledge-Based Intelligent Information and Engineering Systems*, pages 843–849. Springer, 2003.

[3] Y. HaCohen-Kerner, Z. Gross, and A. Masa. Automatic extraction and learning of keyphrases from scientific articles. In *Computational Linguistics and Intelligent Text Processing*, pages 657–669. Springer, 2005.

[4] Q. He, J. Pei, D. Kifer, P. Mitra, and L. Giles. Context-aware citation recommendation. In *Proceedings of the 19th international conference on World wide web*, pages 421–430. ACM, 2010.

[5] J. P. Herrera and P. A. Pury. Statistical keyword detection in literary corpora. *The European Physical Journal B*, 63(1):135–146, 2008.

[6] A. Hulth. Improved automatic keyword extraction given more linguistic knowledge. In *Proceedings of the 2003 conference on Empirical methods in natural language processing*, pages 216–223. Association for Computational Linguistics, 2003.

[7] S. N. Kim and M.-Y. Kan. Re-examining automatic keyphrase extraction approaches in scientific articles. In *Proceedings of the Workshop on Multiword Expressions: Identification, Interpretation, Disambiguation and Applications*, pages 9–16. Association for Computational Linguistics, 2009.

[8] M. Ortuno, P. Carpena, P. Bernaola-Galván, E. Munoz, and A. Somoza. Keyword detection in natural languages and dna. *EPL (Europhysics Letters)*, 57(5):759, 2002.

[9] L. Rokach, M. Kalech, I. Blank, and R. Stern. Who is going to win the next association for the advancement of artificial intelligence fellowship award? evaluating researchers by mining bibliographic data. *Journal of the American Society for Information Science and Technology*, 62(12):2456–2470, 2011.

[10] P. K. Shah, C. Perez-Iratxeta, P. Bork, and M. A. Andrade. Information extraction from full text scientific articles: Where are the keywords? *BMC bioinformatics*, 4(1):20, 2003.

[11] C. Wu, M. Marchese, J. Jiang, A. Ivanyukovich, and Y. Liang. Machine learning-based keywords extraction for scientific literature. *Journal of Universal Computer Science*, 13(10):1471–1483, 2007.

Local Context Modeling with Semantic Pre-filtering

Victor Codina
Universitat Politècnica de Catalunya-BarcelonaTech
Girona 1-3, K2M 201
08034 Barcelona, Spain
vcodina@lsi.upc.edu

Francesco Ricci
Faculty of Computer Science
Free University of Bozen-Bolzano
Piazza Domenicani 3
39100 Italy
fricci@unibz.it

Luigi Ceccaroni
Barcelona Digital Technology Centre
Roc Boronat 117
08018 Barcelona, Spain
lceccaroni@bdigital.org

ABSTRACT

Context-Aware Recommender Systems locally adapt to a specific contextual situation the rating prediction computed by a traditional context-free recommender. In this paper we present a novel semantic pre-filtering approach that can be tuned to the optimal level of contextualization by aggregating contextual situations that are similar to the target one. The similarities of contextual situations are derived from the available contextually tagged users' ratings according to how similarly the contextual conditions influence the user's rating behavior. We present an extensive evaluation of the performance of our pre-filtering approach on several data sets, showing that it outperforms state-of-the-art context-aware Matrix Factorization approaches.

Categories and Subject Descriptors

H.3.3 [**Information Storage and Retrieval**]: Information Search and Retrieval – information filtering.

Keywords

Context-Aware Recommender Systems; Implicit Semantics; Collaborative Filtering; Matrix Factorization

1. INTRODUCTION

Context-Aware Recommender Systems (CARSs) differ from traditional recommenders because they estimate the rating of a target user *u* for an item *i*, not only by using a data set of ratings (of users for items), but also exploiting the knowledge of the contextual situations under which the ratings were acquired and the contextual situation of the target user asking for a recommendation. In this paper we use the term *contextual factor* when referring to a specific *type* of contextual information (e.g. weather), and *contextual condition* when referring to a specific value of a contextual factor (e.g. sunny). The term *contextual situation* refers to a combination of contextual conditions that describe the context in which the user experienced the item.

The main intuition supporting CARS techniques is that, when context matters, the ratings acquired in the target contextual situation should be more relevant for predicting what to recommend in that situation. As we will describe in the next section, in the last years several approaches for exploiting contextual knowledge have been proposed. We view CARS as locally adapted prediction models, i.e., adapted to a local contextual situation. Hence, as in other machine learning tasks, there is the need to judge to what extent the predictive model must fit the local situation. In other words, one must detect the optimal middle point between a global model based on all user preferences (i.e. personalization without context) and a local model just fitting the user preferences in a specific context. This means that one must find the optimal level of contextualization for a given rating data and contextual situation. For instance, a high degree of contextualization may not be appropriate when the contextual situation is too specific and not relevant, or when there are not enough ratings in that situation for generating reliable predictions. Actually, here we present an effective approach to accomplish this task: to find the right level of contextualization.

In a recent work [5] we proposed a flexible pre-filtering approach that exploits the semantic similarities between conditions during rating aggregation in order to find the optimal level of contextualization. Our approach follows a two-step process: (1) we first estimate the similarity of apparently unrelated contextual conditions, by focusing on their effect on user's rating behavior; (2) we exploit these condition-to-condition similarities to estimate the situation-to-situation similarities which are then used to expand the set of ratings for a target contextual situation aggregating the ratings obtained in the most similar situations.

In this work we improve the accuracy and computation efficiency of the proposed semantic pre-filtering approach by redefining its key component: the situation-to-situation similarity computation method. We show that our pre-filtering approach combined with standard Matrix Factorization (MF) is able to outperform, on several contextually tagged data sets, context-free MF (i.e. the global model), *exact* pre-filtering MF (i.e. the local MF models based only on ratings acquired exactly in the recommendation's target situation), and state-of-the-art MF prediction models based on the contextual modeling paradigm. Furthermore, we provide a detailed performance analysis on the considered data sets using different contextualization levels; ranging from context-free MF (global model) to *exact* pre-filtering (perfect local models).

The remainder of this paper is organized as follows. Section 2 positions our work with respect to the state of the art. Section 3 presents our novel semantic pre-filtering approach to CARS. Sections 4 and 5 present the evaluation and its results, and Section 6 draws the main conclusions and describes the future work.

2. RELATED WORK

CARS have been classified into three paradigms [1]: (1) pre-filtering, where context is used for selecting the relevant ratings before computing predictions with a traditional context-free model; (2) contextual post-filtering, where context is used to adjust predictions generated by a context-free model; and (3)

RecSys '13, October 12 - 16 2013, Hong Kong, Hong Kong
Copyright 2013 ACM 978-1-4503-2409-0/13/09...$15.00.
http://dx.doi.org/10.1145/2507157.2507218

contextual modeling, in which contextual information is directly incorporated in a context-free model as additional parameters.

Exact pre-filtering rigidly implements the basic intuition behind CARS: when context matters, generate prediction using only the data acquired in the target contextual situation. Its main limitation is the lack of flexibility: it always uses the maximum level of contextualization, a perfect local model. In the literature, several solutions to this limitation have been proposed. The most popular one is *generalized* pre-filtering [1] that exploits the available hierarchical relations between contextual conditions when searching for the optimal contextual segment (i.e. aggregations of semantically-related situations) for the target contextual situation. However, this solution is computationally expensive and its performance depends on the quality of the context ontology that is often limited to general hierarchical relationships between conditions of the same contextual factor.

Recent solutions have focused on integrating contextualization into a global MF model instead of building several local models. An example is *item splitting* [2], a pre-filtering variant that identifies in a selective way the relevant contextual conditions for the rating prediction of each item. Here ratings' filtering is selectively carried out item by item, for the most relevant contextual condition, and then a prediction model is built using all the data. In the category of contextual modeling, *tensor factorization* [7] extends standard MF to an *n* dimensional model according to the number of contextual factors. Its main limitation is the computational complexity, being applicable only when the number of contextual factors (i.e. dimensions) is small. The authors presented a more scalable approach in [4], which consists of extending standard MF model with contextual baseline predictors modeling the relationships between conditions and items. However, it is effective only when the target contextual situations are described by one or few conditions. Furthermore, all these approaches do not exploit the potential similarities between conditions, and, as we will show in Section 5, this knowledge may be useful to improve the performance of CARS.

3. SEMANTIC PRE-FILTERING

Similarly to *generalized* pre-filtering, we exploit semantic relations between contextual situations to find the optimal level of contextualization for building the local models. But instead of using ontology-based semantic relations, our approach looks for the implicit semantics of contextual conditions that can be estimated from rating data. We deem two contextual conditions *similar* if they influence the users' ratings in a similar way. To compute these similarities from rating data, we adapted Latent Semantic Analysis (LSA) [6] to the task of reducing a context-by-item or context-by-user matrix where entries are real values that measure the influence of conditions on user's rating behavior.

We first measure the influence of a condition on the users' preferences as the aggregated deviation between the actual rating value when the condition holds, and a predicted context-free rating. This aggregation can be based on different perspectives. Here we propose two variants: *user-based*, in which we use a per-user aggregation; and *item-based*, where a per-item aggregation is used. If additional data about the items or the users are available, then other aggregations may be employed, such as those based on item types (e.g. movie genres) or users' groups (e.g. age).

Let us denote with R_{ic} the set of ratings, acquired in contextual condition *c*, for item *i*, and with R_{uc} the set of ratings given by a user *u* in condition *c*. The importance weight of the condition *c* and item *i* (w_{ci}) or user *u* (w_{cu}) is calculated as the average of the deviations between the ratings r_{uic} in R_{ic} or R_{uc}, respectively, and the context-free baseline predictions b_{ui}:

Item-based: $$w_{ci} = \frac{1}{|R_{ic}| + \beta} \sum_{r_{uic} \in R_{ic}} (r_{uic} - b_{ui}) \quad (1)$$

User-based: $$w_{cu} = \frac{1}{|R_{uc}| + \beta} \sum_{r_{uic} \in R_{uc}} (r_{uic} - b_{ui}) \quad (2)$$

where β is used to reduce the estimated weights when R_{ic} or R_{uc} are small. We set the value of β experimentally; in our experiments $\beta \in [0,10]$. In this work we used as baseline predictor the context-free model presented in [8]: $b_{ui} = \mu + b_u + b_i$, where μ is the overall rating average, b_u is the bias associated to the user *u*, and b_i the bias associated to the item *i*. We also tested more sophisticated predictors but no significant differences were observed, hence we decided to use a simple one.

Then, we reduce the dimensionality of the condition-item or condition-user matrix M by using SVD. As a result, we obtain a *l*-dimensional vector of latent features that represents the implicit semantics of a condition *c*:

$$y_c = [f_{c1}, \dots, f_{cl}] \quad (3)$$

The optimal dimensionality *l* depends on data sparsity and was also identified experimentally (see Section 4 for more details about how we have set the model hyper-parameters and Table 3 where we show the optimal *l* values for the considered data sets).

Assume now that there is a training set of rating data provided by users for items in various contextual situations *S*, and, a situation *s* is defined by a vector $s = [c_1, \dots, c_k]$, where, *k* is the number of contextual factors, $c_j = 0,1,\dots,z_j$ are the contextual conditions for the j-th factor, and c_j=0 means that the j-th condition is unknown.

The semantic pre-filtering algorithm is a two-step process. Firstly, given a target contextual situation *s**, for each possible contextual situation *s* in *S*, we measure how similar *s* is to the target situation *s**, *Sim(s, s*)*, by computing the cosine similarity between the vector representations of the two situations y_s and y_{s^*}. If *s* is defined by one condition *c*, then $y_s = y_c$, i.e., it is equal to the *l*-dimensional representation of the contextual condition into the reduced latent feature model representing it, as described in Eq. 3. While if *s* is described by multiple conditions, we define y_s as the average of the vectors y_c of its known conditions C_s:

$$y_s = \frac{1}{|C_s|} \cdot \sum_{c \in C_s} y_c \quad (4)$$

Secondly, all the ratings acquired in a contextual situation *s* where $Sim(s, s^*) \geq t$ (being *t* a similarity threshold) are then aggregated to the training set X_{s^*}, which is used for building the local rating prediction model for the target situation *s**. Denoting with R_s the set of ratings acquired in situation *s*, and with *t* a similarity threshold we have that:

$$X_{s^*} = \bigcup_{s:\, Sim(s,s^*) \geq t} R_s \quad (5)$$

The similarity threshold *t* is a global parameter of the data set: the larger the threshold, the stronger the contextualization level of the local contextual models is, i.e., the local model of each target contextual situation is built aggregating less contextual situations more similar to the target one. When t=1 the local models are those built by *exact* pre-filtering, and only the ratings acquired exactly in the target contextual situation are used. Conversely, when the threshold is set to -1 the local models are all equal and are built using all the rating data, i.e., they are not local anymore and coincide with the context-free model. The goal of our approach is to find the level of contextualization (i.e. a threshold between -1 and 1) that yields the best prediction accuracy. In our experiments all the predictive models are based on MF; they only differ in the set of ratings used for training.

Note that if there is more than one rating for a given user and item acquired in some contextual situations similar to the target one, these ratings are aggregated (averaged) in order to generate a unique rating for user, item and target contextual situation.

4. EXPERIMENTAL SETUP

In order to evaluate our semantic pre-filtering technique we have considered several contextually tagged data sets with different characteristics (see Table 1). Music and Tourism data sets [3] contain ratings for items and users in contextual situations described by one condition only. They also contain ratings not tagged with a specific condition (context-free). Comoda [10] and Adom [1] data sets contain at most one rating per user and movie in a contextual situation that is described by the conjunction of several conditions (e.g. *summer*, *home* and *alone*). LibraryThing and MovieLens are data sets about books and movies, respectively, which contain ratings augmented with user tags (e.g. *funny*), extracted from their respective websites[1]. Here the contextual situation is described by the tags assigned by the users to the rated items: they provide a contextual clue of why the item is important for the user. But given the inherent noise of user-generated tags, we only used those tags that have a statistically significant impact on the user's rating behavior and have been used by a minimum number of users (5 users in MovieLens and 200 in LibraryThing). In particular, as significance test we used Pearson's chi-squared that proved to be an effective method to identify relevant contextual information [10]. We selected the tags with significant dependency on the ratings (99% confidence).

As suggested by [11] we measured the prediction accuracy of the considered models by conducting a per-user evaluation by randomly selecting, for each user, n ratings as test set (n=5 in LibraryThing and n=3 in the others). The remaining ratings were used to acquire the implicit semantics of contextual conditions and train the MF models. We then measured the Mean Absolute Error (MAE) of the predictions on the test items. All the reported results are averages of per-user evaluations, and the statistical significance of the differences between evaluated models has been calculated using the paired Wilcoxon sign rank test.

We evaluated the performance of the two variants of the semantic pre-filtering described in Section 3: using the *item-based* implicit semantics perspective according to Eq. 1 (*Pref-IB*), and using the *user-based* one according to Eq. 2 (*Pref-UB*). To build the local prediction models, with the training ratings identified by each pre-filtering approach, we used a standard MF approach that generates the rating estimation for the user u and item i as the sum of the user and item biases and the dot product between their corresponding vectors of latent features (p_u) and (q_i):

$$\hat{r}_{ui} = \mu + b_u + b_i + q_i^T p_u \quad (6)$$

For comparisons, we also evaluated two variants of the contextual modeling approach presented in [4] and also used in [10], which extends MF by adding baseline parameters that model the influence of the conditions on the items (CAMF-CI) or on the users (CAMF-CU). The parameters of the MF-based models are optimized using stochastic gradient descent. The numeric hyper-parameters of the models were optimized on a single validation set by using the Nelder-Mead search algorithm [9].

[1]See [www.librarything.com] and [www.movielens.org] (accessed August 5th, 2013)

Table 1. Data sets' statistics

Data set	ratings	users	items	density	factors	conditions	scale
Music	4013	43	139	16%	8	26	1-5
Tourism	1679	25	20	48%	14	53	1-5
Adom	1464	84	192	9.1%	4	14	1-13
Comoda	2296	121	1197	1.4%	12	49	1-5
Movie	2190	428	1115	0.4%	29	29	1-10
Library	609K	7192	37K	0.2%	149	149	1-10

5. RESULTS AND DISCUSSION

Here we evaluate the performance of the two variants of the semantic pre-filtering approach (*Pref-IB* and *Pref-UB*) against the context-free model (*MF*), *exact* pre-filtering (*Exact*) and two contextual modeling variants (*CAMF-CI* and *CAMF-CU*). Table 2 shows that the proposed prediction models achieve the best accuracy in most of the data sets. We can observe that in the data sets where contextual situations are described by one or few conditions (viz. Tourism, Music and LibraryThing) the semantic pre-filtering performs similarly to the contextual modeling approach, especially in terms of MAE. However, in data sets where situations are defined by several conditions (viz. Comoda and Adom) our approach clearly outperforms it. Similar results were obtained for Normalized Discounted Cumulative Gain (NDCG) (not shown here for space reasons).

As it can be observed in Table 3 (last two columns) the proposed semantic pre-filtering technique always outperforms *MF* and *Exact*. We can also observe that when the optimal level of contextualization is used (using the optimal threshold shown in the second data column), the average number of ratings increases by several factors with respect to the local models used by *Exact* (sub-column "vs. *Exact*" in "Expansion"), and considerably differs among data sets. In general, the proposed method produces the best results, compared with both *Exact* and *MF*, when the optimal level of contextualization causes a significant increase of the number of ratings that are used to build the local models. This occurs for Music, Tourism, Comoda and LibraryThing data sets where the local models built by our approach are on average 7.9, 7.2, 20 and 677 times larger than those built by *Exact*.

We can also observe that the value of the similarity threshold t is not important, what matters most is the amount of ratings that must be aggregated. For instance, a threshold of 0.9 is much more restrictive in Adom compared to Comoda. This is related to the average similarity of contextual situations in a data set. In fact, in Adom the average similarity between pairs of situations is small, 0.38, while in Comoda is much larger, 0.86; hence in Adom there are much less pairs of situations that are more similar than 0.9, which is the optimal threshold for both data sets.

Table 2. MAE of evaluated models: results in bold are significantly better (95% confidence) than context-free *MF* and results <u>underlined</u> are also significantly better than *Exact*

Models	Tourism	Music	Adom	Comoda	Movie	Library
MF	1.229	1.001	2.249	.760	1.274	1.261
Exact	1.116	1.210	2.213	.828	**1.131**	**1.193**
CAMF-CI	**1.002**	.942	2.291	.749	1.249	1.257
CAMF-CU	**1.031**	.976	2.230	.767	**1.186**	**1.140**
Pref-IB	**1.047**	.934	2.193	**<u>.675</u>**	**1.100**	**<u>1.142</u>**
Pref-UB	**1.009**	.966	2.185	**<u>.651</u>**	**1.116**	**<u>1.136</u>**

Table 3. MAE performance in optimal contextualization level ($l = y_c$ dimensionality (Eq. 3); t = similarity threshold)

Data set	*l*	*t*	Model size		Expansion		Improvement	
			#ratings	vs. *global*	#situations	vs. *Exact*	vs. *Exact*	vs. *MF*
Music	10	0	876	90%	21	7.9	23%	7%
Tourism	10	.24	180	64%	17	7.2	10%	18%
Adom	10	.90	26	1.8%	1.3	1.4	1.5%	3%
Comoda	49	.90	896	39%	730	20	21%	14%
Movie	29	.06	192	8.7%	13	3.3	3%	14%
Library	130	.40	38534	6.3%	2275	677	5%	10%

We note that the effect of the situation-to-situation similarity threshold on the prediction accuracy is similar to the effect of the user-to-user similarity in user-based Collaborative Filtering (CF): using a lower similarity threshold yields to a larger neighbor set and it is well known that it is important to find the right level of locality (neighbor size) in user-based CF.

Figure 1 illustrates the MAE and the level of contextualization in terms of ratings increase (bottom) as functions of the similarity threshold in the Comoda data set. The minimum MAE is obtained when the threshold is 0.9, which causes an aggregation of (on average) 730 situations and produces an increase of 20 times the average model size used by *Exact*.

Compared to the *all-pairs* situation-to-situation similarity strategy presented in [5], the one proposed here always performs better and has a reduced time complexity: its cost is at most O(n) rather than O(n^2), n being the number of contextual factors.

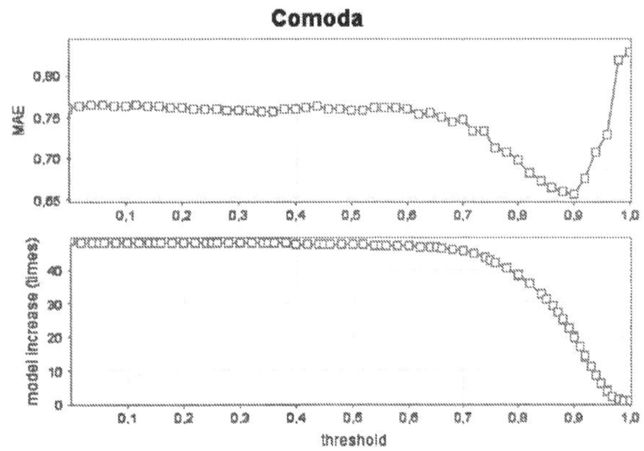

Figure 1. MAE and level of contextualization as functions of the similarity threshold

6. CONCLUSIONS AND FUTURE WORK

We have presented a semantic pre-filtering approach to CARS that can be tuned to find the right level of contextualization. This approach employs a global situation-to-situation similarity threshold that can be used to identify the ratings acquired in situations similar to the target one and that can be effectively used in the given target contextual situation to train the prediction model. The key component of our approach is a novel method for accurately measuring the similarity between contextual situations that is based on how similarly two different situations influence the users' ratings. Therefore, our method does not depend on external knowledge sources as in *generalized* pre-filtering.

The prediction accuracy of the proposed approach has been experimentally compared to state-of-the-art techniques on several contextually tagged data sets. We have shown that the proposed pre-filtering method outperforms both context-free MF and other CARS techniques based on MF as well.

To further improve the proposed semantic pre-filtering technique we will investigate a variant able to fine tune the level of contextualization per contextual situation. We believe that in some data sets where the specificity and relevance of contextual situations considerably differ, this fined-grained tuning may produce even better prediction accuracy.

7. ACKNOWLEDGEMENTS

The research described in this paper is partly supported by the SuperHub and the Citclops European projects (FP7-ICT-2011-7, FP7-ENV-308469), and the Universitat Politècnica de Catalunya-BarcelonaTech (UPC) under an FPI-UPC grant. The opinions expressed in this paper are those of the authors and are not necessarily those of SuperHub or Citclops projects' partners.

8. REFERENCES

[1] Adomavicius, G. and Tuzhilin, A. 2011. Context-aware recommender systems. In *Recommender Systems Handbook*. Springer, 217–256.

[2] Baltrunas, L. and Ricci, F. 2009. Context-based splitting of item ratings in collaborative filtering. In *Proceedings of RecSys '09*, 245–248.

[3] Baltrunas, L., Ludwig, B., Peer, S. and Ricci, F. 2012. Context relevance assessment and exploitation in mobile recommender systems. *Pers. Ubiquit. Comput.* 16(5):507–526.

[4] Baltrunas, L., Ludwig, B. and Ricci, F. 2011. Matrix factorization techniques for context aware recommendation. In *Proceedings of RecSys '11*, 301–304.

[5] Codina, V., Ricci, F. and Ceccaroni, L. 2013. Exploiting the Semantic Similarity of Contextual Situations for Pre-Filtering Recommendation. In *Proceedings of the 21st Conference on User Modeling, Adaptation and Personalization* , 165-177.

[6] Dumais, S. 2006. LSA and information retrieval: Getting back to basics. In Landauer, T.-K., McNamara, D.-S., Dennis, S., Kintsch, W. (Eds.) *LSA: A Road to Meaning*, Lawrence Erlbaum, 293–321.

[7] Karatzoglou, A., Amatriain, X., Baltrunas, L. and Olivier, N. 2010. Multiverse Recommendation: N-dimensional Tensor Factorization for Context-aware Collaborative Filtering. In *Proceedings of RecSys '10*, 79–86.

[8] Koren, Y. and Bell, R. 2011. Advances in Collaborative Filtering. In *Recommender Systems Handbook*, 145–186.

[9] Nelder, A. and Mead, R. 1965. A simplex method for function minimization. In *The Computer Journal*, 7(4).

[10] Odić, A., Tkalčič, M., Tasič, J. and Košir, A. 2013. Predicting and Detecting the Relevant Contextual Information in a Movie Recommender System. *Interact. Comput.* 25(1):74-90.

[11] Shani, G. and Gunawardana, A. 2011. Evaluating Recommendation Systems. In *Recommender Systems Handbook*, Springer, 257–297.

Musical Recommendations and Personalization in a Social Network

[A case study]

Dmitry Bugaychenko
Saint-Petersburg State University
Odnoklassniki LTD
DmitryBugaychenko@gmail.com

Alexandr Dzuba
Saint-Petersburg State University
Odnoklassniki LTD
AlexandrDzuba@gmail.com

ABSTRACT

This paper presents a set of algorithms used for music recommendations and personalization in a general purpose social network `www.ok.ru`, the second largest social network in the CIS visited by more then 40 millions users per day. In addition to classical recommendation features like "recommend a sequence" and "find similar items" the paper describes novel algorithms for construction of context aware recommendations, personalization of the service, handling of the cold-start problem, and more. All algorithms described in the paper are working on-line and are able to detect and address changes in the user's behavior and needs in the real time.

The core component of the algorithms is a *taste graph* containing information about different entities (users, tracks, artists, etc.) and relations between them (for example, user A likes song B with certainty X, track B created by artist C, artist C is similar to artist D with certainty Y and so on). Using the graph it is possible to select tracks a user would most probably like, to arrange them in a way that they match each other well, to estimate which items from a fixed list are most relevant for the user, and more.

In addition, the paper describes the approach used to estimate algorithms efficiency and analyze the impact of different recommendation related features on the users' behavior and overall activity at the service.

Categories and Subject Descriptors

[Information Systems]: Personalization, Collaborative filtering, Social recommendation

General Terms

Algorithms, Case Study

Keywords

musical recommendations, personalization, random walk

RecSys '13, October 12 - 16 2013, Hong Kong, Hong Kong
ACM 978-1-4503-2409-0/13/10 ...$15.00.
http://dx.doi.org/10.1145/2507157.2507192.

1. INTRODUCTION

The success of nearly all Internet projects nowadays highly depends on how much value can they provide for the user requiring as less efforts as possible. Recommender systems are one of the approaches used to increase "value for effort" rate. By analyzing user activity in the past a good recommender selects items which are most relevant to the current user's needs increasing user satisfaction, loyalty and the revenue of the project. Due to the high demand for the recommender systems in the industry, there is a very large field of research works in this area.

The most commonly used recommenders are *collaborative* [2, 6] — they analyze users behavior in the past and mine correlations between items and users. However, there is also a growing interest in the *content based* [7] and *social* [8] recommendation algorithms, in order to address limitation of the collaborative algorithms caused by the data sparsity and the "cold-start problem". It is now clear that none of these approaches is perfect and the best would be to combine benefits from all three worlds.

This paper proposes a composite approach for the recommender systems based on a *taste graph* which combines all data mined from the history of users' activity, content metadata and social network. Vertices of the graph represent different entities: users, tracks, artists, etc. Edges of the graph represent relations between entities: a user likes a track, an artist is similar with another artist and so on. All edges are weighted according to the certainty of the relation and all weights are normalized in order to produce a *stochastic system*.

The algorithms described in the paper are applied for the music service of "OK" (`www.ok.ru`) — a general purpose social network, which is the second largest social network in the CIS used mainly for fun and communication with rich media services. Daily audience of the network is more than 40 millions users mainly from the Russian Federation, Eastern Europe and Middle Asia.

2. TASTE GRAPH AND ALGORITHMS

The taste graph for musical recommendations consists of the following parts: users' preferences, artists' similarity, tracks' similarity and artists' tracks.

Users' preferences, in turn, are composed from different parts. All the history of user playbacks is recorded into a data warehouse and aggregated at a daily basis. Furthermore, there is a running window of the 1000 last played tracks with the time stamps in a real-time storage which is also considered. In addition to the playbacks history there is a real-time storage of the users' custom play lists to consider.

The artists' similarity is created by an analysis of playbacks history. Analysis is done in multiple steps: first of all from a set of all artist's tracks representative tracks are selected, then playbacks for these tracks are aggregated in order to get user–artist matrix. Using a simple correlation measure artist–artist matrix is constructed and then more precise correlation measure is applied iteratively to artist–artist matrix to refine it. Finally, outliers filtration algorithms are applied to the matrix and the top similars are selected.

For the tracks' similarity matrix for each pair of tracks A and B an amount of playbacks from the same user in the scope of limited time window is counted. Than the baselines are applied in order to address tracks popularity and results are normalized. In the end outliers filtration is applied and the top similars are selected.

The artists' works are selected from the music catalog meta data which keeps mapping from track to its main artist and overall rating of the tracks in the system is used as a weighting function. Track ratings are analyzed in dynamics in order to put tracks with higher interest recently above others.

Basic algorithms.

With the taste graph recommendations can be constructed using *random walk with restart* [5]. The main idea is to traverse graph randomly starting from the user's node with the probability α to restart at each step. Given initial vector of the user's preferences random walk recommender finds a fixed point of $x = \alpha \cdot x + (1 - \alpha) \cdot next(x)$ also known as the *steady-state probability distribution*. Items with higher steady-state probability are most likely to be relevant. This approach can be used to solve another recommender's task *extend list*. In this case the content of the list is chosen as the initial state of the walk and personalization technique described below can be used to improve results considering user's preferences.

Taste graph can be used to estimate the relevance of a set of items I (search result, top tracks, etc.) for user u. This could be done by traversing the graph from user preferences vector in a limited number of steps counting all the visits of the vertices from target vector. The vertices with higher number of more probable visits are considered as more relevant for the user.

Randomizing recommended sequence.

Each time user opens the radio he would like to get a new sequence which is relevant, coherent, diverse and novel. In order to achieve that we implemented *random pick with rejection*. Items are picked randomly from the weighted list and each selected item is challenged by a probabilistic rejection algorithm, which depends on multiple factors.

The most important rejection factors are based on the *previous presence*. Presence of item itself can be covered by a simple "yes or no" factor prohibiting repeated inclusion of the item. Presence of other works from the item's artist can be considered in two dimensions: the overall presence and the distance from the previous entry. The overall presence is modeled as an exponentially descending factor and the distance to previous entry factor is modeled as inversed exponential descend.

While previous presence rejection factors increase diversity and novelty of the recommended sequence, coupling with nearest predecessors factors increase coherence of the sequence. The main idea here is to estimate the weight of the paths between item v and its nearest predecessors in the sequence using the taste graph which could be done by using the personalization technique.

Context awareness.

In order to provide value for the user, recommended music must address current context the user is in now (working, having a dinner or playing with his kids). The problem of context awareness is explored in [1] and two techniques were adopted to generate contextual recommendations: contextual pre-filtering of user's preferences and contextual post-filtering of the generated recommendations.

The filtering is done by analyzing all paths of length N starting from the *context set* and ending in the vertices of *filtered set*. Three measures are collected: count of the paths, sum of weights on the all paths and the weight of the best path. Vertices reached high enough limit for at least one of the measures are selected as the input for recommendations generation (when doing pre-filtering) or randomization algorithm (when doing post-filtering).

The selection of the context set is done by the user himself, but he is provided with a bundle of automatically generated sets based on *user preference clustering*. After experimenting with multiple clustering algorithms, we ended up using *affinity propagation* [3] with *common neighborhood subgraph density* [4] as a similarity measure.

Addressing cold-start problem.

When a new user joins the system demographical information is used to support him at the beginning. All users are split into segments depending on their age, sex and region. Behavior of the users in the scope of a demography group is analyzed in order to create a *demography profile*. When a user has no own preferences, best matching demography profile is used instead. Even if user already has some preferences, but not that much, then his own preferences are mixed with demography profile.

When new item is added to the system it becomes the most interesting candidate for being recommended. However, due to the lack of statistics it has only a few links with other items and low overall rating, thus it is unlikely to be recommended. In order to identify relevant new items recently added content is analyzed and activity around them is compared to the time they spent in the system. In order to boost these items in recommendation the weight of the corresponding artist–track link is set to a very high level comparing to other links from this artist.

3. ANALYZING IMPACT

One of the most common approaches to evaluation is the offline analysis based on the historical data [9]. It is simple and cheap, but has an inherent drawback — recommender proposing items user probably knows always get higher score then the recommender proposing relevant items user not likely knows and can't find them himself. An alternative to offline analysis chosen in this work is an online experiment either on a selected subgroup of the users, or on all of them.

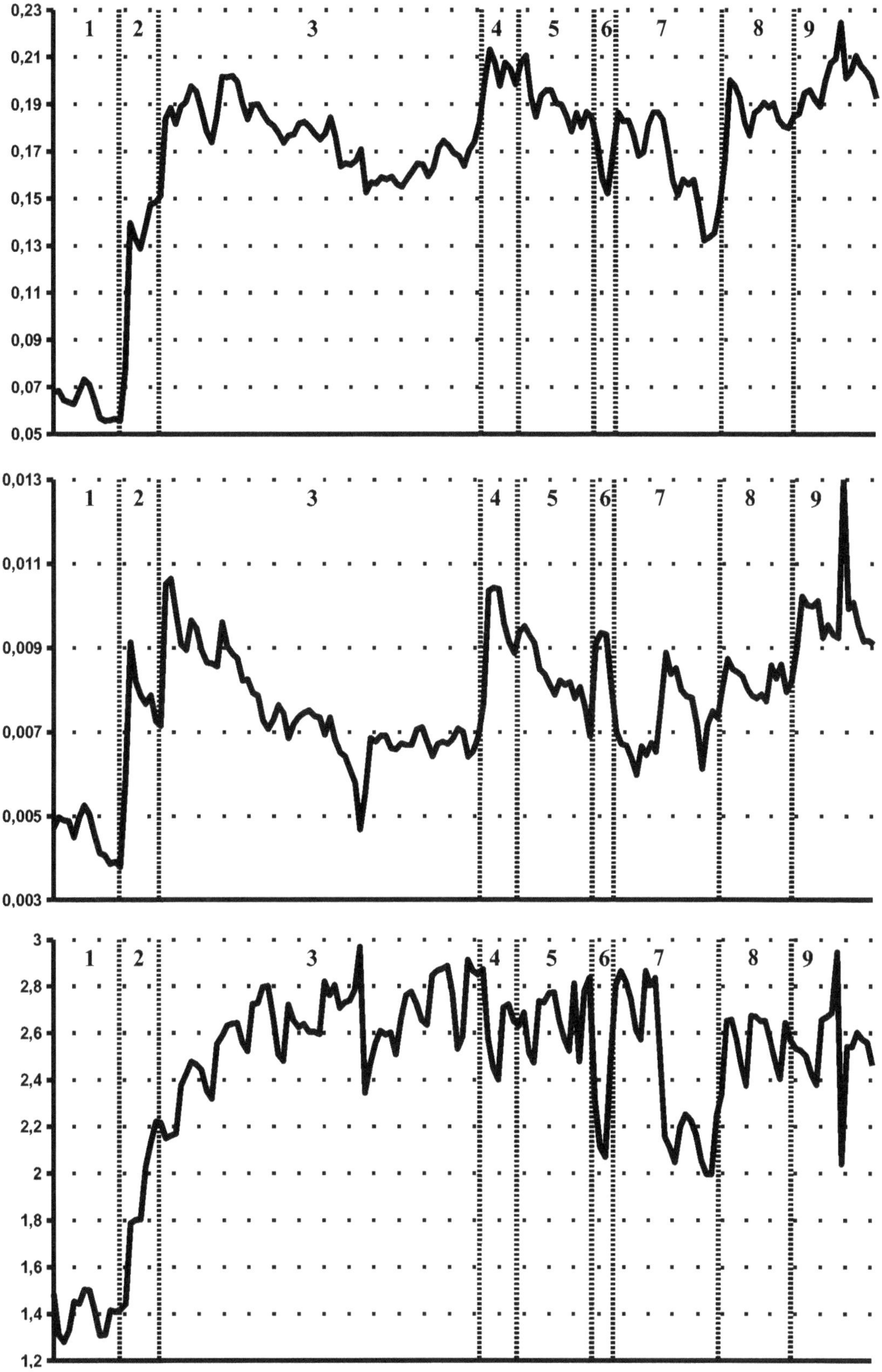

Figure 1: Playback and "likes" from the main page comparing to playbacks from "My music", playbacks from the main page comparing to clicks.

Personalization of the main page (the list of 100 songs user sees after entering the music area) was the first significant feature based on the recommender launched at 2012-11-16. Figure 1 shows user activity trends during the 6 months passed after the launch. Three main indicators are collected:

1. Amount of playbacks from the main page comparing to playbacks from "My music".
2. Amount of "likes" from the main page comparing to playbacks from "My music".
3. Amount of playback from the main page comparing to the amount of clicks at the main page.

"My music" is the list of the user's favorite tracks, it is the most popular list in the system and is used as the measure of overall level of activity. In this perspective the first indicator shows the relevance of the content, the second indicator shows the novelty and the third shows the users' confidence. Following periods are highlighted:

1. Main page contains top tracks based on the all users activity in the system for last 30 days.
2. Personalization enabled selecting top 100 tracks for a user among 1000 top tracks in the system.
3. Size of the underlying list increased to 1500.
4. Enabled suppression of the known items (w_0 set to negative value).
5. Changed the underlying list preparation algorithm.
6. Track known by a user removed from the main page.
7. Full removal disables, Gaussian noise introduced into personalization.
8. Strength of the known tracks suppression decreased, underlying list size increased to 3000.
9. Use of demography data enabled for the new users.

According to the first two charts at the figure 1 personalized main page performs two-three times better then the non-personalized variant. During initial experiments (stages 2-5) each time settings of the personalization were adjusted the user activity at the main page increased (users seen new content there), but a downward trend emerged after few days (users got used to what they see). Stage 6 showed that the strong filtering of known content increases novelty (amount of likes increased), but relevance and the users' interest decreased (playbacks dropped). Replacement of the strong filtering with a lighter suppression (known content still might appear, but with a decreased weight) and introduction of the Gaussian noise at the stage 7 changed trend for likes to upward and for playbacks to sideways. Increasing the underlying list size and using demographical data we achieved upwards trends in both areas.

The third chart at the figure 1 shows the evolution of the users' confidence in the content of the main page. For lists users are confident in they tend to turn playback on with a click and listen, but for the lists with low confidence they tend to control playbacks thoroughly. With the personalization enabled the users' confidence increased slowly and without downward trend. Attempts to increase novelty (at stages 6 and 7) increased the amount of clicks, but it is more an indication of the increased curiosity then of the decreased confidence. The confidence chart also shows that at weekends users tend to produce more clicks.

4. CONCLUSIONS

Recommender systems and personalization are a crucial tool for nearly all kind of web sites. For `www.ok.ru` introduction of personalization for the content of the main page in the music area has increased user activity there threefold. This shows that the common recommender's use case "recommend a sequence" is not the only interesting case. Thus, modern industrial recommender must be flexible enough to address different tasks and to employ the information of the different kinds. Orchestrating multiple recommenders can address this challenge, but at the cost of increased computation complexity.

Taste graph described in this paper has many of the desired properties: it can include data of different kind in a single model and support different kind of algorithms with reasonable computational complexity and immediate reaction to the changes in the user behavior. The results achieved at `www.ok.ru` are very promising in terms of both increased user activity and the recommender's non-functional properties (computational efficiency, scalability and flexibility).

5. REFERENCES

[1] G. Adomavicius and A. Tuzhilin. Context-aware recommender systems. In F. Ricci, L. Rokach, B. Shapira, and P. B. Kantor, editors, *Recommender Systems Handbook*, pages 217–253. Springer US, 2011.

[2] C. Desrosiers and G. Karypis. A comprehensive survey of neighborhood-based recommendation methods. *Recommender Systems Handbook*, pages 107–144, 2011.

[3] D. Dueck. *Affinity propagation: clustering data by passing messages.* PhD thesis, University of Toronto, 2009.

[4] Y. Kang and S. Choi. Common neighborhood sub-graph density as a similarity measure for community detection. In *Neural Information Processing*, pages 175–184. Springer, 2009.

[5] I. Konstas, V. Stathopoulos, and J. M. Jose. On social networks and collaborative recommendation. In *Proceedings of the 32nd international ACM SIGIR conference on Research and development in information retrieval*, SIGIR '09, pages 195–202, New York, NY, USA, July 2009. ACM.

[6] Y. Koren and R. Bell. Advances in collaborative filtering. *Recommender Systems Handbook*, pages 145–186, 2011.

[7] P. Lops, M. Gemmis, and G. Semeraro. Content-based recommender systems: State of the art and trends. *Recommender Systems Handbook*, pages 73–105, 2011.

[8] A. K. Milicevic, A. Nanopoulos, and M. Ivanovic. Social tagging in recommender systems: a survey of the state-of-the-art and possible extensions. *Artificial Intelligence Review*, 33(3):187–209, 2010.

[9] G. Shani and A. Gunawardana. Evaluating recommendation systems. In F. Ricci, L. Rokach, B. Shapira, and P. B. Kantor, editors, *Recommender Systems Handbook*, pages 257–297. Springer US, 2011.

Not by Search Alone: How Recommendations Complement Search Results

Daria Dzyabura & Alex Tuzhilin
Stern School of Business, New York University
{ddzyabur,atuzhili}@stern.nyu.edu

ABSTRACT

This paper presents a novel approach to combining search and recommendations methods into one integrated system to satisfy user information seeking needs. It is shown theoretically and experimentally using simulations that the proposed combined approach outperforms "pure" search and "pure" recommendations in those cases when search is hindered by the user's inability to come up with a complete set of search criteria, and recommendation engine produces mediocre results.

Categories and Subject Descriptors

H.3.3 **[Information Storage and Retrieval]**: Information Search and Retrieval

Keywords: recommender systems, search, hybrid systems.

1. INTRODUCTION

Several prominent recommender systems, such as Netflix and Amazon, support not only recommendations, but also search. For example, 75% of downloads on Netflix come from the recommendation engine and 25% from search [2]. This suggests that neither search nor recommendations alone fully satisfy information seeking needs of these firms' customers and, therefore, the presence of both of them is required. However, recommendations and search are kept separate on Netflix and Amazon without integration of the two into one information seeking mechanism. In this paper, we explore this integration idea, propose one specific approach of how to combine the two mechanisms into one hybrid model, and demonstrate the advantages of the proposed method.

The concept of integration of search and recommendations has been explored before. For example, [7] argues for the need of convergence of search, recommendations and advertising mechanisms into one common information seeking model. Motivations for this type of convergence come from the following considerations. If a user knows what to search for, then search engines would produce good recall results, i.e., would retrieve all or most of the items of interest to the user. However, if the user cannot specify all the relevant search criteria, and only focuses on a fraction of desired attributes [3], then the recall results can be poor since many interesting items will not be retrieved. In these cases, supplementing search engines with recommendations may greatly improve search. Recommendations not only introduce desirable, previously unconsidered items into the consideration set, but also expose the users to new attributes that they can subsequently use in their searches. One of the key advantages of recommender systems over search is that they produce "global" recommendations across the whole item space, thus allowing users to discover serendipitous items which they would not think about searching. However, the recommender system's rating estimates can be noisy, resulting in mediocre recommendations. Users then prefer to manually generate search queries rather than rely only on mediocre recommendations. When neither system works perfectly, a combined system will better satisfy users' information seeking needs, as argued in [7] and attested by the presence of both technologies at Netflix, Amazon and others.

Although [7] argues for the convergence of search and recommendations, the paper presents only a conceptual framework and the need for such a convergence. It does not provide any specific mechanisms of how to combine these two different technologies and does not explore under what circumstances convergence is beneficial. Moreover, some form of combination of search and recommendations has been explored within the framework of flexible, constrained and critique-based recommendations [1, 4, 5, 6, 8, 9]. The key idea behind all of these methods is that recommendations are provided using not the entire item space, but only some subset of items satisfying various types of constraints and queries. These constraints and queries are specified using different mechanisms across various methods. The underlying idea behind these methods is to limit the space of items considered by the recommender system. This is directly related to search, which also finds objects specified by the search query. However, unlike the ideas described in [7] and explored in this paper, those recommendation constraints and queries serve as inputs for recommender systems, making the constraints and queries *tightly integrated* into the recommender system itself. Therefore, all the methods described in [1, 4, 5, 6, 8, 9] can be viewed as a *tight coupling* between search and recommender systems, which is different from the *loose coupling* approach advocated in [7] and in this paper.

In this paper, we show that it is indeed useful to combine search and recommendations in a loosely coupled manner in some cases in order to achieve higher levels of recall (and even the F-measure). We also propose a specific mechanism for doing so and show that it produces better performance results in some cases. In order to demonstrate this, we first present the specific models of search and recommendations, then describe a particular hybrid model combining the two mechanisms in a loosely coupled manner, and then demonstrate theoretically and via simulations that this hybrid approach dominates pure search and pure recommendations in some settings.

RecSys'13, October 12–16, 2013, Hong Kong, China.

http://dx.doi.org/10.1145/2507157.2507231

2. THE MODELS OF SEARCH AND RECOMMENDATIONS

In this paper we focus on specific models of items, search and recommendations. Although we have chosen these very specific models in the paper, we believe that our findings are more general and can be extended to various other models. We plan to work on these extensions in the future, as discussed in Section 5.

2.1. *The Items Model.* We assume that there is a collection of items I, such as books, songs or movies, and that each item has a set of attributes, such as the list of actors, the director and the year of the movie. Further, we assume that all the attributes of all the items come from the universal collection of attributes A, such as all the actors and movie directors in the movie industry. In our model, we do not consider the particular types of these attributes, only their set A. Finally, we assume that each item is characterized by a collection of attributes from A associated with that item, such as the list of actors and the director of a movie. Furthermore, each attribute can be associated with more than one item, e.g., an actor can appear in more than one movie. This means that, in addition to the collection of items I and attributes A, there is also a bipartite graph G specifying which attributes are associated with which items. This bipartite graph can be connected or disconnected, meaning that it can have one or several connected components. An example of such a graph is presented in Figure 1.

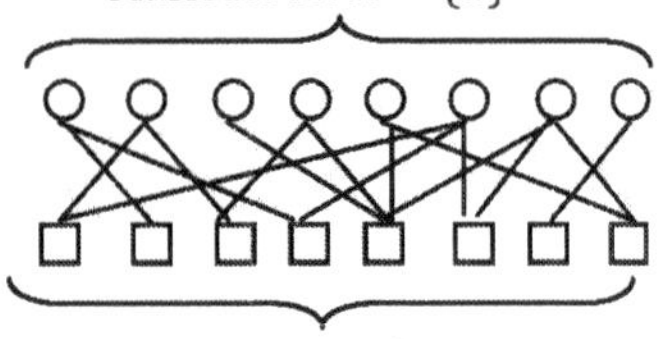

Figure 1: An example of the bipartite graph G.

Let A_i be the set of attributes connected to item i. As is standard in economics and business literature [10], we assume that each item's utility is the sum of the utilities of its attributes:

$$r_{ij} = \sum_{a \in A_i} x_{aj} \quad (1)$$

where x_{aj} is user j's utility for attribute a, and r_{ij} is the overall utility (rating) of item i for user j. An item is considered to be "good" if it's utility is above a threshold value α.

2.2. *Search (S).* Given the bipartite graph presented in Section 2.1, the search process is performed as follows in our model S. First, the user selects a single attribute a from A and submits the search query using this attribute. The search engine returns all the items associated with attribute a in graph G. The user examines all the returned items, identifies those that are of interest to him/her and identifies the criteria for the next search based on this examination of the selected items. Since we have made a simplifying assumption that the search query uses only a single attribute, this means that the user needs to chose only one such attribute for the next search. Although restrictive, we believe that the single attribute simplifying assumption can be lifted in future work and does not restrict the findings of this paper in significant ways.

In this paper, we model this iterative search process and the user's searching behavior as follows. First, we assume that the user selects all the items from the set of items returned by search on attribute a that have utility above the threshold α and "consumes" those items (e.g. adds the selected Netflix movies to the queue). The user then selects the next search attribute probabilistically in our user model from those that occurred in the products that s/he liked from the search results, with probability proportional to the number of times the attribute occurred. For example, if the user searched for "James Bond" at time 1, and one of the films he liked was Casino Royale, he may choose to search for Daniel Craig at time 2. If the search produced n desirable items with a certain feature, the user would be n times more likely to search for that feature in the next period, as if it had occurred only once.

This process of *repeatedly* selecting items and attributes in our model continues until saturation when the point of diminishing returns or a steady state is reached and no more new good items are produced for two periods in a row.

2.3. *Recommendations (R).* In this paper, we do not consider any specific method of estimating unknown ratings. We only assume that the attribute utilities x'_{aj} are estimated somehow using any of the existing techniques proposed in the literature [11] (note that if we know estimates x'_{aj}, then we can compute the ratings r_{ij} using equation (1)). Also, we assume that these estimations, x'_{aj}, are noisy but correlated with their true values x_{aj} and can be modeled as draws from a bivariate normal distribution:

$$\begin{bmatrix} x_{aj} \\ x'_{aj} \end{bmatrix} \sim \mathcal{N}(\mu, \Sigma),$$

where

$$\mu = \begin{bmatrix} 0 \\ 0 \end{bmatrix}, \Sigma = \begin{bmatrix} 1 & \rho \\ \rho & 1 \end{bmatrix}$$

The parameter ρ is crucial because it determines quality of recommendations: larger values of parameter ρ lead to more accurate and lower values to less accurate estimations of unknown ratings. Note that this model R is general because a wide range of existing recommender systems can fit into this generic model.

A "good" item – to be recommended – is one that has utility higher than the threshold value α described in Section 2.1.

2.4. *Combining Search and Recommendations into a Hybrid R+S Model.* The search S and recommendation R models can be combined into a single R+S model in several different ways. In this paper, we focus on one particular hybrid R+S method when certain recommendations are added to the search results. More specifically, we generate a search list using the method described in Section 2.2, produce recommendations as described in Section 2.3, and combine them as follows. When the user selects the attribute for the next search criterion, s/he can choose *either* from the search results, *or* the product recommendations. This way, product recommendations may not only introduce the recommended products into the consideration set, but also influence the *future* search path. For example, a user searching for action films may, if recommended one Hitchcock horror film, search for more Hitchcock and other similar films in the next periods, now that Hitchcock and horror are salient attributes. Understanding attribute salience is critical in connecting user-driven search and recommendation systems: attributes that are made salient to the user by product recommendations can, if the user chooses, be used as search criteria in the future.

3. THE PROBLEM FORMULATION

We want to compare the performance of the hybrid approach with pure recommendations and pure search and demonstrate that in some settings the hybrid approach dominates pure search and pure recommendations. We start with this comparison theoretically and show that there exist some instances of pure search and pure recommendation models where the hybrid approach outperforms them in terms of the recall measure. Then in the next section we demonstrate this further via simulations. We proceed with our theoretical explorations by formulating and proving the following propositions. They compare performance of the hybrid and pure models only in terms of recall since discovery of all the good items was the main motivation of this work. We provide comparisons of precision in the simulation experiments.

Proposition 1. There exists a set of items I, a set of attributes of these items A, and a bipartite graph G of attribute-item features, such that for any starting search query q, pure search (S) retrieves weakly fewer "good" items than the combined R+S model.

Sketch of Proof. Assume that set I consists of N items and these items collectively have N attributes (forming set A). Further, graph G connects each attribute to a single item bijectively, thus producing N clusters, each cluster having only one item. Then any search query q retrieves only 1 item, and no subsequent query generated based on the retrieved list can improve this result. Therefore, the final outcome is that one item is retrieved for any query q if this item is "good", and no items retrieved if it is "bad". In contrast, if we add recommendations to the pure search case, then, if the recommended product turns out to be good, the user will end up with extra good item received. ▮

Proposition 2. There exists a set of items I, a set of attributes of these items A and a bipartite graph G of attribute-item features, such that for any recommendation r generated on graph G and for any search query q, the combined R+S method generates at most as many "good" recommendations as the pure S model.

Sketch of Proof. Assume that graph G is fully connected, i.e., every item is connected to every attribute. It is clear that any search query q will eventually find *all* the good items using the search process (described in Section 2.2) and, therefore, recommendations are superfluous for such graph G. Therefore, the combined R+S model performs at most as well as the S model. ▮

Proposition 2 says that the pure search model is so good on the fully connected graph G that any additional recommendations added to the search model are superfluous because the sequence of iterative item retrievals launched by search query q will eventually find all the good items in the fully connected graph G.

These two propositions theoretically show that the R+S model dominates the pure S model for the recall measure for *some* bipartite graphs. However, the proofs rely on extreme cases (it is unlikely that graph G is either fully connected or disconnected in practice). Thus, it is essential to explore what happens for the whole range of configurations of graph G, as well as compare R+S and R models, which we do in Section 4 using simulations.

4. COMPARING THE R+S MODEL WITH PURE R & S CASES USING SIMULATIONS

We simulate the S, R and the R+S approaches as follows. First, we assume that graph G has 10,000 items in I, 5,000 attributes in A. To generate the edges, we first randomly partition items and attributes into 50 groups, each group representing closely related items. We generate an edge between any item and attribute *within* a group with probability P_w; we generate edges between attributes and items *not* in one group (*across* groups) with probability P_a. In our experiments, we use $P_w = 0.1$ and $P_a \in [0.001, 0.01]$.

Second, we simulate the search process S. We begin with query q having a single attribute a and then iterate through the subsequent searches using the mechanism described in Section 2.2. We stop these iterations when no new "good" items are retrieved after $k = 2$ iterations. The "goodness" of an item (i.e., how valuable it is to the user) is defined with the utility parameter α that takes value of 3.5 in our simulations. Third, we simulate recommendations as described in Section 2.3.We vary the value of parameter ρ from 0 to 1. Finally, we simulate the hybrid R+S model as described in Section 2.4 by doing search and adding recommendations produced by the recommender system.

Based on these simulated data, we compare the performance of the R+S model to that of R and S models for a range of parameter values. The most important parameters that crucially affect the performance results are P_a and ρ. P_a determines the connectivity and "clusteredness" of the graph, and thus controls the quality of search; ρ determines the quality of recommendations.

Fig. 1(*a,b*) present the average recall measure for the R, S and R+S simulations while varying P_a and ρ, respectively and keeping the other parameter constant. The R+S model outperforms the R and S models in the region where R is weak ($\rho < 0.7$). Interesting interactions occur in the region of P_a=0.003, and ρ=0.6, where the respective curves cross. We now focus on this region of P_a and ρ.

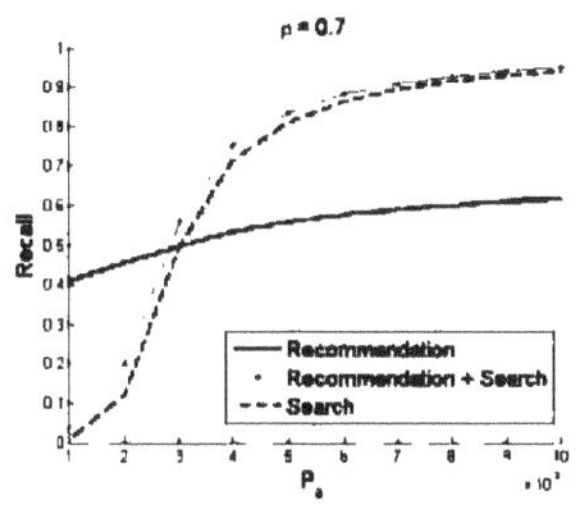

Fig 1a: Recall varying P_a

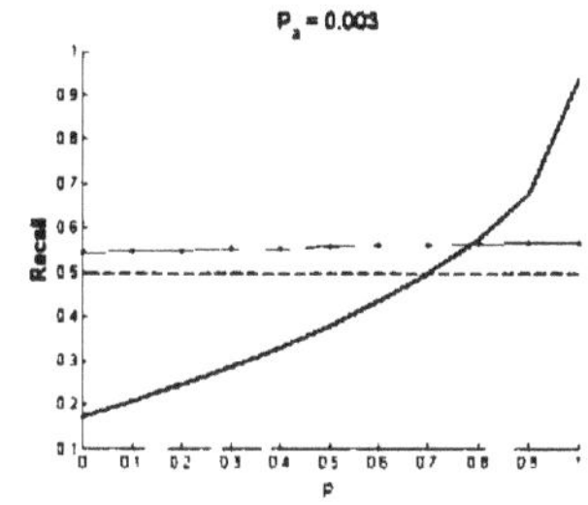

Fig 1b: Recall varying ρ

Fig. 2 presents the probability density functions of the recall measure for the R, S and R+S models computed across 10,000 users for parameter values $P_a = 0.003$ and $\rho = 0.6$. The hybrid R+S model outperforms the pure S and pure R models for these values of parameters. The performance improvement is statistically significant at the highest level. The same result holds for the parameters $P_a = 0.01$ and $\rho = 0.6$ for the recall measure, as shown in Fig. 3, also with a high level of significance. However, this is not true for the case of $P_a = 0.001$ and $\rho = 0.6$, as shown in Fig. 4, where pure R model significantly outperforms both the S and R+S models. This is because when the P_a value is so low the product space is very clustered, which hinders the search process: the user is likely to search only one cluster and stop. Therefore the recall values for the S and R+S cases are diminished, but the pure R system does not suffer from this limitation.

We conclude from these results that the hybrid model R+S does not always outperform the S and R models across all the parameters. Performance improvements for the R+S vs. the R and S cases happen when both search and recommendation results are only mediocre and there is not a big difference in their performance, as in Fig. 2. If either search or recommendations drastically dominates the other, then the hybrid model does not outperform *both* pure search and recommendation cases, as seen in Fig 3 and 4. It is this "middle ground" case of both models performing reasonably well and one model marginally outperforming the other (as in the $P_a = 0.003$ and $\rho = 0.6$ case of Fig. 2) when the R+S model really helps, as Fig. 2 demonstrates.

So far, we have compared the R+S and the R and S models only in terms of the recall measure, which is important, but does not give the full picture of the R+S vs. R and S comparisons. Therefore, Fig. 5 presents the comparison of these models in terms of precision. The pure R model outperforms the R+S and S models in terms of precision in case of parameters $P_a = 0.003$ and $\rho = 0.6$. This is because parameter $\rho = 0.6$ produces fairly precise recommendations, whereas search produces a long and "complete" but not a precise list of outcomes, resulting in low precision values. R also outperforms R+S on the F-measure, but we do not plot it due to space constraints.

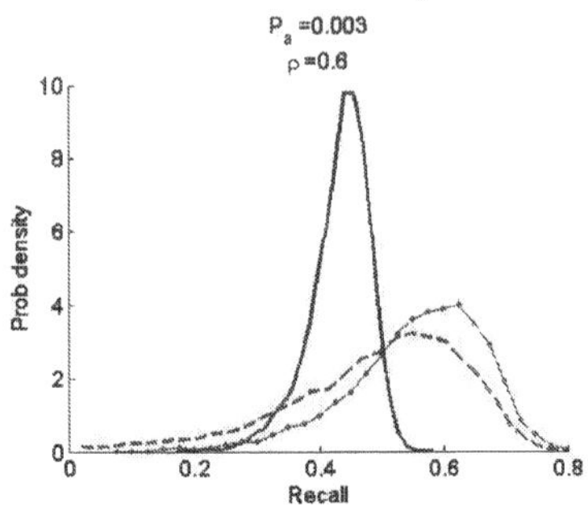

Fig 2: Recall for P_a=0.003,ρ=0.6

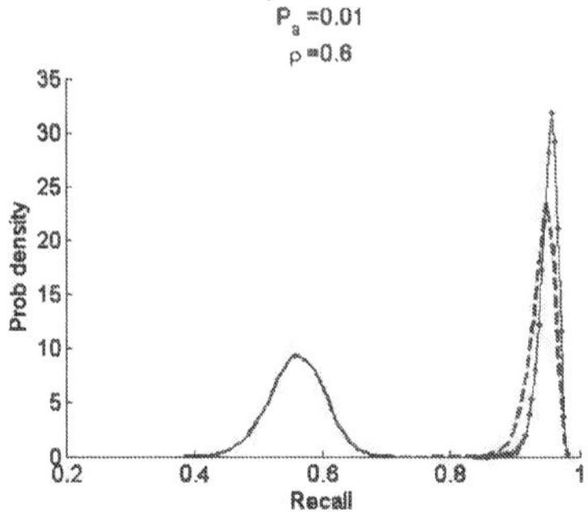

Fig 3: Recall for P_a=0.01, ρ=0.6

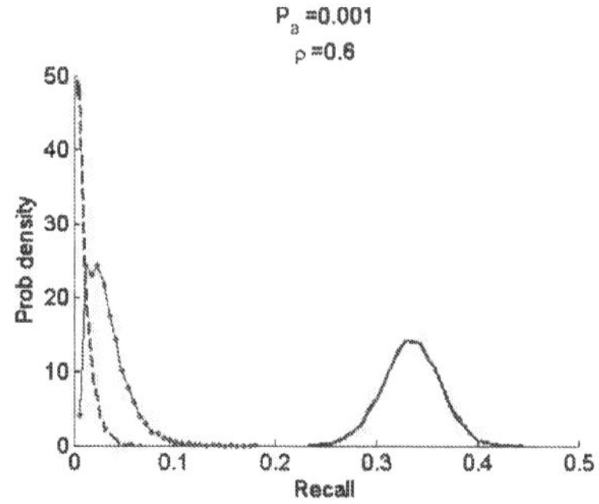

Fig 4: Recall: P_a=0.001,ρ=0.6

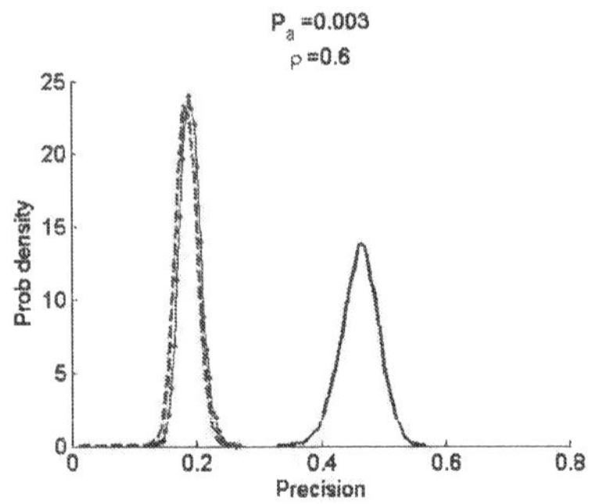

Fig 5: Precision: P_a=0.003, ρ=0.6

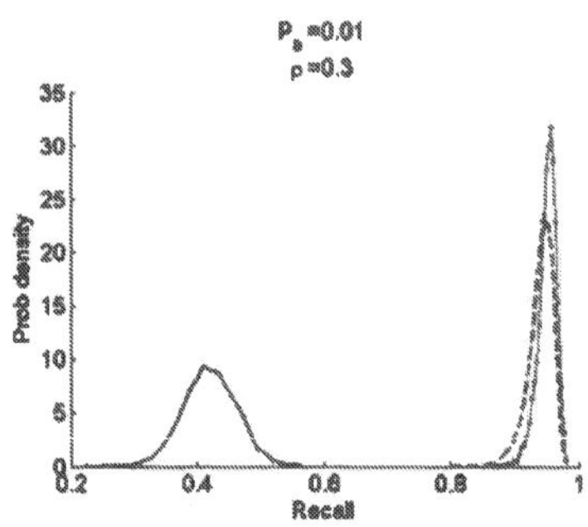

Fig 6: Recall: P_a=0.01,ρ=0.3

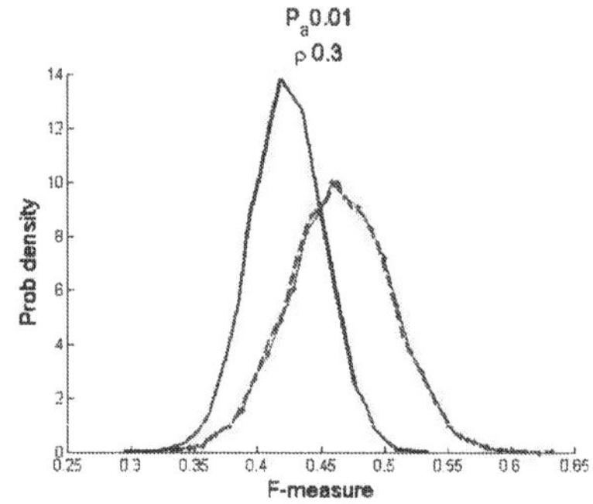

Fig 7: F-measure: P_a=0.01, ρ=0.3

Recommendation — Recommendation + Search — Search

To further explore this phenomenon, we considered less accurate recommendations (ρ = 0.3, P_a = 0.01). The results for recall and the F-measure are presented in Figs 6 and 7, respectively. The R+S model outperforms the R model for P_a = 0.003 and ρ = 0.3 *both* in terms of recall *and* the F-measure. Regarding the R+S vs. S case, the R+S model slightly outperforms the S model in terms of recall *and* achieves practically the same performance results as S in terms of the F-measure. This means that the R+S model performs better or similar than the pure S and R models in terms of not only the recall measure but also the F-measure for some parameter settings.

5. CONCLUSIONS

In this paper, we studied the problem of integrating search and recommendations in a loosely coupled system that combines the search and recommendation results. We proposed a specific method of combining the two approaches and showed that the proposed hybrid R+S model outperforms pure search S and pure recommendation R models in terms of the recall and the F-measures in certain parameter settings, but does not for other settings.

This paper presents our *preliminary* investigations of this important and complex problem. In the future, we plan to conduct experiments on real data and users to investigate if similar results hold on real data. We also plan to study further under which conditions the hybrid approach dominates the pure cases, ideally, trying to formulate the necessary and/or sufficient conditions for such dominance. We also plan to study various other methods of loose coupling of the search and recommendation methods besides the specific one presented in this paper.

6. REFERENCES

[1] Adomavicius, G., Tuzhilin, A. and Zheng, R. REQUEST: A Query Language for Customizing Recommendations. Information Systems Research, 22(1), 2011.

[2] Amatriain, X and Basilico, J. Netflix Recommendations: Beyond the 5 Stars (Part 1), April 2012.

[3] Dzyabura, Daria. The Role of Changing Utility in Product Search. NYU Stern Working Paper, 2013.

[4] Burke, R. Knowledge-based recommender systems, Encyclopedia of Library and Information Sciences, 69(32), 2000.

[5] Chen, L. and Pu, P. Critiquing-based recommenders: survey and emerging trends. User Modeling and User-Adapted Interactions, 22(1-2), 2012.

[6] Felfernig, A., Friedrich, G., Jannach, D., and Zanker, M. Developing Constraint-based Recommenders. Recommender Systems Handbook, Ch. 6, 2011.

[7] Garcia-Molina, H., Koutrika, G., and A. Parameswaran. Information Seeking: Convergence of Search, Recommendations, and Advertising, CACM, Nov. 2011.

[8] Koutrika, G., Ikeda, G., Bercovitz, B. and Garcia-Molina,H. Flexible recommendations over rich data. RecSys 2008.

[9] McCarthy, K., Reilly, J., McGinty, L. and Smyth, B. On the Dynamic Generation of Compound Critiques in Conversational Recommender Systems. Adaptive Hypermedia, 2004.

[10] McFadden, D. Econometric Models for Probabilistic Choice Among Products. Journal of Business, 53(3), 1980.

[11] Ricci, F., Rokach, L., Shapira, B. and Kantor, P. Recommender Systems Handbook, Springer, 2011.

OFF-Set: One-pass Factorization of Feature Sets for Online Recommendation in Persistent Cold Start Settings

Michal Aharon, Natalie Aizenberg, Edward Bortnikov, Ronny Lempel
Yahoo! Labs, Haifa, Israel
{michala,anatalia,ebortnic,rlempel}@yahoo-inc.com

Roi Adadi, Tomer Benyamini, Liron Levin, Ran Roth, Ohad Serfaty
Yahoo! Smart Ad, Tel Aviv, Israel
{roiaddi,tomerb,liron,ranr,ohad}@yahoo-inc.com

ABSTRACT

One of the most challenging recommendation tasks is recommending to a new, previously unseen user. This is known as the *user cold start* problem. Assuming certain features or attributes of users are known, one approach for handling new users is to initially model them based on their features.

Motivated by an ad targeting application, this paper describes an extreme online recommendation setting where the cold start problem is perpetual. Every user is encountered by the system just once, receives a recommendation, and either consumes or ignores it, registering a binary reward.

We introduce One-pass Factorization of Feature Sets, *OFF-Set*, a novel recommendation algorithm based on Latent Factor analysis, which models users by mapping their features to a latent space. OFF-Set is able to model non-linear interactions between pairs of features, and updates its model per each recommendation-reward observation in a pure online fashion. We evaluate OFF-Set against several state of the art baselines, and demonstrate its superiority on real ad-targeting data.

Categories and Subject Descriptors

H.4 [**Information Systems Applications**]: Miscellaneous; D.2.8 [**Software Engineering**]: Metrics—*complexity measures, performance measures*

General Terms

Algorithms, Experimentation

Keywords

Dynamic Ad Optimization, Matrix Factorization, Collaborative Filtering, Persistent cold start problem

1. INTRODUCTION

In recent years, Collaborative Filtering (CF) based recommender systems have gained both commercial success and increased focus from the research community. Generally speaking, CF discovers and exploits recurring consumption patterns of items by users, at scale, in order to recommend items to users. Studied consumption types include ratings of items by users, which explicitly articulate users' likings and dislikings of items; binary indication of users' consumption of items, without explicit evidence regarding the users' opinions on their consumed items; richer implicit interaction settings where users, while still not explicitly providing ratings on items, can perform multiple operations on items (e.g. click or comment on news stories), etc.

In order to provide high-quality recommendations of items to a user, recommender systems must observe some past activity of the user. When new users first arrive to a system, no previous activity is available and they are said to be "cold"; recommending to such users is challenging, and has been coined the "user cold-start problem" [12, 6, 8].

Motivated by an online ad targeting application (Section 3), this paper addresses an extreme online recommendation setting where the cold start problem is perpetual - practically every user encountered by the system is seen just once, i.e. every recommendation request is for a previously unseen user. Nevertheless, certain attributes of the users are known, and those are leveraged for recommendation. For every recommendation made, a binary indication (i.e. reward) is observed. The goal is to maximize the reward.

We introduce One-pass Factorization of Feature Sets - *OFF-Set* a novel recommendation algorithm based on *latent factor analysis* [7], which models both users and items by mapping their features to a latent space. OFF-Set offers a non-linear solution by designing a latent space that models individual as well as pairwise combinations of features. OFF-Set is formulated for purely online recommendation, performing lightweight updates of its model per each recommendation-reward observation. We evaluate OFF-Set against several state of the art baselines, and demonstrate its advantage on real ad-targeting data.

2. RELATED WORK

The ever-growing demand for automated recommendations at scale has prompted the development of a variety of recommendation techniques. Collaborative Filtering (CF) algorithms are often the alternative of choice, among which, the *matrix factorization* (MF) [7] technique is successful and popular [3, 2]. In its most basic form, MF associates each user and each item with a latent factor (vector). The match score between a user and an item is represented as an inner product between the corresponding vectors.

RecSys '13, October 12 - 16 2013, Hong Kong, Hong Kong
ACM 978-1-4503-2409-0/13/10 ...$15.00.

Although collaborative filtering algorithms have been gaining great success in recent years, they are often challenged by the well-known *user cold-start* problem [6] – namely, making recommendations to previously unobserved users. In oder to overcome this problem at scale, reference to user features is often done. One such approach is *factorization machines* (FM), first presented by Rendle [9, 10]. FM is known for its capability to model sparse feature spaces. It is a combination of *support vector machines* (SVM) [4] and matrix factorization, and it closely fits our problem specification. FM was shown to be superior to other approaches, including "regular" matrix factorization [11].

Outside of collaborative filtering there may be found other solutions for feature-based prediction modeling to offer a different approach to the cold-start and sparsity issues. The *gradient-boosted decision trees* (GBDT) algorithm [5] is one such approach. In contrast with linear methods, GBDT models the scoring process as an aggregation over an ensemble of decision trees. GBDT has been shown to be successful in non-latent feature spaces, including those with interdependent features.

Both FM and GBDT are not designed to work in an online setting, as they require several passes over the data in order to converge. In this sense they differ from our approach, as OFF-Set is completely online – i.e., every input element is processed exactly once and the ensuing update of the model is lightweight.

3. DYNAMIC ADVERTISING CAMPAIGNS

Dynamic advertising campaigns are a relatively new form of digital display advertising, where the advertiser offers multiple products or multiple ad creative alternatives (referred to as 'ad variants') to be presented to users. Unlike traditional display advertising settings, where the ad exchange assigns a specific ad to every user impression, in dynamic campaigns the exchange designates a campaign to the impression. It is up to a follow-up process - a selection algorithm - to determine which variant, i.e. which specific ad instance, to actually serve to the user. That decision is based upon data (context) provided to the selection algorithm, e.g. properties about the user, the page content surrounding the ad slot, the time of day, etc. In this work we assume only basic demographic information about the users (age, gender, geographic location) is known.

A typical optimization task in dynamic campaigns is to maximize the campaign's click-through rate (CTR), i.e. the CTR over all user impressions which were served by some ad variant of the campaign. We formulate dynamic ad campaign optimization as a recommendation task which attempts to assign, to each user impression, the variant that a user is most likely to click on.

Display ads, as opposed to content (e.g. articles, search results) and other digital advertising types (e.g. sponsored search) are characterized by very low CTR. In addition, many campaigns *target* (i.e. compete over) the same set of users, resulting in most users being exposed to a campaign no more than once. These two factors lead to an extremely sparse user signal - most users do not register a single click in most campaigns - and impose a great challenge to any recommendation algorithm.

4. NOTATIONS

Our problem is about recommending items, in our case ad

Figure 1: Example of Dynamic Ad Campaign (for Yahoo! Shopping)

variants $\mathbf{A} = \{a_1, a_2, \ldots, a_L\}$, to users $\mathbf{U} = \{u_1, u_2, \ldots, u_M\}$. Each user u_i is associated with a set of feature values $[u_i^1, u_i^2, \ldots, u_i^K]$, where $u_i^k \in \mathbf{F}_k$, and $\mathbf{F}_k$ is the set of available values for feature k (e.g., one feature can be 'gender', where the set of available values is 'male', 'female' and 'unknown'). We now define $\mathbf{C}$ as the set of (user, ad variant) pairs that resulted in a click Similarly, we denote by $\mathbf{NC}$ the set of (user, ad variant) pairs that did not result in a click. Finally, let $\mathbf{N} = \mathbf{C} \bigcup \mathbf{NC}$ be the union of the two sets.

5. THE OFF-SET ALGORITHM

Dynamic ad selection is yet another ranking problem. Given a new user entering the system, we aim at selecting the best possible ad variant that will maximize the probability of a click, thus maximizing the CTR of the overall campaign. Like in many other ranking problems, we chose to use a latent factors approach, where each ad variant and each user are represented by a latent vector, $\mathbf{v}_{a_j} \in R^D$ and $\mathbf{v}_{u_i} \in R^D$ respectively. The score of the match for a pair (u_i, a_j) is defined by the inner product of the two corresponding vectors, $S(u_i, a_j) = \langle \mathbf{v}_{u_i}, \mathbf{v}_{a_j} \rangle = \mathbf{v}_{u_i}^T \cdot \mathbf{v}_{a_j}$, where higher inner products represent better match, or a higher probability of a click. Hence, given a user, the OFF-Set algorithm suggests the ad variant that results in the highest matching score, in order to maximize the CTR of the campaign. As previously mentioned, the user vector is not directly trained by the algorithm, but rather the feature vectors that construct it, as will be detailed in section 6.

5.1 Applying Maximum Log Likelihood

We define the target function for maximization following the approach suggested by Aizenberg et al. [2]. Given the training data described above, that includes $|\mathbf{C}|$ click interactions, we define a multinomial distribution for a click over all our (user, ad variant) pairs as follows:

$$PC(u_i, a_j) = |\mathbf{C}| \cdot \frac{\exp^{S(u_i, a_j)}}{\sum_{(u_k, a_l) \in \mathbf{N}} \exp^{S(u_k, a_l)}}, \qquad (1)$$

where $PC(u_i, a_j)$ is the probability of a click for the (u_i, a_j) pair, and $S(u_i, a_j)$ is the score our model assigns this pair. Note that this is a general definition of probability that satisfies $\sum_{(u_i, a_j) \in \mathbf{N}} PC(u_i, a_j) = |\mathbf{C}|$. Also, it holds that for all i and j, $0 < PC(u_i, a_j) \leq 1$ under the constraint that $|S(u_i, a_j)| \leq \ell$, for $\ell = 0.5 \ln \frac{|\mathbf{N}|}{|\mathbf{C}|}$[1].

Our model's parameters (denoted hereafter by Θ) are now trained in order to maximize the mutual probability of the pairs that actually resulted in a click (assuming independence between all pairs). Using the log likelihood approach,

[1]As the score value is not important by itself, but rather the ranking it derives, scores can always be normalized in order to satisfy this constraint. Therefore, from now on, we will not refer to this constraint.

we get[2]

$$\Theta = \arg\max \log \prod_{(u_i,a_j)\in C} PC(u_i,a_j) = \quad (2)$$
$$\arg\max \sum_{(u_i,a_j)\in C} S(u_i,a_j) - |\mathbf{C}| \cdot \log \sum_{(u_i,a_j)\in \mathbf{N}} \exp^{S(u_i,a_j)}.$$

5.2 Training The Model

We extract Θ using a stochastic gradient ascent method. The derivative of the above target function depends on whether the (user, ad variant) pair resulted in a click or not. Whenever $(u_i, a_j) \in \mathbf{C}$, we get:

$$\Delta\Theta = (1 - PC(u_i,a_j)) \cdot \frac{\partial S(u_i,a_j)}{\partial \Theta}. \quad (3)$$

And when $(u_i, a_j) \in \mathbf{NC}$ we get

$$\Delta\Theta = -PC(u_i,a_j) \cdot \frac{\partial S(u_i,a_j)}{\partial \Theta}. \quad (4)$$

It is clear that a positive reward (a click) will always result in an increase in the value of $S(u_i, a_j)$, and vice versa. However, the increase and decrease step sizes are not equal.

If we begin the training process with random variables, assuming equal probability of a click to all pairs (which equals $\frac{|\mathbf{C}|}{|\mathbf{N}|}$), we get that the ratio (denoted by μ) between the step sizes of a negative and a positive rewards is $\mu = -\frac{|\mathbf{C}|}{|\mathbf{NC}|}$. This implies that for any positive reward we should apply a gradient ascent step that will increase $S(u_i, a_j)$ in some learning step α, while for any negative reward, we apply a gradient ascent step of size $\alpha \cdot \mu$, that will decrease $S(u_i, a_j)$.

Throughout the training process, assuming the model succeeds in representing the user preferences by representing the real probabilities, the step sizes should be decreased in both directions, and dependent on the specific pair. For simplicity reasons, we keep μ as the ratio between the update steps, and update its value throughout the training process, as detailed in Section 5.3.

5.3 Online Training

Up until now we have referred to the training data as a fixed and known set of examples. This, however, does not hold in the real world settings we operate in. The amount of data pairs and the rate in which they are produced are high. On the one hand, the data sparsity issue requires gathering many samples for training. On the other hand, as a single campaign may run for only a few hours, the training must be done with minimal latency. Considering these constraints together, an on-line training scheme is required. In such a solution, each sample updates the model's parameters only once (either positively, or negatively, according to the reward). Furthermore, the update depends only on this single sample, with no reliance on previous data samples. The only accumulative value we aggregate from the collection of data samples is the updated μ factor, the ratio between the step sizes of updates stemming from positive and negative rewards.

6. USER AND ITEM LATENT VECTORS

We now turn to describe the separate latent vector representations that map the ad variants and users into the same latent space. For ad variants which are repeating and stable along the campaign, we simply assign one D-dimensional latent factor per ad variant (item) a_j, $\mathbf{v}_{a_j} \in R^D$.

We offer a novel construction of the latent representation on the user side. Recall that we assume that users are encountered once, and so are perpetually cold. Hence, they must be modeled by their features. Previous works in matrix factorization assigned a latent vector to each feature value, and modeled users (or items) as a linear combination of their features' vectors [2].While this approach can handle sparse user data, it cannot capture any dependencies between the features as the combination between the features is linear. Instead, we construct a more complex latent space over user features, that allows the representation of strong dependencies between each pair of features. Recall that items were mapped into R^D, and assume that each user has some values across K features. We select an *overlap dimension* o and a *standalone dimension* s such that $D = Ks + \binom{K}{2}o$. Each feature value is assigned a d-dimensional vector where $d = s + (K-1)o$, so that $\mathbf{v}^k_{u_i} \in R^d$ is the vector assigned to the kth feature value of user u_i. That vector has s entries that are attributed only to the specific feature, and $K-1$ blocks of o entries that are in overlap with each of the $K-1$ other features[3].

We now compose $\mathbf{v}_{u_i} \in R^D$ from $\binom{K}{2}$ chunks of size o, each holding the products of the values from a pair of feature vectors. The rest of $\mathbf{v}_{u_i}$ holds the Ks standalone values from each of the feature vectors. The process is illustrated in Figure 2. Now, let $\tilde{\mathbf{v}}^j_{u_i} \in R^D$ be an extension of $\mathbf{v}^j_{u_i}$, so that the values of $\mathbf{v}^j_{u_i}$ appear in d of the entries of $\tilde{\mathbf{v}}^j_{u_i}$, according to their indices and the rest of the entries are set to 1 (see middle part of Figure 2). Using this formulation, $\mathbf{v}_{u_i} = \prod_{1\leq j\leq K} \tilde{\mathbf{v}}^j_{u_i}$ (for an element-wise product).

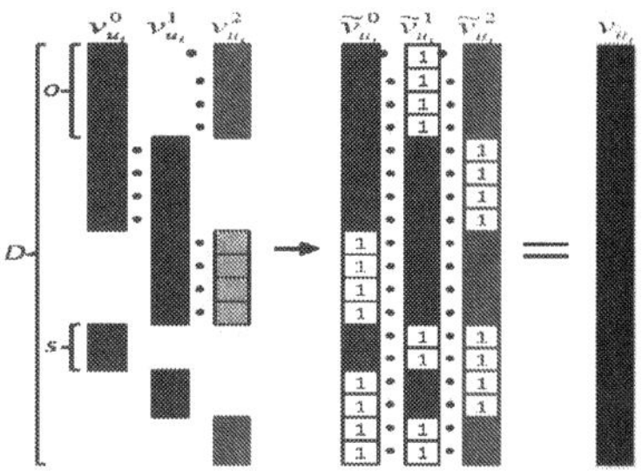

Figure 2: Example of a user latent factor construction from its feature value vectors ($K = 3$). In this example, $D = 18$, $d = 10$, $s = 2$ and $o = 4$. The middle illustration presents the auxiliary vectors $\tilde{\mathbf{v}}^k_{u_i}$

7. EVALUATION

We evaluate OFF-Set against two state-of-the-art methods mentioned in Section 2 as well as a simple 'popularity' algorithm. We use three baselines throughout our experiments: the Factorization Machines (FM) [9, 10] (which is given pairs of features, that allows it to represent dependencies between them), Gradient-Boosted Decision Trees

[2]A more comprehensive technical description was omitted, and can be found at[1]

[3]For simplicity, we assume each feature merits s unique entries and every pair of features merits an overlap of o entries. Non-uniform assignments of entries are possible and have no effect on the rest of the algorithm.

Campaign	clicks in warm-up phase	clicks in test phase	number of ad variants
A	100	2400	14
B	100	900	22

Table 1: Real-life campaign statistics. Significance was computed from Hoeffding's formula with confidence of 95%.

(GBDT) [5] and a global-popularity based algorithm (Popularity), which also follows the trend of the data, by applying a decay factor to the CTR values of all variants[4]

The evaluation metric we used was Mean Reciprocal Rank (mrr), applied only on positive observation (**C**). Formally, for algorithm A,

$$mrr(A) = \frac{1}{|\mathbf{C}|} \sum_{(u_i,a_j)\in\mathbf{C}} \frac{1}{r_A^{u_i}(a_j)}, \quad (5)$$

where the function $r_A^{u_i}(a_j)$ is the rank of the ad variant a_j in algorithm A's computed ranked list for user u_i (1 for the first location). Under the assumption that the presented ad variants appear uniformly at random in the test data (and independently of the user), this metric quantifies well the ability of an algorithm to predict a click.

For evaluation on real data we chose two different dynamic campaigns, henceforth referred to as Campaign A and Campaign B. In order to simulate an on-line setting, the test (on both campaigns) was performed as follows. First, some initial number of observations is used for warm-up training. Subsequently, all remaining observations are iterated over, sorted by time of appearance. Observations that did not result in a click are used for further training. Any observation that resulted in a click is first used for evaluation, by requesting each algorithm to rank the available items for the given user. Afterward, the observation (along with its positive reward) is added as an additional training example. Table 1 provides some statistics on both campaigns, including the number of clicks contained in the warm-up and online test phases described above. Due to business sensitivity, we cannot disclose the exact number of non-clicks in the data. Rather, we roughly disclose that in both campaigns, the number of non-clicks was 2-3 orders of magnitude larger than the number of clicks.

For OFF-Set, being a single pass algorithm, the procedure above is straightforward. FM and GBDT, however, must be retrained from scratch once encountering a click in the online portion of the test[5].

The results are presented in Table 2. We can see a clear and significant advantage to OFF-Set as compared to the baselines (see Table 1 for the significant gap values for each campaign). In addition, its efficiency, being a single pass method, along with its low memory footprint, establish its superiority over the other methods for this problem.

Algorithm	MRR results campaign A	MRR results campaign B
Random	0.2114	0.2255
Popularity	0.2940	0.4360
FM w/paired features	0.3038	0.3824
GBDT	0.2613	0.3193
OFF-Set	0.5993	0.6234

Table 2: MRR results on real (offline) data. MRR differences higher than 0.055 **and** 0.091 **for campaigns** A **and** B **respectively are significant (with 95% confidence).**

8. CONCLUSIONS AND FUTURE WORK

In this work we introduced OFF-Set - an online single-pass algorithm that handles a perpetual user cold start problem. OFF-Set is based on Matrix Factorization, and is motivated by a log-likelihood approach. It exploits repeating user features and captures pairwise feature dependencies. We evaluated OFF-Set on real-life data, and demonstrated its superiority over state-of-the-art methods.

[4]A more detailed evaluation section is given in[1]

[5]Since MRR is only measured on clicks, there is no need to retrain these models, for the purposes of the experiment, on each non-click.

9. REFERENCES

[1] M. Aharon, N. Aizenberg, E. Bortnikov, R. Lempel, R. Adadi, T. Benyamini, L. Levin, R. Roth, and O. Serfaty. Off-set - extended technical report. *arXiv.org:submit/0776700*, 2013.

[2] N. Aizenberg, Y. Koren, and O. Somekh. Build your own music recommender by modeling internet radio streams. *WWW '12 Proceedings of the 21st international conference on World Wide Web*, 2012.

[3] K. Barman and O. Dabeer. Analysis of a collaborative filter based on popularity amongst neighbors. *IEEE Transactions on Information Theory*, 58(12), 2012.

[4] N. Cristianini and J. Shawe-Taylor. *An Introduction to Support Vector Machines and other kernel-based learning methods.* Cambridge University Press, 2000.

[5] J. H. Friedman. Greedy function approximation: A gradient boosting machine. *Ann. Statist.*, 29 (5), 2001.

[6] Z. Gantner, L. Drumond, C. Freudenthaler, S. Rendle, and L. Schmidt-Thieme. Learning attribute-to-feature mappings for cold-start recommendations. *IEEE 10th International Conference on Data Mining (ICDM)*, pages 176 – 185, 2010.

[7] Y. Koren, R. Bell, and C. Volinsky. Matrix factorization techniques for recommender systems. *Published by the IEEE Computer Society*, 42(8), 2009.

[8] S. Park and W. Chu. Pairwise preference regression for cold-start recommendation. *Proceeding RecSys '09 Proceedings of the third ACM conference on Recommender systems*, pages 21–28, 2009.

[9] S. Rendle. Factorization machines. *Proceedings of the 2010 IEEE International Conference on Data Mining (ICDM), Washington, DC, USA*, 2010.

[10] S. Rendle. Social network and clickthrough prediction with factorization machines. In *KDD Cup*, 2012.

[11] S. Rendle. Factorization machines with libfm. *ACM Transactions on Intelligent Systems and Technology*, Volume 3 Issue 3, May 2012.

[12] K. Zhou, S. Yang, and H. Zha. Functional matrix factorizations for cold-start recommendation. *Proceedings of the 34th international ACM SIGIR conference on Research and development in Information Retrieval*, pages 315–324, 2011.

Personalised Ranking with Diversity

Neil Hurley
UCD INSIGHT
University College Dublin
Ireland
neil.hurley@ucd.ie

ABSTRACT

In this paper we discuss a method to incorporate diversity into a personalised ranking objective, in the context of ranking-based recommendation using implicit feedback. The goal is to provide a ranking of items that respects user preferences while also tending to rank diverse items closely together. A prediction formula is learned as the product of user and item feature vectors, in order to minimise the mean squared error objective used previously in the `RankALS` and `RankSGD` methods, but modified to weight the difference in ratings between two items by the dissimilarity of those items. We report on preliminary experiments with this modified objective, in which the minimisation is carried out using stochastic gradient descent. We show that rankings based on the output of the minimisation succeed in producing recommendation lists with greater diversity, with just a small loss in relevance of the recommendation, as measured by the error rate.

Categories and Subject Descriptors

H.3.3 [**Information Storage and Retrieval**]: Information Search and Retrieval

Keywords

Diversity; Implicit Ratings

1. INTRODUCTION

A large amount of research on recommender system algorithms has been driven by the task of predicting ratings for unrated items, given a database of items that have been explicitly rated by users in the past. Matrix factorisation models have proven very successful in minimising the root mean squared prediction error and fast algorithms have been developed to fit these models. However, there is growing interest within the recommender system community in producing recommendation algorithms that optimise for different quality measures in other contexts. One context of particular interest is that of producing personalised *rankings* of items given a database of implicit feedback [2, 4, 5, 3, 6]. For instance, in a music recommendation scenario, implicit positive feedback is gathered in terms of the number of times that a track or an artist has been listened to by a user. In this case, the absence of a rating can be interpreted as negative feedback that should be incorporated into the recommendation algorithm. Of particular interest to the work presented here are the methods of [3, 6], in which a matrix factorisation model is learned by the minimisation of a ranking objective.

Ranking based on relevance only can result in recommendation sets that have low diversity – many of the highly relevant items can be very similar to each other. This has led to interest in diversifying recommendation lists while maintaining high relevance [10, 8, 7]. This paper focuses on this problem. Differently to past work that has focused on diversifying nearest-neighbour algorithms [8, 9] or on selecting diverse subsets of items from a set of relevant items [10], here we examine whether a diversification criterion can be incorporated into a ranking-based objective. Using a matrix factorisation model, user- and item-feature vectors are learned by minimising this objective to produce predicted ratings, that when used to rank the items in the database, result in recommendation sets that are highly diverse, while remaining highly relevant. We present preliminary results that evaluate our *ranking with diversity* model on the Netflix dataset.

RecSys'13, October 12–16, 2013, Hong Kong, China.

http://dx.doi.org/10.1145/2507157.2507226.

2. RANKING WITH IMPLICIT FEEDBACK

Adopting the notation of [6], let U and I be the number of users and items, respectively, in the database and write $\mathcal{U}$ and $\mathcal{I}$ for the sets of users and items. We use $u \in \mathcal{U}$ to index users and $i, j \in \mathcal{I}$ to index items. Implicit ratings are denoted as r_{ui} and the matrix of ratings is denoted as $\mathrm{R} \in \mathbb{R}^{U \times I}$. Predictions are denoted as $\hat{r}_{ui}$. $\mathcal{T}$ denotes the set of (u, i) indices of R where positive feedback is provided. If $(u, i) \notin \mathcal{T}$ then an implicit negative feedback rating of $r_{ui} = 0$ is assumed. $\mathcal{U}_i = \{u | (u, i) \in \mathcal{T}\}$ is the set of users who have given positive feedback on item i.

Our ranking with diversity strategy is based on the objective function proposed originally in [3] and further developed in [6]:

$$f_R(\Theta) = \sum_{u \in \mathcal{U}} \sum_{i \in \mathcal{I}} c_{ui} \sum_{j \in \mathcal{I}} s_j \left[(\hat{r}_{ui} - \hat{r}_{uj}) - (r_{ui} - r_{uj})\right]^2 \quad (1)$$

where Θ are the parameters of the prediction model and c_{ui} and s_j are parameters of the objective function. The key is to find a good ranking by learning the rating difference of two items for a given user u. The parameters c_{ui} select user-item pairs with positive feedback and are taken as $c_{ui} = 1$ if $(u, i) \in \mathcal{T}$ and $c_{ui} = 0$ otherwise. The parameters s_j represent the importance of item j in the objective function. The original KDD 2011 challenge [1] for which the objective was designed, required that items that receive positive feedback from a given user should be distinguished from generally popular items. For this task, an importance weighting of $s_j \propto |\mathcal{U}_j|$ is appropriate.

A matrix factorisation formulation is chosen for the prediction model such that $\hat{r}_{ui} = \mathbf{p}_u^T \mathbf{q}_i$, where $\mathbf{p}$ is an F-dimensional user feature vector associated with user u, $\mathbf{q}$ is an F-dimensional item feature vector associated with item i and F is the number of features. Hence $\Theta = (\mathbf{p}_u, \mathbf{q}_i)$ The computational challenge of minimising $f_R(\Theta)$ is that the objective contains $T \times I$ terms. Originally in [3] a stochastic gradient descent algorithm (SGD), in which the items j of the third summation in (1) are sampled at random, was proposed. This is referred to as the RankSGD algorithm in [6], where an efficient alternating least squares (ALS) algorithm, RankALS, that avoids sampling is proposed. Our focus in not on such computational issues, but rather on exploring whether the ranking objective can be modified to take account of item diversity. In the experiments presented later in this paper, we use RankSGD, although RankALS could also be applied.

3. RANKING WITH DIVERSITY

Assume that we have an $I \times I$ diversity or distance matrix $\mathrm{D} = \{d_{ij}\} \in \mathbb{R}^{I \times I}$ expressing how dissimilar item i is to item j. This matrix may be obtained from any source; it may, for example, represent a content-based dissimilarity of the items. We assume that the dissimilarity is derived from a positive definite, normalised similarity matrix, $\mathrm{S} = \{s_{ij}\}$, with $s_{ii} = 1$, using $d_{ij} = \sqrt{1 - s_{ij}}$.

We wish to form an I-dimensional ranking vector $\mathbf{q}$ based on this dissimilarity matrix. Let π_i denote the item whose rank is i where items are ranked according to $\mathbf{q}$ i.e. $q_{\pi_i} \geq q_{\pi_j}$. Consider an objective that attempts to choose $\mathbf{q}$ so that the squared difference of the difference between two components i and j of the ranking vector and the dissimilarity d_{ij} is minimised:

$$f_1(\mathbf{q}) = \sum_i \sum_j (|q_i - q_j| - d_{ij})^2$$

This objective may be minimised by gradient descent, using:

$$\begin{aligned}\nabla_q(f_1) &= \sum_j (|q_i - q_j| - d_{ij})\mathrm{sgn}(q_i - q_j) - \\ &\quad \sum_j (|q_j - q_i| - d_{ji})\mathrm{sgn}(q_j - q_i) \\ &= 2I(q_i - \bar{q}) - 2\sum_j \mathrm{sgn}(q_i - q_j)d_{ij} \quad \text{(D symmetric)} \\ &= 2I(q_i - \bar{q}) - 2(\sum_{j|q_i > q_j} d_{ij} + \sum_{j|q_i < q_j} d_{ij})\end{aligned}$$

where $\bar{q}$ is the mean of $\mathbf{q}$. We conduct an experiment in which we form a similarity matrix $\mathrm{S} = \mathrm{X}\mathrm{X}^T$ for a random vector X with $I = 100$. We derive the dissimilarity matrix D and minimise $f_1(\mathbf{q})$. The resulting $\mathbf{q}$ is used to sort the items and a set of $N = 10$ items is selected in order, starting

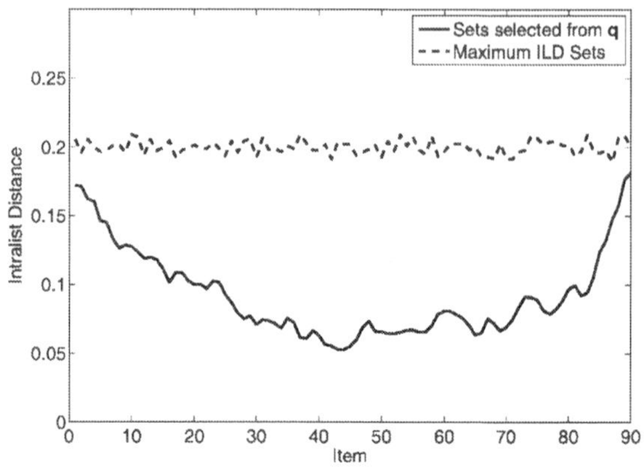

Figure 1: The ILD of a list of $N = 10$ items, consisting of items $\{\pi_i, \ldots, \pi_{i+N-1}\}$, plotted against the item π_i, where ILD $= \frac{2}{N(N-1)} \sum_{i=1}^{N} \sum_{j=i+1}^{N} d_{\pi_i \pi_j}$.

from each item in turn. The intra-list distance (ILD) [10, 8] of the resulting sets is plotted in Figure 1 and compared against sets selected by starting with the same item but greedily maximising the ILD. We note that choosing items from either end of the ordering produced by $\mathbf{q}$ results in sets with high ILD.

3.1 Diversifying Relevance

Of course, if diversity were the only criterion of interest, then we could simply choose sets that maximise the ILD. However, we also want to maximise the relevance of the resulting set. Given ranking vector $\mathbf{r}$, chosen on the basis of relevance, we can ask if we can find a new ranking vector $\mathbf{q}$ which respects the given ranking in $\mathbf{r}$ but otherwise ranks items according to their diversity. To do so, consider the objective

$$f_2(\mathbf{q}) = \sum_i \sum_j ((q_i - q_j) - d_{ij}(r_i - r_j))^2 .$$

Again, computing the gradient, we obtain (assuming symmetric D)

$$\begin{aligned}\nabla_q(f_2) &= 4\sum_j (q_i - q_j) - 2\sum_j (d_{ji} + d_{ij})(r_i - r_j) \quad (2) \\ &= 4I(q_i - \bar{q}) - 4\sum_j (r_i - r_j)d_{ij}\end{aligned}$$

Setting the gradient to zero, we obtain

$$(q_i - \bar{q}) = \frac{1}{I}\sum_j (r_i - r_j)d_{ij} = r_i \bar{d}_i - \frac{1}{I}\sum_j d_{ij} r_j \quad (3)$$

Using the same dissimilarity matrix as the previous experiment with $I = 100$, we now construct a random relevance vector r with each component assigned a number between 1 and 5, with uniform probability. In Figure 2 we show the ILD and the average relevance of sets of $N = 10$ items chosen in order from the ranking derived from $\mathbf{q}$ as computed by (3). We see that, while the ordering of $\mathbf{q}$ respects the order of $\mathbf{r}$ (the average relevance is monotonically decreasing), it also results in sets of high diversity as measured by the ILD.

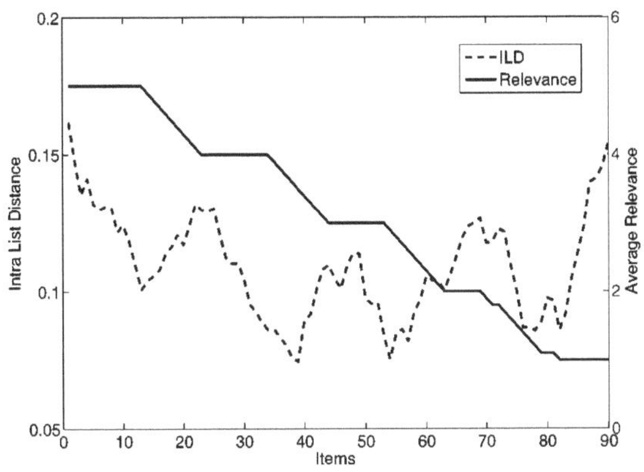

Figure 2: The vector q keeps the same rank order as r when the ratings differ but sets chosen in the rank order of q also have high ILD.

```
Inputs:Learning Rate:  η Num.of features:  F
1. forall (u,i) ∈ T do
2.     draw an item j not rated by u, with
         probability proportional to popularity
3.     r̂_ui ← p_u^T q_i
4.     r̂_uj ← p_u^T q_j
5.     e ← s_j[(r̂_ui − r̂_uj) − d_ij(r_ui − r_uj)]
6.     c = p_u
7.     p_u = p_u − η e (q_i − q_j)
8.     q_i = q_i − η e c
9.     q_j = q_j + η e c
10.end
```

Figure 3: The RankSGD algorithm used to minimize the ranking with diversity objective.

3.2 Optimising for Relevance and Diversity

In the previous section, we assumed that the relevance vector was pre-computed and then modified it to take account of diversity. Now we ask if it is possible to optimise for relevance and diversity simultaneously. To do so, we propose the following modification to the ranking objective function (1), to obtain a *ranking with diversity* objective for implicit feedback systems:

$$f_{RD}(\Theta) = \sum_{u \in \mathcal{U}} \sum_{i \in \mathcal{I}} c_{ui} \sum_{j \in \mathcal{I}} s_j \left[(\hat{r}_{ui} - \hat{r}_{uj}) - d_{ij}(r_{ui} - r_{uj}) \right]^2$$

The RankALS or RankSGD algorithms of [6] and [3] respectively, can be used to minimise this objective to obtain rating estimates $\hat{r}_{ui} = \mathbf{p}_u^T \mathbf{q}$, that are used to rank items to be recommended to each user u. In our experiments, we have employed the RankSGD algorithm with pseudocode shown in Figure 3.

4. EVALUATION

4.1 Datasets

We carry out preliminary evaluation of the ranking with diversity objective on the Netflix dataset. Although this is not an implicit rating dataset, it has previously been used for evaluation of RankALS and RankSGD in [6], so it is possible to compare the results we obtain with these previous results. The Netflix training set consists of 100,480,507 ratings ranging from 1 to 5 from 480,189 users on 17,770 items. Following [6], we defined the implicit rating matrix by assigning 1 to user-items pairs with rating values of 5 and 0 to all other user-item pairs. We trained using the Netflix training set with the probe set removed (containing 22,783,659 implicit ratings) and we tested on the probe set (containing 384,573 implicit ratings).

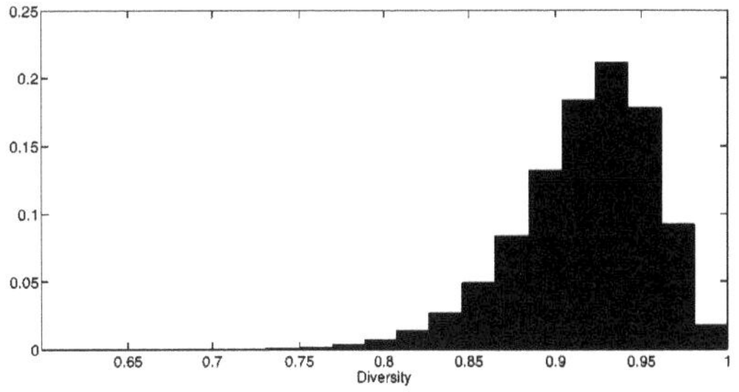

Figure 4: The Distribution of ILD values for $N = 10$ randomly selected items from Netflix

4.2 Performance Measures

To evaluate the performance of the ranking in terms of relevance, we use the `errorrate` metric as proposed in Track 2 of the 2011 KDD cup [1]. To apply this metric, for each user u, the test set consists of two sets of items $\mathcal{I}_u^+$ and $\mathcal{I}_u^-$ containing items for which u has given positive and negative feedback. $\mathcal{I}_u^-$ is created by drawing $|\mathcal{I}_u^+|$ items randomly with probability proportional to $|\mathcal{U}_i|$. The items in $\mathcal{I}_u^+ \cup \mathcal{I}_u^-$ are ranked using the predicted rating and the errorrate is the proportion of the top $|\mathcal{I}_u^+|$ ratings that are not from $\mathcal{I}_u^+$. A lower errorrate implies better performance. To evaluate the diversity of the recommended sets, we use the ILD of the top N items, obtained by ranking all $\mathcal{I} - \mathcal{I}_u^+$ items using the predicted ratings. We evaluate using $N = 10$.

4.3 Pairwise Item Distances

In the presented evaluation, we use a distance matrix D based on item profile distance. In particular, we obtain the similarity matrix S as the normalised dot product of item profiles:

$$\mathrm{S} = (\mathrm{RE}^{-\frac{1}{2}})^T(\mathrm{RE}^{-\frac{1}{2}})$$

where E is a diagonal matrix with diagonal elements $e_i = \sum_u r_{u,i}^2$. Because of the high sparsity of the Netflix dataset, this leads to generally low similarity values (and consequently very high pairwise distances). To obtain a greater spread of diversity values, the similarity values are filtered through the sigmoidal function $\tanh(\alpha s)$, where we take $\alpha = 20$. The resulting distribution of ILD values of sets of $N = 10$ items selected uniformly at random from the 17,770 items in Netflix is shown in Figure 4.

4.4 Results

In [6] it is stated that an item importance weighting proportional to the item popularity is appropriate when the errorrate measure is being optimised. Hence, we take $s_j =$

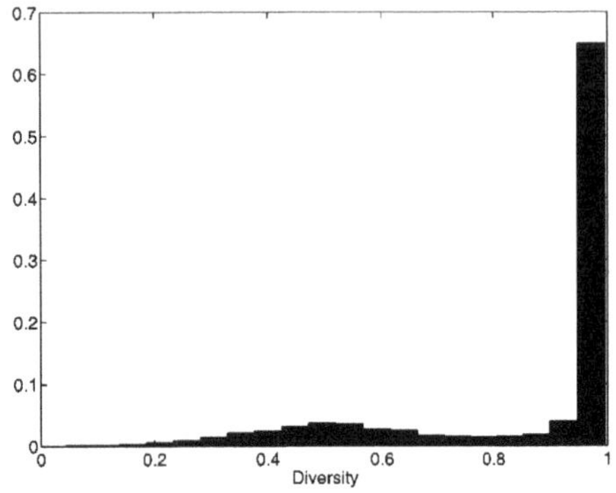

Figure 5: The Distribution of ILD values for $N = 10$ items selected by ranking with diversity $f_{RD}(\Theta)$

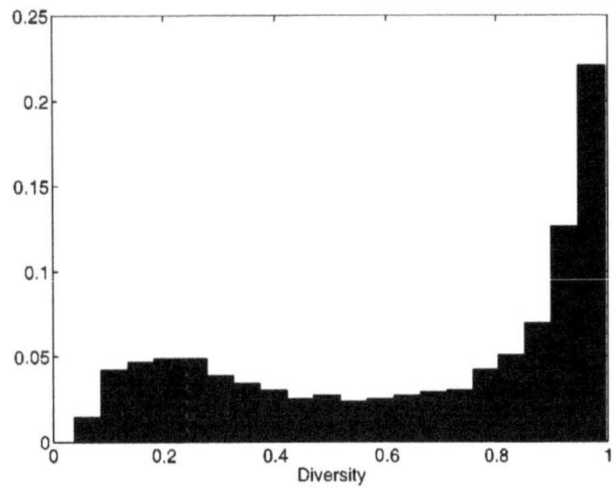

Figure 6: The Distribution of ILD values for $N = 10$ randomly selected by ranking with $f_R(\Theta)$

$|\mathcal{U}_j|/\max|\mathcal{U}_j|$. We compare the RandSGD algorithm run to convergence with $\eta = 0.008$ to minimise the ranking objective $f_R(\Theta)$ with the same algorithm used to minimise the ranking with diversity objective $f_{RD}(\Theta)$. The results are summarised in Table 1. The distribution of ILD values obtained from the ranking with diversity objective is shown in Figure 5 and the distribution obtained from optimising $f_R(\Theta)$ is shown in Figure 6. It is clear that ranking with diversity obtains much more diverse recommendation sets at some cost to performance in terms of relevance. As the raw ILD values are dependent on the distance matrix, it is informative to look at the results in terms of percentiles of the distributions. For instance, the 80th percentile of the distribution of ILD values of randomly selected sets, corresponds to the 79th percentile of the ILD values obtained when only relevance is considered. However, it is only the 36th percentile of the distribution of ILD values obtained by ranking with diversity. Ranking with diversity is highly biased towards highly diverse recommendations.

Table 1: Performance on Netflix Dataset

Obj	Errorrate	Mean ILD
$f_R(\Theta)$	0.25	0.64
$f_{RD}(\Theta)$	0.29	0.84

5. CONCLUSION

Preliminary results with the ranking with diversity objective are encouraging and further evaluations on other datasets will follow. Other formulations for incorporating diversity within ranking objectives will be considered in future work.

6. ACKNOWLEDGEMENTS

This publication has emanated from research conducted with the financial support of Science Foundation Ireland (SFI) under Grant Number SFI/12/RC/2289

7. REFERENCES

[1] G. Dror, N. Koenigstein, Y. Koren, and M. Weimer. The yahoo! music dataset and kdd-cup '11. *Journal of Machine Learning Research - Proceedings Track*, 18:8–18, 2012.

[2] Y. Hu, Y. Koren, and C. Volinsky. Collaborative filtering for implicit feedback datasets. In *Proceedings of the 2008 Eighth IEEE International Conference on Data Mining*, ICDM '08, pages 263–272, Washington, DC, USA, 2008. IEEE Computer Society.

[3] M. Jahrer and A. Töscher. Collaborative filtering ensemble for ranking. *Journal of Machine Learning Research - Proceedings Track*, 18:153–167, 2012.

[4] I. Pilászy, D. Zibriczky, and D. Tikk. Fast als-based matrix factorization for explicit and implicit feedback datasets. In *Proceedings of the fourth ACM conference on Recommender systems*, RecSys '10, pages 71–78, New York, NY, USA, 2010. ACM.

[5] S. Rendle, C. Freudenthaler, Z. Gantner, and L. Schmidt-Thieme. Bpr: Bayesian personalized ranking from implicit feedback. In *Proceedings of the Twenty-Fifth Conference on Uncertainty in Artificial Intelligence*, UAI '09, pages 452–461, Arlington, Virginia, United States, 2009. AUAI Press.

[6] G. Takács and D. Tikk. Alternating least squares for personalized ranking. In *Proceedings of the sixth ACM conference on Recommender systems*, RecSys '12, pages 83–90, New York, NY, USA, 2012. ACM.

[7] S. Vargas and P. Castells. Rank and relevance in novelty and diversity metrics for recommender systems. In *Proceedings of the fifth ACM conference on Recommender systems*, RecSys '11, pages 109–116, New York, NY, USA, 2011. ACM.

[8] M. Zhang and N. Hurley. Avoiding monotony: Improving the diversity of recommendation lists. In *Proceedings of 2nd ACM International Conference on Recommender Systems*, 2008.

[9] M. Zhang and N. Hurley. Niche product retrieval in top-n recommendation. In *2010 IEEE/WIC/ACM International Conference on Web Intelligence, WI 2010, Toronto, Canada, August 31 - September 3, 2010, Main Conference Proceedings*, pages 74–81. IEEE, 2010.

[10] C. Ziegler, S. M. McNee, J. A. Konstan, and G. Lausen. Improving recommendation lists through topic diversification. In *Proceedings of the 14th International Conference on World Wide Web*, pages 22–32, 2005.

Prior Ratings: A New Information Source for Recommender Systems in E-Commerce

Guibing Guo
Nanyang Technological University, Singapore
gguo1@e.ntu.edu.sg

Jie Zhang
Nanyang Technological University, Singapore
zhangj@ntu.edu.sg

Daniel Thalmann
Nanyang Technological University, Singapore
danielthalmann@ntu.edu.sg

Neil Yorke-Smith
American University of Beirut, and University of Cambridge
nysmith@aub.edu.lb

ABSTRACT

Lack of motivation to provide ratings and eligibility to rate generally only after purchase restrain the effectiveness of recommender systems and contribute to the well-known data sparsity and cold start problems. This paper proposes a new information source for recommender systems, called *prior ratings*. Prior ratings are based on users' experiences of virtual products in a mediated environment, and they can be submitted prior to purchase. A conceptual model of prior ratings is proposed, integrating the environmental factor *presence* whose effects on product evaluation have not been studied previously. A user study conducted in website and virtual store modalities demonstrates the validity of the conceptual model, in that users are more willing and confident to provide prior ratings in virtual environments.

Categories and Subject Descriptors

H.5.2 [**Information Interfaces and Presentation**]: User Interfaces—*Evaluation/methodology*

Keywords

Recommender systems, Prior ratings, Data sparsity, Cold start, User study, Virtual product.

1. INTRODUCTION

User ratings are crucial for recommender systems in e-commerce in order to provide quality personalized product recommendations. However, users can lack motivation to provide ratings, and ratings can generally be given only after purchase (how can I share my experience of an item I have not tried?). Without sufficient rating information for preference modelling, the effectiveness of recommender systems is hindered—as seen in well-known problems such as *data sparsity* and *cold start* [3]. Although many approaches have been proposed to address these problems [3, 4], only few researchers have attempted to elicit more user ratings from the perspective of user interfaces, so as to inherently mitigate the severity of these problems.

Contemporary websites, e.g., brides.com and Ray-ban.com are implementing novel interfaces and interactions through which users can virtually try on different wedding dresses and glasses, to better elicit user preferences. However, the available media and interactions are limited in comparison with those of virtual reality (VR), e.g., SecondLife.com which can provide users with immersive virtual product experiences. Users can experience media more richly and can interact in real time with *virtual products*—the 'second existence' of real products in a mediated environment.

While the emergence of 3D VR environments offers more adequate information which can be used to model user preference, research on recommender systems in VR is still in its infancy. Shah et al. [10] recommend to users locations of interest by analyzing users' login data to help them navigate in VR. Hu and Hang [5] design a system to recommend virtual furniture according to users' interest and requirements. Although a controlled prototype was implemented, the features of VR are not exploited to elicit user ratings.

This paper proposes a new information source, called *prior ratings*, built upon virtual product experiences. A conceptual model of prior ratings is proposed to provide a principled foundation, integrating the environmental factor *presence* whose effects on product evaluation have not been studied previously. For evaluation, we conduct user studies in two different modalities. The results demonstrate the validity of the conceptual model under our experimental settings. To our knowledge, this is the first work that defines and investigates the concept of prior ratings.

2. PRIOR RATINGS

We define the term *prior ratings* as users' assessment of products in the light of their *virtual product experiences*, referring to the psychological and emotional states that users undergo while interacting with virtual products in a medi-

RecSys'13, October 12–16, 2013, Hong Kong, China.

ACM 978-1-4503-2409-0/13/10 ...$15.00.
http://dx.doi.org/10.1145/2507157.2507200.

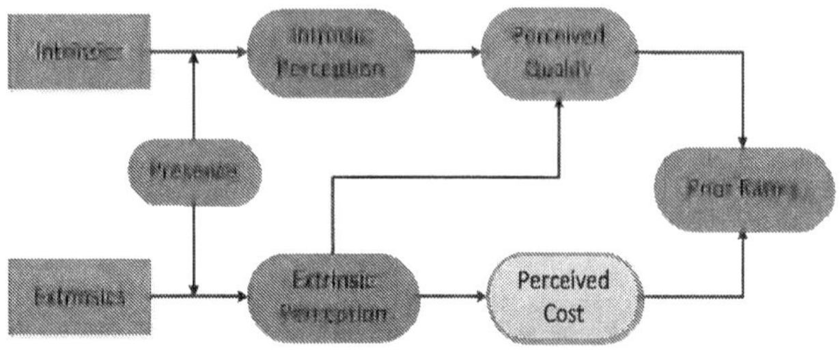

Figure 1: The conceptual model of prior ratings

ated environment [8]. Hence, prior ratings are reported by users based on their interactions with virtual products in a mediated environment, and they can be issued prior to purchase or after purchase (if any). We refer to the 'standard' type of ratings derived from 'posterior' product experiences as *posterior ratings*. By 'posterior', we mean experiences of a tangible product obtained via direct trials or use of the product in a physical environment. Since tangible products can be fully experienced usually only after purchase, posterior ratings are primarily post-purchase ratings. Prior ratings and posterior ratings are distinct and complementary in that they reflect different forms of user experiences.

It is reported that VR real-time interactions enable users to possess a strong sense of being in a mediated environment and gain a lifelike shopping experience [8]. Hence, we draw a hypothesis as follows.

HYPOTHESIS 1. *Users are more willing to provide prior ratings to the items (e.g., products) that they have interacted with in VR than in WS.*

Jiang and Benbasat [7] contend that virtual products in VR help improve the perceived *diagnosticity* of products—the extent to which users believe a particular shopping experience is helpful to understand the quality and performance of a product. Therefore, users may feel more capable of forming direct, intuitive and concrete opinions about products in VR than in WS.

HYPOTHESIS 2. *(a) Users have more confidence in providing prior ratings in VR than in WS; (b) the average value of prior ratings in VR is closer to that of posterior ratings than that of prior ratings in WS.*

Conceptual Model. A conceptual model of prior ratings is illustrated in Figure 1. Such a model allows a principled basis for the elicitation and analysis of prior ratings. For a specific product, a number of intrinsic and extrinsic *attributes* are associated. In different environments, the perceptions of these attributes can differ according to the types of media and interactions that deliver information about them. The intrinsic and extrinsic *perceptions* indicate the quality of products as perceived directly and indirectly, respectively. In contrast, the *perceived cost* (e.g., time, price) refers to the cost that users have to bear in order to obtain the products. A prior rating is an overall evaluation of preference of products in terms of both perceived quality and cost.

Presence is defined as subjects' sense of "being there", the extent to which they experience the virtual environments as real or present and temporarily ignore where they are physically present [11]. In this paper, presence is captured as the extent to which being in a mediated environment feels like being in a real environment[1], given the richness in media and interactions. Since information concerning product attributes is conveyed by media channels and user interactions, presence can be an important environmental factor that will influence the perceptions of product attributes.

HYPOTHESIS 3. *Presence has positive influence on the perceptions of both intrinsic and extrinsic attributes.*

Intrinsic attributes (e.g., workmanship, size) have a direct impact on perceived quality during the goal-directed process of pre-purchase product evaluation [2]. In this paper, we classify intrinsic attributes into three types, namely *appearance*, *material*, and *functionality*. Appearance refers to the attributes related to the superficial representation of products, such as patterns, form, size, etc. Material refers to the attributes associated with what products are made of, such as fabric properties, weight, etc. Functionality refers to the attributes indicating the utility of products or the actions that products can perform or that can be performed on products. For example, an electronic watch contains the functionality of stopwatch and it may 'fit' someone well.

Extrinsic attributes (e.g., price) have no direct indications of perceived quality. Rather, they are often used as cues to infer the quality of products when the information of intrinsic attributes is incomplete [1]. In this case, price is often used by users to infer the quality of products [1]. Brand name serves as a 'shorthand' for perceived quality by providing users with a bundle of product information [6]. In contrast, store name also has a positive but small impact on perceived quality [9]. Other extrinsic attributes (e.g., warranty) may also have effects on perceived quality.

HYPOTHESIS 4. *Users depend more on extrinsic attributes than intrinsic attributes to evaluate the product quality in WS, whereas users depend more on intrinsic attributes than extrinsic attributes to evaluate the product quality in VR.*

Besides quality, extrinsic attributes also contribute to *perceived cost*, a combination of monetary (mainly price) and non-monetary (e.g., time, shipping) attributes.

Prior Ratings. In a pre-purchase phase, users go through a process (perhaps subconscious) of evaluating the benefits that they can get and the cost that they have to incur. The outcome of this process helps determine whether users will like the product in question. Other than perceived quality, we posit that prior ratings could also be positively enhanced if the perceived cost is acceptable. Intuitively, for a specific product interested in by a user in terms of quality, if the price of the product turns out to be acceptable, it is likely that the user will like the product as a whole.

HYPOTHESIS 5. *Perceived quality has significantly positive influence on prior ratings, and perceived cost will also positively influence prior ratings, if the price is acceptable.*

3. USER STUDY

Two kinds of mediated environments are developed: traditional 2D websites (WS) and 3D VR environments. They differ in richness of both media and of interactions through which product information can be delivered. Both user interfaces 'sell' our t-shirts whose source was the real-life commerce website 80stees.com. These 50 t-shirts have average

[1]See question 2 for the tested environments in Figure 2.

To what extent do you agree or disagree with the following statements?

For each t-shirt:

1. The t-shirt has a good looking in terms of color, patterns, style, etc.
2. The t-shirt is made of good material.
3. The t-shirt fits you well.
4. The category of this t-shirt is of your favor.
5. The price of this t-shirt is acceptable, including price and shipping fees.
6. The website (virtual store) is well-designed.
7. In total, the quality of this t-shirt is good.
8. You need to spend a lot to obtain this t-shirt in price, time, effort, etc.
9. In total, this t-shirt is worthy purchasing.
10. Overall, you like this t-shirt.

For each environment:

1. You are confident about your ratings. When you gave ratings, you feel confident and no hesitations to make a judgement.
2. It feels the same that inspecting the t-shirt in the environment is just as if you were in a real store and had a real t-shirt in hand.
3. You are comfortable to give ratings in the tested environment.
4. You are (not) confident in your ratings because (state your reasons)

For willingness (optional):

1. Are you willing to rate the t-shirt of your interest or interacted with?
2. If yes, state your reason and indicate how confident in your ratings?
3. If no, state your reason. In what conditions, you will rate the t-shirts?

Figure 2: Questions in the user study

posterior ratings (on 80stees.com) in the range [3.2, 4.9] (out of 5). The virtual store was built using OpenSimulator.org. T-shirts were displayed and arranged without a predefined order on the walls of virtual store. Users can interact with them by viewing, rotating, zooming, and even virtually trying on and customizing the t-shirts (on their avatar). They can also adjust the avatar's shape as desired. In contrast, no interactions were available in WS: users can only imagine what the t-shirt would be like from text descriptions and static images. Four attributes, namely appearance, material, fit and price are identified as the major concerns of users via a pilot study. Together with attributes store and category, the six attributes are selected for the experiments.

The user study consisted of one session, structured as follows. All subjects started with a tutorial video so as to get familiar with functionalities of user interfaces. Once subjects were comfortable, they proceeded. Each subject experienced and evaluated eight different t-shirts in each environment by giving ratings to the questions about product attributes. Rating values were integers from 1 ("strongly disagree") to 5 ("strongly agree"). Subjects could also add textual comments for each t-shirt. To eliminate the influence of ordering, subjects were randomly determined into two groups. Specifically, of 30 volunteers recruited on a university campus, 16 subjects executed the user study first in WS and then VR, and 14 proceeded inversely. In addition to t-shirts, the subjects were also asked to rate the environment regarding the confidence (and state their reasons) and comfort in giving ratings, and the feelings of sense of presence. Finally, subjects could opt to state whether and in which environment they are willing and prefer to provide prior ratings. The questions are shown in Figure 2.

For Hypothesis 1, of 19 subjects who answered our questions regarding the willingness to rate t-shirts, 18 gave positive responses. More specifically, most subjects preferred to rate products in VR (14) rather than in WS (2). Two other subjects did not explicitly state their preference. Most subjects expressed that the reasons were "it can provide more detail information" and "this environment (VR) has really high engagement. I'd like to share my feeling". Only one subject did not want to provide prior ratings ("time consuming") but did indicate the willingness if "benefits or lucky draw" were offered. Thus, Hypothesis 1 is supported.

Table 1: The evaluations of the environmental factors

	Mean.ws	Mean.vr	Diff	p-value
confidence	3.296	3.778	0.482	**3.300e-3**
comfort	3.444	3.963	0.519	**6.653e-3**
presence	2.185	3.222	1.037	**1.420e-4**

Table 2: The distributions of collected ratings

Scales	R_p	$R.ws$	$R.vr$
1	3.82%	11.63%	3.67%
2	4.08%	18.60%	10.55%
3	7.15%	35.81%	27.52%
4	27.77%	25.12%	42.66%
5	57.18%	8.84%	15.60%
1, 2, 3	15.05%	66.04%	41.74%
4, 5	84.95%	33.96%	58.26%
Total	1469	215	218

For Hypothesis 2(a), we conducted a number of paired two sample t-tests to investigate the mean differences of environmental factors, namely confidence, comfort and presence. Table 1 reports the results. Since all $p < 0.01$, we find that users in VR have greater confidence and feel more comfortable in their prior ratings than in WS. This may be partially explained by the fact that users have stronger sense of presence in VR than in WS. Besides, subjects also commented that the main reasons are due to the fact that they can try t-shirts on their 'own' body rather than have to image the real wearing effect in WS. They also feel stronger sense of presence in VR as if being in a real store. Thus, Hypothesis 2(a) is supported.

For Hypothesis 2(b), the collected data consists of 215 prior ratings in WS ($R.ws$) and 218 records in VR ($R.vr$) (see Table 2). The correlation between posterior ratings (R_p) and $R.ws$, denoted as $corr(R_p, R.ws)$ is -0.42 whereas $corr(R_p, R.vr) = 0.23$, signifying that the distribution of posterior ratings is distinct from prior ratings in WS, but marginally yet positively similar to prior ratings in VR. To have a better viewpoint, we classify rating values (4, 5) larger than median scale (3) as positive, and the remainder (1, 2, 3) as negative. Then we can obtain clearer correlations: $corr(R_p, R.ws) = -1$ and $corr(R_p, R.vr) = 1$. In addition, the average posterior rating is 4.13 whereas the values for $R.ws$ and $R.vr$ are 2.94 and 3.56, respectively. Thus, Hypothesis 2(b) is supported.

For Hypothesis 3, we conducted multiple linear regressions, each of which used 'presence' as independent variable and one of intrinsic or extrinsic attributes in WS and VR as dependent variable. The results are illustrated in Table 3. We see that presence in WS is most influential ($p < 0.01$) on material and store; in VR it is influential ($p < 0.001$) on all attributes except category. Hence, presence in WS has smaller effects on the perceptions of product attributes than that in VR. This can be attributed to the lower level of presence in WS as shown in Table 1. However, for attributes whose information can be adequately communicated by basic media (i.e., text descriptions, static images), such as category, presence may be of limited influence. One possible explanation for the different effects of price in two environments is that price in WS may be ignored as a cue to infer user preference. Thus, Hypothesis 3 is partially supported.

For Hypothesis 4, we conducted a multi-variable linear regression: intrinsic and extrinsic attributes as independent variables and 'perceived quality' as dependent variable. The

Table 3: The influences of presence on attributes

Env.	Attributes	Estimate	T Value	Pr(> $\|t\|$)
WS	appearance	0.142	2.131	0.0342
	material	0.270	3.822	**1.740e-4**
	fit	0.187	2.452	0.0150
	category	0.130	1.880	0.0614
	price	0.0921	1.294	0.197
	store	0.269	3.216	**1.500e-3**
VR	**appearance**	0.0860	1.259	**<2e-16**
	material	0.244	3.388	**8.370e-4**
	fit	0.216	3.349	**9.580e-4**
	category	0.0698	1.092	0.276
	price	0.209	3.295	**1.150e-3**
	store	0.468	7.623	**7.740e-13**

Table 4: The evaluations of perceived quality

Env.	Attributes	Estimate	T Value	Pr(> $\|t\|$)
WS	appearance	-0.06649	-1.152	0.250485
	material	0.28331	5.729	**3.52e-08**
	fit	0.12482	2.130	0.034338
	category	0.31082	5.115	**7.11e-07**
	price	0.04622	0.975	0.330593
	store	0.21357	3.748	**0.000231**
VR	**appearance**	0.1958	3.217	**0.00150**
	material	0.1413	2.941	**0.00363**
	fit	0.2467	4.748	**3.79e-06**
	category	0.1081	2.044	0.04222
	price	0.1999	4.795	**3.07e-06**
	store	-0.0059	-0.126	0.89976

results, presented in Table 4, show that three attributes in WS are the major concerns for product quality, namely material, category and store. In addition, attribute 'fit' is also considered important but has smaller influence. Note that the regression coefficients of category and store are greater than material and fit, which means that perceived quality relies more on extrinsic attributes than on intrinsic attributes. In contrast, the most important attributes in VR are appearance, material, fit and price, and most comments are focused on these four attributes. Hence, subjects relied more on intrinsic attributes than extrinsic attributes to evaluate the quality of t-shirts in VR. Of the four major attributes identified from pilot study, we find that only one of them (material) is recognized in WS whereas all four attributes are correctly recognized in VR. One possible explanation is that when users have less or no direct experiences with products, they may tend to use extrinsic attributes (i.e., category, store, price) as cues to infer the product quality. On the other hand, if users have effective and direct interactions with products and thereby gain sufficient direct product experiences, they may rely more on intrinsic attributes to evaluate products. Thus, Hypothesis 4 is supported.

For Hypothesis 5, we investigated the correlations among prior ratings, perceived quality and cost by applying a linear regression analysis. The results show that the coefficient of perceived quality is positive and large (> 0.6), and that it has a significant influence ($p < 0.001$) on prior ratings. In addition, the cost is demonstrated as relatively small yet positively important in VR ($0.14, p < 0.05$) rather than in WS ($0.06, p > 0.1$). The price of collected t-shirts ranges from US$3.99 to $32.00, indicating that the price is acceptable in general. As a consequence, users are more likely to like products as a whole given good quality estimated. However, as users may not correctly judge the quality of products in WS, the price may fail to be or less considered when assessing their preferences. Thus, Hypothesis 5 is supported.

4. DISCUSSION AND CONCLUSION

There are several potential limitations in our current experiments. First, certain attribute information (e.g., warranty, shipping) was not available for our user study. Although these are less relevant for the product class studied, they may be more important for other kinds of products. Second, due to lack of devices, our prototype implementation uses only visual information in VR: users cannot touch the t-shirts and feel the material. Tactile feedback may be important for user evaluation of preferences. Nevertheless, as aforementioned, this limitation may not greatly influence the general conclusion since we exploited abstract attributes rather than some specific attributes. Third, most subjects were computer or electrical engineering students on a university campus, and the sample size was modest. A larger and more heterogeneous sample may allow for more confident generalization of our research findings. Since higher presence may result in more confident prior ratings, it follows that the design of virtual stores should emphasize the sense of presence by increasing the media richness or the effectiveness of user interactions. The current research focused on the validation of conceptual model of prior ratings. For future work, we intend to investigate the benefits of prior ratings in improving recommendation performance.

Acknowledgement

We thank the support of the Institute for Media Innovation at Nanyang Technological University, Singapore.

5. REFERENCES

[1] W. Dodds, K. Monroe, and D. Grewal. Effects of price, brand, and store information on buyers' product evaluations. *J. of Marketing Research*, 28(3):307–319, 1991.

[2] S. Gardial, D. Clemons, R. Woodruff, D. Schumann, and M. Burns. Comparing consumers' recall of prepurchase and postpurchase product evaluation experiences. *Journal of Consumer Research*, 20(4):548–560, 1994.

[3] G. Guo, J. Zhang, and D. Thalmann. A simple but effective method to incorporate trusted neighbors in recommender systems. In *Proc. UMAP'12*, pages 114–125, 2012.

[4] G. Guo, J. Zhang, and N. Yorke-Smith. A novel bayesian similarity measure for recommender systems. In *Proc. IJCAI'13*, 2013.

[5] X. Hu and K. Wang. Personalized recommendation for virtual reality. In *Proc. ICMT'10*, pages 1–5, 2010.

[6] J. Jacoby, G. Szybillo, and J. Busato-Schach. Information acquisition behavior in brand choice situations. *Journal of Consumer Research*, 3(4):209–216, 1977.

[7] Z. Jiang and I. Benbasat. Virtual product experience: Effects of visual and functional control of products on perceived diagnosticity and flow in electronic shopping. *Journal of Management Information Systems*, 21(3):111–147, 2004.

[8] H. Li, T. Daugherty, and F. Biocca. The role of virtual experience in consumer learning. *Journal of Consumer Psychology*, 13(4):395–407, 2003.

[9] A. Rao and K. Monroe. The effect of price, brand name, and store name on buyers' perceptions of product quality. *J. of Marketing Research*, 26(3):351–357, 1989.

[10] F. Shah, P. Bell, and G. Sukthankar. A destination recommendation system for virtual worlds. In *Proc. FLAIRS'10*, pages 475–476, 2010.

[11] M. Slater, B. Spanlang, and D. Corominas. Simulating virtual environments within virtual environments as the basis for a psychophysics of presence. *ACM Transactions on Graphics (TOG)*, 29(4):92, 2010.

Probabilistic Collaborative Filtering with Negative Cross Entropy

Alejandro Bellogín[a,c], Javier Parapar[b], Pablo Castells[c]
[a]Information Access, Centrum Wiskunde & Informatica
[b]Information Retrieval Lab, Department of Computer Science, University of A Coruña
[c]Information Retrieval Group, Department of Computer Science, Universidad Autónoma de Madrid
alejandro.bellogin@cwi.nl, javierparapar@udc.es, pablo.castells@uam.es

ABSTRACT

Relevance-Based Language Models are an effective IR approach which explicitly introduces the concept of relevance in the statistical Language Modelling framework of Information Retrieval. These models have shown to achieve state-of-the-art retrieval performance in the pseudo relevance feedback task. In this paper we propose a novel adaptation of this language modeling approach to rating-based Collaborative Filtering. In a memory-based approach, we apply the model to the formation of user neighbourhoods, and the generation of recommendations based on such neighbourhoods. We report experimental results where our method outperforms other standard memory-based algorithms in terms of ranking precision.

Categories and Subject Descriptors: H.3.3 [Information Search and Retrieval]: Information Search and Filtering

General Terms: Algorithms, Experimentation, Performance

Keywords: Recommender systems, Collaborative Filtering, Relevance Models

1. INTRODUCTION AND MOTIVATION

Personalised recommendation is a fertile research area with roots in the eighties, which started to attract wider attention in the mid-nineties when the first works on Collaborative Filtering came to light [6]. Three classical approaches to recommendation are distinguished: *content-based recommendation* (CB), based on the user's history and data (descriptions, content, features) of the items; *collaborative filtering* (CF), based on the history of similar users and items; and *hybrid approaches*, based on combining CB and CF recommendation. One of the earliest and most popular CF methods is the so-called k nearest-neighbours (kNN) approach, which is still being used today in many commercial systems.

A common formulation of a user-based kNN method is [6]:

$$\hat{r}(u,i) = C \sum_{v \in N_k(u)} \mathrm{sim}(u,v) r(v,i) \qquad (1)$$

where the known preference of a user u for a particular item i is given by a numeric rating $r(u,i)$, and $\hat{r}(u,i)$ denotes the system's estimate of this value for an item for which the degree of user interest is unknown to the system. To provide that estimation, the method takes into account the ratings $r(v,i)$ provided by the k users v who are most *similar* to u, commonly referred to as neighbours and denoted here as $N_k(u)$. The function $\mathrm{sim}(u,v)$ measures the similarity between two users u and v, and the constant C is a normalisation factor. Thus, the predicted rating of user u for item i is computed as a weighted average of u's neighbours' ratings (deviations with respect to the user and neighbour average can also be considered [6]), where the weights are the similarities between u and her neighbours v.

Relevance-Based Language Models [3] (or Relevance Models for short, RM), on the other hand, are among the best-performing ranking techniques in text retrieval. In this paper, we study how RM can be adapted to rating-based recommendation, and whether they may lead to enhancements in terms of ranking-based metrics such as precision and nDCG. We do so by establishing a mapping between the variables involved in RM and the ones in user-based CF. The mapping is non-trivial as, to begin with, RM is formulated in text IR on a triadic space (query, documents, words), whereas the CF space is typically dyadic (users and items). Based on a proposed mapping, we bring the adaptation to computable terms, giving rise to a workable and effective recommendation framework. The resulting approach comprises two separable subcomponents: a neighbour selection approach and a ranking function, which can be used on their own or together.

In the remaining of this paper, we will answer the following research questions: (**RQ1**) Are the Relevance-Based Language Models useful to identify neighbours in recommendation? (**RQ2**) Is there any advantage in using a complete probabilistic representation of the problem? In other terms, does it make sense to replace the CF weighted average by the RM cross entropy as used in IR, and does this approach work well in practice?

After presenting our proposed method in detail in the next section, we address the research questions experimentally on MovieLens data, testing the effectiveness of our overall approach, and comparing the separate effect of the two subcomponents. As we shall see, the empirical results validate the approach, showing performance improvements over state of the art memory-based alternatives.

2. RELEVANCE MODELLING FOR RECOMMENDATION

Relevance-Based Language Models, as first proposed in [3], view the original user search query Q as a short sample of words obtained from an underlying relevance model R. If one aims to add more words from R to the query then it is reasonable to choose those words with the highest estimated probability given a sample of observed words generated by the relevance model for the query. In [3] two different estimations for RM were originally presented, namely RM1 and RM2 from which, in our present approach, we adopt the former. In RM1 it is assumed that the query words $q_i \in Q$ and the words w in the relevant documents are sampled identically and independently from a unigram distribution (*i.i.d. sampling*).

RecSys'13, October 12–16, 2013, Hong Kong, China.

ACM 978-1-4503-2409-0/13/10 ...$15.00.
http://dx.doi.org/10.1145/2507157.2507191.

RM for Retrieval	RM for Recommendation
query q	target user u
query words $q_1 \dots q_n$	items rated by user $I(u)$
pseudo relevance set PRS	positively rated items $PRS(u)$
candidate expansion terms	candidate user's neighbours

Figure 1: Correspondence between the elements involved in Relevance-Based Language Models for document retrieval and its adaptation to item recommendation

Denoting by R_Q the underlying relevance model from which the words in the query Q were sampled, the relevance language model (i.e. the distribution of words given R_Q) is computed as in Eq. 2:

$$p(w|R_Q) \propto \sum_{d \in C} p(d)p(w|d) \prod_{i=1}^{|Q|} p(q_i|d) \qquad (2)$$

where C is the set of all documents in the search space (the collection). For computational reasons, the top N documents from the initial result set are taken for the estimation, rather than the whole collection C. This set of documents is usually called pseudo relevance set (PRS). Finally, to build the final (expanded) query, the terms with the highest estimated probabilities of relevance with respect to the query are selected, and a second document ranking is produced using the negative cross entropy retrieval function.

2.1 Space Mapping

In order to adapt this framework to the recommendation task, we need to identify the random variables to play the part of queries, documents and words in the above formulation. Our proposed mapping equates, at the top level, users to queries and items to the documents to be retrieved (see Figure 1). Now, words are equated to users or to items, depending on the role they are playing: in assimilating a user u to a query Q, the constituent elements of the latter (the query terms $q_1 \dots q_n$) are mapped to the set of items rated by u – which we shall denote as $I(u)$. However, the words with which queries are expanded are mapped to other users, with similar tastes to the target user, as we shall see. Items as documents play an additional part: that of pseudo-relevant documents. As we just recalled, in RM instead of estimating the Relevance Model R_Q over the whole collection, only a certain top set of documents is commonly used for such task: the pseudo relevant set PRS. In our proposed approach this role is played by the items positively rated by the target user u, which we denote by $PRS(u)$.

Note this last aspect of our approach introduces an interesting difference with respect to RM in IR: while an initial ranking is needed in the IR formulation to select the pseudo relevant documents from, in our adaptation PRS is extracted from readily available data without needing to compute an initial recommendation. This means the resulting approach works as a standalone recommendation algorithm, rather than a query expansion technique.

Other mappings are possible besides the one we investigate here, e.g. words for expansion could be mapped to items instead of users. We leave this possibility as future work. Ratings could also be used as a first-class variable making up a triadic space, apparently easier to match to the IR framework. We think however ratings would be a bad – or at least unpredictable – analogue for words (let alone the query or documents), since ratings are rather a natural equivalent of relevance grades in IR. Log-based recommendation, on the other hand, has a more direct equivalence [8], which is however not applicable to rating data.

The proposed approach allows to decompose the task as follows: a) we compute a relevance model for each user in order to capture how relevant any other user would be as a potential neighbour; and then b) we replace the rating prediction by weighted average in CF with the well-established scoring function (negative cross entropy) used in IR to incorporate the information learnt from the RM. We describe these two parts of our approach in the next two sections.

2.2 Neighbour Selection

The equivalent estimation to RM1 for neighbour selection according to our proposed mapping goes as follows. Modelled after RM1, the probability of a neighbour v under the relevance model R_u for a given user u is estimated as:

$$p(v|R_u) = \sum_{i \in PRS(u)} p(i)p(v|i) \prod_{j \in I(u)} p(j|i) \qquad (3)$$

where $p(i)$ is the probability of the item i in the collection, $p(v|i)$ is the probability of the neighbour v given the item i, and $p(i|j)$ is the conditional probability of item i given another item j. As presented in Figure 1, $I(u)$ corresponds to the set of items rated by user u, and $PRS(u) \subset I(u)$ is the subset of items rated by u above some specific threshold, i.e. items with a favorable rating value indicating the user likes them.

Besides folding a triadic space into a dyadic one, in our formulation the probabilistic RM framework is turned upside down to some extent. The ground probabilistic model upon which RM are formulated in text IR reflects a process in which words are sampled according to a certain (indirectly observed) distribution. While the relevance model steers the generation of words in text IR, in our approach it drives the sampling of users, or to be more specific, user profiles (i.e. a history of item ratings). In this perspective, $p(v|R_u)$ can be read as the probability to observe the ratings entered by user v if her underlying tastes are defined by R_u.

2.3 Item Ranking

In document retrieval, once the terms with the highest estimated probability under the relevance model are selected for expansion, they are used to produce a second ranking by means of the negative cross entropy scoring function. In this paper we propose to use this very same method for ranking the item collection with respect to the preferences of the user u, that is, $\hat{r}(u,i) = H(p(\cdot|R_u); p(\cdot|i)) = \sum_{v \in C_U} p(v|R_u) \log p(v|i)$. With this formulation, we rank the items according to the distance between the item and user probability models, so that the closest – more similar and (hypothetically) more relevant – items are ranked higher. Now, following the kNN CF strategy, we propose to restrict the sum over users v to a subset $N_k(u) \subset C_U$ of k nearest neighbours with most similar tastes to user u. We propose the use of $p(v|R_u)$ as the similarity function, such that we select the neighbourhood for a given user u as the set of k users in the collection with the highest probability to share the user relevance model R_u. The resulting ranking function is:

$$\begin{aligned} \hat{r}(u,i) &= H(p(\cdot|R_u); p(\cdot|i)|N_k(u)) = \qquad (4) \\ &= \sum_{v \in N_k(u)} p(v|R_u) \log p(v|i) \end{aligned}$$

The result of this restriction is that we avoid the residual effect of a long tail of users with a low $p(v|R_u)$ (Eq. 3), whose contribution to the prediction of user tastes does not pay off the incurred computational cost. This conforms to the principle of neighbour selection in kNN CF, but also of keyword selection (a cutoff of most probable words given the relevance model) in query expansion by RM.

2.4 Parameter Estimation

Finally, some estimation details remain to be defined. We initially consider $p(i)$ and $p(u)$ as uniform priors, i.e. every neighbour $v \in N_k(u)$ has the same probability of being sampled, and same for every item in the collection. The conditional distribution $p(j|i)$ is computed by the maximum likelihood estimate $p_{ml}(j|i) = |U(j) \cap U(i)|/|U(i)|$, where $U(i)$ is the set of users who rated the item i. The probability of a user given an item is computed by Bayesian inversion $p(u|i) = p(i|u)p(u)/p(i)$, and the probability of an item given a user is estimated by maximum likelihood smoothed with the probability in the collection (background collection model), using the Jelinek-Mercer smoothing [10]:

$$p_\lambda(i|u) = (1 - \lambda)p_{ml}(i|u) + \lambda p(i|\mathcal{C}) \quad (5)$$

where $p_{ml}(i|u)$ and $p(i|\mathcal{C})$ are estimated as:

$$p_{ml}(i|u) = \frac{r(u,i)}{\sum_{j \in I(u)} r(u,j)}, \quad p(i|\mathcal{C}) = \frac{\sum_{u \in \mathcal{C}_U} r(u,i)}{\sum_{j \in \mathcal{C}_I, u \in \mathcal{C}_U} r(u,j)} \quad (6)$$

where $\mathcal{C}_U$ ($\mathcal{C}_I$) is the set of users (items) in the collection.

3. EMPIRICAL EVALUATION

3.1 Evaluation Methodology

We test the proposed approach on two publicly available datasets[1]. The first one is *MovieLens 100K*, which contains $100,000$ ratings on $1,682$ items by 943 users. We perform a 5-fold cross validation using the data splits contained in the public distribution, which retain 80% of the data for training, and the rest for testing. Using the terminology in [2], we report the results obtained following the *TestItems* evaluation approach described in [1]. In the TestItems methodology, a ranking is generated for each user by predicting a score for every item that has a rating in the test set. We can then compute any standard IR metric on the ranking, such as precision, nDCG or MRR. We report here the values for precision at 5 and 50, and nDCG at 5 and 10. We also report the *user space coverage* metric (cvg) as defined in [7], that is, the number of users for which the system is able to recommend at least one item.

Furthermore, for assessing the robustness of the methods across collections, we took the optimal parameter values for every method in terms of P@5 in the MovieLens 100K dataset, and tested the methods with those values on a second (and disjoint) public dataset, *MovieLens 1M*, containing $1,000,209$ ratings by $6,040$ users to $3,900$ items. We do 5-fold cross validation again in this larger dataset – not with the aim of training the parameters but to enhance the randomisation of the data split, following standard methodology in the evaluation of recommender systems.

3.2 Baselines

We compare our methods against different well-known state-of-the-art recommenders. We take a user-based CF where ratings are predicted as in Eq. 1, with Pearson correlation as similarity measure (**UB** [6]). We also test our methods against the graph partitioning method [2] based on Normalised Cut (NC) with Pearson similarity (**NC+P**) which has demonstrated important improvements for neighbour selection. This method basically clusters the users in the collection by finding the optimal cut (NC) of the computed graph, where Pearson similarity is used to weight the edges between items. Then, it selects a neighbourhood $NC_k(u)$ that outputs those users who belong to the same cluster as the target user u among the k clusters found by the algorithm; finally, the predicted rating is produced like in Eq. 1 with $N_k(u) = NC_k(u)$.

Furthermore, we compare our approach to related work on recommendation algorithms that adapt IR models. Specifically, we compare our methods against the relevance model for log-based CF (**UIR**) proposed in [8], as formulated in the Eq. 16 of that paper:

$$\hat{r}(u,i) \propto \sum_{\substack{v \in U(i) \\ c(u,v)>0}} \log\left(1 + \frac{(1-\lambda)p_{ml}(v|u,r)}{\lambda p(v|r)}\right) + |U(i)| \log \lambda \quad (7)$$

[1]Both available at http://www.grouplens.org/node/73

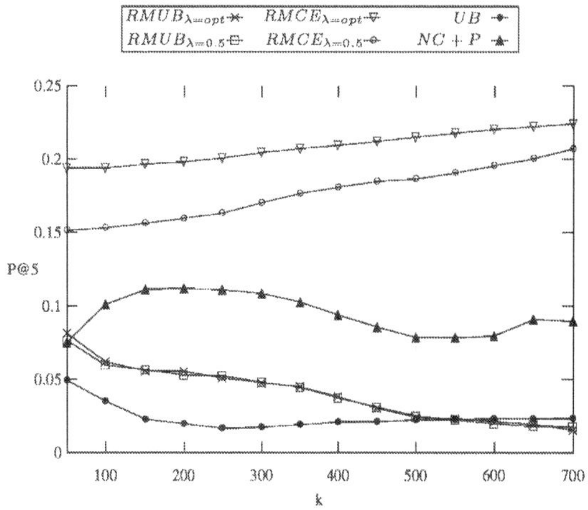

Figure 2: Evolution of the performance of the compared methods in terms of $P@5$ when varying k on the MovieLens 100K collection

where $c(u,v)$ is the number of items rated by both users u and v and the rest of probabilities are estimated as follows:

$$p_{ml}(v|u,r) \propto \frac{c(v,u)}{c(u)}, \quad p(v|r) \propto c(v)$$

We also include as a baseline the unified user-based model (**URM**) presented in [9], which allows for introducing ratings in the probability estimations. More specifically, we use the Eq. 40a from [9] which goes as follows:

$$\hat{r}(u,i) = \frac{\sum_{v \in U(i)} r(v,i) e^{-\frac{1-\cos(u,v)}{h_u^2}}}{\sum_{v \in U(i)} e^{-\frac{1-\cos(u,v)}{h_u^2}}} \quad (8)$$

where $\cos(u,v)$ is a cosine kernel based similarity measure between users u and v represented as vectors in an item space, where the missing ratings can be replaced by a constant value of 0, or by the average rating value. This approach requires a prior learning of the value h_u (the kernel bandwidth window parameter) by expectation-maximisation [9]. In order to provide a fair comparison, we use here the best value $h_u^2 = 0.79$ reported in [9], which was tuned on the very same collection.

3.3 Results and Discussion

We now assess the research questions RQ1 (are RM models useful to identify neighbours in recommendation?) and RQ2 (can we achieve better performance with a complete probabilistic representation of the CF problem?), raised at the beginning of the paper, in light of the results, summarised in Figure 2 and Table 1. Figure 2 shows how sensitive the evaluated methods are to the neighbourhood size (or number of clusters for NC+P). In Table 1 we present the results for different evaluation metrics using the two datasets described previously. For our approaches, we first test a hybrid combination of our neighbour selection approach using Eq. 3 followed by the standard user-based CF formulation with Pearson similarity (Eq. 1); we refer to this method as **RMUB**. Additionally, we denote by RMCE the combination of the relevance model (Eq. 3) followed by the cross entropy ranking function (Eq. 4).

To address **RQ1** we compare the performance of RMUB against that of the other baselines. We observe that the RMUB method clearly outperforms the UB, UIR and URM baselines for P@5, nDCG@5 and nDCG@10, in both MovieLens 100K (see Table 1a) and 1M (Table 1b). Its performance in terms of P@50, however, is similar to some of the baselines, showing that our method is able to rank higher than such baselines interesting items for the user,

Table 1: Summary of comparative effectiveness. Best values for each collection and metric are in bold. Statistical significant improvements w.r.t. UB, NC+P, UIR, URM, RMUB and RMCE are superscripted with a, b, c, d, e and f respectively (Wilcoxon Test with $p < 0.01$). Trained parameter values are $k = 50$; $k = 200$; $h_u^2 = 0.79$; $\lambda = 0.1$; $k = 50$ and $\lambda = 0.1$; and $k = 700$ and $\lambda = 0.9$ respectively.

(a) MovieLens 100K

Method	P@5	nDCG@5	nDCG@10	P@50	cvg
UB	0.049^{cd}	0.041^{cd}	0.047^{cd}	0.056^{ce}	100%
NC+P	0.111^{acde}	0.097^{acde}	0.095^{acde}	0.058^{ce}	83%
UIR	0.004	0.002	0.002	0.002	100%
URM	0.005	0.003	0.018	0.054^{ce}	100%
RMUB	0.081^{acd}	0.064^{acd}	0.062^{acd}	0.050^{c}	60%
RMCE	$\mathbf{0.224}^{abcde}$	$\mathbf{0.204}^{abcde}$	$\mathbf{0.204}^{abcde}$	$\mathbf{0.138}^{abcde}$	100%

(b) MovieLens 1M

Method	P@5	nDCG@5	nDCG@10	P@50	cvg
UB	0.035^{cd}	0.031^{cd}	0.031^{cd}	0.039^{cde}	100%
NC+P	0.037^{acd}	0.033^{acd}	0.036^{acd}	0.048^{acde}	99%
UIR	0.001	0.001	0.001	0.001	100%
URM	0.001	0.001	0.006	0.034^{c}	100%
RMUB	0.075^{abcd}	0.061^{abcd}	0.057^{abcd}	0.038^{c}	41.4%
RMCE	$\mathbf{0.187}^{abcde}$	$\mathbf{0.176}^{abcde}$	$\mathbf{0.168}^{abcde}$	$\mathbf{0.108}^{abcde}$	100%

at least until some reasonable cut-off, which in this case seems to be 50. Moreover, since this method takes two parameters (k and λ), we analyse now its performance sensitivity. Due to space constraints, we only explore in Figure 2 the neighbourhood size k, but we include the performance for two values of λ – the optimal ($\lambda = 0.1$) and neutral ($\lambda = 0.5$) configurations – where a negligible difference is obtained. We can also notice in the same figure that the baseline NC+P obtains a much better performance than RMUB, consistently with results reported in [2]. Table 1 also shows that the coverage results for the NC+P baseline are better than for RMUB in their optimal settings. We further observed (we omit the detailed results here for the sake of space) that the coverage of NC+P decreases with larger k's (as reported in [2]), whereas the coverage of RMUB increases, but at the expense of losing precision. All in all, our answer to RQ1 is that relevance models as a standalone method for neighbour selection are useful but not optimal.

To address **RQ2** we focus on the RMCE approach. In this case our method consistently achieves statistically significant improvements against all the baselines for every reported metric, achieving a 100% improvement with respect to the best baseline (NC+P, which already demonstrated performance superior to a standard Matrix Factorisation baseline [2]). Furthermore, RMCE does not suffer from the coverage problem, although it is highly sensitive to the smoothing parameter, as Figure 2 shows. For this approach, the optimal parameter in MovieLens 100K is 0.9, that is, a configuration which relies heavily on the background collection model. This makes sense since, in such a setting, RMCE promotes popular recommendations which are known to perform very well in this dataset. Furthermore, as the same figure shows, the method outperforms the baselines even for a neutral setting of the smoothing parameter. Thus, we may conclude with a positive answer for RQ2, since the combination of RM-based neighbours and negative cross entropy as scoring function (RMCE) results in important improvements over the existing state-of-the-art CF methods.

Finally, it is interesting to observe how differently the RMUB and RMCE approaches perform, taking into account that the neighbours used for both methods are the same. Our hypothesis is that the classical user-based CF formulation (Eq. 1) has no formal justification to generate item rankings, mainly because it was proposed to predict ratings, not to rank items according to this predictions, in agreement with [4]. By using negative cross entropy as the retrieval function, the ranking shifts from guessing rating values to assessing relevance distribution distances, which proves to reward relevance over rating value accuracy, as we may notice in terms of relevance-oriented ranking metrics; according to the results, we can conclude that like in IR, negative cross entropy maintains its good properties in recommendation tasks.

4. CONCLUSIONS AND FUTURE WORK

We have presented a new approach to collaborative filtering in Recommender Systems. Our approach adapts the negative cross entropy ranking principle from the Relevance-Based Language Models in document retrieval to the item recommendation problem, combined with a neighbour selection step, drawing from the kNN CF principle. We tested our proposal first only for neighbourhood selection and then also for producing the recommendation, finding that the largest improvements are achieved when using the complete probabilistic model. Comparisons of our approach with other highly performing baselines shows consistent significant improvements for every evaluation metric. As future work, we plan to explore the behaviour of our proposal on larger datasets, and study how further the improvements can go with alternative estimation formulations such as different smoothing methods and RM models. We have also researched further alternatives in how the IR and recommendation variables are mapped [5], although more research is still needed on this point.

5. ACKNOWLEDGMENTS

This work was funded by *Secretaría de Estado de Investigación, Desarrollo e Innovación* from the Spanish Government under projects TIN2012-33867 and TIN2011-28538-C02.

6. REFERENCES

[1] BELLOGÍN, A., CASTELLS, P., AND CANTADOR, I. Precision-oriented evaluation of recommender systems: an algorithmic comparison. In *RecSys* (2011), pp. 333–336.

[2] BELLOGÍN, A., AND PARAPAR, J. Using graph partitioning techniques for neighbour selection in user-based collaborative filtering. In *RecSys* (2012), pp. 213–216.

[3] LAVRENKO, V., AND CROFT, W. B. Relevance based language models. In *SIGIR* (2001), ACM, pp. 120–127.

[4] MCLAUGHLIN, M. R., AND HERLOCKER, J. L. A collaborative filtering algorithm and evaluation metric that accurately model the user experience. In *SIGIR* (2004), pp. 329–336.

[5] PARAPAR, J., BELLOGÍN, A., CASTELLS, P., AND BARREIRO, A. Relevance-based language modelling for recommender systems. *Inf. Process. Manage. 49*, 4 (2013), 966–980.

[6] RESNICK, P., IACOVOU, N., SUCHAK, M., BERGSTROM, P., AND RIEDL, J. Grouplens: An open architecture for collaborative filtering of netnews. In *CSCW* (1994), pp. 175–186.

[7] SHANI, G., AND GUNAWARDANA, A. Evaluating recommendation systems. In *Recommender Systems Handbook*. 2011, pp. 257–297.

[8] WANG, J., DE VRIES, A., AND REINDERS, M. A user-item relevance model for log-based collaborative filtering. In *ECIR* (2006), Springer-Verlag, pp. 37–48.

[9] WANG, J., DE VRIES, A. P., AND REINDERS, M. J. T. Unified relevance models for rating prediction in collaborative filtering. *ACM Trans. Inf. Syst. 26*, 3 (June 2008), 16:1–16:42.

[10] ZHAI, C., AND LAFFERTY, J. A study of smoothing methods for language models applied to information retrieval. *ACM Trans. Inf. Syst. 22*, 2 (2004), 179–214.

Recommending Improved Configurations for Complex Objects with an Application in Travel Planning

Amihai Savir, Ronen I. Brafman
Department of Computer Science
Ben-Gurion University
{saviram,brafman}@cs.bgu.ac.il

Guy Shani
Information Systems Engineering
Ben-Gurion University
shanigu@bgu.ac.il

ABSTRACT

Users often configure complex objects with many possible internal choices. Recommendation engines that automatically configure such objects given user preferences and constraints, may provide much value in such cases. These applications generate appropriate recommendations based on user preferences. It is likely, though, that the user will not be able to fully express her preferences and constraints, requiring a phase of manual tuning of the recommended configuration. We suggest that following this manual revision, additional constraints and preferences can be *automatically* collected, and the recommended configuration can be *automatically* improved. Specifically, we suggest a recommender component that takes as input an initial manual configuration of a complex object, deduces certain user preferences and constraints from this configuration, and constructs an alternative configuration. We show an appealing application for our method in complex trip planning, and demonstrate its usability in a user study.

Categories and Subject Descriptors

H.4 [**Information Systems Applications**]: Miscellaneous

Keywords

Recommender Systems, Reconfiguration, Trip planning

1. INTRODUCTION

The configuration of complex objects is known to be a difficult task [1]. Consider the task of constructing a trip to a country, where the goal of such a trip is to visit a set of attractions located in different parts of the country. A configuration of such a trip consists of a set of attractions together with a schedule for visiting them, as well as additional locations for over-night stays and meals.

To find a good travel plan, a traveler may research the destination country thoroughly, reading travel books or talking to past travelers. Although some people enjoy this planning phase, it is clear that constructing a satisfactory trip requires investing significant time and effort. Given limited time, it is impossible to exhaustively search the huge configuration space and design an optimal trip.

Alternatively, a soon-to-be traveler may use a sophisticated recommender system (e.g., [9]) for constructing trips. In these systems the user often answers a set of required questions about her preferences, and receives a recommended plan. This plan is unlikely to be taken as is by the user, and users typically revise the recommended plan manually, by, e.g., switching attractions, changing the schedule, and so forth. This manual revision phase is needed because it is well known that expressing preferences and constraints is difficult and exhausting for users [7]. Thus, one can consider the manual revision phase as implicitly expressing additional preferences and constraints that were not initially inserted.

We propose here a method that can be used to automatically improve such manually constructed or revised plans. We envision our component within a sophisticated travel recommender system, following the manual revision phase.

Our suggested algorithm takes as input a manual configuration from the user, with additional personal preference data. In the trip example, we the user provides an initial planned trip, possibly generated through a manual revision of a previously suggested trip. We also expect numeric ratings for attractions that appear within the trip, reflecting how interesting each chosen attraction seems to the user.

The system then learns from this input the user's preferences over both attraction properties and global trip properties. For example, from a user who rates many museums positively the system may learn that the user likes museums. The system also learns constraints over the relationships between items in the configuration. For example, the system may learn that the user plans a trip with no more than an hour drive between attractions, and hence deduce a constraint of short distances between attractions. The system automatically deduces preferences and constraints about both component classes and the relationship between components. Our algorithm then uses integer programming (IP) to create a better plan, which is returned to the user for inspection. The user may choose to farther revise the trip, and so forth.

We report a user study for trip planning to New Zealand. Participants in the user study, all people who toured New Zealand, provided an initial 5-6 day trip. The study participants clearly preferred the revised trip, and indicated that if a system like that was available, they would have liked to use it.

RecSys'13, October 12–16, 2013, Hong Kong, China.

2. BACKGROUND

Recommender systems [8] are now widely used in many applications. Perhaps the most popular approach for providing recommendations is the collaborative filtering (CF) approach requiring historical usage data. A popular alternative is the content-based (CB) approach [6], where items are described using a set of attributes. For example, trip attractions may be described by their category (e.g. museum, or hiking), by their location, by their price, and so forth.

In some cases, in addition to the information about item attribute values, the system must also maintain information about relationships between items. For example, in the case of attractions we may need to have distance information or public transportation opportunities between attractions. Two attractions in New Zealand, for instance, may be relatively nearby geographically, but due to a mountain range in between may require significant time to travel in between. Also, when visiting an attraction one must plan accommodations, dining, and so forth. The museum, the restaurant, and the hotel must be sufficiently close in order for the user to enjoy them all in one afternoon. Other information may describe how similar two attractions are. For example, two museums may be very similar, making a visit to both less desirable, or they could be distinct, and a visit to both can be interesting for a museum lover.

A system that maintains, in addition to the item attributes, relationships between attributes and items, is often referred to as a knowledge-based recommender system [5]. Such systems are naturally costly to build, as the knowledge must be identified by a domain expert, then collected and inserted into the system. Therefore, they are appropriate mainly to systems that sell relatively profitable items. Indeed, vacation packages are an obvious example of such complex and costly products that require much knowledge to construct properly, and it is no surprise that much work on knowledge-based recommenders considers this domain [9].

A second, orthogonal, research direction considers the interactions of the users with the system [9]. When recommending costly and complex items, it is unlikely that the system will provide good recommendations without collecting preference information from the user by, e.g., filling out a lengthy questionnaire. An alternative to a tiresome questionnaire is to present the user with recommended items after a very brief collection of user goals (e.g. the vacation destination). These recommendations are likely not to be satisfactory, and we must allow the user to criticize them. From the user's response, the system learns additional preference information, and provides improved recommendations.

Such systems provide relatively lengthy interactions between the user and the system to identify good items. Therefore, such systems are useful in the case where a user gains significant value from the items, and is hence willing to invest the required effort in a conversation with the system.

There are a few examples of previous systems designed to recommend travel destinations or plans to users (see, e.g. [4]), in addition to many online travel planning systems with no recommendation component, such as Travelocity or Trip Advisor. These systems typically ask the user to specify many input parameters, such as the destination, the travel party (e.g. couple or family), duration, budget, attraction types and so forth. Then, these systems may use information over the choices of other users to recommend attractions, accommodations and so forth.

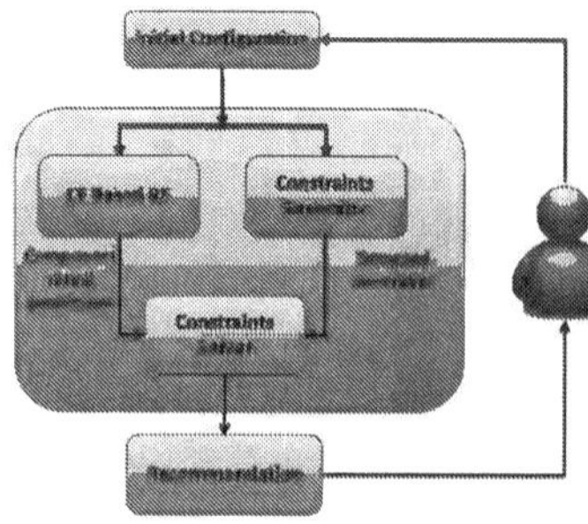

Figure 1: Complex Objects Recommender System.

3. TRAVEL PLANNING RECONFIGURATION

Figure 1 presents our complex objects recommender system, composed of 3 major components — a recommender, a constraint generator, and a constraint solver. The system takes as input an example of a possible configuration of a complex object designed by the user. It is important that the user will provide a sufficiently rich example, because the system then deduces from this example various features. Two separate types of features are learned, the user preference over components, and a set of constraints over the combination of components into a complex object. Then, the system uses the deduced features to compute a recommended complex object. This object is then returned to the user, and she may revise it manually, and provide it as input for a second recommendation.

Recommender: Takes as input a list of preferred or positively rated components and uses some rating prediction approach, such as CF, to predict ratings for other components. These ratings do not take into consideration any constraints or correlations between components.

Constraint generation: Identifies constraints expressed in the given example complex object. Some constraints, such as total price, are global, i.e., apply to the complete complex object. Other constraints apply to subsets of components. For example, the maximal time allotted in the trip to travel between attractions. Finally, there are some constraints that apply to specific components. For example, the user may decide that some attractions must be kept. In our system, all attractions that got the highest possible rating, are considered irreplaceable.

Constraint solver: We now feed the results of the two previous stages to an optimizer, designed to provide a solution that satisfies all constraints while maximizing the sum of predicted ratings. The solution directly corresponds to a complex object that meets all constraints and is considered best in terms of user preferences, e.g., the sum of ratings of all attractions, or some other aggregate measure.

While the system we suggest above is designed generically to fit various types of complex objects, in this paper we focus on a travel planning application. We consider a trip to be a complex object constructed of a sequence of attractions (the components of the complex object). The system's goal is to provide a trip, i.e., a schedule of activities for a 5 day visit to New Zealand. We now explain how the generic phases in the former section manifest themselves in our application.

Database: Our system requires a database consisting of the various possible components (attractions), their attributes, and their relationships. Our database contained 327 attractions, 21 attraction types, and 50 different areas

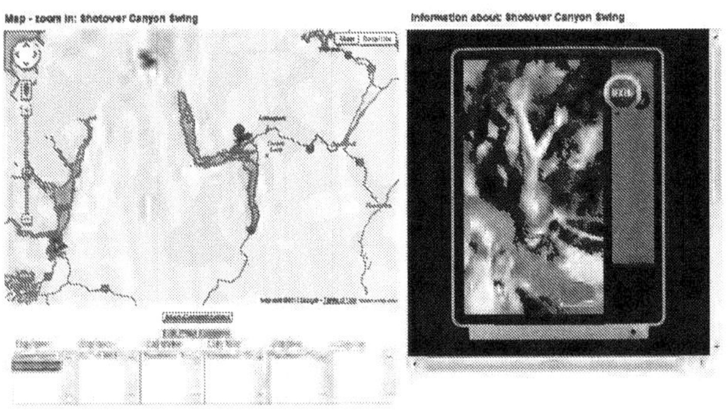

Figure 2: Trip suggestion user interface.

of New Zealand. All the information in the database was taken from the popular Lonely Planet travel guide [2].

Input: The interaction of users with the system begins with inserting information about a possible trip. In our application we asked the user to specify which attractions she would like to visit during each of the 5 days. In addition, the user specified an attraction interest rating, specifying how important is the attraction, on a scale of 1 to 5. Finally, the user was asked to provide information regarding the area where she would like to spend each night.

Attraction Recommender: In order to extrapolate attraction ratings for users, we used a simple CF engine. We constructed a memory-based algorithm, using the popular Pearson correlation to compare user profiles [3]. The algorithm was run on all the users who provided initial ratings for attractions in their input.

Trip constraint generation: We define the following constraints over the revised trip:

- Budget — we computed the overall price of the trip that the user has given us as input. We then require the budget of the revised trip not to exceed this budget by some fixed amount δ (in our experiment we used $\delta = 50NZD$).
- Daily load — the minimal and maximal time required for the attractions that the user chose to visit in a single day. We thus measure whether the user prefers a relaxed trip, or a packed trip, visiting as many attractions as possible.
- Travel distance — the maximal travel distance between attractions. This allows us to measure how much time the user is willing to spend traveling between places.
- Diversity level — input trips contain various types of attractions. We constrain the revised trip to also contain the same attraction types, maintaining the diversity of the trip. For example, even if the recommender predicts higher scores for all hiking attractions than all museum attractions, yet the user entered a few museum attractions in her input trip, we will force the revised trip to also contain some museums. We considered here only attractions rated 3 or higher.
- Preserving important attractions — in the input the user may specify a few attractions as "very important" (a rating of 5). We force the revised trip to contain these attractions.
- Local transportation constraints — while our system does not maintain transportation information between attractions, such as how to get from one museum to another within the same city, we add a fixed transportation time (30 minutes) for travel between attractions in the same city.

Trip constraint optimization: We formulate the problem of optimizing the total value of visited attractions subject to the above constraints using an integer programming (we used http://lpsolve.sourceforge.net/5.5/). To do so, we define two types of boolean variables — $x_{i,j}$ is true whenever attraction j is visited on day i, and $y_{i,l}$ is true whenever area l is visited in day i. We optimize $\sum_{i,j} R_j x_{i,j}$ where R_j is the predicted or specified rating for attraction j. That is, the program optimizes the sum of attraction ratings.

Any solution to the IP problem is mapped directly into a specification of which attractions to visit in each day, using the $x_{i,j}$ boolean parameters.

4. EMPIRICAL EVALUATION

We ran a user study with people who have visited New Zeland within the past 5 years. The users in our study were thus asked to specify a 5 day trip to New Zealand. They were asked to provide a sequence of attractions that they would like to visit in their trip, and to specify in which city they would spend each night. The users also had to add an interest rating for each attraction in the input trip.

These manually constructed trips were run through our system and we computed 3 different suggestions:

1. Best revision: the output of the algorithm of the previous section, within the given time limit.

2. Conservative revision: a revision with an additional set of constraints forcing at most two attractions that were ranked lowest to be replaced.

3. Best attraction list: a list of the attractions with the highest predicted rating, with no trip planning, as is done by simpler recommendation systems.

The alternatives were presented in a random order to reduce biasing due to presentation order. The users could observe the revisions, watch the suggested trip on the map, and request information from Wikipedia concerning the attractions in a separate pane on the user interface (Figure 2). The users were then asked to fill a short survey asking questions about the 3 suggestions.

We collect attraction ratings for our CF component thorough simple online application that allows travelers to New Zealand to provide ratings for attractions that they visited. This application was installed by the owners of a number of guest houses in New Zealand, which are popular among travelers. We collected more than 600 responses of travelers through this online application.

4.1 Experimental Results

We had 19 participants in our user study, ages 20 through 50. All of them have visited New Zealand in the past 5 years. We had 12 male participants and 7 females. Although this is certainly not a large user study, we still got significant results, which further suggests that the differences between the methods are very noticeable. The trips that were inserted were very diverse. Figure 3 shows the distribution of the 5 most popular attraction types. We can observe that the user population had museum lovers, and people who never visit museums, avid hikers alongside people who choose one or less hikes, and so forth. In addition, there were 7 attraction types, such as cruises, fishing, and horse riding, that were selected by only a single person.

As these extracted constraints demonstrate, a personalization approach is needed to understand the different choices that people make when constructing trips, and to be able to automatically construct trip revisions that will be appropriate for their personal taste.

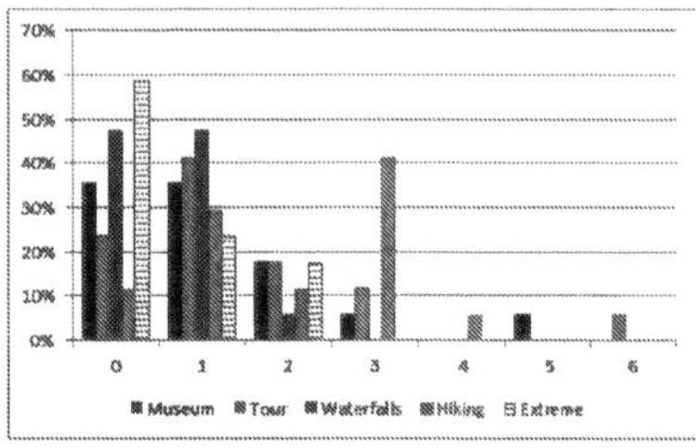

Figure 3: Popular attraction types distribution in input trips. The x-axis shows the number of attractions of that type per trip. The y-axis shows the portion of the user population who chose this number of attractions.

These extracted preferences, along with the attraction ratings that the users supplied, were inserted into the system and the 3 suggestions were computed and presented to the users. After presenting the users with the suggestions, they were asked to fill a short survey.

We asked several general questions regarding the participants' perception of our system: 90% (17) of the participants said that trip planning is difficult and requires much effort, and 95% (18) of them thought that our recommender system for trip planning will be successful, if made available widely. 95% of the users claimed that given the system suggestions they would have made some change to their initial plan.

We now turn to an evaluation of the travel plans and their revisions. Figure 4 shows distribution of grades for the revisions. The average grade for the initial plan was 3.94, while the average for the best revision was 4.45, and the average for the conservative revision was 3.89. In 10 times out of 19, the best revision got a higher grade than the initial plan, and for 6 users both plans got the same grade. Only 3 users gave a higher grade to their initial plan. A sign-test gives a p-value of 0.002 to the null hypothesis that the revised plan is no better than the initial plan.

Only 6 participants marked the conservative revision to be better than the original plan, and 4 gave the original plan higher grades. We allowed the participants to comment on the plans, and we got responses criticizing the conservative plan as being not novel enough.

We also asked the participants which suggestion they preferred. 79% (15) preferred the best revision suggestion over the other two suggestions. 90% preferred a suggestion for a complete plan over a list of interesting attractions. These results demonstrate the value of supplying the actual target object, rather than useful components.

The construction of an initial plan represents a significant effort, and we asked whether the effort was worthwhile. Only one participant claimed that the effort was too high for the given results. One other participant said that the effort is high, but the results are interesting. 26% (5) of the participants said that the effort is considerable, but it is acceptable for trip planning, and the rest 63% (12) of the participants said that the effort is minor given the results.

Although all of our participants already visited New Zealand, 79% of them claimed that the system provided some novel suggestions of places they were unfamiliar with and looked interesting. Some people commented that they recognized some of the suggested attractions and considered them to be good suggestions, indicating the power of our recommender component.

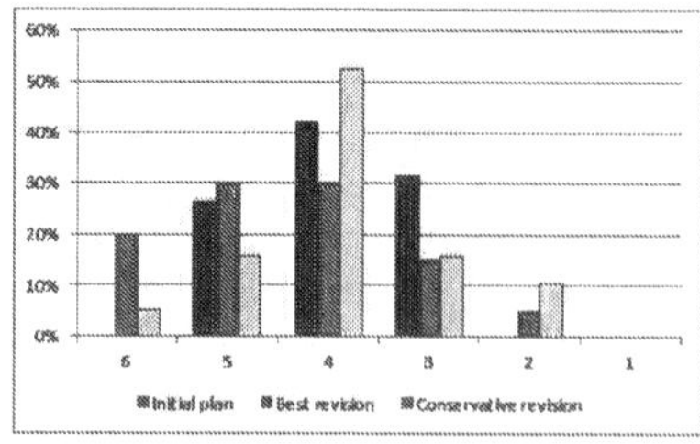

Figure 4: Grades distribution for the initial plan and the two revisions presented to the users.

5. CONCLUSION

We present a recommendation component that takes as input a pre-configured complex object, such as a trip to a country, and some preference data, such as attraction ratings, and produces a better configuration, e.g. an improved trip, taking into account a set of constraints that were extracted from the input example. In a user study over a 5 day trip planning to New Zealand, we produced better trips than manually constructed input trips.

In the future we plan to test our component within a complete recommender system, as an integral part of the trip planning process. In addition, we intend to test our ideas in other domains where complex objects need to be configured, such as configuring an appropriate computer system.

Acknowledgment: This work is partially supported by the Lynn and William Frankel Center for Computer Science.

6. REFERENCES

[1] M. Aldanondo, G. Moynard, and K. Hamou. General configurator requirements and modeling elements. In *ECAI Workshop on Configuration*, pages 1–6, 2000.

[2] C. Bain, G. Dunford, K. Miller, S. O'Brien, and C. Rawlings-Way. *New Zealand — Lonely Planet.* Lonely Planet, 2006.

[3] J. S. Breese, D. Heckerman, and C. M. Kadie. Empirical analysis of predictive algorithms for collaborative filtering. In *UAI*, pages 43–52, 1998.

[4] T. Cao, Q. Nguyen, A. Nguyen, and T. Le. Integrating open data and generating travel itinerary in semantic-aware tourist information system. In *Proceedings of the 13th International Conference on Information Integration and Web-based Applications and Services*, pages 214–221. ACM, 2011.

[5] P. Cunningham and A. Bonzano. Knowledge engineering issues in developing a case-based reasoning application. *Knowl.-Based Syst.*, 12(7):371–379, 1999.

[6] P. Lops, M. de Gemmis, and G. Semeraro. Content-based recommender systems: State of the art and trends. In *Recommender Systems Handbook*, pages 73–105. 2011.

[7] P. Pu, B. Faltings, L. Chen, J. Zhang, and P. Viappiani. Usability guidelines for product recommenders based on example critiquing research. In *Recommender Systems Handbook*, pages 511–545. 2011.

[8] F. Ricci, L. Rokach, and B. Shapira. Introduction to recommender systems handbook. In *Recommender Systems Handbook*, pages 1–35. 2011.

[9] A. Venturini and F. Ricci. Aplying trip@dvice recommendation technology to www.visiteurope.com. In *ECAI*, pages 607–611, 2006.

Recommending Patents based on Latent Topics

Ralf Krestel
Department of Computer Science
University of California, Irvine
krestel@uci.edu

Padhraic Smyth
Department of Computer Science
University of California, Irvine
smyth@ics.uci.edu

ABSTRACT

The availability of large volumes of granted patents and applications, all publicly available on the Web, enables the use of sophisticated text mining and information retrieval methods to facilitate access and analysis of patents. In this paper we investigate techniques to automatically recommend patents given a query patent. This task is critical for a variety of patent-related analysis problems such as finding relevant citations, research of relevant prior art, and infringement analysis. We investigate the use of latent Dirichlet allocation and Dirichlet multinomial regression to represent patent documents and to compute similarity scores. We compare our methods with state-of-the-art document representations and retrieval techniques and demonstrate the effectiveness of our approach on a collection of US patent publications.

Categories and Subject Descriptors

H.3.3 [**Information Search and Retrieval**]: Retrieval Models, Selection Process, Search Process

Keywords

Citation Recommendation, Patent Retrieval, Document Ranking, Topic Models, Language Models

1. INTRODUCTION

Millions of patent documents are publicly available electronically. Analyzing these documents can help in our understanding of technological progress, the evolution of new language and terms, and the emergence of new products. Tools for automated patent analysis also have direct benefits to inventors in terms of finding relevant prior work, for companies wishing to patent new products or ideas, and for patent examiners in deciding which patents to grant.

Being able to efficiently and accurately search large patent databases has been a problem for decades. For example in the early 1950's, a mechanized way of finding relevant patents based on punch cards was developed [3]. Since then, information retrieval techniques have been used to provide more assistance in patent search, allowing for searching of large databases in seconds across multiple languages [15]. Systems that support this type of keyword-based search include both commercial systems such as Dialog or Lexis-Nexis[1], as well as systems used in patent offices[2]. Despite this progress, searching patent databases, either by inventors, lawyers, patent examiners, or analysts, still heavily relies on Boolean keyword queries [2] and often requires considerable legal expertise and domain knowledge.

In the context of patent retrieval, different types of search scenarios are relevant depending on the specific tasks that occur at different stages in the life of a patent [2, 5]:

- When writing a patent a key issue for an inventor is the identification of prior art that needs to be referenced—this motivates the development of automated citation recommendation to support the patent writing process.
- Once a patent is written and submitted to a patent office, a detailed search of relevant prior patents is essential for patent office examiners to decide on a submitted patent's novelty, similarity, relevance, and patentability [8, 11].
- The issue of finding relevant prior art becomes important again if the validity of a patent is evaluated at a later stage (e.g., as part of an infringement lawsuit) to decide whether a similar patent already exists.
- More broadly, commercial entities are often interested in patent analysis for strategic competitive reasons and protecting their intellectual property.

Across all of these tasks, finding patents that are similar to the query patent is a crucial component of the problem. For example, accurately recommending relevant citations could save significant time and resources. In contrast to recommending scientific articles, the problem of automatically recommending patents poses some distinct challenges. For example, language usage in patents tends to be more idiosyncratic and less consistent compared to technical language usage in scientific articles [1]. Furthermore, the citation graph for patents conveys different information than in the case of scientific articles. For example, patent citations do not occur within the text of the patent but are provided as a separate list, often consisting of both inventor-generated and examiner-generated sublists.

RecSys'13, October 12–16, 2013, Hong Kong, China.

ACM 978-1-4503-2409-0/13/10 ...$15.00.
http://dx.doi.org/10.1145/2507157.2507232.

[1]http://www.dialog.com, http://www.lexisnexis.com
[2]e.g. USPTO http://www.uspto.gov

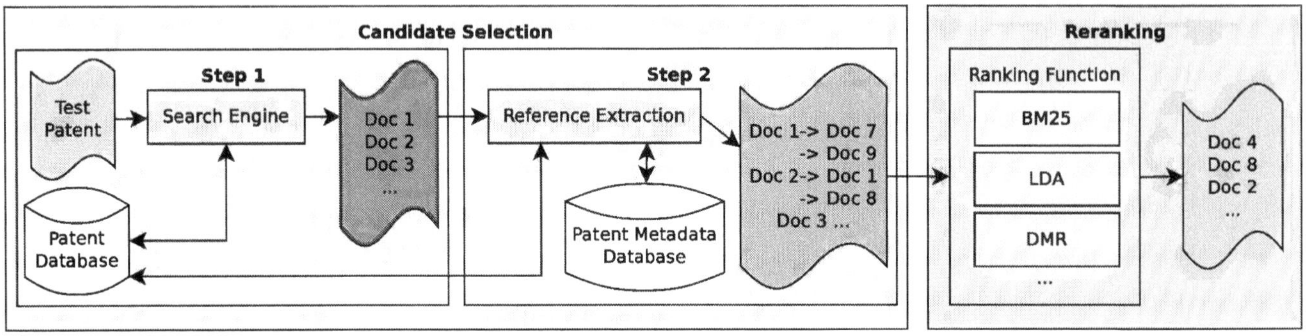

Figure 1: System architecture overview

2. FINDING RELATED PATENTS

We address the problem of finding related or similar patents by investigating a combination of (1) latent Dirichlet allocation (LDA) [4], (2) Dirichlet multinomial regression (DMR) [14], and (3) language models [6]. The combination of topic models and language models, especially when used for document smoothing, has been shown to be beneficial in prior work on document ranking (e.g. [18]). Latent topics can capture concepts and general terms, whereas language models are useful for capturing specific terms and details [10]. In the following we investigate the use of combinations of these models for the specific problem of patent retrieval.

The problem we address is as follows: given a granted patent q, return a ranked list of patents and patent applications $R=\{d_1, d_2, \ldots, d_n\}$, all published before the application date of q, ordered by the degree of similarity to q. The highest ranked patents d_i are considered to be most similar to q.

System Architecture.

Figure 1 shows the overview of our system's architecture. In a manner similar to that of Mase et al. [13], we use a two-stage approach; first generating a list of candidates and then using different ranking functions to determine the most similar patents.

The first stage consists of two steps:

1. To find the candidates we use a search engine to determine the top-K most similar patents to the test patent based on tf-idf.
2. We use the top N terms (with $N=30$)of the summary field of the test document to construct a query to retrieve the top-k most similar patents and patent applications (as suggested by Xue and Croft [17]). To overcome some limitations of this tf-idf based retrieval we extend the list of retrieved documents by extracting citations within the top-K returned documents. If the citation is another USPTO patent document then we add the cited document to our candidate set for ranking.

In the second stage, after the generation of the candidate set in Step 2, we re-rank the candidate patent documents using combinations of language models and topic models. To provide an example of the number of patents returned in a candidate set, when using $K=500$ in step 1, an average candidate set produced from step 2 consists of around 2,700 patents.

Baselines.

We compare our algorithms with two baseline algorithms: (1) BM25 for long queries [12] and (2) language models (LM) [6]. To compute similarity scores for the test patent relative to each candidate we treat the test document as the query q and the candidates from our two-step candidate selection process as our document collection.

For BM25 the similarity score for each candidate d with test document q is computed as:

$$\text{BM25}_d = \sum_{w \in q} \log[\frac{N_c}{df_w}] \cdot \frac{(k_1+1)tf_{wd}}{k_1((1-b)+b\times L)+tf_{wd}} \cdot \frac{(k_3+1)tf_{wq}}{k_3+tf_{wq}}$$

where N_c is the number of documents in the collection, df_w is the document frequency of term w, and L is the length of document d divided by the average document length for all documents in the collection. tf_{wd} is the term frequency of term w in document d. The tuning parameters k_1,k_3, and b are set to 1.5,1.5, and 0.75 respectively, as suggested in [12].

For LM we use a Dirichlet smoothed language model [19]:

$$\text{LM}_d = P_{lm}(q|d) = \prod_{w \in Q} P_{lm}(w|d)$$

$$P_{lm}(w|d) = \frac{N_d}{N_d+\delta} P_{ml}(w|d) + (1 - \frac{N_d}{N_d+\delta}) P_{ml}(w|c)$$

$P_{ml}(w|d)$ is the maximum likelihood estimate of word w in document d, and $P_{ml}(w|c)$ is the maximum likelihood estimate of word w in the entire collection c. N_d is the number of tokens in document d and $\delta=500$.

2.1 LDA and Language Models

We follow Wei and Croft [16], who proposed an LDA-based document model for ad-hoc retrieval where they used topics to smooth a language model representation. To find related documents for a given patent, we compute a similarity score defined as the probability of a query patent q given document d:

$$\text{LDA}_d = P_{lda}(q|d) = \prod_{w \in q} P_{lda}(w|d)$$

$$P_{lda}(w|d) = \sum_{z=1}^{N_z} P(w|z, \hat{\phi}) P(z|\hat{\theta}, d)$$

where z is a latent topic and $\hat{\theta}$ and $\hat{\phi}$ are posterior estimates of θ and ϕ—the inferred topic and word distributions. We use collapsed Gibbs sampling [9] to infer Θ and Φ given the observed words, the model, and the priors.

The number of topics N_z, as well as α and β, are set beforehand. We achieved best results when choosing N_z to be $\sqrt{N_c}$, the square root of the number of documents in the collection. We also used $50/N_z$ for α and $200/N_v$ for β, with N_v being the vocabulary size.

We combine topic and language models by using the latent topics to smooth the language models [16]. The similarity score between the test patent and document d can then be computed as:

$$\text{LM-LDA}_d = P_{lmlda}(q|d) = \prod_{w \in Q} P_{lmlda}(w|d)$$

$$P_{lmlda}(w|d) = \gamma(P_{lm}(w|d)) + (1-\gamma)P_{lda}(w|d)$$

$P_{lm}(w|d)$ is the smoothed language model and $P_{lda}(w|d)$ can be computed using the inferred topic and word distributions as defined earlier. γ is set to 0.3 as suggested in [16] (see Section 3.3 for a discussion of how this parameter influences the retrieval results).

2.2 Dirichlet Multinomial Regression for Patent Retrieval

Mimno and McCallum [14] proposed Dirichlet multinomial regression (DMR), which extends the LDA model to allow the topics to be conditioned on arbitrary features. We can use DMR to model different topical content across different patent sections (abstract, claims, etc.).

The language used in a patent document can vary significantly depending on the section. Different sections can be written by different individuals, e.g. the details of an invention by engineers and the claims by an attorney. By treating sections individually we hope to gain more coherent topics without losing the overall topical context of the patent document as a whole.

In the DMR model the document-topic prior α is a function of the observed document features encoded in a vector x. A 1 in x indicates the presence of a feature in document d and a 0 indicates its absence.

Here we split the patent text into its four sections: *title+abstract*, *claims*, *summary*, and *details*. We model each section as an individual document with two types of metadata information: patent id and section id, where the ids are presented as binary features in the DMR model. The similarity score is then computed as:

$$\text{DMR}_d = P_{dmr}(q|d) = \prod_{w \in q} P_{dmr}(w|d)$$

$$P_{dmr}(w|d) = \sum_{s=1}^{4} \frac{N_s}{N_d} P_{dmr}(w|s)$$

$$P_{dmr}(w|s) = \sum_{z=1}^{N_z} P(w|z,\hat{\phi}) P(z|\hat{\theta}, s)$$

To get $P_{dmr}(w|d)$ we combine the topic models for the different sections s. N_s is the number of words in section s; and N_d is the number of words in the whole patent d. The topic models computed in this way can be used to smooth the language models in a manner analogous to the LDA models:

$$\text{LM-DMR}_d = P_{lmdmr}(q|d) = \prod_{w \in Q} P_{lmdmr}(w|d)$$

$$P_{lmdmr}(w|d) = \gamma(P_{lm}(w|d)) + (1-\gamma)P_{dmr}(w|d)$$

We use the same setting as for LM-LDA with $\gamma = 0.3$.

3. EXPERIMENTS

To evaluate our proposed methods, we use each algorithm to rank patents in terms of similarity to a query patent q, where the set that is ranked is (a) restricted to patents or applications published prior to the date of publication of q, and (b) restricted to the candidates generated by the two-stage candidate set generation process described earlier. We use the citations in a patent q as a proxy for ground truth in terms of determining a set of patents that are relevant to q. This strategy was also used in [17] and in the NTCIR[3] workshop series.

There are a number of drawbacks to using existing citations in a patent as a measure to evaluate patent similarity algorithms. For example, it is quite common in practice that truly relevant patents are not cited, potentially deliberately. In addition, if there exists a published patent application and a granted patent for the same application, only one or the other might have been cited. However, since these limitations affect all of the algorithms, it is reasonable to argue that a patent's citations provide a useful surrogate ground truth by which to compare and evaluate algorithms in the context of patent retrieval.

3.1 Data

For testing, we randomly picked 100 granted utility patents published on November 13th, 2012 by the USPTO[4]. For each of these 100 test patents we selected the top-K=500 patents found by the search engine as candidates (see step one in Figure 1). We expanded these candidate sets by adding the references as described in step two in Figure 1. This resulted in approximately 275,000 patents and patent applications for the 100 test patents in total. For each test patent, the average number of references to US patents published after 1975 was 25.7, of which 9.9 on average were added by the patent examiner. In addition each test patent had on average 4.5 references to non-US patents, old US patents, or other non-patent literature. An average of 18.7 references were present in the citation candidate set whose average size per test patent was 2,772.

3.2 Evaluation Methodology

The US patents cited in the test patents act as our ground truth set. We discard references to non-US patents and non-patent literature. For computation of precision and recall we also do not include references to US patents that are not among the candidates and thus can not be retrieved and ranked by our algorithms.

For each test patent q we generate a ranking of patents to be cited using all the candidates for that patent. We use mean average precision (MAP) [12] to compare the rankings R_i generated by different methods for all test patents $q \in Q$:

$$MAP(Q) = \frac{1}{|Q|} \sum_{j=1}^{|Q|} \frac{1}{m_j} \sum_{k=1}^{m_j} \text{Precision}(R_{jk})$$

where R_{jk} is the set of ranked results from the top of the list down to item k in the list, and the set of relevant items is $\{i_1 \ldots i_{m_j}\}$. If no relevant document is retrieved, precision is taken to be 0.

[3] http://research.nii.ac.jp/ntcir/index-en.html

[4] USPTO patents are publicly available at http://www.google.com/googlebooks/uspto-patents.html

Table 1: Citation Recommendation Results

	Mean Average Precision			
	Total	+/-	Examiner	Others
BM25	0.062	-51.2%	0.048	0.029
LM	0.127	—	0.116	0.066
LDA	0.134	+5.5%	0.106	0.079
DMR	0.143	+12.6%	0.117	0.085
LM-DMR	0.164	+29.1%	0.135	0.090
LM-LDA	0.177	+39.4%	0.147	0.106

3.3 Results and Analysis

The main results from our experiments are summarized in Table 1. We report MAP for the total number of citations and show in the third column the performance difference as a percentage relative to the language model . It is clear from these results that the combination of language model representations with topic model representations (either LDA or DMR) outperforms the individual methods, with LM-LDA yielding the best results. The last two columns in Table 1 show MAP scores considering only the references added by the patent examiner or by others (usually the patent author), respectively. Note that LM on its own performs as well or better than LDA and DMR on their own, for references cited by the examiner, whereas this is not true for references cited by others. (The combination of LM with LDA or DMR is still best overall on both sets). This suggests that references added by examiners tend to contain language that more closely matches the language in the original patent, relative to the references added by non-examiners. This could be due to the fact that patent examiners make more extensive use of keyword-based search, compared to non-examiners, when determining which prior patents should be cited.

4. DISCUSSION AND CONCLUSIONS

In this paper we investigated the application of language modeling and topic modeling to the problem of patent retrieval given a query patent. We conducted experiments on a subset of the USPTO patent corpus using patent citations as ground truth. We found that language models provide systematic improvements in terms of precision and recall over simpler methods such as BM25. Furthermore, our experiments showed that the combination of topic modeling and language modeling provides further significant improvements in performance over either alone. Additional improvements could potentially be gained by incorporating meta-information such as the category information for a patent or citation graphs [7].

5. ACKNOWLEDGEMENT

Supported by the Intelligence Advanced Research Projects Activity (IARPA) via Department of Interior National Business Center contract number D11PC20155. The U.S. government is authorized to reproduce and distribute reprints for Governmental purposes notwithstanding any copyright annotation thereon. Disclaimer: The views and conclusions contained herein are those of the authors and should not be interpreted as necessarily representing the official policies or endorsements, either expressed or implied, of IARPA, DoI/NBC, or the U.S. government.

6. REFERENCES

[1] K. H. Atkinson. Toward a more rational patent search paradigm. In *Proceedings of the 1st ACMWorkshop on Patent Information Retrieval*, pages 37–40, 2008.

[2] L. Azzopardi, W. Vanderbauwhede, and H. Joho. Search system requirements of patent analysts. In *SIGIR'10*, pages 775–776. ACM, 2010.

[3] M. Bailey, B. Lanham, and J. Leibowitz. Mechanized searching in the U.S. Patent Office. *Journal of the Patent Office Society*, 35(7):566–587, 1953.

[4] D. M. Blei, A. Y. Ng, and M. I. Jordan. Latent dirichlet allocation. *Journal of Machine Learning Research*, 3:993–1022, January 2003.

[5] D. Bonino, A. Ciaramella, and F. Corno. Review of the state-of-the-art in patent information and forthcoming evolutions in intelligent patent informatics. *World Patent Inf.*, 32(1):30–38, 2010.

[6] W. B. Croft and J. Lafferty. *Language Modeling for Information Retrieval*. Kluwer Academic Publishers, Norwell, MA, USA, 2003.

[7] A. Fujii. Enhancing patent retrieval by citation analysis. In *SIGIR'07*, pages 793–794. ACM, 2007.

[8] S. Fujita. Technology survey and invalidity search: A comparative study of different tasks for japanese patent document retrieval. *Inf. Process. Manage.*, 43(5):1154–1172, September 2007.

[9] T. L. Griffiths and M. Steyvers. Finding scientific topics. *Proc Natl Acad Sci U S A*, 101 Suppl 1:5228–5235, April 2004.

[10] R. Krestel and P. Fankhauser. Personalized topic-based tag recommendation. *Neurocomputing*, 76(1):61–70, 2012.

[11] R. J. Mann and M. Underweiser. A new look at patent quality: Relating patent prosecution to validity. *Journal of Empirical Legal Studies*, 9(1):1–32, 2012.

[12] C. D. Manning, P. Raghavan, and H. Schütze. *Introduction to Information Retrieval*. Cambridge University Press, Cambridge, UK, July 2008.

[13] H. Mase, T. Matsubayashi, Y. Ogawa, M. Iwayama, and T. Oshio. Proposal of two-stage patent retrieval method considering the claim structure. *TALIP*, 4(2):190–206, June 2005.

[14] D. M. Mimno and A. McCallum. Topic models conditioned on arbitrary features with dirichlet-multinomial regression. In *UAI'08*, pages 411–418. AUAI Press, 2008.

[15] F. Saad and A. Nürnberger. Overview of prior-art cross-lingual information retrieval approaches. *World Patent Inf.*, 34(4):304–314, December.

[16] X. Wei and W. B. Croft. Lda-based document models for ad-hoc retrieval. In *SIGIR'06*, pages 178–185. ACM, 2006.

[17] X. Xue and W. B. Croft. Automatic query generation for patent search. In *CIKM'09*, pages 2037–2040. ACM, 2009.

[18] X. Yi and J. Allan. A comparative study of utilizing topic models for information retrieval. In *ECIR'09*, pages 29–41. Springer-Verlag, 2009.

[19] C. Zhai and J. Lafferty. A study of smoothing methods for language models applied to information retrieval. *Trans. Inf. Syst.*, 22(2):179–214, 2004.

Recommending Scientific Articles Using Bi-Relational Graph-based Iterative RWR

Geng Tian
Beijing Key Lab of Traffic Data Analysis and Mining
Beijing Jiaotong University
11120478@bjtu.edu.cn

Liping Jing
Beijing Key Lab of Traffic Data Analysis and Mining
Beijing Jiaotong University
lpjing@bjtu.edu.cn

ABSTRACT

The overabundance of scientific article information has created much inconvenience to researchers seeking interesting articles online. In this paper, we provide a Bi-Relational graph to represent the heterogenous information of scientific article recommendation system, which includes three parts: the article content similarity, researcher interest correlation, and researcher-article readership. Meanwhile, an iterative random walk with restarts learning method is proposed on the Bi-Relational graph to recommend a researcher rating for each article by making use of the known information. The proposed method has ability to perform both old and new article recommendation. A series of experiments on CiteULike dataset have shown that our method is more effective than other testing methods in the paper.

Categories and Subject Descriptors

H.3 [**Information Storage and Retrieval**]: Information Search and Retrieval—*Information filtering*; I.2 [**Artificial Intelligence**]: Learning

Keywords

Recommending scientific article, Bi-Relational Graph, Iterative RWR, New article recommendation, Old article recommendation

1. INTRODUCTION

With the development of Internet, more and more websites like CiteULike and Mendeley allow researchers to create their own on-line reference libraries for the scientific articles they are interested in. As a consequence, an urgent problem is how to automatically extract the hidden information and effectively recommend an article to the potential relevant researchers.

For finding the interesting articles, keyword searching and citation tracking are popularly used in practice. Both of them are powerful but they have limitations. Recently, recommendation system [6] is applied, where the choice of information sources and the quality of the sources are vital to making recommendation [8].

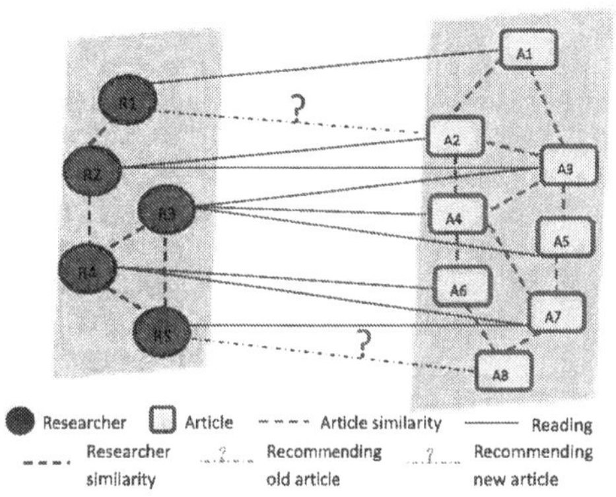

Figure 1: The illustration of Bi-Relation Graph constructed for scientific article recommendation.

In this paper, we focus on the problem of scientific article recommendation. This problem contains two key issues. One is recommending old articles where researchers can understand and learn about the new fields. The other is recommending new articles where researchers can keep up with the state-of-the-art in their discipline. For old article (e.g., A2 in Figure 1), the more researchers read it, the more important it is. Therefore, the opinions of other researchers is important to solve the first issue. However, there is no readership information about any new article (e.g., A8 in Figure 1), in this case, the article content plays an important role in making recommendation.

Generally speaking, recommending scientific article can be taken as a hybrid recommendation [2] problem where both item content and correlation between users and items are known. The typical hybrid recommendation techniques include two categories. One is based on the traditional collaborative filtering (CF) [10] by incorporating item content [1] including item-based CF [7] and CF-Content [13]. The other constructs a general unifying model that incorporates both content and collaborative characteristics. The typical method is collaborative topic regression (CTR) [12] doing collaborative filtering based on latent factor modeling and content analysis based on probabilistic topic modeling.

In order to make use of the existing information sources, a Bi-Relational Graph (BG) is designed to represent recommendation data as shown in Figure 1. The graph contains article similarity subgraph, researcher similarity subgraph, and a bipartite graph connecting articles and researchers. Among them, article similarity is computed based on the article content. The bipartite graph indicates the readership information between articles and researchers, which can also be used to calculate the implicit interest similarity between researchers. Consequently, both articles and researchers are equally regarded as vertices, and scientific article recommendation is transformed to a new problem to measure how closely an article is related to a researcher.

In the literature, random walk with restart (RWR) [11] is a good choice to measure vertex-to-vertex relevance, and has recently applied in recommendation systems [3, 4, 5, 9, 14]. The existing RWR technique is based on a fixed graph, however, the Bi-Relational Graph built for scientific article recommendation could be changed once its subgraph is updated. Thus, we propose an iterative Bi-Relational Graph-based RWR method (BG-IteRWR) to compute the article-researcher relevances with automatical and iterative updating the BG graph. Finally, the weight of dashed line with red question mark in Figure 1 can be predicted for old article recommendation and the weight of dashed line with green question mark can be predicted for new article recommendation. A series of experiments on CiteULike data are conducted to demonstrate that BG-IteRWR outperforms the existing methods for recommending both old and new articles.

2. BI-RELATIONAL GRAPH-BASED RECOMMENDATION

In scientific article recommendation system, we have m researchers $R = \{R_1, R_2, \cdots, R_m\}$ and n articles $A = \{A_1, A_2, \cdots, A_n\}$. Each article has its title and abstract as content, then it can be represented by a feature vector with v vocabulary words, like $A_i = \{A_{i1}, A_{i2}, \cdots, A_{iv}\}$. Then, we can give the pairwise similarities between the articles, denoted as $W_{AA} \in R^{n \times n}$ with $W_{AA}(i1, i2)$ measuring how closely A_{i1} and A_{i2} are related. In experiments, the cosine similarity is used to computer W_{AA}.

Based on the researcher-article readership information, each article is associated with $r_i \le m$ researchers' libraries represented by a binary vector $q_i \in \{0,1\}^m$, such that $q_i(j) = 1$ if A_i appears in R_j researcher's library, otherwise, $q_i(j) = 0$ (empty value) which needs predicting with the recommendation system and let $Q = [q_1, q_2, \cdots, q_m]$. Each column of Q can be taken as an article vector representing the corresponding researcher. The similarity between two columns (e.g., cosine similarity) indicates how these two researchers have the common interests, which is defined as $W_{RR} \in R^{m \times m}$.

2.1 Bi-Relational Graph Construction

Let $\mathcal{G} = (\mathcal{V}_A \bigcup \mathcal{V}_R, \mathcal{E}_{\mathcal{AA}} \bigcup \mathcal{E}_{\mathcal{RR}} \bigcup \mathcal{E}_{\mathcal{AR}})$, where $\mathcal{E}_{\mathcal{AA}} \subseteq \mathcal{V}_A \times \mathcal{V}_A$, $\mathcal{E}_{\mathcal{RR}} \subseteq \mathcal{V}_R \times \mathcal{V}_R$, and $\mathcal{E}_{\mathcal{AR}} \subseteq \mathcal{V}_A \times \mathcal{V}_R$. Among them, $\mathcal{V}_A$ and $\mathcal{V}_R$ indicate the article and researcher vertices set respectively. Obviously, $\mathcal{G}$ covers both article content graph $\mathcal{G}_{\mathcal{A}} = (\mathcal{V}_A, \mathcal{E}_{\mathcal{AA}})$, researcher similarity graph $\mathcal{G}_{\mathcal{R}} = (\mathcal{V}_R, \mathcal{E}_{\mathcal{RR}})$, and they are connected by a bipartite graph $\mathcal{G}_{\mathcal{B}} = (\mathcal{V}_A, \mathcal{V}_R, \mathcal{E}_{\mathcal{AR}})$. $\mathcal{E}_{\mathcal{AA}}$ and $\mathcal{E}_{\mathcal{RR}}$ describe the intra-type relations, while $\mathcal{E}_{\mathcal{AR}}$ describes the inter-type relations, that is why we call $\mathcal{G}$ as Bi-Relational Graph (BG). In order to adopt random walk with restart learning method on BG, we use a matrix to represent $\mathcal{G}$, which can be taken as the transition probability matrix S for a random walk.

In the transition probability matrix S, S_{AA} and S_{RR} are the intra-subgraph transition probability matrices of $\mathcal{G}_{\mathcal{A}}$ and $\mathcal{G}_{\mathcal{R}}$ respectively, and S_{AR} and S_{RA} are the inter-subgraph transition probability matrices between $\mathcal{G}_{\mathcal{A}}$ and $\mathcal{G}_{\mathcal{R}}$. During a random walk process, if the random walker is on a vertex of the article subgraph $\mathcal{G}_{\mathcal{A}}$ that has at least one connection to the researcher subgraph $\mathcal{G}_{\mathcal{R}}$, such as A_2 in Figure 1, it can hop to the researcher subgraph with probability $\beta \in [0, 1]$, or stay on the article subgraph with probability $1-\beta$ and hop to other articles. However, not all articles are associated with researchers, like A_8 in Figure 1. In this case, the random walker has to stay on the article subgraph and hop to other articles, and then hop to researcher subgraph once other articles are connected with researchers. To be more precise, these two situations can be formulated as follows.

- If there is no researcher selecting the ith article, i.e., $\sum_{j=1}^{m} Q(i,j) = 0$, the transition probability in $\mathcal{G}_{\mathcal{A}}$ (i.e., from A_i to A_{i1}) is

$$S_{AA}(i, i1) = W_{AA}(i, i1) / \sum_k W_{AA}(i, k), \quad (1)$$

the transition probability in $\mathcal{G}_{\mathcal{AR}}$ (i.e., from A_i to R_j) is

$$S_{AR}(i, j) = 0. \quad (2)$$

- If some researchers select the ith article, i.e., $\sum_{j=1}^{m} Q(i,j) > 0$, the transition probability in $\mathcal{G}_{\mathcal{A}}$ (i.e., from A_i to A_{i1}) is

$$S_{AA}(i, i1) = (1-\beta) W_{AA}(i, i1) / \sum_k W_{AA}(i, k), \quad (3)$$

the transition probability in $\mathcal{G}_{\mathcal{AR}}$ (i.e., from A_i to R_j) is

$$S_{AR}(i, j) = \beta Q(i, j) / \sum_t Q(i, t). \quad (4)$$

Similarly, a random walker starts with a researcher vertex has the following two situations:

- If there is no article in the jth researcher's library, i.e., $\sum_{i=1}^{n} Q(i,j) = 0$, the transition probability in $\mathcal{G}_{\mathcal{R}}$ (i.e., from R_j to R_{j1}) is

$$S_{RR}(j, j1) = W_{RR}(j, j1) / \sum_k W_{RR}(j, k), \quad (5)$$

the transition probability in $\mathcal{G}_{\mathcal{RA}}$ (i.e., from R_j to A_i) is

$$S_{RA}(j, i) = 0. \quad (6)$$

- If the jth researcher selects some articles, i.e., $\sum_{i=1}^{n} Q(i,j) > 0$, the transition probability in $\mathcal{G}_{\mathcal{R}}$ (i.e., from R_j to R_{j1}) is

$$S_{RR}(j, j1) = (1-\beta) W_{RR}(j, j1) / \sum_k W_{RR}(j, k), \quad (7)$$

the transition probability in $\mathcal{G}_{\mathcal{RA}}$ (i.e., from R_j to A_i) is

$$S_{RA}(j, i) = \beta Q(i, j) / \sum_t Q(t, j). \quad (8)$$

2.2 BG-Based Iterative Recommendation

Once the relatedness between all articles and researchers in BG are known, it is easy to recommend article to the corresponding researchers.

In this paper, we adopt Random Walk with Restart (R-WR) technique to measure the relatedness of two vertices in the graph. In BG graph, the initial researcher correlation subgraph S_{RR} is given, but it is calculated based on Q where the information is incomplete. Thus, a $(n+m)$-dimension column vector p_j^* is constructed for the jth researcher stationary probability to simultaneously update the research-article relation and researcher-researcher correlation, which is defined as

$$P^* = \begin{bmatrix} P_{AR}^* \\ P_{RR}^* \end{bmatrix} \in R^{(n+m)\times m}. \quad (9)$$

In this case, the starting station Y is defined as

$$Y = \begin{bmatrix} Y_{AR} \\ Y_{RR} \end{bmatrix} \in R^{(n+m)\times m}, \quad (10)$$

where $P_{AR}^* \in R^{n\times m}$, $Y_{AR} \in R^{n\times m}$ indicates the relatedness between articles and researchers, and $P_{RR}^* \in R^{m\times m}$, $Y_{RR} \in R^{m\times m}$ for the relatedness between researchers. Among them,

$$Y_{AR}(i,j) = \begin{cases} 1/\sum_t Q(t,j), & if \quad Q(i,j) = 1 \\ 0, & otherwise. \end{cases} \quad (11)$$

$$Y_{RR}(i,j) = \begin{cases} 1, & if \quad i == j \\ 0, & otherwise. \end{cases} \quad (12)$$

Then, the random walk with restart process on S and Y can be defined as

$$P^{(t+1)}(i,j) = (1-\alpha)\sum_{k=1}^{n+m} S(k,i)P^{(t)}(k,j) + \alpha Y(i,j). \quad (13)$$

The stationary probability P^* of random walk process can be determined via the method proposed in [15] as

$$P^*(\cdot,j) = \alpha(I-(1-\alpha)S^T)^{-1}Y(\cdot,j). \quad (14)$$

Since $\max_i \sum_j S(i,j) = 1$, the maximum eigenvalue of S should be less than 1 according to Perron-Frobenius theorem, and then $I-(1-\alpha)S^T$ is positive definite and invertible, thus, P^* is solvable.

The above RWR on S is able to learn a better researcher correlation matrix P_{RR}^* from the original matrix S_{RR} which is directly built from the input data. Thus, it may improve the overall performance by replacing S_{RR} with the learned matrix P_{RR}^*. Repeat this process, we can recommend good articles to the corresponding researchers.

The proposed BG-IteRWR is different from the RWR method in [5] in two facets. Firstly, we constructed different graph by considering the implicit researcher-researcher correlations and explicit article-article correlations, while Konstas et al. [5] ignored the former one which also leads to different RWR learning process. Secondly, the random walker in [5] has the same probability to hop between inter-type and intra-type subgraph (i.e., $\beta = 1/2$), which is not always tenable and may depend on data as shown in next section.

3. EXPERIMENTAL RESULTS

3.1 DataSet

The performance of our proposed method is evaluated on CiteULike data set and the preprocessed version is provided by Wang[1]. There are 5551 researchers and 16980 articles with 204986 observed researcher-article pairs. Each researcher has average 37 articles in the library ranging from 10 to 403, and each article is selected by average 12 researchers ranging from 1 to 321. For all article set, top 8000 distinct words with higher tf-idf value are chosen as the vocabulary, then each article is represented as a vector of vocabulary. The value of each element is in $\{0,1\}$, 1 indicates that the corresponding word occurs in the current article, otherwise the value is 0.

Two recommendation problems, new article and old article recommendation, are tested on CiteULike as follows.

- Recommending old article: we split the researcher-article pairs into 5 folds for each article that appears at least 5 times in the researchers' libraries, iteratively consider each fold as a test set and others as training set, and then record the final average results. The articles appearing fewer than 5 times are always put in the training set.

- Recommending new article: we evenly group all articles into 5 folds, iterative consider each fold as a testing set and others as training set, and then record the final average results. The article appears in training set, all researcher-article pairs information are kept, and the articles in testing set have no researcher information.

3.2 Methodology

In this paper, the aim of recommender system is to find good articles for researchers. Therefore, the well known evaluation metric *Recall@N* [6] is adopted. The higher Recall, the better the recommendation performance.

$$Recall@N = \frac{\text{number of relevant researchers in top N}}{\text{total number of relevant researchers}}$$

Since both article content and researcher-article readership information are used in recommendation system, four popular existing methods are taken as baselines including CF, CF-Content, CTR and RWR. Both CF and CF-Content are item-based collaborative filtering, and we use vector cosine similarity model to compute the item-item similarities. For traditional CF, only article-researcher readership information is used.

In CF-Content, ten β values in $[0,1]$ with step 0.1 are tested and the best one is recorded. In the graphical modeling method CTR [12], we use the best setting for parameters $\lambda_u = 0.01$, $\lambda_v = 100$, $a = 1$, $b = 0.01$, $K = 200$. In [5], RWR model is used to combine social network and user-item interaction information, which can also be adopted to combine article content and researcher-article readership information by setting $UU = 0$ and $TrTr$ as the article similarity in Figure 1 of [5]. Finally, a query vector of articles is returned for each researcher, which provides the recommendation results.

3.3 Comparisons and Discussion

Figure 2 gives the overall performance for old article and new article recommendation. For Recall, we vary the number of returned relevant researchers $N = 5, 10, 20, 40, 60$ re-

[1]http://www.cs.cmu.edu/ chongw/data/citeulike/

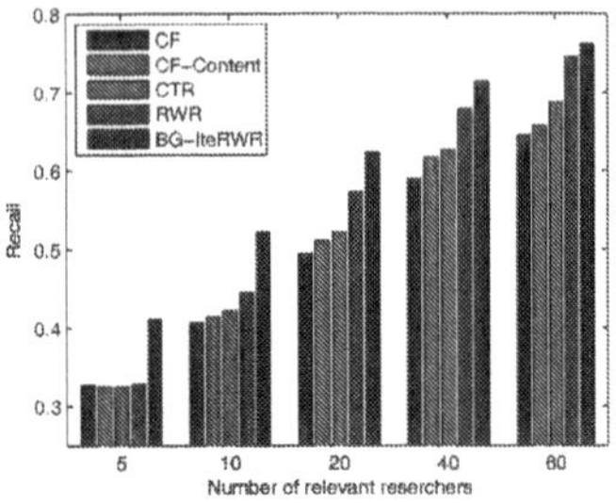

(a) Recall on old article recommendation

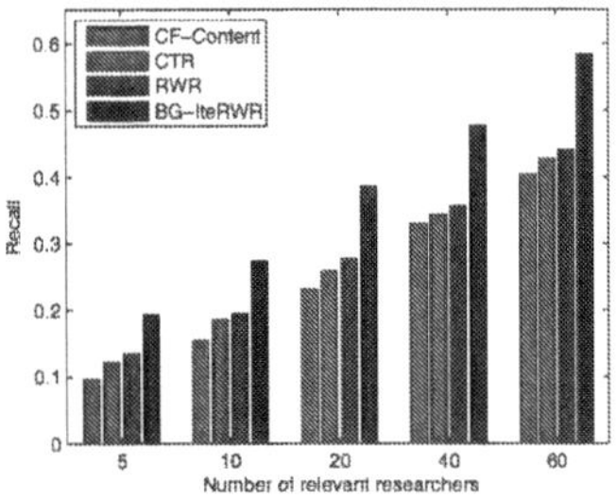

(b) Recall on new article recommendation

Figure 2: Comparison of old/new article recommendation with Recall@N metrics.

spectively. Among them, CF only considers the researcher-article readership information, thus it can not recommend new article because there is no relevant researcher for a new coming article. CF-Content, CTR [12], RWR [5] and BG-IteRWR consider article content except for the readership information, thus they has ability to recommend new article.

It is obvious that BG-IteRWR outperforms the existing methods. For both old and new article recommendation, the improvement is greater when the returned relevant researchers is small on Recall, which indicates that BG-IteRWR is able to find the potential researchers which are really interested in the corresponding articles. One main reason is as follows. BG-IteRWR considers the researcher correlations (sub-matrix S_{RR} in transition probability matrix S) and iteratively updates it, which are helpful to recommend an article to the researchers with similar interest. However, such information is ignored in CF, CF-Content, CTR and RWR.

4. CONCLUSIONS

A novel Bi-Relational Graph model is proposed to combine article content and researcher-article readership information in a unified framework for scientific article recommendation system. Based on BG, we design an iterative random walk with restarts technique to predict both article-researcher relevances and researcher-researcher correlations. The article-researcher relevance can be used to directly recommend both new and old article to the corresponding researchers. Meanwhile, the proposed BG-IteRWR method makes use of the learned researcher-researcher correlations to improve the final recommending performance, and is applied on a real world data set CiteULike. The encouraging experimental results demonstrate the effectiveness of BG-IteRWR.

5. ACKNOWLEDGMENTS

This work was supported by the Fundamental Research Funds for the Central Universities (2011JBM030), NSFC (60905028, 61033013), and Ph.D. Programs Foundation of Ministry of Education of China (20120009110006).

6. REFERENCES

[1] J. Basilico and T. Hofmann. Unifying collaborative and content-based filtering. In *Proc. of ICML*, pages 448–456, 2004.

[2] R. Burk. Hybrid recommender systems: survey and experiments. *User Modeling and User-Adapted Interaction*, 12:331–370, 2002.

[3] F. Fouss, A. Pirotte, J.-M. Renders, and M. Saerens. Random-walk conputation of similarities between nodes of a graph with application to collaborative recommendation. *IEEE Trans. on KDE*, 9(3):355–369, 2007.

[4] M. Jamali and M. Ester. Trustwalker: a random walk model for combining trust-based and item-based recommendation. In *Proc. of ACM SIGKDD*, 2009.

[5] I. Konstas, V. Stathopoulos, and J. M. Jose. On social networks and collaborative recommendation. In *Proc. of ACM SIGIR*, pages 195–202, 2009.

[6] L. Líż, C. H. Yueng, M. Medo, Y.-C. Zhang, Z.-K. Zhang, and T. Zhou. Recommender systems. *Physics Report*, 519:1–49, 2012.

[7] B. Sarwar, G. Karypis, J. Konstan, and J. Riedl. Item-based collaborative filtering recommendation algorithms. In *Proc. of WWW*, pages 285–295, 2001.

[8] B. Schafer, J. A. Konstan, and J. Riedl. E-commerce recommendation applications. *Data Mining and Knowledge Discovery*, 5(1):115–153, 2001.

[9] S. Shang, S. R. Kulkarni, P. W. Cuff, and P. Hui. A random walk based model incorporating social information for recommendations. In *Proc. of Intl. Workshop on Machine Learning for Signal Processing*, 2012.

[10] X. Su and T. M. Khoshgoftaar. A survey of collaborative filtering techniques. *Advances in Artificial Intelligence*, 2009.

[11] H. H. Tong, C. Faloutsos, and J. Y. Pan. Fast random walk with restart and its applications. In *Proc. of ICDM*, pages 613–622, 2006.

[12] C. Wang and D. M. Blei. Collaborative topic modeling for recommending scientific articles. In *Proc. of ACM SIGKDD*, pages 448–456, 2011.

[13] J. Wang, A. de Vries, and M. Reinders. Unifying user-based and item-based collaborative filtering approaches by similarity fusion. In *Proc. of ACM SIGIR*, pages 501–508, 2006.

[14] H. Yildirim and M. S. Krishnamoorthy. A random walk method for alleviating the sparsity problem in collaborative filtering. In *Proc. of ACM RecSys*, pages 131–138, 2008.

[15] D. Zhou, O. Bousquet, T. Lal, J. Weston, and B. Scholkopf. Learning with local and global consistency. In *Proc. of NIPS*, 2004.

Sample Selection for MCMC-based Recommender Systems

Thierry Silbermann
University of Konstanz
78457 Konstanz, Germany
thierry.silbermann@uni-konstanz.de

Immanuel Bayer
University of Konstanz
78457 Konstanz, Germany
immanuel.bayer@uni-konstanz.de

Steffen Rendle
University of Konstanz
78457 Konstanz, Germany
steffen.rendle@uni-konstanz.de

ABSTRACT

Bayesian Inference with Markov Chain Monte Carlo (MCMC) has been shown to provide high prediction quality in recommender systems. The advantage over learning methods such as coordinate descent / alternating least-squares (ALS) or (stochastic) gradient descent (SGD) is that MCMC takes uncertainty into account and moreover MCMC can easily integrate priors to learn regularization values. For factorization models, MCMC inference can be done with efficient Gibbs samplers.

However, MCMC algorithms are not point estimators, but they generate a chain of models. The whole chain of models is used to calculate predictions. For large scale models like factorization methods with millions or billions of model parameters, saving the whole chain of models is very storage intensive and can even get infeasible in practice.

In this paper, we address this problem and show how a small subset from the chain of models can approximate the predictive distribution well. We use the fact that models from the chain are correlated and propose online selection techniques to store only a small subset of the models. We perform an empirical analysis on the large scale Netflix dataset with several Bayesian factorization models, including matrix factorization and SVD++. We show that the proposed selection techniques approximate the predictions well with only a small subset of model samples.

Categories and Subject Descriptors

H.3.3 [**Information Systems**]: Information Search and Retrieval—*Information filtering*

General Terms

Algorithms, Experimentation, Measurement, Performance

Keywords

MCMC, Markov Chain Monte Carlo, Recommender System, Factorization Model, Bayesian Inference

RecSys'13, October 12–16, 2013, Hong Kong, China.
Copyright 2013 ACM 978-1-4503-2409-0/13/10 ...$15.00.
http://dx.doi.org/10.1145/2507157.2507224.

1. INTRODUCTION

Many state-of-the-art recommender systems rely on complex machine learning models. The models usually have a large number of model parameters and several regularization parameters to prevent overfitting. The most common learning algorithms for large scale recommender systems are based on (stochastic) gradient descent (SGD) or alternating least squares (ALS)/ coordinate descent. These algorithms try to find the most probable values for the model parameters. The regularization parameters are mostly searched by external methods, e.g. grid search.

Recently, Bayesian inference with Markov Chain Monte Carlo algorithms (MCMC) has been proposed for learning large scale recommender systems [5]. The advantage of MCMC over SGD and ALS is that MCMC takes the uncertainty in the model parameters into account (resulting often in higher prediction quality) and MCMC allows to jointly make inference over model parameters and regularization values.

SGD and ALS are point estimators and their learning algorithms result in one state of model parameters, which can be used directly for prediction. In contrast to that, the steps ('iterations') in an MCMC algorithm generate samples of the model parameters. Each generated sample is a valid state which should be taken into account for prediction. From a practical point of view, the prediction for an MCMC algorithm is the average prediction of each step, i.e. the model parameters of each step make a prediction and the predictions are averaged. This means for MCMC algorithms, the whole chain of model parameters has to be available when predicting. Whereas the chain can be compressed into a single model state for linear regression models, this is not possible for non-linear models such as factorization models where the full chain has to be considered. Storing the full chain is demanding or even infeasible for models with a large number of model parameters, e.g. factorization models in recommender systems with millions or billions of model parameters.

The contributions of this work are as follows:

1. The important practical problem of handling chains over large models with MCMC inference is raised.
2. Two online-selection algorithms are proposed that make use of the correlation of subsequent chain states.
3. The properties of sample selection algorithms are studied on the large scale Netflix dataset for several state-of-the-art Bayesian recommender models.

2. PROBLEM DESCRIPTION

Recommendation tasks such as rating or click-through prediction can be formalized as a supervised prediction task, where for a case/ data point $\mathbf{x}$, a target variable y should be predicted based on historical observations $S_{\text{train}} = \{(\mathbf{x}_1, y_1), (\mathbf{x}_2, y_2), \dots\}$. To simplify readability, we discuss mostly regression (i.e. $y \in \mathbb{R}$) but our results also hold for classification (i.e. $y \in \{+, -\}$). As common in machine learning, we assume that there exists a function $\hat{y}$ that models the unobserved relation between the target y and the predictor variables $\mathbf{x}$. The model equation $\hat{y}$ typically depends on a set of model parameters Θ.

Bayesian Inference with MCMC.

The model parameters Θ of popular recommender models like matrix factorization (MF), SVD++ [1] or factorization machines (FM) [3] can be learned with several algorithms. Stochastic gradient descent (SGD) or alternating least-squares are popular point estimators, that try to maximize the likelihood $\text{argmax}_\Theta\, p(S_{\text{train}}|\Theta)\, p(\Theta|\Theta_H)$ given the hyperparameters Θ_H (typically the regularization values). Thus, the result of SGD and ALS algorithms is a single state of model parameters Θ. For predicting, the unknown target y of a new case $\mathbf{x}$ the model equation $\hat{y}(\mathbf{x}|\Theta)$ is computed.

In contrast to point estimators, Bayesian inference uses the whole predictive distribution of the target y given the case $\mathbf{x}$ and the whole dataset S_{train}

$$p(y|\mathbf{x}, S_{\text{train}}). \tag{1}$$

With marginalization over model parameters and hyperparameters (Θ, Θ_H) and the typical conditional independence assumptions, the predictive distribution can be written as

$$p(y|\mathbf{x}, S_{\text{train}}) = \int p(y|\mathbf{x}, \Theta, \Theta_H)\, p(\Theta|S_{\text{train}}, \Theta_H)\, p(\Theta_H)\, d(\Theta, \Theta_0). \tag{2}$$

For complex models, this integral cannot be evaluated analytically and it is approximated by samples $\Theta^1, \dots \Theta^M$ drawn from $p(\Theta|S_{\text{train}}, \Theta_H)$

$$p(y|\mathbf{x}, S_{\text{train}}) \approx \frac{1}{M} \sum_{i=1}^{M} p(y|\mathbf{x}, \Theta^i). \tag{3}$$

Given this predictive distribution, one can calculate any statistic of interest. E.g. for a real valued target variable, the prediction (expectation value) of the target y for the case $\mathbf{x}$ is[1]

$$E(y|\mathbf{x}, S_{\text{train}}) \approx \frac{1}{M} \sum_{i=1}^{M} \hat{y}(\mathbf{x}|\Theta^i). \tag{4}$$

Sample Selection for MCMC.

The advantages of MCMC over SGD and ALS come to the prize that the chain of models $\Theta^1, \dots \Theta^M$ has to be available when a case $\mathbf{x}$ is predicted (see eq. 4). Compared to SGD and ALS, the storage and prediction complexity increases linearly in M. Especially if the model has many parameters and the chain is long (i.e. M is large), storing the whole chain can get very expensive or even infeasible.

[1]Here, the likelihood is $y|\mathbf{x}, \Theta^i \sim \mathcal{N}(\hat{y}(\mathbf{x}|\Theta^i), 1/\lambda)$.

In this paper, we investigate techniques to select a subset of states from the chain to reduce the storage and prediction complexity. We will make use of the fact, that samples from MCMC are not i.i.d. but are correlated. Formally, we develop selection methods that select a subset $\mathcal{I} \subset \{1, \dots, M\}$ from the full chain such that the size of the subset $|\mathcal{I}| = m$ is considerably smaller than the full chain: $m \ll M$. The algorithms will decide during MCMC sampling if a sample Θ^i should be kept or discarded. This means in total only $m \ll M$ model states have to be stored and prediction simplifies to

$$E(y|\mathbf{x}, S_{\text{train}}) \approx \frac{1}{m} \sum_{i \in \mathcal{I}} \hat{y}(\mathbf{x}, \Theta^i).$$

Remarks.

For regression with a linear model (e.g. linear regression), one can compress the whole chain into a single state $\overline{\Theta} := \frac{1}{M}\sum_{i=1}^{M} \Theta^i$ because $\frac{1}{M}\sum_{i=1}^{M} \hat{y}(\mathbf{x}|\Theta^i) = \sum_{i=1}^{M} \hat{y}(\mathbf{x}|\overline{\Theta})$. It is very important to note that with non-linear models (e.g. MF, SVD++, FMs) this is not possible and the whole chain is needed for prediction.

3. SAMPLE SELECTION STRATEGIES

In the following, we present algorithms to select a subset $\mathcal{I}$ of m states from the chain of models $\Theta^1, \dots \Theta^M$. Our online algorithm is integrated in the MCMC sampler and has to decide on the fly if a state is selected without knowing any subsequent state.

In practice, there is typically a limited storage for models. We assume that at maximum m models can be stored. With MCMC sampling, long chains $M \gg m$ can be created but in our setting even during sampling at maximum m states (models) can be stored. Thus online selection methods have to decide on the fly if a model should be kept or discarded.

Algorithm 1 shows the basic idea of integrating sample selection in MCMC. The sampler starts with an initial state Θ^0 and an empty set $\mathcal{I}$ of selected states. Then samples are generated iteratively and for each sample an online selection method decides how to refine $\mathcal{I}$. Basically, the online selection algorithm can decide to include or discard the current state Θ^i. If the state is included, the selection method has to make sure that the storage is not exceeded ($|\mathcal{I}| \leq m$) and a previously selected state might have to be discarded – i.e. the current state *overwrites* an existing state.

Algorithm 1 MCMC Sampling with Online Selection

```
1: Θ^0 ← random
2: I ← {}                              ▷ index set for subset to store
3: for i = 1 to M do
4:    sample Θ^i                       ▷ e.g. with Gibbs [5, 3]
5:    I ← onlineSelection(I, i, m)
6:    if i ∈ I then
7:       store Θ^i
8:    end if
9:    discard any Θ^j where j ∉ I      ▷ limit storage to I
10: end for
11: return I
```

Next, we discuss several choices for online selection algorithms (i.e. for line 5 in Algorithm 1).

Early Stopping.

If the samples in the chain would be i.i.d., any subset from $\{1,\ldots,M\}$ could be chosen. Under this assumption, taking the first m samples would be the easiest choice. An advantage of this strategy is that the sampling process could be stopped already after only m steps without the need to sample all M states. Clearly, the assumption of independent samples does not hold for an MCMC algorithm. Nevertheless, we use this strategy as a baseline which more sophisticated selection methods should outperform.

Equidistant Selection.

A basic property of any MCMC algorithm is that each sample is generated from its preceding state – e.g. Θ^i generated from Θ^{i-1}. Thus correlation of neighbors is supposed to be largest. To decrease correlation of selected states, states with maximum distance can be chosen. E.g. if $m = 2$, we may want to choose the two states at position $1/3\,M$ and $2/3\,M$. Or for $m = 10$, the states at position $1/11\,M, \ldots 10/11\,M$. Equidistant selection is an unsupervised strategy which does not take the states of the particular chain into account. E.g. at some position j there might be more correlated states than in other regions – e.g. because the sampler got *stuck* for a short time.

Holdout Selection.

Next, we propose a supervised online sample selection algorithm. The overall goal of sample selection is to find the subset $\mathcal{I}$ of m states with the best predictive accuracy. In general, we are interested in a low error (high quality) on an unknown test set S_{test}. As the test set and especially its labels are unknown, a holdout/ validation set S_{valid} can be used to guide the selection algorithm. Any kind of evaluation function can be used for measuring the quality of the selected size $\mathcal{I}$ on the set S_{valid}, e.g. the root mean square error (RMSE). The selected subset $\mathcal{I}$ can be refined online by trying to replace a state $j \in \mathcal{I}$ with the new sample i if and only if the holdout error decreases for the set $(\mathcal{I} \setminus \{j\}) \cup \{i\}$.

4. EVALUATION

In the evaluation, we study the properties of the selection strategies on four models. We compare online selection strategies among each other and also use basic *backward* and *forward* selections strategies. *Backward* and *forward* are offline selection methods because they have access to all M states – i.e. the full chain. The *backward* method starts with the full chain and removes the state that gives the lowest RMSE after deletion. The *forward* method starts with an empty subset and adds the state that gives the lowest RMSE after addition. Both strategies are used only as lower bounds because we want to avoid to store the whole chain. The overall interest is to examine if the selection strategies succeed in selecting a small portion $m \ll M$ of the whole chain while preserving most of the predictive information.

4.1 Experimental Setup

The proposed selection strategies are evaluated on the Netflix prize dataset. The dataset consists of about 480,000 users and 17,770 movies. We use the official prize split with a training set of $|S_{\text{train}}| = 100,480,507$ observed ratings. As a validation set, the private leaderboard set with $|S_{\text{valid}}| = 1,408,342$ is used. To allow comparing our results to the existing work on the Netflix prize, we report RMSE scores for the public leaderboard set with $|S_{\text{test}}| = 1,408,789$ ratings. All sets (S_{train}, S_{valid}, S_{test}) are disjoint.

Four recommender models are investigated: matrix factorization with biases (MF), SVD++ [1], a time-aware matrix factorization and time-aware SVD++[2]. The smallest model (MF) has already more than 60,000,000 model parameters (for a single state of the chain) which justifies the need for efficient sample selection. All models use Bayesian inference with the Gibbs sampler described in [3] and for each model, a chain of $M = 512$ samples is generated. The sampler is initialized with a randomly generated state ($\Theta^0 \sim \mathcal{N}(0, 0.1)$) and all subsequent 512 samples are used. We use factorization machines from libFM [3] for all experiments. The number of latent dimensions for the four factorization models is $k = 128$.

4.2 Results

Prediction Quality.

The first experiment investigates the prediction quality of the proposed techniques under a varying size of selected states. The experiment allows to compare the selection strategies among each other and allows to investigate how many samples are necessary for a good prediction quality. Figure 1 shows the RMSE on the test set (S_{test}) depending on the size m of the selected subset $\mathcal{I}$. As expected, the error of the selection techniques gets more similar the larger m. For small subsets ($m \ll M$), the differences between the selection techniques become clearly visible.

Online Selection.

Comparing the online selection methods, one can see that early stopping is clearly outperformed by equidistant and greedy holdout selection. This result is in line with our expectation because all states selected by early stopping are correlated whereas equidistant and greedy holdout selection favor uncorrelated states. Secondly, greedy holdout selection outperforms equidistant selection. This indicates that the states of the generated chain are not perfectly equidistant distributed – e.g. because sometimes it takes longer (more states) to move into another region of the posterior distribution. The holdout set seems to be well suited to identify such changes.

Subset Quality.

The experiments show that a small subset of states can approximate the predictive quality of the whole chain very closely. Note that the vertical axis of the plots is scaled under a limit of 0.90 which is known to be a very good result for MF on the Netflix dataset. With 30 states (less than 6% of the 512 states), online holdout selection already achieves a very low error. With 50 states (about 12%), the quality is almost as good as the full chain.

An interest finding is that with backward, forward and holdout selection, the best quality is not achieved with the full chain ($m = M$) but with a subset of models ($m < M$). The reason could be that the validation set is slightly more representative for the test set than the training set. The

[2]The time-aware MF and time-aware SVD++ use a simpler treatment of time than the timeSVD++ model of Koren [2]. See [4] for details about the time-aware MF and time-aware SVD++ used in our experiments.

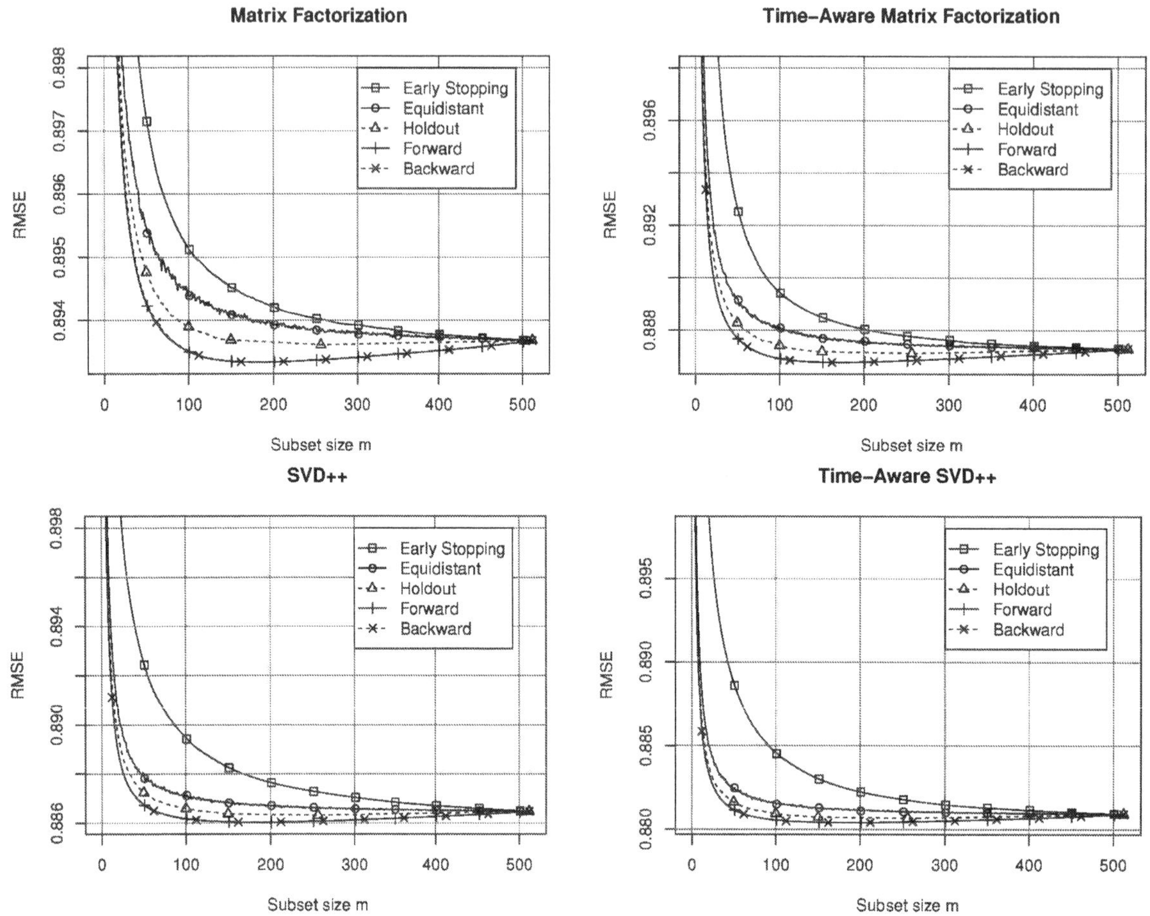

Figure 1: RMSE value on Netflix test set for varying subset size m. Online selection strategies *equidistant* and *holdout* are compared to lower bounds generated by *forward/backward* offline selection and *early stopping* baseline.

results indicate that holdout selection can correct this bias by selecting the right subset. Though due to the scale of the vertical axis, the improvements are only marginal.

5. CONCLUSION

In this paper, we presented the problem of selecting states for MCMC-based models. This problem is very relevant in practice because storing the whole chain of models is impractical for large recommender systems with millions or billions of model parameters. We have proposed subset selection strategies that can select during MCMC sampling whether or not to store a sample. Both equidistant and holdout selection are online methods that can be integrated easily in existing MCMC samplers. We have shown empirically for four state-of-the-art recommender models that the proposed algorithms generate high quality subsets. With less than 10% of the original chain, our best online strategy was able to produce predictions almost as good as the full chain. Moreover, the prediction quality of online holdout selection clearly outperforms early stopping and is almost as good as the offline selection bounds.

Acknowledgement

This work was supported by DFG under grant RE3311/2-1.

6. REFERENCES

[1] Y. Koren. Factorization meets the neighborhood: a multifaceted collaborative filtering model. In *KDD '08: Proceeding of the 14th ACM SIGKDD international conference on Knowledge discovery and data mining*, pages 426–434, New York, NY, USA, 2008. ACM.

[2] Y. Koren. Collaborative filtering with temporal dynamics. In *KDD '09: Proceedings of the 15th ACM SIGKDD international conference on Knowledge discovery and data mining*, pages 447–456, New York, NY, USA, 2009. ACM.

[3] S. Rendle. Factorization machines with libFM. *ACM Trans. Intell. Syst. Technol.*, 3(3):57:1–57:22, May 2012.

[4] S. Rendle. Scaling factorization machines to relational data. In *Proceedings of the 39th international conference on Very Large Data Bases*, Trento, Italy, 2013.

[5] R. Salakhutdinov and A. Mnih. Bayesian probabilistic matrix factorization using Markov chain Monte Carlo. In *Proceedings of the 25th international conference on Machine learning*, ICML '08, pages 880–887, New York, NY, USA, 2008. ACM.

Selecting Content-Based Features for Collaborative Filtering Recommenders

Royi Ronen, Noam Koenigstein, Elad Ziklik and Nir Nice
Microsoft Israel
{royir,noamko,eladz,nicen}@microsoft.com

ABSTRACT

We study the problem of scoring and selecting content-based features for a collaborative filtering (CF) recommender system. Content-based features play a central role in mitigating the "cold start" problem in commercial recommenders. They are also useful in other related tasks, such as recommendation explanation and visualization. However, traditional feature selection methods do not generalize well to recommender systems. As a result, commercial systems typically use manually crafted and selected features. This work presents a framework for automated selection of informative content-based features, that is independent of the type of recommender system or the type of features. We evaluate on recommenders from different domains: books, movies and smart-phone apps, and show effective results on each. In addition, we show how to use the proposed methods to generate meaningful features from text.

Categories and Subject Descriptors

H.2.8 [**Database Management**]: Data Applications - *Data Mining.*

Keywords

Feature Selection, Recommender Systems, Collaborative Filtering, Content Based, Cold Start

1. INTRODUCTION

Collaborative Filtering (CF) recommender systems have become an essential component in many in e-commerce sites and digital markets such as Amazon, Ebay and the Xbox Marketplace [8, 12, 15]. CF algorithms are typically favored over content-based algorithms [11] because of their overall higher accuracy in predicting common purchase patterns. However, by their nature, CF algorithms face challenges in modeling and recommending items with little or no usage (the "cold-start" problem [16]). Items meta-data in the form of content-based features, has been used to alleviate the cold-start problem and improve accuracy [1, 3, 4, 5]. Features are also useful for providing explanations to recommendations [17] and for visualization [7].

RecSys'13, October 12–16, 2013, Hong Kong, China.

ACM 978-1-4503-2409-0/13/09 ...$15.00.
http://dx.doi.org/10.1145/2507157.2507203.

This work studies the problem of evaluating the quality of meta-data features. We present an algorithmic framework which is independent of the specific recommendation algorithm for which the selection is made. Instead, the recommendation algorithm and other parameters are pluggable variables. Two types of selection are discussed: one for scoring meta-data attributes, and another for scoring meta-data labels (to be defined later on). Both have been successfully used to enhance recommendations in the Xbox marketplace, serving recommendations to more then 50 million users worldwide [8, 12, 14, 13].

We evaluate our methods and show their high effectiveness by experimenting with books, movies and data from windows Phone 8 smart-phone apps. In addition, we show how to use the framework to automatically generate informative labels from item descriptions and present the extracted labels for a qualitative evaluation.

1.1 Content-Based Features

Item catalogs in e-commerce marketplaces typically include meta-data features in the form of *attributes*. The attributes may be numerical, categorical, ordinal, binary, etc. For example, some common attributes are *price*, *brand* and *is-on-sale*. Another common type of features are labels, or tags, assigned to items by consumers, experts, or extracted from text by an algorithm. A label is typically a word, an n-gram, or a short phrase describing the item. Labels follow the 'bag-of-words' model. They form a closed dictionary, and every label may or may not be assigned to any item. Some examples of movie labels are: *location-usa*, *horror*, *kids* and *funny*.

In most catalogs there exists a subset of features that is highly informative with regard to the recommendation task at hand. However, many other features are often redundant or irrelevant with regard to CF. For example, in the context of books recommendations, *author* is informative, while *cover-color* is not. Despite a substantial body of work on feature selection for Data Mining algorithms, for most algorithms it is unclear how to extend them to the case of a recommendation system.

1.2 On Feature Selection

We briefly survey the three main categories of feature selection algorithms:

Wrapper methods evaluate different subsets of features by training a model for each subset and then evaluating each subset's contribution on a validation dataset. As the number of all possible subsets is factorial in the number of features, different heuristics are used to choose "promising" subsets (forward-selection, backward-elimination, tree-induction, etc.). Wrapper methods are independent of the prediction algorithm.

Filter methods are typically based on heuristic measures, such as *Mutual Information* or *Pearson Correlation*, to score features based on their information contents w.r.t. the prediction task. Similar to wrapper methods, filter methods are also independent of the algorithm in use. However, they do not require training many models and therefore scale well for large datasets. Yet, filter methods can not be naturally extended to recommender systems, in which the prediction target varies and depends both on the user's history and on the item under consideration. This work proposes a framework and algorithms to address the above difficulties.

Embedded methods are a family of algorithms in which the feature selection is performed in the course of the training phase. Unlike wrapper methods, they are not based on cross-validation and therefore scale with the size of the data. However, since the feature selection is an inherent property of the algorithm, an embedded method is tightly coupled with the specific model: If the recommendation algorithm is replaced, features selection needs to be revisited (e.g., in the context of recommendation systems see [9]).

2. FEATURE SCORING ALGORITHMS

As explained above, we distinct between two types of item features: *attributes* and *labels*. For attributes, we denote by $s.a$ the value that item s has for the attribute a. For labels, we denote by $s.L$ the set of labels associated with the item s ("bag-of-words").

Our algorithms depend on a pluggable features similarity function $sim(\cdot,\cdot)$ between two attribute values or between two labels. The function $sim(\cdot,\cdot)$ may be a content-based function that depends on features values. Alternatively, $sim(\cdot,\cdot)$ can be a CF similarity function based on users who purchased items with features f_1 and f_2. An example of a simple content-based similarity is $sim(f_1, f_2) = \delta(f_1, f_2)$ which equals 1 if $f_1 = f_2$ and 0 otherwise. An example of a CF similarity function is the cosine similarity based on the users of items with f_1 and f_2

We denote by $H_u = \{h_{u1}, h_{u2}, \ldots, h_{un}\}$ the set of n items in user u's history. The set H_u is used by an implicit-feedback recommender to produce a set of k recommended items denoted by $R_k(H_u) = \{r_{u1}, r_{u2}, \ldots, r_{uk}\}$. For the explicit-feedback case, H_u is also associated with numeric ratings.

The recommendation algorithm, $R_k(\cdot)$, is also pluggable to the framework. Different applications may benefit from different $R_k(\cdot)$'s and $sim(\cdot,\cdot)$'s. In Section 3, we discuss some of the concrete similarity measures and the recommender system we use.

2.1 Algorithms

We perform feature selection by computing a relevance score for each feature and then selecting the highest-scoring (i.e., most informative) features. Algorithm 1 and Algorithm 2 describe our algorithms for computing a relevance score for attributes and labels, respectively. Both algorithms are based on the ratio between two variables b_1 and b_2: b_1 is proportional to the similarity of the feature under consideration w.r.t. relevant items according to $R_k(\cdot)$. b_2 is a normalizer which is proportional to the similarity of the feature under consideration w.r.t. random items. The ratio b_1/b_2 measures the *normalized* relevance of the feature with regard to recommended items.

Algorithm 1 ScoreAttribute(Attribute a)

```
Take a sample of n seed user histories {H_1, H_2, ..., H_n};
for each user history H_u do
  Compute k recommended items R_k(H_u) = {r_u1, r_u2, ..., r_uk};
  for each pair (h_ui, r_uj) s.t. h_ui ∈ H_u, r_uj ∈ R_k(H_u) do
    b_1 = b_1 + sim(h_ui.a, r_uj.a);
    Pick a random item r_rand;
    b_2 = b_2 + sim(h_ui.a, r_rand.a);
  end for
end for
return b_1/b_2;
```

Algorithm 2 ScoreLabel(Label l)

```
Take a sample of n seed user histories {H_1, H_2, ..., H_n};
for each user history H_u do
  Compute k recommended items R_k(H_u) = {r_u1, r_u2, ..., r_uk};
  for each pair (h_ui, r_uj) s.t. h_ui ∈ H_u, r_uj ∈ R_k(H_u) do
    Let l_1 be the label in r_uj.L closest to l according to sim(·,·);
    b_1 = b_1 + sim(l, l_1);
    Pick a random item r_rand;
    Let l_2 be the label in r_rand closest to l according to sim(·,·);
    b_2 = b_2 + sim(l, l_2);
  end for
end for
return b_1/b_2;
```

Figure 1: Computing attribute and label scores

2.2 Generalizing Lift

Interestingly, our methods can be seen as a generalization of the lift measure commonly used outside the context of recommendation systems. For the particular case where $sim(v_1, v_2) = \delta(v_1, v_2)$, the parameter b_1 counts co-occurrences of the feature in user histories and in their relevant recommended items. The parameter b_2 counts co-occurrences of the feature in user histories and in random items. Let E_1 be the event where a recommended item r is a "good" recommendation to a user with history H_u (i.e., appears in the top-k recommendations). Let E_2 be the event where a recommended item r, not necessarily "good", has the same feature as an item in H_u. It can be easily shown that under this particular settings, ranking according to b_1/b_2 coincides with the empirical $lift(E_1 \Rightarrow E_2)$:

$$lift(E_1 \Rightarrow E_2) \stackrel{\text{def}}{=} \frac{P_r(E_2|E_1)}{P_r(E_2)} = \frac{b_1}{b_2}. \quad (1)$$

3. IMPLEMENTATION AND EVALUATION

Feature scoring for recommendation systems is not well studied. We thus evaluate the feature scoring algorithm using a novel cold item representation task for Matrix Factorization (MF) models. MF models represent items and users by trait vectors in a low dimensional latent space. The inner product between a user vector and an item vector is

	Author	Publisher	Year of Publication
Score	3.4	1.67	1.15
RMSE	0.98	1.72	2.19

Table 1: Reconstruction results for the books dataset.

proportional to the affinity between the user and the item [10]. We perform our evaluation as follows: After training a MF model we iteratively remove a random item vector from the model and attempt to reconstruct its trait vector based on other item vectors having a similar features (labels or attribute values). We repeat this reconstruction process for N items, each time reconstructing a different item vector.

Formally, let $q_i \in \mathbb{R}^D$ be an item vector of a removed item i from a trained MF model with dimensionality D. We measure the ability of each single feature f to reconstruct q_i based on other items which are similar to i according to the feature f. For each test item i, we find a set of items $S_f(i)$ whose f values are similar to that of item i's value for f. We then compute a reconstructed vector $\hat{q}_i^f$ for i according to $S_f(i)$ as follows:

$$\hat{q}_i^f = \frac{1}{|S_f(i)|} \sum_{j \in S_f(i)} q_j. \quad (2)$$

Finally, we measure the quality of a reconstruction according to the Root Mean Squared Error (RMSE) and score the features quality by averaging all reconstructed item vectors:

$$\text{RMSE}(f) = \sqrt{\frac{1}{N} \sum_{i=1}^{N} ||q_i - \hat{q}_i^f||^2}. \quad (3)$$

where N is the number of reconstructed vectors and $|| \cdot ||^2$ denotes the $\mathcal{L}_2$ norm.

This reconstruction process is designed to cope with the cold-start problem for items. When a new item i is introduced into the catalog, we wish to construct a trait vector in order to integrate i into an existing model even before having any usage data for i. This process is successfully used in the Xbox movies recommender. We note that while this evaluation process is specific to the cold-start representation problem for items in a MF model, the presented feature scoring framework is general to any task and any recommendation algorithm.

3.1 Results

We evaluate with two datasets: The book-crossing dataset [18] and a dataset from the Xbox Movies recommender (smartphone apps are considered in Section 4). As explained, we are interested in implicit-feedback. We use the algorithm of [12] to learn trait vectors for items, as well as for ranking recommended items in Algorithms 1 and 2.

Books: Each book in [18] is associated with three attributes: *author*, *publisher* and *year*. For scoring attributes, we choose $sim(\cdot, \cdot)$ to be the cosine similarity between attribute values. For example, for *author*, $sim(v_1, v_2)$ is the cosine similarity on users who read author v_1 and author v_2. We reconstruct a sample of 500 books based on each of these attributes. Table 1 summarizes the reconstruction results. As intuitively expected, *author* has the highest score, followed by *publisher*, and then *year*. RMSE results coincide with these scores (i.e., higher RMSE for low scores).

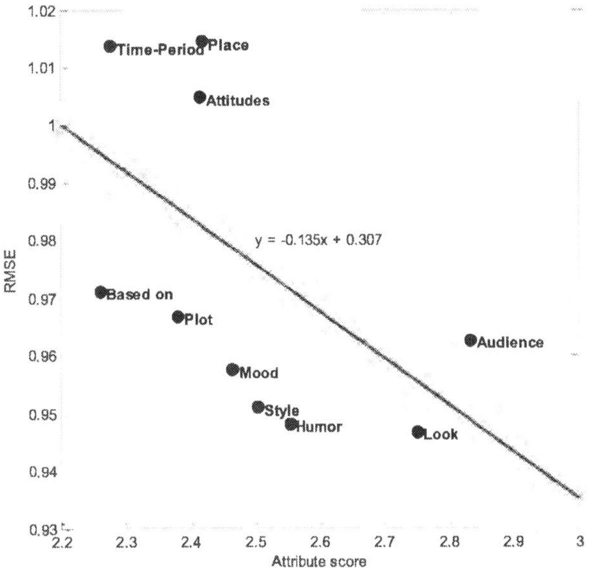

Figure 2: Xbox movies attributes vs. RMSE

Movies: Movies in the Xbox movies dataset are associated with labels. Each label is associated with a category, e.g., *Audience*, *Mood*, *Plot*. Every movie in the catalog has zero or more labels from each category. The *Audience* category has labels such as *Kids*, *Girls Night* and *Family*; The *Look* category has labels such as *3D*, *Black and White* and *Animation*; The *Time-Period* category has labels indicating the time in which the plot takes place. We use this dataset for evaluating both attribute and label ranking as follows:

Movies Attributes. We treat each of the label categories as a distinct attribute, and the unordered set of labels which belong to this category as the attribute value. Here we defined $sim(v_1, v_2)$ to be Jaccard similarity on labels belonging to movies v_1 and v_2. We then reconstruct a sample of 1,500 movies, and compute RMSE for each category. Figure 2 depicts the RMSE results vs. the attribute scores. As expected, categories like *Audience* and *Look* were found to be more informative than categories like *Time-Period*. Notice the negative correlation between the scores and RMSE.

Movies Labels. In this experiment, we evaluate our label scoring algorithm. Our experience shows that different labels from the same category may have a different informative value. For example, the *Place* category is in general non-informative, as for most movies it simply take the label *USA*. Nevertheless, for a small subset of movies, this category carries a more informative label such as *Ghetto* which highly predicts whom might watch the movie. Hence, we evaluate labels separately, ignoring categories. Here, we used $sim(i, j) = \delta(i, j)$. Figure 3 depicts the RMSE results vs. the label scores. Again, we see a clear trend line indicating a negative correlation between the scores and RMSE.

4. GENERATING FEATURES

Crafting a list of descriptive features and assigning them to catalog items is a labor-intensive process, typically performed manually by content specialists. Next, we demonstrate how to use the presented framework to automatically generate (and select) label features extracted from text descriptions of items. We model text descriptions using the

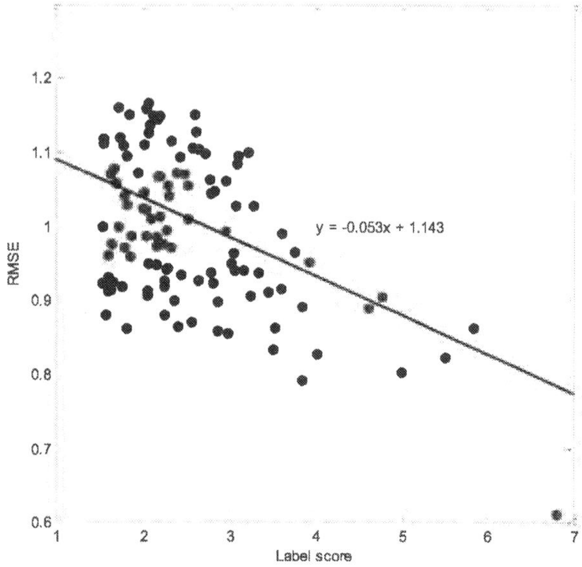

Figure 3: Xbox movies - labels vs. RMSE

Rank	Label feature	Score
1	enemy	2.342
2	ringtone	2.331
3	weapon	2.216
4	girl	2.191
5	youtube	2.183
6	child	2.182
7	kid	2.102
8	music	2.092
9	video	2.092
10	ball	2.086
· · · labels 11 through 1330 · · ·		
1331	version	1.158
1332	add	1.153
1333	time	1.147
1334	simple	1.147
1335	app	1.113

Table 2: Ranked labels from apps descriptions

binary bag of words model, and perform a simple filtering process, in which we remove stop words, words with very high inverse-document frequency, and words with very low frequency [2]. The remaining terms are normalized with a stemmer. We treat each word as a label and perform feature selection using Algorithm 2.

We present a ranked list labels from Windows Phone 8 apps descriptions[1]. After filtering, a total of 1335 labels were scored using Algorithm 2 with $sim(f_1, f_2) = \delta(f_1, f_2)$ and $R_k(\cdot)$ from [12]. Table 4 presents the 10 top ranking and the 5 low ranking labels. Observe that high ranking labels describe apps genres (*music*, *video*, and *ball*, which indicates a game) and demographic features (*kid*, *girl*), that are naturally informative for CF. Labels such as *app*, *version* and *time*, that clearly not informative, are ranked low.

[1] Avail. on `http://www.windowsphone.com/en-us/store`

5. CONCLUSIONS

Feature selection for recommendation systems is a relatively new field. This paper presents a generalized framework for selecting informative features for CF. The framework is successfully utilized to enhance recommendation in the Xbox Marketplace. We hope this work will inspire future research on feature selection for recommendation systems.

6. REFERENCES

[1] Fab: content-based, collaborative recommendation. M. Balabanovic and Y. Shoham. Comm. ACM, 1997.
[2] R. Baeza-Yates and B. Ribeiro-Neto. Modern Information Retrieval, 2011.
[3] Hybrid Recommender Systems: Survey and Experiments. Robin D. Burke. in User Model. User-Adapt. Interact.
[4] Combining content-based and collaborative filters in an online newspaper. M. Claypool and A. Gokhale, et al. Recommender Systems Workshop, 1999.
[5] Yahoo! Music Recommendations: Modeling Music Ratings with Temporal Dynamics and Item Taxonomy. G. Dror, N. Koenigstein, Y. Koren. RecSys 2011.
[6] The Yahoo! Music Dataset and KDD-Cup'11. G. Dror, N. Koenigstein, Y. Koren, M. Weimer. Journal Of Machine Learning Research, 2012.
[7] Map Based Visualization of Product Catalogs. M. Kagie, M. van Wezel and P.J.F. Groenen. Recommender Systems Handbook, 2011.
[8] The Xbox Recommender System. N. Koenigstein, N. Nice, U. Paquet, N. Schleyen. In RecSys 2012.
[9] Xbox Movies Recommendations: Variational Bayes Matrix Factorization with Embedded Feature Selection. N. Koenigstein, U. Paquet. In RecSys 2013.
[10] Matrix Factorization Techniques for Recommender Systems. Y. Koren, R. M. Bell, and C. Volinsky. IEEE Computer, 2009.
[11] Content-based Recommender Systems: State of the Art and Trends. P. Lops, M. de Gemmis, G. Semeraro. Recommender Systems Handbook, 2011.
[12] One-class Collaborative Filtering with Random Graphs. U. Paquet, N. Koenigstein. In WWW 2013, 999–1008.
[13] Sage - Recommender Engine as a Cloud Service. R. Ronen, N. Koenigstein, E. Ziklik, M. Sitruk, R. Yaari, N. Haiby-Weiss. In RecSys 2013.
[14] Automatic Feature Selection for Recommender Systems. R. Ronen, N. Koenigstein, E. Ziklik, N. Nice. Microsoft Patent 339085.01, 2013.
[15] J. B. Schafer, J. A. Konstan, J. Riedl. E-Commerce Recommendation Applications. Data Min. Knowl. Discov. 5(1/2): 115-153 (2001).
[16] Methods and metrics for cold-start recommendations. A. I. Schein, A. Popescul, L. H. Ungar and D. M. Pennock. SIGIR 2002.
[17] Designing and Evaluating Explanations for Recommender Systems. N. Tintarev and J. Masthoff. Recommender Systems Handbook, 2011.
[18] Improving recommendation lists through topic diversification. C. Ziegler, S. M. McNee, J. A. Konstan, G. Lausen. WWW 2005.

Sentimental Product Recommendation

Ruihai Dong†, Michael P. O'Mahony‡, Markus Schaal†, Kevin McCarthy†, Barry Smyth‡
†CLARITY: Centre for Sensor Web Technologies
‡INSIGHT: Centre for Data Analytics
School of Computer Science and Informatics
University College Dublin, Dublin, Ireland
firstname.lastname@ucd.ie

ABSTRACT

This paper describes a novel approach to product recommendation that is based on *opinionated* product descriptions that are automatically mined from user-generated product reviews. We present a recommendation ranking strategy that combines similarity and sentiment to suggest products that are similar but superior to a query product according to the opinion of reviewers. We demonstrate the benefits of this approach across a variety of Amazon product domains.

Categories and Subject Descriptors

H.3.3 [**Information Search and Retrieval**]: Information filtering; H.3.5 [**Online Information Services**]: Web-based services

Keywords

User-generated Reviews; Opinion Mining; Sentiment-based Product Recommendation

1. INTRODUCTION

Consider the *13" Retina MacBook Pro*. At the time of writing its *product features*, as listed by Amazon, cover technical details such as *screen-size*, *RAM*, *processor speed*, and *price*. These are the type of features that one might expect to find in a conventional content-based recommender [9]. Often, such features can be difficult to locate and can be technical in nature, thereby limiting recommendation opportunities and making it difficult for casual shoppers to judge the relevance of suggestions. However, the *MacBook Pro* has more than 70 reviews which encode valuable insights into a great many of its features; from its *"beautiful design"* and *"great video editing"* capabilities to its *"high price"*. These features capture more detail than a handful of technical (catalog) features. They also encode the *opinions* of real users and thus provide a basis for product comparisons.

We consider the following in this paper: can such features be used as the basis for a new type of *experiential* product recommendation, which is based on genuine user experiences? Are these features sufficiently rich to be a viable alternative to more conventional product descriptions based on meta-data or catalog features? And what type of recommendation strategies might be used?

There have been a number of efforts focused on extracting feature-based product descriptions from reviews. The work in [10] is representative in this regard and describes the use of shallow NLP techniques for explicit feature extraction and sentiment analysis; see also [6]. The features extracted, and the techniques used, are similar to those presented in this paper, although in the case of the former there was a focus on the extraction of meronomic and taxonomic features to describe the parts and properties of a product.

Zhang et al. [11] analyze the sentiment of comparative and subjective sentences in reviews on a per-feature basis to create a semi-order of products, but do not consider the recommendation task with respect to a query product. The work in [5] is relevant in that it uses user-generated micro-reviews as the basis for a text-based content recommender, and recently work in [2] has also tried to exploit user-generated content in similar ways. In [1], a manually defined ontology is used to convert opinions extracted from reviews into a structured form. This ontology, which captures both the reviewer's skill level and experience with the product, is then leveraged for recommendation.

The work in this paper uses existing techniques [4, 6–8] to automatically extract rich, opinionated product case representations from user-generated reviews and extends our earlier work [3] by introducing a new approach to sentiment-based recommendation and a hybrid approach for combining similarity and sentiment during recommendation.

2. MINING PRODUCT EXPERIENCES

The reviews for each product, P, are converted into a rich, feature-based, experiential case in 3 steps as follows (Figure 1). See [3] for more details.

Extracting Review Features. Shallow NLP and statistical methods are used to mine features from reviews [6, 7]. We consider *bi-gram* features which conform to one of two part-of-speech co-location patterns: a noun preceded by an adjective (AN) or by a noun (NN). *Single-noun* features which frequently co-occur ($\geq 70\%$ of the time) with sentiment words in the same sentence are also considered [6].

Evaluating Feature Sentiment. We use a version of *opinion pattern mining* to evaluate feature sentiment [8].

RecSys'13, October 12–16, 2013, Hong Kong, China.
Copyright 2013 ACM 978-1-4503-2409-0/13/09 ...$15.00.
http://dx.doi.org/10.1145/2507157.2507199.

For a given feature F_i in sentence S_j of review R_k, we identify the closest sentiment word w_{min} to F_i in S_j; F_i is labeled as *neutral* if no sentiment words are present (sentiment words are those contained in the sentiment lexicon [6]). Next we extract the *opinion pattern*: the part-of-speech tags for w_{min}, F_i and any words that occur between them. After a pass over all features, the frequency of occurrence of all patterns is noted. For valid patterns (those which occur more than once) we assign sentiment to F_i based on that of w_{min} in the sentiment lexicon; sentiment is reversed if S_j contains a negation term within a 4-word distance of w_{min}. Features associated with invalid patterns are labeled as *neutral*.

Generating Experiential Product Cases. For each product P we now have a set of features $F(P) = \{F_1, ..., F_m\}$ extracted from the reviews of P ($Reviews(P)$) and each feature F_i has an associated set of *positive, negative, or neutral* sentiment labels ($L_1, L_2, \ldots$). Features which are mentioned in $\geq$ 10% of reviews for that product are only considered and overall sentiment (Equation 1) and popularity (Equation 2) scores are calculated; $Pos(F_i, P)$ (resp. $Neg(F_i, P)$, $Neut(F_i, P)$) denotes the number of positive (resp. negative, neutral) sentiment labels for feature F_i. The product case, $Case(P)$, is then given by Equation 3.

$$Sent(F_i, P) = \frac{Pos(F_i, P) - Neg(F_i, P)}{Pos(F_i, P) + Neg(F_i, P) + Neut(F_i, P)} \tag{1}$$

$$Pop(F_i, P) = \frac{|\{R_k \in Reviews(P) : F_i \in R_k\}|}{|Reviews(P)|} \tag{2}$$

$$Case(P) = \{[F_i, Sent(F_i, P), Pop(F_i, P)] : F_i \in F(P)\} \tag{3}$$

3. RECOMMENDING PRODUCTS

The above case representation leads to a content-based recommendation approach based on feature similarity to a query product. However, the availability of feature sentiment suggests another approach in which products that offer *better* quality features compared to the query product are recommended. These techniques are described below.

Similarity-Based Recommendation. Each product case is represented as a vector of features, where feature *values* represent their popularity in reviews (Equation 2) as a proxy for their importance. The cosine similarity between query product, Q, and candidate recommendation, C, is given by:

$$Sim(Q, C) = \frac{\sum\limits_{F_i \in F(Q) \cup F(C)} Pop(F_i, Q) \times Pop(F_i, C)}{\sqrt{\sum\limits_{F_i \in F(Q)} Pop(F_i, Q)^2} \sqrt{\sum\limits_{F_i \in F(C)} Pop(F_i, C)^2}} \tag{4}$$

Using this approach, a set of top n recommendations are generated, ranked according to their query product similarity [9].

Sentiment-Enhanced Recommendation. Rather than recommend products using *similarity* alone, feature sentiment can also be used to seek products with *better* sentiment than the query product. Equation 5 computes a score for feature F_i between query product Q and recommendation candidate C; a positive (resp. negative) score means that C has higher (resp. lower) sentiment for F_i compared to Q.

$$better(F_i, Q, C) = \frac{Sent(F_i, C) - Sent(F_i, Q)}{2} \tag{5}$$

Equation 6 computes an average better score at the product level across the *shared* features between Q and C. However, this approach ignores any *residual features* that are unique to Q or C. Thus, Equation 7 computes an average better score across the *union* of features in Q and C; non-shared features are assigned a neutral sentiment score of 0.

$$B1(Q, C) = \frac{\sum_{F_i \in F(Q) \cap F(C)} better(F_i, Q, C)}{|F(Q) \cap F(C)|} \tag{6}$$

$$B2(Q, C) = \frac{\sum_{F_i \in F(Q) \cup F(C)} better(F_i, Q, C)}{|F(Q) \cup F(C)|} \tag{7}$$

Combining Similarity and Sentiment. The sentiment-based approaches above prioritise products that enjoy more positive reviews across a range of features relative to the query product. However, these recommendations may not necessarily be very similar to the query product. Thus, Equation 8 ranks recommendations based on their combined (controlled by w) similarity and sentiment with respect to Q; $B(Q, C)$ denotes $B1$ or $B2$, normalised to [0, 1].

$$Score(Q, C) = (1 - w)\ Sim(Q, C) + w\big(B(Q, C) + 1\big)/2 \tag{8}$$

4. EVALUATION

The above approaches are evaluated using data extracted from Amazon.com during October 2012. We considered 6 product domains; here we present representative results for 3 domains (Table 1). For each product with $\geq$ 10 reviews, we extracted review texts and helpfulness information, and the top n recommendations as suggested by Amazon.

Domain	#Reviews	#Products	#*Features* μ (σ)	Sims. μ (σ)
Tablets	17,936	166	26 (10)	0.6 (0.1)
Phones	14,860	257	9 (5)	0.5 (0.2)
GPS	12,115	119	24 (11)	0.6 (0.2)

Table 1: Dataset statistics.

4.1 Mining Rich Product Descriptions

The success of our approach depends on its ability to translate user-generated reviews into useful product cases. Table 1 shows the mean and standard deviation of the number of features that are extracted for each domain. On average, 9-26 features are extracted per product case, indicating that reasonably feature-rich cases are generated. Table 1 (last column) also shows the mean and standard deviation of the pairwise product cosine similarities. Again the results bode well because they show a relatively wide range of similarity values; very narrow ranges would suggest limitations in the expressiveness of extracted product representations.

4.2 Recommendation Performance

A standard *leave-one-out* approach is used in our evaluation, comparing our recommendations for each product to those produced by Amazon. Thus, for each product (referred to as the *query product*, Q) in a given domain, we generate a set of top 5 recommendations using Equation 8, varying w from 0 to 1 in steps of 0.1. This produces 22 recommendation lists for each Q, 11 each for $B1$ and $B2$, which we compare to Amazon's own recommendations for Q.

4.2.1 Ratings Benefit

We use Amazon's overall product ratings as an independent measure of product quality. The *ratings benefit* metric compares two sets of recommendations based on their ratings (Equation 9), where a ratings benefit of 0.1 means that our recommendations R enjoy an average rating score that is 10% higher that those produced by Amazon (A).

$$Benefit(R, A) = \frac{\overline{Rating(R)} - \overline{Rating(A)}}{\overline{Rating(A)}} \quad (9)$$

We also compute the *query product similarity*, the average similarity based on mined feature representations between our recommendations and the query product. This allows us to evaluate whether our techniques produce recommendations that are related to the query product and also provides a basis for comparison to Amazon's recommendations.

For each domain, Figure 3(a–c) shows $B1$ and $B2$ results for top 5 recommendations. Ratings benefit scores (left y-axis, dashed lines) for $B1$ (circles) and $B2$ (squares) against w (x-axis), along with the corresponding query product similarity values (right y-axis, solid lines), are shown. The average similarity between the query product and the Amazon recommendations is also shown, which is independent of w and so appears as a solid horizontal line in each graph.

4.2.2 Contrasting Sentiment and Similarity

At $w = 0$, Equation 8 is equivalent to a pure similarity-based approach to recommendation using cosine, because sentiment is not contributing to the overall recommendation score. For this configuration there is little or no ratings benefit; the recommendations produced have very similar average ratings to those produced by Amazon. However, the recommendations that are produced are more similar to the query product, in terms of the features mentioned in reviews, than Amazon's own recommendations. For example, in the *Phones* domain (Figure 3(b)) at $w = 0$, recommendations based on cosine have a query product similarity of 0.8 compared to 0.6 for Amazon's recommendations.

At $w = 1$, where recommendations are based solely on sentiment, we see a range of maximum positive ratings benefits (from 0.18 to 0.23) across all 3 product domains. $B2$ outperforms $B1$, except for GPS, indicating that the sentiment associated with residual (non-shared) features is important, at least for two of the three domains considered. Consider again the *Phones* domain (Figure 3(b)). At $w = 1$, we see a ratings benefit of 0.11 and 0.21 for $B1$ and $B2$, respectively. Thus, products recommended by $B2$ enjoy ratings that are 21% higher than Amazon's recommendations, an increase of almost one point on average for Amazon's 5-point scale.

However, these ratings benefits are offset by a drop in query product similarity. At $w = 1$, query product similarity falls below that of the Amazon recommendations. Thus, a tradeoff exists between ratings benefits and query product similarity.

4.2.3 Combining Similarity and Sentiment

The relative contribution of similarity and sentiment is governed by w (Equation 8). As w increases a gradual increase in ratings benefit for $B1$ and $B2$ is seen, especially at larger w, with $B2$ outperforming $B1$ except for GPS. The slope of the ratings benefit curves and the maximum benefit achieved is influenced by the ratings distribution in each domain. For example, $Phones$ and $Tablets$ have ratings distributions with relatively low means and high standard deviations. Thus, more opportunities for improved ratings exist and, indeed, the highest ratings benefits are seen for these domains (above 0.2 at $w = 1$ for $B2$).

Regarding query product similarity, there is little change for $w < 0.7$. But for $w > 0.7$ there is a reduction as sentiment tends to dominate during recommendation ranking. This query product similarity profile is remarkably consistent across all product domains and in all cases $B2$ better preserves query product similarity compared to $B1$.

To better understand the relative performance of $B1$ and $B2$ with respect to the Amazon baseline as w varies, we need a point of reference for the purpose of a *like-for-like* comparison. To do this we compare our techniques by fixing w at the point at which the query product similarity curve intersects with the Amazon query product similarity level and then reading the corresponding ratings benefits for $B1$ and $B2$. This is a useful reference point because it allows us to look at the ratings benefit offered by $B1$ and $B2$ when delivering recommendations that have the same query product similarity as the baseline Amazon recommendations.

Figure 2 shows these ratings benefits and corresponding w values for $B1$ and $B2$. The results clarify the positive ratings benefits that are achieved using sentiment-based recommendation without compromising query product similarity. For $Tablets$ and $Phones$ there are very significant ratings benefits, especially for $B2$ (resp. 15% and 21%). As stated above, $B1$ outperforms $B2$ for GPS, but in a relatively minor way, suggesting that the sentiment associated with residual features is not playing a significant role in this domain.

Finally, note the consistency of the w values at which the query product similarity of the sentiment-based recommendations matches that of Amazon. For each domain, $w \approx 0.9$ (for $B2$) delivers recommendations that balance query product similarity with significant ratings benefits; whether this value of w applies in general we leave to future work.

5. CONCLUSIONS

The objective of this work has been twofold: (1) to convert unstructured reviews into rich product descriptions and (2) to use these product descriptions in a recommender system that combines similarity and sentiment. Our results show clear benefits in terms of recommendation quality compared to Amazon's own recommendations. In this work, we have considered one particular approach to similarity: a cosine metric calculated over the frequency of occurrence of extracted product features. A question arises as to whether this approach indeed reflects an authentic notion of product similarity as judged by human assessment. A detailed exploration of this matter is left to future work; however, we note that preliminary assessments attest to the validity of our approach.

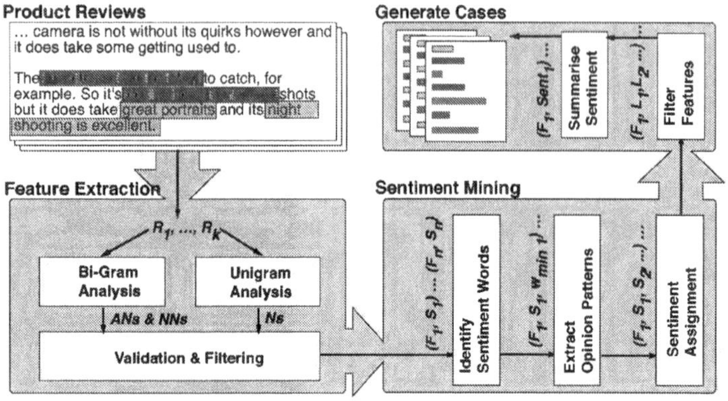

Figure 1: Extracting product cases from user reviews.

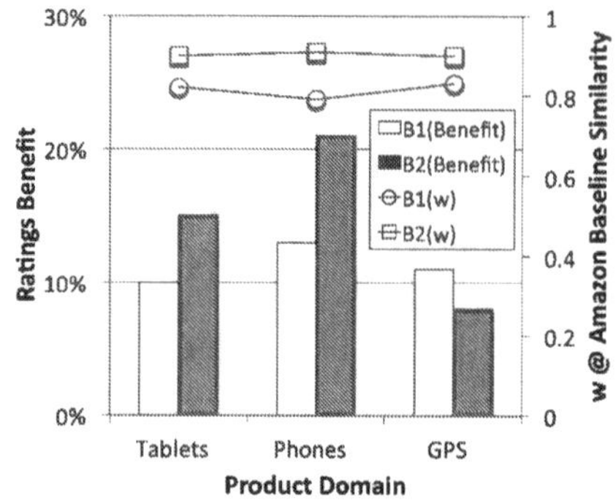

Figure 2: Ratings benefits at Amazon baseline query product similarity.

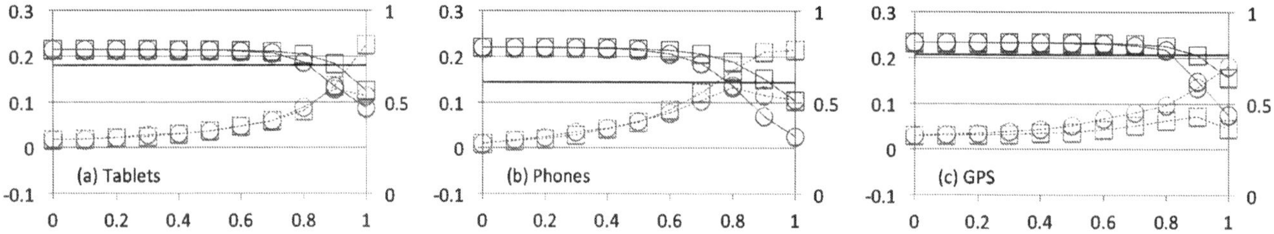

Figure 3: Ratings benefit (left y-axis, dashed lines) and query similarity (right y-axis, solid lines) versus w (x-axis); $B1$ and $B2$ are shown as circles and squares and Amazon query similarity as a solid horizontal line.

6. ACKNOWLEDGEMENTS

This work is supported by Science Foundation Ireland under grant 07/CE/I1147. The INSIGHT Centre for Data Analytics is supported by Science Foundation Ireland under Grant Number SFI/12/RC/2289.

7. REFERENCES

[1] S. Aciar, D. Zhang, S. Simoff, and J. Debenham. Informed recommender: Basing recommendations on consumer product reviews. *Intelligent Systems, IEEE*, 22(3):39–47, 2007.

[2] G. De Francisci Morales, A. Gionis, and C. Lucchese. From chatter to headlines: Harnessing the real-time web for personalized news recommendation. In *Proceedings of the fifth ACM International Conference on Web Search and Data Mining*, WSDM '12, pages 153–162, New York, NY, USA, 2012. ACM.

[3] R. Dong, M. Schaal, M. P. O'Mahony, K. McCarthy, and B. Smyth. Opinionated product recommendation. In *Case-Based Reasoning Research and Development*, volume 7969 of *Lecture Notes in Computer Science*, pages 44–58. Springer Berlin Heidelberg, 2013.

[4] R. Dong, M. Schaal, M. P. O'Mahony, and B. Smyth. Topic extraction from online reviews for classification and recommendation. In *Proceedings of the 23rd International Joint Conference on Artificial Intelligence*, IJCAI '13 (To appear), Menlo Park, California, 2013. AAAI Press.

[5] S. Garcia Esparza, M. P. O'Mahony, and B. Smyth. On the real-time web as a source of recommendation knowledge. In *Proceedings of the fourth ACM Conference on Recommender Systems*, RecSys '10, pages 305–308, New York, NY, USA, 2010. ACM.

[6] M. Hu and B. Liu. Mining and summarizing customer reviews. In *Proceedings of the tenth ACM SIGKDD International Conference on Knowledge Discovery and Data Mining*, KDD '04, pages 168–177, New York, NY, USA, 2004. ACM.

[7] J. S. Justeson and S. M. Katz. Technical terminology: Some linguistic properties and an algorithm for identification in text. *Natural Language Engineering*, 1(1):9–27, 1995.

[8] S. Moghaddam and M. Ester. Opinion digger: An unsupervised opinion miner from unstructured product reviews. In *Proceedings of the 19th ACM International Conference on Information and Knowledge Management*, CIKM '10, pages 1825–1828, New York, NY, USA, 2010. ACM.

[9] M. Pazzani and D. Billsus. Content-based recommendation systems. In *The Adaptive Web*, volume 4321 of *Lecture Notes in Computer Science*, pages 325–341. Springer Berlin Heidelberg, 2007.

[10] A.-M. Popescu and O. Etzioni. Extracting product features and opinions from reviews. In *Natural Language Processing and Text Mining*, pages 9–28. Springer London, 2007.

[11] K. Zhang, R. Narayanan, and A. Choudhary. Voice of the customers: Mining online customer reviews for product feature-based ranking. In *Proceedings of the 3rd Workshop on Online Social Networks*, WOSN '10, Berkeley, CA, USA, 2010.

Set-oriented Personalized Ranking for Diversified Top-N Recommendation

Ruilong Su, Li'Ang Yin, Kailong Chen, Yong Yu
Dept.of Computer Science and Engineering
Shanghai Jiao Tong University
800 Dongchuan Road, Shanghai China, 200240
{rlsu, yinla, chenkl, yyu}@apex.sjtu.edu.cn

ABSTRACT

In this paper, we propose a set-oriented personalized ranking model for diversified top-N recommendation. Users may have various individual ranges of interests. For personalized top-N recommendation task, the combination of relevance and diversity in recommendation results would be desirable. For this purpose, we integrate the concept of diversity into traditional matrix factorization model to construct a set-oriented collaborative filtering model. By optimizing this model with a set-oriented pairwise ranking method, we directly achieve personalized top-N recommendation results which are both relevant and diversified. We also utilize category information explicitly for learning personalized diversity. Experimental results show that our model outperforms traditional models in terms of personalized diversity and maintains good performance on relevance prediction.

Categories and Subject Descriptors

H.3.3 [**Information Systems**]: Information Search and Retrieval—*Information Filtering*

Keywords

Collaborative Filtering, Recommender Systems, Set-oriented Pairwise Ranking, Personalized Diversity

1. INTRODUCTION

Collaborative Filtering (CF) [2] is one of most popular techniques in providing users with personalized suggestions of items or other information. The basic intuition behind CF is that users who had similar ranges of interests in the past are likely to have similar preferences in the future, and the more similar they were in the past, the more likely they will make similar choices in the future.

Top-N recommendation results are often presented to a target user in the form of a rank list according to their predicted relevance scores. In recent years, diversity of the results list has been regarded as another important factor that influences the satisfaction of users to a recommender system significantly. A recommendation list which contains different types of relevant items would be more desirable. In order to achieve this goal, most traditional methods rerank the relevance prediction results to balance relevance and diversity [8, 9]. We believe that relevance and diversity should be considered together. As personalized relevance can be predicted through learning, personalized diversity can be also predicted directly. Unlike relevance, diversity is a set-oriented concept. To quantify this concept, we construct a set-oriented CF model. We optimize this model for ranking by using a set-oriented pairwise ranking method and directly achieve personalized top-N recommendation results which are both relevant and diversified.

The paper is organized as follows: In Section 2, we review some related work briefly. Then in Section 3, we present the details of our set-oriented personalized ranking model. Our experimental results and analysis are reported in Section 4. Finally, Section 5 concludes the paper.

RecSys'13, October 12–16, 2013, Hong Kong, China.

http://dx.doi.org/10.1145/2507157.2507207.

2. RELATED WORK

During the past years, collaborative filtering has been used as an effective technique for recommender systems [2]. In collaborative filtering, latent factor models usually have promising performance on predictive accuracy and scalability. Most latent factor models are based on factorizing the user-item rating matrix, which are known as Singular Value Decomposition (SVD) models [4].

Ranking-oriented models have been proposed recently in order to tackle the task of top-N recommendation more practically. A generic optimization criterion BPR was proposed in [5]. The experiments empirically showed that for the task of personalized ranking, learning a CF model with BPR outperforms other learning methods.

Diversity is regarded as another important aspect for the recommendation quality besides relevance. Previous studies showed that diversity of a recommendation list may hamper relevance to some degree, but will improve user satisfaction as a whole [3]. For traditional work about diversity, the concept of user is usually a generic *average* user, thus the diversified top-N recommendation results are non-personalized. In recent years, many diversification methods have been proposed [8, 9], including some adaptive diversification methods [6]. But most of these methods are two-step methods that consider relevance and diversity separately. In contrast with this, we combine relevance and diversity in a unified model which adaptively balances them for users with different interests in one step.

3. SET-ORIENTED PERSONALIZED RANKING (SPR)

In this section, we present our set-oriented personalized ranking model. The objective of this model is to directly recommend personalized item sets of size N which are both relevant and diversified to users with different ranges of interests. Key notations are shown in Table 1.

3.1 Set-oriented Formalization

Let U be the set of users and I be the set of items. Ratings of U on I are scored in a matrix $R(m \times n)$. Entry r_{ui} in R denotes the rating that user u gives to item i and reflects the preference of user u for item i. Let I_u be the set of items whose ratings are observed in matrix R for user u. We define a subset $I_u^+ \subseteq I_u$ containing items that user u likes.

$$I_u^+ := \{i | i \in I_u, r_{ui} \geq r^+\}$$

Where r^+ represents a rating threshold. We assume that a user prefers all items in I_u^+ over all items in $I_u^- := I \setminus I_u^+$. Previous pairwise ranking approaches use item pairs as training data. In order to quantify the recommendation diversity, in our work we use item set pairs as training data. We define T_u^+ as a candidate positive item set of size N.

$$T_u^+ := \{i | i \in I_u^+\}$$

We denote the set of T_u^+ as $\mathcal{T}_u^+$. Similarly, we define a common item set of size N as:

$$T_u := \{i | i \in I_u\}$$

We also denote the set of T_u as $\mathcal{T}_u$. A training pair (u, S_i, S_j) for user u is constructed by selecting two item sets S_i and S_j from $\mathcal{T}_u^+$ and $\mathcal{T}_u$ respectively, accordingly the set-oriented training collection is formalized as follows:

$$D_S := \{(u, S_i, S_j) | S_i \in \mathcal{T}_u^+ \wedge S_j \in \mathcal{T}_u \wedge (Con1 \vee Con2)\}$$

In which,

$$\begin{aligned} Con1 &:= (r_{s_i} > r_{s_j}) \\ Con2 &:= (r_{s_i} = r_{s_j}) \wedge (d_{s_i} > d_{s_j}) \end{aligned}$$

Where r_s denotes the relevance score of a given item set S and d_s denotes the diversity score of this set. The set S_i is preferred to S_j by considering the two conditions above: 1) the relevance score r_{s_i} of S_i is higher than r_{s_j} of S_j; 2) the diversity score d_{s_i} of S_i is higher than d_{s_j} of S_j, if the relevance scores of S_i and S_j are equal. We will discuss how to calculate the r_s and d_s later.

3.2 Set-oriented Collaborative Filtering Model

As a famous class of latent factor models, SVD models factorize the user-item rating to the inner product of user latent factor p_u and item latent factor q_i, where both of p_u and q_i are f-dimension. In the basic SVD model, the rating that user u gives to item i is predicted as follows:

$$\hat{r}_{ui} = \mu + b_u + b_i + p_u^{\mathrm{T}} q_i \tag{1}$$

In order to learn the diversity together with relevance, we introduce a new concept named "Set Diversity Bias" (SDB) representing the diversification degree of an item set. By combining SDB and the basic SVD model, we propose a set-oriented CF model to directly predict the score of user u on a given item set S_k. The score is decided by both relevance and diversity of S_k. It is formulated as this:

Table 1: Key Notations

Representations	Descriptions
u, i, c	user u, item i, category c
U, I, C	user set, item set, category set
μ	overall average rating
b_u, b_i	users/items bias
$b_d(S_k)$	set diversity bias (SDB)
$bias$	μ, b_u, b_i, $b_d(S_k)$
p_u, q_i	latent factors for user-item affinity
v_i	latent factors for item-item similarity
p_c, w_i	latent factors for category-item relation

$$\hat{r}_{u,S_k} = \mu + b_u + \sum_{i \in S_k} b_i + p_u^{\mathrm{T}} (\sum_{i \in S_k} q_i) + \lambda b_d(S_k) \tag{2}$$

where $b_d(S_k)$ denotes the diversity bias of S_k and λ is a constant to control the weight of diversity in the model.

3.3 Set-oriented AUC Optimization

Many traditional personalized ranking methods maximize the metric of area under the ROC curve (AUC) [1]. In order to learn the set-oriented CF model (2), we maximize a set-oriented AUC. With the notation of D_S, it can be formalized as:

$$AUC(u) := \frac{1}{|D_S|} \sum_{(u,S_i,S_j) \in D_S} \delta(\hat{r}_{u,S_i} - \hat{r}_{u,S_j}) \tag{3}$$

Where $\hat{r}_{u,S_i}$ is the predicted preference score of user u on item set S_i. A value of $(\hat{r}_{u,S_i} - \hat{r}_{u,S_j}) > 0$ means the model predicts that user u prefers item set S_i to item set S_j. We use logistic loss function as $\delta(x)$:

$$\delta(x) = \frac{1}{1 + e^{-x}} \tag{4}$$

Which is a surrogate loss function and corresponds to Bayesian Personalized Ranking (BPR) [5]. Now we can derive our loss function for set-oriented AUC optimization as follows:

$$l(\theta) = \sum_{(u,S_i,S_j) \in D_S} ln(1 + e^{-(\hat{r}_{u,S_i} - \hat{r}_{u,S_j})}) + \lambda_r ||\theta||^2 \tag{5}$$

Where θ represents the unknown parameters in (2) and λ_r is a constant for regularization. We solve this loss function with a stochastic gradient descent algorithm. In every single training step, we use the bootstrap sampling to randomly select a triple (u, S_i, S_j) from D_S for updating our model.

3.4 Set Diversity Bias (SDB)

For the effective learning of diversity, set diversity bias should be able to reflect the diversity of an item set reasonably and easy to learn. A well-known approach proposed is to model diversity as the *average dissimilarity* of all pairs of items in the set [7]. Recently, a new idea has been proposed that the diversity of an item set is associated with the latent factors of items in it [6]. Inspired by this idea, we define v_i as the latent factors of item i for item-item similarity. For any pair of item i and item j, the more similar v_i and v_j are, the greater the inner product of v_i and v_j is. Besides, the categories of items are one kind of important and explicit information related to the diversity of an item set. Let $|C_i|$ be the number of categories item i contains. We also integrate it into SDB to normalize the latent factors, since an item often contains more than one category. With the notations above, our $b_d(S_k)$ is formalized as:

$$b_d(S_k) = -\sum_{i \in S_k} \sum_{j \in S_k, j \neq i} \frac{1}{|C_i||C_j|} v_i^{\mathrm{T}} v_j \quad (6)$$

We also define p_c as the latent factors of category c and w_i as the latent factors of item i for category-item relation, which are estimated by the logistic regression model below.

$$\min_{p_c, w_i} \sum_{i \in I} \sum_{c \in C_i} (1 - \frac{1}{1 + e^{-p_c^{\mathrm{T}} w_i}})^2 \quad (7)$$

The result of this model is that items with common categories have similar w_i, thus we introduce a L2-norm regularizing term $||v_i - w_i||^2$ to help learn SDB.

4. EXPERIMENTAL EVALUATION

In this section, we present a series of experiments to evaluate our proposed set-oriented personalized ranking model.

4.1 Experimental Setup

4.1.1 Dataset

We use the publicly available dataset MovieLen-1M in our experimental evaluation. In our work, we regard items with ratings larger than or equal to 4 as relevant. We randomly split relevant/irrelevant items of each user into the training set and the test set with the ratio of 4:1. Then D_S is constructed on the training set as described in section 3.1. During the training, we define the relevance score r_s of a given item set S as the number of relevant items in it, while the diversity score d_s of set S is measured by $\alpha NDCG_h$@N in (9).

4.1.2 Evaluation Metrics

In our experiments, we adopt the *precision*@N to evaluate the relevance of recommendation sets. The common metric *precision*@N is defined as:

$$precision@N = \frac{H_u}{N} \quad (8)$$

Where H_u is the number of relevant items in a recommendation set for user u. The diversity of recommendation sets can be evaluated by the metric $\alpha NDCG$@N [6]. We use the *highest* $\alpha NDCG@N$ ($\alpha NDCG_h$@N) and the *average* $\alpha NDCG@N$ ($\alpha NDCG_a$@N) instead, since the items in the set have many potential rankings. Let $L_u := \{l_1, l_2, \ldots, l_{N!}\}$ be the set of all potential inner rankings in a given item set of size N for user u, we formulate $\alpha NDCG_h$@N and $\alpha NDCG_a$@N as:

$$\alpha NDCG_h@N = \max_{l_p \in L_u} \alpha NDCG@N \quad (9)$$

$$\alpha NDCG_a@N = \frac{1}{|L_u|} \sum_{l_p \in L_u} \alpha NDCG@N \quad (10)$$

During training, we utilize $\alpha NDCG_h$ to measure the diversity of item sets. We obtain an approximate value of it with greedy algorithm in $O(N^2)$, since the time complexity of calculating exact $\alpha NDCG_h$@N is $O(N|L_u|)$. While in the test, we utilize $\alpha NDCG_a$@N to evaluate the *statistical*

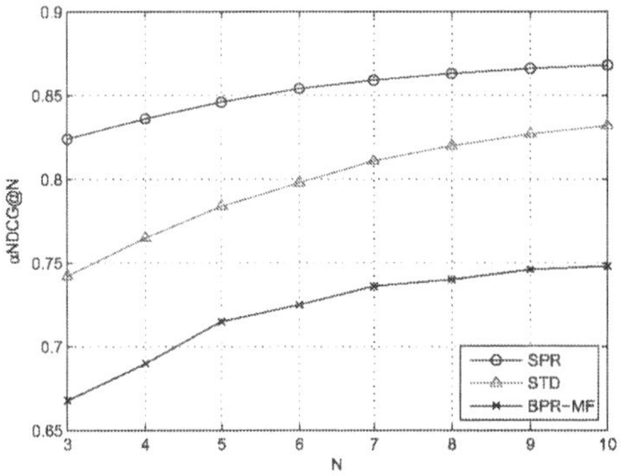

Figure 1: $\alpha NDCG$@N of SPR, STD and BPR-MF on MovieLen-1M

performance of the recommendation sets of size N. For each user u, the recommendation set is approximate optimal recommendation set constructed by greedy selection strategy in $O(a_u N^2)$, where a_u is the amount of items in the test set for user u.

4.1.3 Compared Models

In this paper, we compare our model with several others [5, 9], which are called BPR-MF (Bayesian Personalized Ranking based on Matrix Factorization) and STD (Sequential Topic Diversification) separately in this paper. We refer to the parameters recommended for BPR-MF in [5] and STD in [9].

4.2 Results and Discussion

4.2.1 Performance on Diversity

Figure 1 compares the performance of our model with baselines in terms of diversity on MovieLen-1M. BPR-MF gives the worst performance on diversity, since it only focuses on providing the most relevant results for users without taking the diversity into account. STD gives higher performance than BPR-MF through re-ranking the prediction results based on topic(category) diversification. Our proposed SPR consistently outperforms BPR-MF and STD regarding $\alpha NDCG$@N at any value of $N \in [3, 10]$. Note that for our model, we use $\alpha NDCG_a$@N to evaluate the *statistical* performance of the recommendation sets. Another observation is that our model achieves significant improvement when the size N of recommendation set is small. This result empirically shows that our proposed model is suitable to diversify the top-N recommendation results for a small value of N.

4.2.2 Diversity vs. Relevance

In this section, we conduct experiments in the scenario of top-3 recommendation to explore the relation between relevance and diversity under various settings of λ in (2). Experimental results are shown in Figure 2. In our set-oriented CF model, λ is a constant to balance relevance and diversity for recommendation. We can observe that as the value of λ grows, $\alpha NDCG_a$@3 gradually increases while *precision*@3 decreases. This is consistent to the common intuition that the improvement of diversity weakens the relevance of results. By adjusting λ carefully, a reasonable balance of recommendation relevance and diversity can be achieved.

Table 2: Example top-4 recommendation results for users with *Focused* interests

Type	User with *Focused* interest (userID: 4651)	
ID	**Movies user has seen**	**Categories**
1147	When We Were Kings (4)	7
1192	Paris Is Burning (4)	7
1856	Kurt & Courtney (5)	7, 12
2129	The Saltmen of Tibet (5)	7
ID	**Recommendation Set**	**Categories**
116	Anne Frank Remembered (4)	7
134	Sonic Outlaws (4)	7
162	Crumb (4)	7
2330	Hands on a Hard Body (4)	7

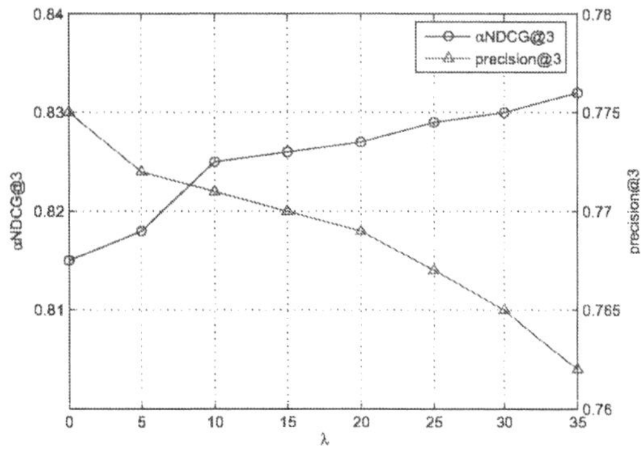

Figure 2: Diversity vs. Relevance

4.2.3 Personalized Diversity

In this section, we demonstrate that recommendation results given by our model achieves good personalized diversity. In Movielen-1M, we regard users who are related to 15 or more categories as "Broad" users and users who are related to 10 or less categories as "Focused" users. We also use numerical id (1-18) to represent different categories in Movielen-1M, such as 1 presents "Action", 7 presents "Documentary" and 17 presents "War".

We conduct experiments for top-4 recommendation. The results are shown in Table 2 and Table 3. In the two tables, movie ratings given by a user are presented in the brackets after movie names. Our model recommends movie sets with category ranges corresponding to different tastes of users. Table 2 shows a "focused" user(id: 4651) case. This user prefers documentary movies suggested by his rating history. Our recommendation set for this user focuses on the same movie type. The relevance of this set is very high with all the movie ratings above 4. Table 3 illustrates a case of the user(id: 406) who has broad interests. The recommendation set for this user covers broad types to meet his taste and also has good performance on relevance. Note that though "Alien" got a rating score 3, it is regarded as a diverse one containing 4 categories related to this user.

We also explore novelty of the recommendation sets for "Broad" users in top-3 recommendation. For this purpose, we consider the number of unique categories that each movie contains in a recommendation set. According to our statistical results, the expectation and variance of this value is 2.3 and 1.3 respectively. This observation means that each movie contains at least one different category from all the others in a recommendation set. This result further supports that our model has good performance in terms of personalized diversity.

Table 3: Example top-4 recommendation results for users with *Broad* interests

Type	User with *Broad* interest (userID: 406)	
ID	**Movies user has seen**	**Categories**
110	Braveheart (4)	1, 8, 17
589	Terminator 2: Judgment Day (4)	1, 15, 16
1183	The English Patient (4)	8, 14, 17
3175	Galaxy Quest (4)	2, 5, 15
ID	**Recommendation Set**	**Categories**
1097	E.T. (4)	4, 8, 9, 15
1210	Star Wars: Episode VI (4)	1, 2, 14, 15, 17
1214	Alien (3)	1, 11, 15, 16
2000	Lethal Weapon (4)	1, 5, 6, 8

5. CONCLUSION

In this paper, we propose a set-oriented personalized ranking model for diversified top-N recommendation. Our experimental results show that our model outperforms traditional models in terms of personalized diversity and maintains good performance on relevance prediction. In future work, we plan to provide a more thoughtful analysis for the potential relation between relevance and diversity in personalized top-N recommendation according to our experimental results.

6. REFERENCES

[1] A. P. Bradley. The use of the area under the roc curve in the evaluation of machine learning algorithms. *Pattern recognition*, 30(7):1145–1159, 1997.

[2] D. Goldberg, D. Nichols, B. M. Oki, and D. Terry. Using collaborative filtering to weave an information tapestry. *Communications of the ACM*, 35(12):61–70, 1992.

[3] N. Hurley and M. Zhang. Novelty and diversity in top-n recommendation–analysis and evaluation. *ACM Transactions on Internet Technology (TOIT)*, 10(4):14, 2011.

[4] Y. Koren. Factorization meets the neighborhood: a multifaceted collaborative filtering model. In *Proceedings of the 14th ACM SIGKDD international conference on Knowledge discovery and data mining*, pages 426–434. ACM, 2008.

[5] S. Rendle, C. Freudenthaler, Z. Gantner, and L. Schmidt-Thieme. Bpr: Bayesian personalized ranking from implicit feedback. In *Proceedings of the Twenty-Fifth Conference on Uncertainty in Artificial Intelligence*, pages 452–461. AUAI Press, 2009.

[6] Y. Shi, X. Zhao, J. Wang, M. Larson, and A. Hanjalic. Adaptive diversification of recommendation results via latent factor portfolio. In *Proceedings of the 35th international ACM SIGIR conference on Research and development in information retrieval*, pages 175–184. ACM, 2012.

[7] B. Smyth and P. McClave. Similarity vs. diversity. In *Proceedings of the International Conference on Case-Based Reasoning and Development (ICCBR)*, volume 2080, pages 347–361. Springer, 2001.

[8] S. Vargas, P. Castells, and D. Vallet. Intent-oriented diversity in recommender systems. In *Proceedings of the 34th international ACM SIGIR conference on Research and development in information retrieval*, pages 1211–1212. ACM, 2011.

[9] C. Ziegler, S. McNee, J. Konstan, and G. Lausen. Improving recommendation lists through topic diversification. In *Proceedings of the 14th international conference on World Wide Web*, pages 22–32. ACM, 2005.

Towards Scalable and Accurate Item-Oriented Recommendations

Noam Koenigstein
School of Electrical Eng., Tel Aviv University
noamk@eng.tau.ac.il

Yehuda Koren
Google, Israel
yehuda.a.koren@gmail.com

ABSTRACT

Most recommenders research aims at personalized systems, which suggest items based on user profiles. However, in reality many systems deal with item-oriented recommendations. In such setups, given a single item of interest, the system needs to provide other related items, following patterns like "people who liked this also liked...".

While item-oriented systems are central in their importance, they have been approached so far using very basic tools. We identify several hurdles faced by standard approaches to the item-oriented task. First, the sparseness of observed activities prevents establishing reliable similarity relations for many item pairs. Second, we address a scalability challenge at the retrieval stage present in many real-world systems: Given an item inventory, which may encompass millions of items, it is desired to identify the most related item pairs in a sub-quadratic time. This work addresses these two challenges, thereby improving both accuracy and scalability of item-oriented recommenders. Additionally, we propose an empirical evaluation scheme for comparing the quality of different solutions with encouraging results.

Categories and Subject Descriptors

H.2.8 [**Database Management**]: Database Applications—*Data Mining*

Keywords

collaborative filtering, item-based recommendation

1. ITEM BASED RECOMMENDATIONS

Most research on recommender systems is focused on modeling relations between users and items. New items are recommended to users based on their past purchases or activities. However, in reality user profiles are often not available (e.g., when a user is new or not logged-in) or irrelevant (e.g., when the current, short-term interest is unrelated to longer term inclinations). Therefore, many industrial systems are based on item-oriented recommendations, where item suggestions are solely based on their relatedness to a small set of currently considered items. Such recommendations aim at highlighting alternative items or items that are often bought together. A well known example of such a recommender is Amazon's shopping cart recommender. Amazon's system capitalizes on customers impulse buying patterns [10] – i.e., when a customer is currently considering a specific book, the system suggests to her more books that are often sold together. This real-world popular recommendation setup is characterized by inferring the recommendations based on the user's current interest rather than on her long term activity history. In general, these item-oriented systems employ signals like "users who liked this product also liked...", which are directly mined from usage logs.

While evidentially used in practice, we are not aware of many published scientific works addressing collaborative-filtering item-oriented recommendations. This is not very surprising as the problem seems rather simplistic compared to personalized recommendations, which indeed may use item-item relations internally. After all, one could argue that simply counting co-usage patterns among items can almost directly deliver the required similarity scores in the form of item-item conditional purchase probabilities, or other pairwise similarity metrics (e.g., cosine and Jaccard similarities, etc.). However, we wish to highlight two shortcomings of such straightforward retrieval techniques. First, pointwise counting of item-item co-occurrences requires an adequate support for both items. Hence, similarities related to items subject to less user activity cannot be estimated reliably. Second, a naïve retrieval of most recommended items requires evaluating all possible items for each target item. Therefore, computing all related item pairs requires a quadratic time which is hard to scale as item inventories grow in size. The scalability issue could be alleviated by different pruning rules or by caching results, yet we suggest a more systematic solution which accounts for both scalability challenges as well accuracy challenges.

We present Euclidean Item Recommender (EIR) which is a new method for identifying related item-pairs while addressing the two aforementioned shortcomings. Instead of determining item-item relations by the limited number of co-occurrences, we represent item-item conditional probabilities through latent factor vectors which are learned using a "global " learning algorithm. Our method is utilizing the entire training data rather than just the pairwise information. Hence, we achieve a smooth estimation of item-to-item relations that facilitates more reliable recommendations even

RecSys'13, October 12–16, 2013, Hong Kong, China.
ACM 978-1-4503-2409-0/13/10.
http://dx.doi.org/10.1145/2507157.2508221.

for rarely co-purchased item pairs. Furthermore, the latent factor vectors are embedded in a Euclidean space, thereby allowing a fast retrieval of most similar items using *metric trees*, without requiring the consideration of all possible item pairs. Finally, another contribution of this work is the establishment of a modeling and experimentation scheme for item-oriented recommendation, which employs existing user preference datasets.

2. RELATED WORK

Item-item neighborhood methods are well studied in the academic literature [10, 13]. We share with these works the need to derive pairwise relations between items. However, our research is item-oriented rather than user-oriented. Unlike previous work, we do not model the users in our dataset. We focus on modeling the item-item relations directly.

Some prior works [9, 12] used latent factors for representing item-item relations. This work also follows this path with several distinctions. First, we aim at item-oriented recommendation dictating a different cost function and training method. In addition, we emphasize fast retrieval which is facilitated by embedding the factor vectors in a Euclidean space, rather than the inner-product space used by others.

Our usage of Euclidean embedding shares some similarities with a recent work on Euclidean matrix factorization [7]. However we model item-item relations and not user-item relations. Beyond this, a fundamental distinction between the works is that we address the implicit feedback case and not explicit ratings, which is in fact the common case in most systems where explicit rating data is not present. Implicit feedback requires a different formulation based on maximizing likelihood rather than squared error minimization [6]. In addition, we propose a novel way of incorporating biases into the model without hindering the effectiveness of the fast retrieval.

3. MODELING PAIRWISE RELATIONS

We represent item-item relations through their conditional probabilities. That is, given items i and j we will estimate $P(j|i)$, the conditional probability that a user consuming item i will consume item j as well. The conditional probabilities will be learned by embedding all items in a low-dimensional Euclidean space. An item k will be represented by a d-dimensional vector $\mathbf{y}_k \in \mathbb{R}^d$, and a scalar bias b_k. The latent item vectors are designed to capture item similarities and the biases capture popularity patterns independently of other co-consumed items. To this end, we define the conditional probability $P(j|i)$ by the multinomial distribution

$$P(j|i) = \frac{\exp(-\|\mathbf{y}_i - \mathbf{y}_j\|^2 + b_j)}{\sum_k \exp(-\|\mathbf{y}_i - \mathbf{y}_k\|^2 + b_k)}. \tag{1}$$

Note that we assure $\sum_j P(j|i) = 1$. Finally, given a training set $\mathcal{D}$, containing item pairs of co-consumed (or co-liked) items, we seek to learn model parameters that maximize the log-likelihood of the training set:

$$\text{log-likelihood}\{\mathcal{D}\} \stackrel{\text{def}}{=} \sum_{(i,j)\in\mathcal{D}} \log P(j|i). \tag{2}$$

3.1 Optimization process

Learning proceeds by stochastic gradient ascent. Given a training pair (i, j) we update each parameter θ (a latent vector component or a bias) by

$$\Delta\theta = \eta\frac{\partial P(j|i)}{\partial\theta} = \eta\left[\frac{\partial}{\partial\theta}\Big(-\|\mathbf{y}_i - \mathbf{y}_j\|^2 + b_j\Big) + \sum_k P(k|i)\frac{\partial}{\partial\theta}\Big(\|\mathbf{y}_i - \mathbf{y}_k\|^2 - b_k\Big)\right], \tag{3}$$

where η is the learning rate. However, such a training scheme would be too slow in practice as each update rule requires summing over all items. We thus resort to sampling the weighted sum in (3) based on the importance sampling idea proposed by Bengio and Senécal [2]; see also Aizenberg et al. [1] for a related usage of the technique.

With importance sampling we draw items according to a *proposal distribution*. In our case we assign each item a probability proportional to its empirical frequency in the training set (fraction of train pairs containing the item), and denote this proposal distribution by $P(i|\mathcal{D})$. Items are sampled with replacement from $P(i|\mathcal{D})$ into a list $\mathcal{L}$. Using $\mathcal{L}$, we approximate $P(k|i)$ for each $k \in \mathcal{L}$ with the weighting scheme

$$w(k|i) = \frac{\exp(-\|\mathbf{y}_i - \mathbf{y}_k\|^2 + b_k)/P(k|\mathcal{D})}{\sum_{l\in\mathcal{L}} \exp(-\|\mathbf{y}_i - \mathbf{y}_l\|^2 + b_l)/P(l|\mathcal{D})}. \tag{4}$$

Consequently, the approximated gradient ascent step given a training pair (i, j) will be

$$\Delta\theta = \eta\left[\frac{\partial}{\partial\theta}\Big(-\|\mathbf{y}_i - \mathbf{y}_j\|^2 + b_j\Big) + \sum_{k\in\mathcal{L}} w(k|i)\frac{\partial}{\partial\theta}\Big(\|\mathbf{y}_i - \mathbf{y}_k\|^2 - b_k\Big)\right]. \tag{5}$$

As mentioned in [2], it is desirable that the size of the set $\mathcal{L}$ grows as the training process proceeds because at later training phases more delicate parameter adjustments are needed. Hence, we employ a simple rule for controlling the sample size ($|\mathcal{L}|$) based on the fitness of the current estimate. Given a training pair (i, j), we keep sampling items into $\mathcal{L}$ until the following condition is satisfied:

$$\sum_{k\in\mathcal{L}} P(k|i) > \alpha \cdot P(j|i). \tag{6}$$

The adaptive sampling automatically lets the sample size grow when parameters are nearing final values and the correct paired item is getting a relatively high probability. In our implementation we used $\alpha = 3$. We impose a minimal size of 5 on the sample size. For efficiency we also limit the maximal sample size to 500.

4. FAST RETRIEVAL

Retrieval time of recommendations is a key factor when designing real-world large-scale systems that need to address tens of thousands of queries per second [8]. A major design goal of EIR is enabling fast pairing of items. In this setting, the task of efficiently retrieving recommendations requires finding items that the user is most likely to purchase given the item she is currently considering. Namely, we wish to find an item j that maximizes:

$$\max_{j\neq i} P(j|i) \quad \Leftrightarrow \quad \max_{j\neq i} -\|\mathbf{y}_i - \mathbf{y}_j\|^2 + b_j. \tag{7}$$

	Items	Users	Training	Test
Netflix	17,749	478,488	53,414,617	941,614
MSD	384,526	1,019,296	45,078,691	2,037,890
YMusic	433,903	497,881	40,362,704	984,162
Books	340,536	103,723	1,068,842	66,306

Table 1: The number of items, users, training-set examples and test-set examples in each dataset.

It is easy to see that by ignoring biases we are left only with the squared Euclidean distance between the two items vectors, and the retrieval is reduced to a simple nearest neighbor task. Nevertheless, biases are a key contributor to recommendations accuracy, and should not be dismissed. We therefore propose a simple transformation to reduce the problem in (7) to that of a simple Euclidean search. For each item vector $\mathbf{y}_j$, we define a concatenated item vector $\hat{\mathbf{y}}_j$ as follows:

$$\hat{\mathbf{y}}_j = [\mathbf{y}_j^\top, \sqrt{M_b - b_j}]^\top \in \mathbb{R}^{d+1}, \quad (8)$$

where M_b is the maximum bias ($M_b = \max_j b_j$). We also define a concatenated query vector as follows:

$$\bar{\mathbf{y}}_i = [\mathbf{y}_i^\top, 0]^\top. \quad (9)$$

It can be easily shown that (7) is equivalent to:

$$\max_{j \neq i} P(j|i) \quad \Leftrightarrow \quad \min_{j \neq i} \|\bar{\mathbf{y}}_i - \hat{\mathbf{y}}_j\|^2. \quad (10)$$

Therefore, this transformation facilitates a variety of Euclidean nearest neighbor algorithms e.g. Metric Trees, or Locality Sensitive Hashing (LSH).

5. EMPIRICAL STUDY

5.1 Dataset Construction

We evaluate our algorithm using four different datasets: Netflix [3], the Million Song Dataset (MSD) [4], Ziegler's books' reviews[1] (Books) [16], and Yahoo! Music (YMusic) [5]. Our work is focused on implicit ratings, however of the four aforementioned datasets only the MSD dataset is implicit. Therefore, we simulated imlicit data from the explicit datasets as follows: In Netflix, we first filtered only the ratings with a value ≥ 4. We then produced a dataset of "co-liked" movies – namely, movies that were liked by the same users. For the YMusic dataset, we repeated the same process for ratings ≥ 80. In the books dataset we simply used all the data-entries in order to create a dataset of co-consumed books that were read and reviewed by the same users (regardless of the review). Finally, in all datasets we generated item pairs as follows: For each user we created a random cyclic order of the items consumed by her. Then, the final dataset is comprised from all the pairs of consecutive items.

We split our datasets into train and test subsets by randomly choosing a subset of users and placing all their item pairs in the test-set. Table 1 summarize the final datasets statistics.

5.2 Baselines

We compared performance against traditional item-item similarity measurements:

- *Empirical Conditional Probability (ECP):* Empirical measurement of the conditional probability $P(j|i)$ defined as
$$P(j|i)_{empirical} = \frac{n_{i,j}}{n_i + 1},$$
where n_i is the total number of occurrences of item i in the dataset, and $n_{i,j}$ is the number co-occurrences of i and j together (counts were smoothed by adding 1).
- *Jaccard Similarity:* Jaccard similarity is a well know similarity measure defined as
$$Jaccard(i,j) = \frac{n_{i,j}}{n_i + n_j - n_{i,j}}.$$
- *Cosine Similarity:* Cosine similarity is another widely used similarity measure defined as
$$Cosine(i,j) = \frac{n_{i,j}}{\sqrt{n_i n_j}}.$$

Note that ranking based on these similarity measures differ in the way of normalizing the co-counts ($n_{i,j}$).

5.3 Accuracy Results

We measure performance in terms of Mean Percentile Rank (MPR). This metric was earlier used in studies of implicit feedback datasets within the context of personalized recommendations [6, 14]. In our item-oriented context, it is defined as follows: For each test pair of related items (i,j) we sample N additional random items. We rank every item k (the N random ones and j) with respect to $P(k|i)$ based on our model. Then, we compute the percentile rank of item j within this ranking. Ranks are averaged over all test pairs. Accordingly, percentile ranks closer to zero indicate better rankings. We used $N = 200$ in our experiments, though results are insensitive to changes in N given the large number of test pairs.

We trained the EIR model with $d = 50$ dimensions. Table 2 presents the MPR results of EIR against the baselines. We were encouraged by the fact that our algorithm outperformed the baselines on the Netflix, MSD and the Books datasets. On the YMusic dataset, our algorithm was second to ECP with a very small difference between the two.

Figure 1 depicts the mean percentile rank of the different algorithms vs. the support (popularity) of the conditioned item i in $P(j|i)$. While all the algorithms perform well on popular items, EIR has a clear advantage in the long tail. This is explained by the fact the EIR employs global optimization that utilize the entire training data rather than just the pairwise information. Among the different baseline algorithms, ECP is most similar to EIR. This is to be expected, as ECP is merely an empirical estimate of $P(j|i)$ – the objective of EIR.

5.4 Fast Retrieval Results

We evaluate the fast retrieval capabilities of EIR using metric trees [11, 15]. Metric trees are binary space-partitioning trees widely used for the task of indexing Euclidean datasets. The tree construction is very fast and space efficient, and the search employs the depth-first branch-and-bound algorithm similar to that of [15]. We quantify the improvement in retrieval time for the task described in (7) when using the

[1] www.informatik.uni-freiburg.de/~cziegler/BX/

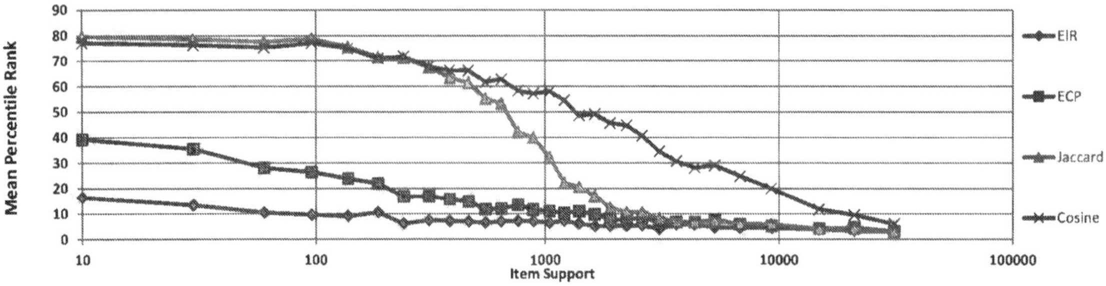

Figure 1: Mean Percentile Rank (MPR) vs. the support of the conditioned item i in $P(j|i)$ in the MSD dataset (lower is better).

	EIR	ECP	Jaccard	Cosine
Netflix	**5.825%**	6.57%	9.728%	8.376%
MSD	**6.602%**	13.663%	35.287%	49.18%
YMusic	2.837%	**2.536%**	9.795%	9.545%
Books	**27.342%**	35.902%	53.896%	61.011%

Table 2: Comparing MPR of EIR against common baselines (lower is better).

	Netflix	MSD	YMusic	Books
Speedup	25.036	21.422	31.219	11.218

Table 3: Speedup values for EIR with 50 dimensions

metric tree compared to a naïve search as follows:

$$\text{Speedup} = \frac{\text{Retrieval Time Using Naive Search}}{\text{Retrieval Time Using Tree}}. \quad (11)$$

The speedup values for each dataset are presented in Table 3.

6. SUMMARY

We tackle *item-oriented* recommendations, where the goal is to find items related to the current item. Our approach is centered around a method embedding items and their biases within a Euclidean space in a way that preserves co-consumption patterns. A unique feature of our embedding is its being Euclidean thereby facilitating fast item retrieval with readily available data structures suitable to the Euclidean space. We demonstrated the efficacy of the method in terms of both accuracy and indexing time.

7. REFERENCES

[1] N. Aizenberg, Y. Koren, and O. Somekh. Build your own music recommender by modeling internet radio streams. In *WWW*, 2012.

[2] Y. Bengio and J.-S. Senécal. Quick training of probabilistic neural nets by sampling. In *Proc. 9th International Workshop on Artificial Intelligence and Statistics (AISTATS'03)*, 2003.

[3] J. Bennett and S. Lanning. The netflix prize. In *Proc. KDD Cup and Workshop*, 2007.

[4] T. Bertin-Mahieux, D. P. Ellis, B. Whitman, and P. Lamere. The million song dataset. In *Proceedings of the 12th International Conference on Music Information Retrieval (ISMIR 2011)*, 2011.

[5] G. Dror, N. Koenigstein, Y. Koren, and M. Weimer. The yahoo! music dataset and kdd-cup'11. *Journal Of Machine Learning Research*, 18:3–18, 2012.

[6] Y. Hu, Y. Koren, and C. Volinsky. Collaborative filtering for implicit feedback datasets. In *ICDM*, pages 263–272, 2008.

[7] M. Khoshneshin and W. N. Street. Collaborative filtering via euclidean embedding. In *RecSys*, pages 87–94, 2010.

[8] N. Koenigstein, P. Ram, and Y. Shavitt. Efficient retrieval of recommendations in a matrix factorization framework. In *CIKM*, 2012.

[9] Y. Koren. Factor in the neighbors: Scalable and accurate collaborative filtering. *TKDD*, 4(1), 2010.

[10] G. Linden, B. Smith, and J. York. Industry report: Amazon.com recommendations: Item-to-item collaborative filtering. *IEEE Distributed Systems Online*, 4(1), 2003.

[11] F. P. Preparata and M. I. Shamos. *Computational Geometry: An Introduction*. Springer, 1985.

[12] S. Rendle, C. Freudenthaler, and L. Schmidt-Thieme. Factorizing personalized markov chains for next-basket recommendation. In *WWW*, pages 811–820, 2010.

[13] B. Sarwar, G. Karypis, J. Konstan, and J. Riedl. Item-based collaborative filtering recommendation algorithms. In *Proceedings of the 10th international conference on World Wide Web*, WWW '01, pages 285–295. ACM, 2001.

[14] H. Steck. Training and testing of recommender systems on data missing not at random. In *KDD*, pages 713–722, 2010.

[15] J. K. Uhlmann. Satisfying general proximity/similarity queries with metric trees. *Inf. Process. Lett.*, 40(4):175–179, 1991.

[16] C.-N. Ziegler, S. M. McNee, J. A. Konstan, and G. Lausen. Improving recommendation lists through topic diversification. In *Proceedings of the 14th international conference on World Wide Web*, WWW '05, pages 22–32, 2005.

Using Geospatial Metadata to Boost Collaborative Filtering

Alexander Ostrikov, Lior Rokach, Bracha Shapira
Department of Information Systems Engineering
Ben-Gurion University of the Negev
Beer-Sheva, Israel
{ostrikov,liorrk,bshapira}@bgu.ac.il

ABSTRACT

In this paper, we present a method for boosting collaborative filtering by integrating spatial information about geo-referenced items (e.g., photos). In particular, we developed a method to estimate missing ratings by propagating an item's neighbor's ratings based on the similarity of geospatial information. An empirical evaluation shows that geospatial information significantly improves recommendation results, and its contribution grows with the ratings data's level of sparseness. We illustrate the usefulness of the method for a photo recommendation task using data obtained from two popular photo-sharing web-sites: Flickr and Panoramio. A comparison with state-of-the-art methods indicates the superiority of the proposed method, implying that geospatial information should be considered, when available.

Categories and Subject Descriptors

H.3.3 [**Information Systems**]: Information Search and Retrieval

General Terms

Algorithms; Modeling; Optimization

Keywords

Context-aware recommender systems; Collaborative filtering

1. INTRODUCTION

Collaborative filtering (CF) -based recommender systems are very popular due to their simplicity and their excellent predictive performance. However, these systems may not be quite as effective if the rating matrix is sparse. Therefore, various methods have been developed to alleviate this sparseness problem (see for example [10]).

The basic idea presented in this paper is to utilize available geographic information, which is attached to the items, to enrich the rating matrix and convert it into a dense matrix. While geo-location data are frequently used for building context-aware recommender systems [2], these systems aim to match the item to the user's current physical location. Here, we focus on a scenario where items from certain locations are of interest to the user, regardless of the user's current location. One motivating example is photo recommendation. In this case, the items are photos taken by other users. We assume that if a user likes a photo taken in a specific location, s/he will probably like other photos taken in locations close-by. Another example is news recommendations: readers may be interested in news from specific locations such as conflict areas.

Our approach is based on the assumption that a user's interest in a specific item is partially based on its geo-location. Thus, we first identify items that lie in the same spatial area and those that are rated by users with similar interests. Then, we propagate ratings between the items that belong to the same geo-interest group. Specifically, the actual ratings of frequently rated items are propagated to items that are sparsely rated in an attempt to create artificial ratings for them. Finally, given the enriched matrix, we can employ the CF method on the dense matrix in order to induce the improved model. Note that genuine ratings should be trusted more than propagated ratings.

These geo-interest groups cannot be detected using the general methods proposed in works dealing with ratings clustering [9], because of the arbitrary shape that objects can form in space. Moreover, different geo-interest groups can be located in the same area and have to be distinguished.

The idea of exploiting geographic information in recommendations is not new. User geographic location is widely used to generate a more relevant result when the user is moving in a mobile environment. The term location-based recommendation is used in the literature to classify this kind of work. Bae-Hee et al. [4] exploit the user's current GPS position to introduce a location context in addition to the personal and the environmental context in the generation of the final recommendation. Horozov et al. [2] reduce the number of possible recommendation candidates using a circular buffer around the present position of the user. Matyas and Schlieder [6] offer an approach for handling users' individual differences by identifying less popular geographic objects that are nevertheless of interest to a specific user. Their approach is based on user-based collaborative filtering in conjunction with geographical partonomy information. Most recently, [5] took a geospatial approach for determining location-based preferences. They proposed capturing the geographic context of user preferences for items using a relational graph, deriving different algorithms for calculating user similarity.

It should be clarified that our work is *not* a context-aware recommender system, because it neither aims to match the user's current location user to the item nor tries to recommend places. Instead, this work uses geographic information attached to the items in an attempt to enrich the rating matrix and improve recommendations.

Currently, no studies exist that tried to alleviate the sparsity problem by using spatial information to enrich the ratings matrix and

RecSys'13, October 12–16, 2013, Hong Kong, China.

http://dx.doi.org/10.1145/2507157.2507201.

make it denser. The goal of this research is to provide a method to boost the performance of CF in the case of sparse data using available spatial metadata regarding the items. The contributions are threefold:

1. A method to enrich the sparse rating matrix using geographical information that is available on the items is introduced.

2. Adjusting Nearest Neighbors Collaboration Filtering (NN CF) methods that consider not only the rating but also its credibility by assigning different weights to genuine rating and propagated rating.

3. The proposed method is evaluated on two real-world datasets; we show that geo-location can actually improve predictive performance.

2. METHODS

While the proposed method can be embedded in any CF-based recommender system, for the sake of clarity, we illustrate our method on the following popular settings: user-to-user NN CF. The main steps of this setting are: 1) Calculating the user-to-user similarity matrix; and 2) recommending items based on the items rated by the top nearest users. Recall that in our approach we enrich the rating matrix by propagating the ratings (Step 1 below). Then, together with the genuine ratings, we calculate the user-to-user similarity matrix (Step 2 below).

2.1 Step 1: Ratings propagation

We present three geo-propagation methods. In the first, most simple method, the propagation is performed within the ratings of the same user based on the geographical distance between items. In our locations clustering-based propagation method, we first cluster the items into spatial groups and then inter-propagate ratings among the items that belong to the same spatial group. In the last method – the locations-users based propagation - we try to detect geo-interest groups by considering both the location and the users' rating patterns. This permitted us to obtain a more fine-grained clustering of the same geographical area based on users' ratings.

Method 1: Direct use of location The provided ratings of items are propagated to closely located items. Specifically, we assign a pair of values to each entry in the user-item matrix. The first value is $V_{ui}(V \geq 0)$, which represents the mean propagated rating. The second value, $W_{ui}(0 \leq W \leq 1)$, refers to the total propagated weights. The values of V_{ui} and W_{ui} are calculated using following equation:

$$V_{ui} = \begin{cases} R_{ui} + \frac{1}{|R_u|-1} \sum_{j \neq i; j \in R_u} \frac{R_{uj}}{(dist(i,j)+\kappa)^2} & \text{if } i \in R_u \\ \frac{1}{|R_u|-1} \sum_{j \neq i; j \in R_u} \frac{R_{uj}}{(dist(i,j)+\kappa)^2} & \text{if } i \notin R_u \end{cases} \quad (1)$$

$$W_{ui} = \begin{cases} 1 + \frac{1}{|R_u|-1} \sum_{j \neq i; j \in R_u} \frac{1}{(dist(i,j)+\kappa)^2} & \text{if } i \in R_u \\ \frac{1}{|R_u|-1} \sum_{j \neq i; j \in R_u} \frac{1}{(dist(i,j)+\kappa)^2} & \text{if } i \notin R_u \end{cases} \quad (2)$$

where $R_u(R \geq 0)$ is the set of items rated by user u and R_{ui} indicates the rating of user u to item i. $dist(i,j)$ is the geographical distance between items i and j (in our case, we calculated the Euclidean distance based on the GPS latitude and longitude coordinates). $\kappa(\kappa > 0)$ is the propagation parameter, which represents the importance of the original rating provided by the user u for item i. A high value of κ indicates that V_{ui} is determined mainly by the original rating provided by the user.

We determine the value of κ through a trial-and-error process and tune its value to the database in hand. More specifically, we started with the value of zero and increased the value while monitoring the recommendation performance. We observed that setting κ to low values provides the best results in terms of recommendation precision. We decided that the propagation weight (strength) will be inversely proportional to the square of the distances between the items' locations in order to emphasize closer items.

Method 2: Locations clustering based propagation: In the previous method, we assumed that propagation can be originated from any item, even from items located far from the target item (toward which the propagation is performed). Moreover, in the previous method, propagation is also performed for target items located in areas that the user has never rated. In the location clustering method, we limit the propagation by first clustering the items based on their location, and then, perform propagation only within the clusters. We do not attempt to enrich items that are located in clusters that were not rated by the user.

For example, pictures taken close to Piazza di Spagna in Rome are interesting because of the historical and architectural sites located in neighboring areas. Therefore, we assume that if users like/dislike an item attributed to this area, they might like/dislike other items located nearby. After grouping items into the same clusters, propagation is performed on them. We use the spatial clustering algorithm DBSCAN [1] to cluster the items based solely on their *density* in the geographical space. DBSCAN it can find arbitrarily shaped clusters and discard isolated items as noise. After cluster detection, the propagating ratings calculation is calculated using Eq. 1 and 2; however, the calculation is performed over the set of clusters to which user u rated items belong, using the set of items that belong to the same cluster as item i.

Method 3: Locations-users based propagation: The previous method clustered items based solely on their location, while ignoring the users' ratings. This may lead to large clusters that include different types of items, some of which the user likes and others s/he dislikes. To demonstrate the problem, recall the Piazza di Spagna in Rome example whose neighborhoods include both historical and architectural sites and also places of leisure, such as shops and cafes. Clearly, some people are more interested in cultural sites than leisure sites and vice versa. Thus, to detect these groups, both spatial and user preferences have to be considered in the cluster-detecting process. After detecting spatial-users clusters, we perform propagation for the items belonging to the same clusters. For each spatial cluster found, we perform the following procedure:

1. Represent each item as a vector of all users' ratings in the cluster, where an entry for every user contains the user's rating or 0 if no rating is available.

2. Blur rating values across the vectors using a Gaussian filter algorithm with a one dimensional kernel. This is inspired by the preprocessing that is frequently done in image processing in an attempt to allow fragment detection and noise reduction.

3. Run the GDBSCAN [7] algorithm, which generalizes clustering of spatial items by considering their non-spatial attributes. The algorithm uses domain custom predicates for determining items neighborhood ($nPred$), and items density ($wCard$). Let D be a cluster in which the user group clusters need to be found. Let p, q be items that belong to D. Thus, the neighborhoods predicate ($Npred$) is set to $true$ if $dist(p,q) < Eps$ and $CosSim(p,q) < MinSim$. The

weight cardinality predicate (*wCard*) is defined by Eq. 3. Literally, $wCard(p)$ is an average of similarities between vector p and its neighbors in radius Eps.

$$wCard\,(p) = \frac{\sum_{q \in N_{Eps}(p)} CosSim(p,q)}{N} \tag{3}$$

We fitted the clustering algorithm parameters heuristically. The parameters Eps and $MinPoints$ should be set to low values for denser spatial distribution of the items. The $WCard$ value was tuned between 0 to 1 by maximizing the recommendation performance.

2.2 Step 2: Calculating user-user similarity

We used an enriched ratings matrix to calculate user-user similarity and find the nearest neighbors. For each pair of users (u, s), we calculated similarity according to the modified Tanimoto similarity function:

$$\frac{\sum_{j \in U \cap S} (V_{uj} W_{uj})(V_{sj} W_{sj})}{\sum_{j \in U} (V_{uj} W_{uj})^2 + \sum_{j \in S} (V_{sj} W_{sj})^2 + \sum_{j \in U \cap S} (V_{uj} W_{uj})(V_{sj} W_{sj})} \tag{4}$$

3. EVALUATION

We evaluated our methods on two recommendation tasks of geo-referenced items: pictures and points of interest. In the first step, we compared our base direct propagation (DP_CF) to the baseline user-user NN CF and the modern state-of-the-art method of recommending items with geo-referenced items' relational neighbors [5]. We used two weighting schemes examined by Marinho – the two layer similarity notated as RN_TL (see [6]) and the CF. In the second step, we compared different propagation approaches – the direct propagation (DP_CF), locations clustering propagation (LP_CF), and locations-users propagation (LUCP_CF).

Our initial datasets were very sparse (>99.99%); thus, so that we could check our hypothesis along different sparsity levels starting from base relatively low sparsity, we selected users who fit the low sparsity profile that was increased by randomly removing parts of the ratings in the training set for each user, by increasing the ratio to achieve a higher actual sparsity. It should be noted that usually in commercial systems sparsity levels tend to be much greater than 95% [8]. The validity of the hypothesis was checked in an off-line evaluation using a repeated random sub-sampling validation. In each of the ten iterations and for each sparsity level, we randomly selected 30% of the users as the test set. Then, since we did not have user transaction times for each user in the test set, we randomly selected 70% of their ratings for training and 30% for testing. To check the significance of our results, we used the Friedman test (α=0.05), and rank sums-based procedure, post-hoc test, for determining the homogeneous subsets (α=0.05).

3.1 Flickr Dataset

Flickr is an image and video hosting website, where comments are posted about shared pictures, which provide valuable information for estimating users' interest in the pictures and their opinions about them. We use a text sentiment analysis algorithm [3] to calculate ratings from sentiment and opinion values refined from bloggers' comments. Each blogger can express his opinion about a particular picture several times resulting in several opinions and sentiment values for one user. We assume that the number of a user's comments about a picture reflects the strength of his opinion about it; thus, the more comments written by the user, the stronger his/her sentiment and opinion expression. Using the above assumption, we calculate a user's rating value for the picture.

We checked our hypothesis for sparsity levels 92%, 95.1%, 99.1% (representing lowest available, middle range, and the highest sparsity), for recall, R-Precision (precision at R, where R is the number of relevant items), and MAP. For all of the metrics and sparsity levels we checked (except R-Precision at 95.1%), we were able to reject the null-hypothesis that there is no difference between the algorithm's performance, using the Friedman test ($p < 0.001$). This indicates that the superiority of our algorithm is statistically significant.

Fig. 1 presents the recall performance for the compared algorithms along the increasing sparsity levels. We got three homogeneous groups, {DP_CF}, {RN_TL, RN_CF}, and {U_CF} for all sparsity levels. Fig. 1 also presents the R-Precision for the compared algorithms along the increasing sparsity levels. At the lowest (92%) level of sparsity, there is no single significant leader; both state-of-the-art approaches RN_TL and collaborative filtering are based on direct ratings propagation (DP_CF), and belong to the same leader homogeneous group as detected by post-hoc tests. The average value of both R-Precision and MAP over the experiments is higher for the RN_TL approach. At a high 95.1% of sparsity, all the algorithms have no significant difference and belong to the same group. At the highest sparsity level of 99%, it can be seen that DP_CF gains a significant advantage over other approaches.

For calculating locations clusters to be used in the LCP_CF method, we used the DBSCAN algorithm with Eps=10 and MinPoints = 4. For detecting user-item clusters to be used in the LUCP_CF method, we used the GDBSCAN algorithm with Eps=3, MinSim=0.6, MinWCard=0.7 and σ=1 for blurring the data.

3.2 Panoramio Dataset

On the Panoramio web-site, many photos illustrate places. This permits the assumption that if a user takes a picture in a specific location, then s/he has some interest in that location. Since the physical POI can be represented by many photos taken by different users in close locations but still in different geographic coordinates, we adopted the same approach as in the compared state-of-the-art approaches, where the authors used geographic clusters to represent POI's. Therefore, instead of recommending individual coordinates represented by photos, we recommended regions where users may be interested in taking photos. Since each user can upload several photos for a single POI, we had to find a way to deal with several users' transactions for one item. In the Panoramio dataset, when a user's transaction is not accompanied by an explicit rating, we assume that the uploading of the photo expresses the users' positive opinion on the item and represent this fact with initial rating of 1. Moreover, we assume that the users' positive opinion is stronger when more images are in a particular POI.

We checked our hypothesis for chosen sparsity levels 95%, 96.9%, 99.3% (representing lowest available, middle range and the highest sparsity), for recall, R-Precision and MAP. The observations are analogous to the results observed for pictures recommendation. In all cases, we were able to reject the null-hypothesis that all algorithms perform the same, using the Friedman test (p <0.001). Fig. 2. presents the recall performance for the compared algorithms along the increasing sparsity levels. We have three homogeneous groups, {DP_CF}, {RN_TL, RN_CF}, {U_CF}, for all sparsity levels. The leading group is the direct propagation approach (DP_CF), obtaining full available recall at all levels, which is explained by recommending based on a 100% populated items-ratings matrix. The relational neighbors approach group (RN_CF, RN_TL), provided better results than the base line unpropagated U_CF, with a quite constant gap along the sparsity levels; the recall of both declined drastically at the highest sparsity. It can be noted that RN_CF and RN_TL obtained exactly the same recall levels.

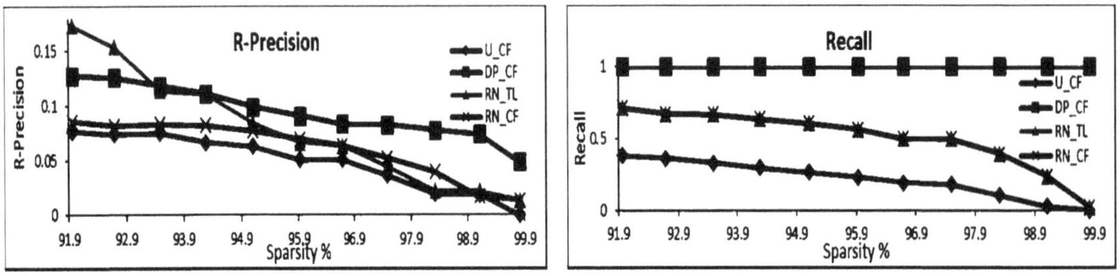

Figure 1: R-Precision and Recall over various sparsity levels for the Flickr Dataset.

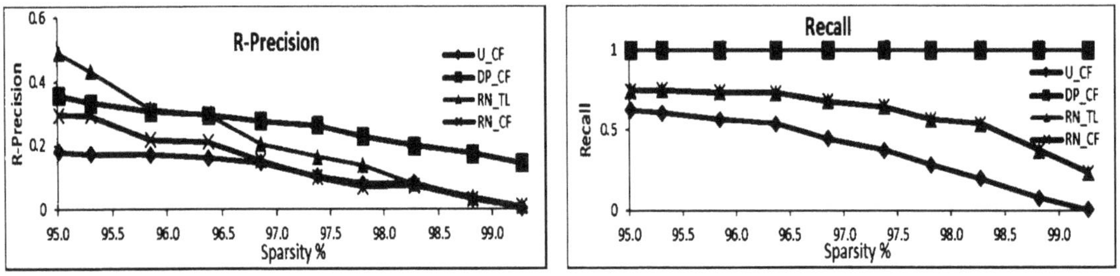

Figure 2: R-Precision and Recall over various sparsity levels for the Panoramio Dataset.

Fig. 2. also presents the R-Precision for the compared algorithms along the increasing sparsity levels. At the lowest (95.0%) level of sparsity, the significant leader is the relational neighbors two layer similarity approach (RN_TL), standing in a separate group, while after increasing sparsity to 96.9% we get quite another picture – the state-of-the-art RN_TL approach and the propagated CF (DP_CF) both stand in the homogeneous leader group, with no significant differences. At the highest sparsity level of 99.3%, the propagated CF (DP_CF) gets the significant advantage at R-Precision and MAP over other approaches, while all the other algorithms drastically plunge to zero levels. For calculating locations clusters to be used in the LCP_CF method, we used the DBSCAN algorithm with Eps=30 and MinPoints = 4. For detecting user-item clusters to be used in the LUCP_CF method, we used the GDBSCAN algorithm with our custom predicates with Eps = 5, MinSim = 0.7, MinWCard = 0.8. For blurring items vectors in the LUCP_CF algorithm, we used σ=1.

4. CONCLUSIONS

In this study, we explored the possibility of boosting the collaborative filtering performance in the case of sparse data in the domain of recommending geo-tagged items by integrating spatial information known about the items. We evaluated the performance of our methods in comparison with the latest state-of-the-art approaches for recommending geo-tagged items, and showed significant advantages of our methods in the case of sparse data, which is the situation in most scenarios. We found that the advantage of our method becomes more significant with the growth of sparsity. We also proposed and evaluated more enhanced propagation approaches intended to improve the precision at lower sparsity levels, but did not get a significant improvement in evaluated datasets over our initially proposed approach. The enhanced approaches of propagation can be valuable in other data scenarios or when more information is available in the ratings matrix. However, since our study was initially oriented to deal with the sparsity problem, we would recommend using our base approach instead.

5. REFERENCES

[1] M. Ester, H.-P. Kriegel, J. Sander, and X. Xu. A density-based algorithm for discovering clusters in large spatial databases with noise. In *KDD*, pages 226–231, 1996.

[2] T. Horozov, N. Narasimhan, and V. Vasudevan. Using location for personalized poi recommendations in mobile environments. In *SAINT*, pages 124–129. IEEE, 2006.

[3] S. Kisilevich, C. Rohrdantz, and D. Keim. Şbeautiful picture of an ugly placeŤ. exploring photo collections using opinion and sentiment analysis of user comments. In *IMCSIT*, pages 419–428, 2010.

[4] B.-H. Lee, H.-N. Kim, J.-G. Jung, and G.-S. Jo. Location-based service with context data for a restaurant recommendation. In *Database and Expert Systems Applications*, pages 430–438. Springer, 2006.

[5] L. B. Marinho, T. Sandholm, C. de Souza Baptista, I. Nunes, C. Nóbrega, and J. Araújo. Extracting geospatial preferences using relational neighbors. *JIDM*, 3(3):364–377, 2012.

[6] C. Matyas and C. Schlieder. A spatial user similarity measure for geographic recommender systems. In *GeoSpatial Semantics*, pages 122–139. Springer, 2009.

[7] J. Sander, M. Ester, H.-P. Kriegel, and X. Xu. Density-based clustering in spatial databases: The algorithm gdbscan and its applications. *Data Mining and Knowledge Discovery*, 2(2):169–194, 1998.

[8] B. Shapira, L. Rokach, and S. Freilikhman. Facebook single and cross domain data for recommendation systems. *User Model. User-Adapt. Interact.*, 23(2-3):211–247, 2013.

[9] A. Shepitsen, J. Gemmell, B. Mobasher, and R. Burke. Personalized recommendation in social tagging systems using hierarchical clustering. In *Proceedings of the 2008 ACM conference on Recommender systems*, pages 259–266, 2008.

[10] H. Yildirim and M. S. Krishnamoorthy. A random walk method for alleviating the sparsity problem in collaborative filtering. In *Proceedings of the 2008 ACM conference on Recommender systems*, pages 131–138, 2008.

When Power Users Attack: Assessing Impacts in Collaborative Recommender Systems

David C. Wilson and Carlos E. Seminario
Software and Information Systems Department
University of North Carolina at Charlotte
davils@uncc.edu cseminar@uncc.edu

ABSTRACT

Power users, in a Collaborative Filtering (CF) Recommender System (RS) context, are those who can exert considerable influence over the recommendation outcomes presented to other users. RS operators encourage the existence of power user communities and leverage them to help fellow users make informed purchase decisions. Thus, RS research in this area has focused on power user identification and utilization to address challenges such as rating sparsity for new items or users. But, as ever, there remains the potential for corruption of power. Alongside accuracy and efficiency measures, RS robustness to manipulation or 'attack' has been studied using injection of false user profiles. Our research is investigating the impact on RS predictions and top-N recommendation lists when simulated power users provide biased ratings for new items. In this study, we introduce the notion of a 'Power User Attack' for RS robustness analysis, as well as a novel use of social networking degree centrality concepts for identifying RS power users. Initial results show that power users identified using in-degree centrality, compared to other techniques, can be more influential as reflected by accuracy and robustness impacts before and after power user attacks.

Categories and Subject Descriptors

H.3.3 [**Information Storage and Retrieval**]: Information Search and Retrieval–*Information filtering*

Keywords

Recommender Systems; Power User; Attacks; Evaluation

1. INTRODUCTION

In a Collaborative Filtering (CF) Recommender System (RS) context, *power users* are those who can exert considerable influence over the recommendations presented to other users. Previous research has indicated that power users can have major impacts on RS ratings predictions and top-N recommendations lists, especially when the underlying RS algorithms are neighborhood-based [10]. However, recommender system operators encourage the existence of power user communities; e.g., Amazon Vine^{TM}invites the most trusted reviewers on Amazon to post opinions about new and pre-release items to help their fellow users make informed purchase decisions[1]. Furthermore, new items can sometimes pose significant market acceptance challenges to producers of goods and services; in order to address this issue, marketers may rely on the influence that power users have in recommending items to other users [4, 1]. And given the influence that power users can have over others, what happens when power users provide biased ratings for new items?

To address this issue, we investigate the identification/selection and attack impacts of RS power users. We define and study a novel "Power User Attack" as a set of power user profiles that influence the results presented to other users by providing biased ratings. This attack is distinct from previously studied types of RS attacks [12, 9, 11] (e.g., "random", "average", "bandwagon", etc.) that rely on a set of carefully configured false user profiles which are injected into the dataset to mount the attack. Power User Attack analyses rely critically on power user identification, so we develop and evaluate a novel use of degree centrality concepts from social network analysis [18], for identifying the most influential RS power users for attack purposes.

In this paper we develop hypotheses for, and present initial results of, experiments designed to answer several questions related to RS power users and attacks on new items using power user profiles: (1) How are power users best identified in a RS? (2) What happens to the accuracy and robustness of the RS rating predictions when power user profiles contain biased ratings for new items? (3) How do the popular RS algorithms compare in their robustness against power user attacks?

2. RELATED WORK

In the RS context, power users are of interest to system operators and their client companies when launching a new item because a positive endorsement (high rating) can translate into item recommendations to a large number of users. This is known as market-based use of RS and has been previously promoted as a solution to the "cold-start" or "new item" problem [1]. However, identifying power users remains an active research topic. Rashid et al [14] developed a RS algorithm-independent approach based on the number of unique prediction differences observed when an active user is removed from the prediction calculation. Viral marketing to exploit the network value of customers was studied by [4]. Maximizing the spread of influence through a social network was further studied by [8] who found the problem to be NP-hard and provided the first provable approximate guarantees for efficient algorithms. More recently, [5] has analyzed several heuristic ap-

[1]http://www.amazon.com/gp/vine/help

RecSys'13, October 12–16, 2013, Hong Kong, China.

ACM 978-1-4503-2409-0/13/10 ...$15.00.
http://dx.doi.org/10.1145/2507157.2507220 .

proaches to power user selection. Power user selection techniques have been evaluated using various methods such as shifts in prediction values [14, 5], accuracy and coverage measures [1], and expected lift in profit [4]. Although robustness measures such as Hit Ratio and Rank (see Evaluation Metrics in §4) have not been used previously to evaluate power user selection methods, we use them here because we believe that true power users are in some sense defined by their capacity for impact on system outcomes.

Social Network Analysis affords well-known concepts that can be readily applied to RS power users and their influence in the underlying RS social graph. The concept of Degree Centrality [18] indicates that nodes (users) who have more edges (connections) to other nodes may have advantages; high in-degree refers to nodes that many other nodes connect to and corresponds to high prominence, prestige, or popularity and high out-degree refers to nodes that connect to many other nodes and corresponds to high expansiveness. Furthermore, collaborative relationships in recommender systems can be represented as a social network [13], where, in-degree represents the number of contact lists a user appears in and out-degree indicates the number of users on a contact list that can be used to ask opinions or advice. Neighborhood characteristics and power user selection in recommender systems were analyzed in [10] as part of study on temporal social networks.

Attempts to influence recommender system results by providing false ratings are known as "shilling attacks" [9], or "profile injection attacks" [11]. A user profile contains the set of ratings a user has made using the recommender system. The intent of an attack is to either promote ("push") a target item by setting the rating to the maximum value or demote ("nuke") a target item by setting the rating to the minimum value; furthermore, attackers will submit one or more user profiles containing item ratings (called attack user profiles) that push or nuke a specific item. Research in attacks on recommender systems began in 2002 [12] and has continued to be studied, especially in the areas of attack detection and improvements in algorithm robustness; a more recent summary on RS attacks can be found in [2]. This research has revealed that knowledge of the underlying RS algorithms and dataset characteristics can enhance the effectiveness of an attack even though this knowledge may be difficult to obtain. With today's level of user sophistication, however, attackers can obtain this knowledge either indirectly (e.g., scraping/data-mining, social engineering well-known users via side channels) or even directly (e.g., leak, insider, system breach). Uncovering, in part or full, the social network of interest that underlies such RS can leave systems vulnerable to exploitation from more subtle, yet powerful, attacks by highly-influential power users. And this vector of attack remains an open question in RS robustness research that we begin to explore in this study.

3. POWER USER ATTACK

We define the *Power User Attack* (PUA) as a new attack model where power users bias the results of the RS predictions and top-N recommendation lists with targeted fake ratings. Like other attack models, PUA profiles contain target items that are set to the maximum or minimum rating depending on attack intent. However, unlike classic attack models (e.g., random, average, bandwagon) that employ straightforward statistical templates (e.g., average rating, popularity, and likability) to generate synthetic attack profile filler (non-target) items [11], very little is known about the profile characteristics of power users. And without this knowledge, it is difficult to generate synthetic power user profiles. So, in order to evaluate this attack model, our initial foray into studying the impact of a PUA uses selected power user profiles that already exist in the dataset as simulated injected attack user profiles; we recognize this as a limitation in our initial work and will be addressed in the future with the use of synthetic power user attack profiles. Thus, to implement our initial attack, a group of power users are selected (see §3.1), the attack intent and target item(s) are specified, and the remainder of the profile for the PUA (the filler) remains unchanged for each power user in the attack. By keeping the power users' profiles the same and then adding the target item rating for the attack, the power users' connections to other users, from a social network standpoint, remain essentially the same[2]. The number of power users participating in the attack defines the attack size; the larger the attack size, the larger the expected disruption in RS predictions and top-N recommendation lists.

3.1 Power User Selection

Power users in the RS context have been referred to as users with a large number of ratings [7] as well as those that are able to influence the largest number of other users [4, 14, 1, 5]. To measure influence, [14] used the number of prediction differences above a prediction threshold when a user is removed from the dataset, [5] used the number of users that had the prediction for a target item shifted sufficiently above a threshold so that the item appears in their top-N list, [1] used MAE and coverage to evaluate various seed (influential user) selection algorithms, and [4] used the expected lift in profit earned by influencing other users, recursively. Although maximizing the spread of influence through a social network is an NP-hard problem to solve optimally [8], several heuristics were analyzed by [5] in order to select groups of influential users including Most Central (those with highest aggregate similarity to other users), Most Positive (those with the highest positive average rating), Most Active (those who have rated the highest number of items), and Random (a control group comprised of randomly selected users).

We have developed an approach to power user selection for attack purposes, based on social network analysis concepts of Degree Centrality [18, 10]. Specifically, we use In-Degree Centrality (users who appear in the highest number of other users' neighborhoods) with significance weighting [6] because when using similarity and neighborhood-based methods to select power users, significance weighting encourages strong connections between users who have rated many items in common. In an initial study, we found that both our approach and the Most Central heuristic [5] performed significantly better using significance weighting.

4. EXPERIMENTAL DESIGN

To address our research questions we test the following Hypotheses: (1) Using Degree Centrality to select a set of power users results in a more effective attack than using either Aggregated Similarity or Number of Ratings, (2) A small number of power users can have significant effects on RS predictions and top-N lists of recommendations for new items, and (3) User-based CF is more vulnerable to the power user attack than item-based CF algorithms.

Evaluation Metrics: We use Mean Absolute Error and prediction coverage for accuracy and coverage [7, 17] using a holdout-partitioned 70/30 train/test dataset. We also use Hit Ratio, Prediction Shift, and Rank robustness measures [11, 2] where a high Hit Ratio and a low Rank indicates that the attack was successful (from the attacker's standpoint). Since the PUA being evaluated here is for new items (zero rating value), the Prediction Shift is expected to be close to the maximum rating as defined by the RS.

[2]In a few cases, power user profiles that already had a target item rating were updated in certain attack scenarios and, although the target item rating change might alter their neighborhoods, we believe the impact to this initial analysis is not an issue.

Datasets and Algorithms: The data used in this study were the MovieLens[3] 100K[4] and 1M[5] datasets, with item ratings from 1 (did not like) to 5 (liked very much). For the user-based CF algorithm [15, 6, 3], we used Pearson Correlation similarity (with significance weighting of $n_{ci}/50$, where n_{ci} is the number of co-rated items), Neighborhood formation (similarity thresholding = 0.0 and kNN = 25 and 50), and Mean-centered prediction. For the item-based CF algorithm [16], we used Adjusted Cosine similarity (with significance weighting of $n_{ci}/50$), Neighborhood formation (similarity thresholding = 0.0), and Weighted prediction. Following earlier studies evaluating power user influence [4, 14, 5], we focus on traditional user-based and item-based CF algorithms for this analysis. We plan to use matrix factorization approaches as a next step.

Power User Selection: The following methods were used:
InDegree (ID2550 and ID5050): Our method is based on the in-degree centrality concept from social network analysis — power users are those who participate in the highest number of neighborhoods. For each user i compute its similarity with every other user j applying significance weighting $n_{ci}/50$, then discard all but the top-n neighbors for each user i (we used n=25 for ID2550 and n=50 for ID5050). Count the number of similarity scores for each user j (# neighborhoods user j is in) and select the top 50 user j's.
AggregatedSimilarity (AS25NO): This is the Most Central heuristic from [5]. The top 50 users with the highest aggregate similarity scores become the selected set of power users. This method requires at least 5 co-rated items between user i and user j and does not use significance weighting[6].
NumberRatings (NR): This method is based on [7] where "power user" refers to users with the highest number of ratings; it also is called the Most Active heuristic in [5]. We selected the top 50 users based on the total number of ratings they have in their user profile.

Target Item Selection: For each dataset, 50 target items with no more than one rating, regardless of their rating value, were selected randomly, given our objective to attack only 'new' items.

Attack Parameter Selection: The Attack Intent is Push, i.e., target item rating is set to max (= 5). The Attack Size or number of power users in each attack is 50, 40, 30, 20, 10, 5, 3, and 2; 50 power user profiles equate to a 5% attack for ML100K and a 1% attack for ML1M. The Attack profiles used were actual power user profiles and we added the target item rating. The Filler size is determined by each power users' profile size.

Test Variations: Two prediction algorithms, two datasets, four power user selection methods, and eight attack sizes. Each test variation was executed once for each of the 50 target items and data results were averaged over the 50 target items.

5. RESULTS AND DISCUSSION

(1) How are power users best identified in a RS? How much influence power users can exert on other users, before and after an attack, would indicate the best identification method. **Before the power user attack**, one measure of influence is the negative impact on RS accuracy when removing power users. We removed from 1 to 50 power users from datasets of user-item ratings before any attacks took place for all three methods of power user selection. The results for InDegree (Figure 1) show that as power users are removed, accuracy impacts are more significant on user-based recommenders (p <0.001 when the number of power users removed is > 10) than on item-based recommenders (p <0.025 when the number of power users removed is = 30) across both dataset sizes. Similar (ML1M) and weaker (ML100K) results occurred for AggregatedSimlarity and NumberRatings methods. Coverage results (not shown) also indicate significant impacts as more power users are removed, especially for user-based CF. The accuracy and coverage results for the InDegree method and user-based CF are consistent with results found in [10]. **After the attack**, we believe that the method that selects the most influential set of power users is the one producing the highest Hit Ratio and lowest Rank. Both InDegree and NumberRatings power user selection methods dominated (attack was more successful) the AggregatedSimilarity method as indicated by the Average Hit Ratio and Rank results for user-based CF using ML1M (Figure 2). While Hit Ratio and Rank results for InDegree and NumberRatings were about the same for ML100K (not shown), InDegree performed better than NumberRatings on the ML1M dataset (p<0.05). For item-based CF, none of the power user selection methods tested here produced a major impact to Hit Ratio or Rank using ML1M (Figure 3) or ML100K. From the attacker's perspective, the AggregatedSimilarity method was slightly more effective than InDegree and NumberRatings.

Therefore, using In Degree Centrality to select a set of power users results in a more effective attack than using either Aggregated Similarity or Number of Ratings, confirming our first Hypothesis for user-based CF only. Impacts to the accuracy metrics (Figure 1) and robustness metrics (Figure 2) indicate that a small number of power users[7] can have significant effects on RS predictions and top-N recommendation lists for new items, confirming our second Hypothesis for user-based CF only.

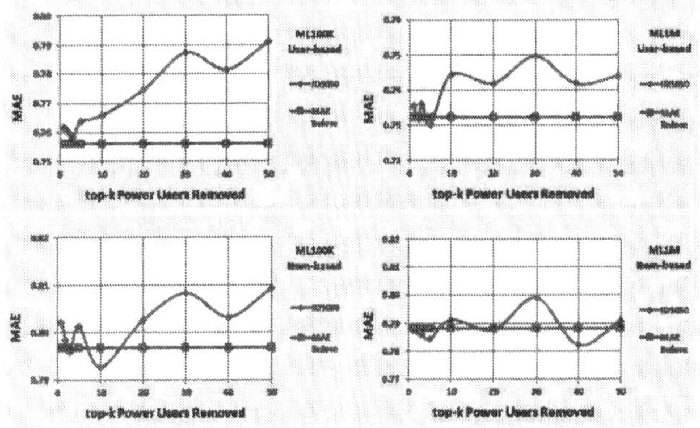

Figure 1: MAE impacts, before and after removing Power Users – In Degree using ML100K and ML1M

(2) What happens to the accuracy and robustness of the RS rating predictions when power user profiles contain biased ratings for new items? Accuracy and robustness metrics were negatively impacted due to the PUA. Accuracy results were mixed across datasets, CF algorithms, selection methods, and size of attack. Notably after attack, all four selection methods yielded MAE values significantly higher (p <0.05) for ML1M user-based CF and 30 or more power users, and the InDegree method yielded MAE values significantly higher (p <0.05) for ML1M item-based CF with 30 or 40 power users. As noted above, robustness results (Figures 2 and 3) indicate that InDegree and NumberRatings impact user-based CF recommenders more significantly than AggregatedSimilarity; however, we found the reverse to be true for item-based CF recommenders.

(3) How do the popular RS algorithms (user-based and item based CF) compare in their robustness against power user attacks?

[3]http://www.grouplens.org
[4]100,000 ratings, 1,682 movies, 943 users, 93.7% sparsity.
[5]1,000,209 ratings, 3,883 movies, 6,040 users, 95.7% sparsity.
[6]Based on personal communication with the authors.
[7]Note that 50 power users is < 1% of the ML1M user base.

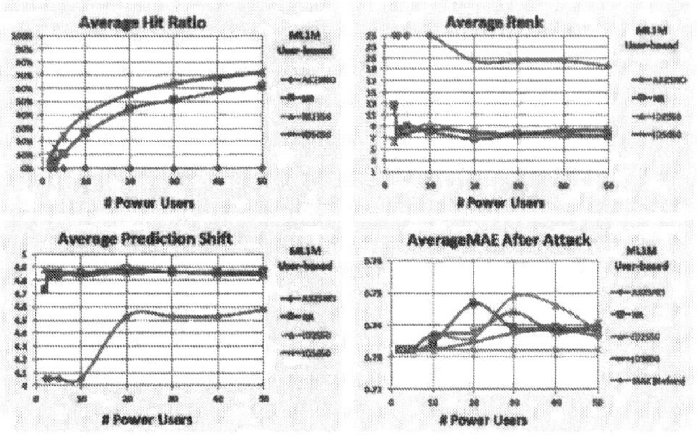

Figure 2: ML1M – User-based Results

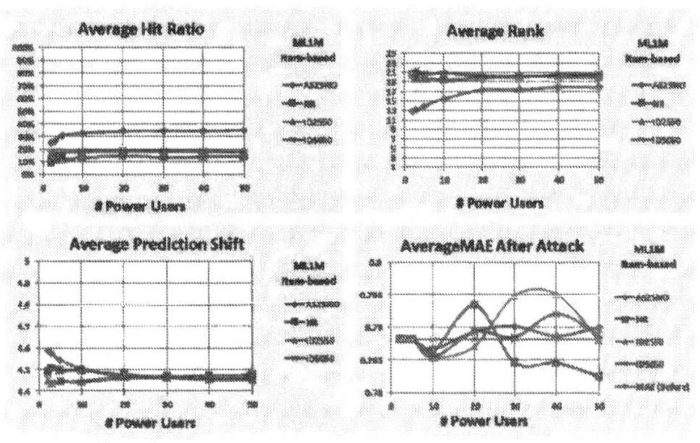

Figure 3: ML1M – Item-based Results

User-based CF is significantly more vulnerable to the power user attack than Item-based CF, confirming our third Hypothesis, and is also consistent with previous findings [9, 11, 2] because the PUA, like the random and average attacks, are able to exploit the similarity between the attackers and non-attackers to favor the target item. For item-based CF, the AggregatedSimilarity method produced a more effective set of power users for the attack as compared to InDegree and NumberRatings across both datasets (ID5050 and AS25NO Hit Ratio difference was significant at $p < 0.001$ for ML1M); however, the impact of the attack was weak, i.e. relatively low Hit Ratio and high Rank, compared to user-based CF.

6. CONCLUSION

Power users are important to recommender systems and contribute to their improved prediction accuracy; however, we have found that power user attacks can be effective against recommender systems. In this initial study, we have shown that a relatively small number of power users can have significant effects on RS predictions and top-N recommendation lists for new items. We have also shown that the InDegree method of power user selection produces a set of power users that are able to mount more effective attacks than the AggregatedSimilarity and NumberRatings methods.

Our contributions have been to provide a novel attack model called Power User Attack and to evaluate a novel use of a social network analysis method for selecting top-k influential power users for attack purposes. To further strengthen our work, in the future we plan to research the use of (1) power user profile characteristics to enable us to build synthetic power user attack profiles to formally mount the PUA, (2) other RS algorithms, such as SVD, (3) target items other than new items, and (4) other domains/datasets.

7. REFERENCES

[1] S. S. Anand and N. Griffiths. A market-based approach to address the new item problem. In *Proceedings of the 5th ACM Recommender Systems Conference*, 2011.

[2] R. Burke, M. P. O'Mahony, and N. J. Hurley. Robust collaborative recommendation. In F. Ricci, L. Rokach, B. Shapira, and P. B. Kantor, editors, *Recommender Systems Handbook*. Springer, 2011.

[3] C. Desrosiers and G. Karypis. A comprehensive survey of neighborhood-based recommendations methods. In F. Ricci, L. Rokach, B. Shapira, and P. B. Kantor, editors, *Recommender Systems Handbook*. Springer, 2011.

[4] P. Domingos and M. Richardson. Mining the network value of customers. In *Proceedings of KDD'01*. ACM, 2001.

[5] A. Goyal and L. V. S. Lakshmanan. Recmax: Exploiting recommender systems for fun and profit. In *Proceedings of KDD'12*, 2012.

[6] J. L. Herlocker, J. A. Konstan, A. Borchers, and J. Riedl. An algorithmic framework for performing collaborative filtering. In *Proceedings of the ACM SIGIR Conference*, 1999.

[7] J. L. Herlocker, J. A. Konstan, L. G. Terveen, and J. Riedl. Evaluating collaborative filtering recommender systems. *ACM Transactions on Information Systems*, 22(1), 2004.

[8] D. Kempe, J. Kleinberg, and E. Tardos. Maximizing the spread of influence through a social network. In *Proceedings of KDD'03*, 2003.

[9] S. K. Lam and J. Riedl. Shilling recommender systems for fun and profit. In *WWW '04: Proceedings of the 13th international conference on World Wide Web*. ACM, 2004.

[10] N. Lathia, S. Hailes, and L. Capra. knn cf: A temporal social network. In *Proceedings of the 2nd ACM Recommender Systems Conference (RecSys '08)*, 2008.

[11] B. Mobasher, R. Burke, R. Bhaumik, and C. Williams. Toward trustworthy recommender systems: An analysis of attack models and algorithm robustness. *ACM Trans. Internet Technol.*, 7(4):23, 2007.

[12] M. P. O'Mahony, N. Hurley, and G. C. M. Silvestre. Promoting recommendations: An attack on collaborative filtering. In *Proceedings of DEXA'02*, 2002.

[13] J. Palau, M. Montaner, B. Lopez, and J. L. D. L. Rosa. Collaboration analysis in recommender systems using social networks. In *Cooperative Information Agents VIII: 8th International Workshop, CIA 2004*.

[14] A. Rashid and J. Karypis, G.and Riedl. Influence in ratings-based recommender systems: An algorithm-independent approach. In *Proceedings of the SIAM International conference on Data Mining, 2005*.

[15] P. Resnick, N. Iacovou, M. Suchak, P. Bergstrom, and J. Riedl. GroupLens: an open architecture for collaborative filtering of netnews. In *Proceedings of CSCW'94*, 1994.

[16] B. Sarwar, G. Karypis, J. Konstan, and J. Riedl. Item-based collaborative filtering recommendation algorithms. In *Proceedings of the World Wide Web Conference*, 2001.

[17] G. Shani and A. Gunawardana. Evaluating recommendation systems. In F. Ricci, L. Rokach, B. Shapira, and P. B. Kantor, editors, *Recommender Systems Handbook*. Springer, 2011.

[18] S. Wasserman and K. Faust. *Social Network Analysis: Methods and Applications*. Cambridge University Press, New York, NY, 1994.

xCLiMF: Optimizing Expected Reciprocal Rank for Data with Multiple Levels of Relevance

Yue Shi[a], Alexandros Karatzoglou[b], Linas Baltrunas[b], Martha Larson[a], Alan Hanjalic[a]
[a]Delft University of Technology, Netherlands; [b]Telefonica Research, Spain
[a]{y.shi, m.a.larson, a.hanjalic}@tudelft.nl, [b]{alexk, linas}@tid.es

ABSTRACT

Extended Collaborative Less-is-More Filtering *xCLiMF* is a learning to rank model for collaborative filtering that is specifically designed for use with data where information on the level of relevance of the recommendations exists, e.g. through ratings. *xCLiMF* can be seen as a generalization of the Collaborative Less-is-More Filtering (*CLiMF*) method that was proposed for top-N recommendations using binary relevance (implicit feedback) data. The key contribution of the *xCLiMF* algorithm is that it builds a recommendation model by optimizing Expected Reciprocal Rank, an evaluation metric that generalizes reciprocal rank in order to incorporate user feedback with multiple levels of relevance. Experimental results on real-world datasets show the effectiveness of *xCLiMF*, and also demonstrate its advantage over *CLiMF* when more than two levels of relevance exist in the data.

Categories and Subject Descriptors

H.3.3 [**Information Storage and Retrieval**]: Information Search and Retrieval—*Information Filtering*

Keywords

Collaborative filtering, expected reciprocal rank, graded relevance, top-N recommendation, ranking

1. INTRODUCTION

The purpose of a recommender system is, typically, to generate a ranked item list (or top-N item list) that is tailored to the preferences of each individual user [1, 8]. Collaborative Filtering (CF) is one of the most successful techniques for recommender systems [6], the core concept of which is to provide recommendations to a user based on the common interest between this user and other users.

Learning to rank techniques originated in the Information Retrieval (IR) and Machine Learning communities [3].

RecSys'13, October 12–16, 2013, Hong Kong, China.

http://dx.doi.org/10.1145/2507157.2507227.

One main branch of learning to rank techniques is to directly optimize a IR measure such as Mean Average Precision (MAP), Area Under the ROC Curve (AUC), Mean Reciprocal Rank (MRR) , or Normalized Discounted Cumulative Gain (NDCG), e.g., [2, 15]. Learning to rank techniques have been recently used to optimize CF models. CF models for ranking binary relevance data are based on optimizing a smooth version of binary relevance measures for IR such as AUC in the case of Bayesian Personalized Ranking (BPR) [10], MAP for the TFMAP algorithm [12] and MRR for *CLiMF* [13]. Note that in this paper we use the term binary relevance to refer to data where users provide implicit feedback about their preferences (e.g., clicks, purchases, views etc.) *not* the case where there is explicit feedback on a binary scale (e.g., like/dislike). When multiple levels of relevance exist in the data, e.g., rating levels assigned by users can be productively treated as grades of relevance, these methods cannot be easily used since that would require an arbitrary threshold to binarize the relevance. In this way though fine-grained rating information is thrown out that actually may be helpful.

Ranking methods for CF have been also developed for multiple level relevance data which typically come in the form of ratings, for example, CoFiRank [14] optimized an upper bound of a NDCG loss function. One of the main disadvantage of NDCG is the underlying assumption that the usefulness of a document at rank i is independent of the usefulness of the documents at rank less than i. Thus a single perfectly relevant item in the top of a recommendation list might get less NDCG score than a list with several lower scored relevant items in the top positions.

The *Expected Reciprocal Rank* (ERR) [4] measure was recently introduced to deal with these shortcomings. ERR is a generalized version of RR designed to be used with multiple relevance level data (e.g., ratings). It has similar properties to RR in that it strongly emphasizes the relevance of results returned at the top of the list. Importantly, ERR, like RR, imposes the assumption that the user scans the results list from top to bottom, and stops when a result is found that fully satisfies the user's information need. This model of user behavior provides a particularly good fit with top-N recommender use scenarios. In such scenarios, the user is often looking for a single item/product and is completely satisfied after having found it in the list. This work builds upon our previous contribution of *CLiMF* [13], which aimed at optimizing Reciprocal Rank (RR), for top-N recommendation in domains with binary relevance data. It extends our initial experimentation with exploiting graded relevance for top-N recommendation [11]. Its critical contribution is the focus on the benefits of ERR within top-N recommendation use scenarios. We propose a new CF approach, *Extended Collaborative Less-is-More Filtering (xCLiMF)*, which aims at directly optimizing ERR, for top-N recommendation in domains with graded relevance data. We derive an optimization procedure that is linear to the number of relevance data (i.e., ratings), and show that *xCLiMF* outperforms a few baseline methods on two datasets.

The remainder of the paper is structured as follows. In the next section, we present the technical detail of *xCLiMF*, after which we demonstrate the experimental evaluation in Section 3. Finally, Section 4 summarizes the key aspects of this work and briefly addresses the directions for future work

2. EXTENDED CLIMF

Using the definition of ERR in [4], we can express ERR for a ranked item list of user m as follows:

$$ERR_m = \sum_{i=1}^{N} \frac{r_{mi}}{R_{mi}} \prod_{j=1}^{N} (1 - r_{mj}\mathbb{I}(R_{mj} < R_{mi})) \quad (1)$$

$\mathbb{I}(\cdot)$ is an indicator function, which is equal to 1 if the condition is true, and otherwise 0. R_{mi} denotes the rank position of item i for user m, when all items are ranked in descending order of the predicted relevance values. r_{mi} denotes the probability that user m finds the item i is relevant. We use a mapping function similar to the one used in [4], to convert ratings (or levels of relevance in general) to probabilities of relevance, as shown below:

$$r_{mi} = \begin{cases} \frac{2^{y_{mi}}-1}{2^{y_{max}}}, & I_{mi} > 0 \\ 0, & I_{mi} = 0 \end{cases} \quad (2)$$

where y_{mi} denotes the rating given by user m to item i, and y_{max} is the highest rating. Note that $I_{mi} > 0$ ($I_{mi} = 0$) indicates that user m's preference to item i is known (unknown). We employ factor models and in particular matrix factorization where the relevance between user m and item i is modeled by the inner product of U_m and V_i (i.e., the latent factors of user m and item i), as follows:

$$f_{mi} = \langle U_m, V_i \rangle = \sum_{d=1}^{D} U_{md} V_{id} \quad (3)$$

Note that the value of rank R_{mi} depends on the value of f_{mi}. For example, if the predicted relevance value f_{mi} of item i is the second highest among all the items for user m,then we will have $R_{mi} = 2$.

Similar to other ranking measure such as RR, ERR is also non-smooth with respect to the latent factors of users, items, i.e., U and V, it is thus impossible to optimize ERR directly using conventional optimization techniques. We thus employ smoothing techniques that where also used in *CLiMF* [13], to attain a smoothed version of ERR. In particular we approximate the rank-based terms $1/R_{mi}$ and $\mathbb{I}(R_{mj} < R_{mi})$ in Eq. (1) by smooth functions with respect to the model parameters U and V, as shown below

$$\mathbb{I}(R_{mj} < R_{mi}) \approx g(f_{mj} - f_{mi}) \quad (4)$$

$$\frac{1}{R_{mi}} \approx g(f_{mi}) \quad (5)$$

where $g(x)$ is a logistic function, i.e., $g(x) = 1/(1 + e^{-x})$.

Substituting Eq. (4) and (5) into Eq. (1), we obtain a smoothed approximation of ERR_m:

$$ERR_m = \sum_{i=1}^{N} r_{mi} g(f_{mi}) \prod_{j=1}^{N} (1 - r_{mj} g(f_{m(j-i)})) \quad (6)$$

Note that for notation convenience, we make use of the substitution $f_{m(j-i)} := \langle U_m, V_j \rangle - \langle U_m, V_i \rangle$.

Using Jensen's inequality and exploiting the concavity of the *log* function in a similar manner to [13], we can derive a lower bound of ERR_m in Eq.(6) :

$$L(U_m, V) = \sum_{i=1}^{N} r_{mi} \big[\ln g(f_{mi}) + \sum_{j=1}^{N} \ln (1 - r_{mj} g(f_{m(j-i)})) \big] \quad (7)$$

Using the lower bound we can optimize a factor model with respect to ERR. Taking into account all M users and using the Frobenius norm of the latent factors for regularization, we obtain the objective function of *xCLiMF*:

$$\begin{aligned} F(U, V) = & \sum_{m=1}^{M} \sum_{i=1}^{N} r_{mi} \big[\ln g(f_{mi}) \\ & + \sum_{j=1}^{N} \ln (1 - r_{mj} g(f_{m(j-i)})) \big] \\ & - \frac{\lambda}{2} (\|U\|^2 + \|V\|^2) \end{aligned} \quad (8)$$

We can now maximize the objective function (8) with respect to the latent factors $argmax_{U,V} F(U, V)$. Note that $F(U, V)$ represents an approximation of the mean value of ERR across all the users, we can thus remove the constant coefficient $1/M$, since it has no influence on the optimization of $F(U, V)$. Since the objective function is smooth we can use gradient ascent for the optimization. The gradients can be derived in a similar manner to *CLiMF* [13], as shown below:

$$\begin{aligned} \frac{\partial F}{\partial U_m} = & \sum_{i=1}^{N} r_{mi} \big[g(-f_{mi}) V_i \\ & + \sum_{k=1}^{N} \frac{r_{mk} g'(f_{mk} - f_{mi})}{1 - r_{mk} g(f_{mk} - f_{mi})} (V_i - V_k) \big] - \lambda U_m \end{aligned} \quad (9)$$

$$\begin{aligned} \frac{\partial F}{\partial V_i} = & r_{mi} \big[g(-f_{mi}) \\ & + \sum_{k=1}^{N} r_{mk} g'(f_{mi} - f_{mk}) \Big(\frac{1}{1 - r_{mk} g(f_{mk} - f_{mi})} \\ & - \frac{1}{1 - r_{mi} g(f_{mi} - f_{mk})} \Big) \big] U_m - \lambda V_i \end{aligned} \quad (10)$$

Note that *xCLiMF* can be seen as a generalized version of the *CLiMF* algorithm. We can derive *CLiMF* from the *xCLiMF* algorithm as a special case when r_{mi} is binary, i.e., 1 for relevant items and 0 otherwise. The overall complexity of the optimization procedure is in the order of $O(d\tilde{n}^2 M)$, where $\tilde{n}$ the average number of items per user. Note that we have $\tilde{n}M = S$, in which S denotes the number of non-zeros in the user-item matrix. The complexity of the learning algorithm is then $O(d\tilde{n}S)$. Since we usually have $\tilde{n} << S$,

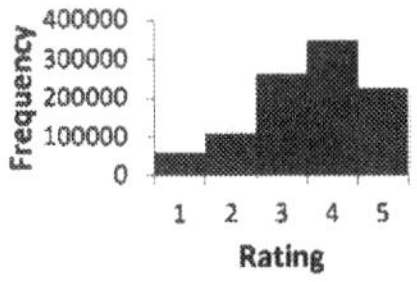

(a) ML1m

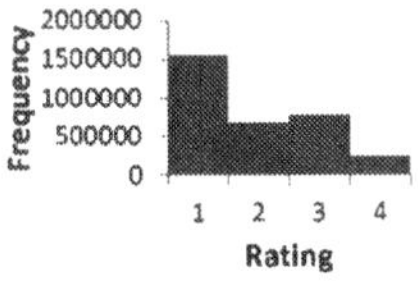

(b) TVid

Figure 1: The distributions of ratings in ML1m and TVid datasets.

the complexity is $O(dS)$ even in the case that $\tilde{n}$ is large, i.e., being linear to the number of non-zeros (i.e. relevant observations in the data).

3. EXPERIMENTAL EVALUATION

In this section we present a series of experiments for the evaluation of *xCLiMF*. We are trying to address the following two research questions:

1. Does *xCLiMF* outperform state-of-the-art CF approaches for top-N recommendation in the domains with explicit feedback data?
2. How does *xCLiMF* perform compared to *CLiMF*?

3.1 Experimental Setup

3.1.1 Datasets

We use two datasets for the experiments: The first is the MovieLens 1 million dataset[1] (ML1m) [7], which contains ca. 1M ratings (1-5 scale) from ca. 6K users and 3.7K movies. The sparseness of the ML1m dataset is 95.53%. The second dataset was collected from the video watching data in the Tuenti social network[2]. In the experiments, we convert the count of video-watching into four levels: 1 if a user did not watched a video completely; 2 if a user watching a video only once; 3 if a user watching a video 2-5 times; 4 if a user watched a video more than 5 times. Those levels (similar to ratings) are defined to indicate different levels of user preference to videos, and used as explicit feedback data in the experiments. In the following, we denote this dataset as TVid, it contains ca. 3.2 million rating levels from ca. 55.5K users and 51.1K videos with 99.89% data sparseness. The distributions of ratings in the two datasets are presented in Figure 1.

3.1.2 Experimental Protocol

For each dataset, we randomly selected 5 rated items (movies or videos) for each user to form a test set. We then randomly selected a varying number of rated items from the rest to form a training set. For example, under the condition of "Given 5", we randomly select 5 rated items (disjoint to the items in the test set) for each user in order to generate a training set. We investigated a variety of "Given" conditions for the training sets, i.e., 5, 10 and 15 for the ML1m dataset and 5, 15, 25 for the TVid dataset. Generated recommendation lists for each user are compared to the ground truth in the test set in order to measure the performance. Apart from ERR, we also measure the recommendation performance by NDCG, a well-known evaluation metric for measuring the performance of ranked results with graded judgments. Since in recommender systems the user's satisfaction is dominated by only a few items on the top of the recommendation list, our evaluation in the following experiments focuses on the performance of top-5 recommended items, i.e., ERR@5 and NDCG@5. Note that in the evaluation we cannot treat all the unrated items as irrelevant to a given user. For this reason, we apply a widely-used practical strategy, as suggested in literature [5, 9], which is to first randomly select 1000 unrated items (which are assumed to be irrelevant to the user) in addition to the ground truth (i.e., rated items) for each user in the test set, and then evaluate the performance of the recommendation list that consists of only the selected unrated items and the ground truth items. In addition, considering the domination effect of top popular items [13], we exclude the top-3 most popular items in each dataset from recommendations for the evaluation in the test set. The parameters in *xCLiMF* are tuned so as to yield the best balance between performance and computational cost based on a validation set of each dataset, i.e., D=10, λ=0.001 and learning rate 0.001.

[1]http://www.grouplens.org/node/73

[2]https://www.tuenti.com/

3.2 Performance Comparison

We compare the performance of *xCLiMF* with that of two baseline algorithms. The approaches we compare against are listed below:

- **PopRec**. A naive baseline that recommends items based on the number of times of being rated.
- **CofiRank**. A state-of-the-art CF approach that optimizes the NDCG measure [14] for domains with explicit feedback data (ratings). The implementation is based on the publicly available software package from the authors[3].

The results of the experiments are shown in Table 1 and 2, from which we obtain two observations.

First, *xCLiMF* outperforms the baseline approaches in terms of both ERR and NDCG in most of the cases. The improvements against baselines are all statistically significant according to the Wilcoxon signed rank test with p<0.05. The results also show that the improvement of ERR aligns consistently with the improvement of NDCG, indicating that optimizing ERR would not degrade the utility of recommendations that are captured by the NDCG measure.

Second, the relative performance of *xCLiMF* improves as the number of observed ratings from the users increases. This result indicates that *xCLiMF* can learn better top-N recommendation models if more observations of the graded relevance data from users can be used. The results also reveal that it is difficult to model user preferences encoded in multiple levels of relevance with limited observations, in particular, when the number of observations is lower than the number of relevance levels.

3.3 xCLiMF vs. CLiMF

We compare the performance between *xCLiMF* and *CLiMF*. We use *CLiMF* on the explicit feedback datasets by binarizing the rating values with different thresholds. On the ML1m dataset, we take rating 4 and 5 (the highest two relevance levels), respectively, as the relevance threshold for

[3]http://www.cofirank.org/

Table 1: Performance comparison of *xCLiMF* and the baseline approaches on the ML1m dataset

	Given 5		Given 10		Given 15	
	NDCG	ERR	NDCG	ERR	NDCG	ERR
PopRec	0.024	0.023	0.030	0.029	0.025	0.025
CofiRank	0.031	0.037	0.035	0.040	0.036	0.042
xCLiMF	**0.035**	**0.038**	**0.037**	**0.044**	**0.043**	**0.054**

Table 2: Performance comparison of *xCLiMF* and the baseline approaches on the TVid dataset

	Given 5		Given 15		Given 25	
	NDCG	ERR	NDCG	ERR	NDCG	ERR
PopRec	0.120	0.059	0.160	0.079	0.203	0.107
CofiRank	**0.148**	**0.097**	0.169	0.096	0.205	0.124
xCLiMF	0.121	0.063	**0.229**	**0.164**	**0.337**	**0.241**

training the *CLiMF* model and measure the performance using Mean Reciprocal Rank (MRR). On the TVid dataset, we take rating 3 and 4 (the highest two relevance levels), respectively, as the relevance threshold. The results are shown in Table 3 and 4. We observe that, although *CLiMF* is trained to optimize RR, it suffers from the additional data sparseness as a result of the binarization of the multi-level relevance data. *CLiMF* is outperformed by *xCLiMF* in terms of both MRR and ERR, across all the settings of relevance thresholds and datasets. The results indicate that the information loss from binarizing multi-level relevance data would inevitably make recommendation models based on binary relevance data, such as *CLiMF*, suboptimal for the use cases with explicit feedback data. We can thus conclude that, *xCLiMF* is addressing the top-N recommendation problem for multiple-level relevance data.

Table 3: *xCLiMF* vs. *CLiMF* on the ML1m dataset

	Threshold 4		Threshold 5	
	MRR	ERR	MRR	ERR
CLiMF	0.088	0.032	0.062	0.043
xCLiMF	**0.104**	**0.054**	**0.064**	**0.054**

Table 4: *xCLiMF* vs. *CLiMF* on the TVid dataset

	Threshold 3		Threshold 4	
	MRR	ERR	MRR	ERR
CLiMF	0.234	0.161	0.065	0.133
xCLiMF	**0.348**	**0.241**	**0.080**	**0.241**

4. CONCLUSIONS AND FUTURE WORK

We have presented *xCLiMF*, an extended version of *CLiMF* that can be used with multi-level relevance data for the purpose of top-N recommendation. Compared to *xCLiMF*, which optimizes RR, *xCLiMF* learns latent factors of users and items by optimizing ERR, a measure of quality of ranked results with multiple relevance levels. The experiments demonstrate the competitive performance of *xCLiMF* for top-N recommendation in the domains with multi-level relevance data. We also demonstrate the specific advantage of *xCLiMF* compared to *CLiMF* when used on multi-level relevance data.

There are several possibilities for future work. One is to investigate the relationship between ERR optimization and diversification. Another interesting topic is to compare the recommendation models that are designed for optimizing different ranking measures, and to investigate the possibility of optimizing recommendation results for multiple criteria.

5. ACKNOWLEDGEMENTS

This work is funded as part of a Marie Curie Intra European Fellowship for Career Development (IEF) award (CARS, PIEF-GA-2010-273739) held by Alexandros Karatzoglou.

6. REFERENCES

[1] G. Adomavicius and A. Tuzhilin. Toward the next generation of recommender systems: A survey of the state-of-the-art and possible extensions. *IEEE Transactions on Kowledge and Data Engineering*, 17(6):734–749, 2005.

[2] C. J. C. Burges, R. Ragno, and Q. V. Le. Learning to rank with nonsmooth cost functions. NIPS '06, pages 193–200, 2006.

[3] O. Chapelle, Y. Chang, and T.-Y. Liu. Future directions in learning to rank. *Journal of Machine Learning Research - Proceedings Track*, 14:91–100, 2011.

[4] O. Chapelle, D. Metlzer, Y. Zhang, and P. Grinspan. Expected reciprocal rank for graded relevance. In *Proceedings of the 18th ACM conference on Information and knowledge management*, CIKM '09, pages 621–630, New York, NY, USA, 2009. ACM.

[5] P. Cremonesi, Y. Koren, and R. Turrin. Performance of recommender algorithms on top-n recommendation tasks. RecSys '10, pages 39–46. ACM, 2010.

[6] M. D. Ekstrand, J. T. Riedl, and J. A. Konstan. Collaborative filtering recommender systems. *Foundations and Trends in Human-Computer Interaction*, 4(2):81–173, 2011.

[7] J. L. Herlocker, J. A. Konstan, A. Borchers, and J. Riedl. An algorithmic framework for performing collaborative filtering. SIGIR '99, pages 230–237. ACM, 1999.

[8] J. Konstan and J. Riedl. Recommender systems: from algorithms to user experience. *User Modeling and User-Adapted Interaction*, 22:101–123, 2012. 10.1007/s11257-011-9112-x.

[9] Y. Koren. Factorization meets the neighborhood: a multifaceted collaborative filtering model. KDD '08, pages 426–434. ACM, 2008.

[10] S. Rendle, C. Freudenthaler, Z. Gantner, and S.-T. Lars. Bpr: Bayesian personalized ranking from implicit feedback. UAI '09, pages 452–461. AUAI Press, 2009.

[11] Y. Shi, A. Karatzoglou, L. Baltrunas, M. Larson, and A. Hanjalic. GAPfm: Optimal top-n recommendations for graded relevance domains. CIKM '13. ACM, 2013.

[12] Y. Shi, A. Karatzoglou, L. Baltrunas, M. Larson, A. Hanjalic, and N. Oliver. TFMAP: optimizing map for top-n context-aware recommendation. SIGIR '12, pages 155–164. ACM, 2012.

[13] Y. Shi, A. Karatzoglou, L. Baltrunas, M. Larson, N. Oliver, and A. Hanjalic. CLiMF: learning to maximize reciprocal rank with collaborative less-is-more filtering. RecSys '12, pages 139–146. ACM, 2012.

[14] M. Weimer, A. Karatzoglou, Q. Le, and A. Smola. Cofirank - maximum margin matrix factorization for collaborative ranking. NIPS'07, pages 1593–1600, 2007.

[15] Y. Yue, T. Finley, F. Radlinski, and T. Joachims. A support vector method for optimizing average precision. SIGIR '07, pages 271–278. ACM, 2007.

Evolving Friend Lists in Social Networks

Jacob Bartel, Prasun Dewan
University of North Carolina
Chapel Hill, NC
{bartel,dewan}@cs.unc.edu

ABSTRACT

In a social network, users can sort members of their social graph into friend lists to both understand the social structures within the graph and control the flow of incoming and outgoing information. To reduce the user-effort required to create these lists, previous work has developed techniques for generating friend-lists in a static social graph. This paper considers the user effort required to create friend lists in an evolving graph. We have developed several new initial quantitative metrics to capture this effort, and identified an initial technique for modeling graph growth. We have used these metrics and model to compare two techniques for evolving friend lists when the social graph grows: manual evolution – the user evolves friend lists using no external tools – and full recommendation – an existing state of the art tool recommends a whole new set of friend lists. In these comparisons, we used the friend lists of 12 individuals, and simulated the growth of their social graphs and friend lists using our graph-growth model. Intuitively, when the graph evolves by a small (large) amount, the manual (automatic) approach should perform better. Our experiments show that full recommendation performs better than manual when the social graph changes by more than 1%, and yields an almost complete reduction in effort in the best cases.

Categories and Subject Descriptors

H.5.3 **[Information Systems]** Group and Organization Interfaces – *computer-supported cooperative work, evaluation/methodology*

General Terms

Algorithms, Management, Measurement, Experimentation, Security, Human Factors.

Keywords

Evolution; social networks; Facebook; friend lists; refactoring.

1. INTRODUCTION

Currently, social network users have a large number of friends with whom they share large amounts of information in a variety of forms, such as posts, messages, photos, and links. One recent statistic stated that the average Facebook user has 130 friends and shares 90 pieces of content with those friends per month [8]. With such broad and varied forms of communication, certain tasks become difficult. A user must be able to organize their friends to understand the social structures to which they belong, filter out and sort incoming information, and control where outgoing information is directed.

RecSys'13, October 12–16, 2013, Hong Kong, China.

http://dx.doi.org/10.1145/2507157.2507194

One approach to reduce this difficulty is to group users sharing some characteristic(s) and apply the same information controls to each member of a group., Several popular social networks today allow an arbitrary number of friend lists as they are called in Facebook (and tags, groups, or circles in Renren, LinkedIn, and Google+). Previous studies have found that users either do not know how to create these lists [13] or are not willing to put the time and effort required to create them [3, 8, 9, 13]. In one health study [10], people who wished to share their medical problems with others did not use Facebook to do so because of the fear that this information may reach unintended ears. This is consistent with a more general problem of the high effort cost in access control lists [10],

The question then becomes how to reduce the costs of creating these friend lists. One approach is to create a recommendation tool to generate these lists [2, 3, 6, 9]. With such a tool, the user only has to approve, disapprove, or modify a recommended list rather than learn how to create a list and then generate a list from scratch, leading to significantly less learning and effort costs. Previous research has shown that the cost of manually editing recommended lists is a small fraction of the effort required to manually create the lists from scratch. However, current friend list recommendation tools make recommendations only when a friend list is initially created [3, 6, 12], or are limited to recommendations for two lists [7]. How this arbitrary number of lists should evolve as the social graph changes has been explicitly stated as an open problem by authors of these tools [2, 3, 9].

This paper takes a first stab at addressing this problem. It identifies initial new quantitative metrics to capture the effort a user has to exert to manually edit, accept, or reject recommendations In addition, it derives an initial technique for modeling graph growth It uses these metrics and model to compare two approaches for friend list evolution: manual evolution - the user evolves (manually or automatically generated) friend lists using no tools and full recommendation – a state of the art friend list recommendation tool is used to recommend a whole new set of friend lists.

2. FRIEND LIST RECOMMENDATION DESIGN SPACE

Our problem is a sub-problem of the general problem of finding communities in a network of nodes [3]. Our focus is on recommending classification of friends of a particular user into (potentially overlapping) friend lists. There have been a variety of diverse approaches to this problem in previous work. To combine the ideas in these approaches and to better understand and describe our own work, we have developed a design space of friend list recommendations, which is a contribution in its own right. These approaches can be divided into two broad schemes, member suggestion [2, 12] and group creation [3, 6, 8, 9] .

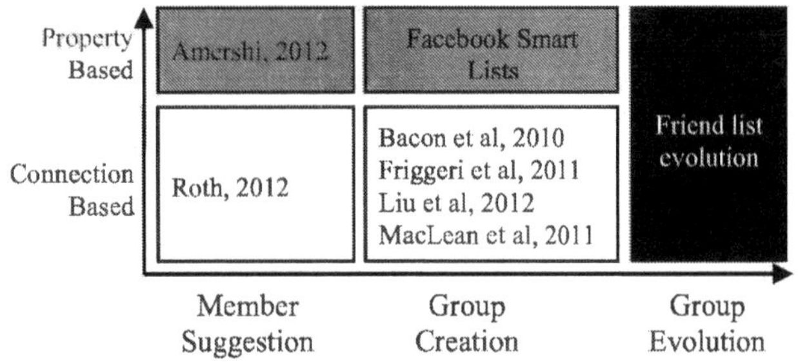

Figure 2. Design space of friend list recommendations

Member suggestion recommends friends who should be added to a new friend list. A user initially has an unpublished empty friend list, for which a recommender suggests new members. From those suggestions, the user selects appropriate additions to the friend list. The user then may accept this list or request more recommendations, forming a cycle in the work flow where each iteration of the cycle requires user input. This process is then carried out for other friend lists.

In group creation, the user starts with no friend lists. The recommender suggests a set of new friend lists by determining clusters within the user's set of friends, each of which the user can edit or reject. The edited friend lists are then published. As opposed to the incremental member suggestion approach, which may require user input multiple times for recommendations for each friend list, the "batch" group creation approach requires user input at only one point for all recommendations.

Recommendation schemes can be further categorized based on how they group users. Again, there are two main approaches. The first is property-based clustering, which clusters individuals based on shared values of associated attributes such as age, sex, or location. The second is connection-based, which clusters individuals based on subsets of vertices in the social graph that are highly connected. Each of these approaches has its strengths and weaknesses. The property-based approach uses more information, and thus, is likely give predictions that are at least as precise as those of the connection-based approach. On the other hand, because it is dependent on the individuals' properties, it is restricted to systems and users where these properties are available and correct. Some systems may grant limited access to these properties due to privacy or security reasons, and many users may specify an incorrect or incomplete set of properties, thus limiting this technique to subset of social networks.

These different techniques can be sorted into the design space, shown in Figure 2. As indicated, there has been work in all points involving member suggestion and group creation in this space.

3. FRIEND LIST EVOLUTION

Previous approaches offer recommendations only at a friend list's creation time. However, social networks can gain and lose members and connections, which would require the evolution of friend lists. Such evolution is not restricted to social networks. It occurs in any system that can be improved or expanded while retaining some of its old functionalities, and is often tool-supported. For example, database refactoring systems restructure databases as they grow to improve the architecture while retaining the original information, and code refactoring systems update code to improve organization and readability while retaining the original behavior. Our contribution is to consider this issue in the context of friend lists.

There are three ways that a social graph can change: members can be added, members can be removed, and connections can be changed. In this first cut at friend list evolution, we address only adding individuals and connections to a user's social graph and friend lists. Thus, our work applies directly to only those users who do not do "garbage" collection to delete connections or regroup users in a social graph.

To illustrate this evolution, we introduce a running example illustrated in Figure 1. In the past (time t_{k-1}) Joe's social graph contained a 6 friends, Alice, Bob, Carol, David, Eva, and Frank, and two friend lists, Research Group and Social Group (Figure 1 (a)). Between time t_{k-1} and t_k, Joe's company hired two people, Greg and Hal, and Joe's social graph grew to include them (Figure 1(b)). Joe also wants each of his friend lists to grow to include his new friends (Figure 1 (c)).

One way Joe could reach these ideal lists is the manual approach, where he determines what has changed in the social graph between time t_{k-1} and t_k and evolve the friend lists accordingly. This approach has the possibility of being the most precise because it takes all of a user's intentions into account. However, it requires significant work if the number of friends or friend lists is significantly large or there are significant changes to the social graph. Moreover, this approach requires that the user identify changes between the different states of the social graph, which may not be feasible if the social graph is significantly large or has changed a significant amount.

Full recommendation uses a friend list recommendation tool, or a recommender engine, to generate a new set of friend lists from the evolved graph, which the user then edits and labels. As mentioned earlier, friend list recommendation can be divided into member suggestion and group creation. Each of these approaches has its pros and cons in terms of group evolution. To illustrate, we

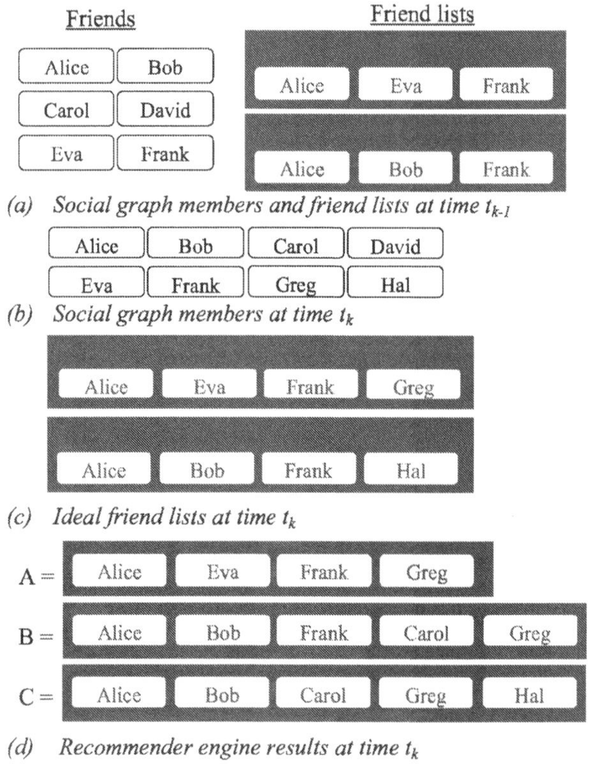

Figure 1. Example of friend list growth

continue with our running example where the social a recommender engine generates the new friend lists in Figure 1(d).

Consider the scenario where Greg and Hal are added to `Social Group` and `Research Group` remains unchanged. In general, member suggestion, the user may first unnecessarily ask for recommendations for `Research Group`. Alternatively, group creation may only present the user recommended changes to `Social Group`. If the recommendations made using member suggestion and group creation are both perfectly effective, then it can be assumed that in group creation a user will only handle friend lists that change, leading to possibly fewer steps.

However, group creation cannot use feedback to adjust recommendations, while member suggestion's iterative nature allows feedback throughout the recommendation process, which can be used to improve future recommendations. Consider the situation in which Greg and Hal should be added to `Research Group` and `Social Group`, respectively. Let us assume that without user feedback, both approaches predict the incorrect list for each user. After the user overrides its first wrong suggestion, member suggestion can correct its second prediction. Group prediction would require the user to correct both predictions.

In this paper, we focus on group creation because it has been more extensively covered by past work (including our own). We present the intuitive analysis above to show that it would be useful to also look at member suggestion in future work.

Thus, in our comparison of the two evolution approaches, manual and full recommendation, we assume that the recommender engine uses group creation. Assuming such an engine is effective, which has been shown to be true in past work by ourselves and others, full recommendation could work better than the manual approach. However, the recommender engine may reintroduce previously rejected recommendations a cost not incurred in the manual approach. Thus, it is difficult to predict which of these approaches will require less effort. If the social graph has changed by a small amount, the effort required to manually add the members might be less than that required to correct and label the predictions of a friend list recommender.

4. EVALUATION AND ANALYSIS

In order to test our scheme, we analyzed a variety of methods for evaluating our work. The first option we investigated was to generate artificial networks. However, such an option may not match reality. The most realistic option, of course, is to use a field study observing how users actually evolve their friend lists. However, such a study would possibly take years to complete and, more importantly, due to the limited control it allows, it would be unable to compare different approaches using the same users. A third option would be to perform a lab study at a single point of time. Such an approach, however, requires us to model friend list and social graph growth.

This is the approach we took. We used data from a previous study in which 12 users were asked to create friend lists from their current social graph [3], and generated previous evolutions of friend lists and social graphs. There has been a large amount of work on modeling future graph growth, but little done to model how a graph may have grown to its current state.

We looked at these various alternative approaches to modeling future graph growth to see if any are applicable to our own problem domain. One such approach, which is used for modeling remote sensor networks, randomly distributes nodes on a plane or

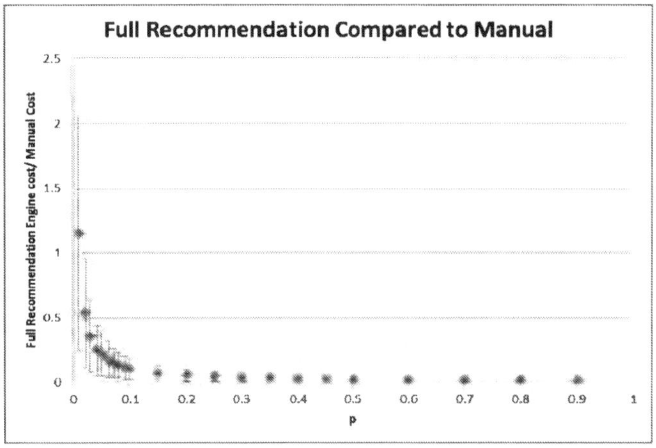

Figure 3. Cost of full recommendation compared to manual

three-dimensional surface. Then based on the how close two nodes are to each other, an edge may be formed between the two nodes [5]. This approach is not compatible with our domain as edges are not dependent on the closeness of the nodes they are connecting. In a social graph, two nodes that are a large distance apart when plotted geometrically may still have an edge connecting them, or, similarly, two nodes that have a small geometric distance may not have an edge between them.

There has also been work modeling graph growth based on the power law, which states that the number of nodes with degree d is proportional to the value $1/d^{\alpha}$ where $\alpha \geq 0$. Using this relationship, when a vertex is added to a graph at time t, it will connect to some existing vertex with probability $d_{v,t}/2e_t$ where $d_{v,t}$ is the degree of vertex v at time t and e_t is the number of edges at time t [1, 4]. Existence of the power law has been shown in large graph representations, such as citation networks [11] or collaboration graphs of movie actors [4] and thus such graphs have been effectively modeled using the above technique. However, smaller graphs have been shown to be more difficult to approximate with the power-law [4], and since our graphs are only one-hop sub-graphs of the global social graph, our graphs are not large enough to be appropriately modeled using the power-law. Moreover, upon analyzing our user study data, the social graphs for our users did not display an adherence to the power law.

Because of the failure of these modeling techniques to map to our problem domain, we used a randomized approach to model past graph evolution. To model an evolution at time t_{k-1}, we assumed there is a set of new members ($M_{new,k}$) for our social graph at time t_k (S_k)., where each of these new members would have been added to the social graph after time t_{k-1}. We can then subtract this new set of members from the social graph (S_k) and friend lists at time t_k (F_k) to find the respective S_{k-1} and F_{k-1}.

With this model of group growth, we can model the growth of both the social graph and friend lists between time t_{k-1} and t_k and vary growth rates by adjusting the size of $M_{new,k}$. Specifically, we modeled these growth rates as a proportion of the size of global social graph by defining a proportion $p = |M_{new,k}|/|S_k|$ and varied p over a wide range of values as shown in Figure 3's x-axis.

This approach is limited in that it cannot model member deletion. Because we only have friend lists and social graphs from a single time slice, our data does not give us any information of individuals that are currently missing from the S_k but were contained in some previous S_j where $t_j < t_k$. For this reason, we restricted ourselves to only growing social graph and friend lists.

The next issue is how to measure the user effort required to grow friend lists generated using this model. One alternative is to ask each user to actually use each of the compared approaches. This is the approach used, for instance, in [9], where users were asked to create initial friend lists either manually or by editing generated friend lists. The experimenters found that the manual task was so tedious that few subjects completed it. This problem would be exacerbated in work that addresses evolution of friend lists, because each user would be required to evolve a friend list by different degrees. Therefore, we used an analytical approach to measuring user effort.

When evolving friend lists or using recommended evolutions, the user can exert effort by adding or removing members of a friend list or recommendation. Therefore we approximated the cost of an approach as the total number of additions and deletions that would be required to transform the old or recommended friend lists to the ideal friend lists. We then compared approaches by comparing their total costs. If there are huge differences in the costs of two approaches, then we assume that a user study would show that users prefer the approach with the lower cost.

This metric also captures the importance of the classical metrics precision, or the number of correct recommendations, and recall, or the number of times that recommendations are generated. If there is low precision, many of the recommendations will be incorrect and therefore the user will need to perform many additions and deletions during editing. Moreover, if there is low recall, there will be many failed recommendations, and thus there will be many friend lists which will require manual evolutions, which will likely require many more additions and deletions. Therefore, if user effort is shown to be low in terms of the number of required additions and deletions, we assume the precision and recall will be sufficiently high such that the user does not become frustrated to the point to stop using the recommender system.

Using the techniques for modeling evolution and user effort, we compared the full recommendation and manual approaches, which is shown in Figure 3. In this figure we plotted the average relative costs with bars marking values one standard deviation away. As shown, full recommendation performs better than manual in all cases except when the graph grew by 1%. This aligns with the results of previous work which showed the effectiveness of a recommender recommending friend list creation [2, 3, 9]. What is surprising is that such a recommender is also effective when the graph grows by a very small amount.

5. CONCLUSION AND FUTURE WORK

This paper has made multiple contributions. First of all, we have developed a design space of different approaches for recommending friend lists in social networks. This design space allows an easier comparison of past approaches and determination of which areas may be explored in future work.

We have also identified how recommender engines may be applied to evolve friend lists. To analyze this approach, we have identified a method for modeling social graph and friend list growth and identified metrics applicable towards gauging user effort. Our results show that the full recommendation approach outperforms the manual approach by reducing required additions and deletions in all but the smallest of social graph growths.

Our results are not limited to Facebook. To apply our techniques, a social network needs to be able to represent a user and his friends in a graph, with vertices representing individuals in the network, and edges representing connections between them. This social graph also needs to be able to evolve by at least allowing a user to add friends and connections to his social graph. Furthermore, the user must also be allowed to sort any of their friends into non-static friend lists. Renren, LinkedIn, and Google+ are additional systems fulfilling these requirements.

Of course, our results have limitations. We have restricted our recommendations to friend list growth. It is important to model deletions, which can make certain friend lists disappear. In addition, full recommendation forces users to rename their friend lists for each evolution. We have not modeled the cost of such renaming, which may be significant in some cases. It may also be possible to predict how friend lists should change rather than predict a new set of friend lists, which may allow such a system to automatically associate names with the recommended friend list evolutions.

We have only addressed evolutions in terms of the membership of friend lists. It may be possible to evolve access rights as the members evolve. Future work could address how to evolve rights alongside the social graph and friend lists. Our work provides a basis for investigating these unresolved issues.

6. ACKNOWLEDGEMENT

This research was supported in part by NSF grant IIS-0810861. We thank the reviewers for their in-depth comments.

7. REFERENCES

[1] Aiello, W. et al. 2001. Random Evolution in Massive Graphs. *Proc. FOCS.* (2001).

[2] Amershi, S. et al. 2012. ReGroup: Interactive Machine Learning for On-Demand Group Creation in Social Networks. *Proc. CHI* (2012).

[3] Bacon, K. and Dewan, P. 2011. Mixed-Initiative Friend-List Creation. *Proc. ECSCW* (2011).

[4] Barabási, A.-L. and Albert, R. 1999. Emergence of scaling in random networks. *Science*. 286, (1999), 509–512.

[5] Dowell, L.J. and Bruno, M.L. 2001. Connectivity of random graphs and mobile networks: validation of Monte Carlo simulation results. *Proc. SAC* (2001).

[6] Friggeri, A., G. Chelius and Fleury, E. 2011. Triangles to Capture Social Cohesion. *The Third IEEE International Conference on Social Computing* (2011).

[7] Hannon, J. et al. 2010. Recommending twitter users to follow using content and collaborative filtering approaches. *Proc. RecSys* (2010).

[8] Liu, Y. et al. 2012. Simplifying Friendlist Management. *Proc. WWW* (2012).

[9] MacLean, D. et al. 2011. Groups without tears: mining social topologies from email. *Proc. IUI* (2011).

[10] Newman, M.W. et al. 2011. "'It's not that I don't have problems, I'm just not putting them on Facebook': Challenges and Opportunities in Using Online Social Networks for Health". *Proc. CSCW* (2011).

[11] Redner, S. 2004. *Citation statistics from more than a century of physical review.* Technical Report #0407137. physics.

[12] Roth, M. et al. 2010. Suggesting Friends Using the Implicit Social Graph. *Proc. KDD* (2010).

[13] Skeels, M. and Grudin, J. 2009. When Social Networks Cross Boundaries: A Case Study of Workplace Use of Facebook and LinkedIn. *Proc. Group* (2009).

Exploratory and Interactive Daily Deals Recommendation

Anisio Lacerda[1] Adriano Veloso[1] Nivio Ziviani[1,2]

[1]Universidade Federal de Minas Gerais
Computer Science Department
Belo Horizonte, Brazil
{anisio, adrianov, nivio}@dcc.ufmg.br

[2]Zunnit Technologies
Belo Horizonte, Brazil
nivio@zunnit.com

ABSTRACT

Daily deals sites (DDSs), such as Groupon and LivingSocial, attract millions of customers in the hunt for products and services at significantly reduced prices. A typical approach to increase revenue is to send email messages featuring the deals of the day. Such daily messages, however, are usually not centered on the customers, instead, all registered users typically receive similar messages with almost the same deals. Traditional recommendation algorithms are innocuous in DDSs because: (i) most of the users are sporadic bargain hunters, and thus past preference data is extremely sparse, (ii) deals have a short living period, and thus data is extremely volatile, and (iii) user taste and interest may undergo temporal drifts. In order to address such particularly challenging scenario, we propose new algorithms for daily deals recommendation based on the explore-then-exploit strategy. Users are split into exploration and exploitation sets – in the exploration set the users receive non-personalized messages and a co-purchase network is updated with user feedback for purchases of the day, while in the exploitation set the updated network is used for recommending personalized messages for the remaining users. A thorough evaluation of our algorithms using real data obtained from a large daily deals website in Brazil in contrast to state-of-the-art recommendation algorithms show gains in precision ranging from 18% to 34%.

Categories and Subject Descriptors

H.3.3 [**Information Storage and Retrieval**]: Information Filtering

General Terms

Algorithms, Experimentation, Measurement, Performance

Keywords

Daily Deals, Recommendation, Exploration-Exploitation

1. INTRODUCTION

The daily deals business is a group-buying concept based on a synergistic view: helping small-businesses to advertise their products and services, while also helping customers to access significantly discounted offers (aka. deals). Typically, potential customers register as members of a daily-deals website and receive online offers and invitations, mostly by email. This concept has gained popularity over the last years, leading to myriad *daily-deals sites* (DDSs) and making web-based group-buying discount market extremely competitive. This forced top players, such as Groupon and LivingSocial, to shift their tatics towards providing more relevant and appealing deals, instead of non-personalized and ineffective email messages which are commonly viewed as spam.

In this paper we propose novel algorithms specifically devoted to daily-deals recommendation. The algorithms are based on the explore-then-exploit strategy. In our context, exploration is related to the "pursuit of information" that might come to be known, while exploitation is related to the "use" of the acquired information. Thus, we separate a fraction of the users to receive non-personalized messages (with non-biased deals) during the exploration phase. Rather than suggesting personalized deals, exploration focuses on capturing user interaction by gathering the most recent feedback (i.e., the purchases of the day). Then, in a posterior phase, feedback captured during exploration is exploited for suggesting personalized deals to the remaining users.

We employ a co-purchase network structure which evolves as users purchase deals. In this case, each node represents a user, and an edge between two nodes is created once the corresponding users purchase the same deal. Intuitively, a deal becomes more likely to be relevant to a particular user if he/she is close to users that have also purchased this deal recently.

We conducted a systematic evaluation involving real data obtained from PeixeUrbano,[1] the largest DDS in Brazil. The experiments showed that the proposed explore-then-exploit algorithms are extremely effective for daily-deals recommendation, providing precision improvements that range from 18% to 34%, when compared against existing recommendation algorithms.

The major contributions of this paper are:

- We propose explore-then-exploit algorithms and investigate the dilemma between exploration and exploitation under the daily-deals recommendation scenario.
- We propose criteria based on network centrality so that users are sorted in a way that increases the amount of feedback gathered during exploration, and also the amount of feedback indeed used during exploitation.
- We thoroughly evaluate the proposed explore-then-exploit algorithms using real data from a large DDS in contrast to state-of-the-art recommendation algorithms.

[1]`www.peixeurbano.com.br`

RecSys '13, October 12–16, 2013, Hong Kong, China.

http://dx.doi.org/10.1145/2507157.2507228 .

The remainder of this paper is organized as follows. In Section 2, we review the related literature on DDSs and on exploration-exploitation recommendation strategies. In Section 3, we describe our explore-exploit algorithms. In Section 4, we describe the dataset, baselines, evaluation methodology and the results of the experimental evaluation of the explore-exploit algorithms. Finally, in Section 5, we present our concluding remarks.

2. RELATED WORK

The two most popular problems related to daily deals recommendation are: (i) deal-size estimation [3], and (ii) deal ordering for revenue maximization [7]. The first problem refers to the number of coupons that a DDS is expecting to sell for a given deal. The second algorithmic problem can be stated as: given a set of candidate deals, which are the ones that a DDS should feature as daily-deals in order to maximize its revenue. In both scenarios, the focus is to maximize the benefit of the DDS. In this sense, our work is closer related to [7].

Also related to our work are exploration-exploitation strategies applied to recommender systems [8] and related problems [11]. Usually, authors consider the multi-armed bandit setting [9, 8]. Under this setting, basically, we must simultaneously attempt to acquire new knowledge and optimize decisions based on existing knowledge. Therefore, it is necessary to maximize reward based on the knowledge already acquired, while attempting new actions to further increase knowledge. While we could have modeled the daily-deals recommendation problem under the bandit setting, we took other direction and propose alternate heustistics specifically devised to the problem.

3. EXPLORE-EXPLOIT ALGORITHMS

In this section we introduce algorithms for daily-deals recommendation based on the explore-then-exploit strategy [6]. Exploration is related to the pursuit of information that might come to be known, while exploitation is related to the use of the acquired information in order to improve a particular objective. More specifically, we take advantage from controling the order in which users receive email messages featuring the deals of the day. During the exploration phase, a subset of users receive non-personalized messages, and we acquire information regarding deals recently purchased by users that have a similar taste. We follow a $\epsilon-$first strategy, in which a pure exploration phase is followed by a pure exploitation phase. In this case, given a total of N users, the exploration phase occupies $\epsilon \times N$ users, while the exploitation phase occupies the remaining $(1 - \epsilon) \times N$ users. Figure 1 describes the entire process of daily-deals recommendation based on the explore-then-exploit strategy. balancing exploration and exploitation.

3.1 The Exploration Phase

The exploration phase consists of picking a particular recommendation algorithm, and following the deals it suggests based on the past preference data collected so far. Thus, a fraction ϵ of the users will receive email messages featuring the k deals suggested by the recommendation algorithm. During this process users provide feedback when a suggested deal is indeed purchased, and this feedback is embedded into a structure we call *co-purchase network*.

The co-purchase network is an undirected and unweighted graph used to represent users that have purchased at least one deal in common, that is, nodes are users and an edge is created between two users if they have purchased a deal in common at least once. The co-purchase network makes evident users sharing similar tastes recently, and therefore it provides important information for the sake of personalized daily-deals recommendations. During the exploration phase, the co-purchase network is updated with the most recent purchases.

3.2 The Exploitation Phase

The exploitation phase consists of picking a particular recommendation algorithm, and following the deals it suggests based not only on past preference data, but also on current taste information. More specifically, we modified the recommendation algorithm so that it becomes aware of the proximity between users in the current co-purchase network. Then, we force the algorithm to weight more heavily deals that were recently purchased by nearby users. Thus, a fraction $(1 - \epsilon)$ of the users will receive email messages featuring the k deals suggested by the recommendation algorithm, but these users are likely to benefit from more appealing and relevant deals that were recently purchased by users sharing similar tastes.

3.3 Splitting Users

At some point during the explore-then-exploit process, the set of users must be split into two partitions – the partition composed of users $\{u_1, u_2, \ldots, u_{b-1}\}$ is devoted to exploration, while the partition composed of users $\{u_b, u_{b+1}, \ldots, u_N\}$ is devoted to exploitation. We may apply some criteria in order to sort users, and separate a fraction ϵ for exploration, and a fraction $(1 - \epsilon)$ for exploitation. Ideally we should explore users that: (i) are more likely to provide feedback (i.e., to purchase a suggested deal), and (ii) share similar tastes with many other users. These two properties are more apparent in users that are more central in the co-purchase network. Therefore, we employ different centrality measures [4, 2] in order to sort users, as discussed next.

- Degree: given an arbitrary user in the co-purchase network, centrality is defined as the number of users having similar taste, that is, the number of edges focusing on the user.
- Betweeness: given an arbitrary user in the co-purchase network, centrality is defined as the number of times the user acts as a bridge along the shortest path between two other users in the network.
- PageRank: given an arbitrary user in the co-purchase network, centrality is defined as the number of all users that can be connected to the user through a path, while the contribution of a distant user is penalized by an attenuation factor.

Splitting by exploring central users. Our first splitting strategy directs most central users to receive recommendations during the exploration phase. Clearly, exploring central users has some advantages: (i) central users are likely to provide feedback, and (ii) many other users may share the same taste of central users.

4. EXPERIMENTAL EVALUATION

In this section we empirically analyze the recommendation performance of our explore-then-exploit algorithms. We employ MAP (mean average precision). All experiments were performed on a 1.93 GHz Core i7 machines with 8GB of memory.

4.1 Dataset

We employ real data obtained from PeixeUrbano, the largest DDS in Brazil. Our dataset comprises two months of information about deals, users and purchases. Specifically, during this 2-month period, 31,642 users purchased at least one out of 455 deals, resulting in a total number of 43,274 purchases. On average, each

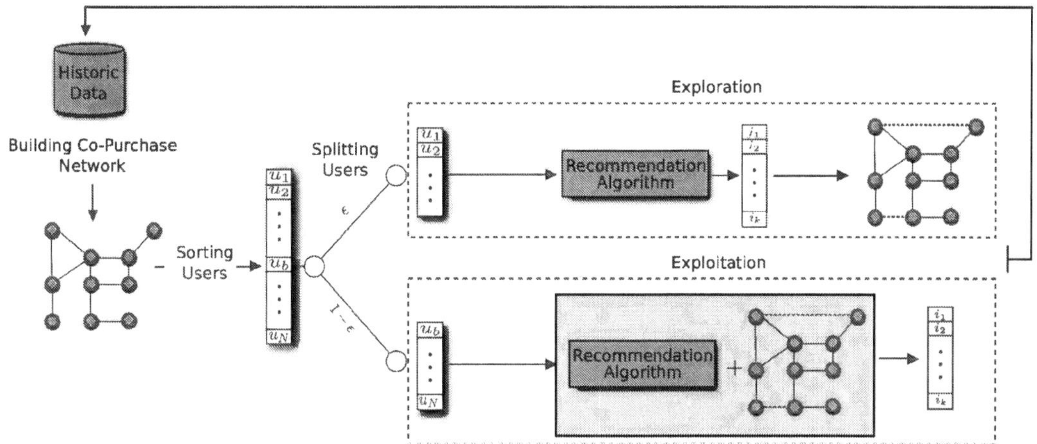

Figure 1: The daily-deals recommendation process. A fraction of the users are separated for exploration, and the co-purchase network is updated with the most recent purchases. The remaining users are benefited during exploitation. This process is repeated on a daily basis.

user purchases 1.36 deals, and thus the data is extremely sparse if compared with more studied recommendation scenarios, such as NetFlix (with 208 ratings per user) and MovieLens (with 166 ratings per user). Also, each deal remains valid, on average, for only 4 days.

4.2 Baselines

We used several recommendation algorithms as baselines. Most-Popular is a simple algorithm which recommends deals based on their popularity considering all previously purchased deals. In this case, the algorithm always suggests the same deal, no matter the target user. We also employ more sophisticated algorithms, including WRMF [5], a state-of-the-art matrix factorization algorithm, and BPR-MF [10], as a representative of collaborative filtering algorithms for binary relevance data.

4.3 Evaluation Methodology

Our evaluation follows the Interleaved Test-Then-Train methodology [1], in which each all recommendations user u_i receives on day t are evaluated, and then all deals purchased by user u_i on day t are included into the historical data available at day $t+1$. The results to be reported correspond to an average over all days. Significance tests were performed (p<0.05) and the best results, including statistical ties, are shown in bold. Our evaluation takes three dimensions into account: (i) the fraction ϵ of users to be explored, (ii) the recommendation algorithm used during the process, (iii) the criterion used to sort users.

4.4 Results and Discussions

Our first experiment concerns the study of lower and upper bounds for the recommendation performance using the proposed explore-then-exploit strategy. Specifically, we executed 1,000 runs for each ϵ value, and in each run we randomly split users into exploration and exploitation. Therefore, we have 1,000 results for each ϵ value, from which we calculate the average, the best and the worst performance numbers for each ϵ value, as shown in Figure 2. The performance numbers shown in the figure will serve as lower and upper bounds for the recommendation performance.

The next experiment involves a detailed analysis of a very simple recommendation algorithm – the Most-Popular algorithm – when coupled with the proposed explore-then-exploit strategy. Table 1 shows performance numbers in terms of MAP. The analysis

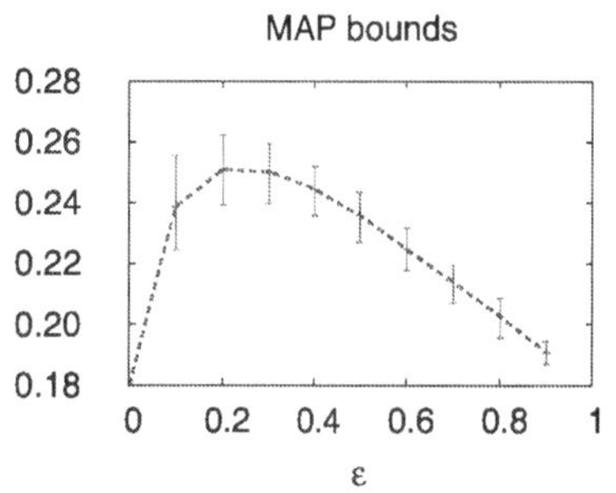

Figure 2: (Color online) Users were randomly split into exploration and exploitation (1,000 runs). Empirical lower and upper are derived from the worst and best results, respectively.

consists in evaluating the different sorting network-centrality criteria. The best performance numbers with each sorting criteria are underlined, and the best overall numbers are shown in bold. The first row, for which $\epsilon = 0$, shows the performance numbers obtained with no exploration, and this is equivalent to running the original Most-Popular algorithm (i.e., with no feedback information), and thus we consider the first row as baseline numbers. In terms of MAP, improvements over the baseline range from 29% to 34%. The recommendation performance of the Most-Popular algorithm is always close (and many times surpasses) the empirical upper bound shown in Figure 2, no matter the evaluation measure employed. In almost all cases, sorting users according to their betweeness leads to higher improvements over the baseline.

Figure 3 shows MAP numbers for the WRMF algorithm (top) and BP-RMF algorithm (bottom). Each plot shows the MAP performance during the exploration, exploitation and overall (i.e., the entire process) phases. The plots also show MAP numbers obtained by Most-Popular (symbol •) and the (empirical) upper bound for MAP (symbol ▲). From the plots, the trade-off between exploration and exploitation is clear, and the best value for ϵ is usually around 0.3 (i.e., the best overall performance). Notice that Most-Popular is the best performer in all cases, no matter the criterion used to sort users. Algorithms WRMF and BP-RMF show similar

ϵ	Degree Explore	Betweeness Explore	PageRank Explore
0.00	0.199 •	0.199 •	0.199 •
0.01	0.201 ↑	0.214 ↑	0.203 ↑
0.05	0.202 ↑	0.224 ↑	0.204 ↑
0.10	0.206 ↑	0.240 ↑	0.213 ↑
0.20	0.213 ↑	0.258 ↑	0.222 ↑
0.30	0.224 ↑	**0.264** ↑	0.237 ↑
0.40	0.231 ↑	0.255 ↓	0.237 •
0.50	0.228 ↓	0.252 ↓	0.240 ↑
0.60	0.227 ↓	0.244 ↓	0.235 ↓
0.70	0.224 ↓	0.233 ↓	0.232 ↓
0.80	0.213 ↓	0.221 ↓	0.221 ↓
0.90	0.204 ↓	0.207 ↓	0.205 ↓
avg.	7.5%	17.6%	10.6%

Table 1: MAP numbers, considering the Most-Popular algorithm. Symbol ↑ indicates that the corresponding result is an improvement over the result obtained using the previous ϵ value. The last row shows the average improvement considering all ϵ values.

MAP numbers, with WRMF being slightly superior in most of the cases.

5. CONCLUSIONS

This paper focused on the important problem of suggesting relevant and appealing products and services to potential customers, considering the particularly challenging scenario of daily-deals recommendation. Specifically, we consider the task of sending personalized email messages featuring potentialy relevant deals to users. In this case, we can impose a restriction on the order that users receive their messages, that is, some users receive their messages before others. We propose explore-then-exploit recommendation algorithms that are devised to: (i) gather feedback from users that receive their messages first (i.e., during the exploration phase), and (ii) use the gathered feedback in order to send personalized messages to the remaining users (i.e., during the exploitation phase).

There is a trade-off between exploration and exploitation, in the sense that the more users are explored, more feedback is gathered but less feedback is indeed used. To deal with this trade-off, we propose sorting users according to their centrality in an evolving co-purchase network, so that more central users are those that share the same taste with more users. We employ a 2-month real data snapshot obtained from PeixeUrbano, the largest daily-deals website in Brazil, and show that: (i) the recommendation performance of existing algorithms is no better than the naive strategy of suggesting non-personalized deals for all users (i.e., all users receive the same message featuring the same deals), and (ii) the proposed explore-then-exploit algorithms are very effective and well-suited to the daily-deals recommendation scenario, providing improvements ranging from 18% to 34%.

Acknowledgments

This work is partially supported by the National Institute of Science and Technology for the Web, MCT/CNPq grant 57.3871/2008-6, and by the authors' individual grants and scholarships from CAPES and CNPq. We thank PeixeUrbano for providing the data used in the experiments.

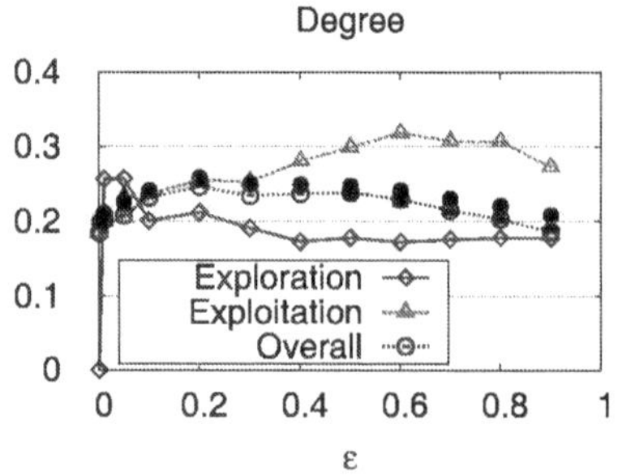

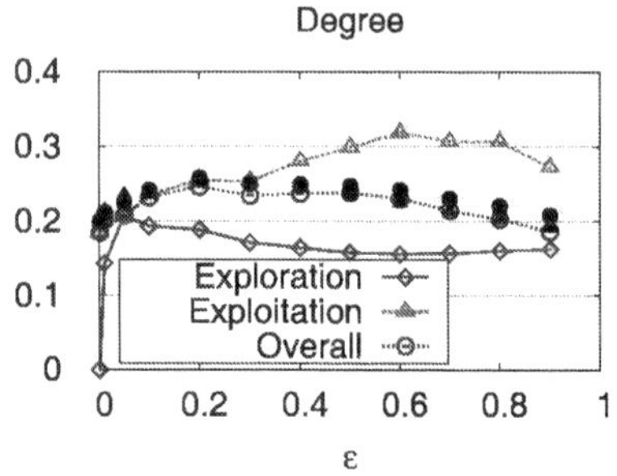

Figure 3: (Color online) MAP numbers obtained considering: (i) only the exploration phase (red curve), (ii) only the exploitation phase (green curve), and (iii) overall (blue curve). Symbol • indicates the corresponding MAP numbers for Most-Popular. Symbol ▲ indicates the (empirical) upper bound for MAP. The plot at the top corresponds to the WRMF algorithm and the plot at the bottom corresponds to the BP-RMF algorithm.

6. REFERENCES

[1] A. Bifet, G. Holmes, R. Kirkby, and B. Pfahringer. MOA: Massive online analysis. *Journal of Machine Learning Research*, 11:1601–1604, 2010.

[2] P. Bonacich. Power and centrality:a family of measures. *The American Journal of Sociology*, 92(5):1170–1182, 1987.

[3] J. Byers, M. Mitzenmacher, and G. Zervas. Daily deals: prediction, social diffusion, and reputational ramifications. In *WSDM*, pages 543–552, 2012.

[4] L. Freeman. Centrality in social networks: Conceptual clarification. *Social Networks*, 1(3):215–239, 1979.

[5] Y. Hu, Y. Koren, and C. Volinsky. Collaborative filtering for implicit feedback datasets. In *ICDM*, pages 263–272, 2008.

[6] L. Kaelbling, M. Littman, and A. Moore. Reinforcement learning: A survey. *J. Artif. Intell. Res.*, 4:237–285, 1996.

[7] T. Lappas and E. Terzi. Daily-deal selection for revenue maximization. In *CIKM*, pages 565–574, 2012.

[8] L. Li, W. Chu, J. Langford, and R. Schapire. A contextual-bandit approach to personalized news article recommendation. In *WWW*, pages 661–670, 2010.

[9] F. Radlinski, R. Kleinberg, and T. Joachims. Learning diverse rankings with multi-armed bandits. In *ICML*, pages 784–791, 2008.

[10] S. Rendle, C. Freudenthaler, Z. Gantner, and L. Schmidt-Thieme. Bpr: Bayesian personalized ranking from implicit feedback. In *UAI*, pages 452–461, 2009.

[11] Z. Xu, K. Kersting, and T. Joachims. Fast active exploration for link-based preference learning using gaussian processes. In *ECML/PKDD (3)*, pages 499–514, 2010.

Dynamic Generation of Personalized Hybrid Recommender Systems

Simon Dooms
iMinds-Ghent University
G. Crommenlaan 8, box 201, Ghent, Belgium
simon.dooms@intec.ugent.be

ABSTRACT

The problem of information overload has been a relevant and active research topic for the past twenty years. Since then, numerous algorithms and recommendation approaches have been proposed, which gives rise to a new type of problem: recommendation algorithm overload. Although hybrid recommendation techniques, which combine the strengths of individual recommenders, have become well-accepted, the procedure of building and tuning a hybrid recommender is still a tedious and time-consuming process. In our work, we focus on dynamically building personalized hybrid recommender systems on an individual user basis. By means of a dynamic online learning strategy we combine the most appropriate recommendation algorithms for a user based on realtime relevance feedback. Learning effectiveness of genetic algorithms, machine learning techniques and other optimization approaches will be studied in both an offline and online setting.

Categories and Subject Descriptors

H.3.3 [**Information Search and Retrieval**]: Information filtering, Relevance feedback, User-centered design

General Terms

Algorithms, Design, Human Factors

Keywords

Recommender systems, hybrid recommender system, self-learning

1. INTRODUCTION

Since the introduction of the collaborative filtering principle by Resnick et al. [1] in 1994, numerous algorithms and recommendation approaches have been proposed to tackle the information overload problem. Every one of these algorithms in its own way attempts to connect users to relevant content. Roughly classified, recommendation algorithms are typically divided into categories based on the data they exploit. Collaborative algorithms use rating behavior of the community (i.e., other users or items), content-based algorithms process available content data (e.g., item features) and knowledge-based algorithms exploit general knowledge available in the domain of the recommendation use case.

In recent years however, rather than focussing on mathematically improving classic algorithms to squeeze out every last bit of recommendation accuracy, new types of algorithms are on the rise. New trends as social media and smartphones are increasingly providing new and complexer types of user data like social data (e.g., friend connections) and context (e.g., location, time of day, mood, etc.), which results in new categories of recommendation algorithms that specifically target these kinds of data.

While recommendation algorithms used to be competing against each other, nowadays it has been generally accepted that every algorithm has its own focus, optimal use cases, advantages and disadvantages and that hybrid recommenders, which combine multiple recommenders, are able to further increase recommendation quality and overcome individual drawbacks [2, 3, 4]. Although hybrid recommenders are well-accepted and have shown their merits in multiple competitions (such as the Netflix prize), the procedure of actually building and tweaking the hybrid recommender is still a tedious and time-consuming process.

In our work, we focus on building a future-proof hybrid recommendation platform that can seamlessly integrate existing recommendation algorithms and dynamically combine them into a best-fit hybrid recommender. While most mainstream recommendation algorithms typically start from the notion that users in a system behave similarly [5], recent research is turning more towards the idea that every user is unique and (combinations of) different algorithms may be best for different users [4, 6, 7]. Therefore, every user would probably benefit from a uniquely tailored hybrid recommender system. A self-learning hybrid platform could prove to be of great value for e.g., industrial use cases where often different algorithms are experimented with simultaneously, and both users and industry would benefit from the improved user experience.

We define the following research questions:

- Do (all) users benefit from personalized hybrid recommender systems?
- How can a hybrid recommender be dynamically adjusted?

RecSys'13, Oct 12–16, 2013, Hong Kong, China.
ACM 978-1-4503-2409-0/13/09.
http://dx.doi.org/10.1145/2507157.2508069.

- What kind of artificial intelligence techniques can be applied to this problem?
- What kind of evaluation metrics should be considered?
- How can we measure and take into account online user relevance feedback?

To address the stated research questions, the problem of building a hybrid recommender system will be reformulated as an optimization task to which known techniques from the domain of machine learning can then be applied.

2. RELATED WORK

Hybrid recommender systems were first categorized by Burke et al. [2] in function of how they combine individual recommenders (e.g., weighted, cascade, mixed, etc.). Early hybrid recommender systems often internally merged two classical algorithms e.g. a form of collaborative filtering (CF) with content-based filtering (CBF) to cope with specific failing use cases. Cornelis et al. [8] for example combined elements of CF and CBF to recommend time-specific items (i.e., events), which get rated only after users have consumed (i.e., visited) the items. Since in these types of hybrids, specific properties of the individual algorithms are exploited, they lack extendibility and easy integration of more and other types of algorithms.

Hybrid recommenders regarding individual recommendation algorithms as black boxes, are more interesting because they easily allow to extend their models with other algorithms of any type. One famous example of such a system is the winning submission to the Netflix prize. Belkor et al. [9] blended 107 individual recommenders into one weighted hybrid model to achieve an optimal RMSE value. Their optimization target however was overall RMSE, and so the weights for the individual algorithms were the same for every user (i.e., static hybrid).

The AdaRec system [10] proposed a dynamic hybrid strategy that modifies its prediction strategy at runtime to cope with unique domains, trends and user interests. Focus however, is on a switching strategy that selects the most suitable recommendation algorithm rather than composing a dynamic weighted hybrid that incorporates input from all algorithms.

Closely related to this work, is the work of Bellogin et al. [4] where the problem of dynamic weighting of ensemble recommenders was analyzed from an information retrieval (IR) perspective. They proposed adaptations of query performance techniques from ad-hoc IR to define performance predictors in recommender systems. These performance predictors could then be used to dynamically adapt the recommendation strategy to the situation at hand. Our work differs from theirs, in that we do not adapt our system to predicted accuracy, but rather to realtime relevance feedback collected through a user-system interaction process. We furthermore investigate the dynamic ensemble weighting problem from a machine learning perspective and observe a black box approach for individual recommendation algorithms allowing easy integration of numerous algorithms regardless of complexity or type.

3. DYNAMIC FRAMEWORK

To be able to empirically experiment with various strategies and settings, we built a dynamic framework that provides some basic recommendation functionality. Figure 1 visualizes the conceptual layout of our framework. In our research we focus on movies as recommendable items because of the wildly available datasets and easily interpretable domain. To avoid any cold start problems, we start from the MovieLens (1M) dataset but integrate also rating data collected from popular social media platforms to also feature new and relevant items (the most recent movie in the MovieLens 1M dataset is from the year 2000). The rating data is then provided to multiple recommendation algorithms which run in parallel and isolated from each other. Individual algorithms are considered black boxes, and so only their inputs and outputs are being taken into account. Because the system does not rely on any internal properties of the algorithms, new algorithms can easily be 'plugged in'. This approach even allows to add all sorts of hybrid algorithms e.g. cascading algorithms to be integrated without any additional effort (displayed as the '×' algorithm in Figure 1). We currently integrated over 20 algorithms from the recommendation framework MyMediaLite [11] but plan on integrating more from other recommendation frameworks (like LensKit [12], Duine [13] and Mahout[1]) as well.

The output (i.e., predictions) of the algorithms serve as input to the learning module of the system, which then generates final predictions for a user. Interactively a user is able to provide relevance feedback (i.e., how good are these recommendations?) while providing new ratings. The relevance feedback is propagated back to the learning module which adapts in realtime and new results can be made available to the user. New ratings in their turn are propagated to the backend of the system where they are merged with the original dataset and provide new data for the recommendation algorithms.

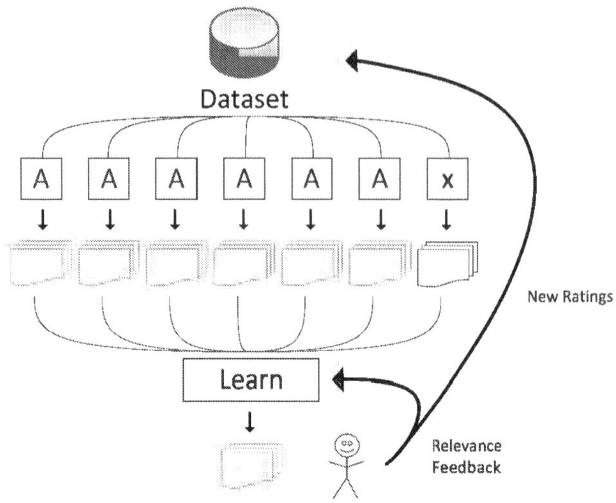

Figure 1: The layout of our dynamic framework. Data is fed to multiple recommendation algorithms in parallel, which are then combined into one hybrid set of recommendations by a self-learning online module that processes user relevance feedback.

[1]http://mahout.apache.org

4. LEARNING APPROACH

The learning approach, or *module* as referred to in the previous section, is the very heart of this research. We want to dynamically combine predictions made by multiple algorithms and use reinforcement learning strategies to adapt in realtime to user feedback. To do so, we will be redefining our problem as an optimization task. We adopt the notation from [14] to define a dynamic ensemble recommender as:

$$g(u,i) = \gamma_{a_1}(u) * g_{a_1}(u,i) + \ldots + \gamma_{a_n}(u) * g_{a_n}(u,i)$$

where γ is a weighting factor indicating the importance value of the contribution for every algorithm a to the final prediction score g for a user u and item i. We now define an objective function:

$$f(\gamma(u))$$

where

$$\gamma(u) = (\gamma_{a_1}(u), \ldots, \gamma_{a_n}(u))$$

with n the total number of algorithms. By choosing an objective function f, we can now minimize (or maximize) f by creating an appropriate vector of algorithm weights $\gamma(u)$. Interesting choices for objective functions are for example typical evaluation metrics in the recommendation domain like RMSE, MAE, etc. When the objective function is selected, known optimization techniques can be applied to generate good choices for the weight vector $\gamma(u)$. The implied research challenge for the learning module will be twofold. First, we must define what we want to optimize. Do we want minimal RMSE? Maximum precision or recall? Or even other metrics as 'number of user clicks', as long as they are measurable, can be optimized for. Secondly, an appropriate optimization technique must be selected to generate a good solution in an appropriate time frame. Since we want to update the hybrid recommendations for a user dynamically while user feedback is provided, the appropriate time frame in this context is 'almost realtime'.

We are currently investigating the applicability of genetic algorithms which, according to our earliest experiments, are able to rapidly provide near-optimal solutions to our problem when properly tuned.

Figure 2 shows the results of a small experiment where we test our dynamic hybrid approach on 10 randomly selected users from the MovieLens 1M dataset. For these users, we trained our genetic algorithm to optimize their algorithm weight vectors (optimizing for RMSE) for 25 individual recommendation algorithms. We compared our dynamic hybrid recommender with a baseline switching strategy that for each user selects the best algorithm (i.e., lowest RMSE). While the difference varies from user to user, an overall advantage of our weighted hybrid approach (over the switching approach) can be observed.

When we manually inspect the generated algorithm weight vectors, we find them to be very different for each user and so our early results seem to confirm that it makes sense to personalize these weights on an individual user level.

We plan on expanding our experiments to other machine learning techniques and to do more formal evaluations, first focusing on offline testing, where user data is simulated or *replayed*, but gradually moving to online testing where actual users can become involved in the evaluation process.

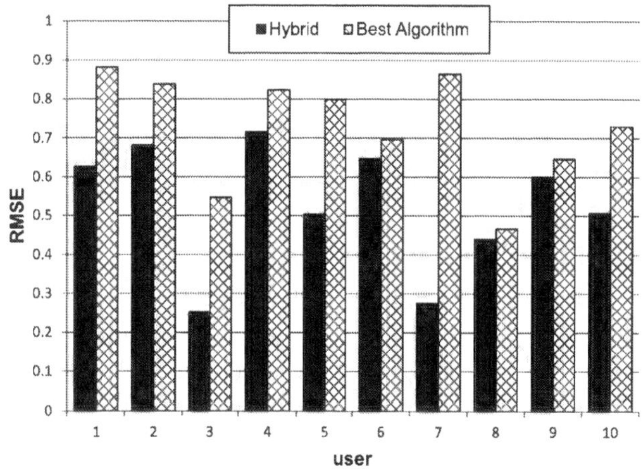

Figure 2: RMSE comparison of our dynamic hybrid recommender, optimized by a genetic algorithm, and a baseline hybrid switching strategy for 10 random MovieLens users.

5. AVOIDING FILTER BUBBLES

In 2011, Eli Pariser caused a stir in the recommender systems domain when he introduced the concept of the *Filter Bubble*[2]. He claimed that, because of personalization, more and more users of online platforms will be trapped in their own separate, filtered *bubbles* of information. Such a bubble would virtually surround users with content tailored to their interests and therefore at the same time also keeps them from thinking outside the 'bubble'. They are no longer able to learn new things, evolve and change interests. A panel in the RecSys 2011 conference discussed the topic, and the take-away message was that personalization is fine as long as users can be given a certain amount of control (e.g., choose to disable personalized results) and recommender systems can be made as transparent as possible (e.g., explain the origin of a recommendation).

In our work, we intend to avoid bubble issues by allowing users to take control of their recommendations. In the context of dynamic ensembles, being in control could mean for example being able to manipulate the weight vector that controls the importance of underlying algorithms. Transparency can also be easily provided by allowing users to inspect their weight vector. Whether these functionalities should be available for all users, or for power users only (e.g., recommendation administrators) may differ, and depends largely on the intended use case.

6. DISCUSSION

We aim for our work to be a usable blue print for real-life recommender system applications. Especially in industry, content providers are not so much interested in what recommendation algorithm is deployed as long as it delivers the expected quality. Therefore, a self-learning system that automatically assemblies good hybrids from individual 'plugged-in' algorithms could be of great value. Furthermore, it allows to introduce new trending algorithms at production time without fundamentally disrupting previous user experience. If newly introduced algorithms turn out to

[2]http://www.thefilterbubble.com/ted-talk

deliver good predictions, their importance weights can gradually increase and thereby also their contribution to the final user recommendations.

Some recommendation algorithms, such as neighborhood-based algorithms, can be run with a variety of different settings such as different neighborhood sizes, different similarity metrics, etc. Our hybrid approach, makes it very easy to empirically test appropriate settings, by plugging in multiple versions of the same algorithm in the system, each time with different settings. The best settings will then automatically prevail.

Scalability issues are avoided in the system by the decoupling of the individual recommendation calculation and the final hybrid visualization of the results to users. While a slow calculation backend can periodically re-run the individual recommendation algorithms in batch, a fast online learning module on the frontend can provide users with an interactive and realtime feeling by instantly adapting to user feedback. Finally, we note that because the vector of algorithm weights can be made manipulable to the user, the system is able to account for some very user-specific situations. By for example including a recommendation algorithm that predicts ratings proportional to how recent movies are, the manipulation of the weight of this algorithm allows users to choose for themselves how much they want the recentness of movies to contribute their recommendations. Another interesting example is the random recommender. By including the random recommender as one of the individual recommendation algorithms, users may introduce an appropriate value of randomness thereby manipulating the serendipity (and diversity) of their recommendations.

7. CONCLUSIONS AND PLANNED WORK

In this work, we wish to solve the problem that emerged from solving the information overload problem: the recommendation algorithm overload problem. Instead of focusing on quality improvement of individual algorithms, we turn towards hybrid recommendation to combine the advantages and surpass the quality of its individual components. We propose a future-proof, dynamic weighted ensemble approach that allows to generate hybrid recommenders on an individual user basis. To aid our research task, we have implemented a basic recommendation platform that integrates numerous and widely differing algorithms and supports a self-learning strategy to dynamically combine them in an optimal way. We are currently experimenting with genetic algorithms, but plan on involving and comparing multiple types of optimizing techniques like neural nets and other machine learning strategies.

In ongoing work we intend to explore an evaluation strategy, both in an offline and online context, to assess the quality of developed methods and eventually address the research questions proposed in this work.

8. ACKNOWLEDGMENTS

The described research activities were funded by a PhD grant to Simon Dooms of the Agency for Innovation by Science and Technology (IWT Vlaanderen).

9. REFERENCES

[1] Paul Resnick, Neophytos Iacovou, Mitesh Suchak, Peter Bergstrom, and John Riedl. Grouplens: an open architecture for collaborative filtering of netnews. In *Proc. 1994 ACM Conf. Computer supported cooperative work*, pages 175–186. ACM, 1994.

[2] Robin Burke. Hybrid recommender systems: Survey and experiments. *User modeling and user-adapted interaction*, 12(4):331–370, 2002.

[3] Gediminas Adomavicius and Alexander Tuzhilin. Toward the next generation of recommender systems: A survey of the state-of-the-art and possible extensions. *Knowledge and Data Engineering, IEEE Transactions on*, 17(6):734–749, 2005.

[4] Alejandro Bellogín. *Performance prediction and evaluation in Recommender Systems: An Information Retrieval perspective*. PhD thesis, Universidad Autonoma de Madrid, November 2012.

[5] Dietmar Jannach, Markus Zanker, Alexander Felfernig, and Gerhard Friedrich. *Recommender systems: an introduction*. Cambridge University Press, 2010.

[6] Michael Ekstrand and John Riedl. When recommenders fail: predicting recommender failure for algorithm selection and combination. In *Proc. 6th ACM Conf. Recommender systems (RecSys 2012)*, pages 233–236. ACM, 2012.

[7] Benjamin Kille and Sahin Albayrak. Modeling difficulty in recommender systems. In *Workshop on Recommendation Utility Evaluation: Beyond RMSE (RUE 2011)*, page 30, 2012.

[8] Chris Cornelis, Xuetao Guo, Jie Lu, and Guanquang Zhang. A fuzzy relational approach to event recommendation. In *Proc. Indian Int. Conf. Artificial Intelligence*, 2005.

[9] Robert M Bell, Yehuda Koren, and Chris Volinsky. The bellkor solution to the netflix prize. *KorBell Team?s Report to Netflix*, 2007.

[10] Fatih Aksel and Aysenur Birtürk. An adaptive hybrid recommender system that learns domain dynamics. In *Int. Workshop on Handling Concept Drift in Adaptive Information Systems: Importance, Challenges and Solutions (HaCDAIS-2010) at the European Conference on Machine Learning and Principles and Practice of Knowledge Discovery in Databases*, page 49, 2010.

[11] Zeno Gantner, Steffen Rendle, Christoph Freudenthaler, and Lars Schmidt-Thieme. MyMediaLite: A free recommender system library. In *Proc. 5th ACM Conf. Recommender Systems (RecSys 2011)*, 2011.

[12] Michael D Ekstrand, Michael Ludwig, Joseph A Konstan, and John T Riedl. Rethinking the recommender research ecosystem: reproducibility, openness, and lenskit. In *Proc. 5th ACM Conf. Recommender systems (RecSys 2011)*, pages 133–140. ACM, 2011.

[13] M. van Setten. *Supporting People in Finding Information: Hybrid Recommender Systems and Goal-Based Structuring*. PhD thesis, Telematica Instituut, Enschede, December 2005.

[14] Alejandro Bellogín. Predicting performance in recommender systems. In *Proc. 5th ACM Conf. Recommender systems (RecSys 2011)*, pages 371–374. ACM, 2011.

Accuracy and Robustness Impacts of Power User Attacks on Collaborative Recommender Systems

Carlos E. Seminario
Software and Information Systems Department
University of North Carolina at Charlotte
cseminar@uncc.edu

ABSTRACT

Power users, in a Collaborative Filtering (CF) Recommender System (RS) context, are those who can exert considerable influence over the recommendation outcomes presented to other users. RS operators encourage the existence of power user communities and leverage them to help fellow users make informed purchase decisions. Thus, RS research in this area has focused on power user selection and utilization to address challenges such as rating sparsity for new items or users. But, as ever, there remains the potential for corruption by power users who provide biased ratings. And because of the influence that power users wield, biased ratings they provide can have significant impacts on RS accuracy and robustness. In order to better understand this problem and develop solution strategies, our research is investigating the impact on RS predictions and top-N recommendation lists when power users provide biased ratings. The open areas of research we have explored are analyzing and evaluating power user selection techniques, statistically characterizing power users in order to create attack profiles, mounting power user attacks on new items, and using accuracy and robustness metrics to evaluate power user attacks. In the future, we plan to extend our initial research in power user selection, characterization, and evaluation, as well as generate attack profiles based on power user characteristics, mount power user attacks on user-based, item-based, and SVD-based CF systems, evaluate power user attacks, and generalize our work across different domains.

Categories and Subject Descriptors

H.3.3 [**Information Storage and Retrieval**]: Information Search and Retrieval–*Information filtering*

Keywords

Recommender Systems; Power User; Attacks; Evaluation

1. INTRODUCTION

In a Collaborative Filtering (CF) Recommender System (RS) context, *power users* are those who can exert considerable influence over the recommendations presented to other users. Previous research has indicated that power users can have major impacts on RS ratings predictions and top-N recommendations lists, especially when the underlying RS algorithms are neighborhood-based [9]. However, recommender system operators encourage the existence of power user communities; e.g., Amazon Vine™invites the most trusted reviewers on Amazon to post opinions about new and pre-release items to help their fellow users make informed purchase decisions[1]. Furthermore, new items can sometimes pose significant market acceptance challenges to producers of goods and services; in order to address this issue, marketers may rely on the influence that power users have in recommending items to other users [3, 1]. But given the influence that power users can have over others, what happens when power users provide biased ratings?

To address this issue, we define a novel "Power User Attack" as a set of power user profiles that influence the results presented to other users by providing biased ratings. This attack is distinct from previously studied types of RS attacks [11, 8, 10] (e.g., "random", "average", "bandwagon", etc.) that rely on a set of carefully configured false user profiles, which are injected into the dataset to mount the attack. Power User Attack analyses rely critically on power user selection, so we use degree centrality concepts from social network analysis [16] for identifying the most influential RS power users for attack purposes and develop a novel approach for evaluating power user selection that gathers metrics before and after a power user attack.

Our progress to date (see §3 and §4) has been to analyze and evaluate power user selection techniques, characterize power users in order to create attack profiles, mount power user attacks on new items, and evaluate power user attacks. To advance this work, my dissertation proposal investigates several questions related to RS power users and attacks mounted using synthetic power users:

1. How are power users best identified in a RS and what evaluation metrics are best suited to make that determination?
2. What is the value of the social network analysis approach as opposed to other, more simpler approaches?
3. How are power users best characterized using their rating history and how are they localized in the social network?
4. What happens to RS accuracy and robustness when synthetic power users provide biased item ratings?
5. Can a novel attack be crafted to achieve power user capability with strong influence and "low" cost of attack?
6. Can power user attacks be configured to be effective across several popular collaborative RS algorithms?
7. Do similar accuracy and robustness results hold across different domains?

The open problem is to understand the vulnerability of collabo-

[1]http://www.amazon.com/gp/vine/help

RecSys'13, October 12–16, 2013, Hong Kong, China.
ACM 978-1-4503-2409-0/13/10.
http://dx.doi.org/10.1145/2507157.2508070.

rative RSs to manipulation by power users. In order to address the problem, my research objectives are to:

1. Evaluate various power user selection techniques including approaches for identifying RS power users based on social networking degree centrality concepts and select approaches that yield the most influential power users.
2. Determine power user characteristics based on statistical features and clustering in order to better understand who the power users are within a collaborative filtering dataset.
3. Develop a novel 'Power User Attack' for RS, generate attack profiles based on power user characteristics, and mount attacks across different domains.
4. Evaluate impacts of the power user attack using accuracy and robustness metrics, for user-based, item-based, and matrix factorization (Singular Value Decomposition - SVD) CF RS.
5. Develop a novel power user selection evaluation approach based on accuracy metrics (before the attack) and robustness metrics (after the attack).

Initial results (see §4) indicate that degree centrality offers significant improvements over existing techniques for power user selection and that power user attacks have significant accuracy and robustness impacts on RS predictions and recommendations, especially for new items in user-based CF systems.

2. RELATED WORK

In the RS context, power users are of interest to system operators and their client companies when launching a new item because a positive endorsement (high rating) can translate into item recommendations to a large number of users. This is known as market-based use of RS and has been previously promoted as a solution to the "cold-start" or "new item" problem [1]. However, identifying power users remains an active research topic. Rashid et al [13] developed a RS algorithm-independent approach based on the number of unique prediction differences observed when an active user is removed from the prediction calculation. Viral marketing, to exploit the network value of customers, was studied by [3]. Maximizing the spread of influence through a social network was further studied by [7] who found the problem to be NP-hard and provided the first provable approximate guarantees for efficient algorithms. More recently, [4] has analyzed several heuristic approaches to power user selection. Power user selection techniques have been evaluated using various methods such as shifts in prediction values [13, 4], accuracy and coverage measures [1], and expected lift in profit [3]. Although robustness measures such as Hit Ratio and Rank (see Evaluation Metrics in §3.2) in the context of RS attacks have not been used previously to evaluate power user selection methods, we use them here because we believe that true power users are in some sense defined by their capacity for impact on system outcomes.

Social Network Analysis affords well-known concepts that can be readily applied to RS power users and their influence in the underlying RS social graph. The concept of Degree Centrality [16] indicates that nodes (users) who have more edges (connections) to other nodes may have advantages; high in-degree refers to nodes that many other nodes connect to and corresponds to high prominence, prestige, or popularity and high out-degree refers to nodes that connect to many other nodes and corresponds to high expansiveness. Furthermore, collaborative relationships in recommender systems can be represented as a social network [12], where, in-degree represents the number of contact lists a user appears in and out-degree indicates the number of users on a contact list that can be used to ask opinions or advice. Neighborhood characteristics and power user selection in recommender systems were analyzed in [9] as part of a study on temporal social networks.

Attempts to influence recommender system results by providing false ratings are known as "shilling attacks" [8], or "profile injection attacks" [10]. A user profile contains the set of ratings a user has made using the recommender system. Attacks are used to either promote ("push") a target item by setting the rating to the maximum value or demote ("nuke") a target item by setting the rating to the minimum value; furthermore, attackers will submit one or more user profiles containing item ratings (called attack user profiles) that push or nuke a specific item. Research in attacks on recommender systems began in 2002 [11] and has continued to be studied, especially in the areas of attack detection and improvements in algorithm robustness; a more recent summary on RS attacks can be found in [2]. This research has revealed that knowledge of the underlying RS algorithms and dataset characteristics can enhance the effectiveness of an attack even though this knowledge may be difficult to obtain. With today's level of user sophistication, however, attackers can obtain this knowledge either indirectly (e.g., scraping/data-mining, social engineering well-known users via side channels) or even directly (e.g., leak, insider, system breach). Uncovering, in part or full, the social network of interest that underlies such RS can leave systems vulnerable to exploitation from more subtle, yet powerful, attacks by highly-influential power users. And this vector of attack remains an open question in RS robustness research that is explored in my dissertation.

3. POWER USER ATTACK

We define the *Power User Attack* (PUA) as a novel attack model[2] where power users bias the results of the RS predictions and top-N recommendation lists with targeted fake ratings. Like other attack models, PUA profiles contain target items that are set to the maximum or minimum rating depending on attack intent. However, unlike classic attack models such as random, average, and bandwagon, that employ straightforward statistical templates, e.g., average rating, popularity, and likability, to generate attack profile "filler" (non-target) items [10], very little is known about the profile characteristics of power users. And without this knowledge, it is difficult to generate synthetic power user profiles. So, in order to evaluate this attack model, our initial foray into studying the impact of a PUA uses selected power user profiles that already exist in the dataset as simulated injected attack user profiles; we recognize this as a limitation in our initial work and will be addressed in the future with the use of synthetic power user attack profiles.

3.1 Power User Selection

Power users in the RS context have been referred to as users with a large number of ratings [6] as well as those that are able to influence the largest number of other users [3, 13, 1, 4]. To measure influence, [13] used the number of prediction differences above a prediction threshold when a user is removed from the dataset, [4] used the number of users that had the prediction for a target item shifted sufficiently above a threshold so that the item appears in their top-N list, [1] used MAE and coverage to evaluate various seed (influential user) selection algorithms, and [3] used the expected lift in profit earned by influencing other users. Although maximizing the spread of influence through a social network is an NP-hard problem to solve optimally [7], several heuristics were analyzed by [4] in order to select groups of influential users including Most Central

[2]Described in a short paper to appear in RecSys 2013; excerpts from that paper were used in this abstract. Also, new results using ML10M and SVD are provided in §4.1 of this abstract.

(those with highest aggregate similarity to other users), Most Positive (those with the highest positive average rating), Most Active (those who have rated the highest number of items), and Random (a control group comprised of randomly selected users).

We have developed an approach to power user selection for attack purposes called *InDegree*, based on social network analysis concepts of Degree Centrality [16, 9]. Specifically, we use In-Degree Centrality (users who appear in the highest number of other users' neighborhoods) with significance weighting [5]; in an initial study, we found that both our approach and the Most Central heuristic [4] performed significantly better selecting power users when using significance weighting. Our selection process is such that for each user i we compute its similarity with every other user j applying significance weighting $n_{ci}/50$, then discard all but the top-n neighbors for each user i (we used n=25 for ID2550 and n=50 for ID5050), count the number of similarity scores for each user j (# neighborhoods user j is in), and select the top k users.

Other approaches were implemented for comparative purposes:
Aggregated Similarity (AS25NO): This is the Most Central heuristic from [4] that selects the top users with the highest aggregate similarity scores; this method requires at least 5 co-rated items between user i and user j and does not use significance weighting[3].
Number of Ratings (NR): This method, based on power user definition in [6] and Most Active heuristic in [4], selects the top users based on the total number of ratings they have in their user profile.

3.2 Power User Analysis Environment Setup

Our initial analyses for power user selection, characterization, and power user attack on new items use the following setup:
Datasets and Algorithms: We used MovieLens[4] ML100K[5], ML1M[6], and ML10M[7] datasets. Following earlier studies evaluating power user influence [3, 13, 4], we use traditional CF algorithms. For the user-based CF algorithm [14, 5], we used Pearson Correlation similarity with significance weighting, neighborhood formation, and mean-centered prediction. For the item-based CF algorithm [15], we used Adjusted Cosine similarity, neighborhood formation, and weighted prediction. We also use SVD with 50 features and 50 iterations for the power user selection analysis (see §4.1).
Attack-related Target Item Selection: For each dataset, fifty target items were selected randomly from a set of items with no more than one rating, because our initial intent was to attack only 'new' items.
Attack Parameter Selection: The Attack Intent used is Push, i.e., target item rating is set to max (= 5). The Attack Size or number of power users in each attack varies from 2 to 50, where 50 power user profiles equate to a 5% attack for ML100K and a 1% attack for ML1M; ML10M was not used for attack analysis. The attack profiles used were actual power user profiles with the target item rating inserted[8]; the filler size is determined by each power users' profile size.
Evaluation Metrics: We use Mean Absolute Error and prediction coverage [6] for accuracy and coverage using a holdout-partitioned 70/30 train/test dataset, and Hit Ratio, Prediction Shift, and Rank robustness measures [10, 2] where high Hit Ratio and low Rank indicate that the attack was successful (from attacker's perspective).

[3]Based on personal communication with the authors.
[4]http://www.grouplens.org
[5]nominal 100,000 ratings, 1,682 movies, and 943 users.
[6]nominal 1,000,209 ratings, 3,883 movies, 6,040 users.
[7]nominal 10,000,054 ratings, 10,676 movies, 69,878 users.
[8]In a few cases, power user profiles that already had a target item rating were updated in certain attack scenarios and, although the target item rating change might alter their neighborhoods, we believe the impact to this initial analysis is not an overriding issue.

4. INITIAL RESULTS

4.1 Power User Selection and Evaluation

Our approach to evaluating selection of power users and their influence is to use accuracy metrics (before the attack) and robustness metrics (after the attack). **Before the attack**, the measure of influence is the negative impact on RS accuracy when removing power users. Prior to attack, we incrementally removed power users from the datasets for each method of power user selection. The results for ML10M[9] (Figure 1) show that as power users are removed, MAE is negatively impacted in all CF algorithms tested; this is also the case for ML100K and ML1M (not shown) and these results are consistent with those observed in [9]. Compared to a baseline where no power users are removed, InDegree selection impacts MAE by an average high of 2.2% across all three CF algorithms, Number of Ratings by 1.8%, and Aggregated Similarity by 0.5%; all these impacts were significant (p <0.02). InDegree selection, compared to the other methods, has a higher MAE impact in User-based CF. Both InDegree and Number of Ratings methods are better at selecting power users than Aggregated Similarity, i.e., they have the most significant impacts on MAE with removal of fewer power users, especially in SVD-based and User-based CF. The Number of Ratings method performs relatively well across all CF algorithms and begs the question of whether having a large number of ratings is really the only requirement to become a power user. **After the attack**, the most influential set of power users is the one producing the highest Hit Ratio and lowest Rank (see results in §4.3).

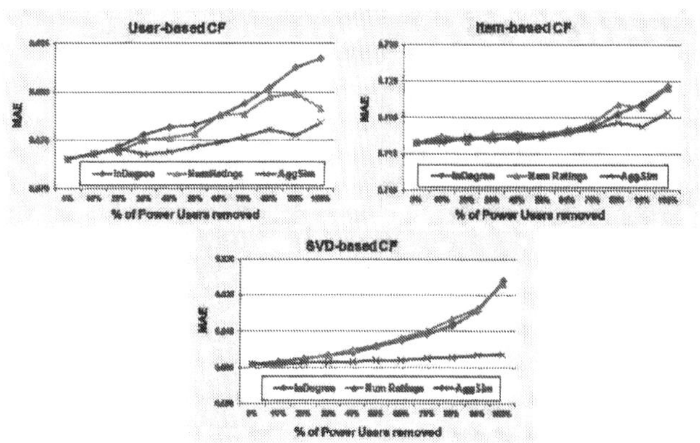

Figure 1: ML10M MAE impacts after removing Power Users

4.2 Power User Characterization

In order to understand the differences between power and non-power user groups within a given dataset, identified using InDegree, we have collected various statistical measures for each group across ML100K, ML1M, and ML10M. Notably for InDegree across these datasets, a statistically significant (p <0.02) pattern is emerging: power users have a lower average rating, higher average number of ratings, higher average number of co-rated items, and higher rating entropy when compared to the non-power user group and the entire dataset of users. Although the absolute number for each measure varies according to the dataset, the pattern is consistent.

4.3 Power User Attack on New Items

Accuracy and robustness metrics (Figures 2 and 3) were negatively impacted due to the PUA. Although accuracy results varied, all of the selection methods yielded MAE values significantly

[9]We selected 3500 power users or about 5% of all ML10M users.

higher ($p < 0.05$) for ML1M User-based CF and 30 or more power users, and the InDegree selection method yielded MAE values significantly higher ($p < 0.05$) for ML1M Item-based CF with 30 or 40 power users. Robustness results indicate that InDegree and Number of Ratings impact User-based CF recommenders more significantly than Aggregated Similarity; however, we found the reverse to be true for Item-based CF recommenders. For User-based CF, InDegree performed better than Number of Ratings on the ML1M dataset ($p < 0.05$) as indicated by Hit Ratio and Rank results; InDegree and Number of Ratings were about the same for ML100K (not shown). Impacts to robustness metrics indicate that a small number of power users[10] can have significant effects on RS predictions and top-N recommendation lists for new items; User-based CF is significantly more vulnerable to this power user attack than Item-based CF and is consistent with previous findings [8, 10, 2].

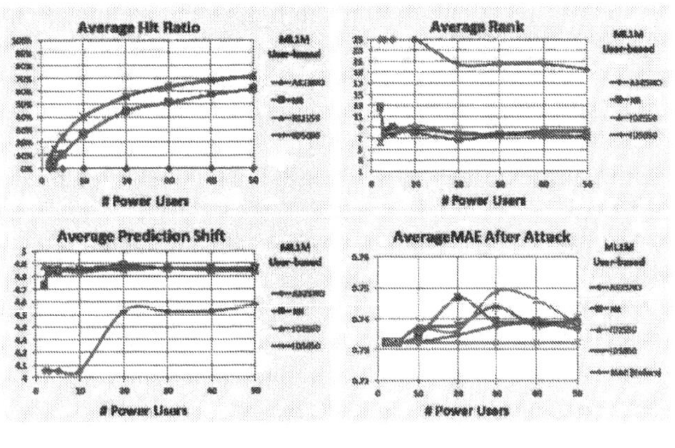

Figure 2: ML1M – User-based Results

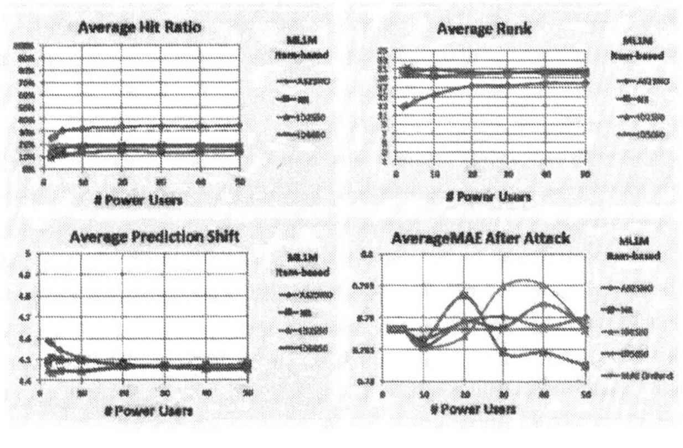

Figure 3: ML1M – Item-based Results

5. DISCUSSION AND FUTURE WORK

To the best of our knowledge, this is the first definition, analysis, and evaluation of the PUA and its impacts on RS. Addressing this problem will allow us to understand the vulnerability of collaborative RSs to manipulation by power users as well as to enable development of attack detection and mitigation methods. Our initial analysis indicates that power users identified using social network degree centrality can have significant effects on accuracy and robustness measures and that the PUA can mount effective attacks against user-based CF systems. In the future, we plan to extend this work by: (1) Completing the characterization of power users using additional statistical and clustering methods to refine our definition of a power user, (2) Generating PUA profiles based on our knowledge of power user characteristics, inject those profiles into datasets, and evaluate attacks across different domains using accuracy and robustness metrics, (3) Developing PUA models that are effective for user-based, item-based, and SVD-based CF systems, and (4) Refining our power user selection evaluation approach using accuracy and robustness metrics.

[10]Note that 50 power users is < 1% of the ML1M user base.

6. REFERENCES

[1] S. S. Anand and N. Griffiths. A market-based approach to address the new item problem. In *Proceedings of the 5th ACM Recommender Systems Conference*, 2011.

[2] R. Burke, M. P. O'Mahony, and N. J. Hurley. Robust collaborative recommendation. In F. Ricci, L. Rokach, B. Shapira, and P. B. Kantor, editors, *Recommender Systems Handbook*. Springer, 2011.

[3] P. Domingos and M. Richardson. Mining the network value of customers. In *Proceedings of KDD'01*. ACM, 2001.

[4] A. Goyal and L. V. S. Lakshmanan. Recmax: Exploiting recommender systems for fun and profit. In *Proceedings of KDD'12*, 2012.

[5] J. L. Herlocker, J. A. Konstan, A. Borchers, and J. Riedl. An algorithmic framework for performing collaborative filtering. In *Proceedings of the ACM SIGIR Conference*, 1999.

[6] J. L. Herlocker, J. A. Konstan, L. G. Terveen, and J. Riedl. Evaluating collaborative filtering recommender systems. *ACM Transactions on Information Systems*, 22(1), 2004.

[7] D. Kempe, J. Kleinberg, and E. Tardos. Maximizing the spread of influence through a social network. In *Proceedings of KDD'03*, 2003.

[8] S. K. Lam and J. Riedl. Shilling recommender systems for fun and profit. In *WWW '04: Proceedings of the 13th international conference on World Wide Web*. ACM, 2004.

[9] N. Lathia, S. Hailes, and L. Capra. knn cf: A temporal social network. In *Proceedings of RecSys '08*, 2008.

[10] B. Mobasher, R. Burke, R. Bhaumik, and C. Williams. Toward trustworthy recommender systems: An analysis of attack models and algorithm robustness. *ACM Trans. Internet Technol.*, 7(4):23, 2007.

[11] M. P. O'Mahony, N. Hurley, and G. C. M. Silvestre. Promoting recommendations: An attack on collaborative filtering. In *Proceedings of DEXA'02*, 2002.

[12] J. Palau, M. Montaner, B. Lopez, and J. L. D. L. Rosa. Collaboration analysis in recommender systems using social networks. In *Cooperative Information Agents VIII: 8th International Workshop, CIA 2004.*

[13] A. Rashid and J. Karypis, G.and Riedl. Influence in ratings-based recommender systems: An algorithm-independent approach. In *Proceedings of the SIAM International conference on Data Mining, 2005.*

[14] P. Resnick, N. Iacovou, M. Suchak, P. Bergstrom, and J. Riedl. GroupLens: an open architecture for collaborative filtering of netnews. In *Proceedings of CSCW'94*, 1994.

[15] B. Sarwar, G. Karypis, J. Konstan, and J. Riedl. Item-based collaborative filtering recommendation algorithms. In *Proceedings of the World Wide Web Conference*, 2001.

[16] S. Wasserman and K. Faust. *Social Network Analysis: Methods and Applications*. Cambridge Univ Press, 1994.

Integrating Trust and Similarity to Ameliorate the Data Sparsity and Cold Start for Recommender Systems

Guibing Guo
School of Computer Engineering
Nanyang Technological University, Singapore
gguo1@e.ntu.edu.sg

ABSTRACT

Our research aims to tackle the problems of data sparsity and cold start of traditional recommender systems. Insufficient ratings often result in poor quality of recommendations in terms of accuracy and coverage. To address these issues, we propose three different approaches from the perspective of preference modelling. Firstly, we propose to merge the ratings of trusted neighbors and thus form a new rating profile for the active users, based on which better recommendations can be generated. Secondly, we aim to make better use of user ratings and introduce a novel Bayesian similarity measure by taking into account both the direction and length of rating vectors. Thirdly, we propose a new information source called *prior ratings* based on virtual product experience in virtual reality environments, in order to inherently resolve the concerned problems.

Categories and Subject Descriptors

H.3.3 [**Information Storage and Retrieval**]: Information Search and Retrieval—*Information filtering*; H.5.2 [**Information Interfaces and Presentation**]: User Interfaces—*Evaluation/methodology*

Keywords

Similarity, Trust, Similarity measure, Prior ratings

1. INTRODUCTION

Collaborative filtering (CF) [1] is an effective technique for recommender systems to provide users with high quality items of interest, tackling the problem of *information overload*. It makes use of the heuristic that the preferences of like-minded users are similar. However, CF inherently suffers from two issues, namely *data sparsity* and *cold start* [1]. The former issue refers to the difficulty in finding reliable similar users, given the fact that users only rate a small portion of items, while the latter refers to the difficulty in modelling user preference due to only few items rated by the active users (known as *cold users*). Our research aims to resolve these issues by better modelling user preferences from both user behaviors (i.e., ratings) and social connections (i.e., trusted friends).

Trust has been extensively exploited to improve the predictive performance and ameliorate the concerned issues, given the strong and positive correlation with preference [21]. Trust is defined as one's belief towards the ability of others in providing valuable ratings. For example, users in Epinions.com can specify other users as trustworthy (to the 'web of trust') or untrustworthy (to the 'block list). Massa and Anesani [16] substitute similarity with trust in predicting items' ratings. Trust is allowed to propagate through the trust networks in order to incorporate more trusted neighbors and hence alleviate the data sparsity and cold start problems. It shows that more robust recommendations are obtained without significant loss in accuracy. Chowdhury et al. [5] suggest to evaluate a value for the similar users who have not rated the given item, according to the ratings of their trusted neighbors. In this way, more similar users can be involved in generating prediction. However, it is hard for cold users to find many reliable similar users in the first place. Ray and Mahanti [17] argue that trusted neighbors may have different preferences and by removing the trust links with low similarity can further improve the performance. The drawback is that only few items can be predicted. Although empirical studies [5, 17] show that better performance can be obtained, it seems not far that we have achieved in trust-aware recommender systems [20].

Another line of research is to design new similarity measures to make better use of existing user ratings, given the ineffectiveness of the traditional approaches [14] such as Pearson correlation coefficient and cosine similarity. It has been shown that they cannot function well when only few ratings are available or the length of rating vectors is ignored [15]. Lathia et al. [13] find the proportion of agreement and estimate the correlation between two users based on the number of concordant, discordant and tied pairs of common ratings. However, user similarity is not computable in the cases where ratings are flat or only a single rating pair is available. Ahn [2] suggests to highlight the importance of semantic differences between rating scales. The author introduces three semantic heuristics through which user similarity is obtained. The drawback is that the obtained value is not bounded (often greater than 1) and lack of meaningful indications. Bobadilla et al. [4] identify *singularity* as a critical element to distinguish user similarity, based on the intuition that users with high singularity from the majority are more

RecSys'13, October 12–16, 2013, Hong Kong, China.

ACM 978-1-4503-2409-0/13/09 ...$15.00.
http://dx.doi.org/10.1145/2507157.2508071.

Table 1: The predictive performance on the Flixster data set

Views	Approaches measured in MAE, RC and F1									
	CF	MT1	MT2	MT3	RN	TCF1	TCF2	Merge1	Merge2	Merge3
All Users	0.928	1.060	0.932	0.862	0.858	0.870	**0.850**	0.890	0.877	**0.875**
	68.56%	12.36%	71.37%	90.71%	0.38%	80.92%	**85.23%**	89.64%	94.90%	**95.04%**
	0.7357	0.2128	0.7512	0.8549	0.0076	0.8079	**0.8312**	0.8466	0.8690	**0.8719**
Cold Users	1.153	1.127	1.005	0.934	NaN	1.047	**0.923**	1.008	0.960	0.949
	3.27%	8.11%	52.69%	**79.55%**	0.00%	12.97%	21.41%	63.03%	83.11%	**85.15%**
	0.0626	0.1464	0.6279	**0.7939**	NaN	0.2219	0.3373	0.6956	0.8083	**0.8191**

similar than those whose ratings are consistent with the others. However, the length of rating vectors is ignored, and the effectiveness is only verified on a single data set.

In addition, most current research focus on building advanced recommendation algorithms to exploit existing (behavioral or contextual) data, but only a few works have attempted to elicit more user ratings from the perspective of user interfaces. We argue that eliciting more user ratings can inherently mitigate the concerned issues. The emergence of 3D virtual reality (VR) environments such as SecondLife.com offers more useful information (than traditional website environments) that can be used to model user preference. In particular, products could be represented in the form of 3D models which allow users to interact efficiently and effectively and thereby gain intuitive, direct and concrete first-hand experience prior to purchase. Hence, it has great potential to better model user preference in VR. However, the research on recommender systems is still in its infancy. Eno et al. [6] analyze the content of 3D objects and the locations that users visited in VR environments from which user preference can be modelled. Shah et al. [18] propose a location recommender system by analyzing users' login data, and thus help users navigate in VR. Hu and Wang [11] implement a controlled prototype of a system to recommend virtual furniture according to users' interest and requirements. However, the features of VR are not well exploited to elicit more user ratings.

2. RESEARCH PROGRESS TO DATE

Following these research lines described in the previous section, we have conducted three different approaches to resolve the data sparsity and cold start problems. We will elaborate them in subsequent sections.

2.1 The Merge Method

Our work [8] aims to form a new rating profile for the active users, especially for the cold users who have only rated few items, by merging the ratings of trusted neighbors. Specifically, the ratings for a given item reported by trusted neighbors will be aggregated by:

$$\tilde{r}_{u,i} = \frac{\sum_{v \in TN_u} t_{u,v} r_{v,i}}{\sum_{v \in TN_u} t_{u,v}}, \tag{1}$$

where $\tilde{r}_{u,i}$ is the merged rating for the active user u on a given item i, and $r_{v,i}$ is the rating reported by a trusted user v. User u is also regarded as a trusted neighbor in the trust neighborhood TN_u, and $t_{u,v} \in [0,1]$ is the trustworthiness of user v from u's point of view (hence $t_{u,u} = 1$). The quality of a merged rating $\tilde{r}_{u,i}$ is measured as the certainty by taking into account two factors, namely the number of ratings and the conflicts between positive and negative opinions:

$$c_{u,i} = \frac{1}{2} \int_0^1 \left| \frac{x^{p_{u,i}}(1-x)^{n_{u,i}}}{\int_0^1 x^{p_{u,i}}(1-x)^{n_{u,i}} dx} - 1 \right| dx, \tag{2}$$

where $c_{u,i}$ is the certainty of merged rating $\tilde{r}_{u,i}$ as a function of $p_{u,i}$ and $n_{u,i}$, referring to the number of positive and negative ratings used for the merging, respectively. A rating is defined as *positive* if its value is greater than the median rating scale; otherwise, it is *negative*. Hence, the more number of and the less conflicts among ratings, the more certain that the merged rating represents the collective opinion. Only the ratings whose certainty is greater than a predefined threshold will be adopted as a useful merged rating. This procedure is continued until all the ratings of the items rated by the trusted neighbors are merged. As a result, a new rating profile is generated to represent the preferences of the active users. Based on the new rating profile, a traditional CF is then employed to make recommendations.

The effectiveness of our Merge approach is evaluated on three real-world data sets and compare with a batch of comparative methods as shown in Table 1[1]: **MT**x is the method proposed by Massa and Anesani [16] where x is the length of trust propagation; **RN** is the method of Ray and Mahanti [17]; **TCF**x is reported by Chowdhury et al. [5] where x is the number of iterations; **Merge**x is our method where x denotes the length of trust propagation. Table 1 shows that our method generally and consistently achieves the best performance: the relatively low *mean absolute errors* (MAE) and the highest *rating coverage* (RC) as well as the best F-measure (F1) of MAE and RC, especially in the view of *cold users*. Principally, the Merge method is capable of handling two extreme cold scenarios where (1) only trust is available; and (2) only ratings are available. Our method can survive in either case[2] to form an effective rating profile for the cold users. Although it fails to function if neither trust nor ratings are present, this is beyond the scope of our discussion. In summary, our method shades light on a new way to utilize social trust and alleviate the concerned problems.

2.2 Bayesian Similarity Measure

In the work of [10], we propose a novel Bayesian similarity measure by taking into account both the direction and length of rating profiles (vectors), with the aims to solve the issues of traditional approaches. Our approach consists of three components: *overall similarity* ($s'_{u,v}$), *chance correlation* ($s''_{u,v}$) and the *user bias* (δ). Formally, the user similarity between users u and v is computed by removing the

[1]The other two data sets are Epinions and FilmTrust, where similar results are obtained.

[2]In the second case, our method will be equivalent with CF since the only trusted neighbors are active users themselves.

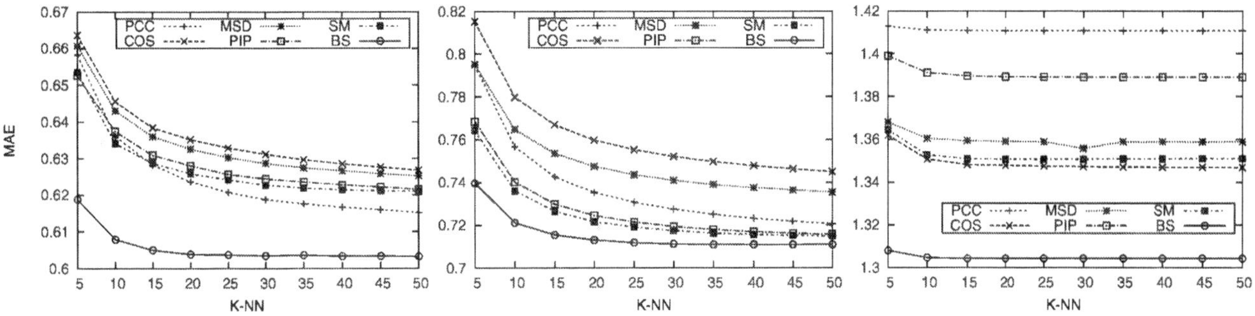

(a) FilmTrust (b) MovieLens 1M (c) BookCrossing

Figure 1: The predictive accuracy of comparative approaches

chance correlation and user bias from the overall similarity:

$$s_{u,v} = \max(s'_{u,v} - s''_{u,v} - \delta, 0). \quad (3)$$

For the overall similarity, the Dirichlet distribution is adopted to accommodate the multinomial rating distances. The underlying assumption is that rating evidences (i.e., a pair of ratings from two users) towards different items are not equally useful in computing similarity. We also claim that realistic value can be derived from consistent item ratings, which is determined by two factors: (1) the standard deviation of ratings on a specific item; and (2) the rating tendency of all users. As new evidence arrives, the posterior probability density is updated. Therefore, we define the *user distance* as the average of rating distances weighted by their respective importance weights which reflect the extent to which evidences fall in such a rating distance. Lastly, the overall similarity is computed by inversely normalizing user distance. In practice, two users may be regarded as 'similar' if they happen to have small rating distances, especially when there are only a small number of user ratings. Hence, the chance correlation is defined as the probability that the amount of evidences fall in different distance levels independently. In addition, by investigating the nature (mean and standard deviation) of traditional and our approaches, we note that our method will generally hold a limited (yet much smaller) user bias, i.e., $\delta = 0.04$. We empirically demonstrate that removing chance correlation and user bias is helpful for similarity computation.

Six real-world data sets are used to evaluate the effectiveness of our approach (denoted by **BS**) in comparison with a number of benchmarks: three traditional approaches (PCC, COS, MSD) and two recently proposed approaches (PIP, SM). In particular, **PCC**, **COS**, **MSD** [19] refer to Pearson correlation coefficient, cosine similarity and mean square distance, respectively; **PIP** is proposed by Ahn [2] based on three semantic heuristics; **SM** is the singularity similarity introduced by Bobadilla et al. [4]. Due to space limitation, the results on three data sets are illustrated in Figure 1 which are similar with other data sets. It is concluded that our approach consistently outperforms the other counterparts in terms of MAE, i.e., better accuracy.

2.3 Prior Ratings

Our recent works [7, 9] introduce a new direction of research to inherently resolve the concerned problems by eliciting more kinds of user ratings. Traditional ratings are usually reported by users who purchased a product according to their after-use experience. However, users are not well-motivated to provide their ratings and hence result in the data sparsity problem. In contrast, we propose a new information source called *prior ratings* which are based on virtual product experience gained via real-time interactions with virtual products—the second presence of products in VR environments which allow users to view, rotate, zoom in and out, and virtually try on, etc. Accordingly, we term the traditional ratings as 'posterior ratings'.

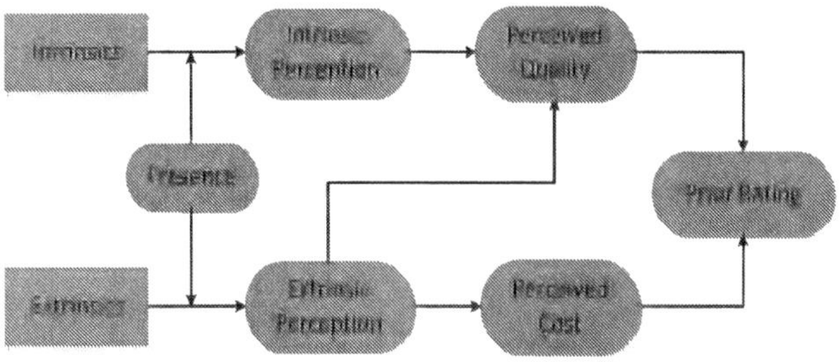

Figure 2: The conceptual model of prior ratings

Prior and posterior ratings differ in reflecting different forms of user experience. Posterior ratings are usually post-purchase ratings whereas prior ratings are likely to be prior-purchase ratings. The major difference lies in the confidence that users have. Specifically, posterior ratings may have higher confidence due to the experience derived from tangible products. However, prior ratings are more dense since users are more willing to provide their ratings partially due to the fact more types of media and interactions are supported in VR environments and hence more pleasant experience could be received. In addition, it is well understood that users browse or experience more products than they actually purchase, especially in the virtual environments where product information is easy to reach. Therefore, prior ratings could be greatly complementary to posterior ratings, and by leveraging both prior and posterior ratings, the concerned problems can be inherently alleviated.

To provide a principled foundation, we propose a conceptual model for prior ratings, as shown in Figure 2. For a specific product, a number of intrinsic and extrinsic *attributes* are associated. In different environments, the perceptions of these attributes could vary according to the types of media and interactions that deliver information about them. The intrinsic and extrinsic *perceptions* indicate the quality of products as perceived directly and indirectly, respectively.

In contrast, the *perceived cost* (e.g., time, price) refers to the cost that users have to bear in order to obtain the products. A prior rating is an overall evaluation of preference of products in terms of both perceived quality and cost. Five hypotheses are proposed regarding the relations among the components in the conceptual model.

A user study was designed in order to validate the proposed conceptual model and hypotheses. In particular, two user interfaces—a 2D website (WS) and 3D virtual store—were designed to represent two different kinds of virtual environments with distinct sense of presence. A number of subjects were recruited in the user study. The results demonstrated the validity of the conceptual model. Specifically, we found that presence has positive influence on the perceptions of some intrinsic and extrinsic attributes; perceived quality in VR mainly depends on intrinsic attributes while in WS it rests more on extrinsic attributes; both perceived quality and cost have a positive impact on prior ratings, if the price is acceptable. Further, the stronger sense of presence a virtual environment is, the more confident prior ratings will be and the closer to posterior ratings. Hence, it indicates that the design of virtual environments should enhance the sense of presence by increasing the media richness or the effectiveness of user interactions.

3. FUTURE RESEARCH

One potential drawback of our current research is the dependency on explicit trust. In most applications, users may not share or be willing to expose such information due to the concerns of, for example, privacy. Thus, we intend to infer users' trust from historical user behaviors and ensure that such modelling can approach explicit trust as close as possible. For this purpose, we may need to model and learn the trust factors from explicit trust information. On the other hand, dimension reduction-based approaches (e.g., matrix factorization [12]) have also been proposed to investigate the utility of trust. Hence, we intend to focus on model-based approaches to further resolve the concerned problems. In particular, clustering-based approaches will be our main focus due to its efficiency and scalability. The main issues for clustering-based approaches are the relatively low accuracy and coverage. However, recent research [3] has indicated that superior accuracy can be achieved if more sophisticated clustering methods are applied. To our knowledge, no dedicated approaches have been proposed to resolve the cold start problem for clustering-based approaches. We plan to incorporate both trust and similarity to better cluster users and improve the recommendation performance by alleviating the cold start problem.

4. REFERENCES

[1] G. Adomavicius and A. Tuzhilin. Toward the next generation of recommender systems: A survey of the state-of-the-art and possible extensions. *IEEE Transactions on Knowledge and Data Engineering*, 17(6):734–749, 2005.

[2] H. Ahn. A new similarity measure for collaborative filtering to alleviate the new user cold-starting problem. *Information Sciences*, 178(1):37–51, 2008.

[3] A. Bellogín and J. Parapar. Using graph partitioning techniques for neighbour selection in user-based collaborative filtering. In *Proceedings of the 6th ACM Conference on Recommender Systems*, RecSys, pages 213–216, 2012.

[4] J. Bobadilla, F. Ortega, and A. Hernando. A collaborative filtering similarity measure based on singularities. *Information Processing & Management*, 48(2):204–217, 2012.

[5] M. Chowdhury, A. Thomo, and B. Wadge. Trust-based infinitesimals for enhanced collaborative filtering. In *Proceedings of the 15th International Conference on Management of Data*, COMAD, 2009.

[6] J. Eno, G. Stafford, S. Gauch, and C. Thompson. Hybrid user preference models for Second Life and opensimulator virtual worlds. In *Proceedings of the 19th International Conference on User Modeling, Adaption and Personalization*, UMAP, pages 87–98, 2011.

[7] G. Guo and M. Elgendi. A new recommender system for 3D e-commerce: An EEG based approach. *Journal of Advanced Management Science*, 1(1), 2013.

[8] G. Guo, J. Zhang, and D. Thalmann. A simple but effective method to incorporate trusted neighbors in recommender systems. In *Proceedings of the 20th International Conference on User Modeling, Adaptation and Personalization*, UMAP, 2012.

[9] G. Guo, J. Zhang, D. Thalmann, and N. Yorke-Smith. Prior ratings: A new information source for recommender systems in e-commerce. In *Proceedings of the 7th ACM Conference on Recommender Systems*, RecSys, 2013.

[10] G. Guo, J. Zhang, and N. Yorke-Smith. A novel bayesian similarity measure for recommender systems. In *Proceedings of the 23rd International Joint Conference on Artificial Intelligence*, IJCAI, 2013.

[11] X. Hu and K. Wang. Personalized recommendation for virtual reality. In *Proceedings of the 2010 International Conference on Multimedia Technology*, ICMT, pages 1–5, 2010.

[12] Y. Koren, R. Bell, and C. Volinsky. Matrix factorization techniques for recommender systems. *Computer*, 42(8):30–37, 2009.

[13] N. Lathia, S. Hailes, and L. Capra. Private distributed collaborative filtering using estimated concordance measures. In *Proceedings of the 2007 ACM Conference on Recommender Systems*, RecSys, pages 1–8, 2007.

[14] N. Lathia, S. Hailes, and L. Capra. The effect of correlation coefficients on communities of recommenders. In *Proceedings of the 23rd Annual ACM Symposium on Applied Computing*, SAC, pages 2000–2005, 2008.

[15] H. Ma, I. King, and M. Lyu. Effective missing data prediction for collaborative filtering. In *Proceedings of the 30th Annual International ACM SIGIR Conference on Research and Development in Information Retrieval*, SIGIR, pages 39–46, 2007.

[16] P. Massa and P. Avesani. Trust-aware recommender systems. In *Proceedings of the 2007 ACM Conference on Recommender Systems*, RecSys, pages 17–24, 2007.

[17] S. Ray and A. Mahanti. Improving prediction accuracy in trust-aware recommender systems. In *Proceedings of the 43rd Hawaii International Conference on System Sciences*, HICSS, pages 1–9, 2010.

[18] F. Shah, P. Bell, and G. Sukthankar. A destination recommendation system for virtual worlds. In *Proceedings of the 21st International Florida Artificial Intelligence Research Society Conference*, FLAIRS, pages 475–476, 2010.

[19] U. Shardanand and P. Maes. Social information filtering: algorithms for automating âĂIJword of mouthâĂİ. In *Proceedings of the SIGCHI Conference on Human Factors in Computing Systems*, SIGCHI, pages 210–217, 1995.

[20] Y. Shi, M. Larson, and A. Hanjalic. How far are we in trust-aware recommendation? In *Proceedings of the 33rd European Conference on Advances in Information Retrieval*, ECIR, pages 704–707. Springer, 2011.

[21] P. Singla and M. Richardson. Yes, there is a correlation: from social networks to personal behavior on the web. In *Proceedings of the 17th International Conference on World Wide Web*, WWW, pages 655–664, 2008.

Agent-based Computational Investing Recommender System

Mona Taghavi [1] Kaveh Bakhtiyari [2] Edgar Scavino [3]

[1, 2, 3] Department of Electrical, Electronics and Systems Engineering
Faculty of Engineering and Built Environment
Universiti Kebangsaan Malaysia (The National University of Malaysia)
43600 UKM, Bangi, Selangor Darul Ehsan, Malaysia

[2] Department of Computer & Cognitive Science, Faculty of Engineering
University of Duisburg-Essen
47048 Duisburg, North Rhine-Westphalia (NRW), Germany

mona.taghavi@gmail.com academic@bakhtiyari.com scavino@eng.ukm.my

ABSTRACT

The fast development of computing and communication has reformed the financial markets' dynamics. Nowadays many people are investing and trading stocks through online channels and having access to real-time market information efficiently. There are more opportunities to lose or make money with all the stocks information available throughout the World; however, one should spend a lot of effort and time to follow those stocks and the available instant information. This paper presents a preliminary regarding a multi-agent recommender system for computational investing. This system utilizes a hybrid filtering technique to adaptively recommend the most profitable stocks at the right time according to investor's personal favour. The hybrid technique includes collaborative and content-based filtering. The content-based model uses investor preferences, influencing macro-economic factors, stocks profiles and the predicted trend to tailor to its advices. The collaborative filter assesses the investor pairs' investing behaviours and actions that are proficient in economic market to recommend the similar ones to the target investor.

Categories and Subject Descriptors

H.3.3 [INFORMATION STORAGE AND RETRIEVAL] : Information Search and Retrieval - *Information filtering*

Keywords

Recommender system, computational investing, stock market, multi-agent system, hybrid filtering.

1. INTRODUCTION

The rapid evolving development of communication and computing has significantly changed the dynamics of financial markets. These days, people prefer to trade online through the Web rather than using full-service brokerages [2]. Online financial services have provided new opportunities for investors to access real-time data of financial market to trade stocks efficiently. There are more threats or opportunities to lose or make money, with all the available stocks through the World, but merely if one has energy and time to follow the stocks. The stocks' data change continuously, while trading information and news regarding financial status of the companies are instantly available. All these make it difficult to choose the most profitable stocks at the right time and right place.

Volatility modelling and forecasting are critically important to financial market investors. Financial volatility forecasts enable the farsighted investors to adjust their investment portfolios to mitigate investment risk and to modify their investing strategies align with the upcoming market movements [10].

1.1 Agent-based Computational Investing

Agent-based Computational Investing (ACI) is a complex, dynamic and adaptive system where agents are interacting with each other based on rules to process economic data, perceive the environment and take action [12]. Starting from preliminary conditions which is identified by the modeller, computational investing changes over time when its resident agents interact frequently together and learn from each other through the processes of interactions. Therefore, ACI is a bottom-up culture-dish approach to economic systems studies. In a very new research area of agent-based computational economics or investing, researchers utilize computational frameworks to find out the market economies evolution under supervised conditions of experiments [9].

There are some fully automated trading systems, but they are totally automatic and independent from human decisions. These electronic systems are not completely reliable, and it is difficult for investors to let a machine take over their money and trades without their intervention. They prefer to know the procedure and to be involved into the process and the reason of what is being recommended. For this reason we are going to use a recommender system which proposes best stock options available to buy or even sell, but not to be replaced with human judgment and decisions. Therefore, it can attract their trust as well as make them confident about their decisions with letting them know why the system is recommending a specific stock.

RecSys'13, October 12–16, 2013, Hong Kong, China.
ACM 978-1-4503-2409-0/13/10.
http://dx.doi.org/10.1145/2507157.2508072.

1.2 Recommender Systems

In overall, recommender systems are employed to help people to select and make their choices based on the knowledge which they have [3]. In the beginning, the majority of recommender systems were mainly a basic query-based information retrieval system, which named content-based recommender system. Just like the way that search engines act, they were bringing up those web pages with contents similar to users' queries. Later, a more sophisticated approach was proposed by Goldberg which called collaborative filtering [6]. Collaborative recommender systems accumulate items ratings from other users and make recommendations depending on those ratings. They are widely applied in many fields in academic and commercial context, such as Amazon which uses for proposing books and MovieLens which proposes movies on this basis.

Although collaborative recommender systems are still quite successful, they fail when requested items have no recorded history or when individual preferences are determinant for selection, such as a movie's cast or genre. Additionally, it relies only on other users and the quality recommendation is completely depending on the user rating rather than the information content.

To overcome the limitations of content-based and collaborative approaches, hybrid approaches were proposed to benefit user preferences and content at the same time. Proposed approaches to hybrid system can be classified into two clusters. The first cluster is the linear combination of collaborative and content-based filtering results as is illustrated in Figure 1. As an example, Wasfi [1] developed ProfBuilder which recommends web pages utilizing both collaborative and content-based filters, and each provides a separate recommendation list without merging them to make a combined prediction.

The second cluster combines sequentially the content-based filtering and collaborative filtering as is presented in Figure 2. In this approach, at first, content-based filtering is applied to identify users who have similar interests. Then, a collaborative algorithm is employed to generate predictions.

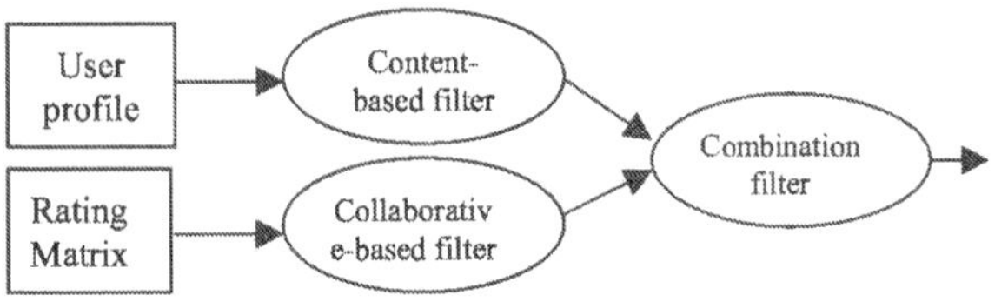

Figure 1. Linear combination in hybrid approach

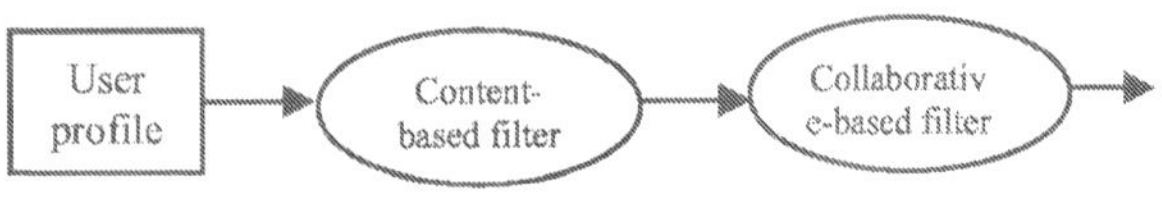

Figure 2. Sequential combination in hybrid approach

2. RELATED WORK AND PROBLEM STATEMENT

In today's stock market, there are huge numbers of competing investments and the prices of stocks change intensely. In such a situation, practitioners try to guide the timing and selection process of investment typically relying on one of two available main frameworks, called technical analysis and fundamental analysis. Technical analysis deals with patterns of price volume for individual stocks. But fundamental analysis is a technique where the stock is studied by itself for its fundamentals such as DIVIDEND YIELD, P/E, PRICE/BOOK VALUE, etc. These traditional techniques enable investors to manage their investment by predicting stocks prices with some tools. So far, experimental studies have adequately shown that stocks price prediction is very non-stationary and time-varying [10], and none of these is sufficient and absolutely superior to the others [7].

Volatility modelling and forecasting of financial time series is regarded as one of the most confronting applications of modern time series forecasting. Financial time series are inherently forceful, noisy and deterministically chaotic [2].

The stock market specialists are not able to come to an agreement regarding whether or not there are strategies which can consistently beat the market. The economic situation, which has been developed since 2008, has made this lack of forecasting precision quite clear. Not even the top financial analysts could predict such a serious economic crisis. Financial markets are too sensitive; and they are affected by so many elements (such as government policies, sanctions, international dependencies, etc.) that it is quite impossible to realize predictions with enough confidence. For example, the Malaysia stock market has experienced a very large drop since September 2011 which is attributed to uncertainties over Malaysia's Election 2013 and a perception of political instability, it is expected to have even greater impact after the election [4]. Past research in this area did not consider any of these influencing elements.

Many high-return projects need long-term commitment of capital. Meanwhile, most of the investors are reluctant to invest in a project for a long period and are not enough confident; therefore less investment goes to the high return project which requires a long-term commitment [12]. This imbalance funding may harm economic growth.

Users mainly are not happy with the recommendations which are not of their interest. This recommendation error is called false positive and it will lower their trusts in the future. So this is the most important error which has not received enough attention from researchers [5].

Moreover, each trader has different style of investment from another investor, some of them are concerned about long term returns and some are more aggressive risk takers. Some may prefer to know what the other investors with the same favour are investing for, or there may be some novice investors who would like to know the professional investor's profile.

As an example, Schelling [8] showed how patterned social behaviour can evolve as the unintentional consequence of repeated local interactions among agents who follow simple behavioural rules. For example, he proves how exclusion by race can arise through local chain reactions if agents have a moderate preference for avoiding small-minority status, since they favour more of their neighbours to have the same race as themselves. Existing systems and services commonly do not take these individual preferences [11].

3. AGENT-BASED COMPUTATIONAL INVESTING RECOMMENDER SYSTEM (ACIRS)

ACIRS has adopted a hybrid approach with combination of collaborative and content-based filtering in a new style which is different with *linear* and *sequential*. As Figure 3 illustrates, it utilizes separated as well as mixed recommendations from both content-based and collaborative filtering. Through content-based filtering, ACIRS recommends stocks relying on *Trend prediction*, *Macro-economic factors* and *User profile*. On the other hand, it is also interested to apply content-based filtering algorithm and to identify users with same interests, then combine with collaborative algorithm to make suggestions.

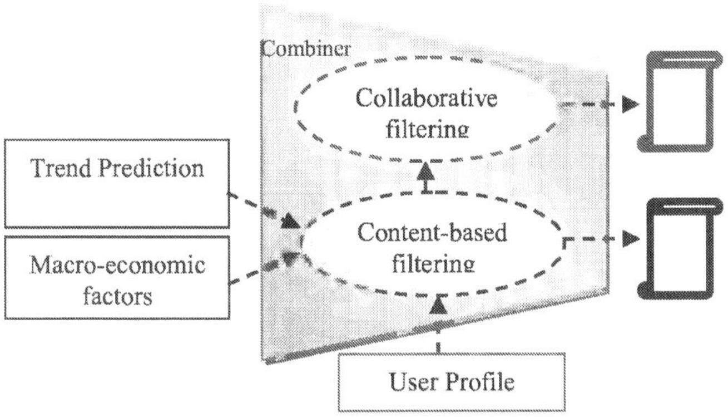

Figure 3. A hybrid approach with new combination

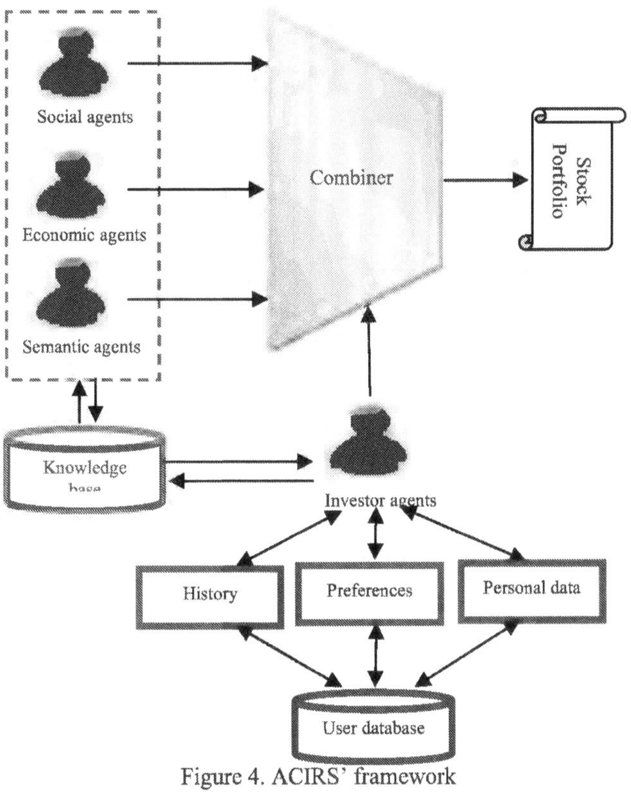

Figure 4. ACIRS' framework

Intelligent agents are the agents who are able to *react* to their environment's changes, have communication and *social ability*, and they are also able to employ computational intelligence to achieve their objectives through *proactive* actions [3].

Agent-based computational investing is defined as the computational investigation of economies which are simulated as autonomous agents interacting in an evolving system. It starts from preliminary condition which is specified by the modeller. Over time, the computational economy grows when its resident agents interact together frequently and learn from each other in these interactions.

The Framework of ACIRS is shown in Figure 4. The ACIRS modeller starts by constructing a stock market trading environment consisting of primary agents. These agents include economic agents (e.g., price trend prediction, companies/producers, intermediaries and so on.), social agents which represent various social and environmental events (e.g., market inter-relations, governmental policies, regulatory, sanctions and so on) and investor agents.

The ACIRS modeller initializes the market state through recognizing the starting attributes belong to the agents. The agent's primary attributes may contain form characteristics, internalized behavioural rules, inner modes of behaviour (comprising communication and learning norms), and knowledge and information of itself and other agents which is stored internally. The market later gets involve over time without more modeller intervention. All consequent events that happen should arise from the historical time-line of agent-agent interactions. To reason and justify the environmental factors and stocks and user priorities, a knowledge-base is needed for semantic agents. The ACIRS' knowledge-base is based on OWL (Web Ontology Language) which is a knowledge representation language for authoring ontologies. It allows sharing and reusing of the information sufficiently in an agent-based system architecture.

For fully automated economic computational models, an investigator may reason to identify a universal learning scheme with appropriate personal tactics of the computational agents which mutually change to fulfil their needs and desired following globally specified goals (e.g., productive efficiency). Whereas, ACIRS already considers users preferences and utilizes their strategies in providing the recommendations. Besides, the user plays the final role in decision making and ordering what to sell or to buy.

4. PROTOTYPE AND EVALUATION

We plan to train the system using Artificial Neural Network machine learning technique and develop a prototype using Object Oriented Programming and Swarm which is an agent-based software library. Another possibility is development of Computational Laboratories (CL) which are pre-built computational frameworks with employing a Graphical User Interface (GUI) that permit systematically experimentation for a domain of particular problem. It also allows a researcher to use a CL to easily evaluate the system sensitivity to changes with various main parameters.

The required data for training and testing is supposed to be collected from Bursa Malaysia, and the data regarding investors is to be collected using a global survey asking about their personal information, interests and behaviours of trading and preferences.

We are going to evaluate the system in a real stock market using several samples of investors and stock. We will compare the ACIRS's recommendations, investors satisfaction and actual purchase or sell of the stocks through a survey.

Open issues: we may not be able to gather all investors' personal details and their attitudes, and it can be done for a small size of users. Another issue is investors' emotions of fear and greed which mainly drive their decision to buy or sell a stock and this is not an emotional intelligent system, so it may alter the evaluation results. Additionally, the macro-economic factors are mainly very difficult to predict precisely, although this system tries to consider them, it may fail to receive and to analyse them on time (real-time), correctly and precisely.

5. CONCLUSION

In this research proposal, we bridged the concept of agent-based computational economics with recommender systems. Recommender systems can address the problem of financial market data overload by reducing the amount of data that investors should examine and recommend the best opportune options to invest. This paper introduced and clarified the potential advantages of application of recommender systems in computational investing through providing a practical system framework. ACIRS uses a new hybrid approach in combination of content-based filtering and collaborative filtering. We plan to develop a prototype and to evaluate the system with real stock market data.

6. REFERENCES

[1] AHMAD WASFI, A.M., 1998. Collecting user access patterns for building user profiles and collaborative filtering. In *Proceedings of the 4th international conference on Intelligent user interfaces* ACM, 57-64.

[2] BATAINEH, E., AL AMIR, F., IBRAHEEM, H., MESMAR, H., and AL MUTAWA, S., 2008. A Framework for Smart e-Trader System for UAE Stock Markets.

[3] BIRUKOU, A., BLANZIERI, E., and GIORGINI, P., 2012. Implicit: a multi-agent recommendation system for web search. *Autonomous Agents and Multi-Agent Systems 24*, 1, 141-174.

[4] CHANG, Y.B. and GURBAXANI, V., 2012. Information Technology Outsourcing, Knowledge Transfer, and Firm Productivity: An Empirical Analysis. *MIS Quarterly-Management Information Systems 36*, 4, 1043.

[5] GAY JR, R.D., 2011. Effect of macroeconomic variables on stock market returns for four emerging economies: Brazil, Russia, India, and China. *International Business & Economics Research Journal (IBER) 7*, 3.

[6] GOLDBERG, D., NICHOLS, D., OKI, B.M., and TERRY, D., 1992. Using collaborative filtering to weave an information tapestry. *Communications of the ACM 35*, 12, 61-70.

[7] JASEMI, M., KIMIAGARI, A.M., and MEMARIANI, A., 2011. A modern neural network model to do stock market timing on the basis of the ancient investment technique of Japanese Candlestick. *Expert Systems with Applications 38*, 4, 3884-3890.

[8] SCHELLING, T.C., 2006. *Micromotives and macrobehavior.* WW Norton.

[9] TEGLIO, A., RABERTO, M., and CINCOTTI, S., 2010. Balance Sheet Approach to Agent-Based Computational Economics: The EURACE Project. In *Combining Soft Computing and Statistical Methods in Data Analysis* Springer, 603-610.

[10]TUNG, W. and QUEK, C., 2011. Financial volatility trading using a self-organising neural-fuzzy semantic network and option straddle-based approach. *Expert Systems with Applications 38*, 5, 4668-4688.

[11]YOO, J., GERVASIO, M., and LANGLEY, P., 2003. An adaptive stock tracker for personalized trading advice. In *Proceedings of the Proceedings of the 8th international conference on Intelligent user interfaces* (2003), ACM, 197-203.

[12]ZAFFAR, M.A., KUMAR, R.L., and ZHAO, K., 2011. Diffusion dynamics of open source software: An agent-based computational economics (ACE) approach. *Decision Support Systems 51*, 3, 597-608.

Beyond Rating Prediction Accuracy: On New Perspectives in Recommender Systems

Panagiotis Adamopoulos
Department of Information, Operations and Management Sciences
Leonard N. Stern School of Business, New York University
padamopo@stern.nyu.edu

ABSTRACT

This paper proposes a number of studies in order to move recommender systems beyond the traditional paradigm and the classical perspective of rating prediction accuracy. We contribute to existing helpful but less explored paradigms and also propose new approaches aiming at more useful recommendations for both users and businesses. Working toward this direction, we discuss the studies we have conducted so far and present our future research plans. In particular, we move our focus from even more accurate rating predictions and aim at offering a holistic experience to the users by avoiding the over-specialization of generated recommendations and providing the users with sets of non-obvious but high quality recommendations that fairly match their interests and they will remarkably like.

Categories and Subject Descriptors

H.1.2 [**Models and Principles**]: User/Machine Systems - Human Factors; H.3.3 [**Information Storage and Retrieval**]: Information Search and Retrieval - Information filtering, Selection process; H.4.m [**Information Systems Applications**]: Miscellaneous

General Terms

Algorithms, Design, Experimentation, Human Factors, Measurement, Performance, Theory

Keywords

Item Accuracy; Unexpectedness; Novelty; Serendipity; Diversity; Recommendation Opportunities; Recommendation Sets; Recommender Systems

1. INTRODUCTION

Over the last two decades, a wide variety of different types of recommender systems (RSs) has been developed and successfully used across several domains [6]. During this time, many researchers have focused mainly on the development and improvement of efficient algorithms for more accurate rating prediction. Although the recommendations of the latest class of systems are significantly more accurate than they used to be a decade ago [7] and the broad social and business acceptance of RSs has already been achieved, there is still a long way to go in terms of satisfaction of users' actual needs [14]. This is due, primarily, to the fact that many existing RSs focus on providing more accurate rather than more useful recommendations. Some of the main problems pertaining to this narrow rating prediction accuracy-based focus of many existing RSs [8] and the ways to broaden the current approaches have been discussed in [18].

Even though the aforementioned rating prediction perspective is the prevailing paradigm in recommender systems, there are other perspectives that try to alleviate the problems pertaining to this narrow rating prediction accuracy-based focus and have been gaining significant attention in the field of RS [10]. In particular, some of the most recent perspectives maintain that RSs should make the users familiar with the various product categories and the whole product catalog. In addition, recommender systems should provide personalized recommendations from a wide range of items and should also enable the users to find relevant items that might be hard to discover. Also, they should increase user satisfaction and engagement and offer a superior user experience. Moreover, RSs should also be able to reduce user search costs, improve the quality of decisions that consumers make, and increase their welfare. Besides, from a business perspective, RSs should increase the sales volume and conversion rates, as well as promote items from the long tail that usually exhibit significantly lower marginal cost and, at the same time, higher marginal profit.

Moving beyond the classical perspective of the rating prediction accuracy, the main objective of this stream of research is to contribute to existing helpful but less explored paradigms of RSs as well as to propose new approaches that will result in more useful recommendations for both users and businesses. Working toward this direction, we discuss the studies we have conducted so far and present our future research plans. In particular, we move our focus from even more accurate rating predictions and aim at offering a holistic experience to the users by avoiding the over-specialization of recommendations and providing the users with non-obvious but high quality recommendation sets (not restricted to simple lists of individual items) that fairly match their interests and they will remarkably like.

Other streams of research that improve recommender systems going beyond rating prediction accuracy include work on *human-computer interaction* (HCI), which involves the

RecSys'13, October 12–16, 2013, Hong Kong, China.
ACM 978-1-4503-2409-0/13/09.
http://dx.doi.org/10.1145/2507157.2508073.

study and design of the interaction between users and RSs, *diversification*, which maximizes the variety of items in a recommendation list, *group recommenders* [19], which recommend items for groups of people, rather than individuals, and recommendation *sequences* [17], where sequences of ordered items are recommended instead of single items.

2. RESEARCH STUDIES

In this stream of research, we are moving beyond the classical perspective of the rating prediction accuracy and we are aiming at providing even more useful recommendations for both users and businesses. Working toward this direction, we designed a number of research studies to explore issues related to several new approaches for providing recommendations. In particular, Section 2.1 proposes a concept of *unexpectedness* and specific metrics to measure both unexpectedness and quality of recommendations, as well as algorithms for generating such recommendations. Then, Section 2.2 introduces a method for generating recommendations based on *recommendation opportunities* using higher *weighted percentiles*. Finally, Section 2.3 discusses *recommendation sets* where the generated recommendation lists are based on sets of candidate items, rather than just individual items, also taking into account various interactions among items, such as complementarity and substitution effects. All these research studies go beyond the classical perspective of RSs and aim at providing the users with non-obvious but high quality recommendation sets that fairly match their interests and they will remarkably like. Thorough discussions of these concepts, implementation details, and experimental results are provided in [2, 5, 4, 3].

2.1 Beyond over-specialization

Sections 2.1.1 and 2.1.2 address the over-specialization problem in recommender systems focusing on *unexpectedness* and the related concepts of coverage, novelty, serendipity, and diversity of recommendation lists.

2.1.1 Expecting the Unexpected

In [2, 3], we propose a concept of unexpected recommendations as recommending those items that significantly depart from the expectations of the users and suggest a method for generating such recommendations, based on the utility theory of economics, as well as specific metrics to measure the unexpectedness of recommendation lists.

In particular, we formally define the concept of *unexpectedness* in recommender systems taking into account the actual *expectations* of the users and discuss how the concept of unexpectedness is differentiated from various related notions, such as novelty, serendipity, and diversity. Following the Greek philosopher Heraclitus, we approach this difficult problem of finding and recommending unexpected items by first capturing the items expected by the users. Toward this direction, we suggest several mechanisms for specifying users' expectations that can be applied across various domains. Such mechanisms include the past transactions performed by the users, knowledge discovery and data mining techniques, and experts' domain knowledge. Besides, we formulate and fully operationalize the notion of unexpectedness and present an algorithm for providing unexpected recommendations of high quality that are hard to discover but fairly match the users' interests, based on the *utility theory* of economics. Moreover, we propose specific performance metrics to measure the unexpectedness of the generated recommendation lists taking into account also the usefulness of individual items.

Using "real-world" data sets, various examples of sets of expected recommendations, and different utility functions and distance metrics, we were able to test the proposed method under a large number of experimental settings including various levels of sparsity, different mechanisms for specifying users' expectations, and different cardinalities of these sets of expectations. The empirical study showed that all the examined variations of the proposed method significantly outperformed in terms of unexpectedness the standard baseline algorithms, including item-based and user-based k-Nearest Neighbors [13], Slope One [16], and Matrix Factorization [15]. This demonstrates that the proposed method indeed effectively captures the concept of unexpectedness since, in principle, it should do better than unexpectedness-agnostic methods. Furthermore, the proposed method for unexpected recommendations performed at least as well as, and in some cases even better than, the baseline algorithms in terms of the classical accuracy-based measures, such as root-mean-square error (RMSE) and the F-measure, as well as other popular performance measures, such as catalog coverage, aggregate diversity, serendipity, and the Gini coefficient. In addition, we presented a number of actual recommendation examples generated by the proposed method and the employed baseline approaches and provided insightful qualitative comments.

One of the main premises of the proposed method is that the users' expectations should be explicitly considered in order to provide the users with unexpected recommendations of high quality that are hard to discover but fairly match their interests. Hence, the greatest improvements both in terms of unexpectedness and accuracy vis-à-vis all other approaches were observed in the experiments using the more accurate sets of expectations. Moreover, the use of a utility function of standard form illustrates that the proposed method can be easily implemented in existing recommender systems as a new component that enhances unexpectedness of recommendations, without the need to further modify the current rating prediction procedures.

2.1.2 Probabilistic Neighborhoods

In [4], we propose a new probabilistic method for neighborhood selection in collaborative filtering (CF) models. In particular, we illustrate the practical implementation of the proposed approach presenting a specific variation of the classical k-nearest neighbors (k-NN) CF method in which the neighborhood selection is based on an underlying probability distribution instead of just the k neighbors with the highest similarity level to the target user. For the probabilistic neighborhood selection, we use an efficient method for weighted sampling [21] of k neighbors without replacement that also takes into consideration the similarity levels between the target user and the n candidate neighbors. The key intuition for this *probabilistic nearest neighbors* collaborative filtering method is two-fold. First, using the neighborhood with the most similar users to estimate unknown ratings and recommend candidate items, the generated recommendation lists usually consist of known items with which the users are already familiar. Second, because of the multi-dimensionality of users' tastes, there are many items that the target user may like and are unknown to the k most similar users to her/him. Thus, we propose the use of probabilistic neighborhood selection in order to alleviate the aforementioned problems and move beyond the limited focus of rating prediction accuracy.

To investigate this claim, we conducted an empirical study and we tested the proposed method under a large number of experimental settings. In detail, we used a large number of probability distributions from different families of distributions with various location and shape parameters, in order to compare the proposed probabilistic method for neighborhood selection against the standard collaborative filtering approach in terms of popular evaluation metrics for item prediction accuracy, utility-based ranking, coverage, diversity, unexpectedness, and dispersion of recommendations.

The experimental results illustrate that the proposed approach indeed generates recommendations that are orthogonal to the classical CF method. We also demonstrated that the proposed method performs at least as well as, and in some cases even better than, the standard user-based CF approach in terms of popular item prediction accuracy and utility-based ranking measures, such as the F-measure and the normalized cumulative discounted gain, across various experimental settings. Besides, we showed that the performance improvement is not achieved at the expense of some other popular performance measures that go beyond the rating prediction accuracy, such as catalog coverage, aggregate diversity, and recommendation dispersion and mobility.

2.2 Recommendation Opportunities

In [5], under a definition of a *recommendation opportunity* as how much a user *could* realistically like an item, we aim at recommending items that the users will remarkably like. Moving beyond the standard perspective of rating prediction accuracy and exploring such recommendation opportunities can increase user satisfaction and engagement and offer a superior user experience through the discovery of items that the users will really like.

In particular, we illustrate the practical implementation of the proposed approach presenting a certain variation of the classical user-based k-NN collaborative filtering method in which the estimation of an unknown rating of the target user for an item is based not on the weighted averages of the k nearest neighbors but on the *weighted percentile* of the ratings of these k neighbors. For the estimation of the weighted percentile of the distribution of the ratings in the neighborhood of the target user, an efficient method is used that does not increase the computational complexity of the classical k-NN method. The key intuition behind the weighted percentile method, instead of using weighted averages, is that high percentiles (such as in the 70% to 90% range) constitute more realistic estimates of how much a targeted user *could* possibly like the candidate item. As a consequence, the proposed approach not only provides more useful for the users recommendations of items that they remarkably like but also has the potential to let us better identify and serve any specific niches of the market.

To support this claim, we conducted an empirical study and showed that the proposed percentile method outperforms by a wide margin, across various experimental settings, the standard user-based CF approach in terms of item prediction accuracy measures, such as precision, recall, and the F-measure, and also utility-based ranking metrics, such as normalized cumulative discounted gain and mean reciprocal rank. Finally, we demonstrated that this performance improvement is not achieved at the expense of some other popular performance measures, such as catalog coverage, aggregate diversity, and the Gini coefficient. This illustrates that our proposed weighted percentile method for *recommendation opportunities* performs at least as well as, or even significantly better than, the classical user-based collaborative filtering method in terms of these important measures, in most of the experiments.

Nevertheless, apart from the user-based and item-based k-NN CF approaches, other popular RSs methods that can be easily extended, with the use of quantile regression [12], in order to allow us both to build models that predict high percentiles and to evaluate them with regard to the goal of predicting percentiles of estimated ratings, include content-based methods and Matrix Factorization [11].

2.3 Recommendation Sets

In the classical recommendation system paradigms, the generated recommendation lists are based on the top-N items with the highest estimated ratings regardless of the possible interaction effects among the candidate items. One exception of this paradigm is the concept of diversity, according to which the variety of items in a recommendation list is maximized. However, in many recommendation settings there are important interactions among the candidate items that should be explicitly considered. For instance, in a clothing on-line retail setting the utility of recommending to a user a specific pair of pants depends on whether a matching shirt is also included in the same recommendation list or not. Similarly, in the case of a RS for a supermarket, the utility of recommending olive oil to a user might depend on whether feta cheese and tomatoes are recommended as well.

In our next study, moving beyond the classical recommendation lists of individual items with the highest estimated ratings and working toward our objective of providing the users with non-obvious but high quality recommendation sets that fairly match their interests and they will really like, we will propose to generate *recommendation sets*, rather than individual items, taking into account various interactions effects among the candidate items [9], the potential prerequisites and constraints of the items [20], and the limited budget of the users [22]. In particular, we will focus on co-occurrence interaction effects, such as complementarity and substitution effects, aiming at developing effective methods for both accurately estimating the various effects and efficiently recommending such sets of items.

To experimentally test the proposed approach we plan to conduct a live experiment involving human subjects. In detail, we plan to design an on-line experiment and examine the proposed paradigm in the context of massive open online courses (MOOCs) [1]. As part of the experiment, we will generate personalized recommendations for MOOCs taking into account the academic major of the human subject, the various dependencies among the courses, such as the complementarity and substitution effects, and different prerequisites and constraints, such the difficulty and the estimated workload of each recommended course.

3. DISCUSSION AND FUTURE WORK

Successfully completing the aforementioned work will help the recommender systems field move further beyond the perspective of rating prediction accuracy. Following the proposed stream of research and adhering to our main objective of providing more useful recommendations for both users and businesses, we both contribute to existing helpful but less explored paradigms for recommender systems and propose new valuable approaches and perspectives. Working toward this direction of providing more useful recommendations for both users and businesses, we discussed the studies we have conducted so far and also presented in detail some of our future research plans. In particular, the studies discussed in Section 2 move our focus from even more accurate rating predictions and aim at offering a holistic experience to the users by avoiding the over-specialization of recommendations and providing the users with non-obvious but high quality recommendation sets that fairly match their interests and they will remarkably like.

In detail, Section 2.1 proposes a concept of *unexpectedness* and specific metrics to measure both unexpectedness and quality of recommendations, as well as algorithms for generating such recommendations, Section 2.2 introduces a method for generating recommendations that the users will remarkably like based on *recommendation opportunities* using higher *weighted percentiles*, and Section 2.3 discusses *recommendation sets*, rather than individual items, taking into account various interactions among items, such as complementarity and substitution effects.

As part of the future work, we would like to implement and evaluate the proposed approaches in a traditional on-line retail setting as well as in a platform for massive open on-line courses (MOOCs) [1]. Besides, we would like to conduct a series of live controlled experiments with human subjects in order to study the on-line user behavior, examine and actively adjust the trade-off between exploration (e.g. unexpectedness, serendipity, diversity, etc.) and exploitation (e.g. accuracy) of recommender systems, and better evaluate the proposed perspectives in a user-centric framework. In addition, we plan to investigate how the proposed recommendation approaches and perspectives can be effectively combined with traditional approaches in hybrid recommender systems aiming at accurate and non-obvious recommendation sets that the users will remarkably like.

Furthermore, the generated recommendations should be useful for both users and businesses and, hence, as part of our future work, we would also like to focus more on the business perspective and the business value aspects of recommender systems. Thus, we would like to design an empirical study in order to examine the economic impact of the proposed recommender system approaches and perspectives across various domains and recommendation settings. In particular, we would like to study and estimate the economic impact of both the direct effect of offering recommendations from a wider range of items that are harder to discover and the indirect effect of recommending items from the long tail and not focusing mostly on bestsellers that usually exhibit higher marginal cost. Such a research study can shed more light on the usefulness of recommender systems for businesses and further promote the use of non-classical perspectives and approaches that go beyond the traditional paradigm of rating prediction accuracy.

Moreover, the proposed program of research can be extended in various other valuable directions. For instance, the main strengths and weaknesses of the different existing recommender system algorithms, in terms of the multiple objectives of the aforementioned perspectives and metrics, should be thoroughly examined and, if possible, the "best" mixture in each context among all the existing and proposed approaches should be identified. Finally, the possible spillover effects of the proposed approaches on other important objectives and properties of recommender systems, such as the trustworthiness and persuasiveness of recommendations, should be extensively examined as well.

4. ACKNOWLEDGMENTS

I would like to thank my advisor and co-author, Prof. Alexander Tuzhilin, for his support, guidance, and valuable feedback.

5. REFERENCES

[1] P. Adamopoulos. What Makes a Great MOOC? An Interdisciplinary Analysis of Online Course Student Retention. In *Proceedings of the 34th International Conference on Information Systems*, ICIS '13, 2013.

[2] P. Adamopoulos and A. Tuzhilin. On Unexpectedness in Recommender Systems: Or How to Expect the Unexpected. In *DiveRS 2011*, RecSys '11. ACM, 2011.

[3] P. Adamopoulos and A. Tuzhilin. On Unexpectedness in Recommender Systems: Or How to Better Expect the Unexpected. *Working Paper: CBA-13-03, New York University*, 2013. http://hdl.handle.net/2451/31801.

[4] P. Adamopoulos and A. Tuzhilin. Probabilistic k-NN: Improving Item Prediction and Diversity Using Probabilistic Neighborhood Selection in Collaborative Filtering Systems. *Working Paper: New York University*, 2013.

[5] P. Adamopoulos and A. Tuzhilin. Recommendation Opportunities: Improving Item Prediction Using Weighted Percentile Methods in Collaborative Filtering Systems. In *Proceedings of RecSys '13*. ACM, 2013.

[6] G. Adomavicius and A. Tuzhilin. Toward the next generation of recommender systems: A survey of the state-of-the-art and possible extensions. *IEEE Trans. on Knowl. and Data Eng.*, 17(6):734–749, June 2005.

[7] R. M. Bell, J. Bennett, Y. Koren, and C. Volinsky. The million dollar programming prize. *IEEE Spectr.*, 46(5):28–33, 2009.

[8] P. Cremonesi, F. Garzotto, S. Negro, A. V. Papadopoulos, and R. Turrin. Looking for "good" recommendations: a comparative evaluation of recommender systems. In *INTERACT '11*, 2011.

[9] D. L. Hansen and J. Golbeck. Mixing it up: recommending collections of items. In *Proceedings of CHI '09*. ACM, 2009.

[10] D. Jannach, M. Zanker, A. Felfernig, and G. Friedrich. *Recommender systems: an introduction*. Cambridge University Press, 2010.

[11] A. Karatzoglou and M. Weimer. Quantile matrix factorization for collaborative filtering. *In Proceedings of EC-Web '10*, 2010.

[12] R. Koenker. *Quantile Regresssion*. Wiley Online Library, 2005.

[13] J. A. Konstan, B. N. Miller, D. Maltz, J. L. Herlocker, L. R. Gordon, and J. Riedl. Grouplens: applying collaborative filtering to usenet news. *Comm. of the ACM*, 40(3), 1997.

[14] J. A. Konstan and J. T. Riedl. Recommender systems: from algorithms to user experience. *User Modeling and User-Adapted Interaction*, 22:101–123, 2012.

[15] Y. Koren, R. Bell, and C. Volinsky. Matrix factorization techniques for recommender systems. *Computer*, 42(8), 2009.

[16] D. Lemire and A. Maclachlan. Slope one predictors for online rating-based collaborative filtering. *CoRR*, abs/cs/0702144, 2007.

[17] J. Masthoff. Group recommender systems: Combining individual models. In *Recommender Systems Handbook*, pages 677–702. Springer, 2011.

[18] S. M. McNee, J. Riedl, and J. A. Konstan. Being accurate is not enough: how accuracy metrics have hurt recommender systems. In *Proceedings of CHI '06*, pages 1097–1101. ACM, 2006.

[19] M. O'Connor, D. Cosley, J. A. Konstan, and J. Riedl. Polylens: a recommender system for groups of users. In *Proceedings of ECSCW '01*. Kluwer Academic Publishers, 2001.

[20] A. G. Parameswaran and H. Garcia-Molina. Recommendations with prerequisites. In *Proceedings of RecSys '09*. ACM, 2009.

[21] C.-K. Wong and M. C. Easton. An efficient method for weighted sampling without replacement. *SIAM Journal on Computing*, 9(1):111–113, 1980.

[22] M. Xie, L. V. Lakshmanan, and P. T. Wood. Breaking out of the box of recommendations: from items to packages. In *Proceedings of RecSys '10*. ACM, 2010.

Anytime Algorithms for Top-N Recommenders

David Ben-Shimon
Ben-Gurion University of the Negev, Beer-Sheva, Israel
dudibs@post.bgu.ac.il

ABSTRACT

Many small and mid-sized e-businesses use the services of recommender system (RS) provider companies to outsource the construction and maintenance of their RS. The fees that RS providers charge their clients must cover the computation costs for constructing and updating the recommendation model. By using anytime algorithms, a RS provider can control the computation costs and still offer a system capable of delivering reasonable recommendations. Thus, a RS provider should be able to stop the construction of a recommendation model once the cost for computing it reaches the amount the customer has agreed to pay.

In this research we suggest anytime algorithms as a possible solution to a problem that RS providers face. We demonstrate how certain existing recommendation algorithms can be adjusted to the anytime framework. We focus on the case of item-item algorithms, showing how the anytime behavior can be improved using different ordering methods of computations. We conduct a comparative study demonstrating the benefits of the proposed methods for top-N item-item recommenders.

Categories and Subject Descriptors

H.4 [**Information Systems Applications**]: Miscellaneous

Keywords

Anytime Algorithms, Collaborative Filtering, Item-Based, Locality Sensitive Hashing

1. INTRODUCTION

Many e-commerce businesses record users' activities in order to enable personalization and to recommend items to view or purchase. The decision of an e-business to apply personalization and integrate recommendations into their existing systems can be challenging and even risky since the expected return on investment (ROI) is difficult to predict. As for small and medium e-businesses, the required knowledge, expertise, and resources needed for implementing a personalized recommender system may be beyond their reach.

To minimize the investment and risk, many small or medium e-businesses, prefer to purchase the recommender system as a service. Such services allow an e-business to request recommendations online for the active customer through a remote server, which the e-business neither owns nor operates. In case of an unsuccessful deployment in which the system does not meet the goals of the e-business owner, the service can be easily terminated without any major financial losses to the business owner. In other words, recommender system services can reduce the required initial investment and present very little risk to the e-business.

The providers of such services, often called recommender system (RS) providers, offer a set of pre-made solutions that can be adjusted to specific website needs at a low cost. The solutions offered by the RS providers are generally hosted on remote servers, where the website data is also maintained, prediction models are constructed, and recommendation queries are handled. While the RS provider may own and operate these servicers, growing cloud computing framework services [1], such as Amazon and Microsoft providing, are offering alternative storage and computation possibilities. In such a case, building models for customers may incurs substantial costs to the RS provider. We are motivated by that specific problem that RS providers face, namely, the balancing of model computation costs and quality.

One possible approach for controlling the balance between computation cost and recommendation quality is through the use of anytime algorithms (AA) [5]. An anytime algorithm provides a trade-off between computation time and the quality of the solution it provides. The more the computation time, the better the predictive performance that is achieved. Such algorithms can be stopped at any point in the course of the computation and still yield solutions. Given sufficient time, the solution becomes optimal.

This research makes two contributions to the field of RS. First, it is presenting the RS provider business model and the problems that these providers face. Second, it shows how anytime algorithms can address some of these problems by presenting two techniques for adapting nearest neighborhood CF algorithms to act as anytime algorithms. Experiments show that these techniques can be used to provide a better time-quality trade-off

2. BACKGROUND

2.1 Recommender Systems Providers

In the past, recommender systems were employed mainly by large scale e-businesses, such as Amazon. The main reasons for this phenomenon are that implementing recommendation algorithms can involve substantial investments; require certain expertise; programming effort; high computational power; and suitable infrastructure. In many cases, particularly for mid-sized and small e-businesses, these substantial investments cannot be justified by the added value. That is because the cost of realizing such a solution will be much larger than the income which will come out of it. On the other hand, the integration of a ready-made recommender engine into a website requires a set of skills that are commonly found in companies constructing web pages, and less initial investment, except for the needed integration, is required.

Consequently, a feasible RS alternative is to outsource the RS to a company that specializes in this area and consume it as a service. Companies providing recommendation systems as a service are often called RS providers. By exposing application program interface (API), the RS providers are storing recorded users' activities, computing models, and delivering list of

RecSys '13, October 12–16, 2013, Hong Kong, China.

http://dx.doi.org/10.1145/2507157.2508074

recommendations on demand. Since recommendation services should be inexpensive, a RS provider must be able to support many clients to be profitable. It cannot afford to offer its clients a tailor-made solution. Providers typically select the most suitable solution for a customer from a set of pre-made generic methods.

While the quality of the recommendations may vary, an obvious restriction is that the on-line recommendations have to be provided very rapidly. It is unacceptable for a system to wait more than a fraction of a second for the computation of a recommendation. To ensure that, the RS providers is using Model-Based [2] approach and typically sign a service level agreement (SLA) that defines the required response time.

The RS provider may build its own infrastructure for computing recommendation models and answering recommendation requests rapidly. The cost of this infrastructure and its maintenance, however, may become too high for a RS provider given the low fees it charges its clients. Another alternative is to use cloud computing services [1]. Amazon, as well as other companies, maintain large server farms, and allow users to store data and to run computation processes on these servers. The users pay a fee proportional to the amount of storage, time and computation power they use. Given such cloud computing services, it is easy for the RS provider to estimate the cost of the required computations, such as models building, and charge the e-business accordingly.

2.2 Anytime Algorithms

To maintain profitability when using existing recommender methods, RS providers can offer either simple, low-cost models which are optimal but can be trained rapidly e.g., a Naïve Bayes Classifier, or expensive more popular models (such as SVD) that require heavy computational resources. However, those existing methods do not allow direct control over the accuracy-cost trade-off. Given the RS provider scenario, that provides RS as a service, it is difficult or even impossible to determine in advance the required time and computational resources needed to generate models offering a suitable level of cost and accuracy for handling unseen data of an e-business.

A more compelling approach would be to make use of an algorithm to be constructed in such a way so that it builds the best model possible under the constraint of limited computation time. Standard algorithms for model building do not offer this option. Many of the algorithms for model building in RS, when interrupted before termination, will not have an available model to return. To enable interruption, an algorithm must be designed to allow intermediate result snapshots. Such algorithms are typically called anytime algorithms [5].The accuracy that anytime algorithms provide always improve or stay the same over the time, but never decrease. In this research we propose that applying anytime algorithms to the recommendation problem is adequate for RS provider business model.

Anytime algorithms have been used in various areas such as data mining [4] decision support systems [8]; and for various intelligent systems [11]. Little research exists on the application of anytime algorithms to recommender systems. One particularly interesting line of research has been the application of efficient anytime methods to sequential association rules models [3]. In such a models, the anytime approach was used to limit the latency of computing recommendations online and not to the model building process. While this approach is interesting, especially in the case of memory-based algorithms, it is different from the scenario that we are interested in, where the approach is model-based and the recommendations must be computed in constant time.

3. CASE STUDY - ANYTIME TOP-N RECOMMENDERS OVER IMPLICIT FEEDBACK DATASETS

In the neighborhood-based item-item model, the goal is to find the nearest neighbors of each item. A neighborhood is defined as being based on similarity score between items. These similarities are cached in a model that is, in turn, used online to provide recommendations. In a CF approach for implicit datasets, two items may be considered to be similar, if users tend to consume them together. A simple example of a similarity function for implicit datasets is the Jaccard coefficient [9]:

$$J(i,j) = \frac{|U_i \cap U_j|}{|U_i \cup U_j|} \qquad (1)$$

where U_i and U_j are the sets of users that consumed items i, and j respectively.

3.1 Methods for Ordering Item Pairs in Nearest Neighbor Search Methods

In an anytime setting, we can compute item pair statistics until a predefined time limit has been reached. When computing recommendations online, the recommendation algorithm can only use the statistics it has computed within the given time. As we show below, in such a setting, the order by which item pairs are investigated can greatly influence the quality of the recommendations.

We suggest two methods for deciding on the order of pairwise similarity computation. An essential property of such methods is that they must be computed very rapidly. Otherwise, we might spend more time on the initialization of the method than on constructing the model. We use a data structure that allows us to rapidly access all the users who have used an item and all the items that a given user has used.

3.1.1 Locality Sensitive Hashing Tree

Locality sensitive hashing (LSH) [6] is a technique for rapidly computing the similarity of items. We apply the LSH technique to provide us with an anytime approach for the item pair computations. To generate our signatures matrix (reduced representation of the user-item input matrix) over the data, we adapted the idea of LSH Google news personalization [5] where the hash value for an item in a given dimension in the signature of an item, is the first user ID that consumed this item in a random permutation of the user ID list. We generated P permutations over the user IDs and applied this hash function on each permutation to end up with an item signatures matrix of the size PxN. This P defines the number of dimensions in the signatures matrix.

We now wish to split the item signatures set into two disjoint subsets such that the items in each subset will most likely be more similar to one another than to items in the other subset. We split the items in the signatures matrix based on the medians of the various dimensions. Given an item signature matrix, we first compute a median for each dimension independently. Then, for each item in the set, we compute the portion of its dimension entries whose value is higher than the median of that dimension. If this portion is lower than 0.5, the item is placed in the left child subset; otherwise it is placed in the right child subset. We use a top-down approach, starting with all item signatures and splitting them into equally sized subsets. We continue recursively until we reach a predefined minimum number of items in a subset. This splitting approach creates a balanced binary tree, where every two disjoint subsets created through the splitting process are always the full set of their related parent. Figure 1 illustrates the tree construction and the number of items in each node and leaf.

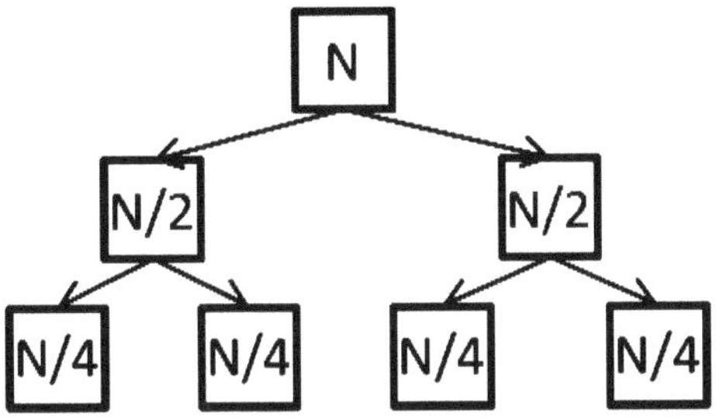

Figure 1: The N items divided evenly on each level using the medians.

Beginning with the leaves of the tree, we first compute for each leaf the pairwise Jaccard similarities of items in the leaf. After all leaves are computed, we move up a level, and compute the pairwise similarities of items that belong to sibling leaves. Moving up levels in the tree, the process is continued, until all pairwise similarities have been computed.

Assuming that the signatures matrix maintains the Jaccard similarities and that the median splits the items into two homogenous groups during the construction of the tree, we expect that items with high similarity will be computed first with high probability, and that a good anytime performance will be achieved.

3.1.2 The Most Popular First

The second method is based on the assumption that popular items provide information to the model, and thus should be computed first. As popular items appear in many users' profiles, they can be utilized for rapidly computing personalized recommendations for most users.

This approach can be implemented efficiently by sorting items according to decreasing consumption set cardinality (i.e., popularity). We then compute for each item its similarity to the most popular item, its similarity to the second most popular item, etc. Following is a pseudo code of the popular first approach.

```
L ← items sorted by decreasing popularity
For i = 1 to |L|
  For each user U who consumed item i
    For each item j consumed by user U
          compute J(Li, Lj)
```

3.2 Initialization Complexity

Let I be the number of items, A be the average number of users who have chosen each item, and P be the reduced dimension in the LSH reduction.

The initialization complexity for the '*LSH Tree*' requires $O(P \cdot I \cdot A)$ for computing the signatures matrix. Then, constructing the tree requires $O(I \cdot P \log I)$ operations, for finding the medians in each level in the tree, and there are at most $O(\log I)$ levels. Hence, assuming that A and P are much smaller than I, the computation time is dominated by $O(I \cdot \log I)$.

The initialization complexity of the '*Most Popular*' method is $O(I \cdot \log I)$ for sorting the items by the number of users who consumed them.

In the results below this initialization time is included, but for both methods it required no more than a few hundreds of milliseconds and is therefore negligible.

3.3 Comparative Experiments

To compare and analyze the anytime behavior of the '*LSH Tree*' and the '*Most Popular*' method, we carried out a series of experiments. As a baseline we present the Amazon approach [10] that computes item pairs in an arbitrary order.

All three methods for ordering the items pairs leverage the symmetry in the Jaccard coefficient. That is, if $J(i,j)$ was computed, then $J(j,i)$ is also known, and not computed again. The algorithms compute the similarities only for pairs of items which were consumed together by at least one user yielding a score greater than zero. The baseline method, the Amazon approach, is somewhat anytime in nature due to its iterative computation.

We conducted experiments on three datasets: buying events from a music web shop: buying events from a software games web shop; and Movie-Lens, described in Table 1.For Movie-Lens, we attempted to recommend movies that the user might rate, given other movies she has rated. To model this scenario, we ignored the actual ratings and used a dataset where users either rated or didn't rate a movie. The music dataset contains real data, capturing buying events in a music portal over several consecutive months during 2010. The games dataset is also a real dataset and derives from an online shop selling software games over the past few years. In the music and the games datasets we computed a list of recommended items given other items that the user has bought.

Table 1. The benchmark datasets used in the experiments

Name	#events	# items	# users	Sparsity
Movie-Lens	100,000	1682	943	0.9369
Music	458,131	116,583	9901	0.9996
Games	320,641	3304	72,347	0.9986

Each users' consumption set is divided randomly into a train and test set. We executed the three algorithms on all three datasets, stopping them at each predefined interval time to measure the performance of the currently computed model. The interval time was 5 seconds for the Movie-Lens; 30 seconds for the games dataset; and 60 seconds for the music dataset. Since the task is to provide top-N recommendations, we found *precision@N* [7] to be the most appropriate metric for evaluating model performances. Below, we provide results for $N=5$, i.e., we directed the algorithm to supply us with 5 recommendations. We also experimented with different values of N (10, 15, and 25), but found no sensitivity to N. We ran all algorithms 5 times, and report the average results. The standard error of the 5 runs was well below 10^{-5} and is not shown in the graphs. All algorithms use the same train-test split, allowing us to measure paired statistical significance over the different users.

3.4 Results

Figures 2, 3, and 4 present precision as a function of computation time for the Movie-lens, Music and Games datasets respectively.

Each point in a curve represents the average precision of a model at a certain time during the learning phase, and is averaged over five different train-test splits.

The '*Most Popular*' technique shows superiority in the Movie lens and in the music datasets, while the '*LSH Tree*' shows superiority also in the Movie-Lens and in the games datasets. The

Amazon baseline method demonstrates moderate anytime performance.

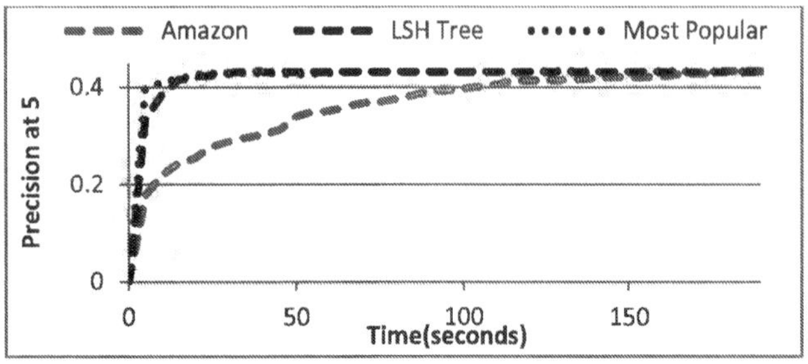

Figure 2: Anytime results for the Movie-Lens dataset

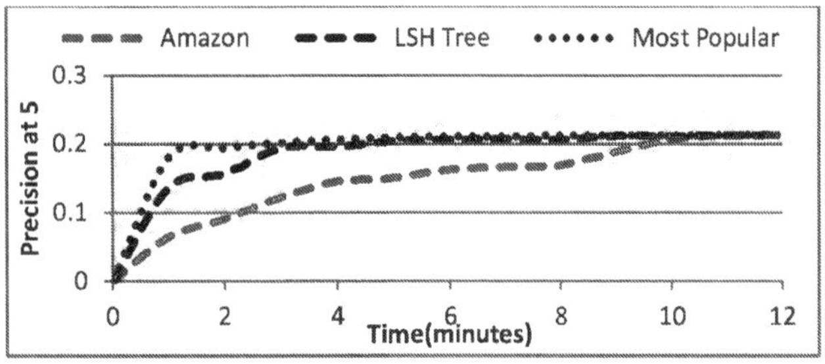

Figure 3: Anytime results for the music dataset

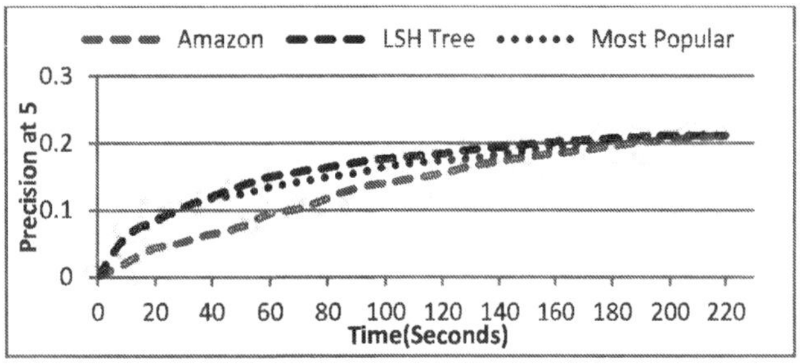

Figure 4: Anytime results for the software games dataset

Table 2 presents the area under the curve (AUC) for all three approaches on the three datasets. Each value in the table is the average over the five different train-test splits. The standard deviation of each value is also presented. AUC provides a comparison of the entire running process.

Table 2. Area under the curve (AUC) for both domains

Method	Movie-Lens	Music	Games
Amazon	68.18±1.71	1.78±0.02	29.4±1.48
Tree LSH	79.18±1.44	2.24±0.02	36.1±0.5
Most Popular	80.34±1.47	2.36±0.03	34.5 ±0.7

These results demonstrate that the anytime behavior of standard recommendation approaches can be improved. Simple technique, such as the *'Most Popular'* orders the item pairs so that the models present better precision faster than standard methods. While the *'LSH Tree'* method may not seem the best in our experiments, we believe that compared to the popularity technique, it is more general and less tailored to the Jaccard-based similarity algorithm that we employ.

4. CONCLUSIONS AND FUTURE RESEARCH

We described the problem of RS providers who need to balance the computation time of recommendation models with the fees they collect from customers. We have suggested that anytime algorithms, which support interrupting the computation after a given time, may provide an adequate solution to this problem. RS providers can stop the algorithm once the cost for computation time reaches the payment the RS provider agreed upon with the customer. We claim that typical model-based CF algorithms display poor anytime behavior. Using public and real life buying events datasets, we demonstrated this on the well-known Amazon approach. Consequently it is necessary to either construct new algorithms or to adapt existing algorithms to provide better anytime behavior. We view this research as the starting point for further exploration of anytime algorithms for constructing recommendations models. In the future we will investigate anytime techniques for the gradient descent SVD, improving on both the latent factors learning phase as well as the recommendation computation phase.

5. ACKNOWLEDGMENTS

I would like to thank my advisors, Prof. Lior Rokach and Prof. Bracha Shapira for their valuable instruction, ideas and feedbacks on this work, and to Dr. Guy Shani for the insightful discussions.

6. REFERENCES

[1] M. Armbrust, A. Fox, R. Griffith, A. D. Joseph, R. H. Katz, A. Konwinski, G. Lee, D. A. Patterson, A. Rabkin, I. Stoica, M. Zaharia (2009). Above the Clouds: A Berkeley View of Cloud computing. Technical Report No. UCB/EECS-2009.

[2] J.S Breese. D. Heckerman, C. Kadie (1998). Empirical analysis of predictive algorithms for collaborative filtering. In Proceedings of the 14th Conference on Uncertainty in Artificial Intelligence (UAI-98). G. F. Cooper, and S. Moral, Eds. Morgan-Kaufmann, San Francisco, Calif., 43–52.

[3] A. Brun, A. Boyer (2009). Towards Privacy Compliant and Anytime Recommender Systems. Proceedings of 10th International Conference on Electronic Commerce and Web Technologies. Pages 276-287.

[4] D. Dash, M. Druzdzel (1999). A hybrid anytime algorithm for the construction of causal models from sparse data, Proceedings of the fifteenth international conference on uncertainty in artificial intelligence.

[5] T. Dean (1987). Intractability and Time-Dependent Planning. In Proceedings of the 1986 Workshop on Reasoning about Actions and Plans. eds. M. P. Georgeff and A. L. Lansky. San Francisco, Calif.: Morgan Kaufmann.

[6] P. Gionis, P. Indyk, R. Motwani (1999). Similarity search in high dimensions via hashing. Proceedings of VLDB, pp. 518–529.

[7] J.L. Herlocker, J.A. Konstan, L.G Terveen, J.T. Riedl (2004). Evaluating Collaborative Filtering Recommender Systems. ACM Trans. Information Systems, vol. 22, no. 1, pp. 5-53, 2004.

[8] M.C. Horsch, D. Poole (1998). An anytime algorithm for decision making under uncertainty, in: Proceedings of the14th Annual Conference on Uncertainty in Artificial Intelligence, Morgan Kaufmann, San Francisco, 1998, pp. 246–255.

[9] P. Jaccard (1901). Étude comparative de la distribution florale dans une portion des Alpes et des Jura. Bulletin de la Société Vaudoise des Sciences Naturelles 37: 547–579.

[10] Linden, B. Smith, J. York (2003). Amazon.com recommendations: Item-to-item collaborative filtering. IEEE Internet Computing, 7, 76-80.

[11] S. Zilberstein (1996). Using anytime algorithms in intelligent systems. AI Magazine, 17(3), 73-83.

GAIN: Web Service for User Tracking and Preference Learning – a SMART TV Use Case

Jaroslav Kuchař*
Web Engineering Group
Faculty of Information Technology, Czech Technical University, Prague
jaroslav.kuchar@fit.cvut.cz

Tomáš Kliegr†
Department of Information and Knowledge Engineering
University of Economics, Prague
tomas.kliegr@vse.cz

ABSTRACT

GAIN (**inbeat.eu**) is a web application and service for capturing and preprocessing user interactions with semantically described content. GAIN outputs a set of instances in tabular form suitable for further processing with generic machine-learning algorithms. GAIN is demoed as a component of a "SMART-TV" recommender system. Content is automatically described with DBpedia types using a Named Entity Recognition (NER) system. Interest is determined based on explicit user actions and user's attention computed by 3D head pose estimation. Preference rules are learnt with an association rule mining algorithm. These can be e.g. deployed to a business rules system, acting as a recommender.

Categories and Subject Descriptors

H.4 [**Information Systems Applications**]: Miscellaneous

Keywords

preference learning, entity classification, association rules

Introduction

An important part of the personalization process is the capture of user interaction and preprocessing the recorded data to a form that can be handled by the preference learning algorithm of choice. GAIN[1] (**inbeat.eu**) captures user interaction with a video player. The text of the video is automatically semantically annotated and linked to the DBpedia ontology with the **entityclassifier.eu** service. GAIN output, the aggregated user data, is subject to preference (association rules) learning using **easyminer.eu**.

*Also affiliated with the Dep. of Information and Knowledge Engineering, University of Economics, Prague

†Also affiliated with the Multimedia and Vision Research Group, Queen Mary, University of London

[1]General Analytics INterceptor and INterest Aggregator

RecSys'13, October 12–16, 2013, Hong Kong, China.
ACM 978-1-4503-2409-0/13/10.
http://dx.doi.org/10.1145/2507157.2508217.

1. SYSTEM OVERVIEW

The input of GAIN is a variable number of *interest clues* and a *semantic description of content*. Interest clues are user interactions, which can be either explicit (clicking a button) or implicit (attention level). Content is described in terms of *views*, the smallest amount of content to which the interest clue can be related to. View can contain multiple *objects* linked to a domain ontology by Linked Open Data (LOD) identifiers. Objects are described by attributes, properties which influence user interest in the object. Their values might be literals, or LOD identifiers. Domain ontology can be loaded to GAIN allowing computation of relatedness between attribute values.

GAIN output is a set of instances in a tabular form suitable for processing with generic machine-learning algorithms. Each mining instance relates to one view and is described by a fixed-length vector of weighted classes from the domain ontology, created by an aggregation of content of objects in the view, and a scalar value of *interest*, aggregation of all preference clues related to the view.

To foster integration with other components of a recommender system, GAIN is encapsulated into a REST web service interface. In the remainder of this section, the internals of GAIN are described.

Tracking module is integrated into the user interface with which the users interact. It is responsible for capturing interest clues and forwarding them in the form of events to the Application module. There are two version: modified Google Analytics (GA) JavaScript tracking code (`ga.js`) for web analytics and a REST API for other domains.

Application module contains the GAIN core logic. GAIN is implemented on the Node.js (`http://nodejs.org/`), a lightweight scalable platform with event-driven, non-blocking I/O model. After processing, the data are passed to the storage module. API for importing and exporting data at multiple processing stages is also available.

Storage module is implemented as a NoSQL document-oriented database MongoDB (`http://www.mongodb.org/`). The key advantage of this solution is a schema-less design, which fosters the attachment of semantic description to objects, with which the user interacted.

Aggregation module combines the interest clues from the Tracking module with description of content interacted with into fixed-length vectors suitable for machine learning. Content annotation is sent to the tracking module simultaneously with each interaction or added during the aggregation.

Figure 1: An extended version of the YouTube player used for the SmartTV demo

2. GAIN IN SMART TV RECOMMENDER

The LinkedTV project (`linkedtv.eu`) develops a recommender system for "Smart TV", which gathers data on televiewers behaviour and uses them to learn their preferences. These are then used to choose links to content on the web related to the video being played that will be recommended to the user. GAIN is used for capturing and preprocessing user feedback during video playback. For easy accessibility, this usecase is demoed with the YouTube player.

User Tracking

There are two sources of interaction: remote control and user behaviour feedback. These two types of interaction are depicted at Fig. 1 as "Basic controls" and "Behaviour controls". Within the LinkedTV project, the latter type of interaction comes from 3D head pose estimation [2]. Every user interaction is immediately sent by the player via the REST API component to GAIN server along with the time in the video and video identification.

Consider example televiewer watching news. During a spot covering a football match, the user clicks on a bookmark button and behaviour tracking records "Looking at screen".

Ontology-based Content Description

The video is fragmented into smaller time-intervals in order to relate user feedback more precisely to what is on the screen at the time the feedback is recorded. This segmentation is performed from start and stop time of subtitles, in the LinkedTV platform, shot detection algorithms are used. The result of segmentation are *views.*

To identify salient objects, the text of the video, as extracted from subtitles, is processed with entity recognition tool THD [1]. The THD tool also assigns each object with several *type attributes* corresponding to one or more DBpedia Ontology classes.

Example: if entity dbpedia:Ronaldinho is recognized in the subtitle, the type assigned is dbpedia-owl:SoccerPlayer.

Aggregation

Multidimensional semantic (taxonomical) description of tracked objects are processed along with user feedback to the lower-dimensional output representation, with a tabular form suitable for analysis with mainstream data mining algorithms.

Content Description. Each *view* contains a varying number of objects. First, the domain ontology is used to expand the *type* attributes to a *class membership vector.*

Next, the class membership vectors of all objects within a view are aggregated into a single class membership vector.

The "dbpedia-owl:SoccerPlayer" type attribute value is expanded to subvector containing non-zero values also for its superclasses: dbpedia-owl:Athlete and dbpedia-owl:Person.

User feedback. None to multiple user actions are recorded during a view. These are aggregated into a single *interest value*, which ranges from -1 (maximum disinteret) to 1 (maximum interest). The impact of individual types of actions is determined by a custom set of rules, such as *if user clicks on bookmark, the interest is increased by 0.5* or *if user looks at the screen, the interest is increased by 0.3. Our user's bookmark and look at screen actions resulted in a total 0.8 interest for the view.*

Learning preference rules with EasyMiner

For a given user, GAIN outputs one table, where rows correspond to views recorded for the user. The Table has $n+m+1$ columns, where n is the number of classes in the domain ontology, m number of unique objects and the last column is the estimated value of interest. User preferences are discovered with EasyMiner [5], a web sevice and web application for association rule discovery based on LISp-Miner [4].

Mining interactions of our user yields rules such as:
∘*dbpedia-owl:Athlete*$\wedge$*dbpedia:Brazil* $\rightarrow$ *interest* $= \langle 0.3; 0.5)$
∘*dbpedia:Ronaldinho* $\rightarrow$ *interest* $= (0.5; 1\rangle$.

Content recommendation with Business Rules

EasyMiner allows to export selected rules to a Business Rules Engine [3]. There is an ongoing work on using this engine as a recommender system. Input is a description of a candidate content item with an $n+m$ dimensional vector of concepts. The output is the predicted interest.

Acknowledgment. This research was supported by the EU via the LinkedTV project (FP7-287911), CTU in Prague grant (SGS13/100/OHK3/1T/18) and VSE by grant IGA 20/2013. The content in Fig. 1 was adapted from Wikipedia.

3. REFERENCES

[1] M. Dojchinovski and T. Kliegr. Entityclassifier.eu: real-time classification of entities in text with Wikipedia. In *ECML'13*, pages 654–658. Springer.

[2] J. Leroy, F. Rocca, M. Mancas, and B. Gosselin. Second screen interaction: an approach to infer tv watcher's interest using 3d head pose estimation. In *LiME-2013*, WWW '13 Companion, ACM, pages 465–468, 2013.

[3] S. Vojíř, T. Kliegr, A. Hazucha, R. Škrabal, and M. Šimůnek. Transforming association rules to business rules: EasyMiner meets Drools. In *RuleML-2013 Challenge*. CEUR-WS.org, 2013.

[4] M. Šimůnek. Academic KDD project LISp-Miner. In *Advances in Soft Computing - Intelligent Systems Design and Applications*, pages 263–272. Springer, 2003.

[5] R. Škrabal, M. Šimůnek, S. Vojíř, A. Hazucha, T. Marek, D. Chudán, and T. Kliegr. Association rule mining following the web search paradigm. In *ECML'12*, pages 808–811. Springer, 2012.

PEN recsys: a Personalized News Recommender Systems Framework

Florent Garcin   Boi Faltings

Artificial Intelligence Lab
Ecole Polytechnique Fédérale de Lausanne
Switzerland
firstname.lastname@epfl.ch

ABSTRACT

We present the Personalized News (PEN) recommender systems framework[1], currently in use by a newspaper website to evaluate various algorithms for news recommendations. We briefly describe its system architecture and related components. We show how a researcher can easily evaluate different algorithms thanks to a web-based interface.

Categories and Subject Descriptors

H.3.3 [**Information Storage and Retrieval**]: Information Search and Retrieval—*Information filtering*

Keywords

recommender system, news, online evaluation

1. INTRODUCTION

Researchers in the recommender systems community have developed open-source platforms which try to bring a growing number of recommender algorithms under one roof. Most of these platforms are designed for research purposes to conduct offline evaluations and only a few target online evaluations on production websites.

In this paper, we are interested in *online* evaluation of state-of-the-art algorithms for *news* recommendations. Unfortunately, it is not possible to use current open-source platforms because they are not tailored to the specific needs of news recommendations and thus are difficult to adapt to the news domain [1].

To this end, we present the PEN recsys framework for online evaluation of news recommender systems. PEN recsys is designed with 4 criteria in mind. First, it has to be *fast*. The framework must provide real-time recommendations as soon as possible, without making the users wait. Second, it must be *reliable*. It is not acceptable for a newspaper website to suffer from crashes. Third, a *flexible* design is important. It should be easy to add new components or extend recommender systems. Finally, it must be *scalable*. News websites are subject to unpredictable visit peaks and the framework must be able to handle them by delivering recommendations on time and without problems.

[1]Note that this paper is an extended abstract of [2].

RecSys'13, October 12–16, 2013, Hong Kong, China.
Copyright 2013 ACM 978-1-4503-2409-0/13/09 ...$15.00.
http://dx.doi.org/10.1145/2507157.2508218.

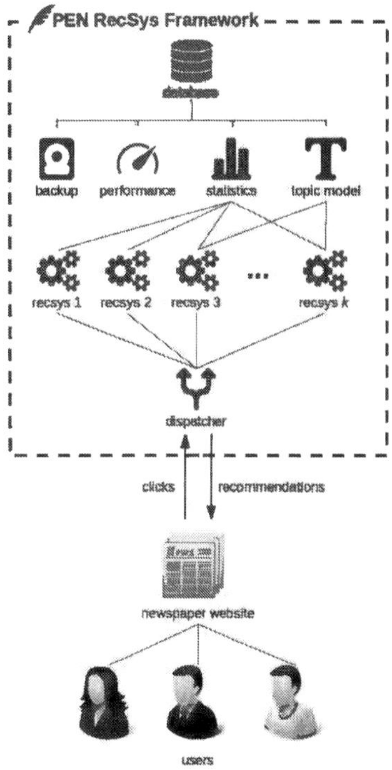

Figure 1: System architecture and components

2. SYSTEM ARCHITECTURE

Figure 1 gives a brief overview of the main components in the PEN recsys framework. When a user clicks on a news story, she is assigned to a recommender system which will provide recommendations.

The *dispatcher* randomly assigns a recommender system to a user, performing A/B or multivariate testing. The *recsys* $1, 2, 3, ..., k$ are the different algorithms to evaluate (See Section 3 for more details). Some algorithms relies on click statistics. The component *statistics* gathers click statistics about the stories. Other recommender systems needs the content of news articles, or more specifically to its topic distribution. The component *topic model* is in charge of keeping the topic model up-to-date.

The *performance* component generates performance reports of the algorithms under evaluation. The *database* stores the clicks, statistics and performance reports for offline analysis.

Finally, the *backup* component periodically triggers backup to the hard disk of the various states of the system such as the current topic model and click statistics. This is useful if we want to roll back to a previous set of parameters.

It is important to deliver recommendations to the user as soon as possible. With this in mind, the platform is designed to reduce this latency to the minimum. Hence tasks that are not essential for generating recommendations are run in the background. For instance, the database is known to be a bottleneck. Thus statistics are first cached in memory and later stored in the database when resources are available.

The PEN recsys framework follows the software-as-a-service paradigm and is implemented using Java EE technologies. It scales very well since each component can be physically located on different sites.

3. RECOMMENDER SYSTEMS

The framework contains various recommender systems such as the 4 versions of context-tree recommender systems [1], a simple collaborative filtering, a content-based approach, most popular articles, and random articles. We plan to implement more algorithms in the future.

To add a new algorithm, we just need to implement a single method `getRecommendations`. If required, the algorithm can have access to the click statistics, fresh news stories, or topic model via the specific components.

4. INTERFACES

The PEN recsys framework has a web-based control panel (Fig. 2). The researcher can configure the general behaviour of the framework, enable/disable an algorithm, fine tune its parameters (see Fig. 3).

The researcher can also check the performance of the enabled algorithms. Figure 4 shows the performance panel with 3 metrics: success@5, mean average precision and the average clicks per visit.

5. CONCLUSION

We presented the PEN recsys framework which aims at helping researchers and practitioners to evaluate algorithms for news recommendations. The PEN recsys framework is fast, reliable, flexible and scalable. With the help of a simple control interface, it is possible to fine tune each recommender system and have a direct feedback of their performance.

In the future, we plan to increase the set of recommender systems available on this platform.

6. REFERENCES

[1] F. Garcin, C. Dimitrakakis, and B. Faltings. Personalized news recommendation with context trees. In *Int. Conf. on Recommender Systems*, 2013.

[2] F. Garcin and B. Faltings. Pen recsys: a personalized news recommender systems framework. In *News Recommender Systems Workshop*, 2013.

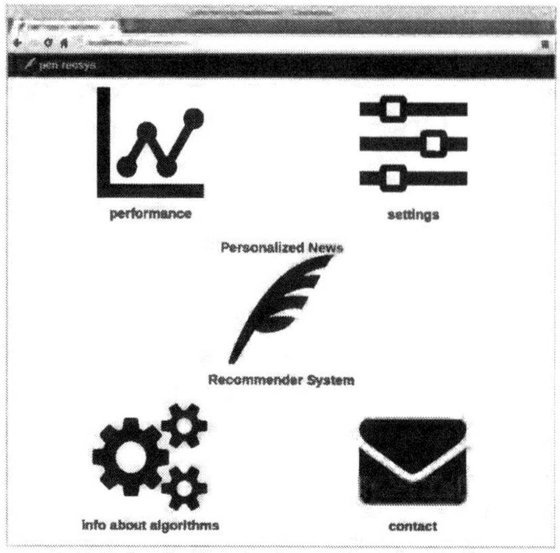

Figure 2: screenshot of the main panel

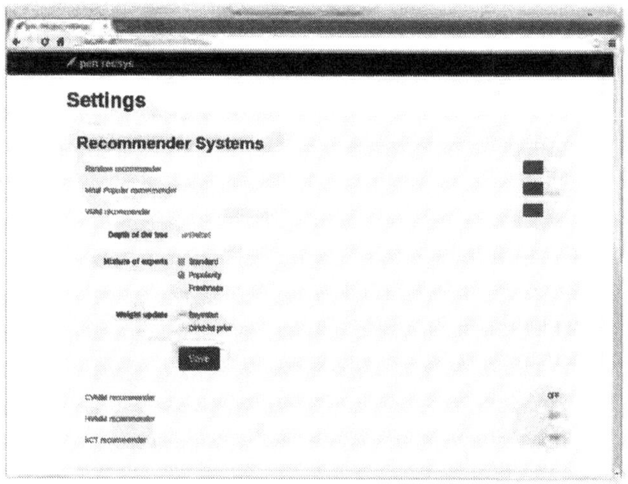

Figure 3: screenshot of the setting panel (partial)

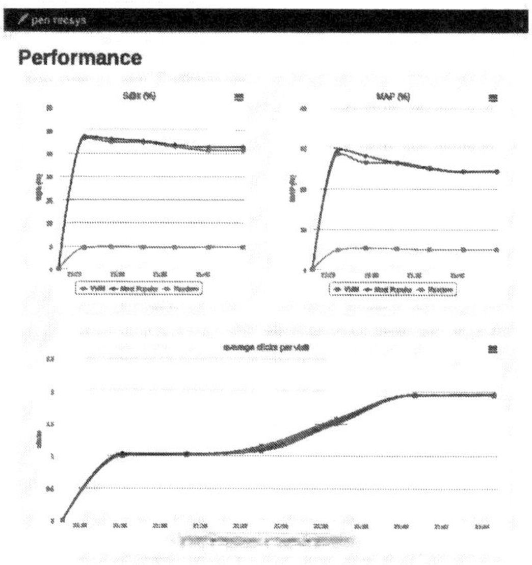

Figure 4: screenshot of the performance panel

A Heterogeneous Graph-based Recommendation Simulator

Yeonchan Ahn[*] Sungchan Park[*] Sangkeun Lee[**] Sang-goo Lee[*]
[*]School of Computer Science and Engineering
Seoul National University
Seoul, Korea
{acha21, baksalchan, sglee}@europa.snu.ac.kr
[**]Computer Science and Engineering Division
Oak Ridge National Laboratory
Oak Ridge, United States
lee4@ornl.gov

ABSTRACT
Heterogeneous graph-based recommendation frameworks have flexibility in that they can incorporate various recommendation algorithms and various kinds of information to produce better results. In this demonstration, we present a heterogeneous graph-based recommendation simulator which enables participants to experience the flexibility of a heterogeneous graph-based recommendation method. With our system, participants can simulate various recommendation semantics by expressing the semantics via meaningful paths like $User \xrightarrow{like} Movie \xrightarrow{likedBy} User \xrightarrow{like} Movie$. The simulator then returns the recommendation results on the fly based on the user-customized semantics using a fast Monte Carlo algorithm.

Categories and Subject Descriptors
H.5.0 [**Information Interfaces and Presentation**]: General; H.3.5 [**Information Search and Retrieval**]: Online Information Services

General Terms
Algorithms, Human Factors

Keywords
Graph-based recommendation, Graph algorithm

1. INTRODUCTION
The heterogonous graph-based recommendation framework PathRank [2] provides obvious benefits in terms of flexibility. It is not only able to simulate various recommendation semantics, but can also adopt various types of input and output. By making use of these advantageous properties, recommendation service providers can test the various algorithms or plan new recommendation services that adopt customized recommendation semantics without the need for code-level modification. In the PathRank framework, the recommendation semantics of the recommendation algorithms are represented as semantic paths. For example, collaborative filtering can be expressed as the semantic path $User \xrightarrow{like} Movie \xrightarrow{likedBy} User \xrightarrow{like} Movie$. Furthermore, this framework can easily incorporate various types of information such as time, location, and metadata related to items. Despite these obvious benefits, it is difficult to show its superiority in terms of flexibility through experiments.

RecSys'13, October 12–16, 2013, Hong Kong, China.
ACM 978-1-4503-2409-0/13/10.
http://dx.doi.org/10.1145/2507157.2508219

In this demonstration, in order to show the flexibility of the PathRank framework, we present a heterogonous graph-based recommendation simulation tool that allows participants to add their own customized recommendation semantics via intuitive interface. They can also instantly see how the paths contribute to the recommendation results via a comprehensive visualization. The flexible PathRank framework and fast Monte Carlo algorithm enable such functionalities.

2. A HETEROGENEOUS GRAPH-BASED RECOMMENDATION SIMULATOR
Our proposed system is composed of two components, a graph-based online recommendation engine and a web-based user interface. Our recommendation engine is based on S. Lee et al.'s framework [2]. In order to allow the user to see the effects of different semantic recommendations, the system should provide the results quickly. Thus the system is implemented as a simulation algorithm using the Monte Carlo method so that the given semantic paths can be quickly reflected in the recommender system. The web-based user interface provides an intuitive semantic path interface and recommendation result visualizer. We will describe the design of the entire system in detail. In our demonstration, the HetRec 2011 MovieLens dataset[1] published by the GroupLens research group was used.

2.1 Graph-based recommendation engine
Our recommendation engine ranks items according to their PathRank [2] score. PathRank is defined via iterative matrix operations like Personalized PageRank. Meanwhile, computing the PathRank score via matrix multiplications or other similar techniques is time consuming and does not provide a prompt output. To solve this problem, we apply the Monte Carlo method in computing the PathRank scores. Our recommendation algorithm is described as follows.

Algorithm 1: Computing PathRank using the Monte Carlo method

N random walkers are initiated at the query nodes. Let each of them iteratively do an operation among the following three options: 1) move to one of the adjacent nodes with the transition probability, 2) follow one of given paths with the path following probability, and 3) stop with the restart probability. The PathRank score of each node is computed by transforming the number of random walkers stopped at the node to the probability.

In our implementation, we confirmed that the estimated PathRank scores can be generated in a few seconds when the number of sample size N is about ten thousands in the HeteRec 2011 MovieLens dataset on a laptop.

[1] http://www.grouplens.org/node/462

2.2 User Interface

The web-based user interface provides a tool for defining the semantic paths along with path recommendation functionality and visualizations of the recommendation process of the top-k results to help the user choose the best path for the user's needs.

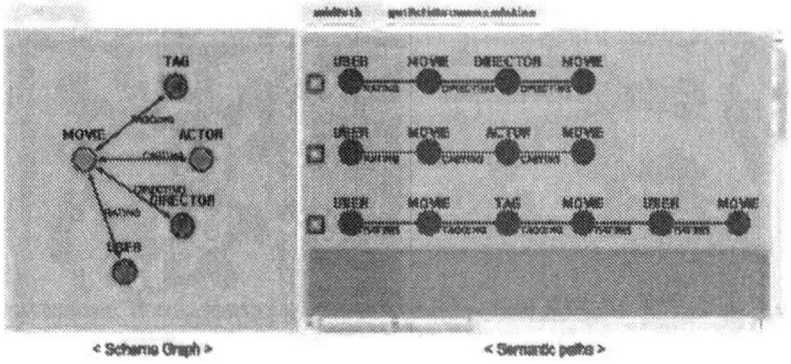

(a) User interface for defining the paths

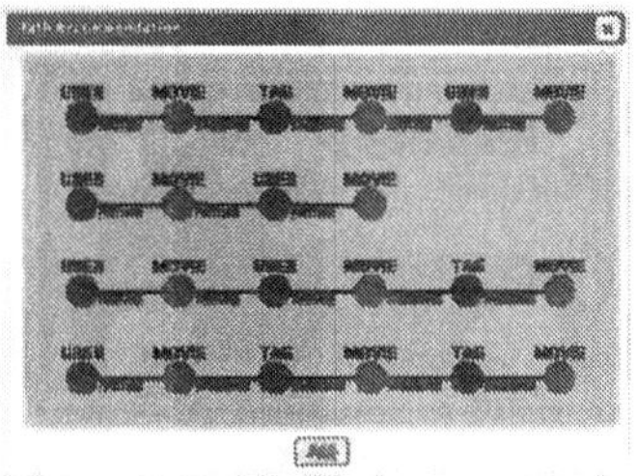

(b) Recommended paths

Figure 1. GUI interface for inputting paths

The schema graph and the chosen semantic paths are depicted in Figure 1(a). By using Aditva et al.'s method [1], the heterogeneous graph is constructed from the data stored in the relational database. Once the heterogeneous graph is constructed, the user can define and test various recommendation semantics by defining semantic paths through the web interface. The user can input semantic paths in two ways; they can define semantic paths by clicking the nodes in the schema graph window or choose a predefined path from an automatically generated list of recommended paths. The recommended paths are selected from all possible paths by evaluating each path on a sample graph using F-measure. In Figure 1(a), the first path, which means "*recommend a movie directed by the same director of the movie that a target user liked,*" is manually inserted. The third long path was selected from the recommended path list in Figure 1(b). It is difficult to understand the implications of the path, but it could possibly increase performance factors such as precision.

In the visualization area, the top-k recommendation results produced using the given semantic paths and queries are presented to provide understanding of how the results are generated by the algorithms. For this step, the user should enter a query node manually or use automatically sampled query nodes. The recommendation results are then represented in the form of a graph where each of the nodes is represented by a pie graph with different colors. Each portion of pie graph is proportional to the number of random walkers that passed through each of the semantic paths, and the radius of the pie graph is proportional to the PathRank score. This visualization tells the user whether the node is popular or semantic-biased. The trace of a single Monte Carlo sample per each top-k result is animated with pursuant information such as the title of the movie to show how the item is recommended.

Figure 2 shows an example of a recommendation of a movie for a user. In this figure, the user can see that the movie titled "Memento" is recommended because a number of random walkers have passed through the semantic path.

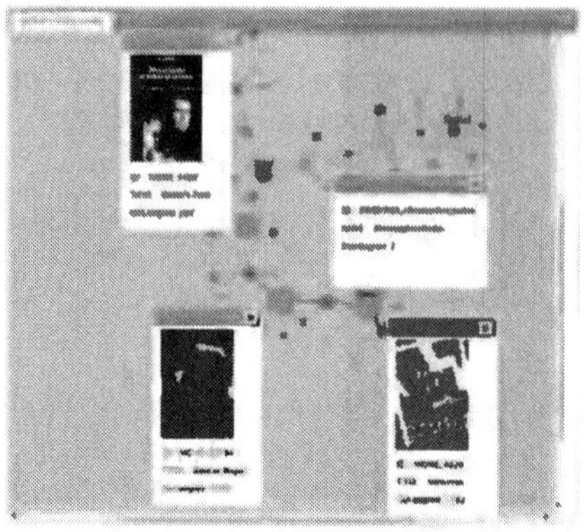

Figure 2. Example of the visualization of a recommendation

Finally, a report on the evaluation metrics such as precision is given for each semantic path entered. This report can tell the user which path has more contributions to the accurate recommendation. We look forward to this report helping the service provider to select the semantic paths that result in more accurate recommendation results.

3. CONCLUSION & FUTURE WORK

In this demonstration, we present a novel simulation tool that enables participants to experience the flexibility of a heterogeneous graph-based recommendation framework. In future works, we plan to find the paths that most successfully satisfy diverse aspects of requirements such as novelty and context-awareness.

4. ACKNOWLEDGMENTS

This work was supported by the National Research Foundation of Korea(NRF) grant funded by the Korea government(MEST) (No. 20110017480).

5. REFERENCES

[1] B. Aditya, G. Bhalotia, S. Chakrabarti, A. Hulgeri, C. Nakhe, P. Parag, and S. Sudarshan. 2002. Banks: Browsing and keyword searching in relational databases. In *Proceedings of the 28th International Conference on Very Large Data Bases*, pp. 1083-1086.

[2] S. Lee, S. Park, M. Kahng, and S.-g. Lee, 2012. PathRank: a novel node ranking measure on a heterogeneous graph for recommender systems, In *Proceedings of the 21st ACM International Conference on Information and Knowledge Management*, Maui, Hawaii, USA, pp. 1637-1641. DOI= http://dx.doi.org/10.1145/2396761.2398488

Design and Evaluation of a Client-side Recommender System

Chris Newell
BBC Research & Development
56 Wood Lane
London W12 7SB UK
+44 3030 409747
chris.newell@bbc.co.uk

Libby Miller
BBC Research & Development
56 Wood Lane
London W12 7SB UK
+44 3030 409747
libby.miller@bbc.co.uk

ABSTRACT

Most recommender systems found on the web are server-based and centralised. However, it can be difficult to maintain the responsiveness with this approach when there are large numbers of concurrent users. In this demonstration we present an alternative approach where major parts of the recommender system are implemented in scripts run by the user's client system.

Categories and Subject Descriptors

H.3.3 [**Information Systems**]: Information Search and Retrieval

Keywords

Recommender Systems, Distributed Systems, Client-side

1. INTRODUCTION

Our previous work involving a user centric study of recommender systems [1] indicated that users valued the ability to explicitly influence the behavior of recommender systems. This encouraged us to pursue research on conversational recommender systems where users are able to steer the recommendations to suit their current mood and interests. However, to provide a satisfactory user experience these systems need to be responsive. This led us to explore the feasibility of a client-side approach which could provide low latency whilst supporting many concurrent users.

In our approach all tasks except model training are implemented on the client system using two components downloaded from the server:

1. A recommender model which is trained and rebuilt at periodic intervals by the server.
2. A recommender engine which implements prediction, ranking and filtering.

Since both of these components are static files, which can be cached, the approach is easily scalable to a large number of users. The recommender system is also easier to manage and deploy as the complexity and processing requirements of the server are reduced. The responsiveness becomes independent of the load on the server and the round-trip delay to the server is eliminated.

RecSys '13, October 12–16, 2013, Hong Kong, China.
ACM 978-1-4503-2409-0/13/10.
http://dx.doi.org/10.1145/2507157.2508220

However, the client-side approach is only practical when there is a limited number of recommendable items since the model size generally scales with the number of items. Consideration must also be given to the fact that the recommender model would be in the public domain and whether it contains any sensitive data.

2. IMPLEMENTATION

The context of our work is an online TV and radio catch-up service where programmes are available on demand for 7 days after broadcast. In this application the number of programmes available at any one time is relatively small so the client-side approach is very practical.

Theoretically, any algorithm which supports the incremental addition of new users and their feedback would be suitable. For our initial implementations we have used either the Weighted Item k-NN or the Weighted Item Attribute k-NN algorithm as implemented in the MyMediaLite Recommender System Library [2] which is used to produce the required recommender models. We use a k value of 20 as this gave good results in our quantitative evaluations. The recommender model in this algorithm is a sparse correlation matrix which lists the nearest neighbors for each item and their weights.

In our prototype implementation the recommender model is embedded in a JavaScript file. This file also carries some basic metadata for each programme (e.g. title, locator and genre) which is provided for filtering and presentation purposes. The model describes around 700 programmes and is typically about 120 KB including metadata. However the size could be reduced substantially by using a binary format.

The recommender engine is also implemented in JavaScript. It accepts positive and negative binary user preferences, as these match the requirements of our applications, but could be adapted to other rating schemes. The recommendations can be filtered by genre or media type (i.e. TV or radio) and are typically produced in around 20 milliseconds. An open source implementation of this recommender engine is available with tools for producing the required model file [1].

3. EVALUATION

The client-side recommender is currently under evaluation in user trials of two prototype applications.

[1] http://github.com/bbcrd/clientside-recommender

3.1 Drag and Drop Recommender

The first application is a TV and radio programme recommender system designed for tablets and personal computers[2]. It provides a simple drag-and-drop user interface as shown in Figure 1.

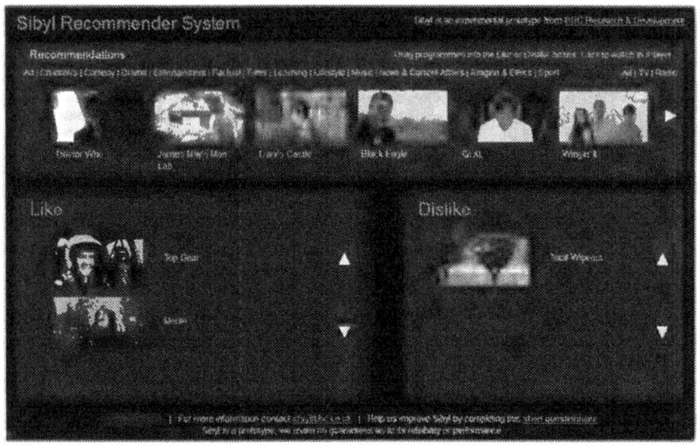

Figure 1. Drag-and-drop recommender system.

Users are presented with a scrollable list of programme recommendations which they can filter by genre and media type. The initial ordering of the list is determined by the overall popularity of each programme. The user is able to express explicit preferences by dragging individual programmes into "like" and "dislike" boxes positioned below. These preferences are immediately used by the client-side recommender to re-rank the programmes and refresh the recommendation list.

Initially, the application was implemented using a server-based recommender system and there was a noticeable and variable lag between each user input and the refresh process. With the client-side approach the delay is imperceptible.

Participants in the trial are asked to find programmes to watch using the application and then complete the associated questionnaire.

3.2 ViSTA-TV Clip-based Recommender

The second application is a TV programme recommender system which provides a continuous sequence of programme clips. The user can either skip or add each programme to their playlist for later consumption. These two user actions are interpreted as negative and positive user feedback respectively. The recommender engine uses this implicit user feedback to update the ranking of the clips and select the next clip to be presented. The mobile version of this application is shown in Figure 2.

In the present implementation the programme clips are streamed by the server. However, the clips could also be downloaded, allowing the application to function when the user is offline. This offline capability would only be possible with a client-side recommender.

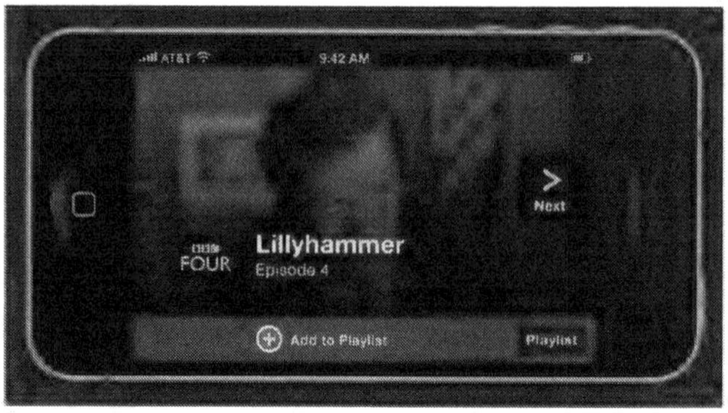

Figure 2. Clip-based recommender system.

This application was developed within the ViSTA-TV EU-funded collaborative research project[3] which is developing a stream processing engine to provide recommendations based on a real-time analysis of IPTV viewing data and media content.

4. CONCLUSIONS

An alternative, client-side approach to the implementation of web-based recommender systems has been presented which can be used to create highly responsive and easily scalable systems. The approach is highly effective in conversational recommender systems, which require a high degree of interaction with the user. It supports the possibility of privacy-preserving recommender systems, where the user can choose to retain all personal data on the client, and would allow personalised recommendations to be provided in unidirectional broadcast systems, where there is no return path.

5. ACKNOWLEDGMENTS

The authors would like to thank Anthony Onumonu, Dan Nuttall and Andrew Wood for their design and development work. The research leading to these results has received funding from the European Union Seventh Framework Programme FP7/2007-2011 under grant agreement n° 296126.

6. REFERENCES

[1] Knijnenburg, B. P., Willemsen, M. C., Gantner, Z., Soncu, H. and Newell, C. 2012. Explaining the user experience of recommender systems. *User Modeling and User-Adapted Interaction*. 22, 4-5 (Oct. 2012), 441-504. DOI= http://dx.doi.org/10.1007/s11257-011-9118-4

[2] Gantner, Z., Rendle, S., Freudenthaler, C. and Schmidt-Thieme, L. 2011. MyMediaLite: a free recommender system library. *Proceedings of the 5th ACM conference on Recommender Systems*, RecSys 2011. 305-308. DOI= http://dx.doi.org/10.1145/2043932.2043989

---

[2] http://sibyl.prototyping.bbc.co.uk/

[3] http://vista-tv.eu

Sage: Recommender Engine as a Cloud Service

Royi Ronen, Noam Koenigstein, Elad Ziklik, Mikael Sitruk, Ronen Yaari, Neta Haiby-Weiss
Microsoft Israel
{royir,noamko,eladz,mikaels,royaari,netahw}@microsoft.com

ABSTRACT

Project Sage is Microsoft's all-purpose recommender system, designed and deployed as an ultra-high scale cloud service. Sage focuses on both state of the art research and high scale robust implementation. In the research front, we demonstrate new pre-processing and cleaning techniques, a novel probabilistic matrix factorization model for implicit one-class data, and a relatively new evaluation framework. In the engineering front, we present a working service deployed on the Microsoft Azure cloud, which provides easy-to-use interfaces to integrate a recommendation service into any website.

Categories and Subject Descriptors

H.2.8 [**Database Management**]: Data Applications - *Data Mining.*

Keywords

Recommender Systems, Cloud Services

1. INTRODUCTION

Personalized recommendation systems are becoming increasingly popular in many websites and online stores. While there is a clear demand for such systems, there are only few high-scale implementations to choose from. A notable example is *Apache Mahout*, which provides source code for several well-established recommendation algorithms. As opposed to Mahout, Sage is a live service on the Microsoft Azure cloud, which exposes easy-to-use interfaces and a dashboard to design and train models, as well as to explore personalized recommendations and item-to-item relations. Our service integrates several novel algorithms, to form an all-purpose recommender, based on one-class implicit feedback.

Figure 1 depicts our system overview. There are 5 main stages: (1) Data collection; (2) Data cleaning and feature selection; (3) Variational Bayes matrix factorization; (4) Qualitative and quantitative evaluation; (5) Online service.

RecSys'13, October 12–16, 2013, Hong Kong, China.
ACM 978-1-4503-2409-0/13/10.
http://dx.doi.org/10.1145/2507157.2508221.

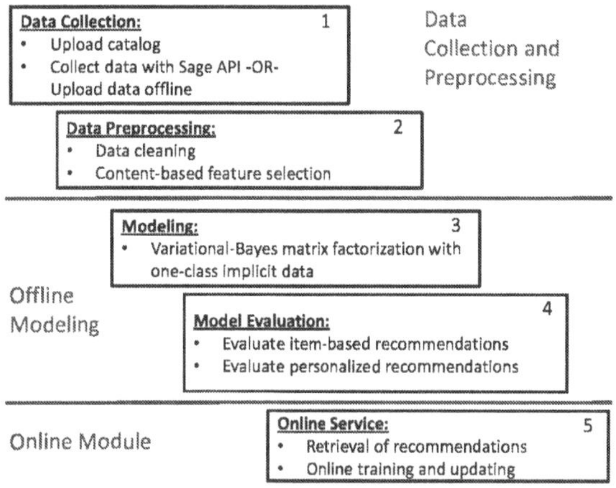

Figure 1: Sage System Overview

2. SAGE OVERVIEW

We present an overview of Sage, by describing each of the aforementioned stages in terms of user flow and back-end algorithms.

Data Collection and Preprocessing. While much research into recommender systems is focused on numeric ratings, the common case in most real-world systems is non-numeric implicit data. Under this setting, only positive observations are available – hence the name *one-class* data [6]. Sage recommendations are based on implicit one-class data, e.g., purchase history, movies watched, etc. We do not assume the presence of numeric ratings or even binary ratings.

Data collection requires uploading an items catalog. The catalog may also include item meta-data features. The training data can be either dynamically collected from a website using embedded scripts or uploaded offline as a file. The preprocessing consists of data cleaning, in which non-informative data rows are pruned, e.g., items that were purchased only few times and alone. If item meta-data is included in the catalog, we also employ a novel feature selection algorithm in order to choose a subset of meta-data features which are most informative with regard to collaborative filtering. Our feature selection algorithm is described in [8].

Offline Modeling. Recommender systems based on Matrix Factorization (MF) models have repeatedly demonstrated better accuracy than other methods, such as nearest neighbor models and restricted Boltzmann machines [1, 4]. How-

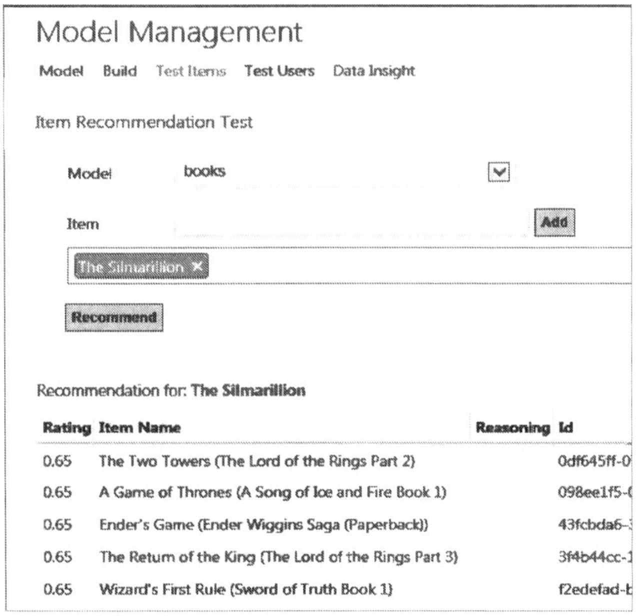

Figure 2: Qualitative evaluation dashboard (with books recommendations)

ever, MF models based on one-class data are relatively new. Sage uses a novel in-house probabilistic Bayesian algorithm that was recently published in [7]. Based on this model, Sage computes probabilities p_{mn} – the probability that user m will consume item n. In this process, Sage also employs items meta-data in a similar fashion to [5]. At the modeling stage, we also extract item-to-item relations (similarities) for common co-occurring item pairs.

After the training stage, Sage performs an evaluation process. A quantitative evaluation is computed in terms of *Mean Percentile Rank* (MPR), a relatively new metric in studies of implicit feedback recommenders [9]. Qualitative evaluation is also provided in the form of an interactive dashboard. The dashboard allows users to choose any subset of items, and generate appropriate recommendations as well as explore item-to-item relations (see Figure 2).

Online Module. The online module enables retrieving recommendations either for existing users or for new users (i.e., users not present in the training data). In the former case, recommendations are based on past interactions collected during the data collection stage. In the latter case, Sage quickly trains the model, on the fly, to include new users based on a short list of items that the new user is currently considering (click log, shopping cart, etc.). Similarly, Sage can update existing users online, based on new observations.

The Sage APIs. As discussed above, an API is provided to allow simple embedding of the recommender service in a live website. Figure 3 shows an example of the Sage API. The reader will notice methods to build a model and to retrieve item-to-item relations and personalized recommendations (*I2IRecommendation* and *U2I Recommendation*, respectively). Automatic data collection is performed by embedding a Javascript snippet on each item page. Usage information about the item (purchases, views, etc.) is collected and uploaded directly to Sage.

```
//-------------
// Sage API
//-------------
Gate.Login(http, userName, password);
var model = Models.CreateModel(http, modelName);
Models.UploadCatalogFileForAModel(http, model.Id, catalogPath);
Models.UploadUsageFileForAModel(http, model.Id, usagePath);
Models.ListModels(http);
Build.BuildModel(http, model);
Build.ReportModelsProgress(http);
Models.DeleteModel(http, model.Id);

Recommend.I2IRecommendation(http, modelId, itemId);
Recommend.I2IRecommendationWithListOfItems(http, modelId, history);
Recommend.U2IRecommendation(http, modelId, userId);
Recommend.U2IRecommendationWithHistory(http, modelId, userId, history);
```

Figure 3: Using Sage API in C# code: upload data, build model and retrieve recommendations.

3. FUTURE WORK

Research and development at Sage are planned to be extended in several directions. We wish to implement additional recommendation algorithms. In some scenarios, we believe that users may benefit from other algorithms, such as non-probabilistic matrix factorization, neighborhood-based recommender systems, content-based filtering, and hybrid models [2].

Real world models are best evaluated against real-world results. We also plan to develop an experimentation framework [3] to evaluate different models based on metrics such as Click-Through Rate (CTR), or conversion rate, rather than just offline metrics such as MPR.

4. REFERENCES

[1] Lessons from the Netflix prize challenge. R. M. Bell and Y. Koren. SIGKDD Explor. Newsl. 2007.

[2] Hybrid Recommender Systems: Survey and Experiments. Robin D. Burke. In User Model. User-Adapt. Interaction, 2002.

[3] Online Experiments: Practical Lessons. R. Kohavi, R. Longbotham. T. Walker. Online Experiments: Practical Lessons, 2010.

[4] The Yahoo! Music Dataset and KDD-Cup'11. G. Dror, N. Koenigstein, Y. Koren, M. Weimer. Journal Of Machine Learning Research, 2012.

[5] Xbox Movies Recommendations: Variational Bayes Matrix Factorization with Embedded Feature Selection. N. Koenigstein, U. Paquet. In ACM RecSys 2013.

[6] One-Class Collaborative Filtering. R. Pan, Y. Zhou, B. Cao, N.N. Liu, R. Lukose, M. Scholz, Q. Yang. IEEE International Conference on Data Mining, 2008.

[7] One-class Collaborative Filtering with Random Graphs. U. Paquet, N. Koenigstein. In Proc. WWW 2013, 999–1008.

[8] Selecting Content-Based Features for Collaborative Filtering Recommenders. R. Ronen, N. Koenigstein, E. Ziklik and N. Nice. In ACM RecSys 2013.

[9] Training and testing of recommender systems on data missing not at random. H. Steck. In KDD, 2010.

The Fifth ACM RecSys Workshop on Recommender Systems and the Social Web

Bamshad Mobasher
School of Computing
DePaul University, USA
mobasher@cs.depaul.edu

Dietmar Jannach
Dept. of Computer Science
TU Dortmund, Germany
dietmar.jannach@udo.edu

Werner Geyer
IBM Research
Cambridge, MA,USA
werner.geyer@us.ibm.com

1. WORKSHOP SUMMARY

The emergence of what is called the social web and the continuing stream of new applications and community-based platforms including Facebook, Twitter, LinkedIn and others had a substantial impact on recommender systems research and practice over the last years in different ways.

First, today's web users are more willing to share more about themselves than before the Web 2.0, thus providing more information sources that can be leveraged in the user modeling and recommendation process. Furthermore, the newly available information sources can not only be used to optimize the recommendations for an individual user, but can also help to identify more general patterns and trends in the behavior of the community that can be exploited by other applications.

Second, personalization, information filtering and recommendation are often the central functionality of many of these social web based applications. On typical social networks, users for example get recommendations for news to read, songs to listen to, groups to join, friends to follow, people to connect or jobs that might be interesting.

These developments lead to different challenges to be addressed in recommender systems research. On the one hand, for example, the question arises of how to effectively combine the huge variety of information sources for improved recommendations. On the other hand, regarding the new opportunities for applying recommender systems in social web environments, in many cases new techniques are required to address the particularities of the domain or to deal with scalability issues.

The *ACM RecSys 2013 Workshop on Recommender Systems and the Social Web* aims to be a platform for researchers from academia and industry as well as for practitioners to present and discuss the various challenges and possible solutions related to all aspects of social web recommendations. The call for papers correspondingly covered a variety of topics in this area including all sorts of applications of recommender systems technology and their interfaces; collective knowledge creation and topic emergence; context-aware and group recommendation approaches; and case studies and empirical evaluations.

This year's workshop is already the fifth in a series of successful workshops co-located with the ACM Conference on Recommender Systems since 2009. Overall, we received 17 submissions from authors of 13 different countries, which demonstrates the continuing interest of the community in this field.

The submitted papers were thoroughly reviewed and selected for presentation at the workshop by a program committee of international experts in the field. The papers addressed a number of different topics and contained proposals for a number of new approaches to build better social web recommender systems. In the context of the novel applications areas for recommenders on social web platforms, the papers for example dealt with the recommendation of messages (posts), events, locations, tags as well as general information items based on social web information. Beside these already "traditional" types of social web recommender applications, some of the papers also introduced very novel areas in which social web information can be leveraged for recommendations such as for investment decisions or the problem of group formation. Other papers finally focused on approaches to further improve the quality of recommendations based on social network information, the social graph as well as sensor information.

2. ADDITIONAL AUTHORS

Jill Freyne, CSIRO ICT Center, Australia,
`jill.freyne@csiro.au`
Andreas Hotho, Universität Würzburg, Germany,
`hotho@informatik.uni-wuerzburg.de`
Sarabjot Singh Anand, Algorithmic Insight, India,
`sarabjot.singh@gmail.com`
Ido Guy, IBM Research, Haifa, Israel,
`ido@il.ibm.com`

3. WORKSHOP WEB SITE

The workshop web site can be found at:
`http://ls13-www.cs.uni-dortmund.de/homepage/rsweb2013`

Categories and Subject Descriptors

H.3.3 [**Information Search and Retrieval**]; H.4.2 [**Decision Support Systems**]

Keywords

Recommender Systems, Personalization, Social Web

RecSys '13, October 12–16 2013, Hong Kong, China.
ACM ACM 978-1-4503-2409-0/13/09.
http://dx.doi.org/10.1145/2507157.2508001 .

Workshop on Human Decision Making in Recommender Systems: Decisions@RecSys'13

Li Chen
Hong Kong Baptist University
224 Waterloo Road, Hong Kong, China
lichen@comp.hkbu.edu.hk

Marco de Gemmis
University of Bari Aldo Moro
Via Orabona 4, Bari, Italy
marco.degemmis@uniba.it

Alexander Felfernig
Graz University of Technology
Inffeldgasse 16b/2, Graz, Austria
alexander.felfernig@ist.tugraz.at

Pasquale Lops
University of Bari Aldo Moro
Via Orabona 4, Bari, Italy
pasquale.lops@uniba.it

Francesco Ricci
Free University of Bozen-Bolzano
Piazza Domenicani 3, Bolzano, Italy
fricci@unibz.it

Giovanni Semeraro
University of Bari Aldo Moro
Via Orabona 4, Bari, Italy
giovanni.semeraro@uniba.it

Martijn C. Willemsen
Eindhoven University of Technology
P.O. Box 513, Eindhoven, The Netherlands
M.C.Willemsen@tue.nl

ABSTRACT

A primary function of recommender systems is to help their users to make better choices and decisions. The overall goal of the workshop is to analyse and discuss novel techniques and approaches for supporting effective and efficient human decision making in different types of recommendation scenarios. The submitted papers discuss a wide range of topics, from core algorithmic issues to the management of the human computer interaction.

Categories and Subject Descriptors

H.4.2 [**Information Systems Applications**]: Types of Systems—*Decision support*; H.3.3 [**Information Storage and Retrieval**]: Information Search and Retrieval—*Information filtering*

General Terms

Algorithms, Experimentation, Human Factors, Theory

Keywords

Decision Making; Decision Psychology; Recommendation Algorithms; Decision Biases

RecSys'13, October 12–16, 2013, Hong Kong, China.
ACM 978-1-4503-2409-0/13/10.
http://dx.doi.org/10.1145/2507157.2508002.

1. OVERVIEW

Users interact with recommender systems to obtain useful information about products or services that may be of interest for them. But, while users are interacting with a recommender system to fulfill a primary task, which is usually the selection of one or more items, they are facing several other decision problems. For instance, they may be requested to select specific feature values (e.g., camera's size, zoom) as criteria for a search, or they could have to identify features to be used in a critiquing based recommendation session, or they may need to select a repair proposal for inconsistent user preferences when interacting with a recommender. In all these scenarios, and in many others, users of recommender systems are facing decision tasks.

The complexity of decision tasks, limited cognitive resources of users, and the tendency to keep the overall decision effort as low as possible is modeled by theories that conjecture "bounded rationality", i.e., users are exploiting decision heuristics rather than trying to take an optimal decision [4]. Furthermore, preferences of users will likely change throughout a recommendation session, i.e., preferences are constructed in a specific decision context and users may not fully know their preferences beforehand [2]. Within the scope of a decision process, preferences are strongly influenced by the goals of the customer, existing cognitive constraints, and the personal experience of the customer [6]. Due to the fact that users do not have stable preferences, the interaction mechanisms provided by a recommender system and the information shown to a user can have an enormous impact on the outcome of a decision process [3]. For example, some authors analyzed the existence of anchoring effect in recommender systems and show the impacts of different types of rating drifts on a user's rating behavior [1, 7].

Theories from decision psychology and cognitive psychology have already elaborated a number of methodological tools for explaining and predicting the user behavior in these scenarios. In [5], the authors pointed out their importance for recommender systems research, but current systems hardly integrate this knowledge in the computational model. The major goal of this workshop is to establish a platform for industry and academia to present and discuss new ideas and research results that are related to the topic of human decision making in recommender systems. The workshop is focused on the role of decision theories in advancing recommender systems research and applications. The main topics of the workshop are:

- Theories, algorithms and applications
  - Decision theories in recommender systems (e.g., priming, framing, and decoy effects)
  - Trust inspiring recommendation
  - Persuasive recommendation (e.g., argumentation-aware recommendation)
  - The role of emotions and personality in recommender systems
  - Detection and avoidance of decision biases
- User modeling and preference elicitation
  - Modeling user information search and decision making processes in recommender systems
  - Active approaches to preference elicitation
- User interfaces
  - User interfaces for decision making
  - Explanations in Recommender Systems
- Evaluation
  - User perceptions leading to the acceptance of recommendations
  - Empirical studies and innovative metrics of system performance

In particular, papers submitted to this third edition of the workshop have focused on:

- Preference and recommendation aggregation techniques for group recommender systems;
- The role of emotions in recommender systems;
- Interaction design for better decision support in recommender systems;
- Techniques for detecting relevant contextual conditions which influence the users' decision making process;
- Algorithms for avoiding biased recommendations and avoid the Filter Bubble;
- User profiles based on explicit knowledge rather than latent factors;
- Hybrid approaches for improved accuracy and efficiency;
- Analysis of the usage of gestural interaction patterns for mobile recommender systems.

2. FURTHER INFORMATION

The workshop material (list of accepted papers, invited talk, and the workshop schedule) can be found at the Decisions@RecSys 2013 workshop webpage: http://recex.ist.tugraz.at.

3. REFERENCES

[1] G. Adomavicius, J. Bockstedt, S. Curley, and J. Zhang. Recommender systems, consumer preferences, and anchoring effects. In *RecSys 2011 Workshop on Human Decision Making in Recommender Systems*, pages 35–42, 2011.

[2] J. Bettman, M. Luce, and J. Payne. Constructive consumer choice processes. *Journal of Consumer Research*, 25(3):187–217, 1998.

[3] D. Cosley, S. Lam, I. Albert, J. Konstan, and J. Riedl. Is seeing believing?: how recommender system interfaces affect users' opinions. In *Proceedings of the SIGCHI Conference on Human Factors in Computing Systems*, CHI '03, pages 585–592, New York, NY, USA, 2003. ACM.

[4] D. Kahneman. Maps of bounded rationality: psychology for behavioral economics. *The American Economic Review*, 93(5):1449–1475, 2003.

[5] M. Mandl, A. Felfernig, E. Teppan, and M. Schubert. Consumer decision making in knowledge-based recommendation. *Journal of Intelligent Information Systems*, 37(1):1–22, Aug. 2011.

[6] C. Warren, A. McGraw, and L. VanBoven. Values and preferences: defining preference construction. *Wiley Interdisciplinary Review: Cognitive Science*, 2(2):193–205, 2010.

[7] J. Zhang. Anchoring effects of recommender systems. In *Proceedings of the fifth ACM conference on Recommender systems*, RecSys '11, pages 375–378, New York, NY, USA, 2011. ACM.

Workshop and Challenge on News Recommender Systems

Mozhgan Tavakolifard[1], Jon Atle Gulla[1], Kevin C. Almeroth[2], Frank Hopfgartner[3]
Workshop organizers
[1]Norwegian University of Science & Techn.
{mozhgan, jag}@idi.ntnu.no
[2]University of California, Santa Barbara,
almeroth@cs.ucsb.edu
[3]Technische Universität Berlin,
frank.hopfgartner@tu-berlin.de

Benjamin Kille[1], Till Plumbaum[1], Andreas Lommatzsch[1], Torben Brodt[2], Arthur Bucko[2], Tobias Heintz[2]
Challenge organizers
[1]Technische Universität Berlin
{firstname.lastname}@tu-berlin.de
[2]Plista GmbH, {tb, ab, thz}@plista.com

ABSTRACT

Recommending news articles entails additional requirements to recommender systems. Such requirements include special consumption patterns, fluctuating item collections, and highly sparse user profiles. This workshop (NRS'13@RecSys) brought together researchers and practitioners around the topics of designing and evaluating novel news recommender systems. Additionally, we offered a challenge allowing participants to evaluate their recommendation algorithms with actual user feedback.

Categories and Subject Descriptors

H.3.3 [**Information Search and Retrieval**]

Keywords

News; Recommender Systems

1. OVERVIEW

News article recommendation differs in several ways from other well-known types of recommender systems such as for music and movies: 1) **Freshness** represents an important aspect. Sometimes, freshness is deemed more important than relevancy. On one hand, users are usually interested in most recent news. On the other hand, users sometimes are interested to read previous relevant articles [4, 9, 10, 12, 17, 18], 2) **Large volume** of news articles make this domain different from other types of Web objects. News articles tend to be in flood within a short period of time, requiring much more computation for recommendation [3, 6, 10, 14, 15], 3) Similarity between news articles does not necessarily reflect their **relatedness**. For instance, two news articles might share a majority of words. Still, their actual topic might differ [13], 4) News are typically published in a rather unstructured format [15]. In contrast, structured data such as social graphs facilitate pre-processing steps, 5) Most news articles describe the occurring of specific events. Online news readers' interests are highly correlated to so-called named entities. Such named entities describe who was involved in the event. News readers might have special **entity preferences** on some particular events which recommender systems can barely predict. Still, we struggle detecting such preferences due to little information on the user available, 6) **Serendipities** (i. e., variety in recommended news articles) represent a crucial property of a news recommender system. Contrarily to music recommendations, users avoid to re-consume an item. Thus, news recommender systems are required to provide diverse sets of items in order to assure not to recommend monotonously. Users might have great interest in news articles for which the content does not match with the information the system has gathered about the user [2, 5, 7, 16], 7) **Breaking or trendy news** might have a high relevance even though the appear completely unrelated to the individual user profile [12]. Popularity and recency of news articles change dramatically along with the time, which differentiates other news items, such as products and movies, rendering traditional recommendation methods ineffective, 8) it has not yet established consensus on how to **evaluate** news recommender systems. We typically observe implicit preferences as users interact with news portals. Those preferences do not exhibit a graded relevance. Thus, well-established evaluation criteria based on ratings (e.g., root mean squared error) cannot be applied, 9) Recommender systems are known to struggle with so-called **"cold-start users"** (i. e., users form whom no preferences are available yet). News portals typically refrain to require users to login prior to read news articles. Hence, there is a large fraction of users who appear to be "cold-start users" [4, 6, 9, 10, 11]. 10) The lack of sufficiently many interaction to established trustworthy **user profiles** entails further challenges. Inferring interest signals suffers from incomplete profiles. News providers do generally not require their users to create own user profiles and users consume news articles anonymously. Therefore, news recommender systems have to cope without explicit user profiles. Tracking users suffers from changing session identifiers, access limiting browser setups, and shared computers. This increases the sparsity of data as well [3, 10, 15].

Another challenge related to the context arises from the increasingly frequent use of mobile devices to read news articles such as tablets and smart phones [1]. Those have a limited space available to display news and related recommendations. News recommender systems have to deal with this issue thus applying suited layout mechanisms to fit the content to the available screen.

Finally, news recommender systems face numerous technical challenges. Those challenges include minimizing response time improve user experience, scaling to the large amount of requests

RecSys'13, October 12–16, 2013, Hong Kong, China.
ACM 978-1-4503-2409-0/13/10.
http://dx.doi.org/10.1145/2507157.2508004.

to avoid time outs, providing flexibility to incorporate new recommendation methods or adjust parameter settings for existing implementations, and guarantee a reliable service whom user can access at any time.

2. SCOPE

This workshop aimed at creating an interdisciplinary community focusing on the design issues for news recommender systems and promoting collaboration opportunities between researchers and practitioners. We brought together researchers as well as practitioners around the topics of designing and evaluating novel news recommender systems in order to: (1) share research on news recommendation techniques and evaluation methodologies, (2) explore key challenges in the area, and (3) identify emerging topics.

2.1 Workshop

The topics of papers submitted to the workshop can be summarized as follows: recommendation techniques suited for news recommendation, tracking the evolution of news over time, evaluation approaches, the interplay of news and social-media data, user interface for news portals and their implications to news recommendation, news mining and analytics, news reader behavioral models, semantic and news context analysis, user profiling and preference elicitation, news recommendations on mobile platforms, and information retrieval in news collections. The papers covered a wide range of different perspective on the field. The accepted papers included a practitioners perspective based on an actual news recommender systems and their data on the one hand. On the other hand, a survey on the state-of-the-art of news recommender systems and their inherent challenges was conducted to illustrate the research perspective.

2.2 Challenge

Prior to the workshop, we offered researchers as well as practitioners the chance to interact with a real-time news recommender system. We released an off-line data set [8] for bootstrapping purposes. This data set contained more than 84 million interactions recorded over a 4 week period. Subsequently, participants could directly interact with a news recommender system providing news on several news portals in the time frame from August 15 - September 15, 2013. The participants received actual recommendation request and transmit recommendations. Thus, we were able to mimic the actual requirements for news recommender systems. Those requirements included to handle a large amount of request in real-time with a fixed response time limit. At the workshop we presented evaluation results of the challenge.

3. FURTHER INFORMATION

The workshop material (list of accepted papers, invited talk, and the workshop schedule) can be found at the workshop webpage: `https://sites.google.com/site/newsrec2013/home`. The workshop proceedings are published in the ACM International Conference Proceedings Series (ICPS). Papers related could not be submitted before the conference deadline. The challenge-related papers which have been accepted are published as CEUR proceedings.

4. REFERENCES

[1] D. Billsus and M. Pazzani. User modeling for adaptive news access. *User modeling and user-adapted interaction*, 10(2):147–180, 2000.

[2] H. L. Borges and A. C. Lorena. A survey on recommender systems for news data. In *Smart Information and Knowledge Management*, pages 129–151. Springer, 2010.

[3] A. S. Das, M. Datar, A. Garg, and S. Rajaram. Google news personalization: scalable online collaborative filtering. In *Proceedings of the 16th international conference on World Wide Web*, pages 271–280. ACM, 2007.

[4] B. Fortuna, C. Fortuna, and D. Mladenić. Real-time news recommender system. In *Machine Learning and Knowledge Discovery in Databases*, pages 583–586. Springer, 2010.

[5] E. Gabrilovich, S. Dumais, and E. Horvitz. Newsjunkie: providing personalized newsfeeds via analysis of information novelty. In *Proc. of the 13th int. conf. on WWW*, pages 482–490. ACM, 2004.

[6] F. Garcin, C. Dimitrakakis, and B. Faltings. Personalized news recommendation with context trees. *arXiv preprint arXiv:1303.0665*, 2013.

[7] L. Iaquinta, M. De Gemmis, P. Lops, G. Semeraro, M. Filannino, and P. Molino. Introducing serendipity in a content-based recommender system. In *HIS*, pages 168–173. IEEE, 2008.

[8] B. Kille, F. Hopfgartner, T. Brodt, and T. Heintz. The plista dataset. In *Proc. International News Recommender Systems Workshop and Challenge*, 2013. to appear.

[9] H. J. Lee and S. J. Park. Moners: A news recommender for the mobile web. *Expert Systems with Applications*, 32(1):143–150, 2007.

[10] L. Li, D. Wang, T. Li, D. Knox, and B. Padmanabhan. Scene: a scalable two-stage personalized news recommendation system. In *SIGIR*, pages 125–134, 2011.

[11] C. Lin, R. Xie, L. Li, Z. Huang, and T. Li. Premise: personalized news recommendation via implicit social experts. In *Proc. of the 21st ACM int. conf. on Information and knowledge management*, pages 1607–1611. ACM, 2012.

[12] J. Liu, P. Dolan, and E. R. Pedersen. Personalized news recommendation based on click behavior. In *Proceedings of the 15th international conference on Intelligent user interfaces*, pages 31–40. ACM, 2010.

[13] Y. Lv, T. Moon, P. Kolari, Z. Zheng, X. Wang, and Y. Chang. Learning to model relatedness for news recommendation. In *Proc. WWW*, pages 57–66. ACM, 2011.

[14] P. Resnick, N. Iacovou, M. Suchak, P. Bergstrom, and J. Riedl. Grouplens: an open architecture for collaborative filtering of netnews. In *CSCW*, pages 175–186. ACM, 1994.

[15] Saranya.k.g and G. S. Sadhasivam. A personalized online news recommendation system. *International Journal of Computer Applications*, 57(18):6–14, November 2012.

[16] V. Vinod, R. A. Jim, and C. P. S. George. News sync: Three reasons to visualize news better. *HCIR 2010*, page 45, 2010.

[17] H. Wen, L. Fang, and L. Guan. A hybrid approach for personalized recommendation of news on the web. *Expert Systems with Applications*, 39(5):5806–5814, 2012.

[18] K. F. Yeung and Y. Yang. A proactive personalized mobile news recommendation system. In *Developments in E-systems Engineering*, pages 207–212. IEEE, 2010.

Prior Ratings: A New Information Source for Recommender Systems in E-Commerce

Guibing Guo
Nanyang Technological University, Singapore
gguo1@e.ntu.edu.sg

Jie Zhang
Nanyang Technological University, Singapore
zhangj@ntu.edu.sg

Daniel Thalmann
Nanyang Technological University, Singapore
danielthalmann@ntu.edu.sg

Neil Yorke-Smith
American University of Beirut, and University of Cambridge
nysmith@aub.edu.lb

ABSTRACT

Lack of motivation to provide ratings and eligibility to rate generally only after purchase restrain the effectiveness of recommender systems and contribute to the well-known data sparsity and cold start problems. This paper proposes a new information source for recommender systems, called *prior ratings*. Prior ratings are based on users' experiences of virtual products in a mediated environment, and they can be submitted prior to purchase. A conceptual model of prior ratings is proposed, integrating the environmental factor *presence* whose effects on product evaluation have not been studied previously. A user study conducted in website and virtual store modalities demonstrates the validity of the conceptual model, in that users are more willing and confident to provide prior ratings in virtual environments.

Categories and Subject Descriptors

H.5.2 [**Information Interfaces and Presentation**]: User Interfaces—*Evaluation/methodology*

Keywords

Recommender systems, Prior ratings, Data sparsity, Cold start, User study, Virtual product.

1. INTRODUCTION

User ratings are crucial for recommender systems in e-commerce in order to provide quality personalized product recommendations. However, users can lack motivation to provide ratings, and ratings can generally be given only after purchase (how can I share my experience of an item I have not tried?). Without sufficient rating information for preference modelling, the effectiveness of recommender systems is hindered—as seen in well-known problems such as *data sparsity* and *cold start* [3]. Although many approaches have been proposed to address these problems [3, 4], only few researchers have attempted to elicit more user ratings from the perspective of user interfaces, so as to inherently mitigate the severity of these problems.

RecSys'13, October 12–16, 2013, Hong Kong, China.

ACM 978-1-4503-2409-0/13/10 ...$15.00.
http://dx.doi.org/10.1145/2507157.2507200.

Contemporary websites, e.g., brides.com and Ray-ban.com are implementing novel interfaces and interactions through which users can virtually try on different wedding dresses and glasses, to better elicit user preferences. However, the available media and interactions are limited in comparison with those of virtual reality (VR), e.g., SecondLife.com which can provide users with immersive virtual product experiences. Users can experience media more richly and can interact in real time with *virtual products*—the 'second existence' of real products in a mediated environment.

While the emergence of 3D VR environments offers more adequate information which can be used to model user preference, research on recommender systems in VR is still in its infancy. Shah et al. [10] recommend to users locations of interest by analyzing users' login data to help them navigate in VR. Hu and Hang [5] design a system to recommend virtual furniture according to users' interest and requirements. Although a controlled prototype was implemented, the features of VR are not exploited to elicit user ratings.

This paper proposes a new information source, called *prior ratings*, built upon virtual product experiences. A conceptual model of prior ratings is proposed to provide a principled foundation, integrating the environmental factor *presence* whose effects on product evaluation have not been studied previously. For evaluation, we conduct user studies in two different modalities. The results demonstrate the validity of the conceptual model under our experimental settings. To our knowledge, this is the first work that defines and investigates the concept of prior ratings.

2. PRIOR RATINGS

We define the term *prior ratings* as users' assessment of products in the light of their *virtual product experiences*, referring to the psychological and emotional states that users undergo while interacting with virtual products in a medi-

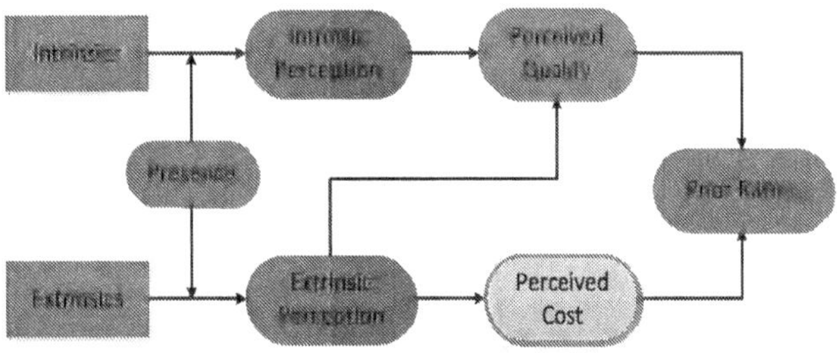

Figure 1: The conceptual model of prior ratings

ated environment [8]. Hence, prior ratings are reported by users based on their interactions with virtual products in a mediated environment, and they can be issued prior to purchase or after purchase (if any). We refer to the 'standard' type of ratings derived from 'posterior' product experiences as *posterior ratings.* By 'posterior', we mean experiences of a tangible product obtained via direct trials or use of the product in a physical environment. Since tangible products can be fully experienced usually only after purchase, posterior ratings are primarily post-purchase ratings. Prior ratings and posterior ratings are distinct and complementary in that they reflect different forms of user experiences.

It is reported that VR real-time interactions enable users to possess a strong sense of being in a mediated environment and gain a lifelike shopping experience [8]. Hence, we draw a hypothesis as follows.

HYPOTHESIS 1. *Users are more willing to provide prior ratings to the items (e.g., products) that they have interacted with in VR than in WS.*

Jiang and Benbasat [7] contend that virtual products in VR help improve the perceived *diagnosticity* of products—the extent to which users believe a particular shopping experience is helpful to understand the quality and performance of a product. Therefore, users may feel more capable of forming direct, intuitive and concrete opinions about products in VR than in WS.

HYPOTHESIS 2. *(a) Users have more confidence in providing prior ratings in VR than in WS; (b) the average value of prior ratings in VR is closer to that of posterior ratings than that of prior ratings in WS.*

Conceptual Model. A conceptual model of prior ratings is illustrated in Figure 1. Such a model allows a principled basis for the elicitation and analysis of prior ratings. For a specific product, a number of intrinsic and extrinsic *attributes* are associated. In different environments, the perceptions of these attributes can differ according to the types of media and interactions that deliver information about them. The intrinsic and extrinsic *perceptions* indicate the quality of products as perceived directly and indirectly, respectively. In contrast, the *perceived cost* (e.g., time, price) refers to the cost that users have to bear in order to obtain the products. A prior rating is an overall evaluation of preference of products in terms of both perceived quality and cost.

Presence is defined as subjects' sense of "being there", the extent to which they experience the virtual environments as real or present and temporarily ignore where they are physically present [11]. In this paper, presence is captured as the extent to which being in a mediated environment feels like being in a real environment[1], given the richness in media and interactions. Since information concerning product attributes is conveyed by media channels and user interactions, presence can be an important environmental factor that will influence the perceptions of product attributes.

HYPOTHESIS 3. *Presence has positive influence on the perceptions of both intrinsic and extrinsic attributes.*

Intrinsic attributes (e.g., workmanship, size) have a direct impact on perceived quality during the goal-directed process of pre-purchase product evaluation [2]. In this paper, we classify intrinsic attributes into three types, namely *appearance*, *material*, and *functionality*. Appearance refers to the attributes related to the superficial representation of products, such as patterns, form, size, etc. Material refers to the attributes associated with what products are made of, such as fabric properties, weight, etc. Functionality refers to the attributes indicating the utility of products or the actions that products can perform or that can be performed on products. For example, an electronic watch contains the functionality of stopwatch and it may 'fit' someone well.

Extrinsic attributes (e.g., price) have no direct indications of perceived quality. Rather, they are often used as cues to infer the quality of products when the information of intrinsic attributes is incomplete [1]. In this case, price is often used by users to infer the quality of products [1]. Brand name serves as a 'shorthand' for perceived quality by providing users with a bundle of product information [6]. In contrast, store name also has a positive but small impact on perceived quality [9]. Other extrinsic attributes (e.g., warranty) may also have effects on perceived quality.

HYPOTHESIS 4. *Users depend more on extrinsic attributes than intrinsic attributes to evaluate the product quality in WS, whereas users depend more on intrinsic attributes than extrinsic attributes to evaluate the product quality in VR.*

Besides quality, extrinsic attributes also contribute to *perceived cost*, a combination of monetary (mainly price) and non-monetary (e.g., time, shipping) attributes.

Prior Ratings. In a pre-purchase phase, users go through a process (perhaps subconscious) of evaluating the benefits that they can get and the cost that they have to incur. The outcome of this process helps determine whether users will like the product in question. Other than perceived quality, we posit that prior ratings could also be positively enhanced if the perceived cost is acceptable. Intuitively, for a specific product interested in by a user in terms of quality, if the price of the product turns out to be acceptable, it is likely that the user will like the product as a whole.

HYPOTHESIS 5. *Perceived quality has significantly positive influence on prior ratings, and perceived cost will also positively influence prior ratings, if the price is acceptable.*

3. USER STUDY

Two kinds of mediated environments are developed: traditional 2D websites (WS) and 3D VR environments. They differ in richness of both media and of interactions through which product information can be delivered. Both user interfaces 'sell' our t-shirts whose source was the real-life commerce website 80stees.com. These 50 t-shirts have average

[1] See question 2 for the tested environments in Figure 2.

To what extent do you agree or disagree with the following statements?

For each t-shirt:

1. *The t-shirt has a good looking in terms of color, patterns, style, etc.*
2. *The t-shirt is made of good material.*
3. *The t-shirt fits you well.*
4. *The category of this t-shirt is of your favor.*
5. *The price of this t-shirt is acceptable, including price and shipping fees.*
6. *The website (virtual store) is well-designed.*
7. *In total, the quality of this t-shirt is good.*
8. *You need to spend a lot to obtain this t-shirt in price, time, effort, etc.*
9. *In total, this t-shirt is worthy purchasing.*
10. *Overall, you like this t-shirt.*

For each environment:

1. *You are confident about your ratings. When you gave ratings, you feel confident and no hesitations to make a judgement.*
2. *It feels the same that inspecting the t-shirt in the environment is just as if you were in a real store and had a real t-shirt in hand.*
3. *You are comfortable to give ratings in the tested environment.*
4. *You are (not) confident in your ratings because (state your reasons)*

For willingness (optional):

1. *Are you willing to rate the t-shirt of your interest or interacted with?*
2. *If yes, state your reason and indicate how confident in your ratings?*
3. *If no, state your reason. In what conditions, you will rate the t-shirts?*

Figure 2: Questions in the user study

posterior ratings (on 80stees.com) in the range [3.2, 4.9] (out of 5). The virtual store was built using OpenSimulator.org. T-shirts were displayed and arranged without a predefined order on the walls of virtual store. Users can interact with them by viewing, rotating, zooming, and even virtually trying on and customizing the t-shirts (on their avatar). They can also adjust the avatar's shape as desired. In contrast, no interactions were available in WS: users can only imagine what the t-shirt would be like from text descriptions and static images. Four attributes, namely appearance, material, fit and price are identified as the major concerns of users via a pilot study. Together with attributes store and category, the six attributes are selected for the experiments.

The user study consisted of one session, structured as follows. All subjects started with a tutorial video so as to get familiar with functionalities of user interfaces. Once subjects were comfortable, they proceeded. Each subject experienced and evaluated eight different t-shirts in each environment by giving ratings to the questions about product attributes. Rating values were integers from 1 ("strongly disagree") to 5 ("strongly agree"). Subjects could also add textual comments for each t-shirt. To eliminate the influence of ordering, subjects were randomly determined into two groups. Specifically, of 30 volunteers recruited on a university campus, 16 subjects executed the user study first in WS and then VR, and 14 proceeded inversely. In addition to t-shirts, the subjects were also asked to rate the environment regarding the confidence (and state their reasons) and comfort in giving ratings, and the feelings of sense of presence. Finally, subjects could opt to state whether and in which environment they are willing and prefer to provide prior ratings. The questions are shown in Figure 2.

For Hypothesis 1, of 19 subjects who answered our questions regarding the willingness to rate t-shirts, 18 gave positive responses. More specifically, most subjects preferred to rate products in VR (14) rather than in WS (2). Two other subjects did not explicitly state their preference. Most subjects expressed that the reasons were "it can provide more detail information" and "this environment (VR) has really high engagement. I'd like to share my feeling". Only one subject did not want to provide prior ratings ("time consuming") but did indicate the willingness if "benefits or lucky draw" were offered. Thus, Hypothesis 1 is supported.

Table 1: The evaluations of the environmental factors

	Mean.ws	Mean.vr	Diff	p-value
confidence	3.296	3.778	0.482	**3.300e-3**
comfort	3.444	3.963	0.519	**6.653e-3**
presence	2.185	3.222	1.037	**1.420e-4**

Table 2: The distributions of collected ratings

Scales	R_p	$R.ws$	$R.vr$
1	3.82%	11.63%	3.67%
2	4.08%	18.60%	10.55%
3	7.15%	35.81%	27.52%
4	27.77%	25.12%	42.66%
5	57.18%	8.84%	15.60%
1, 2, 3	15.05%	66.04%	41.74%
4, 5	84.95%	33.96%	58.26%
Total	1469	215	218

For Hypothesis 2(a), we conducted a number of paired two sample t-tests to investigate the mean differences of environmental factors, namely confidence, comfort and presence. Table 1 reports the results. Since all $p < 0.01$, we find that users in VR have greater confidence and feel more comfortable in their prior ratings than in WS. This may be partially explained by the fact that users have stronger sense of presence in VR than in WS. Besides, subjects also commented that the main reasons are due to the fact that they can try t-shirts on their 'own' body rather than have to image the real wearing effect in WS. They also feel stronger sense of presence in VR as if being in a real store. Thus, Hypothesis 2(a) is supported.

For Hypothesis 2(b), the collected data consists of 215 prior ratings in WS ($R.ws$) and 218 records in VR ($R.vr$) (see Table 2). The correlation between posterior ratings (R_p) and $R.ws$, denoted as $corr(R_p, R.ws)$ is -0.42 whereas $corr(R_p, R.vr) = 0.23$, signifying that the distribution of posterior ratings is distinct from prior ratings in WS, but marginally yet positively similar to prior ratings in VR. To have a better viewpoint, we classify rating values (4, 5) larger than median scale (3) as positive, and the remainder (1, 2, 3) as negative. Then we can obtain clearer correlations: $corr(R_p, R.ws) = -1$ and $corr(R_p, R.vr) = 1$. In addition, the average posterior rating is 4.13 whereas the values for $R.ws$ and $R.vr$ are 2.94 and 3.56, respectively. Thus, Hypothesis 2(b) is supported.

For Hypothesis 3, we conducted multiple linear regressions, each of which used 'presence' as independent variable and one of intrinsic or extrinsic attributes in WS and VR as dependent variable. The results are illustrated in Table 3. We see that presence in WS is most influential ($p < 0.01$) on material and store; in VR it is influential ($p < 0.001$) on all attributes except category. Hence, presence in WS has smaller effects on the perceptions of product attributes than that in VR. This can be attributed to the lower level of presence in WS as shown in Table 1. However, for attributes whose information can be adequately communicated by basic media (i.e., text descriptions, static images), such as category, presence may be of limited influence. One possible explanation for the different effects of price in two environments is that price in WS may be ignored as a cue to infer user preference. Thus, Hypothesis 3 is partially supported.

For Hypothesis 4, we conducted a multi-variable linear regression: intrinsic and extrinsic attributes as independent variables and 'perceived quality' as dependent variable. The

Table 3: The influences of presence on attributes

Env.	Attributes	Estimate	T Value	Pr(> |t|)
WS	appearance	0.142	2.131	0.0342
	material	0.270	3.822	**1.740e-4**
	fit	0.187	2.452	0.0150
	category	0.130	1.880	0.0614
	price	0.0921	1.294	0.197
	store	0.269	3.216	**1.500e-3**
VR	**appearance**	0.0860	1.259	**<2e-16**
	material	0.244	3.388	**8.370e-4**
	fit	0.216	3.349	**9.580e-4**
	category	0.0698	1.092	0.276
	price	0.209	3.295	**1.150e-3**
	store	0.468	7.623	**7.740e-13**

Table 4: The evaluations of perceived quality

Env.	Attributes	Estimate	T Value	Pr(> |t|)
WS	appearance	-0.06649	-1.152	0.250485
	material	0.28331	5.729	**3.52e-08**
	fit	0.12482	2.130	0.034338
	category	0.31082	5.115	**7.11e-07**
	price	0.04622	0.975	0.330593
	store	0.21357	3.748	**0.000231**
VR	**appearance**	0.1958	3.217	**0.00150**
	material	0.1413	2.941	**0.00363**
	fit	0.2467	4.748	**3.79e-06**
	category	0.1081	2.044	0.04222
	price	0.1999	4.795	**3.07e-06**
	store	-0.0059	-0.126	0.89976

results, presented in Table 4, show that three attributes in WS are the major concerns for product quality, namely material, category and store. In addition, attribute 'fit' is also considered important but has smaller influence. Note that the regression coefficients of category and store are greater than material and fit, which means that perceived quality relies more on extrinsic attributes than on intrinsic attributes. In contrast, the most important attributes in VR are appearance, material, fit and price, and most comments are focused on these four attributes. Hence, subjects relied more on intrinsic attributes than extrinsic attributes to evaluate the quality of t-shirts in VR. Of the four major attributes identified from pilot study, we find that only one of them (material) is recognized in WS whereas all four attributes are correctly recognized in VR. One possible explanation is that when users have less or no direct experiences with products, they may tend to use extrinsic attributes (i.e., category, store, price) as cues to infer the product quality. On the other hand, if users have effective and direct interactions with products and thereby gain sufficient direct product experiences, they may rely more on intrinsic attributes to evaluate products. Thus, Hypothesis 4 is supported.

For Hypothesis 5, we investigated the correlations among prior ratings, perceived quality and cost by applying a linear regression analysis. The results show that the coefficient of perceived quality is positive and large (> 0.6), and that it has a significant influence ($p < 0.001$) on prior ratings. In addition, the cost is demonstrated as relatively small yet positively important in VR ($0.14, p < 0.05$) rather than in WS ($0.06, p > 0.1$). The price of collected t-shirts ranges from US$3.99 to $32.00, indicating that the price is acceptable in general. As a consequence, users are more likely to like products as a whole given good quality estimated. However, as users may not correctly judge the quality of products in WS, the price may fail to be or less considered when assessing their preferences. Thus, Hypothesis 5 is supported.

4. DISCUSSION AND CONCLUSION

There are several potential limitations in our current experiments. First, certain attribute information (e.g., warranty, shipping) was not available for our user study. Although these are less relevant for the product class studied, they may be more important for other kinds of products. Second, due to lack of devices, our prototype implementation uses only visual information in VR: users cannot touch the t-shirts and feel the material. Tactile feedback may be important for user evaluation of preferences. Nevertheless, as aforementioned, this limitation may not greatly influence the general conclusion since we exploited abstract attributes rather than some specific attributes. Third, most subjects were computer or electrical engineering students on a university campus, and the sample size was modest. A larger and more heterogeneous sample may allow for more confident generalization of our research findings. Since higher presence may result in more confident prior ratings, it follows that the design of virtual stores should emphasize the sense of presence by increasing the media richness or the effectiveness of user interactions. The current research focused on the validation of conceptual model of prior ratings. For future work, we intend to investigate the benefits of prior ratings in improving recommendation performance.

Acknowledgement

We thank the support of the Institute for Media Innovation at Nanyang Technological University, Singapore.

5. REFERENCES

[1] W. Dodds, K. Monroe, and D. Grewal. Effects of price, brand, and store information on buyers' product evaluations. *J. of Marketing Research*, 28(3):307–319, 1991.

[2] S. Gardial, D. Clemons, R. Woodruff, D. Schumann, and M. Burns. Comparing consumers' recall of prepurchase and postpurchase product evaluation experiences. *Journal of Consumer Research*, 20(4):548–560, 1994.

[3] G. Guo, J. Zhang, and D. Thalmann. A simple but effective method to incorporate trusted neighbors in recommender systems. In *Proc. UMAP'12*, pages 114–125, 2012.

[4] G. Guo, J. Zhang, and N. Yorke-Smith. A novel bayesian similarity measure for recommender systems. In *Proc. IJCAI'13*, 2013.

[5] X. Hu and K. Wang. Personalized recommendation for virtual reality. In *Proc. ICMT'10*, pages 1–5, 2010.

[6] J. Jacoby, G. Szybillo, and J. Busato-Schach. Information acquisition behavior in brand choice situations. *Journal of Consumer Research*, 3(4):209–216, 1977.

[7] Z. Jiang and I. Benbasat. Virtual product experience: Effects of visual and functional control of products on perceived diagnosticity and flow in electronic shopping. *Journal of Management Information Systems*, 21(3):111–147, 2004.

[8] H. Li, T. Daugherty, and F. Biocca. The role of virtual experience in consumer learning. *Journal of Consumer Psychology*, 13(4):395–407, 2003.

[9] A. Rao and K. Monroe. The effect of price, brand name, and store name on buyers' perceptions of product quality. *J. of Marketing Research*, 26(3):351–357, 1989.

[10] F. Shah, P. Bell, and G. Sukthankar. A destination recommendation system for virtual worlds. In *Proc. FLAIRS'10*, pages 475–476, 2010.

[11] M. Slater, B. Spanlang, and D. Corominas. Simulating virtual environments within virtual environments as the basis for a psychophysics of presence. *ACM Transactions on Graphics (TOG)*, 29(4):92, 2010.

First Workshop on Large-Scale Recommender Systems: Research and Best Practice (LSRS 2013)

Tao Ye
Pandora Inc.
2101 Webster St., 16th Fl
Oakland, CA 94612
(+1) 510-451-4100
tye@pandora.com

Danny Bickson
GraphLab Inc.
4000 Mason Rd
Seattle, WA 98195
(+1)425-615-3777
bickson@graphlab.com

Quan Yuan
Alimama Inc, Alibaba Group
12#, West DaWang Rd
Chaoyang district, Beijing, China
100022
(+86)10-80775638
yuanquan.yq@taobao.com

ABSTRACT
With the increase of data collected and computation power available, modern recommender systems are ever facing new challenges. While complex models are developed in academia, industry practice seems to focus on relatively simple techniques that can deal with the magnitude of data and the need to distribute the computation. The first workshop on large-scale recommender systems (LSRS) is a meeting place for industry and academia to discuss the current and future challenges of applied large-scale recommender systems.

Categories and Subject Descriptors
H.2.8 [Database Management]: Database Applications – *data mining*. H.3.4 [Database Management]: System and Software – *distributed systems*.

Keywords
Recommendation systems, big data.

1. BACKGROUND AND MOTIVATION
As we enter the era of Big Data, the modern Recommender System faces greatly increased data volume and complexities. Previous computational models and experience on small data may not hold today, thus, how to build an efficient and robust system has become an important issue for many practitioners. Meanwhile, there is an increasing gap between academia research of recommendation systems focusing on complex models, and industry practice focusing on solving problems at large scale using relatively simple techniques.

RecSys'13, October 12–16 2013, Hong Kong, China.
ACM 978-1-4503-2409-0/13/09.
http://dx.doi.org/10.1145/2507157.2508007

Chances favor connected minds. The motivation of this workshop is to bring together researchers and practitioners working on large-scale recommender system in order to: (1) share experience, techniques and methodologies used to develop effective large-scale recommender, from architecture, algorithm, programming model, to evaluation (2) identify key challenges and promising trends in the area, and (3) identify collaboration opportunities among participants.

2. OBJECTIVES
This workshop aims to foster discussions in several fields that are of interest to our growing community of recommendation system builders. On the practical side, we would like to encourage sharing of architecture best practices in large-scale recommender systems as they are practiced in industry, as well as particular challenges and pain points. We hope this will guide future research that is system aware. On the research side, we focus on bringing in ideas and evaluations on scaling beyond the current generation of big data systems, with improved recommendation metrics. We believe the brightest minds from both sides will mutually benefit from the discussions and accelerate problem solving.

3. TOPICS OF INTEREST
We solicited submissions from industrial level recommendation system practitioners in either a short paper or slides formats on large scale system practice, as well as from recommendation systems researchers on their new research related to system aspect of recommendation with Big Data.

We focused on the following topics:

Systems of Large-scale RS:

- Architecture
- Programming Model
- Distributed systems
- Real-time recommendation
- Online learning for recommendation
- Scalability and Robustness

Data & Algorithms in Large-scale RS:

- Big data processing in offline/near-line/online modules

- Streaming data for recommendation
- Data platforms for recommendation
- Large, unstructured and social data for recommendation
- Heterogeneous data fusion
- Sampling techniques
- Parallel algorithms
- Incremental algorithms
- Algorithm validation and correctness checking

Application & Evaluation of Large-scale RS:

- Emerging applications
- Explanations in Large-scale RS
- Anti-attack of Large-scale RS
- Large data and privacy issue
- Evaluation methodology
- Large user studies
- Measurement platforms
- Visualization

4. PROGRAM COMMITTEE

We are grateful for the help of our program committee to review submissions:

Udi Weinsberg, Technicolor Labs

Noam Koenigstein, Microsoft

Yong Liu, NYU/Polytech

Lei Tang, Walmart Labs

Jan Neumann, Comcast

Edo Liberty, Yahoo! Labs

Qiang Yan, Chinese Academy of Science

Sebastian Schelter, Apache Mahout

Yang-qiu Song, HKUST

Yi Wang, Tecent

Hua Zheng, Hulu

Shou-kun Wang, Douban

Wen-dong Gu, Cutt.com

Olfa Nasraoui, University of Louisville

Dionysios Logothetis, Telefonica I+D

Yi Zhang, UC Santa Cruz

Mingxuan Sun, Pandora

Jason Zhao, Douban

Shai Fine, Intel

Ranjit Desai, Adobe

Linas Baltrunas, Telefonica I+D

Ron Karidi, Outbrain

5. WORKSHOP FORMAT

The workshop will feature two keynotes and three presentation sessions. We clustered the presentations to: (1) systems of large-scale recommenders, (2) data and algorithms, and (3) applications and evaluations. We plan to schedule a discussion period following each presentation session, where the participants will breakout into groups to discuss with the presenters and each other.

Our industry keynote is from lead researcher Justin Basilico at Netflix, titled "Recommendation at Netflix Scale". Our academic keynote is from Aapo Kyrola (author of Graphchi) of Carnegie Melon University, titled "Large-scale recommender systems on just a PC".

6. ACKNOWLEDGMENTS

We thank the RecSys 2013 organizing committee for giving us the opportunity to host this workshop in conjunction with RecSys 2013.

RecSys Challenge 2013

Jim Blomo
Yelp
San Francisco, CA, USA
jblomo@yelp.com

Martin Ester
Simon Fraser University
School of Computing Science
Burnaby, BC, Canada
ester@cs.sfu.ca

Marty Field
Yelp
San Francisco, CA, USA
mfield@yelp.com

Categories and Subject Descriptors
H.2.8 [**Database Applications**]: Data mining

General Terms
Algorithms, Design, Experimentation.

Keywords
Recommender systems, online reviews, business recommendation, feature extraction, model building, end-to-end system.

1. CONTEST

The 2013 Recommender Systems Challenge is associated with ACM RecSys 2013. Known as RecSys Challenge 2013, this is a LBS contest organized by Yelp. The theme of this year's competition is personalized business recommendations for Yelp users. We provide a dataset on over 10,000 businesses, eight thousand check-in sites, 40 thousand users and 200 thousand reviews. Contestants are asked to predict the users' future ratings on businesses. The competition starts on May 3, 2013 and ends on August 31, 2013.

The leaderboard for the competition is open and more detailed information is available at https://www.kaggle.com/c/yelp-recsys-2013. A $500 prize will be presented to the winners at the RecSys 2013 conference.

RecSys'13, October 12–16, 2013, Hong Kong, China.
ACM 978-1-4503-2409-0/13/10.

2. WORKSHOP

After the competition closes, we will hold a full-day workshop, co-located with the ACM RecSys 2013 conference, to discuss interesting approaches to the competition problem as well as lessons learned. We invite all contest participants to present their approach to building business recommendations. Contributions may focus on any individual step such as feature extraction or model building; or describe an end-to-end system to predict business ratings.

Submissions are welcome in the form of extended abstracts of proposed presentations. These extended abstract should give overviews on the approaches used in the competition problem. One submission type is accepted: short manuscripts of 2 to 4 pages. The extended abstracts will be evaluated for originality, contribution significance, and overall quality. Submissions should be in the form of a PDF attachment to a contest submission on Kaggle on August 31, 2013.

Accepted speakers will be invited to submit a short paper that describes their approach and results. The short papers will be distributed at the workshop and made available online afterwards.

Recommendation in Social Networks

Martin Ester
Simon Fraser University
School of Computing Science
001-778 782 4411
ester@cs.sfu.ca

Categories and Subject Descriptors

H.2.8 [**Database Applications**]: Data mining

Keywords

Recommender systems, social networks, social influence, collaborative filtering, matrix factorization.

1. TUTORIAL DESCRIPTION

With the emergence of online social networks, academia and industry have explored ways to exploit the information in social networks to improve the quality of recommendations and to support new recommendation tasks. The underlying motivation is to capture the effects that govern the evolution of social networks, i.e. social influence, selection, correlational influence and transitivity, to enhance the typically very sparse rating matrix. Recommender systems exploiting a social network promise to outperform traditional recommenders in particular for cold-start (new) users who have not yet provided enough information about their preferences. After introducing the motivation and some of the practical applications, we discuss social networks and the main factors affecting their evolution. We then review state-of-the-art methods for item recommendation in social networks, both memory-based approaches and model-based approaches, in particular matrix factorization. We discuss friend recommendation, an important recommendation task that is unique to the context of social networks. We conclude the tutorial with a discussion of future research directions such as privacy-preserving recommendations and social recommendation in distributed/peer-to-peer networks.

RecSys'13, October 12–16, 2013, Hong Kong, China.
ACM 978-1-4503-2409-0/13/10.
http://dx.doi.org/10.1145/2507157.2508062

2. TUTORIAL OUTLINE

The outline of the tutorial is as follows:

1. Introduction
2. Social networks and the effects that govern their evolution
3. Memory-based approaches for item recommendation in social networks
4. Model-based approaches for item recommendation in social networks
5. Friend recommendation
6. Future directions

3. PREREQUISITES

This tutorial targets researchers who want to get up to speed in this emerging research area as well as practitioners who are interested in developing their own applications. The tutorial assumes familiarity with the common methods of recommender systems. Some background in data mining and social network analysis will be helpful, but is not required.

Learning to Rank for Recommender Systems

Alexandros Karatzoglou[1], Linas Baltrunas[1], Yue Shi[2]
[1]Telefonica Research, Spain; [2]Delft University of Technology, Netherlands;
[1]{alexk, linas}@tid.es, [2]y.shi@tudelft.nl

ABSTRACT

Recommender system aim at providing a personalized list of items ranked according to the preferences of the user, as such ranking methods are at the core of many recommendation algorithms. The topic of this tutorial focuses on the cutting-edge algorithmic development in the area of recommender systems. This tutorial will provide an in depth picture of the progress of ranking models in the field, summarizing the strengths and weaknesses of existing methods, and discussing open issues that could be promising for future research in the community. A qualitative and quantitative comparison between different models will be provided while we will also highlight recent developments in the areas of Reinforcement Learning.

Categories and Subject Descriptors

H.3.3 [**Information Storage and Retrieval**]: Information Search and Retrieval—*Information Filtering, Retrieval Models*

Keywords

Collaborative filtering, learning to rank, ranking, recommender systems

1. INTRODUCTION

Recommender systems aim to provide users with personalized items, which are typically ranked in a descending order of predicted relevance [1]. Learning the personalized recommendation list can be cast as a ranking problem. Naturally this cutting-edge research topic, *Learning to Rank* (LtR) [4], has already attracted a lot of attention in the Information Retrieval and Machine Learning communities. Recent contributions to collaborative filtering (CF) have exploited LtR techniques for improving the ranking of the top-N recommendations. In this tutorial, we present the key ideas of different categories of learning to rank approaches, and demonstrate examples that extend these ideas to specific CF methods. We also discuss a few open issues that remain challenging for future research in this direction.

RecSys'13, October 12–16, 2013, Hong Kong, China.
ACM 978-1-4503-2409-0/13/10.

2. OVERVIEW

2.1 Background

The tutorial briefly introduces the background of recommender systems and CF techniques. In particular, conventional CF methods target the rating prediction problem, such as the problem defined in Netflix Prize contest [1]. However, we emphasize that the more important objective in recommender systems is *ranking*, or the *top-N recommendation*. We also review some conventional ranking methods for recommendation, such as item-based CF [8].

2.2 LtR for Recommender Systems

We introduce the concept of LtR in the area of information retrieval, and explain its usefulness for recommender systems based on the analogy between query-document search and user-item recommendation. Then, we review three types of LtR techniques, i.e., point-wise, pair-wise and list-wise LtR.

CF methods that learn a ranking model based on the preference scores of individual items can are considered point-wise ranking methods [3]. With pair-wise LtR, CF methods can be developed to take into account the preferences of each user to a pair of items. A typical example of CF with paire-wise LtR is Bayesian personalized ranking [7]. CF methods based on list-wise LtR model the list-wise preferences of each user to a list of items (usually the rated items). An important branch of CF methods in this category are designed to directly optimize the evaluation metrics, such as mean average precision (MAP), Mean Reciprocal Rank (MRR) and Normalized Discounted Cumulative Gain (NDCG), which are usually list-wise ranking measures. Typical examples of those methods are CofiRank [12], CLiMF [10] and TFMAP [9].

2.3 Implicit and Explicit Feedback

The core idea behind CF is that users whose past interests were similar will also share common interests in future. The user's interest is inferred by the user interaction patterns with the items either explicitly or implicitly. In explicit feedback, users are asked/allowed to explicitly rate the items that have been purchased/consumed, using a pre-defined Likert scale (graded relevance), e.g., 1-5 stars in

[1]http://www.netflixprize.com/

Netflix movie recommendation site. Higher grade indicates higher preference/relevance of the item. In implicit feedback [2], users interact with items by downloading, purchasing, and their preferences are deduced from the interaction patterns. In this paper we propose a new model for the case of explicit/graded relevance data.

Various models for implicit feedback data use learning to rank [4] techniques to optimize binary relevance data ranking metrics. For example, several CF models [7, 9, 10] compute near optimal ranked lists with respect to the Area Under the Curve (AUC), Average Precision (AP) [5] and Reciprocal Rank [11] metrics. However, metrics that are defined to handle binary relevance data are not directly suitable for graded relevance data. Binary metrics, and CF methods that optimize for these metrics can be used on graded relevance data if it is converted to binary relevance by e.g., imposing a threshold (e.g., setting rating 4 as the threshold for the 1-5 scale so that items rated 4 and 5 are treated as relevant). This process has two major drawbacks: 1) we *lose grading information* within the rated items, e.g., items rated with a 5 are more relevant then items rated with a 4. This information is crucial in building precise models. 2) the choice of the *thresholding relevance is arbitrary* and will have an impact on the performance of different recommendation approaches.

2.4 Interactive Recommendation

In many recommendation domains the content is often dynamic and/or short lived such as video, news recommendation and computational advertising. In these domains it is often difficult to collect enough information in the form of clicks or ratings to recommend an item accurately using standart CF methods. Exploration/exploitation methods from reinforcement learning such as Multi-armed Bandits are particularly well suited for these domains. LtR techniques can be also used for Multi-armed Bandits [6].

2.5 Open Issues

While there has been significant progress in the development of novel ranking methods one significant issue in CF methods and recommender systems in general is modeling the dependencies of the items in a recommendation list. Modeling the dependencies within a recommendation list can potentially produce more accurate ranking, increased diversity and novelty. Other open issues despite significant progress include the efficient modeling of context (e.g. location) and item content information in ranking models.

3. OBJECTIVES

The topic of this tutorial focuses on the cutting-edge algorithmic development in the area of recommender systems. This tutorial would bring a big picture of the progress of ranking models in the field, summarizing the strengths and weaknesses of existing methods, and discussing open issues that would be promising for the future research in the community. The tutorial is intended for researchers and practitioners in the area of recommender systems, especially those who are interested in recommendation algorithms.

4. ACKNOWLEDGEMENTS

This work is funded as part of a Marie Curie Intra European Fellowship for Career Development (IEF) award (CARS, PIEF-GA-2010-273739) held by Alexandros Karatzoglou.

5. REFERENCES

[1] G. Adomavicius and A. Tuzhilin. Toward the next generation of recommender systems: A survey of the state-of-the-art and possible extensions. *IEEE Transactions on Kowledge and Data Engineering*, 17(6):734–749, 2005.

[2] Y. Hu, Y. Koren, and C. Volinsky. Collaborative filtering for implicit feedback datasets. ICDM '08, pages 263–272. IEEE Computer Society, 2008.

[3] Y. Koren and J. Sill. Ordrec: an ordinal model for predicting personalized item rating distributions. In *Proceedings of the fifth ACM conference on Recommender systems*, RecSys '11, pages 117–124, New York, NY, USA, 2011. ACM.

[4] T.-Y. Liu. Learning to rank for information retrieval. *Foundations and Trends in Information Retrieval*, 3(3):225–331, 2009.

[5] C. D. Manning, P. Raghavan, and H. Schütze. *Introduction to information retrieval.* Cambridge Univ. Press, Cambridge [u.a.], 1. publ. edition, 2008.

[6] F. Radlinski, R. Kleinberg, and T. Joachims. Learning diverse rankings with multi-armed bandits. In *Proceedings of the 25th international conference on Machine learning*, ICML '08, pages 784–791, New York, NY, USA, 2008. ACM.

[7] S. Rendle, C. Freudenthaler, Z. Gantner, and S.-T. Lars. Bpr: Bayesian personalized ranking from implicit feedback. UAI '09, pages 452–461. AUAI Press, 2009.

[8] B. Sarwar, G. Karypis, J. Konstan, and J. Reidl. Item-based collaborative filtering recommendation algorithms. WWW '01, pages 285–295. ACM, 2001.

[9] Y. Shi, A. Karatzoglou, L. Baltrunas, M. Larson, A. Hanjalic, and N. Oliver. TFMAP: optimizing map for top-n context-aware recommendation. SIGIR '12, pages 155–164. ACM, 2012.

[10] Y. Shi, A. Karatzoglou, L. Baltrunas, M. Larson, N. Oliver, and A. Hanjalic. CLiMF: learning to maximize reciprocal rank with collaborative less-is-more filtering. RecSys '12, pages 139–146. ACM, 2012.

[11] E. M. Voorhees. The trec-8 question answering track report. In *TREC-8*, 1999.

[12] M. Weimer, A. Karatzoglou, Q. Le, and A. Smola. Cofirank - maximum margin matrix factorization for collaborative ranking. NIPS'07, pages 1593–1600, 2007.

Beyond Friendship: The Art, Science and Applications of Recommending People to People in Social Networks

Luiz Augusto Pizzato
School of Information Technologies
The University of Sydney, NSW 2006, Australia
luiz.pizzato@sydney.edu.au

Anmol Bhasin
LinkedIn Corp
Mountain View, CA 94043, USA
abhasin@linkedin.com

ABSTRACT

While Recommender Systems are powerful drivers of engagement and transactional utility in social networks, People recommenders are a fairly involved and diverse subdomain. Consider that movies are recommended to be watched, news is recommended to be read, people however, are recommended for a plethora of reasons – such as recommendation of people to befriend, follow, partner, targets for an advertisement or service, recruiting, partnering romantically and to join thematic interest groups.

This tutorial aims to first describe the problem domain, touch upon classical approaches like link analysis and collaborative filtering and then take a rapid deep dive into the unique aspects of this problem space like reciprocity, intent understanding of recommender and the recomendee, contextual people recommendations in communication flows and social referrals – a paradigm for delivery of recommendations using the social graph. These aspects will be discussed in the context of published original work developed by the authors and their collaborators and in many cases deployed in massive-scale real world applications on professional networks such as LinkedIn.

Categories and Subject Descriptors

H.3.3 [**Information Storage and Retrieval**]: Information Search and Retrieval—*Information filtering*

General Terms

Algorithms, Experimentation, Human Factors

Keywords

People Recommenders, Social Networks

1. PEOPLE RECOMMENDERS

Recommending new connections to establish is one of the core practical applications of Recommender Systems in social networks. Recently, Social Network utility however has evolved tremendously from simply following and connecting to friends to now covering a host of business applications such as hiring, dating, partnering and advertising. People connect to other people on these networks for these aforementioned reasons. While the core ideological aspect of making a "connection" stands intact, the semantics of the nature of the connection (e.g. hiring, business partners) go beyond classical graph mining approaches. When cast in a Recommender System lens, thematic People Recommenders present a unique graph mining, collaborative filtering and content filtering hybrid landscape which deserves a deep dive session tailored to the Recommender Systems and Social Network Analysis community alike. First hand information from creators and operators of real-life ginormous scale implementations of the ideas in this space at top online social networks should be a compelling session for this community to attend.

2. TUTORIAL OVERVIEW

1. Introduction
    - The basics of Social Recommenders
    - People recommender systems
2. Special Topics in People Recommenders
    - Why reciprocal (people) recommenders are different to traditional (product) recommendations
    - Multi-Objective Optimization
    - Intent Understanding
    - Feature Engineering
    - Social Referral
    - Pathfinding
3. Concluding remarks

3. TARGET AUDIENCE

This tutorial is aimed at Recommender Systems and Social Network Analysis research community, Data and Graph miners, Machine Learning practitioners and computational advertising enthusiasts alike. Since, this is a relatively new and specialized area in and of itself, most participants should find the material fresh, insightful and educational.

The material presented in the tutorial ranges from foundational aspects of People Recommender Systems to the specialized variants thereof in the viewed with the business applications in a social network lens, especially, large industrial

RecSys'13, October 12–16, 2013, Hong Kong, China.
ACM 978-1-4503-2409-0/13/10.
http://dx.doi.org/10.1145/2507157.2508064.

scale deployments of such systems. The audience can expect to walk away with a thorough overview of the problem domain, subtleties and applications of people recommenders. In addition, algorithmic and mathematical formulations of Multi-objective optimization, Reciprocity and Behavioural Intent modelling and Social referrals will be discussed which should provide a compelling preview into building real world applications using these techniques for both enterprise and consumer industrial applications. The pre-requisites for this tutorial is some familiarity with foundational Recommender Systems, Data Mining, Machine Learning and Social Network Analysis literature, however, since introductory material will be covered as well, so the talk should cater to a wide audience at the conference.

4. TUTORS' BIOGRAPHY

Luiz Augusto Pizzato is a research fellow with the University of Sydney. He works closely with the Smart Services Cooperative Research Centre on projects related to services on personalisation, mobile personalisation, new media, and multi-channel content delivery. He has a PhD from Macquarie University in Sydney, Australia for work related natural language processing and information retrieval. Luiz has done extensive work in the area of reciprocal recommender and have implemented and evaluated a number of reciprocal recommender algorithms to match people to people for a large online dating website. These algorithms have been successfully trialled in a large scale user experiment and have since then been used to find dating partners.

Anmol Bhasin is the Director of Engineering for Recommendations, Personalization and A/B testing systems at LinkedIn. His team's contributions include LinkedIn's various personalized recommendation products (e.g., *Jobs You Might Be Interested In*), social news (*LinkedIn Today*), and systems for ad targeting and click through rate prediction. He and his team also work on enterprise People Recommenders in LinkedIn's product suite such as *People You May Hire* and *Talent Match* for LinkedIn's recruiter product. His team operates the content processing pipeline and online experimentation (A/B) framework used for LinkedIn's suite of data products. Prior to LinkedIn, Anmol worked at business search engine Business.com, where he developed the crawler, indexing systems, and retrieval algorithms. Anmol has also authored mobile gaming applications, including the award-winning Tecmo Bowl. Anmol received a Masters in Computer Science from the State University of New York at Buffalo, where he focused on text mining and applied machine learning for cross document learning.

5. RELATED WORK

[1] J. Akehurst, I. Koprinska, K. Yacef, L. Pizzato, J. Kay, and T. Rej. CCR - a content-collaborative reciprocal recommender for online dating. In *IJCAI* 2011.

[2] M. S. Amin, B. Yan, S. Sriram, A. Bhasin, and C. Posse. Social referral: leveraging network connections to deliver recommendations. In RecSys'12, 2012.

[3] J. Chen, W. Geyer, C. Dugan, M. Muller, and I. Guy. Make new friends, but keep the old: recommending people on social networking sites. In *CHI*, 2009.

[4] F. Diaz, D. Metzler, and S. Amer-Yahia. Relevance and ranking in online dating systems. In *33rd ACM conf. on Research and development in information retrieval*, SIGIR'10, pages 66–73, 2010.

[5] M. Fazel-Zarandi, H. J. Devlin, Y. Huang, and N. Contractor. Expert recommendation based on social drivers, social network analysis, and semantic data representation. In *HetRec*, 2011.

[6] D. Gale and L. S. Shapley. College admissions and the stability of marriage. *The American Mathematical Monthly*, 69(1):9–15, 1962.

[7] W. H. Hsu, A. L. King, M. S. Paradesi, T. Pydimarri, and T. Weninger. Collaborative and structural recommendation of friends using weblog-based social network analysis. In *AAAI Spring Symposium: Computational Approaches to Analyzing Weblogs*, 2006.

[8] Z. Huang, X. Li, and H. Chen. Link prediction approach to collaborative filtering. In *5th ACM/IEEE-CS joint conf. on Digital libraries*, JCDL'05, 2005.

[9] S. Kamat, A. Hill, C. Posse, A. Bhasin, and C. Chen. Referring members of a social network as job candidates. Europe Patent 13/678,236, Nov. 15 2012.

[10] J. Kunegis, G. Gröner, and T. Gottron. Online dating recommender systems: The split-complex number approach. In *4th ACM RecSys workshop on Recommender systems and the social web*, 2012.

[11] H. Liu, M. Amin, B. Yan, and A. Bhasin. Generating supplemental content information using virtual profiles. In RecSys'13, 2013.

[12] J. Malinowski, T. Keim, O. Wendt, and T. Weitzel. Matching people and jobs: A bilateral recommendation approach. In *39th Hawaii International Conf. on System Sciences*, volume 6 of *HICSS'06*, 2006.

[13] I. Paparrizos, B. B. Cambazoglu, and A. Gionis. Machine learned job recommendation. In *RecSys*, 2011.

[14] L. Pizzato, J. Akehurst, C. Silvestrini, K. Yacef, I. Koprinska, and J. Kay. The effect of suspicious profiles on people recommenders. In *20th International Conf. on User Modeling, Adaptation and Personalization*, UMAP'12, pages 225–236, 2012.

[15] L. Pizzato, T. Rej, J. Akehurst, I. Koprinska, K. Yacef, and J. Kay. Recommending people to people: the nature of reciprocal recommenders with a case study in online dating. *User Modeling and User-Adapted Interaction*, pages 1–42, 2012.

[16] L. Pizzato, T. Rej, T. Chung, I. Koprinska, and J. Kay. RECON: a reciprocal recommender for online dating. In *RecSys*, pages 207–214, 2010.

[17] L. Pizzato, T. Rej, K. Yacef, I. Koprinska, and J. Kay. Finding someone you will like and who won't reject you. In *19th Conf. on User Modeling, Adaptation and Personalization*, UMAP'11, pages 269–280, 2011.

[18] C. Posse, A. Gupta, A. Bhasin, and M. Rogati. Methods and systems for identifying similar people via a business networking service Patent 20,130,031,090, 2013.

[19] M. Rodriguez, C. Posse, and E. Zhang. Multiple objective optimization in recommender systems. In *RecSys*, 2012.

[20] J. Wang, Y. Zhang, C. Posse, and A. Bhasin. Is it time for a career switch? In WWW'13, 2013.

Tutorial on Preference Handling

Alexis Tsoukiàs
LAMSADE - CNRS
Université Paris Dauphine
alexis.tsoukias@dauphine.fr

Paolo Viappiani
LIP6 - CNRS
Université Pierre et Marie Curie
paolo.viappiani@lip6.fr

Categories and Subject Descriptors

I.2 [**Artificial Intelligence**]: Miscellaneous; H.3.3 [**Information Storage and Retrieval**]: Information Search and Retrieval-Information Filtering; H.3.4 [**Information Technology and Systems Applications**]: Decision Support; G.m [**Mathematics of Computing**]: Miscellaneous

Keywords

preferences, utility theory, decision-making under uncertainty, representation languages, preference elicitation, preference aggregation, preference learning, argumentation

ABSTRACT

This tutorial, addressed to researchers and practitioners in the area of recommendation systems, reviews the foundations of decision theory and utility theory, focusing on methods for representing, learning and reasoning with preferences. Recent advances on handling preferences will also be discussed, with a focus on preference learning, preference aggregation and preferences in argumentation. Finally, we will show how these techniques can be used in a practice in recommender systems.

1. TUTORIAL DESCRIPTION

The tutorial aims at introducing the general field that deals with techniques for representing, learning and reasoning with preferences. While the community of Recommender Systems have recently done extensive work in techniques for providing user recommendations in different settings, preferences have been formally studied since several decades (the community that studies preferences from a formal algorithmic point of view is now often called *algorithmic decision theory*).

Preferences are a basic concept for several research fields such as economics, decision theory, game theory, artificial intelligence, classification, data bases, etc.; preferences constitute a key concept for the development of recommender systems since they represent the elementary information upon which recommendations are constructed. The tutorial will introduce both the formalisms more widely used to model and represent preferences as well as the procedures aimed at learning preferences and at producing a recommendation for an end-user (decision maker).

RecSys'13, October 12–16, 2013, Hong Kong, China.
Copyright 2013 ACM 978-1-4503-2409-0/13/09
http://dx.doi.org/10.1145/2507157.2508065 .

More precisely the tutorial will cover the following topics.

1. General introduction, Historical Perspective
2. Axiomatic, Behavioural and Prescriptive approaches
3. Binary Relations, Languages for preferences
4. Preference Modelling, representation theorems, foundations of utility theory
5. Decision-making under certainty and uncertainty
6. Measuring Preferences, Compact representations
7. Preference Learning, utility elicitation
8. Preference Aggregation
9. Constructing a recommendation
10. Preferences in Argumentation
11. Applications and Discussion

The tutorial is mainly addressed to researchers in the area of recommendation systems. Practitioners willing to understand how to use correctly preferences as well as the algorithmic challenges may also be interested in attending. Basic notions of discrete mathematics and probability theory are the only prerequisite.

Short Biographies of Tutorial Presenters

Alexis Tsoukiàs (Greece, 1959) is a CNRS research director at LAMSADE, Université Paris Dauphine. He holds (1989) a PhD in Computer Science and Systems Engineering from Politecnico di Torino (Italy) where he also graduated engineering studies. His research interests include subjects such as: multiple criteria decision making, non conventional preference modelling, governance support, applied non classical logics, ordinal mathematical programming, artificial intelligence and decision theory. He is the co-author of two books and more than 70 journal articles and book contributions. He has been vice-president of ROADEF (the french OR society) as well as President of EURO (the European association of OR societies). Since 2007 he was coordinator of the European COST Action IC0602, Algorithmic Decision Theory funded within the FP7. He served the Research Administration in several positions, the last being the National Committee of the CNRS (elected member since 2008). Presently he is the Director of the LAMSADE. Besides teaching to several post-graduate classes in Paris and world wide, he occasionally practices decision support. He has been invited to more than 30 Universities world wide. He is member of several editorial boards, besides editing special issues of journals and conference volumes. He has been involved in the Programme and Organisation Committee of several conferences in Decision Analysis, OR and AI. His most recent invited tutorial was in IJCAI 2009 on Algorithmic Decision Theory. Personal web page: *http://www.lamsade.dauphine.fr/~tsoukias*

Paolo Viappiani is a researcher of the French Centre National de la Recherche Scientifique (CNRS) affiliated with the LIP6 laboratory of Univ. Pierre et Marie Curie (UPMC). He holds a PhD in Computer Science from EPFL (2007). His research interests include recommender systems, preference elicitation, mathematical models for social networks, interactive optimization and machine learning. He often publishes in venues such as AAAI, JAIR, ICML and NIPS. He often serves as a PC member of conferences such as AAAI, IJCAI, WWW, ACM EC; he is a member of the editorial board of the Journal of Artificial Intelligence Research (JAIR). He has been co-organizer of the workshop "Choice Models and Preference Learning" co-located with NIPS 2011 and co-organizer of the Multidisciplinary Workshop on Advances in Preference Handling (MPREF) in 2012 and 2013. Personal web page: *http://www-desir.lip6.fr/~viappianip*

Author Index

www.ingramcontent.com/pod-product-compliance
Ingram Content Group UK Ltd.
Pitfield, Milton Keynes, MK11 3LW, UK
UKHW051415290926
15471UKWH00009B/1612

9 781450 326780